W9-DDP-469

Writing Analytically with Readings

Georgia State University Edition

Rosenwasser | Stephen

With materials prepared by Diana Eidson

CENGAGE
Learning·

Australia • Brazil • Japan • Korea • Mexico • Singapore • Spain • United Kingdom • United States

CENGAGE
Learning·

Writing Analytically with Readings: Georgia State University Edition

Writing Analytically with Readings, 2nd Edition
David Rosenwasser, Jill Stephen
© 2012 Cengage Learning. All rights reserved.

Executive Editors:

Maureen Staudt
Michael Stranz

Senior Project Development Manager:

Linda deStefano

Marketing Specialist:

Courtney Sheldon

Senior Production/
Manufacturing Manager:

Donna M. Brown

Production Editorial Manager:
Kim Fry

Sr. Rights Acquisition
Account Manager:

Todd Osborne

ALL RIGHTS RESERVED. No part of this work covered by the copyright herein may be reproduced, transmitted, stored or used in any form or by any means graphic, electronic, or mechanical, including but not limited to photocopying, recording, scanning, digitizing, taping, Web distribution, information networks, or information storage and retrieval systems, except as permitted under Section 107 or 108 of the 1976 United States Copyright Act, without the prior written permission of the publisher.

For product information and technology assistance, contact us at
Cengage Learning Customer & Sales Support, 1-800-354-9706
For permission to use material from this text or product,
submit all requests online at **cengage.com/permissions**
Further permissions questions can be emailed to
permissionrequest@cengage.com

This book contains select works from existing Cengage Learning resources and was produced by Cengage Learning Custom Solutions for collegiate use. As such, those adopting and/or contributing to this work are responsible for editorial content accuracy, continuity and completeness.

Compilation © 2012 Cengage Learning.

ISBN-13:   978-1-285-14288-3

ISBN-10:   1-285-14288-8

Cengage Learning
5191 Natorp Boulevard
Mason, Ohio 45040
USA

Cengage Learning is a leading provider of customized learning solutions with office locations around the globe, including Singapore, the United Kingdom, Australia, Mexico, Brazil, and Japan. Locate your local office at:
international.cengage.com/region.

Cengage Learning products are represented in Canada by Nelson Education, Ltd.

For your lifelong learning solutions, visit **www.cengage.com/custom.**
Visit our corporate website at **www.cengage.com.**

Printed in the United States of America

Brief Contents

Contents

PART 2   THE READINGS

Preface

Writing Analytically with Readings is two books in one. Part One (chapters 1 - 19) is the latest version of our stand- alone writing text, *Writing Analytically*, now in its sixth edition. Part Two (chapters 20 - 24), which contains exercises and writing assignments keyed to Part One, is a revised collection (second edition) of topic-centered readings and images for students to analyze and to use as models and lenses for analyzing other materials.

Our original book, *Writing Analytically*, grew out of our experience as directors of a Writing Across the Curriculum program and Writing Center at a small liberal arts college and out of our writing pedagogy workshops for faculty at our own and other colleges and universities. Since the beginning of our work on *Writing Analytically* in the early 1990s, we have studied what faculty say about their goals for student writing and used this information to develop a book that would allow faculty to talk to each other across disciplinary lines. Two decades later, we are still working on that goal and learning about what college students need in order to succeed at academic writing both in first-year composition courses and in the various discourse communities they migrate among during their undergraduate careers and beyond.

We learned from faculty across the curriculum that what they wanted from student writing was not passive summary, not personal narrative, not opinions and debate-style argument, but analysis, with its patient and methodical inquiry into the meaning of information. They wanted writing aimed at understanding rather than at promoting a particular point of view. They wanted students to think on the page about what things mean—which is our primary definition of analysis. Among the reader reports that we pondered for this edition, we found faculty reporting that students are coming to them prepared to write five-paragraph themes and arguments but radically unprepared to think and write analytically.

Most books of writing instruction devote only a chapter, if that, to analysis. This book is organized entirely around analytical writing. We acknowledge that analytical essays inevitably make arguments, but we think there is value in distinguishing between argument and analysis, and we think that students learn to write better arguments when they are taught first to analyze and to dwell more comfortably with uncertainty. *Writing Analytically with Readings* offers alternatives to oversimplified thinking of the like/dislike, agree/disagree variety. It argues that an idea is not the same thing as an opinion and teaches students how to respect the complexity of subjects where there is no single right answer.

This edition of *Writing Analytically with Readings* remains committed to the goal of giving students the tools they need in order to engage in the analytical habits of mind that will be expected of them in their courses and in the world they encounter after graduation. Students who learn to analyze information and who know how to use writing in order to discover and develop ideas will continue to be in demand in the workplace, regardless of the forms they find themselves writing in or the medium in which their writing appears.

As the book seeks to demonstrate, the analytical process is surprisingly formulaic: it consists of a fairly limited set of moves. People who think well have these moves at their disposal, whether they are aware of using them or not. Analysis, the book argues, is a frame of mind, a set of habits for observing and making sense of the world.

CULTIVATING THE ANALYTICAL FRAME OF MIND

Entering this analytical frame of mind requires specific tasks that will reduce students' anxiety for instant answers, impede the reflex move to judgments, and encourage a more hands-on engagement with materials. *Writing Analytically with Readings* supplies these tasks for each phase of the writing and idea-generating process: making observations, inferring implications, and making the leap to possible conclusions. The root issue here is the writer's attitude towards evidence. The book argues that the ability of writers to discover ideas and improve on them in revision depends largely on their ability to use evidence as a means of testing and revising ideas rather than just supporting them.

This book's employment of verbal prompts like "So what?" and its recommendation of step-by-step procedures, such as the procedure for making a thesis evolve, should not be confused with prescriptive slot-filler formulae for writing. Our book does not prescribe a fill-in-the-blank grid for producing papers. Instead it offers schematic descriptions of what good thinkers do—as acts of mind—when they are confronted with data.

We continue to have faith in the book's heuristics for their ability to spur more thoughtful writing but also for the role they can play in making the classroom a more collaborative space. When students and teachers can share the means of idea production, reading and writing and class discussion become better connected, and students can more easily learn to see that good ideas don't just happen—they're made.

PART TWO: THE ANTHOLOGY OF READINGS

The readings in Part Two of *Writing Analytically with Readings* aim to complement the rhetoric by

- providing students with essays that prompt and model writing that is primarily analytical rather than argumentative
- providing students with a mix of imitable academic writing and smart contemporary journalism

The essays in each of the book's five chapters of readings serve as primary material for analytical summary, comparative analysis, and synthesis, but also as lenses and models for student application to other materials.

THE THREE LIVES OF A READING

At the heart of *Writing Analytically with Readings* is the notion that readings function in three ways in a writing course:

- As Objects for Analysis
- As Lenses for Viewing Other Material
- As Models for Imitating

As Object: the readings offer interesting and relatively sophisticated primary material for students to analyze. Writing tasks attached to the readings teach readers to use writing in order to read more deeply and reflectively.

As Lens: the readings contain theories and analytical methods that students can extract and use for viewing other materials, both verbal and nonverbal. The ability to apply theories and information in other settings is a critical skill in college writing.

As Model: the readings demonstrate ways of approaching a topic. Tasks linked to specific readings show writers how to emulate the ways that effective analytical writing operates.

PRINCIPLES OF SELECTION FOR THE READINGS

We kept asking ourselves as we read a range of possible materials for the book, what would our students *do* with this reading? How could they *use* it? How could they turn it into a lens? Where might they locate a complication that would give them something to say about it—and not just repeat what it already says?

We think we have put together a collection of readings and images that are informative and interesting but most important, thought-provoking and imitable. Each of the book's five topic categories contains essays of sufficient depth and complexity to comprise an interpretive context to guide readers' own analyses as they move from writing about the reading to applying the reading to other readings, and to their observations about the world.

The selections are not ideological in the sense of essays having been chosen to move readers toward a particular point of view. Instead we have aimed for serious writing on matters of interest and importance now, such as

changing habits of communication in a technological world

public and private space in America today

cities and suburbs: the way we live now

race, ethnicity, and "the melting pot"

political labels: liberal, conservative and other semantically challenging key words

visual rhetoric: interpreting images

The selections are moderate in length and difficulty: not byte-sized but also not graduate school level pieces on cultural theory. We have kept in mind that the primary audience for the anthology consists of reasonably engaged first-year students.

Most selections are fairly current—since 2000—though there are some classic essays, often serving as theoretical frames [e.g., Jane Jacobs (1962), John Berger (1972), Susan Sontag (1977)]. In some cases the older selections will offer writers the challenging opportunity to update these classic pieces and assess them from the perspective of the present.

LINKS TO WRITING ACROSS THE CURRICULUM (WAC)

Writing Analytically with Readings developed from our backgrounds as WAC directors. The book does not, however, aim *primarily* to introduce students to the academic disciplines as different discourse communities, each with its own characteristic vocabulary, rhetoric, and epistemology. Although readings are included from a number of disciplines—for example, political science, history, media and communications, American studies, photography, film studies—we do not emphasize these as disciplinary templates for writing. We do hope, however, that the readings might acquaint students with the diverse vocabularies, protocols, and mindsets of the different academic disciplines. Primarily, though, we intend the rhetoric and readings to teach students the habits of mind that serious, intellectually stimulating academic writing across the disciplines shares and to give students the information they need to understand disciplinary styles and protocols—especially those of the natural and social sciences—rhetorically.

Two essays that appear among the readings were written especially for our book. One, an interview we did with a photography professor whose photographs document the almost vanished world of American steel-making, offers his historical and theoretical framework for understanding contemporary American photography. The other piece, by a political science professor who is also a well-known pollster, addresses the history, use and abuse of political labels in contemporary culture.

WHAT'S NEW IN THIS EDITION OF *WRITING ANALYTICALLY WITH READINGS*

Readers familiar with the first edition of *Writing Analytically with Readings* will find it paired with a substantially revised version of the rhetoric wherein the book's key concepts and heuristics remain the same but are, we think, clearer, better illustrated, easier to find, and easier to use.

The accompanying anthology of readings contains some new pieces and more attention—in the ordering of chapters and in accompanying introductions and assignments—to ways that the readings might work together to provide coherent sequences of assignments for a semester-long or year-long writing course.

The anthology of readings now ends with the "Seeing" chapter on visual rhetoric, where it is positioned for easy reference in relation to topics addressed in the previous four reading chapters—inviting students to visit these topics again through the lens of visual media, both "high culture" (art photography) and popular (images from advertising and film).

As in the first edition, the anthology of readings begins with a chapter on technology, communication, and manners, which are treated as a related set of concerns. This chapter sets up a major binary and connecting theme for the readings as a whole— public vs. private. To this opening chapter we have added an essay on a topic much addressed in both academic and more popular writing: the impact of the internet on the way people think and feel about themselves and the world.

The writing assignments throughout have been clarified in order to suggest topics for short analytical papers on each reading and topics that locate interesting points of contact among the readings.

The "for further research" sections have been revised and updated by reference librarian Kelly Cannon. These sections also contain more opportunities for writing.

Part One of the book now has two "toolkit" chapters of analytical methods (chapters 2 and 4), making the book's primary heuristics more prominent, more accessible, and more clearly arranged in a hierarchy of increasingly sophisticated skills. The first toolkit includes strategies for helping student writers to become more observant and to focus on patterns of significant detail. The second toolkit pulls uncovering assumptions, reformulating binaries, passage-based focused freewriting, difference within similarity, and "seems to be about X" out of chapters in which they have been embedded and uses them to set up the Writing about Reading chapter, which follows.

The book's discussion of counterproductive habits of mind (much shorter and less like a jeremiad) now appears at the end of the first toolkit (chapter 2), so that the chapter leads with concrete activities and positive advice before we supply rationale and admonitions.

We have added many new examples of student and professional writing that use the book's heuristics.

The book's treatment of discipline-specific writing, especially writing in the natural and social sciences, is now more fully described and theorized, and is supported by many new examples of student and professional writing in disciplines outside the humanities, as well as by new Voices from Across the Curriculum sections.

We have aimed overall for shorter paragraphs and more heads. We sought to make individual chapters browseable by putting the chapters' key advice in heads and bullet lists and by locating in chapter openings a PowerPoint-like "slide" that lists the key writing procedures in the chapter.

The book has a new opening chapter comprised of fourteen short-takes— previews of key topics in writing and writing instruction that are particularly useful to discuss early in a writing course. Among the chapter's topics are writing in the disciplines, academic vs. non-academic writing, writing about reading, rhetoric, argument, analysis, freewriting, our critique of five-paragraph form, and the place of the traditional essay in the digital age. Because the chapter's organization is modular, students and faculty can take from it what they need when they need it. Cumulatively, the short-takes tell a story about making the transition to college writing.

All of the book's heuristics are designed to deepen students' engagement with written texts. To clarify this fact, we have given our Writing about Reading chapter a new subtitle—"more moves to make with written texts."

Chapter 9, Analyzing Arguments has been rewritten and includes new sections on Rogerian argument and practical reasoning as well as figurative logic. The brief glossary of common logical errors has also been significantly expanded with many new examples. The book is aligned with the thinking of Carl Rogers and others on the goal of making argument less combative and more inclined toward negotiation among competing points of view and the evolution of new ideas from the pressure of one idea against another.

Chapter 14, Finding, Citing, and Integrating Sources, much of which was written by college reference librarian, Kelly Cannon, has been updated and revised and also features a much expanded treatment of the four documentation styles—APA, Chicago, CSE, and MLA.

ACKNOWLEDGMENTS

First and foremost, thanks to our students who testdrive and troubleshoot the book's writing advice. Thanks especially to our wonderful cadre of writing tutors who have developed workshops for students and faculty based on our book.

How fortunate we have been for the many years of support offered by our publishers. In particular, let us single out our developmental editor, Mary Beth Walden, for her sound advice, patience, and good cheer. Thanks too to Margaret Leslie, Leslie Taggart and to a host of others, past and present: Karl Yambert, Michael Rosenberg, Dickson Musslewhite (who persuaded us to take on this project initially), John Meyers, Michell Phifer, Karen R. Smith, Julie McBurney, Ellen Shraim, Kevin Loane, and Dan Silverberg (go Sox).

We are very grateful to our faculty colleagues at Muhlenberg who created workshops for our writing tutors on writing in their disciplines and then contributed expanded versions of these materials for the book: Keri Colabroy, Christopher Borick, Thomas Cragin, and Mark Sciutto. Boundless thanks as well to Kelly Cannon, reference librarian extraordinaire, for his expanded contributions on how to think and act like a researcher.

Writing Analytically with Readings owes much to two former students and five of our colleagues. Former students Sarah Kersh and Robbie Saenz de Viteri spent a summer gleaning cool readings to get us started. Kelly Cannon contributed all of the For Further Research sections, bringing his inimitable combination of skills as reference librarian, offbeat intellectual, and English PhD to the task. Jack Gambino and Jim Peck, admired colleagues and friends, generously agreed to let us include their work among our reading selections. For Chris Borick and Joe Elliott, who spent a semester producing pieces for us to include in key locations in the anthology, we reserve particular thanks. Thanks for taking the time to think with us and write for us, Chris; and thanks for those memorable Friday morning interviews, Joe, where you taught us how to look at photographs.

The cross-curricular dimension of this book would be sadly impoverished without the interest and support of an enviable range of colleagues who participate in the writing cohort at our college. They have shared with us examples of good student and professional writing in their fields, writing assignments from their writing-intensive classes, and examples of their own writing: Linda Bips, Pearl Rosenberg, Jefferson Pooley, Jeremy Teissere, Brian Mello, Christopher Borick, Marcia Morgan, Susan Clemens-Bruder, Amy Corbin, and William "Chip" Gruen. Special thanks goes to Ted Conner for being a new Voice from Across the Curriculum. We are also grateful to Katherine Kibblinger Gottschalk of Cornell University for permission to quote her unpublished 4 C's paper on the correspondence of E.B. White.

Thanks to Kate Christein, Assistant Director of the Writing Center, for keeping everything up and running while we were stuck in front of our computer screens producing this revision. And thanks also to our colleague Linda Bips, with whom we co-direct the Writing Program. We and it would be much less sane without her. Grace Gardella has looked out for us in the English department. And we are grateful for the support provided by the folks at Pistachios--Colleen Hauck, Sidney Stecher, and Eric Serrano.

Deep thanks are due to Eddie Singleton, Scott DeWitt, Wendy Hesford and their graduate students at the Ohio State University: our annual visits there have nourished our thinking about writing in countless ways. Christine Farris at Indiana University has been a friend of the book from its earliest days, and we cannot imagine sitting down to revise without the trenchant advice she offers us. Thanks too to her colleague, the unsinkable John Schilb and to Ted Leahey, teacher of teachers, who produced the instructor's manual for this book and its previous edition. And for the many conversations about teaching and writing that have sustained us we thank Richard Louth, Dean Ward, Kenny Marotta, Alec Marsh, Matthew Johnson, Matthew Hollrah, and Miles McCrimmon. We also thank Muhlenberg College for continuing to support our participation at national conferences.

A number of past and present students have also graciously allowed us to use their materials in this edition: Bob Tarby and Anna Whiston for their major contributions, along with Emily Petchler Herstoff, Michelle Bielko, Molly Harper, Melissa Bressler, Sean Heron,Lauren Artiles, Elissa Davidowitz, and Christa Carlstrand.

We are grateful to the many reviewers who took the time to offer their input on Writing Analytically with Readings:

Dan Albergotti, *Elon University*
Stephanie Almagno, *Piedmont College*
Joyce Anderson, *Millersville University*
Paul Aviles, *Onondaga Community College*
Dr. Diana Badur, *Black Hawk College*
Donna Bauerly, *Loras College*
Rebecca Baumann, *Indiana University*
Linda Bips, *Muhlenberg College*
Beau Black, *Weatherford College*
Margaret D. Bonesteel, *Syracuse University*

Margot Boyer, *North Seattle Community College*
Norman Boyer, *Saint Xavier University*
Melanie Brezniak, *Indiana University Bloomington*
Cheryl Brown, *Towson University*
Jessica Brown, *City College of San Francisco*
Robin Bryant, *Phillips Community College*
Patricia Burdette, *Ohio State-Mansfield*
Melissa Burley, *University of Miami*
Susan Callaway, *University of St. Thomas*
Alexandria Casey, *Graceland University*
Anita P. Chirco, *Keuka College*
Wayne Christensen, *Florida Memorial University*
J.C. Clapp, *North Seattle Community College*
Michelle *Collins-Sibley Mount Union College*
Innam Dajany, *North Country Community College*
Susan Davis, *Indiana University*
Kate Dobson, *McDaniel College*
Victoria Dowling, *University of Massachusetts*
Jayme Duncan Eveland, *Indiana University*
Dr. Chitralekha Duttagupta, *Arizona State University*
Sharyn Emery, *Indiana University*
Mary Ertel, *Medaille College*
Rebecca Fast, *The Ohio State University Mansfield*
Dr. Patricia Feito, *Barry University/ ACE*
Karen Feldman, *University of California, Berkeley*
Fran Ferrante, *University of San Francisco*
Judy Fowler, *Fayetteville State University*
Sue Frankson, *College of DuPage*
Erica Frisicaro, *University of St. Thomas*
Ryan Futrell, *Cedarville University*
Greta Gard, *Indiana University*
Margaret V. Gardineer, *Felician College*
Jill Gatlin, *University of Washington*
Mary A. Gervin, *Albany State University*
Sue Granger-Dickson, *Bakersfield College*
Sally Green, *University of Colorado at Boulder*
Jane Hammons, *University of California, Berkeley*
Corliss Harmer, *Antioch University*
Suzanne Harper, *Penn State Worthington*
Jennifer Hellwarth, *Allegheny College*
Scott Hermanson, *Dana College*
Margaret Hermes, *Indiana University*
Lisa Hermsen, *Rochester Institute of Technology*
Nels P. Highberg, *University of Hartford*

Mica Hilson, *Indiana University*
Matt Hollrah, *University of Central Oklahoma*
Catherine Imbriglio, *Brown University*
Susan Isaac, *Georgia Military College*
Dawnelle A. Jager, *Syracuse University*
Jacqueline Jenkins-Glymph, *Stanford University*
Rick Johnston, *Indiana University*
Gail Jones, *University of Texas at San Antonio*
Jason B. Jones, *Central Connecticut State University*
Justin A. Joyce, *University of Illinois at Chicago*
Erick Kelemen, *Columbia College*
Karalyn Kendall, *Indiana University, Bloomington*
Jessica Ketcham, *Louisiana State University*
Melissa Korber, *Las Positas College*
Anne Langendorfer, *The Ohio State University*
Kathy Lattimore, *SUNY Cortland*
Melissa Lingle-Martin, *Indiana University*
Debra Lohe, *Washington University in St. Louis*
Stephanie M. Loomis, *Boston College*
Michael Lueker, *Our Lady of the Lake University*
Sonja Lynch, *Wartburg College*
Renee Major, *Louisiana State University*
Ann Marshall, *Weatherford College*
David W. Marshall, *Indiana University-Bloomington*
Kim Martin, *Fort Lewis College*
David McAvoy, *Indiana University, Bloomington*
Laura McCracken, *North Seattle Community College*
Susanne Meslans, *Edmonds Community College*
Michael Moghtader, *James Madison University*
Deborah Montuori, *Shippensburg University*
Gwendolyn Morgan, *Montana State University*
Jane Mueller Ungari, *Robert Morris College*
Sean P. Murphy, *College of Lake County*
Debbie Olson, *Central Washington University*
Elizabeth Passmore, *University of Connecticut*
Velvet Pearson, *Long Beach City College*
Adrienne Peek, *Modesto Junior College*
Kate Pluta, *Bakersfield College*
Kelli Prejean, *Marshall University*
Donna Qualley, *Western Washington University*
Deborah Renville, *Kankakee Community College*
Celia Rasmussen, *Indiana University, Bloomington*
Kathleen Riley, *Ohio Dominican University*
Rochelle Rodrigo, *Mesa Community College*

Cheryl Ronish, *Lower Columbia College*
Margaret Rozga, *University of Wisconsin-Waukesha*
Paul Sanchez, *Fresno City College*
Heather Schell, *George Washington University*
Dr. Laine Scott, *LaGrange College*
Rachella Sinclair, *University of San Francisco*
Virginia Skinner-Linnenberg, *Nazareth College*
Harvey Solganick, *LeTourneau University*
Jean Sorensen, *Grayson County College*
Randolph Splitter, *De Anza College*
Melissa Storms, *North Seattle Community College*
Karen J. Strewler, *University of Wisconsin-Superior*
Liz Stringer, *East Mississippi Community College*
Nicole Tobin, *Indiana University*
Dorothy Turuta, *San Francisco State University*
Joseph Viera, *Nazareth College*
Robin Vogelzang, *Indiana University*
Courtney Weikle, *Ohio State University*
Stephanie Wells, *Orange Coast*
Laura Wilder, *SUNY Albany*
April Witt, *Indiana University*
Sarah Wolf Newlands, *Portland State University*
Monica Zewe, *Mercyhurst North East College.*

Finally, for their understanding: our spouses, Mark and Debby, our children, Lesley, Sarah, and Lizzie—and the dogs.

Part 1

THE RHETORIC

UNIT I

THE ANALYTICAL FRAME OF MIND: INTRODUCTION TO ANALYTICAL METHODS

Finding Your Way in This Book:
A Note to Readers

WRITING ANALYTICALLY'S CHAPTERS can stand alone and can be used in any order, but there are organizing principles that determine the sequence of chapters.

The book's overall method is **recursive**. In addition to moving to increasingly complex writing tasks, the book assumes you will keep using the tools from Unit I as habitual practices in the writing you are invited to do in later chapters.

- Unit I (Chapters 1–7), The Analytical Frame of Mind: Introduction to Analytical Methods, concentrates on ways of training yourself to be more observant and to push observations to implications and conclusions.

- Unit II (Chapters 8–14), Writing Analytical Papers: How to Use Evidence, Evolve Claims, and Converse with Sources, incorporates the essential methods of Unit I into strategies for writing various kinds of analytical papers, including papers that require you to synthesize secondary sources and orchestrate a conversation among them. Thesis and evidence are key terms of Unit II.

- Unit III (Chapters 15–19), Matters of Form: The Shapes That Thought Takes, addresses such topics as organization, disciplinary formats, introductions and conclusions, and grammar and style. The emphasis throughout is rhetorical, focusing on the relationship between forms and the thinking these forms enable.

The book provides a view of writing in different academic disciplines and how they vary in their expectations of student writing. Interspersed throughout the text are sections labeled Voices from Across the Curriculum—discussions of disciplinary practices solicited from our colleagues in a variety of disciplines. Although the book respects stylistic difference, we argue that there is an underlying purpose and thought structure that the disciplines share.

Chapter 1

Introduction: Fourteen Short Takes on Writing and the Writing Process

THIS IS A "HOW TO THINK ABOUT ..." and "Where to Look for ..." chapter, consisting of a sequence of short takes on topics that are especially helpful to understand at the beginning of a writing course. Although you will find more extended discussions of most of these topics later in the book, we think you will find it useful to have them assembled here in compact, browseable form. Learning to be a better writer is not just a matter of acquiring skills. To a significant extent it involves learning new ways of thinking about what writing is and what it does.

Because the organization of the chapter is modular, you can easily skip around in it to sample what it has to offer. There is, however, a logic to the order of the short takes, which is why the chapter is not arranged alphabetically. Typically, each short take triggers the next. Cumulatively, the short takes tell a story about making the transition to college writing. Some of the entries will be more pertinent for you now than others. Return to the chapter from time to time and browse for concepts and key terms you have come to need.

ORDER OF THE SHORT TAKES

- Thinking About Writing as a Tool of Thought
- Analysis: A Quick Definition
- What Do Faculty Want from Student Writing?
- Breaking Out of 5-Paragraph Form
- Writing Traditional Papers in the Digital Age
- What's Different About Writing Arguments in College?
- Rhetoric: What It Is and Why You Need It
- Writing about Reading: Beyond "Banking"
- Freewriting: How and Why to Do It
- Process and Product: Some Ways of Thinking About the Writing Process

- How to Think About Grammar and Style (Beyond Error-Catching)
- A Quick Word on Style Guides
- How to Think About Writing in the Disciplines
- Academic vs. Nonacademic Writing: How Different Are They?

THINKING ABOUT WRITING AS A TOOL OF THOUGHT

Learning to write well means more than learning to organize information in appropriate forms and construct clear and grammatically correct sentences. Learning to write well means learning ways of using writing in order to think well.

The achievement of good writing does, of course, require attention to form, but writing is not just a thing, a container for displaying already completed acts of thinking—it is also a mental activity. Through writing, we figure out what things mean, which is this book's definition of analysis.

The book will make you much more aware of your own acts of thinking and will show you how to experiment more deliberately with ways of having ideas—for example, by sampling kinds of informal and exploratory writing that will enhance your ability to learn.

As the next few chapters will show, the analytical process is surprisingly formulaic. It consists of a fairly limited set of basic moves. People who think well have these moves at their disposal, whether they are aware of using them or not. Analysis, the book argues, is a frame of mind, a set of habits for observing and making sense of the world.

ANALYSIS: A QUICK DEFINITION

Just about all of the reading and writing you will do in college is analytical. Such writing is concerned with accurate description and with thinking collaboratively (rather than combatively) with readers about ways of understanding what things might mean. The problem is that much of what we hear on television or read online seems to be primarily devoted to bludgeoning other people into submission with argumentative claims. The book's analytical methods provide a set of moves that derail more unproductive responses, such as agree/disagree, like/dislike, and other forms of gladiatorial opinion-swapping.

Chapter 2 offers the first set of methods, along with discussion of the counterproductive habits of mind they are designed to deflect. Chapter 3 defines analysis in detail (in what we call the five analytical moves) and shows you how it operates differently from other forms of thinking and writing. For now, we offer the following list on the goals of analysis and its identifying traits:

Analysis Defined

1. Analysis seeks to discover what something means. An analytical argument makes claims for how something might be best understood and in what context.
2. Analysis deliberately delays evaluation and judgment.

3. Analysis begins in and values uncertainty rather than starting from settled convictions.

4. Analytical arguments are usually pluralistic; they tend to try on more than one way of thinking about how something might be best understood.

WHAT DO FACULTY WANT FROM STUDENT WRITING?

Here is a list of faculty expectations based on what faculty across the curriculum say at our seminars on writing:

- Analysis rather than passive summary, personal reaction and opinions
- Analysis before argument, understanding in depth before taking a stand
- Alternatives to agree-disagree & like-dislike responses
- Tolerance of uncertainty
- Respect for complexity
- Ability to apply theories from reading, using them as lenses
- Acquiring and understanding the purpose of disciplinary conventions
- Ability to use secondary sources in ways other than plugging them in as "answers"

Overall, what faculty across the curriculum want is for students to learn to do things with course material beyond merely reporting it on the one hand, and just reacting to it with personal response on the other. This is the crux of the issue that *Writing Analytically* addresses: how to locate a middle ground between passive summary and personal response. We call that middle ground analysis.

To these expectations, we would add that the ability to cultivate interest and curiosity is a great desideratum of faculty across the curriculum. They want students to understand that interest need not precede writing; interest is more often a product of writing.

BREAKING OUT OF 5-PARAGRAPH FORM

The shift from high school to college writing is not just a difference in degree but a difference in kind. The changes it requires in matters of form and style are inevitably also changes in thinking. In order to make these changes in thinking, you may need to "unlearn" some practices you've previously been taught. At the top of the unlearning list for many entering college students is 5-paragraph form—the rigid, one-size-fits-all organizational scheme that is still taught in many high schools.

If you have come to rely on this form, giving it up can be anxiety-producing. This is especially so when you are asked to abandon an all-purpose form and replace it with a set of different forms for different situations. But it's essential to let go of this particular security blanket.

So, what's wrong with 5-paragraph form? Its rigid, arbitrary and mechanical organizational scheme values structure over just about everything else, especially in-depth thinking.

The formula's defenders say that essays need to be organized and that the simple three-part thesis and three-body paragraphs (one reason and/or example for each) and repetitive conclusion meets that need. They also say that 5-paragraph form is useful for helping writers to get started. The problem with treating 5-paragraph form as a relatively benign aid to clarity is that like any habit it is very hard to break.

Students who can't break the habit remain handicapped because 5-paragraph form runs counter to virtually all of the values and attitudes that they need in order to grow as writers and thinkers—such as respect for complexity, tolerance of uncertainty, and the willingness to test and complicate rather than just assert ideas.

The form actually discourages thinking by conditioning writers to be afraid of looking closely at evidence. If they look too closely, they might find something that doesn't fit, at which point the prefabricated organizational scheme falls apart. But it is precisely the something-that-doesn't-seem-to-fit, the thing writers call a "complication," that triggers good ideas.

Finally, what about the perception that students need to master 5-paragraph form in order to do well on SAT exams and other forms of standardized testing? Standardized tests in writing usually don't encourage writers to take the kinds of risks in both form and content that good writers must learn to take. But it is a myth that SAT evaluators reward 5-paragraph form. In fact, the two criteria that most often earn high scores from graders are length (yes, length) and vocabulary (Michael Winerip, "SAT Essay Test Rewards Length and Ignores Errors," the *New York Times*, May 4, 2005, On Education). Readers of writing-based college entrance exams give high marks not to writing that has a tidy structure but to writing that avoids clichés and overstated claims and that employs sentence and essay structures capable of accommodating complex ideas. (*See Chapter 10 for alternatives to 5-paragrah form that can accommodate complexity. See especially the Template for Using 10 on 1.*)

ON WRITING TRADITIONAL ESSAYS
IN THE DIGITAL AGE

You might be wondering why it is that colleges and universities continue to ask students to write traditional essays in an age when so much communication is dominated by the short and often multi-modal forms of the Internet. Does the arrival of the Internet with its blogs and web pages and YouTube clips mean that the traditional essay is rapidly becoming extinct? Why shouldn't college students spend their time learning to write exclusively in these new forms rather than learning to do a kind of writing they might not use after college?

There are several answers to these questions. First and most importantly, learning to write the traditional essay is the only way to develop the skills and habits of mind necessary for engaging in acts of sustained, in-depth reflection. Nor does it matter if you never write essays or lab reports or academic articles after college. It is not the presentation that matters—the forms of college writing—so much as what the forms allow you to do as a thinker.

In this chapter's short take on the writing process (*See Process and Product: Some Ways of Thinking About the Writing Process*), we point out that the form of a finished piece of writing does not disclose the process that would allow a writer to produce it. The necessarily concise lists of PowerPoints and of some kinds of writing on the Web don't just spring into being in that form. The careful compression in such forms is typically the product of writing as a tool of thought.

Finally, we are advising that traditional forms and formats are only a part of what you need to learn in order to grow as a writer and thinker. The first unit of this book, for example, although its assignments can lead to traditional essays, focuses primarily on ways of using writing in order to improve your ability to observe. This kind of writing—exploratory writing, writing to help you discover ideas—can fuel various formats, including multi-modal ones.

WHAT'S DIFFERENT ABOUT WRITING ARGUMENTS IN COLLEGE?

Insofar as you will be asked to write arguments in college, they will differ in significant ways from what you hear on crossfire-style talk shows and "news" programs. In made-for-TV arguments, people set out to defeat other people's positions and thus "win." Arguments in college are more *exploratory*—aimed at locating new ways of understanding something or at finding a tentative solution to a problem. Such arguments lead with analysis rather than position-taking. The claims you arrive at in an analysis are, in fact, arguments—analytical arguments.

Here are some of the differences between argument as it is too often conducted in the media and argument of the type cultivated by college writing:

- has more than two sides
- moves from much more carefully defined and smaller (less global) claims
- seeks out common ground between competing points of view rather than solely emphasizing difference
- uses potentially contradictory evidence to test and qualify claims rather than ignoring such evidence or housing it solely as concessions ("okay, I'll give you that point, but …") and refutations ("here is why you are wrong!")
- adopts a civil and nonadversarial **ethos** (self-presentation) and **rhetorical stance** (relationship with the audience) (*see Chapter 3*)
- avoids stating positions as though they were obviously and self-evidently true
- avoids cheap tricks such as straw man—misrepresenting or trivializing another's position so that it is easy to knock down and blow away—and name calling and other of the logical fallacies (*see Chapter 9*)
- includes much more evidence and careful analysis of that evidence

Targeting the Opinionated and the Argumentative We can cap this brief discussion of modes of argument in college by targeting two words that are sometimes misunderstood—**opinionated** and **argumentative**. These are not neutral terms. Saying that someone is opinionated is not the same as saying that he or she has opinions, nor is an argumentative person simply one who offers arguments. The opinionated person has too many opinions—a firmly held view on virtually everything, and the argumentative person is one for whom argument is a form of interpersonal warfare and for whom relationships tend to be competitive and adversarial. Both terms are associated with being close-minded and uncivil.

Although members of the academic world frequently disagree with each other and call attention to those disagreements, they do not lead with conflict and criticism. For knowledge to grow in the academic world, people have to continue to talk with each other and hear what each other has to say. *(See* Naturalizing Our Assumptions and "I Didn't Know You Wanted My Opinion" *in Chapter 2.)*

RHETORIC: WHAT IT IS AND WHY YOU NEED IT

Long before there were courses on writing, people studied a subject called rhetoric—as they still do. Rhetoric is a way of thinking about thinking. It offers ways of generating and evaluating arguments as well as ways of arranging them for maximum effect in particular situations. This book is a rhetoric in the sense that it offers methods for observing all manner of data and arriving at ideas. The division of rhetoric devoted to the generation of ideas is called "invention." *Writing Analytically* is an invention-oriented rhetoric.

In ancient Greece, where rhetoric was first developed as a systematic body of knowledge, emphasis was on public speaking. When Aristotle trained his students in rhetoric, he was preparing them to make arguments in the *agora*, the central assembly place in Athens where social, political, and religious issues of the day were decided. A person well-trained in rhetoric was adept at finding available arguments on the spot. Rhetorical training provided its practitioners with particular habits of mind.

Today, training in rhetoric continues to be especially helpful for all people who wish to enter public discourse and contribute to civil debate on key issues. In one of the best current textbooks on classical rhetoric, *Ancient Rhetorics for Contemporary Students* (Pearson/Longman 2004), authors Sharon Crowley and Debra Hawhee say about rhetoric that "its use allows people to make important choices without resorting to less palatable means of persuasion—coercion or violence" (2).

Unfortunately, the word "rhetoric" has suffered a serious decline in popular perception. To some people, rhetoric has come to mean something like empty, willfully deceitful, and sometimes just plain dishonest uses of language. People who think of rhetoric in this way will say things like "It was all just rhetoric," that is, all talk and no substance.

In order to make use of all that a rhetorical orientation toward writing and thinking can offer, you will first need to understand rhetoric as something other than a way of dressing up lies and making poor decisions sound respectable. We offer the following two ways of thinking about rhetoric—not just the rhetorics of the ancient Greeks, but the various kinds of rhetorics that have been invented since:

1. a rhetoric is a systematic body of techniques for coming to understand and find things to say about a subject (invention), and

2. rhetoric is also the term used to describe a speaker's or writer's way of using language to appeal to a particular audience.

It is from the second definition—rhetoric as a means of arranging language in order to persuade—that the negative definition of rhetoric has come. But finding a way of saying something so that others might hear and consider it does not necessarily mean that people skilled at rhetoric are puffed up tricksters.

The various academic disciplines you will study have rhetorics, which is a very helpful way to understand them. The struggles we all have with writing are to a significant extent rhetorical, because writers are concerned not just with what they want to say but with how to say it so as to be best understood by their target audiences.

It follows that stylistic decisions are always also rhetorical decisions. This is why writers cannot rely on a single set of style prescriptions for all occasions. Different styles have different rhetorical implications and effects. *(See the short take on Style Guides.)*

Two Key Terms

Here are two key terms from classical rhetoric that you will encounter in this book:

Heuristic: Although this word has other meanings in disciplines such as engineering, in classical rhetoric a heuristic was an aid to discovery. It comes from the Greek word *heuriskein*, which means "to find out" or "discover." *Heuriskein* is the Greek equivalent of the Latin word, *invenire,* which means "to find" or "to come upon" (Crowley 20). This book's analytical methods, such as the ones you will find in the two Toolkits (Chapters 2 and 4), are heuristics.

Commonplace: Rhetorical training provided rhetors—those who were skilled at public speaking—with pre-determined arguments called places that might fit any number of situations. The Greek word for "place"—*topoi*—gives us our word topic. Our word "commonplace" is descended from the way classical rhetoric treats commonplaces: as commonly held beliefs.

Here is a 20th-century definition of the term commonplace from an essay by David Bartholomae called "Inventing the University." Bartholomae argues that college writing—especially writing in the academic disciplines—requires students to learn not just forms and styles, but disciplinary commonplaces, the commonly held ways of thinking in the various academic communities that make up the university:

> A 'commonplace,' then, is a culturally or institutionally authorized concept or statement that carries with it its own necessary elaboration. We all use commonplaces to orient ourselves

in the world; they provide a point of reference and a set of 'prearticulated' explanations that are readily available to organize and interpret experience" (24).

This is a useful way of understanding what you are being asked to acquire in a college or graduate school education, the commonly held concepts that each discipline accepts as givens.

A rhetorical orientation is especially prominent in the following places in *Writing Analytically*:

- short take on Writing in the Disciplines in this chapter, which explains why you should think about disciplinary formats rhetorically
- Chapter 3, where analysis is defined rhetorically
- Chapters 15 and 16, where paper organization and types of introductory and concluding paragraphs are explained rhetorically
- Chapters 17 and 18, where word choice and sentence structure are treated rhetorically

WRITING ABOUT READING: BEYOND "BANKING"

Both the amount of reading and what you are expected to do with it will undergo significant upgrades in college. It is fairly common for those new to college writing to expect to write about reading in one of three ways: by handing it back on tests, by agreeing or disagreeing with it, or by registering a more elemental personal response, which is a common student misunderstanding triggered by the so-called "reaction paper." Much of the writing about reading you will be asked to do in college will move you beyond these three responses.

The Banking Model of Education—and Beyond

You will of course be responsible for retaining what you have read and "handing it back" on examinations. This is known as the **banking** model of education. The learner (in the banking model) is mostly a passive conduit taking things in and spitting them back out. Educational theorist Paolo Freire mounted a famous attack on this model, arguing that an education consisting entirely of "banking"—information in/information out—does not teach thinking. Being able to recite the ideas of others does not automatically render a person capable of thinking about these ideas or producing them.

Banking is not limited to quizzes and exams. It also occurs when teachers, through the best of intentions, do too much of the thinking for you. When there is discussion of the reading in class, for example, it often moves from a teacher's questions. If you write about the reading, this often takes place after the teacher has presented his or her explanations in lectures, maybe even with PowerPoints that foreground the teacher's selection of important points. In these ways, you are "protected" from the task of treating the reading as raw material, so to speak.

At some point, however, you have to figure out how to "process" complex course information for yourself. It is hard to learn to do a cartwheel solely by watching someone else do one. And the best way to learn is to write about the reading, not after the teacher has banked it for you but before.

Why write about reading? It will teach you how to do the things with readings that your teachers know how to do—how to find the questions rather than just the answers, how to make connections between one reading and another, how to bring together key passages from readings and put these into conversation with each other, and how to apply an idea or methodology in a reading to understanding something else.

Virtually all of the methods and procedures in this book can help you to write analytically about reading. See especially:

- Chapters 2 and 4, the two Toolkits of Analytical Methods, offer heuristics that are essential for analyzing reading
- Chapter 5, Writing About Reading: More Moves to Make with Written Texts, shows you how to use a reading as a lens
- Chapter 13, Using Sources Analytically: The Conversation Model, shows you how to put readings into conversation with each other and how to find your own voice in the conversation
- Chapter 7, Making Common Topics More Analytical, helps you with traditional assignments that involve writing about reading such as summary, comparison/contrast, and the so-called "reaction" paper

FREEWRITING: HOW AND WHY TO DO IT

Freewriting is a method of arriving at ideas by writing continuously about a subject for a limited period of time without pausing to edit or revise. The rationale behind this activity can be understood through a well-known remark by the novelist E.M. Forster (in regard to the "tyranny" of prearranging everything): "How do I know what I think until I see what I say?" Freewriting gives you the chance to see what you'll say.

Author Anne Lamott writes eloquently (in *Bird by Bird*) about the censors we all hear as nasty voices in our heads that keep us from writing. These are the internalized voices of past critics whose comments have become magnified to suggest that we will never get it right. Freewriting allows us to tune out these voices long enough to discover what we might think.

There aren't many rules to freewriting—just that you have to keep your pen (or fingers on the keyboard) moving. Don't reread as you go. Don't pause to correct things. Don't cross things out. Don't quit when you think you have run out of things to say. Just keep writing.

There are various forms of freewriting. For academic and other analytical projects, we recommend **passage-based focused freewriting**. In passage-based focused freewriting (*see Chapters 4 and 5*), class members embark from and attempt to stay grounded in some short passage or single sentence (usually their choice) from the day's reading. In this way, they learn to choose and develop starting points for discussion, rather than rely on a teacher's questions.

The practice of freewriting has long been advocated by writer, teacher, and writing theorist Peter Elbow who argues that poor writing occurs when writers try to draft and edit at the same time. There are sound psychological and cognitive reasons for trying not to get too bogged down in "fixing" things in the early drafting stages. First, it is hard to keep your larger purpose in sight if you constantly worry about making mistakes or being wrong. You need to keep moving, even when you know parts of what you have written are not yet good enough. Second, it is hard to discover where to go next if you keep looking back. Some people keep reading what they've just written, hoping to find the next move. But when you instead try to write fast—to forge ahead without looking back—you are more likely to discover a new leaping-off point, some connection to another and possibly better idea. Freewriting lets this process happen. Give it the chance to surprise you.

Here are some of the things that regular freewriting accomplishes:

- develops fluency
- deters writer's block
- encourages experimentation
- requires you to find your own starting points for writing and run with them
- provides a nurturing alternative to rigidly format-driven writing
- allows you to observe your characteristic ways of moving as a thinker, your habits of mind

Some Useful Techniques for Freewriting

Here are some analytical methods from later in the book that work especially well to generate freewrites:

- Paraphrase × 3, Notice and Focus, and So What? from Chapter 2
- Making the Implicit Explicit from Chapter 3
- Uncovering Assumptions, Reformulating Binaries, Seems to Be About X, and Difference within Similarity from Chapter 4
- 10 on 1 in Chapter 10

PROCESS AND PRODUCT: SOME WAYS OF THINKING ABOUT THE WRITING PROCESS

Process and **product** are the usual terms for thinking about the relation between exploratory writing (such as freewriting) and the more finished kinds of assignments to which it may lead. The **process** includes everything you needed to do in order to get to the finished draft, which is known as the **product**. In classical rhetoric, the terms are **invention** and **arrangement** *(See the short take on*

Rhetoric). In the invention stage, you follow prescribed methods for coming up with things to say, material which can then be arranged into the most effective form (presentation).

Writing is a recursive, not a linear process. Generation and presentation require different kinds of writing and thinking activities, though in practice these phases overlap. Writers do not simply finish a rough draft, then revise it, and then edit it in the tidy three-stage process commonly taught in school. They might, for example, make several different starts at the same writing task, then revise it, then learn from these revisions that they need to do more drafting, and so on.

Your goal is to generate enough material to locate your best options. Even in disciplines that do not encourage forms of exploratory writing (such as psychology and the natural sciences), because they concentrate instead on the forms of finished products, you can make use of your own informal writing, dwelling longer in the process, so as to learn how to arrive at more thoughtful products.

To a significant extent, the final draft re-creates for the reader the writer's experience of arriving at his or her key ideas. Good analytical writing, at whatever stage, has an exploratory feel. It shares its discovery process with the reader. This is true, by the way, even in such tightly predetermined forms as that of the scientific lab report. The report format actually requires the writer to recreate the steps that took him or her to conclusions.

Tips for Managing the Writing Process

Start anywhere that gets you going. The writing process is nonlinear. Very few writers simply begin at the beginning and write straight through to the end. Sometimes your best bet is to write individual paragraphs and then arrange them later.

Allow yourself to write a crummy first draft if that is how you work best. Get something on paper before worrying about what others might think of it. A writer's assumptions about his or her audience can help to generate writing but can also create writer's block. When you get stuck or frustrated, don't worry—just keep writing.

If you draft on a computer, try not to hit delete prematurely. Instead, rename each of your drafts. Hang on to false starts; they may help you later.

Postpone anxiety about grammar and spelling and style. You can revise and correct your draft once you have given yourself the opportunity to discover what you want to say.

Know that what works for one writer might not work for another. There is no one right way to conduct the writing process. Some writers need to outline; other writers need to write first and then might use outlining later to figure out what is going on in their drafts. Some writers absolutely must write an introduction before they can move forward. Others need to jump in elsewhere and write the introduction last. Experiment! Devote some time to finding out what works for you.

Put your unconscious on the job. You can't always write through an act of will. Sometimes, when the words aren't coming, it helps to go do something else—take a shower, go for a walk. Often you will find that a part of your brain has remained on the job. We call this resource in the writing process **the back-burner**—the place where things keep quietly stewing while you are thinking about something else. If you are really stuck, take some notes right before bedtime and write as soon as you wake in the morning.

HOW TO THINK ABOUT GRAMMAR AND STYLE (BEYOND ERROR-CATCHING)

A mantra of the book is that a sentence is the shape that thought takes. The goal of the book's treatment of grammar and style is to get you to refocus your attention from anxiety about error-detection to particular interest in the structures of sentences.

Many people are unduly anxious about grammar—so much so that they have trouble writing. Error-avoidance is important in the final stages of drafting, but it is also a very limited and limiting perspective on sentences. Instead, look at sentences in terms of logic and rhetoric. Ask yourself, "So what that the sentence is constructed in the way that it is? How does this shape relate to the way of thinking that the sentence contains?"

You need at least a minimal amount of grammatical terminology for understanding the shapes of sentences. Try to acquire this vocabulary as early in a writing course as you can. You need to be able to recognize and construct the following: **dependent clause, independent clause, simple sentence, compound sentence, complex sentence, compound-complex sentence, cumulative sentence, periodic sentence.** (*See Chapter 18.*)

Because punctuation makes sentence shapes visible, you should also know the basics of punctuation. In particular, learn the primary rules governing commas. (No, the fact that you pause is not a reliable indicator.) *See the short guide to punctuation early in Chapter 19.*

Once you orient yourself toward thinking about the shapes of sentences, you will be able to use sentences that clarify for readers the way you organize your ideas and place emphasis. You will maximize your choices and increase your persuasive power. When analyzing the sentences of others, this knowledge will give you insight into the writer's thinking: how the ideas are ranked and connected.

As for error-catching, you can revise and correct your draft once you've given yourself the opportunity to discover what you want to say. And, as we have been suggesting here, instead of dwelling on errors, try to cultivate an interest in the shapes of good sentences. *See "go-to" sentence in Chapter 2*, which will tell you how to use the grammar and style unit to start recognizing the connections between the characteristic shapes of a writer's sentences and the way he or she thinks.

A QUICK WORD ON STYLE GUIDES

Style guides are fine, provided they don't acquire the status of law, which is to say that you shouldn't take them as offering the last word. Some style guides have acquired almost cult status—Strunk and White's *Elements of Style*, for example. Among E.B.

White's letters, now collected at Cornell University, are many in which White is clearly responding with discomfort to letter writers appealing to him as the ultimate authority on style.

In one letter, he writes, "There are no rules of writing (who could possibly invent them?); there are only guidelines, and the guidelines can, and should be, chucked out the window whenever they get in your way or in your hair. I have never paid the slightest attention to 'The Elements of Style' when I was busy writing. [...] If the book inhibits you or constrains you, you should build a bonfire and throw the book into the flames" (qtd. in "The Phenomenon of the Little Book: Letters to E.B. White on *The Elements of Style*," an unpublished talk by Katherine K. Gottschalk, given at the 2010 Conference on College Composition and Communication, pp. 5–6).

In an entertaining article by Catherine Prendergast, we also learn that *Elements of Style* was found among other do-it-yourself manuals on the bookshelf of Theodore Kaczynski, the Unabomber ("The Fighting Style: Reading the Unabomber's Strunk and White," *College English,* Volume 72, Number 1, September 2009).

The problem with subscribing to one set of style "rules" is that this practice ignores rhetoric and context. There simply is no one set of rules that is appropriate for all occasions. In his essay, "Style and Good Style," philosophy professor Monroe Beardsley takes this point one step further. He writes: "Many charming, clever, and memorable things have been said about style—most of which turn out to be highly misleading when subjected to analysis"(4). Changes in style, says Beardsley, always produce changes in meaning: "If the teacher advises a change of words, or of word order, he is recommending a different meaning" (13).

Here is one of the examples Beardsley offers in his measured attack on the rules in Strunk and White's *Elements of Style*. Strunk and White, offering the common stylistic advice that writers should seek to replace forms of "to be" with active verbs, suggest that the sentence "There were a great number of dead leaves lying on the ground" should be replaced with "Dead leaves covered the ground." Of this suggested change, Beardsley observes, "But isn't that a difference in meaning? For one thing, there are more leaves in the second sentence. The second one says that the ground was covered; the first one only speaks of a great number. Stylistic advice is a rather odd sort of thing if it consists in telling students to pile up the leaves in their descriptions" (6).

Similarly, the usual advice that writers should avoid the "not-un" formation produces not just a change in style but a change in meaning. Saying "I am not unhappy" is not the same thing as saying "I am happy"—which is the kind of bolder, more decisive statement that *Elements of Style* recommends.

So, style guides are useful provided you recognize that style guidelines always carry with them an unstated preference for a certain kind of approach to the world—a certain kind of speaking persona, which may or may not be suited to what you wish to say. Richard Lanham's very useful "paramedic method," which we discuss in Chapter 18, puts a lot of emphasis on active verbs, the active voice, and on reducing "Latinate" diction. This emphasis produces a vigorous style but one that is not consistent, for example, with the stylistic conventions of science writing.

HOW TO THINK ABOUT WRITING IN THE DISCIPLINES

There will be days when you feel that each classroom you walk into is asking you to learn a different language. To some extent you're right. To navigate your way across the curriculum successfully, you will need to recognize that matters of form are also matters of epistemology, which is to say that they are indicative of each discipline's ways of knowing. Embedded in a discipline's ways of writing—its key terms and stylistic conventions—are its primary assumptions about thinking, how it should be done and toward what end.

No single book or course can equip you with all that you will need to write like a scientist or a psychologist or an art historian. What this book can do is teach you how to think about discipline-specific writing practices and how to analyze them for their logic and rhetoric. Once you acquire these skills, you will find it easier to adapt to the different kinds of writing you will encounter in college. You will also learn to see the common ways of thinking that underlie stylistic differences. For now, let's focus briefly on some interesting differences.

Here are three brief examples of significant stylistic differences. Think about what makes each difference more than simply superficial. Contemplate what these rules reveal about the particular discipline's values. And how do these rules implicitly define the relationship of the writer to his or her subject matter and assumed audience?

A. In psychology and some other social and natural sciences, writers paraphrase and cite other writers but do not include the language being paraphrased. In English, religion, and other disciplines in the humanities, writers also paraphrase, but they quote the language being paraphrased.

B. It is still largely true that in the sciences, particularly the natural sciences, writers use the passive rather than the active voice. So, the scientist would write: "The air was pumped out of the chamber" (passive voice, which leaves out the person performing the action, leading with the action instead) rather than "We pumped the air out of the chamber" (active voice, which includes the person performing the action).

C. In the sciences, writers typically do not criticize other scientists' work, although in the opening section of lab reports they survey other relevant studies and use these to explain the need for their current research. By contrast, writers in the humanities and some social sciences commonly build a piece of writing and research upon the discovery of a problem—that will be stated explicitly—in someone else's writing and research.

At the end of the chapter, we suggest that you interview a professor (perhaps from your major) to collect brief examples of what he or she considers good writing in his or her academic discipline. Some disciplines accept a wider variety of suitable forms and styles than others. There are lots of acceptable ways to write a history, English, or economics paper but only one way to write an acceptable lab report in biology. Your best bet is to study examples of what different disciplines think of as good writing, especially in disciplines where there is no rulebook for matters of form.

For the book's specific advice on writing in the disciplines plus discussion of common denominators, see the following:

- Chapters 15 and 16, the opening chapters of Unit III, entitled Matters of Form: The Shapes That Thought Takes
- Voices from Across the Curriculum (interspersed throughout the text), written by professors in various disciplines who offer their perspective on such matters as introductions and determining what counts as evidence

ACADEMIC VS. NONACADEMIC WRITING: HOW DIFFERENT ARE THEY?

We conclude this chapter with some final reflections on what it means to call writing "academic." Not all writing that has proved central to academic disciplines—such as works by philosophers, novelists, or world leaders—was written by academic writers. And not all writing by academics is meant only for other academics. This is especially the case when academics are engaged in problem solving outside the university—in public policy or government, for example—or when they write for popular audiences. Scientists, such as Steven Pinker and Simon Baron-Cohen, for example, publish in both scientific journals and in more popular publications.

Nonetheless, academic writers are typically cautious about trying to translate their work into forms suitable for consumption by nonacademics. This is not just in-group behavior but a product of the nature of academic research and writing.

Scientists, for example, typically focus on very small, narrowly defined questions, such as the function of a single receptor in the brain or a single kind of cellular reaction. Also, much scientific research goes on for a long time. Public radio recently interviewed a scientist who is involved in a 40-year-long study of a particular small mammal, looking for changes in size and breeding habits in response to such factors as global warming. In science in particular and in academic fields more generally, the results don't come quickly or easily and are often necessarily uncertain.

Translating these carefully contextualized, narrowly focused, and often long-term studies in a way that would make them interesting and available to a general audience is difficult. This is so not only because nonscientists have trouble with scientific language but because nonacademic readers often distort or overextend the science writing they take in.

The single biggest difference between academic and nonacademic writing is the size of the claims. General audiences often expect bigger and more definitive claims than carefully qualified academic writing is willing to make. The desire for overly authoritative claims and immediate answers that characterizes mainstream media produces an appropriate wariness among scientists and other academics.

In any case, learning to write in one or more of the academic disciplines will change the way you think. The analytical habits of mind you will have acquired inside of your chosen disciplines will grant you confidence and independence as a learner. They will cause you to see more in whatever you read, to arrive at more carefully limited claims about it, and to have more patience with yourself and others as thinkers.

Assignments

1. **Write a Literacy Narrative.** Write a short autobiographical piece that presents a chapter in your history as a writer. Describe what you now take to be an especially formative experience in how you came to be the writer you are today. What practices and ideas has this experience or set of related experiences led to? You might begin by freewriting a draft for 15 minutes in class. This narrative offers a good way to begin exploring your ways of thinking about writing and about yourself as a writer. The early lessons we take in about writing—sometimes accidentally—affect many of us more than we recognize.

2. **Collect Samples of Good Writing**. Begin collecting examples of good writing in a discipline of your choice from a professor of your choice. You might, for example, begin a collection of introductory and concluding paragraphs because these are critical sites in all writing and are especially useful in understanding the ways different disciplines frame and present information.

3. **Experiment with the Five-Finger Exercise.** The primary shift in thinking that the book promotes is from the general and global to the particular and local—to a focus on words and sentences and details, rather than on the large (general) picture. In order to introduce this re-orientation, we offer a writing activity taken from a famous fiction writer, Ernest Hemingway. He called it his "five-finger exercise," probably by analogy with the exercises that piano players do in order to make certain ways of moving their fingers more automatic.

   Read the passage below, wherein Hemingway (calling himself "Your Correspondent") offers advice to a young writer (referred to as "Mice") who has come to him for advice. Then start practicing Hemingway's recommended exercise of *tracing impressions back to the details that caused them.*

   Everything we have to say in the book relates in one way or another to Hemingway's advice, which is relevant to writing of all kinds, not just fiction. To become more aware—which is key to becoming a better writer—we have to train ourselves to notice more: both our impressions of things and how these are formed. Becoming more aware of our own responses is step one. Step two is tracing these impressions back to the particular details of experience that caused them.

   Mice: How can a writer train himself?

   Your Correspondent: Watch what happens today. If we get into a fish see exactly what it is that everyone does. If you get a kick out of it while he is jumping, remember back until you see exactly what the action was that gave you the emotion. Whether it was the rising of the line from the water and the way it tightened like a fiddle string until drops started from it, or the way he smashed and threw water when he jumped. Remember what the noises were and what was said. Find what gave you the emotion; what the action was that gave you the excitement. Then write it down, making it clear so the reader will see it too and have the same feeling you had. That's a five finger exercise.

Mice: All right. [....]

Your Correspondent: Listen now. When people talk, listen completely. Don't be thinking what you're going to say. Most people never listen. Nor do they observe. You should be able to go into a room and when you come out know everything that you saw there and not only that. If that room gave you any feeling, you should know exactly what it was that gave you that feeling. Try that for practice. When you're in town stand outside the theater and see how the people differ in the way they get out of taxis and motor cars. There are a thousand ways to practice. And always think of other people. (Ernest Hemingway, "Monologue to the Maestro: A High Seas Letter," *Esquire*: October 1935 rpt. in *ByLine*)

Start practicing by doing the exercise aloud with others. Write down the three details you think contributed most to your response to a particular setting, such as a classroom or other place on campus. Then share these with the class or in a small group. Next, use the exercise to produce a short piece of descriptive writing about some location of your choice or that the class might visit as a group. Take time to just observe the scene, register your responses to it and write down details. Then recast your writing into a descriptive paragraph. Keep revising your description until you have a rendering of your "data"—the details—that will cause your readers to think and feel about the scene as you do. Try to limit the number of evaluative adjectives you use—words like *ugly, beautiful, depressing,* and so on. Let the details do most of the work.

Chapter 2

Toolkit of Analytical Methods I: Seeing Better, Seeing More

"Reserving judgments is a matter of infinite hope." Fitzgerald, *The Great Gatsby*

"See better, Lear." Shakespeare, *King Lear*

FOCUS ON THE DETAILS

This chapter offers a set of tools for training your ways of seeing and making sense of things—the world, images, and especially written texts. Rhetoricians call these tools *heuristics*, from the Greek word for discovery. Heuristic has the same root as Eureka— "I've found it!" All of the heuristics in this chapter seek to help you to discover things to say about whatever you are studying. The final third of the chapter surveys the counterproductive habits of mind that these activities seek to replace.

NOTICING

- Noticing significant detail is a skill that can be improved through practice.
- The ability to notice is blocked by common habits of mind: judging and generalizing and leaping prematurely to conclusions.
- One solution: experiment with eliminating the words *like, dislike, agree,* and *disagree* from your vocabulary, at least for a while.
- Another solution: slow down. Dwell longer in the open-ended, exploratory, information-gathering stage.

A. The Heuristics

There are two broad categories of heuristics in this chapter—observation strategies and interpretive prompts. Both seek to retrain the way you focus your attention from the global (general) to the local. Here is a list of the chapter's heuristics, each with a very brief summary of what it involves. We will then go on to explain each in more detail.

HEURISTICS

1. Notice and Focus + Ranking
    (select a few details as most important: What do you find most "Interesting" or "Strange"?)

2. The Method: Looking for Patterns of Repetition and Contrast
    (organize details into groupings based on similarity or opposition)

3. Asking So What?
    (make the leap from observing X to querying what X means)

4. Paraphrase × (times) 3
    (recast the key words in new language to question what they mean)

5. Identifying a "Go To" Sentence
    (locate the sentence shape a writer habitually uses; then ponder how that shape reveals the writer's habitual ways of seeing)

Note: these heuristics are not formulae for organizing papers. They are "thinking moves" designed to produce higher quality material that will eventually go into an essay or argument or report. The heuristics lend themselves to group work, to collaborative thinking, as well as individual work. The best way to get good at these observation and thinking skills is to try them out repeatedly with other writers. In Unit II, you'll be invited to put them to work in writing papers and other kinds of assignments.

1. NOTICE AND FOCUS + RANKING

RULES OF NOTICE & HABITS OF MIND: SLOW DOWN

Not "What do you think?" &
Not "What do you like or dislike?"
                    but
          "What do you notice?"
A few prompts:
                    What do you find most INTERESTING?
                    What do you find most STRANGE?
                    What do you find most REVEALING?

The activity called Notice and Focus guides you to dwell longer with the data before feeling compelled to decide what the data mean. Repeatedly returning to the question, "What do you notice?" is one of the best ways to counteract the tendency to generalize too rapidly. "What do you notice?" redirects attention to the subject matter itself and delays the pressure to come up with answers.

Start by noticing as much as you can about whatever it is you are studying. Next, narrow your scope to a representative portion of your evidence, and then dwell with the data. Record what you see. Don't move to generalization, or worse, to judgment.

What this procedure will begin to demonstrate is how useful description is as a tool for arriving at ideas. If you stay at the description stage longer, deliberately delaying leaps to conclusions, you are more likely to arrive at better ideas. Training yourself to notice will improve your memory and your ability to think.

Step 1: Cast a wide net by continuing to **list details** you notice. Go longer than you normally would before stopping—often the tenth or eleventh detail is the one that will eventually lead to your best idea.

Step 2: Focus inside what you've noticed. **Rank** the various features of your subject you have noticed. Answer the question "What details (specific features of the subject matter) are most interesting (or significant or revealing or strange)?" The purpose of relying on *interesting* or one of the other suggested words is that these will help to deactivate the like/dislike switch of the judgment reflex and replace it with a more analytical perspective.

Step 3: Say why three things you selected struck you as the most interesting (or revealing or significant or strange). Saying why will trigger interpretive leaps to the possible meaning of whatever you find most interesting in your observations.

Discussion   Let's pause a moment to ponder the key words in step 2: interesting, revealing, strange. What does it mean to find something *interesting?* Often, we are interested by things that have captured our attention without our clearly knowing why. Interest and curiosity are near cousins. To say that something is interesting is not the end but the beginning of analysis: then you figure out what is interesting about this feature of your subject and why.

The word *strange* is a useful prompt because it gives us permission to notice oddities and things that initially seem not to fit. Strange, in this context, is not a judgmental term but one denoting features of a subject or situation that aren't readily explainable. Where you locate something strange, you have isolated something to interpret—to figure out what makes it strange and why.

Along similar lines, the words *revealing* and *significant* work by requiring you to make choices that can lead to interpretive leaps. If something strikes you as revealing or significant, even if you're not yet sure why, you will eventually begin producing some explanation. What is revealed, and why is it revealing?

Troubleshooting Notice and Focus

In the Noticing phase of Notice and Focus, you will be tempted to begin having ideas and making claims about your subject. Resist this temptation. Many of those first stabs at ideas will be overly general, fairly obvious, and they will block further noticing.

A Quick Note on 10 on 1

In later chapters (4 & 10), you will encounter a key heuristic that is the cousin of Notice and Focus. It is called "10 on 1"—based on the notion that it is productive to say more about less, to make ten points or observations about a single example rather than making the same overly general or obvious point about ten related examples. Like Notice and Focus, 10 on 1 depends on extended observation but it reduces scope to a single representative piece of evidence.

Try This 2.1: Doing Notice and Focus with a Room

Practice this activity as a class or in small groups with the room you're in. List a number of details about it, then rank the three most important ones. Use as a focusing question any of the four words suggested above—*interesting, significant, revealing,* or *strange.* Or come up with your own focus for the ranking, such as the three aspects of the room that seem most to affect the way you feel and behave in the space. Then you might go home and repeat the exercise alone in the room of your choice. Start out not with "what do I think?" but with "what do I notice?" And remember to keep the process going longer than might feel comfortable: "what else do I notice?"

Try This 2.2: Notice and Focus Fieldwork

Try this exercise with a range of subjects: an editorial, the front page of a newspaper, a website, a key paragraph from something you are reading, the style of a favorite writer, conversations overheard around campus, looking at people's shoes, political speeches, a photograph, a cartoon, and so forth. (The speech bank at americanrhetoric.com is an excellent source.) Remember to include all three steps: notice, rank, and say why.

---

2. THE METHOD: WORK WITH PATTERNS OF REPETITION AND CONTRAST

THE METHOD

What repeats?

What goes with what? (strands)

What is opposed to what? (binaries)

> (for all of these questions) ---> *SO WHAT?*

What doesn't fit? (anomalies) So what?

"The Method" is our shorthand for a systematic procedure for analyzing evidence by looking for patterns of repetition and contrast. It offers a way to get the big picture without overgeneralizing—it is insistently empirical. It also has an uncanny ability to help you figure out what is most important in anything you read.

Using The Method induces you to get physical with the data—literally, for you will find yourself circling, underlining, and listing. Although you will thus descend from the heights of abstraction to the realm of concrete detail, the point of tallying repetitions and strands and binaries and then selecting the most important and interesting ones is to trigger ideas. The discipline required to notice patterns in the language will produce more specific, more carefully grounded conclusions than you otherwise might have made.

Like Notice and Focus, The Method orients you toward significant detail; but whereas Notice and Focus is a deliberately unstructured activity, The Method applies a matrix or grid of observational moves to a subject.

Step 1: List exact **repetitions** and the number of each (words, details). For example, if forms of the word *seems* repeat three times, write "seems × 3." With images, the repeated appearance of high foreheads would constitute an exact repetition.

Concentrate on substantive (meaning-carrying) words. Only in rare cases will words like "and" or "the" merit attention as a significant repetition. At the most literal level, whatever repeats is what the thing is about.

Step 2: List repetitions of the same or similar kind of detail or word—which we call **strands** (for example, *polite, courteous, decorous*). Be able to explain the strand's connecting logic with a label: manners.

Step 3: List details or words that form or suggest **binary oppositions**—pairs of words or details that are opposites—and select from these the most important ones, which function as **organizing contrasts** (for example, *open/closed, ugly/beautiful, global/local*). Binaries help you locate what is at stake in the subject—the tensions and issues it is trying to resolve.

Step 4: Choose ONE repetition or strand or binary as most important or interesting and explain in one healthy paragraph why you think it's important. (This ranking, as in Notice and Focus, prompts an interpretive leap.)

Step 5: Locate **anomalies:** exceptions to the pattern, things that seem not to fit. Anomalies become evident only after you have discerned a pattern, so it is best to locate repetitions, strands, and organizing contrasts—things that fit together in some way—before looking for things that seem not to fit. Once you see an anomaly, you will often find that it is part of a strand you had not detected (and perhaps one side of a previously unseen binary).

Discussion The method of looking for patterns works through a series of steps. Hold yourself initially to doing the steps one at a time and in order. Later, you will be able to record your answers under each of the three steps simultaneously. Although the steps of The Method are discrete and modular, they are also consecutive. They proceed by a kind of narrative logic. Each step leads logically to the next, and then to various kinds of regrouping, which is actually rethinking.

Tip: Expect ideas to suggest themselves to you as you move through the steps of The Method. Strands often begin to suggest other strands that are in opposition to them. Words you first took to be parts of one strand may migrate to different strands. This process of noticing and then relocating words and details into different patterns is one aspect of doing The Method that can push your analysis to interpretation.

The Method can be applied to virtually anything you wish to analyze—an essay, a political campaign, a work of visual or verbal art, a dense passage from some secondary source you feel is important but can't quite figure out, and—last but not least—your own writing.

It may be helpful to think of this method of analysis as a form of mental doodling. Rather than worrying about what you are going to say, or about whether or not you understand, you instead get out a pencil and start tallying up what you see. Engaged in this process, you'll soon find yourself gaining entry to the logic of your subject matter. To some extent, doing The Method is archaeological. It digs into the language or the material details of whatever you are analyzing in order to unearth its thinking. This is most evident in the discovery of organizing contrasts.

Binary oppositions often indicate places where there is struggle among various points of view. And there is usually no single "right" answer about which of a number of binaries is *the* primary organizing contrast. One of the best ways to develop your analyses is to try on different possible oppositions as the primary one. A related technique is to repeatedly recast the key terms in the binaries. *(For more on this technique, see "reformulating binaries" in Chapter 4: Toolkit of Analytical Methods II.)*

Two Examples of The Method Generating Ideas

Try noticing repetitions and contrasts in your own writing. This will help you to recognize and develop your ideas. In the paragraph below, you can see how the writer's noticing strands and binaries directs his thinking.

> The most striking aspect of the spots is how different they are from typical fashion advertising. If you look at men's fashion magazines, for example, at the advertisements for the suits of Ralph Lauren or Valentino or Hugo Boss, they almost always consist of a beautiful man, with something interesting done to his hair, wearing a gorgeous outfit. At the most, the man may be gesturing discreetly, or smiling in the demure way that a man like that might smile after, say, telling the supermodel at the next table no thanks he has to catch an early-morning flight to Milan. But that's all. The beautiful face and the clothes tell the whole story. The Dockers ads, though, are almost exactly the opposite. There's no face. The camera is jumping around so much that it's tough to concentrate on the clothes. And instead of stark simplicity, the fashion image is overlaid with a constant, confusing patter. It's almost as if the Dockers ads weren't primarily concerned with clothes at all—and in fact that's exactly what Levi's intended. What the company had discovered,

in its research, was that baby-boomer men felt that the chief thing missing from their lives was male friendship. Caught between the demands of the families that many of them had started in the eighties and career considerations that had grown more onerous, they felt they had lost touch with other men. The purpose of the ads—the chatter, the lounging around, the quick cuts—was simply to conjure up a place where men could put on one-hundred-percent-cotton khakis and reconnect with one another. In the original advertising brief, that imaginary place was dubbed Dockers World.

—Malcolm Gladwell, "Listening to Khakis"

First, Gladwell notes the differences in two kinds of fashion ads aimed at men. There are the high fashion ads and the Dockers ads. In the first of these, the word "beautiful" repeats twice as part of a strand (including "gorgeous," "interesting," "supermodel," "demure"). The writer then poses traits of the Dockers ads as an opposing strand. Instead of beautiful face there is no face, instead of "gorgeous outfit," "it's tough to concentrate on the clothes." These oppositions cause the writer to make his interpretive leap, that the Dockers ads "weren't primarily concerned with clothes at all" and that this was intentional.

In the student essay below, Lesley Stephen develops a key contrast between two thinkers, Sigmund Freud and Michel Foucault, by noticing the different meanings that each attaches to some of the same key words. The Method helps to locate the key terms and to define them by seeing what other words they suggest (strands).

> Freud defines civilization as serving two main purposes. The first is to protect men against nature, and the second is to adjust their mutual relations. Freud seems to offer returning to nature as a possible solution for men's sexual freedom. I think Freud might believe that returning to nature by rejecting civilization could bring about sexual freedom, but that sexual freedom does not necessarily equal happiness.
>
> Foucault completely defies Freud's idea that sexuality is natural and that repression exists as anti-sexuality. He believes that everything is created from discourse; nothing is natural. And because nothing is natural, nothing is repressed. There is no such thing as a natural desire; if the desire exists, it is because it is already part of the discourse.

By focusing on repetitions of the words "nature" and "natural" and then seeing what goes with what, the writer creates a succinct and revealing comparison.

Doing The Method on a Poem

Here is an example of how one might do The Method on a piece of text—in this case, a student poem. We use a poem because it is compact and so allows us to illustrate efficiently how The Method works. See also the use of The Method on a visual image in Chapter 6, Making Interpretations Plausible.

Brooklyn Heights, 4:00 A.M.
Dana Ferrelli

sipping a warm forty oz.

Coors Light on a stoop in

Brooklyn Heights. I look

across the street, in the open window;

Blonde bobbing heads, the

smack of a jump rope, laughter

of my friends breaking

beer bottles. Putting out their

burning filters on the #5 of

a hopscotch court.

We reminisce of days when we were

Fat, pimple faced—

look how far we've come. But tomorrow

a little blonde girl will

pick up a Marlboro Light filter, just to play.

And I'll buy another forty, because

that's how I play now.

Reminiscing about how far I've come

Doing the Method on a Poem: Our Analysis

1. *Words that repeat exactly*: forty × 2, blonde × 2, how far we've (I've) come × 2, light × 2, reminisce, reminiscing × 2, filter, filters × 2, Brooklyn Heights × 2

2. *Strands*: jump rope, laughter, play, hopscotch (connecting logic: child-hood games representing the carefree worldview of childhood) Coors Light, Marlboro Light filters, beer bottles (connecting logic: drugs, adult "games," escapism?)

   Smack, burning, breaking (violent actions and powerful emotion: burning)

3. *Binary oppositions*: how far we've come/how far I've come (a move from plural to singular, from a sense of group identity to isolation, from group values to a more individual consideration)

   Blonde bobbing heads/little blonde girl

   Burning/putting out

Coors Light, Marlboro Lights/jump rope, hopscotch

How far I've come (two meanings of *far*?, one positive, one not)

Heights/stoop

Present/past

4. *Ranked repetitions, strands and binaries plus paragraph explaining the choice of one of these as central to understanding.*

Most important repetitions: forty, how far we've/I've come

Most important strands: jump rope, laughter, play, hopscotch, Coors Light, Marlboro Light filters, beer bottles

Most important binaries: jump rope, laugher, play, hopscotch versus Coors Light, Marlboro Light filters, beer bottles; burning/putting out

Analysis (Healthy Paragraphs) The repetition of *forty* (forty ounce beer) is interesting. It signals a certain weariness—perhaps with a kind of pun on forty to suggest middle age and thus the speaker's concern about moving toward being older in a way that seems stale and flat. The beer, after all, is warm—which is not the best state for a beer to be in, once opened, if it is to retain its taste and character. Forty ounces of beer might also suggest excess—"supersizing."

The most important (or at least most interesting) binary opposition is *burning versus putting out.* This binary seems to be part of a more intense strand in the poem, one that runs counter to the weary prospect of moving on toward a perhaps lonely ("how far *I've* come") middle-aged feeling. Burning goes with breaking and the smack of the jump rope, and even putting out (a strand), if we visualize putting out not just as fire extinguished but in terms of putting a cigarette out by pushing the burning end of it into something (the number 5 on the Hopscotch court). The poem's language has a violent and passionate edge to it, even though the violent words are not always in a violent context (for example, the smack of the jump rope).

This is a rather melancholy poem in which, perhaps, the speaker is mourning the passing, the "putting out" of the passion of youth ("burning"). In the poem's more obvious binary—the opposition of childhood games to more "adult" ones—the same melancholy plays itself out, making the poem's refrain-like repetition of "how far I've come" ring with unhappy irony. The little blonde girl is an image of the speaker's own past self (since the poem talks about reminiscing), and the speaker mourns that little girl's (her own) passing into a more uncertain and less carefree state. It is 4:00 A.M. in Brooklyn Heights—just about the end of night, the darkest point perhaps before the beginning of morning. But windows are open, suggesting possibility, so things are not all bad. The friends make noise together, break bottles together, revisit hopscotch square 5 together, and contemplate moving on.

Why Do The Method?

It does take some getting used to, working with The Method. It fragments everything; it can appear as if you are ignoring the usual cues by which you make sense of things, such as reading consecutively, from a to b to c, rather than looking for and tabulating all of the a's, all of the b's and so forth. And why read for pattern in the first place? Two answers are:

- The Method can help you to control in condensed form a wealth of information. The organizational grids will bring out the features of the subject that are most important, what the reading or image is most concerned with (which repeats), and what it is concerned or worried about (what is opposed to what).

- The Method can spur you to discover things to say about whatever you are analyzing. In the normal process of observing, and especially of reading, we are often not attending to what repeats or contrasts. We're just taking in the information—not *doing* anything with it. But when you do things with information, that promotes thinking; it makes you an active learner.

Try This 2.3: Experiment in a Group Setting with The Method—Use a Visual Image by Adrian Tomine

Often, it will seem strange at first to read or analyze in the somewhat mechanical form that The Method prescribes, so it makes sense to work collaboratively at first, in small groups or with everyone in the class, to collect the data. Appoint one group member as scribe. Keep each other on task—do each step discretely. As with Notice and Focus, prolong the observation phase and refrain from judgments and big claims, at least until you begin writing about what is important (step 4).

Try an image by Adrian Tomine—a frequent contributor to *The New Yorker* magazine and a graphic novelist. Just use Google Images for "New Yorker covers + Tomine" to obtain a range of possibilities. We suggest his August 24, 2009 cover, "Double Feature"—an image of a crowd at dusk beneath the Brooklyn Bridge. Then, for homework, repeat the exercise alone, using a second Tomine cover—we suggest the November 8, 2004 cover, "Missed Connection," featuring a man and a woman looking at each other from passing subway cars.

Try This 2.4: Apply The Method to Arts & Letters Daily

Select any article from our favorite website, Arts & Letters Daily (aldaily.com), and do The Method on it. You can actually apply The Method to anything you are reading, especially a piece you wish to understand better. You can use the front page of the newspaper, a speech from the American Rhetoric website, perhaps a series of editorials on the same subject, an essay, one or more poems by the same author (because The Method is useful for reading across texts for common denominators), and so on. You can work with as little as a few paragraphs or as much as an entire article or chapter or book. The key is to practice the procedure so that it becomes familiar: so that you will begin to look for repetitions and contrasts almost naturally.

3. ASKING "SO WHAT?"

PUSHING OBSERVATIONS TO CONCLUSIONS: ASKING SO WHAT?

(shorthand for)
What does the observation imply?
Why does this observation matter?
Where does this observation get us?
How can we begin to theorize the significance of the observation?

Asking So what? is a universal prompt for spurring the move from observation to implication and ultimately interpretation. Asking So what?—or its milder cousin, And so?—is a calling to account, a way of pressing yourself to confront that essential question, "Why does this matter?" It is thus a challenge to make meaning through a creative leap—to move beyond the patterns and emphases you've been observing in the data to tentative conclusions about what these observations suggest. In step 4 of The Method, when you select a single repetition, strand, or contrast and write about why it's important, you are essentially asking So what? and answering that question.

Step 1: describe significant evidence, paraphrasing key language and looking for interesting patterns of repetition and contrast.

Step 2: begin to query your own observations by making what is implicit explicit.

Step 3: push your observations and statements of implications to interpretive conclusions by again asking So what?

Discussion First, a note on implication—crucial to step 2, and a subject treated at length in the next chapter. For now, it is enough to know that implications are suggested meanings. We look at the evidence and draw a conclusion that is not directly stated but that follows from what we see.

For example, a recent article in *Foreign Policy* entitled "Bury the Graveyard" demonstrates that the reputation of Afghanistan as "the graveyard of empires" is a "bogus history," or myth. So what? The *implication*, unstated but palpable, is that the makers of U.S. foreign policy should seek out another version of the history of military intervention in Afghanistan—one that might put current military efforts there in a better light. When you ask So what? you are looking to make overt (direct, clear) what is at present indirect.

The tone of So what? can sound rude or at least brusque, but that directness can be liberating. Often, writers will go to great lengths to avoid stating what they take something to mean. After all, that leaves them open to attack, they fear, if they get it wrong. But asking So what? is a way of forcing yourself to take the plunge without too much hoopla. And when you are tempted to stop thinking too soon, asking So what? will press you onward.

For example, let's say you make a number of observations about the nature of e-mail communication—it's cheap, informal, often grammatically incorrect, full of abbreviations ("IMHO"), and ephemeral (impermanent). You rank these and decide that its ephemerality is most interesting. So what? Well, that's why so many people use it, you speculate, because it doesn't last. So what that its popularity follows from its ephemerality? Well, apparently we like being released from the hard-and-fast rules of formal communication; e-mail frees us. So what? Well, . . .

The repeated asking of this question causes people to push on from and pursue the implications of their first responses; it prompts people to reason in a chain, rather than settling prematurely for a single link, as the next example illustrates.

MOVING FORWARD

Observation --> So what? --> Implications

Implications --> So what? --> Conclusions

Asking So What?: An Example

The following is the opening paragraph of a talk given by a professor of Political Science at our college, Dr. Jack Gambino, on the occasion of a gallery opening featuring the work of two contemporary photographers of urban and industrial landscapes. We have located in brackets our annotations of his turns of thought, as these pivot on "strange" and "So what?" (Note: images referred to in the example are available from Google Images—type in Camilo Vergara Fern Street 1988, also Edward Burtynsky.)

> If you look closely at Camilo Vergara's photo of Fern Street, Camden, 1988, you'll notice a sign on the side of a dilapidated building:
>
> ### Danger: Men Working
> ### W. Hargrove Demolition
>
> Perhaps that warning captures the ominous atmosphere of these very different kinds of photographic documents by Camilo Vergara and Edward Burtynsky: "Danger: Men Working." Watch out—human beings are at work! But the work that is presented is not so much a building-up as it is a tearing-down—the work of demolition. *[strange: tearing down is unexpected; writer asks So what? and answers:]* Of course, demolition is often necessary in order to construct anew: old buildings are leveled for new projects, whether you are building a highway or bridge in an American city or a dam in the Chinese countryside. You might call modernity itself, as so many have, a process of creative destruction, a term used variously to describe modern art, capitalism, and technological innovation. The photographs in this exhibit, however, force us to pay attention to the "destructive" side of

this modern equation. *[strange: photos emphasize destruction and not creation; writer asks So what? and answers]* What both Burtynsky and Vergara do in their respective ways is to put up a warning sign—they question whether the reworking of our natural and social environment leads to a sustainable human future. And they wonder whether the process of creative destruction may not have spun recklessly out of control, producing places that are neither habitable nor sustainable. In fact, a common element connecting the two photographic versions is the near absence of people in the landscape. *[writer points to supporting feature of evidence, which he will further theorize]* While we see the evidence of the transforming power of human production on the physical and social environment, neither Vergara's urban ruins nor Burtynsky's industrial sites actually show us "men working." *[writer continues to move by noticing strange absence of people in photographs of sites where men work]* Isolated figures peer suspiciously out back doors or pick through the rubble, but they appear out of place. *[writer asks a final So what? and arrives at a conclusion:]* It is this sense of displacement—of human beings alienated from the environments they themselves have created—that provides the most haunting aspect of the work of these two photographers.

The Gambino paragraph is a good example of how asking So what? generates forward momentum for the analysis. Notice the pattern by which the paragraph moves: the observation of something strange, about which the writer asks and answers So what? several times until arriving at a final So what?—the point at which he decides what his observations ultimately mean. We call the final So what? in this chain of thinking **"the ultimate So what?"** because it moves from implications to the writer's culminating point.

Try This 2.5: Track the "So What?" Question

The aim of this exercise is to sensitize you to the various moves a writer makes when he or she presents and analyzes information. Locate any piece of analytical prose—an article from Arts & Letters Daily online, a passage from a textbook, a paper you or a friend has written. Focus on how it proceeds more than on what it says. That is, look for places where the writer moves from presenting evidence (step 1) to formulating that evidence into patterns of connection or contrast (step 2) and then asking So what? about it (step 3). Identify these moves in the margin as we have done inside brackets in the Gambino example.

4. PARAPHRASE × (TIMES) 3

PARAPHRASE × 3: HOW TO DO IT

Locate a short key passage.

Assume you <u>don't</u> understand it completely.

Substitute other concrete language for ALL of the key words.

Repeat the paraphrasing several (3) times.

Ponder the differences in implication among the versions. Return to the original passage and interpret its meanings: what do the words imply?

Paraphrasing is one of the simplest and most overlooked ways of discovering ideas and stimulating interpretation. Once you begin paraphrasing regularly, you will swiftly understand why: paraphrasing inevitably discloses that what is being paraphrased is more complicated than it first appeared. And so it will get you to start questioning what important passages and key details mean rather than assuming you understand them.

The word *paraphrase* means to put one phrase next to ("para") another phrase. When you recast a sentence or two—finding the best synonyms you can think of for the original language, translating it into a parallel statement—you are thinking about what the original words mean. (Paraphrasing stays much closer to the actual words than summarizing.) The use of "× 3" (times 3) in our label is a reminder to paraphrase key words more than once, not settling too soon for a best synonym.

Note: You should also be aware that different academic disciplines treat paraphrase somewhat differently. In the humanities, it is essential first to quote an important passage and then to paraphrase it. In the social sciences, however, especially in psychology, you paraphrase but never quote another's language.

Step 1: Select a short passage (as little as a single sentence or even a phrase) from whatever you are studying that you think is interesting, perhaps puzzling, and especially useful for understanding the material. Assume you *don't* understand it completely, even if you think you do.

Step 2: Find synonyms for all of the key terms. Don't just go for the gist, a loose approximation of what was said. Substitute language virtually word-for-word to produce a parallel version of the original statement.

Step 3: Repeat this entire rephrasing several times (we suggest three). This will produce a range of possible implications that the original passage may possess.

Step 4: Contemplate the various versions you have produced. Which seem most plausible as restatements of what the original piece intends to communicate? Where can you not determine which of two restatements might win out as most accurate?

Step 5: Return to the original passage and reflect: what do you now recognize about the passage on the basis of your repeated restatements? What does it appear to mean? What else might it mean?

Discussion Like the other heuristics in this chapter, Paraphrase × 3 seeks to locate you in the local, the particular, and the concrete rather than the global, the overly general and the abstract. Rather than make a broad claim about what a sentence or passage says, a paraphrase stays much closer to the actual words. Most students think of paraphrase in the context of avoiding plagiarism ("putting it in your own words") and demonstrating their understanding of assigned reading. In more advanced writing, paraphrase serves the purpose of producing the literature review—survey of relevant research—that forms the introduction to reports in the sciences. Paraphrase as an act of analytical translation, however, goes further.

Why is paraphrasing useful? When you paraphrase language, whether your own or language you encounter in your reading, you are not just defining terms but opening out the wide range of implications those words inevitably possess. When we read, it is easy to skip quickly over the words, assuming we know what they mean. Yet when people start talking about what particular words mean—the difference, for example, between *assertive* and *aggressive* or the meaning of ordinary words such as *polite* or *realistic* or *gentlemanly*—they usually find less agreement than expected.

Here's a theory that underlies paraphrase as an interpretive tool. What we see as reality is shaped by the words we use. What we say is inescapably a product of how we say it. This idea is known as the constitutive theory of language. It is opposed to the so-called "transparent" theory of language—that we can see through words to some meaning that exists beyond and is independent of them. The transparent theory of language, which assumes that the meanings of words are obvious and self-evident, is rejected by linguists and other language specialists. They know that to change a word is inevitably to change meaning. So, to make paraphrase work for you:

- don't assume you know the meanings of words you encounter
- assume instead that words may have more than one clear meaning, depending on context.

How Paraphrase × 3 Unlocks Implications: An Example

Like the "So what?" question, paraphrasing is an effective way of bringing out implications, meanings that are there in the original but not overt. And especially if you paraphrase the same passage repeatedly, you will discover which of the words are most "slippery"—elusive, hard to define simply and unambiguously.

Let's look at a brief example of Paraphrase × 3. The sentence comes from a book entitled *The Literature Workshop* by Sheridan Blau.

> "A conviction of certainty is one of the most certain signs of ignorance and may be the best operational definition of stupidity" (213).

1. Absence of doubt is a clear indication of cluelessness and is perhaps the top way of understanding the lack of intelligence.

2. A feeling of being right is one of the most reliable indexes of lack of knowledge and may show in action the meaning of mental incapacity.

3. Being confident that you are correct is a foolproof warning that you don't know what's going on, and this kind of confidence may be an embodiment of foolishness.

Having arrived at these three paraphrases, we can use them to explore what they suggest—i.e., their implications. Here is a short list. Once you start paraphrasing, you discover that there's a lot going on in this sentence.

- One implication of the sentence is that as people come to know more and more, they feel less confident about what they know.
- Another is that ignorance and stupidity are probably not the same thing though they are often equated.
- Another is that there's a difference between feeling certain about something and being aware of this certainty as a conviction.
- Another implication is that stupidity is hard to define—perhaps it can only be defined in practice, "operationally," and not as an abstract concept.

As we paraphrased, we were struck by the repetition of "certainty" in "certain," which led us to wonder about the tone of the passage. Tone may be understood as the implicit point of view, the unspoken attitude of the statement towards itself and its readers. The piece overtly attacks "a conviction of certainty" as "a sign of ignorance" and perhaps ("may be") "a definition of stupidity." So by implication, being less sure you are right would be a sign of wisdom. But the statement itself seems extremely sure of itself, brimming with confidence: it asserts "a certain sign."

One implication of this apparent contradiction is that we are meant to take the statement with a grain of salt; read it as poking fun at itself (ironically)—demonstrating the very attitude it advises us to avoid.

Try This 2.6: Experiment with Paraphrase × 3

Recast the substantive language of the following statements using Paraphrase × 3:

- "I am entitled to my opinion."
- "We hold these truths to be self-evident."
- "That's just common sense."

What do you come to understand about these remarks as a result of paraphrasing? Which words, for example, are most slippery (that is difficult to define and thus rephrase), and why?

It is interesting to note, by the way, that Thomas Jefferson originally wrote the words "sacred and undeniable" in his draft of the Declaration of Independence, instead of "self-evident." So what?

Try This 2.7: Paraphrase and Implication

Two recent books on Abraham Lincoln offer a fascinating conflict in their accounts of the president's death. Use paraphrase to discuss the difference between these two accounts.

a. "Now he belongs to the ages"—Edwin Stanton, Lincoln's Secretary of War, as Lincoln expired, according to Doris Kearns Goodwin in *Team of Rivals*.

versus

b. "Now he belongs to the angels"—Edwin Stanton, Lincoln's Secretary of War, as Lincoln expired, according to James L. Swanson in *Manhunt*.

You might also consider for a moment an assignment a student of ours, Sean Heron, gave to a class of high school students he was student-teaching during a unit on the Civil War. He asked students to paraphrase three times the following sentence: "The South left the country." His goal, he reported, was to get them to see that "because language is open to interpretation, and history is conveyed through language, history must also be open to interpretation." Use paraphrase × 3 to figure out how Sean's sentence slants history.

5. IDENTIFYING THE "GO TO" SENTENCE

Every writer has a "go to" sentence, a characteristic way of putting things. With a little practice, you can learn to spot writers' "go to" sentences. These can reveal a lot about how the writer thinks and the ways he or she approaches the world.

Once you've acquired some of the specialized vocabulary of grammar and style, you will be able to see the shapes of sentences more easily and to understand what those shapes tell you about both the writer and his or her point of view on the subject at hand. But you don't need a lot of specialized vocabulary to begin; this exercise is based on careful description. (To acquire the terms and concepts you need, see Chapter 18, The Rhetoric of the Sentence and The Glossary of Grammatical Terms at the end of Chapter 19.)

Step 1: Select a single characteristic sentence from your own writing or from a reading—a sentence shape that repeats frequently or at certain habitual spots (such as the beginnings or ends of paragraphs).

Step 2: Describe the structure of the sentence: its basic shape. Identify what you think are the sentence's most distinctive features.

Step 3: Decide how this particular sentence shape reveals tendencies of the way the writer thinks. Consider sentence structure, word order, kinds of words, etc.

Discussion All of us have "go to" sentences that we fall back on in daily life—in speaking as well as writing. It is illuminating (and fun) to try to become aware of these. Our choice of sentence shapes is influenced by how we tend to think, but the shape we go to also varies according to the subjects we are writing and talking about and the rhetorical situation in which we are doing so.

A sentence is the shape thought takes. That is a mantra already offered in the discussions of grammar and style in Chapter 1, and it bears repeating. The particular ways of ordering words that each of us habitually goes to are actually features of who we are; our "go to" sentences embody how we characteristically respond to the world.

Some Examples of "Go To" Sentences

For example, if a person's "go to" sentence takes the form "Not only x, but y," he or she is inclined to define things thoroughly by contrasting what something is with what it is not. A person who says "I am not unhappy" is a person who wishes to avoid blunt claims and prefers subtler descriptions of mental states. A person who is not unhappy differs from a person who is happy and willing to say so. Note, by the way, how little technical vocabulary you actually need to talk about the shape and effect of these sentences.

Here's another example: "Although x, the fact is that y,"

> Although the President raised the number of troops in
> Afghanistan, the fact is that he presented a timetable for
> complete troop withdrawal.

> Although the show Cupcake Wars on the Food Network
> decadently panders to pop culture, the fact is that I cannot watch
> it without wanting to bake cupcakes.

With this sentence type, some technical vocabulary would help. The sentence begins with what is known as a subordinate or dependent clause. Subordination usually indicates a desire to qualify (put limits on) one's claims. The use of the phrase "the fact is" in the second half of the sentence, the independent clause, indicates a less qualified and more certain way of thinking. This is an interesting tension between the two halves of the sentence and thus the two different ways of thinking they suggest.

Here's one more example, taken from a student's memoir, of how sentence shape matches subject matter:

> I wish I could tell you more about that night, but it's kind of blurry.
> What do I remember? My father's voice, "Mommy passed away."
> I know I cried, but for how long I don't remember. My boyfriend
> was there; he only heard my end of the conversation. He drove
> me home from college. I guess that took a couple of hours. There
> was a box of tissues on my lap, but I didn't use any. He smoked
> a cigarette at one point, and opened up a window. The black air
> rushed in and settled on me like a heavy cloak.

Notice how flat and largely unembellished these statements are: "He drove me home from college"; "He smoked a cigarette at one point, and opened the window." Here again it is useful if you have a little technical vocabulary, but you don't need much.

It will help if you know the difference between *coordinate* sentences, in which everything is treated at one level of importance, and *subordinate* sentences in which some things depend upon and are set up as less important than other things. This writer and her sentences are shell-shocked by an unexpected tragedy that renders everything that happens the same, basically meaningless. The passage contains virtually no subordination and instead a number of short declarative sentences.

Try This 2.8: Identify the Features of "Go To" Sentences

Below are examples of "go to" sentences contributed by colleagues at our institution, taken from their own professional writing. What features do you see as distinguishing the shapes of these sentences, and so what? That is, (1) describe the shape of each sentence, and (2) suggest what the shapes "say" about the kind of thinker each writer is, and why you think so.

a. Earlier steel studies compared work, family, and community in ethnically defined neighborhoods surrounding the mills—in the case of Bethlehem within the "shadow of the steel stacks—until the lure of suburbia disrupted working class living patterns, changed neighborhood ethnic composition, and dispersed extended families, thereby complicating the very nature and definition of a steel community." (Susan Clemens, Professor of History)

b1. But there is another burden which, although also strongly related to the external political and historical events of the time, is internal to the text itself.

b2. But it is evident that, after the arguments that Adorno presents against Kierkegaard have been examined, Adorno's claims have less to do with Kierkegaard than with a desire to read something else into and against Kierkegaard. (Marcia Morgan, Professor of Philosophy)

c1. BCM 441 is a course concerned with the content, presentation, and evaluation of modern biochemistry.

c2. It is through metabolism that stored nutrients, ingested foods, and the energy of light are converted to complex biomolecules and the energy to drive cellular processes.

c3. As part of the project, Joe and his lab partner performed a pull down assay to detect stable protein-protein interactions, a chemical cross linking assay to detect transient interactions, and then prepared target protein bands for analysis by mass spectrometry. (Keri Colabroy, Professor of Biochemistry)

Try This 2.9: Find One of Your Own "Go To" Sentences

Locate a sentence in something you have written. Reading for repetition will help you find a characteristic sentence shape. You might try looking for key connecting words, such as "and" or "but" or "however" or "because" or for characteristic ways that your sentences begin and end. Remember that you are not looking for bad examples or to criticize your own writing. You're looking to identify and understand the sentence shapes you rely on. This exercise is useful to do in small groups. When time allows, we like having students present their "go to" sentence and analysis to the class.

B. Counterproductive Habits of Mind

Analysis, we have been suggesting, is a frame of mind, a set of habits for observing and making sense of the world. There is also, it is fair to say, an anti-analytical frame of mind with its own set of habits. These shut down perception and arrest potential ideas at the cliché stage.

So far, you have been working through the solutions. For the rest of the chapter, we will spell out in more detail the problems. Here's a quick review of the solutions.

***

SOLUTIONS THE CHAPTER HAS OFFERED:

Slow down: describe what you are studying; give yourself more chances to see what you think.

Start your thinking with the local rather than the global; trace impressions back to causes; apply the heuristics

Recognize and reject the reflex move to generalization and judgment

Assume you don't completely understand what you are studying; look for questions rather than answers; invite rather than flee uncertainty

THE PROBLEM

leaps to

data (words, images, other detail) ---------> broad generalization

leaps to

data -----------> evaluative claims (like/dislike; agree/disagree)

* * *

REACTING IS NOT THINKING

A lot of what passes for thinking is merely reacting. Ask someone for a description of a place, a movie, a new CD, and see what you get: good/bad, loved it/hated it, couldn't relate to it, boring. Responses like these are habits, reflexes of the mind. And they are surprisingly tough habits to break. All of the tools in the toolkit seek to slow down unthinking (reflex) reactions.

We live in a culture of inattention and cliché. It is a world in which we are perpetually assaulted with mind-numbing claims (Arby's offers "a baked potato so good you'll never want anyone else's"), flip opinions ("The Republicans/Democrats are idiots") and easy answers ("Be yourself"; "Provide job training for the unemployed, and we can do away with homelessness"). We're awash in such stuff.

On this note, we turn to a closer examination of four of the most stubbornly counterproductive habits of mind: (1) premature leaps, (2) the judgment reflex, (3) generalizing, and (4) naturalizing assumptions (overpersonalizing).

1. PREMATURE LEAPS

In a way, the premature leap is the most fundamental bad habit. The others—reflex judgments, generalizing, and overpersonalizing—are all versions of leaping too quickly to conclusions.

A classic example of the premature leap is the one that inexperienced writers make to arrive at a thesis statement before they have observed enough and reflected enough to find one worth using. These writers end up clinging to the first idea that they think might serve as a thesis, with the result that they stop looking at anything in their evidence except what they want and expect to see. Typically, they find themselves proving the obvious—some too general and superficial idea. Worse, they miss opportunities for the better paper lurking in the more complicated evidence screened out by the desire to make the thesis "work."

You'll know you are becoming a more accomplished analytical writer when the meaning of your evidence starts to seem less rather than more clear to you, perhaps even strange—and you don't panic. Then you will begin to see details you hadn't seen before and a range of competing meanings where you had thought there was only one.

Make It Strange

Making it strange rather than trying to normalize what you see and read is a productive habit of mind. It opposes our more usual habit to quickly render things familiar by locating them in comfortable and habitual categories. One purpose of writing, as the writer David Lodge suggests, "is to overcome the deadening effects of habit by representing familiar things in unfamiliar ways." *Defamiliarization* is a term used by artists, philosophers and psychologists to talk about the need to fight against the deadening effects of habit. The man who coined the term defamiliarization, Victor Shklovsky, wrote, "Habitualization devours works, clothes, furniture, one's wife, and the fear of war. . . . And art exists that one may recover the sensation of life" (David Lodge, *The Art of Fiction*. New York: Penguin, 1992, p.53).

The following quotation from an article entitled "The Transition to College Reading" remarks on the need for defamiliarizing in its account of students' misunderstandings of readings:

> "I find that [students] are most inclined to substitute what they generally think a text should be saying for what it actually says [. . . .] They want to read every text as saying something extremely familiar that they might agree with".
> Robert Scholes, "The Transition to College Reading,"
> *Pedagogy*, volume 2, number 2, Duke UP, 2002, page165.

What is interesting here is the idea that people actually substitute something they already think, their habitual frames of reference, for what is actually on the page.

Get Comfortable with Uncertainty

To short-circuit premature leaps and see though the veil of familiarity, you'll need to find ways of becoming more comfortable with uncertainty. In fact, it's a healthy practice to assume you're missing something, always. Prepare to be surprised at how difficult this can be. Why? Most of us learn early in life to pretend that we understand things even when we don't. Rather than ask questions and risk looking foolish, we nod our heads. Soon, we even come to believe that we understand things when really we don't, or not nearly as well as we think we do.

The nineteenth-century American poet Emily Dickinson, writes about this problem in her poem that begins "Perception of an object/Costs precise the object's loss." The point of the Dickinson poem is a paradox: when we think we understand something, we in a sense cease to see it. Our idea of the thing has replaced the thing itself, producing a form of mental blindness—loss of the object.

By training yourself to be more comfortable with not knowing, you give yourself license to start working with your material, the data, *before* you try to decide what you think it means. Only then will you be able to *see the questions,* which are usually much more interesting than the temporary stopping points you have elected as answers.

2. THE JUDGMENT REFLEX

In its most primitive form—most automatic and least thoughtful—judging is like an on/off switch. When the switch gets thrown in one direction or the other—good/bad, right/wrong, positive/negative—the resulting judgment predetermines and overdirects any subsequent thinking we might do. Rather than thinking about what X is or how X operates, we lock ourselves prematurely into proving that we were right to think that X should be banned or supported.

It would be impossible to overstate the mind-numbing effect that the judgment reflex has on thinking. The psychologist Carl Rogers has written at length on the problem of the judgment reflex. He claims that our habitual tendency as humans—virtually a programmed response—is to evaluate everything and to do so very quickly.

Walking out of a movie, for example, most people will immediately voice their approval or disapproval, usually in either/or terms: I liked it *or* didn't like it; it was right/wrong, good/bad, interesting/boring. The other people in the conversation will then offer their own evaluation plus their judgment of the others' judgments: I think it was a good movie and you are wrong to think it was bad. And so on. Like the knee jerking in response to the physician's hammer, such reflex judgments are made without conscious thought (the source of the pejorative term "knee-jerk thinking").

This is not to say that all judging should be avoided. Obviously, we all need to make decisions: whether we should or shouldn't vote for a particular candidate, for instance. Analytical thinking does need to arrive at a point of view—which is a form of judgment—but analytical conclusions are usually not phrased in terms of like/dislike or good/bad. They disclose what a person has come to understand about X rather than how he or she rules on the worth of X.

Three Cures for the Judgment Reflex

- Neither agree nor disagree with another person's position until you can repeat that position in a way the other person would accept as fair and accurate. Carl Rogers recommends this strategy to negotiators in industry and government.
- Try eliminating the word "should" from your vocabulary for a while. Judgments often take the form of *should* statements.
- Try eliminating evaluative adjectives—those that offer judgments with no data. "Jagged" is a descriptive, concrete adjective. It offers something we can experience. "Beautiful" is an evaluative adjective. It offers only judgment. Sometimes the concrete-abstract divide is complicated. Consider for example the word "green," a literal color with figurative associations (envious, innocent, ecological, etc.).

Try This 2.10: Distinguishing Evaluative from Nonevaluative Words

The dividing line between judgmental and nonjudgmental words is often more difficult to discern in practice than you might assume. Categorize each of the terms in the following list as judgmental or nonjudgmental, and be prepared to explain your reasoning: monstrous, delicate, authoritative, strong, muscular, automatic, vibrant, tedious, pungent, unrealistic, flexible, tart, pleasing, clever, slow.

Try This 2.11: Experiment with Adjectives and Adverbs

Write a paragraph of description—on anything that comes to mind—without using any evaluative adjectives or adverbs. Alternatively, analyze and categorize the adjectives and adverbs in a piece of your own recent writing.

3. GENERALIZING

Vagueness and generality are major blocks to learning because, like the other habits of mind discussed so far, they allow you to dismiss virtually everything you've read and heard except the general idea you've arrived at: What it all boils down to is . . . What this adds up to is . . . The gist of her speech was . . .

Most of us tend to remember our global impressions and reactions. The dinner was dull. The house was beautiful. The music was exciting. But we forget the specific, concrete causes of these impressions (if we ever fully noticed them). As a result, we deprive ourselves of material to think with—the data that might allow us to reconsider our initial impressions or share them with others.

Often, the generalizations that come to mind are so broad that they tell us nothing. To say, for example, that the economy of a particular emerging nation is inefficient, accomplishes very little, since the generalization could fit almost any economy.

Take My Word for It?

Generalizing is not always a bad habit. We generalize from our experience because this is one way of arriving at ideas. Summary writing, which you will do a lot of in college, is a useful form of generalizing. Summarizing materials helps you to learn and to share information with others.

The problem comes when generalizations omit any supporting details. Consider for a moment what you are actually asking others to do when you offer them a generalization such as "The proposed changes in immigration policy are a disaster." Unless the recipient of this observation asks a question—such as "Why do you think so?"—he or she is being required to take your word for it: the changes are a disaster because you say so.

What happens instead if you offer a few details that caused you to think as you do? Clearly, you are on riskier ground. Your listener might think that the details you cite lead to different conclusions and a different reading of the data, but at least conversation has become possible.

Antidotes to Habitual Generalizing

- Trace your general impressions back to the details that caused them. This tracing of attitudes back to their concrete causes is one of the most basic and necessary moves in the analytical habit of mind. Train yourself to become more conscious about where your generalizations come from (see the Five-Finger Exercise at the end of Chapter 1).
- Think of the words you use as steps on an abstraction ladder, and consciously climb down the ladder from abstract to concrete. "Mammal," for example, is higher on the abstraction ladder than "cow." A concrete word appeals to the senses. Abstract words are not available to our senses of touch, sight, hearing, taste, and smell.

"Peace-keeping force" is an abstract phrase. It conjures up a concept, but in an abstract and general way. "Submarine" is concrete. We know what people are talking about when they say there is a plan to send submarines to a troubled area. We can't be so sure what is up when people start talking about peace-keeping forces.

Try This 2.12: Locating Words on the Abstraction Ladder

Find a word above (more abstract) and a word below (more concrete) for each of the following words: society, food, train, taxes, school, government, cooking oil, organism, story, magazine.

Try This 2.13: Distinguishing Abstract from Concrete Words

Make a list of the first 10 words that come to mind and then arrange them from most concrete to most abstract. Then repeat the exercise by choosing key words from a page of something you have written recently.

4. NATURALIZING OUR ASSUMPTIONS (OVERPERSONALIZING)

It is surprisingly difficult to break the habit of treating our points of view as self-evidently true—not just for us but for everyone. The overpersonalizer assumes that because he or she experienced or believes X, everyone else does, too.

What is "common sense" for one person and so not even in need of explaining can be quite uncommon and not so obviously sensible to someone else. More often than not, "common sense" is a phrase that really means "what seems obvious to me and therefore should be obvious to you." This way of thinking is called **"naturalizing our assumptions."** The word *naturalize* in this context means we are representing—and seeing—our own assumptions as natural, as simply the way things are *and ought to be*.

Writers who naturalize their own assumptions tend to make personal experiences and prejudices an *unquestioned* standard of value. A person who has a nightmarish experience in the emergency room may lead him to reject a plan for nationalized health care, but his writing needs to examine in detail the holes in the plan, not simply evoke the three hours waiting to get seen by a doctor.

Try This 2.14: Fieldwork: Looking for Naturalized Assumptions

Take a day to research just how pervasive a habit of mind naturalizing assumptions is in the world around you. Start listening to the things people say in everyday conversation. (Lunch lines are a choice site for a little surreptitious overhearing.) Or read some newspaper editorials with your morning coffee (a pretty disturbing way to start the day in most cases). Jot down examples of people naturalizing their assumptions.

"I Didn't Know You Wanted My Opinion"

We cannot leave the topic of naturalizing assumptions—assuming our way of seeing the world is the only way—without contemplating the key term at the heart of the subject: opinions. Over the years, those of us who teach have heard our students say a million times, "I didn't know you wanted my opinion."

This classic student/teacher miscommunication warrants some analysis. What, in this context, does the word "opinion" mean? You may have already done some thinking on opinions and people's attitude toward them in the paraphrase × 3 section of this toolkit. There we asked you to paraphrase the assertion "I am entitled to my opinion." Now let's pursue the implications (which is what analysis does) of the exclamation—or complaint—"I didn't know you wanted my opinion."

- Paraphrase #1: You should have told me sooner that it is okay for me to talk about my personal beliefs!
- Paraphrase #2: I am pleasantly surprised to find that you are interested in my feelings and experience.
- Paraphrase #3: I had not anticipated that you might expect me to say what I think.

Paraphrases 1 and 2 reveal a common but problematic definition of opinion as personal beliefs and feelings. This way of thinking leads to the implicit ground rule that when a teacher asks for personal opinion, students believe they do not need to provide evidence or reasoning. They're in a "free zone," which is why another ground rule seems to be that "opinion pieces" should be graded more leniently or not at all.

The problem with this way of understanding opinion is that it assumes our opinions are merely personal. In fact, our opinions are never just our opinions. They are deeply embedded in the conceptual fabric of a culture, and they are always learned.

As contemporary cultural theorists are fond of pointing out, the "I" is not a wholly autonomous free agent who writes from a unique point of view. Rather, the "I" is shaped by forces outside the self—social, cultural, educational, historical, and so on. Chronic naturalizers will not see the extent to which they are socially constructed, sites through which dominant cultural ways of understanding the world (ideologies) circulate. To put it perhaps too strongly, they're like actors who don't know they're actors, reciting various cultural scripts they don't realize are scripts.

What about the third paraphrase, "I had not anticipated that you might expect me to say what I think"? Paraphrase #3 reveals a person who recognizes that she is being asked to share her thinking, not just her views.

She is ready to think more about what opinion means. Is an opinion the same as an idea or theory? Are most ideas just opinions? How do I figure out what I think about things other than simply consulting my ready store of familiar views?

What do faculty *really* want when they make assignments to which students respond, "I didn't know you wanted my opinion?" Faculty at our college tell us they want two things:

(1) for students to do more than merely transmit information

(2) for students to do more than merely react and instead find thoughtful ways to engage the information and develop a stake in it.

Opinions: Are They Counterproductive Habits of Mind?

So: are opinions counterproductive habits of mind? Not necessarily. It would be naïve to say that each of us should get rid of our opinions in order to think well. This simply is not possible nor is it desirable. To see opinions only in the negative would be to diminish the important role that they play in the lives of individuals and of cultures. Rather than trying to suppress opinions, we need to take responsibility as thinkers for having opinions about things and for respecting the fact that other people have opinions too. It's a civic duty.

We should examine our opinions, not primarily to assert and defend them, but to explore them for what they might reveal about ourselves and the communities to which we belong. Opinions as kneejerk reactions—reflexes—cannot help us. But thoughtful examination of our opinions can.

Habits of Mind in Psychology: A Psychologist Speaks

In the following Voice from Across the Curriculum, clinician and psychology professor Mark Sciutto notes that the problematic habits of mind identified in this chapter are also recognized as problems in the discipline of psychology. In cognitive behavior therapy, these habits are called automatic thoughts.

Voices From Across the Curriculum

Readers should not conclude that the "Counterproductive Habits of Mind" presented in this chapter are confined to writing. Psychologists who study the way we process information have established important links between the way we think and the way we feel. Some psychologists such as Aaron Beck have identified common "errors in thinking" that parallel the habits of mind discussed in this chapter. Beck and others have shown that falling prey to habits of mind is associated with a variety of negative outcomes. For instance, a tendency to engage in either/or thinking, overgeneralization, and personalization has been linked to higher levels of anger, anxiety, and depression. Failure to attend to these errors in thinking chokes off reflection and analysis. As a result, the person becomes more likely to "react" rather than think, which may prolong and exacerbate the negative emotions.

—Mark Sciutto, Professor of Psychology

To familiarize yourself further with the thinking errors identified by cognitive therapy, one place to look is *Cognitive Therapy: Basics and Beyond* by Judith S. Beck (the daughter of Aaron) (NY: The Guilford Press, 1995). There Dr. Beck lists 12 of the most common "automatic thoughts" that she labels "mistakes in thinking." These include "Emotional reasoning," about which she writes,

> "You think something must be true because you 'feel' (actually believe) it so strongly, ignoring or discounting evidence to the contrary'" (119).

Opinions—A Democratic Disease? A Political Science Professor Speaks

As a final word for the chapter, we turn to our colleague, Jack Gambino, who offers the view of a social scientist that everything is not opinion, nor are all opinions equal in weight.

Voices From Across the Curriculum

Many students taking political science courses come with the assumption that in politics, one opinion is as good as another. (Tocqueville thought this to be a peculiarly democratic disease.) From this perspective, any position a political science professor may take on controversial issues is simply his or her opinion to be accepted or rejected by students according to their own beliefs/prejudices. The key task, therefore, is not so much substituting knowledge for opinions, but rather substituting well-constructed arguments for unexamined opinions.

What is an argument, and how might it be distinguished from opinions? Several things need to be stressed: (1) The thesis should be linked to evidence drawn from relevant sources: polling data, interviews, historical material, and so forth. (2) The thesis should make as explicit as possible its own ideological assumptions. (3) A thesis, in contrast to mere statement of opinion, is committed to making an argument, which means that it presupposes a willingness to engage with others. To the extent that writers operate on the assumption that everything is an opinion, they have no reason to construct arguments; they are locked into an opinion.

—Jack Gambino, Professor of Political Science

Assignments: Using the Toolkit

1. **Do The Method on a Reading**. Look for repetitions, strands, and binaries in the paragraphs below, the opening of an article entitled "The End of Solitude" by William Deresiewicz, which appeared in *The Chronicle of Higher Education* on January 30, 2009 and at http://chronicle.com/article/The-End-of-Solitude/3708. After selecting the repetition, strand, or organizing contrast you find most important, try writing several paragraphs about it.

What does the contemporary self want? The camera has created a culture of celebrity; the computer is creating a culture of connectivity. As the two technologies converge—broadband tipping the Web from text to image, social-networking sites spreading the mesh of interconnection ever wider—the two cultures betray a common impulse. Celebrity and connectivity are both ways of becoming known. This is what the contemporary self wants. It wants to be recognized, wants to be connected: It wants to be visible. If not to the millions, on Survivor or Oprah, then to the hundreds, on Twitter or Facebook. This is the quality that validates us, this is how we become real to ourselves—by being seen by others. The great contemporary terror is anonymity. If Lionel Trilling was right, if the property that grounded the self, in Romanticism, was sincerity, and in modernism it was authenticity, then in postmodernism it is visibility.

So we live exclusively in relation to others, and what disappears from our lives is solitude. Technology is taking away our privacy and our concentration, but it is also taking away our ability to be alone. Though I shouldn't say taking away. We are doing this to ourselves; we are discarding these riches as fast as we can. I was told by one of her older relatives that a teenager I know had sent 3,000 text messages one recent month. That's 100 a day, or about one every 10 waking minutes, morning, noon, and night, weekdays and weekends, class time, lunch time, homework time, and toothbrushing time. So on average, she's never alone for more than 10 minutes at once. Which means, she's never alone.

2. **Paraphrase a Complicated Passage**. Paraphrasing can help you to understand sophisticated material by uncovering the implications of the language. As a case in point, consider this passage from an article about *Life* magazine by Wendy Kozol entitled, "The Kind of People Who Make Good Americans: Nationalism and *Life*'s Family Ideal." Rather than simply skipping those passages that seem unclear, the savvy analytical writer could confront them head-on through paraphrase. Try Paraphrase $\times$ 3 with this passage, from page 186:

> Traditional depictions of the family present it as a voluntary site of intimacy and warmth, but it also functions as a site of consumption. At the same time capitalism lauds the work ethic and the family as spheres of morality safe from the materialism of the outside world. These contradictions produce a 'legitimation crisis' by which capitalist societies become ever more dependent for legitimacy on the very sociocultural motivations that capitalism undermines. (186; rpt in *Rhetorical Visions* by Wendy Hesford, pp. 177–200).

3. **Experiment with Notice and Focus and The Method**. Find a subject to analyze using Notice and Focus and then The Method. Your aim here initially is not to write a formal paper but to do data-gathering on the page. Notice as much as you can about it. Then organize your observations using The Method: What details repeat? What is opposed to what?

   After you have written the paragraph that is the final part of The Method, revise and expand your work into a short essay. Don't worry too much at this point about form (introductory paragraph, for example) or thesis. Just write at greater length about what you noticed and what you selected as most revealing or interesting or strange or significant, and why.

   You can do this writing with either print or nonprint materials. For some suggestions, see Try This 2.2 and 2.4. The Method could yield interesting results applied to the architecture on your campus, the student newspaper, campus clothing styles, or the latest news about the economy.

4. **Analyze an Image in Relation to Text**. The Adrian Tomine *New Yorker* covers that we referred to in Try This 2.3 could produce a good short paper. You could do The Method on the two covers in order to write a comparative paper. Or, you could do The Method on the Tomine cover called "Double Feature" and the two paragraphs from "The End of Solitude" above, and write about them comparatively. (Note: the entire article is available online.)

What do you think Tomine's cover says about the issues raised in "The End of Solitude" by William Deresiewicz? How might Tomine see the issues differently? And how might Deresiewicz interpret Tomine's cover, and so what?

Chapter 3

Analysis: What It Is and What It Does

NOW THAT YOU HAVE acquired an overview of the study of writing (Chapter 1) and an acquaintance with some essential tools for doing analysis (Chapter 2), it is time to focus in on the process of analysis itself—how a writer uses these tools to produce better, smarter, more interesting thinking on the page.

This chapter defines analysis as the search for meaningful pattern. It asks how something does what it does or why it is as it is. Analysis is a form of detective work that typically pursues something puzzling, something you seek to understand rather than something you believe you already know. Analysis finds questions where there seemed not to be any, and it makes connections that might not have been evident at first. Analysis is, then, more than just a set of skills: it is a frame of mind, an attitude toward experience.

A. Five Analytical Moves

At the heart of this chapter are what we call the Five Analytical Moves. These represent our attempt to present a template for the analytical frame of mind.

Move 1: Suspend judgment (understand before you judge).

Move 2: Define significant parts and how they are related.

Move 3: Look for patterns of repetition and contrast and for anomalies (aka The Method).

Move 4: Make the implicit explicit (convert to direct statement meanings that are only suggested—make details "speak").

Move 5: Keep reformulating questions and explanations (what other details seem significant? what else might they mean?).

We have seized upon analysis as the book's focus because it is the skill most commonly called for in college courses and beyond. When asked in faculty writing seminars to talk about what they want from student writing, faculty say that they want students to be able to arrive at ideas about information, rather than merely report it (neutral summary) or try to match information with personal experience. Control of information matters; engagement with the information also matters, but neither extreme is enough. Analysis occupies the middle ground between these two extremes.

What Faculty Seek in Student Writing

HAVING IDEAS
(doing something with the material)

versus

RELATING ←— —→ REPORTING
(personal experience   (information
matters, but . . .)   matters, but . . .)

Metacognition

The word *metacognition* means thinking about thinking. The first step in improving as a writer is to press yourself to become more aware of your own thinking, not just *what* you think—your "database" of customary convictions—but *how* you think. Interestingly, most of us don't pay much attention to how we think. It just happens. Or does it?

An obstacle in learning to think well is that we are accustomed to being rewarded for having answers. This was the view advanced by one of America's greatest metacognitive philosophers, John Dewey, in his book *How We Think* (1933, rev. ed.). Dewey:

- located the origin of thinking in uncertainty and doubt;
- worked to understand understanding—the meaning-making process; and
- defined thinking as "systematic reflection and inquiry."

In this context, let's now return to the five analytical moves in more detail. These will add to the repertoire of observation and interpretation strategies you learned in Chapter 2—enhancing your ability to engage in what Dewey calls "systematic reflection."

MOVE 1: SUSPEND JUDGMENT

The first of these five moves, *suspending judgment*, is really more a pre-condition than an actual activity. We include it as an analytical move, however, because suspending judgment takes an act of will, and we need then to consciously substitute other ways of thinking.

As we suggested in our critique of the Judgment Reflex in Chapter 2, the tendency to judge everything—to respond with likes and dislikes, with agreeing and disagreeing—shuts down our ability to see and to think. Just listen in on the next three conversations around you to be reminded of the pervasiveness of this phenomenon.

Consciously leading with the word interesting (as in "What I find most interesting about this is …") tends to deflect the judgment response into a more exploratory state of mind, one motivated by curiosity. As a general rule, you should seek to understand the subject you are analyzing before deciding how you feel about it. (*See the discussion of interesting, revealing, and strange under Notice and Focus in Chapter 2.*)

MOVE 2: DEFINE SIGNIFICANT PARTS AND HOW THEY'RE RELATED

Whether you are analyzing an awkward social situation, an economic problem, a painting, a substance in a chemistry lab, or your chances of succeeding in a job interview, the process of analysis is the same:

- Divide the subject into its defining parts, its main elements or ingredients.
- Consider how these parts are related, both to each other and to the subject as a whole.

One common denominator of all effective analytical writing is that it pays close attention to detail. We analyze because our global responses—to a play, for example, or to a speech or a social problem—are too general. Let's say you hear a local environmentalist give a public lecture on pollution. Afterward, you tell your friend, "I heard this great talk." This kind of generic response one could offer about almost anything. Such "one-size-fits-all" comments don't tell us much, except that you liked what you heard.

In order to say more, you'd need to become more analytical: you'd shift your attention to different elements of the talk and how they fit together. You might note that the talk began with a slide show of polluted creeks and that the speaker explained how different kinds of drain lines—sewer lines and storm water lines—are connected, so that when there are not enough water treatment plants in an area, a storm can cause the drains to overflow capacity and force officials to use "direct release," thus easing the pressure on the facility but fouling the creeks.

This move from generalization to analysis, from the larger subject to its key components, is characteristic of good thinking. To understand a subject, we need to get past our first, generic, evaluative response in order to discover what the subject is "made of," the particulars that contribute most strongly to the character of the whole.

The tendency of analysis to break things down into their component parts is sometimes thought of as destructive—as murdering to dissect (to paraphrase a famous poet). This point of view, however, fails to recognize that when people analyze, they break things down in order to see them more clearly and *construct* their understandings of the world they inhabit.

Some Everyday Examples   If you find yourself being followed by a large dog, your first response, other than breaking into a cold sweat, will be to analyze the situation. What does being followed by a large dog mean for me, here, now? Does it mean the dog is vicious and about to attack? Does it mean the dog is curious and wants to play?

Similarly, if you are losing a game of tennis or you've just left a job interview or you are looking at a painting of a woman with three noses, you will begin to analyze. How can I play differently to increase my chances of winning? Am I likely to get the job, and why (or why not)? Why did the artist give the woman three noses?

In the case of the large dog, you might notice that he's dragging a leash, has a ball in his mouth, and is wearing a bright red scarf. Having broken your larger subject into these defining parts, you would try to see the connection among them and determine what they mean, what they allow you to decide about the nature of the dog: apparently somebody's lost pet, playful, probably not hostile, unlikely to bite me.

Analysis of the painting of the woman with three noses, a subject more like the kind you might be asked to write about in a college course, would proceed in the same way. Your result—ideas about the nature of the painting—would be determined, as with the dog, not only by your noticing its various parts but also by your familiarity with the subject. If you knew very little about art history, scrutinizing the painting's parts would not tell you, for instance, that it is an example of the movement known as Cubism. Even without this context, however, you would still be able to draw some analytical conclusions—ideas about the meaning and nature of the subject. You might conclude, for example, that the artist is interested in perspective or in the way we see, as opposed to realistic depictions of the world.

Try This 3.1: Description as a Form of Analysis

Describe something you wish to better understand. Initially, don't interpret; just record significant detail. Say what is there, what details you notice in your subject. Then write a paragraph in which you say what the description revealed to you about the nature of your subject. You might describe, for example, a painting or a photograph, a current event as reported in a newspaper or another source, a conversation overheard, a local scene (such as the college bookstore or a place where students congregate), a math problem, or your favorite song off a new CD.

Description as a Form of Analysis: Some Academic Examples

The act of describing is just as important to analytical writing—in fact to all kinds of writing—as it is to the writing of poems or fiction. Browse, for example, a history book, an economics textbook, the newspaper, any collection of essays, including those on scientific subjects, and you will find description (and narrative as well, since the two so often go hand in hand). We simply cannot think well without it. Although academic disciplines vary in the ways they use description, all of them call for keeping thinking in touch with telling detail.

It is also essential to recognize that virtually all forms of description are implicitly analytical. When we select particular details and call attention to them by describing them, we are more likely to begin noticing what these details suggest about the character of the whole. Description presents details so that analysis can make them speak.

Here are three excerpts of student papers from different academic disciplines, followed by one evocative example from a professional writer.

The first example, from a draft of an undergraduate honors thesis in biology, shows how a writer uses Move 2—defining significant parts and how they are related—to analyze the relationship between two kinds of aquatic snails. The writer, Emily Petchler Herstoff seeks to understand why a type of snail, *Crepidula adunca*, attaches itself selectively to one kind of grazing snail, *Calliostoma ligatum*, and not to other, similar snails.

> Studying the effects of predation on host choice can shed insight onto the symbiotic relationship between *Calliostoma ligatum* and *Crepidula adunca*, and may illuminate why *Calliostoma ligatum* is the preferred host for *Crepidula adunca* in the San Juan Islands. My first experimental goal was to determine if *Crepidula adunca* confers any benefits to *Calliostoma ligatum* in the form of predator defense. As *Crepidula adunca* has already been proven to harm its host *Calliostoma ligatum* (Vermeij et al, 1987), it may be that *Crepidula adunca* is in a parasitic, rather than mutualistic relationship with its host. To determine if *Crepidula adunca* may be mutualistic, I performed predation tests to see if *C. adunca* conferred any advantages, in the form of defense, to its host *Calliostoma ligatum*. I performed a series of predator preference experiments to determine if predators more frequently consumed *Calliostoma ligatum* without *Crepidula adunca*.

Here is another example, a rhetorical analysis of a commencement address delivered by novelist David Foster Wallace at Kenyon College in 2005 (later published as "This Is Water"). Notice how the writer isolates parts of the speech, such as its apologies and denials, in order to arrive at claims about the rhetoric of the speech as a whole. *(See Chapter 1, the short take called Rhetoric: What It Is and Why You Need It.)* The writer begins by listing four quotations from the address.

> "I am not the wise old fish" (1).
> "Please don't worry that I am getting ready to lecture you about compassion" (2)
> "Please don't think that I am giving you moral advice" (5).
> "Please don't dismiss it as just some finger-wagging Dr. Laura sermon" (7)
> A recurrent feature of the address is the author's imploring his audience ("Please") not to assume that he is offering moral instruction. The sheer repetition of this pattern suggests that he is worried about sounding like a sermonizer, that the writer is anxious about the didacticism of his speech.
> But obviously the piece does advance a moral position; it does want us to think about something serious, which is part of its function as a commencement address. What's most interesting is

the final apology, offered just as the piece ends (7). Here Wallace appears to shift ground. Rather than denying that he's "the wise old fish" (1), he denies that he is Dr. Laura, or rather, he pleads not to be dismissed as a Dr. Laura. So he's saying, in effect, that we should not see him as a TV personality who scolds ("finger wagging") and offers moral lessons for daily life ("sermon").

Why is he so worried about the didactic function? Obviously, he is thinking of his audience, fearful of appearing to be superior, and fearful that his audience does not want to be preached at. But he cannot resist the didactic impulse the occasion bestows. In these terms, what is interesting is the divided nature of the address: on the one hand, full of parables—little stories with moral intent—and on the other hand, full of repeated denials of the very moral impulse his narratives and the occasion itself generically decree.

In our next example, Michelle Bielko, a history and English major, isolates details in the writing of 19th-century poet Walt Whitman to theorize his celebratory treatment of the Civil War.

Of interest is the fact that an analysis of Whitman's poems and journalistic works from the period suggest that for the artist the Civil War was in some way a continuation of the noble   . Revolutionary War, providing Americans with the opportunity to exhibit heroism in the likeness of the fathers of the nation. A close examination of the language Whitman used in his Civil War poetry anthology *Drum Taps* and in *Memoranda During the War* demonstrates that the poet consciously sought ways to cast President Lincoln as the George Washington of the Civil War, *both* northerners and southerners as the virtuous patriots of the Civil War, and to curiously leave the loathsome loyalist of the American Revolution without a corresponding double in his literary representation of the 1861–1865 conflict. In doing so, Whitman was ironically able to reinvent the so called "Secession War," which threatened to divide and destroy the United States, as a unifying conflict as worthy of celebration as the American War for Independence from Britain.

Two parallel features drive this writer's analysis of Whitman: that he treats both northerners and southerners as Civil War patriots and that he focuses only on patriots in the Revolutionary War, ignoring colonists who remained loyal to the crown.

We take our final example from a classic early text in Urban Studies, *The Death and Life of Great American Cities* (1961), by Jane Jacobs. Notice how she weaves a pattern of descriptive detail to build her implicit argument that sidewalks in cities are sites where people police themselves, providing safety not only for friends but for strangers.

When I get home after work, the ballet is reaching its crescendo. This is the time of roller skates and stilts and tricycles, and games in the lee of the stoop with bottle tops and plastic cowboys; this is the time of bundles and packages, zigzagging from the drugstore to the fruit stand and back over to the butcher's; this is the time when teenagers, all dressed up, are pausing to ask if their slips show or their collars look right; this is the time when beautiful girls get out of MG's; this is the time when the fire engines go through; this is the time when anybody you know around Hudson Street will go by.

As darkness thickens and Mr. Halpert moors the laundry cart to the cellar door again, the ballet goes on under lights, eddying back and forth but intensifying at the bright spotlight pools of Joe's sidewalk pizza dispensary, the bars, the delicatessen, the restaurant and the drug store. The night workers stop now at the delicatessen, to pick up salami and a container of milk. Things have settled down for the evening but the street and its ballet have not come to a stop.

I know the deep night ballet and its seasons best from waking long after midnight to tend a baby and, sitting in the dark, seeing the shadows and hearing the sounds of the sidewalk. Mostly it is a sound like infinitely pattering snatches of party conversation and, about three in the morning, singing, very good singing. Sometimes there is sharpness and anger or sad, sad weeping, or a flurry of search for a string of beads broken. One night a young man came roaring along, bellowing terrible language at two girls whom he had apparently picked up and who were disappointing him. Doors opened, a wary semicircle formed around him, not too close, until the police came. Out came the heads, two, along Hudson Street, offering opinion, "Drunk . . . Crazy . . . A wild kid from the suburbs."

Writing that is not markedly academic in style, such as these paragraphs from Jane Jacobs, often makes its way into academic discussions. Descriptive detail is as valuable in academic writing as it is in more popular forms.

MOVE 3: LOOK FOR PATTERNS OF REPETITION AND CONTRAST AND FOR ANOMALIES (AKA THE METHOD)

We have been defining analysis as the understanding of parts in relation to each other and to a whole. But how do you know which parts to attend to? What makes some details in the material you are studying more worthy of your attention than others?

The heuristic we call The Method offers a tool for uncovering significant patterns. In its most reduced form, The Method organizes observation and then prompts interpretation by asking the following sequence of questions. (*See Chapter 2, The Method.*)

THE METHOD

What repeats?

What goes with what? (strands)

What is opposed to what? (binaries)

(for all of these questions) ---> *SO WHAT?*

What doesn't fit? (anomalies) So what?

In virtually all subjects, repetition and close resemblance (strands) are signs of emphasis. In a symphony, for example, certain patterns of notes repeat throughout, announcing themselves as major themes. In Shakespeare's *King Lear*, references to seeing and eyes call attention to themselves through repetition, causing us to recognize that the play is *about* seeing. Binary oppositions, which often consist of two strands or repetitions in tension with each other, suggest what is at stake in a subject. We can understand *King Lear* by the way it opposes kinds of blindness to ways of seeing.

Along with looking for pattern, it is also fruitful to attend to anomalous details—those that seem not to fit the pattern. Anomalies help us to revise our assumptions. Picture a baseball player reading Dostoyevsky in the dugout: a TV commercial that did that to advertise a team was working through anomaly. In this case, the anomaly, a baseball player who reads serious literature, is used to subvert (question, unsettle) the stereotypical assumption that sports and intellectualism don't belong together.

People tend to avoid information that challenges (by not conforming to) views they already hold. Screening out anything that would ruffle the pattern they've begun to see, they ignore the evidence that might lead them to a better theory. Most advances in thought, for example, have arisen when someone has observed some phenomenon that does not fit with a prevailing theory.

Looking for Patterns: An Example

Examine the following excerpt from a draft of a paper about Ovid's *Metamorphoses*, a collection of short mythological tales dating from ancient Rome. We have included annotations in boldface to suggest how a writer's ideas evolve as she looks for pattern, contrast, and anomaly, constantly remaining open to reformulation.

The draft begins with two loosely connected observations: that males dominate females and that many characters in the stories lose the ability to speak and thus become submissive and dominated. In the excerpt, the writer begins to connect these two observations and speculate about what this connection means.

> 1. There are many other examples in Ovid's *Metamorphoses* that show the dominance of man over woman through speech control. In the Daphne and Apollo story, Daphne becomes a tree to escape Apollo, but her ability to speak is destroyed. Likewise, in the Syrinx and Pan story, Syrinx becomes a marsh reed, also a life form that cannot talk, although Pan can make it talk by playing it. *[The writer establishes a pattern of similar detail.]* Pygmalion and

Galatea is a story in which the male creates his rendition of the perfect female. The female does not speak once; she is completely silent. Also, Galatea is referred to as "she" and never given a real name. This lack of a name renders her identity more silent. *[Here the writer begins to link the contrasts of speech/silence with the absence/presence of identity.]*

2. Ocyrhoe is a female character who could tell the future but who was transformed into a mare so that she could not speak. One may explain this transformation by saying it was an attempt by the gods to keep the future unknown. *[Notice how the writer's thinking expands as she sustains her investigation of the overall pattern of men silencing women: here she tests her theory by adding another variable—prophecy.]* However, there is a male character, Tiresias, who is also a seer of the future and is allowed to speak of his foreknowledge, thereby becoming a famous figure. (Interestingly, Tiresias during his lifetime has experienced being both a male and a female.) *[Notice how the Ocyrhoe example has generated a contrast based on gender in the Tiresias example. The pairing of the two examples demonstrates that the ability to tell the future is not the sole cause of silencing because male characters who can do it are not silenced—though the writer pauses to note that Tiresias is not entirely male.]* Finally, in the story of Mercury and Herse, Herse's sister, Aglauros, tries to prevent Mercury from marrying Herse. Mercury turns her into a statue; the male directly silences the female's speech.

3. The woman silences the man in only two stories studied. *[Here the writer searches out an anomaly—women silencing men—that grows in the rest of the paragraph into an organizing contrast.]* In the first, "The Death of Orpheus," the women make use of "clamorous shouting, Phrygian flutes with curving horns, tambourines, the beating of breasts, and Bacchic howlings" (246) to drown out the male's songs, dominating his speech in terms of volume. In this way, the quality of power within speech is demonstrated: "for the first time, his words had no effect, and he failed to move them [the women] in any way by his voice" (247). Next the women kill him, thereby rendering him silent. However, the male soon regains his temporarily destroyed power of expression: "the lyre uttered a plaintive melody and the lifeless tongue made a piteous murmur" (247). Even after death Orpheus is able to communicate. The women were not able to destroy his power completely, yet they were able to severely reduce his power of speech and expression. *[The writer learns, among other things, that men are harder to silence; Orpheus's lyre continues to sing after his death.]*

4. The second story in which a woman silences a man is the story of Actaeon, in which the male sees Diana naked, and she transforms him into a stag so that he cannot speak of it: "he tried to say 'Alas!' but no words came" (79). This loss of speech leads to Actaeon's inability to inform his own hunting team of his true identity; his loss of speech leads ultimately to his death. *[This example reinforces the pattern that the writer had begun to notice in the Orpheus example.]*

These paragraphs exemplify a writer in the process of discovering a workable idea. They begin with a list of similar examples, briefly noted. Notice, as the examples accumulate, how the writer begins to make more connections and to formulate trial explanations. In turn, the emerging patterns help her to see more significant details.

MOVE 4: MAKE THE IMPLICIT EXPLICIT

This move and the one that follows it (Keep reformulating questions and explanations) are the ones that push observations toward conclusions (the "So what?" part of the process).

One of the central activities and goals of analysis is to make explicit—overtly stated—what is implicit (suggested). When we do so, we are addressing such questions as "What follows from this?" and "If this is true, what else is true?" The pursuit of such questions—drawing out implications—moves our thinking and our writing *forward*.

We have already introduced in Chapter 2 several of the tools that spur the quest for implication: Asking So What? and Paraphrase × 3. Both of these heuristics enable a writer to examine evidence and draw conclusions about it that are not literally present but that follow from what the writer sees.

The word *implication* comes from the Latin *implicare*, which means "to fold in." The word *explicit* is in opposition to the idea of implication. It means "folded out." An act of mind is required to take what is folded in and fold it out for all to see. Paraphrasing is an especially useful tool in uncovering implications precisely because restating things in other words widens the range of meanings (folds them out) that are embedded in (folded in) the language and details under scrutiny.

This process of drawing out implications is also known as making inferences. *Inference* and *implication* are related but not synonymous terms. The term *implication* describes something suggested by the material itself; implications reside in the matter you are studying. The term *inference* describes your thinking process. In short, you infer what the subject implies.

Implication: An Example   Now, let's move on to an example, which will suggest not only how the process of making the implicit explicit works, but also how often we do it in our everyday lives. Imagine you are driving down the highway and find yourself analyzing a billboard advertisement for a brand of beer. Such an analysis might begin with your noticing what the billboard photo contains, its various "parts"—six young, athletic, and scantily clad men and women drinking beer while pushing kayaks into a fast-running river. At this point, you have produced not an analysis but a summary—a description of what the photo contains. If, however, you go on to consider what the particulars of the photo imply, your summary would become analytical.

You might infer, for example, that the photo implies that beer is the beverage of fashionable, healthy, active people. Your analysis would lead you to convert to direct statement meanings that are suggested but not overtly stated, such as the advertisement's goal of attacking common stereotypes about its product (that only lazy, overweight men drink beer). By making the implicit explicit (inferring what the ad implies) you can better understand the nature of your subject.

Try This 3.2: Making Inferences

This activity is suitable for in-class writing or small group work or to a longer writing assignment. Locate any magazine ad you find interesting. Ask yourself, *"What is this a picture of?"* Use our hypothetical beer ad as a model for rendering the implicit explicit. Don't settle for just one answer. Keep answering the question in different ways, letting your answers grow in length as they identify and begin to interpret the significance of telling details. Ask the implication-question: If the picture gives us this, what else is it asking us to believe? Also make sure to ask, after you have done some analysis, the *rhetoric*-question: "Why did the advertiser choose this particular image or set of images?" This question will help you to think about how the ad has been fashioned for consumption by a particular audience. You might then examine a second advertisement for the same product. Is there a pattern in the way certain items are marketed?

Then shift gears a bit by considering the implications of significant detail in the cover of a high-end magazine such as *The New Yorker*. First, describe the cover using analytical moves 2 and 3; then consider what the moves imply. You can easily find these covers online either by visiting *The New Yorker*'s website or by going to the websites of particular artists who regularly produce *New Yorker* covers. You may have already experimented with a cover by Adrian Tomine in Chapter 2, Try This 2.3. You could look at more of his covers and read for patterns of subject matter and implication. You might also look at the covers of Harry Bliss—such as "Son of Kong," from August 1, 2005, cover #3632 at *The New Yorker* cover browser online.

Implications Versus Hidden Meanings

Two familiar phrases that reveal people's anxiety toward making the implicit explicit are *hidden meanings* and *reading between the lines*. Both phrases imply that meanings exist in places other than the literal words on the page: they are to be found either "under" or between the lines of text.

This is not a wholly unreasonable response because it recognizes that meanings are not always overt. But responding with these phrases does misrepresent the process of making inferences. It can also suggest some skeptical assumptions that a person may hold without fully realizing them. Let's spell some of these out.

For example, the charge that the meaning is hidden can imply for some people an act of conspiracy on the part of either an author, who chooses to deliberately obscure his or her meaning, or on the part of readers, who conspire to "find" things lurking below the surface that other readers don't know about and are unable to see. Another implicit assumption is that people probably know what they mean most of the time but, for some perverse reason, are unwilling to come out and say so.

"Reading between the lines" is a version of the hidden meaning theory in suggesting that we have to look for meanings elsewhere than in the lines of text themselves. At its most skeptical, the phrase "reading between the lines" means that an interpretation has come from nothing at all, from the white space between the lines and therefore has been imposed on the material by the interpreter.

Proponents of these views of analysis are, in effect, committing themselves to the position that everything in life means what it says and says what it means. It is probably safe to assume that most writers try to write what they mean and mean what they say. That is, they try to control the range of possible interpretations that their words could give rise to, but there is always more going on in a piece of writing (as in our everyday conversation) than can easily be pinned down and controlled. It is, in fact, an inherent property of language that it always means more than and thus other than it says.

The best evidence for the presence of implication in language itself (not under it or inserted into the white space) can be found by pondering statements that are rich in implication, for their unstated suggestions. We urge you take the time to work through Try This 3.3 below, an exercise demonstrating that implicit meanings are "really there."

Try This 3.3: Inferring Implications from Observations

Each of the statements below is rich in implication. Write a list of as many plausible implications as you can think of for each of the statements. After you have made your list of implications for each item, consider how you arrived at them. You might find it useful to do this exercise along with other people because part of its aim is to reveal the extent to which different people infer the same implications.

1. The sidewalk is disappearing as a feature of the American residential landscape. [Here are a couple of implications to prime the pump: people don't walk anywhere anymore; builders lack much sense of social responsibility.]

2. New house designs are tending increasingly toward open plans in which the kitchen is not separated from the rest of the house.

3. "Good fences make good neighbors."—Robert Frost

4. In the female brain, there are more connections between the right hemisphere (emotions, spatial reasoning) and the left hemisphere (verbal facility). In the male brain, these two hemispheres remain more separate.

5. In America, an increasing number of juveniles—people under the age of 18—are tried and convicted as adults, rather than as minors, resulting in more minors serving adult sentences for crimes they committed while still in their teens.

6. Neuroscientists tell us that the frontal cortex of the brain, the part responsible for judgment and especially for impulse control, is not fully developed in humans until roughly the age of 21. What are the implications of this observation relative to observation 5?

7. Linguists have long commented on the tendency of women's speech to use rising inflection at the end of statements as if the statements were questions. An actual command form—Be home by midnight!—thus becomes a question instead. What are we to make of the fact that in recent years, younger men (under 30) have begun to end declarative statements and command forms with rising inflections?

8. Shopping malls and grocery stores rarely have clocks.

9. List as many plausible implications as you can for this statement (which has been contested by other researchers).

> "In the eye-tracking test, only one in six subjects read Web pages linearly, sentence by sentence. In this study, Nielsen found that people took in hundreds of pages 'in a pattern that's very different from what you learned in school.' It looks like a capital letter F. At the top, users read all the way across, but as they proceed their descent quickens and horizontal sight contracts, with a slowdown around the middle of the page. Near the bottom, eyes move almost vertically, the lower-right corner of the page largely ignored."
>
> —Mark Bauerlein, "Online Literacy Is a Lesser Kind," *The Chronicle Review,* 9/19/08, http://chronicle.com/free/v55/i04/04b01001.htm.

(For an extended example of a writer who moves from implications, see "2:30," the commencement address by Bob Tarby, which is located after Move 5 on page 67.)

MOVE 5: KEEP REFORMULATING QUESTIONS AND EXPLANATIONS

Analysis, like all forms of writing, requires a lot of experimenting. Because the purpose of analytical writing is to figure something out, you shouldn't expect to know at the start of your writing process exactly where you are going, how all of your subject's parts fit together, and to what end. The key is to be patient and to know that there are procedures— in this case, questions—you can rely on to take you from uncertainty to understanding.

The following three groups of questions (organized according to the analytical moves they're derived from) are typical of what goes on in an analytical writer's head as he or she attempts to understand a subject. These questions will work with almost anything you want to think about. As you will see, the questions are geared toward helping you locate and try on explanations for the meaning of various patterns of details.

Which details seem significant? Why?

What does the detail mean?

What else might it mean?

(Moves: Define Significant Parts; Make the Implicit Explicit)

How do the details fit together? What do they have in common?

What does this pattern of details mean?

What else might this same pattern of details mean? How else could it be explained?

(Move: Look for Patterns)

What details don't seem to fit? How might they be connected with other details to form a different pattern?

What does this new pattern mean? How might it cause me to read the meaning of individual details differently?

(Moves: Look for Anomalies and Keep Asking Questions)

The process of posing and answering such questions—the analytical process—is one of trial and error. One of the main things you acquire in the study of an academic discipline is knowledge of the kinds of questions the discipline typically asks. For example, an economics professor and a sociology professor might observe the same phenomenon, such as a sharp decline in health benefits for the elderly, and analyze its causes and significance in different ways. The economist might consider how such benefits are financed and how changes in government policy and the country's population patterns might explain the declining supply of funds for the elderly. The sociologist might ask about attitudes toward the elderly and about the social structures that the elderly rely on for support.

Science as a Process of Argument: A Biologist Speaks

In the following Voice from Across the Curriculum, molecular biologist Bruce Wightman argues that, as in other disciplines, scientific ideas are constantly tested and reformulated. He is responding to the misconception that science is all about facts and thus does not require analysis and interpretation.

Voices from Across the Curriculum

I find it ironic that the discipline of science, which is so inherently analytical, is so difficult for students to think about analytically. Much of this comes from the prevailing view of society that science is somehow factual. Science students come to college to learn the facts. I think many find it comforting to think that everything they learn will be objective. None of the wishy-washy subjectivity that many perceive in other disciplines.

Anyone who has ever done science knows that nothing could be further from the truth. Just like other academics, scientists spend endless hours patiently arguing over evidence that seems obscure or irrelevant to laypeople. There is rarely an absolute consensus. Science is an endless process of argument, obtaining evidence, analyzing evidence, and reformulating arguments. To be sure, we all accept gravity as a "fact." But to Newton, gravity was an argument for which evidence needed to be produced, analyzed, and discussed. It's important to remember that a significant fraction of his intellectual contemporaries were not swayed by his argument. Equally important is that many good scientific ideas of today will eventually be significantly modified or shown to be wrong.

—Bruce Wightman, Professor of Biology

"2:30": An Example of the Five Analytical Moves in Action

Printed below is a commencement address given on May 27, 2010 at Harvard University to medical and dentistry students and their families and friends. Students in both programs take their courses together for the first two years and then pursue separate tracks in the final two years before coming together again at graduation. The speaker, Bob Tarby, was a biology and English major at our college before going on to Harvard. HSDM is the Harvard School of Dental Medicine.

Study how this speech develops as a piece of thinking from its initial observation that "dentistry is the butt of a lot of jokes." Concentrate on moves 4 and 5—making the implicit explicit and reformulating questions. Throughout the piece, you will also notice how the writer has set up his primary questions by employing moves 1–3. He suspends judgment to explore a question. He locates significant parts and finds patterns, both in people's responses to dentists and in the way people think and feel about teeth.

Mark specific sentences in which the speaker makes the implicit explicit. Also mark places where he pauses to formulate and to reformulate questions. We have included a few analytical observations in square brackets to help you shift your attention from what the speech says to what it does—how it operates and moves.

2:30
by Bob Tarby

[1] Distinguished guests, deans, faculty, staff, and of course classmates, friends, and families—welcome! Welcome to the 138th HSDM-HMS Class Day. To my classmates— my friends and now my colleagues—thank you for the privilege to represent our class today.

[2] I'm not the most doggedly determined dental student that's graced Harvard's hallways. Therefore, as my classmates would only expect, I would like to start with an old joke:

[3] What's the best time to go see the dentist? Tooth hurty.

[4] If you didn't get it, just give it a few seconds to sink in. If you still don't get it, I can explain it later, although I'm pretty sure it's not going to be funny. But maybe it's better that way, because to all the dentists in the room, dental jokes are *never* funny. Anyone who's seen Seinfeld remembers the episode where Jerry tells another dental wisecrack: what's the difference between a dentist and a sadist? – Newer magazines.

His dentist, Dr. Whatley, seeks his revenge in an unnecessarily prolonged and painful procedure that is peppered with question upon question requiring narrative answers... Why is it, by the way, that dentists never ask simple yes or no questions when they've got their hands in your mouth?

[5] I'm sorry that Jerry's procedure was painful... but what do you think dentist jokes are to Dr. Whatley, or to us, the thirty-something individuals with purple lapels walking across the stage in about 20 minutes? "What do you call a doctor that didn't get into medical school? A dentist!?" Ouch.

[6] I'm certainly not here today solely to tell dentist jokes. Instead, I want to pose a nuanced idea about the intersection of humor and dentistry. Over the past couple of weeks, I've been thinking seriously about what makes dentistry unique. As we often cite, dentistry is a subspecialty of medicine, and our first two years in the medical school have been invaluable to who we have become as professionals. We are not medical doctors but doctors of dental medicine, and there is an important difference. Two things set dentistry apart from all other medical specialties:

   1) dentistry deals (almost exclusively) with the oral cavity and maxillofacial region, and

   2) dentistry is the butt of a lot of jokes

[7] There are plenty of other doctor jokes—I think proctology and urology probably bear the brunt of these—but I'll refrain from discussing other specialties and other orifices. Why do we care so much about the mouth? *[= primary question essay will explore]*

[8] Dentistry is not a contemporary construct. Thousands of years ago, Incans placed shell implants, and Egyptians inlaid their teeth with precious metals. Even the institution has been important enough to differentiate its educational system— dental school is different than medical school. History aside, the mouth is the only orifice that smiles back at us in the mirror every morning, indicating the implicit importance of dentistry. A smile goes beyond simply anatomy; its esthetic quality communicates health, well-being, and even status. This makes the mouth and the face—the orofacial structures, in dental lingo—important.

[9] As student clinicians, my classmates and I saw evidence of this everyday in the dental clinic: our patients sit in the chair, fidget anxiously, and say, apologetically, "I just ate lunch" or "I didn't have a chance to brush" or "I *try* to floss regularly". They

are embarrassed to open their mouths in front of people who chose mouths and teeth as their professional undertaking. Judging by their reticence to "open up", we can safely assume that this is an intensely personal space: the mouth runs the gamut from function and survival to social hierarchy. Put differently, you can't eat without teeth, and you can't get a job at a Top 10 company without a flawless line of pearly whites. Or at least that's the conception.

[10] If teeth serve such important functions, where do all these dental jokes come from? Everything is Freudian, and jokes are no exception. Among other ideas on humor, Freud presents a theory that jokes are structured like an inverted triangle: a straight line at the top and two sides coming down to a point. At each of the three points is a character: the teller, the witness, and at the bottom, the "butt." I know I promised not to speak on behalf of the proctologists, so we'll keep this brief.

[11] Looking at the language of jokes, especially ones that involve a butt, we see that the butt gets "sent up" or "knocked down a peg". Up or down, there is social movement implicit in the work of a joke. According to Freud, a joke is serious and subversive—read another way, it works to elevate the teller and denigrate the butt.

[12] So I pose a question: why are we constantly denigrating dentists? It might be because they cause us pain, but more likely, it's because they have a bizarre and special permission to probe one of our most personal anatomic spaces. We let dentists put needles, crowns and dentures, not to mention their hands, into a space that serves the dual function of nourishing our bodies and expressing our social status.

[13] More than just a highly sensitive observer, though, the dentist takes ownership of another person's mouth. By extension, he or she has control over the oral functions that make the mouth such an important orifice: the ability to eat, the ability to communicate and to express, and, perhaps most important for our argument here, the dentist has control over the esthetics of the mouth, which dictate so much of how we understand each other, and how we understand ourselves. Imposing on the oral cavity in such a way gives the dentist a transgressive power over our mouths, and a strange ownership of a very intimate space. No wonder dentists make us anxious.

[14] *[qualifies claim:]* But there are doctors who do the same thing—cardiac surgeons, for example, invade and transgress, and probably most people would be more than a little

anxious about having open-heart surgery. It would not, however, be a joking matter—a heart is among the few organs that are crucial for the very basis of life. Teeth on the other hand – well, who wants to admit that teeth are important? Certainly not as important as a heart, right?

[15] So we are anxious about the dentist smelling our breath or discovering bits of food stuck between our teeth, about having a smile that indicates social order, and, to further complicate matters, we are anxious about admitting all this. *[= ultimate claim]* Because teeth shouldn't be *that* important.

[16] Out of this anxiety, dentist jokes are born. Comedy is often a vehicle for truth: dentist jokes indicate that our fear of the dentist—physical discomfort or pain, the power the dentist holds over an important part of our body—is real. And jokes are a way to ease that fear, to make dentistry accessible and, occasionally, even funny.

[17] So today, on our inaugural day as dentists, let's embrace the dentist joke! Teeth are important, and we like them! We're going out into the world to change smiles and lives. And we're going to make jokes when opportunities arise—not because what we do isn't serious, but because we can't and shouldn't take ourselves too seriously.

Try This 3.4: Apply the Five Analytical Moves to a Speech

Speeches provide rich examples for analysis, and they are easily accessible on the Internet and on You Tube. We especially recommend a site called American Rhetoric (You can Google it for the URL). Choose any speech and analyze it for its use of the five analytical moves. Where, for example, does the speech locate pattern? How does it define significant parts and locate them in relation to the whole? Where does the speaker make inferences? To what extent does it reformulate its questions and explanations?

On the basis of your results, draw a few conclusions about the speech's point of view and its way of presenting that point of view, which is to say its rhetoric. Try to get beyond the obvious and the general. What does applying the moves cause you to notice that you might not have noticed before?

WHAT IT MEANS TO HAVE AN IDEA

In the final sections of this chapter, we will go on to distinguish analysis from other forms of writing: argument, summary, and personal response. We conclude this opening section of the chapter, on the Five Analytical Moves, with discussion of what counts as an idea in analytical writing.

Thinking, as opposed to reporting or reacting, should lead you to ideas. But what does it mean to have an idea? It's one thing to acquire knowledge, but you also need to learn how to produce knowledge, to think for yourself. The problem is that people get daunted when asked to arrive at ideas. They dream up ingenious ways to avoid the task. Or they get paralyzed with anxiety.

What is an idea? Must an idea be something entirely "original"? Must it revamp the way you understand yourself or your stance toward the world?

Such expectations are unreasonably grand. Clearly, a writer in the early stages of learning about a subject can't be expected to arrive at an idea so original that, like a Ph.D. thesis, it revises complex concepts in a discipline. Nor should you count as ideas only those that lead to some kind of life-altering discovery. Ideas are usually much smaller in scope, much less grand, than people seem to expect.

Some would argue that ideas are discipline-specific, that what counts as an idea in Psychology differs from what counts as an idea in History or Philosophy or Business. Surely the context does affect the way ideas are shaped and expressed. This book operates on the premise, however, that ideas across the curriculum share common elements. All of the items in the list below, for example, are common to ideas and to idea-making in virtually any context.

It is easiest to understand what ideas are by considering what ideas do and where they can be found. Most strong analytical ideas launch you in a process of resolving problems and bringing competing positions into some kind of alignment. They locate you where there is something to negotiate, where you are required not just to list answers but also to ask questions, make choices, and engage in reasoning about the significance of your evidence.

Here is a partial list of what it means to have an idea:

1. An idea usually starts with an observation that is puzzling, with something you want to figure out rather than something you think you already understand.

2. An idea may be the discovery of a question where there seemed not to be one.

3. An idea answers a question; it explains something that needs to be explained or provides a way out of a difficulty that other people have had in understanding something.

4. An idea may make explicit and explore the meaning of something implicit—an unstated assumption upon which an argument rests, or a logical consequence of a given position.

5. An idea may connect elements of a subject and explain the significance of that connection.

6. An idea often accounts for some *dissonance*, that is, something that seems to not fit together.

B. Distinguishing Analysis from Argument, Summary, and Expressive Writing

How does analysis differ from other kinds of thinking and writing? A common way of answering this question is to think of communication as having three possible centers of emphasis—the writer, the subject, and the audience. Communication, of course, involves all three of these components, but some kinds of writing concentrate more on one than on the others. Autobiographical writing, for example, such as diaries or memoirs or stories about personal experience, centers on the writer and his or her desire for self-expression. Argument, in which the writer takes a stand on an issue, advocating or arguing against a policy or attitude, is reader-centered; its goal is to bring about a change in its readers' actions and beliefs. Analytical writing is more concerned with arriving at an understanding of a subject than with either self-expression or changing readers' views.

These three categories of writing are not mutually exclusive. So, for example, expressive (writer-centered) writing is also analytical in its attempts to define and explain a writer's feelings, reactions, and experiences. And analysis is a form of self-expression since it inevitably reflects the ways a writer's experiences have taught him or her to think about the world. But even though expressive writing and analysis necessarily overlap, they also differ significantly in both method and aim. In expressive writing, your primary subject is your self, with other subjects serving as a means of evoking greater self-understanding. In analytical writing, your reasoning may derive from your personal experience, but it is your reasoning and not you or your experiences that matter. Analysis asks not just "what do I think?" but "how good is my thinking? how well does it fit the subject I am trying to explain?"

In its emphasis on logic and the dispassionate scrutiny of ideas ("what do I think about what I think?"), analysis is a close cousin of argument. But analysis and argument are not the same.

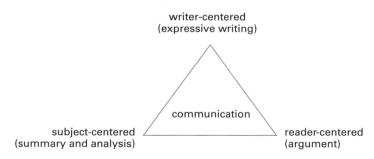

Figure 3.1
Diagram of Communication Triangle

ANALYSIS AND ARGUMENT

Analysis and argument proceed in the same way. They offer evidence, make claims about it, and supply reasons that explain and justify the claims. In other words, in both analysis and argument, you respond to the questions "what have you got to go on?" (supply evidence) and "how did you get there?" (supply the principles and reasons that caused you to conclude what you did about the evidence).

Although analysis and argument proceed in essentially the same way, they differ in the kinds of questions they try to answer. Argument, at its most dispassionate, asks, "what can be said with truth about x or y?" In common practice, though, the kinds of questions that argument more often answers are more committed, directive, and should-centered, such as "which is better, x or y?," "how can we best achieve x or y?," and "why should we stop doing x or y?"

Analysis, by contrast, asks, "what does x or y mean"? In analysis of the evidence (your data) is something you wish to understand, and the claims are assertions about what that evidence means. The claim that an analysis makes is usually a tentative answer to a what, how, or why question; it seeks to explain why people watch professional wrestling or what a rising number of sexual harassment cases might mean, or how certain features of government health care policy are designed to allay the fears of the middle class.

The claim that an argument makes is often an answer to a "should" question: for example, readers should or shouldn't vote for bans on smoking in public buildings, or they should or shouldn't believe that gays can function effectively in the military. The writer of an analysis is more concerned with discovering how each of these complex subjects might be defined and explained than with convincing readers to approve or disapprove of them.

Analysis Versus Debate-Style Argument

A factor that sometimes separates argument and analysis is the closer association of argument with the desire to persuade. When the aim of argument is persuasion—to get the audience to accept the writer's position on a given subject—argument is likely to differ significantly from analysis. For one thing, a writer concerned with persuading others may feel the need to go into the writing process with considerable certainty about the position he or she advocates. The writer of an analysis, on the other hand, usually begins and remains for an extended period in a position of uncertainty.

Analytical writers are frequently more concerned with persuading themselves, with discovering what they believe about a subject, than they are with persuading others. The writer of an analysis is thus more likely to begin with the details of a subject he or she wishes to better understand, rather than with a position he or she wishes to defend.

Many of you may have been introduced to writing arguments through the debate model—arguing pro or con (for or against) on a given position, with the aim of defeating an imagined opponent and convincing your audience of the rightness of your position. The agree/disagree mode of writing and thinking that you often see in editorials, hear on radio or television, and even practice sometimes in school may incline you to focus all your energy on the bottom line—aggressively advancing a claim for or against some view—without first engaging in the exploratory interpretation of evidence that is so necessary to arriving at thoughtful arguments. But as the American College Dictionary says, "to argue implies reasoning or trying to understand; it does not necessarily imply opposition." It is this more exploratory, tentative, and dispassionate mode of argument that this book encourages you to practice.

Adhering to the more restrictive, debate-style definition of argument can create a number of problems for careful analytical writers:

1. By requiring writers to be oppositional, debate-style argument inclines them to discount or dismiss problems in the side or position they have chosen; they cling to the same static position rather than testing it as a way of allowing it to evolve.

2. It inclines writers toward either/or thinking rather than encouraging them to formulate more qualified (carefully limited, acknowledging exceptions, etc.) positions that integrate apparently opposing viewpoints.

3. It overvalues convincing someone else at the expense of developing understanding.

As should now be clear, the aims of analysis and argument can sometimes be in conflict. Nevertheless, it's important to remember that in practice, analysis and argument are inevitably linked. Even the most tentative and cautiously evolving analysis is ultimately an argument; it asks readers to accept a particular interpretation of a set of data.

Similarly, even the most passionately committed argument is an analysis. If you approach an argument with the primary goals of convincing others that you are right and defeating your opponents, you may neglect the more important goal of arriving at a fair and accurate assessment of your subject. In fact, you will be able to argue much more effectively from evidence if you first take the time to really consider what that evidence means, and thereby, to find valid positions to argue about it.

ETHOS AND ANALYSIS

Analysis, as we have been arguing, is interested in how we come to know things, how we make meaning. This focus privileges not just conclusions about a subject but sharing with readers the thought process that led to those conclusions. Rather than telling other people what to think, the best analytical writers encourage readers to think collaboratively with them. This is true of the best writers in the civic forum as well as in colleges and universities. *(See Chapter 1, the short take called "What's Different About Writing Arguments in College?)*

It follows that the character of the speaker (ethos) in an analysis will serve to create a more collaborative and collegial relationship with readers than might be the case in other kinds of writing.

Classical rhetoric thought of the impact that writers/speakers had on audiences in terms of three categories: logos, pathos, and ethos. These categories are very useful, especially as you go about trying to construct a written version of yourself that will allow you to succeed and grow as a college writer. The word *logos* (from Greek) refers to the logical component of a piece of writing or speaking. *Pathos* refers to the emotional component in writing, the ways it appeals to feelings in an audience. *Ethos* will be familiar to you as a term because of its relation to the word ethics. In classical rhetoric, ethos is the character of the speaker, which is important in determining an audience's acceptance or rejection of his or her arguments.

Much of this book is concerned with the logos of academic writing, with ways of deriving and arguing ideas in colleges, universities, and the world of educated discourse. Ethos matters, too. The thinking you do is hard to separate from the sense the audience has of the person doing the thinking. In fact, the personae (versions of ourselves) we assume when we write have a formative impact on what we think and say. Ethos is not just a mask we assume in order to appeal to a particular audience. The stylistic and thinking moves prescribed by the ethos of particular groups become, with practice, part of who we are and thus of how we think and interact with others.

Eventually, college writers need to learn how to adopt different self-presentations for different academic disciplines. The acceptable ethos of a Chemistry lab report differs in significant ways from the one you might adopt in a Political Science or English paper. For present purposes, we'll note that the ethoi of most analytical writing across the curriculum share certain significant traits:

- nonadversarial tone—is not looking for a fight
- collaborative and collegial—treats readers as colleagues who are worthy of respect and who share your interest
- carefully qualified—does not making overstated claims
- relative impersonality in self-presentation—keeps focus primarily on the subject, not the writer

ANALYSIS VERSUS SUMMARY: THE EXAMPLE OF *WHISTLER'S MOTHER*

One of the most common kinds of writing you'll be asked to do in college, other than analysis, is summary. Summary differs from analysis, because the aim of summary is to recount, in effect, to reproduce someone else's ideas. But summary and analysis are also clearly related and usually operate together. Summary is important to analysis because you can't analyze a subject without laying out its significant parts for your reader. Similarly, analysis is important to summary because summarizing is more than just copying someone else's words. To write an accurate summary, you have to ask analytical questions such as:

- Which of the ideas in the reading are most significant? Why?
- How do these ideas fit together? What do the key passages in the reading mean?

Summary Is a Focused Description

Like an analysis, an effective summary doesn't assume that the subject matter can speak for itself: the writer needs to play an active role. A good summary provides perspective on the subject as a whole by explaining, as an analysis does, the meaning and function of each of that subject's parts. Moreover, like an analysis, a good summary does not aim to approve or disapprove of its subject: the goal, in both kinds of writing, is to understand rather than to evaluate. *(For more on summary, see Chapter 7, Making Common Topics More Analytical, and Chapter 5, Writing About Reading.)*

So, summary, like analysis, is a tool of understanding and not just a mechanical task. But a summary stops short of analysis because summary typically makes much smaller interpretive leaps. A summary of the painting popularly known as *Whistler's Mother,* for example, would tell readers what the painting includes, which details are the most prominent, and even what the overall effect of the painting seems to be. A summary might say that the painting possesses a certain serenity and that it is somewhat spare, almost austere. This kind of language still falls into the category of *focused description,* which is what a summary is.

Analysis Makes an Interpretive Leap

An analysis would include more of the writer's interpretive thinking. It might tell us, for instance, that the painter's choice to portray his subject in profile contributes to our sense of her separateness from us and of her nonconfrontational passivity. We look at her, but she does not look back at us. Her black dress and the fitted lace cap that obscures her hair are not only emblems of her self-effacement, shrouds disguising her identity like her expressionless face, but also the tools of her self-containment and thus of her power to remain aloof from prying eyes. What is the attraction of this painting (this being one of the questions that an analysis might ask)? What might draw a viewer to the sight of this austere, drably attired woman, sitting alone in the center of a mostly blank space? Perhaps it is the very starkness of the painting, and the mystery of self-sufficiency at its center, that attracts us (see Figure 3.2).

Laying out the data is key to any kind of analysis not simply because it keeps the analysis accurate but also because, crucially, it is *in the act of carefully describing a subject that analytical writers often have their best ideas.* Observations of the sort just offered go beyond describing what the painting contains and enter into the writer's ideas about what its details imply, what the painting invites us to make of it and by what means. Notice in our analysis of the painting how intertwined the description (summary) is with the analysis.

REUNION DES MUSEES NATIONAUX, ART RESOURCE, NY. James Abbott McNeil Whistler.

Figure 3.2
Arrangement in Grey and Black: The Artist's Mother by James Abbott McNeill Whistler, 1871.

The writer who can offer a careful description of a subject's key features is likely to arrive at conclusions about possible meanings that others would share. You may not agree with the terms by which we have summarized the painting, and thus you may not agree with such conclusions as "the mystery of self-sufficiency." Nor is it necessary that you agree because there is no single, right answer to what the painting means. The absence of a single right answer does not, however, mean that all possible interpretations are equal and equally convincing to readers.

Here are two guidelines to be drawn from this discussion of analysis and summary:

1. Describe with care. The words you choose to summarize your data will contain the germs of your ideas about what the subject means.

2. In moving from summary to analysis, scrutinize the language you have chosen, asking, "why did I choose this word?" and "what ideas are implicit in the language I have used?"

Data	Analytical Moves	Interpretive Leaps (So What?)
subject in profile, not looking at us	make implicit explicit (speculate about what the detail might suggest)	figure strikes us as separate, nonconfrontational, passive
folded hands, fitted lace cap, contained hair, expressionless face	locate pattern of same or similar detail; make what is implicit in pattern of details explicit	figure strikes us as self-contained, powerful in her separateness and self-enclosure—self-sufficient?
patterned curtain and picture versus still figure and blank wall; slightly frilled lace cuffs and ties on cap versus plain black dress	locate organizing contrast; make what is implicit in the contrast explicit	austerity and containment of the figure made more pronounced by slight contrast with busier, more lively, and more ornate elements and with little picture showing world outside
slightly slouched body position and presence of support for feet	anomalies; make what is implicit in the anomalies explicit	these details destabilize the serenity of the figure, adding some tension to the picture in the form of slightly uneasy posture and figure's need for support: she looks too long, drooped in on her own spine

Figure 3.3
Summary and Analysis of *Whistler's Mother* Diagram

ANALYSIS AND PERSONAL ASSOCIATIONS

Although observations like those offered in the "Interpretive Leaps" column in Figure 3.3 go beyond simple description, they stay with the task of explaining the painting, rather than moving to private associations that the painting might prompt, such as effusions about old age, or rocking chairs, or the character and situation of the writer's own mother. Such associations could well be valuable as a means of prompting a searching piece of expressive writing. They might also help a writer to interpret some feature of the painting that he or she was working to understand. But the writer would not be free to use pieces of his or her personal history as conclusions about what the painting communicates, unless these conclusions could also be reasonably inferred from the painting itself.

Analysis is a creative activity, a fairly open form of inquiry, but its imaginative scope is governed by logic. The hypothetical analysis we have offered is not the only reading of the painting a viewer might make because the same pattern of details might lead to different conclusions. But a viewer would not be free to conclude anything he or she wished, such as that the woman is mourning the death of a son or is patiently waiting to die. Such conclusions would be unfounded speculations, since the black dress is not sufficient to support them. Analysis often operates in areas where there is no one right answer, but like summary and argument, it requires the writer to reason from evidence.

A few rules are worth highlighting here:

1. The range of associations for explaining a given detail or word must be governed by context.

2. It's fine to use your personal reactions as a way into exploring what a subject means, but take care not to make an interpretive leap stretch farther than the actual details will support.

3. Because the tendency to transfer meanings from your own life onto a subject can lead you to ignore the details of the subject itself, you need always to be asking yourself: "what other explanations might plausibly account for this same pattern of detail?"

As we began this chapter by saying, analysis is a form of detective work. It can surprise us with ideas that our experiences produce once we take the time to listen to ourselves thinking. But analysis is also a discipline; it has rules that govern how we proceed and that enable others to judge the validity of our ideas. A good analytical thinker needs to be the attentive Dr. Watson to his or her own Sherlock Holmes. That is what the remainder of this book will teach you to do. *(See Chapter 6, Making Interpretations Plausible, for more on the rules governing interpretation, again using* Whistler's Mother *as a primary example.)*

Rhetorical Analysis of an Advertisement: An Example

We have demonstrated how the five moves might work in the analysis of a painting. Our final example addresses a more popular form: advertising. The example is a student paper that uses the moves to produce a rhetorical analysis of a perfume advertisement that appeared in a magazine aimed at young women. Locate the Five Analytical Moves, especially making the implicit explicit.

The visual imagery of advertisements offers instructive opportunities for rhetorical analysis because advertising is a form of persuasion. Advertisers attend carefully to rhetoric by carefully targeting their audiences. This means advertisements are well suited to the questions that rhetorical analysis typically asks: how is the audience being invited to respond and by what means (in what context)? You'll notice that in the rhetorical analysis of the magazine ad, the writer occasionally extends her analysis to evaluative conclusions about the aims and possible effects (on American culture) of the advertisement.

Marketing the Girl Next Door: A Declaration of Independence?

[1] Found in *Seventeen* magazine, the advertisement for "tommy girl," the perfume manufactured by Tommy Hilfiger, sells the most basic American ideal of independence. Various visual images and text suggest that purchasing tommy girl buys freedom and liberation for the mind and body. This image appeals to young women striving to establish themselves as unbound individuals. Ironically, the advertisement uses traditional American icons as vehicles for marketing to the modern woman. Overall, the message is simple: American individualism can be found in a spray or nonspray bottle.

[2] Easily, the young woman dominates the advertisement. She has the look of the all-American "girl next door." Her appeal is a natural one, as she does not rely on makeup or a runway model's cheekbones for her beauty. Freckles frame her eyes that ambitiously gaze skyward; there are no limits restricting women in capitalist America. Her flowing brown hair freely rides a stirring breeze. Unconcerned with the order of a particular hairstyle, she smiles and enjoys the looseness of her spirit. The ad tells us how wearing this perfume allows women to achieve the look of self-assured and liberated indifference without appearing vain.

[3] The second most prevalent image in the advertisement is the American flag, which neatly matches the size of the young woman's head. The placement and size of the flag suggest that if anything is on her cloudless mind, it is fundamental American beliefs that allow for such self-determination. The half-concealed flag is seemingly continued in the young woman's hair. According to the ad, American ideals reside well within the girl as well as the perfume.

[4] It is also noticeable that there is a relative absence of all land surrounding the young woman. We can see glimpses of "fruited plains" flanking the girl's shoulders. This young woman is barely bound to earth, as free as the clouds that float beneath her head. It is this liberated image Americans proudly carry that is being sold in the product.

[5] The final image promoting patriotism can be found in the young woman's clothing. The young woman is draped in the blue jean jacket, a classic symbol of American ruggedness and originality. As far as we can see, the jacket is spread open, supporting the earlier claim of the young women's free and independent spirit. These are the very same ideals that embody American pride and patriotism. The ad clearly employs the association principle in linking the tommy girl fragrance with emotionally compelling yet essentially unrelated images of American nationalism and patriotism.

[6] A final obvious appeal to American nationalism is the tagline of the advertisement, the underlying message being "a declaration of independence." The young woman has already declared her independence, and now it is your turn. Doesn't every young woman want to be in that green field, hair blowing in the wind, wearing a confident look outlined against an American flag and clean, carefree, endless blue sky?

[7] Lastly, the advertisement utilizes several implicit arrows that point to the actual product of tommy girl perfume. The white writing against the dark blue jean jacket catches the eye first, encouraging the reader to continue in the traditional, left to right order. When the writing stops, we are naturally pointed

toward the product. In addition, the young woman's hair, seen earlier as an extension of the American flag, is flurrying out and somewhat downward. We follow the hair to its end, where it seemingly kisses the product's cap. All visual indications of direction in the advertisement lead the viewer to an inevitable end: the irresistible scent of tommy girl perfume.

[8] But we might also look beyond the ad's overt messages, and examine its effects on the viewer and our society as a whole. Returning to the ad's portrayal of the young woman, we are shown a girl with a natural beauty, free of worries or cares about conforming to the pressures of society as a female. Jean Kilbourne (2003) argues that countless ads tell women to search for freedom and independence through being thin, as echoed in the ad's skinny and attractive young woman. Kilbourne actually refers to another tommy girl ad that uses the same tagline: "'A declaration of independence,' proclaims an ad for perfume that features an emaciated model, but in fact the quest for a body as thin as the model's becomes a prison for many women and girls" (p. 263). She argues that ads encouraging a search for feminine independence often promote the worship of the thinness ideal, as well as the dilemma of being a successful and powerful woman while remaining "feminine" and unthreatening (pp. 262–264).

[9] Additionally, the ad for tommy girl perfume is also effective because it "takes on the trappings of a movement for social justice," according to Thomas Frank (1997, p. 187). Frank describes how advertisers constantly link products with the rebellious, revolutionary political and social movements of the past in order to conjure the vehement emotions associated with their resounding emotional content. The tommy girl ad emphasizes typical patriotic American images—like the American flag and denim clothing—as well as the phrase *a declaration of independence,* which explicitly creates a connection between the perfume and the American colonists' revolutionary pursuit of liberty in their beliefs and behavior during the American Revolution.

[10] Yet in reality, this marketing of liberation is paradoxical; although this freeing message promotes rebellion and nonconformity, it actually supports the market economy and feeds into capitalism and conformity. When advertisers employ political protest messages to be associated with products, they imply that buying the product is a form of political action.

[11] But lastly, the ad gives another paradoxical message with the portrayal of the beauty of the American, unspoiled, natural environment. Another typical American image is of the untouched landscapes, green pastures, and cloudless blue skies of the open frontier, which serves as the ad's backdrop.

The ad's clear blue sky with the American flag flying freely in the wind encourages the viewer to link the beauty of the natural American landscape with the purchase of tommy girl. Sut Jhally, editor of the video *Advertising and the End of the World* (1998), would argue that the ad's purpose—the consumption of the product—is paradoxically putting the environment at risk. Our "freedom" to buy all of what we need (and especially, what we don't need) is essentially spoiling the natural surroundings that we romanticize. And so the viewers are simply left to decide: Does this tommy girl ad truly portray a declaration of independence, or of *dependence?*

REFERENCES

Frank, T. (1997). Liberation marketing and the culture trust. In E. Barnouw et al. (Ed.), *Conglomerates and the media* (pp. 173–190). New York: The New Press.

Jhally, S. (Ed.). (1998). *Advertising and the end of the world* [Videotape]. Northampton, MA: Media Education Foundation.

Kilbourne, J. (2003). The more you subtract, the more you add: Cutting girls down to size. In G. Dines & J. Humez (Eds.), *Gender, race and class in media* (pp. 258–267). Thousand Oaks, CA: Sage.

GUIDELINES FOR ANALYSIS: WHAT IT IS AND WHAT IT DOES

1. Avoid deciding what your subject means before you analyze it, and remember that analysis often operates in areas where there is no one right answer.

2. As a general rule, analysis favors live questions—where something remains to be resolved—over inert answers, places where things are nailed down and don't leave much space for further thinking.

3. As you analyze a subject, ask not just "What are its defining parts?" but also "How do these parts help me to understand the meaning of the subject as a whole?"

4. Look for patterns of repetition and organizing contrasts in the data, as well as anomalies, and ask yourself questions about what these mean.

5. Make the implicit explicit: convert the suggested meanings of particular details into overt statements.

6. When you describe and summarize, attend carefully to the language you choose, since the words themselves will usually contain the germs of ideas.

7. The analytical process is one of trial and error. Learning to write well is largely a matter of learning how to frame questions. Whatever questions you ask, the answers will often produce more questions.

Assignments

1. **Expand a Try This into a Longer Essay**. Two of the Try This exercises in this chapter are suitable for more extended pieces of writing: Try This 3.2: Making Inferences and Try This 3.4: Apply the Five Analytical Moves to a Speech. Develop either into a piece of several pages in length.

2. **Analyze a Portrait or Other Visual Image**. Locate any portrait, preferably a good reproduction from an art book or magazine, one that shows detail clearly. Then do a version of what we've done with *Whistler's Mother*.

   Your goal is to produce an analysis of the portrait with the steps we included in analyzing *Whistler's Mother*. First, summarize the portrait, describing accurately its significant details. Do not go beyond a recounting of what the portrait includes; avoid interpreting what these details suggest.

   Then use the various methods offered in this chapter to analyze the data. What repetitions (patterns of same or similar detail) do you see? What organizing contrasts suggest themselves? In light of these patterns of similarity and difference, what anomalies do you then begin to detect? Move from the data to interpretive conclusions. This process will produce a set of interpretive leaps, which you may then try to assemble into a more coherent claim of some sort—a short essay about what the portrait "says."

3. **Describe a Neighborhood**. Revisit the paragraphs from Jane Jacobs' book, *The Death and Life of Great American Cities* (1961), which are offered earlier in this chapter under the heading Description as a Form of Analysis: Some Academic Examples. These paragraphs offer an implicitly analytical description of city life in Greenwich Village, a neighborhood in New York City, in the 1950s. Use these paragraphs as the basis of a writing assignment to be done in two steps.

   First, find an example of Jacobs' "go-to sentence," following the instructions offered in Chapter 2, the section entitled Identifying the "Go To" Sentence. Be sure to relate the shape of the sentence you select to Jacobs' way of thinking and of communicating her point of view in the piece.

   Second, write several descriptive paragraphs of your own in which you try to capture the character of a neighborhood by presenting significant detail.

   * * *

   We are offering you two further assignments, both taken from our colleagues. Either assignment might be adapted to materials in your writing course, but at least in part we share them with you to provide a glimpse of real life analytical assignments in writing-intensive courses in two different academic disciplines.

   * * *

4. **Analyze Two Representations of Inner City Life**. This assignment was designed by Political Science Professor Brian Mello for his course entitled *The Wire: Money, Drugs, & Life in Urban America*. You can adapt this assignment for your own use by comparing two representations of inner city life: photographs,

videos, songs, and so forth. Analyze these by locating patterns of significant detail and by making the implicit explicit. Dr. Mello's assignment follows:

Your task is to find your own representation of inner city life, and bring it to the last week of class where you will be asked to share this with your peers. This representation could come in the form of a photograph (or series of photographs), a song (or a music video), a poem, a passage from a work of literature, or a passage from a non-fiction text.

This assignment points us back to the central theme of this course— examining what assumptions are made by, and what implications should be drawn from the representation of socioeconomic concerns in *The Wire.* As Thomas Bender pointed out in his lecture, representations of urban life are never apolitical—they always create for the viewer certain assumptions and interpretations about life in urban America.

Compare the story that gets expressed in the representation of urban life that you have selected to the story that gets told in any one of the following course texts— *The Wire, The Corner, Cop in the Hood, or Gang Leader for a Day.* You should focus in on specific passages or scenes from these texts. Insofar as a different interpretation of urban life emerges from the representations that you bring into class, what explains this difference? How can or should one reconcile these different interpretations? Insofar as there are similarities, what are they, and why might it be interesting or important that common representations emerge in multiple contexts? What do these representations tell us about who gets to represent urban life?

5. **Compare Two Cultural Documents That Reveal a Current Cultural Divide**. Here is an assignment designed by Communications Professor Dr. Jefferson Pooley for his writing-intensive course, *1968*. You can adapt this assignment by locating two contemporary documents that reveal a cultural divide in America now. Be sure to explain *how* the details of the documents disclose this cultural rift. You could also choose two political cartoons from different points of view on the same subject. Note: please refrain from taking a stand on the cultural divide that your documents embody. Focus instead on careful description and inferring implications. Here is the original assignment:

In a three-page paper use the attached transcript from the "Chicago Seven" trial—the circus-like prosecution of prominent DNC protestors— to support the thesis that the exchange between Abbie Hoffman (Yippie leader) and Julius Hoffman (judge) represents, in microcosm, the cultural divide then gripping America. (The excerpt is a verbatim transcript from the infamous 1969 trial of Hoffman and six other New Left leaders.)

Your task in this paper is to organize your evidence in some coherent way. The legal theatrics of the Hoffman-Hoffman exchange provide you with an abundance of material to work with. A strong paper will discuss the trial transcript according to some organizing logic, though the specific structure is up to you.

Chapter 4

Toolkit of Analytical Methods II: Going Deeper

A TEACHER COMMENT found in the margins of many essays and famous for bewildering students is the single word "develop"—or just "dev." Faculty who write that term seem to be saying they want more thinking, that what's on the page is too simple or uncomplicated. But it's no easy matter to develop your ideas. This chapter offers you tools for doing so—hence, the chapter's subtitle, Going Deeper.

This chapter is the logical next step to be taken. Where Chapter 2 equips you with foundational observational skills, and Chapter 3 incorporates them into a five-step analytical sequence, Chapter 4 offers you a set of analytical activities that can enable you to extend, complicate, and deepen your understanding of whatever you are analyzing. In effect, this new set of strategies seeks to give you more concrete ways of carrying out the last two of the five analytical moves featured in Chapter 3—to make what is implicit explicit and to reformulate questions and explanations.

Here is the list of the chapter's heuristics, each with a very brief summary of what it involves. We will go on to explain each in more detail.

1. Passage-Based Focused Freewriting

   (analyze a representative passage to understand better how the whole works)

2. Uncovering Assumptions

   (determine the givens, what must be believed first in order to posit what the thing you are analyzing has said)

3. Reformulating Binaries

   (question the accuracy of a basic contrast and determine the extent to which one side prevails over the other)

4. [Looking for] Difference within Similarity and Similarity Despite Difference

   (move beyond a mechanical matching exercise by exploring how two things are alike, and So What, and then different, and So What)

5. "Seems to Be About X, but Could Also Be (or Is 'Really') about Y"

   (assume that you got it wrong the first time to get somewhere new and interesting the second time)

Note: these heuristics, although not intended as formulae for organizing papers, can to some extent function in this way. They are primarily "thinking moves" designed to produce better, more in-depth thinking for essays, arguments or reports. The best way to learn these thinking skills is to practice them out repeatedly in your own work and with other writers.

1. PASSAGE-BASED FOCUSED FREEWRITING

WHAT IT DOES

Find an interesting passage
Sketch its context
Target and paraphrase key words and phrases
Explore why (so what that) the passage is interesting
Draw out implications
Ask how the passage is representative of the larger reading

WHAT IT DOES NOT DO

Voice reactions and criticisms
Free-associate with other subjects

Passage-based focused freewriting increases your ability to learn from what you read. The passage-based version differs from regular freewriting by limiting the focus to a piece of text. It prompts in-depth analysis of a representative example, on the assumption that you'll attain a better appreciation of the whole after you've explored how a piece of it works. (*Please review the short take from Chapter 1, Freewriting: How and Why to Do It.*)

The impromptu nature of passage-based focused freewriting encourages you to take chances, to think out loud on the page. It invites you to notice what you notice in the moment and take some stabs at what the passage might mean without having to worry about formulating a weighty thesis statement or maintaining consistency. It allows you to worry less about what you don't understand and instead start to work things out as you write.

A lot of great papers start as in-class writings—not as outlines.

Step 1: Choose a limited piece of concrete evidence to focus on and write about it without stopping for 10 to 20 minutes. Pick a passage you find interesting and that you probably don't quite understand. Copy out the passage at the beginning of your freewrite. This act will encourage attention to the words and induce you to notice more about the particular features of your chosen passage.

Step 2: Contextualize the evidence. Where does the passage come from in the text? Of what larger discussion is it a part? Briefly answering these questions will prevent you from taking things out of context.

Step 3: Focus on what the text is inviting you to think—its point of view—not on what you think, your point of view of that subject.

Step 4: Make observations about the evidence. Stay close to the data you've quoted, paraphrasing key phrases in the passage and teasing out the possible meanings of these words. Then reflect on what you've come to better understand through paraphrasing.

Step 5: Share your reasoning about what the evidence means. As you move from observation to implication, remember that you need to explain how the data mean what you claim they mean.

Step 6: Address how the passage is representative, how it connects to broader issues in the reading. Move from your analysis of local details to consider what the work as a whole may plausibly be "saying" about this or that issue or question. It's okay to work with the details for almost the entire time and then press yourself to an interpretive leap with the prompt, "I'm almost out of time but my big point is. . . ."

Discussion Passage-based focused freewriting is probably the single best way to arrive at ideas about what you are reading. The more you practice it, the better you will get—the easier you will find things to say about your chosen passage. Ask yourself:

- "What one passage in the reading do you think most needs to be discussed—is most useful and interesting for understanding the material?"
- "What one passage seems puzzling, difficult to pin down, anomalous, or even just unclear—and how might this be explained?"

The best passage-based focused freewrites usually do one or more of the following:

- **Interpretation**, which moves from restatement to what the sentence from the text means.
- **Implication**. A useful (and logical) next step is to go after implication. If X or Y is true, then what might follow from it? (Or "So what?")
- **Application**. A passage that is resonant in some way for the reader might lead him or her to write about some practical way of applying the reading—for example, as a lens for understanding other material *(see Chapter 5, Writing About Reading)*.
- **Assumptions**. We lay out implications by moving forward (so to speak). We unearth assumptions by moving backward. If a text asks us to believe X, what else must it already believe? From what unstated assumptions, in other words, would X follow?
- **Queries**. What questions, interpretive difficulties, and struggles are raised by the reading?

As the short take Freewriting: How and Why to Do It in Chapter 1 discusses, passage-based focused freewriting incorporates a number of the methods introduced in the opening chapters. So, for example:

- it often starts with observations discovered by doing Notice and Focus;
- it grows out of doing The Method, further developing the paragraph that explains why you chose one repetition, strand or binary as most important;

- in analyzing the chosen passage, writers normally paraphrase key words; and
- they keep the writing going by insistently asking "So what?" at the ends of paragraphs.

Notice how the writers use these tools in the examples that follow.

Passage-based Focused Freewriting: An Example

Sometimes, in-class writings are done in class in response to a prompt. The prompt for this freewrite was, "how does Obama's inaugural address compare with his election night victory speech?" Notice how the writer chooses to find most interesting.

> What was most interesting to me about Obama's inaugural speech was his use of the collective first person—"we," "our," "us," etc.—as opposed to the singular "I." This is especially different from his victory speech, which did not make use of the singular "I" and addressed the audience as "you." These pronoun choices are actually very conducive to the tone of each speech. Obama's victory speech was a *victory* speech—it was meant to be joyful, hopeful, optimistic, and of course thankful...so every use of "you" is not accusatory by rather congratulatory and proud—e.g., "this is because of you," "you have done this," "this is your victory."
>
> On the other hand, Obama's inaugural speech was by and large a more somber piece of writing—as the President said to George Stephanopolous, he wanted to capture that moment in history as exactly as possible. "You" here is not the American public as in the victory speech; rather, "you" is any "enemy" of America. And "I," it seems, has become "we." This choice automatically makes Obama the voice of society, as though speaking for every American. This is a really subtle but smart choice to make, because the listener or reader is hearing everything he says as his or her own position. Using that collective first person also puts Obama on the same level as everyone else, and when he does blame America for its own problems, the "our's" and "we's" soften the blow. The "you's" here are harsh and accusatory but meant for that great, terrible, unnamed enemy to "our" freedom and happiness.
>
> I found a lot more obvious echoes to Lincoln in this speech as compared to the victory speech, coupled with earth imagery—for example, "we cannot hallow this ground" (Lincoln) vs. "what the cynics fail to understand is that the ground has shifted" (Obama). This ties America to the actual physical land. It romanticizes and makes permanent the ideas of our country—a nice setting behind all of the nation's troubles—while simultaneously adding to the so-desired degree of "timelessness" of Obama's first inaugural address.

You can sense the writer, Molly Harper, gathering steam here as she begins to make connections in her evidence, yet her rhetorical analysis seems to spring naturally from simple observation of Obama's pronouns and then the significance of the contrast between them in the two speeches she is comparing.

Passage-based Focused Freewriting: Another Example

Below is an example of a student's exploratory writing on an essay by the twentieth-century African-American writer Langston Hughes. The piece is a twenty-minute reflection on two excerpts. Most notable about this piece, perhaps, is the sheer number of interesting ideas. That may be because the writer continually returns to the language of the original quotes for inspiration. She is not restricted by maintaining a single and consistent thread. It is interesting though, how as the freewrite progresses, a primary focus (on the second of her two quotes) seems to emerge.

Passages from "The Negro Artist and the Racial Mountain" by Langston Hughes

"But jazz to me is one of the inherent expressions of negro life in America; the eternal tom-tom beating in the Negro soul—the tom-tom of revolt against weariness in a white world, a world of subway trains, and work, work, work; the tom-tom of joy and laughter, and pain swallowed in a smile. Yet the Philadelphia clubwoman is ashamed to say that her race created it and she does not like me to write about it. The old subconscious "white is best" runs through her mind. . . . And now she turns up her nose at jazz and all its manifestations—likewise almost everything else distinctly racial."

"We build our temples for tomorrow, strong as we know how, and we stand on top of the mountain, free within ourselves."

Langston Hughes's 1926 essay on the situation of the Negro artist in America sets up some interesting issues that are as relevant today as they were in Hughes's time. Interestingly, the final sentence of the essay ("We build our temples. . .") will be echoed some four decades later by the Civil Rights leader, Martin Luther King, but with a different spin on the idea of freedom. Hughes writes "we stand on top of the mountain, free within ourselves." King says, "Free at last, free at last, my God almighty, we're free at last." King asserts an opening out into the world—a freeing of black people, finally, from slavery and then another century of oppression.

Hughes speaks of blacks in a more isolated position—"on top of the mountain" and "within ourselves." Although the mountain may stand for a height from which the artist can speak, it is hard to be heard from the top of mountains. It is one thing to be free. It is another to be free within oneself. What does this phrase mean? If I am free within myself I am at least less vulnerable to those who would restrict me from without. I can live with their restrictions. Mine is an inner freedom. Does inner freedom empower artists? Perhaps it does. It may allow them to say what they want and not worry about what others say or think. This is one thing that Hughes seems to be calling for. But he is also worried about lack of recognition of Negro artists, not only by whites but by blacks. His use of the repeated phrase, tom-tom, is interesting in this respect. It, like the word "mountain," becomes a kind of refrain in the essay—announcing both a desire to rise above the world and its difficulties (mountain) and a desire to be heard (tom-tom and mountain as pulpit).

The idea of revolt, outright rebellion, is present but subdued in the essay. The tom-tom is a "revolt against weariness" and also an instrument for expressing "joy and laughter." The tom-tom also suggests a link with a past African and probably Native American culture—communicating by drum and music and dance. White culture in the essay stands for a joyless world of "work work work." This is something I would like to think about more, as the essay seems to link the loss of soul with the middle and upper classes, both black and white.

And so the essay seeks to claim another space among those he calls "the low down folks, the so-called common element." Of these he says ". . . they do not particularly care whether they are like white folks or anybody else. Their joy runs, bang! into ecstasy. Their religion soars to a shout. Work maybe a little today, rest a little tomorrow. Play awhile. Sing awhile. O, let's dance!" In these lines Hughes the poet clearly appears. Does he say then that the Negro artist needs to draw from those of his own people who are the most removed from middle class American life? If I had more time, I would start thinking here about Hughes's use of the words "race" and "racial" . . . .

Try This 4.1: Do a Passage-based Focused Freewrite

Select a passage from any of the material you are reading and copy it at the top of the page. Remember to choose the passage in response to the question, "What is the single sentence that I think it is most important for us to discuss and why?" Then do a twenty-minute focused freewrite, applying the steps offered above. Discover what you think by seeing what you say.

It is often productive to take the focused freewrite and type it, revising and further freewriting until you have filled the inevitable gaps in your thinking that the time limit has created. (One colleague of ours has students revise and expand in a different font, so both can see how the thinking is evolving.) Eventually, you can build up, through a process of accretion, the thinking for an entire paper in this way.

An especially useful way of making pbff (as we shorthand it) productive academically is to freewrite for fifteen minutes every day on a different passage as you move through a book. If, for example, you are discussing a book over four class periods, prepare for each class by giving 15 minutes to a passage before you attend. You will not only discover things to say; you will begin to write your way to an essay.

2. UNCOVERING ASSUMPTIONS

WHAT IS AN ASSUMPTION?

An assumption is an underlying belief from which other statements spring.

Virtually all statements have underlying assumptions—especially claims.

Assumptions are usually unstated, which is why they need to be uncovered.

We generally reason forward to implications (what follows from X), but we reason backward to assumptions (what has led to X), which are a particular kind of implicit meaning.

The ability to uncover assumptions is a powerful analytical procedure to learn. It gives you insight into the root, the basic givens that a piece of writing has assumed are true. When you locate assumptions in a text, you understand the text better—where it's coming from, what else it believes that is more fundamental than what it is overtly declaring.

You also find things to write about. When analyzing the work of others, you are likely to discover related ideas or positions, and sometimes these are positions of which the writer is not aware. The same goes for developing and revising your own work. When you work back to your own premises from some statement you like that you have written, you will often find what else you believe, at a more basic level, that you did not realize you believed.

Step 1: Paraphrase the explicit statement. This will produce a range of related ideas and highlight the key terms in the original statement (*see Chapter 2, Paraphrase x 3*).

Step 2: List the implicit ideas that the statement seems to assume to be true. Ask yourself, "Given what is overtly stated, what must the writer also *already* believe?"

Step 3: Further analyze the original claim by drawing out implications of the underlying assumptions. What do you now recognize about the statement?

Discussion   Uncovering assumptions is a version, with a difference, of Move 4 of the Five Analytical Moves from Chapter 3: it renders the implicit explicit. But in this case, what it is revealing is not what follows from a given statement, but rather, what precedes.

You should be aware that this tool gets used for different purposes. In argument, it is often used (and abused) to catch out the other guy: your opponent's undiscerned assumption is exposed in order to be attacked. But in analysis, the goal is not attack; as Chapter 1 discusses in the short takes entitled Analysis: A Quick Definition and What's Different About Writing Arguments in College, analysis can lead *eventually* to making an argument or claim, but it does not generally conduct search-and-destroy missions. It seeks instead primarily to understand other positions, and in this context, uncovering the assumptions of other writers can be an essential move in helping everyone comprehend more clearly what is involved in accepting or negotiating with another point of view.

Uncovering Assumptions: An Example

In the reference application sent to professors at our college for students seeking to enter the student-teaching program, the professor is asked to rank the student from one to four (unacceptable to acceptable) on the following criterion: *"The student uses his/her sense of humor appropriately."*

Step 1: To uncover the assumptions in that statement, we might first paraphrase it a few times:

> The student makes jokes in a way that is right for the situation.
>
> The student creates situations that invite others to laugh in ways that are not socially indecorous.
>
> The student has good manners in the way he or she does things that are funny.

The paraphrasing helps identify the key terms in the original statement that are open to interpretation: "uses" and "sense of humor" and especially, "appropriately."

Step 2: What are the implicit ideas that the claim assumes to be true? And what must the writers of the form also already believe if they have asked that question? Here is a partial list:

> students have a sense of humor;
>
> students use their sense of humor in class;
>
> some senses of humor are appropriate, and others are not;
>
> the teacher, the one asked to fill out the evaluation, can distinguish appropriate from inappropriate uses of humor in the classroom by students; and
>
> the teacher probably shares the values and attitudes of the teachers who sent out the form, and by extension, teachers in general have a consensus view on this issue.

Step 3: Let's return to analyze the original claim, drawing out implications of these underlying assumptions.

Interestingly, the predictive tool that the Education Department has devised to screen its applicants targets humor as a charged site—a classroom space in which a would-be teacher is likely to demonstrate his or her ability to conduct himself or herself modestly, to remain within the bounds of good taste as defined by the educational institution. Further, we see that the Education Department has done some thinking: they've figured out that humor is a site of potential danger and subversion. But they have also seen that humor is inevitable, and therefore that they can test their candidates' adequacy through this convenient focus. If there is going to be a problem, it's likely to show up there.

Uncovering Assumptions: Another Quick Example

Consider the claim, "Tax laws benefit the wealthy."

We might paraphrase the claim as "The rules for paying income tax give rich people monetary advantages" or "The rules for paying income tax help the rich get richer."

Now let's look at the implicit ideas that the claim assumes to be true. Because this sentence has been offered out of context, let's supply a range of possibilities:

Tax laws don't treat people equally.

Tax laws may have unintended consequences.

If we assume the speaker is worried about tax laws possibly benefitting the wealthy, then a few more assumptions can be inferred:

Tax laws shouldn't benefit anybody.

Tax laws shouldn't benefit those who are already advantaged.

This process of definition will help you see the key concepts upon which the claim depends. Regardless of the position you might adopt—attacking tax laws, defending them, showing how they actually benefit everyone, or whatever—you would risk arguing blindly if you failed to question what the purpose of tax law is in the first place. How does the writer intend "benefit"? Does he or she mean that tax laws benefit only the wealthy and presumably harm those who are not wealthy? Note by the way that the assumptions we might infer would differ depending on context. If this statement appeared at a rally for the Tea Party, it would suggest one set of underlying assumptions; if it appeared at the Democratic National Convention, it would suggest another set.

The wording of this claim seems to conceal an egalitarian premise: the assumption that tax laws should not benefit anyone, or, at least, that they should benefit everyone equally. But what is the purpose of tax laws? Should they redress economic inequities? Should they spur the economy by rewarding those who generate capital? Our point here is that you would need to move your thesis back to this point and test the validity of the assumptions upon which it rests.

Try This 4.2: Uncover Assumptions in Reviews

Say you read a review that praises a television show or film for being realistic but faults it for setting a bad example for the kids who watch it. What assumptions might we infer from such a review? Here is an example of one underlying assumption: Good and bad examples are clear and easily recognizable by everyone. List at least three more.

Then locate a review of any other cultural product—a film, a show, a CD, a book, a concert, and so forth. Isolate key claims and uncover assumptions, that is, reason back to premises.

Uncovering Assumptions: An Economist Speaks

In the following Voice from Across the Curriculum, economics professor James Marshall foregrounds the importance of uncovering assumptions in designing and answering research questions.

Voices From Across the Curriculum

What's beneath the question? On some occasions, students find that they have confronted an issue that cannot be resolved by the deductive method. This can be exciting for them. Will cutting marginal tax rates cause people to work more? The answer is yes or no, depending on the premises underlying the work-leisure preferences incorporated into your model.

—James Marshall, Professor of Economics

Try This 4.3: Uncovering Assumptions: Fieldwork

You can practice uncovering assumptions with all kinds of material—newspaper editorials, statements you see on billboards, ideas you are studying in your courses, jokes, and so forth. Try a little fieldwork: spend a week jotting down in your notebook interesting statements you overhear. Choose the best of these from the standpoint of the implied (but unstated) premises upon which each statement seems to rest. Then make a list of the uncovered assumptions.

---

3. REFORMULATING BINARIES

HOW TO REFORMULATE BINARIES

Step 1: Locate a range of opposing categories.
Step 2: Define and analyze the key terms.
Step 3: Question the accuracy of the binary and rephrase the terms.
Step 4: Substitute "to what extent?" for "either/or."

Binaries are an essential component of thinking and writing analytically. They have already figured significantly in earlier chapters—as part of The Method after locating repetitions and strands, and as Move 3 of the Five Analytical Moves, in searching for patterns. We wish now to focus on a new use of binaries, one that takes place in higher order analysis, when you are "going deeper." This move is reformulating binaries.

First, here is a quick reprise on the benefits and dangers of binary thinking. When you run into a binary opposition in your thinking, it is like a fork in the road, a place where two paths going in different directions present themselves and you pause to choose the direction you will take. Binary oppositions are sites of uncertainty, places where there is struggle among various points of view. As such, binaries are the breeding ground of ideas. And, as we suggested in our discussion of The Method in Chapter 2, when you determine the organizing contrast in whatever you are analyzing, you have found the structural beam that gives conceptual shape to a piece.

If you leap too quickly to a binary, however, one that is too general or inaccurate, you can get stuck in oversimplification, in rigidly dichotomized points of view. At that point, you are in the grasp of a reductive habit of mind called either/or thinking.

The solution is to remember that, when you find a binary opposition in an essay, film, political campaign, or anything else, you have located the argument that the film, essay, or campaign is having with itself, the place where something is at issue. Your next step is to immediately begin to ask questions about and complicate the binary. To "complicate" a binary is to discover evidence that unsettles it and to formulate alternatively worded binaries that more accurately describe what is at issue in the evidence.

Step 1: Locate a range of **opposing categories** (binaries). Finding binaries will help you find the questions around which almost anything is organized. Use The Method to help you uncover the binary oppositions in your subject matter that might function as organizing contrasts.

Step 2: Define and analyze the **key terms**. By analyzing the terms of most binaries, you should come to question them and ultimately arrive at a more complex and qualified position.

Step 3: Question the **accuracy** of the binary and **rephrase** the terms. Think of the binary as a starting point—a kind of deliberate overgeneralization—that allows you to set up positions you can then test in order to refine.

Step 4: Substitute **"to what extent?"** for "either/or." The best strategy in using binaries productively is usually to locate arguments **on both sides** of the either/or choice that the binary poses and then choose a position somewhere between the two extremes. Once you have arrived at what you consider the most accurate phrasing of the binary, you can rephrase the original either/or question in the more qualified terms that asking "To what extent?" allows. Making this move does not release you from the responsibility of taking a stand and arguing for it.

Discussion Thinking is not simply linear and progressive, moving from point A to point B to point C like stops on a train. Careful thinkers are always retracing their steps, questioning their first—and second—impressions, assuming that they've missed something. All good thinking is *recursive;* that is, it repeatedly goes over the same ground, rethinking connections. And that's why reformulating binaries is an essential analytical move.

As a general rule, analysis favors live questions over inert answers. It thrives where something remains to be resolved, not where things are already pretty much nailed down and don't leave much space for further thinking.

Reformulating binaries will cause you to do one or more of the following:

- Discover that you have not named the binary adequately and that another formulation of the opposition would be more accurate.

- Weigh one side of your binary more heavily than the other, rather than seeing the issue as all or nothing.

- Discover that the two terms of your binary are not really so separate and opposed after all but are actually parts of one complex phenomenon or issue. (This is a key analytical move known as "collapsing the binary.")

There is usually no single "right" answer about which of a number of binary oppositions is the primary organizing contrast. This is because analytical thinking involves interpretation. Interpretive conclusions are not matters of fact, but theories. It is in the nature of theories to be tentative and open to alternative readings of the same information. This is why good analytical thinking takes time and is inevitably open-ended.

Reformulating Binaries: An Example

Suppose you are analyzing the following topic in a management course: *Would the model of management known as Total Quality Management (TQM) that is widely used in Japan function effectively in the American automotive industry?*

Step 1: There are a range of opposing categories suggested by the language of the topic, the most obvious being function versus not function. But there are also other binaries here: Japanese versus American, and TQM versus more traditional and more traditionally American models of management. These binaries imply further binaries. The question requires a writer to consider the accuracy and relative suitability of particular traits commonly ascribed to Japanese versus American workers, such as communal and cooperative versus individualistic and competitive.

Step 2: Questions of definition might concentrate on what it means to ask whether TQM *functions effectively* in the American automotive industry? Does that mean "make a substantial profit"? "Produce more cars more quickly"? "Improve employee morale"? You would drown in vagueness unless you carefully argued for the appropriateness of your definition of this key term.

Step 3: How accurate is the binary? To what extent do American and Japanese management styles actually differ? Can you locate significant differences between these management styles that correspond to supposed differences between Japanese and American culture that might help you formulate your binary more precisely?

Step 4: To complicate the either/or formulation, you might suggest the danger of assuming that all American workers are rugged individualists and all Japanese workers are communal bees. Insofar as you are going to arrive at a qualified claim, it would be best stated in terms of the extent to which TQM might be adaptable to the auto industry.

Collapsing the Binary: A Brief Example

Let's consider a brief example in which a writer starts with the following binary: was the poet Emily Dickinson psychotic, or was she a poetic genius? This is a useful, if overstated, starting point for prompting thinking. Going over the same ground, the writer might next decide that the opposing terms *insanity* and *poetic genius* don't accurately name the issue. He or she might decide, as the poet Adrienne Rich did, that poetic genius is often perceived as insanity by the culture at large and, thus, it's not a viable either/or formulation. This move is known as *collapsing the binary:* coming to see that what had appeared to be an opposition is really two parts of one complex phenomenon.

Perhaps the insanity/poetic genius binary would be better reformulated in terms of conventionality/unconventionality—a binary that might lead the writer to start reappraising the ways in which Dickinson is not as eccentric as she at first appears to be.

Reformulating Binaries: Two More Examples

In the following two examples, writers Jonathan Franzen and James Howard Kunstler define a problem by locating, defining, analyzing, and reformulating binaries. The thinking in the Franzen paragraph moves by inverting readers' usual expectations. Notice how he does this with the binary public versus private. Kunstler's paragraph takes on the same issue but sets it up in slightly different terms. Notice how Kunstler reformulates the binary public versus private.

I. Walking up Third Avenue on a Saturday night, I feel bereft. All around me, attractive young people are hunched over their StarTacs and Nokias with preoccupied expressions, as if probing a sore tooth, or adjusting a hearing aid, or squeezing a pulled muscle; personal technology has begun to look like a personal handicap. All I really want from a sidewalk is that people see me and let themselves be seen, but even this modest ideal is thwarted by cell-phone users and their unwelcome privacy. They say things like "Should we have couscous with that?" and "I'm on my way to Blockbuster." They aren't breaking any laws by broadcasting these breakfast-nook conversations. There's no PublicityGuard that I can buy, no expensive preserve of public life to which I can flee. Seclusion, whether in a suite at the Plaza or in a cabin in the Catskills, is comparatively effortless to achieve. Privacy is protected as both commodity and right; public forums are protected as neither. Like old-growth forests, they're few and irreplaceable and should be held in trust by everyone. The work of maintaining them gets only harder as the private sector grows ever more demanding, distracting, and disheartening. Who has the time and energy to stand up for the public sphere? What rhetoric can possibly compete with the American love of "privacy"? [From Jonathan Franzen, "Imperial Bedroom" in *How to Be Alone* (Farrar, Straus, and Giroux, 2003)]

II. Civic life is what goes on in the public realm. Civic life refers to our relations with our fellow human beings—in short, our roles as citizens. Sometime in the past forty years we ceased to speak of ourselves as citizens and labeled ourselves consumers. That's what we are today in the language of the evening news—*consumers*—in the language of the Sunday panel discussion shows—*consumers*—in the blizzard of statistics that blows out of the U.S. Department of Commerce every month. Consumers, unlike citizens, have no responsibilities, obligations, or duties to anything larger than their own needs and desires, certainly not to anything like the common good. How can this be construed as anything other than an infantile state of existence? In degrading the language of our public discussion this way—labeling ourselves consumers—have we not degraded our sense of who we are? And is it any wonder that we cannot solve any of our social problems, which are problems of the public realm and the common good? [From James Howard Kunstler, *Home From Nowhere: Remaking Our Everyday World for the Twenty-First Century*, (Simon & Schuster, 1996)]

Try This 4.4: Reformulating Binaries in a Familiar Expression

Write a few paragraphs in which you work with the binaries suggested by the following familiar expression: "School gets in the way of one's education." Keep the focus on working through the binaries implicit in the quotation. What other terms would you substitute for "school" and "education"? Coming up with a range of synonyms for each term will clarify what is at stake in the binary. Remember to consider the accuracy of the claim. To what extent, and in what ways, is the expression both true and false?

Try This 4.5: Reformulating Binaries: More Practice

Apply the Strategies for Using Binaries Analytically to analyze the following statements (or questions), as we did with the TQM example. This does not mean that you must proceed step-by-step through the strategies, but, at the least, you should list all of the binaries you can find, isolate the key terms, and reformulate them. Even if the original formulation looks okay to you, assume that it is an overgeneralization that needs to be refined and rephrased.

a. It is important to understand why leaders act in a leadership role. What is the driving force? Is it an internal drive for the business or group to succeed, or is it an internal drive for the leader to dominate others?

b. Is nationalism good for emerging third-world countries?

c. The private lives of public figures should not matter in the way they are assessed by the public. What matters is how competently they do their jobs.

d. The Seattle sound of rock and roll known as Grunge was not original; it was just a rehash of Punk and New Wave elements.

Try This 4.6: Reformulating Binaries: Fieldwork

Locate some organizing contrasts in anything—something you are studying, something you've just written, something you saw on television last night, something on the front page of the newspaper, something going on at your campus or workplace, and so forth. Binaries pervade the way we think; therefore, you can expect to find them everywhere. Consider, for example, the binaries suggested by current trends in contemporary music or by the representation of women in birthday cards. Having selected the binaries you want to work with, pick one and transform the either/or thinking into a more qualified thinking using the extent to which formula.

4. DIFFERENCE WITHIN SIMILARITY

> When A & B are obviously similar,
> > look for unexpected difference.
> When A & B are obviously different,
> > look for unexpected similarity.

Too often, writers notice a fundamental similarity and stop there. But ideas tend to arise when a writer moves beyond this basic demonstration and complicates (or "qualifies") the basic similarity by also noting areas of difference, and accounting for the significance of that difference.

Step 1: Decide whether the similarities or differences are most obvious and easily explained.

Step 2: Briefly explain the relatively obvious similarity or difference by asking "So what?" Why is this similarity or difference significant?

Step 3: Then focus your attention on the less obvious but revealing difference within the similarity or similarity despite the difference.

Discussion The phrase "difference within similarity" is to remind you that once you have started your thinking by locating apparent similarities, you can usually refine that thinking by pursuing significant, though often less obvious, distinctions among the similar things. In Irish studies, for example, scholars characteristically acknowledge the extent to which contemporary Irish culture is the product of colonization. To this extent, Irish culture shares certain traits with other former colonies in Africa, Asia, Latin America, and elsewhere. But instead of simply demonstrating how Irish culture fits the general pattern of colonialism, these scholars also isolate the ways that Ireland *does not fit* the model. They focus, for example, on how its close geographical proximity and racial similarity to England, its colonizer, have distinguished the kinds of problems it encounters today from those characteristic of the more generalized model of colonialism. In effect, looking for difference within similarity has led them to locate and analyze the anomalies.

A corollary of the preceding principle is that you should focus on *unexpected similarity rather than obvious difference*. The fact that in the Bush presidency Republicans differed from Democrats on environmental policy was probably a less promising focal point than their surprising agreement on violating the so-called lockbox policy against tapping Social Security funds to finance government programs. Most readers would expect the political parties to differ on the environment, and a comparison of their positions could lead you to do little more than summarizing. But a surprising similarity, like an unexpected difference, necessarily raises questions for you to pursue: do the parties' shared positions against the lockbox policy, for example, share the same motives?

Looking for Difference Within Similarity: An Example

Notice how in the following example, taken from an essay on George Orwell's book on the Spanish Civil War, *Homage to Catalonia:*, Lauren Artiles notes differences among political parties that shared an essential position.

> The forces that united against Franco in favor of the government were ragtag and unlikely; the resistance was made up of a slew of different factions of the political left, anarchists and socialists and communists all fighting together against the threat of a Fascist Spain. As Orwell said of the groups and their various acronyms, "It looked at first sight as though Spain was suffering from a plague of initials. I knew that I was serving in something called the P.O.U.M. but I did not realize that there were serious differences between the political parties. [...] I thought it idiotic that people fighting for their lives should *have* separate political parties; my attitude always was, 'Why can't we drop all this political nonsense and get on with the war?'" (47). [. . .]

> The conflict between the P.O.U.M. and the rest of the Communist parties was that the P.O.U.M. was staunchly dissident; they were anti-Stalinist and criticized his Purge Trials of the late '30s, a huge issue considering that the Soviet Union's support of the Spanish Communists' efforts was deemed so crucial. In addition, unlike their counterparts in the P.S.U.C. or Socialist Party of Catalonia, they were very much supporters of the revolution and believed it was a necessary end to the war already underway. The Communists' aim was to win the war and suppress the coming revolution, believing military efficiency to be superior to revolutionary chaos. These ideological differences, which seem so small to an outsider unfamiliar with party politics, led to the eventual persecution of the P.O.U.M. when the Communists seized power.

> [. . .] The question of revolution or no revolution became the biggest issue within the resistance movement and the failure to reach a consensus combined with the vicious power struggle this resulted in weakened the left critically; the war was no longer about defeating the evil of Fascism, but about petty ideological differences between those who were united by that noble, all-consuming cause.

Try This 4.7: Looking for Significant Difference or Unexpected Similarity

Choose any item from the list. After you've done the research necessary to locate material to read and analyze, list as many similarities and differences as you can: go for coverage. Then, review your list, and select the two or three most revealing similarities and the two or three most revealing differences. At this point, you are ready to write a few paragraphs in which you argue for the significance of a key difference or similarity. In so doing, try to focus on an *unexpected* similarity or difference—one that others might not initially notice.

1. accounts of the same event from two different newspapers or magazines or textbooks

2. two CDs (or even songs) by the same artist or group

3. two ads for the same kind of product, perhaps aimed at different target audiences

4. the political campaigns of two opponents running for the same or similar office

5. courtship behavior as practiced by men and by women

6. two clothing styles as emblematic of class or sub-group in your school, town, or workplace

5. SEEMS TO BE ABOUT X BUT COULD ALSO BE (IS "REALLY") ABOUT Y

> Be suspicious of your first responses.
>
> Use the formula "seems to be about X"
> to try on alternative ways of understanding.

This is a useful freewriting prompt that helps students get beyond their first impressions and helps them to see that meanings are inevitably plural and that things mean differently in different contexts.

Like the other heuristics in this toolkit, this last one, "Seems to be about X," prompts you to move beyond potentially superficial explanations—to go deeper. When we begin to interpret something, we usually find that less obvious meanings are cloaked by more obvious ones, and so we are distracted from seeing them. In most cases, the less obvious and possibly unintended meanings are more telling and more interesting than the obvious ones we have been conditioned to see.

The person doing the interpreting too often stops with the first "answer" that springs to mind as he or she moves from observation to implication, usually landing upon a cliché. If this first response becomes the X, then he or she is prompted by the formula to come up with other, probably less commonplace interpretations as the Y.

Step 1: Start the interpretive process by filling in the blank (the X) in the statement "This subject seems to be about X." X should be an interpretive leap, not just a summary or description.

Step 2: Next, pose another interpretive possibility by finishing the sentence, "but it could also be (or is really) about Y."

Step 3: It's essential to repeat this process a number of times to provoke new, interpretive leaps. In effect, you are brainstorming alternative explanations for the same phenomenon.

Step 4: Choose what you think is the best formulation for Y, and write a paragraph or more explaining your choice.

Discussion This prompt is based on the conviction that understandings are rarely simple and overt. Completing the formula by supplying key terms for X and Y, writers get practice in making the implicit explicit and accepting the existence of multiple plausible meanings for something. "Seems to be about X" is especially useful when considering the *rhetoric* of a piece: its complex and various ways of targeting and appealing to an audience. It's also useful for "reading against the grain"—seeking out what something is about that it probably does not know it's about *(see Chapter 5, Writing About Reading).*

Note: Don't be misled by our use of the word *really* in this formula ("Seems to be about X, is really about Y") into thinking that there should be some single, hidden, right answer. Rather, the aim of the formula is to prompt you to think recursively, to come up, initially, with a range of landing sites for your interpretive leap, rather than just one.

Seems to Be About X . . .: An Example

A classic and highly successful television ad campaign for Nike Freestyle shoes contains 60 seconds of famous basketball players dribbling and passing and otherwise handling the ball in dexterous ways to the accompaniment of court noises and hip-hop music. The ad seems to be about X (basketball or shoes) but could also be about Y. Once you've made this assertion, a rapid-fire (brainstormed) list might follow in which you keep filling in the blanks (X and Y) with different possibilities. Alternatively, you might find that filling in the blanks (X and Y) leads to a more sustained exploration of a single point. This is your eventual goal, but doing a little brainstorming first would keep you from shutting down the interpretive process too soon.

Here is one version of a rapid-fire list, any item of which might be expanded:

Seems to be about basketball but is "really" about dance

Seems to be about selling shoes but is "really" about artistry

Seems to be about artistry but is "really" about selling shoes

Seems to be about basketball but is "really" about race

Seems to be about basketball but is "really" about the greater acceptance of black culture in American media and society

Seems to be about the greater acceptance of black culture in American media but is "really" about representing black basketball players as performing seals or freaks

Seems to be about individual expertise but is "really" about working as a group

Here is one version of a more sustained exploration of a single Seems-to-Be-About-X statement.

> The Nike Freestyle commercial seems to be about basketball but is really about the greater acceptance of black culture in American media. Of course it is a shoe commercial and so aims to sell a product, but the same could be said about any commercial.
>
> What makes the Nike commercial distinctive is its seeming embrace of African-American culture. The hip-hop sound track, for example, which coincides with the rhythmic dribbling of the basketball, places music and sport on a par, and the dexterity with which the players (actual NBA stars) move with the ball—moonwalking, doing 360s on it, balancing it on their fingers, heads, and backs—is nothing short of dance.
>
> The intrinsic cool of the commercial suggests that Nike is targeting an audience of basketball lovers, not just African-Americans. If I am right, then it is selling blackness to white as well as black audiences. Of course, the idea that blacks are cooler than whites goes back at least as far as the early days of jazz and might be seen as its own strange form of prejudice. . . . In that case, maybe there is something a little disturbing in the commercial, in the way that it relegates the athletes to the status of trained seals. I'll have to think more about this.

Try This 4.8: Apply the Formula "Seems to Be About X, But Could Also Be (Is "Really") About Y"

As we have been saying, this formula is useful for quickly getting past your first responses. An alternative version of this formula is "Initially I thought X about the subject, but now I think Y." Take any reading or viewing assignment you have been given for class, and write either version of the formula at the top of a page. Fill in the blanks several times, and then explain your final choice for X and Y in a few paragraphs. You might also try these formulae when you find yourself getting stuck while drafting a paper. Seems to Be About X . . . is a valuable revision as well as interpretive tool.

Assignment: Using the Toolkit

Putting the Tools to Work: Composing an Analytical Portfolio. The heuristics introduced in this chapter have been included in the toolkit because they are "all-purpose" analytical moves. In a more extended assignment, try using several of them together. First, review the Try This exercises through the chapter, which suggest a variety of subjects to which you might apply the heuristics. Once you have selected a subject—which could be a film, an advertising campaign, a political campaign, a television series, something you are currently reading for a course or on your own, and so forth—do a series of passage-based focused freewritings as a way of generating ideas.

Try to use both reformulating binaries and uncovering assumptions in the same or consecutive freewrites. Alternatively, try to shake up your thinking by doing Seems to Be About X or Difference Within Similarity in the same or subsequent free writes.

Once you have produced at least four 20-minute free writes, survey them and choose the one you find most interesting. Then do the following:

*Type up three of the free writes, spending 10 or 15 minutes polishing each to achieve some kind of focus and coherence.

*Spend an hour or more expanding and revising your most interesting free write (or some combination of them) into a longer piece, perhaps 3–4 pages. Place this document at the front of the portfolio.

Chapter 5

Writing About Reading: More Moves to Make with Written Texts

THIS BOOK IS ABOUT ANALYZING two kinds of subjects, one of which we might call "the world" (anything and everything you want to better understand), and the other, the world of reading—that is, other people's ideas as these are developed in writing. Throughout the book's first four chapters, we have been concentrating, implicitly or explicitly, on ways of analyzing both worlds. In this chapter, we dwell on this second world—the world of reading.

Here is a list of the chapter's strategies for writing about reading, each with a brief summary of what it involves. We will then go on to explain each in more detail.

READING ANALYTICALLY

1. Find alternatives to reading for the gist: become conversant with the reading.
2. Go local—start with sentences (pointing, passage-based focused freewriting, paraphrasing, commonplace book)
3. Situate the reading rhetorically—find what it seeks to accomplish and what it is set against: the pitch, the complaint, and the moment
4. Seek to understand the reading fairly on its own terms—track the thinking of the piece as it moves through complication and qualification
5. Use the reading as a model
6. Apply the reading as a lens

THE THREE LIVES OF A READING

This chapter focuses on how to approach readings analytically, especially the kinds of complex reading you are likely to encounter in college and ultimately in the workplace. The chapter offers you ways to accomplish two primary tasks: (1) how to **own** a difficult reading, that is, how to make the thinking in a reading yours; and (2) how to use the reading, once you own it.

In practical terms, this chapter will focus on writing about reading in three contexts, which we refer to as the three lives of a reading. These are

- As an Object for Analysis
- As a Model for Imitating
- As a Lens for Viewing Other Material

For More on Writing About Reading Inevitably, not everything that we have to say about reading can be included in this chapter. The chapter assumes, first of all, that you will be using the heuristics in Chapters 2, 3, and 4 when you read. So, for example, when you read virtually anything, you will want to:

- look for patterns of repetition and contrast (aka The Method, Chapter 2),
- paraphrase (Chapter 2),
- make the implicit explicit (Chapter 3),
- uncover assumptions and reformulate binaries (Chapter 4), and
- do passage-based focused freewriting (Chapter 4).

Other essential reading-related skills will be treated in later chapters. These include

- writing analytical summaries (in Chapter 7, Making Common Topics More Analytical),
- writing reaction papers (also in Chapter 7),
- putting readings into conversation with other readings—research-based writing (in Chapter 13, Using Sources Analytically), and
- decoding disciplinary formats (in Chapter 15, Forms and Formats Across the Curriculum)

HOW TO READ: WORDS MATTER

The greatest enemies of reading analytically are "reading for the gist" and the transparent theory of language. Reading for the gist causes readers to leap to global (and usually unsubstantiated) impressions, attending only superficially to what they are reading. The transparent theory of language (first introduced in the discussion of paraphrase in Chapter 2) has a similar effect. This theory invites readers to see through the words as if they were clear windows, suggesting that there is a meaning that can be accessed without the language. Failure to arrest attention on the words causes readers to miss all but the vaguest impression of the ideas that the words embody.

Any child psychology textbook will tell you that as we acquire language, we acquire categories that shape our understanding of the world. Words allow us to ask for things, to say what's on our mind. This is not to say that words are the only reality, but to an enormous extent, we understand the world and our relation to it by working through language.

Considering how central language is in our lives, it's amazing how little we think about words. We tend to assume things mean simply or singly, but virtually all words have multiple meanings, and words mean differently depending on context. Consider the following examples of memorably silly headlines: "Teacher Strikes Idle Kids," "New Vaccines May Contain Rabies," "Local High School Drop-outs Cut in Half," and "Include Your Children When Baking Cookies" (or if you prefer, "Kids Make Nutritious Snacks"). Language is always getting away from us—in such sentences as "The bandage was wound around the wound," or in the classic, "Time flies like an arrow; fruit flies like a banana." The meanings of words and the kinds of sense a sentence makes are rarely stable.

BECOME CONVERSANT INSTEAD OF READING FOR THE GIST

Many readers operate under the mistaken impression that they are to read for the gist—for the main point, to be gleaned through a speed-reading. Although there are virtues to skimming, the vast majority of writing tasks you will encounter in college and in the workplace require your *conversancy* with material you have read. To become conversant means that

- after a significant amount of work with the material, you should be able to talk about it conversationally with other people and answer questions about it without having to look everything up; and
- you should be able to converse with the material—to be in some kind of dialogue with it, to see the questions the material asks, and to pose your own questions about it.

Few people are able to really understand things they read or see without making the language of that material in some way their own. We become conversant, in other words, by finding ways to actively engage material rather than moving passively through it.

Owning the Reading

The short take in Chapter 1, "Writing About Reading: Beyond Banking," lists four tasks that writing about reading at the college level normally requires:

- finding the questions rather than just the answers,
- putting key passages from a reading into conversation with each other,
- using an idea or methodology in a reading in order to generate thinking about something else, and
- gaining control of complex ideas on your own rather than expecting others (such as teachers) to do this work for you.

These tasks require you to change your orientation to reading. How, you might ask, do I make this change, given that I am reading difficult material produced by experts?

What does it mean to read actively and critically when I do not yet have enough knowledge to take issue with what the readings are saying?

There are two key acts of mind—positions you must accept—if you are to play this more active role in writing about reading:

1. *Learn to speak the language of the text.* Every course is in some sense a foreign language course: if a writer wishes to be heard, he or she needs to acquire the vocabulary of the experts. That's why it's so important to pay attention to the actual words in a reading and to use them when you write.

2. *Accept that good reading is a physical as well as a mental activity.* Passing your eyes or highlighter over the text or generalizing about it or copying notes from someone else's PowerPoint will not teach you the *skills* to become an independent thinker. These activities are too passive; they don't trigger your brain into engaging the material. To get physical with the reading, focus on particular words and sentences, copy them out, restate them, and clarify for yourself what you do and do not understand.

FOCUS ON INDIVIDUAL SENTENCES

GOING LOCAL

Pointing
Passage-based focused freewriting
Paraphrasing
Keep a commonplace book

Analyzing needs to be anchored, and anchoring to a general impression, a global sense of what the reading is about, is like putting a hook in a cloud. There is nothing specific to think about, to rephrase, to nudge towards implications or back to assumptions. The best way to remember what you read, and to have ideas about it, is to start with the local—individual sentences and short passages—and build up a knowledge base from there.

It does not matter which sentences you start with. What matters is to choose sentences that strike you as especially revealing, significant, or strange *(see Notice and Focus, Chapter 2).* Good reading is *slow* reading: it stops your forward momentum long enough to allow you to dwell on individual sentences and make the effort necessary to understand them.

A second and related way that people neglect the actual words is that they approach the reading *looking to react.* They are so busy looking to respond to other people's statements that they don't listen to what the other person is saying. A recent article on reading by the literary and educational theorist Robert Scholes suggests that people read badly because they substitute for the words on the page some association or predetermined idea that the words accidentally trigger in them. As a result, they rehearse their own gestalts rather than taking in what the writer is actually saying (see Robert Scholes, "The Transition to College Reading," *Pedagogy*, volume 2, number 2, Duke UP, 2002, pp. 165–172).

We will now survey a few techniques for focusing on individual sentences.

Pointing

Pointing is a practice (associated with two writing theorists and master teachers, Peter Elbow and Sheridan Blau) in which members of a group take turns reading sentences aloud. Pointing provides a way of summarizing without generalizing, and it is one of the best ways to build community and to stimulate discussion.

1. Select sentences from a reading you are willing to voice.
2. Take turns reading aloud without raising hands. Read only one of your chosen sentences at a time. Later in the session, you may read again. Pointing usually lasts about five minutes and ends more or less naturally, when people no longer have sentences they wish to read.
3. No one comments on the sentences in any way during the pointing.
4. Some sentences in the reading repeat as refrains; others segue or answer the previously articulated line.

Pointing stirs our memories about the particular language of a piece. In reading aloud and hearing others do it, you hear key words and discover questions you'd not seen before; and the range of possible starting points for getting at what is central in the reading inevitably multiplies. Pointing is an antidote for the limiting assumption that a reading has only one main idea. It also remedies the tendency of group discussion to veer into general impressions and loose associations.

Passage-Based Focused Freewriting (PBFF)

Passage-based focused freewriting is probably the single best way to arrive at ideas about what you are reading. It is discussed at length in Chapter 4. Here is a quick reprise of the procedure.

PASSAGE-BASED FOCUSED FREEWRITING: WHAT IT DOES

Find an interesting passage
Sketch its context
Target and paraphrase key words and phrases
Explore why the passage is interesting
Draw out implications
Ask how the passage is representative of the larger reading

WHAT IT DOES NOT DO

Voice reactions and criticisms
Free-associate with other subjects

We cannot overstate how important we think it is to do this activity frequently. The practice will enhance your fluency and help you to trust writing as a tool of thought. It is the best place to practice the heuristics in this book. *(Also see the short take, Freewriting: How and Why to Do It, in Chapter 1.)*

Paraphrasing

Paraphrasing is an essential skill in reading closely. It is discussed at length in Chapter 2. Here is a quick reprise of the procedure.

PARAPHRASE FOR IMPLICATION

Locate a short key passage
Assume you **don't** understand it completely
Substitute other concrete language for **all** of the key words
Repeat the paraphrasing several times
Ponder the differences in implication among the versions
Return to the original passage and interpret its meanings

Successive restatement allows you to arrive at your own sense of the significance of the sentence. An essential last step in paraphrasing is to return to the original statement and take stock: "This is what I now understand the passage to mean, having done the paraphrase."

Keep a Commonplace Book

Professional writers have long kept commonplace books—essentially, records of their reading. Most such books consist primarily of quotations the writers have found striking and memorable. The goal of keeping a commonplace book in a course is to bring you closer to the language you find most interesting, which you inscribe in your memory as you copy it onto the page. It's remarkable what you will notice about a sentence (and the ideas in it) if you copy it out rather than just underline or highlight it. Moreover, you will find yourself remembering *the original language* that has struck you most forcefully in the reading. That way you can continue to ponder key words and phrases and to stay engaged, almost physically, with what the writers have said.

When we assign commonplace books in our courses, we stipulate that everyone copy at least two quotations (with citation) from each reading. (These often anchor pointing and passage-based focused freewriting—see the Try This on the next page.) By the end of the semester, every student will have produced a compressed history of his or her reading to supplement class notes and others' commentaries. Note: segregate your commonplace book, whether on paper or online, into a separate notebook or file. This makes the book sequential and browseable.

Try This 5.1: Writing & Reading with Others: A Sequence of Activities

We use this sequence of writing-about-reading activities regularly in our classes. It also works in small, self-directed groups, both in and outside the classroom.

1. Spend 5–10 minutes pointing on some piece of reading. Remember: no one should comment on his or her choice of sentences during the pointing exercise.

2. Without pausing for discussion, spend 10 minutes doing a passage-based focused freewrite on a sentence or several similar sentences from the reading. It is important to write nonstop and to keep writing throughout the appointed time.

3. Volunteers take turns reading all or part of their freewrites aloud to the group without comment. It is essential that people read rather than describe or summarize what they wrote. As each person reads, listeners should jot down words and phrases that catch their attention.

4. Listeners call out what they heard in the freewrite by responding to the question, "What did you hear?"

SITUATE THE READING RHETORICALLY: FIND THE PITCH, THE COMPLAINT, AND THE MOMENT

There is no such thing as "just information." Virtually all readings possess what speech-act theorists call "illocutionary force"—the goal of an utterance. Everything you read, to varying degrees, is aware of you, the audience, and is dealing with you in some way.

One of the most productive ways of analyzing a reading is to consider the frame within which a piece is presented: who its intended audience is, what it seeks to persuade that audience about, and how the writer presents himself or herself to appeal to that audience. Readings virtually never treat these questions explicitly, and thus, it is a valuable analytical move to infer a reading's assumptions about audience *(see the short take, Rhetoric: What It Is and Why You Need It, in Chapter 1).*

An element of situating a reading rhetorically is to locate what it seeks to accomplish and what it is set against at a given moment in time. We address these concerns as a quest to find what we call the pitch, the complaint, and the moment:

- the **pitch**, what the piece wishes you to believe;
- the **complaint**, what the piece is reacting to or worried about; and
- the **moment**, the historical and cultural context within which the piece is operating.

Here's a bit more on each.

The pitch: A reading is an argument, a presentation of information that makes a case of some sort, even if the argument is not explicitly stated. Look for language that reveals the position or positions the piece seems interested in having you adopt.

The complaint: A reading is a reaction to some situation, some set of circumstances, that the piece has set out to address, even though the writer may not say so openly. An indispensable means of understanding someone else's writing is to figure out what seems to have caused the person to write the piece in the first place. Writers write, presumably, because they think *something* needs to be addressed. What is that something? Look for language in the piece that reveals the writer's starting point. If you can find the position or situation he or she is worried about and possibly trying to correct, you will more easily locate the pitch, the position the piece asks you to accept.

The moment: A reading is a response to the world conditioned by the writer's particular moment in time. In your attempt to figure out not only what a piece says but where it is coming from (the causes of its having been written in the first place and the positions it works to establish), history is significant. When was the piece written? Where? What else was going on at the time that might have shaped the writer's ideas and attitudes?

The Pitch, the Complaint, and the Moment: Two Brief Examples

Here are two examples of student writing in response to the request that they locate the pitch, the complaint, and the moment for a famous essay in the field of Composition and Rhetoric, "Inventing the University" by David Bartholomae.

> Bartholomae's complaint seems to center around the idea that writing is typically taught at a grammatical, not intellectual level. 'Basic' writers are identified by their sentence level compositional errors, not by the content of their ideas or ability to present a complex argument. Bartholomae argues that students must be drawn into the language and mindset of academia before they have the authority to confidently expand upon more complicated ideas. Students are expected to fluently participate in academic discourse long before they have the authority to pull it off with ease. Therefore, students should be familiarized with the world of academia and led through the preliminary steps towards becoming proficient in its language. This is the only way to make them more authoritative writers.

And here is another example that treats the moment in particular:

> The moment, or the specific time in which the essay was written, offers some valuable insight into what might have shaped Bartholomae's perspective. First, it is important to note the other writers and thinkers Bartholomae cites throughout the essay. Take the author's frequent mention of writer Pat Bizzell whom Bartholomae deems "one of the most important scholars now writing on 'basic writers'" and whom he recognizes as "owing a

great debt to." He credits Bizzell with seeing how difficult it is for young writers to learn the complex vocabularies and conventions of academic discourse.

There are most likely other, more broadly cultural influences at work as well, such as the American political scene in 1985. In 1984 Ronald Reagan was re-elected president. His presidency and the conservative climate it fostered sparked change in Americans' attitude toward education. Reagan's policies mandated spending cuts and, it can reasonably be assumed, invited certain anti-academic and more pre-professional attitudes. In this moment, then, Bartholomae's concerns about higher education and the need for students to gain access into the privileged world of the educated begins to make more sense.

Audience Analysis: A Brief Example

Consider the following paragraph of student writing on the same essay, this time focused on how the essay's author establishes his relationship with his target audience. Here is the assignment the writer was responding to: Write a brief analysis of the essay's rhetoric—the various methods it employs to gain acceptance with its target audience. (a) Who is the target audience? How can you tell? Cite and analyze evidence. (b) What decisions has the author made on how best to "sell" his argument to this audience? How do you know?

Bartholomae often uses the inclusive "us" to describe academia, putting the reader (presumably, academics) above the level of those being discussed. Students must be taught "to speak our language, to speak as we do, to try on the peculiar ways of knowing, selecting, evaluating, reporting, concluding and arguing that define the discourse of our community" (3). He effectively builds up the reader, perhaps making him or her more open to absorbing the argument that follows. He refrains from criticizing, including his audience in his idea and putting them on the same level as he is. He refers to the students as 'our students' and writes almost as though the reader is separate from any flaws in the current system. He writes to colleagues, with the tone of one sharing something new and interesting.

Try This 5.2: Locating the Pitch and the Complaint

Go to aldaily.com (Arts & Letters Daily, the website sponsored by the Chronicle of Higher Education). Locate an article on a topic you find interesting. It should be a substantive piece of thinking, as opposed to an editorial or a piece of popular commentary.

It is easier to find the pitch if you first look for language that reveals the position or situation the writer is trying to correct. Once you have done this, find language that reveals the position or positions the piece seems interested in having you adopt. Type out these sentences, and be ready to explain your choices.

SEEK TO UNDERSTAND THE READING FAIRLY ON ITS OWN TERMS

Most good reading starts by giving the reading the benefit of the doubt: this is known as producing a *sympathetic reading*, or *reading with the grain*. This advice applies whether or not you are inclined to agree with the claims in the reading. When you are seeking to entertain the reading on its own terms, first you have to decide to suspend judgment as an act of mind, trying instead to think *with* the piece.

While giving the piece its most sympathetic reading, you may find yourself occasionally confused by disagreements that the reading appears to be having with itself. The back-and-forth movement of claims and qualifications can often be mistaken for contradiction or inconsistency. Rather than sit in judgment, follow the movement of mind in the writing as it tries to make sense of something complicated.

Notice, by the way, that this is a place where skimming for overall shape ("fast reading") is appropriate as a starting point. Browse first and last sentences of paragraphs, the introduction and conclusion, and transitional words such as "but" and "however."

ENTERING THE THINKING IN A READING: UNCOVERING ASSUMPTIONS AND REFORMULATING BINARIES (A REPRISE)

Here, we briefly revisit two items from Toolkit II, heuristics essential to seeing the thinking in a reading *(see Chapter 4)*.

UNCOVERING ASSUMPTIONS

Isolate the key terms in the statement.
Ask what the statement rests on, the ideas underlying it.
Draw out implications of the underlying ideas.

All readings—virtually all statements—are built on assumptions. Uncovering the assumptions in a reading, also known as reasoning back to premises, enables you to understand the text better—where it's coming from, what else it believes that is more fundamental than what it is overtly declaring. The essential move is to ask, *"Given its overt claim, what must this reading also already believe?"* To answer this question, you need to make inferences from the primary claims to the ideas that underlie them. In effect, you are working backward, reinventing the chain of thinking that led the writer to the position you are now analyzing.

Once you begin looking at chains of thought, you will often discover that key binaries rise to the surface and need to be reconsidered. You will see examples of this phenomenon in two examples that follow: Christopher Borick's consideration of the term "liberal" and Anna Whiston's analysis of self-deprecation on late night talk shows.

REFORMULATING BINARIES

Step 1: Locate a range of opposing categories

Step 2: Define and analyze the key terms

Step 3: Question the accuracy of the binary and rephrase the terms

Step 4: Substitute "to what extent?" for "either/or"

At the heart of most seriously reflective thinking is some organizing binary. This is to say that thinking rarely looks like a steamroller paving the writer's way from a clear beginning to a predestined end. Rather, it consists of key terms in tension with each other, the tension providing organization and structure for the thought. Thus, the swiftest way to apprehend what's at stake in a reading is to discern its organizing contrasts. Analysis progresses when writers consider how accurately they have named the oppositions in their thinking and whether these should be named otherwise.

Tracking the Thinking Through Complication and Qualification: An Example

Notice how the writer of the following piece—an excerpt from "On Political Labels" by political scientist Christopher Borick—complicates the definition of liberalism by tracking it historically. Look in the first paragraph for the historical roots of liberalism as favoring public control over government actions. Then, in the second paragraph, see how this emphasis moves almost to its opposite—the belief that "government intervention in society is necessary." You'll learn a lot from the excerpt by seeing how it pivots around more than one sense of the word "freedom."

> Let's look at liberalism for a start. The term liberal can be traced at least back to17th-Century England, where it evolved from debates dealing with the voting franchise among English citizens. Proponents of including greater numbers of Englishmen in elections came to be known as liberals, thanks in part to the writings of John Locke, whose ideas about the social contract helped to build the philosophical underpinnings of this political ideology. Over time, liberalism has maintained its focus on public control over government actions, but there have been splits that have led to its current manifestation. In the 18th and 19th Centuries, liberalism began to stress the importance of individual freedom

and broader rights of the citizenry in terms of limits on government. In essence, this type of liberalism focused on "negative rights" or the restrictions on what government could do to its citizens. The First Amendment of the Constitution includes numerous examples of negative rights. The granting of the right to freedom of speech or the press is achieved through the prohibition of government from creating laws that abridge such freedoms. Thus negating an action of government creates rights for the people.

In the 20th Century, however, liberalism became synonymous with the view that government had to be much more active in helping citizens get to the point where they would be able to truly live a free life. In this expanding view of liberalism, government intervention in society is necessary to create a more level playing field on which individuals can then use their freedom to achieve desired goals. Such beliefs have been at the roots of government expansion into social welfare policies such as public housing, food stamps, and affirmative action, and have formed the core of government agendas such as Franklin Roosevelt's New Deal and Lyndon Johnson's Great Society.

As this piece progresses, you can expect that it will either resolve the significant gap between the two historical definitions of liberalism or that it will in various ways show us how the gap has continued to produce tensions or misunderstandings.

In the case of most academic writing, it is usually a mistake to assume that the piece is making a single argument. A smarter assumption is that the piece is interested in exploring an issue or a problem from multiple points of view.

THE PROBLEM OF CRITIQUE

Although you should not be expected simply to go along with all that you read, neither should you jump in and try to critique an expert from your too limited experience. So how do you go about doing the thing that people call "critical reading"?

1. Ultimately, your aim is to put the reading into conversation with other readings on the same subject. In this situation, you speculate, making inferences about what writer X would say about the position of writer Y, and vice versa, establishing a critical conversation in which you cast yourself as referee *(see Chapter 13, Using Sources Analytically for ways of making this move).*

2. Usually, it is more important to learn how to use a complex theoretical lens than it is to arrive at a point from which you can launch an extended critique.

3. Even when an academic reading offers a single dominant claim, in most cases the writing will focus on limiting and qualifying that claim—categorizing it, dividing it into parts, tracing its implications, and so forth. So instead of approaching the reading with the question, "Where might this be wrong?", ask yourself, "How is the argument presented, and why is it presented in this way?"

What Do We Mean by Critical Reading? A Music Professor Speaks

In the following Voice from Across the Curriculum, music professor Ted Conner discusses ways of helping students develop more sophisticated reading skills.

Voices From Across the Curriculum

As a first step, we consider what we mean by a "critical reading." Because the term itself has become so ingrained in our consciousness, we rarely think critically about what it means. So, we discuss moving beyond a summary of the content and cursory judgment. I ask students to take notes on each reading (content and commentary) and conclude with three points. These points may include a main idea of the article or a part of the author's argument they found particularly interesting. We try to locate insights into the author's reason for writing the essay and rhetorical gestures or techniques used by the author to influence the reader.

Does the author make his or her objectives and biases explicit? If not, we examine the rhetorical strategies authors employ to convince us of their objectivity. We observe the ways that language colors the presentation of facts— how "a bitter civil war that pitted the slave-holding Southern states against the rest of the country" was probably not written by an author sympathetic to the Confederacy.

Much of our time is spent investigating how authors construct their narratives: the mode of emplotment (comedy, tragedy, romance, satire), the way the argument is formed, and its ideological position—liberal, conservative, radical, anarchist. These various frames for viewing the reading help us to move beyond content, delay judgment, and evaluate readings on a more sophisticated level.

—Ted Conner, Professor of Music

READING AGAINST THE GRAIN

When we ask ourselves what a work (and, by implication, an author) might not be aware of communicating, we are *reading against the grain*. When we ask ourselves what a work seems aware of, what its (and, by implication, its author's) conscious intentions are, we are *reading with the grain*.

Surely you have had the experience of looking back on something you wrote and wondering where it came from. You didn't plan to say it that way ahead of time. This suggests that writers can never be fully in control of what they communicate—that words always, inescapably, communicate more (and less) than we intend. Any of us who has had what we thought a perfectly clear and well-intentioned letter misinterpreted (or so we thought) by its recipient can understand this idea. When we look at the letter again, we usually see what it said that we hadn't realized (at least not consciously) we were saying.

Communication of all kinds takes place both directly and indirectly. Reading against the grain—looking for what a work is saying that it might not know it is saying, that it might not mean to say—requires us to notice and emphasize implicit patterns and make their significance explicit. So, for example, in the classic novel *Jane Eyre*, the narrator Jane repeatedly remarks on her own plain appearance, with the implication that physical beauty is transient and relatively insignificant. Reading against the grain, we'd see the novel's very obsession with plainness as a symptom of how worried it is about the subject, how much it actually believes (but won't admit) that looks matter. *(See also Chapter 9 for methods of analyzing the logic of an argument.)*

USE A READING AS A MODEL

Most of the critical activities with readings involve assimilating and thinking about the information conveyed. But to use a reading as a model is to focus instead on presentation. This represents a change in orientation for most readers, and it takes a little practice to learn how to do it. A useful guideline to remember is *look beyond content* (or subject matter). To focus on presentation is to focus on what a piece of writing *does* rather than just on what it *says*.

There are two primary reasons for using a reading as a model:

1. It can provide a way of approaching and organizing your own material.
2. Additionally, it can lead you to see features of a reading that you might otherwise overlook. We are, for the most part, "seduced" by the content of what we read, and so we do not see how the piece is "behaving"—how it sets us up, how it repeats certain phrases, how it is patterned.

If, for example, you were to do an analysis of programs designed to help smokers quit by using an analysis of programs designed to help drinkers quit, the latter might be used as a model for the former. And, if the drinking cessation piece began with a long anecdote to phrase some central problem in program design, and you then began your piece with an analogous problem serving the same aim for your piece, that would represent a still closer use of a reading as a model.

To use a reading as a model, detach your attention from the pure information-assimilation mode to observe *how* the reading says *what* it says. Where does it make claims? What kind of evidence does it provide? Does the writer overtly reveal his or her premises? How and when does she use metaphors or analogies?

And what about the overall organization of the piece you are reading? Not all reading proceeds in a straight narrative line from A to B to C. Some pieces are organized like quilts, a series of patches or vignettes operating as variations on a theme. Others favor a radial organization—locating some central issue or example in the center, and then spiraling out to connect it to other matters, then returning to it again and spiraling out again.

APPLY A READING AS A LENS

This final section of the chapter shows how to apply a reading to other material you are studying. Using a reading as a lens means literally looking at things as the reading does, trying to think in its terms.

As with using a reading as a model, when you use a reading as a lens, you first need to separate its analytical method from the particular argument to which it leads.

Not that the argument should be ignored, but your emphasis rests on *extracting the methodology* in order to apply it to your own analytical ends. For example, you can learn a lot about looking at spaces from one of Mike Davis' urban studies articles on the relocation of the homeless in Los Angeles without necessarily focusing on either L.A. or the homeless. Most college campuses, for example, offer significant opportunities to observe the manipulation of public space either to encourage or deter use by certain populations.

Your first goal when working with a reading as a lens is to fully explore its usefulness for explaining features of your subject. Of course, the match between lens and new material will never be perfect. Thus, you need to remember that whenever you apply the lens A to a new subject B, you are taking lens A from its original context and using its ideas in somewhat different circumstances for at least somewhat different purposes. Using the lens in a different context on a different kind of information will often require you to adjust the lens—to refocus it a bit to bring this new content into clear focus.

Let's say, for example, that you read a smart review essay on the representation of black/white race relations in contemporary films in the 1970s, and you decide to use the review as a lens for exploring the spate of black/white buddy films that emerged in the 1990s.

"Yes, but …," you find yourself responding: there are places where the 1990s films appear to fit within the pattern that the article claims, but there are also exceptions to the pattern. What do you do? What *not* to do is either choose different films that "fit better" or decide that the article is wrong-headed. Instead, start with the "yes": talk about how the film accords with the general pattern. Then focus on the "but," the claims in the reading (the lens) that seem not to fit, or material in your subject not adequately accounted for by the lens.

Because cultural climates and trends are constantly shifting and reconfiguring themselves, particularly in popular culture, you will learn from examining the films how the original review might be usefully extended to account for phenomena that were not present when it was originally written.

Using a Reading as a Lens: "Self-Deprecation on Late Night Television"

The following student paper by Anna Whiston was a culminating project for a first-year seminar. The assignment was to use concepts from two books by sociolinguist Deborah Tannen—*You Just Don't Understand: Women and Men in Conversation* and *That's Not What I Meant: How Conversational Style Makes or Breaks Relationships*—to explore a conversational topic of the student's choice, in this case, conversations among male celebrities on late night talk shows. The essay won an award at our college for best writing by a first-year student. The faculty reviewers praised the essay for its analytical depth, its respect for complexity, and its sophisticated use of secondary sources as lenses.

Throughout the essay, the writer deliberately seeks out evidence that might initially seem to contradict theories supplied by her lens. But rather than finding fault with the lens or dismissing the apparent contradictions, she deftly locates the complexity in Tannen's thinking and in her primary material, refusing to oversimplify either.

As you read the essay (which we have excerpted slightly), notice how the writer

- locates significant patterns in her primary material (her transcripts of conversations on late night talk shows) and asks "So what?";
- uses restatement to infer implications;
- uncovers assumptions;
- formulates and reformulates binaries; and
- uses both data and lens to repeatedly qualify and complicate her claims.

We have included annotations in square brackets to suggest how the writer uses various analytical methods for writing about reading.

"I think my cooking, uh, sucks": Self-Deprecation on Late Night Television
by Anna Whiston

Low confidence is not exactly typical in Hollywood. Celebrities are known just as much for their egos as they are for the movies that they headline and the scandals that they induce. And yet, late night talk shows, such as *The Tonight Show with Jay Leno, Late Night with Conan O'Brien, The Late Show with David Letterman,* and *Jimmy Kimmel Live*, include endless examples of self-deprecation on the parts of both the male hosts and the male celebrity guests. Self-deprecation is, on the surface, a way of belittling oneself. However, examination of the conversations that take place on these television programs helps show that this strand of apparent humility is actually a much more nuanced conversational technique. Conversations on late night talk shows reveal that self-deprecation does not necessarily pit one man as inferior to another.

In *You Just Don't Understand*, linguist Deborah Tannen explores conversation as a process affected largely by the gender of the speaker. For men, according to Tannen, "...life is a contest in which they are constantly tested and must perform, in order to avoid the risk of failure" (178). This sense of competition often manifests itself in "one-upsmanship," a strategy in which men attempt to outdo each other in order to achieve a hierarchical position within a conversation (Tannen 26). However, there are certain situations in which hierarchy is not necessarily desirable. The interactions between men on late night talk shows serve as one example of this situation.

In another one of her works on conversation, *That's Not What I Meant*, Tannen discusses framing, the idea that "everything about the way we say something contributes to establishing the footing that frames our relationships to each other "(75).

The guests on talk shows are entering a frame, or conversational alignment, that is inherently asymmetrical. Though both guest and host are technically celebrities, the guest is presented as the centerpiece of the program, the man who answers the questions, while the host is simply the asker. This frame is not always one that is appealing for the guest, who may want to create a persona that is not that of an elite star, but of a likable and approachable everyman. In order to cultivate this persona, the guest can use conversation to downplay his star status and success in order to establish a more symmetrical alignment to the host, thereby changing the frame of the conversation. As we will see, however, this reframing is complicated, since it essentially shifts the asymmetry to a different ground. An example of this technique can be found in actor Paul Rudd's interview with NBC late night talk show host Conan O'Brien:

Rudd: I'm great, how are you?
O'Brien: I'm very good. You know things are going very well for you. You've been in so many successful movies. You have this new film *Role Models*. People love this movie, very funny, big hit for you, you've gotta be excited. I mean you you're a big, big star.
Rudd: It...I don't know about that, but it's very exciting. Oh God, I'm still out of breath! I swear to God.

By negating O'Brien's compliment, Rudd downplays his fame and thus reframes the conversation. By saying, "Oh God, I'm still out of breath," Rudd draws attention away from his stardom to some goofy dancing that O'Brien and Rudd did at the beginning of the interview. When O'Brien again tries to draw attention to Rudd's star power, Rudd again dodges the compliment.

O'Brien: But I would have to think by now that it's reaching critical mass, so many successful movies you must be getting the star treatment now. I bet you're treated like—
Rudd: I met Bruce Springsteen. I met him but it wasn't a...I snuck backstage at a Police concert and he was there.

Rudd's move, which allows him to segue into a self-deprecating anecdote about his encounter with Bruce Springsteen, represents an effort to resist the frame that O'Brien attempts to establish. Instead of accepting the frame that situates Rudd as a star and O'Brien as an average fan, Rudd strategically reframes the conversation by invoking a third party, a star whom both O'Brien and Rudd admire. Now, the conversation is not taking place between a "big star" and his fan, but rather between two fans.

[The writer sets up and queries binaries:] To help understand Rudd's move, we can use Tannen's conversational categories of "report-talk" and "rapport-talk," the former being a way of "exhibiting knowledge and skill" and the latter being a way of "establishing connections" by "displaying similarities and matching experiences" (*Understand* 77). While men are generally associated with report talk rather than rapport talk, the two categories are not necessarily gender exclusive. Humility, which often takes the form of self-deprecation, can help to remove asymmetry from a conversation. Such a move allows the men to capitalize on their similarities rather than emphasize their differences. We see Rudd do just that by transforming his conversational role from that of the star to that of the fan, a fan that must sneak backstage to meet his musical idols, just like the proverbial rest of us.

[The writer uses her lens to reformulate binaries and uncover assumptions:] If the goal of a conversation is to achieve a sense of equality between speakers, one speaker reinforcing the other's self-deprecation may appear to be detrimental to a relationship. Surely, if one makes a comment that he or she is not funny enough, not smart enough, or not brave enough, it is only polite for the other speaker to contradict this statement. However, when the conversation is between men, such a negation would likely be interpreted as sympathy, and may actually undermine rapport. According to Tannen, "Showing elaborate concern for others' feelings frames you as the social worker who has it all together, and them as your patients" (*Understand* 173). Sympathy or pity, as a result, creates a conversational hierarchy. The sympathizer is in a superior position; he is the one with answers while the other man is the one with the problems.

The men conversing on late night talk shows, rather than offering sympathy on hearing another man's self-deprecating anecdote, frequently endorse and even augment the other's self-deprecation. Take, for example, Rudd's story about a wedding he attended, paying special attention to O'Brien's responses.

Rudd: I had a horrible one happen a few years ago where I actually got, um, thrown out of a wedding.
O'Brien: You got thrown out of a wedding?
Rudd: Yeah.
O'Brien: Did you know the people well, I mean these were friends of yours?
Rudd: Yeah, um—
O'Brien: And they threw you out?

Rudd goes on to describe a slightly embarrassing but very humorous video that he made for the bride and groom, with the conversation continuing as follows:

O'Brien: But you didn't think—you didn't know they were gonna show it at the wedding? And so all these people are there, hundreds of people?
Rudd: Well yeah...and uh, uh I'm not even gonna...yeah.
O'Brien: And what happened?
Rudd: Well I—she like, you know—people got kind of freaked out and the bride ran out. I mean it's not the way you imagine your wedding day—
O'Brien: The bride ran away?! That's terrible!
Rudd: I felt horrible.

O'Brien does nothing to soothe Rudd's worries about Rudd's disastrous experience; he urges his guest to divulge all the painful details and seems to relish Rudd's embarrassment. But then, Rudd's purpose was probably not to earn sympathy. O'Brien supported Rudd by *not* showing sympathy, as "refraining from giving sympathy is generous, insofar as it [sympathy] potentially condescends" (*Understand* Tannen 61). Had O'Brien responded that he was sure that Rudd's friends would forgive him and that the incident was not remarkably embarrassing, he would have undermined the purpose of Rudd's story. Instead, O'Brien complies with Rudd by emphasizing the "terrible" nature of his guest's experience. [...]

*[The writer moves next to another of Tannen's theories, which reformulate the binaries in the Rudd and O'Brien example:]*Tannen suggests that while women look for understanding for their problems, men look for solutions: "Yet another man commented that women seem to wallow in their problems, wanting to talk about them forever, whereas he and other men want to get them out and be done with them, either by finding a solution or by laughing them off" (*Understand* 52). The men in these examples did not want sympathy for their problems, nor did they want their problems dismissed—they sought validation. But, unlike the women Tannen described, such validation does not come from sympathy or identification, but from laughter and reinforcement. The self-deprecator is laughing at a problem of his own, and needs the other man to acknowledge that his problem is funny, and is, indeed, a problem, for the two men to achieve equal status within the conversation.

[The writer then moves on to another pattern in her data, instances where two men in a conversation both use self-deprecation:] Self-deprecation is not always used by only one party; it is also sometimes used by both parties to negotiate footing within a conversation. The following excerpt comes from a conversation between ABC late night host Jimmy Kimmel and comedian Artie Lange in which the two men discuss a celebrity wedding both men attended.

Kimmel: I know, right. Well you said something—
Lange: Wasn't that a great event though?
Kimmel: It was great and you did a great job with the toast. What was it you said with the toast about—
Lange: Well it's a, it's an older guy marrying a model way too young for him…

Notice how Lange attempts to avoid accepting Kimmel's assertion that Lange said something funny at the wedding, drawing attention instead to the event as a whole when he senses that Kimmel is about to be complimentary. Later in the same conversation, Lange retaliates and attempts to reframe the conversation.

Lange: But you upstaged me because you—when—I didn't know—I didn't know any other funny people were gonna talk. And then you went up and killed it before they married each other and—
Kimmel: Well you should have known about that. They asked me to do a little thing at the ceremony—
Lange: Right.
Kimmel: Like the day before so I did a little prayer for them.
Lange: That was nice—it was—you were funny.
Kimmel: I didn't mean to, uh, step on your toes there, I didn't want to ruin it. But you do owe me and I'll tell you why…

Lange attempts to reframe the conversation by saying that Kimmel upstaged him. Kimmel, like Lange, dismisses the praise, saying that the prayer that Lange labeled "very funny" was really a "little thing" that he had put together the "day before." Kimmel then clumsily changes the subject in order to draw attention away from himself. This presents a case in which a compliment comes across more as an accusation than a statement of praise. *[The writer has offered an alternative explanation for a possible contradiction with her lens:]* One possible explanation for the desire to dismiss and minimize praise is that compliment-giving is not the selfless act in may appear to be, but is, in fact, pure one-upmanship.

[The writer locates a theory in her lens that would support the explanation:] According to Tannen, "Giving praise, like giving information is also inherently asymmetrical. It too frames the speaker as one-up, in a position to judge someone else's performance" (*Understand* 69). Thus, accepting praise may force the man on the receiving end of the praise to surrender supremacy to the praise-giver. By negating or avoiding praise, hierarchy can be reserved.

The type of combative self-deprecation that Kimmel and Lange display in this conversation, in which one man accuses the other of "upstaging" him, also indicates that self-deprecation is used to display magnanimity. In *That's Not What I Meant*, Tannen writes, "It's an ironic twist by which you want to be magnanimous but want credit for it too—and taking credit for being magnanimous reframes the other person's behavior as depriving you" (89). Self-deprecating humor operates in a similar way. One is not merely telling an embarrassing personal anecdote or using himself as the target of a joke, but, on the "metamessage" level, which looks beyond the surface of a statement to determine "what we're doing when we speak" (*Understand* 32), he is telling his partner (and in the case of talk shows, the audience as well) that he is being generous, sacrificing his own pride in order to compliment the other man. This is evident in Kimmel and Lange's conversation. Both men combine compliments of the other man with denunciations of themselves, suggesting that such a combination is a generous and giving gesture. *[The writer ably concludes her analysis with a compressed restatement about competition:]* The real competition is not about which man was funnier at the wedding, but over which man can better compliment the other's performance.

In Conan O'Brien's conversation with actor Kiefer Sutherland, O'Brien repeatedly pokes fun at his own weakness in order to emphasize Sutherland's toughness, a trait for which the actor is known. It may appear that O'Brien is putting himself down, but at the same time he displays one-upmanship. When O'Brien is being self-deprecating, downplaying his own skills in relation to Sutherland's, Sutherland becomes the recipient of O'Brien's generosity. O'Brien, thus, comes out of the conversation in a hierarchical position to Sutherland, for he was the one giving, and not receiving, the praise and generosity.

[The writer now extends her category of self-deprecation to include another form, teasing:] Teasing and self-deprecation may appear to go hand-in-hand. In teasing, man A makes fun of man B, and in self-deprecation, man B makes fun of man B. Either

way, man B is made fun of. However, the target of the humor is not always as important as the source. If man A teases man B, man A has the upper hand. But if man B teases himself, it is man B who gains dominance in the conversation. On the topic of the wedding that Jimmy Kimmel and Artie Lange attended, Lange says, "Um, but I was glad you were at my table, man, cause it was all good looking people. You uglied it up a bit." Kimmel responds, "I know, yeah. That's uh…yeah we make quite an imposing pair." The men go on, both making fun of what they describe as mutual ugliness. Later in the conversation, Lange begins to tease Kimmel about the host's girlfriend, saying that the couple was engaging in frequent displays of public affection at the wedding. In this situation, Kimmel does *not* transform Lange's teasing into self-deprecation, but instead tries to remove the teasing altogether.

Lange: And so I'm thinking I'm not gonna be the only single loser there and then you and Sarah—I look over and it's like you were shooting *Nine and a Half Weeks* or something.
Kimmel: Oh, no it wasn't.
Lange: You oughta, you oughta see these two.
Kimmel: That's not true.
Lange: "So Jim there's a broad over there we could dance with" he's like (kissing face).
Kimmel: Stop it. That wasn't me—
Lange: I'm telling you, she—
Kimmel: That's really embarrassing cause that wasn't me. Maybe you're confusing me with Corolla, people do that from time to time.

In this excerpt, Lange shatters the mutual self-deprecation that the two had been enjoying earlier, teasing Kimmel about something that Kimmel is clearly not comfortable being teased nor teasing himself about. As a result, Lange has dominance in this conversation. Kimmel struggles to recapture a sense of control, telling Lange that *he* is the one who should be embarrassed, at which point he bring ups a third party, actor Adam Corolla, to be the subject of the teasing. *[The writer is seeing the questions and making them explicit; then characteristically, she seeks out points of connection with the lens:]* Why did Kimmel choose to be self-deprecating about his looks but not his relationship? One possibility, as Tannen suggests, is that men are uncomfortable discussing "personal relationships and feelings" (*Understand* 276). Whatever Kimmel's reasons were, his shifting behavior in this conversation depicts the varying forms and uses of teasing. Teasing can be transformed into self-deprecation, providing the self-deprecator with dominance. But, when the teasing is resisted, the teaser has the opportunity to gain the upper hand. This sheds light on the nature of teasing as a move that provides the teaser with control, regardless of if the teaser is another man or the target of the teasing himself.

Perhaps, then, self-deprecating humor also functions as a sort of pre-emptive move in which one man points out his own flaws before the other man has the chance to do so. If a man makes fun of himself, he still has control. He refuses to surrender this power to another man and thus surrender a hierarchical position in the conversation. Take, for example, this excerpt from Senator John McCain's conversation with NBC host Jay Leno:

Leno: And you went up to the mountains too?
McCain: We went up to our place near Sedona and had a very nice time and—
Leno: Now which house is that, number twel—
McCain: You know that's uh let's see it's a very...let's see... twenty-seven.

Leno was on the verge of making a dig about the senator's many homes, but McCain, seeing this coming, beat Leno to the punch, cutting him off before he even finished the word "twelve." McCain then goes on to exaggerate the number of homes that he owns. This shows that McCain not only understands the public's perception of him, he also is aware that his surplus of homes is a funny, and perhaps even embarrassing, subject. Thus, McCain uses self-deprecation to control the conversation, taking away Leno's opportunity to laugh at him before he laughs at himself.

Perhaps the most frequent and telling place in which self-deprecation pops up is in stories. Late night television is an excellent medium through which to study storytelling; in addition to the release dates of the projects they are promoting, celebrities always come equipped with an anecdote or two. Tannen includes a study of the differences found in stories told by men from those told by women. Her findings indicated that "the stories the men told made them look good" while the women were more likely to tell stories "in which they [women] violate social norms and are scared or embarrassed as a result" (*Understand* 177). The behavior of men on late night talk shows would seem to contradict these findings: the men's stories usually involve them telling of an incident in which, they were, indeed, "embarrassed as a result." However, when we look at the content of these stories, it becomes apparent that these stories function on a more sophisticated level than simple self-effacement.

[This paragraph begins the writer's summation and culmination of her analysis. Notice how deftly she uses Tannen's key terms rather than just relying on quotation.]

Whether it is Paul Rudd's story about showing an embarrassing movie at a friend's wedding or Steve Carrell's anecdote about his parents flying on a plane with a Thanksgiving turkey because his cooking "sucks," the men doing the self-deprecating do not ultimately portray themselves in an embarrassing or pathetic light. The stories that they tell at their own expense draw laughs—and the story teller is laughing with them. In this regard, the stories told are actually more flattering than they are embarrassing. The stories send the message, or metamessage, that the storyteller is able not only to laugh at himself, but also to draw laughs from his audience, all the while coming across as likable and humble. What appears to be humility or lack of self-confidence actually serves a purpose more akin to a joke. And when a joke is told, conversational asymmetry is unavoidable as one man is doing the joke telling while the other functions as the audience (*Understand* 90). Thus, what seems like a way to put one's self down is, in fact, one-upmanship.

Self-deprecation is a complex conversational tool. On the surface, it seems to be simply a way for the speaker to disparage himself. It also, however, can function as a tool for humility and compromise, a way to create conversational symmetry from a situation of asymmetry. The most subtle and fascinating way in which self-deprecation functions, however, is a bit of a paradox: by putting himself down, a man can actually build himself up. This is revealing of the extent to which conversation operates in ways that can be very deceptive. People, whether rich and famous or otherwise, can use conversation not just as a way to transmit information, but as a means to an end. Although this study involved individuals whose job it is to use words to play a character or keep a reputation in check, one need not be an Oscar-winning actor to reap the benefits of being a smart conversationalist. Conversation is not merely a straightforward exchange of words; it is a skill, that when used strategically and with great awareness, can help a speaker to get ahead—often without anyone else realizing that he is doing it.

GUIDELINES FOR WRITING ABOUT READING

1. Get beyond reading for the gist. Always mark a few key passages in whatever you read.

2. Whenever you read critically, actively look for the pitch and the complaint—what the writer wants to convince you of, and the position that he or she is reacting against. Also be aware of the moment—how the historical context qualifies the way we interpret the reading.

3. Experiment with passage-based focused freewriting. Find out what you think by seeing what you say.

4. Alternatively, keep a commonplace book. The act of copying out key sentences from a reading and perhaps jotting a few notes will inevitably lead you to remember more and discover more about what you are reading.

5. Paraphrase key passages to open up the language and reveal complexities you may not have noticed. Paraphrasing three times is sure to help get you started interpreting a reading, moving you beyond just repeating pieces of it as answers.

6. In applying a reading as a lens, think about how lens A both fits and does not fit subject B: use the differences to develop your analysis.

7. Uncover unstated assumptions by asking, "Given its overt claim, what must this reading also already believe?"

8. A provocative way to open up interpretation is to try reading against the grain of a reading. Ask, "what does this piece believe that it does not know it believes?" Using The Method to uncover obsessive repetitions will sometimes provide the evidence to formulate against-the-grain claims.

Assignments: Writing Analytically About Reading

1. **Apply a Reading as a Lens**. Use a reading as a lens for examining a subject. For example, look at a piece of music or a film through the lens of a review that does not discuss the particular piece or film you are writing about. Or you might read about a particular theory of humor and use that as a lens for examining a comic play, film, story, television show, or stand-up routine.

2. **Analyze a Challenging Paragraph and Apply It as a Lens**. In a recent book on representations of the public and the private in contemporary American life, law professor Jeffrey Rosen offers the following discussion of political scientist Daniel Boorstin's analysis of heroes and celebrities:

> In *The Image*, Daniel Boorstin explored the way the growth
> of movies, radio, print, and television had transformed the
> nature of political authority, which came to be exercised
> not by distant and remote heroes but instead by celebrities,

whom Boorstin defined as 'a person who is known for his well-knownness.' 'Neither good nor bad,' a celebrity is 'morally neutral,' 'the human pseudo-event,' who has been 'fabricated on purpose to satisfy our exaggerated expectations of human greatness' (11). While the heroes of old exercised authority by being remote and mysterious, modern celebrities exercise authority by being familiar and intelligible, creating the impression—but not the reality—of emotional accessibility. Heroes were distinguished by their achievement, celebrities by their image or trademarks or 'name brands' (*The Naked Crowd*, Random House, 2004).

Bring the tools for reading analytically to bear on this passage in the following sequence:

a. Use paraphrase to restate both Boorstin's claims and Rosen's exposition of it.

b. Then locate the dominant binaries in the paragraph and articulate these to help you determine what is at stake there.

c. Once you've done these tasks, take Boorstin's theory and use it as a lens to examine the presentation of a public figure of your choice, whether a politician, a contemporary hero, a celebrity, a musician, a sports star, and so forth. As you write about this figure, seek to explore not only how your subject fits the lens but also how he or she does not fit. Use the Whiston essay on talk shows as a model for negotiating complication in both the lens and the primary material.

3. **Apply the Lens of Ritual to Daily Life**. In her book, *The Rituals of Dinner* (1991), Margaret Visser discusses table manners as a form of ritual:

> Rules of politeness tend to cluster round moments of transition, of meeting others, making decisions, conferring, parting, commemorating. Rituals are there to make difficult passages easier. They include the gestures—waving, nodding, smiling, speaking set phrases—which daily smooth our meetings with other people; the attitudes and postures we adopt when standing or sitting in the presence of others, especially when we are talking to them; the muttering of 'excuse me' when interrupting others or squeezing past them. Full-dress celebrations of coming together, of marking transitions and recollections, almost always require food, with all the ritual politeness implied in dining—the proof that we all know how eating should be managed. We eat whenever life becomes dramatic: at weddings, birthdays, funerals, at parting and at welcoming home, or at any moment which a group decides is worthy of remark. Festivals and feasts are solemn or holy days; they are so regularly celebrated by people meeting for meals that 'having a feast' has actually come to mean 'eating a lot.'

As this paragraph suggests, rituals depend on rules and conventional behaviors that provide order and stability, thereby easing "difficult passages." Use the tools you've acquired in this and previous chapters to uncover the implications in this paragraph. Then use it as a lens to analyze some ritual from everyday life. Obviously, Visser is concentrating on the ritual functions surrounding food—which you can use as a model for your investigation of some other ritual, perhaps one that you never noticed as a ritual before. It could be any system regulated by manners:

- handling a pet in public,
- ordering drinks for a group of friends,
- visiting a professor during office hours,
- participating in class discussion,
- attending a baseball game, or
- socializing in the library.

And the list is endless. Choose any ritual activity, and use Visser as a model and a lens to analyze it. Describe carefully its rules, and explore what these rules control and why such control is useful.

Chapter 6

Making Interpretations Plausible

IN THIS CHAPTER, we focus on the move from description to interpretation and address some of the issues that interpretation typically raises. What makes some interpretations better than others? What makes interpretations more than a matter of personal opinion?

The book has so far offered two kinds of prompts for making interpretive leaps: ranking (what is most important, or interesting, or revealing and why?) and asking "So what?" We've also demonstrated that the writer who can offer careful description of a subject's key features is likely to arrive at conclusions about possible meanings that others would share. We will now add another necessary move: specifying and arguing for a context in which the evidence might be best understood—the **interpretive context**.

Here are two key principles:

- *Everything means*; that is, everything in life calls on us to interpret—even when we are unaware of doing so.
- *Meaning is contextual*; that is, meaning-making always occurs inside of some social or cultural or other frame of reference.

WHAT INTERPRETATION DOES

Offers a theory of what X means, not fact

Supplies a context for understanding X that is suggested by the details

Strives for the plausible, not the certain: explains individual details and patterns of evidence

Supplies reasons for why evidence means what you claim it means

MOVING FROM DESCRIPTION TO INTERPRETATION

Throughout this book, we have been defining analysis as a search for meaning, a search conducted primarily through discovery of significant patterns in your evidence. In Chapter 3, Analysis: What It Is and What It Does, we noted that the process of noticing, of recording selected details and patterns of detail (analysis), is already the beginning of interpretation. Analysis differs from description and summary because it triggers larger interpretive leaps.

As we also argued in Chapter 3, the first step toward arriving at and persuading others to accept your interpretation is to make the most of the observation stage by following these two rules:

1. **Describe with care.** The words you choose to summarize your data will contain the germs of your ideas about what the subject means.

2. **In moving from summary to analysis and interpretation, look consciously at the language you have chosen,** asking, "Why did I choose this word? What ideas are implicit in the language I have used?"

Your readers' willingness to accept an interpretation is powerfully connected to their ability to see its *plausibility*, that is, how it follows from both the supporting details you selected and the language you used in characterizing those details. *An interpretive conclusion is not a fact, but a theory.* Interpretive conclusions stand or fall not so much on whether they can be proved right or wrong, but on whether they are demonstrably plausible. Often, the best you can hope for with interpretive conclusions is not that others will say, "Yes, that is obviously right," but "Yes, I can see where it might be possible and reasonable to think as you do."

A major point of this chapter is that interpretive contexts are suggested by the material you are studying; they aren't simply imposed on it by a writer. Explaining why you think a subject should be seen through a particular interpretive "lens" is an important part of making interpretations reasonable and plausible. Our discussion will illustrate how, once an interpretive context is selected, a writer goes about analyzing evidence to test—as well as support—the usefulness of that context.

Different interpretations will account better for some details than others, which is why it enriches our view of the world to try on different interpretations. Ultimately, you will have to decide which possible interpretation, as seen through which plausible interpretive context, best accounts for what you think is most important and interesting to notice about your subject.

HOW TO INTERPRET

Organize the data (do The Method)
Move from observation to implication (ask So what?)
Select an appropriate interpretive context
Determine a range of plausible interpretations
Assess the extent to which one interpretation explains the most

MAKING INTERPRETATIONS PLAUSIBLE ACROSS THE CURRICULUM

As we note at various points in this book, the practices governing data gathering, analysis, and interpretation differ as you move from one academic division to another. In the humanities, the data to be analyzed are usually textual—visual or verbal details.

In the social sciences, data are sometimes textual, as would be the case, for example, if you were analyzing the history of a particular political theory or practice such as free speech. But much analytical thinking in the social sciences and the natural sciences involves arriving at plausible conclusions about the significance of quantitative (numerical) and experimental data. This book's primary interpretive prompt, "So what?" (where do these research data get me, and why does this data set mean what I say it means?) still applies in the sciences, though the interpretive leaps are typically worded differently.

Interpretation in the natural and social sciences considers the extent to which data either confirm or fail to confirm the expectations defined in a hypothesis, which is a theory the writer proposes in response to a research question. This chapter's examples demonstrate analytical thinking as it typically operates in the humanities. The emphases, however, on careful description of evidence and on arguing for the appropriateness of a particular interpretive context are common to all three academic divisions. *(For more on the language and methods of interpretation in the natural and social sciences, see Chapter 15, Forms and Formats Across the Curriculum.)*

PLAUSIBLE VERSUS IMPLAUSIBLE INTERPRETATIONS: THE SOCIAL CONTEXT

Meanings must be reasoned from sufficient evidence if they are to be judged plausible. Meanings can always be refuted by people who find fault with your reasoning or can cite conflicting evidence. Let's refer back briefly to a hypothetical question raised in Chapter 3's discussion of *Whistler's Mother*—that the woman in the painting who is clad in black is mourning the death of a loved one, perhaps a person who lived in the house represented in the painting on the wall. It is true that black clothes often indicate mourning. This is a culturally accepted, recognized sign. But with only the black dress, and perhaps the sad facial expression (if it is sad) to go on, this "mourning theory" gets sidetracked from what is actually in the painting into storytelling. Insufficient evidence would make this theory implausible.

Now, what if another person asserted that Whistler's mother is an alien astronaut, for example, her long black dress concealing a third leg? Obviously, this interpretation would not win wide support, and for a reason that points up another of the primary limits on the meaning-making process: meanings, to have value outside one's own private realm of experience, have to make sense to other people. The assertion that Whistler's mother is an alien astronaut is unlikely to be deemed acceptable by enough people to give it currency.

This is to say that the relative value of interpretive meanings is to some extent socially (culturally) determined. Although people are free to say that things mean whatever they want them to mean, saying doesn't make it so. The mourning theory has more evidence than the alien astronaut theory, but it still relies too heavily on what is not there, on a narrative for which there is insufficient evidence in the painting itself.

In experimental science, it is especially important that a writer/researcher can locate his or her work in the context of other scientists who have achieved similar results. Isolated results and interpretations, those that are not corroborated by others' research, have much less credibility. In this respect, the making of meaning is collaborative and communal. The collaborative nature of scientific and scholarly work is one of the reasons that writing about reading is so important in college-level writing. In order to interpret evidence in a way that others will find plausible, you first have to have some idea of what others in the field are talking about.

INTERPRETIVE CONTEXTS AND MULTIPLE MEANINGS

There are, however, other possible interpretations that would satisfy the two criteria of sufficient evidence and broad cultural acceptance. And it is valuable to recognize that evidence usually will support more than one plausible interpretation. Consider, for example, a reading of *Whistler's Mother* that a person might produce if he or she began with noticing the actual title, *Arrangement in Grey and Black: The Artist's Mother*. From this starting point, a person might focus observation on the disposition of color exclusively and arrive at an interpretation that the painting is about painting (which might then explain why there is also a painting on the wall).

The figure of the mother then would have meaning only insofar as it contained the two colors mentioned in the painting's title, black and gray, and the painting's representational content (the aspects of life that it shows us) would be assigned less importance. This is a promising and plausible idea for an interpretation. It makes use of different details from previous interpretations that we've suggested, but it would also address some of the details already targeted (the dress, the curtain) from an entirely different context, focusing on the use and arrangement of color.

To generalize: two equally plausible interpretations can be made of the same thing. It is not the case that our first reading (in Chapter 3), focusing on the profile view of the mother and suggesting the painting's concern with mysterious separateness, is right, whereas the painting-about-painting (or aesthetic) view, building from the clue in the title, is wrong. They operate within different contexts.

An interpretive context is a lens. Depending on the context you choose—preferably a context suggested by the evidence itself—you will see different things. Regardless of how the context is arrived at, an important part of getting an interpretation accepted as plausible is to argue for the appropriateness of the interpretive context you use, not just the interpretation it takes you to.

Specifying an Interpretive Context: A Brief Example

Notice how, in the following analysis, the student writer's interpretation relies on his choice of a particular interpretive context, post–World War II Japan. Had he selected another context, he might have arrived at some different conclusions about the same details. Notice also how the writer perceives a pattern in the details and queries his own observations ("So what?") to arrive at an interpretation.

The series entitled "Kamaitachi" is a journal of the photographer Hosoe's desolate childhood and wartime evacuation in the Tokyo countryside. He returns years later to the areas where he grew up, a stranger to his native land, perhaps likening himself to the legendary Kamaitachi, an invisible sickle-toothed weasel, intertwined with the soil and its unrealized fertility. "Kamaitachi #8" (1956), a platinum palladium print, stands alone to best capture Hosoe's alienation from and troubled expectation of the future of Japan. *[Here, the writer chooses the photographer's life as his interpretive context.]*

The image is that of a tall fence of stark horizontal and vertical rough wood lashed together, looming above the barren rice fields. Straddling the fence, half-crouched and half-clinging, is a solitary male figure, gazing in profile to the horizon. Oblivious to the sky above of dark and churning thunderclouds, the figure instead focuses his attentions and concentrations elsewhere. *[The writer selects and describes significant detail.]*

It is exactly this *elsewhere* that makes the image successful, for in studying the man we are to turn our attention in the direction of the figure's gaze and away from the photograph itself. He hangs curiously between heaven and earth, suspended on a makeshift man-made structure, in a purgatorial limbo awaiting the future. He waits with anticipation—perhaps dread?—for a time that has not yet come; he is directed away from the present, and it is this sensitivity to time which sets this print apart from the others in the series. One could argue that in effect this man, clothed in common garb, has become Japan itself, indicative of the post-war uncertainty of a country once-dominant and now destroyed. What will the future (dark storm clouds) hold for this newly-humbled nation? *[Here, the writer notices a pattern of in-between-ness and locates it in an historical context in order to make his interpretive leap.]*

Remember that regardless of the subject you select for your analysis, you should directly address not just "What does this say?" but also, as this writer has done, "*What are we invited to make of it, and in what context?*"

The Role of Context in Interpreting Numerical Data

In the previous example, the writer chose an interpretive context that seemed to best explain a pattern of detail in his evidence. In order to make a case for his interpretation, the writer needed to demonstrate the appropriateness and relevance of his chosen context, including his reasons for choosing one possible interpretive context over another.

The process is similar when a writer seeks to interpret numerical data. The writer must decide the extent to which his or her numerical data confirm or fail to confirm an expectation defined in the study's hypothesis. Here is a brief example of statistical analysis from a political science course on public opinion research. The study uses a data set generated to test the hypothesis that "Republican defectors who have been members of the party for over 11 years are less likely to change party affiliation to Democrat because of the Republican Party's policies than Republican defectors registered with the party for under 10 years." Note how the writer integrates quantitative data into her discussion of the findings, a move characteristic of interpretation in the social sciences, and how she establishes the context in which this data might be best understood. Notice too how her findings complicate her original research question.

> The data suggest that the longer a Republican defector was a member of the Republican Party, the more likely that person was to switch party affiliation to Democrat because of the Republican Party's policies as opposed to changes in his or her own belief system. For example, 35% of Republican defectors who had been members of the party for 1-5 years agreed with the statement 'the Republican Party's policies led me to leave the party,' while 35% said it was due to changes in their personal beliefs. Thus, it appears as though both reasons have equal influence on an individual's decision to switch parties.
>
> However, when you look at the defectors who were members of the party for over 6 years, roughly 20% more of them left because of the party's policies than because of a change in their personal beliefs. This suggests that people don't change their views—it is the party's change of views that prompts defection by even long-time members.

In the case of statistical data, an interpretive problem arises when writers attempt to determine whether a statistical correlation between two things—blood cholesterol level and the likelihood of dying of a heart attack, for example—can be interpreted as causal. Does a statistical correlation between high cholesterol levels and heart attack suggest that higher levels of cholesterol cause heart attacks, or might it only suggest that some other factor associated with cholesterol is responsible? Similarly, if a significantly higher percentage of poor people treated in hospital emergency rooms die than their more affluent counterparts, do we conclude that emergency room treatment of the poor is at fault? What factors, such as inability of poor people to afford regular preventive health care, might need to be considered in interpretation of the data? *(For more on interpreting numerical data, see "Interpreting the Numbers: A Psychology Professor Speaks" in Chapter 8, Reasoning from Evidence to Claims.)*

INTENTION AS AN INTERPRETIVE CONTEXT

An interpretive context that frequently creates problems in analysis is intention. People relying on authorial intention as their interpretive context typically assert that the author—not the work itself—is the ultimate and correct source of interpretations.

©The Dancers, by Sarah Kersh. Pen and ink drawing, 6″ × 13.75″.
Used by Permission of Sarah Kersh.

FIGURE 6.1
The Dancers **by Sarah Kersh. Pen-and-Ink Drawing, 6″ × 13.75″**

Look at the drawing titled *The Dancers* in Figure 6.1. What follows is the artist's statement about how the drawing came about and what it came to mean to her.

> This piece was created completely unintentionally. I poured some ink onto paper and blew on it through a straw. The ink took the form of what looked like little people in movement. I recopied the figures I liked, touched up the rough edges, and ended with this gathering of fairy-like creatures. I love how in art something abstract can so suddenly become recognizable.

In this case, interestingly, the artist initially had no intentions beyond experimenting with materials. As the work evolved, she began to arrive at her own interpretation of what the drawing might suggest. Most viewers would probably find the artist's interpretation plausible, but this is not to say that the artist must have the last word and that it is somehow an infraction for others to produce alternative interpretations.

Suppose the artist had stopped with her first two sentences. Even this explicit statement of her lack of intention would not prohibit people from interpreting the drawing in some of the ways that she later goes on to suggest. The artist's initial absence of a plan doesn't require viewers to interpret *The Dancers* as only ink on paper.

Whenever an intention is ascribed to a person or an act or a product, this intention contributes significantly to meaning; but the intention, whatever its source, does not outrank or exclude other interpretations. It is simply another context for understanding.

Why is this so? In our earlier discussion of personalizing, we suggested that people are not entirely free agents, immune to the effects of the culture they inhabit. It follows that when people produce things, they are inevitably affected by that culture in ways of which they are both aware and unaware. The culture, in other words, speaks through them. In the early 1960s, for example, a popular domestic sitcom, *Leave It to Beaver,* portrayed the mother, June Cleaver—usually impeccably dressed in heels, dress, and pearls—doing little other than dusting the mantle and making tuna fish sandwiches for her sons. Is the show then intentionally implying that the proper role for women is that of domestic helper? Well, in the context of post–women's movement thinking, the show's representation of Mrs. Cleaver might plausibly be read this way, but not as a matter of intention. To conclude that *Leave It to Beaver* promoted a particular stereotype about women does not mean that the writers got together every week and thought out ways to do so.

It is interesting and useful to try to determine from something you are analyzing what its makers might have intended. But, by and large, you are best off concentrating on what the thing itself communicates as opposed to what someone might have wanted it to communicate.

WHAT IS AND ISN'T "MEANT" TO BE ANALYZED

What about analyzing things that were not intended to "mean" anything, like entertainment films and everyday things like blue jeans and shopping malls? Some people believe it is wrong to bring out unintended implications. Let's take another example: Barbie dolls. These are just toys intended for young girls, people might say. Clearly, the intention of the makers of Barbie is to make money by entertaining children. Does that mean Barbie must remain outside of interpretive scrutiny for such things as her built-in earrings, high-heeled feet, and heavily marketed lifestyle?

What the makers of a particular product or idea intend is only a part of what that product or idea communicates. The urge to cordon off certain subjects from analysis on the grounds that they weren't meant to be analyzed unnecessarily excludes a wealth of information—and meaning—from your range of vision. It is right to be careful about the interpretive contexts we bring to our experience. It is less right—less useful—to confine our choice of context in a too literal-minded way to a single category. To some people, baseball is only a game and clothing is only there to protect us from the elements.

What such people don't want to admit is that things communicate meaning to others whether we wish them to or not; that is, the meanings of most things are socially determined. What, for example, does the choice of wearing a baseball cap to a staff meeting or to a class "say"? Note, by the way, that a communicative gesture such as the wearing of a hat need not be premeditated to communicate something to other people. The hat is still "there" and available to be "read" by others as a sign of certain attitudes and a culturally defined sense of identity—with or without intention.

Meaning and Social Contexts

Baseball caps, for example, carry different associations from berets or wool caps because they come from different social contexts. Baseball caps convey a set of attitudes associated with the piece of American culture they come from. They suggest, for example, popular rather than high culture, casual rather than formal, young—perhaps defiantly so, especially if worn backward—rather than old, and so on.

We can, of course, protest that the "real" reason for turning our baseball cap backward is to allow more light in, making it easier to see than when the bill of the cap shields our faces. This practical rationale makes sense, but it does not explain away the social statement that the hat and a particular way of wearing it might make, whether or not this statement is intentional. Because meaning is, to a significant extent, socially determined, we can't entirely control what our clothing, our manners, our language, or even our way of walking communicates to others.

The social contexts that make gestures like our choice of hats carry particular meanings are always shifting, but some such context is always present. As we asserted at the beginning of this chapter, everything means, and meaning is always contextual.

We turn now to two common problems writers encounter in interpretation. These problems are so widespread that we have fancifully labeled them "schools."

THE FORTUNE COOKIE SCHOOL OF INTERPRETATION

The theory of interpretation that we call the Fortune Cookie School believes that things have a single, hidden, "right" meaning, and that if a person can only "crack" the thing, it will yield an extractable and self-contained "message." There are several problems with this conception of the interpretive process *(see Chapter 3, Implications Versus Hidden Meanings)*.

First, the assumption that things have single hidden meanings interferes with open-minded and dispassionate observation. Adherents of the Fortune Cookie School look solely for clues pointing to *the* hidden message and, having found these clues, discard the rest, like the cookie in a Chinese restaurant once the fortune has been extracted. The fortune cookie approach forecloses on the possibility of multiple plausible meanings, each within its own context. When you assume only one right answer exists, you are also assuming there is only one proper context for understanding and, by extension, that anybody who happens to select a different starting point or context and who thus arrives at a different answer is necessarily wrong.

Most of the time, practitioners of the fortune cookie approach aren't even aware they are assuming the correctness of a single context because they don't realize a fundamental truth about interpretations: they are always limited by contexts. In other words, we are suggesting that claims to universal truths are always problematic. Things don't just mean in some simple and clear way for all people in all situations; they always mean within a network of beliefs, from a particular point of view. The person who claims to have access to some universal truth, beyond context and point of view, is either naïve (unaware) or, worse, a bully—insisting that his or her view of the world is obviously correct and must be accepted by everyone.

THE ANYTHING GOES SCHOOL OF INTERPRETATION

At the opposite extreme from the single-right-answer Fortune Cookie School lies the completely relativist Anything Goes School. The problem with the Anything Goes approach is that it tends to assume that *all* interpretations are equally viable, and that meanings are simply a matter of individual choice, regardless of evidence or plausibility. Put another way, it overextends the creative aspect of interpretation to absurdity, arriving at the position that you can see in a subject whatever you want to see. But such unqualified relativism is not logical. It is simply not the case that meaning is entirely up to the individual; some readings are clearly better than others. The better interpretations have more evidence and rational explanation of how the evidence supports the interpretive claims—qualities that make these meanings more public and negotiable.

MAKING AN INTERPRETATION: THE EXAMPLE OF A *NEW YORKER* COVER

A major point of this section is that interpretive contexts are suggested by the material you are studying; they aren't simply imposed. Explaining why you think a subject should be seen through a particular interpretive "lens" is an important part of making interpretations reasonable and plausible. Our discussion illustrates a writer's decision-making process in choosing an interpretive context and how, once that context has been selected, the writer goes about analyzing evidence to test as well as support the usefulness of that context.

The example on which we focus is a visual image, a cover from the *New Yorker* magazine (see Figure 6.2). The cover of the October 9, 2000 issue is by Ian Falconer and is entitled "The Competition." To see the image in color, you can easily access it online by following these steps: (1) visit the *New Yorker* store website; (2) click on Browse by Artist; (3) choose Ian Falconer; and (4) page forward to October 9, 2000.

Producing a close description of anything you analyze is one of the best ways to begin because the act of describing causes you to notice more and triggers analytical thinking. Here is our description of the *New Yorker* cover:

The picture contains four women, visible from the waist up, standing in a row in semi-profile, staring out at some audience other than us, since their eyes look off to the side. All four gaze in the same direction. Each woman is dressed in a bathing suit and wears a banner draped over one shoulder in the manner of those worn in the swimsuit competition at beauty pageants. Three of the women are virtually identical. The banners worn by these three women show the letters *gia, rnia,* and *rida,* the remainder of the letters being cut off by the other women's shoulders, so that we have to fill in the missing letters to see which state each woman represents.

The fourth woman, who stands third from the left in line, tucked in among the others who look very much alike, wears a banner reading *york.* This woman's appearance is different in just about every respect from the other three. Whereas they are blonde with long flowing hair, she is dark with her hair up in a tight bun. Whereas their mouths are wide open, revealing a wall of very white teeth, her mouth is closed, lips drawn together. Whereas their eyes are wide open and staring, hers, like her mouth, are nearly closed, under deeply arched eyebrows.

The dark woman's lips and eyes and hair are dark. She wears dark eye makeup and has a pronounced dark beauty mark on her cheek. Whereas the other three women's cheeks are high and round, hers are sharply angular. The three blonde women wear one-piece bathing suits in a nondescript gray color. The dark-haired woman, whose skin stands out in stark contrast to her hair, wears a two-piece bathing suit, exposing

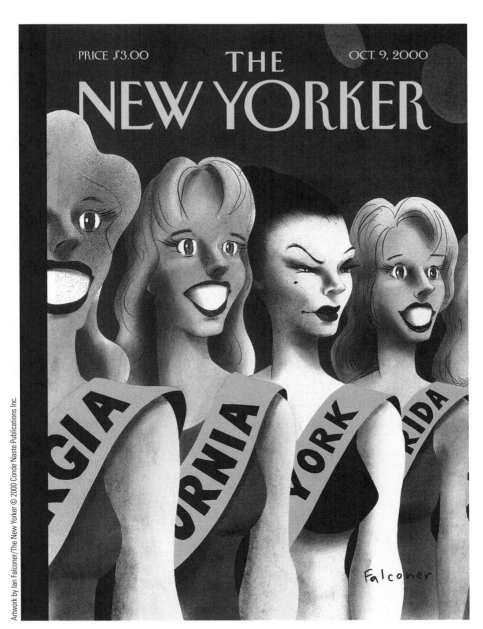

Artwork by Ian Falconer/The New Yorker © 2000 Conde Naste Publications Inc.

FIGURE 6.2
"The Competition" by Ian Falconer

her midriff. Like her face, the dark-haired woman's breast, sticking out in half profile in her bathing suit, is pointed and angular. The other three women's breasts are round and quietly contained in their high-necked gray bathing suits.

Using the Method to Identify Patterns of Repetition and Contrast

As we discussed in Chapter 2, looking for patterns of repetition and contrast (aka The Method) is one of your best means of getting at the essential character of a subject. It will prevent you from generalizing, instead involving you in hands-on engagement with the details of your evidence. Step 1, looking for things that repeat exactly, tends to suggest items for step 2, repetition of the same or similar kinds of words or details (strands), and step 2 leads naturally to step 3, looking for binary oppositions and organizing contrasts.

Here are our partial lists of exact repetitions and strands and binary oppositions in the *New Yorker* cover:

Some Details That Repeat Exactly

Large, wide open, round eyes (3 pairs)

Long, blonde, face-framing hair (3)

Small, straight eyebrows (3 pairs)

Wide-open (smiling?) mouths with expanses of white teeth (3)
    (but individual teeth not indicated)

banners (4) but each with different lettering

round breasts (3)

states that end in *a* (3)

Some Strands (groups of the same or similar kinds of details)

Lots of loose and flowing blonde hair/large, fully open, round eyes/large, open, rather round (curved) mouths:

Connecting logic = open, round

Skin uniformly shaded on three of the figures/minimal color and shading contrasts/mouths full of teeth but just a mass of white without individual teeth showing:

Connecting logic = homogenous, undifferentiated, indistinct

Binary Oppositions

Blonde hair/black hair

Open mouths/closed mouth

Straight eyebrows/slanted (arched) eyebrows

Round breasts/pointed breast

Covered midriff/uncovered midriff

Notice that we have tried hard to stick with "the facts" here—concrete details in the picture. If we were to try, for example, to name the expression on the three blonde women's faces and the one on the black-haired woman (expressionless versus knowing? vapid versus shrewd? trusting versus suspicious? and so on), we would move from data gathering—direct observation of detail—into interpretation. The longer you delay interpretation in favor of noticing patterns of like and unlike detail, the more thoughtful and better grounded your eventual interpretation will be.

Anomalies

Miss New York

Pushing Observations to Conclusions: Selecting an Interpretive Context

As we argued throughout this chapter, the move from observations to conclusions depends on context. You would, for example, come up with different ideas about the significance of particular patterns of detail in the *New Yorker* cover if you were analyzing them in the context of the history of the *New Yorker* cover art than you might if your interpretive context was other art done by Ian Falconer, the cover's artist. Both of these possibilities suggest themselves, the first by the fact that the title of the magazine, the *New Yorker*, stands above the women's heads, and the second by the fact that the artist's last name, Falconer, runs across two of the women.

What other interpretive contexts might one plausibly and fairly choose, based on what the cover offers us? Consider the cover's date—October 9, 2000. Some quick research into what was going on in the country in the early fall of 2000 might provide some clues about how to read the cover in a **historical context**. November 2000 was the month of a presidential election. At the time the cover was published, the long round of presidential primaries, with presidential hopefuls courting various key states for their votes, had ended, but the last month of campaigning by the presidential nominees—Al Gore and George W. Bush—was in full swing.

You might wish to consider whether and how the cover speaks to the country's political climate during the Gore/Bush competition for the presidency. The banners and the bathing suits and the fact that the women stand in a line staring out at some implied audience of viewers, perhaps judges, reminds us that the picture's narrative context is a beauty pageant, a competition in which women representing each of the states compete to be chosen the most beautiful of them all. Choosing to consider the cover in the context of the presidential campaign would be reasonable; you would not have to think you were imposing a context on the picture in an arbitrary and ungrounded way. Additionally, the table of contents identifies the title of Falconer's drawing as "The Competition."

Clearly, other information on the cover might allow you to interpret the picture in some kind of political and/or **more broadly cultural context**. A significant binary opposition is New York versus Georgia, California, and Florida. The three states having names ending in the same letter are represented by look-alike, virtually identical blondes. The anomalous state, New York, is represented by a woman, who, despite standing in line with the others, is about as different from them as a figure could be.

So what that the woman representing New York looks so unlike the women from the other states? And why those states?

If you continued to pursue this interpretive context, you might want more information. Which presidential candidate won the primary in each of the states pictured? How were each of these states expected to vote in the election in November? Since timing would matter in the case of a topical interpretive context, it would also be interesting to know when the cover art was actually produced and when the magazine accepted it. If possible, you could also try to discover whether other of the cover artist's work was in a similar vein. (He has a website.)

Making the Interpretation Plausible

As we have been arguing, the picture will "mean" differently, depending on whether we understand it in terms of American presidential politics in the year 2000, or in terms of American identity politics at the same point, specifically attitudes of and about New Yorkers, and the *New Yorker* magazine's place among these attitudes—and influence on them. Analytical thinking involves interpretation, and interpretive conclusions are tentative and open to alternative possibilities.

What makes an interpretation plausible? Your audience might choose not to accept your interpretation for a number of reasons. They might, for example, be New Yorkers and, further, inclined to think that New Yorkers are cool and that this is what the picture "says." They might be from one of the states depicted on the cover in terms of look-alike blondes and, further, inclined to think that New Yorkers are full of themselves and forever portraying the rest of the country as shallowly conformist and uncultured.

But none of these personal influences ultimately matters. What matters is that you share your data, show your reasons for believing that it means what you say it means, and do this well enough for a reader to find your interpretation reasonable (whether he or she actually believes it or not).

Arriving At an Interpretive Conclusion: Making Choices

Let's try on one final interpretive context, and then see which of the various contexts (lenses) through which we have viewed the cover produces the most credible interpretation, the one that seems to best account for the patterns of detail in the evidence. We will try to push our own interpretive process to a choice by selecting one interpretive context as the most revealing: the *New Yorker* magazine itself.

In this context, the dark-haired figure wearing the New York banner stands, in a sense, for the magazine or, at least, for a potential reader—a representative New Yorker. What, then, does the cover "say" to and about New Yorkers and to and about the magazine and its readers?

So what that the woman representing New York is dark when the other women are light, is closed (narrowed eyes, closed mouth, hair tightly pulled up and back) when the others are open (wide-open eyes and mouths, loosely flowing hair), is pointed and angular when the others are round, sports a bared midriff when the others are covered?

As with our earlier attempt to interpret the cover in the context of the 2000 presidential campaign, interpreting it in the context of other *New Yorker* covers would require a little research. How do *New Yorker* covers characteristically represent New Yorkers? What might you discover by looking for patterns of repetition and contrast in a set of *New Yorker* covers rather than just this one?

The covers are all online. A cursory review of them would make evident the magazine's fondness for simultaneously sending up and embracing the stereotype of New Yorkers as sophisticated, cultured, and cosmopolitan. How does the cover read in the context, for example, of various jokes about how New Yorkers think of themselves relative to the rest of the country, such as the cover depicting the United States as two large coastlines, east and west, connected by an almost nonexistent middle?

Armed with the knowledge that the covers are not only characteristically laughing at the rest of the country but also at New Yorkers themselves, you might begin to make explicit what is implicit in the cover.

Here are some attempts at making the cover speak. Is the cover in some way a "dumb blonde" joke in which the dark woman with the pronounced beauty mark and calculating gaze participates in but also sets herself apart from some kind of national "beauty" contest? Are we being invited (intentionally or not) to invert the conventional value hierarchy of dark and light so that the dark woman—the sort that gets represented as the evil stepmother in fairy tales such as "Snow White"—becomes "the fairest of them all," and nobody's fool?

Let's end this sample analysis and interpretation with two possibilities—somewhat opposed to each other, but both plausible, at least to certain audiences (East and West Coast Americans, and readers of the *New Yorker*). At its most serious, the *New Yorker* cover may speak to American history in which New York has been the point of entry for generations of immigrants, the "dark" (literally and figuratively) in the face of America's blonde northern European legacy. Within the context of other *New Yorker* covers, however, we might find ourselves wishing to leaven this dark reading with comic overtones—that the magazine is also admitting, yes America, we do think that we're cooler and more individual and less plastic than the rest of you, but we also know that we shouldn't be so smug about it.

GUIDELINES FOR MAKING INTERPRETATIONS PLAUSIBLE

1. Laying out the data is key to any kind of analysis, not simply because it keeps the analysis accurate but because, crucially, it is in the act of carefully describing a subject that analytical writers often have their best ideas. The words you choose to summarize your data will contain the germs of your ideas about what the subject means.

2. All explanations and interpretations occur in a context, which functions like a lens for focusing your subject. An important part of getting an interpretation accepted as plausible is to *argue for the appropriateness of the interpretive context you use,* not just the interpretation it takes you to.

3. Look for a range of plausible interpretations rather than assuming only one right answer exists. Control the range of possible interpretations by attending carefully to context.

4. It is interesting and sometimes useful to try to determine from something you are analyzing what its makers might have intended. But, by and large, you are best off concentrating on what the thing itself communicates as opposed to what someone might have wanted it to communicate. Besides, intentions can rarely be known with much accuracy.

Assignments: Making Interpretations Plausible

1. **Build a Paper from Implications**. Begin this assignment by making observations and drawing out implications for one of the topics below. Then use your list as the starting point for a longer paper.

   Having done the preceding exercise with inferring implications, you could now make up your own list of observations and pursue implications. Make some observations, for example, about the following, and then suggest the possible implications of your observations:

   • changing trends in automobiles today;

   • what your local newspaper chooses to put on its front page (or editorial page) over the course of a week;

   • shows (or advertisements) that appear on network television (as opposed to cable) during one hour of evening prime time; and

   • advertisements for scotch whiskey in highbrow magazines.

2. **Analyze a Magazine Cover by Researching an Interpretive Context**. Choose a magazine that, like *The New Yorker*, has interesting covers. Write an analysis of one such cover by studying other covers from the same magazine. Follow the model offered at the end of this chapter:

   a. Apply The Method—looking for patterns of repetition and contrast—to the cover, so that you arrive at key repetitions, strands, and organizing contrasts and begin to ponder a range of possible interpretive leaps to what they signify.

   b. Use these data to suggest plausible interpretive contexts for the cover. Remember that interpretive contexts are not simply imposed from without; they're suggested by the evidence.

   c. Then move to the other covers. Perform similar operations on them to arrive at an awareness of common denominators among the covers, and to analyze what those shared traits might reveal or make more evident in the particular cover you are studying. You will be trying to figure out how the magazine conceives of itself and its audience by the way it characteristically represents its "face."

It might be illuminating to survey a range of covers by a single artist, such as Ian Falconer, who created the cover we analyze in the chapter.

3. **Write an Essay in Which You Make Observations About Some Cultural Phenomenon, Some Place and Its Social Significance, or an Event** (in terms of its significance in some context of your choice) and then push these observations to tentative conclusions by repeatedly asking "So what?"

   Be sure to query your initial answers to the "So what?" question with further "So what?" questions, trying to push further into your own thinking and into the meaning of whatever it is you have chosen to analyze. Trends of some sort are good to work with. Marketing trend? So what? Trends in movies about unmarried women or married men or... So what? And so forth.

   Since the chapter offers sample analyses of paintings and advertisements, you might choose one of these. Cartoons are interesting subjects. Here you would really have to think a lot about your choice of interpretive context. Gender? Politics? Humor? Family life? American stereotypes? What are we invited to make of this, by what means, and in what context?

Chapter 7

Making Common Topics More Analytical

THE FIRST UNIT OF THIS BOOK, The Analytical Frame of Mind, has sought to persuade you that analysis is worth the challenge—that you can unlearn less productive ways of thinking and take on fresh habits that will make you smarter. In this final chapter of Unit 1, we offer concrete advice about how to succeed in creating writing that fulfills some of the most common basic writing tasks you will be asked to produce at the undergraduate level and beyond.

A unifying element of the chapters in this unit is their focus on the stage of the composing process that rhetoricians call *invention*. This chapter takes up several of classical rhetoric's "topics of invention." These are "places" (from the Greek *topoi*) from which a writer or orator might discover the things he or she needs to say. These topics include comparison/contrast and definition to which we have added summary, reaction papers, and agree/disagree topics because these are such common forms in college and other writing settings. The chapter offers you strategies for making the best use of these topics as analytical tools.

The remainder of the chapter offers strategies for upping the analytical quotient of the staple forms of academic and so-called "real world" writing. We can't guarantee these strategies will succeed, but if you follow them, you are likely to have more and better ideas and to achieve greater success in writing inside the traditional forms.

COMMON TOPICS

Summary
Personal Response: The Reaction Paper
Agree/Disagree
Comparison/Contrast
Definition

SUMMARY

Summary and analysis go hand-in-hand; the primary goal for both is to understand rather than evaluate. Summary is a necessary early step in analysis because it provides perspective on the subject as a whole by explaining the meaning and function of each of that subject's parts. Within larger analyses—papers or reports—summary performs the essential function of contextualizing a subject accurately. It creates a fair picture of what's there.

Summarizing isn't simply the unanalytical reporting of information; it's more than just shrinking someone else's words. To write an accurate summary, you have to ask analytical questions, such as the following:

- Which of the ideas in the reading are most significant? Why?
- How do these ideas fit together?
- What do the key passages in the reading mean?

Summarizing is, then, like paraphrasing, a tool of understanding and not just a mechanical task.

When summaries go wrong, they are just lists, a simple "this and then this" sequence. Often lists are random, as in a shopping list compiled from the first thing you thought of to the last. Sometimes they are organized in broad categories: fruit and vegetables here, dried goods there. At best, they do very little logical connecting among the parts beyond "next." Summaries that are just lists tend to dollop out the information monotonously. They omit the *thinking* that the piece is doing—the ways it is connecting the information, the contexts it establishes, and the implicit slant or point of view.

Writing analytical summaries can teach you how to read for the connections, the lines that connect the dots. And when you're operating at that level, you are much more likely to have ideas about what you are summarizing.

Strategies for Making Summaries More Analytical

Strategy 1: Look for the underlying structure. Use The Method to find patterns of repetition and contrast (*see Chapter 2*). If you apply it to a few key paragraphs, you will find the terms that get repeated, and these will suggest strands, which in turn make up organizing contrasts. This process works to categorize and then further organize information and, in so doing, to bring out its underlying structure.

Strategy 2: Select the information that you wish to discuss on some principle other than general coverage. Use Notice and Focus to rank items of information in some order of importance (*see Chapter 2*). Let's say you are writing a paper on major changes in the tax law or on recent developments in U.S. policy toward the Middle East. Rather than simply collect the information, try to arrange it into hierarchies. What are the least or most significant changes or developments, and why? Which are most overlooked or most overrated or most controversial or most practical, and why? All of these terms—significant, overlooked, and so forth—have the effect of focusing the summary, guiding your decisions about what to include and exclude.

Strategy 3: Reduce scope and say more about less. Both The Method and Notice and Focus involve some loss of breadth; you won't be able to cover everything. But this is usually a trade-off worth making. Your ability to rank parts of your subject or choose a revealing feature or pattern to focus on will give you surer control of the material than if you just reproduce what is in the text. You can still begin with a brief survey of major points to provide context, before narrowing the focus. Reducing scope is an especially efficient and productive strategy when you are trying to understand a reading you find difficult or perplexing. It will move you beyond passive summarizing and toward having ideas about the reading.

If, for example, you are reading Chaucer's *Canterbury Tales* and start cataloguing what makes it funny, you are likely to end up with unanalyzed plot summary—a list that arranges its elements in no particular order. But narrowing the question to "How does Chaucer's use of religious commentary contribute to the humor of 'The Wife of Bath's Tale'"? reduces the scope to a single tale and the humor to a single aspect of humor. Describe those as accurately as you can, and you will begin to notice things.

Strategy 4: Get some detachment: shift your focus from what? to how? and why? Most readers tend to get too single-minded about absorbing the information. That is, they attend only to the *what*: what the reading is saying or is about. They take it all in passively. But you can deliberately shift your focus to *how* it says what it says, and *why*.

To focus on how and why something is presented in a given way—whether it be a sign on a subway or the language of a presidential speech—is to focus rhetorically. Like analysis in general, rhetorical analysis asks what things mean, why they are as they are and do what they do. But rhetorical analysis asks these questions with one primary question always foregrounded: how does the thing achieve its effects on an audience? Rhetorical analysis asks not just what do I think, but *what am I being invited to think (and feel) and by what means?*

One way to distinguish a summary is to concentrate on rhetorical matters. If, for example, you were asked to discuss the major discoveries that Darwin made on *The Beagle,* you could avoid simply listing his conclusions by redirecting your attention to *how* he proceeds. You could choose to focus, for example, on Darwin's use of the scientific method, examining how he builds and, in some cases, discards hypotheses. Or you might select several passages that illustrate how Darwin proceeded from evidence to conclusion and then *rank* them in order of importance to the overall theory. Notice that in shifting the emphasis to Darwin's thinking—the how and why—you would not be excluding the what (the information component) from your discussion.

PERSONAL RESPONSE: THE REACTION PAPER

The biggest advantage of reaction papers is that they give you the freedom to explore where and how to engage your subject. They bring to the surface your emotional or intuitive response, allowing you to experiment with placing the subject in various contexts.

Interestingly, a response paper is not actually asking for your response, at least not primarily. Instead, it is asking you to locate something you think is interesting, revealing, especially significant, and/or perhaps difficult (and thus in need of discussion) in the reading (or observing), and to analyze what you locate. You are allowed to talk about how you responded to the subject, but you are expected to do so in terms of how you found a way to understand and think about the material—as opposed to your gut-level evaluative judgment (like/dislike) of it.

Personal response becomes a problem, however, when it distracts you from analyzing the subject. When you are invited to respond personally, you are being asked for more than your endorsement or critique of the subject. If you find yourself constructing a virtual list—I agree with this point, or I disagree with that point—you are probably doing little more than matching your opinions with the points of view encountered in a reading. At the very least, you should look for places in the reaction paper where you find yourself disagreeing with yourself.

In most cases, you will be misinterpreting the intent of a personal response topic if you view it as an invitation either to

1. assert your personal opinions unreflectively, or
2. substitute narratives of your own experience for careful consideration of the subject. In an academic setting, an opinion is more than simply an expression of your beliefs; it's a conclusion that you earn the rights to through a careful examination of evidence.

Strategies for Making Personal Responses More Analytical

Strategy 1: Trace your responses back to their causes. As we noted in the first two chapters, tracing your impressions back to their causes is the key to making personal response analytical—because you focus on the details that gave you the response rather than on the response alone. In the planning stage, you may find it useful to brainstorm some of your reactions/responses—the things you might say about the material if asked to talk about it with a sympathetic friend. You would then take this brainstorm and use it to choose the key sentences, passages, and so forth in the reading that you want to focus on in your analysis.

Let's say you are responding to an article on ways of increasing the numbers of registered voters in urban precincts. You find the article irritating; your personal experience working with political campaigns has taught you that getting out the vote is not as easy as this writer makes it seem. From that starting point, you might analyze one (to you) overly enthusiastic passage, concentrating on how the writer has not only overestimated what campaign workers can actually do but also condescends to those who don't register—assuming, perhaps, that they are ignorant rather than indifferent or disillusioned. Tracing your response back to its cause may help to defuse your emotional response and open the door to further investigation of the other writer's rationale. You might, for example, discover that the writer has in mind a much more long-term effect or that urban models differ significantly from the suburban ones of your experience.

Strategy 2: Assume that you may have missed the point. It's difficult to see the logic of someone else's position if you are too preoccupied with your own. Similarly, it is difficult to see the logic, or illogic, of your own position if you already assume it to be true. Although an evaluative response (approve/disapprove) can sometimes spur analysis, it can also lead you to prejudge the case. If, however, you habitually question the validity of your own point of view, you will sometimes recognize the possibility of an alternative point of view, as was the case in the voter registration example (see Figure 7.1). Assuming that you have missed the point is a good strategy in all kinds of analytical writing. It causes you to notice details of your subject that you might not otherwise have registered.

Strategy 3: Locate your response within a limiting context. Suppose you are asked in a religion course to write your religious beliefs. Although this topic would naturally lead you to think about your own experiences and beliefs, you would probably do best to approach it in some more limiting context. The reading in the course could provide this limit. Let's say that thus far you have read two modern religious thinkers, Martin Buber and Paul Tillich. Using these as your context, "What do I believe?" would become "How does my response to Buber and Tillich illuminate my own assumptions about the nature of religious faith?" An advantage of this move, beyond making your analysis less general, is that it would help you to get perspective on your own position.

Another way of limiting your context is to consider how one author or recognizable point of view you have encountered in the course might respond to a single statement from another author or point of view. If you used this strategy to respond to the topic "Does God exist?" you might arrive at a formulation such as "How would Martin Buber critique Paul Tillich's definition of God?" Although this topic appears to exclude personal response entirely, it does not. Your opinion would necessarily enter because you would be actively formulating something not already evident in the reading (how Buber might respond to Tillich).

Evaluative Personal Response: *"The article was irritating."* This response is too broad and dismissively judgmental. Make it more analytical by tracing the response back to the evidence that triggered it.

A More Analytical Evaluative Response: *"The author of the article oversimplifies the problem by assuming the cause of low voter registration to be voters' ignorance rather than voters' indifference."* Although still primarily an evaluative response, this observation is more analytical. It takes the writer's initial response ("irritating") to a specific cause.

A Non-evaluative Analytical Response: *"The author's emphasis on increased coverage of city politics in local/neighborhood forums such as the churches suggests that the author is interested in long-term effects of voter registration drives and not just in immediate increases."* Rather than simply reacting ("irritating") or leaping to evaluation ("oversimplifies the problem"), the writer here formulates a possible explanation for the difference between his or her point of view on voter registration drives and the article's.

FIGURE 7.1
Making Personal Response More Analytical

AGREE/DISAGREE

We offer here only a brief recap of this kind of topic because it is discussed at length in earlier chapters. *(In particular, see the discussion of the Judgment Reflex Under Counterproductive Habits of Mind in Chapter 2.)* Topics are frequently worded as agree/disagree, especially on essay exams, but the wording is potentially misleading because you are rarely being asked for as unqualified an opinion as agree or disagree.

In most cases, your best strategy in dealing with agree/disagree questions is to choose *neither* side. Instead, question the terms of the binary so as to arrive at a more complex and qualified position to write about. In place of choosing one side or the other, decide to what extent you agree and to what extent you disagree. You are still responsible for coming down more on one side than the other, but this need not mean that you have to locate yourself in a starkly either/or position. The code phrase for accomplishing this shift *(as we've suggested in the discussion of Reformulating Binaries in Chapter 4)* is "the extent to which": "To what extent do you agree (or disagree)?"

COMPARISON/CONTRAST

Although comparison/contrast is meant to invite analysis, it is too often treated as an end in itself. The fundamental reason for comparing and contrasting is that you can usually discover ideas about a subject much more easily when you are not viewing it in isolation. When executed mechanically, however, without the writer pressing to understand the significance of a similarity or difference, comparison/contrast can suffer from pointlessness. The telltale sign of this problem is the formulaic sentence beginning, "Thus we see there are many similarities and differences between X and Y"—as "chaos" and "cream cheese" might fit that formula (both begin with the letter "c").

Comparison/contrast topics produce pointless essays if you allow them to turn into matching exercises—that is, if you match common features of two subjects but don't get beyond the equation stage (a, b, c = x, y, z). Writers fall into this trap when they have no larger question or issue to explore and perhaps resolve by making the comparison. If, for example, you were to pursue the comparison of the representations of the Boston Tea Party in British and American history textbooks, you would begin by identifying similarities and differences. But simply presenting these and concluding that the two versions resemble and differ from each other in some ways would be pointless. You would need to press your comparisons with the So what? question *(see Chapter 2)* in order to give them some interpretive weight.

Strategies for Making Comparison/Contrast More Analytical

Strategy 1: Argue for the significance of a key comparison. Rather than simply covering a range of comparisons, focus on a key comparison. Although narrowing the focus might seem to eliminate other important areas of consideration, it usually allows you to incorporate at least some of these other areas in a more tightly connected, less list-like fashion. So, for example, a comparison of the burial rites of two

cultures will probably reveal more about them than a much broader but more superficial list of cultural similarities and differences. In the majority of cases, covering less
is covering more.

You can determine which comparison is key by ranking—designating one part
of your topic as especially important or revealing. Suppose you are asked to compare
General David Petraeus's strategy in the current Afghanistan conflict with General
Douglas MacArthur's strategy in World War II. As a first move, you could limit the
comparison to some revealing parallel, such as the way each man dealt with the media,
and then argue for its significance above other similarities or differences. You might,
for instance, claim that in their treatment of the media, we get an especially clear or
telling vantage point on the two generals' strategies. At this point, you are on your
way to an analytical point—for example, that because MacArthur was more effectively
shielded from the media at a time when the media was a virtual instrument of propa-
ganda, he could make choices that Petraeus might have wanted to make but could not.

Strategy 2: Use one side of the comparison to illuminate the other. Usually, it is not
necessary to treat each part of the comparison equally. It's a common misconception
that each side must be given equal space. In fact, the purpose of your comparison governs the amount of space you'll need to give to each part. Often, you will use one side
of the comparison primarily to illuminate the other. For example, in a course on contemporary military policy, the ratio between the two parts would probably be roughly
70 percent on Petraeus to 30 percent on MacArthur rather than 50 percent on each.

**Strategy 3: Imagine how one side of your comparison might respond to the
other.** This strategy, a variant of the preceding one, is a particularly useful way of
helping you to respond to comparison/contrast topics more purposefully. This
strategy can be adapted to a wide variety of subjects. If you were asked to compare
Sigmund Freud with one of his most important followers, Jacques Lacan, you would
probably be better off focusing the broad question of how Lacan revises Freud by considering how and why he might critique Freud's interpretation of a particular dream
in *The Interpretation of Dreams*. Similarly, in the case of the Afghanistan example, you
could ask yourself how MacArthur might have handled some key decision in dealing
with Kabul and why. Or you might consider how he would have critiqued Petraeus's
decisions and why.

**Strategy 4: Focus on difference within similarity (or similarity within
difference).** The typical move when you are asked to compare two subjects is to collect a number of parallel examples and show how they are parallel, which can lead
to bland tallying of similarities without much analytical edge. In the case of obvious
similarities, you should move quickly to significant differences within the similarity
and the implications of these differences. In this way, you will better define your subject, and you will be more likely to offer your readers something that is not already
clear to them. For example, the Carolingian and Burgundian Renaissances share an
emphasis on education, but if you were asked to compare them, you could reveal the
character of these two historical periods more effectively by concentrating on the

different purposes and origins of this emphasis on education. *(Here we are reprising the final heuristic presented in Chapter 4, Toolbox II.)*

A corollary of the difference-within-similarity formula is that you can focus on unexpected similarity rather than obvious difference. So, for example, we would probably expect that, given the vast differences in terrain and in government between Iraq and Afghanistan, significant differences would exist in the United States' military campaigns in these two locales. But as David Petraeus used to command forces in Iraq and now does so in Afghanistan, we might productively look for some revealing similarities despite obvious differences.

DEFINITION

Definition becomes meaningful when it serves some larger purpose. You define "rhythm and blues" because it is essential to any further discussion of the evolution of rock-and-roll music or because you need that definition in order to discuss the British Invasion spearheaded by groups such as the Beatles, the Rolling Stones, and the Yardbirds in the late 1960s, or because you cannot classify John Lennon or Mick Jagger or Eric Clapton without it.

Like comparison/contrast, definition can produce pointless essays if the writer gets no further than assembling information. Moreover, when you construct a summary of existing definitions with no clear sense of purpose, you tend to list definitions indiscriminately. As a result, you are likely to overlook conflicts among the various definitions and overemphasize their surface similarities. Definition is in fact a site at which there is some contesting of authorities—different voices who seek to make their definition triumph.

Strategies for Making Definition More Analytical

Strategy 1: Test the definition against evidence. One common form of definition asks you to apply a definition to a body of information. It is rare to find a perfect fit. Therefore, as a general rule, you should use the data to assess the accuracy and the limitations of the definition, rather than simply imposing it on your data and ignoring or playing down the ways in which it does not fit. Testing the definition against evidence will evolve your definition. The definition, in turn, will serve as a lens to better focus your thinking about the evidence.

Suppose you were asked to define capitalism in the context of third world economies. You might profitably begin by matching some standard definition of capitalism with specific examples from one or two third-world economies, with the express purpose of detecting where the definition does *and does not* apply. In other words, you would respond to the definition topic by assaying the extent to which the definition provides a tool for making sense of the subject.

Strategy 2: Use a definition from one source to critique and illuminate another. As a general rule, you should attempt to identify the points of view of the sources from which you take your definitions, rather than accepting them as uncontextualized answers. It is essential to identify the particular slant because otherwise you will tend to overlook the conflicting elements among various definitions of a key term.

A paper on alcoholism, for example, will lose focus if you use all of the definitions available. If, instead, you convert the definition into a comparison and contrast of competing definitions, you can more easily generate a point and purpose for your definition. By querying, for example, whether a given source's definition of alcoholism is moral or physiological or psychological, you can more easily problematize the issue of definition.

Strategy 3: Problematize as well as synthesize the definition. To explore competing definitions of the same term requires you to attend to the difficulties of definition. In general, analysis achieves direction and purpose by locating and then exploring a problem. You can productively make a problem out of defining. This strategy is known as *problematizing*, which locates and then explores the significance of the uncertainties and conflicts. It is always a smart move to problematize definitions, as this tactic reveals complexity that less careful thinkers might miss.

The definition of capitalism that you might take from Karl Marx, for example, will differ in its emphases from Adam Smith's. In this case, you would not only isolate the most important of these differences but also try to account for the fact that Marx's villain is Smith's hero. Such an accounting would probably lead you to consider how the definition has been shaped by each of these writers' political philosophies or by the culture in which each theory was composed.

Strategy 4: Shift from "what?" to "how?" and "why?" questions. It is no accident that we earlier offered the same strategy for making summary more analytical: analytical topics that require definition also depend on "why?" or "how?" questions, not "what?" questions (which tend simply to call for information).

If, for example, you sought to define the meaning of darkness in Joseph Conrad's *Heart of Darkness* and any two other modern British novels, you would do better to ask why the writers find darkness such a fertile term than simply to accumulate various examples of the term in the three novels. You might start by isolating the single best example from each of the works, preferably ones that reveal important differences as well as similarities. Then, in analyzing how each writer uses the term, you could work toward some larger point that would unify the essay. You might show how the conflicts of definition within Conrad's metaphor evolve historically, get reshaped by woman novelists, change after World War I, and so forth.

GUIDELINES FOR MAKING COMMON TOPICS MORE ANALYTICAL

1. Find ways to move beyond passive summary (what questions). Use information to develop some idea (how and why questions) rather than just repackaging what others have written.

2. Drastically reduce scope. Concentrate on what seems the most important or revealing part of your subject (ranking) rather than trying to cover everything.

3. Avoid turning comparisons into pointless matching exercises. Only set up similarities and differences in order to discuss the significance of that comparison.

4. You needn't devote equal space to both sides of a comparison. If one side is used primarily to illuminate the other, a 30–70 ratio (or 20–80 or 40–60) makes more sense than 50–50.

5. Rather than answering a question of definition with inert summary, test the definition against evidence and/or explore its competing parts.

6. For agree/disagree questions, the best move is to choose *neither* side. Question the terms of the binary so as to arrive at a more complex and qualified position. Decide to what extent you agree and to what extent you disagree.

Assignments: Making Common Topics More Analytical

1. **Write Two Summaries of the Same Article or Book Chapter**. Make the first one consecutive (the so-called "coverage" model), that is, try to cover the piece by essentially listing the key points as they appear. Limit yourself to a typed page. Then rewrite the summary, doing the following:

   - rank the items in order of importance according to some principle that you designate, explaining your rationale;
   - eliminate the last few items on the list, or at most, give each a single sentence; and
   - use the space you saved to include more detail about the most important item or two.

   The second half of this assignment will probably require closer to two pages.

2. **Explore Significant Differences and Similarities**. This assignment first appeared as a Try This in Chapter 4. If you did not do it then, try it now.

   Use any item from the list below. List as many similarities and differences as you can: go for coverage. Then review your list and select the two or three most revealing similarities and the two or three most revealing differences. At this point, you are ready to write a few paragraphs in which you argue for the significance of a key difference or similarity. In so doing, you may find it interesting to focus on an *unexpected* similarity or difference—one that others might not initially notice.

   1. Accounts of the same event from two different newspapers or magazines or textbooks;
   2. two CDs (or even songs) by the same artist or group;
   3. two ads for the same kind of product, perhaps aimed at different target audiences;
   4. the political campaigns of two opponents running for the same or similar office;

5. courtship behavior as practiced by men and by women; or

6. two clothing styles as emblematic of class or sub-group in your school, town, or workplace.

3. **Write a Comparative Definition**. Seek out different and potentially competing definitions of the same term or terms. Begin with a dictionary such as the *Oxford English Dictionary* (popularly known as the *OED*, available in most library reference rooms or online) that contains both historically based definitions tracking the term's evolution over time and etymological definitions that identify the linguistic origins of the term (its sources in older languages). Be sure to locate both the etymology and the historical evolution of the term or terms.

Then look up the term in one or preferably several specialized dictionaries. We offer a list of some of these in Chapter 14, "Finding, Citing, and Integrating Sources," but you can also ask your reference librarian for pertinent titles. Generally speaking, different disciplines generate their own specialized dictionaries.

Summarize key differences and similarities among the ways the dictionaries have defined your term or terms. Then write a comparative essay in which you argue for the significance of a key similarity or difference, or an unexpected one.

Here is the list of words: hysteria, ecstasy, enthusiasm, witchcraft, leisure, gossip, bachelor, spinster, romantic, instinct, punk, thug, pundit, dream, alcoholism, aristocracy, atom, ego, pornography, conservative, liberal, entropy, election, tariff. Some of these words are interesting to look at together, such as ecstasy/enthusiasm or liberal/conservative or bachelor/spinster. Feel free to write on a pair instead of a single word.

UNIT II

WRITING ANALYTICAL PAPERS: HOW TO USE EVIDENCE, EVOLVE CLAIMS, AND CONVERSE WITH SOURCES

Chapter 8

Reasoning from Evidence to Claims

> Most of what goes wrong in using a thesis is the result of a writer leaping too quickly to a generalization that would do as a thesis, and then treating evidence only as something to be mustered in support of that idea.

THIS CHAPTER IS ABOUT EVIDENCE—what it is, what it is meant to do, and how to recognize when you are using it well. The chapter's overall argument is that you should use evidence to test, refine, and develop your ideas, rather than just to prove they are correct.

Evidence is usually suggestive rather than conclusive. The interesting and important questions are to be found not in the facts but in our hypotheses about what the facts mean. Finding solid evidence—the facts—is only part of the problem. The larger question is always interpretive: what do the facts really tell us?

Theories—ways of seeing and understanding things—are what cause us to accept some things as facts. So, for example, once observers and theorists had demonstrated that the sun rather than the earth was at the center of the (then) known universe, people had to reconsider what was and wasn't a fact. This is why good writing uses evidence to test and qualify claims as well as support them. And this is also why this book argues against the narrow view of evidence as "the stuff that proves I'm right." Rather than arriving at demonstrably true claims from definite facts, writers more often arrive at plausible theories about evidence. Most thinking about evidence, in other words, is inevitably interpretive and tentative (*see Chapter 6, Making Interpretations Plausible*).

THE FUNCTIONS OF EVIDENCE

To substantiate claims

To test and refine ideas

To define key terms more precisely

To qualify (restrict the scope) of claims, making them more accurate

The chapter's first section addresses two common problems: claims without evidence (unsubstantiated claims) and evidence without claims (pointless evidence). The chapter's second section then offers examples of the kinds of evidence most commonly encountered in academic writing.

HOW TO MAKE EVIDENCE SPEAK

Select telling pieces of concrete data
Explain clearly what you take the data to mean
Show why the evidence might support the claim
Focus on how the evidence complicates (qualifies) the claim

A. Linking Evidence and Claims

Evidence matters because it always involves authority: the power of evidence is, well, *evident* in the laboratory, the courtroom, the classroom, and just about everywhere else. Your SAT scores are evidence, and they may have worked for or against you. If they worked against you—if you believe yourself smarter than the numbers on this standardized test indicate—then you probably offered alternative evidence, such as class rank or extracurricular achievements when you applied to college. As this example illustrates, there are many kinds of evidence; and whether or not something qualifies as acceptable evidence, as well as what it may show or prove, is often debatable. Are high school grades a more reliable predictor of success in college than a 600 on the Verbal? What exactly is an SAT score evidence of?

The types and amounts of evidence necessary for persuading readers and building authority also vary from one discipline to another, as does the manner in which the evidence is presented. While some disciplines—the natural sciences, for example—require you to present your evidence first and then interpret it, others (the humanities and some social sciences) will expect you to interpret your evidence as it is presented. But in all disciplines, and virtually any writing situation, it is important to support claims with evidence, to make your evidence lead to claims, and especially to be explicit about *how you've arrived at the connection between your evidence and your claims* (see Figure 8.1).

The relationship between evidence and claims is rarely self-evident: that relationship virtually always needs to be explained. The word *evident* comes from a Latin verb meaning "to see." To say that the truth of a statement is "self-evident"

FIGURE 8.1
Linking Evidence and Claims.

means that it does not need proving because its truth can be plainly seen by all. One of the Five Analytical Moves discussed in Chapter 3 was making the implicit explicit. This move is critical for working with evidence. The thought connections that have occurred to you about what the evidence means will not automatically occur to others. Persuasive writing always makes the connections between evidence and claim overt.

The first step in learning to explain the connection between your evidence and your claims is to remember that *evidence rarely, if ever, can be left to speak for itself.* When you leave evidence to speak for itself, you are assuming it can be interpreted in only one way and that others will necessarily think as you do.

Writers who think that evidence speaks for itself generally do very little with it. Sometimes they will present it without making any overt claims, stating, for example, "There was no alcohol at the party," and expecting the reader to understand this statement as a sign of approval or disapproval. Alternatively, they may simply place the evidence next to a claim: "The party was terrible—there was no alcohol," or "The party was great—there was no alcohol." Juxtaposing the evidence with the claim (just putting them next to each other) leaves out the thinking that connects them, thereby implying that the logic of the connection is obvious. But even for readers prone to agreeing with a given claim, simply pointing to the evidence is rarely enough.

Of course, before you can attend to the relationship between evidence and claims, you first have to make sure to include both of them. But before we examine the problems posed by leaving either one out (evidence or claims), let's first consider what it is that evidence is meant to do.

THE FUNCTION OF EVIDENCE

A common assumption about evidence is that it is "the stuff that proves I'm right." Although this way of thinking about evidence is not wrong, it is much too limited. Corroboration (proving the validity of a claim) is one of the functions of evidence— but not the only one.

It helps to remember that the word *prove* actually comes from a Latin verb meaning "to test." The noun form of prove, proof, has two meanings: (1) evidence sufficient to establish a thing as true or believable and (2) the act of testing for truth or believability. When you operate on the first definition of proof alone, you are far more likely to seek out evidence that supports only your point of view, ignoring or dismissing other evidence that could lead to a different and possibly better idea. You might also assume that you can't begin writing until you have arrived at an idea you're convinced is right, since only then could you decide which evidence to include. Both of these practices close down your thinking instead of leading you to a more open process of formulating and testing ideas.

The advantage to following the second definition of the word proof—in the sense of testing—is that you will be better able to negotiate among competing points of view. Doing so will predispose your readers to consider what you have to say because you are offering them not only the thoughts a person has had, but also a person in the act of thinking. Writing well means sharing your thought process with your readers, telling them why you believe the evidence means what you say it does.

"BECAUSE I SAY SO": UNSUBSTANTIATED CLAIMS

Problem: Making claims that lack supporting evidence.

Solution: Use concrete details to support and sharpen the claim.

Unsubstantiated claims occur when a writer concentrates only on conclusions, omitting the evidence that led to them. At the opposite extreme, pointless evidence results when a writer offers a mass of detail attached to an overly general claim. Both of these problems can be solved by offering readers the evidence that led to the claim and explaining how the evidence led there.

The word *unsubstantiated* means "without substance." An unsubstantiated claim is not necessarily false; it just offers none of the concrete "stuff" upon which the claim is based. When a writer makes an unsubstantiated claim, he or she has assumed that readers will believe it just because the writer put it out there.

Perhaps more important, unsubstantiated claims deprive you of details. If you lack some actual "stuff" to analyze, you tend to overstate your position and leave your readers wondering exactly what you mean. The further away your language gets from concrete, physical details—things that you can see, hear, count, taste, smell, and touch—the more abstract it becomes.

You can see the problem of unsubstantiated assertions not only in papers but in everyday conversation. It occurs when people get in the habit of leaping to conclusions—forming impressions so quickly and automatically that they have difficulty even recalling what triggered a particular response. Ask such people why they thought a new acquaintance is pretentious, and they will rephrase the generalization rather than offer the evidence that led to it: the person is pretentious because he puts on airs.

Rephrasing your generalizations rather than offering evidence starves your thinking; it also shuts out readers. If, for example, you defend your judgment that a person is pretentious by saying that he puts on airs, you have ruled on the matter and dismissed it. (You have also committed a logical flaw known as a circular argument; because "pretentious" and "putting on airs" mean virtually the same thing, using one in support of the other is arguing in a circle.) If, by contrast, you include the grounds upon which your judgment is based—that he uses words without regard to whether his listeners will understand or that he always wears a bow tie—you have at least given readers a glimpse of your evaluative criteria. Readers are far more likely to accept your views if you give them the chance to think with you about the evidence. The alternative—offering groundless assertions—is to expect them to take your word for it.

There is, of course, an element of risk in providing the details that have informed your judgment. You leave yourself open to attack if, for example, your readers wear bow ties. But this is an essential risk to take, for otherwise, you leave your readers wondering why you think as you do, or worse, unlikely to credit your point of view.

Most importantly, taking care to substantiate your claims will make you more inclined to think openly and carefully about your judgments. And precisely because what people have taken to be common knowledge ("women can't do math," for example, or "men don't talk about their feelings") so often turns out to be wrong, you should take care to avoid unsubstantiated claims.

DISTINGUISHING EVIDENCE FROM CLAIMS

To check your drafts for unsubstantiated assertions, you first have to know how to recognize them. It is sometimes difficult to separate facts from judgments, data from interpretations of the data. Writers who aren't practiced in this skill can believe that they are offering evidence when they are really offering only unsubstantiated claims. In your own reading and writing, pause once in a while to label the sentences of a paragraph as either evidence (E) or claims (C). What happens if we try to categorize the sentences of the following paragraph in this way?

> The owners are ruining baseball in America. Although they claim they are losing money, they are really just being greedy. Some years ago, they even fired the commissioner, Fay Vincent, because he took the players' side. Baseball is a sport, not a business, and it is a sad fact that it is being threatened by greedy businessmen.

The first and last sentences of the paragraph are claims. They draw conclusions about as yet unstated evidence that the writer will need to provide. The middle two sentences are harder to classify. If particular owners have said publicly that they are losing money, the existence of the owners' statements is a fact. But the writer moves from evidence to unsubstantiated claims when he suggests that the owners are lying about their financial situation and are doing so because of their greed. Similarly, it is a fact that Commissioner Fay Vincent was fired, but it is only an assertion that he was fired "because he took the players' side," an unsubstantiated claim. Although many of us might be inclined to accept some version of this claim as true, we should not be asked to accept his opinion as self-evident truth. What is the evidence in support of the claim? What are the reasons for believing that the evidence means what he says it does?

The writer of the baseball paragraph, for example, offers as fact that the owners claim they are losing money. If he were to search harder, however, he would find that his statement of the owners' claim is not entirely accurate. The owners have not unanimously claimed that they are losing money; they have acknowledged that the problem has to do with poorer "small-market" teams competing against richer "large-market" teams. This more complicated version of the facts might at first be discouraging to the writer, since it reveals his original thesis ("greed") to be oversimplified. But then, as we have been saying, the function of evidence is not just to corroborate your claims; it should also help you to *test* and *refine* your ideas and to *define* your key terms more precisely.

Try This 8.1: Distinguishing Evidence from Claims

Take an excerpt from your own writing, at least two paragraphs in length—perhaps from a paper you have already written, or a draft you are working on—and, at the end of every sentence, label it as either evidence (E) or claim (C). For sentences that appear to offer both, determine which parts of the sentence are evidence and which are claim, and then decide which one, E or C, predominates. What is the ratio of evidence to claim, especially in particularly effective or weak paragraphs? This is also an instructive way of working with other writers in small groups or pairs. It is often much easier to distinguish (E) from (C) in someone else's writing first.

If none of your writing is immediately handy, try this exercise with a few paragraphs of Anna Whiston's essay on talk shows included in Chapter 5, the section entitled "Using a Reading as a Lens: An Extended Example."

GIVING EVIDENCE A POINT: MAKING DETAILS SPEAK

Problem: Presenting a mass of evidence without explaining how it relates to the claims.

Solution: Make details speak. Explain how evidence confirms and qualifies the claim.

Your thinking emerges in the way that you follow through on the implications of the evidence you have selected. You need to interpret it for your readers. You have to make the details speak, conveying to your readers why they mean what you claim they mean. The following example illustrates what happens when a writer leaves the evidence to speak for itself.

> Baseball is a sport, not a business, and it is a sad fact that it is being threatened by greedy businessmen. For example, Eli Jacobs, the previous owner of the Baltimore Orioles, recently sold the team to Peter Angelos for one hundred million dollars more than he had spent ten years earlier when he purchased it. Also, a new generation of baseball stadiums have been built in the last few decades—in Baltimore, Chicago, Arlington (Texas), Cleveland, San Francisco, Milwaukee, Houston, Philadelphia, and most recently, in Washington. These parks are enormously expensive and include elaborate scoreboards and luxury boxes. The average baseball players, meanwhile, now earn more than a million dollars a year, and they all have agents to represent them. Alex Rodriguez, the third baseman for the New York Yankees, is paid more than twenty million dollars a season. Sure, he continues to set records for homers by a player at his age, but is any ballplayer worth that much money?

Unlike the previous example, which was virtually all claims, this paragraph, except for the opening claim and the closing question, is all evidence. The paragraph presents what we might call an "evidence sandwich": it encloses a series of facts between two claims. (The opening statement blames "greedy businessmen," presumably owners, and the closing statement appears to indict greedy, or at least overpaid, players.) Readers are left with two problems. First, the mismatch between the opening and concluding claims leaves it not altogether clear what the writer is saying that the evidence suggests. And second, he has not told readers why they should believe that the evidence means what he says it does. Instead, he leaves it to speak for itself.

If readers are to accept the writer's implicit claims—that the spending is too much and that it is ruining baseball—he will have to show how and why the evidence supports these conclusions. The rule that applies here is that *evidence can almost always be interpreted in more than one way.*

We might, for instance, formulate at least three conclusions from the evidence offered in the baseball paragraph. We might decide that the writer believes baseball will be ruined by going broke or that its spirit will be ruined by becoming too commercial. Worst of all, we might disagree with his claim and conclude that baseball is not really being ruined, since the evidence could be read as signs of health rather than decay. The profitable resale of the Orioles, the expensive new ballparks (which, the writer neglects to mention, have drawn record crowds), and the skyrocketing salaries all could testify to the growing popularity rather than the decline of the sport.

How to Make Details Speak: A Brief Example

The best way to begin making the details speak is to take the time to look at them, asking questions about what they imply.

1. Say explicitly what you take the details to mean.
2. State exactly how the evidence supports your claims.
3. Consider how the evidence complicates (qualifies) your claims.

The writer of the baseball paragraph leaves some of his claims and virtually all of his reasoning about the evidence implicit. What, for example, bothers him about the special luxury seating areas? Attempting to uncover his assumptions, we might speculate that he intends it to demonstrate how economic interests are taking baseball away from its traditional fans because these new seats cost more than the average person can afford. This interpretation could be used to support the writer's governing claim, but he would need to spell out the connection, to reason back to his own premises. He might say, for example, that baseball's time-honored role as the all-American sport—democratic and grassroots—is being displaced by the tendency of baseball as a business to attract higher box office receipts and wealthier fans.

The writer could then make explicit what his whole paragraph implies, that baseball's image as a popular pastime in which all Americans can participate is being tarnished by players and owners alike, whose primary concern appears to be making money. In making his evidence speak in this way, the writer would be practicing step 3 above—using the evidence to complicate and refine his ideas. He would discover which specific aspect of baseball he thinks is being ruined, clarifying that the "greedy businessmen" to whom he refers include both owners and players.

Let's emphasize the final lesson gleaned from this example. When you focus on tightening the links between evidence and claim, the result is almost always a "smaller" claim than the one you set out to prove. This is what evidence characteristically does to a claim: it shrinks and restricts its scope. This process, also known as *qualifying a claim*, is the means by which a thesis develops.

Sometimes it is hard to give up on the large, general assertions that were your first responses to your subject. But your sacrifices in scope are exchanged for greater accuracy and validity. The sweeping claims you lose ("Greedy businessmen are ruining baseball") give way to less resounding but also more informed, more incisive, and less judgmental ideas ("Market pressures may not bring the end of baseball, but they are certainly changing the image and nature of the game").

B. Kinds of Evidence: What Counts?

Thus far, this chapter has concentrated on how to use evidence after you've gathered it. In many cases, though, a writer has to consider a more basic and often hidden question before collecting data: what counts as evidence? This question raises two related concerns:

Relevance: in what ways does the evidence bear on the claim or problem you are addressing? Do the facts really apply in this particular case, and if so, how?

Framing assumptions: in what ways is the evidence colored by the point of view that designated it as evidence? At what point do these assumptions limit its authority or reliability?

To raise the issue of framing assumptions is not to imply that all evidence is merely subjective, somebody's impressionistic opinion. We are implying, however, that even the most apparently neutral evidence is the product of some way of seeing that qualifies the evidence as evidence in the first place. In some cases, this way of seeing is embedded in the established procedure of particular disciplines. In the natural sciences, for example, the actual data that go into the results section of a lab report or formal paper are the product of a highly controlled experimental procedure. As its name suggests, the section presents the results of seeing in a particular way.

The same kind of control is present in various quantitative operations in the social sciences, in which the evidence is usually framed in the language of statistics. And in somewhat less systematic but nonetheless similar ways, evidence in the humanities and in some projects in the social sciences is always conditioned by methodological assumptions. A literature student cannot assume, for example, that a particular fate befalls a character in a story because of events in the author's life (it is a given of literary study that biography may inform but does not explain a work of art). As the professors' comments in this section of the chapter make clear, evidence is never just some free-floating, absolutely reliable, objective entity for the casual observer to sample at random. It is always a product of certain starting assumptions and procedures that readers must take into account.

Questions of Relevance and Methodology: A Political Science Professor Speaks

In the following Voice from Across the Curriculum, political science professor Jack Gambino suggests that it is always useful to try to figure out the methodological *how* behind the *what,* especially since methodology is always based in certain assumptions as opposed to others.

Voices from Across the Curriculum

What counts as evidence? I try to impress upon students that they need to substantiate their claims with evidence. Most have little trouble with this. However, when I tell them that evidence itself is dependent upon methodology— that it's not just a question of gathering "information," but also a question of how it was gathered—their eyes glaze over. Can we trust the source of information? What biases may exist in the way questions are posed in an opinion poll? Who counts as an authority on a subject? (No, Rush Limbaugh cannot be considered an authority on women's issues, or the environment, or, for that matter, anything else!) Is your evidence out of date? (In politics, books on electoral behavior have a shelf life only up to the next election. After two years, they may have severe limitations.)

Methodological concerns also determine the relevance of evidence. Some models of, say, democratic participation define as irrelevant certain kinds of evidence that other models might view as crucial. For instance, a pluralist view of democracy, which emphasizes the dominant role of competitive elites, views the evidence of low voter turnout and citizen apathy as a minor concern. More participatory models, in contrast, interpret the same evidence as an indication of the crisis afflicting contemporary democratic practices.

In addition to this question of relevance, methodology makes explicit the game plan of research: how did the student conduct his or her research? Why did he or she consider some information more relevant than others? Are there any gaps in the information? Does the writer distinguish cases in which evidence strongly supports a claim from evidence that is suggestive or speculative?

Finally, students need to be aware of the possible ideological nature of evidence. For instance, Americans typically seek to explain such problems as poverty in individualistic terms, a view consistent with our liberal heritage, rather than in terms of class structure, as a Marxist would. Seeking the roots of poverty in individual behavior simply produces a particular kind of evidence different from that which would be produced if we began with the assumption that class structure plays a decisive influence in shaping individual behavior.

—Jack Gambino, Professor of Political Science

The preferences of different disciplines for certain kinds of evidence notwithstanding, most professors share the conviction that the evidence you choose to present should not be one-sided. They also understand that the observation and use of evidence is never completely neutral.

A useful example for thinking about evidence-gathering in this context is Werner Heisenberg's famous formulation, the Uncertainty Principle. A theoretical physicist, Heisenberg hypothesized a subatomic particle orbiting the nucleus of an atom that could be observed only when it passed through a concentrated beam of light. At the instant of its illumination, however, the direction of the particle would necessarily be skewed by the beam. From this model, Heisenberg concluded that the act of observation invariably alters whatever is observed.

This insight has made its way across the academic disciplines. In anthropology, for example, Clifford Geertz has written extensively on the ways that researchers into other cultures not only impose their own cultural assumptions onto their subjects, but also, by their very presence, cause change in the behavior of the people they are observing.

The challenge of determining what counts as evidence is also at issue when you start with a given problem or question and then must decide what you should look at. Say you are looking into the causes of child abuse. How do you decide what to look at? How do you even define what it is you are studying, since what conceivably constitutes child abuse now might have been considered normal child-rearing practices in the past? If you are searching for causes, what is the important evidence? In the past, the physical environment lay outside what sociologists usually considered, but what if the height of buildings in which child abuse occurs provides better data than the size of families? As this hypothetical example suggests, the relationship between cause and effect is always slippery, and the assumptions about what is and isn't evidence are potentially blinding.

We are, to a significant degree, a society obsessed with evidence—from UFO fanatics to conspiracy theorists to those who avidly follow the latest leaks in the press about the peccadilloes of the famous. This raises the question of the kinds of evidence that can be used to support claims.

MORE THAN JUST THE FACTS

As we have been suggesting for most of this chapter, evidence is virtually never simply a matter of "the facts." It is no accident that one often hears the phrase "questions of evidence" because evidence is perennially subject to question—for its accuracy, its veracity, and so forth. When we hear that mellifluous voiceover in the TV commercial assuring us that "3 out of 4 dentists recommend a fluoride toothpaste," how are we to take that remark? Why are lie detector tests "inadmissible as evidence" in some cases?

Nor is established practice a guarantee that the evidence is reliable. About 15 years ago, sportswriter Bill James levied a powerful attack on the accepted way of providing data for assessing a baseball player's fielding—the fielding average, which was a ratio of the total number of balls hit to a fielder (his "chances") as against his errors. James pointed out that fielding percentage didn't take into account the greater number of balls that a superior fielder might get to in the first place, adding that the more difficult the chance, the more likely the player was to make an error. So the number of errors was not a reliable index of a player's proficiency. Consequently, James invented a new statistical measure, the range factor, which more heavily weights the number of chances and devalues the number of errors. In effect, he redefines the pool of evidence.

What follows are some passages from student and professional writing, each of which illustrates a different kind of evidence. The list is not comprehensive, but we have tried to select a few of the most common categories.

STATISTICAL EVIDENCE

Statistics are a primary tool—a virtual language—for those writing in the natural and especially the social sciences. They have the advantage of greater objectivity, and, in the social sciences, of offering a broad view of a subject. Remember, though, that like other forms of evidence, statistics do not speak for themselves; their significance must be overtly elucidated. And, as the fielding average example suggests, it should never simply be assumed that statistics are valid representations of the reality they purport to measure.

The following brief excerpt is from a study of factors that determine Americans' views on global warming, written by Christopher Borick and Barry Rabe (in *Issues in Governance Studies*, No.18, July, 2008).

Excerpt from "A Reason to Believe: Examining the Factors That Determine Americans' Views on Global Warming"

Since the 1980s, there has been a growing body of data that examines the perceptions of Americans regarding the issue of global warming. This data paints a picture of generally increasing recognition, acceptance, and concern in the United States regarding atmospheric heating of the earth (Nisbet and Myers, 2007).

In the past two decades, the number of Americans who have heard of the "greenhouse effect" has steadily increased. In 1986, less than one in four respondents said they had heard of global warming. By 2006, over nine out of ten recognized the issue (Nisbet and Myers, 2007). A growing number of Americans believe that the Earth is already experiencing increased heating as Table One shows. [...]

Public opinion research shows Americans are increasingly acknowledging global warming (Nisbet and Myers, 2007); however, what isn't seen are the underlying causes of these beliefs. In particular, what type of evidence do Americans cite as having an important effect on their perceptions of global warming? Recent Pew Research Center polls have shown fairly significant short-term shifts in the number of Americans who believe there is evidence of global warming. Between June 2006 and January 2007, there was a 7% increase (70% to 77%) among U.S. residents who indicated there was "solid evidence" that the Earth is warming. However, between January 2007 and April 2008, the percentage decreased by 6% (77% to 71%). This decline in public acceptance of the evidence of global warming may be an aberration in a long-term trend of increasing belief. However, the shift does raise questions regarding the underlying factors affecting public acknowledgement of global warming. What types of evidence are individuals reacting to? *[The writers note a significant short-term shift in views of Americans on global warming but then go on to frame a new research question about the kinds of evidence upon which individuals are basing their claims. This will in turn lead to further opinion polling and statistical analysis.]*

Interpreting the Numbers: A Psychology Professor Speaks

In the following Voice from Across the Curriculum, psychology professor Laura Edelman offers advice on how to read statistically. She expresses respect for the value of numbers as evidence, as opposed to relying on one's own experience or merely speculating. But she also advises students to be aware of the various problems of interpretation that statistical evidence can invite.

Voices from Across the Curriculum

The most important advice we offer our psychology students about statistical evidence is to look at it critically. We teach them that it is easy to misrepresent statistics and that you really need to evaluate the evidence provided. Students need to learn to think about what the numbers actually mean. Where did the numbers come from? What are the implications of the numbers?

In my statistics course, I emphasize that it is not enough just to get the "correct" answer mathematically. Students need to be able to interpret the numbers and the implications of the numbers. For example, if students are rating satisfaction with the textbook on a scale of one (not at all satisfied) to seven (highly satisfied) and we get a class average of 2.38, it is not enough to report that number. You must interpret the number (the class was generally not satisfied) and again explain the implications (time to choose a new text).

Students need to look at the actual numbers. Let's say I do an experiment using two different stat texts. Text A costs $67 and text B costs $32. I give one class text A and one class text B, and at the end of the semester I find that the class using text A did statistically significantly better than the class using text B. Most students at this point would want to switch to the more expensive text A. However, I can show them an example where the class using text A had an average test grade of 87 and the class with text B had an average test grade of 85 (which can be a statistically significant difference): students see the point that even though it is a statistical difference, practically speaking it is not worth double the money to improve the class average by only two points.

There is so much written about the advantages and limitations of empirical information that I hardly know where to begin. Briefly, if it is empirical, there is no guesswork or opinion (Skinner said "the organism is always right"—that is, the data are always right). The limitations are that the collection and/or interpretation can be fraught with biases and error. For example, if I want to know if women still feel that there is gender discrimination in the workplace, I do not have to guess or intuit this (my own experiences are highly likely to bias my guesses): I can do a survey. The survey should tell me what women think (whether I like the answer or not). The limitations occur in how I conduct the survey and how I interpret the results. You might remember the controversy over the Hite Report on sexual activities (whom did she sample, and what kind of people answer those kinds of questions, and do they do so honestly?).

Despite the controversy over the problems of relying on empirical data in Psychology, I think that it is the only way to find answers to many fascinating questions about humans. The patterns of data can tell us things that we have no other access to without empirical research. It is critically important for people to be aware of the limitations and problems, but then to go on and collect the data.

—Laura Edelman, Professor of Psychology

EXPERIMENTAL EVIDENCE

Experimental evidence is a form of empirical evidence. Empirical evidence is derived from experience, the result of observation and experiment, as opposed to theory. It is usually associated with the bodily senses; the word *empirical* means "capable of being observed, available to the senses," and the word comes from the Greek word for experience.

Experimental evidence is usefully distinguished from other forms of evidence by the careful attention to procedure it requires. Evidence in the sciences is usually recorded in particular predetermined formats, both because of the importance of methodology, and because the primary test of validity in the sciences is that the experiment must be repeatable, so that another experimenter can follow the same procedure and achieve the same results *(see Chapter 15, Forms and Formats Across the Curriculum).*

The concern with procedure is present throughout writing in the sciences, though, not just in the Methods section of a lab report. Scientific writing constantly begins by asking the question, "How do we know what we think we know?" And, since experiments inevitably take a scientist into the unknown, it then asks, "On the basis of what we know, what else might be true, and how can we find out?" The concern with procedure in scientific writing is ultimately, then, a matter of clearly articulating the means of verifying and explaining what we think we know.

The treatment of evidence in the following example of scientific writing, a review of existing research on a given phenomenon, explores the adequacy of competing hypotheses.

Excerpt from "Hypotheses about Rev Function"

Two major hypotheses for Rev function have been proposed. One is that Rev may inhibit splicing or interfere with the assembly of the spliceosome. This hypothesis would imply that inhibiting spliceosome activity would release pre-mRNA for transport to the cytoplasm (Fischer et al. 1995). The other hypothesis is that Rev might directly target viral pre-mRNA to the cytoplasm through the interaction of its domains with cellular cofactors. *[States hypotheses and their implications]* While there is evidence to support both models, there seems to be stronger support in favor of the second hypothesis. The finding that functional inactivation of the Rev activation domain always resulted in the inability of the protein to exit the nucleus provides significant evidence that the activation domain is a nuclear export signal (NES) and Rev is indeed actively involved in the direct transport of viral mRNAs (Meyer et al. 1996). *[Offers as rationale for preferred hypothesis that it better explains evidence]* Additionally, Rev was able to directly promote nuclear export of RRE-containing mRNAs after nuclear injection into Xenopus oocytes independently of the presence of introns in these RNAs and thus presumably in the absence of spliceosome formation (Fischer et al. 1994). *[Adds additional evidence from second source to support preferred hypothesis]*

USING AUTHORITIES AS EVIDENCE

A common way of establishing support for a claim is to invoke an authority—to call in as evidence the thinking of an expert in the subject area you are writing about. The practice of invoking authorities as evidence can be heard in TV advertising ("three out of four doctors recommend…," etc.) as well as in scholarly books and articles, where a writer may offer as partial support for a claim the thinking of a better-known writer. Much academic writing consists of evaluating and revising views that people have come to believe are authoritative. The building of knowledge involves in large part the ongoing consideration of who or what will be accepted as authoritative.

Later in this unit of the book, we offer a whole chapter on the matter of using authorities as evidence *(Chapter 13, Using Sources Analytically: The Conversation Model)*. In that chapter, we explain how to use—rather than just include and agree with—other writers on your subject. In the meantime, we offer the following passage from a student paper on ancient art. In it, you will see how the writer calls on the authority of his sources, putting them into evidence for his case, but also how he offers alternatives to their claims on the basis of his own review of the primary evidence (the art objects themselves).

Note that he does not simply import his sources' claims but their evidence as well. Calling in the support of an authority, an expert witness, can be very useful, but it's no substitute for logic: the fact that somebody has gotten a claim printed doesn't mean it's a good conclusion. Sharing the source's evidence and reasoning with your readers will help them to understand your use of the source.

Notice as well how the writer is refereeing a range of possible interpretations by juxtaposing the ways that different experts theorize the significance of empirical evidence—such as their all having ears and all being naked females. (As noted earlier, the word "empirical" means capable of being observed, available to the senses; the word comes from the Greek word for experience.)

The paper from which we took the following excerpt is a study of a group of white marble statues from the Cycladic Islands in the Aegean Sea. Designated as part of the "Early Spedos" stylistic group, the statues date from 2700–2500 B.C. After a careful description of the figures themselves, the writer uses a blend of his own analysis and theories by art history authorities to speculate about the significance of the figures.

Excerpt from "Early Spedos Cycladic Idols"

The function of the figurines is still unclear; there is no specific accepted doctrine or theory on why these figures were created, though many hypotheses and interpretations have been offered. *[Writer states problem.]* It is commonly known that statues were placed facing the deceased, or the deceased were placed facing the statues in the tomb itself. Most statues are female in the folded arm pose, about hand size for perhaps a daily use, like a child's doll, and accompanied tools and jewelry in the tomb. *[Writer offers empirical analysis by summarizing potentially revealing details in the evidence. He next begins to cite the theories of three authorities on the function of the figures.]*

Bigwood notes that, "The different qualities of the carving suggest that the sculptures were not just in the possession of an elite but were accessible to the whole culture" (250–251). Along with a widespread class base, figures occurred in tombs regardless of a person's sex. With these facts in mind, a few theories on function seem more acceptable than others. Take Fitton, who states in her book,

> Figures were put into graves for a variety of reasons. They [may have been] servants who would attend the dead in the after-life, sometimes with special roles—female figures [may have been] concubines, musicians who played for the deceased, and so on. Alternatively, they [may have been] personal possessions, thought to protect the owner in life before accompanying him or her to the grave. As such, they may represent their owners, or a deity (67).

In his book, Thimme suggests that the figures were conceived as images of divine beings and specifically intended for the grave: the female figures represent a divine mistress of life and death who will secure for the deceased rebirth in another world (42).

The occurrence of female figures in both women's and men's graves best suits Thimme's hypothesis that the figures represent a being quite independent of the deceased, a divine or daemonic being (Thimme 43). *[Writer cites empirical evidence to support one of his authority's claims.]* Fitton offers some words on the attractive possibility of the female deity theory:

> A female deity, perhaps with worshippers represented in her own image, is an attractive possibility. While the once-fashionable assumption that the prehistoric Aegean peoples worshipped a 'Great Mother' goddess is demonstrably simplistic, there can be no doubt that some explanation is needed to account for the fact

that the majority of Cycladic figures are in the form of a naked female, and a female deity remains a possible identification (69). *[Includes not just another authority's claim but also the supporting evidence]*

The theories put forth by Fitton and Thimme seem to be most confirming since other interpretations, including substitute mother, nurse mother, concubine, and magical midwife are weakened by our knowledge that, for the first two mother theories, there was a rarity of child tombs and, with the last two sexual/procreative theories, the inclusion of figurines in graves occurred irrespective of the individual's sex. *[Writer uses empirical evidence to dismiss claims of authorities conflicting with those he is advocating.]* In respect to the particular figurines examined above, the presence of ears suggests a divine being who was designed to listen to prayers, a point to reinforce the validity of a female mother goddess theory. *[Writer uses more empirical evidence to justify chosen claim]*

ANECDOTAL EVIDENCE

An anecdote is a little story (a narrative), a piece of experience. The word comes from a Greek term meaning "things unpublished." At its best, anecdotal evidence involves the close examination of particular instances. At its worst, it misrepresents fairly isolated anecdotes as if they were truly representative instances, but without any substantiating evidence. In effect, these inadequately contextualized examples take cheap shots at others' positions—a common practice during political campaigns.

Often it includes the writer/researcher's own experience with whatever he or she is studying. So, for example, a historian wishing to understand the origins and development of the Latino community in a small east coast American city might use as a large part of her evidence interviews that she has conducted with local Latino residents.

Anecdotal evidence is in some ways at the opposite extreme from statistical evidence. Statistical research often attempts to locate broad trends and patterns by surveying large numbers of instances and tries to arrive at reliable information by deliberately controlling the kind and amount of questions it asks. In fact, one of the most important tasks for someone using statistical research is the careful crafting of the questions to guarantee that they don't, for example, predispose the respondent to choose a particular response. By contrast, the kind of thinking based on anecdotal evidence is less concerned with verifiable trends and patterns than with a more detailed and up-close presentation of particular instances.

Given the difficulty of claiming that a single case (anecdote) is representative of the whole, researchers using anecdotal evidence tend to achieve authority through a large number of small instances, which begin to suggest a trend. Authority can also be acquired through the audience's sense of the analytical ability of the researcher—her skill, for example, at convincingly connecting the evidence with the claim.

Sometimes, statistical and anecdotal evidence operate hand-in-hand; they tend to need each other. A certain number of closely examined particular instances may be necessary in order to determine what questions to ask for a larger statistical survey. Statistical evidence is occasionally seen as incomplete and can even be misleading without more in-depth examination. Thus, for example, one of the most popular research tools in both business and the academic world is the combining of a questionnaire with follow-up discussion by a focus group. The focus group usually consists of a representative sample of respondents to a questionnaire who are selected for a more detailed follow-up discussion of the questions than the statistical format could ever allow. Often the researcher will learn from the focus group that the questionnaire was asking the wrong questions, or that respondents had been generally misunderstanding the questions.

While it is a central claim of this book that evidence cannot and should not be expected to speak for itself, and thus needs analysis, there is another side to this argument, especially in certain kinds of research. Historians, for example, are especially sensitive to the problem of distorting evidence by offering too much interpretation of it before they have adequately presented it—in effect, filtering it prematurely though their own conclusions. While they take care to frame the evidence in a context that makes its range of meanings apparent, they try not to put too much of themselves between the reader and the data. Rather than speaking for their subjects, such historians give them a space to speak.

Here is an example in which a historian presents the experience of a representative individual, one of the first Puerto Rican immigrants to Allentown, Pennsylvania. Note that she allows us to hear his "voice"—his experience—more than hers, although, if you look for it, you will see her presence as well.

Excerpt from *Hidden from History: The Latino Community of Allentown, PA* by Anna Adams

Jesus Ramos, the oldest of nine children of a Puerto Rican migrant worker, came to New Jersey in the early 1950s to pick fruit. He worked in the fields for two summers, returning to Puerto Rico for the winters. After visiting a Puerto Rican friend who had settled in Allentown, Ramos decided to move there himself. He recalls that by the late 1950s there were approximately 500 Latinos living in Allentown with no place to buy Spanish foods. *[Writer uses subject as statistical source]* Ramos and Juan Acevedo opened La Famosa grocery store where he sold Goya products upstairs and had pool tables in the basement. When Puerto Ricans began to congregate and socialize in the store, the police accused them of loitering and arrested Mr. Ramos for running a gambling establishment. *[Writer embeds narrative of racism without commenting on it; notice that she sticks to the vividly evoked facts]* After clearing himself of those charges, he went to work in the cutoff department of the Greif/Genesco Corporation where he stayed for twenty-eight years. He and his wife Carmen have raised nine children in Allentown. As one of the pioneers of the Puerto Rican community, Jesus tried to smooth the way for others. *[Here, the writer generalizes about her subject, turning him into a representative figure]* He lobbied for Genesco to hire more Spanish speaking people and was one of the founders of Casa Guadalupe, a community center dispensing social services. Despite his efforts, things weren't always easy. "As long as you spoke Spanish, they looked at you different, and you had to work three times harder than the others," he says in fluent, heavily accented English. *[Notice the implied commentary in the fact that after 40 years Ramos continues to sound Puerto Rican but also to speak his new language fluently: he inhabits two worlds, whether out of reluctance to deny his Puerto Rican heritage or inability to do so]* He recalls one occasion when a subordinate co-worker quit rather than take orders from a Puerto Rican. *[Although use of the word "recalls" tells us that the whole account was told to the writer by Ramos, she is selective about what she actually quotes and exerts her influence in this way]*

Try This 8.2: Finding Kinds of Evidence

Find and examine a piece of writing that makes use of anecdotal evidence. Such evidence can take the form of stories or brief story-like examples in which the writer reports his or her own or others' experience and observations. You might look for examples of this kind of evidence in a magazine like *the New Yorker*, in a feature article of a newspaper's Sunday magazine section, in a chapter from a nonfiction book on some feature of contemporary life and culture, in a historical account (since history-writing often makes use of anecdotal evidence), in a transcript of a radio interview such as the kind Terry Gross conducts in her program "Fresh Air" on public radio, and so forth.

You could also look at a textbook you are using, or seek out a textbook on economics or sociology or anthropology. Try to determine what in a given section of the book might be categorized as anecdotal evidence. Also try to name and categorize the other kinds of evidence the book uses.

Remember that there are more kinds of evidence than we have named and illustrated in this chapter. Start getting into the habit of asking yourself, "What kind of evidence is this, and how is it used?"

Case Studies: Two Examples

The case study is a cousin of anecdotal evidence in that it relies on in-depth and careful description of a particular case in point. The case study is a common form of what is known as qualitative research, as opposed to quantitative (numerical) research, in the social sciences. Each discipline has its own rules governing the method of conducting a case study.

The first example is a piece of what's called ethnographic writing wherein the writer uses description to come to terms with and understand some kind of cultural experience. This piece, by Elissa Davidowitz, was written for a course on research methodologies in education. Notice how, in the words of her professor, Pearl Rosenberg, the excerpt combines "ongoing data collection, self-reflexive thinking, and socio-cultural analysis" and captures "her humility in the face of an unfamiliar task in relation to real people."

I didn't understand how Kent could give the other students such a hard time for dropping out of school when he did the same thing. Yes, they dropped out of school, but they are here five days a week at 8:30 in the morning to get their GED. Doesn't that make them somewhat credible? I thought so. After working with Kent I was left with many questions. I knew from my short time with him that he was a man struggling to maintain his self-worth and self-respect. His constant need to "prove" himself made it clear that he thought of me as someone who held power over him. What did it mean for me to take on the role of educator and Kent to be the student? *[Writer frames the case—helping to teach a GED class to inner city people]*

As Kent felt the need to prove himself to me, I felt the need to prove to Kent that the teaching in that room was going both ways. Anne Ferguson describes in her ethnography, *Bad Boys*, the need for teachers to classify students as "good" or "bad." Ferguson goes on to explain that, "Even though we treat it this way, the category 'child' does not describe and contain a homogeneous and naturally occurring group of individuals at a certain stage of human development . . . What it means to be a child varies dramatically by virtue of location in cross-cutting categories of class, gender, and race" (Ferguson, 81). The same can be said for adults. We cannot classify all adults in one way. Yes, it may be easy to say that all of the adult learners attending the GED class dropped out of school because they were lazy kids, but it is never that simple. Each individual is a complex being filled with multiple dimensions living in a world where people are constantly trying to simplify things. As an educator, it is crucial to understand the many aspects that make up a child or person. Coming to terms with the truth of the complexity of people's lives is the first step towards helping them grow both as an individual and a student. *[Writer uses secondary source to contextualize the study and foreground her assumptions about complexity]*

Throughout my time volunteering at the GED class, I have learned how motivation varies greatly from individual to individual. I always knew that people were motivated by different factors, internal or external, sometimes both. It became clear to me that Vissilios and Kent were internally motivated. Although Kent was affected by the need to provide for his family, he was also getting his GED to prove to himself that he was capable. In my interview with Vissilios the same idea of "proving oneself" became evident. Vissilios told me that he was not pushed by his mother to stay in school when he was younger, and was not pushed to go back to school. He explained that he wanted his GED to prove to people that it wasn't lack of ability that kept him from getting a high school diploma; rather it was his own laziness as a kid. After talking with Mrs. Cooper about the issue of motivation for adult learners, I gained a new insight into the field. Mrs. Cooper explained to me from the beginning that this is a GED class, and that her students are adults. They are not required to show up to class; they come by choice. She explained that there is an attendance policy and if the students are falling below the amount of hours they are required to attend, it is the teacher's choice whether or not to drop the student from the class. Mrs. Cooper said that in her 15 years of teaching at the Literacy Center she has never officially dropped a student. She explained that in order to keep her students motivated she feels that focusing on their personal needs is the most effective. She makes a point to make herself available for extra help as often as possible. Mrs. Cooper also tries to make the class interesting by discussing current events when relevant. *[Writer presents the point of view of one of her students and then quotes an authority to help her assess his motives]*

The second example is a case study in which psychology students were asked to analyze data suggestive of particular kinds of mental illnesses as they are represented in contemporary films. The difference between the following case study and the preceding one is that the psychology case study has prescribed categories (subheads) under which the information is recorded. The assignment here is to give examples of some of the behaviors exhibited by the character Roy in *Matchstick Men* that might lead to a diagnosis of obsessive-compulsive disorder.

Matchstick Men

Patient Evaluation: Roy

Presenting Problem:

Patient describes extreme discomfort when placed in outdoor settings. He fears dirt, germs, insects, and pollen. He becomes extremely distracted by these fears when he is outdoors. Patient also reports that he feels the need to open and close each door through which he enters or leaves a room three times while counting out loud (often in a language other than English).

He reports extreme anxiety at the thought of his home being anything less than perfectly clean and is plagued by constant thoughts of cleanliness. Patient fears shoes on the carpet of his home and is at times overwhelmed by anxiety if in fact someone walks on the carpet with shoes on. Patient reports muscular ticks in his face, neck and head in certain situations. These often become prominent when he is nervous, outdoors, or in a new or unfamiliar setting.

History of Present Illness:

Patient reports that he has noticed his symptoms and has attempted to self-medicate utilizing illegally obtained prescription drugs. He does not know the name of this medication. Symptoms seem to have been present for at least fifteen years but may stretch as far back as adolescence. Patient reports that on one occasion he felt suicidal because of his overwhelming feelings about his symptoms but that fear of staining his carpet prevented him from taking his own life with a handgun.

Past Psychiatric Illness, Treatments, Outcomes:

No known history

Medical History:

Patient reports anxiety-induced spells of hyperventilation and lightheadedness.

Psychosocial History:

Patient reports that his last romantic relationship ended nearly fifteen years ago. He describes this relationship as abusive and states that he was physically aggressive toward his ex-wife Heather. At the end of this relationship Heather was pregnant; patient knows nothing about the whereabouts of the child. Patient's only close relationship is that which he holds with his "business partner" Frank with whom he conducts illegal and fraudulent business endeavors. Although he works with Frank on a daily basis and considers him a close partner, Roy claims that he does not fully trust Frank because of their line of work.

Drug and Alcohol History:

Patient reports that he has a history of alcoholism beginning over fifteen years ago. Patient is known to have utilized some sort of illegally conjured prescription drug to self medicate for his symptoms. Patient smokes as many as eight packs of cigarettes each day.

Behavioral Observations:

Patient is alert and coherent however, he displays nervous behavior, fidgeting and ticks in his face and neck. Patient seems eager to leave the office and his eyes repeatedly dart around the room. He repeatedly and urgently requests a prescription for his symptoms and is hesitant to answer questions.

Mental Status Exam:

Speech pattern is urgent. Patient refuses to answer questions but seems capable of doing so when pressed. Patient seems to have high intellectual capacity and is completely conscious of his surroundings. Patient seems to have no control over obsessive thoughts.

Functional Assessment:

Patient does not recognize the severity of his illness. He believes that he must live with his illness but that only medication has the capability to help him. The patient is involved with illegal activity and has very little social interaction beyond that with his partner Frank. He does not function well in new environments and cannot go outside without becoming extremely uncomfortable. Without treatment the patient may be a suicide risk.

Strengths:

Patient is extremely intelligent and creative. He is organized, meticulous, and values cleanliness. Although his work is criminal, he excels in his ability to talk to people and persuade them into doing what he wants them to do.

Diagnosis:

Obsessive Compulsive Disorder

Treatment Plan:

It is recommended that patient begin a carefully monitored drug therapy and Cognitive therapy program. Patient will be strongly encouraged in therapy to withdraw from his criminal lifestyle in order to apply his talents and strengths toward more productive work.

Prognosis:

If the patient is treated cognitively and chemically through drug therapy, vast improvement may be achieved. However, if criminal behavior persists, treatment may not be as effective. Similarly, if patient does not continue consistent treatment indefinitely, a relapse of symptoms is highly probable.

TEXTUAL EVIDENCE

Types of evidence, as we've been noting, can be divided into two broad categories: quantitative (numerically based) and qualitative (based on interviews and other kinds of non-numerical data). Those who work with qualitative data tend to focus closely on words. We are using the term "textual evidence" to designate instances in which the language itself is of fundamental importance: both how things are worded and the range of meanings that key words might possess. Insofar as the actual language of a document counts, you are in the domain of textual evidence.

Perhaps the profession that most commonly uses textual evidence is the law, which involves interpreting the language of contracts, wills, statutes, statements of intention, etc. Similarly, diplomats, accountants, people in business—all those who must rely on written documents to guarantee understanding—need to be adept at textual analysis. People in such fields as literary study, media studies, and public relations also engage in textual analysis.

Notice in the following excerpt from a student paper how the writer focuses on particular words as evidence.

Excerpt from "Women and Nature in Lessing and Chopin"

Susan tends to fear everything connected to the natural world *[General claim about feature of text she wishes to understand]*. The heroine first shows signs of irrationality as she refuses to sit in her garden. Lessing describes, "She was filled with tension, like a panic: as if an enemy was in the garden with her" (Doris Lessing, "To Room 19" 2306) *[Writer selects evidence]*. This "enemy" is a threat to Susan's carefully planned and structured life, and so she attempts to avoid nature. This becomes an interesting idea as the story clearly shows that Susan longs to yield to that "enemy" and to destroy her ordered existence. *[Explains quoted evidence, selecting a particular word that organizes thinking in the text and that she proceeds to apply to the text as a whole]* Susan decides she must have a holiday to free herself from the bondage that her children represent, and so she goes on a walking tour of Wales. But she never can truly be unfettered; even on a mountainside, her family is capable of dragging her back to her obligations. In this case, the telephone becomes Susan's downfall, as Lessing writes, "Susan prowled over wild country with the telephone wire holding her to her duties like a leash" (2313). *[Distinguishes organizing contrast in the language of additional evidence (freedom in nature vs. entrapment in domesticity) and uses it to develop claim]* [...] Susan is forced to deal with an unfaithful spouse instead of being the adulterous one herself. In her mind, sex does have close ties to nature, but she chooses to ignore it as her husband has hurt her by acting upon his passions. It does not seem to be a coincidence that room 19 is entirely green; the curtains, the bed, and the wicker chair all share the same hue. And when Matthew practically forces Susan to create an imaginary lover, she selects the name Michael Plant, an obvious reference to the natural equaling the sensual. *[Locates additional evidence to confirm the pattern and further develop her claim]*

Try This 8.3: Using Textual Evidence

Here is another excerpt from the paper on women and nature. Study the passage and answer the following questions. Where do we see the writer's general claim about the evidence? Where does she select the feature of the text she wants to focus on? How does the cited evidence organize her thinking—on what pattern or organizing contrast?

Chopin also applies the imagery of birds to her heroine, symbolically alluding to Edna's wish to fly, in a sense, from all her responsibilities. Edna refers to her new home as the "pigeon house," a place where she thinks she has evaded her husband and children. She asserts her independence in this new dwelling, throwing parties and working on her art. Perhaps the greatest reference to Edna's tie to birds occurs right before she kills herself. Chopin portrays the scene on page 108, "A bird with a broken wing was beating the air above, reeling, fluttering, circling disabled down, down to the water." This bird comes to represent everything Edna has endured up until her breakdown, her suicide "down, down to the water." Edna can never reconcile her natural sexual instincts, her "broken wing," with the civilized world she inhabits; society will not let her merge the two domains, and so she resolves to die.

WHAT DO THE FACTS REALLY TELL US?

In the realm of analysis, there are precious few smoking guns and absolutely reliable eyewitnesses. When there are, you have an open-and-shut case that probably does not need to be argued. It makes sense, then, to avoid thinking that a particular use of evidence is strong and good because the evidence is clearly true and factual, whereas another use of evidence is weak and inadequate because it's possibly untrue and not factual. Most analytical uses of evidence are a matter of making inferences, interpreting the evidence with subtlety and respect.

To a significant extent, decisions about the value of evidence depend on the kind of claim you are making (how broad, for example, and how conclusive) and the genre you are writing in. What could be appropriate and valid for writing a magazine profile of residents trying to rebuild a poor urban neighborhood might not be appropriate and valid for supporting policy decisions or sociological theories about people in such neighborhoods. The strength of such a profile, however, should not be under-estimated, because it may be rich in suggestion, in questions and angles of approach for further research.

Whatever kind of evidence you're using, the emphasis rests on how you use what you have: how you articulate what it means and how carefully you link the evidence to your claims. When you find yourself asking, "How good is my argument?" here are two working criteria from the chapter:

- Am I oversimplifying the implications of my evidence?
- Does my use of evidence go beyond mere corroboration of an overly general claim?

Another guiding principle, perhaps the chapter's most important point, is to think with the evidence; keep it before you. If you start to move too far afield, return to the source, the evidence itself, to refresh your thinking.

GUIDELINES FOR REASONING FROM EVIDENCE TO CLAIMS

1. Learn to recognize unsubstantiated assertions, rather than treating claims as self-evident truths. Whenever you make a claim, offer your readers the evidence that led you to it.

2. Make the evidence speak. Explain how it supports the claim; offer your reasons for believing the evidence means what you say it does.

3. Use evidence to advance your claim, not just confirm it. Explore how the evidence does not fit the claim, and use what you learn to reshape the claim, making it more accurate.

4. Consider what counts as evidence in a given field or context, or as one of the Voices puts it, remember that "evidence itself is dependent upon methodology—that it's not just a question of gathering 'information,' but also a question of how it was gathered."

5. Most professors agree that evidence is never completely neutral, simply a matter of "the facts," so you need to determine the slant—the principles of selection—that have produced this evidence. And as a corollary, try to gather evidence from more than one side of a topic.

Assignments: Reasoning from Evidence to Claims

1. **Distinguishing Evidence from Claims.** Take an excerpt from your own writing, at least two paragraphs in length—perhaps from a paper you have already written or a draft you are working on—and at the end of every sentence label the sentence as either evidence (E) or claim (C). For sentences that appear to

offer both, determine which parts of the sentence are evidence and which are claim, and then decide which one, E or C, predominates. What is the ratio of evidence to claim, especially in particularly effective or weak paragraphs?

2. **Find Examples of Using Authorities as Evidence**. How are the authorities used? What other kinds of evidence appear in the piece? It might be interesting with this assignment to compare a piece of academic writing with a piece of nonacademic writing on the same subject.

3. **Linking Evidence with Claims**. Study a piece of writing, yours or something you come across in your reading. Locate the places where the writer explicitly explains the connection between the evidence and the claim. If you are studying your own writing, this exercise could be the basis of a revision in which you more fully explain the thought process that caused you to say your evidence means what you say it does.

Chapter 9

Analyzing Arguments

THIS CHAPTER addresses different schools of thought on the nature and purpose of argument along with a brief introduction to the rules of argument through which the linking of evidence and claims has traditionally been tested. The chapter ends with a glossary of the most common logical fallacies.

THREE VIEWPOINTS ON ARGUMENT
- Formal Argument Analysis: The Syllogism and the Toulmin Model
- Rogerian Argument and Practical Reasoning
- Figurative Logic: Reasoning with Metaphors

Argument analysis and the definition of argument depend on what a person wants to know, and by what means. In some academic disciplines, the means are primarily quantitative. In most disciplines, the means are empirical in one way or another—based on observation.

As this chapter and later ones (*especially Chapter 15, Forms and Formats Across the Curriculum*) demonstrate, each division and discipline of the academic world has its own way of knowing. This way of knowing—called an *epistemology*—carries with it a particular way of assessing the value of evidence and of determining the relative validity of claims. No one discipline has the last word on thinking.

Psychology departments, for example, concentrate much less on the soundness of an argument than they do on factors that influence the way people think. We offer one example of thinking about thinking in psychology in the Voice from Across the Curriculum appearing at the end of Chapter 2. There psychologist Mark Sciutto speaks about cognitive behavior therapy and the problem of various kinds of automatic thoughts, such as globalizing and fortune-telling, that distort the way people think. In Chapter 2, we argue that the deeply ingrained habits of overgeneralizing, judging, and leaping prematurely to conclusions are the most fundamental causes of poor thinking.

Neuroscience departments study thinking in a more materially empirical way, by trying to isolate the various biochemical and other mechanisms in the brain that determine how we process experience. History, religion, English, and art history departments, among others, study the various traditions of thought, including traditions in language that shape and condition thinking in individuals and cultures.

We now turn to the long tradition of analyzing arguments that has evolved from the thinking of Aristotle and other early Greek philosophers. This necessarily brief discussion cannot do justice to the methods of argument analysis employed by philosophers, especially logicians. But it is possible to provide a skeletal version of how these methods operate and also to locate them in the context of other ways of thinking about argument.

THE RULES OF ARGUMENT: SYLLOGISM AND ENTHYMEME

Philosophers have long quested for forms that might lend to human argument some greater clarity and certainty, more like what is possible with formulas in math. As you will see and as most philosophers readily admit, the reality of evaluating arguments in day-to-day life is necessarily a less tidy process than the rules of argument might make it seem. The kinds of certainty that are sometimes possible with formulas in math are not so easily available when using words to make claims about human experience. Nevertheless, the rules of argument described here offer a set of specific guidelines for discovering things that go right—and wrong—in the construction of an argument.

Probably the most common way of talking about logical argumentation goes back to Aristotle. This approach doesn't always have direct applications in the kinds of analytical writing described in this book, but knowing the ways that philosophers have devised for evaluating arguments can expand your ability to assess your own and others' reasoning about claims and evidence.

There are a number of rules for evaluating the validity of a syllogism's conclusion. In this short section, we cannot offer enough of the details about argument analysis to equip you with the necessary skills. But we will give you enough detail so that you can understand the basic principles and methods of this way of thinking about argument.

At the heart of the Aristotelian model is the syllogism, which consists of three parts:

1. Major premise: a general proposition presumed to be true;
2. Minor premise: a subordinate proposition also presumed to be true; and
3. Conclusion: a claim that follows logically from the two premises, if the argument has been properly framed.

Here is a frequently cited example of a syllogism:

All men are mortal (major premise).

Socrates is a man (minor premise).

Therefore, Socrates is mortal (conclusion).

A premise is a proposition (assumption) upon which an argument is based and from which a conclusion is drawn. In the syllogism, if both of the premises have been stated in the proper form (both containing a shared term), then the conclusion must be valid.

An important thing to know about syllogisms is that they are only as true as the premises they are made of. It is not, however, the business of the syllogism to test the truth of the premises. Syllogisms can only demonstrate that the form of the argument is valid. As you will see, this word "valid" is a key term in argument evaluation, a term that does not mean the same thing as right or true.

If a writer follows the prescribed steps of the syllogism without violating any of the rules on proper wording and on the way the steps may be put together, then the conclusion arrived at in step 3 is valid. An argument evaluated in this way can be valid and still be false. For example:

All politicians are corrupt.

The mayor of Chicago is a politician.

Therefore, the mayor of Chicago is corrupt.

The problem here is not with the form of the syllogism but with the fact that the major premise is untrue.

To make good use of syllogistic reasoning, you need to get into the habit of recasting arguments that you write or read or hear into the proper syllogistic form. The way most people articulate claims—often without even recognizing that they are making claims—is rarely if ever syllogistic. Claims, for example, if they are to be most easily assessed for validity, usually need to be recast using forms of "to be" rather than other kinds of verbs (as in the Chicago example above).

While arguments as formulated in formal logic are grounded in abstract, universal terms, most arguments as we encounter them in daily life involve statements about values and beliefs. These real-life arguments typically appear in a form that philosophers call the "enthymeme." An enthymeme is an incomplete syllogism. One of its premises has been left unstated, usually because the person offering the argument takes the unstated assumption to be a given, something so obviously true that it doesn't even need to be made explicit.

Sample Enthymeme: Cats make better pets than dogs because cats are more independent.

Unstated Assumption: Independent animals make better pets.

Sample Enthymeme: Charter schools will improve the quality of education because they encourage competition.

Unstated Assumption: Competition improves the quality of education.

TOULMIN'S ALTERNATIVE MODEL OF THE SYLLOGISM

British philosopher Steven Toulmin offered a competing model of argument in his influential book, *The Uses of Argument* (1958). Toulmin's model was motivated by his belief that the philosophical tradition of formal logic, with its many rules for describing and evaluating the conduct of arguments, conflicts with the practice and idiom (ways of phrasing) of arguers. To radically simplify Toulmin's case, it is that the

FIGURE 9.1
The Toulmin Model.

syllogism does not adequately account for what really happens when thinkers try to frame and defend various claims. Toulmin tried to describe the structure of argument in a way that he thought came closer to what actually happens in practice when we try to take a position.

The Toulmin model of argument renames and reorders the process of reasoning described in the Aristotelian syllogism as follows:

1. Data: the evidence appealed to in support of a claim; data respond to the question "What have you got to go on?"

2. Warrant: a general principle or reason used to connect the data with the claim; the warrant responds to the question "How did you get there?" (from the data to the claim).

3. Claim: a conclusion about the data (see Figure 9.1).

Consider this model in terms of the chapter's opening discussion of linking evidence and claims. In the Toulmin model, the warrant is the link. It supplies the reasoning that explains why the evidence (support) leads to the conclusion (claim).

Let's look briefly at how this reasoning structure works in practice by looking at one of Toulmin's examples.

data: Harry was born in Bermuda.

warrant: The relevant statutes provide that people born in the colonies of British parents are entitled to British citizenship (reason for connecting data to claim);

claim: So, presumably, Harry is a British citizen. (conclusion)

We can now follow Toulmin a little further in his critique and revision of syllogistic ways of describing thinking. A syllogism, as you saw above, is designed to reveal its soundness through the careful framing and arrangement of its terms:

All men are mortal. (All x's are y.)

Socrates is a man. (Socrates is an x.)

Therefore, Socrates is mortal. (Socrates is a y.)

At what price, asks Toulmin, do we simplify our phrasing of complex situations in the world in order to gain this appearance of truth? In how many situations, he asks, can we say that "all x's are y"?

The strictness of the rules necessary for guaranteeing formal validity, Toulmin argues, leaves out the greater amount of uncertainty that is a part of reasoning about most questions, issues, and problems. Toulmin observes, using his own argument structure as a case in point, that as soon as an argument begins to add information in support of its premises, the complexity and inevitable tentativeness of the argument become apparent, rather than its evident truth.

Here is Toulmin's explanation of what must happen to the form of an argument when a person begins to add more supporting information, which Toulmin calls *backing.* The backing for the warrant in the example above about the British citizenship of people born in Bermuda would inevitably involve mentioning "the relevant statutes"—acts of Parliament, statistical reports, and so forth—to prove its accuracy. The addition of such information, says Toulmin, would "prevent us from writing the argument so that its validity shall be manifest from its formal properties alone" (*The Uses of Argument,* 123).

Not everyone agrees with Toulmin's revision or his reasoning. The rhetorician Edward Corbett, for example, argues that the Toulmin system lacks rules and guidelines for assessing the "logicality of the argument" (*The Elements of Reasoning,* Macmillan, 1991, p. 44). Corbett also argues that Toulmin's system is less easy to use than it appears, noting that recognizing claims, data, warrants, and backing in an argument may not be any easier than finding conclusions, minor premises, and major premises in a syllogism.

The rules of argument are important for clarifying and testing our thinking. And, of course, many more forms and structures are available in logic than this brief account could begin to suggest. There are, for example, a number of rules for arriving at claims about evidence inductively. Syllogistic reasoning is deductive; it works by bringing premises into accord with some larger governing premise.

To use an analogy, if the Aristotelian syllogism appears to offer us the promise of never mistaking the forest for the trees, Toulmin's revision of that model is to never let us forget that the forest is in fact made up of trees.

As a writer, you will naturally want some guidelines and workable methods for selecting evidence and linking it to claims. But what you can't expect to find is a set of predetermined slots into which you can drop any piece of evidence and find the truth. Rather, analyses and arguments operate within the complex set of details and circumstances that are part of life as we live it. An argument depends not only on whether or not its premises follow logically but on the quality of the thinking that produces those premises in the first place and painstakingly tests their accuracy. This is the job of analysis.

ROGERIAN ARGUMENT AND PRACTICAL REASONING

Most people want to be reasonable and have others think of them as reasonable. It has long been hoped by some people that we might devise a foolproof system for demonstrating that one person's argument is clearly right and another's is clearly wrong. Certainty is an attractive goal for many people.

The kind of formal argument analysis we have been considering is a piece of this hope. The rules of argument—whichever model you try to apply—do have a significant capacity for discriminating sound arguments from less sound ones. Moreover, the challenge of translating real world propositions into the forms required by this or that argumentative system is not insurmountable. A number of books out there can teach you to do it.

Our discussion, however, has disclosed the problems that logical analysis of the forms of argument faces. It is difficult to incorporate into the prescribed forms much of the detail that is actually significant in making the argument sound. Even these problems can be negotiated, though, if you don't expect too much and if you take a practical approach, such as focusing on enthymemes (the form that everyday arguments most often take) and learning to supply the missing assumptions.

There are, however, other objections to prioritizing the rules of argument. These objections come from contemporary rhetoricians who are less concerned about testing the adequacy of arguments than they are with making argument better serve the needs of people in everyday life and in the larger arena of public discourse. The view of argument offered throughout this book—for example, in the discussion of counterproductive habits of mind in the latter half of Chapter 2—is aligned with the thinking of two such rhetoricians, Carl Rogers and Wayne Booth. For these rhetoricians, the aim is not primarily to defeat opponents but to locate common ground. (Many have noticed the presence of militaristic rhetoric in argument analysis.)

Both Rogers and Booth place their emphasis on listening. They stress the need to be able to understand and accurately represent the positions of "opponents" in an argument. This goal is very much the norm in academic writing, where people try to put different points of view into conversation rather than set out to have one view defeat another. As Zachary Dobbins has argued, "For Booth, reasoning equates not just with rational thought but instead with inquiry, a term that more expansively describes the process all of us are daily engaged in to shape and make sense of the world—a process the ends of which are seldom certain or empirically measurable" ("Wayne Booth, Narrative, and the Rhetoric of Empathy"—an unpublished talk delivered at the 2010 Conference on College Composition and Communication). Dobbins quotes Booth to the effect that "The supreme purpose of persuasion [...] should not be to talk someone else into a preconceived view; rather it must be to engage in mutual inquiry or exploration [...]" (*Modern Dogma and the Rhetoric of Dissent*).

TWO WAYS TO IMPROVE AN ARGUMENT: CHECK FOR UNSTATED ASSUMPTIONS AND QUALIFY CLAIMS

Many of the arguments we encounter in daily life succumb to overly rigid and unqualified categorical thinking. Of course, putting things into categories is not unto itself a bad practice. In order to generalize from particular experiences, we try to put those experiences into meaningful categories. Analytical thought is quite unthinkable without categories. But these can mislead us into oversimplification when the categories are too broad or too simply connected.

This is especially the case with the either/or choices to which categorical thinking is prone: approve/disapprove, real/unreal, accurate/inaccurate, believable/unbelievable. The writer who evaluates leadership in terms of its selflessness/selfishness, for example, needs to pause to consider why we should evaluate leadership in these terms in the first place.

We will refer to the following two examples to illustrate how (1) qualifying your claims and (2) checking for the unstated assumptions upon which your claims depend can remedy the two primary problems created by categorical thinking: unqualified claims and overstated positions. *(For more on methods of uncovering unstated assumptions and reformulating binaries, see Chapter 4, Toolkit of Analytical Methods II.)*

> **Example I:** I think that there are many things shown on TV that are damaging for people to see. But there is no need for censorship. No network is going to show violence without the approval of the public, obviously for financial reasons. What must be remembered is that the public majority will see what it wants to see in our mass society.

> **Example II:** Some members of our society feel that [the televised cartoon series] *The Simpsons* promotes wrong morals and values for our society. Other members find it funny and entertaining. I feel that *The Simpsons* has a more positive effect than a negative one. In relation to a real-life marriage, Marge and Homer's marriage is pretty accurate. The problems they deal with are not very large or intense. As for the family relationships, the Simpsons are very close and love each other.

The main problem with Example I is the writer's failure to qualify his ideas, a problem that causes him to generalize to the point of oversimplification. Note the writer's habit of stating his claims absolutely (we have italicized the words that make these claims unqualified):

"there is *no* need for censorship"

"*no* network is going to show violence without"

"*obviously* for financial reasons"

"what *must* be remembered"

"the majority *will* see"

Such broad, pronouncement-like claims cannot be supported. The solution is to more carefully limit the claims, especially the key premise about public approval. The assertion that a commercial television industry will, for financial reasons, give the public "what it wants" is true *to an extent* (our key phrase for reformulating either/ors)—but it is not true as globally as the writer wishes us to believe.

Couldn't it also be argued, for example, that given the power of television to shape people's tastes and opinions, the public sees not just what it wants but what it has been taught to want? This complication of the writer's argument about public approval undermines the credibility of his global assertion that "there is no need for censorship."

Example II would appear to be more qualified than Example I because it acknowledges the existence of more than one point of view. Rather than broadly asserting that the show is positive and accurate, she tempers these claims (as italics show): "I *feel* that *The Simpsons* has a *more* positive effect *than* a negative one"; "Marge and Homer's marriage is *pretty* accurate." These qualifications, however, are superficial.

Before she could convince us to approve of *The Simpsons* for its accuracy in depicting marriage, she would have to convince us that accuracy is a reasonable criterion for evaluating TV shows (especially cartoons) rather than assuming the unquestioned value of accuracy. Would an accurate depiction of the life of a serial killer, for example, necessarily make for a "positive" show? Similarly, if a fantasy show has no interest in accuracy, is it necessarily "negative" and without moral value?

When writers present a debatable premise as if it were self-evidently true, the conclusions built upon it cannot stand. At the least, the writer of Example II needs to recognize her debatable premise, articulate it, and make an argument in support of it. She might also precede her judgment about the show with more analysis. Before deciding that the show is "more positive than negative" and thus does not promote "wrong morals and values for our society," she could analyze what the show says about marriage and how it goes about saying it.

Likewise, if the writer of Example I had further examined his own claims before rushing to argue an absolute position on censorship, he would have noticed how much of the thinking that underlies them remains unarticulated and thus unexamined. It would also allow him to sort out the logical contradiction with his opening claim that "there are many things shown on TV that are damaging for people to see." If television networks will only broadcast what the public approves of, then apparently the public must approve of being damaged or fail to notice that it is being damaged. If the public either fails to notice it is being damaged or approves of it, aren't these credible arguments for rather than against censorship?

FIGURATIVE LOGIC: REASONING WITH METAPHORS

To understand reasoning only in terms of propositional logic is to ignore how much of our day-to-day thinking is conducted indirectly, not in the form of explicit claims but in metaphors. Many people assume that figurative thinking—the kind conducted in metaphors and similes—is confined only to poems and that it is not really thinking but is instead primarily emotional and irrational.

There are some problems with these charges against figurative thinking that lie beyond the scope of this discussion—for example, that emotions are the enemy of rationality, an assumption that neuroscience researchers like Antonio Damasio have challenged. What is important for present purposes is to consider challenges that can reasonably be made to the assumption that one of our most common ways of thinking is not, in fact, a way of reasoning about evidence.

THE LOGIC OF METAPHOR

- Metaphors pervade our ways of thinking
- Metaphor is a way of thinking by analogy
- The logic of metaphors is implicit

- The implicit logic of metaphors can be made explicit by scrutinizing the language
- We can recast figurative language to see and evaluate its arguments just as we recast language to examine its logic in syllogistic form

Everyday Thinking

Metaphors are deeply engrained in the language we use everyday; they are far from being solely the concern of poets. George Lakoff, professor of linguistics and cognitive science, and English professor Mark Turner, among others, have demonstrated that metaphors are built into the way we think. (See Lakoff and Turner's book, *More than Cool Reason, a Field Guide to Poetic Metaphor*, University of Chicago Press, 1989.) As such, metaphors routinely constitute our assumptions about the world and our place in it. Life, for example, is a journey. To become successful, you climb a ladder. Being up is a good thing. To be down is to be unhappy and blue. These are all metaphors. If we accept their implicit arguments in an unexamined way, they call the shots in our lives more than we should allow them to.

Although figurative logic does not operate in the same way as claims-based (propositional) logic, it nevertheless produces arguments, the reasoning of which can be analyzed and evaluated. Let's start with a definition. A metaphor works by **analogy**—a type of comparison that often finds similarities between things that are otherwise unlike. Consider the simile "My love is like a red red rose." A simile, identifiable by its use of the words "like" or "as," operates like a metaphor except that both sides of the analogy are explicitly stated. The subject of the simile, love, is called the tenor; the comparative term brought in to think about love, rose, is called the vehicle.

In metaphors, the thought connection between the vehicle (rose) and the tenor (my love) is left unstated. But for our purposes, the clearer and more explicit simile will do. It is the nature of the resemblance between the speaker's "love" and roses that we are invited to infer.

What are the characteristics of red roses—especially red red (very red) roses—that might be relevant in this piece of thinking by analogy? Well, most people find roses to be beautiful. Most people associate red with passion. In fact, science can now measure the body's response to different colors. Red produces excitement. Red can even make the pulse rate go up. Roses are also complicated flowers. Their shape is convoluted. Roses are thought of as female. Rose petals are fragile. Many roses have thorns. So, the simile is actually a piece of thinking about love and about women.

It is not a very deep piece of thinking, and probably many women would prefer that the thorn part not be made too prominent. In fact, a reader would have to decide in the context of other language in the poem whether thorniness, as a characteristic of some roses, is significant and ought to be considered. The point is that the simile does make an argument about women that could be stated overtly, analyzed, and evaluated. The implication that women, like roses, might have thorns—and thus be hard to "pick," defending them from male intruders, and so forth is part of the argument.

Here is the procedure for exploring and decoding the logic of metaphor—what we have to do, more or less automatically, to understand the thinking that the metaphor suggests.

Step 1: Isolate the vehicle—the language in the metaphor that states one side of the analogy.

Step 2: Articulate the characteristics of the vehicle, its defining traits.

Step 3: Select the characteristics of the vehicle that seem most significant in context.

Step 4: Use these significant characteristics of the vehicle to prompt interpretive leaps to what the metaphor communicates. Make the implicit explicit.

Notice how, in the rose example, our recasting of the original simile has made explicit the implicit meanings inside the figurative language. This recasting is a useful act of thinking, one that makes evident the thought process that a metaphor sets in motion.

What such recasting reveals is not only that metaphors do, in fact, make claims, but that they are remarkably efficient at doing so. A metaphor can say a lot in a little by compressing a complex amalgam of thought and feeling into a single image.

What objections might remain to thinking that figurative language has an implicit logic and is a way of thinking and making arguments? People who pride themselves on being logical thinkers and place great value on rationality are inclined to think of metaphorical language as imprecise and too little available to any systematic way of arriving at meaning that all who encounter the metaphor might share. This is a reasonable objection, but one that can be answered in the terms that we introduced in our discussion of Practical Reasoning above.

As we argue at some length in Chapter 6, Making Interpretations Plausible, certainty and single right answers are very rarely available, especially when our evidence consists of words. Even in areas, however, where it is not possible to prove beyond a doubt that one statement of meaning is truer and more accurate than another, people will usually accept some reasoning from evidence as better—truer to the meaning of the words in context—than others. The meaning-making process is social and consensual. To put a Rogerian slant on this point, understanding figurative logic involves careful listening to language, an openness to multiple possibilities, and it also requires empathy—much like what is required of us in understanding people's arguments in everyday life.

Skepticism about the logic and usefulness of metaphorical language is especially common among people who like to think of themselves as completely out-front (a metaphor!) and practical—always saying what they mean, as though it were possible for everything that mattered to be made entirely overt and equally understandable by all, regardless of background and experience.

The fact that metaphors require interpretation—as do most uses of language—does not take away from the fact that metaphors are a way of thinking. Being able to articulate the implicit arguments embodied in metaphors, making their meanings explicit so that they can be opened to discussion with others—is an important thinking and language skill to acquire.

A BRIEF GLOSSARY OF COMMON LOGICAL FALLACIES

This last section of the chapter offers a brief discussion of common fallacies—false moves—that can subvert argument and interpretation. If you can recognize these fallacies, you can more easily avoid them both in constructing arguments and in analyzing the arguments of others.

The logical fallacies share certain characteristics. First of all, they are forms of cheating in an argument, which is to say that, however false and misleading they may be, and however intentional or unintentional, these tactics are often quite successful. They offer cheap and unethical ways of "winning" an argument—usually at the cost of shutting down the possibility of negotiation among competing views and discovery of common ground that are the goals of Rogerian argument.

The most noticeable feature of arguments based on the logical fallacies is sloganizing—or slogan-slinging, which is a suitably graphic way of putting it. In sloganizing, each side tries to lay claim to various of a culture's honorific words, which then are repeated so often and so much out of context that they evoke little more than a warm glow that each side hopes to attach to its cause. Words and phrases often used in this way are "liberty," "freedom," "the individual," and "the American people," to name a few.

Words like these are sometimes referred to as "weasel" words, along with words like "natural" and "real." The analogy with weasels goes to the notion that weasels suck out the contents of eggs, leaving empty shells behind.

The sloganizing move gets made when each side tries to attach to the other side various labels that evoke fear, even though the words have been repeated so often, in reference to so many different things, that they have become virtually meaningless. This type of sloganizing almost always takes complex circumstances and reduces them to clear-cut goods and evils. Prominent examples in the current contentious political environment are "socialist," "big government," and "capitalist."

It is usual to organize the fallacies into the categories Pathos, Ethos, and Logos from classical rhetoric *(see Chapter 3, the section on Analysis and Argument)*. Appeals to the audience's emotions, for example, such as the fallacy called "bandwagon," fall under pathos. Attacks on the character of one's opponent, such as the fallacy called *ad hominem*, are located under ethos. Various kinds of deceptive and erroneous thinking, such as *post hoc ergo propter hoc*, come under Logos.

Here is another useful way to think about the fallacies. The categories overlap somewhat, but it is helpful to differentiate diversionary tactics from moves that misrepresent the issues.

- Fallacies that derail an argument by distracting audience attention to a mostly irrelevant topic (e.g., red herring, *ad hominem*)
- Fallacies that oversimplify and polarize positions, often through the use of slogans or scare words (e.g., slippery slope, equivocation, false dichotomies, false analogies, straw man).

Some of the fallacies in this second category appear to make a show of substantiality and logicality, while actively misrepresenting things (e.g., simple cause/complex effect, confusing a correlation with a cause—especially when statistics are involved).

Recognizing fallacies in other people's arguments all too often leads to games of "gotcha." Pointing out others' dubious moves can help you "win;" A better alternative is the Rogerian one, to restate what another person is saying in a manner that he or she is willing to accept. This difficult but rewarding tactic can bring both sides in the argument out from behind the barriers, so to speak, where real discussion might be possible. As you will see, many of these errors involve the root problem of oversimplification.

1. ***Ad hominem***. Literally, the Latin phrase means "to the person." When an argument is aimed at the character of another person rather than at the quality of his or her reasoning or performance, we are engaging in an *ad hominem* argument. If a political candidate is attacked because he or she is rich, rather than on the basis of his or her platform, he or she is the victim of an ad hominem attack. In some cases, an *ad hominem* argument is somewhat pertinent—e.g., if a political candidate is discovered to have mob connections.

2. **Bandwagon (*ad populum*)**. Bandwagon arguments appeal to the emotions of a crowd, as in "everyone's doing it." A bandwagon argument is a bad argument from authority, because no reasons are offered to demonstrate that "everybody" is an informed and reliable source.

3. **Begging the question (circular reasoning)**. When you beg the question, you attempt to prove a claim by offering an alternative wording of the claim itself. To beg the question is to argue in a circle by asking readers to accept without argument a point that is actually at stake. This kind of fallacious argument hides its conclusion among its assumptions. For example, "*Huckleberry Finn* should be banned from school libraries as obscene because it uses dirty language" begs the question by presenting as obviously true issues that are actually in question: the definition of obscenity and the assumption that the obscene should be banned because it is obscene.

4. **Equivocation**. Equivocation confuses an argument by using a single word or phrase in more than one sense. For example: "Only man is capable of religious faith. No woman is a man. Therefore, no woman is capable of religious faith." Here the first use of "man" is generic, intended to be gender neutral, while the second use is decidedly masculine.

5. **False analogy**. A false analogy misrepresents matters by making a comparison between two things that are more unlike than alike. The danger that arguing analogically can pose is that an inaccurate comparison, usually one that oversimplifies, prevents you from looking at the evidence. Flying to the moon is like flying a kite? Well, it's a little bit like that, but . . . in most ways that matter, sending a rocket to the moon does not resemble sending a kite into the air.

   An analogy can also become false when it becomes overextended: there is a point of resemblance at one juncture, but the writer then goes on to assume that the two items compared will necessarily resemble each other in most other respects. To what extent is balancing your checkbook really like juggling? On the other hand, an analogy that first appears overextended may not be: how far, for example, could you reasonably go in comparing a presidential election to a sales campaign, or an enclosed shopping mall to a village main street?

When you find yourself reasoning by analogy, ask yourself two questions: (1) are the basic similarities greater and more significant than the obvious differences? and (2) am I over-relying on surface similarities and ignoring more essential differences?

6. **False cause**. This is a generic term for questionable conclusions about causes and effects. Here are three versions of this fallacy:

   a. **Simple cause/complex effect**. This fallacy occurs when you assign a single cause to a complex phenomenon that cannot be so easily explained. A widespread version of this fallacy is seen in arguments that blame individual figures for broad historical events, for example, "Eisenhower caused America to be involved in the Vietnam War." Such a claim ignores the cold war ethos, the long history of colonialism in Southeast Asia, and a multitude of other factors. When you reduce a complex sequence of events to a simple and single cause—or assign a simple effect to a complex cause—you will virtually always be wrong.

   b. ***Post hoc, ergo proctor hoc***. This term is the Latin for **after this, therefore because of this**. The fallacy rests in assuming that because *A* precedes *B* in time, *A* causes *B*. For example, it was once thought that the sun shining on a pile of garbage caused the garbage to conceive flies.

      This error is the stuff that superstition is made of. "I walked under a ladder, and then I got hit by a car" becomes "Because I walked under a ladder, I got hit by a car." A more dangerous form of this error goes like this:

      Evidence: A new neighbor moved in downstairs on Saturday. My television disappeared on Sunday.

      Conclusion: The new neighbor stole my TV.

      As this example also illustrates, typically in false cause some significant alternative has not been considered, such as the presence of flies' eggs in the garbage. Similarly, it does not follow that if a person watches television and then commits a crime, television watching necessarily causes crime; there are other causes to be considered.

   c. **Mistaking correlation for cause**. This fallacy occurs when a person assumes that a correlation between two things—some kind of connection—is necessarily causal. Philosopher David Hume called this problem "the constant conjunction of observed events." If you speed in a car and then have a minor accident, it does not follow that speeding caused the accident. If an exit poll reveals that a large number of voters under the age of 25 voted for candidate X, and X loses, it does not follow that X lost because he failed to appeal to older voters. There is a correlation, but the candidate may have lost for a number of reasons.

7. **False dilemma**. When the options are reduced to only two often sharply opposed alternatives, you have committed a false dilemma. An obvious example appears

in the case often made for Intelligent Design: because the universe is very complexly organized, it had to have been created by an intelligent life force. Are there no alternative explanations?

8. **Hasty generalization**. A conclusion derived from only one or two examples produces the fallacy known as hasty generalization. It is also known as an unwarranted inductive leap because the conclusion lacks sufficient evidence. When a child concludes that all orange food tastes bad because he dislikes carrots, he has run afoul of this fallacy. Give him an orange popsicle.

9. *Non sequitur*. Latin for "it does not follow," *non sequiturs* skip logical steps in arriving at a conclusion. For example: "If we mandate a new tax on people who work downtown but do not live there, businesses will all leave the city." Really?

10. **Oversimplification/overgeneralization** is an inadequately qualified claim. It may be true that some heavy drinkers are alcoholics, but it would not be fair to claim that all heavy drinking is or leads to alcoholism. As a rule, be wary of "totalizing" or global pronouncements; the bigger the generalization, the more likely it will admit of exceptions.

11. **Poisoning the well**. This fallacy occurs when a person uses loaded language to trivialize or dismiss an argument before even mentioning it. For example: "No reasonable person would swallow that left-wing, tax-and-spend position."

12. **Red herring**. The name comes from the practice of using herring, a smelly fish, to distract dogs from the scent they are supposed to be tracking. A red herring diverts the attention of the audience from the matter at hand, often by provoking them with some loaded or controversial topic not really related to the matter at hand. For example, if you are talking about the quality of different kinds of computers, the issue of whether or not they were made in America would be a red herring.

13. **Slippery slope**. This error is based on the fear that once a move is made in one direction, we will necessarily continue to "slide" in that direction. So, for example, if the U.S. approves medicinal uses of marijuana, soon there will be no control of what is now illicit drug use across the nation. A classic case is offered by the Vietnam War: if a single country was allowed to fall under communist rule, soon all the other countries in the region would follow.

14. **Straw man**. This move involves oversimplifying and even caricaturing another person's argument or position in order to make it easier to refute. For example, opponents of health care reform treat it as a straw man when they claim that such reform would deny benefits to the elderly and perhaps even result in so-called "death panels"—groups who would choose which people will live and which will die.

15. **Weasel word**. A specialized form of equivocation results in what are sometimes called weasel words. As we note earlier, a weasel word is one that has been used so much and so loosely that it ceases to have much meaning (the term derives from the weasel's reputed practice of sucking the contents from an egg without destroying the shell). The word "natural," for example, can mean good, pure, and unsullied, but it can also refer to the ways of nature (flora and fauna). Such

terms ("love," "reality," and "experience" are others) invite equivocation because they mean so many different things to different people.

GUIDELINES FOR ANALYZING ARGUMENTS

1. Make unstated premises (assumptions) explicit.
2. Look for the general principle or reason (warrant) that connects your data ("what have I got to go on?") with your claim.
3. Remember that argument need not be mortal combat: "mutual inquiry or exploration" (as Wayne Booth puts it) is a constructive goal.
4. Be able to state another's position to his or her satisfaction before you agree or disagree with it, as Carl Rogers counsels.
5. Beware of excessively categorical thinking, which produces overstated claims. To remedy, make sure to qualify your claims and check for unstated assumptions.

Assignments: Analyzing Arguments

1. **Find Examples of Any Two of the Logical Fallacies**. You might look in newspapers, online web pages, blogs, and so forth. Copy out the language that contains the fallacy and explain why it is what you say it is.
2. **Find Examples of Figurative Thinking**. Look at prose rather than poetry so that you can locate figurative thinking as it operates in everyday writing. You can choose a piece of academic writing to see how figurative thinking operates there. Or you might look at a magazine feature article or other essay or even in your college catalog. Copy out the relevant language and explain how the figurative thinking works. Use the four-step procedure for exploring the logic of metaphor.
3. **Apply Toulmin's Scheme to an Editorial**. Choose any editorial from your local newspaper and run it through Toulmin's scheme, which we have repeated below:

   - Data: what evidence does the editorial offer in support of its position? (Data respond to the question "What have you got to go on?")
   - Warrant: what general principle or reason is used to connect the data with the claim? (The warrant responds to the question "How did you get there?")
   - Claim: what conclusion does the writer draw?

   After you have anatomized the editorial in these terms, assess its strength more carefully. What do you find most and least convincing about it, and why? Do you detect any logical lapses—into categorical thinking, say, if not actual logical fallacies? Write up your assessment in a few paragraphs.

Chapter 10

Using Evidence to Build a Paper: 10 on 1

IN THIS CHAPTER, WE ARGUE for the importance of saying more about less. The phrase we use for this idea is 10 on 1. The term 10 on 1 was briefly mentioned in Chapter 2, Toolkit of Analytical Methods I, as a variant of Notice and Focus, an observation strategy. In this chapter, 10 on 1 is used to talk about essay structure as well as the analysis of selected data.

The phrase 10 on 1 stands for the principle that it is better to make 10 observations or points about a single representative issue or example (10 on 1) than to make the same basic point about 10 related issues or examples (1 on 10). Doing 10 on 1 teaches writers to narrow their focus and then analyze in depth, drawing out as much meaning as possible from their best examples.

ORGANIZING PAPERS USING 10 ON 1

1. Use The Method or Notice and Focus to find a revealing pattern or tendency in your evidence (see Chapter 2).
2. Select a representative example.
3. Do 10 on 1 to produce an in-depth analysis of your example.
4. Test your results in similar cases.

DEVELOPING A THESIS IS MORE THAN REPEATING AN IDEA

When the time comes to compose a formal paper with a thesis, it is very common for writers to abandon the wealth of data and ideas they have accumulated in the exploratory writing stage, panic, and revert to old habits: "Now I better have my one idea and be able to prove to everybody that I'm right." Out goes careful attention to detail. Out goes any evidence that doesn't fit. Instead of analysis, they substitute the kind of paper we call a *demonstration;* that is, they cite evidence to prove that a generalization is generally true. The problem with the demonstration lies with its too limited notions of what a thesis and evidence can do in a piece of analytical thinking.

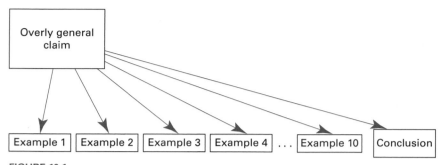

FIGURE 10.1

Doing 1 on 10. The horizontal pattern of 1 on 10 (in which "10" stands arbitrarily for any number of examples) repeatedly makes the same point about every example. Its analysis of evidence is superficial.

A paper produced by repeating a single unchanging idea generally follows the form we call 1 on 10: the writer makes a single and usually very general claim ("History repeats itself," "Exercise is good for you," and so forth) and then proceeds to affix it to 10 examples (see Figure 10.1). A writer who reasserts the same idea about each example is going to produce a list, not a piece of developed thinking. By contrast, in nearly all good writing the thesis evolves by gaining in complexity and, thus, in accuracy as the paper progresses.

The 1 on 10 demonstration results from a mistaken assumption about the function of evidence, that it exists only to demonstrate the validity of (corroborate) a claim. Beyond corroborating claims, evidence should serve to test and develop and evolve the thesis. This is one of the most important points of this chapter.

When and How to Use 1 on 10

Doing 1 on 10 is not always a counterproductive habit of mind. Although collecting a bunch of similar examples of the same phenomenon is unlikely to produce an analytically acute paper, there are occasions when gathering evidence to develop a thesis is essential. It makes sense to do 1 on 10 in order to find an example worth developing because in effect you will be locating a pattern of evidence. The search for repetition that is the first step in The Method is essentially a form of doing 1 on 10.

Noticing a repetition is a key way of ascertaining if a particular kind of evidence is important. If, for example, you discover that revolutionary movements at vastly different historical moments and geographical locales produce similar kinds of violence, it would be essential to demonstrate that pattern before you settled down to analyze one such instance as exemplary. Similarly, when a writer is trying to determine whether there is sufficient evidence to make a claim, it is useful to collect a group of related examples before focusing on the most interesting or revealing ones. If, for example, you were writing about the failure of faith in the biblical book of Exodus, you would do well to chart repeated instances of its failure to substantiate that it is a recurrent feature. But to get beyond this general demonstration, you would need to look more closely at a representative instance.

Sometimes doing 1 on 10 can be valuable in itself, not just as a step in some larger analytical procedure. Demonstrations have their place—short speeches, for example, in situations where the audience has to follow a chain of thought in spite of interference from noise or other distractions.

STUCK IN 1 ON 10: THE PROBLEM OF FIVE-PARAGRAPH FORM

In Chapter 1, we argued that five-paragraph form, an organizational scheme still taught in many high schools, blocks thought. In this chapter, we will be more specific about why this happens and how you can move on to better organizational schemes. *(See Chapter 1, the short take entitled Breaking Out of 5-Paragraph Form.)*

Perhaps the best way to explain the problem with 5-paragraph form can be found in Greek mythology. On his way to Athens, the hero Theseus encounters a particularly surly host, Procrustes, who offers wayfarers a bed for the night but with a catch. If they do not fit his bed exactly, he either stretches them or lops off their extremities until they do. This story has given us the word "procrustean," which the dictionary defines as "tending to produce conformity by violent or arbitrary means." Five-paragraph form is a procrustean formula that most students learn in high school. Although it has the advantage of providing a mechanical format that will give virtually any subject the appearance of order, it usually lops off a writer's ideas before they have the chance to form, or it stretches a single idea to the breaking point.

A complex idea is one that has many sides. To treat such ideas intelligently, writers need a form that will not require them to cut off all of those sides except the one that most easily fits the bed. Most of you will find the basic 5-paragraph form familiar:

1. An introduction that ends with a thesis listing three points (the so-called tripartite thesis)
2. Three body paragraphs, each supporting one of the three points
3. A conclusion beginning "Thus, we see" or "In conclusion" that essentially repeats the thesis statement as it was in paragraph one.

Here is an example in outline form:

Introduction: The food in the school cafeteria is bad. It lacks variety, it's unhealthy, and it is always overcooked. In this essay, I will discuss these three characteristics.

Paragraph 2: The first reason cafeteria food is bad is that there is no variety. (Plus one or two examples—no salad bar, mostly fried food, and so forth)

Paragraph 3: Another reason cafeteria food is bad is that it is not healthy. (Plus a few reasons—high cholesterol, too many hot dogs, too much sugar, and so forth)

Paragraph 4: In addition, the food is always overcooked. (Plus some examples—the vegetables are mushy, the "mystery" meat is tough to recognize, and so forth)

Conclusion: Thus, we see … (Plus a restatement of the introductory paragraph)

Most high school students write dozens of themes using this basic formula. They are taught to use 5-paragraph form because it seems to provide the greatest good—a certain minimal clarity—for the greatest number of students. But the form does not promote logically tight and thoughtful writing. It is a meat grinder that can turn any content into sausages.

The two major problems it typically creates are easy to see.

1. *The introduction reduces the remainder of the essay to redundancy.* The first paragraph tells readers, in an overly general and list-like way, what they're going to hear; the succeeding three paragraphs tell the readers the same thing again in more detail, carrying the overly general main idea along inertly; and the conclusion repeats what the readers have just been told (twice). The first cause of all this redundancy lies with the thesis. As in the example above, the thesis (cafeteria food is "bad") is too broad—an unqualified and obvious generalization—and substitutes a simple list of predictable points for a complex statement of idea.

2. *The form arbitrarily divides content:* why are there three points (or examples or reasons) instead of five or one? A quick look at the three categories in our example reveals how arbitrarily the form has divided the subject. Isn't overcooked food unhealthy? Isn't a lack of variety also conceivably unhealthy? The format invites writers to list rather than analyze, to plug supporting examples into categories without examining them or how they are related. Five-paragraph form, as is evident in our sample's transitions ("first," "second," "in addition"), counts things off but doesn't make logical connections. At its worst, the form prompts the writer to simply append evidence to generalizations without saying anything about it.

The subject, on the other hand, is not as unpromising as the format makes it appear. It could easily be redirected along a more productive pathway. (If the food is bad, what are the underlying causes of the problem? Are students getting what they ask for? Is the problem one of cost? Is the faculty cafeteria better? Why or why not?)

Now let's look briefly at the introductory paragraph from a student's essay on a more academic subject. Here we can see a remarkable feature of 5-paragraph form— its capacity to produce the same kind of say-nothing prose on almost any subject.

> Throughout the film *The Tempest*, a version of Shakespeare's play *The Tempest*, there were a total of nine characters. These characters were Calibano, Alonso, Antonio, Aretha, Freddy, the doctor, and Dolores. Each character in the film represented a person in Shakespeare's play, but there were four people who were greatly similar to those in Shakespeare, and who played a role in symbolizing aspects of forgiveness, love, and power.

The final sentence of the paragraph reveals the writer's addiction to 5-paragraph form. It signals that the writer will proceed in a purely mechanical and superficial way, producing a paragraph on forgiveness, a paragraph on love, a paragraph on power, and a conclusion stating again that the film's characters resemble Shakespeare's in these three aspects. The writer is so busy *demonstrating* that the characters are concerned with forgiveness, love, and power that she misses the opportunity to analyze the significance of her own observations. Instead, readers are drawn wearily to a conclusion; they get no place except back where they began. Further, the demonstration mode prevents her from analyzing connections among the categories. The writer might consider, for example, how the play and the film differ in resolving the conflict between power and forgiveness (focusing on difference within similarity) and to what extent the film and the play agree about which is the most important of the three aspects (focusing on similarity despite difference).

These more analytical approaches lie concealed in the writer's introduction, but they never get discovered because the 5-paragraph form militates against sustained analytical thinking. Its division of the subject into parts, which is only one part of analysis, has become an end unto itself. The procrustean formula insists on a tripartite list in which each of the three parts is separate, equal, and above all, inert.

Here are two quick checks for whether a paper of yours has closed down your thinking through a scheme such as 5-paragraph form:

1. *Look at the paragraph openings.* If these read like a list, each beginning with an additive transition like "another" followed by a more or less exact repetition of your central point ("another example is…," "yet another example is…"), you should suspect that you are not adequately developing your ideas.

2. *Compare the wording in the last statement of the paper's thesis (in the conclusion) with the first statement of it in the introduction.* If the wording at these two locations is virtually the same, you will know that your thesis has not responded adequately to your evidence.

ANALYZING EVIDENCE IN DEPTH: "10 ON 1"

The practice called 10 on 1 focuses analysis on a representative example. In doing 10 on 1, you are taking one part of the whole, putting it under a microscope, and then generalizing about the whole on the basis of analyzing a single part.

- The phrase 10 on 1 means 10 observations and implications about one representative piece of evidence (where 10 is an arbitrary number meaning "many").
- The phrase 1 on 10 means one general point attached to 10 pieces of evidence.

As a guideline, 10 on 1 will lead you to draw out as much meaning as possible from your best example—a case of narrowing the focus and then analyzing in depth (see Figure 10.2). Eventually, you will move from this key example to others that usefully extend and qualify your point, but first you need to let analysis of your representative example produce more thinking.

You can use 10 on 1 to accomplish various ends: (1) to locate the range of possible meanings your evidence suggests; (2) to make you less inclined to cling to your first

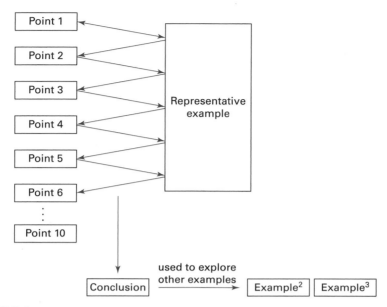

FIGURE 10.2
Doing 10 on 1. The pattern of 10 on 1 (in which "10" stands arbitrarily for any number of points) successively develops a series of points about a single representative example. Its analysis of evidence is in depth.

claim; (3) to open the way for you to discover the complexity of your subject; and (4) to slow down the rush to generalization and thus help to ensure that when you arrive at a working thesis, it will be more specific and better able to account for your evidence.

Demonstrating the Representativeness of Your Example

Focusing on your single best example has the advantage of economy, cutting to the heart of the subject, but it runs the risk that the example you select might not in fact be representative. Thus, to be safe, you need to demonstrate its representativeness overtly. This means showing that your example is part of a larger pattern of similar evidence and not just an isolated instance. To establish that pattern, it is useful to do 1 on 10—locating 10 examples that share a trait—as a preliminary step and then select one of these for in-depth analysis.

In terms of logic, the problem of generalizing from too little and unrepresentative evidence is known as an unwarranted inductive leap. The writer leaps from one or two instances to a broad claim about an entire class or category. Just because you see an economics professor and a biology professor wearing corduroy jackets, for example, you would not want to leap to the conclusion that all professors wear corduroy jackets. Most of the time, unwarranted leaps result from making too large a claim and avoiding examples that might contradict it.

10 on 1 and Disciplinary Conventions

In some cases, the conventions of a discipline appear to discourage doing 10 on 1. The social sciences in particular tend to require a larger set of analogous examples to prove a hypothesis. Especially in certain kinds of research, the focus of inquiry rests on discerning broad statistical trends over a wide range of evidence. But some trends deserve more attention than others, and some statistics similarly merit more interpretation than others. The best writers learn to choose examples carefully—each one for a reason—and to concentrate on developing the most revealing ones in depth.

For instance, proving that tax laws are prejudiced in particularly subtle ways against unmarried people might require a number of analogous cases along with a statistical summary of the evidence. But even with a subject such as this, you could still concentrate on some examples more than others. Rather than moving through each example as a separate case, you could use your analyses of these primary examples as lenses for investigating other evidence.

PAN, TRACK, AND ZOOM: USING 10 ON 1 TO BUILD A PAPER

How can 10 on 1 generate the form of a paper? The language of filmmaking offers a useful way for understanding the different ways a writer can focus evidence. The writer, like the director of a film, controls the focus through different kinds of shots.

The pan—The camera pivots around a stable axis, giving the viewer the big picture. Using a pan, we see everything from a distance. Pans provide a context, some larger pattern, the "forest" within which the writer can also examine particular "trees." Pans establish the representativeness of the example the writer later examines in more detail, showing that it is not an isolated instance.

The track—The camera no longer stays in one place but follows some sequence of action. For example, whereas a pan might survey a room full of guests at a cocktail party, a track would pick up a particular guest and follow along as she walks across the room, picks up a photograph, proceeds through the door, and throws the photo in a trash can. Analogously, a writer tracks by moving in on selected pieces of the larger picture and following them to make telling connections among them.

The zoom—The camera moves in even closer on a selected piece of the scene, allowing us to notice more of its details. For example, a zoom might focus in on the woman's hand as she crumples the photograph she's about to throw away or on her face as she slams the lid on the trash can. A writer zooms in by giving us more detail on a particular part of the evidence and making the details say more. The zoom is the shot that enables you to do 10 on 1.

In a short paper (three to five pages), you might devote as much as 90 percent of your writing to exploring what one example (the "1"—your zoom) reveals about the larger subject. Even in a paper that uses several examples, however, as much as 50 percent might still be devoted to analysis of and generalization from a single case. The remaining portion of the paper would make connections with other examples, testing and applying the ideas you arrived at from your single case. In-depth analysis of your best example thus creates a center from which you can move in two directions: (1) toward generalizations about the larger subject and (2) toward other examples, using your primary example as a tool of exploration.

Doing 10 on 1: A Brief Example (Tiananmen Square)

Note how the writer of the following discussion of the people's revolt in China in 1989 sets up his analysis. He first explains how his chosen example—a classic photograph (shown in Figure 10.3) from the media coverage of the event—illuminates his larger subject. The image is of a Chinese man in a white shirt who temporarily halted a line of tanks on their way to quell a demonstration in Tiananmen Square in Beijing.

> The tank image provided a miniature, simplified version of a larger, more complex revolution. The conflict between man and tank embodied the same tension found in the conflict between student demonstrators and the Peoples' Army. The man in the white shirt, like the students, displayed courage, defiance, and rebellious individuality in the face of power. Initially, the peaceful revolution succeeded: the state allowed the students

© Jeff Widener/AP

FIGURE 10.3
Tiananmen Square, Beijing, 1989.

to protest; likewise, the tank spared the man's life. Empowered, the students' demands for democracy grew louder. Likewise, the man boldly jumped onto the tank and addressed the soldiers. The state's formerly unshakable dominance appeared weak next to the strength of the individual. However, the state asserted its power: the Peoples' Army marched into the square, and the tanks roared past the man into Beijing.

The image appeals to American ideology. The man in the white shirt personifies the strength of the American individual. His rugged courage draws on contemporary heroes such as Rambo. His defiant gestures resemble the demonstrations of Martin Luther King Jr. and his followers. American history predisposes us to identify strongly with the Chinese demonstrators: we have rebelled against the establishment, we have fought for freedom and democracy, and we have defended the rights of the individual. For example, the *New York Times* reported that President George [H. W.] Bush watched the tank incident on television and said, "I'm convinced that the forces of democracy are going to overcome these unfortunate events in Tiananmen Square." Bush represents the popular American perspective of the Chinese rebellion; we support the student demonstrators.

This analysis is a striking example of doing 10 on 1. In the first paragraph, the writer constructs a detailed analogy between the particular image and the larger subject of which it was a part. The analogy allows the writer not just to describe but also to interpret the event. In the second paragraph, he develops his focus on the image as an image, a photographic representation tailor-made to appeal to American viewing audiences. Rather than generalizing about why Americans might find the image appealing, he establishes a number of explicit connections (does 10 on 1) between the details of the image and typical American heroes. By drawing out the implications of particular details, he manages to say more about the significance of the American response to the demonstrations in China than a broader survey of those events would have allowed.

Try This 10.1: Doing 10 on 1 with Newspaper Visuals

Search out photographs in the newspaper and do 10 on 1. Or alternatively, spend some time doing 10 on 1 on a comic strip. What perspectives emerge once you have restricted the focus? List details, but also list multiple implications. Remember to ask not just What do I notice? but What else do I notice? And not just What does it imply? but What else might it imply?

Try This 10.2: Doing 10 on 1 with a Reading

Take a piece of reading—a representative example—from something you are studying and do 10 on 1. The key to doing 10 on 1 successfully is to slow down the rush to conclusions so that you can allow yourself to notice more about the evidence and make the details speak. The more observations you assemble about your data before settling on your main idea, the better that idea is likely to be. Remember that a single, well-developed paragraph from something you are reading can be enough to practice on, especially because you are working on saying more about less rather than less about more.

CONVERTING 1 ON 10 INTO 10 ON 1: A STUDENT PAPER (FLOOD STORIES)

The following student paper, about the recurrence of flood stories in religious texts and myth, shows what happens when a writer falls into doing 1 on 10. That is, rather than zooming in on representative examples to test and refine his ideas, he attaches the same underdeveloped point to each of his examples. Typical of the 1-on-10 pattern, the flood paper views everything from the same relatively unrevealing distance.

In the essay that follows, we have used boldface to track the "one" point—the as-yet-underdeveloped thesis idea—that the writer has attached to each of his examples (1 on 10). Brackets and ellipses [...] indicate where we have abridged the essay.

Flood Stories

[1] **The role of people**, as reflected in Genesis, Ovid's *Metamorphoses*, and the *Epic of Gilgamesh*, **is solely to please the gods.** Men, as the gods' subordinates, exist to do right in the gods' eyes **and make them feel more like gods**; for without men, whom could the gods be gods of? [...]

[2] In Genesis, for example, God created humans in his own image or likeness, and **when they displeased Him**, He destroyed them. If God could see wickedness in his creations, perhaps it was like seeing wickedness in himself. Further, the idea of having evidence of God being able to create an imperfect, "wicked" race of humans may have been a point God wasn't willing to deal with: "The Lord saw that the wickedness of man was great in the earth, and that every imagination of the thoughts of his heart was only evil continually. And the Lord was sorry that he had made man on the earth and it grieved him to his heart." It seems as though **God had become unhappy with his creations** so they

were to be destroyed. Like a toy a child no longer has use for, humankind was to be wasted.

[3] Similarly, in Ovid's *Metamorphoses*, God made humanity and "fashioned it into the image of the all-governing gods." Again here, humans were made in the gods' image to serve as an everlasting monument of their glorification, to honor them and do good by them. In other words, **humans spent less time making the gods happy and therefore made them unhappy.** Some men even questioned the reality of the gods' existence and the strength of their power. Lyacon, for example, had a driving tendency to try to belittle the gods and make them look like fools. **The gods were very displeased** with this trend, and now the entire race had to be destroyed. A flood would be sent to wipe out the race of men. *[The writer then summarizes several examples in which the wicked are destroyed and a few upstanding citizens are preserved and arrives at the following conclusion:]*Thus, the justification of yet another flood to appease the gods' egos.

[4] Further evidence of **humans as being a mere whim of the gods to make them happy** lies in the flood story in the *Epic of Gilgamesh.* It is obvious **the gods weren't concerned with humankind, but rather with their own comfort.** As the story goes, Enlil, the god of earth, wind, and air, couldn't bear the noise humans were making while he tried to sleep, so he gathered all the gods together, and thus they jointly decided to get rid of their grief of having all the humans around by destroying them. Ea [the god of wisdom], however, warned one man (Utnapishtim) of the flood to come. He told him to build a boat for himself and his wife and for the "seeds of all living creatures." [...]

[5] Enlil later repented the harshness of his actions, deified Utnapishtim and his wife and then had the two live far away "on the distance of the rivers' mouths." It possibly **could have been belittling** to have Utnapishtim and his wife speaking to the new race of humans in terms of how rash and mindlessly the gods were capable of acting, so he immortalized them and had them live far out of the reach of human ears—"the secret of the gods."

[6] It seems that the **main objective of the gods was to remain gods; for that is what made them happy. And humanity's role, then, was as the gods' stepping-stone to their happiness.** [...] Witnessing the fall of humankind, for the gods, was like witnessing imperfection in themselves, and thus their fall;

anything causing these feelings didn't do the gods any good
and therefore could be terminated without a second thought.
It was the job of human beings to make the gods happy, and
upon failure at this task, they could be "fired" (death), only to
be replaced later—it wasn't a position which the gods could
hold vacant for long. Thus were the great flood stories.

The essay starts with a pan on the "big picture." Panning on all three stories has
allowed the writer to discover similarities among his blocks of evidence and to demonstrate that the examples he has chosen are representative of his generalization—his
claim—that in all three flood stories men exist "solely to please the gods."

The writer then constructs a series of tracks, summaries of each of the three stories
that isolate some interesting parallels for readers to ponder. But at this point, rather
than allowing his tracks to set up zooms, the writer returns again and again to versions
of his original pan. In other words, a reflex move to 1-on-10 leads him to repeatedly
match the evidence to his one governing claim.

To develop his central claim, the writer needs to devote much less space to repeating that claim, and more to actually looking at key pieces of evidence, zooming in on
significant variations within the general pattern. In his second paragraph, for example,
the writer allows the 1-on-10 pattern to rush his thinking and distract him from his
evidence. He claims that the God of Genesis "had become unhappy with his creations
so they were to be destroyed. Like a toy a child no longer has use for, humankind was
to be wasted."

This claim fits Enlil, the god in *Gilgamesh* who, as we are later told, decides to
get rid of humans because they make too much noise. But it does not so easily fit
the God of Genesis, about whom the writer has just told us that "the wickedness of
man...grieved him to his heart." If he did 10 on 1 on this passage, slowing down to
think about the evidence, the writer would likely see that the difference between the
two gods is significant. The grief that his evidence mentions suggests that God's decision to flood the earth was possibly ethical rather than childishly selfish and rash. And
the statement from Genesis that "every imagination of the thoughts of [man's] heart
was only evil continually" might lead him to see that humans were not simply victims
of divine prerogative, but rather that they deserved punishment.

The writer doesn't consider these other possible interpretations because his reliance on pans—the general pattern—has predisposed him to see his evidence only as
another sign of the gods' egotism, their desire to remain "happy" at any cost.

Revising the Draft Using 10 on 1 and Difference Within Similarity

How might the writer make better use of the evidence he has collected, using the
principle of looking for difference within similarity?

Revision Strategy 1: *Assume that the essay's "answer"—its conclusion about the evidence—does not yet go far enough.* Rather than having to throw out his thinking,
the writer should consider, as is almost always the case in revision, that he hasn't

refined his initial idea enough. As an interpretation of the evidence, it leaves too much unaccounted for.

Revision Strategy 2: *Find a "1" to use with 10 on 1—a piece of the evidence sufficiently revealing to be analyzed in more detail; then zoom in on it.* In the case of the writer of "Flood Stories," that 1 might be a single story, which he could examine in more detail. He could then test his claims about this story through comparison and contrast with the other stories. In the existing draft, the writer has not used comparison and contrast to refine his conclusion; he has just imposed the same conclusion on the other stories. Alternatively, the 1 might be the single most interesting feature that the three stories share.

Revision Strategy 3: *To find the most revealing piece or feature of the evidence, keep asking, What can be said with some certainty about the evidence?* This question will induce a writer to rehearse the facts to keep them fresh, so that his or her first impressions don't "contaminate" or distort consideration of subsequent evidence.

If the writer were to apply these strategies, he might have a conversation with himself that sounded something like this:

"What can I say with some certainty about my evidence?"

"In all three of these stories, a first civilization created by a god is destroyed by the same means—a flood."

Notice that this is a factual description of the evidence rather than a speculation about it. You are always better off to report the facts in your evidence carefully and fully before moving to conclusions. (This is harder to do than you might think.)

"What else is certain about the evidence?"

"In each case the gods leave a surviving pair to rebuild the civilization rather than just wiping everybody out and inventing a new kind of being. Interestingly, the gods begin again by choosing from the same stock that failed the first time around."

Mulling over the evidence in this way—taking care to lay out the facts and distinguish them from speculation—can help you decide what evidence to zoom in on. One of the chief advantages of zooms is that they get you in close enough to your evidence to see the questions its details imply.

Revision Strategy 4: *Examine the evidence closely enough to see what questions the details imply and what other patterns they reveal.* So far, the writer has worked mostly from two quite general questions: Why did the gods decide to wipe out their creations? And why do the gods need human beings? But there are other questions his evidence might prompt him to ask. In each story, for example, the gods are disappointed by humankind, yet they don't invent submissive robots who will dedicate their lives to making the deities feel good about themselves. Why not? This question might cause the writer to uncover a shared feature of his examples (a pattern) that he has thus far not considered—the surviving pairs.

Revision Strategy 5: *Uncover implications in your zoom that can develop your interpretation further.* Having selected the surviving pairs for more detailed examination, what might the writer conclude about them? One interesting fact that the surviving pairs reveal is that the flood stories are not only descriptions of the end of a world but also creation accounts, because they also tell us how a new civilization, the existing one, got started.

Revision Strategy 6: *Look for difference within similarity to better focus the thesis.* Given the recurrence of the survival pairs in the three stories, where might the writer locate a significant difference? One potentially significant difference involves the survival pair in the story of Gilgamesh, who are segregated from the new world and granted immortality. Perhaps this separation suggests that the new civilization will not be haunted by the painful memory of a higher power's intervention, leaving humans less fearful of what might happen in the future. This distinction could focus the argument in the essay; it does not distract from the writer's overall generalization but rather develops it.

Revision Strategy 7: *Constellate the evidence to experiment with alternative thesis options.* Notice how the hypothetical revision we've been producing has made use of looking for difference within similarity to explore alternative ways of connecting the evidence—a selected set of zooms—into an overall explanation. We call this activity *constellating the evidence*: like the imaginary lines that connect real stars into a recognizable shape, your thinking configures the examples into some larger meaning. In this case, instead of repeatedly concluding that the gods destroy humans when humans fail to make them happy, the writer might be on his way to a thesis about the relative optimism or skepticism of the way the flood stories represent change.

- Possible thesis #1: The flood stories propose the view that real change is necessarily apocalyptic rather than evolutionary.

- Possible thesis #2: The flood stories present qualified optimism about the possibility of new starts.

Try This 10.3: Describing Evidence

Have a conversation with yourself (on paper) about some piece of evidence you are studying. Start with the question we proposed for the student writer of the flood stories essay: What can be said with some certainty about this evidence? What, in other words, is clearly true of the data? What can be reported about it as fact without going on to interpretation of the facts?

This distinction between fact and interpretation can be a tricky one, but it is also essential because, if you can't keep your data separate from what you've begun to think about them, you risk losing sight of the data altogether. Press yourself to keep answering the same question—What can be said with some certainty about this evidence? or a variant of the question, such as What's clearly true of this evidence is....

You may find it helpful to do this exercise with a partner or in a small group. If you work in a small group, have one member record the results as these emerge. You might also try this exercise as a freewrite and then share your results with others by reading aloud your list of facts or putting them on a blackboard along with other people's results. Once you've assembled a list of what can fairly be stated as fact about your evidence, you are ready to start on some version of the question, What do these facts suggest? or What features of these data seem most to invite/require interpretation?

DOING 10 ON 1: A STUDENT PAPER (*GOOD BYE LENIN!*)

The essay below is an exploratory draft on a film, using a single scene to generate its thinking. As you read the essay, watch how the writer uses 10 on 1. Unlike "Flood Stories," in which the writer felt compelled to make all of his evidence fit a narrow thesis, here the writer repeatedly tests her tentative conclusions against the evidence until she arrives at a plausible *working thesis* that might organize the next draft.

Think of the working thesis as an ultimate So what?—the product of other, smaller interpretive leaps along the way. As we did in Chapter 6 Interpretation, we have written in the So what? prompt where the writer has used it to move from observation to implication to conclusions. Notice how the writer allows her evidence to complicate and stimulate her thinking rather than just confirm (corroborate) her general idea.

On the Edge: A Scene from *Good Bye Lenin!*

[1] The movie shows us Alex and Lara's first date, which is to a sort of underground music club where the performers wear costumes made of plastic tubing and leather, and play loud hard-core rock music. At first, the musicians look surreal, as though they are part of a strange dream from which, at any moment, Alex will awake. The Western rock is real, though, as are the sci-fi costumes, and the scene moves forward to show Alex and Lara climbing a stairway out onto what looks like a fire escape and then through a window and into an apartment.

[2] Here, Alex and Lara settle down into conversation. The young couple sits, hand in hand, and gazes together into the night sky; yet, as the camera pans away, we see that the apartment where the two have retreated is missing its façade. Inside, three walls are still decorated, complete with furniture, wallpaper, and even working lamps; yet, the two sit on the ledge of the fourth wall, which has crumbled away completely.

[3] *[So what?:]* On the surface, I think the movie invites us to read this as a visual representation of the new lives Alex, Lara, and the other characters face now that the wall has fallen. As a Westerner, at first I read this scene as a representation of the

new relationship between Lara and Alex. In other words, I imagined the movie's placement of the couple on the ledge of a domestic space as a representation of where their lives were going together—toward some shared domestic life, toward living together, toward becoming a family. I also thought this was a clever representation of the collapse of communism—this wall has also fallen down.

[4] *[Complicating evidence:]* I don't think, however, that the movie lets us entertain this one romanticized reading of the scene for long—the image is too frightening. As the camera pans away, we see that this isn't a new Westernized apartment; this is an East German flat decorated in much the same way as Alex's home was only months before. The image is alarming; the wall here has been ripped down, *[so what?:]* and we are forced to ask, did the fall of communism violently blow apart domestic and daily living of East German people?

[5] The movie allows us this dichotomy and, I think, fights to sustain it. On one hand, Alex and Lara would not be on this date if the wall hadn't come down, and yet the scene is more than just another representation of East Germany torn between Communism and the new Westernization. *[Working thesis:]* The movie tries hard to remind us that the rapid Westernization of East Germany devastated while it liberated in other ways. This scene uses space to represent Alex and Lara's (and East Germany's) dilemma: Alex and Lara gaze out at the night sky but only because the wall has been blown apart. The exposed apartment is uninhabitable and yet the lights still work, the pictures are still hung, and a young couple leans against one another inside.

This draft is a good example of a writer using evidence to complicate as well as support her claims. Her thinking evolves through successive complications; that is, she complicates a previous claim that was a complication. When the writer arrives at tentative answers, she tests them rather than just adding more evidence to prove she is right.

Try This 10.4: Marking Claims, Evidence, and Complications in a Draft

As a check on the range of concepts that this and the previous chapter have introduced, mark the student draft as follows:

- *Mark claims—assertions made about the evidence—with the letter C.* Claims are ideas that the evidence seems to support. An example of a claim is in paragraph 4: "I don't think, however, that the movie lets us entertain this one romanticized reading of the scene for long."

- *Underline evidence.* The evidence is the pool of primary material (data)—details from the film, rather than the writer's ideas about it. An example of evidence is in paragraph 2: "The young couple sits, hand in hand, and gazes together into the night sky; yet, as the camera pans away, we see that the apartment where the two have retreated is missing its façade." This piece of evidence is the 1 of the 10 on 1. In effect, the whole draft goes after the range of possible implications that may be inferred from the image of the young couple sitting at the edge of an apartment that is missing one of its walls, presumably a result of war damage.

- *Circle complications.* Complications can be found both in the evidence a writer cites and in the claims a writer makes about it. Complicating evidence is evidence that does not fit the claims the writer has been making. For example, in paragraph 4: "As the camera pans away, we see that this isn't a new Westernized apartment; this is an East German flat decorated in much the same way as Alex's home was only months before. The image is alarming; the wall here has been ripped down." This evidence causes the writer to reconsider an earlier claim from paragraph 3, that the scene is about the couple moving "toward some shared domestic life, toward living together, toward becoming a family."

A TEMPLATE FOR ORGANIZING PAPERS USING 10 ON 1: AN ALTERNATIVE TO FIVE-PARAGRAPH FORM

Here is a template for writing papers using 10 on 1. It brings together much of the key terminology introduced in this chapter. Think of it not as a rigid format but as an outline for moving from one phase of your paper to the next. Unlike five-paragraph form, the template will give you room to think and to establish connections among your ideas.

1. In your introduction, start by noting (panning on) an interesting pattern or tendency you have found in your evidence. (As explained at the beginning of the chapter, you may find it useful to do 1 on 10 in order to discover the pattern.) Explain what attracted you to it—why you find it potentially significant and worth looking at. This paragraph would end with a tentative theory (working thesis) about what this pattern or tendency might reveal or accomplish.

2. Zoom in on your representative example, some smaller part of the larger pattern and argue for its representativeness and usefulness in coming to a better understanding of your subject.

3. Do 10 on 1—analyze your representative example—sharing with your readers your observations (what you notice) and your tentative conclusions (answers

to the So what? question). Then use complicating evidence to refine your claims.

4a. In a short paper, you might at this point move to your conclusion, with its qualified, refined version of your thesis and brief commentary on what you've accomplished, that is, the ways in which your analysis has illuminated the larger subject.

4b. In a longer paper, you would begin constellating—organizing the essay by exploring and elaborating the connections among your representative examples analyzed via 10 on 1. In the language of the film analogy, you would move from your initial zoom to another zoom on a similar case, to see the extent to which the thesis you evolved with your representative example needed further adjusting to better reflect the nature of your subject as a whole. This last move is a primary topic of our next chapter.

GUIDELINES FOR USING EVIDENCE TO BUILD A PAPER: 10 ON 1

1. Learn to recognize unsubstantiated assertions, rather than treating claims as self-evident truths. Whenever you make a claim, offer your readers the evidence that led you to it.

2. Make details speak. Explain how evidence confirms or qualifies your claim, and offer your reasons for believing the evidence means what you say it does.

3. Say more about less rather than less about more, allowing a carefully analyzed part of your subject to provide perspective on the whole.

4. It is generally better to make ten points on a representative issue or example than to make the same basic point about ten related issues or examples; this axiom we call 10 on 1.

5. Argue overtly that the evidence on which you choose to focus is representative. Be careful not to generalize on the basis of too little or unrepresentative evidence.

6. Use your best example as a lens through which to examine other evidence. Analyze subsequent examples to test and develop your conclusions, rather than just confirming that you are right.

7. Look for difference within similarity as a way of doing 10 on 1. Rather than repeating the same overly general claim (i.e., doing 1 on 10), use significant variation within the general pattern to better develop your claim.

8. To find the most revealing piece or feature of the evidence, keep asking yourself, "What can I say with some certainty about the evidence?" If you continually rehearse the facts, you are less likely to let an early idea blind you to subsequent evidence.

Assignment: Writing a Paper Using the 10 on 1 Template

Write a paper in which you do 10 on 1 with a single representative example of something you are trying to think more carefully about. The template should work with virtually any content. It could be an in-depth look at a particular kind of film (vampire films or feel-good sports stories or tragic death at an early age films), or the advertisements for a particular product (cars, make-up, hair care, sports equipment, suntan lotion). It could be a more academic subject: economic stimulus packages, government bail-outs, intelligence tests, failed revolutions, successful fascist dictatorships. You might choose a representative passage from a story or a representative story from a volume of stories by a single author—or a representative poem from a short volume of poetry or a representative passage from a nonfiction book or article. It could be a passage from a favorite columnist or a single representative song from a CD. It could be a single scene or moment or character from a film or play or other performance. It could be one picture or work of art that is representative of a larger exhibit.

Brainstorm your "1" on the page, making observations and asking, So what? Draw out as much meaning as possible from your representative example. Go for depth. Then use this example as a lens for viewing similar examples. Remember to use the template in the previous section as a model for organizing the paper.

Chapter 11

Making a Thesis Evolve

THIS CHAPTER IS AT THE HEART of what we have to say about essay writing, especially about the function of thesis statements. The chapter argues that even in a final draft a thesis develops through successive complications; it doesn't remain static, as people tend to believe. Even in cases such as the report format of the natural and social sciences, where the thesis itself cannot change, there is still development between the beginning of the paper and the end. The thesis, usually called a hypothesis, is tested in various ways in order to evaluate its adequacy.

Formulating a claim, seeking conflicting evidence, and then using these conflicts to revise the claim is a primary movement of mind in analytical writing. Here's the mantra: *the complications you encounter are an opportunity to make your thesis evolve*, not a problem. An evolving thesis is one that responds more fully and accurately to evidence.

This chapter contains one heuristic, Six Steps for Making a Thesis Evolve Through Successive Complications. Here is a skeletal version of this process, which the chapter will demonstrate and define in more detail.

SIX STEPS FOR MAKING A THESIS EVOLVE THROUGH SUCCESSIVE COMPLICATIONS

1. Formulate an idea about your subject, a working thesis.
2. See how far you can make this thesis go in accounting for confirming evidence.
3. Locate evidence that is not adequately accounted for by the thesis.
4. Make explicit the apparent mismatch between the thesis and selected evidence, asking and answering "so what?"
5. Reshape your claim to accommodate the evidence that hasn't fit.
6. Repeat steps 2, 3, 4, and 5 several times.

Your ability to discover ideas and improve on them in revision, as we've argued in the preceding chapters, depends largely on your attitude toward evidence—on your ability to use it as a means of testing and developing your ideas rather than just (statically) confirming and reasserting them.

MOVING FROM IDEA TO THESIS STATEMENT: WHAT A GOOD THESIS LOOKS LIKE

Considerable misunderstanding exists about thesis statements among students—and among many teachers. We have chosen to use the term "thesis" because, by and large, it is the most common term across the academic disciplines for what might otherwise be called a "controlling idea" or "primary claim" or "hypothesis." The term has a long history, going back to classical rhetoric wherein a thesis involved taking a position on some subject. The term "thesis" named general questions with wide applications. The term "hypothesis" was used "to name a specific question that involved actual persons, places, or events" (Crowley 57). (For an excellent discussion of the history of these terms, see Sharon Crowley and Debra Hawhee, *Ancient Rhetorics for Contemporary Students*.)

This idea of "taking a position," as in an argument, is what some faculty members dislike about the term, mistaking it perhaps for an invitation to writers to express their views on a subject rather than closely examining it. For every faculty member who wishes student writers to organize their thinking around a clearly-defined central claim (thesis), other faculty members argue that thesis-driven writing and reflective writing differ in methods and goals.

In the meantime, we will continue to use the term thesis, though not in the way it is often described in writing textbooks, where it is presented as a static idea that a writer sets out to prove. Our use of the term is probably closer to the idea of a "hypothesis," which has come to mean a theory to be tested.

Arriving at Thesis Statements: When and Where

The most disabling misunderstanding for students is that a writer needs to have a thesis before he or she begins writing. Good thesis statements are the product of writing, not its precursor. Worrying about having a thesis statement too early in the writing process will just about guarantee papers that support overly general and often obvious ideas. Arriving prematurely at claims also blinds writers to complicating evidence (evidence that runs counter to the thesis) and so deprives them of their best opportunities to arrive at better ideas.

Another disabling assumption is that the thesis of a paper must always appear at or near the end of the first paragraph, preferably in the form of a single-sentence claim. The fact is that the governing idea of most analytical writing is too complex to be asserted as a single-sentence claim that could be understood at the beginning of the paper. *Nevertheless*, it is true that a writer has not moved from the exploratory writing phase to the writing of a paper until he or she has discovered an idea around which his or her thinking can cohere. Without a governing idea to hold onto, readers will not understand why you are telling them what you are telling them. In order for a paper to make sense to readers, a thesis, or, in the case of inductively organized papers, a thesis "trail" (some sense of the issues and questions that are generating the paper's forward momentum) must be evident. (See *The Shaping Force of Common Thought Patterns: Deduction and Induction* in Chapter 15.)

The best way to learn about thesis statements is to look for them in published writing. You will find that the single-sentence thesis statement as prescribed in writing textbooks is a rather rare specimen. It is most common in argument, wherein a writer has a proposition that he or she wants readers to either adopt or dismiss. In analytical writing, the thesis is more likely to become evident in phases, guided by some kind of opening claim sufficient to get the paper started. This claim is commonly known as the **working thesis**. Sometimes as much as the first third of a paper will explore an idea that the rest of the paper will subsequently replace with a different, though not necessarily opposing perspective. If you look closely, however, you will see the trail that lets readers anticipate a shift from one possible way of seeing things to another.

Strong versus Weak Thesis Statements

A thesis is an idea. It is a thought that you have arrived at about your evidence, rather than something you can expect to find, ready-made, in whatever you are studying. A strong thesis is a theory about the meaning and significance of your evidence that would not have been immediately obvious to your readers. A weak thesis either makes no claim or makes a claim that doesn't need proving, such as a statement of fact or an opinion with which virtually all of your readers would most likely agree before reading your essay (for example, "exercise is good for you").

Analytical writing begins with something puzzling that the writer wishes to better understand. Strong thesis statements enable exploration. Weak thesis statements disable exploration by closing things down way too tightly at the outset.

Here are two characteristics that an idea needs to possess in order to work as a thesis.

- the thesis of an analytical paper is an idea about what some feature or features of your subject *means*
- a thesis should be an idea in need of argument; that is, it should not be a statement of fact or an idea with which most readers would already agree.

Finding the Tension in Good Thesis Statements

In the Try This on the next page are six examples of good thesis statements, that is, good translations of ideas into forms that could direct the development of an essay. The first thing you should notice about all of these thesis statements is the presence of tension—the pressure of one idea against another idea, of one potentially viable way of seeing things against another viable, but finally less satisfactory way of seeing things. Good ideas usually take place with the aid of some kind of back pressure, by which we mean that the idea takes shape by pushing against (so to speak) another way of seeing things. This is not the same as setting out to overturn and completely refute one idea in favor of another (although thesis statements sometimes work in this way too). More often what happens is that the thesis statement's primary idea emerges as some kind of clarification or reworking of another idea. The forward momentum of the thesis comes from playing the newer idea off of the older one.

Try This 11.1: Spotting the Tension in Good Thesis Statements

Look at the thesis statements below, all of which were taken from published analytical essays. Find the tension in each, or the defining pressure of one idea against another possibility. In the first thesis sentence, for example, the primary idea is that the new advertising campaign for Docker trousers is radical. The back pressure against which this idea takes shape is that this new campaign may not seem radical. The writer will demonstrate the truth of both of these claims, rather than overturning one and then championing the other. The same can be said of the parts of the second thesis statement. The primary idea, recognizable by the syntax of the second sentence, is that cosmetic surgery will make life worse for everyone. The back pressure against which this idea will take shape is the claim that cosmetic surgery has psychologicial benefits; it makes individual people happier.

Notice that the thesis statement does not simply say: "Cosmetic surgery is bad." The writer's job will be to demonstrate that the potential harm of cosmetic surgery outweighs the benefits, but the benefits won't be just summarily dismissed. Both of the two ideas are to some extent true. Neither idea, in other words, is **a straw man**—the somewhat deceptive argumentative practice of setting up a dummy position solely because it is easy to knock down. A straw man does not strengthen a thesis statement because it fails to provide genuine back pressure.

1) It may not seem like it, but "Nice Pants" is as radical a campaign as the original Docker series.

2) If opponents of cosmetic surgery are too quick to dismiss those who claim great psychological benefits, protesters are far too willing to dismiss those who raise concerns. Cosmetic surgery might make individual people happier, but in the aggregate it makes life worse for everyone.

3) The history of thought in the modern era of history of thinking about the self may be an exaggeration, but the consequences of this vision of a self set apart have surely been felt in every field of inquiry.

4) We may join with the modern builders in justifying the violence of means—the sculptor's hammer and chisel—by appealing to ends that serve the greater good. Yet too often modern planners and engineers would justify the creative destruction of habitat as necessary for doubtful utopias.

5) The derogation of middlebrow, in short, has gone much too far. It's time to bring middlebrow out of its cultural closet, to hail its emollient properties, to trumpet its mending virtues. For middlebrow not only entertains, it educates—pleasurably training us to appreciate high art.

6) There is a connection between the idea of place and the reality of cellular telephones. It is not encouraging. Places are unique—or at least we like to believe they are—and we strive to experience them as a kind of engagement with particulars. Cell phones are precisely the opposite.

If you have been taught to write in 5-paragraph form in school, you will initially have some difficulty writing thesis statements of the sort you have just seen. This is because the "thesis statement plus three supporting paragraphs" format of 5-paragraph form invites listing rather than the articulation of ideas. The typical three-part thesis of 5-paragraph form offers a short list of broadly stated topics (rather than well-defined claims about the topics) and then offers examples of each of these in the body paragraphs.

There is nothing wrong with partitioning the development of a subject into manageable parts, but there is a lot wrong with a thesis that makes no claim or an overly general and obvious claim such as "Television causes adolescents to become violent, lazy, and ill-read." All three parts of this general claim may be true, but nothing much of substance can be said about them in a short paper that is trying to cover all three. And notice the lack of tension in this sample thesis statement. Try writing a better thesis statement—one that has tension—about the impact of some aspect of television on teenagers.

A Note on the Syntax of Good Thesis Statements

Before we move on to concentrated applications of the procedure for making a thesis evolve, take a look at the shape of imprecise thesis statements:

Environmentalism prevents economic growth.

Tax laws benefit the wealthy.

The economic situation today is bad.

Women in contemporary films are more sensitive than men.

All four are simple, declarative sentences that offer very broad assertions. They are both grammatically and conceptually simple. More than that, they're *slack*—especially the first three, in which the primary claim stands alone, not in relation to anything else.

The very *shape* of these weak thesis statements is a warning sign. Most effective working theses, though they may begin more simply, achieve both grammatical and conceptual complexity as they evolve. Such theses contain tension in their syntax, the balance of this against that. Thus, they begin with "although" or incorporate "however" or use an "appears to be about *x* but is actually about *y*" kind of formulation. *(See "Appears to be about X..." in Chapter 4.)*

Here, by contrast, are three possible versions of the fourth weak thesis above:

Although women more readily cry in contemporary films, the men, by not crying, seem to win the audience's favor.

The complications that fuel the plots in today's romantic comedies arise because women and men express their sensitivity so differently; the resolutions, however, rarely require the men to capitulate.

A spate of recent films has witnessed the emergence of the new "womanly" man as hero, and not surprisingly, his tender qualities seem to be the reason he attracts the female love interest.

THE RECIPROCAL RELATIONSHIP BETWEEN THESIS AND EVIDENCE: THE THESIS AS LENS

What we have said so far about the thesis does not mean that all repetition of ideas in an essay is bad or that a writer's concluding paragraph should have no reference to the way the paper began. One function of the thesis is to provide the connective tissue, so to speak, that holds together a paper's three main parts—beginning, middle, and end. Periodic reminders of your paper's thesis, its unifying idea, are essential for keeping both you and your readers on track.

As we've also argued, though, developing an idea requires more than repetition. It is in light of this fact that the analogy of thesis to connective tissue proves inadequate. A better way of envisioning how a thesis operates is to think of it as a camera lens. This analogy more accurately describes the relationship between the thesis and the subject it seeks to explain. While the lens affects how we see the subject (what evidence we select, what questions we ask about that evidence), the subject we are looking at also affects how we adjust the lens.

Here is the principle that the camera lens analogy allows us to see: the relationship between thesis and subject is *reciprocal.* In good analytical writing, especially in the early, investigatory stages of writing and thinking, the thesis not only directs the writer's way of looking at evidence; the analysis of evidence should also direct and redirect (bring about revision of) the thesis. Even in a final draft, writers are usually fine-tuning their governing idea in response to their analysis of evidence. (See Figure 11.1.)

The enemy of good analytical writing is the fuzzy lens—imprecisely worded thesis statements. Very broad thesis statements, those that are made up of imprecise (fuzzy) terms, make bad lenses. They blur everything together and muddy important distinctions. If your lens is insufficiently focused, you are not likely to see much in your evidence. If you say, for example, that the economic situation today is bad, you will at least have some sense of direction, but the imprecise terms "bad" and "economic situation" don't provide you with a focus clear enough to distinguish significant detail in your evidence. Without significant detail to analyze, you can't develop your thesis, either by showing readers what the thesis is good for (what it allows us to understand and explain) or by clarifying its terms.

Thesis

Evidence

FIGURE 11.1

The Reciprocal Relationship Between Thesis and Evidence. Like a lens, the thesis affects the way a writer sees evidence. Evidence should also require the writer to readjust the lens.

A writer's thesis is usually fuzzier in a paper's opening than it is in the conclusion. As we argued in our critique of five-paragraph form in Chapter 10, a paper ending with a claim worded almost exactly as it was in the beginning has not made its thesis adequately responsive to evidence. The body of the paper should not only substantiate the thesis by demonstrating its value in selecting and explaining evidence, but also bring the opening version of the thesis into better focus.

Making a Thesis Evolve: A Brief Example

More often than not, when inexperienced writers face a situation in which evidence seems to be unclear or contradictory, they tend to make one of two unproductive moves: they either ignore the conflicting evidence, or they abandon the problem altogether and look for something more clear-cut to write about. Faced with evidence that complicates your thesis, the one thing not to do is run away.

The savvy writer will actively seek out complicating evidence, taking advantage of chances to bring out complications in order to make the thesis more fully responsive to evidence. Let's revisit a sample thesis from the discussion of uncovering assumptions in Chapter 4, "tax laws benefit the wealthy." If you were to seek out data that would complicate this overstated claim, you would soon encounter evidence that would press you to make some distinctions that the initial formulation of this claim leaves obscure. You would need, for example, to distinguish different sources of wealth and then to determine whether all or just some wealthy taxpayers are benefited by tax laws.

Do people whose wealth comes primarily from investments benefit less (or more) than those whose wealth comes from high wages? Evidence might also lead you to consider whether tax laws, by benefiting the wealthy, also benefit other people indirectly. Both of these considerations would necessitate some reformulation of the thesis. By the end of the paper, the claim that tax laws benefit the wealthy would have evolved into a more carefully defined and qualified statement that would reflect the thinking you have done in your analysis of evidence. This, by and large, is what good concluding paragraphs do—they reflect back on and reformulate your paper's initial position in light of the thinking you have done about it. (See Figure 11.2.)

But, you might ask, isn't this reformulating of the thesis something a writer does before he or she writes the essay? Certainly some of it is accomplished in the early exploratory writing and note-taking stage. But your finished paper will necessarily do

FIGURE 11.2
A strong thesis evolves as it confronts and assimilates evidence; the evolved thesis may expand or restrict the original claim. The process may need to be repeated a number of times.

more than list conclusions. Your revision process will have weeded out various false starts and dead ends that you may have wandered into on the way to your finished ideas, but the main routes of your movement from a tentative idea to a refined and substantiated theory should remain visible for readers to follow. To an extent, all good writing reenacts the chains of thought that led you to your conclusions.

Try This 11.2: Qualifying Overstated Claims

Making a thesis evolve is to make that thesis more accurate. To do so is almost always to qualify (limit) the claim. Using the model of inquiry in the treatment of the example "Tax laws benefit the wealthy," seek out complications in one of the overstated claims listed below. These complications should include conflicting evidence (which you should specify) and questions about the meaning or appropriateness of key terms. Illustrate a few of these complications, and then reformulate the claim in language that is more carefully qualified and accurate.

Welfare encourages recipients not to work.

Religious people are more moral than those who are not.

Herbal remedies are better than pharmaceutical ones.

The book is always better than the film.

Women are more sensitive than men.

We learn from the lessons of history.

The Evolving Thesis as Hypothesis and Conclusion in the Natural and Social Sciences

A thesis functions differently depending on the academic discipline—whether it must be stated in full at the outset, for example, and what happens to it between the beginning of the paper and the end. The differences appear largest as you move back and forth between courses in the humanities and courses in the natural and certain of the social sciences.

The natural and social sciences generally use a pair of terms, *hypothesis* and *conclusion,* for the single term *thesis.* Because writing in the sciences is patterned according to the scientific method, writers in disciplines such as biology and psychology must report how the original thesis (hypothesis) was tested against empirical evidence and then conclude on this basis whether or not the hypothesis was confirmed.

The gap between this way of thinking about the thesis and the concept of an evolving thesis is not as large as it may seem. The scientific method is in sync with one of the chapter's main points—that something must happen to the thesis between the introduction and the conclusion—so that the conclusion does more than just restate what had already been claimed in the beginning.

Analogously, in a scientific paper, the hypothesis is tested against evidence, the results of which allow the writer to draw conclusions about the hypothesis's validity. Although the hypothesis does not change (or evolve), the testing of it and subsequent interpretation of those results produce commentary on and, often, qualifications of the paper's central claim.

In the natural and social sciences, successive reformulations of the thesis are less likely to be recorded and may not even be expressly articulated. But, as in all disciplines, the primary analytical activity in the sciences is to repeatedly reconsider the assumptions on which a conclusion is based. *(See Chapter 15, Forms and Formats Across the Curriculum.)*

The Hypothesis in the Natural and Social Sciences: Four Professors Speak

The following Voices from Across the Curriculum explain how a hypothesis functions in writing in their disciplines. Notice that in each case, although the hypothesis itself does not change, something does happen to it between introduction and conclusion.

Voices from Across the Curriculum

If the empirical evidence doesn't confirm your hypothesis, you rethink your hypothesis, but it's a complex issue. Researchers whose hypotheses are not confirmed often question their *method* ("if I had more subjects," or "a better manipulation of the experimental group," or "a better test of intelligence," etc.) as much as their hypothesis. And that's often legitimate. Part of the challenge of psychological research is its reliance on a long array of assumptions. Failure to confirm a hypothesis could mean a problem in any of that long array of assumptions. So failure to confirm your hypothesis is often difficult to interpret.

—Alan Tjeltveit, Professor of Psychology

The thesis in experimental psychology papers is the statement of the hypothesis. It is always carefully and explicitly stated in the last few sentences of the introduction. The hypothesis is usually a deductive statement such as: if color does influence mood, then an ambiguous picture printed on different colors of paper should be interpreted differently, depending on the color of the paper. Specifically, based on the results of Jones (1997), the pink paper should cause participants to perceive the picture as a more calm and restful image, and the green paper should cause the picture to be interpreted as a more anxious image.

—Laura Edelman, Professor of Psychology

The thesis is usually presented in the abstract and then again at the end of the introduction. Probably the most frequent writing error is not providing a thesis at all. Sometimes this is because the student doesn't *have* a thesis; other times, it is because the student wants to maintain a sense of mystery about the paper, as if driving toward a dramatic conclusion. This actually makes it harder to read. The best papers are clear and up front about what their point is, then use evidence and argument to support and evaluate the thesis. I encourage students to have a sentence immediately following their discussion of the background on the subject that can be as explicit as: "In this paper, I will argue that while research on toxic effects of methyl bromide provides troubling evidence for severe physiological effects, conclusive proof of a significant environmental hazard is lacking at this time."

I try to avoid the use of the term "hypothesis." I think it gives the false sense that scientists always start with an idea about how something works. Frequently, that is not the case. Some of the best science has actually come from observation. Darwin's work on finches is a classic example. His ideas about adaptation probably derived *from* the observation.

—Bruce Wightman, Professor of Biology

Economists do make pretense to follow scientific methodology. Thus, we are careful not to mix hypothesis and conclusion. I think it's important to distinguish between what is conjectured, the working hypothesis, and what ultimately emerges as a result of an examination of the evidence. Conclusions come only after some test has been passed.

—James Marshall, Professor of Economics

So, in the natural and social sciences, successive reformulations of the thesis are less likely to be recorded and may not even be expressly articulated. But, as in all disciplines, the primary analytical activity in the sciences is to repeatedly reconsider the assumptions on which a conclusion is based.

SIX STEPS FOR MAKING A THESIS EVOLVE

As an overarching guideline, *acknowledge the questions that each new formulation of the thesis prompts you to ask.* The thesis develops through successive complications. Allowing your thesis to run up against potentially conflicting evidence ("but what about this?") enables you to build on your initial idea, extending the range of evidence it can accurately account for by clarifying and qualifying its key terms.

1. Formulate an idea about your subject. This working thesis should be some claim about the meaning of your evidence that is good enough to get you started.

2. See how far you can make this thesis go in accounting for evidence. Use the thesis to explain as much of your evidence as it reasonably can. Try it on.

3. Locate evidence that is not adequately accounted for by the thesis. Actively search for such evidence because the initial version of the thesis will incline you to see only what fits and not to notice the evidence that doesn't fit.

4. Make explicit the apparent mismatch between the thesis and selected evidence. Explain how and why some pieces of evidence do not fit the thesis.

5. Reshape your claim to accommodate the evidence that hasn't fit. This will mean rewording your thesis to resolve or explain apparent contradictions.

6. Repeat steps two, three, four, and five several times, until you are satisfied that the thesis statement accounts for your evidence as fully and accurately as possible.

EVOLVING A THESIS IN AN EXPLORATORY DRAFT: THE EXAMPLE OF *LAS MENINAS*

The example is a student writer's exploratory draft on a painting called *Las Meninas* (Spanish for "the ladies-in-waiting") by the seventeenth-century painter Diego Velázquez. The method of analysis used here will, however, work with anything, print or non-print.

Look at the painting in Figure 11.3, and then read the student's draft. As you read, you will notice that much of the essay consists of list-like description, which leaves it somewhat unfocused. But careful description is a necessary stage in moving toward interpretations of evidence, especially in an exploratory draft where the writer is not yet committed to any single position. Notice how the writer's word choice in her

FIGURE 11.3
Las Meninas by Diego Velázquez, 1656 Approximately 10'5" x 9'. Museo del Prado, Madrid.

descriptions prompts various kinds of interpretive leaps. We have added in brackets our observations about how the writer's thinking is proceeding, and we have used underlining to track her various attempts at formulating a thesis.

Velázquez's Intentions in *Las Meninas*

[1] Velázquez has been noted as being one of the best Spanish artists of all time. It seems that as Velázquez got older, his paintings became better. Toward the end of his life, he painted his masterpiece, *Las Meninas*. Out of all his works, *Las Meninas* is the only known self-portrait of Velázquez. There is much to be said about *Las Meninas*. The painting is very complex, but some of the intentions that Velázquez had in painting *Las Meninas* are very clear. *[The writer opens with background information and a broad working thesis (underlined).]*

[2] First, we must look at the painting as a whole. The question that must be answered is, Who is in the painting? The people are all members of the Royal Court of the Spanish monarch Philip IV. In the center is the king's daughter, who eventually became Empress of Spain. Around her are her *meninas* or ladies-in-waiting. These *meninas* are all daughters of influential men. To the right of the *meninas* are dwarfs who are servants, and the family dog who looks fierce but is easily tamed by the foot of the little dwarf. The more unique people in the painting are Velázquez himself, who stands to the left in front of a large canvas; the king and queen, whose faces are captured in the obscure mirror; the man in the doorway; and the nun and man behind the *meninas*. To analyze this painting further, the relationship between characters must be understood. *[The writer describes the evidence and arrives at an operating assumption—focusing on the relationship among characters.]*

[3] Where is this scene occurring? Most likely it is in the palace. But why is there no visible furniture? Is it because Velázquez didn't want the viewers to become distracted from his true intentions? I believe it is to show that this is not just a painting of an actual event. This is an event out of his imagination. *[The writer begins pushing observations to tentative conclusions by asking So what?]*

[4] Now, let us become better acquainted with the characters. The child in the center is the most visible. All the light is shining on her. Maybe Velázquez is suggesting that she is the next light for Spain and that even God has approved her by shining all the available light on her. Back in those days there was a belief in the divine right of kings, so this just might be what Velázquez is saying. *[The writer starts ranking evidence for importance and continues to ask,*

So what?; she arrives at a possible interpretation of the painter's intention.]

[5]   The next people of interest are the ones behind the *meninas*. The woman in the habit might be a nun and the man a priest.

[6]   The king and queen are the next group of interesting people. They are in the mirror, which is to suggest they are present, but they are not as visible as they might be. Velázquez suggests that they are not always at the center where everyone would expect them to be. *[The writer continues using Notice and Focus plus asking So what?; the writer has begun tackling evidence that might conflict with her first interpretation.]*

[7]   The last person and the most interesting is Velázquez. He dominates the painting along with the little girl. He takes up the whole left side along with his gigantic easel. But what is he painting? As I previously said, he might be painting the king and queen. But I also think he could be pretending to paint us, the viewers. The easel really gives this portrait an air of mystery because Velázquez knows that we, the viewers, want to know what he is painting. *[The writer starts doing 10 on 1 with her selection of the most significant detail.]*

[8]   The appearance of Velázquez is also interesting. His eyes are focused outward here. They are not focused on what is going on around him. It is a steady stare. Also interesting is his confident stance. He was confident enough to place himself in the painting of the royal court. <u>I think that Velázquez wants the king to give him the recognition he deserves by including him in the "family."</u> And the symbol on his vest is the symbol given to a painter by the king to <u>show that his status and brilliance have been appreciated by the monarch.</u> It is unknown how it got there. It is unlikely that Velázquez put it there himself. That would be too outright, and Velázquez was the type to give his messages subtly. Some say that after Velázquez's death, King Philip IV himself painted it to finally <u>give Velázquez the credit he deserved for being a loyal friend and servant.</u> *[The writer continues doing 10 on 1 and asking So what?; she arrives at three tentative theses (underlined).]*

[9]   I believe that Velázquez was very ingenious by putting his thoughts and feelings into a painting. He didn't want to offend the king who had done so much for him. It paid off for Velázquez because he did finally get what he wanted, even if it was after he died. *[The writer concludes and is now ready to redraft to tighten links between evidence and claims, formulate a better working thesis, and make this thesis evolve.]*

Description to Analysis: The Exploratory Draft

The purpose of an exploratory draft is to use writing as a means of arriving at a working thesis that the next draft can more fully evolve. Most writers find that potential theses emerge near the end of the exploratory draft—which is the case in this student draft (see the three claims underlined in paragraph 8).

This is a good exploratory draft. The writer has begun to interpret details and draw plausible conclusions from what she sees, rather than just describing (summarizing) the scene depicted on the canvas or responding loosely to it with her unanalyzed impressions.

The paper is typical of an early draft in several ways:

- It is written more for the writer as a form of inquiry than for readers. The writer reports her thoughts as they occur, but she doesn't always explain how she arrived at them or how they connect to each other.

- recognizable thesis doesn't emerge until near the end (in paragraph 8).

- The paper contains more than one potential thesis. The paper ignores the conflicts among its various theses and some of its evidence.

- The writer tends to end paragraphs with promising observations and then walk away, leaving the observations undeveloped. Rather than draw out the implications of her observations, she halts her thinking too soon in order to move on to the next piece of evidence. See, for example, this writer's repeated return to paragraph openings using "next" and "also," which traps her into listing parallel examples rather than building connections among them. As we will illustrate later, the writer can remedy this problem by querying her observations with the question "So what?"

What is especially good about the draft is that it reveals the writer's willingness to push on from her first idea (reading the painting as an endorsement of the divine right of kings, expressed by the light shining on the princess) by seeking out complicating evidence. This first idea does not account for enough of the evidence and is undermined by evidence that clearly doesn't fit, such as the small size and decentering of the king and queen, and the large size and foregrounding of the painter himself.

Rather than ignoring these potentially troublesome details, the writer instead zooms in on them, making the painter's representation of himself and of his employers the 1 for doing 10 on 1 (making a number of observations about a single representative piece of evidence and analyzing it in depth).

Starting a Revision by Looking Again at the Details: The Method

Now what? The writer is ready to rewrite the paper in order to choose and better define her thesis. She might first wish to step back a bit from her initial formulations by using The Method to again survey the details of the painting, looking for patterns of repetition and contrast.

Examples of exact or nearly exact **repetitions**:

the pictures in the background

the fact that both the dwarf and the painter, each on his own side of the painting, stare confidently and directly at the viewer

Examples of **strands** (repetition of the same or similar kind of detail):

details having to do with family

servants: dwarf, *meninas*, dog? painter?

details having to do with art and the making of art: easel, brush, paintings on wall

Examples of organizing **contrasts**—binaries:

royalty/commoners

employers/servants

large/small

foreground/background

central (prominent)/marginalized (less prominent)

Having used The Method to see the evidence anew, the writer would be ready to try the Six Steps for Making the Thesis Evolve. She'd begin by noticing that, as is the case in most exploratory drafts, she has several potential thesis statements vying for control of the paper.

Applying the Six Steps to *Las Meninas*

Step 1: *Formulate a working thesis.*

As a general rule, you should *assume the presence of multiple, often competing theses*, some of which you may not have yet detected. In the *Las Meninas* paper, as is often the case in early drafts, no single idea emerges clearly as the thesis. Instead, we get three related but not entirely compatible ideas vying for control of the paper (all in paragraph 8):

"I think that Velázquez wants the king to…"

Thesis 1: give Velázquez "the recognition he deserves by including him in the 'family.'"

Thesis 2: "show that his [Velázquez's] status and brilliance [as an artist] have been appreciated."

Thesis 3: give Velázquez "the credit he deserved for being a loyal friend and servant."

These three ideas about the painter's intentions could be made to work together, but at present the writer is left with an uneasy fit among them.

Step 2: *See how far you can make each thesis go in accounting for evidence.*

Each of the three potential thesis ideas explains some of the evidence. The writer should try on each one to see what it helps to explain.

Thesis 1: painting as bid for inclusion in the family

> **Evidence:** the painter's inclusion of himself with the family—the king, queen, and princess—in a fairly domestic scene

Thesis 2: painting as bid for appreciation of painter's status and brilliance as an artist

> **Evidence:** prominence of easel and brush and painter himself in the painting; painter's confident stare and the apparent decentering of king and queen; painting set in artist's studio—his space

Thesis 3: painting as bid for credit for being loyal friend and servant

> **Evidence:** painter's location of himself among other loyal servants at court (ladies in waiting, dog, and large dwarf)

Step 3: *Locate evidence that is not adequately accounted for by each thesis.*

Step 4: *Make explicit the apparent mismatch between the thesis and selected evidence.*

What happens when the writer begins to search for evidence that doesn't seem to be adequately accounted for by her various thesis formulations?

Thesis 1: painting as bid for inclusion in the family

> **Evidence mismatches:** presence of painter among servants; foregrounding of servants in image and in painting's title *(The Ladies in Waiting)*—painter's large size (larger than king and queen) does not go with the idea of "inclusion," and emphasis on servants does not go with inclusion in royal family

Thesis 2: painting as bid for appreciation of painter's status and brilliance as an artist

> **Evidence mismatches:** prominence of other servants in the painting; emphasis on family as much as or more than on artist himself—if bidding for status, painter would not present himself as just one of the servants, nor might he give so much attention to the princess (and the king and queen's regard for her)

Thesis 3: painting as bid for credit for being loyal friend and servant

> **Evidence mismatches:** painter's prominence; his confident stare; prominence of easel and brush; small size of king and queen (smaller than servants)—if painter wished to emphasize loyalty and service, his subordinate relationship to the more powerful at court, he would have made himself and the tools of his trade less important

Step 5: *Choose the claim that seems to account for the most evidence and then reshape that claim to better accommodate evidence that doesn't fit.*

When you've found conflicting or inadequately explained evidence, try using it to evolve your existing thesis rather than beating a too-hasty retreat. The direction in which the writer's thinking is moving—that the painting asks for someone's strengths to be recognized—is not an entirely new start. The shift she is apparently making but not yet overtly articulating is from the painting as showcase of royal power to the painting as showcase of the painter's own power.

In order to better formulate this claim, the writer should query what she is emphasizing as the primary feature of her evidence: size, especially that of the king and queen versus the painter. She could do this by pushing her thinking with the question So what?

- **So what** that the king and queen are small, but the painter, princess, and dwarf (another servant) are all large and fairly equal in size and/or prominence?
- **So what** that there are size differences in the painting? What might large or small size mean?

Here are possible answers to the "So what?" questions:

- Perhaps the relative size and/or prominence of figures in the painting can be read as indicators of their importance or of what the painter wants to say about their importance.
- Perhaps the king and queen have been reduced so that Velázquez can showcase their daughter, the princess.
- Perhaps the size and physical prominence of the king and queen are relatively unimportant. In that case, what matters is that they are a presence, always overseeing events (an idea implied but not developed by the writer in paragraph 6).
- Perhaps the painter is demonstrating his own ability to make the king and queen any size—any level of importance—he chooses. Although the writer does not overtly say so, the king and queen are among the smallest as well as the least visible figures.

Given these answers to the So what? questions, the writer should probably choose Thesis 2—that the painting is a bid for recognition of the painter's status and brilliance as an artist—because this thesis explains more of the evidence than anything else the writer has come up with so far. It explains, for example, the painter's prominence and the relative insignificance of the monarchs: that the painter, in effect, creates their stature (size, power) in the world through his paintings. Framed in a mirror and appearing to hang on the wall, the king and queen are, arguably, suspended among the painter's paintings, mere reflections of themselves—or, rather, the painter's reflection of them.

Step 6: *Repeat steps 2 through 5 as necessary.*

The writer would probably want to concentrate on repeating Step 2, seeing how far she can go in making her revised thesis account for additional evidence.

Thesis: painting as bid for appreciation of painter's status and brilliance as an artist

Step 2 repeated: *See how far you can make each thesis go in accounting for evidence.*

Evidence:

- The painter is demonstrating that he can make the members of the royal family any size he wants, then the painting not only is a bid for recognition, but also can be seen as a playful though not-so-subtle threat: be aware of my power and treat me well, or else suffer the consequences. As an artist, the painter decides how the royal family will be seen. The king and queen depend on the painter, as they do in a different way on the princess, with whom Velázquez makes himself equal in prominence, to extend and perpetuate their power.

- In subverting viewers' expectations both by decentering the monarchs and concealing what is on the easel, the painter again emphasizes his power, in this case, over the viewers (among whom might be the king and queen if their images on the back wall are mirror reflections of them standing, like us, in front of the painting). He is not bound by their expectations and in fact appears to use those expectations to manipulate the viewers: he can make them wish to see something he has the power to withhold.

- The presence of the large dwarf in the right-hand foreground is positioned in a way that links him with the painter. The dwarf arguably furthers the painting's message and does so, like much else in the painting, in the form of a loaded joke: the small ("dwarfed" by the power of others) are brought forward and made big.

Knowing When to Stop: How Much Revising Is Enough?

We emphasize before leaving this example that the version of the thesis we have just proposed is not necessarily the "right" answer. Looked at in a different context, the painting might have been explained primarily as a demonstration of the painter's mastery of the tools of his trade—light, for example, and perspective. But our proposed revision of the thesis for the *Las Meninas* paper meets two important criteria for evaluating thesis statements:

1. It unifies the observations the writer has made.
2. It is capable of accounting for a wide range of evidence.

The writer has followed through on her original desire to infer Velázquez's intentions in the painting. As we argued in Chapter 6 (Making Interpretations Plausible), whether or not Velázquez consciously intended to make his painting a tongue-in-cheek self-advertisement, there is clearly enough evidence to claim plausibly that the painting can be understood in this way.

How do you know when you've done enough reformulating of your thesis and arrived at the best possible idea about your evidence? Getting the thesis to account for (respond to) all rather than just some of your evidence does not mean you need to discuss every detail of the subject. Writers must take care not to ignore important evidence, especially if it would alter their "case," but no analysis can address everything—nor should it. Your job as a writer is to select those features of your subject that seem most significant and to argue for their significance. An analysis says to readers, in effect, "These are the details that best reveal the nature and meaning of my subject, or at least the part of the subject that I am trying to address."

EVOLVING A THESIS IN A LATER-STAGE DRAFT: THE EXAMPLE OF *EDUCATING RITA*

In this example, we will apply the Six Steps in order to make a thesis evolve within the draft, rather than to select among various as yet unformed competitors for the role of thesis (as was the case with *Las Meninas*). The process of thesis evolution we will trace here would remain visible in the writer's final draft as a means of sharing her thought processes with her readers. By contrast, the writer of *Las Meninas* would probably not include in her final draft the competition among her three potential thesis statements—only the evolution of the "winning" one.

In the film *Educating Rita*, a working-class English hairdresser (Rita) wants to change her life by taking courses from a professor (Frank) at the local university, even though this move threatens her relationship with her husband (Denny), who burns her books and pressures her to quit school and get pregnant. Frank, she discovers, has his own problems: he's a divorced alcoholic who is bored with his life, bored with his privileged and complacent students, and bent on self-destruction. The film follows the growth of Frank's and Rita's friendship and the changes it brings about in their lives. By the end of the film, each has left a limiting way of life behind and has set off in a seemingly more promising direction. Rita leaves her constricting marriage, passes her university examinations with honors, and begins to view her life in terms of choices; Frank stops drinking and sets off, determined but sad, to make a new start as a teacher in Australia.

Step 1: *Formulate an idea about your subject, a working thesis.*

Working thesis: *Educating Rita* celebrates the liberating potential of education. The film's relatively happy ending and the presence of the word *educating* in the film's title make this thesis a reasonable opening claim.

Step 2: *See how far you can make this thesis go in accounting for evidence.*
The working thesis seems compatible, for example, with Rita's achievement of greater self-awareness and independence. She becomes more articulate, which allows her to free herself from otherwise disabling situations. She starts to think about other kinds of work she might do, rather than assuming that she must continue in the one job she has always done. She travels, first elsewhere in England and then to the Continent. So, the thesis checks out as viable: there is enough of a match with evidence to stick with and evolve it.

Steps 3 & 4: *Locate evidence that is not adequately accounted for by the thesis, and ask So what? about the apparent mismatch between the thesis and selected evidence.*
Some evidence reveals that the thesis as stated is not the whole picture. Rita's education causes her to become alienated from her husband, her parents, and her social class; at the end of the film, she is alone and unsure about her direction in life. In

Frank's case, the thesis runs into even more problems. His boredom, drinking, and alienation seem to have been caused, at least in part, by his education rather than by his lack of it. He sees his book-lined study as a prison, not a site of liberation. Moreover, his profound knowledge of literature has not helped him control his life: he comes to class drunk, fails to notice or care that his girlfriend is having an affair with one of his colleagues, and asks his classes whether it is worth gaining all of literature if it means losing one's soul.

Step 5: *Reshape your claim to accommodate the evidence that hasn't fit.*
The idea that the film celebrates the liberating potential of education still fits a lot of significant evidence. Rita is arguably better off at the end of the film than at the beginning: we are not left to believe that she should have remained resistant to education, like her husband, Denny, whose world doesn't extend much beyond the corner pub. But the thesis also leaves some significant evidence unaccounted for, so the writer would need to bring out the complicating evidence—the film's seemingly contradictory attitudes about education—and then modify the wording of the thesis in a way that might resolve or explain these contradictions.

Education as represented by the film seems to be of two kinds: enabling and stultifying. The next step in the development of the thesis would be to elaborate on how the film seeks to distinguish enabling forms of education from debilitating ones (as represented by the self-satisfied and status-conscious behavior of the supposedly educated people at Frank's university). Perhaps this difference is what the film is primarily interested in—not just education's potential to liberate.

Revised thesis: *Educating Rita* celebrates the liberating potential of enabling—in contrast to stultifying—education.

Step 6: *Repeat steps 2, 3, 4, and 5.*
Having refined the thesis in this way, the writer would then repeat the step of seeing what the new wording allows him or her to account for in the evidence. The revised thesis would foreground a contest in the film between two different kinds of and attitudes toward education. This thesis as lens would cause us to see Frank's problems as being less a product of his education than of the cynical and pretentious versions of education that surround him in his university life. It would also explain the film's emphasis on Frank's recovery of at least some of his idealism about education, for which Rita has provided the inspiration.

What else does this revised thesis account for in the evidence? What about Frank's emigration to Australia? If we can take Australia to stand for a newer world, one where education would be less likely to become the stale and exclusive property of a self-satisfied elite, then the refined version of the thesis would seem to be working well. In fact, given the possible thematic connection between Rita's working-class identity and Australia (associated, as a former frontier and English penal colony, with lower-class vitality as opposed to the complacency bred of class privilege), the thesis about the film's celebration of the contrast between enabling and stultifying forms of education could be sharpened further. It might be proposed, for example, that the film presents institutional education as desperately in need of frequent doses of "real life" (as represented by Rita and Australia)—infusions of working-class pragmatism, energy, and optimism—if it is to remain healthy and open, as opposed to becoming the oppressive property of a privileged social class. This is to say that the film arguably exploits stereotypical assumptions about social class.

Revised thesis: *Educating Rita* celebrates the liberating potential of enabling education, defined as that which remains open to healthy doses of working-class, real-world infusions.

Repeat steps 3 and 4, locating evidence not adequately accounted for and ask so what?

At the end of the film, Frank and Rita walk off in opposite directions down long, empty airport corridors. Though promising to remain friends, the two do not become a couple. This closing emphasis on Frank's and Rita's alienation from their respective cultures, and the film's apparent insistence on the necessity of each going on alone, significantly qualifies the happiness of the "happy ending."

Having complicated the interpretation of the ending, the writer would again need to modify the thesis in accord with new observations. Does the film simply celebrate education if it also presents it as being, to some degree, incompatible with conventional forms of happiness? By emphasizing the necessity of having Frank and Rita each go on alone, the film may be suggesting that to be truly liberating, education—as opposed to its less honest and more comfortable substitutes—inevitably produces and even requires a certain amount of loneliness and alienation. Shown in Figure 11.4 are the successive revisions of the thesis.

Repeat step 5, reshaping the claim.

Final version of thesis: *Educating Rita* celebrates the liberating potential of enabling education (kept open to real-world, working-class energy) but also acknowledges its potential costs in loneliness and alienation.

Note: this last version of the thesis is the one that would appear in the writer's final paragraph, the product of qualifying and refining the paper's claim by repeatedly confronting and assimilating complicating evidence. In effect, the Six Steps have produced a reasonably complete draft in outline form.

Try This 11.3: Tracking a Thesis

As should be clear now, various versions of the thesis recur throughout a piece of writing, usually with increasing specificity, complication, and grammatical complexity. The four evolutions of the thesis statement on *Educating Rita* illustrate this pattern of recurrence clearly. One of the best ways to teach yourself how and where to locate statements of the thesis in your own writing is to track the thesis in a piece of reading. Use a highlighter to mark the evolutions. Where in the essay do you find the thesis? How has it changed in each recurrence? In response to what complication?

FIGURE 11.4
Successive Revisions of a Thesis. An initial thesis about *Educating Rita*
evolves through successive complications as it reexamines evidence in the
film.

The Evolving Thesis in Outline Form: Superman

We borrow this example from the website of the First Year Writing Program at Ohio State University, for which we offer much thanks. Like the evolving thesis in *Educating Rita*, some of the various reformulations of the thesis would appear in the final draft.

Original Thesis:

"Superman is an unchanging icon because he stands for Truth, Justice, and the American way."

Complicating Evidence:

Superman has made dramatic body-image changes in his "career."

Revised Thesis: "Though Superman's body-image has changed, his status as an icon and his message have remained steady."

Complicating Evidence:

Older body-images are met with boredom and distaste by the new generation of viewers. He has become younger and more sexual.

Revised Thesis:

"The new young, sexy Superman liberates him from past images, and caters his message to a new, more sexually sophisticated generation of viewers."

Complicating Evidence:

If Superman's body-image changes so much, doesn't this change his message automatically? What does his body-image say? Does his body speak loader than his message?

Revised Thesis:

"A young, sexy Superman liberates his image from a wholesome, community-oriented image and celebrates more explicitly a message of individuality and sexual power."

Complicating Evidence:

It is the viewers who place these demands on Superman's image. He is the "offspring" of consumers.

Revised Thesis:

"A younger and more sexualized generation of consumers has liberated Superman's image from a wholesome, community-oriented image to reflect more readily its own values of individuality and sexual power."

LOCATING THE EVOLVING THESIS IN THE FINAL DRAFT

Having achieved a final version of a thesis, what next? Why wouldn't a writer just relocate the last and fullest statement of the thesis to his or her first paragraph and then prove it?

Usually it's neither possible nor desirable to encapsulate in the opening sentences what it will take the whole paper to explain. The position articulated in the fully evolved thesis is typically too complex to be stated intelligibly and concisely in the introduction. If you approach an essay as an act of thinking, then the evolutions of the thesis record the history of your various changes in thinking as you encounter evidence. If your readers get to see these, they are far more likely to go along with you, literally to follow your trains of thought. Rather than imposing your conclusions, you will be sharing your thought process with the reader, which is what good writing does.

Normally, you lead (usually at the end of the first paragraph or at the beginning of the second) with the best version of your thesis you can come up with that will be understandable to your readers without a lengthy preamble. If you find yourself writing a page-long introductory paragraph to get to your initial statement of thesis, try settling for a simpler articulation of your central idea in its first appearance.

The first paragraph does not need to—and usually can't—offer your conclusion; it will take the body of your paper to accomplish that. It should, however, provide a quick look at particular details that set up the issue. Use these details to generate a theory, a working hypothesis, about whatever it is you think is at stake in the material. The rest of the paper will test and develop this theory.

The *Educating Rita* paper might open, for example, by using a version of the Seems-to-Be-About-X gambit (see Chapter 4), claiming that at first glance the film seems to celebrate the liberating potential of education. You could then lay out the evidence for this view and proceed to complicate it in the ways we've discussed.

Your concluding paragraph should offer the more carefully qualified and evolved version of your thesis that the body of your paper has allowed you to arrive at. Rather than just summarize and restate what you said in your introduction, the concluding paragraph leaves readers with what you take to be your single best insight. It should put what you have had to say into some kind of perspective.

Recognizing and Relocating Your Thesis: A History Professor Speaks

In the following Voice from Across the Curriculum, history professor Ellen Poteet offers suggestions on how writers might best prompt themselves to arrive at and recognize a thesis in their writing.

Voices from Across the Curriculum

For an analytical or interpretive historical essay, *thesis* is a conventional term and one of much value. The thesis usually is that point of departure from the surfaces of evidence to the underlying significance, or problems, a given set of sources reveal to the reader and writer. In most cases, the thesis is best positioned up front, so that the writer's audience has a sense of what lies ahead and why it is worth reading on. I say *usually* and *in most cases* because the hard and fast rule should not take precedence over the inspirational manner in which a thesis comes to be formulated and recognized by the writer. It is my experience, in fact, that if inspiration strikes, one realizes it only after the fact.

Recognizing a thesis can be extremely difficult. It can often be a lot easier to talk "about" what one is writing than to say succinctly what the thrust of one's discussion is. I sometimes ask students to draw a line at the end of a paper after they have finished it, and then write one, at most two sentences, saying what they most want to tell their readers. My comment on that postscript frequently is "Great statement of your thesis. Just move it up to your first paragraph where it could begin to develop."

—Ellen Poteet, Professor of History

Try This 11.4: Moving from Observations to a Thesis

The following piece of writing is a student's exploratory draft analyzing a place—a chain restaurant located in a Boston shopping mall. It is an early draft; the writer has not yet been expected to attend to organization, style, and so on. One purpose of such idea-gathering drafts is to survey the data in order to discover one or more possible working theses.

For our purposes, the draft offers an opportunity to identify claims and assess how they connect to the evidence presented. It can also give you practice in reformulating claims on the basis of careful examination of evidence. The steps listed below are a version of the Six Steps for Making a Thesis Evolve. These steps also work well for pairs or small groups of writers working on each others' drafts.

1. Underline all of the paper's claims about the meaning of the details the writer has noticed. Star the claims that seem to be potential thesis formulations.

2. Examine the match between evidence and claims, focusing on the claims. Where do you find mismatches? Try in a sentence or two to explain the mismatch.

3. Reformulate one of the writer's potential thesis statements in a way that better accounts for the evidence. Be sure that the thesis has tension—that it generates forward momentum by casting its primary claim against another possibility. Try starting the thesis with the word "although" or use the formulation, "Seems to be about X, but is also (or really) about Y."

Mall Cuisine

[1] At the outer reaches of an enclosed shopping mall near downtown Boston's Copley Square there is an interesting restaurant named Bon Marche. The mall is huge, connecting several high-rise hotels, and it offers dozens of upscale shops.

[2] My friend and I entered Bon Marche just to look around; we were hungry for some breakfast, and it looked promising. Almost immediately a Latino guy about twenty wearing a green beret stopped us to give us a check. He told us that there was one for take-out and one for eating there, and then he explained how the restaurant worked. There were a number of different stations serving food, and you were supposed to give them your ticket to be stamped when you got food there. The ticket, by the way, which was designed to look like a passport, included a comical warning that if you lost it, you would be required to wash dishes there for two days.

[3] The stations were scattered all over this enormous room, and each one offered a different kind of food. (We later learned that they had a market downstairs too, where they sold the food uncooked.) A lot of the foods were international in flavor. There was lots of seafood, especially

shellfish of various kinds. Other stations offered omelettes, sushi, wood-oven cooked pizza, fresh squeezed juices (including carrot!), soups such as chowders and bouillabaisse, crepes, Oriental stir fries, and various kinds of bread and pastries. I did notice, though, that there was no lox, though plenty of fresh salmon they would cook for you.

[4] I noticed that at a number of these stations, you could basically design your food choice. For example, you would choose what "innards" you wanted in your omelette from a variety of ingredients in silver bowls at the front of the station. The same went for the stir fry station and the pizza station, where you chose among toppings. And most of the stations also offered vegetarian options.

[5] We decided to have breakfast, and that's when we discovered one drawback to this station idea. We had to wait in line for about fifteen minutes before we were able to order our omelettes. They looked and smelled great, and they came with hash browns, but when we asked for some bacon, the Latina girl who was cooking told us that we had to go to another station where they cook breakfast meats. That would mean waiting in line again, while our food was getting cold. And then we'd have to wait in line again if we wanted juice, which was at another station.

[6] Just as there is a great variety of exotic foods, there are a lot of diverse seating areas at Bon Marche. One area was glassed-in, like a French bistro, with small white tables that had multicolored umbrellas in them. Another seemed Indonesian—rattan furniture and hay bales. We chose an area by the windows looking out over downtown Boston. It was decorated with lattices like a grape arbor at an Italian villa.

[7] Once we noticed the international character of Bon Marche's food and settings, we began to see it in other aspects of the place. First of all, there's the French name of the place. And virtually all of the staff were members of ethnic minorities—especially Latinos, African-Americans, and Asians. Plus the place was awash in the upbeat rhythms of Latino music—a kind of nouveau sound. While most of the staff were young, the sushi counter proved an exception. That station featured two middle-aged Asian women, bent over their sushi mats, making mostly Boston rolls and California rolls, one after another after another. We were struck with how boring the job must be. How many omelettes was that woman cooking an hour, with the line getting longer every minute?

[8] Still, the food was tasty (and inexpensive!), and the atmosphere was really interesting. I had the overall impression that Bon Marche was all about youth and choice and feeling optimistic. Considering its great location and how busy it was, the staff must make pretty good money, and so they are getting to participate in the American dream of opportunity and freedom as well.

[9] That's when I realized that maybe what makes Bon Marche so great is that it embodies democracy. It has everything for everybody, and the individual gets to choose what he or she wants, down to the last

detail. And the whole place was just bursting with food—there seemed to be abundance for all. It makes available to everyone the experience of international cuisines at affordable prices, whereas in the past you would have had to travel abroad, or at least to expensive restaurants all over the city, to get this diversity. Mall culture offers the world in one convenient location, as Bon Marche exemplifies.

[10] As we were leaving, we saw more evidence for this democracy idea in the uniforms that the staff were wearing. They all had full-length aprons matching the color of their berets—the men all wore green berets while the women wore red ones. This uniform was bright and happy, and the berets seemed to symbolize that everyone was equal. Also the berets seem to go with the restaurant's French name, except that the berets themselves had these fitted leather bases that made them seem stiffer than traditional French berets.

[11] The cashier was located at the front of the restaurant, and when she gave us our receipts, we also received what they called "exit visas" that we then had to hand to a guy standing about four feet away, just at the interface of the restaurant and the rest of the mall. It was as if we were leaving this fantasy world behind.

GUIDELINES FOR FINDING AND DEVELOPING A THESIS

1. A thesis offers a theory about the meaning of evidence that would not have been immediately obvious to your readers.

2. A thesis is made, not found. It is the result of a process of thinking of about the evidence but is not itself present in the evidence, like a golden egg.

3. Treat your thesis as a hypothesis to be tested rather than an obvious truth.

4. Most effective theses contain tension. They are conceptually complex, and that is reflected in their grammatical shape—often they will begin with "although" or incorporate "however."

5. The body of your paper should serve not only to substantiate the thesis by demonstrating its value in selecting and explaining evidence, but also to evolve the thesis—move it forward—by uncovering the questions that each new formulation of it prompts you to ask.

6. When you encounter potentially conflicting evidence (or interpretations of that evidence), don't simply abandon your thesis. Use the complications to refine your thesis until you arrive at the most accurate explanation of the evidence that you can manage.

7. To check that your thesis has evolved, locate and compare the various versions of it throughout the draft. Have you done more than demonstrate the general validity of an unqualified claim?

Assignment: Making a Thesis Evolve

Formulate and Evolve a Thesis on a Film, Painting, or Other Visual Image.
Using the models of either *Las Meninas* or *Educating Rita*, produce an interpretation of the film or painting or other visual image of your choice.

First, begin by formulating a variety of possible statements about the film or painting that could serve as a working thesis. These might be in answer to the question "What is the film/painting about?" or "What does it 'say'?" Or you might begin by doing The Method to uncover pattern of repetition or contrast you have observed and can then explain.

Obviously, this assignment could be adapted to other subjects—an essay, the coverage of a current event, and so forth. Here are some specific suggestions:

- The contemporary appeal of a cartoon or other popular television character
- Differences in political rhetoric between Democrats and Republicans on the same issue
- The rhetoric of a popular print or television ad campaign for a familiar product, such as an insurance company or a soft drink or an automobile

Next, follow the procedure for making the thesis evolve, listed again here for convenience:

1. Formulate an idea about your subject, a working thesis.
2. See how far you can make this thesis go in accounting for confirming evidence.
3. Locate evidence that is not adequately accounted for by the thesis.
4. Make explicit the apparent mismatch between the thesis and selected evidence, asking and answering "So what?"
5. Reshape your claim to accommodate the evidence that hasn't fit.
6. Repeat steps 2, 3, 4, and 5 several times.

Chapter 12

Recognizing and Fixing Weak Thesis Statements

BY WAY OF REVIEW, a strong thesis makes a claim that (1) requires analysis to support and evolve it and (2) offers some point about the significance of your evidence that would not have been immediately obvious to your readers. By contrast, a weak thesis either makes no claim or makes a claim that does not need proving. This chapter offers advice on how to recognize a weak thesis statement—and how to fix it. The chapter consists largely of examples of weak thesis statements taken from actual student papers, followed by discussion of how to recognize and rethink and rephrase them.

Weak thesis statements don't give the writer enough to do in his or her essay. Typically, a weak thesis is an unproductive claim because it doesn't actually require further thinking or proof, as, for example, "An important part of one's college education is learning to better understand others' points of view" (a piece of conventional wisdom that most people would already accept as true, and thus not in need of arguing).

FIVE KINDS OF WEAK THESIS STATEMENTS

1. A thesis that makes no claim ("This paper examines the pros and cons of . . .")
2. A thesis that is obviously true or a statement of fact ("Exercise is good for you")
3. A thesis that restates conventional wisdom ("Love conquers all")
4. A thesis that offers personal conviction as the basis for the claim ("Shopping malls are wonderful places")
5. A thesis that makes an overly broad claim ("Individualism is good")

Solutions? Be suspicious of your first responses to a subject. Privilege live questions over inert answers. Find ways to bring out the complexity of your subject. Look again at the What It Means to Have an Idea section in Chapter 3, which tells you to start with something puzzling that you want to figure out rather than with something you already believe to be clearly and obviously true. Look back as well to Chapter 11, which guides you to use evidence to complicate your claims and to compose thesis statements that contain inherent tension. When in doubt, do more exploratory writing to trigger better ideas.

FIVE KINDS OF WEAK THESIS STATEMENTS AND HOW TO FIX THEM

WEAK THESIS TYPE 1: THE THESIS MAKES NO CLAIM

Problem Examples

> I'm going to write about Darwin's concerns with evolution in *The Origin of Species.*

> This paper addresses the characteristics of a good corporate manager.

Both problem examples name a subject and link it to the intention to write about it, but they don't make any claim about the subject. As a result, they direct neither the writer nor the reader toward some position or plan of attack. Even if the second example were rephrased as "This paper addresses why a good corporate manager needs to learn to delegate responsibility," the thesis would not adequately suggest why such a claim would need to be argued or defended. *There is, in short, nothing at stake, no issue to be resolved.*

Solution: Raise specific issues for the essay to explore.

Solution Examples

> Darwin's concern with survival of the fittest in *The Origin of Species* initially leads him to neglect a potentially conflicting aspect of his theory of evolution—survival as a matter of interdependence.

> The very trait that makes for an effective corporate manager—the drive to succeed—can also make the leader domineering and, therefore, ineffective.

Some disciplines expect writers to offer statements of method and/or intention in their papers' openings. Generally, however, these openings also make a claim: for example, "In this paper, I examine how Congressional Republicans undermined the attempts of the Democratic administration to legislate a fiscally responsible health care policy for the elderly," *not* "In this paper, I discuss America's treatment of the elderly."

WEAK THESIS TYPE 2: THE THESIS IS OBVIOUSLY TRUE OR IS A STATEMENT OF FACT

Problem Examples

> The jean industry targets its advertisements to appeal to young adults.

> The flight from teaching to research and publishing in higher education is a controversial issue in the academic world. I will show different views and aspects concerning this problem.

A thesis needs to be an assertion with which it would be possible for readers to disagree.

In the second example, few readers would disagree with the fact that the issue is "controversial." In the second sentence of that example, the writer has begun to identify a point of view—that the flight from teaching is a problem—but her declaration that she will "show different views and aspects" is a broad statement of fact, not an idea. The phrasing of the claim is noncommittal and so broad that it prevents the writer from formulating a workable thesis.

Solution: Find some avenue of *inquiry*—a question about the facts or an issue raised by them. Make an assertion with which it would be possible for readers to disagree.

Solution Examples

> By inventing new terms, such as "loose fit" and "relaxed fit," the jean industry has attempted to normalize, even glorify, its product for an older and fatter generation.

> The "flight from teaching" to research and publishing in higher education is a controversial issue in the academic world. As I will attempt to show, the controversy is based to a significant degree on a false assumption, that doing research necessarily leads teachers away from the classroom.

WEAK THESIS TYPE 3: THE THESIS RESTATES CONVENTIONAL WISDOM

Problem Examples

> An important part of one's college education is learning to better understand others' points of view.

> "*I was* supposed to bring the coolers; *you* were supposed to bring the chips!" exclaimed ex-Beatle Ringo Starr, who appeared on TV commercials for Sun County Wine Coolers a few years ago. By using rock music to sell a wide range of products, the advertising agencies, in league with corporate giants such as Pepsi, Michelob, and Ford, have corrupted the spirit of rock and roll.

"Conventional wisdom" is a polite term for cultural cliché. Most clichés were fresh ideas once, but over time they have become trite, prefabricated forms of nonthinking. Faced with a phenomenon that requires a response, inexperienced writers sometimes resort to a small set of culturally approved "answers." Because conventional wisdom is so general and so commonly accepted, however, it doesn't teach anybody—including the writer—anything. Worse, because the cliché looks like an idea, it prevents the writer from engaging in a fresh exploration of his or her subject.

There is some truth in both of the preceding problem examples, but neither complicates its position. A thoughtful reader could, for example, respond to the advertising example by suggesting that rock and roll was highly commercial long before it colonized the airwaves. The conventional wisdom that rock and roll is somehow pure and honest while advertising is phony and exploitative invites the savvy writer to formulate a thesis that overturns these clichés. It could be argued that rock has actually improved advertising, not that ads have ruined rock—or, alternatively, that rock has shrewdly marketed idealism to gullible consumers. At the least, a writer committed to the original thesis would do better to examine what Ringo was selling—what he/wine coolers stand for in this particular case—than to discuss rock and advertising in such predictable terms.

> **Solution:** Seek to complicate—see more than one point of view on—your subject. Avoid conventional wisdom unless you can qualify it or introduce a fresh perspective on it.

Solution Examples

> While an important part of one's college education is learning to better understand others' points of view, a persistent danger is that the students will simply be required to substitute the teacher's answers for the ones they grew up uncritically believing.

> While some might argue that the presence of rock and roll soundtracks in TV commercials has corrupted rock's spirit, this point of view not only falsifies the history of rock but also blinds us to the ways that the music has improved the quality of television advertising.

WEAK THESIS TYPE 4: THE THESIS BASES ITS CLAIM ON PERSONAL CONVICTION

Problem Examples

> Sir Thomas More's *Utopia* proposes an unworkable set of solutions to society's problems because, like communist Russia, it suppresses individualism.

> Although I agree with Jeane Kirkpatrick's argument that environmentalists and business should work together to ensure the ecological future of the world, and that this cooperation is beneficial for both sides, the indisputable fact is that environmental considerations should always be a part of any decision that is made. Any individual, if he looks deeply enough into his soul, knows what is right and what is wrong. The environment should be protected because it is the right thing to do, not because someone is forcing you to do it.

Like conventional wisdom, personal likes and dislikes can lead inexperienced writers into knee-jerk reactions of approval or disapproval, often expressed in a moralistic tone. The writers of the preceding problem examples assume that their primary job is to judge their subjects, or testify to their worth, not to evaluate them analytically. They have taken personal opinions for self-evident truths. *(See Naturalizing Our Assumptions in Chapter 2.)*

The most blatant version of this tendency occurs in the second problem example, which asserts, "Any individual, if he looks deeply enough into his soul, knows what is right and what is wrong. The environment should be protected because it is the right thing to do." Translation (only slightly exaggerated): "Any individual who thinks about the subject will obviously agree with me because my feelings and convictions feel right to me and therefore they must be universally and self-evidently true." Testing an idea against your own feelings and experience is not an adequate means of establishing whether something is accurate or true.

It is fine, of course, to write about what you believe and to consult your feelings as you formulate an idea. But the risk you run in arguing from your unexamined feelings and convictions is that you will continue to play the same small set of tunes in response to everything you hear. And without the ability to think from multiple perspectives, you are less able to defend your convictions against the ideas that challenge them because you won't really have examined the logic of your own beliefs—you just believe them.

> **Solution:** Try on other points of view honestly and dispassionately; treat your ideas as hypotheses to be tested rather than obvious truths. In the following solution examples, we have replaced opinions (in the form of self-evident truths) with ideas—theories about the meaning and significance of the subjects that are capable of being supported and qualified by evidence.

Solution Examples

> Sir Thomas More's *Utopia* treats individualism as a serious but remediable social problem. His radical treatment of what we might now call "socialization" attempts to redefine the meaning and origin of individual identity.

> Although I agree with Jeane Kirkpatrick's argument that environmentalists and business should work together to ensure the ecological future of the world, her argument undervalues the necessity of pressuring businesses to attend to environmental concerns that may not benefit them in the short run.

WEAK THESIS TYPE 5: THE THESIS MAKES AN OVERLY BROAD CLAIM

Problem Examples

> Violent revolutions have had both positive and negative results for man.

> There are many similarities and differences between the Carolingian and the Burgundian Renaissances.
>
> *Othello* is a play about love and jealousy.

Overly generalized theses avoid complexity. Such statements usually lead either to say-nothing theses or to reductive either/or thinking. Similar to a thesis that makes no claim, theses with overly broad claims say nothing in particular about the subject at hand and so are not likely to guide a writer's thinking beyond the listing stage. One of the best ways to avoid drafting overly broad thesis statements is to sensitize yourself to the characteristic phrasing of such theses: "both positive and negative," "many similarities and differences," or "both pros and cons." Virtually everything from meatloaf to taxes can be both positive and negative.

Solution: Convert broad categories and generic claims to more specific, more qualified assertions; find ways to bring out the complexity of your subject.

Solution Examples

> Although violent revolutions begin to redress long-standing social inequities, they often do so at the cost of long-term economic dysfunction and the suffering that attends it.
>
> The differences between the Carolingian and Burgundian Renaissances outweigh the similarities.
>
> Although *Othello* appears to attack jealousy, it also supports the skepticism of the jealous characters over the naïveté of the lovers.

Getting Beyond the All-Purpose Thesis: A Dance Professor Speaks

In the following Voice from Across the Curriculum, dance professor Karen Dearborn offers examples of thesis statements that do more than offer standard "different but alike" phrasing.

Voices from Across the Curriculum

Making the Thesis Specific

Not so good thesis/question: "What were Humphrey's and Weidman's reasons behind the setting of *With My Red Fires,* and of what importance were the set and costume design to the piece as a whole?"

Good thesis: "While Graham and Wigman seem different, their ideas on inner expression (specifically subjectivism versus objectivism) and the incorporation of their respective countries' surge of nationalism bring them much closer than they appear."

What I like about the good thesis is that it moves beyond the standard "they are different, but alike" (which can be said about anything) to actually tell the reader what specific areas the paper will explore. I can also tell that the subject is narrow enough for a fairly thorough examination of one small slice of these two major choreographers' work rather than some over-generalized treatment of these two historic figures.

—Karen Dearborn, Professor of Dance

Try This 12.1: Revising Weak Thesis Statements

You can learn a lot about writing strong thesis statements by analyzing and rewriting weak ones. For the following example, first identify the type of problem for each thesis. Then rewrite them, providing solutions as we have done. Revising will require you to add information and thinking—to come up with some interesting claims that most readers would not already have thought of.

1. In this paper, I discuss police procedures in recent domestic violence cases.
2. The way that the media portrayed the events of April 30, 1975, when Saigon fell, greatly influenced the final perspectives of the American people toward the end result of the Vietnam War.
3. From cartoons in the morning to adventure shows at night, there is too much violence on television.
4. The songs of the punk rock group Minor Threat relate to the feelings of individuals who dare to be different. Their songs are just composed of pure emotion. Pure emotion is very important in music because it serves as a vehicle to convey the important message of individuality. Minor Threat's songs are meaningful to me because I can identify with them.
5. It is important to understand why leaders act in a leadership role. What is the driving force? Is it an internal drive for the business or group to succeed, or is it an internal drive for the leader to dominate over others?

HOW TO REPHRASE THESIS STATEMENTS: SPECIFY AND SUBORDINATE

Weak thesis statements can be quickly identified by their word choice and syntax (sentence structure). Each of the first three problem examples for Weak Thesis Type 5, for example, relies mostly on nouns rather than verbs; the nouns announce a broad heading, but the verbs don't do anything with or to the nouns. In grammatical terms, these thesis statements don't *predicate* (affirm or assert something about the subject of a proposition). Instead, they rely on anemic verbs like *is* or *are*, which function as equal signs that link general nouns with general adjectives rather than specify more complex relationships.

By replacing the equal sign with a more active verb, you can force yourself to advance some sort of claim, as in one of our solutions: "The differences between the Carolingian and Burgundian Renaissances *outweigh* the similarities." While this reformulation remains quite general, it at least begins to direct the writer along a more particular line of argument. Replacing *is* or *are* (verbs that function only as equal signs) with stronger verbs usually impels you to rank ideas in some order of importance and to assert some conceptual relation among them.

The best way to remedy the problem of overgeneralization is to move toward specificity in word choice, in sentence structure, and in idea. If you find yourself writing "The economic situation is bad," consider revising it to "The tax policies of the current administration threaten to reduce the tax burden on the middle class by sacrificing education and health care programs for everyone."

Here's the problem/solution in schematic form:

Broad Noun	+ Weak Verb	+ Vague, Evaluative Modifier
economic situation	is	bad

Specific Noun	+ Active Verb	+ Specific Modifier
(The) tax policies (of the current administration)	threaten to reduce (the tax burden on the middle class)	by sacrificing education and health care programs for everyone

By eliminating the weak thesis formula—broad noun plus *is* plus vague evaluative adjective—a writer is compelled to qualify, or define carefully, each of the terms in the original proposition, arriving at a more particular and conceptually rich assertion.

A second way to rephrase overly broad thesis statements, in tandem with adding specificity, is to *subordinate* one part of the statement to another. The both-positive-and-negative and both-similarity-and-difference formulae are recipes for say-nothing theses because they encourage pointless comparisons. Given that it is worthwhile to notice both strengths and weaknesses—that your subject is not all one way or all another—what, then, can you do to convert the thesis from a say-nothing to a say-something claim? Generally, there are two strategies for this purpose that operate together. The first we have already discussed.

1. *Specify:* Replace the overly abstract terms—terms like *positive* and *negative* (or *similar* and *different*)—with something specific; *name* something that is positive and something that is negative instead.

2. *Subordinate:* Rank one of the two items in the pairing underneath the other.

   When you subordinate, you put the most important, pressing, or revealing side of the comparison in what is known as the main clause and the less important side in what is known as the subordinate clause, introducing it with a word like *while* or *although. (See Glossary of Grammatical Terms in Chapter 19 for the definitions of main and subordinate clauses.)*

In short, specify to focus the claim, and subordinate to qualify (further focus) the claim still more. This strategy produces the remedies to both the *Othello* and the violent revolution examples in Weak Thesis Type 5. As evidence of the refocusing work that fairly simple rephrasing accomplishes, consider the following version of the violent revolution example, in which we merely invert the ranking of the two items in the pair.

Although violent revolutions often cause long-term economic dysfunction and the suffering that attends it, such revolutions at least begin to redress long-standing social inequities.

Is it Okay to Phrase a Thesis as a Question?

A question frequently asked about thesis statements is: Is it okay to phrase a thesis as a question? The answer is both yes and no. Phrasing a thesis as a question makes it more difficult for both the writer and the reader to be sure of the direction the paper takes because a question doesn't make an overt claim. Questions, however, can clearly imply claims. And many writers, especially in the early, exploratory stages of drafting, begin with a question, as we note in the discussion of What It Means to Have an Idea in Chapter 3.

As a general rule, use thesis questions cautiously, especially in final drafts. Although a thesis question often functions well to spark a writer's thinking, it can too often muddy the thinking by leaving the area of consideration too broad. Make sure that you do not let the thesis-question approach allow you to evade the responsibility of making some kind of claim. Especially in the drafting stage, a question posed overtly by the writer can provide focus, but only if he or she then proceeds to answer it with what would become a first statement of thesis.

Try This 12.2: Determining What the Thesis Requires You to Do Next

Learning to diagnose the strengths and weaknesses of thesis statements is a skill that comes in handy as you read the claims of others and revise your own. A good question for diagnosing a thesis is *What does the thesis require the writer to do next?* This question should help you to figure out what the thesis actually wants to claim, which can then direct you to possible rephrasings that would better direct your thinking.

Using this question as a prompt, list the strengths and weaknesses of the following two thesis statements, and then rewrite them. In the first statement, just rewrite the last sentence (the other sentences have been included to provide context).

1. Many economists and politicians agree that, along with the Environmental Protection Agency's newest regulations, a global-warming treaty could damage the American economy. Because of the great expense that such environmental standards require, domestic industries would financially suffer. Others argue, however, that severe regulatory steps must be taken to prevent global warming, regardless of cost. Despite both legitimate claims, the issue of protecting the environment while still securing our global competitiveness remains critical.

2. Regarding promotion into executive positions, women are continually losing the race because of a corporate view that women are too compassionate to keep up with the competitiveness of a powerful firm.

GUIDELINES FOR RECOGNIZING AND FIXING WEAK THESIS STATEMENTS

1. Your thesis should make a claim with which it would be possible for readers to disagree. In other words, move beyond defending statements that your readers would accept as obviously true.

2. Be skeptical of your first (often semiautomatic) response to a subject: it will often be a cliché (however unintentional). Avoid conventional wisdom unless you introduce a fresh perspective on it.

3. Convert broad categories and generic (fits anything) claims to more specific assertions. Find ways to bring out the complexity of your subject.

4. Submit the wording of your thesis to this grammatical test: if it follows the "abstract noun + is + evaluative adjective" formula ("The economic situation is bad"), substitute a more specific noun and an active verb that will force you to predicate something about a focused subject ("Tax laws benefit the rich").

5. Routinely examine and question your own key terms and categories rather than simply accepting them. Assume that they mean more than you first thought.

6. Always work to uncover and make explicit the unstated assumptions (premises) underlying your thesis. Don't treat debatable premises as givens.

7. As a rule, be suspicious of thesis statements that depend on words such as "real," "accurate," "believable," "right," and "good." These words usually signal that you are offering personal opinions—what "feels" right to you—as self-evident truths for everybody.

8. One way to assess the adequacy of a thesis statement is to ask yourself where the writer would need to go next to develop his or her idea. If you can't answer that question, then the thesis is still too weak.

9. Qualify your claims; you will avoid the global pronouncements—typical of the dangers of overly categorical thinking—that are too broad to be of much use (or true).

Assignment: Recognizing and Fixing Weak Thesis Statements

Analyzing Cliches: "Love Is the Answer"

Clichés are not necessarily untrue; they just are not worth saying (even if you're John Lennon, who offered this sodden truism in one of his more forgettable tunes).

One of the best ways to inoculate yourself against habitually resorting to clichés to provide easy and safe answers to all the problems of the planet—easy because they fit so many situations generically, and safe because, being so common, they *must* be true—is to go out and collect them, and then use this data-gathering to generate a thesis. Spend a day doing this, actively listening and looking for clichés—from overheard conversations (or your own), from reading matter, from anywhere (talk radio and TV are exceptionally rich resources) that is part of your daily round.

Compile a list, making sure to write down not only each cliché but the context in which it is used. From this data, and applying what you have learned from the chapters in this unit, formulate a thesis and write a paper about one or more of the clichés that infect some aspect of your daily life. You might find it useful to use The Method to identify key shared traits among the clichés and/ or among the contexts in which you have discovered them. And you might apply the advice provided under Weak Thesis Type 3 to work out alternative formulations to certain clichés to discover what that might teach us about the ways clichés function in given situations—how, for example, they do and don't fit the facts of the situation. If you can find a copy of Paul Muldoon's short poem, "Symposium," which is composed entirely of clichéd expressions, it might anchor an analysis or provide a lens for uncovering aspects of your data.

Chapter 13

Using Sources Analytically: The Conversation Model

THIS CHAPTER SHOWS you how to integrate secondary sources into your writing. That is often a daunting task because it requires you to negotiate with authorities who generally know more than you do about the subject at hand. Simply ignoring sources is a head-in-the-sand attitude and, besides, you miss out on learning what people interested in your subject are talking about. But what role can you invent for yourself when the experts are talking? Just agreeing with a source is an abdication of your responsibility to present your thinking on the subject. But taking the opposite tack by disagreeing with an expert who has studied your subject and written books about it would also appear to be a fool's game. So what are you to do?

This chapter attempts to answer that question. It lays out the primary trouble spots that arise when writers use secondary materials, and it suggests remedies—ways of using sources as points of departure for your own thinking rather than using them as either "The Answer" or a straw man. We call this approach *conversing with sources.*

Six Strategies for Analyzing Sources

Strategy 1: Make Your Sources Speak

Strategy 2: Attend Carefully to the Language of Your Sources by Quoting or Paraphrasing

Strategy 3: Supply Ongoing Analysis of Sources (Don't Wait until the End)

Strategy 4: Use Your Sources to Ask Questions, Not Just to Provide Answers

Strategy 5: Put Your Sources into Conversation with One Another

Strategy 6: Find Your Own Role in the Conversation

The kind of writing you are doing will affect the way you use sources. Analytical writing uses sources to expand understanding—often to allow readers to view a subject from a range of plausible points of view. This approach differs from the kind of research based writing wherein the goal is to locate a single position that beats out the others in a combative mode. One way sources are often used in an academic setting is as lenses for examining other sources and primary materials. *(For using a source as a lens, see Chapter 5, Writing About Reading: More Moves to Make with Written Texts.)*

We use the terms *source* and *secondary source* interchangeably to designate ideas and information about your subject that you find in the work of other writers. Secondary sources allow you to gain a richer, more informed, and complex vantage point on your *primary sources*. Here's how primary and secondary sources can be distinguished: if you were writing a paper on the philosopher Nietzsche, his writing would be your primary source, and critical commentaries on his work would be your secondary sources. If, however, you were writing on the poet Yeats, who read and was influenced by Nietzsche, a work of Nietzsche's philosophy would become a secondary source on your primary source, Yeats's poetry.

"SOURCE ANXIETY" AND WHAT TO DO ABOUT IT

Typically, inexperienced writers either use sources as "answers"—they let the sources do too much of their thinking—or ignore them altogether as a way of avoiding losing their own ideas. Both of these approaches are understandable but inadequate.

Confronted with the seasoned views of experts in a discipline, you may well feel there is nothing left for you to say because it has all been said before or, at least, it has been said by people who greatly outweigh you in reputation and experience. This anxiety explains why so many writers surrender to the role of conduit for the voices of the experts, providing conjunctions between quotations. So why not avoid what other people have said? Won't this avoidance ensure that your ideas will be original and that, at the same time, you will be free from the danger of getting brainwashed by some expert?

The answer is no. If you don't consult what others have said, you run at least two risks: you will waste your time reinventing the wheel, and you will undermine your analysis (or at least leave it incomplete) by not considering information and ideas commonly discussed in the field. By remaining unaware of existing thinking, you choose, in effect, to stand outside of the conversation that others interested in the subject are having.

It is possible to find a *middle ground* between developing an idea that is entirely independent of what experts have written on a subject and producing a paper that does nothing but repeat other people's ideas. A little research—even if it's only an hour's browse in the relevant databases on your library's website—will virtually always raise the level of what you have to say above what it would have been if you had consulted only the information and opinions that you carry around in your head.

A good rule of thumb for coping with source anxiety is to formulate a tentative position on your topic before you consult secondary sources. In other words, give yourself time to do some preliminary thinking. Try writing informally about your topic, analyzing some piece of pertinent information already at your disposal. That way, you will have your initial responses written down to weigh in relation to what others have said.

THE CONVERSATION ANALOGY

Now, let's turn to the major problem in using sources—a writer leaving the experts he or she cites to speak for themselves. In this situation, the writer characteristically makes a generalization in his or her own words, juxtaposes it to a quotation or other reference from a secondary source, and assumes that the meaning of the reference will be self-evident. This practice not only leaves the connection between the writer's thinking and his or her source material unstated but also substitutes mere repetition of someone else's viewpoint for a more active interpretation. The source has been allowed to have the final word, with the effect that it stops the discussion and the writer's thinking.

First and foremost, then, you need *to do something* with the reading. Clarify the meaning of the material you have quoted, paraphrased, or summarized and explain its significance in light of your evolving thesis.

It follows that the first step in using sources effectively is to reject the assumption that sources provide final and complete answers. If they did, there would be no reason for others to continue writing on the subject. As in conversation, we raise ideas for others to respond to. Accepting that no source has the final word does not mean, however, that you should shift from unquestioning approval to the opposite pole and necessarily assume an antagonistic position toward all sources. Indeed, a habitually antagonistic response to others' ideas is just as likely to bring your conversation with your sources to a halt as is the habit of always assuming that the source must have the final word.

Most people would probably agree on the attributes of a really good conversation. There is room for agreement and disagreement, for give and take, among a variety of viewpoints. Generally, people don't deliberately misunderstand each other, but a significant amount of the discussion may go into clarifying one's own as well as others' positions. Such conversations construct a genuinely collaborative chain of thinking: Karl builds on what David has said, which induces Jill to respond to Karl's comment, and so forth.

There are, of course, obvious differences between conversing aloud with friends and conversing on paper with sources. As a writer, you need to construct the chain of thinking, orchestrate the exchange of views with and among your sources, and give the conversation direction. A good place to begin in using sources is to recognize that you need not respond to everything another writer says, nor do you need to come up with an entirely original point of view—one that completely revises or refutes the source. You are using sources analytically, for example, when you note that two experiments (or historical accounts, or whatever) are similar but have different priorities or that they ask similar questions in different ways. Building from this kind of observation, you can then analyze what these differences imply.

TWO METHODS FOR CONVERSING WITH SOURCES

- Choose one sentence from a secondary source and one from a primary source, and put these into conversation. What does each reveal about the other?
- Pick one sentence from one source (A) and one from another (B): how does A speak to B? How does B speak to A?

Remember: go local, not global. You will be better off if you bring together two representative moves or ideas from the sources rather than trying to compare a summary of one source with a summary of another. A useful phrase here is "points of contact": look for ways that an idea or observation in source A appears to intersect with one in source B. Then stage the conversation you can imagine taking place between them.

Conversing with a Source: A Brief Example

Consider, for example, the following quotation, the opening sentences of an essay, "Clichés," by Christopher Ricks, which is ostensibly a review of a reissued book on the subject:

> The only way to speak of a cliché is with a cliché. So even the best writers against clichés are awkwardly placed. When Eric Partridge amassed his *Dictionary of Cliches* in 1940 (1978 saw its fifth edition), his introduction had no choice but to use the usual clichés for clichés. Yet what, as a metaphor, could be more hackneyed than *hackneyed,* more outworn than *outworn,* more tattered than *tattered?* Is there any point left to—or in or on—saying of a cliché that its "original point has been blunted"? Hasn't this too become blunted? (Christopher Ricks, "Cliches" in *The State of the Language,* University of California Press, 1980, p. 54)

A writer would not want to cite this passage simply to illustrate that clichés are "bad"—language uses to be avoided—or to suggest, as a dictionary might, that a cliché is a form of expression one might call "hackneyed" or "outworn" or "tattered," even though this information is clearly included in Ricks's sentences. Nor would a writer simply want to reiterate Ricks's leading claim, that "The only way to speak of a cliché is with a cliché," because Ricks already said that.

Instead, you'd need to talk about how Ricks treats the topic—that he has uncovered a paradox, for example, in that first sentence. You might go on to say that his point of view provides a useful warning for those who wish to talk about clichés. And then you might make some inferences you could build on: that simply dismissing clichés on vaguely moral grounds as unoriginal (hackneyed) does not add anything to our knowledge, and so perhaps, it's time to rethink our usual response to clichés and to see them afresh. In any case, as a rule of thumb, only include a quotation if you plan to say something about it.

WAYS TO USE A SOURCE AS A POINT OF DEPARTURE

There are many ways of approaching secondary sources, but these ways generally share a common goal: to use the source as a point of departure. Here is a partial list of ways to do that.

- Make as many points as you can about a single representative passage from your source, and then branch out from this center to analyze other passages that "speak" to it in some way. (*See 10 on 1 and Pan, Track and Zoom in Chapter 10.*)

- Use Notice and Focus to identify what you find most strange in the source; this will help you cultivate your curiosity about the source and find the critical distance necessary to thinking about it.

- Use The Method to identify the most significant organizing contrast in the source; this will help you see what the source itself is wrestling with, what is at stake in it.

- Apply an idea in the source to another subject. (*See Applying a Reading as a Lens in Chapter 5.*)

- Uncover the assumptions in the source, and then build upon the source's point of view, extending its implications. (*See Uncovering Assumptions in Chapter 4.*)

- Agree with most of what the source says, but take issue with one small part that you want to modify.

- Identify a contradiction in the source, and explore its implications, without necessarily arriving at a solution.

In using a source as a point of departure, you are in effect using it as a stimulus to have an idea. If you quote or paraphrase a source with the aim of conversing rather than allowing it to do your thinking for you, you will discover that sources can promote rather than stifle your ability to have ideas. Try to think of sources not as answers but as voices inviting you into a community of interpretation, discussion, and debate.

SIX STRATEGIES FOR ANALYZING SOURCES

Many people never get beyond like/dislike responses with secondary materials. If they agree with what a source says, they say it's "good," and they cut and paste the part they can use as an answer. If the source somehow disagrees with what they already believe, they say it's "bad," and they attack it or—along with readings they find "hard" or "boring"—discard it. As readers, they have been conditioned to develop a point of view on a subject without first figuring out the conversation (the various points of view) that their subject attracts. They assume, in other words, that their subject probably has a single meaning—a gist—disclosed by experts, who mostly agree. The six strategies that follow offer ways to avoid this trap.

Strategy 1: Make Your Sources Speak

Quote, paraphrase, or summarize *in order to* analyze—not in place of analyzing. Don't assume that either the meaning of the source material or your reason for including it is self-evident. Stop yourself from the habit of just stringing together citations for which you provide little more than conjunctions. Instead, explain to your readers what the quotation or paraphrase or summary of the source means. What elements of it do you find interesting or revealing or strange? Emphasize how those affect your evolving thesis.

In making a source speak, focus on articulating how the source has led to the conclusion you draw from it. Beware of simply putting a generalization and a quotation next to each other (juxtaposing them) without explaining the connection. Instead, fill the crucial site between claim and evidence with your thinking. Consider this problem in the following paragraph from a student's paper on political conservatism.

> Edmund Burke's philosophy evolved into contemporary American conservative ideology. There is an important distinction between philosophy and political ideology: philosophy is "the knowledge of general principles that explain facts and existences." Political ideology, on the other hand, is "an overarching conception of society, a stance that is reflected in numerous sectors of social life" (Edwards 22). Therefore, conservatism should be regarded as an ideology rather than a philosophy.

The final sentence offers the writer's conclusion—what the source information has led him to—but how did it get him there? The writer's choice of the word "therefore" indicates to the reader that the idea following it is the result of a process of logical reasoning, but this reasoning has been omitted. Instead, the writer assumes the reader will be able to connect the quotations with his conclusion. The writer needs to make the quotation speak by analyzing its key terms more closely. What is "an overarching conception of society," and how does it differ from "knowledge of general principles"? More important, what is the rationale for categorizing conservatism as either an ideology or a philosophy?

Here, by contrast, is a writer who makes her sources speak. Focus on how she integrates analysis with quotation.

> Stephen Greenblatt uses the phrase "self-fashioning" to refer to an idea he believes developed during the Renaissance—the idea that one's identity is not created or born but rather shaped, both by one's self and by others. The idea of self-fashioning is incorporated into an attitude toward literature that has as its ideal what Greenblatt calls "poetics of culture." A text is examined with three elements in mind: the author's own self, the cultural self-fashioning process that created that self, and the author's reaction to that process. Because our selves, like texts, are "fashioned," an author's life is just as open to interpretation as that of a literary character.
>
> If this is so, then biography does not provide a repository of unshakeable facts from which to interpret an author's work. Greenblatt criticizes the fact that the methods of literary interpretation are applied just to art and not to life. As he observes, "We wall off literary symbolism from the symbolic structures operative elsewhere, as if art alone were a human creation" (Begley 37). If the line between art and life is indeed blurred, then we need a more complex model for understanding the relationship between the life and work of an author.

In this example, the writer shows us how her thinking has been stimulated by the source. At the end of the first paragraph and the beginning of the second, for example, she not only specifies what she takes to be the meaning of the quotation but also draws a conclusion about its implications (that the facts of an author's life, like his or her art, require interpretation). And this manner of proceeding is habitual: the writer repeats the pattern in the second paragraph, moving beyond what the quotation says to explore what its logic suggests.

Strategy 2: Attend Carefully to the Language of Your Sources by Quoting or Paraphrasing Them

Rather than generalizing broadly about ideas in your sources, you should spell out what you think is significant about their keywords. In those disciplines in which it is permissible, *quote sources if the actual language they use is important to your point.* Generally, disciplines in the humanities expect you to quote as well as paraphrase, while in the social sciences, students are encouraged to paraphrase, not quote.

Quoting and paraphrasing has the benefit of helping writers to represent the views of their sources fairly and accurately. In situations where quoting is not allowed—such as in the report format in psychology—you still need to attend carefully to the meaning of keywords in order to arrive at a summary or paraphrase that is not overly general. As we have suggested repeatedly, paraphrasing provides an ideal way to begin interpreting because the act of careful rephrasing usually illuminates attitudes and assumptions implicit in a text. It is almost impossible not to have ideas and not to see the questions when you start paraphrasing.

Another reason quoting and paraphrasing are important is because your analysis of a source will nearly always benefit from attention to the way the source represents its position. Although focusing on the manner of presentation matters more with some sources than with others—more with a poem or scholarly article in political science than with a paper in the natural sciences—the information is never wholly separable from how it is expressed. If you are going to quote *Newsweek* on Pakistan, for example, you will be encountering not "the truth" about American involvement in this Asian nation but rather one particular representation of the situation—in this case, one crafted to meet or shape the expectations of mainstream popular culture. Similarly, if you quote President Bush on terrorism, what probably matters most is that the president chose particular words to represent—and promote—the government's position. It is not neutral information. The person speaking and the kind of source in which his or her words appear usually acquire added significance when you make note of these words rather than just summarizing them.

Strategy 3: Supply Ongoing Analysis of Sources (Don't Wait Until the End)

Unless disciplinary conventions dictate otherwise, analyze *as* you quote or paraphrase a source, rather than summarizing everything first and leaving your analysis for the end. A good conversation does not consist of long monologues alternating among the speakers. Participants exchange views, query, and modify what other speakers have said. Similarly, when you orchestrate conversations with and among your sources, you need to integrate your analysis into your presentation of them.

In supplying ongoing analysis, you are much more likely to explain how the information in the sources fits into your unfolding presentation, and your readers will be more likely to follow your train of thought and grasp the logic of your organization. You will also prevent yourself from using the sources simply as an answer. A good rule of thumb in this regard is to force yourself to ask and answer "So what?" at the ends of paragraphs. In laying out your analysis, however, take special care to distinguish your voice from the sources'.

Bringing Sources Together: A Psychology Professor Speaks

In the following Voice from Across the Curriculum, psychology professor Alan Tjeltveit offers a tip about how members of his discipline orchestrate a number of sources on more than one topic.

Voices from Across the Curriculum

Avoid serial citation summaries; that is, rather than discussing what Author A found, then what Author B found, then what Author C found, and so forth, *integrate* material from all of your sources. For instance, if writing about the cause and treatment of a disorder, discuss what all authors say about cause, then what all authors say about treatment, and so forth, addressing any contradictions or tensions among authors.

—Alan Tjeltveit, Professor of Psychology

Strategy 4: Use Your Sources to Ask Questions, Not Just To Provide Answers

Use your selections from sources as a means of raising issues and questions. Avoid the temptation to plug in such selections as answers that require no further commentary or elaboration. You will no doubt find viewpoints you believe to be valid, but it is not enough to drop these answers from the source into your own writing at the appropriate spots. You need to *do* something with the reading, even with those sources that seem to have said what you want to say.

As long as you consider only the source in isolation, you may not discover much to say about it. Once you begin considering it in other contexts and with other sources, you may begin to see aspects of your subject that your source does not adequately address. Having recognized that the source does not answer all questions, you should not conclude that the source is "wrong"—only that it is limited in some ways. Discovering such limitations is in fact advantageous because it can lead you to identify a place from which to launch your own analysis.

It does not necessarily follow that your analysis will culminate in an answer to replace those offered by your sources. Often—in fact, far more often than many writers suspect—it is enough to discover issues or problems and raise them clearly. Phrasing explicitly the issues and questions that remain implicit in a source is an important part of what analytical writers do, especially with cases in which there is no solution, or at least none that can be presented in a relatively short paper. Here, for example, is how the writer on Stephen Greenblatt's concept of self-fashioning concludes her essay:

It is not only the author whose role is complicated by New Historicism; the critic also is subject to some of the same qualifications and restrictions. According to Adam Begley, "it is the essence of the new-historicist project to uncover the moments at which works of art absorb and refashion social energy, an endless process of circulation and exchange" (39). In other words, the work is both affected by and affects the culture. But if this is so, how then can we decide which elements of culture (and text) are causes and which are effects? If we add the critic to this picture, the process does indeed appear endless. The New Historicists' relationship with their culture infuses itself into their assessment of the Renaissance, and this assessment may in turn become part of their own self-fashioning process, which will affect their interpretations, and so forth....

Notice that this writer incorporates the quotation into her own chain of thinking. By paraphrasing the quotation ("In other words"), she arrives at a question ("how then") that follows as a logical consequence of accepting its position ("but if this is so"). Note, however, that she does not then label the quotation right or wrong. Instead, she tries to figure out to what position it might lead and to what possible problems.

By contrast, the writer of the following excerpt, from a paper comparing two films aimed at teenagers, settles for plugging in sources as answers and consequently does not pursue the questions implicit in her quotations.

In both films, the adults are one-dimensional caricatures, evil beings whose only goal in life is to make the kids' lives a living hell. In *Risky Business,* director Paul Brickman's solution to all of Joel's problems is to have him hire a prostitute and then turn his house into a whorehouse. Of course, as one critic observes, "the prostitutes who make themselves available to his pimply faced buddies are all centerfold beauties: elegant, svelte, benign and unquestionably healthy (after all, what does V.D. have to do with prostitutes?)" (Gould 41)—not exactly a realistic or legal solution. Allan Moyle, the director of *Pump Up the Volume,* provides an equally unrealistic solution to Mark's problem. According to David Denby, Moyle "offers self-expression as the cure to adolescent funk. Everyone should start his own radio station and talk about his feelings" (59). Like Brickman, Moyle offers solutions that are neither realistic nor legal.

This writer is having a hard time figuring out what to do with sources that offer well-phrased and seemingly accurate answers (such as "self-expression is the cure to adolescent funk"). She settles for the bland conclusion that films aimed at teenagers are not "realistic"—an observation that most readers would already recognize as true. But unlike the writer of the previous example, she does not ask herself, "If this is true, then what follows?" Some version of the *So what?* question might have led her to inquire how the illegality of the solutions is related to their unrealistic quality. So what, for example, that the main characters in both films are not marginalized as criminals and made to suffer for their illegal actions, but rather are celebrated as heroes? What different kinds of illegality do the two films apparently condone, and how might these be related to the different decades in which each film was produced? Rather than use her sources to think with, in order to clarify or complicate the issues, the writer has used them to confirm a fairly obvious generalization.

Strategy 5: Put Your Sources Into Conversation with One Another

Rather than limiting yourself to agreeing or disagreeing with your sources, aim for conversation with and among them. Although it is not wrong to agree or disagree with your sources, it is wrong to see these as your only possible moves. This practice of *framing the discussion* typically locates you either for or against some well-known point of view or frame of reference; it's a way of sharing your assumptions with the reader. You introduce the source, in other words, to succinctly summarize a position that you plan to develop or challenge in a qualified way. This latter strategy—sometimes known as straw man, because you construct a "dummy" position specifically in order to knock it down—can stimulate you to formulate a point of view, especially if you are not accustomed to responding critically to sources.

As this boxing analogy suggests, however, setting up a straw man can be a dangerous game. If you do not fairly represent and put into context the straw man's argument, you risk encouraging readers to dismiss your counterargument as a cheap shot and to dismiss you for being reductive. On the other hand, if you spend a great deal of time detailing the straw man's position, you risk losing momentum in developing your own point of view.

In any case, if you are citing a source in order to frame the discussion, the more reasonable move is both to agree *and* disagree with it. First, identify shared premises; give the source some credit. Then, distinguish the part of what you have cited that you intend to develop or complicate or dispute. This method of proceeding is obviously less combative than the typically blunt straw man approach; it verges on conversation.

In the following passage from a student's paper on Darwin's Theory of Evolution, the student clearly recognizes that he needs to do more than summarize what Darwin says, but he seems not to know any way of conversing with his source other than indicating his agreement and disagreement with it.

> The struggle for existence also includes the dependence of one being on another being to survive. Darwin also believes that all organic beings tend to increase. I do not fully agree with Darwin's belief here. I cannot conceive of the fact of all beings increasing in number. Darwin goes on to explain that food, competition, climate, and the location of a certain species contribute to its survival and existence in nature. I believe that this statement is very valid and that it could be very easily understood through experimentation in nature.

This writer's use of the word "here" in his third sentence is revealing. He is tagging summaries of Darwin with what he seems to feel is an obligatory response—a polite shake or nod of the head: "I can't fully agree with you there, Darwin, but here I think you might have a point." The writer's tentative language lets us see how uncomfortable, even embarrassed, he feels about venturing these judgments on a subject too complex for this kind of response. It's as though the writer moves along, talking about Darwin's theory for a while, and then says to himself, "Time for a response," and lets a particular summary sentence trigger a yes/no switch. Having pressed that switch, which he does periodically, the writer resumes his summary, having registered but not analyzed his own interjections. There is no reasoning in a chain from his own observations, just random insertions of unanalyzed agree/disagree responses.

Here, by contrast, is the introduction of an essay that uses summary to frame the conversation that the writer is preparing to have with her source.

> In *Renaissance Thought: The Classic, Scholastic and Humanist Strains,* Paul Kristeller responds to two problems that he perceives in Renaissance scholarship. The first is the haze of cultural meaning surrounding the word "humanism": he seeks to clarify the word and its origins, as well as to explain the apparent lack of religious concern in humanism. Kristeller also reacts to the notion of humanism as an improvement upon medieval Aristotelian scholasticism.

Rather than leading with her own beliefs about the source, the writer emphasizes the issues and problems she believes are central in it. Although the writer's position on her source is apparently neutral, she is not summarizing passively. In addition to making choices about what is especially significant in the source, she has also located it within the conversation that its author, Kristeller, was having with his own sources—the works of other scholars whose view of humanism he wants to revise ("Kristeller responds to two problems").

As an alternative to formulating your opinion of the sources, try constructing the conversation you think the author of one of your sources might have with the author of another. How might they recast each other's ideas, as opposed to merely agreeing or disagreeing with those ideas? Notice how, farther on in the paper, the writer uses this strategy to achieve a clearer picture of Kristeller's point of view:

> Unlike Kristeller, Tillyard [in *The Elizabethan World Picture*] also tries to place the seeds of individualism in the minds of the medievals. "Those who know most about the Middle Ages," he claims, "now assure us that humanism and a belief in the present life were powerful by the 12th century" (30). Kristeller would undoubtedly reply that it was scholasticism, lacking the humanist emphasis on individualism that was powerful in the Middle Ages. True humanism was not evident in the Middle Ages.
>
> In Kristeller's view, Tillyard's attempts to assign humanism to medievals are not only unwarranted, but also counterproductive. Kristeller ends his chapter on "Humanism and Scholasticism" with an exhortation to "develop a kind of historical pluralism. It is easy to praise everything in the past that appears to resemble certain favorable ideas of our own time, or to ridicule and minimize everything that disagrees with them. This method is neither fair nor helpful" (174). Tillyard, in trying to locate humanism within the medieval world, allows the value of humanism to supersede the worth of medieval scholarship. Kristeller argues that there is inherent worth in every intellectual movement, not simply in the ones that we find most agreeable.
>
> Kristeller's work is valuable to us primarily for its forthright definition of humanism. Tillyard has cleverly avoided this undertaking: he provides many textual references, usually with the companion comment that "this is an example of Renaissance humanism," but he never overtly and fully formulates the definition in the way that Kristeller does.

As this excerpt makes evident, the writer has found something to say about her source by putting it into conversation with another source with which she believes her source, Kristeller, would disagree ("Kristeller would undoubtedly reply"). Although it seems obvious that the writer prefers Kristeller to Tillyard, her agreement with him is not the main point of her analysis. She focuses instead on foregrounding the problem that Kristeller is trying to solve and on relating that problem to different attitudes toward history. In so doing, she is deftly orchestrating the conversation between her sources. Her next step would be to distinguish her position from Kristeller's. Having used Kristeller to get perspective on Tillyard, she now needs somehow to get perspective on Kristeller. The next strategy addresses this issue.

Strategy 6: Find Your Own Role in the Conversation

Even in cases in which you find a source's position entirely congenial, it is not enough simply to agree with it. This does not mean you should feel compelled to attack the source but rather that you need to find something of your own to say about it.

In general, you have two options when you find yourself strongly in agreement with a source. You can (1) apply it in another context to qualify or expand its implications. Or you can (2) seek out other perspectives on the source in order to break the spell it has cast on you. To break the spell means you will necessarily become somewhat disillusioned but not that you will then need to dismiss everything you previously believed.

How, in the first option, do you take a source somewhere else? Rather than focusing solely on what you believe your source finds most important, locate a lesser point, not emphasized by the reading, that you find especially interesting and develop it further. This strategy will lead you to uncover new implications that depend on your source but lie outside its own governing preoccupations. In the preceding humanism example, the writer might apply Kristeller's principles to new geographic (rather than theoretical) areas, such as Germany instead of Italy.

The second option, researching new perspectives on the source, can also lead to uncovering new implications. Your aim need not be simply to find a source that disagrees with the one that has convinced you and then switch your allegiance because this move would perpetuate the problem from which you are trying to escape. Instead, you would use additional perspectives to gain some critical distance from your source. An ideal way of sampling possible critical approaches to a source is to consult book reviews on it found in scholarly journals. Once the original source is taken down from the pedestal through additional reading, there is a greater likelihood that you will see how to distinguish your views from those it offers.

You may think, for example, that another source's critique of your original source is partly valid and that both sources miss things you could point out; in effect, you *referee* the conversation between them. The writer on Kristeller might play this role by asking herself: "So what that subsequent historians have viewed his objective—a disinterested historical pluralism—as not necessarily desirable and in any case impossible? How might Kristeller respond to this charge, and how has he responded already in ways that his critics have failed to notice?" Using additional research in this way can lead you to situate your source more fully and fairly, acknowledging its limits as well as its strengths.

In other words, this writer, in using Kristeller to critique Tillyard, has arrived less at a conclusion than at her next point of departure. A good rule to follow, especially when you find a source entirely persuasive, is that if you can't find a perspective on your source, you haven't done enough research.

Evaluating Sources in the Sciences: A Biology Professor Speaks

In the following Voice from Across the Curriculum, molecular biologist Bruce Wightman suggests the range of tasks he expects students to do when they engage a source—not only to supply ongoing analysis of it and to consider its contributions in light of other research, but also to locate themselves in relation to the questions their analysis of the source has led them to discover.

Voices from Across the Curriculum

One of the problems with trying to *read* critical analyses of scientific work is that few scientists want to be in print criticizing their colleagues. That is, for political reasons, scientists who write reviews are likely to soften their criticism or even avoid it entirely by reporting the findings of others simply and directly.

What I want from students in molecular biology is a critical analysis of the work they have researched. This can take several forms.

First, *analyze* what was done. What were the assumptions (hypotheses) going into the experiment? What was the logic of the experimental design? What were the results?

Second, *evaluate* the results and conclusions. How well do the results support the conclusions? What alternative interpretations are there? What additional experiments could be done to strengthen or refute the argument? This is hard, no doubt, but it is what you should be doing every time you read anything in science or otherwise.

Third, *synthesize* the results and interpretations of a given experiment in the context of the field. How does this study inform other studies? Even though practicing scientists are hesitant to do this in print, everyone does it informally in journal clubs held usually on a weekly basis in every lab all over the world.

—Bruce Wightman, Professor of Biology

USING SOURCES ANALYTICALLY: AN EXAMPLE

In a recent article on thinking entitled "The Other You" that appeared in the journal *New Scientist*, the writer introduces sources in sequence, wherein each source offers a different researcher's angle on the same central question: how is the subconscious related to the conscious activities of the mind? The writer, Kate Douglas, discusses the implications of each source without choosing any one as "the answer":

- "Shadlin sees the subconscious and conscious as two parts of the same system, rather than two separate thought processors working in the same machine" (45).

- "Others want to further subdivide conscious and subconscious thought and have come up with alternative descriptions to replace the old two-part model" (45)

- "Peter Dayan [and colleagues] see the mind as comprising four systems."
- "Dayan says that our behavior is often driven by more than one of the four controllers."

At the end of this phase of the article, Douglas then states, "Importantly, the subconscious isn't the dumb cousin of the conscious, but rather a cousin with different skills" (Kate Douglas, "The Other You," *New Scientist*, December 1–7, 2007. vol. 196, no. 2632, p. 45).

As this example demonstrates, often in conversing with sources, a writer is not staging conflicts or debates, but bringing together multiple points of view and offering a final synthesis. Those familiar with the popular journalist Malcolm Gladwell may recognize that he is fond of this method. In books such as *Blink*, Gladwell presents one piece of research, and in making inferences about it, leads us to the next and often unexpectedly related piece of research. Part of the appeal of Gladwell's method is how he quilts together a range of disparate voices into one unfolding narrative. The thinking in a Gladwell piece is presented in the way he connects the parts, not in the way that he is critiquing them, finding shortcomings, or emphasizing the differences.

GUIDELINES FOR CONVERSING WITH SOURCES

1. Avoid the temptation to plug in sources as answers. Aim for a *conversation* with them. Think of sources as voices inviting you into a community of interpretation, discussion, and debate.

2. Quote, paraphrase, or summarize *in order to* analyze. Explain what you take the source to mean, showing the reasoning that has led to the conclusion you draw from it.

3. Quote sparingly. You are usually better off centering your analysis on a few quotations, analyzing their key terms, and branching out to aspects of your subject that the quotations illuminate. Remember that not all disciplines allow direct quotation.

4. Don't underestimate the value of close paraphrasing. You will almost invariably begin to interpret a source once you start paraphrasing its key language.

5. Locate and highlight what is at stake in your source. Which of its points does the source find most important? What positions does it want to modify or refute, and why?

6. Look for ways to develop, modify, or apply what a source has said, rather than simply agreeing or disagreeing with it.

7. If you challenge a position found in a source, be sure to represent it fairly. First, give the source some credit by identifying assumptions you share with it. Then, isolate the part that you intend to complicate or dispute.

8. Look for sources that address your subject from different perspectives. Avoid relying too heavily on any one source. Aim at the end to synthesize these perspectives: what is the common ground?

9. When your sources disagree, consider playing mediator. Instead of immediately agreeing with one or the other, clarify areas of agreement and disagreement among them.

Assignments: Conversing with Sources

1. **Make One Source Speak to Another**. Choose two articles or book chapters by different authors or by the same author at different points in his or her career. The overriding aim of the assignment is to give you practice in getting beyond merely reacting and generalizing, and instead, participating in your sources' thinking.

   Keep in mind that your aim is not to arrive at your opinion of the sources, but to construct the conversation you think the author of one of your sources might have with the author of another. How might they recast each other's ideas, as opposed to merely agreeing or disagreeing with those ideas? It's useful to confine yourself to thinking as impartially as you can about the ideas found in your two sources.

2. **Use Passage-Based Focused Freewriting to Converse with Sources**. Select a passage from a secondary source that appears important to your evolving thinking about a subject you are studying, and do a passage-based focused freewrite on it. You might choose the passage in answer to the question "What is the one passage in the source that I need to discuss, that poses a question or a problem or that seems, in some way difficult to pin down, anomalous or even just unclear?" Copy the passage at the top of the page, and write without stopping for 20 minutes or more. As noted in the discussion of freewriting in Chapter 4, paraphrase key terms as you relentlessly ask "So what?" about the details.

3. **Use a Source as a Lens on Another Source**. Apply a brief passage from a secondary source to a brief passage from a primary source, using the passage from the secondary source as a lens. Choose the secondary source passage first—one that you find particularly interesting, revealing, or problematic. Then locate a corresponding passage from the primary source to which the sentence from the first passage can be connected in some way. Copy both passages at the top of the page, and then write for 20 minutes. You should probably include paraphrases of key phrases in both—not just the primary text—but your primary goal is to think about the two together, to allow them to interact.

Chapter 14

Finding, Citing, and Integrating Sources

THIS CHAPTER SHIFTS ATTENTION to more technical matters associated with writing the researched paper. More than just mechanically gathering information, research continues to be a primary means of discovering the ongoing conflicts about a subject and having ideas about it. Engaging the information sparks thinking—not just arranging.

THIS CHAPTER IS DIVIDED INTO FIVE SECTIONS

A. Research Methods

B. Plagiarism and the Logic of Citation

C. Citing Sources: Four Documentation Styles

D. Integrating Quotations Into Your Paper

E. Preparing an Abstract

The core of this chapter is a discussion of research methods written by a reference librarian at our college, Kelly Cannon. It offers a wealth of insider's tips for making more productive use of your research time.

A. A Guided Tour of Research Methods by Reference Librarian Kelly Cannon

THREE RULES OF THUMB FOR GETTING STARTED

- A half-hour spent with a reference librarian can save you half a day wandering randomly through the stacks selecting sources.
- Start your research in the present and work backward. Usually the most current materials include bibliographical citations that can help you identify the most important sources in the past. Along the same lines, you are usually better off starting with journal articles rather than books because articles are more current.

- Consistently evaluate the reliability of the source, looking for its potential bias or agenda. Evidence is always qualified by how it is framed. For example, *Newsweek* can be a useful source if you want evidence about popular understanding of a subject or issue. The fact that the material comes from *Newsweek* and thus represents a position aimed at a mainstream, nonacademic audience provides the central reason for citing it.

The challenge of doing research in the Information Age is that there is so much information available. How do you know which information is considered authoritative in a particular discipline and which isn't? How can you avoid wasting time with source materials that have been effectively refuted and replaced by subsequent thinking? A short answer to these questions is that you should start in the reference room of your library or with its electronic equivalent. Many if not all of the resources listed below are now available online through your college library website. Your reference librarian can advise you on availability.

Start with Indexes, Specialized Dictionaries, Abstracts, and Bibliographies

These reference sources can rapidly provide you with both a broad perspective on your subject and a summary of what particular sources contain. An **index** offers a list of titles directing you to scholarly journals; often this list is sufficient to give you a clearer idea of the kinds of topics about which writers in the field are conversing. **Compilations of abstracts** and **annotated bibliographies** provide more information—anywhere from a few sentences to a few pages that summarize each source. *(See the section at the end of this chapter on abstracts and how to write them.)*

Here are a few of the most commonly used indexes, bibliographies, and abstracts:

Art Abstracts

Business Source Elite

ERIC (Education)

MLA (Modern Language Association)

PubMed

SocAbs

Specialized dictionaries and encyclopedias are sometimes extraordinarily useful in sketching the general terrain for a subject, and they often include bibliographical leads as well. Here are some titles, ranging from the expected to the eccentric:

Dictionary of the History of Ideas	*Encyclopedia of Economics*
Dictionary of Literary Biography	*Encyclopedia of Native American Religions*
Encyclopedia of American History	
Encyclopedia of Bioethics	*Encyclopedia of Philosophy*
Encyclopedia of Crime and Justice	*Encyclopedia of Psychology*

Encyclopedia of Unbelief

Encyclopedia of World Art

Encyclopedic Dictionary of Mathematics

Macmillan Encyclopedia of Computers

Encyclopedia of Medical History

McGraw Hill Encyclopedia of Science and Technology

New Grove Dictionary of Music and Musicians

Oxford English Dictionary

Most of the resources just listed also include book reviews. In addition, the *Reader's Guide to Periodical Literature* locates reviews as well as articles in popular—general audience—publications such as *Time* and *Newsweek*. For a broader range of titles, you might also consult *Book Review Index, Book Review Digest,* and *Subject Guide to Books in Print.*

Indexes of Scholarly Journals

Nearly every discipline has its own major index, one most consulted by scholars. Here are just a few: *MLA* (literary criticism), *ERIC* (education), *PsycInfo* (psychology), *Historical Abstracts* (non-U.S. history), *Sociological Abstracts* (sociology), and *PubMed* (medicine).

When professors refer to bibliographic research, they probably mean research done with indexes. Again, these indexes are specific to particular subject areas. Their coverage is not broad, but deep and scholarly. These are the indexes to consult when seeking the most scholarly information in your area of study. Although the full text is often not included, the indexing provides information sufficient to track down the complete article.

These indexes are a great aid in evaluating the scholarly merit of a publication, as they usually eliminate any reference that isn't considered scholarly by the academy. For example, *MLA* only indexes literary criticism that appears in peer-reviewed journals and academically affiliated books. So, consider the publications that appear in these indexes to have the academic "seal of approval."

For more information on this crucial aspect of research, see the headings later in this chapter entitled "Subscriber-Only Databases" and "Four Steps Toward Productive Research Across the Disciplines."

Finding Your Sources: Articles and Books

The resources above will not only provide you with an excellent overview of your topic, but also direct you to authoritative books and journal articles. The next step is to find out how to access the full text of those books and articles online or in print form. Your library's online catalog will direct you to books in your local library. You may wish to take advantage of this time in the catalog to run a keyword search on your topic. Watch the subject headings that appear at the bottom of catalog records. You can click on these subject headings to guide you to more books highly relevant to your topic.

Don't be concerned if many of the books that have been recommended in specialized dictionaries, encyclopedias, and indexes don't appear in your library's online catalog. The reference librarian can direct you to *WorldCat,* where you can request on interlibrary loan any book to be sent to you from another library for your perusal. This is a valuable service, as it makes available to you the research collections of large universities, all with the stroke of a key.

Journal articles are likely to be the next step in your research. You will need to find which articles are available in-house, online or in print, and which you will need to submit an interlibrary loan request for (in this case, unlike with books, you will receive a photocopy of the interlibrary loaned article to keep—no need to return it to the lending library). Your library's online catalog will generally—though not always—provide you with a complete list of journals available electronically or in print. Just title search on the journal name, not the article title, in order to locate the journal. Ask a reference librarian for assistance in locating journals. He or she can also assist you in requesting on interlibrary loan any articles from journals your library does not have.

Finding Quality Sources: Two Professors Speak

In the following Voices from Across the Curriculum, a business professor and a psychology professor offer useful tips for searching under more than one heading in order to find more information.

Voices from Across the Curriculum

A critical part of the bibliographic effort is to find a topic on which materials are available. Most topics can be researched. The key is to choose a flexible keyword/phrase and then try out different versions of it. For example, a bibliography on "women in management" might lead you to look up *women, females, business* (women in), *business* (females in), *gender in the workplace, sexism and the workplace, careers* (of men, of women, in business), *women and CEOs, women in management, affirmative action and women, women in corporations, female accountants,* and so forth. Be imaginative and flexible. A little bit of time with some of the indexes will provide you with a wealth of sources.

Here is a sampling of indexes heavily used in the social sciences, for instance: *Social Science Index, SocAbs, Wall Street Journal Index* (for *WSJ* stories), *New York Times Index* (for *NYT* stories), *Business Source Elite,* and the *Public Affairs Information Service (PAIS).*

—Frederick Norling, Professor of Business

Use quality psychological references, that is, use references that professional psychologists use and regard highly. *Psychology Today* is not a good reference; *Newsweek* and *Reader's Digest* are worse. APA journals, such as the *Journal of Abnormal Psychology,* on the other hand, are excellent.

In looking for reference material, be sure to search under several headings. For example, look under *depression, affective disorders,* and *mood disorders.* Books (e.g., *The Handbook of Affective Disorders*) are often very helpful, especially for giving a general overview of a topic. Books addressing a professional audience are generally preferable to those addressing a general, popular audience.

Finally, references should be reasonably current. In general, the newer, the better. For example, with rare exceptions (classic articles), articles from before 1970 are outdated and so should not be used.

—Alan Tjeltveit, Professor of Psychology

FINDING QUALITY ON THE WEB

Imagine a megalibrary to which anyone has access any time of day or night and to which anyone can contribute material, to inform, but perhaps more so to sell and to promote, no matter how questionable the cause or idea. So it is with the web. A general caveat to this "library of the Internet" might well be User Beware.

Take as an example the website *Martin Luther King: A True Historical Examination* (www.martinlutherking.org). This site appears prominently in any web search for information about Martin Luther King, Jr. The site is visually appealing, claiming to include "essays, speeches, sermons, and more." But who created the site? As it turns out, after a little digging (see Tips #1 and #2 later in the chapter), the site is sponsored by Stormfront, Inc. (http://stormfront.org), an organization out of West Palm Beach, Florida, serving "those courageous men and women fighting to preserve their White Western culture, ideals and freedom of speech." This author is concealed behind the work, a ghost writer of sorts. While the site is at one's fingertips, identifying the author is a challenge, more so than in the world of conventional publishing, where protocols are followed such as author and publisher appearing on the same pages as the title. For those websites with no visible author, no publishing house, no recognized journal title, no peer-review process, and no library selection process (the touchstones of scholarship in the print world), seemingly easy Internet research is now more problematic: the user must discern what is—and is not—authoritative information.

Understanding Domain Names

But how is the user to begin evaluating a web document? Fortunately, there are several clues to assist you through the Internet labyrinth. One clue is in the web address itself. For example, the *Internet Movie Database* has www.imdb.com as its web address (also known as URL, or uniform resource locator). One clue lies at the very end of the URL, in what is known as the domain name, in this case the abbreviation ".com." Websites ending in .com are commercial, often with the purpose of marketing a product. Sites ending in .org generally signal nonprofits, but many have a veiled agenda, whether it is marketing or politics. Like the .coms, .org addresses are sold on a first-come first-served basis. (The organization that oversees the many vendors of .com and .org domain names is The Internet Corporation for Assigned Names and Numbers, or ICANN [www.icann.org/].)

On the other hand, .edu and .gov sites may indicate less bias, as they are ostensibly limited exclusively to educational and government institutions, and they are often the producers of bonafide research. In particular, .gov sites contain some of the best information on the Internet. This is in part because the U.S. government is required by an act of Congress to disseminate to the general public a large portion of its research.

The U.S. government, floated by tax dollars, provides the high-quality, free websites reminiscent of the precommercial Internet era. This means that government sites offer high-quality data, particularly of a statistical nature. Scholars in the areas of business, law, and the social sciences can benefit tremendously, without subscription fees, from a variety of government databases. Prime examples are the legislative site known as *Thomas* (http://thomas.loc.gov) and data gathered at the website of the Census Bureau (www.census.gov).

Print Corollaries

But a domain name can be misleading; it is simply one clue in the process of evaluation. Another clue is the correlation between a website and the print world. Many websites correlate with a print edition, such as the web version of the *Economist* (economist.com), offering some unique information, some identical, as that offered in the print subscription. (Access to some web articles may be limited to subscribers.) Moreover, some websites are the equivalents of their print editions. For example, Johns Hopkins University Press now publishes its journals, known and respected for years by scholars, in both print and electronic formats. Many college and university libraries subscribe to these Johns Hopkins journals electronically, collectively known as *Project Muse* (http://muse.jhu.edu). In both cases—the *Economist* and *Project Muse*—the scholar can expect the electronic form of the publication to have undergone the same editorial rigor as the print publication.

Web-Published Gems

Building a reputation of high quality takes time. But the Internet has been around long enough now that some publications with no pre-web history have caught the attention of scholars who turn to these sites regularly for reliable commentary on a variety of subject areas.

These high-quality sites can best be found by tapping into scholarly web directories such as the *ipl2* (www.ipl.org) and *intute* (www.intute.ac.uk) that work like mini search engines but are managed by humans who sift through the chaff, including in these directories only what they deem to be gems.

The student looking specifically for free, peer-reviewed journals original to the web can visit a highly specific directory called the *Directory of Open Access Journals* (www.doaj.org), listing several hundred journals in a variety of subject areas. Many libraries have begun to link to these journals to promote their use by students and faculty.

Then there are the web treasures that compare to highbrow magazines or newspapers such as *The New Yorker*. Two celebrated examples are *Salon.com* (salon.com) and *Slate* (slate.com), both online literary reviews. Once tapped into, these sites do a good job of recommending other high-quality websites. Scholars are beginning to cite from these web-based publications just as they would from any print publication of long-standing reputation.

An excellent site for links to all kinds of interesting articles from journals and high level general interest magazine is *Arts and Letters Daily.com* (http://aldaily.com), sponsored by *The Chronicle of Higher Education*. You should also be aware of websites run by special interest organizations, such as the *American Academy of Poets* (http:// poets.org), which offers bibliographic resources, interviews, reviews, and the like.

Wikipedia, Google, and Blogs

Three tools have in recent years dramatically altered the nature of web-based research. First and foremost, the search engine *Google*, through a proprietary search algorithm, has increased the relevance and value of search results. Relevance in *Google* is determined by text-matching techniques, while value is determined by a unique "PageRank" technology that places highest on the list those results that are most often linked to from other websites.

However, the determination of value is by no means fool-proof. *Google*'s ranking of value assesses less a website's authoritativeness than its popular appeal. For example, a recent search on "marijuana" yielded as its second result (*Wikipedia*'s entry on marijuana is first) a private website promoting the use of marijuana and selling marijuana paraphernalia. This site could be useful in any number of ways in a research paper (i.e., as a primary resource reflecting public perceptions and use of marijuana in the United States). That it appears so high on the list suggests *Google*'s algorithm of popularity over authoritativeness. This is not necessarily a bad thing, just something to be aware of. It is a little like picking a pebble off the ground. Its value is not inherent: responsibility rests with the user to discover its value. Finding information in *Google* is never the challenge. Discerning appropriateness and authoritativeness is the bigger task.

High on the list of most search results in *Google*—if not first—is *Wikipedia*. Is this an authoritative source? Certainly, *Wikipedia* has revolutionized the way web pages are authored. The world is the author of every entry. That is the beauty and the hazard and the secret to its broad scope and thus to its popularity. Anyone can write and edit in *Wikipedia*. In this way, *Wikipedia* is infinitely democratic. All opinions count equally, for better or worse—while authority languishes. Consequently, *Wikipedia* is likely to contribute little to a scholarly research project. In fact, it could detract from an assertion of authority. In short, use *Wikipedia* entries judiciously. Like any encyclopedia, *Wikipedia* will be viewed by the informed reader as introductory, not as the hallmark of thorough research.

Just as *Wikipedia* invites all of us to be writers, so too do blogs. But unlike *Wikipedia*, blogs typically reveal the identity or at least the assumed identity of the author, and are written by a closed group of people, often one individual. As such, over time the identity and politics of the author(s) show through. In the best tradition of the World Wide Web, blogs have extended the sphere of publication, inviting everyone to be published authors, possibly achieving popularity and authority on a topic no matter how narrow by being at the right place at the right time, with access to the right information written in a voice of confidence. Blogs invite outside comment, but lack the formal structure of a peer review. As such, use blogs sparingly in academic research, being attentive to the credentials of the author(s), and to the wider acceptance of a particular blog in the scholarly community.

Asking the Right Questions

In the end, it is up to the individual user to evaluate each website independently. Here are some critical questions to consider:

Question: Who is the author?

Response: Check the website's home page, probably near the bottom of the page.

Question: Is the author affiliated with any institution?

Response: Check the URL to see who sponsors the page.

Question: What are the author's credentials?

Response: Check Google Scholar (scholar.google.com) to see if this person is published in scholarly journals or books.

Question: Has the information been reviewed or peer-edited before posting?

Response: Probably not, unless the posting is part of a larger scholarly project; if so, the submission process for publication can be verified at the publication home page.

Question: Is the page part of a larger publication that may help to assess authoritativeness?

Response: Try the various links on the page to see if there is an access point to the home page of the publication. Or try the backspacing technique mentioned later in the chapter.

Question: Is the information documented properly?

Response: Check for footnotes or methodology.

Question: Is the information current?

Response: Check the "last update," usually printed at the bottom of the page.

Question: What is the purpose of the page?

Response: Examine content and marginalia.

Question: Does the website suit your purposes?

Response: Review what the purpose of your project is. Review your information needs: primary vs. secondary, academic vs. popular. And always consult with your instructor.

Subscriber-Only Databases

An organized and indexed collection of discreet pieces of information is called a *database*. Two examples of databases are a library's card catalogue and online catalogue. The World Wide Web is full of databases, though they are often restricted to subscribers. Subscription fees can be prohibitive, but fortunately for the average researcher, most college and university libraries foot the bill. The names of these databases are now well known and, arguably, contain the most thoroughly reviewed (i.e., scholarly) full text available on the web. Inquire at your library to see if you have access to these databases:

Academic Search Premier from EBSCO (www.ebscohost.com)

Academic ASAP/Onefile from Gale, Cengage Learning (www.gale.cengage.com)

JSTOR from ITHAKA (www.jstor.org)

Project Muse from Johns Hopkins (muse.jhu.edu/)

Proquest Central from ProQuest (www.proquest.com)

Omnifile from Wilson (www.hwwilson.com).

Each of these databases contains its own proprietary search engine, allowing refinement of searches to a degree unmatched by search engines on the Internet at large. More is not better in an information age. The fact that information is at your fingertips, and sometimes "in your face," can be a problem. Well-organized databases are shaped and limited by human hands and minds, covering only certain media types or subject areas.

Second, databases allow searching by subject heading, in addition to keyword searching. This means that a human has defined the main subject areas of each entry, consequently allowing the user much greater manipulation of the search. For example, if I enter the words "New York City" in a simple keyword search, I will retrieve everything that simply mentions New York City even once; the relevance will vary tremendously. On the other hand, if subject headings have been assigned, I can do a subject search on New York City and find only records that are devoted to my subject. This may sound trivial, but in the age of information overload, precision searching is a precious commodity.

The most specialized databases are those whose primary purpose is not to provide full text but to index all of the major journals, along with books and/or book chapters, in a discipline, regardless of where the full text to that journal can be found. These electronic indexes provide basic bibliographic information and sometimes an abstract (summary) of the article or book chapter. (*See Scholarly Indexes earlier in the chapter.*)

Try This 14.1: Tuning in to Your Research Environment: Four Exercises

Every university and college is different, each with its own points of access to information. Following are some exercises to help you familiarize yourself with your own scholarly environment.

Exercise #1: Go to your library's reference desk and get a list of all the scholarly journal indexes available electronically at your school. Then get a list of all online, full-text databases available to you.

Exercise #2: Contact your reference librarian to get a list of all the journals the library subscribes to electronically. Then get a list of all journals available at your library either in print or electronically in your major area of study.

Exercise #3: Ask the reference librarian about web access in general for your major area of study. What tips can the librarian give you about doing electronic research at your academic institution? Are there any special databases, web search engines/directories, or indexes you should consult in your research?

Exercise #4: Try out some or all of the full-text databases available on your campus. Now try the same searches in a scholarly index. What differences do you see in the quality/scope of the information?

Eight Tips for Locating and Evaluating Electronic Sources

Tip #1: Backspacing "Backspacing" a URL can be an effective way to evaluate a website. It may reveal authorship or institutional affiliation. To do this, place the cursor at the end of the URL and then backspace to the last slash and press Enter. Continue backspacing to each preceding slash, examining each level as you go.

Tip #2: Using WHOIS *WHOIS* (www.networksolutions.com/whois/index.jsp) is an Internet service that allows anyone to find out who's behind a website.

Tip #3: Beware of the ~ in a Web Address Many educational institutions allow the creation of personal home pages by students and faculty. While the domain name remains .edu in these cases, the fact that they are personal means that pretty much anything can be posted and so cannot assure academic quality.

Tip #4: Phrase Searching Not finding relevant information? Try using quotation marks around key phrases in your search string. For example, search in *Google* for this phrase, enclosed in quotation marks: "whose woods these are I think I know."

Tip #5: Title Searching Still finding irrelevant information? Limit your search to the titles of web documents. A title search is an option in several search engines, among them *Yahoo* (advanced search) (http://search.yahoo.com) and *Google* (advanced search) (www.google.com).

Tip #6: *Wikipedia* Discussion Tab Use *Wikipedia* to full advantage by clicking on the discussion tab located at the top of *Wikipedia* entries. The discussion tabs expose the often intense debates that rage behind the scenes on topics like marijuana, genocide, and Islam. The discussion tab is an excellent source for locating paper topics because it highlights ongoing sources of controversy—those areas worthy of additional writing and research. To find the most controversial topics at any given moment, visit *Wikipedia*'s Controversial Issues page (http://en.wikipedia.org/wiki/Wikipedia:List_of_controversial_issues).

Tip #7: Full Text The widest selection of previously published full text (newspapers, magazines, journals, book chapters) is available in subscription databases via the web.

Inquire at your library to see if you have access to *Academic Search Premier* from EBSCO(www.ebscohost.com), *Academic ASAP/Onefile* from Gale Cengage (www. gale.cengage.com), *JSTOR* from ITHAKA (www.jstor.org), *Project Muse* from Johns Hopkins (muse.jhu.edu/), *Proquest Central* from ProQuest (www.proquest.com), *Omnifile* from Wilson (www.hwwilson.com), or other full-text databases.

The leading free full-text site for magazines and newspapers is BNET's *FindArticles* (http://findarticles.com). This database of "hundreds of thousands of articles from more than 300 magazines and newspapers" can be searched by all magazines, magazines within categories, or specific magazine or newspaper.

For the full text of books, try the *Internet Archive Text Archive* (hwww.archive.org/details/texts)), pointing to the major digital text archives.

Tip #8: Archives of Older Published Periodicals Full text for newspapers, magazines, and journals published prior to 1990 is difficult to find on the Internet. One subscription site your library may offer is *JSTOR* (www.jstor.org), an archive of scholarly full-text journal articles dating back in some cases into the late 1800s. *LexisNexis Academic* (www. lexisnexis.com), also a subscription service, includes the full text of popular periodicals such as the *New York Times* as far back as 1980.

Two free sites offer the full text of eighteenth- and nineteenth-century periodicals from Great Britain and the United States, respectively: *Internet Library of Early Journals* (www.bodley.ox.ac.uk/ilej) and *Nineteenth Century in Print* (http://memory. loc.gov/ammem/ndlpcoop/moahtml/snchome.html).

Use your library's interlibrary loan service to acquire articles from periodicals not freely available on the web. Electronic indexing (no full text) for older materials is readily available, back as early as 1900, sometimes earlier. Inquire at your library.

Four Steps Toward Productive Research Across the Disciplines

The steps below include a few of the sites most relied on by academic librarians. For the subscription databases, you will need to inquire at your library for local availability.

Step 1: search at least one of these multidisciplinary subscription databases; check your library's website for availability.

- *Academic Search Premier* (EBSCOhost) for journals
- *Academic ASAP/Onefile* (Gale Cengage) for journals
- *JSTOR* for journals
- *Omnifile* (WilsonWeb) for journals
- *Project Muse* for journals
- *Proquest Central* for journals
- *WorldCat* (OCLC FirstSearch) for books

Step 2: search subject-specific databases. These too are mostly subscription databases; check your library's website for availability.

- Anthropology: *Anthropological Abstracts*
- Art: *Art Abstracts*
- Biology: *Biological Abstracts, Biological and Agricultural Index*
- Business: *ABI Inform, Business Source Elite/Premier, Business & Company Resource Center, Dow Jones Factiva, LexisNexis*
- Chemistry: *SciFinder Scholar, Science Direct*
- Communication: *Communication and Mass Media, Communication Abstracts*
- Computer Science: *Inspec*
- Economics: *EconLit*
- Education: *ERIC* (free)
- Film Studies: *MLA*
- Geography/Geology: *GEOBASE*
- History: *America History and Life, Historical Abstracts*
- Language, Literature: *MLA, Literature Online*
- Law: *LexisNexis, Westlaw*
- Mathematics: *MathSciNet*
- Medicine: *PubMed, Science Direct* (free)
- Music: *RILM*
- Philosophy: *Philosopher's Index*
- Physics: *Inspec*
- Political Science: *PAIS*
- Psychology: *PsycINFO*
- Religion: *ATLA Religion*
- Sociology: *Sociological Abstracts*

Step 3: visit these not-to-be-missed free websites and meta-sites that lead to a variety of materials relevant to a discipline:

- All subjects: *Google Scholar* scholar.google.com (books and journals)
- Anthropology: *Anthropological Index Online* http://aio.anthropology.org.uk/ aiosearch/ (journals) *Anthropology Resources on the Internet* www.anthropology-resources.net
- Art: *ArtCyclopedia* www.artcyclopedia.com (images and critical bibliographies)
- Biology: *Biology Browser* www.biologybrowser.org (gateway to digital archives of colleges and universities, *Agricola* http://agricola.nal.usda.gov (journals)
- Business: *EDGAR* www.sec.gov/edgar.shtml (company annual reports), *Hoover's Online* www.hoovers.com/free (company reports)
- Chemistry: *Chemdex.org* www.chemdex.org (chemical compounds), *World of Chemistry* scienceworld.wolfram.com/chemistry (encyclopedia)

- Communication: *Television News Archive: Vanderbilt University* tvnews.vanderbilt.edu (index to television news)
- Computer Science: *arXiv.org* arxiv.org/ non-peer-reviewed but moderated scholarly e-print submissions), *CompInfo* www.compinfo-center.com (magazines and downloads)
- Economics: *Intute: Economics* www.intute.ac.uk/economics/ (reviewed websites associated with economics)
- Education: *Educator's Reference Desk* eduref.org (resource guides and lesson plans)
- Film Studies: *Film Studies Resources* www.lib.berkeley.edu/MRC/filmstudies/index.html (index to reviews and criticism)
- Geography/Geology: *GeoSource* www.library.uu.nl/geosource (gateway to reviewed web resources)
- History: *American Memory* memory.loc.gov/ammem/index.html (primary documents)
- Language, Literature: *Online Literary Criticism Collection* www.ipl.org/div/litcrit (biography and criticism)
- Law: *FindLaw* www.findlaw.com (free legal information)
- Mathematics: *arXiv.org* arxiv.org/ (non-peer-reviewed but moderated scholarly e-print submissions), Mathworld mathworld.wolfram.com (encyclopedia),
- Medicine: *BioMed Central* www.biomedcentral.com (journals)
- Music: *Online Resources for Music Scholars* hcl.harvard.edu/research/guides/music/resources/index.html (gateway to music resources on the web)
- Philosophy: *Stanford Encyclopedia of Philosophy* plato.stanford.edu
- Physics: *arXiv.org* arxiv.org/ (non-peer-reviewed but moderated scholarly e-print submissions), *World of Physics* http://scienceworld.wolfram.com/physics
- Political Science: *Intute: Politics* www.intute.ac.uk/politics/ (web resources), *THOMAS* http://thomas.loc.gov (U.S. government documents)
- Psychology: *Intute: Psychology* www.intute.ac.uk/psychology/ (web resources)
- Religion: *Religion Online* http://www.religion-online.org/ (articles and book chapters), *Hartford Institute forReligion Research* www.hartfordinstitute.org (surveys and statistics)
- Sociology: *Intute: Sociology* www.intute.ac.uk/sociology (web resources)

Step 4: search the web using these selective search engines:

- *Intute* www.intute.ac.uk/

Intute is arguably the most academically oriented of all the search engines. The creators of *Intute* have carefully screened and summarized websites for inclusion.

- *ipl2* www.ipl.org/

ipl2 contains a lower percentage of academic websites than *Intute*.

B. Plagiarism and The Logic of Citation

It is impossible to discuss the rationale for citing sources without reference to plagiarism, even though the primary reason for including citations is not to prove that you haven't cheated. It's essential that you give credit where it's due as a courtesy to your readers. Along with educating readers about who has said what, citations enable them to find out more about a given position and to pursue other discussions on the subject. Nonetheless, plagiarism is an important issue: academic integrity matters. And because the stakes are very high if you are caught plagiarizing, we will now offer some guidelines on how to avoid it.

In recent years, there has been a significant rise in the number of plagiarism cases nationally. Many commentators blame the Internet, with its easily accessible, easy to cut-and-paste information, for increasing the likelihood of plagiarism. Others cite a lack of clarity about what plagiarism is and why it is a serious problem. So, let's start by clarifying.

Most people have some idea of what plagiarism is. You already know that it's against the rules to buy a paper from an Internet "paper mill" or to download others' words verbatim and hand them in as your own thinking. And you probably know that even if you change a few words and rearrange the sentence structure, you still need to acknowledge the source. Plagiarism gives the impression that you have written or thought something you have in fact borrowed from someone else. It is a form of theft and fraud. Borrowing from someone else, by the way, also includes taking and not acknowledging words and ideas from your friends or your parents. Put another way, any assignment with your name on it signifies that you are the author—that the words and ideas are yours—with any exceptions indicated by source citations and, if you're quoting, by quotation marks.

Knowing what plagiarism is, however, doesn't guarantee that you'll know how to avoid it. Is it okay, for example, to cobble together a series of summaries and paraphrases in a paragraph, provided you include the authors in a bibliography at the end of the paper? Or how about if you insert a single footnote at the end of the paragraph? The answer is that both are still plagiarism because your reader can't tell where your thinking starts and others' thinking stops. As a basic rule of thumb, readers must be able to distinguish your contribution from that of your sources, and exactly which information came from which source.

WHY DOES PLAGIARISM MATTER?

A recent survey indicated that 53 percent of Who's Who High Schoolers thought that plagiarism was no big deal (Sally Cole and Elizabeth Kiss, "What Can We Do About Student Cheating?" *About Campus*, May–June 2000, p. 6). So why should institutions of higher learning care about it? Here are two great reasons:

- Plagiarism poisons the environment. Students who don't cheat are alienated by students who do and get away with it, and faculty can become distrustful of students and even disillusioned about teaching when constantly driven to track down students' sources. It's a lot easier, by the way, than most students think for faculty to recognize language and ideas that are not the student's own. And now there are all those search engines provided by firms like Turnitin.com that have been generated in response to the Internet paper-mill boom. Who wants another cold war?

- Plagiarism defeats the purpose of going to college, which is learning how to think. You can't learn to think by just copying others' ideas; you need to learn to trust your own intelligence. Students' panic about deadlines and their misunderstandings about assignments sometimes spur plagiarism. It's a good bet that your professors would much rather take requests for help and give extra time on assignments than have to go through the anguish of confronting students about plagiarized work.

So, plagiarism gets in the way of trust, fairness, intellectual development, and, ultimately, the attitude toward learning that sets the tone for a college or university community.

FREQUENTLY ASKED QUESTIONS (FAQS) ABOUT PLAGIARISM

Is it still plagiarism if I didn't intentionally copy someone else's work and present it as my own; that is, if I plagiarized it by accident?
Yes, it is still plagiarism. Colleges and universities put the burden of responsibility on students for knowing what plagiarism is and then making the effort necessary to avoid it. Leaving out the quotation marks around someone else's words or omitting the attribution after a summary of someone else's theory may be just a mistake—a matter of inadequate documentation—but faculty can only judge what you turn in to them, not what you intended.

If I include a list of works consulted at the end of my paper, doesn't that cover it?
No. A works-cited list (bibliography) tells your readers what you read but leaves them in the dark about how and where this material has been used in your paper. Putting one or more references at the end of a paragraph containing source material is a version of the same problem. The solution is to cite the source at the point that you quote or paraphrase or summarize it. To be even clearer about what comes from where, also use what are called in-text attributions. See the next FAQ on these.

What is the best way to help my readers distinguish between what my sources are saying and what I'm saying?
Be overt. Tell your readers in the text of your paper, not just in citations, when you are drawing on someone else's words, ideas, or information. Do this with phrases like "According to X" or "As noted in X"—called in-text attributions.

Are there some kinds of information that I do not need to document?
Yes. Common knowledge and facts you can find in almost any encyclopedia or basic reference text generally don't need to be documented (such as, John F. Kennedy became president of the United States in 1960). This distinction can get a little tricky because it isn't always obvious what is and is not common knowledge. Often, you need to spend some time in a discipline before you discover what others take to be known to all. When in doubt, cite the source.

If I put the information from my sources into my own words, do I still need to include citations?
Yes. Sorry, but rewording someone else's idea doesn't make it your idea. Paraphrasing is a useful activity because it helps you to better understand what you are reading, but paraphrases and summaries have to be documented and carefully distinguished from ideas and information you are representing as your own.

If I don't actually know anything about the subject, is it okay to hand in a paper that is taken entirely from various sources?
It's okay if (1) you document the borrowings and (2) the assignment called for summary. Properly documented summarizing is better than plagiarizing, but most assignments call for something more. Often comparing and contrasting your sources begins to give you ideas so that you can have something to contribute. If you're really stumped, go see the professor.
    You also reduce the risk of plagiarism if you consult sources after—not before—you have done some preliminary thinking on the subject. If you have become somewhat invested in your own thoughts on the matter, you will be able to use the sources in a more active way, in effect, making them part of a dialogue.

Is it plagiarism if I include things in my paper I thought of with another student or a member of my family?
Most academic behavior codes, under the category called "collusion," allow for students' cooperative efforts only with the explicit consent of the instructor. The same general rule goes for plagiarizing yourself—that is, for submitting the same paper in more than one class. If you have questions about what constitutes collusion in a particular class, be sure to ask your professor.

What about looking at secondary sources when my professor hasn't asked me to? Is this a form of cheating?
It can be a form of cheating if the intent of the assignment was to get you to develop a particular kind of thinking skill. In this case, looking at others' ideas may actually retard your learning process and leave you feeling that you couldn't possibly learn to arrive at ideas on your own.

Professors usually look favorably on students who are willing to take the time to do extra reading on a subject, but it is essential that, even in class discussion, you make it clear that you have consulted outside sources. To conceal that fact is to present others' ideas as your own. Even in class discussion, if you bring up an idea you picked up on the Internet, be sure to say so explicitly.

C. CITING SOURCES: Four Documentation Styles by Reference Librarian Kelly Cannon

The four most common styles of documentation are those established by:

- the *American Psychological Association (APA),*
- the *Council of Science Editors (CSE),*
- the *University Press of Chicago,* and
- the *Modern Language Association (MLA).*

Note: The University of North Carolina at Chapel Hill Libraries offer authoritative examples of basic citations of electronic and print resources in all four styles at http://www.lib.unc.edu/instruct/citations/.

For citation examples not given at the University of North Carolina at Chapel Hill Libraries website, it is advisable to consult the various organizations' printed manuals—*Publication Manual of the American Psychological Association* (6th edition), the *Chicago Manual of Style* (15th edition), *Scientific Style and Format: The CSE Manual for Authors, Editors, and Publishers,* and the *MLA Handbook for Writers of Research Papers* (7th edition). It is important to use the most recent edition available of each of these manuals.

You have probably already discovered that some professors are more concerned than others that students obey the particulars of a given documentation style. Virtually all faculty across the curriculum agree, however, that *the most important rule for writers to follow in documenting sources is formal consistency.* That is, all of your in-text citations or footnotes/endnotes should follow the same format, and all of your end-of-text citations should follow the same format.

Once you begin doing most of your writing in a particular discipline, you may want to purchase or access on the Internet the more detailed style guide adhered to by that discipline. Because documentation styles differ not only from discipline to discipline but also even from journal to journal within a discipline, you should consult your professor about which documentation format he or she wishes you to use in a given course.

THE FOUR DOCUMENTATION STYLES: SIMILARITIES AND DIFFERENCES

The various styles differ in the specific ways that they organize the bibliographical information, but they also share some common characteristics.

1. They place an extended citation for each source, including the author, title, date, and place of publication, at the end of the paper (though in *Chicago*, this end-of-text list is optional when employing footnotes/endnotes: consult with your professor). These end-of-text citations are organized in a list, usually alphabetically.

2. All four styles distinguish among different kinds of sources—providing slightly differing formulas for citing books, articles, encyclopedias, government documents, interviews, and so forth.

3. They all ask for these basic pieces of information to be provided whenever they are known: author, title of larger work along with title of article or chapter as appropriate, date of publication, and publisher or institutional affiliation.

To briefly distinguish the styles:

- the APA style employs the author-date format of parenthetical in-text citation and predominates in the social sciences;
- the *Chicago* style, best known for its use of footnotes or endnotes, is employed in history, the fine arts, and some other humanities disciplines;
- the CSE (aka CBE) style, which employs alternately the citation-sequence system and the name-year system, is commonly used throughout the sciences, especially the natural sciences; and
- the MLA style, which uses the author-page format of parenthetical in-text citation, prevails in the humanities disciplines of language, literature, film, and cultural studies.

Here are a few basic examples of in-text and end-of-text citations in the four most commonly used styles, followed by a brief discussion of the rules that apply.

1. *APA* STYLE

> **In-text citation:** Studies of students' changing attitudes toward the small colleges they attend suggest that their loyalty to the institution declines steadily over a four-year period, whereas their loyalty to individual professors or departments increases "markedly, by as much as twenty-five percent over the last two years" (Brown, 1994, p. 41).

For both books and articles, include the author's last name, followed by a comma, and then the date of publication. If you are quoting or referring to a specific passage, include the page number as well, separated from the date by a comma and the abbreviation "p." (or "pp."), followed by a space. If the author's name has been mentioned in the sentence, include only the date in the parentheses immediately following the author's name.

> **In-text citation:** Brown (1992) documents the decline in students' institutional loyalty.

End-of-text book citation: Tannen, D. (1991). *You just don't understand: Women and men in conversation.* New York: Ballantine Books.

End-of-text journal article citation: Baumeister, R. (1987). How the self became a problem: A psychological review of historical research. *Journal of Personality and Psychology, 52,* 163–176.

End-of-text website citation: Hershey Foods Corporation. (2001, March 15). *2001 Annual Report.* Retrieved from http://www. hersheysannualreport.com/2000/index.htm

End-of-text citation of a journal article retrieved from a website or database: Paivio, A. (1975). Perceptual comparisons through the mind's eye. *Memory & Cognition, 3,* 635-647. doi:10.1037/0278-6133.24.2.225

Note that citations of journal articles retrieved on the web include a DOI, a unique code that allows easy retrieval of the article. The DOI is typically located on the first page of the electronic journal article near the copyright notice. When a DOI is used in your citation, no other retrieval information is needed. Use this format for the DOI in references: doi:xxxxxxx

If no DOI has been assigned to the content, provide the home page URL of the journal or report publisher. If you retrieve an article from a library (subscription) database, in general it is not necessary to include the database information in the citation. Do not include retrieval dates unless the source material has changed over time.

APA style requires an alphabetical list of references (by author's last name, which keys the reference to the in-text citation). This list is located at the end of the paper on a separate page and entitled "References." Regarding manuscript form, the first line of each reference is not indented, but all subsequent lines are indented three spaces.

In alphabetizing the references list, place entries for a single author before entries he or she has co-authored, and arrange multiple entries by a single author by beginning with the earliest work. If there are two or more works by the same author in the same year, designate the second with an "a," the third with a "b," and so forth, directly after the year. For all subsequent entries by an author after the first, substitute three hyphens followed by a period [---.] for his or her name. For articles by two or more authors, use commas to connect the authors, and precede the last one with a comma and an ampersand (&).

The APA style divides individual entries into the following parts: author (using initials only for first and middle names), year of publication (in parentheses), title, and publication data. Each part is separated by a period from the others. Note that only the first letter of the title and subtitle of books is capitalized (although proper nouns would be capitalized as necessary).

Journal citations differ from those for books in a number of small ways. The title of a journal article is neither italicized (nor underlined) nor enclosed in quotation marks, and only the first word in the title and subtitle is capitalized. The name of the journal is italicized (or underlined), however, and the first word and all significant words are capitalized. Also, notice that the volume number (which is separated by a comma from the title of the journal) is italicized (or underlined) to distinguish it from the page reference. Page numbers for the entire article are included, with no "p." or "pp." and are separated by a comma from the preceding volume number. If the journal does not use volume numbers, then p. or pp. is included.

2. *CHICAGO* STYLE

Footnote or endnote citation: The earliest groups to explore that part of the country spent much of their time finding out of the way places to "hide their families and cache their grain."[1]

The raised numeral indicates a footnote at the bottom of the page or an endnote at the conclusion of a chapter. Following is an example of what that note would look like, assuming this is the first note to have appeared in the paper, thus listed as note number one:

Footnote/endnote book citation: 1. Juanita Brooks, *The Mountain Meadows Massacre* (Norman, OK: University of Oklahoma Press), 1991, 154.

Here are some examples of other types of notes, numbered consecutively as if each were appearing in the same paper, in this order:

Footnote/endnote journal article citation: 2. Richard Jackson, "Running Down the Up-Escalator: Regional Inequality in Papua New Guinea," *Australian Geographer* 14 (May 1979): 180.

Footnote/endnote website citation: 3. Baha'i International Community. "The Baha'i Faith." *The Baha'i World*. http://www. bahai.org/article1201.html (accessed July 20, 2010).

Footnote/endnote citation of a journal article retrieved from a website: 4. Linda Belau, "Trauma and the Material Signifier," *Postmodern Culture* 11, no. 2 (2001): par. 6, http://www.iath. virginia.edu/pmc/text-only/issue.101/11.2belau.txt (accessed July 20, 2010).

Footnote/endnote library (subscription) database journal article citation: 5. Ilan Rachun, "The Meaning of 'Revolution' in the English Revolution (1648–1660)," *Journal of the History of Ideas* 56, no. 2, 196, http://www.jstor.org (accessed July 10, 2010).

In addition to footnotes/endnotes, the *Chicago* style recommends but does not require an alphabetical list of references (by author's last name). This list is located at the end of the paper on a separate page and is entitled "Bibliography." Listed below are the same references employed above, formatted for the bibliography:

End-of-text book citation: Brooks, Juanita. *The Mountain Meadows Massacre.* Norman, OK: University of Oklahoma Press, 1991.

End-of-text journal article citation: Jackson, Richard. "Running Down the Up-Escalator: Regional Inequality in Papua New Guinea." *Australian Geographer* 14 (May 1979): 175–84.

End-of-text website citation: Baha'i International Community. "The Baha'i Faith." *The Baha'i World.* http://www.bahai.org/ article1201.html (accessed July 20, 2010).

End-of-text citation of a journal article retrieved from a website: Belau, Linda. "Trauma and the Material Signifier." *Postmodern Culture* 11, no. 2 (2001), http://www.iath.virginia.edu/pmc/text-only/issue.101/11.2belau.txt (accessed July 20, 2010).

End-of-text library (subscription) database journal article citation: Rachun, Ilan. "The Meaning of 'Revolution' in the English Revolution (1648-1660)." *Journal of the History of Ideas* 56, no. 2 (1995):195–215. http://www.jstor.org (accessed July 10, 2010).

Each entry in the bibliography is divided into three parts: author, title, and publication data. Each of these parts is separated by a period from the others. Titles of book-length works are italicized. Journal citations differ slightly: article names go inside quotations, no punctuation follows the titles of journals, and a colon precedes the page numbers when pagination is known.

3A. *CSE* STYLE EMPLOYING NAME-YEAR (AUTHOR-DATE) SYSTEM

In-text citation: Soap works as a cleaning agent because of the distinctiveness of each end of the soap molecule, that is their "opposing tendencies" (McMurry and others 2010, p 768).

For both books and articles, include the author's last name followed by the date of publication. For two authors, include the two last names (Smith and Jones 2009). For more than two authors, as in the case above, employ the phrase "and others." If you are quoting or referring to a specific passage, include the page number as well, separated from the date by a comma and the abbreviation "p" (or "pp") followed by a space. If the author's name has been mentioned in the sentence, include only the date in the parentheses immediately following the author's name wherever it appears in the sentence.

In-text citation: Romero (2008) reviews the transformation of scientific knowledge about the polymer.

End-of-text book citation: McMurry J, Castellion ME, Ballantine DS. 2010. **Fundamentals of general, organic, and biological chemistry.** New York: Prentice Hall.

End-of-text journal article citation: Healy R, Cerio R, Hollingsworth A, Bewley A. 2010. Acquired perforating dermatosis associated with pregnancy. Clin Exp Dermatol 35(6): 621–623.

End-of-text website citation: Hilton-Taylor C, compiler. 2000. 2000 IUCN red list of threatened species [Internet]. Gland, Switzerland and Cambridge, UK: IUCN. [cited 2002 Feb 12]. Available from: http://www.redlist.org/

End-of-text citation of journal article retrieved from a website: Philippi TE, Dixon PM, Taylor BE. 1998. Detecting trends in species composition. Ecol Appl [Internet]. [cited 2010 Feb 12]; 8(2): 300–308. Available from: http://www.esajournals.org/esaonline/?request=get-pdf&file=i1051-0761-008-02-0300.pdf

End-of-text library (subscription) database journal article citation: Kenny G, Yardley J, Brown C, Sigal R, Jay O. 2010. Heat stress in older individuals and patients with common chronic diseases. Can Med Assoc J [Internet]. [cited 2010 June 12]; 182(10): 1053–1060. Available from Health Source: Academic/Nursing Edition: http://0-search.ebscohost.com.library.muhlenberg.edu/login.aspx?direct=true&db=hch&AN=522266 11&site=ehost-live&scope=site. System requirements: Adobe Acrobat. Subscription required for access.

CSE style requires an alphabetical list of references (by author's last name, which keys the reference to the in-text citation). This list is located at the end of the paper on a separate page and is titled "Cited References." Regarding manuscript form, the first line of each reference is not indented, but all subsequent lines are indented three spaces.

In alphabetizing the references list, place entries for a single author before entries that he or she has co-authored, and arrange multiple entries by a single author by beginning with the earliest work.

The *CSE* style divides individual entries into the following parts: author (using initials only for first and middle names), year of publication, title, and publication data. Each part is separated by a period from the others. Note that only the first letter of the title and subtitle of books is capitalized (although proper nouns would be capitalized as necessary).

Journal citations differ from those for books in a number of small ways. The title of a journal article is neither italicized (nor underlined) nor enclosed in quotation marks, and only the first word in the title and subtitle is capitalized. CSE style requires that journal titles be abbreviated in the standard manner used by science researchers, found at ISI Journal Title Abbreviations http://www.efm.leeds.ac.uk/~mark/ISIabbr/. This is followed by a volume number and an issue number if available. Page numbers for the entire article are included, with no "p." or "pp.," and are separated by a colon from the preceding volume or issue number.

3B. *CSE* STYLE EMPLOYING CITATION SEQUENCE SYSTEM

In-text citation: Soap works as a cleaning agent because of the distinctiveness of each end of the soap molecule, that is their "opposing tendencies."[1]

Page numbers are generally not included in this system of CSE, but point to the source generally.

End-of-text book citation: 1. McMurry J, Castellion ME, Ballantine DS. Fundamentals of general, organic, and biological chemistry. New York: Prentice Hall; 2010.

End-of-text journal article citation: 2. Healy R, Cerio R, Hollingsworth A, Bewley A. 2010. Acquired perforating dermatosis associated with pregnancy. Clin Exp Dermatol. 2010; 35(6): 621–623.

End-of-text website citation: 3. Hilton-Taylor C, compiler. 2000 IUCN red list of threatened species [Internet]. Gland, Switzerland and Cambridge, UK: IUCN; 2000 [cited 2002 Feb 12]. Available from: http://www.redlist.org/

End-of-text citation of journal article retrieved from a website: 4. Philippi TE, Dixon PM, Taylor BE. Detecting trends in species composition. Ecol Appl [Internet]. 1998 [cited 2010 Feb 12]; 8(2): 300–308. Available from: http://www.esajournals.org/esaonline/?request=get-pdf&file=i1051-0761-008-02-0300.pdf

End-of-text library (subscription) database journal article citation: 5. Kenny G, Yardley J, Brown C, Sigal R, Jay O. Heat stress in older individuals and patients with common chronic diseases. Can Med Assoc J [Internet]. 2010 [cited 2010 June 12]; 182(10): 1053–1060. Available from Health Source: Academic/Nursing Edition: http://0-search.ebscohost.com.library.muhlenberg.edu/login.aspx?direct=true&db=hch&AN=52226611&site=ehost-live&scope=site. System requirements: Adobe Acrobat. Subscription required for access.

In the CSE style, end-of text citations appear in a list titled "Cited References," and correspond to the superscript numeral appearing in the text, in the order of their introduction in the text.

The *CSE* style in according to this system divides individual entries into the following parts: author (using initials only for first and middle names), title, and publication data. Each part is separated by a period from the others. Note that only the first letter of the title and subtitle of books is capitalized (although proper nouns would be capitalized as necessary).

Journal citations differ from those for books in a number of small ways. The title of a journal article is neither italicized (nor underlined) nor enclosed in quotation marks, and only the first word in the title and subtitle is capitalized. *CSE* style requires that journal titles be abbreviated in the standard manner used by science researchers, found at ISI Journal Title Abbreviations http://www.efm.leeds.ac.uk/˜mark/ISIabbr/. This is followed by a volume number and an issue number if available. Page numbers for the entire article are included, with no "p." or "pp." and are separated by a colon from the preceding volume or issue number.

4. *MLA* STYLE

> **In-text citation:** The influence of Seamus Heaney on younger poets in Northern Ireland has been widely acknowledged, but Patrick Kavanagh's "plain-speaking, pastoral" influence on him is "less recognized" (Smith 74).

"(Smith 74)" indicates the author's last name and the page number on which the cited passage appears. If the author's name had been mentioned in the sentence—had the sentence begun "According to Smith"—you would include only the page number in the citation. Note that there is no abbreviation for "page," that there is no intervening punctuation between name and page, and that the parentheses precede the period or other punctuation. If the sentence ends with a direct quotation, the parentheses come after the quotation marks but still before the closing period. Also note that no punctuation occurs between the last word of the quotation ("recognized") and the closing quotation mark.

> **End-of-text book citation:** Douglas, Ann. *Terrible Honesty: Mongrel Manhattan in the 1920s*. New York: Farrar, Straus, and Giroux, 1995. Print.
>
> **End-of-text journal article citation:** Cressy, David. "Foucault, Stone, Shakespeare and Social History." *English Literary Renaissance* 21 (1991): 121–33. Print.
>
> **End-of-text website citation:** Landow, George, ed. *Contemporary Postcolonial and Postimperial Literature in English*. Brown University, 2002. Web. 25 June 2010.
>
> **End-of-text citation of a journal article retrieved from a website:** Nater, Miguel. "El beso de la Esfinge: La poética de lo sublime en *La amada inmóvil* de Amado Nervo y en los *Nocturnos* de José Asunción Silva." *Romanitas* 1.1 (2006): n. pag. Web. 25 June 2010.
>
> **End-of-text library (subscription) database journal article citation:** Arias, Judith H. "The Devil at Heaven's Door." *Hispanic Review* 61.1 (Winter 1993): n. pag. *Academic Search Premier*. Web. 25 June 2010.

Note that the above citations all indicate a format type (print or web) and the web citations end with the date the researcher accessed the website or database.

MLA style stipulates an alphabetical list of references (by author's last name, which keys the reference to the in-text citation). This list is located at the end of the paper on a separate page and entitled "Works Cited."

Each entry in the Works Cited list is divided into three parts: author, title, and publication data. Each of these parts is separated by a period from the others. Titles of book-length works are italicized, unless your instructor prefers underlining. (Underlining is a means of indicating italics.) Journal citations differ slightly: article names go inside quotations, no punctuation follows the titles of journals, and a colon precedes the page numbers when pagination is known.

D. Integrating Quotations into Your Paper

Writers lose authority and readability when they fail to correctly integrate quotations into their own writing. The following guidelines should help, but keep in mind that not all disciplines encourage (or even permit) writers to include quotations. In those disciplines, such as psychology and the natural sciences, the comments below would then apply to integrating paraphrase or summary.

1. **Acknowledge sources in your text, not just in citations.** When you incorporate material from a source, attribute it to the source explicitly in your text—not just in a citation. In other words, when you introduce the material, *frame* it with a phrase such as "according to Marsh" or "as Gruen argues."

   Although it is not required, you are usually much better off making the attribution overtly, even if you have also cited the source within parentheses or with a footnote at the end of the last sentence quoted, paraphrased, or summarized. If a passage does not contain an attribution, your readers will not know that it comes from a source until they reach the citation at the end. Attributing upfront clearly distinguishes what one source says from what another says and, perhaps more important, what your sources say from what you say. Useful verbs for introducing attributions include the following: notes, observes, argues, comments, writes, says, reports, suggests, and claims. Generally speaking, by the way, you should cite the author by last name only—as "Gruen," not as "William Gruen" or "Mr. Gruen."

2. **Splice quotations onto your own words.** Always attach quotations to some of your own language; don't let them sit in your text as independent sentences with quotation marks around them. You can normally satisfy this rule with an attributive phrase—commonly known as a tag phrase—that introduces the quotation.

   According to Paul McCartney, "All you need is love."

   Note that the tag phrase takes a comma before the quote.
   Alternatively, you can splice quotations into your text with a setup: a statement followed by a colon.

> Patrick Henry's famous phrase is one of the first that American schoolchildren memorize: "Give me liberty, or give me death."

The colon, you should notice, usually comes at the end of an independent clause (that is, a subject plus verb that can stand alone), at the spot where a period normally goes. It would be incorrect to write "Patrick Henry is known for: 'Give me liberty, or give me death.'"

The rationale for this guideline is essentially the same as that for the previous one: if you are going to move to quotation, you first need to identify its author so that your readers will be able to put it in context quickly.

Spliced quotations frequently create problems in grammar or punctuation for writers. Whether you include an entire sentence (or passage) of quotation or just a few phrases, you need to take care to integrate them into the grammar of your own sentence.

One of the most common mistaken assumptions is that a comma should always precede a quotation, as in "A spokesperson for the public defender's office demanded, 'an immediate response from the mayor.'" The sentence structure does not call for any punctuation after "demanded."

3. **Cite sources after quotations.** In MLA style, locate citations in parentheses after the quotation and before the final period. This information appears at the end of the sentence, with the final period following the closing parenthesis.

> A recent article on the best selling albums in America claimed that "Ever since Elvis, it has been pop music's job to challenge the mores of the older generation" (Hornby 168).

Note that in MLA style there is normally *no punctuation* at the end of the quotation itself, either before or after the closing quotation mark. A quotation that ends either in a question mark or an exclamation mark is an exception to this rule because the sign is an integral part of the quotation's meaning.

> As Hamlet says to Rosencrantz and Guildenstern, "And yet to me what is this quintessence of dust?" (2.2.304–05).

See the section entitled "How to Cite Sources" earlier in this chapter for the appropriate formats for in-text citations in various documentation styles.

4. **Use ellipses to shorten quotations.** Add ellipses to indicate that you have omitted some of the language from within the quotation. Form ellipses by entering three dots (periods) with spaces in between them, or use four dots to indicate that the deletion continues to the end of the sentence (the last dot becomes the period). Suppose you wanted to shorten the following quotation from a recent article about Radiohead by Alex Ross:

> The album "OK Computer," with titles like "Paranoid Android," "Karma Police," and "Climbing Up the Walls," pictured the onslaught of the information age and a young person's panicky embrace of it (Ross 85).

Using ellipses, you could emphasize the source's claim by omitting the song titles from the middle of the sentence:

> The album "OK Computer" … pictured the onslaught of the information age and a young person's panicky embrace of it (Ross 85).

In most cases, the gap between quoted passages should be short, and in any case, you should be careful to preserve the sense of the original. The standard joke about ellipses is helpful here: A reviewer writes that a film "will delight no one and appeal to the intelligence of invertebrates only, but not average viewers." An unethical advertiser cobbles together pieces of the review to say that the film "will delight … and appeal to the intelligence of … viewers."

5. **Use square brackets to alter or add information within a quotation.** Sometimes it is necessary to change the wording slightly inside a quotation to maintain fluency. Square brackets indicate that you are altering the original quotation. Brackets are also used when you insert explanatory information, such as a definition or example, within a quotation. Here are a few examples that alter the original quotations previously cited.

> According to one music critic, the cultural relevance of Radiohead is evident in "the album 'OK Computer' … [which] pictured the onslaught of the information age and a young person's panicky embrace of it" (Ross 85).

> Popular music has always "[challenged] the mores of the older generation," according to Nick Hornby (168).

Note that both examples respect the original sense of the quotation; they have changed the wording only to integrate the quotations gracefully within the writer's own sentence structure.

E. Preparing an Abstract

There is one more skill essential to research-based writing that we need to discuss: how to prepare an abstract. The aim of the nonevaluative summary of a source known as an abstract is to represent a source's arguments as fairly and accurately as possible, not to critique them. Learning how to compose an abstract according to the conventions of a given discipline is a necessary skill for academic researched writing. Because abstracts differ in format and length among disciplines, you should sample some in the reference section of your library or via the Internet to provide you with models to imitate. Some abstracts, such as those in *Dissertation Abstracts,* are very brief—less than 250 words. Others may run as long as two pages.

Despite disciplinary differences, abstracts by and large follow a generalizable format. The abstract should begin with a clear and specific explanation of the work's governing thesis (or argument). In this opening paragraph, you should also define the work's purpose, and possibly include established positions that it tries to refine, qualify, or argue against. What kind of critical approach does it adopt? What are its aims? On what assumptions does it rest? Why did the author feel it necessary to write the work—that is, what does he or she believe the work offers that other sources don't? What shortcomings or misrepresentations in other criticism does the work seek to correct? *(For specifics on writing abstracts in the Natural Sciences, see Chapter 16, Introductions and Conclusions Across the Curriculum.)*

You won't be able to produce detailed answers to all of these questions in your opening paragraph, but in trying to answer some of them in your note-taking and drafting, you should find it easier to arrive at the kind of concise, substantive, and focused overview that the first paragraph of your abstract should provide. Also, be careful not to settle for bland, all-purpose generalities in this opening paragraph. And if you quote there, keep the selections short, and remember that quotations don't speak for themselves.

In summary, your aim in the first paragraph is to define the source's particular angle of vision and articulate its main point or points, including the definition of key terms used in its title or elsewhere in its argument.

Once you've set up this overview of the source's central position(s), you should devote a paragraph or so to the source's *organization* (how it divides its subject into parts) and its *method* (how it goes about substantiating its argument). What kind of secondary material does the source use? That is, how do its own bibliographic citations cue you to its school of thought, its point of view, its research traditions?

Your concluding paragraph should briefly recount some of the source's conclusions (as related to, but not necessarily the same as, its thesis). In what way does it go about culminating its argument? What kind of significance does it claim for its position? What final qualifications does it raise? The following model is a good example of an abstract:

Abstract of "William Carlos Williams," *An Essay*

By Christopher MacGowan in The Columbia History of American Poetry, pp. 395–418, Columbia University Press, 1993.

MacGowan's is a chronologically organized account of Williams' poetic career and of his relation to both modernism as an international movement and modernism as it affected the development of poetry in America. MacGowan is at some pains both to differentiate Williams from some features of modernism (such as the tendency of American writers to write as well as live away from their own cultural roots) and to link Williams to modernism. MacGowan argues, for example, that an essential feature of Williams's commitment as a poet was to "the local—to the clear presentation of what was under his nose and in front of his eyes" (385).

But he also takes care to remind us that Williams was in no way narrowly provincial, having studied in Europe as a young man (at Leipzig), having had a Spanish mother and an English father, having become friendly with the poets Ezra Pound and H. D. while getting his medical degree at the University of Pennsylvania, and having continued to meet important figures in the literary and art worlds by making frequent visits to New York and by traveling on more than one occasion to Europe (where Pound introduced him to W. B. Yeats, among others). Williams corresponded with Marianne Moore, he continued to write to Pound and to show Pound some of his work, and he wrote critical essays on the works of other modernists. MacGowan reminds us that Williams also translated Spanish works (ballads) and so was not out of contact with European influences.

Williams had a long publishing career—beginning in 1909 with a self-published volume called *Poems* and ending more than fifty years later with *Pictures from Brueghel* in 1962. What MacGowan emphasizes about this career is not only the consistently high quality of work, but also its great influence on other artists (he names those who actually corresponded with Williams and visited with him, including Charles Olson, Robert Creeley, Robert Lowell, Allen Ginsberg, and Denise Levertov). MacGowan observes that Williams defined himself "against" T. S. Eliot—the more rewarded and internationally recognized of the two poets, especially during their lifetimes—searching for "alternatives to the prevailing mode of a complex, highly allusive poetics," which Williams saw as Eliot's legacy (395). MacGowan depicts Williams as setting himself "against the international school of Eliot and Pound—Americans he felt wrote about rootlessness and searched an alien past because of their failure to write about and live within their own culture" (397).

GUIDELINES FOR FINDING, CITING, AND INTEGRATING SOURCES

1. Examine bibliographies at the end of the articles and books you've already found. Remember that one quality source can, in its bibliography, point to many other resources.

2. Citing sources isn't just about acknowledging intellectual or informational debts; it's also a courtesy to your readers, directing them how to find out more about the subjected cited.

3. Before you settle in with one author's book-length argument, use indexes and bibliographies and other resources to achieve a broader view.

4. URLs with domain names ending in .edu and .gov usually offer more reliable choices than the standard .com.

5. When professors direct you to do bibliographic research, they usually are refer- ring to research done with indexes; these are available in print, online, and CD-ROM formats.

6. In evaluating a website about which you don't know much, try "backspacing" a URL to trace back to its authorship or institutional affiliation.

7. Tell your readers in the text of your paper, not just in citations, when you are using someone else's words, ideas, or information; rewording someone else's idea doesn't make it your idea.

8. Always attach a quotation to some of your own language; never let it stand as its own sentence in your text. Attribution—"According to Walden"—before the quote fulfills this function nicely.

Assignments: A Research Sequence

The traditional sequence of steps for building a research paper—or for any writ- ing that relies on secondary materials—is *summary, comparative analysis, and synthesis.* The following sequence of four exercises addresses the first two steps as discrete activities. (You might, of course, choose to do only some of these exercises.)

1. **Compose an Informal Prospectus.** Formulate your initial thinking on a subject before you do more research. Include what you already know about the topic, especially what you find interesting, particularly signifi- cant, or strange. This exercise helps deter you from being overwhelmed by and absorbed into the sources you later encounter.

2. **Conduct a "What's Going on in the Field" Search, and Create a Preliminary List of Sources.** This exercise is ideal for helping you to find a topic or, if you already have one, to narrow it. The kinds of bibliographic materials you consult for this portion of the research project depend on the discipline within which you are writing. Whatever the discipline, start in the reference room of your library with specialized indexes (such as the *Social Sciences Index* or the *New York Times Index*), book review indexes, specialized encyclopedias and dictionaries, and bibliographies (print ver- sion or CD-ROM) that give you an overview of your subject or topic. If you have access to databases through your school or library, you should also search them. (See the section in this chapter entitled Electronic Research: Finding Quality on the Web.)

   The "what's going on in the field" search has two aims:

   1. to survey materials to identify trends—the kinds of issues and questions that others in the field are talking about (and, thus, find important)

   2. to compile a bibliography that includes a range of titles that interest you, that could be relevant to your prospective topic, and that seem to you representative of research trends associated with your subject (or topic)

You are not committed at this point to pursuing all of these sources but rather to reporting what is being talked about. You might also compose a list of keywords (such as Library of Congress headings) that you have used in conducting your search. If you try this exercise, you will be surprised how much value there is in exploring indexes *just for titles,* to see the kinds of topics people are currently conversing about. And you will almost surely discover how *narrowly* focused most research is (which will get you away from global questions).

Append to your list of sources (a very preliminary bibliography) a few paragraphs of informal discussion of how the information you have encountered (the titles, summaries, abstracts, etc.) has affected your thinking and plans for your paper. These paragraphs might respond to the following questions:

a. In what ways has your "what's going on in the field" search led you to narrow or shift direction in or focus your thinking about your subject?

b. How might you use one or more of these sources in your paper?

c. What has this phase of your research suggested you might need to look for next?

3. **Write an Abstract of an Article (or Book Chapter).** Use the procedure offered in the preceding section, "How to Prepare an Abstract." Aim for two pages in length. If other members of your class are working on the same or similar subjects, it is often extremely useful for everyone to share copies of their abstracts. Remember, your primary concern should lie with representing the argument and point of view of the source as fairly and accurately as possible.

Append to the end of the abstract a paragraph or two that addresses the question, "How has this exercise affected your thinking about your topic?" Objectifying your own research process in this way helps move you away from the cut-and-paste–provide-only-the-transitions mode of writing research papers.

4. **Write a Comparative Summary.** Choose two reviews of a single source. Most writers, before they invest the significant time and energy required to study a book-length source, take the much smaller amount of time and energy required to find out more about the book. Although you should always include in your final paper your own analytical summary of books you consult on your topic, it's extremely useful also to find out what experts in the field have to say about the source.

Select from your "what's going on" list one book-length source that you've discovered is vital to your subject or topic. As a general rule, if a number of your indexes, bibliographies, and so forth, refer you to the same book, it's a good bet that this source merits consultation.

Locate two book reviews on the book, and write a summary that compares the two reviews. Ideally, you should locate two reviews that diverge in their points of view or in what they choose to emphasize. Depending on the length and complexity of the reviews, your comparative summary should require two or three pages.

In most cases, you will find that reviews are less neutral in their points of view than are abstracts, but they always do more than simply judge. A good review, like a good abstract, should communicate the essential ideas contained in the source. It is the reviewer's aim also to locate the source in some larger context, by, for example, comparing it to other works on the same subject and to the research tradition the book seeks to extend, modify, and so forth. Thus, your summary should try to encompass how the book contributes to the ongoing conversation on a given topic in the field.

Append to your comparative summary a paragraph or two that explains how this exercise has affected your thinking about your topic.

Obviously, you could choose to do a comparative summary of two articles, two book chapters, and so forth, rather than two book reviews. But in any event, if you use books in your research, you should always find a means of determining how these books are received in the relevant critical community.

The next step, if you were writing a research paper, would involve the task known as *synthesis,* in which you essentially write a comparative discussion that includes more than two sources. Many research papers start with an opening paragraph that synthesizes prevailing, perhaps competing, interpretations of the topic being addressed. Few good research papers consist only of such synthesis, however. Instead, writers use synthesis to frame their ideas and to provide perspective on their own arguments; the synthesis provides a platform or foundation for their own subsequent analysis.

It is probably worth adding that bad research papers fail to use synthesis as a point of departure. Instead, they line up their sources and agree or disagree with them. To inoculate you against this unfortunate reflex, review the section in Chapter 13 entitled Six Strategies for Analyzing Sources, especially Strategy 6: Find Your Own Role in the Conversation.

UNIT III

MATTERS OF FORM:
THE SHAPES
THAT THOUGHT TAKES

Chapter 15

Forms and Formats Across the Curriculum

THIS IS A CHAPTER ABOUT ORGANIZATION—the forms and formats writers use to structure their ideas. The first section of the chapter concentrates on *disciplinary formats*—the prescribed structures for finished papers in the academic disciplines. The best way to learn these formats is from professors in specific disciplines, but this book can teach you what these look like, their purpose, and more generally, how to analyze them so you can better understand what they do.

The rest of the chapter will then broaden the focus from specific disciplinary formats to more general matters of form:

- ways of grasping the overall shape of a paper
- how and where to locate the thesis
- how and where to use transitions
- ways of organizing paragraphs

Overall, the chapter seeks to increase your **rhetorical awareness**, that is, your awareness of how an audience's attitudes and needs can affect the shape of your writing.

It's important to recognize that all organizational schemes are conventional—which is to say, they are agreed-upon protocols with social functions. They show you how to write in a way that will allow you to be heard by others in a particular discourse community, such as an academic discipline. But it's also important to recognize that these protocols embody ways of thinking that help people to arrive at ideas. Formats are not just containers for information; they are tools of invention. They show you the accepted ways of finding things out in a discipline.

A. Disciplinary Forms and Formats

Two Functions of Formats: Rhetorical and Heuristic

- Rhetorical: formats make communication among members of a discipline easier and more efficient.
- Heuristic: formats offer writers a means of finding and exploring ideas.

THE TWO FUNCTIONS OF DISCIPLINARY FORMATS

Most of the writing (and thinking) we do is generated by some kind of format, even if we are not aware of it. Writers virtually never write in the absence of conventions. Accordingly, you should not regard the formats you encounter simply as *prescriptive* (that is, strictly required) sets of artificial rules. Rather, try to think of them as descriptive accounts of the various *heuristics*—sets of questions and categories—that humans typically use to guide and stimulate their thinking.

Because formats offer a means not only of displaying thinking in a discipline but also of shaping it, the format a discipline requires (whether tacitly or overtly) conditions its members to think in particular ways. Learning to use the format that scientists use predisposes you to think like a scientist. Although knowing the required steps of a discipline's writing format won't write your papers for you, not knowing how writers in that discipline characteristically proceed can keep you from being read.

Academic disciplines differ in the extent to which they adhere to prescribed organizational schemes. In biology and psychology, for example, formal papers and reports generally follow an explicitly prescribed pattern of presentation. Some other disciplines are less uniform and less explicit about their reliance on formats, but writers in these fields—economics, for example, or history—usually operate within fairly established forms as well. Thus, we also use the term "format" for organizational schemes that lay out the form of prospective papers in a series of steps.

The writing strategies and heuristics in this book are formats in the sense that most prescribe a series of steps. Our emphasis rests more on the process of invention than it does on the organization of the finished paper, but, as we have been suggesting, the two are not really separate. See, for example, "A Template for Organizing Papers Using 10 on 1: An Alternative to 5-Paragraph Form" (end of Chapter 10) and "Six Steps for Making a Thesis Evolve Through Successive Complications" (Chapter 11). The book's heuristics can be used as organizational models and can be adapted to disciplinary forms. They are especially useful in the many disciplines that do not prescribe a specific format.

USING FORMATS HEURISTICALLY: AN EXAMPLE

To lose sight of the heuristic value of formats is to become preoccupied with formats merely as disciplinary etiquette. The solution to this problem probably sounds easier than it is: you need to find the spaces in a format that will allow it to work as a heuristic. Consider how you might go about using even a highly specified organizational scheme like the following:

1. State the problem.
2. Develop criteria of adequacy for a solution.
3. Explore at least two inadequate solutions.
4. Explicate the proposed solution.
5. Evaluate the proposed solution.
6. Reply to anticipated criticisms.

The best reason not to ignore any of the six steps in this problem/solution format is that the format does have a logic, although it leaves that logic unstated. The purpose of including at least two inadequate solutions (step 3), for example, is to protect the writer against moving to a conclusion too quickly on the basis of too little evidence. The requirements that the writer evaluate the solution and reply to criticisms (steps 5 and 6) press the writer toward complexity, preventing a one-sided and uncritical answer. In short, heuristic value in the format is there for a writer to use if he or she doesn't allow a premature concern with matters of form to take precedence over thinking. It would be a mistake, in other words, to assume that one must move through the six steps consecutively; the writer would only need to arrange his or her thinking in that order when putting together the final product.

FORMS AND FORMATS ACROSS THE CURRICULUM: SOME COMMON ELEMENTS

As you read this chapter's discussion of differences among disciplinary formats, also look for features they share. Differences in surface features—sentence style, organization—tend to obscure the fact that a common underlying structure and set of aims unites most kinds of academic writing across the curriculum.

You can train yourself to start seeing this underlying structure by first recognizing that academic writing in all disciplines is **problem-oriented**, which is to say that academic writing typically starts by noting something that is missing from previous writing and research. As you will see, disciplines differ in how overtly writers may single out problems in other writers' thinking. And yet, in one way or another, most academic writing begins by locating something that needs to be done—why there is a need for more study—and why this new work might matter. The introductory sections of most kinds of academic writing tell readers what the writer found interesting, worth pursuing, and why.

Science Format (IMRAD) Compared with Other Academic Formats

Here is a quick overview of the organizational scheme prescribed in the natural sciences and for some kinds of papers in the social sciences, such as reports on research in psychology and political science. Although not all writing in these disciplines follows this format, most does—especially lab reports and articles based on the experimental method and quantitative research. The structure is commonly referred to as IMRAD:

I   introduction

M   methods

R   results

A

D   discussion

You can think of this format as two descriptions of the research (methods and results) framed by two sections (introduction and discussion) that locate it in the context of existing knowledge in the field. The introduction locates the new work in terms of what has already been done (which points to what still needs to be done). The discussion section considers how knowledge in the field might be changed by addition of the new results. (See LabWrite Program sponsored by NSF at www.ncsu.edu/labwrite. Also see advice from the Council of Science Editors—CSE.)

The IMRAD format, which we will define in more detail in a moment, lays out a sequence that you can locate as the underlying structure of much academic writing. Here is a restatement of the format that makes the common denominators easier to recognize.

The Common Format of Academic Writing

1. Begin with some kind of problem or question or uncertainty. Say why the new study might matter, why it needs doing. Offer a theory to be tested (working thesis/hypothesis).
2. Test the adequacy of the theory by conducting some kind of experimental procedure or other way of analyzing evidence.
3. Report resulting data—what was revealed by the experiment or other analytical method such as close reading of textual evidence or statistical analysis.
4. Interpret the results and draw conclusions about their significance. How might the results change current thinking and/or open the way to new questions and further study?

If you are just learning to write and think in an academic discipline, you cannot be expected to offer in the opening paragraph the state of knowledge in the field on a particular question. Nor can you be expected to arrive at something that will alter thinking in a discipline—although sometimes this does in fact happen. Nevertheless, college writers and their teachers across the curriculum write with similar goals: *ask and answer a new question, offer alternatives to existing ideas or evidence, or provide a new perspective or better evidence on something already known.*

Writing in the Sciences: A Biochemistry Professor Speaks

The following Voice from Across the Curriculum is taken from a presentation that biochemistry professor Keri Colabroy delivered to a group of undergraduate writing tutors at our college. The talk aimed at enabling the tutors, many of whom are not science majors, to work more confidently with writing that science students bring to the college's Writing Center. We are grateful to Professor Colabroy for making her material available to us and to the tutors we train. You will find more of this material in the next chapter, Introductions and Conclusions Across the Curriculum.

Voices From Across the Curriculum

The lab report as taught in college science courses teaches students to mimic the process of thinking required to write a scientific paper. The governing question of the lab report is, "To what extent is my data consistent with what I was supposed to get?" Like most scientific writing, the lab report has four parts (five if you include the abstract):

The Parts of Lab Reports and Scientific Papers

Abstract
The short synoptic version of essentially the entire paper: What you did, what you found and how you did it

Introduction/Purpose/Objective
What you are trying to accomplish and why it is important

Methods/Experimental Procedures
The details of how you performed the experiments

Results/Data
Reporting of the data without commentary, often done with tables, graphs and figures rather than text

Primarily summative and descriptive, like a Notice and Focus exercise without the implications (See *Writing Analytically,* Chapter 2)

Discussion/Conclusions
This is where the analysis happens. Cite the data, then make qualified, evidence-based claims from the data; draw implications.

In the written accounts of scientific experiments, some information is repeated across sections. This repetition is deliberate. No scientist reads a paper in order, and so every section has to stand by itself.

In scientific papers, introductions serve two purposes:

(1) to orient your readers to the scientific context of your work while showing them the inherent need for new (your) information to solve an *uncertainty* or *problem*, something you or the community doesn't quite understand (in *Writing Analytically,* the prompts "interesting, significant or strange" focus writers on problems and areas of uncertainty); and

(2) to state succinctly what the paper/study has accomplished and what that means for the big picture you outlined in point #1.

The introduction of a scientific paper is full of references to primary literature (other scientific papers). In most undergraduate science courses, students are not asked to write the introduction section. Instead, the professor provides a paraphrase of the question/problem that the experiment is meant to solve.

It is not until the discussion section that the science writer analyzes the data. The discussion section is not a summary; rather, the writer makes qualified claims and backs them up with evidence. The discussion section completes the frame set up by the introduction by arguing for the significance of the study within its scientific context. A discussion section concludes by looking backwards to summarize implications, then looking forward to articulate what this particular study means for the whole field.

The conclusion explains how questions have been answered and how knowledge in the field might be changed because of the new information.

Word choice in scientific papers—especially the choice of verbs—is important. Scientific writing never "proves," for example. It "implies" and "indicates." The science writer chooses verbs to make carefully qualified claims based on an accumulation of evidence.

Scientific writing is corporate, by which I mean that scientific writers speak to and about the community of other science writers. To name a particular scientist is considered pretentious. It is appropriate to point out inconsistencies in thinking as in, "a lot of work has been done here, but we still don't understand X." It is not considered appropriate to locate shortcomings in the work of particular scientists.

—Keri Colabroy, Professor of Biochemistry

How to Write—and Read—Scientific Formats: Three Professors Speak

Note that the observations in the following Voices from Across the Curriculum apply to much but certainly not all of the writing that goes on in the sciences. Writing in physics, for example, where research is more theoretical, often takes a different form. There are other exceptions. Writing in psychology can appear in the form of the case study rather than in reports on experiments.

It is necessary, a biology professor asserts, to recognize the need for flexibility when using the scientific format. Although the format has a clear defining logic, the distinctions among the various parts are not always as clear-cut as some students may think they are. (*For examples of science writing, see Chapter 16, Introductions and Conclusions Across the Curriculum.*)

Voices From Across the Curriculum

In writing in the social sciences, there is a standard plot with three alternative endings. The "Introduction" (a standard section of APA style) sets forth the problem, which the "Methods" section promises to address. The "Results" section "factually" reports the outcome of the study, with the "Discussion" section interpreting the results. "The data" are given the starring role in determining which ending is discussed in the "Discussion" section: hypothesis confirmed, hypothesis rejected, or hard to say. (I would say "which ending the author chooses" versus "which ending is discussed," but the data are supposed to be determinative, and the role of the author/investigator neutral.) Analytical thinking comes in setting up the problem and making sense of the results in conjunction with existing literature on the subject.

—Alan Tjeltveit, Professor of Psychology

○ Experimental Psychology uses a very rigid format. I explain to the students the functions of the different sections for the reader. Once students start to read journal articles themselves, the functions of the sections become clear. Readers do not always want to read or reread the whole article. If I want to replicate someone's research, I may read just the "Methods" section to get the technical details I need. I may read just the "Results" section to get a sense of the numerical results I might expect. On the other hand, I may not care about the details of how the experiment was run. I might just want to know if it worked, in which case I would read the first few sentences of the "Discussion" section. The format lets me know exactly where to find whatever I might be looking for, without having to read through the whole article.

—Laura Edelman, Professor of Psychology

○ Scientific format appears highly formulaic at first glance. Papers are generally broken into four sections: "Introduction" (What is this all about, what do we already know, why do we care?), "Experimental Procedures" (What did you actually do?), "Results" (What happened in your experiments?), and "Discussion" (What do you think it means, what are the remaining questions?). This breakdown is useful because it emphasizes the process of argument (introduction and results), providing evidence (results), and analysis (discussion). However, although this may seem different from writing in other disciplines, I think of it as a codification of basic analytical writing that is common in most disciplines.

A common mistake made by beginning and intermediate students is taking this breakdown too literally. In order to be comprehensible, the rules must be broken periodically. For example, results frequently must be referred to in the "Experimental Procedures" section in order to understand *why* the next procedure was performed. Similarly, the "Results" section frequently must include some discussion, so that the reader understands the immediate significance of the results, if not the broader implications. For example, the following sentences might appear in a "Results" section: "These data suggest that the p53 protein may function in repressing cell division in potential cancer cells. In order to test this possibility, we overexpressed p53 protein in a transformed cell line." The first sentence provides an interpretation of the results that is necessary to understand why the next experiment was performed.

—Bruce Wightman, Professor of Biology

B. The Shaping Force of Common Thought Patterns

DEDUCTION AND INDUCTION

According to the usual definitions of the terms deduction and induction, you might expect that a fairly full-fledged version of the thesis would appear at the beginning of a deductive paper but at the end of an inductive one. But as we will go on to show, papers don't neatly fit these two abstract models of thinking. In practice, all writing combines the two patterns. In virtually all essays, the paper

(A) Deduction

(B) Induction

(C) Blend: Induction to Deduction

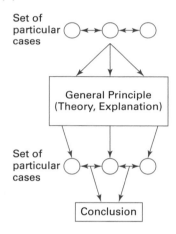

(D) Blend: Deduction to Induction

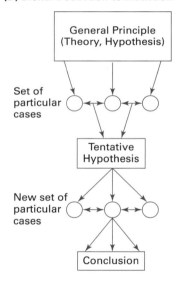

FIGURE 15.1

Deduction and Induction. Deduction (A) uses particular cases to exemplify general principles and analyze their implications. Induction (B) constructs general principles from the analysis of particular cases. In practice, analytical thinking and writing blend deduction and induction and start either with particular cases (C) or a general principle (D).

begins with some kind of organizing claim; this is not delayed until the end. And in virtually all essays, the opening claim is not simply repeated at the end but occurs there in its duly tested and evolved form. To clarify these claims we need to offer some definitions. (See Figure 15.1, A and B).

Deduction

As a thought process, deduction reasons from a general principle (assumed to be true) to the particular case. It introduces this principle up front and then uses it to select and interpret evidence. For example, a deductive paper might state in its first paragraph that attitudes toward and rules governing sexuality in a given culture can be seen, at least in part, to have economic causes. The paper might then apply this principle, already assumed to be true, to the codes governing sexual behavior in several cultures or several kinds of sexual behavior in a single culture.

A good deductive argument is, however, more than a mechanical application or matching exercise of general claim and specific details that are explained by it. Deductive reasoning uses the evidence to draw out the implications—what logicians term *inferring the consequences*—of the claim. The general principle explains selected features of particular cases, and *reciprocally,* the evidence brings out implications in the principle.

Thus, the general principle stated at the beginning of the paper and the idea stated as the paper's conclusion are not the same. Rather, the conclusion presents the (evolved) idea that the writer has arrived at through the application of the principle.

Induction

An inductively organized paper typically begins not with a principle already accepted as true but with particular data for which it seeks to generate some explanatory principle. Whereas deduction moves by applying a generalization to particular cases, induction moves from the observation of individual cases to the formation of a general principle. Because all possible cases can obviously never be examined— every left-handed person, for example, if one wishes to theorize that left-handed people are better at spatial thinking than right-handers—the principle (or thesis) arrived at through inductive reasoning always remains open to doubt.

Nevertheless, the thesis of an inductive paper is generally deemed acceptable if a writer can demonstrate that the theory is based on a reasonably sized sampling of representative instances. Suffice it to say that a child who arrives at the thesis that all orange food tastes bad on the basis of squash and carrots has not based that theory on an adequate sampling of available evidence.

The Overlap

In most cases, induction and deduction operate in tandem (see Figure 15.1, C and D). Analysis by nature moves between the particular and the general, regardless of which comes first. Whether the overall shape of the analysis—its mode of progression—is primarily inductive or deductive, it will still gain in complexity from beginning to end as it confronts evidence.

It's true that in some disciplines (philosophy, for example) the deductive pattern of argument prevails, but not exclusively. The analysis of evidence, though clearly designed to reflect a general principle, will also lead to new formulations that will modify the general principle in various ways.

THESIS SLOTS

Even in the most inductive forms of essay development, readers are guided by various formulations of the thesis. Here is a short list of the places in an essay that readers typically expect some version of the thesis to occur:

- The first articulation of the working thesis usually occurs late in the opening paragraph or early in the second paragraph of a piece. This first articulation comes after the writer has presented the problem or question that establishes the tension the thesis aims to resolve, and after he or she has provided some kind of context for it.

- Subsequent articulations of the thesis usually occur at points of transition, typically at paragraph openings following the analysis of complicating evidence. This kind of updating has the added benefit of providing unity to the essay, using the thesis as a kind of spine.

- The final statement of the thesis occurs in the concluding paragraph, or perhaps the next to last one. It is usually offered in clear relationship to the terms offered in the introduction, so the reader is offered a last vision of where the essay has traveled.

THE SHAPING FORCE OF THESIS STATEMENTS

A sentence is the shape that thought takes. The shape of the thought in thesis statements has shaping force in the way the paper develops. Some thesis shapes are more effective than others.

- A strong thesis usually contains **tension**, the balance of this against that

- Thesis statements often begin with a grammatically subordinate idea that will get outweighed by a more pressing claim: "Although X appears to account for Z, Y accounts for it better."

- A less effective thesis shape is the *list*

The order of clauses in a thesis statement often predicts the shape of the paper. A thesis that begins with a subordinate clause ("Although X ....."), for example, might lead to a paper in which the first part of the paper deals with the claims for X and then moves to a fuller embrace of Y.

The advantage of the subordinate construction (and the reason that so many theses are set up this way) is that the subordinate idea helps you to define your own position by giving you something to define it against. The subordinate clause of a thesis helps you to demonstrate that there is in fact an issue involved—that is, more than one possible explanation exists for the evidence you are considering. In practice, using this shape will often lead you to arrive at some compromise position between the claims of both X and Y. What appeared to be a *binary opposition*—"not X but Y"—emerges as a more complex combination of the two.

A less effective thesis shape that can predict the shape of a paper is the *list*. This shape, in which a writer might offer three points and then devote a section to each, often leads to sloppier thinking than one having a thesis statement containing both subordinate and independent clauses, because the list often does not sufficiently specify the connections among its various components. As a result, it fails to assert a relationship among ideas.

Try This 15.1: Predicting Essay Shapes from Thesis Shapes

It is a useful skill, both in reading and writing, to predict paper shapes from thesis shapes. For each of the theses below, what shape is predicted? That is, what will probably be discussed first, what second, and why? Which words in the thesis are especially predictive of the shape the paper will take?

1. The reforms in education, created to alleviate the problems of previous reforms, have served only to magnify the very problems they were meant to solve.

2. Although women more readily cry in contemporary films, the men, by not crying, seem to win the audience's favor.

3. The complications that fuel the plots in today's romantic comedies arise because women and men express their sensitivity so differently; the resolutions, however, rarely require the men to capitulate.

THE SHAPING FORCE OF TRANSITIONS

The linkage between where you've been and where you're going is usually a point in your writing at which thinking is taking place. This is especially the case in the evolving rather than the static model of thesis development in which the writer continually *updates* the thesis as it moves through evidence.

- Thinking tends to occur at points of transition.
- A good transition articulates a paper's logical links—how each phase of the paper leads to the next.
- Too many additive transitions ("also," "another example of") produce papers that list, an overly loose form of organization

It is useful to think of transitions as *directional indicators*, especially at the beginnings of paragraphs but also within them. "And," for example, is a plus sign. It indicates that the writer will add something, continuing in the same direction. The words "but," "yet," "nevertheless," and "however" are among the many transitional words that alert readers to changes in the direction of the writer's thinking. They might indicate the introduction of a qualification, or a potentially contradictory piece of evidence, or an alternative point of view.

Some additive transitions do more work than "also" or "another." The word "moreover" is an additive transition, but it adds emphasis to the added point. The transitional sequence "not only... but also" restates and then adds information in a way that clarifies what has gone before.

Too many additive transitions can pose a problem for your writing. A list is a slack form of organization, one that fails to identify how this is related to that. Although transitional wording such as "another example of" or "also" at the beginning of paragraphs does tell readers that a related point or example will follow, it does not specify that relationship beyond piling on another "and." Essentially, these words just list.

If you find yourself relying on "another" and "also" at points of transition, force yourself to substitute other transitional wording that indicates more precisely the nature of the relationship with what has gone before in the paper. Language such as "similarly" and "by contrast" can sometimes serve this purpose. Often, some restatement is called for to keep your reader on track—brief repetition is not necessarily redundant. A good transition reaches backward, telling where you've been, as the grounds for making a subsequent move forward.

The first step toward improving your use of transitions (and thereby, the organization of your writing) is to become conscious of them. If you notice that you are beginning successive paragraphs with "Another reason," for example, you can probably conclude that you are listing rather than developing your ideas. If you notice a number of sentences that start with the vague referent "This," you probably need to name the thing "This" refers to.

Think of transitions as echoes in the service of continuity. If you study the transitions in a piece, you will usually find that they echo either the language or the ideas of something that precedes them as they point to what is ahead.

Try This 15.2: Tracking Transitions

As an exercise in becoming more conscious of how transitions shape thinking, track the transitions in a piece of writing. Take a few pages of something you are reading (preferably a complete piece, such as a short article) and circle or underline all of the directional indicators. Remember to check not only the beginnings of paragraphs but within them. Then, survey your markings. What do you notice now about the shape of the piece? This exercise is also useful for expanding your repertoire of transitional words to use in your own writing. As an alternative, track the transitional wording in the next section of this chapter.

C. The Rhetoric of Form

Thus far, we have talked about form primarily in relation to the search for meaning. We've demonstrated that some forms of arranging ideas (5 paragraph form, for example) interfere with a writer's ability to have ideas in the first place. Whatever form one uses, we've argued, it has to be flexible enough to allow ideas to evolve. The point is that there are various factors influencing a writer's decisions about forms and formats. These include both the demands of the subject itself and those of the discourse community within which the writing seeks to communicate.

We now wish to expand on the role that a writer's sense of his or her *audience* plays in determining the formal presentation of ideas. We have entitled this section "The Rhetoric of Form" to emphasize the effects that a chosen form has on an audience—on its receptiveness to a writer's ideas, for example.

The study of rhetoric is primarily concerned with the various means at a writer's (or speaker's) disposal for influencing the views of an audience. In early rhetorics, Greek and Roman writers divided these means into three large categories—ethos, logos, and pathos—that you encountered earlier in this book in our definition of analysis (*see Chapter 3*). We'll use these categories for organizing what we wish to say about the relationship between formal structures and audience.

1. **Ethos** refers to the character of the speaker or writer. If an audience perceives a speaker to be ethical and rational, it will be inclined to perceive her or his argument as ethical and rational too. Thus, writers attend to the kind of *persona* they become on the page, the personality conveyed by the words and the tone of the words. In classical orations—the grandparent of virtually all speech and essay formats—the first section was always allotted to particular means of establishing an appealing persona, one whom an audience would want to listen to and believe. *(See the next section, "The Classical Oration Format".)*

2. **Logos** refers to the character of the thinking itself: the rational component, evident in the presence and development of the ideas.

3. **Pathos** includes appeals to the audience's emotions—which writing does all of the time, whether a writer wants it to or not. It is possible to think of the form of a paper in terms of how it might negotiate the likes and dislikes, the hopes and fears, of its assumed audience. If, for instance, you were to present an argument in favor of a position with which you knew in advance that your audience was predisposed to disagree, you would probably choose to delay making a case for this position until you had found various ways of earning that audience's trust. By contrast, when presenting an argument to an audience of like-minded people, you would be much more likely to start out with the position you planned to advance.

THE CLASSICAL ORATION FORMAT

All-purpose formats have been around a long time. Some are very simple. Others are more elaborate. The simplest organizing scheme consists of three parts: introduction, body, and conclusion. The format of the classical oration has a more elaborate form:

- *exordium*, introduction
- *narratio*, statement of facts
- *divisio*, outline of the points or steps in the argument
- *confirmatio*, proof of the case
- *confutatio*, refutation of opposing arguments
- *peroratio*, conclusion

If you read or listen to (for example) political speeches, you will find that many of them follow this order. This is because the form of the classical oration is suited primarily to argument—to the kind of writing in which the writer makes a case for or against something and refutes opposing arguments. As we have been demonstrating throughout this book, analytical thinking does not fit well into formats calling for an upfront statement of a predetermined claim, which is then simply proven to be correct. And so the book offers alternative organizational schemes that allow the space necessary for the recursive (back and forth between evidence and claims) thinking that analytical writing involves. These forms include some of the elements of the classical oration but without its emphasis on proof and refutation.

THREE COMMON ORGANIZING STRATEGIES

The following organizational patterns are determined more by rhetorical considerations—the desired effect on an audience—than by their idea-generating potential. As you will see, however, each also has potential for shaping thought. The first two patterns, climactic order and comparison/contrast, are common in all forms of writing. The third pattern, which concerns locating refutations and concessions, is particular to argument.

Climactic Order: Saving the Best for Last

Climactic order arranges elements from least to most important. The idea is to build to your best points, rather than leading with them and thereby allowing the paper to trail off from your more minor and less interesting observations. But what are your best points? A frequent mistake writers make in arranging their points climactically— and one that has much to do with the rhetoric of form—is to assume that the best point is the most obvious, the one with the most data attached to it and the one least likely to produce disagreement with readers. Such writers end up giving more space than they should to ideas that really don't need much development because they are already evident to most readers.

If you follow the principle of climactic order, you would begin with the most obvious and predictable points—and ones that, psychologically speaking, would get readers assenting—and then build to the more revealing and less obvious ones. So, for example, if the comparisons between film A and film B are fairly mundane but the contrasts are really provocative, you'd get the comparisons out of the way first and build to the contrasts, exploiting difference within similarity (see Chapter 4).

If, for example, there are three important reasons for banning snowmobiling in your town, you might choose to place the most compelling one last. If you were to put it first, you might draw your readers in quickly (a principle used by news stories) but then lose them as your argument seemed to trail off into less interesting rationales.

Comparisons/Contrasts: Two Formats

In Chapter 7, we discuss comparison as an invention strategy. We now want to address this subject from the perspective of organizing a paper. The first decision a writer has to make when arranging comparisons and contrasts is whether to address the two items being compared and contrasted in sequential blocks (A and then B) or point by point

- Organize by subjects being compared (subject A and then subject B), or
- Organize the comparison under a series of topics (Topic 1: A and B, Topic 2: A and B, etc.)

If you are comparing subject A with subject B, you might first make all the points you wish to make about A and then make points about B by explicitly referring back to A as you go. The advantage of this format is that it will allow you to use comparing and contrasting to figure out what you wish to say as you are drafting.

The disadvantage of this "subject-A-then-subject-B" format is that it can easily lose focus. If you don't manage to keep the points you raise about each side of your comparison parallel, you may end up with a paper comprised of two loosely connected halves. The solution is to make your comparisons and contrasts in the second half of the paper connect explicitly with what you said in the first half. What you say about subject A, in other words, should set the subtopics and terms for discussion of subject B.

The alternative pattern of organization for comparisons and contrasts is to organize by topic—not A and then B but A1 and B1, A2 and B2, A3 and B3, and so forth. That is, you talk about both A and B under a series of subtopics. If, for example, you were comparing two films, you might organize your work under such headings as directing, script, acting, special effects, and so forth.

The advantage of this format is that it better focuses the comparisons, pressing you to use them to think with. The disadvantage is that organizing in this way is sometimes difficult to manage until you've already done quite a bit of thinking about the two items you're comparing. The solution, particularly in longer papers, is sometimes to use both formats. You begin by looking at each of your subjects separately to make the big links and distinctions apparent and then focus what you've said by further pursuing selected comparisons one topic at a time.

Concessions and Refutations: Giving and Taking Away

In the language of argument, you *concede* whenever you acknowledge that a position at odds with your own does indeed have merit, even though you continue to believe that your position overall is the more reasonable one. When making a concession, a writer needs to represent this competing point of view as genuinely creditable—rather than only seemingly creditable until he or she lays out a means of opposing it. Another option is to argue against these views so as to *refute* their reasonableness. (*For a misuse of concessions and refutations, see Straw Man under Logical Fallacies in Chapter 9, Analyzing Arguments.*)

As a rule of thumb, avoid making your readers wait too long before you either concede or refute a view that you can assume will already have occurred to them. If you delay too long, you may inadvertently suggest either that you are unaware of the competing view or that you are afraid to bring it up.

In the case of short and easily managed concessions and refutations, you can often house these within the first several paragraphs and, in this way, clear a space for the position you wish to promote. In the case of more complicated and potentially more threatening alternative arguments, you may need to express your own position clearly and convincingly first. But to avoid the rhetorical problem of appearing to ignore the threat, you will probably need to give it a nod, telling readers that they will return to a full discussion of it later, once you have laid out your own position in some detail.

The placement of arguments has much to do with their relative complexity. Reasonably straightforward and easily explained concessions and refutations can often all be grouped in one place, perhaps as early as the second or third paragraph of a paper. The approach to concession and refutation in more complex arguments does not allow for such grouping. For each part of your argument, you will probably need to concede and refute as necessary, before moving to the next part of your argument and repeating the procedure.

Try This 15.3: Locating Concessions and Refutations

The following passage from a student essay on the relation between gender inequality and language makes skillful use of concessions and refutations. The excerpt is part of an introductory paragraph, after the writer has set up the issue: whether or not the elimination of sexism in language (the use of male pronouns and words like "mankind," for example, in circumstances applying to both men and women) through the use of generic pronouns (those that do not indicate gender, such as "they" rather than "he") can help to eliminate gender exclusion in the culture. The paragraph names the two sides of the issue and moves from there to a tentative thesis.

Study the paragraph to answer the following questions: (1) What language functions as concession? (2) What language functions as refutation? (3) What part of the competing argument does the refutation still appear willing to concede? (4) How is the refutation that the writer offers different from the position to which he concedes?

Gender Inequality and Linguistic Bias

The more conservative side on this issue questions whether the elimination of generic pronouns can, in fact, change attitudes, and whether intentionally changing language is even possible. The reformist side believes that the elimination of generic pronouns is necessary for women's liberation from oppression and that reshaping the use of male pronouns as generic is both possible and effective. Although the answer to the debate over the direct link between a change in language and a change in society is not certain, it is certain that the attitudes and behaviors of societies are inseparable from language. Language conditions what we feel and think. The act of using "they" to refer to all people rather than the generic "he" will not automatically change collective attitudes toward women. These generic pronouns should be changed, however, because 1) the struggle itself increases awareness and discussion of the sexual inequalities in society, and subsequently, this awareness will transform attitudes and language, and 2) the power of linguistic usage has been mainly controlled by and reserved for men. Solely by participating in linguistic reform, women have begun to appropriate some of the power for themselves.

D. The Idea of the Paragraph

Throughout this section of the chapter, we will focus on what are sometimes called "body" paragraphs, as opposed to the more special-function paragraphs that serve as the beginning and end of papers. *(For discussion of introductory and concluding paragraphs, see the next chapter, Introductions and Conclusions Across the Curriculum.)*

HOW A PARAGRAPH SAYS

It is useful to think of any piece of writing as consisting of parts or blocks. The paragraph is a fundamental building block, bigger than the sentence, smaller than the section or paper. Paragraphs can be thought of by analogy with the paper. Like papers, paragraphs have parts: they make opening gambits, they put forward evidence and analyze it, and they arrive at some kind of summarizing or culminating closure. They have, in short, a beginning, a middle, and an end. But unlike the paper, the paragraph does not stand alone as an independent entity. For a paragraph to be effective, readers need to be able to understand its role in unfolding the thinking of the paper as a whole.

The two primary characteristics of virtually all strong paragraphs are unity and development.

- **unity**: all the sentences in the paragraph should be related to some central idea or focus. Normally, the sentence that serves this function in the paragraph is the topic sentence.

- **development**: the sentences in a paragraph need to connect to each other in some way; a paragraph needs to go somewhere, to build. Normally, the sentences in a paragraph either offer a series of observations about the main idea or build one upon the next to offer a more sustained analysis of one element of the main idea.

Notice that we don't say here that a paragraph offers a claim plus examples and reasons. This model of the paragraph is true in some cases, but paragraphs typically do more than make simple claims and then back them up with one or more examples.

Once you begin paying attention to paragraphs, you will see that they are far less uniform in their shapes and procedures than you may have been asked to believe. The paragraph police will not haul you away for producing a paragraph that lacks a topic sentence, or places it at the end of the paragraph instead of the front, or contains several claims instead of one, or delays the substantiating evidence till later. Nonetheless, most of the paragraphs you encounter—and most that you should write—have unity and development. They are about one thing, and they tell you why it is important.

HOW LONG? PARAGRAPHS, READERS, AND WRITERS

Paragraphing is a kindness to your reader, since it divides your thinking into manageable bites. If you find a paragraph growing longer than half a page—particularly if it is your opening or second paragraph—find a place to make a paragraph break. More frequent paragraphing provides readers with convenient resting points from which to relaunch themselves into your thinking.

Long paragraphs are daunting—rather like mountains—and they are easy to get lost in, for both readers and writers. When writers try to do too much in a single paragraph, they often lose focus and lose contact with the larger purpose or point that got them into the paragraph in the first place. Remember that old rule about one idea to a paragraph? Well, it's not a bad rule, though it isn't exactly right because sometimes you need more space than a single paragraph can provide to lay out a complicated phase of your overall argument. In that case, just break wherever it seems reasonable to do so in order to keep your paragraphs from becoming ungainly. Two paragraphs can be about the same thing, the first half and then the second half. This paragraph, for example, might have been easier to process if we had broken it right before the question about that old rule.

Paragraphs are a relief not just for your readers: they also give the writer a break. When you draft, start a new paragraph whenever you feel yourself getting stuck: it's the promise of a fresh start. Paragraph breaks are like turning a corner to a new view, even when the thinking is continuous. They also force the writer to make transitions, overt connections among the parts of his or her thinking, and to state or restate key ideas. Paragraph indentations allow readers to scan essays, searching for connecting words and important ideas.

It can be extraordinarily useful to draft a paper in phases, as a series of paragraphs:

- Break up the larger interpretation or argument into more manageable pieces.
- Give yourself space to think in short sections that you can then sequence.
- When you revise, use paragraphs to clean up your thinking by dividing it into its most logical parts.

A short paragraph will always provide emphasis, for which most readers will thank you. (You should, however, use very short paragraphs sparingly.)

Paragraphs need to justify their existence. A paragraph break should remind you to check that you have suggested to the readers why they need to know this information. Ask yourself why you are telling them what you are telling them. How does the thinking in the paragraph relate to the overall idea that your paper is developing?

A good way to check if your paragraph is really advancing your claims is to ask and answer "So what?" at the end of the paragraph.

PARAGRAPHS ACROSS THE CURRICULUM: SOME COMMON PATTERNS

The simplest way of thinking about paragraph organization draws on a slightly extended version of what is known as the traditional rhetorical modes: Exemplification, Narration, Description, Process, Comparison/Contrast, Classification/Division, Definition, Cause/Effect, Problem/Solution, and, of course, Analysis.

You have been studying the characteristic shape of analytical thinking throughout this book. It consists of seeing the parts of something in relation to the whole. In practice, this means finding a significant pattern of detail and explaining what this pattern reveals about the nature and purpose of whatever it is you are studying. The practice we call 10 on 1 (see Chapter 10) is typical of analytical paragraphs. It consists of close scrutiny of a single representative example wherein the writer notices as much as possible about the example and then interprets his or her observations by asking and answering the question "So what?"

Because analysis typically focuses on relationships among the parts and between those parts and the whole, classification and division are well-suited to analytical writing. In the organizational pattern called division, the writer breaks a subject into its component parts. Classification explains how the parts relate to each other by putting them into categories. In practice, classification and division tend to occur together, often in conjunction with definition. When we define something we locate its defining traits, the features that make it what it is.

Here is a brief example of classification and division going on in the same paragraph:

> The United States has never had a pure growth-directed model of education. Some distinctive and by-now-traditional features of our system resist being cast in those terms. Unlike virtually every nation of the world, we have a liberal-arts model of university education: instead of entering college to study a single subject, students are required to take a wide range of courses in their first two years, prominently including courses in the humanities. That model influences secondary education: nobody is tracked too early into a nonhumanities stream. (Martha C. Nussbaum, "The Liberal Arts Are Not Elitist," *The Chronicle of Higher Education*, February 28, 2010).

Although most paragraphs employ a mix of these modes of organization, the patterns are usually easy to see. For purposes of illustration, we will focus on narrative organization. A surprising amount of writing in the disciplines is **narrative**; that is, writers often find themselves needing to explain sequences of action (as in the methods and results sections of a scientific paper or lab report) or events or behaviors or ideas. Notice, for example, how profoundly narrative the writing is in the following excerpt from a lab report.

A set of electrophilic aromatic substitution reactions was performed using two monosubstituted benzenes so as to describe substitution patterns as a function of substrate. Samples of toluene and ethylbenzene each underwent a nitration via a 1:1 mixture of sulfuric and nitric acid. The acid mixture formed a strongly electrophilic nitronium ion which attacked the mono-substituted benzene ring and replaced a proton. Upon mixing the reagents, both nitration reactions turned yellow. The toluene reaction darkened somewhat over the reaction period, while the ethylbenzene reaction turned brown. The color change is evidence of a reaction occurring. The products of each reaction were iso-lated via a liquid extraction with MTBE and dried. The isolated products were analyzed via GC-MS (gas chromatography – mass spectroscopy) which separates compounds based on their vola-tility. This was used to both identify the products and determine their respective ratios.

A good piece of writing—at the level of the paragraph as well as at the level of the paper as a whole—tells a story. It explains how and why the writer came to focus on an issue or question or problem. It also narrates for readers how the writer came to understand the meaning and significance of his or her evidence.

LINKING THE SENTENCES IN PARAGRAPHS: MINDING THE GAPS

It helps to think of the space between the period at the end of a sentence and the beginning of the next sentence as a gap that the reader has to cross. Start thinking in this way as you follow the train of thought in this paragraph and those that follow it. Keep asking yourself: what is the connection between each sentence and the one that follows it? What keeps the reader from falling out of the paper at the gaps between sentences, losing sight of the thought connections that make a paragraph more than just a collection of sentences?

In many paragraphs, the connections between and among sentences are made apparent by the repetition of **key words**. This idea of key words brings us back to a core principle of this book: that both writers and readers make meaning by locat-ing significant patterns of repetition and contrast. What is the pattern of repeated words in the paragraph above this one, for example? Notice the repetition of the key word "gap," which goes with the idea of falling and which is in opposition to such words as "connection" and "train of thought." The other connecting feature of the paragraph comes with its repeated use of questions. The paragraph you are now reading gets its sense of purpose from the previous paragraph's questions. Here we start answering them.

Sometimes (but not always) the connecting logic that helps readers negotiate the gaps between sentences must be made explicit. So, for example, some sentences begin with the words, "So, for example." The function of this type of connection is illustration. Some other words that operate in this gap-bridging way are "thus," "furthermore," "in addition," "similarly," "in other words," and "on the contrary."

When the organizing principle of a paragraph is sufficiently evident, explicit transitional words are often not needed. If parallelism is the paragraph's organizing principle, for example, readers will be able to see the relationship among the paragraph's sentences without a lot of repetition of connecting words.

WHAT A PARAGRAPH DOES: THE PARAGRAPH AS MOVEMENT OF MIND

The key to understanding how to write paragraphs, as well as how to analyze what you read in them, is to focus on what the various sentences in a paragraph *do*. To follow what a paragraph *does* is to follow its succession of sentences as a movement of mind, an unfolding of consciousness on the page that conveys to readers the relationships among its various pieces of information. If you can keep this idea in mind, seeing paragraphs as possessing behavior—actively shaping thought and communicating it to imagined readers—your writing will improve.

The sentences in a paragraph have different jobs; there is a distribution of labor. To see this element of paragraphing, it is essential that you "look beyond content"; that is, you need to focus on what the sentences are doing, not just on what they are saying. In Chapter 8, Reasoning from Evidence to Claims, we ask you to distinguish which sentences in a paragraph were evidence and which were claims, and to mark these with an E or a C. Those are two functions of sentences in paragraphs—two tasks that sentences in a paragraph can perform.

As this chapter has already suggested, there are other functions as well. Here are some roles sentences play in paragraphs:

- link one idea to another
- link evidence to a claim
- qualify the major claim (the thesis)
- paraphrase the major claim (restating and querying the key terms in order to figure out what they imply)
- operate as transitions, linking the paragraph to the one that precedes it and to the overall idea the paper is developing

Paragraph Structure #1: Topic Sentence, Restriction, Illustration

One model for thinking about paragraph structure comes from the rhetorician Alton Becker: Topic sentence (T), Restriction (R) and Illustration (I). The topic sentence states some kind of claim—an idea that the paragraph will develop in some way. This may or may not appear as the first sentence of the paragraph, and there may be more than one claim in the paragraph, although one of these is usually primary. Restriction limits the claim in some way. Illustration supplies examples in support of the claim.

As our earlier discussions of thesis and evidence have suggested, evidence does more than just support claims; when we consider how evidence does not match the claim, we are led to qualify (shrink, restrict) the claim. This process of asserting ideas and then restricting them also goes on, often repeatedly, at the level of the paragraph.

The TRI model does not cover everything that goes on in various kinds of paragraphs, but it is a good way to start looking at paragraphs in order to begin thinking about what the sentences do. Here is a somewhat expanded list of jobs that sentences may do inside paragraphs.

What Sentences Do Inside Paragraphs

T = topic sentence -> announces the main idea of the paragraph

R = restriction -> qualifies, further defines, limits claims; happens at various points in the paragraph

P = paraphrasing -> restates claims and evidence to analyze them

I = illustration -> provides substantiating evidence

EXP = explains the illustrations, draws out meaning of evidence

Th = thesis restatement -> offers versions of an evolving thesis

Tr = transitional wording -> links sentences, connects ideas inside paragraph but also connects paragraph to what precedes and follows it

SW = answers "So what?"-> tells readers the purpose of the paragraph, why the writer bothered to tell them this

Let's look at a paragraph to see what some of the sentences are doing. We have labeled some of the sentences (in square brackets) according to our expanded version of Becker's marking scheme.

[T:] Armin Schnider, a neurologist from the Cantonal University Hospital in Geneva, Switzerland, says that the vast majority of confabulations he has heard from his patients over the years relate directly to their earlier lives. [I:] One of his patients, a retired dentist, worried while in hospital that he was keeping his patients waiting. [I:] Another, an elderly woman, talked regularly about her baby in the present tense. [EXP:] Most of these patients had damage to the temporal lobes of the brain, particularly the memory regions of the hippocampus, so it seemed likely that they had somehow lost the ability to make new memories and were retrieving old ones instead. [EXP:]The intriguing thing was that they didn't realize these memories were old — they seemed convinced by their stories, and sometimes even acted on them. [SW:] So Schnider decided to study their memory in more detail. (Helen Phillips, "Everyday Fairytales," New Scientist, 7 October 2006)

Try This 15.4: Label the Function of the Sentences in a Paragraph

One of the best ways to understand how paragraphs work—to apprehend them as tools of thought and to be able to deploy them to work for you—is to assign the abbreviations in our list above to any paragraph in anything you have written or read, including this book.

Paragraph Structure #2: Observation -> Implication -> Conclusion

One of the models described in this book for the analytical movement of mind is as follows: *Observation → So what? → implication → So what? → tentative conclusions.* This sequence goes beyond the simplest kind of paragraph development—idea + illustration—because it contains more of the writer's thinking on how he or she reasons to the claim from evidence. Explicitly drawing out the implications of evidence complicates, but also more accurately represents the process of thinking, than does simply attaching examples to the idea they support.

One example of this model of mental movement appears earlier in this book, in the section of Chapter 2 entitled "Asking So What?" Not all paragraphs in an analytical paper move in this way, but a significant number of them do. We reprint the paragraph here, adding annotations about what the paragraph does.

[Paragraph opens with empirical observation:] If you look closely at Camilo Vergara's photo of Fern Street, Camden, 1988, you'll notice a sign on the side of a dilapidated building that reads "Danger: Men Working - W. Hargrove Demolition."

[Implication:] Perhaps that warning captures the ominous atmosphere of these very different kinds of photographic documents by Camilo Vergara and Edward Burtynsky: "Danger: Men Working." Watch out—human beings are at work! *[Topic sentence:]* But the work that is presented is not so much a building-up as it is a tearing-down—the work of demolition. *[Qualification of claim:]* Of course, demolition is often necessary in order to construct anew: old buildings are leveled for new projects, whether you are building a highway or bridge in an American city or a dam in the Chinese countryside.

[Paraphrasing—interpretive restatement:] You might call modernity itself, as so many have, a process of creative destruction, a term used variously to describe modern art, capitalism, and technological innovation. *[Topic sentence:]* The photographs in this exhibit, however, force us to pay attention to the "destructive" side of this modern equation. *[Writer asks So what? and concludes:]* What both Burtynsky and Vergara do in their respective ways is to put up a warning sign—they question

whether the reworking of our natural and social environment leads to a sustainable human future. *[Restatement:]* And they wonder whether the process of creative destruction may not have spun recklessly out of control, producing places that are neither habitable nor sustainable. *[Supporting observation:]* In fact, a common element connecting the two photographic versions is the near absence of people in the landscape. *[Observation:]* While we see the evidence of the transforming power of human production on the physical and social environment, neither Vergara's urban ruins nor Burtynsky's industrial sites actually show us "men working." *[Observation:]* Isolated figures peer suspiciously out back doors or pick through the rubble, but they appear out of place. *[Writer asks So what? and concludes in reference to the paragraph's opening observation:]* It is this sense of displacement—of human beings alienated from the environments they themselves have created—that provides the most haunting aspect of the work of these two photographers. (Jack Gambino, "Demolition Zones: Contemporary Photography by Edward Burtynsky and Camilo Jose Vergara")

Paragraph Structure #3: Coordinate and Subordinate Paragraphs

Here is a third way of thinking about how paragraphs develop. In his influential essay, "A Generative Rhetoric of the Paragraph," Francis Christensen defines the topic sentence as "the one the other sentences depend from, the one they develop or amplify, the one they are a comment on" (*Notes Toward a New Rhetoric*, 1967, page 80). Christensen posits two kinds of paragraphs: coordinate and subordinate. In coordinate structures, all of the sentences following the topic sentence are equal in weight, or as he puts it, "all children of the same mother" (61).

Consider the following example of a (primarily) coordinate paragraph, taken from earlier in this chapter. Most of the sentences relate back to the topic sentence in some way. A number 1 indicates that the sentence is coordinate with the topic sentence, operating on the same level of importance and repeatedly clarifying the topic sentence. The number 2 indicates that the sentence is a subordinate structure, which will be explained below.

> [T:] Paragraphs are a relief not just for your readers: they also give the writer a break.
>
> 1 When you draft, start a new paragraph whenever you feel yourself getting stuck: it's the promise of a fresh start.
>
> 1 Paragraph breaks are like turning a corner to a new view, even when the thinking is continuous.
>
> 1 They also force the writer to make transitions, overt connections among the parts of his or her thinking, and to state or restate key ideas.
>
> 1 Paragraph indentations allow readers to scan essays, searching for connecting words and important ideas.

The paragraph above best fits the pattern that Christensen calls coordinate because all of the sentences that come after the topic sentence "develop or amplify" it. Each offers reasons for thinking that paragraphs are a relief not just for readers but also for writers.

In what Christensen identifies as subordinate structures, each sentence clarifies or comments on the one before it, as for example in this short sequence that he cites:

1 The process of learning is essential to our lives.

  2 All higher animals seek it deliberately.

    3 They are inquisitive and they experiment.

      4 An experiment is a sort of harmless trial run...(60).

Note how each sentence generates the one that follows it, rather than primarily relating back to the topic sentence.

Here is another example of a subordinate paragraph to contemplate:

1 Another startling conclusion from the science of consciousness is that the intuitive feeling we have that there's another executive "I" that sits in a control room of our brain, scanning the screens of the senses and pushing the buttons of the muscles, is an illusion.

  2 Consciousness turns out to consist of a maelstrom of events distributed across the brain.

    3 These events compete for attention, and as one process outshouts the others, the brain rationalizes the outcome after the fact and concocts the impression that a single self was in charge all along. (Steven Pinker, "The Mystery of Consciousness," *Time*, January 19, 2007)

Go back now and look at our first example (above) of a coordinate paragraph—the one about paragraph breaks being a relief. Are there any sentences in that paragraph that we might have classified as subordinate? What about the last sentence, for example? Notice that it clearly refers back to the topic sentence because it explains what paragraph indentations do to help readers. But it is also true that this last sentence evolves out of the sentence that immediately precedes it by developing the idea of transitions ("connecting words" "overt connections") and restatement of "key ideas." So we might have labeled that last sentence as level 2.

This kind of ambiguity should not concern you. It is less important to be able to accurately and precisely locate each sentence in a paragraph as coordinate or subordinate than it is to begin to recognize that most paragraphs are some kind of mix of these two thought patterns. In practice, as Christensen observes, most paragraphs combine coordinate and subordinate sequences, although one of the two structures often predominates. Consider, for example, the following paragraph, where we have explained in square brackets our reasons for labeling the sentences as we did.

[Topic sentence:] Imagery may be necessary for human imagination.

1 It has been suggested that all the products of the imagination are derived from imagery, following some transformation of the basic imagery. *[restates and slightly expands topic sentence]*

1 For example, Rutgers' psychologist Alan Leslie, when he worked in London in the 1980s, proposed that imagination essentially involves three steps: *[sets up example of the transformation process that is necessary for the human imagination]*

[The next moves in the paragraph lay out the psychologist's three steps; they are still supporting the topic sentence, but refer back more directly to the sentence immediately above them. Christensen describes this move as a subordinate sequence.]

2 Take what he called a 'primary' representation (which, as we have already established, is an image that has truth relations to the outside world).

2 Then make a copy of this primary representation (Leslie calls this copy a 'second-order' representation).

2 Finally, one can then introduce some change to this second-order representation, playing with its truth relationships to the outside world without jeopardising the important truth relationships that the original, primary representation needs to preserve.

1 For Leslie, when you use your imagination, you leave your primary representation untouched (for important evolutionary reasons that we will come onto), but once you have a photocopy of this (as it were), you can do pretty much anything you like with it." *[Having laid out the transformative process in the middle of the paragraph, the writer is now free to finish the paragraph with a summative sentence that more fully spells out why imagery is necessary to the imagination.]* (Simon Baron-Cohen, "The Biology of Imagination," Entelechy: Mind & Culture summer/fall 2007 no. 9)

You do not need to ponder these relationships each time you write a new sentence in a paragraph, but, when you find yourself getting stuck in your writing, you can help yourself to move forward by thinking about which sentence in the paragraph is the actual generator (or jumping off point) for the next one.

Try This 15.5: Arrange Coordinate and Subordinate Sequences

Go back to the paragraph on page 338 that we used to illustrate our expanded version of Becker's TRI model. Try to arrange the sentences according to levels—coordinate and subordinate. Which sentences in the paragraph form a coordinate sequence with the topic sentence? Are there any sentences in the paragraph that, rather than being generated by the topic sentence instead clarify or comment on the one that precedes it?

Try This 15.6: Identify the Structure of Paragraphs

Take each of the paragraphs below and apply the terms offered in this section to describe what various sentences do. Look for coordinate versus subordinate structures, but more specifically, label the mental moves performed by individual sentences. We have numbered the sentences to make the paragraphs easier to work with.

Paragraph A:

1. What does it mean for a nation to advance?
2. In one view, it means to increase its gross domestic product per capita.
3. For decades that measure has been the standard used by development economists, as if it were a proxy for a nation's overall quality of life.
4. Never mind about distribution and social equality; never mind about the preconditions of stable democracy; never mind about the quality of race and gender relations; never mind about the improvement of other aspects of a human being's quality of life that are not well linked to economic growth.
5. (Empirical studies have by now shown that political liberty, health, and education are all poorly correlated with growth.)
6. One sign of what that model leaves out is the fact that South Africa under apartheid used to shoot to the top of development indexes.
7. There was a lot of wealth in the old South Africa, and the old model of development rewarded that achievement (or good fortune), ignoring the staggering distributional inequalities, the brutal apartheid regime, and the health and educational deficiencies that went with it.

(Martha C. Nussbaum, "The Liberal Arts Are Not Elitist" *The Chronicle of Higher Education*, February 28, 2010)

Paragraph B:

1. What does the contemporary self want?
2. The camera has created a culture of celebrity; the computer is creating a culture of connectivity.
3. As the two technologies converge—broadband tipping the Web from text to image, social-networking sites spreading the mesh of interconnection even wider—the two cultures betray a common impulse.
4. Celebrity and connectivity are both ways of becoming known.
5. This is what the contemporary self wants.
6. It wants to be recognized, wants to be connected: it wants to be visible.
7. If not to the millions, on Survivor or Oprah, then to the hundreds, on Twitter or Facebook.

8. This is the quality that validates us, this is how we become real to ourselves—by being seen by others.

9. The great contemporary terror is anonymity.

10. If Lionel Trilling was right, if the property that grounded the self, in Romanticism, was sincerity, and in modernism it was authenticity, then in postmodernism it is visibility.

(William Deresiewicz, "The End of Solitude," *The Chronicle of Higher Education*, January 30, 2009)

Paragraph C:

1. White might not have succeeded in completely ridding his life of modern civilization, but Strunk's manual in White's hands became a successful *primitivist* tract.

2. Perhaps that seems like an overstatement, but in fact what counts as primitivist is flexible, Marianna Torgovnick reminded us, entirely dependent on what bugs one about the modern.

3. The key feature of primitivism, Torgovnick offered, is defining the primitive in reaction to the present: "Is the present too majestic? Primitive life is not—it is a precapitalist utopia in which only use value, never exchange value, prevails. Is the present sexually repressed? Not primitive life—primitives live life whole, without fear of the body" (8).

4. For Strunk and White, modern life was verbose and obscure, so primitive life must be brief, direct, and clear.

5. New things are bad things, new words the worst of all.

6. The words *offputting* and *ongoing* appear in the third and subsequent editions of The *Elements of Style* as "newfound adjectives, to be avoided because they are inexact and clumsy" (*Third Edition* 54).

7. The suffix oriented is lambasted as "a clumsy, pretentious device, much in vogue" (*Third Edition* 55).

8. *The Elements of Style* thus had become, over a period of nearly unprecedented technological progress, the perfect complement to the manual typewriter—a deliberate rejection of "books with permissive steering and automatic transitions" that made our lives easier but rendered our prose impotent and our character lax (xvi).

9. For impotence and laxity, *The Elements of Style* offers a program of stylistic and moral restitution, word by word.

(Catherine Prendergast, "The Fighting Style: Reading the Unabomber's Strunk and White," *College English*, Volume 72, No 1, September 2009)

FINDING THE SKELETON OF AN ESSAY: AN EXAMPLE

We end this chapter with a skeletal version of an essay by one of our colleagues (available in the anthology version of this text). We have included only the first sentence of each paragraph, and in some cases the last, the working thesis as it appears at the end of paragraph 2, and the evolved thesis as it appears in the next to final paragraph. As you will see, each paragraph does begin with some kind of assertion. You will also see that writers allow themselves some flexibility on where they locate the working thesis and its later evolution. This way of looking at essays is a practice we recommend: it can teach you a lot about paragraphing and essay structure in a hurry.

September 11th: A National Tragedy?

By James Peck

Paragraph 1, sentence 1: Since the events of September 11th, I've been pursued by thoughts and images of tragedy.

Paragraph 1, last sentence: A voluminous literature theorizes the limits of tragic form, and I admit it rankles me to hear the word "tragic" used as a generic modifier for anything really bad that happens.

Paragraph 2, sentence 1: With the events of September 11th, however, I have found myself using the language of tragedy pretty indiscriminately.

Paragraph 2, last two sentences [Working thesis]: But I am coming to the conviction that tragedy offers a demanding, stark paradigm that at least accounts for some of the emotional force of these events and may even suggest some generative ways to think about them. Beyond simply capturing a bit of the devastation wrought by the attacks, can the form of tragedy help us narrate, image, or otherwise represent these horrors?

Paragraph 3, sentence 1: I acknowledge that it may seem frivolous, even blasphemous, to discuss these overwhelming and all too real events in a matrix borrowed from the relatively rarified topic of dramatic form.

Paragraph 4, sentence 1: I'm suggesting that the form of tragedy might accommodate some of the affective power of September 11th, and even point towards some of its moral claims.

Paragraph 5, sentence 1: I think this ought to be the tenor of our discourse in the wake of September 11th.

Paragraph 6, sentence 1: A tragic witnessing of September 11th must also preserve outrage at these callous acts.

Paragraph 7, sentence 1: Finally, a tragic witnessing of these events should squarely face some awful truths, dwell in the full weight of those truths, and try to see ourselves anew as a result of doing so.

Paragraph 8, sentence 1: The cornerstone of Aristotle's theory of tragedy is the dual principle of peripety and recognition.

Paragraph 9, sentence 1: I worry that my discussion may seem tasteless, or worse, coy.

Paragraph 10, sentence 1: I don't want to live in a melodrama.

Paragraph 11, sentence 1: It deeply worries me that the dominant national discourse in the aftermath of September 11th is melodramatic.

Paragraph 12, sentence 1: I'd like to close by evoking the function of tragedy in Athenian democracy.

Paragraph 13, sentence 1: Given this avowedly patriotic context, the most remarkable thing about the City Dionysia was its frank criticism of Athenian public life.

Paragraph 13, final sentence [The evolved thesis]: In this moment of national crisis, I think we would benefit from bringing the same questioning, restless, self-critical spirit to our own national conversation.

Paragraph 14 (entire): I hope we take seriously our casual language, and witness September 11th as a tragedy. Remember the dead. Pursue their killers. Interrogate ourselves.

GUIDELINES FOR FORMS AND FORMATS ACROSS THE CURRICULUM

1. Find the space in a format that will allow it to work as a heuristic, a set of steps designed not just to organize but to stimulate and guide your thinking. Avoid the slot-filler mentality.

2. Look for and expect to find the common denominators among the various formats you learn to use across the curriculum. You can master—and benefit from—virtually any format if you approach it not as a set of arbitrary and rigid rules, but as a formalized guide to having ideas.

3. Don't make your readers wait too long before you concede or refute a view that you can assume will already have occurred to them. Otherwise, they may assume you are unaware of the competing view or afraid to bring it up.

4. Always treat opposing views fairly. A good strategy is to concede their merits but argue that, in the particular context you are addressing, your position is more important or appropriate.

5. Use climactic order to organize your points, building to your best ones. The best ones are usually the most revealing and thought-provoking, not the most obvious or commonly agreed upon.

6. Phrasing your thesis to include a subordinate construction—"although X appears to account for Z, Y accounts for it better"—will give your paper a ready-made organizational shape, along with giving you something to define your own position against.

7. A good transition reaches backward, telling where you've been, as the grounds for making a subsequent move forward. Opt for "similarly" and "by contrast," for example, which specify connections for your readers, rather than merely additive transitions such as "another" and "also."

8. Half a page is a healthy length for most paragraphs, long enough to launch an idea but short enough to give your reader time to rest.

9. To keep your paragraphs healthy, focus at some point in your writing process on what they do—not just what they say. Here are five questions to ask yourself:

   - Do your readers know why you are telling them what you are telling them?
   - Can readers see the connection between the paragraph and your evolving thesis?
   - Has your paragraph moved backwards before moving forward?
   - Have you buried your best ideas, the main claims of the paragraph, in the middle, rather than leading or concluding with them?
   - Have you asked and answered "so what?" at the end of the paragraph?

Assignments: Forms and Formats

1. **Infer the Format of a Published Article.**
   Often the format governing the organization of a published piece is not immediately evident. That is, it is not subdivided according to conventional disciplinary categories that are obeyed by all members of a given discourse community. Especially if you are studying a discipline in which the writing does not follow an explicitly prescribed format, such as history, literature, or economics, you may find it illuminating to examine representative articles or essays in that discipline, looking for an implicit format. In other words, you can usually discern some underlying pattern of organization: the formal conventions, the rules that are being followed even when these are not highlighted.

   The following assignment works well whether you tackle it individually or in a group. It can lead to a paper, an oral report, or both. First, you need to assemble several articles from the same or a similar kind of journal or magazine. "Journal" is the name given to publications aimed at specialized, usually scholarly, audiences, as opposed to general or popular audiences. *Time, Newsweek,* and the *New Yorker* are called "magazines" rather than "journals" because they are aimed at a broader general audience. *Shakespeare Quarterly* is a journal; *Psychology Today* is a magazine.

   Having found at least three journal or magazine articles, study them in order to focus on the following question: *Insofar as there appears to be a format that articles in this journal adhere to, what are its parts?*

   How, for example, does an article in this journal or magazine typically begin and end? Does there seem to be a relatively uniform place in which these articles include opposing arguments? You will, in other words, be analyzing the articles inductively (reasoning from particular details to general principles). Begin with the product and reason backward to the skeleton beneath the skin.

Note that if your professor directs you to work with magazines rather than journals, you should probably further narrow the focus—to a *Time* cover story, to the *New Yorker*'s "Letter from [the name of a city]," or another such recurring feature. Even gossip columns and letters of advice to the lovelorn in teen magazines adhere to certain evident, though not explicitly marked, formats.

Write up your results. Cite particular language from at least two articles in support of your claims about the implicit format. In presenting your evidence, keep the focus on the underlying form, showing how the different articles proceed in the same or similar ways. Don't let yourself get too distracted by the articles' content, even though there may be similarities here as well. Instead, work toward formulating a rationale for the format—what you take to be its rhetoric of form. You will need, for example, both to lay out the typical form of the introduction and to account for its taking that typical form. Devote several paragraphs to this rationale, either at the end of your report or integrated within it.

2. **Find the Organizing Principles of an Essay**
   Excerpt a skeletal version of an essay, using the model of the 9/11 essay by James Peck located at the end of the chapter. Copy out the opening sentence of each paragraph as well as sentences that state the essay's working thesis and its final form in or near the concluding paragraph. Your aim is to discern the shape of the thinking in the essay at a glance.

3. **Practice Induction**
   Study a group of like things inductively. You might, for example, use greeting cards aimed at women versus greeting cards aimed at men, a group of poems by one author, or ads for one kind of product (jeans) or aimed at one target group (teenage girls).

   Compile a set of significant details about the data, and then leap to a general claim about the group that you think is interesting and reasonably accurate. This generalization is your inductive principle. Then use the principle to examine deductively more data of the same kind, exploring its implications as you evolve it more accurately.

Chapter 16

Introductions and Conclusions Across the Curriculum

THIS CHAPTER ADDRESSES two perennial trouble-spots in all kinds of writing—introductions and conclusions. The chapter gives special attention to strategies for solving two problems: trying to do too much in the introduction and not doing enough in the conclusion.

There are no absolute rules for writing introductions and conclusions, but there does seem to be a consensus across the disciplines that introductions should raise issues rather than settle them and that conclusions should go beyond merely restating what has already been said. Insofar as disciplinary conventions permit, in introductions you should play an ace but not your whole hand; and in conclusions, don't just summarize—culminate.

Throughout the chapter, we will point to differences in the language that the various disciplines use in their prescriptions for introductions and conclusions, but once you have learned to see past differences in style, you will recognize that the jobs introductions and conclusions do are actually quite similar across the curriculum.

> The introduction isolates a specific question or issue and explains why, in a specified context, this question or issue matters.
>
> Think of the concluding paragraph as the site of the paper's final So what?, which is shorthand for "Where does this get us?" or "Why does this matter?"
>
> Rather than just restate and summarize, the concluding paragraph should leave readers with your single best insight and put it into some kind of broader perspective.

INTRODUCTIONS AND CONCLUSIONS AS SOCIAL SITES

When you read, you enter a world created of written language—a textual world—and to varying degrees, you leave the world "out there." Even if other people are around, we all read in relative isolation; our attention is diverted from the social and physical world upon which the full range of our senses normally operates.

Your introduction takes the reader from the everyday world of sights and sounds and submerges him or her into a textual one. And your conclusion returns the reader to his or her nonwritten reality. Introductions and conclusions **mediate**—they carry the reader from one way of being to another. They function as the most social parts of any written communication, the passageways in which you need to be most keenly aware of your reader.

At both sites, there is a lot at stake. The introduction gives the reader his or her first impression, and we all know how indelible that can be. The conclusion leaves the reader with a last—and potentially lasting—impression of the written world you have constructed.

HOW MUCH TO SAY UPFRONT

Most of the difficulties in composing introductions and conclusions arise in deciding how you should deal with the thesis. How much of it should you put in the introduction?

The first paragraph does not need to—and usually can't—offer your conclusion; it will take the body of your paper to accomplish that. It should, however, provide a quick look at particular details that set up the issue. Use these details to generate a theory, a working hypothesis, about whatever it is you think is at stake in the material. The rest of the paper will test and develop this theory.

The most important thing to do in the introductory paragraph of an analytical paper is to lay out a genuine issue, something that seems to be at stake in whatever it is you are studying. Preferably, you should select a complex issue—one not easily resolved, seeming to have some truth on both sides—and not an overly general one. Otherwise, you run the risk of writing a paper that proves the obvious or radically oversimplifies.

Set up this issue as quickly and concretely as you can. As a general rule, you should assume that readers of your essay will need to know on page one—preferably by the end of your first paragraph—what your paper is attempting to resolve or negotiate.

In the sciences, the standard instructions for composing an introduction are worded somewhat differently, but with similar intent: create a context by citing all previous work relevant to your study, show the need for new information by pointing to an uncertainty or problem in existing knowledge, and say what you are trying to accomplish and why it is important.

WHAT INTRODUCTIONS DO: "WHY WHAT I'M SAYING MATTERS"

The primary challenge in writing introductions lies in occupying the middle ground between saying too much too soon (overassertive prejudgment) and saying too little upfront (avoidance of taking a position).

A rule of thumb is *start fast*. The introduction should give your reader a quick (a third of a typed page or a half-page at most) sampling of some feature or features in your evidence that initially aroused your curiosity. Avoid unnecessary throat-clearing, and cut immediately to something interesting that you have observed and that your paper will put into context and explain. Your introduction is saying: "Look at this, reader; it is worth thinking about, and here's why."

As the Latin roots of the word suggest—*intro*, meaning "within," and *ducere*, meaning "to lead or bring"—an introduction brings the reader into a subject. Its length varies, depending on the scope of the writing project. An introduction may take a paragraph, a few paragraphs, a few pages, a chapter, or even a book. In most academic writing, one or two paragraphs is a standard length. In that space, you should try to accomplish some or all of the following objectives:

- Define your topic—the issue, question, or problem—and say why it matters.
- Indicate your method of approach to the topic.
- Provide necessary background or context.
- Offer the working thesis (hypothesis) your paper will develop.

An objective missing from this list that you might expect to find is the directive to engage the reader. Clearly, all introductions need to engage the reader, but this advice is too often misinterpreted as an invitation to be entertaining or cute. In academic writing, you don't need a gimmick to engage your readers; you can assume they care about the subject. You will engage them if you can articulate why your topic matters, doing so in terms of existing thinking in the field.

Especially in a first draft, the objectives just listed are not so easily achieved, which is why many writers wisely defer writing the polished version of the introduction until they have completed at least one draft of the paper. At that point, you will usually have a clearer notion of why your subject matters and which aspect of your thesis to place first. Often, the conclusion of a first draft becomes the introduction to the second draft.

In any case, the standard shape of an introduction is a *funnel*. It starts wide, providing background and generalization and then narrows the subject to a particular issue or topic. Here is a typical example from an essay entitled "On Political Labels" by Christopher Borick.

> One of the first things you should think about when you see or hear a political label is where it came from. Common political labels such as "liberal" or "conservative" have long histories that shed light on their contemporary use. It's important to recognize that a label's meaning differs from place to place and over time. A conservative in Texas may believe much differently from a conservative in New York, just as an American conservative varies in view points from a conservative in Norway. Similarly, someone calling herself a conservative in 2005 would significantly differ from someone calling himself a conservative in 1905 or even 1975. You may wonder, with such variation over time and place, how can we attach meaning to key political terms at all? While not always easy to see, at least part of the answer can be discovered through an examination of the history of the terms.

The paragraph begins with a generalization in the first sentence (about standard responses to the subject at hand) and funnels down in the last sentence to a qualified working thesis (that some of the meaning lies in the linguistic history of the terms themselves). This does not mean that the first sentence of the paragraph is a throwaway, something broad and bland. Make the first sentence count. Say something incisive and substantive.

PUTTING AN ISSUE OR QUESTION IN CONTEXT

Rather than leaping immediately to the paper's issue, question, or problem, most effective introductions provide some broader context to indicate why the issue matters. Although the various models we offer here differ in small ways from discipline to discipline, the essential characteristics they share suggest that most professors across the curriculum want the same things in an introduction: the locating of a problem or question within a context that provides background and rationale, culminating in a working thesis.

It is important for writers to be conscious of their choice of interpretive context. As we argued in Chapter 6, things don't just "mean" in the abstract; they mean in particular contexts. Thus, to a significant extent, context shapes and determines what we see. Whether we are aware of it or not, we are always locating things in some context. An interpretive context is a lens through which we scrutinize what we are trying to understand. The best writers defend their choice of interpretive context and make their readers aware of it from the start.

Providing an Introductory Context: A Political Science Professor Speaks

In the following Voice from Across the Curriculum, political science professor Jack Gambino notes the usefulness of anomalies for contextualizing papers in his discipline. The discovery of an anomaly, something that does not fit with conventional ways of thinking, can serve as a useful point of departure in a paper that goes on to revise an existing theory or opinion.

Voices from Across the Curriculum

An introduction is not simply the statement of a thesis but also the place where the student needs to set a context, a framework that makes such a thesis statement interesting, timely, or in some other way important. It is common to see papers in political science begin by pointing out a discrepancy between conventional wisdom (what the pundits say) and recent political developments, between popular opinion and empirical evidence, or between theoretical frameworks and particular test cases. Papers, in other words, often begin by presenting *anomalies*.

I encourage students to write opening paragraphs that attempt to elucidate such anomalies by:

1. Stating the specific point of departure: Are they taking issue with a bit of conventional wisdom? Popular opinions? A theoretical perspective? This provides the context in which a student is able to "frame" a particular problem, issue, and so forth.

2. Explaining why the wisdom/opinion/theory has become problematic or controversial by focusing on a particular issue, event, test case, or empirical evidence.

3. Formulating a brief statement of the tentative thesis/position to be pursued in the paper. This can take several forms, including the revising of conventional wisdom/theory/opinion, discarding it in favor of alternative conceptions, or calling for redefinition of an issue and question.

—Jack Gambino, Professor of Political Science

INTRODUCTIONS AND ABSTRACTS IN THE SCIENCES

The natural and social sciences both rely on a fairly tightly defined format for reports on research. The professors quoted in the remainder of this chapter emphasize the importance of isolating a specific question or issue and locating it within a wider context. Notice, as you read these voices, how little the model for an introduction changes in moving from social science to natural science.

In the sciences, the introduction is an especially important and somewhat challenging section of the report to compose because it requires a writer not merely to assemble but also to assimilate the background of information and ideas that frame his or her hypothesis.

One distinctive feature of scientific papers is that a separate prefatory section called the *abstract* precedes the introduction. Authors also produce abstracts for papers in many other disciplines, but these are usually published separately—for example, in a bibliography, in a journal's table of contents, and so forth.

The abstract provides a very concise summary of the paper. Here is a brief definition from a professor of biochemistry at our college, Keri Colabroy: "what you did (experimental approach), why you did it (the problem, some background), and what you found (major findings and conclusions). You might want to know that there are subtle differences in the format of abstracts depending on the journal." *(For more on science writing, see Chapter 15, Forms and Formats Across the Curriculum.)*

Introductions in the Sciences: Three Professors Speak

In the following Voices from Across the Curriculum, biology professor Richard Niesenbaum and psychology professors Laura Edelman and Mark Sciutto address the challenges of introducing and contextualizing research in science writing. Introductions in the IMRAD format (Introduction, Methods, Results, and Discussion/Conclusions), the standard form for lab reports and other kinds of science writing, must do a lot of work in a small space.

Voices from Across the Curriculum

A paper usually starts by making some general observation or a description of known phenomena and by providing the reader with some background information. The first paragraphs should illustrate an understanding of the issues at hand and should present an argument for why the research should be done. In other words, a context or framework is established for the entire paper. This background information must lead to a clear statement of the objectives of the paper and the hypothesis that will be experimentally tested. This movement from broad ideas and observations to a specific question or test starts the deductive scientific process.

—Richard Niesenbaum, Professor of Biology

The introduction is one of the hardest sections to write. In the introduction, students must summarize, analyze, and integrate the work of numerous other authors and use that to build their own argument.

The task is to read each article and *summarize* it in their own words. The key is to analyze rather than just repeat material from the articles so as to make clear the connections among them. (It is important to note that experimental psychologists almost never use direct quotes in their writing. Many of my students have been trained to use direct quotation for their other classes, and so I have to spend time explaining how to summarize without directly quoting or plagiarizing the work that they have read.)

Finally, in the introduction the students must show explicitly how the articles they have summarized lead to the hypothesis they have devised. Many times the students see the connection as implicitly obvious, but I require that they explicitly state the relationships between what they read and what they plan to do.

—Laura Edelman, Professor of Psychology

The format of the empirical paper in psychology resembles an hourglass. It starts reasonably broad, narrows, and then broadens again to the larger perspective: "Now that we know this, where can we go with it? What are the implications?" As in other kinds of science writing, the empirical psychology paper consists of abstract, introduction, methods, results, and discussion. The introduction is especially difficult to write because it must contextualize the new research by pulling together a lot of reading from a variety of sources. This part of the introduction, the literature review, answers the question, "What do we know?"

In order to efficiently locate the new study in the context of others' work on the subject, writers must **integrate** citations. Rather than summarize what Johnson found and then what Smith found and then what Moore found, the writer needs to bring these together into a more concise summary. All three studies might be summarized and cited in one paragraph or even a single sentence. As a rule of thumb, citations should include more than one source. Single citations don't allow enough integration.

—Mark Sciutto, Professor of Psychology

Integration of Citations in a Literature Review: A Brief Example

Note in the following paragraph—from a 1999 article in *Personality and Social Psychology Bulletin*—how the citations (in parentheses) include more than one study:

Self-presentational motives play a role in a variety of potentially dangerous health-related behaviors, including behaviors that lead to risk of HIV infection; accidental death and injury; and alcohol, tobacco, and drug use (Leary, Tchividjian, & Kraxberger, 1994; Martin, Leary, & Rejeski, in press). The desire to be perceived as a risk-taker, brave, or one of the crowd (or conversely, concerns about being viewed as overly cautious or neurotic) may lead people to take chances with their health to create the desired image (Denscombe, 1993; Finney, 1978).

Introductions in Scientific Papers: A Brief Example

The following example comes from a set of excerpted introductions that biochemistry professor Keri Colabroy uses to teach her students how to write concise, focused sentences of two types: Type #1: sentences that orient readers to the scientific context of a new study while also showing the need for it, and Type #2: sentences that succinctly state what the paper/study has accomplished. The sentences come from a paper published in *Nature Chemical Biology* 2006.

> #1 Although the antitumor activity of these two compounds has been shown to involve binding to microtubules, the targets and modes of actions for many other bioactive cyanobacterial metabolites remain elusive.

Dr. Colabroy comments: *This is a great sentence. You can see the tension. Some activity has been shown, but there is still something we don't understand . . . and that is the problem this paper will solve.*

> #2 Here we examine the mode of action of apratoxin A using a number of approaches based on functional genomics, including mRNA expression analysis and genome-wise, arrayed cDNA overexpression. These and other studies suggest that apratoxin A acts in part by blocking the FGFR signaling pathway.

Dr. Colabroy comments: *The use of "here" focuses your attention on the action that immediately follows—"we examine." That is different from "we found" or "we propose," and it implies that the authors didn't really have a hypothesis going in. They were just trying to learn some stuff, and in the process, they came up with some "implications" from the data.*

Framing Research Questions and Hypotheses: A Political Science Professor Speaks

In the following Voice from Across the Curriculum, political science professor Chris Borick explains effective and less effective ways of stating research questions and hypotheses in the introduction.

Voices from Across the Curriculum

Different fields within political science—legal writing, political theory, political policy and behavior—prescribe different forms of writing. Political policy and political behavior papers adhere to a version of the format used in science writing. This format has six parts: statement of the research question, literature review (context), statement of hypothesis, measurement of variables, description of tests, and analysis of findings. The literature review describes the conversation that is going on in the field on the paper's topic. It explains what others know. The research question tells readers what the writer is trying to do. The hypothesis states a claim that is specific enough to test.

The research question sets up the hypothesis; it is the point from which everything flows. Consider the following two versions of a research question on capital punishment. 1) In this study I seek to examine the capital punishment laws used at the state level. 2) In this study I seek to explain why some states adopt capital punishment and others do not. The second version is clearly better. It gives much better direction.

The hypothesis needs to indicate some direction for the research. Although general in scope, it must be specific enough to test. Here again are two examples. Which do you think would make the better hypothesis? 1) The greater the percentage of college educated individuals in a state, the more likely that state will be to allow same sex marriage. 2) The more educated a society, the more liberal it will be.

—Chris Borick, Professor of Political Science

INTRODUCTIONS IN THE HUMANITIES

We have devoted considerable attention in this chapter and the previous one to the prescribed formats for writing lab reports, scientific articles, and empirical studies in the social sciences. As we have suggested throughout these chapters, the surface differences you will encounter as you move across the curriculum can too easily obscure the underlying structure that the disciplines share.

Nevertheless, there are some striking differences. In the sciences, for example, it is inappropriate to name and especially to criticize particular pieces of research or their authors. Writers in the humanities are much more likely to name names, to quote other studies, and to be explicit on where these studies seem to fall short. Relatively broad claims about consensus views on the writer's topic are okay. In fact, papers in the humanities often begin that way. But these highly compressed generalizations are typically followed with more detail on who said what, why they may have said it, and what needs revising.

Because most writing in the humanities is grounded in textual analysis, humanities writers think it important to attend to the actual language of other people's writing. Words and their meanings are data to humanities writers. For this reason, writers in the humanities quote and then paraphrase key statements, rather than summarizing and paraphrasing without the original language, as is the rule in psychology and other science and social science writing. It is a habit of mind in the humanities to share the evidence—the language being phrased and cited—with readers, rather than asking them to take the writer's word for it.

As in the sciences, methods of analysis in the humanities are empirical—grounded in close observation of evidence. But, as we argued in Chapter 6, "Making Interpretations Plausible," the authority of a writer's interpretation of evidence relies on other scholars accepting it as plausible. This is true in the sciences as well, a fact somewhat hidden by the nature of scientific evidence and the very detailed character of the process of investigation.

Here is a typical set of guidelines for writing introductory paragraphs in a humanities paper—in this case, in English. Introductions are not the same across all disciplines in the humanities, but much in the following guidelines is representative.

1. **An introduction is not a conclusion**. You do not need to announce, in short form, your whole argument. In English papers, the intro paragraph is an opening gambit. The thesis you state at the end of paragraph one should be an idea, not a statement of fact. For example, you might offer an idea about what you think is the most important difference and/or similarity between the poem you have chosen to analyze and "Ode to a Nightingale." This statement will get qualified and expanded and tested in the paper. You should not simply march the statement through the paper and prove you are right.

2. **The intro offers readers some representative piece of your evidence**—some data from your poem: perhaps a binary that you see in both poems or some other tendency of the language in both that you found interesting and that you think is worth exploring. *The reader should come away from your opening paragraph knowing what you found interesting and worth pursuing and why.*

3. **Resist dumping a great lump of background into the intro**. You should do some contextualizing in the opening, but don't overdo it. Stay focused on the poem and what you notice about the kind of thinking it is inviting us to do.

4. **Resist what is known as "freshman omniscience"**—recognizable by sweeping claims and a grandiose tone . . . "Since the beginning of time poets have been . . ."

5. **The last sentence of the paragraph should make some kind of claim**. It should not be the standard tri-partite thesis of the 5-paragraph form essay.

HOW MUCH TO INTRODUCE UPFRONT: TYPICAL PROBLEMS

Introductions need to do a lot in a limited space. To specify a thesis and locate it within a larger context, to suggest the plan or outline of the entire paper, and to negotiate first relations with a reader—that's plenty to pack into a paragraph or two. In deciding how much to introduce up front, you must make a series of difficult choices about what to include and exclude.

The danger is trying to turn the introduction into a miniature essay. Consider the three problems discussed next as symptoms of overcompression, telltale signs that you need to reconceive, and probably reduce, your introduction.

Digression

Digression results when you try to include too much background. If, for example, you plan to write about a recent innovation in video technology, you'll need to monitor the amount and kind of technical information you include in your opening paragraphs. You'll also want to avoid starting at a point that is too far away from your immediate concerns, as in "Communication has always been a necessary part of being human."

As a general rule in academic writing, don't assume your readers know little or nothing about the subject. Instead, use the social potential of the introduction to set up your relationship with your readers and make clear what you are assuming they do and do not know.

Incoherence

Incoherence results when you try to preview too much of your paper's conclusion in the introduction. Such introductions move in too many directions at once, usually because the writer is trying to conclude before going through the discussion that will make the conclusion comprehensible. The language you are compelled to use in such cases tends to be too dense, and the connections between the sentences tend to get left out, because there isn't enough room to include them. After having read the entire paper, your readers may be able to make sense of the introduction, but in that case, the introduction has not done its job.

The following introductory paragraph is incoherent, primarily because it tries to include too much. It neither adequately connects its ideas nor defines its terms.

> Twinship is a symbol in many religious traditions. The significance of twinship will be discussed and explored in the Native American, Japanese Shinto, and Christian religions. Twinship can be either in opposing or common forces in the form of deities or mortals. There are several forms of twinship that show duality of order versus chaos, good versus evil, and creation versus destruction. The significance of twinship is to set moral codes for society and to explain the inexplicable.

Prejudgment

Prejudgment results when you appear to have already settled the question to be pursued in the rest of the paper. The problem here is logical. In an effort to preview your paper's conclusion at the outset, you risk appearing to assume something as true that your paper will in fact need to test. In most papers in the humanities and social sciences, where the thesis evolves in specificity and complexity between the introduction and conclusion, writers and readers can find such assumptions prejudicial. Opening in this way, in any event, can make the rest of the paper seem redundant. Even in the sciences, where a concise statement of objectives, plan of attack, and hypothesis are usually required up front, separate "Results" and "Discussion" sections are reserved for the conclusion.

Avoiding Strong Claims in the Introduction: An Economics Professor Speaks

In the following Voice from Across the Curriculum, economics professor James Marshall argues that strong claims in the form of conclusions don't belong in the introduction.

Voices from Across the Curriculum

I might be careful about how tentative conclusions should play in the opening paragraph, because this can easily slide into a prejudging of the question at hand. I would be more comfortable with a clear statement of the prevailing views held by others. For example, a student could write on the question, "Was Franklin Delano Roosevelt a Keynesian?" What purpose would it serve in an opening paragraph to reveal without any supporting discussion that FDR was or was not a Keynesian?

What might be better would be to say that in the public mind FDR is regarded as the original big spender, that some people commonly associate New Deal policies with general conceptions of Keynesianism, but that there may be some surprises in store as that common notion is examined.

In sum, I would discourage students from making strong claims at or near the beginning of a paper. Let's see the evidence first. We should all have respect for the evidence. Strong assertions, bordering on conclusions, too early on are inappropriate.

—James Marshall, Professor of Economics

USING PROCEDURAL OPENINGS

In the interests of clear organization, some academic disciplines require students to include in the introduction an explanation of how the paper will proceed. Such a general statement of method and/or intention is known as a *procedural opening*. Among the disciplines in which you are most likely to find this format are philosophy, political science, and sociology. The danger of procedural openings is that the writer will avoid making a claim at all.

The statement of a paper's plan is not and cannot take the place of a thesis (an idea about the topic that the paper will explore and defend). Consider the deficiencies of the following procedural opening.

> In this paper I will first discuss the strong points and weak points in America's treatment of the elderly. Then I will compare this treatment with that in other industrial nations in the West. Finally, I will evaluate the various proposals for reform that have been advanced here and abroad.

This paragraph identifies the subject, but it neither addresses why the subject matters nor suggests the writer's approach. Nor does it provide background to the topic or suggest a hypothesis that the paper will pursue. In some kinds of essays, especially those that move (inductively) from specific observations to more general claims, there is little need for procedural openings, with their declaration of intention and method at the outset. As the following Voice from Across the Curriculum reveals, however, there is real difference on this matter across disciplines.

Using Procedural Openings: A Political Science Professor Speaks

In the following Voices from Across the Curriculum box, political science professor Jack Gambino explains a common organizational strategy used to orient readers, particularly in social science papers.

Voices from Across the Curriculum

I encourage students to provide a "road map" paragraph early in the paper, perhaps the second or third paragraph. (This is a common practice in professional journals.) The "road map" tells the reader the basic outline of the argument. Something like the following: "In the first part of my paper I will present a brief history of the issue. . . . This will be followed by an account of the current controversy. . . . Part III will spell out my alternative account and evidence. . . . I then conclude. . . ." I think such a paragraph becomes more necessary with longer papers.

—Jack Gambino, Professor of Political Science

GOOD WAYS TO BEGIN

All of the following ways to begin a paper enable you to play an ace, establishing your authority with your readers, without having to play your whole hand. They offer a starting position rather than a miniaturized version of the entire paper. Remember that the aim of the introduction is to answer the question, Why does what I'm about to say matter? What makes it especially interesting or revealing, and in what context? Here are a few methods of accomplishing this aim.

Challenge a Commonly Held View

This move provides you with a framework against which to develop your ideas; it allows you to begin with some back pressure, which will help you to define your position. Because you are responding to a known point of view, you have a ready way of integrating context into your paper. As the economics professor notes of the FDR example, until we understand what the prevailing view is on FDR, it is pointless to start considering whether or not he was a Keynesian.

Begin with a Definition

Beginning with a definition is a reliable way to introduce a topic, so long as that definition has some significance for the discussion to follow. If the definition doesn't do any conceptual work in the introduction, the definition gambit becomes a pointless cliché.

You are most likely to avoid a cliché if you cite a source other than a standard dictionary for your definition. The reference collection of any academic library contains a range of discipline-specific lexicons that provide more precise and authoritative definitions than Webster ever could. A useful alternative is to quote a particular author's definition of a key term because you want to make a point about his or her particular definition: for example, "Although the *Dictionary of Economics* defines Keynesianism as *XYZ*, Smith treats only *X* and *Y*" (or substitutes *A* for *Z*, and so forth).

Lead with Your Second-Best Example

Another versatile opening gambit, where disciplinary conventions allow, is to use your *second-best example* to set up the issue or question that you later develop in depth with your best example. This gambit is especially useful in papers that proceed inductively on the strength of representative examples, an organizational pattern common in the humanities. As you are assembling evidence in the outlining and prewriting stage, in many cases you will accumulate a number of examples that illustrate the same basic point. For example, several battles might illustrate a particular general's military strategy; several political primaries might exemplify how a particular candidate tailors his or her speeches to appeal to the religious right; several scenes might show how a particular playwright romanticizes the working class, and so on.

Save the best example to receive the most analytical attention in your paper. If you were to present this example in the introduction, you would risk making the rest of the essay vaguely repetitive. A quick close-up of another example will strengthen your argument or interpretation. By using a different example to raise the issues, you suggest that the phenomenon exemplified is not an isolated case and that the major example you will eventually concentrate on is indeed representative.

Exemplify the Topic with a Narrative

An occasional gambit in the humanities and social sciences, the narrative opening introduces a short, pertinent, and vivid story or anecdote that exemplifies a key aspect of a topic. Although generally not permissible in the formal reports assigned in the natural and social sciences, narrative openings turn up in virtually all other kinds of writing across the curriculum.

As the introduction funnels to its thesis, the readers receive a graphic sense of the issue that the writer will now develop nonnarratively. Nonnarrative treatment is necessary because by itself anecdotal evidence can be seen as merely personal. Storytelling is suggestive but usually does not constitute sufficient proof; it needs to be corroborated.

WHAT CONCLUSIONS DO: THE FINAL "SO WHAT?"

Like the introduction, the conclusion has a key social function: it escorts the readers out of the paper, just as the introduction has escorted them in. What do readers want as they leave the textual world you have taken them through? The concluding paragraph presents the paper's final "So what?"

Implicit here is the notion that conclusions always state (or restate) the thesis in its most fully evolved form. (See Chapter 11.) In addition, the conclusion usually makes all of the following moves:

- *It comes full circle.* That is, it creates a sense of closure by revisiting the way the paper began. Often, it returns to some key phrase from the context established in the introduction and updates it.

- *It pursues implications.* That is, it reasons from the particular focus of the essay to broader issues, such as the study's practical consequences or applications, or future-oriented issues, such as avenues for further research. To unfold implications in this way is to broaden the view from the here and now of the paper by looking outward to the wider world and forward to the future.

- *It identifies limitations.* That is, it acknowledges restrictions of method or focus in the analysis, and qualifies the conclusion (and its implications) accordingly.

These moves are quite literally movements—they take the thinking in the essay, and the readers with it, both backward and forward. The backward thrust we call *culmination*; the forward thrust we call *send-off*.

When you culminate a paper, you bring together things you have already said, establishing their connection and ascending to one final statement of your thinking. The word *culminate* is derived from the Latin "*columen*," meaning "top or summit." To culminate is to reach the highest point, and it implies a mountain (in this case, of information and analysis) you have scaled.

The climactic effects of culmination provide the basis for the send-off. The send-off is both social and conceptual, a final opening outward of the topic that leads the reader out of the paper with something further to think about. Here, the thinking moves beyond the close analysis of data that has occupied the body of the paper into a kind of speculation that the writer has earned the right to formulate. Simply put, you culminate with the best statement of your big idea, and your send-off gets you and the reader out of the paper.

Beyond Restatement: Two Professors Speak

The professors in the following Voices from Across the Curriculum suggest ways of ending on a note of expanded implication, bringing the paper's more focused analysis to a larger perspective.

Voices from Across the Curriculum

I tell my students that too many papers "just end," as if the last page or so were missing. I tell them the importance of ending a work. One could summarize main points, but I tell them this is not heavy lifting.

I believe the ending should be an expansion of possibilities, sort of like an introduction to some much larger "mental" paper out there. I sometimes encourage students to see the concluding section as an option to introduce ideas that can't be dealt with now. Sort of a "Having done this, I would want to explore boom, boom, boom if I were to continue further." Here the students can critique and recommend ("Having seen 'this,' one wonders 'that'").

—Frederick Norling, Professor of Business

The conclusion does not appear simply as a restatement of a thesis, but rather as an attempt to draw out its implications and significance (the "So what?"). This is what I usually try to impress upon students. For instance, if a student is writing on a particular proposal for party reform, I would expect the concluding paragraph to consider both the significance of the reform and its practicality.

I should note that professional papers often indicate the tentativeness of their conclusions by stressing the need for future research and indicating what these research needs might be. Although I haven't tried this, maybe it would be useful to have students conclude papers with a section entitled "For Further Consideration" in which they would indicate those things that they would have liked to have known but couldn't, given their time constraints, the availability of information, and lack of methodological sophistication. This would serve as a reminder of the tentativeness of conclusions and the need to revisit and revise arguments in the future (which, after all, is a good scholarly habit).

—Jack Gambino, Professor of Political Science

CONCLUSIONS IN THE SCIENCES: THE DISCUSSION SECTION

As is the case with introductions, the conclusions of reports written in the natural and in some social sciences are regulated by formalized disciplinary formats. Conclusions, for example, occur in a section entitled "Discussion." There, the writer analyzes conclusions and qualifies them in relation to some larger experimental context, "the big picture."

First, specific results are interpreted (but not restated), and then their implications and limitations are discussed. At the end, the writer should rephrase the original research question and discuss it in light of the results presented. It is at this point that alternative explanations may be considered and new questions posed.

Writing Conclusions in the Sciences: Two Professors Speak

In the following Voices from Across the Curriculum, a psychology professor and a biochemistry professor explain how the discussion section of a scientific paper locates its conclusions in the context of other research—that which came before and that which will follow.

Voices from Across the Curriculum

The conclusion occurs in a section labeled "Discussion" and, as specified by the *Publication Manual of the American Psychological Association*, is guided by the following questions:

- What have I contributed here?
- How has my study helped to resolve the original problem?
- What conclusions and theoretical implications can I draw from my study?

In a broad sense, a particular research report should be seen as but one moment in a broader research tradition that *preceded* the particular study being written about and that will *continue after* this study is published. And so the conclusion should tie this particular study into both previous research considering implications

for the theory guiding this study and (when applicable) practical implications of this study. One of the great challenges of writing a research report is thus to place this particular study within that broader research tradition. That's an analytical task.
—Alan Tjeltveit, Professor of Psychology

The Discussion section is where the scientist finally gets to analyze the data. The previous two sections of a science paper—Methods and Results—report rather than analyze. In the Discussion section, the writer makes claims and backs them with evidence (data). Analysis of the data tells readers what the study found in the context of current knowledge in the field and the researcher's expectations. The paper's conclusions, which usually appear in the last paragraph of the Discussion, always look back and then forward—first back to previous research and then forward to remaining questions.
—Keri Colabroy, Professor of Biochemistry

Conclusions in Scientific Papers: A Brief Example

As you read this sample Discussion/Conclusion section of a scientific paper, refer back to Dr. Colabroy's preceding comments.

> The rapid and sustained elevations in 2-AG induced by JZL 184 were accompanied by an array of CB1-dependent behavioral effects, including analgesia, hypomotility and hypothermia. This collection of phenotypes qualitatively resembles those induced by direct CB1 agonists. Overall these data suggest that MAGL-regulated 2-AG pathways endogenously modulate several behavioral processes classically associated with the pharmacology of cannabinoids . . . .
> In summary, we believe that the properties of JZL184 warrant inclusion of this compound among the growing arsenal of efficacious and selective pharmacological probes used to examine the endocannabinoid system. JZL184 could itself serve as a lead scaffold for the development of such dual inhibitors, given that at high concentrations this compound inhibited both MAGL and FAAH without affecting other brain serine hydrolases.

SOLVING TYPICAL PROBLEMS IN CONCLUSIONS

The primary challenge in writing conclusions, it should now be evident, lies in finding a way to culminate your analysis without claiming either too little or too much. There are a number of fairly common problems to guard against if you are to avoid either of these two extremes.

Redundancy

In Chapter 10, we lampooned an exaggerated example of the 5-paragraph form for constructing its conclusion by stating "Thus, we see" and then repeating the introduction verbatim. The result is redundancy. It's a good idea to refer back to the opening, but it's a bad idea just to reinsert it mechanically. Instead, reevaluate what you said there in light of where you've ended up, repeating only key words or phrases from the introduction. This kind of selective repetition is a desirable way of achieving unity and will keep you from making one of two opposite mistakes—either repeating too much or bringing up a totally new point in the conclusion.

Raising a Totally New Point

Raising a totally new point can distract or bewilder a reader. This problem often arises out of a writer's praiseworthy desire to avoid repetition. As a rule, you can guard against the problem by making sure you have clearly expressed the conceptual link between your central conclusion and any implications you may draw. An implication is not a totally new point but rather one that follows from the position you have been analyzing.

Similarly, although a capping judgment or send-off may appear for the first time in your concluding paragraph, it should have been anticipated by the body of your paper. Conclusions often indicate where you think you (or an interested reader) may need to go next, but you don't actually go there. In a paper on economist Milton Friedman, for example, if you think another economist offers a useful way of critiquing him, you probably should not introduce this person for the first time in your conclusion.

Overstatement

Many writers are confused over how much they should claim in the conclusion. Out of the understandable (but mistaken) desire for a grand (rather than a modest and qualified) culmination, writers sometimes overstate the case. They assert more than their evidence has proven or even suggested. Must a conclusion arrive at some comprehensive and final answer to the question your paper has analyzed?

Depending on the question and the disciplinary conventions, you may need to come down exclusively on one side or another. In a great many cases, however, the answers with which you conclude can be more moderate. Especially in the humanities, good analytical writing seeks to unfold successive layers of implication, so it's not even reasonable for you to expect neat closure. In such cases, you are usually better off qualifying your final judgments, drawing the line at points of relative stability.

Anticlimax

The end of the conclusion is a "charged" site because it gives the reader a last impression of your paper. If you end with a concession—an acknowledgement of a rival position at odds with your thesis—you risk leaving the reader unsettled and possibly confused. The term for this kind of letdown is "anticlimax." In most cases, you will flub the send-off if you depart the paper on an anticlimax.

There are many forms of anticlimax besides ending with a concession. If your conclusion peters out in a random list or an apparent afterthought or a last-minute qualification of your claims, the effect is anticlimactic. And for many readers, if your final answer comes from quoting an authority in place of establishing your own, that, too, is an anticlimax.

At the beginning of this section, we suggested that a useful rule for the introduction is to play an ace but not your whole hand. In the context of this card-game analogy, it is similarly effective to save an ace for the conclusion. In most cases, this high card will provide an answer to some culminating "So what?" question—a last view of the implications or consequences of your analysis.

Try This 16.1: Analyze Paired Introductions and Conclusions

The best way to learn about introductions and conclusions is to study them separated out from the larger articles or essays they frame. Once they are isolated in this way, you can begin to focus on the form, noticing how the introductions raise an issue, provide minimal context, and perhaps start down a particular thesis path. And looking at the paired conclusion, you can see where each writer ends up and how he or she gets us there, culminating the journey in the context of its beginning.

What follows are eight introductions paired with their conclusions, taken from various kinds of published writing. Study the pairings to identify how particular sentences function, in terms of both organization and rhetoric. The following questions should help.

- Where in each of the introductions does the working thesis or other indication of the paper's probable direction appear?
- Which words and sentences in each of the conclusions bring the paper full circle?
- What seems to have happened to the paper's opening claims by the time the writer arrives at his or her conclusion?
- What strategies does each writer use to begin and end his or her writing?
- Where and how do the concluding paragraphs seem to culminate and provide readers with some kind of send-off?

Your goal is to get in the practice of noticing what writers do in their introductions and conclusions.

1. From Jessica Love, "They Get to Me" in *The American Scholar* (July 2, 2010). [http://www.theamericanscholar.org/they-get-to-me/]

Introduction:

I used to be a normal psycholinguistics graduate student. I wanted to study how the mind parses improbable metaphors, unintelligible accents, and quirky syntax. Sexy things. Things that would play out well at parties. I imagined myself magnanimously explaining how sentences like "The bartender served the bourbon fell down the stairs" were truly grammatical. I imagined myself dropping newspaper headlines like "Iraqi Head Seeks Arms" into conversations with beautiful people. I would defend Internet chatroom slang on local radio. I would exchange holiday cards with Steven Pinker.

But something has happened. I am in my third year of graduate school, and I have fallen in love. I have fallen for pronouns. It's hard to shut me up about them.

Conclusion:

Lucky for me, there are plenty of pronouns in need of more study—the diectics (here, there), the reflexives (himself, themselves), the interrogatives (who, what), the possessives (his, mine), the indefinites (somebody, anything)—each with its own relatively unexamined life. Or, for the freshest pronoun around, I could always coin one myself.

In Baltimore, some teenagers already have: their candidate, yo, is a new gender-neutral third-person personal pronoun. As in Yo was tuckin' in his shirt or Yo sucks at magic tricks. If yo sticks around—and if it spreads—maybe we can put the ever-awkward he or she to rest forever. And what would that mean? What consequences could that have for how we think about our world? Empirical question. Send in the psycholinguists.

2. From "Energy in the European Union, Gas Wars" in *The Economist* 390.8613 (January 10, 2009). (*The Economist* does not publish the names of the authors of its articles.)

Introduction:

A gas row between Russia and Ukraine has become a Christmas ritual. That may explain why, until this week, the European Union seemed to pay the latest tiff so little heed. Indeed, the people in Brussels talked of it as a normal bilateral commercial dispute in which the EU should neither interfere nor take sides. Yet Russia's abrupt decision on January 5th to cut off almost all the gas it supplies to the EU countries via Ukraine has sharply raised the stakes, inviting the Europeans to intervene more directly. The shutdown should force a rethink of the EU's overall energy policy as well.

Conclusion:

Beyond this, Europe needs to work harder to diversify its sources of energy, something that it must do anyway if it is to meet its ambitious climate-change targets. And it cannot be repeated too often that a fully liberalized energy market, with better linkages between countries, offers all of Europe not only a more efficient energy future but also a more secure one.

3. From Germaine Greer, "Beaten to the Punchline" in *The Guardian* (February 3, 2009). [http://www.guardian.co.uk/stage/2009/mar/02/germaine-greer-comedy-women]

Introduction:

I should probably not have said, in so few words on television recently, that women aren't as funny as men. Put so baldly, the observation sounds like deliberate provocation, as if I was baiting feminists, or looking for some kind of a knee-jerk response. I was actually trying to present an aspect of the psychopathology of everyday life that strikes me as interesting and important. Women are at least as intelligent as men, and they have as vivid and ready a perception of the absurd; but they have not developed the arts of fooling, clowning, badinage, repartee, burlesque and innuendo into a semi-continuous performance as so many men have.

Conclusion:

At the heart of the judgment that women are not as funny as men is another far less inflammatory observation: that women are less competitive. Competition drives men to more and more outrageous and bizarre mental acrobatics, to stay ahead of the game and have the last laugh. The greater the pressure, the faster the firing of neurons in the male brain. You get your best results from women when you take the pressure off. Men do the inspired lunacy; women do droll.

4. From Robert Kagan, "Why the United States and Europe See the World Differently" in *Policy Review* 113 (2002). [http://www.hoover.org/publications/policyreview/3460246.html] Accessed March 10, 2009.

Introduction:

It is time to stop pretending that Europeans and Americans share a common view of the world, or even that they occupy the same world. On the all-important question of power—the efficacy of power, the morality of power, the desirability of power—American and European perspectives are diverging. Europe is turning away from power, or to put it a little differently, it is moving beyond power into a self-contained world of laws and rules and transnational negotiation and cooperation. It is entering a post-historical paradise of peace and relative prosperity, the realization of Kant's "Perpetual Peace." The United States, meanwhile, remains mired in history, exercising power in the anarchic Hobbesian world where international laws and rules are unreliable and where true security and the defense and promotion of a liberal order still depend on the possession and use of military might. That is why on major strategic and international questions today, Americans are from Mars and Europeans are from Venus: They agree on little and understand one another less and less. And this state of affairs is not transitory—the product of one American election or one catastrophic event. The reasons for the transatlantic divide are deep, long in development, and likely to endure. When it comes to setting national priorities, determining threats, defining challenges, and fashioning and implementing foreign and defense policies, the United States and Europe have parted ways.

Conclusion:

These are small steps, and they will not address the deep problems that beset the transatlantic relationship today. But, after all, it is more than a cliché that the United States and Europe share a set of common Western beliefs. Their aspirations for humanity are much the same, even if their vast disparity of power has now put them in very different places. Perhaps it is not too naïvely optimistic to believe that a little common understanding could still go a long way.

5. From Jerry A. Coyne, " in *The New Republic* (February 4, 2009). [http://www. tnr.com/article/books/seeing-and-believing] Accessed February 23, 2011

Introduction:

Charles Darwin was born on February 12, 1809—the same day as Abraham Lincoln—and published his magnum opus, On the Origin of Species, fifty years later. Every half century, then, a Darwin Year comes around: an occasion to honor his theory of evolution by natural selection, which is surely the most important concept in biology, and perhaps the most revolutionary scientific idea in history. 2009 is such a year, and we biologists are preparing to fan out across the land, giving talks and attending a multitude of DarwinFests. The melancholy part is that we will be speaking more to other scientists than to the American public. For in this country, Darwin is a man of low repute. The ideas that made Darwin's theory so revolutionary are precisely the ones that repel much of religious America, for they imply that, far from having a divinely scripted role in the drama of life, our species is the accidental and contingent result of a purely natural process.

Conclusion:

This disharmony is a dirty little secret in scientific circles. It is in our personal and professional interest to proclaim that science and religion are perfectly harmonious. After all, we want our grants funded by the government, and our schoolchildren exposed to real science instead of creationism. Liberal religious people have been important allies in our struggle against creationism, and it is not pleasant to alienate them by declaring how we feel. This is why, as a tactical matter, groups such as the National Academy of Sciences claim that religion and science do not conflict. But their main evidence—the existence of religious scientists—is wearing thin as scientists grow ever more vociferous about their lack of faith. Now Darwin Year is upon us, and we can expect more books like those by Kenneth Miller and Karl Giberson. Attempts to reconcile God and evolution keep rolling off the intellectual assembly line. It never stops, because the reconciliation never works.

6. From John Cassidy, "Harder Times" in *The New Yorker* (March 16, 2009).

Introduction:

As an exercise in political symbolism, the release of the White House's $3.6-trillion budget for 2010 was an important moment. President Obama, by putting some numbers behind his plans to reform health care, limit carbon emissions, and tackle rising inequality, confirmed his intention to lead the country in a new direction. Republican jibes that the budget was "socialist" should be treated with the respect they deserve, which is to say none: after a major rise in outlays this year, due to the stimulus package, federal spending as a share of the gross domestic product is projected to fall back to twenty-two percent by 2013, which represents a rise of just one percent over last year's figure.

Conclusion:

Last week, Christina Romer, the head of the Council of Economic Advisers, expressed the hope that the Administration's policies would lead to a "Rooseveltian moment," by which she meant a sharp economic upturn, like the one that occurred from 1933 to 1937. Acting in a Rooseveltian manner involves defying orthodoxy, challenging powerful interests, and giving voice to the public's disgust at the corrupt financial establishment. F.D.R. was called a lot worse names than socialist. He didn't let it stop him.

7. From Blight S. K., Larue R. C., Mahapatra A., Longstaff D. G., Chang E., Zhao G., Kang P. T., Green-Church K. B., Chan M. K., Krzycki J. A., "Direct Charging of tRNAcua with pyrrolysine in vitro and in vivo" in *Nature* 439 (2004).

Introduction:

Most organisms employ UAG as a stop codon, but translation is not terminated at in-frame UAGs in some methyltransferases of methanogenic Archaea. Rather, these codons serve as sense codons and,

as determined by crystal structure analysis, UAG encodes pyrrolysine, that is, lysine with the epsilon nitrogen in amide linkage to (4R,
5R)-4-substituted-pyrroline-5-carboxylate, the 22nd amino acid found
to be genetically encoded in nature. A key question is whether the
UAG-translating tRNAcua is first charged with lysine and then modified to pyrrolysine for incorporation into the growing polypeptide or
whether pyrrolysine is attached as the fully synthesized amino acid
to tRNAcua. Here we show that the latter possibility is feasible by
demonstrating the direct pyrrolysylation of tRNAcua in vitro. This is
the first example found in nature of specific aminoacylation of tRNA
with a non-canonical amino acid. The results reported show further
that the expression of only two genes, pylT and pylS, which encode
tRNAcua and pyrrolysyl-tRNAsynthetase, can expand the genetic
code of E. coli to include pyrrolysine. This procedure could potentially be used to immediately expand the genetic code of any species
that can incorporate exogenously added pyrrolysine.

Conclusion:

The current data indicate that pyrrolysine is encoded in DNA using
the general mechanism employed for the common set of 20 amino
acids. Direct charging of pyrrolysine onto tRNAconstrasts with
selenocysteine, a genetically encoded non-canonical amino acid
synthesized only on tRNA. Several systems have been recently
developed to expand and manipulate the genetic code to generate
recombinant proteins containing unnatural amino acids. By adding
pylS and pylT genes, it should now be possible to generate proteins
with the 22nd amino acid incorporated at UAG targeted sites in any
species that can incorporate added pyrrolysine, thereby adding a
unique natural amino acid with electrophilic properties. We are now
focusing on the pyrrolysine biosynthetic pathway, which offers the
possibility of also adding genes that will generate pyrrolysine internally in recombinant organisms.

8. From Aviya Kushner, "McCulture" in *The Wilson Quarterly* (2009).

Introduction:

As a child, I lived in a house where we spoke only Hebrew. I remember relatives from the American side of the family complaining
about my parents' language policy when they visited our house in
NewYork. "She'll suffer if she doesn't speak English at home," one
worried. "She won't be able to write well enough to get into college." But something unexpected happened as my Israeli mother
sang the Psalms to my siblings and me while we bathed: empires
fell. The Berlin Wall literally came down. Droves of immigrants and

refugees—huddled masses who had long yearned to be free—
changed London, Berlin, Tel Aviv, and New York. India rose, China
skyrocketed, and four young Israelis invented instant messaging.
Bilingual kids like me, toting odd foods at lunch and speaking with
their mothers in something unintelligible, were suddenly not the
problem, but the glittering future.

Conclusion:

This is not to discount the value of bilingual writers. There are bilingual writers who feel a special freedom in English: a rebirth, they
say, without the weight of culture or history, the taste of prayer or
the memory of genocide. Olga Grushin, at the end of our conversation, quoted Charlemagne, who said that to have a second language
is to possess a second soul.

I was moved by the idea of another soul. But then I thought it
over, as reader instead of writer. As praise is heaped on people who
have mastered English, we are rewarding writers for selling their
first soul. A culture with a healthier translation climate would create a space between languages, a space between souls. As readers,
we'd win. We'd be able to hear the sound of all sorts of souls on the
page—whether a first soul or, as Charlemagne claimed, a second
soul, trying to speak, or perhaps, with luck, sing.

GUIDELINES FOR WRITING INTRODUCTIONS AND CONCLUSIONS

Introductions

1. The introduction seeks to raise the issue, not settle it. Articulate why, in the context of existing thinking on the subject, your topic matters.

2. Don't try to do too much. Offer only the most relevant context, the most essential parts of your road map, and (disciplinary conventions permitting) a first rather than last claim.

3. Always introduce a working (hypo)thesis, frame it with (appropriately cited) background or other context, and indicate your method or angle of approach.

4. Especially in longer papers, you can use a procedural opening to forecast the organization clearly, but don't let it distract you from also stating your claim.

5. Experiment with opening gambits: challenge a common view, use your second best example to set up the issue, or exemplify the problem with a narrative opening.

Conclusions

6. Culminate—don't just summarize. Offer your most fully evolved and qualified statement of the thesis or your final judgment on the question posed in the introduction.

7. Come full circle: revisit the introductory hypothesis and context. This strategy will unify your paper and locate it within an ongoing conversation on your topic.

8. Your conclusion should not unqualifiedly claim more than your evidence has established, but it should leave the reader with further implications or speculations to ponder (a send-off).

9. Let your conclusion gradually escort the reader out of the paper. Like the introduction, it is a social site, so try to leave the reader with a positive last impression.

Assignments: Analyzing Introductions and Conclusions

1. **Introductions and Audience.** Compare and contrast introductory paragraphs from a popular magazine with those from an academic journal aimed at a more specialized audience. Select one of each and analyze them to determine what each author assumes the audience knows. Where in each paragraph are these assumptions most evident? If you write out your analysis, it should probably take about a page, but this exercise can also be done productively with others in a small group.

2. **Analyzing Introductions.** One of the best ways to learn about introductions is to gather some sample introductory paragraphs and, working on your own or in a small group, figure out how each one works, what it accomplishes. Here are some particular questions you might pose:

   • Why does the writer start in this way—what is accomplished?

   • What kind of relationship does this opening establish with the audience and to what ends?

   • How does the writer let readers know why the writing they are about to read is called for, useful, and necessary?

   • Where and by what logic does the introduction funnel?

3. **Analyzing Conclusions.** Find some examples of concluding paragraphs from published writing. First, compare the conclusion with the introduction, looking for the way the conclusion comes full circle. Which elements of the

introduction are repeated to accomplish this? Then look for the statement of the essay's thesis in its final, culminating form. Finally, locate the send-off by finding implications and limitations that the writer has noted as part of his final So what? On the basis of your findings, write a few paragraphs in which you describe the writer's approach to conclusions.

At this point, you will be ready to repeat this exercise with some of your own work. Only this time, rather than describing the writer's approach, write an improved version of one of your conclusions based on what you learned from your analysis.

Chapter 17

Revising for Style: Word Choice

THIS FIRST CHAPTER ON STYLE ADDRESSES WORD CHOICE, also known as diction, and its effect on style. The chapter seeks to make you more self-conscious about the kinds of words you habitually use and to expand your range of choices. Chapter 18 attempts to do the same with sentence shapes (syntax). The unit's final chapter moves from stylistic questions—a matter of choice—to common grammatical errors, a matter of correct versus incorrect forms. For this chapter and the next, we'll be asking you to think rhetorically, that is, in terms of appropriate choices for particular contexts rather than right versus wrong.

Most people simply don't pay attention to words. They use words as if their sounds were inaudible, their shapes were invisible, and their meanings were single and self-evident. One goal of this chapter is to interest you in words themselves—as *things* with particular qualities, complex histories, and varied shades of meaning.

> **STYLE: THE BASICS**
>
> Style is not merely decorative.
> Simplicity does not necessarily equal clarity.
> A matter of words is always a matter of meaning.

STYLE IS MEANING

A key concept throughout this unit is that style is not merely decorative. It is often mistakenly assumed that style is separate from meaning and in that sense largely cosmetic. From this perspective, paying close attention to style seems finicky, or worse, cynical—a way of dressing up the content to sell it to readers or listeners. The problem with this perspective is that it subscribes to what we have earlier referred to as *the transparent theory of language.* This is the idea that meaning exists outside of language—that we somehow see *through* words to meaning and can then address that meaning without addressing the words that embody it. In the transparent theory of language, words are merely pointers to get past.

Another key concept of this unit is that simplicity does not necessarily equal clarity. This chapter targets the unexamined cultural bias in favor of "straight talk." The assumption seems to be that people who use too many words, especially big ones, are needlessly complicating what would otherwise be obvious to anyone's common sense. *Not so.* (Those imperious arbiters of style, Strunk and White, are sometimes correct when they say in *The Elements of Style*—"Never use six words when three will do"—but not always.) Strunk and White also say, for example, never to use the "not un-" formation. So they summarily rule that it is always better to say "I am happy" rather than "I am not unhappy." The second sentence, however, does not mean the same thing as the first. The difference is not just a matter of words but of meaning. This chapter seeks to persuade you that a matter of words is always a matter of meaning.

STYLE: A MATTER OF CHOICES

And what is style? Well, it's not just icing on the cake—cosmetic, a matter of polishing the surface. Broadly defined, *style* refers to all of a writer's decisions in selecting, arranging, and expressing what he or she has to say. Many factors affect your style: your aim and sense of audience, the ways you approach and develop a topic, the kinds of evidence you choose, and, particularly, the kinds of syntax (word order) and diction (word choice) you characteristically select.

In this sense, style is personal. The foundations of your style emerge in the dialogue you have with yourself about your topic. When you revise for style, you consciously reorient yourself toward communicating the results of that dialogue to your audience. Stylistic decisions, then, are a mix of the unconscious and conscious, of chance and choice. You don't simply impose style onto your prose; it's not a mask you don or your way of icing the cake. Revising for style is more like sculpting. As a sculptor uses a chisel to "bring out" a shape from a block of walnut or marble, a writer uses style to bring out the shape of the conceptual connections in a draft of an essay. This bringing out demands a certain detachment from your own language. It requires that you become aware of your words as words and of your sentences as sentences.

You may have been taught that you should always avoid the first-person *I* in academic writing, steer clear of jargon, and never start a sentence with *and* or *but.* There are occasions when all three rules, and others like them, should be rejected. These are matters of usage, not hard-and-fast rules of grammar. This chapter seeks to persuade you that all writing is *contextual,* its appropriateness dependent on the rhetorical situation.

It is commonly assumed that "getting the style right" is a task that begins at the editing stage of producing a paper, as part of polishing the final draft. This assumption is only partly true. Getting the style right is not as simple as proofreading for errors in grammar or punctuation. Proofreading occurs in the relatively comfortable linguistic world of simple right and wrong. Stylistic considerations, by contrast, take place in the more exploratory terrain of *making choices* among more and less effective ways of formulating and communicating your meaning. Most writers do delay a full-fledged stylistic revision until a late stage of drafting, but that doesn't mean that they totally ignore stylistic questions as they draft. The decisions you make about how to phrase your meaning inevitably exert a powerful influence on the meaning you make.

If stylistic considerations are not merely cosmetic, then it follows that rethinking the way you have said something can lead you to rethink the substance of what you have said.

HOW STYLE SHAPES THOUGHT: A BRIEF EXAMPLE

How does the difference in sentence structure affect the meaning of the following two sentences?

> **Draft:** The history of Indochina is marked by colonial exploitation as well as international cooperation.

> **Revision:** The history of Indochina, *although* marked by colonial exploitation, testifies to the possibility of international cooperation.

In the draft, the claim that Indochina has experienced colonial exploitation is equal in weight to the claim that it has also experienced international cooperation. But the revision ranks the two claims. The "although" clause makes the claim of exploitation secondary to the claim of cooperation. The first version of the sentence would probably lead you to a broad survey of foreign intervention in Indochina. The result would likely be a static list in which you judged some interventions to be "beneficial" and others "not beneficial." The revised sentence redirects your thinking, tightens your paper's focus to prioritize evidence of cooperation, and presses you to make decisions, such as whether the positive consequences of cooperation outweigh the negative consequences of colonialism. In short, the revision leads you to examine the dynamic relations between your two initial claims.

Rethinking what you mean is just as likely to occur when you attend to word choice. Notice how the change of a single word in the following sentences could change the entire paper.

> **Draft:** The president's attitude toward military spending is ambiguous.

> **Revision:** The president's attitude toward military spending is ambivalent.

In the draft, the use of the word "ambiguous" (meaning "open to many interpretations") would likely lead to a paper on ways that the president's decisions are unclear. If the president's policies aren't unclear—hard to interpret—but are conflicted over competing ways of thinking, then the writer would want the word "ambivalent." This recognition would lead not only to reorganizing the final draft but also to refocusing the argument, building to the significance of this ambivalence (that the president is torn between adopting one of two stances) rather than to the previous conclusion (that presidential policy is incoherent).

"RIGHT" AND "WRONG" WORDS: SHADES OF MEANING

The nineteenth-century English statesman Benjamin Disraeli once differentiated between *misfortune* and *calamity* by using these words in a sentence describing his political rival William Gladstone: "If Mr. Gladstone fell into the Thames, it would be a misfortune; but if someone dragged him out, it would be a calamity." Misfortune and calamity might mean the same thing to some people, but in fact the two words allow a careful writer to discriminate fine shades of meaning.

One of the best ways to pay attention to words as words is to practice making subtle distinctions among related words. The "right" word contributes accuracy and precision to your meaning. The "wrong" word, it follows, is inaccurate or imprecise. The most reliable guide to choosing the right word and avoiding the wrong word is a dictionary that includes not only concise definitions but also the origin of words (known as their *etymology*). A dicey alternative is a thesaurus (a dictionary of synonyms, now included in most word processing software). A thesaurus can offer you a host of choices, but you run a fairly high risk of choosing an inappropriate word because the thesaurus lists words as synonyms that really have different shades of meaning and connotation.

Many of the most common diction errors happen because the writer has not learned the difference between similar terms that actually have different meanings. A common error of this kind is use of the word "notorious" when what the writer means to say is "famous." A *notorious* figure is widely but unfavorably known, whereas a *famous* person is usually recognized for accomplishments that are praiseworthy. Referring to a famous person as notorious—a rather comic error—could be an embarrassing mistake.

A slightly less severe version of getting the wrong word occurs when a writer uses a word with a shade of meaning that is inappropriate or inaccurate in a particular context. Take, for example, the words *assertive* and *aggressive*. Often used interchangeably, they don't really mean the same thing—and the difference matters. Loosely defined, both terms mean forceful. But assertive suggests being bold and self-confident, whereas aggressive suggests being eager to attack. In most cases, you compliment the person you call assertive but raise doubts about the person you call aggressive (whether you are giving a compliment depends on the situation: aggressive is a term of praise on the football field but less so if used to describe an acquaintance's behavior during conversation at the dinner table).

One particularly charged context in which shades of meaning matter involves the potentially sexist implications of using one term for women and another for men. If, for example, in describing a woman and a man up for the same job, the employer were to refer to the woman as *aggressive* but the man as *assertive,* his diction would deservedly be considered sexist. It would reveal that what is perceived as poised and a sign of leadership potential in a man is construed as unseemly belligerence in a woman. The sexism enters when word choice suggests that what is assertive in a man is aggressive in a woman.

Word Histories and the *OED*

In choosing the right shade of meaning, you will get a sharper sense for the word by knowing its etymological history—the word or words from which it evolved. In the preceding example, *aggressive* derives from the Latin *aggressus,* meaning "to go to or approach"; and *aggressus* is itself a combination of *ad,* a prefix expressing motion, and *gradus,* meaning "a step." An aggressive person, then, is "coming at you." *Assertive,* on the other hand, comes from the Latin *asserere,* combining *ad* and *serere,* meaning "to join or bind together." An assertive person is "coming to build or put things together"—certainly not to threaten.

The best dictionary for pursuing word histories, by the way, is the *Oxford English Dictionary,* which commonly goes by its initials, *OED.* Available in every library reference collection and usually online at colleges and universities as well, it provides examples of how words have been used over time.

Try This 17.1: Tracing Word Histories

One of the best ways to pay attention to words as words is to practice making fine distinctions among related words, as we did with aggressive and assertive. The following exercise will not only increase your vocabulary but also acquaint you with that indispensable reference work for etymology: the *OED.*

Look up one of the following pairs of words in the *OED.* Write down the etymology of each word in the pair, and then, in a paragraph for each, summarize the words' linguistic histories—how their meanings have evolved across time. (The *OED*'s examples of how the word has been used over time will be helpful here.)

ordinal/ordinary

explicate/implicate

tenacious/stubborn

induce/conducive

enthusiasm/ecstasy

adhere/inhere

monarchy/oligarchy

overt/covert

What's Bad About "Good" and "Bad"

Broad evaluative terms such as *good* and *bad* can seduce you into stopping your thinking while it is still too general and ill-defined—a matter discussed at length in The Judgment Reflex section of Chapter 2. If you train yourself to select more precise words whenever you encounter *good* and *bad* in your drafts, not only will your prose become clearer but also the search for new words will probably start you thinking again, sharpening your ideas. If, for example, you find yourself writing a sentence such as "The subcommittee made a *bad* decision," ask yourself *why* you called it a bad decision. A revision to "The subcommittee made a *shortsighted* decision" indicates what in fact is bad about the decision and sets you up to discuss why the decision was myopic, further developing the idea.

Be aware that often evaluative terms are disguised as neutrally descriptive ones—*natural,* for instance, and *realistic.* Realistic according to whom, and defined by what criteria? Something is natural according to a given idea about nature—an assumption—and the same goes for *moral*. These are not terms that mean separately from a particular context or ideology, that is, an assumed hierarchy of value. Similarly, in a sentence such as "Society disapproves of interracial marriage," the broad and apparently neutral term *society* can blind you to a host of important distinctions about social class, about a particular culture, and so on.

Concrete and Abstract Diction

At its best, effective analytical prose uses both concrete and abstract words. Simply defined, concrete diction brings things to life by offering readers words that play on their senses. *Telephone, eggshell, crystalline, azure, striped, kneel, flare,* and *burp* are examples of concrete diction. You need concrete language whenever you are describing what happens or what something looks like—in a laboratory experiment, in a military action, in a painting or film sequence. The language of evidence consists of concrete diction. It allows us to see for ourselves the basis of a person's convictions in the stuff of lived experience.

By contrast, abstract diction refers to words that designate concepts and categories. *Virility, ideology, love, definitive, desultory, conscientious, classify,* and *ameliorate* are examples of abstract diction. So are *democracy, fascism, benevolence,* and *sentimentality.* Abstract words give us the language of ideas. We cannot do without abstract terms, and yet writing made up only of such words loses contact with experience, with the world that we can apprehend through our senses.

The line between abstract and concrete is not always as clear as these examples may suggest. You may recall the ladder of abstraction that we discuss in the section entitled Generalizing in Chapter 2. There, we propose that abstract and concrete are not hard-and-fast categories so much as a continuum, a sliding scale. Word A (for example, machine) may be more abstract than word B (computer) but more concrete than word C (technology).

Concrete and abstract diction need each other. Concrete diction illustrates and anchors the generalizations that abstract diction expresses. Notice the concrete language used to define the abstraction *provinciality* in this example:

> There is no cure for *provinciality* like traveling abroad. In America, the waiter who fails to bring the check promptly at the end of the meal we rightly convict for not being watchful. But in England, after waiting interminably for the check and becoming increasingly irate, we learn that only an ill-mannered waiter would bring it without being asked. We have been rude, not he.

In the following example, the abstract terms *causality, fiction,* and *conjunction* are integrated with concrete diction in the second sentence:

> According to the philosopher David Hume, *causality* is a kind of *fiction* that we ascribe to what he called "the constant *conjunction* of observed events." If a person gets hit in the eye and a black semicircle develops underneath it, that does not necessarily mean the blow caused the black eye.

A style that omits concrete language can leave readers lost in a fog of abstraction that only tangible details can illuminate. The concrete language helps readers see what you mean, much in the way that examples help them understand your ideas. Without the shaping power of abstract diction, however, concrete evocation can leave you with a list of graphic but ultimately pointless facts. The best writing integrates concrete and abstract diction, the language of showing and the language of telling (explaining).

Try This 17.2: Two Experiments with Abstract and Concrete Diction

1. Compose a paragraph using only concrete diction and then one using only abstract diction. Compare results with another person who has done the same task, as this can lead to an interesting discussion of kinds of words, where they reside on the ladder of abstraction, and why.

2. Rewrite the sentences listed below, substituting more concrete language and/or more precise abstractions. Support any abstractions you retain with appropriate detail. Just for the challenge, try to rewrite so that your sentences include no abstract claims, that is, use only concrete details to convey the points.

> It was a great party; everybody had fun.
>
> It was a lousy party; everybody disliked it.
>
> The book was really boring.
>
> The film was very interesting.
>
> His morals were questionable.
>
> Social Security is not an entitlement.
>
> He became extraordinarily angry.

Latinate Diction

One of the best ways to sensitize yourself to the difference between abstract and concrete diction is to understand that many abstract words are examples of what is known as Latinate diction. This term describes words in English that derive from Latin roots, words with such endings as *–tion, –ive, –ity, –ate,* and *–ent.* (Such words are designated by an *L* in the etymological section of dictionary definitions.) Taken to an extreme, Latinate diction can leave your meaning vague and your readers confused. This is not because there is something dubious about words that come into English from Latin. A large percentage of English words have Latin or Greek roots, words like *pentagon* (Greek for five sides), *anarchy* (Latin for without order), and *automobile* (Latin for self-moving).

The problem with Latinate diction lies in the way it is sometimes used. Latin endings such as *–tion* make it too easy for writers to construct sentences made up of a high percentage of vague nouns, as in the following example:

> The examination of different perspectives on the representations of sociopolitical anarchy in media coverage of revolutions can be revelatory of the invisible biases that afflict television news.

This sentence actually makes sense, but the demands it makes on readers will surely drive off most of them before they have gotten through it. Reducing the amount of Latinate diction can make it more readable:

> Because we tend to believe what we see, the political biases that afflict television news coverage of revolutions are largely invisible. We can begin to see these biases when we focus on how the medium reports events, studying the kinds of footage used, for example, or finding facts from other sources that the news has left out.

Although the preceding revision retains a lot of Latinate words, it provides a ballast of concrete, sensory details that allows readers to follow the idea. Although many textbooks on writing argue against using Latinate terms where shorter, concrete terms (usually of Anglo-Saxon origin) might be used instead, such an argument seems needlessly limiting in comparison with the advantages offered by a thorough mixture of the two levels of diction. It's fine to use Latinate diction; just don't make it the sole staple of your verbal diet.

CHOOSING WORDS: SOME RHETORICAL CONSIDERATIONS

We don't wish to make too firm a distinction between writing to make things clear and writing that is considerate of the needs of an audience beyond just clarity. And yet it is the case that when you begin to imagine the response of an audience, an actual listener to or reader of your prose, some additional considerations do come into play. The most important of these is tone.

Tone

Tone is the *implied attitude* of a piece of language toward its subject and audience. Whenever you revise for style, your choices in syntax and diction affect the tone. There are no hard-and-fast rules to govern matters of tone, and your control of it depends on your sensitivity to the particular context—your understanding of your own intentions and your readers' expectations.

Let's consider, for example, the tonal implications of the warning signs in the subways of London as compared with New York.

London: Leaning out of the window may cause harm.

New York: Do not lean out of the window.

Initially, you may find the English injunction laughably indirect and verbose in comparison with the shoot-from-the-hip clarity of the American sign. But that is to ignore the very thing we are calling *style*. The American version appeals to authority, commanding readers what not to do without telling them why. The English version, by contrast, appeals to logic; it is more collegial toward its readers and assumes they are rational beings rather than children prone to misbehave.

In revising for tone, you need to ask yourself if the attitude suggested by your language is appropriate to the aim of your message and to your audience. Your goal is to keep the tone *consistent* with your rhetorical intentions. The following paragraph, from a college catalogue, offers a classic mismatch between the overtly stated aim and the tonal implications:

> The student affairs staff believes that the college years provide a growth and development process for students. Students need to learn about themselves and others and to learn how to relate to individuals and groups of individuals with vastly different backgrounds, interests, attitudes and values. Not only is the tolerance of differences expected, but also an appreciation and a celebration of these differences must be an outcome of the student's experience. In addition, the student must progress toward self-reliance and independence tempered by a concern for the social order.

The explicit content of this passage—*what* it says—concerns tolerance. The professed point of view is student-friendly, asserting that the college exists to allow students "to learn about themselves and others" and to support the individual in accord with the "appreciation . . . of . . . differences." But note that the implicit tone—*how* the passage goes about saying *what* it says—is condescending and intolerant. Look at the verbs. An imperious authority lectures students about what they "*need* to learn," that tolerance is "*expected*," that "celebration . . . *must* be an outcome," and that "the student *must* progress" along these lines. Presumably, the paragraph does not intend to adopt this high-handed manner, but its deafness to tone subverts its desired meaning.

Try This 17.3: Analyzing Tone-Deaf Prose

Using the example from the college catalogue as a model, locate and bring to class examples of tonal inconsistency or inappropriateness that you encounter in your daily life. If you have difficulty finding examples, try memos from those in authority at your school or workplace, which often contain excruciating examples of officialese. Type one of your passages, and underneath it compose a paragraph of analysis in which you single out particular words and phrases and explain how the tone is inappropriate. Then rewrite the passage to remedy the problem.

Formal and Colloquial Styles: Who's Writing to Whom, and Why Does It Matter?

Generalizations About Style

- There are many ways of conveying a message.
- The way you phrase a message constitutes a significant part of its meaning.
- Your phrasing gives your reader cues that suggest your attitude and your ways of thinking.
- There are no transparent (absolutely neutral) delivery systems.
- All stylistic decisions depend on your sensitivity to context— who's talking to whom about what subject and with what aims.

The last of these generalizations concerns what is called the *rhetorical situation*. *Rhetoric* is the subject that deals with how writers and speakers behave in given situations and, more specifically, how they can generate language that produces the effects they desire on a particular audience. Obviously, as you make stylistic choices, you need to be aware of the possible consequences of making certain statements to a certain audience in a certain fashion.

How you say something is always a significant part of *what* you say. To look at words as words is to focus on the *how* as well as the *what*. Imagine that you call your friend on the phone, and a voice you don't recognize answers. You ask to speak with your friend, and the voice responds, "With whom have I the pleasure of speaking?" By contrast, what if the voice instead responds, "Who's this?" What information do these two versions of the question convey, beyond the obvious request for your name?

The first response—"With whom have I the pleasure of speaking?"—tells you that the speaker is formal and polite. He is also probably fastidiously well educated: he not only knows the difference between "who" and "whom" but also obeys the etiquette that outlaws ending a sentence with a preposition ("Whom have I the pleasure of speaking *with*?"). The very formality of the utterance, however, might lead you to label the speaker pretentious. His assumption that conversing with you is a "pleasure" suggests empty flattery. On the other hand, the second version—"Who's this?"—while also grammatically correct, is less formal. It is more direct but also terse to a fault; the speaker does not seem particularly interested in treating you politely.

The two hypothetical responses represent two different levels of style. Formal English obeys the basic conventions of standard written prose, and most academic writing is fairly formal. An informal style—one that is conversational and full of slang—can have severe limitations in an academic setting. The syntax and vocabulary of written prose aren't the same as those of speech, and so attempts to import the language of speech into academic writing can result in your communicating less meaning with less precision. Let's look at one brief example:

Internecine quarrels within the corporation destroyed morale and sent the value of the stock plummeting.

The phrase "internecine quarrels" may strike some readers as a pretentious display of formal language, but consider how difficult it is to communicate this concept economically in more colloquial (talk-like, conversational) terms. "Fights that go on between people related to each other" is awkward; "brother against brother" is sexist and a cliché; and "mutually destructive disputes" is acceptable but long-winded and less precise.

It is arguably a part of our national culture to value the simple and the direct as more genuine and democratic than the sophisticated, which is supposedly more aristocratic and pretentious. This "plain-speaking" style, however, can hinder your ability to develop and communicate your ideas. In the case of internecine, the more formal diction choice actually communicates more, and more effectively, than the less formal equivalents.

When in doubt about how your readers will respond to the formality or informality of your style, you are usually better off opting for some version of "With whom have I the pleasure of speaking?" rather than "Who's this?" The best solution usually lies somewhere in between: "May I ask who's calling?" would protect you against the imputation of either priggishness or piggishness.

Try This 17.4: Analyzing Effective Tone

Find an example of tone that you think is just about perfect for the message and audience. Type it, and underneath discuss why it succeeds. Be as specific as you can about how the passage functions stylistically. Talk about particular phrasings and the match between what is being said and how it is said. Factor into your discussion the relationship between levels of style in the example and its presumed audience.

First Person, Second Person or Third Person?

The person question concerns which of the three basic forms of the pronoun you should use when you write. Here are the three forms, with brief examples.

First person: I believe Heraclitus is an underrated philosopher.

Second person: You should believe that Heraclitus is an underrated philosopher.

Third person: He or she believes that Heraclitus is an underrated philosopher.

Which person to use is a stylistic concern because it involves a writer's *choices* as regards to level of formality, the varying expectations of different audiences, and overall tone.

As a general rule, in academic writing you should discuss your subject matter in the third person and avoid the first and second person. There is logic to this rule: most academic analysis focuses on the subject matter rather than on you as you respond to it. If you use the third person, you keep the attention where it belongs.

"I": Pro and Con

Using the first-person "I" can throw the emphasis on the wrong place. Repeated assertions of "in my opinion" actually distract your readers from what you have to say. Omit them except in the most informal cases. You might, however, consider using the first person in the drafting stage if you are having trouble bringing your own point of view to the forefront. In this situation, the "I" becomes a strategy for loosening up and saying what you really think about a subject rather than adopting conventional and faceless positions. In the final analysis, though, most analytical prose is more precise and straightforward in the third person. When you cut "I am convinced that" from the beginning of any claim, what you lose in personal conviction you gain in concision and directness by keeping the focus on the main idea in a main clause.

Using the First-Person "I": Three Professors Speak

Are there cases when you should use "I"? Contrary to the general rule, some professors actually prefer the first-person pronoun in particular contexts, as noted in the accompanying Voices from Across the Curriculum. It is a general rule, however, in the formal products of science and social science writing, to avoid personal pronouns. (*See Chapter 15, Forms and Formats Across the Curriculum.*)

Voices From Across the Curriculum

○   Avoid phrases like "*The author* believes (or will discuss)." Except in the paper's abstract, "*I* believe (or will discuss)" is okay, and often best.
—Alan Tjeltveit, Professor of Psychology

○   I prefer that personal opinion or voice (for example, "I this" or "I that") appear throughout. I like the first person. No "the author feels" or "this author found that," please! Who is the author? Hey, it's you!
—Frederick Norling, Professor of Business

○   The biggest stylistic problem is that students tend to be too personal or colloquial in their writing, using phrases such as the following: "Scientists all agree," "I find it amazing that," "The thing that I find most interesting." Students are urged to present data and existing information in their own words, but in an objective way. My preference in writing is to use the active voice in the past tense. I feel this is the most direct and least wordy approach: "I asked this," "I found out that," "These data show."
—Richard Niesenbaum, Professor of Biology

Note that these are not blanket endorsements; they specify a limited context within which "I" is preferred. The biology professor's cautioning against using an overly personal and colloquial tone is also probably the consensus view.

Although a majority of professors may prefer the first-person "I think" to the more awkward "the writer (or 'one') thinks," we would point out that, in the service of reducing wordiness, you can often avoid both options. For example, in certain contexts and disciplines, the first-person-plural, we, is acceptable usage: "The president's speech assumes that *we* are all dutiful but disgruntled taxpayers." The one case in which the first person is particularly appropriate occurs when you are citing an example from your own experience. Otherwise, if you are in doubt about using I or we, avoid these first-person pronouns.

"You": Pro and Con

Proceed with caution. Using "you" is a fairly assertive gesture. Many readers will be annoyed, for example, by a paper about advertising that states, "When you read about a sale at the mall, you know it's hard to resist." Most readers resent having a writer airily making assumptions about them or telling them what to do. Some rhetorical situations, however, call for the use of "you." Textbooks, for example, use "you" frequently because it creates a more direct relationship between authors and readers. Yet, even in appropriate situations, directly addressing readers as "you" may alienate them by ascribing to them attitudes and needs they may not have.

The conventional argument for using the first and second person is that "I" and "you" are personal and engage readers. It is not necessarily the case, however, that the third person is therefore impersonal. Just as film directors put their stamps on films by the way they organize the images, move among camera viewpoints, and orchestrate the sound tracks, so writers, even when writing in the third person, have a wide variety of resources at their disposal for making the writing more personal and accessible for their audiences. See, for example, the discussion of the passive voice in Chapter 18.

Jargon

Many people assume that all jargon—the specialized vocabulary of a particular group—is bad: pretentious language designed to make most readers feel inferior. Many writing textbooks attack jargon in similar terms, calling it either polysyllabic balderdash or a specialized, gate-keeping language designed by an in-group to keep others out.

Yet, in many academic contexts, jargon is downright essential. It is conceptual shorthand, a technical vocabulary that allows the members of a group (or a discipline) to converse with one another more clearly and efficiently. Certain words that may seem odd to outsiders in fact function as connective tissue for a way of thought shared by insiders.

The following sentence, for example, although full of botanical jargon, is also admirably cogent:

> In angiosperm reproduction, if the number of pollen grains deposited on the stigma exceeds the number of ovules in the ovary, then pollen tubes may compete for access to ovules, which results in fertilization by the fastest growing pollen tubes.

We would label this use of jargon acceptable because it is written, clearly, *by* insiders *for* fellow insiders. It might not be acceptable language for an article intended for readers who are not botanists, or at least not scientists.

The problem with jargon comes when this insiders' language is directed at outsiders as well. The language of contracts offers a prime example of such jargon at work:

> The Author hereby indemnifies and agrees to hold the Publisher, its licensees, and any seller of the Work harmless from any liability, damage, cost, and expense, including reasonable attorney's fees and costs of settlement, for or in connection with any claim, action, or proceeding inconsistent with the Author's warranties or representations herein, or based upon or arising out of any contribution of the Author to the Work.

Run for the lawyer! What does it mean to "hold the Publisher . . . harmless"? To what do "the Author's warranties or representations" refer? What exactly is the author being asked to do here—release the publisher from all possible lawsuits that the author might bring? We might label this use of jargon obfuscating; although it may aim at precision, it leaves most readers bewildered. Although nonprofessionals are asked to sign them, such documents are really written by lawyers for other lawyers.

As the botanical and legal examples suggest, the line between acceptable and obfuscating jargon has far more to do with the audience to whom the words are addressed than with the actual content of the language. Because most academic writing is addressed to insiders, students studying a particular area need to learn its jargon. Using the technical language of the discipline is a necessary skill for conversing with others in that discipline. Moreover, by demonstrating that you can "talk the talk," you will validate your authority to pronounce an opinion on matters in the discipline.

Here are two guidelines that can help you in your use of jargon: (1) when addressing *insiders,* use jargon accurately ("talk the talk"); and (2) when addressing *outsiders*—the general public or members of another discipline—either define the jargon carefully or replace it with a more generally known term, preferably one operating at the same level of formality.

The Politics of Language

We cannot leave this chapter without reflecting on its place in what we earlier labeled the culture of inattention and cliché that surrounds us. Style has political and ethical implications. A little over a half-century ago, in his famous essay "Politics and the English Language," George Orwell warns of the "invasion of one's mind by ready-made phrases... [which] can only be prevented if one is constantly on guard against them." The worst modern writing, he declares, "consists in gumming together long strips of words which have already been set in order by someone else, making the results presentable by sheer humbug."

Insofar as style is an expression of the writer's self, Orwell implies, (1) we are under attack from broad cultural clichés and sentimental nostrums that do our thinking for us, and (2) it is thus a matter of personal integrity and civic responsibility to ask ourselves a series of questions about the sentences that we write. As Orwell says,

What am I trying to say? What words will express it? What image or idiom will make it clearer? Is this image fresh enough to have an effect? [...] Could I put it more shortly? Have I said anything that is avoidably ugly?

Words matter. They matter in how we name things, in how we phrase meanings—but also in how we are shaped by the words we read and hear in the media. Words don't simply reflect a neutral world that is out there in some objective way that offers self-evident meanings we can universally agree upon. Words don't reflect—they constitute; they call the world into being. They call us into being when we write them.

Earlier in this chapter we noted, for example, that the decision to call a woman "aggressive" as opposed to "assertive" matters. There are examples all around you of language creating rather than merely reflecting reality. Start looking for these on the front page of your newspaper, in political speeches, in advertising, even in everyday conversation. Does it matter, for instance, that there are no equivalents to the words "spinster" or "whore" for men? Does it change things to refer to a bombing mission as a "containment effort" or, by way of contrast, to call an enthusiastic person "a fanatic"?

An article in the journal *Foreign Affairs* by Peter van Ham (October 2001) offers one last dispatch from the frontier of the culture of inattention and cliché. The article is about the rise of the so-called brand state—about how nations market themselves not only to consumers but to other nations. A brand, defined as "a customer's idea about a product," is a powerful tool to replace what a thing is with what other people, for reasons of their own, would have you think it is. This is the world we inhabit, and style can be its adversary or its accomplice. In the last analysis, that's what's at stake in choosing to care about style.

GUIDELINES FOR WORD CHOICE

1. Remember first and foremost that revision is not merely cosmetic: to change the words is to change the meaning.

2. Strive for distance from your own prose as you edit for diction: place yourself in the position of the audience. Is the tone appropriate to the rhetorical context?

3. There are always shades of meaning. Strive to choose the best—the most accurate and appropriate—word for the situation. When in doubt, consult etymology, the history of the word, as the most reliable guide to its usage.

4. Avoid "good," "bad," "real," and other broad, judgmental terms that prematurely close off analysis.

5. Blend concrete and abstract diction, which is generally the language of details and the language of abstractions, respectively. In particular, go easy on those Latinate–*tion* words.

6. In given contexts, jargon is useful shorthand, but there is always the danger of getting used by it. Make sure you know what the words mean, and don't over-rely on them.

Assignment: Thinking About Word Choice

Analyze the Style of a Particular Group Write a paper that analyzes the style of a particular group or profession (for example, sports, advertising, bureaucracy, show business, or music reviewing). Or as an alternative, adopt the voice of a member of this group, and write a parody that critiques or analyzes the language practices of the group. If you choose the latter, be aware that there is always a risk in parody of belittling in an unduly negative way a style that is not your own.

Obviously, you will first need to assemble and make observations about a number of samples of the style you are analyzing or parodying. Use The Method to help you uncover the kinds of words that are repeated, the most common strands, and so forth. Look at the level of formality, the tone, the use of concrete and abstract diction, and the predilection for Latinate as opposed to Anglo-Saxon words. Who's writing to whom about what, and so what that the writing adopts this style? Also, see the assignments at the end of Chapter 18.

Chapter 18

Revising for Style: The Rhetoric of the Sentence

ONE OF THE MOST DISTINCTIVE WAYS of identifying a really good writer is by the way he or she puts together a sentence. A writer who understands how to build sentences is a writer who understands the key concept of sentence style: that there is a powerful link between the shape of a sentence and the shape of a thought. We summarize this key idea with the phrase, *a sentence is the shape thought takes*. The slide below bullets what shape can do.

A SENTENCE IS THE SHAPE THOUGHT TAKES

What the shape can do:
- indicate where to find the important meanings in the sentence
- reveal how the other information in the sentence is related to the most important meanings
- get readers to follow you and understand you in the way you desire
- slow readers down when they need the extra time to understand more complex points
- keep them on track, so they know where they are going and they remember where they've come from

OPERATING ASSUMPTIONS

In order to compose sentences that will work for you and help your readers access your meaning as you wish them to, it's necessary for many writers to re-orient the way they think about sentences. This means unlearning some old habits—discarding some unhelpful beliefs—that interfere with writing fluent sentences and replacing these habits with new assumptions about how to construct sentences. The following three "laws" are corollaries of our primary mantra—that every sentence is a shape thought takes.

- **Every sentence is a delivery system**. *Stop thinking that a sentence is a neutral carrier of meanings.* There's a good chance you've never really thought much about your sentences as sentences—that is, as arrangements of words that always carry rhythm and emphasis, whether you intend them to or not. The sentence always affects, is always part of the content it carries. If you care about the meanings you are asking your sentences to convey, don't let yourself look past them; train yourself to *see* them. This takes practice, but it is a very worthwhile skill to acquire.

- **Every sentence possesses style**. *Start focusing on what makes sentences right rather than on what makes them wrong.* Yes, it matters if you commit lots of sentence-level errors, but temporarily stop worrying about such errors and the rules of grammar (which the next chapter will focus on). Instead, focus on style, the choices a writer makes as he or she fashions meaning for a particular purpose in a particular setting. Start looking actively for sentences you like. Then analyze what you like about them. Imitate them. Try making one a go-to sentence. *(See Chapter 2, Toolkit I on Go-To Sentences.)*

- **Every sentence is composed of interchangeable parts**. *And you can rearrange the parts.* This rearranging lies at the heart of revision—a process of seeing again to make your meanings more accurate or clear or memorable. Assembling and reassembling the parts is not a cosmetic act. It is an act of thinking.

There's a surprisingly small amount of specialized vocabulary to master in order to see and talk about sentence shapes. We can best illustrate this vocabulary and how it works by looking at one comma rule and then four basic sentence shapes. We will then build on this foundation for the rest of the chapter, adding more technical terms as we need them.

Please be aware that all of these terms have been collected in the Glossary of Grammatical Terms located at the end of Chapter 19. In particular, see entries for the following terms: *clause, conjunction, conjunctive adverb, coordination, direct object, phrase, preposition, subject, subordination,* and *verbals.* Earlier in that chapter, you will also find a brief guide to punctuation entitled "What Punctuation Marks Say: A Quick-Hit Guide." Punctuation makes sentence shapes visible.

THE PRIMARY COMMA RULE: IDENTIFYING THE MAIN CLAUSE

The main idea of most sentences resides in the main clause, the subject + verb that can stand by itself (aka independent clause). The main clause generally gets the most emphasis and carries the most meaning. Sentences are built around main clauses, and writers (as well as readers) will benefit from developing the ability to find the main clause in any sentence. Here's one:

The cat / was happy.

The diagonal line separates the subject from the predicate. "Cat" is the subject, "was" is the verb, and "happy" is an adjective that modifies (describes) "cat."

Let's say we wish to add some modifying information to this sentence, such as "despite not having enough for breakfast." There are three places (slots) in sentences where this modifying phrase might be added. In each sample sentence below we have underlined the main clause and italicized the modifying information.

> **beginning:** *Despite not having enough for breakfast,* <u>the cat was happy.</u>
>
> **middle:** <u>The cat,</u> *despite not having enough for breakfast,* <u>was happy.</u>
>
> **end:** <u>The cat was happy,</u> *despite not having enough for breakfast.*

These "slots" for adding information at the beginning, middle, and end are generally separated from the main clause by commas. *The commas are there to help the reader easily find and recognize the main clause.*

The first example, with the modifying phrase at the end, doesn't absolutely need a comma; we won't misread the sentence without it, though the comma does help to clarify matters. And, what if we raise the level of complexity by adding more modifiers to a more complicated idea?

> **modifying phrase at beginning:** *Although both candidates claimed to be running clean races and blamed the other for the mud-slinging,* <u>the campaign was ugly.</u>
>
> **modifying phrase at middle:** <u>The campaign,</u> *although both candidates claimed to be running clean races and blamed the other for the mud-slinging,* <u>was ugly.</u>
>
> **modifying phrase at end:** <u>The campaign was ugly,</u> *although both candidates claimed to be running clean races and blamed the other for the mud-slinging.*

Now let's build on this primary comma rule by applying it to the four basic sentence shapes.

HOW TO RECOGNIZE THE FOUR BASIC SENTENCE TYPES & WHAT THEY DO

To see sentence shapes, always start by finding the clauses. A clause is any subject + verb combination. There are two types of clauses:

- **independent clauses,** which can stand alone, such as <u>The dog was depressed</u>
- **dependent clauses,** which cannot stand alone, such as <u>Because the dog was depressed</u>. A dependent clause literally depends (hangs on) another clause.

Sentences can be divided into four basic types depending on the kind and relation of clauses.

> Consumers shop.
>
> Consumers shop, and producers manufacture.
>
> Consumers shop in predictable ways, so producers manufacture with different target groups in mind.

> Consumers shop in ways that can be predicted by such determinants as income level, sex, and age; consequently, producers use market research to identify different target groups for their products.

These four sentences become progressively longer, and the information they contain becomes increasingly detailed, but they also differ in their structure—specifically, in the number of independent and dependent clauses they contain.

The Simple Sentence: One Statement at a Time

How and why to use the simple sentence: The *simple sentence* consists of a single independent clause. Simple sentences are the most effective choice when you wish to say something clearly and forcefully. They are especially effective in contrast to longer and more complicated sentences that may surround them. They give the reader—and the writer—a chance to get grounded. It's as if the sentence structure itself—the **syntax**—says: "simply put." If you find yourself getting confused while writing something complicated, it's probably time for a simple sentence. On the other hand, if you string together too many simple sentences in a row, you are probably not adequately connecting your ideas. At its most basic, the simple sentence contains a single subject and verb.

> Consumers shop.

Other words and phrases can be added to this sentence, but it will remain simple so long as "Consumers shop" is the only clause.

> Most consumers shop unwisely.

Even if the sentence contains more than one grammatical subject or more than one verb, it remains simple in structure.

> Most consumers **shop** unwisely and **spend** more than they can afford. *[two verbs]*

> Both female **consumers** and their **husbands** shop unwisely. *[two subjects]*

The sentence structure in the example that uses two verbs ("shop" and "spend") is known as a *compound predicate*. The sentence structure in the example that uses two subjects ("consumers" and "husbands") is known as a *compound subject*. If, however, you were to add both another subject and another verb to the original simple sentence, you would have the next sentence type, a compound sentence.

The Compound Sentence: Two Items of Equal Weight

How and why to use the compound sentence: The *compound sentence* consists of at least two independent clauses and no subordinate clauses. The information conveyed in these clauses should be of roughly equal importance. Use compound sentences when you are grouping in twos, both pairing likes and balancing oppositions. There should probably be some kind of conceptual linkage between the two clauses. Using compound sentences helps both you and your readers to organize the information.

In most cases, the two independent clauses in a compound sentence are bound by a *coordinating conjunction* (*and, or, but* are the most common), preceded by a comma. This comma is extremely useful, for it lets your readers know as they move across the sentence that you are about to add a second independent clause. Compound sentences put equal grammatical weight on each independent clause.

> Producers manufacture, and consumers shop.

As with the simple sentence, you can also add qualifying phrases to the compound sentence, and it will remain compound, as long as no dependent clauses are added.

> Consumers shop in predictable ways, so producers manufacture with different target groups in mind.

> Consumers shop recklessly during holidays; marketers are keenly aware of this fact.

Note that a compound sentence can connect its independent clauses with a semicolon as an alternative to the comma + coordinate conjunction. This is the primary use of the semicolon—to link two independent clauses that are closely related in some way. *(See What Punctuation Marks Say: A Quick-Hit Guide in Chapter 19.)* If you were to substitute a **subordinating conjunction** for either of these connectors, however, you would have a sentence with one independent clause and one dependent clause. For example:

> *Because consumers shop in predictable ways,* <u>producers manufacture</u> with different target groups in mind.

This revision changes the compound sentence into the next sentence type, the complex sentence.

The Complex Sentence: Ranking the Value of Ideas or Information

How and why to use the complex sentence: The *complex sentence* consists of a single independent clause and one or more dependent clauses: "Before the President did X, he did Y, because he was forced to do so." The information conveyed in the dependent clauses are subordinated to the more important independent clause. Complex sentences are invaluable when you are establishing emphasis and assigning different values to different pieces of information. In the following example, the subject and verb of the main clause are underlined, and the subordinating conjunctions are italicized:

> *Although mail-order merchandising has increased,* most <u>consumers</u> still <u>shop</u> unwisely, buying on impulse rather than deliberation.

This sentence contains one independent clause ("consumers shop"). Hanging on it are one introductory dependent clause ("although merchandising has increased") and one participial phrase ("buying on impulse"). If your sentence had two independent clauses (compound) and one or more dependent clauses, it would become the next sentence type: compound-complex. In the following example, the subjects and verbs of the two main clauses are underlined, and the conjunctions are italicized:

> Mail-order <u>merchandising</u>—*which* generally saves shoppers
> money—<u>has</u> <u>increased</u>, *but* <u>consumers</u> still <u>shop</u> unwisely, buying
> on impulse rather than deliberation.

The Compound-Complex Sentence: Using Syntax to Convey Complexity

How and why to use the compound-complex sentence: The *compound-complex sentence* consists of two or more independent clauses and one or more dependent clauses. This syntactic shape is essential in representing complex relationships and so is frequently put to use in various forms of analytical writing, especially in academic writing. It is also probably true that the ability to use compound-complex sentences elevates a writer's credibility: it demonstrates that he or she can bring together in a single sentence a range of different pieces of information and order them in relationship to each other. This is not to say that the compound-complex sentence invites confusion: on the contrary, when handled carefully, it has the opposite effect—it clarifies the complexity and enables readers to see it clearly. See the discussion of parallel structure later in this chapter for one mode of achieving this clarity when you build complicated sentences.

See if you can find and identify the parts of the following compound-complex sentence. List separately the main clauses, the subordinate clauses, and the various coordinating and subordinating conjunctions. (See the *conjunction* entry in the Glossary of Grammatical Terms at the end of Chapter 19 for a list of these.)

> Consumers shop in ways that can be predicted by such
> determinants as income level, sex, and age; consequently,
> producers use market research that aims to identify different
> target groups for their products.

As we end this survey of the four sentence types, let us reinforce a key point about sentence style: it is not simply good or bad. Every stylistic choice a writer makes (consciously or not) has implications. This chapter aims to equip you with the information you need in order to see the range of your choices and thus make appropriate decisions.

Try This 18.1: Compose the Four Sentence Types

As we have done with the consumers-shop example, compose a simple sentence and then a variety of expansions: a compound subject, a compound predicate, a compound sentence, a complex sentence, and a compound-complex sentence.

To prevent this exercise from becoming merely mechanical, keep in mind how different sentence shapes accomplish different ends. In other words, make sure your compound sentence balances two items of information, that your complex sentence emphasizes one thing (in the main clause) over another (in the subordinate clause), and that your compound-complex sentence is capable of handling and organizing complexity.

Try This 18.2: Identify the Four Sentence Types in Sentences You Like

As one of the operating assumptions for this chapter, we suggested that "Every sentence possesses style" and so you should "*Start focusing on what makes sentences right rather than on what makes them wrong.*" We use these propositions as the basis for an exercise in which we direct students to locate in their reading any sentences whose shape they like, and to use these as the basis for practicing their ability to name sentence features.

In the following list of sentences, all taken from our students' lists, do the following:

- identify which of the four types it is
- underline the subject and verb of the main clause(s)
- double-underline the subordinate clauses
- circle the coordinating conjunctions and subordinating conjunctions

1. "Since the Martians were evidently, in spite of their repulsive forms, intelligent creatures, it had been resolved to show them, by approaching them with signals, that we too were intelligent." (H. G. Wells, *The War of the Worlds*)

2. "Latin American societies have not transcended racism by embracing indigenous American and African elements in their national mix, but they have gotten further than many other multiracial societies, including, many believe, the United States." (John Charles Chasteen, *Born in Blood and Fire*)

3. "Chwa was in her late eighties at the time of the interview, had poor eyesight, though good hearing, and could still walk." (Richard B. Lee, *The Dobe Ju/'hoansi*)

4. "John Darnielle, leader of a veteran band called the Mountain Goats, writes songs that unspool like short stories, and his new album, "Heretic Pride," is full of desperate characters and evocative settings." (John Jurgensen, *The Washington Post*)

5. "As it is undeniable that portions of the human family have existed in a state of savagery, other portions in a state of barbarism, and still other portions in a state of civilization, it seems equally so that these three distinct conditions are connected with each other in a natural as well as necessary sequence of progress." (R. Jon McGee and Richard L. Warms, *Anthropological Theory: An Introductory History*)

Alternatively, you might do these operations on sentences of your own choice. Also please note that there will be an opportunity to repeat and expand this Try This in the end-of-chapter assignments. We recommend, in any case, that you might start your own list of sentences you like. It's one of the very best ways to learn about style.

USING COORDINATION AND SUBORDINATION TO EMPHASIZE MEANINGS

As we trust you are beginning to see, sentence structure operates as a form of implicit logic. The syntax defines relationships among the clauses—subject + verb combinations—in a sentence according to the choices you make about coordination and subordination. A third factor in according emphasis is the order of clauses, as we shall discuss in what follows. All three—coordination, subordination, and the order of clauses—are tools of logic and emphasis that help to rank your meanings and convey this ranking to the reader.

Using Coordination to Balance This with That

Coordination uses grammatically equivalent constructions to link ideas. These ideas should carry roughly equal weight as well. Sentences that use coordination connect clauses with coordinating conjunctions (such as *and, but,* and *or*). Here are two examples.

Historians organize the past, *and* they can never do so with absolute neutrality.

Homegrown corn is incredibly sweet, *and* it is very difficult to grow.

If you ponder these sentences, you may begin to detect the danger of the word *and*. It does not specify a precise logical relationship between the things it connects but instead simply adds them. Notice that the sentences get more precise if we substitute *but* for *and*.

Historians organize the past, *but* they can never do so with absolute neutrality.

Homegrown corn is incredibly sweet, *but* it is very difficult to grow.

These sentences are still coordinate in structure; they are still the sentence type known as compound. But they achieve more emphasis than the *and* versions. In both cases, the *but* clause carries more weight, because *but* always introduces information that qualifies or contradicts what precedes it.

Emphasis Rests at the End of Coordinate Clauses

In both the *and* and *but* examples of coordinate clauses, the second clause tends to be stressed. The reason is simple: *the end is usually a position of emphasis.* You can see the effect of clause order more starkly if we reverse the clauses in our examples.

> Historians are never absolutely neutral, but they organize the past.

> Homegrown corn is very difficult to grow, but it is incredibly sweet.

Note how the meanings have changed in these versions because emphasis tends to fall on whatever comes last in a sentence. Rather than simply having their objectivity undermined ("Historians are never absolutely neutral"), historians are now credited with at least providing organization ("they organize the past"). Similarly, whereas the previous version of the sentence about corn was likely to dissuade gardeners from trying to grow it ("it is very difficult to grow"), the new sentence is more likely to lure them to nurture corn ("it is incredibly sweet").

Nonetheless, all of these sentences are examples of coordination because the clauses are grammatically equal. As you revise, notice when you use coordinate syntax, and think about whether you really intend to give the ideas equal weight. Consider as well whether reversing the order of clauses will more accurately convey your desired emphasis to your readers.

Try This 18.3: Rearrange Coordinate Clauses for Emphasis

Rearrange the parts of the following coordinate sentence, which is composed of four sections, separated by commas. Construct at least three versions, and jot down how the meaning changes in each version.

> I asked her to marry me, two years ago, in a shop on Tremont Street, late in the fall.

Then subject two sentences of your own, perhaps taken from your papers, to the same treatment. Make sure to describe how the meaning changes in each case, because it will get you accustomed to seeing the effects of the rearrangements.

Using Subordination to Adjust Emphasis

In sentences that contain *subordination,* there are two "levels" of grammar—the main clause and the subordinate clause—that create two levels of meaning. When you put something in a main clause, you emphasize its significance. When you put something in a subordinate clause, you make it less important than what is in the main clause.

As noted in the discussion of complex sentences, a subordinate clause is linked to a main clause by words known as *subordinating conjunctions.* Here is a list of the most common ones: *after, although, as, as if, as long as, because, before, if, rather than, since, than, that, though, unless, until, when, where, whether,* and *while.* All of these words define something *in relation to* something else:

> *If* you study hard, you will continue to do well.
>
> You will continue to do well, *if* you study hard.

In both of these examples, *if* subordinates "you study hard" to "you will continue to do well," regardless of whether the *if* clause comes first or last in the sentence.

How the End Affects Emphasis When Using Subordinate Clauses

Unlike the situation with coordinate clauses, the emphasis in sentences that use subordination virtually always rests on the main clause, regardless of the clause order. Nevertheless, the principle of end-position emphasis still applies, though to a lesser extent than among coordinate clauses. Let's compare two versions of the same sentence.

> Although the art of the people was crude, it was original.
>
> The art of the people was original, although it was crude.

Both sentences emphasize the idea in the main clause ("original"). Because the second version locates the "although" clause at the end, however, the subordinated idea ("crude") has more emphasis than it does in the first version.

You can experiment with the meaning and style of virtually any sentence you write by reversing the clauses. Here, taken almost at random, is an earlier sentence from this chapter, followed by two such transformations.

> When you put something in a subordinate clause, you make it less important than what is in the main clause.
>
> Put information in a subordinate clause if you want to make it less important than what is in the main clause.
>
> If you want to make information less important than what is in the main clause, put it in a subordinate clause.

As we hope you can see, the ordering of clauses is one way of according emphasis, the decision to subordinate or coordinate is another, and the two modes of emphasizing can work in tandem. Thus, a sentence that ends with a subordinate clause gives that clause more force than a sentence that contains a subordinate clause but does not end with it.

Try This 18.4: Experiment with Coordination, Subordination, and the Order of Clauses

Do two rewritings of the following sentence, changing the order of clauses and subordinating or coordinating as you wish. We recommend that you make one of them end with the word *friendly.*

> Faculty members came to speak at the forum, and they were friendly, but they were met with hostility, and this hostility was almost paranoid.

How does each of your revisions change the meaning and emphasis?

Parallel Structure: Put Parallel Information into Parallel Form

One of the most important and useful devices for shaping sentences is *parallel structure* or, as it is also known, *parallelism.* Parallelism is a form of symmetry: it involves placing sentence elements that correspond in some way into the same (that is, parallel) grammatical form. Consider the following examples, in which the parallel items are underlined or italicized:

> The three kinds of partners in a law firm who receive money from a case are popularly known as finders, binders, and grinders.

> The Beatles acknowledged their musical debts to American rhythm and blues, to English music hall ballads and ditties, and later to classical Indian ragas.

> There was no way that the President could gain the support of party regulars *without alienating* the Congress, and no way that he could appeal to the electorate at large *without alienating* both of these groups.

> In the entertainment industry, the money that goes out to hire *film stars* or *sports stars* comes back in increased ticket sales and video or television rights.

As all of these examples illustrate, at the core of parallelism lies repetition—of a word, a phrase, or a grammatical structure. Parallelism uses repetition to organize and emphasize certain elements in a sentence, so that readers can perceive more clearly the shape of your thought. In the Beatles example, each of the prepositional phrases beginning with *to* contains a musical debt. In the President example, the repetition of the phrase *no way that* emphasizes his entrapment.

Parallelism has the added advantage of economy: each of the musical debts or presidential problems might have had its own sentence, but in that case the prose would have been wordier and the relationships among the parallel items more obscure. Along with this economy come balance and emphasis. The trio of rhyming words (finders, binders, and grinders) that concludes the law-firm example gives each item equal weight; in the entertainment-industry example, "comes back" answers "goes out" in a way that accentuates their symmetry.

Try This 18.5: Find Examples of Parallelism

List all of the examples of parallelism in the following famous passage from the beginning of the Declaration of Independence:

> We hold these truths to be self-evident: that all men are created equal; that they are endowed by their Creator with certain inalienable rights; that, among these, are life, liberty, and the pursuit of happiness.

Remember that parallelism can occur with clauses and phrases, especially prepositional phrases. You might find it useful to review the entries for these three terms in the glossary in Chapter 19. After you have completed your list, what do you notice about the way that the parallel structures accumulate? And what is the effect of the placement and phrasing of these parallelisms? In other words, try to describe how this famous passage develops stylistically.

When you employ parallelism in revising for style, there is one grammatical rule to obey. It is important to avoid what is known as *faulty parallelism*, which occurs when the items that are parallel in content are not placed in the same grammatical form.

Faulty: *To study* hard for four years and then *getting* ignored once they enter the job market is a hard thing for many recent college graduates to accept.

Revised: *To study* hard for four years and then *to get* ignored once they enter the job market is a hard thing for many recent college graduates to accept.

Try This 18.6: Correct Errors in Parallelism

Rewrite the following examples of faulty parallelism using correct parallel structure. In the last of these sentences, you will need to contemplate the thinking behind it as well as its form.

1. The problems with fast food restaurants include the way workers are exploited, eating transfatty acids, and that the food can damage your liver.

2. Venus Williams likes to play tennis and also designing clothes.

3. In the 1960s the use of drugs and being a hippie were ways for some people to let society know their political views and that they were alienated from the mainstream.

Two Powerful Forms of Parallelism: Antithesis and Chiasmus

One particularly useful form of balance that parallel structure accommodates is known as *antithesis* (from the Greek word for "opposition"), a conjoining of contrasting ideas. Here, the pattern sets one thing against another thing, as in the following example:

> Where bravura failed to settle the negotiations, tact and patience succeeded.

"Failed" is balanced antithetically against "succeeded," as "bravura" against "tact and patience." Antithesis commonly takes the form of "if not *x*, at least *y*" or "not *x*, but *y*."

Another specialized form of parallelism known as *chiasmus* is a rhetorical pattern that organizes elements in an ABBA structure. The most famous chiasmus known to most Americans comes from a speech by John F. Kennedy: "Ask not [A] what your country can do for you [B]; ask what you [B] can do for your country [A]."

Note how this form also uses antithesis—the JFK example moves from "ask not" to "ask"—which is why it is known as a form of inverted parallelism, the second half of the expression balanced against the first, with the parts reversed. You can more easily remember the term chiasmus once you realize that it derives from the Greek letter *chi*, meaning X, as that is the shape of the AB -> BA structure. Here is another example of chiasmus from Matthew 19:30: "But many that are *first* shall be *last*; and the *last* shall be *first*." The effect is memorable.

As you write, and especially as you revise for style, search for opportunities to place sentence elements in parallel structure. Remember that parallelism can occur with *clauses and phrases, especially prepositional phrases*. Often, the parallels will be hidden in the sentences of your draft, but they can be brought out with a minimum of labor. After you've acquired the habit of casting your thinking in parallel structures, they will rapidly become a staple of your stylistic repertoire, making your prose more graceful, clear, and logically connected.

PERIODIC AND CUMULATIVE SENTENCES: TWO EFFECTIVE SENTENCE SHAPES

The shape of a sentence governs the way it delivers information. The order of clauses, especially the placement of the main clause, affects what the sentence means.

There are two common sentence shapes defined by the location of their main clauses; these are known as *periodic* and *cumulative* sentences. The periodic sentence is built on suspense and delay: it puts maximum emphasis on the way the sentence ends. The cumulative sentence aims for upfront impact; there is no suspense, but rather, the rolling momentum of an extended follow-through.

The Periodic Sentence: Delay Closure to Achieve Emphasis

The main clause in a periodic sentence builds to a climax that is not completed until the end. Often, a piece of the main clause (such as the subject) is located early in the sentence, as in the example on the next page.

> The <u>way</u> that beverage companies market health—"No
> Preservatives," "No Artificial Colors," "All Natural," "Real
> Brewed"—<u>is</u> often, because the product also contains a high
> percentage of sugar or fructose, <u>misleading</u>.

We have underlined parts of the main clause to clarify how various modifiers interrupt it. The effect is suspenseful: not until the final word does the sentence consummate its fundamental idea. Pieces of the main clause are spread out across the sentence.

Another version of the periodic sentence locates the entire main clause at the end, after introductory modifiers.

> Using labels that market health—such as "No Preservatives,"
> "No Artificial Colors," "All Natural," and "Real Brewed"—while
> producing drinks that contain a high percentage of sugar or
> fructose, <u>beverage companies are misleading</u>.

As previously discussed, the end of a sentence normally receives emphasis. When you use a periodic construction, the pressure on the end intensifies because the sentence needs the end to complete its grammatical sense. In both of the preceding examples, the sentences "snap shut." They string readers along, delaying *grammatical closure*—the point at which the sentences can stand alone independently—until they arrive at climactic ends. (Periodic sentences are also known as *climactic sentences*.)

You should be aware of one risk that accompanies periodic constructions. If the delay lasts too long because there are too many "interrupters" before the main clause gets completed, your readers may forget the subject being predicated. To illustrate, let's add more subordinated material to one of the preceding examples.

> The way that beverage companies market health—"No
> Preservatives," "No Artificial Colors," "All Natural," "Real
> Brewed"—is often, because the product also contains a high
> percentage of sugar or fructose, not just what New Agers
> would probably term "immoral" and "misleading" but what a
> government agency such as the Food and Drug Administration
> should find illegal.

Arguably, the additions (the "not just" and "but" clauses after "fructose") push the sentence into incoherence. The main clause has been stretched past the breaking point. If readers don't get lost in such a sentence, they are at least likely to get irritated and wish the writer would finally get to the point.

Nonetheless, with a little care, periodic sentences can be extraordinarily useful in giving emphasis. If you are revising and want to underscore some point, try letting the sentence snap shut upon it. Often the periodic *potential* will already be present in the draft, and stylistic editing can bring it out more forcefully. Note how minor the revisions are in the following example:

> **Draft:** The novelist Virginia Woolf suffered from acute anxieties for most of her life. She had several breakdowns and finally committed suicide on the eve of World War II.

> **Revision:** Suffering from acute anxieties for most of her life, the novelist Virginia <u>Woolf</u> not only <u>had</u> several <u>breakdowns</u> <u>but</u>, finally, on the eve of World War II, <u>committed suicide</u>.

This revision has made two primary changes. It has combined two short sentences into a longer sentence, and it has made the sentence periodic by stringing out the main clause (italicized). What is the effect of this revision? Stylistically speaking, the revision radiates a greater sense of its writer's authority. The information has been arranged for us. After the opening dependent clause ("Suffering..."), the subject of the main clause ("Woolf") is introduced, and the predicate is protracted in a *not only/ but* parallelism. The interrupters that follow "had several breakdowns" ("finally, on the eve of World War II") increase the suspense, before the sentence snaps shut with "committed suicide."

In general, when you construct a periodic sentence with care, you can give readers the sense that you are in control of your material. You do not seem to be writing off the top of your head, but rather from a position of greater detachment, rationally composing your meaning.

The Cumulative Sentence: Start Fast to Build Momentum

The cumulative sentence is in many respects the opposite of the periodic. Rather than delaying the main clause or its final piece, the cumulative sentence begins by presenting the independent clause as a foundation and then *accumulates* a number of modifications and qualifications. As the following examples illustrate, the independent clause provides quick grammatical closure, freeing the rest of the sentence to amplify and develop the main idea.

> <u>Robert F. Kennedy was assassinated</u> by Sirhan B. Sirhan, a twenty-four-year-old Palestinian immigrant, prone to occultism and unsophisticated left-wing politics and sociopathically devoted to leaving his mark in history, even if as a notorious figure.

> <u>There are two piano concerti</u> composed solely for the left hand, one by Serge Prokofiev and one by Maurice Ravel, and both commissioned by Paul Wittgenstein, a concert pianist (and the brother of the famous philosopher Ludwig Wittgenstein) who had lost his right hand in combat during World War I.

Anchored by the main clause, a cumulative sentence moves serially through one thing and another thing and the next thing, close to the associative manner in which people think. To an extent, then, cumulative sentences can convey more immediacy and a more conversational tone than can other sentence shapes. Look at the following example:

> The film version of *Lady Chatterley's Lover* changed D. H. Lawrence's famous novel a lot, omitting the heroine's adolescent experience in Germany, making her husband much older than she, leaving out her father and sister, including a lot more lovemaking, and virtually eliminating all of the philosophizing about sex and marriage.

Here, we get the impression of a mind in the act of thinking. Using the generalization of changes in the film as a base, the sentence then appends a series of parallel participial phrases ("omitting," "making," "leaving," "including," "eliminating") that moves forward associatively, gathering a range of information and laying out possibilities. Cumulative sentences perform this outlining and prospecting function very effectively. On the other hand, if we were to add four or five more changes to the sentence, readers would likely find it tedious, or worse, directionless. As with periodic sentences, overloading the shape can short-circuit its desired effect.

Try This 18.7: Write Periodic and Cumulative Sentences

If you consciously practice using periodic and cumulative constructions, you will be surprised how quickly you can learn to produce their respective effects in your own writing. You will also discover that both of these sentence shapes are already present in your prose in some undiscovered and thus unrefined way. It is often simply a case of bringing out what is already there. Try including at least one of each in the next paper you write.

Toward that end, compose a simple sentence on any subject, preferably one with a direct object. Then construct two variations expanding it, one periodic and one cumulative. Here, as a model, is an example using the core sentence "James Joyce was a gifted singer."

> **Periodic:** Although known primarily as one of the greatest novelists of the twentieth century, James Joyce, the son of a local political functionary who loved to tip a few too many at the pub, was also a gifted—and prizewinning—singer.

> **Cumulative:** James Joyce was a gifted singer, having listened at his father's knee to the ballads sung in pubs, having won an all-Ireland prize in his early teens, and having possessed a miraculous ear for the inflections of common speech that was to serve him throughout the career for which he is justly famous, that of a novelist.

Can't think of a core sentence? Okay, here are a few:

> Why do airlines show such mediocre films?

> Madison Bumgarner and friends brought a flag to San Francisco.

> Every senator is a millionaire.

CUT EXTRA WORDS TO ACHIEVE GREATER DIRECTNESS

If you can reduce verbiage, your prose will communicate more directly and effectively. In cutting the fat, you need to consider both the diction and the syntax. When it comes to diction, the way to eliminate superfluous words is deceptively simple: ask yourself if you need all of the words you've included to say what you want to say. Such revision requires an aggressive attitude. *Expect* to find unnecessary restatements or intensifiers such as "quite" and "very" that add words but not significance.

Sometimes, by the way, the problem is not just a matter of syntax but a matter of confidence. A lot of writing becomes obscure because the writer is trying to hide what he or she has to say with various "throat clearings" and other defensive verbiage. If you don't say anything clearly enough to be understood, you can't be accused of being wrong. If you find yourself bogged down in language, take a moment to write as directly as possible an answer to the question, "What I'm really trying to say here is…"

BEGINNING WITH "IT IS" OR "THERE IS": ADVANTAGES AND DISADVANTAGES

Sentences that begin with "It is" or "There is" are known as *expletive* constructions. The term *expletive* comes from a Latin word that means "serving to fill out." Most of the time, you can streamline your prose by getting rid of expletive constructions. Consider how the expletives function in the following examples:

> *There* are several prototypes for the artificial heart.

> *It* is obvious that the American West exerted a profound influence on the photography of Ansel Adams.

Compare these with versions that simply eliminate the expletives.

> The artificial heart has several prototypes.

> The American West exerted a profound influence on the photography of Ansel Adams.

The "It is obvious that" opening, for example, causes the grammar of the sentence to subordinate its real emphasis.

In some cases, though, an expletive can provide useful emphasis, as in the following example: "There are three primary reasons that you should avoid litigation." Although this sentence grammatically subordinates its primary content (avoiding litigation), the expletive provides a useful frame for what is to follow.

In an excellent book entitled *Rhetorical Grammar* (Longman, 2009), Martha Kolln and Loretta Gray make the case for using what they term "the there-transformation" as a strategy for adding emphasis. They do so by focusing on what they call "the rhythm pattern" of the sentence. Compare "There's a stranger standing on the porch," where the accent falls on "stranger," with the end focus of "The stranger stands on the porch." Here are two more examples of their advice on using rhythm patterns to provide emphasis, which we offer in part to demonstrate how easily you can begin attuning yourself to shapes:

- **End focus:** a common rhythm pattern in which, if you read aloud, you can hear the stress near the end, in the last or next to last unit of information. Kolln offers as examples "Barbara wrecked her motorcycle yesterday" and "My book for chemistry class cost almost 60 dollars." Note how the pressure falls on the "yes" in yesterday and the "six" in sixty and "dol" in dollars.
- **Interrupting the rhythm pattern:** a sentence marked by an inserted interrupter—Kolln offers "Other ways, in fact, are much more common." Here, the interrupter attracts emphasis by standing out.

STATIC VERSUS ACTIVE VERBS: "TO BE" OR "NOT TO BE"

Verbs energize a sentence. They do the work, connecting the parts of the sentence with each other. In a sentence of the subject–verb–direct object pattern, the verb— known as a *transitive verb*—functions as a kind of engine, driving the subject into the predicate, as in the following examples.

> John F. Kennedy effectively *manipulated* his image in the media.

> Thomas Jefferson *embraced* the idea of America as a country of yeoman farmers.

By contrast, "is" and other forms of the verb "to be" provide an equal sign between the subject and the predicate but otherwise tell us nothing about the relationship between them. "To be" is an *intransitive* verb; it cannot take a direct object. Compare the two preceding transitive examples with the following versions of the same sentences using forms of the verb "to be."

> John F. Kennedy *was* effective at the manipulation of his image in the media.

> Thomas Jefferson's idea *was* for America to be a country of yeoman farmers.

Rather than making things happen through an active transitive verb, these sentences let everything just hang around in a state of being. In the first version, Kennedy did something—*manipulated* his image—but in the second he just *is* (or *was*), and the energy of the original verb has been siphoned into an abstract noun, "manipulation." The revised Jefferson example suffers from a similar lack of momentum compared with the original version: the syntax doesn't help the sentence get anywhere.

Certain situations, however, dictate the use of forms of "to be." For definitions in particular, the equal sign that an "is" provides works well. For instance, "Organic gardening *is* a method of growing crops without using synthetic fertilizers or pesticides." As with choosing between active and passive voices, the decision to use "to be" or not should be just that—a conscious decision on your part.

Table 18.1 Static and Active Verbs

Action Hidden in Nouns and "To Be" Verbs	Action Emphasized in Verbs
The <u>cost</u> of the book *is* ten dollars.	The book *costs* ten dollars.
The <u>acknowledgment</u> of the fact *is* increasingly widespread that television *is* a <u>replacement</u> for reading in American culture.	People increasingly *acknowledge* that television *has replaced* reading in American culture.
A computer *is* ostensibly a labor-<u>saving</u> device— until the hard drive *is* the victim of a <u>crash</u>.	A computer ostensibly *saves* labor— until the hard drive *crashes*.
In the <u>laying</u> of a flagstone patio, the important preliminary steps to remember *are* the <u>excavating</u> and the <u>leveling</u> of the area and then the <u>filling</u> of it with a fine grade of gravel.	To *lay* a flagstone patio, first *excavate* and *level* the area and then *fill* it with a fine grade of gravel.

If you can train yourself to eliminate every unnecessary use of "to be" in a draft, you will make your prose more vital and direct. In most cases, you will find the verb that you need to substitute for "is" lurking somewhere in the sentence in some other grammatical form. In the preceding sentence about Kennedy, "manipulate" is implicit in "manipulation." In Table 18.1, each of the examples in the left-hand column uses a form of "to be" for its verb (italicized) and contains a potentially strong active verb lurking in the sentence in some other form (underlined). These "lurkers" have been converted into active verbs (italicized) in the revisions in the right-hand column.

Clearly, the examples in the left-hand column have problems other than their reliance on forms of "to be"—notably wordiness. But as Richard Lanham first articulated in his excellent *Revising Prose* (Longman, 2006), "to be" syntax tends to encourage circumlocution and verbosity. Lanhan named this kind of writing "The Official Style," and he attacked it for its flabbiness, which he traced to its addiction to forms of "to be," the passive voice, and strings of prepositions in place of concrete verbs in the active voice (see the next section). Lanham's proposes a series of steps, which he calls The Paramedic Method, for doing triage on Official Style sentences. He instructs writers to mark all of the prepositions, identify the forms of *to be*, find the action buried in the sentence and make it into an active verb.

Try This 18.8: Finding the Active Verb

Take a paper you've written and circle the sentences that rely on forms of "to be." Then, examine the other words in these sentences, looking for "lurkers." Rewrite the sentences, converting the lurkers into vigorous verbs. You will probably discover many lurkers, and your revisions will acquire more energy and directness.

ACTIVE AND PASSIVE VOICE: EMPHASIZING THE DOER OR THE ACTION

In the *active voice,* the grammatical subject acts; in the *passive voice,* the subject is acted upon. Here are two examples.

Active: Adam Smith wrote *The Wealth of Nations* in 1776.

Passive: *The Wealth of Nations* was written by Adam Smith in 1776.

The two sentences convey identical information, but the emphasis differs—the first focuses on the author, the second on the book. As the examples illustrate, using the passive normally results in a longer sentence than using the active. If we consider how to convert the passive into the active, you can see why. In the passive, the verb requires a form of "to be" plus a past participle. (For more on participles, see the Glossary of Grammatical Terms in Chapter 19.) In this case, the active verb "wrote" becomes the passive verb "was written," the grammatical subject ("Smith") becomes the object of the preposition "by," and the direct object ("*The Wealth of Nations*") becomes the grammatical subject.

Now consider the activity described in the two versions of this example: a man wrote a book. That's what happened in life. The grammar of the active version captures that action most clearly: the grammatical subject ("Smith") performs the action, and the direct object *("The Wealth of Nations")* receives it, just as in life. By contrast, the passive version alters the close link between the syntax and the event: the object of the action in life *("The Wealth of Nations")* has become the grammatical subject, whereas the doer in life ("Smith") has become the grammatical object of a prepositional phrase.

Note, too, that the passive would allow us to omit "Smith" altogether: "*The Wealth of Nations* was written in 1776." A reader who desired to know more and was not aware of the author would not appreciate this sentence. More troubling, the passive can also be used to conceal the doer of an action—not "I made a mistake" (active) but rather "A mistake has been made" (passive).

In sum, there are three reasons for avoiding the passive voice when you can: (1) it's longer, (2) its grammatical relationships often reverse what happened in life, and (3) it can omit the performer responsible for the action.

On the other hand, sometimes there are good reasons for using the passive. If you want to emphasize the object or recipient of the action rather than the performer, the passive will do that for you: "*The Wealth of Nations* was written in 1776 by Adam Smith" places the stress on the book. The passive is also preferable when the doer remains unknown: "The president has been shot!" is probably a better sentence than "Some unknown assailant has shot the president!"

Especially in the natural sciences, the use of the passive voice is a standard practice. There are sound reasons for this disciplinary convention: science tends to focus on what happens to something in a given experiment, rather than on the person performing the experiment. Compare the following sentences.

Passive: Separation of the protein was achieved by using an electrophoretic gel.

Active: The researcher used an electrophoretic gel to separate the protein.

If you opted for the active version, the emphasis would rest, illogically, on the agent of the action (the researcher) rather than on what happened and how (electrophoretic separation of the protein).

More generally, the passive voice can provide a way to avoid using the pronoun "I," whether for reasons of convention, as indicated earlier, or for other reasons. For example, the following passive sentence begins a business memo from a supervisor to the staff in her office.

> The Inventory and Reprint departments have recently been restructured and merged.

Like many passive sentences, this one names no actor; we do not know for sure who did the restructuring and merging, though we might imagine that the author of the memo is the responsible party. The supervisor might, then, have written the sentence in the active voice.

> I have recently restructured and merged the Inventory and Reprint departments.

But the active version is less satisfactory than the passive one for two reasons: one of practical emphasis and one of sensitivity to the audience (tone). First, the fact of the changes is more important for the memo's readers than is the announcement of who made the changes. The passive sentence appropriately emphasizes the changes; the active sentence inappropriately emphasizes the person who made the changes. Second, the emphasis of the active sentence on "I" (the supervisor) risks alienating the readers by taking an autocratic tone and by seeming to exclude all others from possible credit for the presumably worthwhile reorganization.

On balance, "consider" is the operative term when you choose between passive and active as you revise the syntax of your drafts. Recognize that you do have choices—in emphasis, in relative directness, and in economy. All things being equal and disciplinary conventions permitting, the active is usually the better choice.

Try This 18.9: Converting Passive to Active

Identify all of the sentences that use the passive voice in one of your papers. Then, rewrite these sentences, converting passive into active wherever appropriate. Finally, count the total number of words, the total number of prepositions, and the average sentence length (words per sentence) in each version. What do you discover?

For more practice, here's another exercise. Compose a paragraph of at least half a page in which you use only the passive voice and verbs of being, followed by a paragraph in which you use only the active voice. Then, rewrite the first paragraph using only active voice, if possible, and rewrite the second paragraph using only passive voice and verbs of being as much as possible. How do the paragraphs differ in shape, length, and coherence?

Sentence Style in Science Writing: A Biochemistry Professor Speaks

Most of the advice offered in this chapter also applies to the very specialized writing style expected in lab reports and other formal science writing. Like academic style in general, science writing is concerned with combining ideas in order to locate emphasis appropriately and to create greater concision than a string of simple sentences would allow. The voice, ethos, and tone of science writing is typically quite muted. Active verbs appear, but the style goes out of its way to not call attention to itself, and especially not to the writer. This muted quality is, in fact, true of most academic writing, but it is markedly so in the sciences.

   In the following Voice from Across the Curriculum, biochemistry professor Keri Colabroy shares the basic guidelines for constructing sentences in scientific style that she provides for her science majors.

Voices from Across The Curriculum

o   Subjects (the "actor" is absent)

  - Passive voice

      Yes: The gel was run; No: I ran the gel.

      Better: The protein migrated at a molecular weight of... (data first, not procedure)

  - Pronouns—it's safer to avoid them

Verbs (qualify, qualify, qualify...)

  - Do: demonstrate, indicate, suggest, construct, deliver, observe
  - Don't: show, prove, make

Sentences

  - Don't say in two sentences what you can say with one (embedding).
  - Subordinate and coordinate.

Words

  - Data are plural.
  - When making observations, use academic, not conversational language.
  - Choose words for precision and tone (qualify your verbs, not your adjectives).

                                   —Keri Colabroy, Professor of Biochemistry

ABOUT PRESCRIPTIVE STYLE MANUALS: A WORD OF WARNING

Every change in style is a change in meaning. Although style guides can be very useful when they illuminate the range of choices a writer has and the implications of those choices, they often value one style and tone over another as self-evidently good and right. In so doing, they imply a rhetorical preference for a particular way of approaching the world in speech, a preference that may not actually match your style or the style of a particular discipline in which you are writing.

Despite Strunk & White's rule (in *Elements of Style*), three words are not better than six in every rhetorical situation. And their edict against it notwithstanding, passive voice has its place, its own special advantages. As we hope you have seen from the foregoing discussion, active is not always better. Much depends on context. The key to growing as a stylist is learning to see the choices. *(See Chapter 1, the Short Take entitled "A Quick Word on Style Guides".)*

EXPERIMENT!

A key idea of this chapter is that there are not necessarily right and wrong choices when it comes to sentence style but instead better and best choices for particular situations. The from-the-hip plain style of a memo or a set of operating instructions for your lawnmower is very likely not the best style choice for a good-bye letter to a best friend, a diplomatic talk on a sensitive political situation, or an analysis of guitar styles in contemporary jazz.

Is style a function of character and personality? Is it, in short, personal, and thus something to be preserved in the face of would-be meddlers carrying style manuals and grammar guides? Well, as you might guess at this point in the book, the answer is yes and no. We all need to find ways of using words that do not succumb to the mind-numbing environment of verbal cliché in which we dwell. It helps then, to become more self-conscious about style and not assume that it is inborn. Staying locked into one way of writing because that is "your style" is as limiting as remaining locked into only one way of thinking.

This chapter has presented some terms and techniques for experimenting with sentence styles. Equipped with these, you might profitably begin to read and listen for style more self-consciously. Find models. When a style appeals to you, figure out what makes it work. Copy sentences you like. Try imitating them. Know, by the way, that imitation will not erase your own style—it will allow you to experiment with new moves, new shapes into which to cast your words.

GUIDELINES FOR THE RHETORIC OF THE SENTENCE

1. Revise sentences to clarify their meaning by revealing the organization of thought. Align like with like, set difference against difference, and in general use form to emphasize what's important and demote what is not.

2. Become aware of your own syntactic habits. What is your "go-to sentence" and how might you build upon it to extend your range and force?

3. Cut the fat. Don't use five words ("due to the fact that") when one will do ("because"). Root out expletives that needlessly subordinate ("It is true that..."). Avoid redundancy.

4. Tighten the syntax of your sentences by energizing the verbs. The active voice generally achieves directness and economy; it will promote clarity and cut fat.

5. Look for potentially strong active verbs "lurking" in sentences that use a form of *to be*. Beware habitual use of *to be* and passives, since these forms tend to blur or submerge the action, omit its performers, and generally lack momentum.

6. Look at the order and arrangement of clauses. Are ideas of equal importance in coordinate constructions? Have you used subordination to rank ideas? Have your sentences exploited the end as a position of emphasis?

7. Look at the shapes of your sentences. Do they use parallelism to keep your ideas clear? Where do you find opportunities for composing periodic and cumulative sentences that revision can bring out?

Assignments: Stylistic Analyses—The Rhetoric of the Sentence

1. **Compare the Style of Two Writers**. Analyze the style—the syntax but also the diction—of two writers doing a similar kind of writing; for example, two sportswriters, two rock music reviewers, or two presidents. Study first the similarities. What style characteristics does this type of writing seem to invite? Then study the differences. How is one writer recognizable through his or her style? The American Rhetoric website is a wonderful place to go hunting.

2. **Analyze Your Own Style**. Assemble some pieces you have written, preferably of a similar type, and study them for style. Do you have some favorite stylistic moves? What sentence shapes (simple, compound, complex, compound-complex, highly parallel, periodic, or cumulative) dominate in your writing? What verbs? Do you use forms of "to be" a lot, and so forth?

3. **Find Go-To Sentences**. As we discuss in Chapter 2, whether we recognize it or not, most of us have a "go-to" sentence—the sentence shape we repeatedly go to as we write and talk. If a person's "go-to" sentence takes the form "Although _____, the fact is that _____," we might see that person as inclined to qualify his or her thoughts ("Although") and disinclined to immediately impose his or her ideas on others ("the fact that" comes in the second half of the sentence, where it gets a lot of emphasis but is also delayed and qualified by the sentence's opening observation).

   First, select one sentence in something you've been reading that you think is typical of that writer's way of putting sentences together. Describe that sentence shape and speculate about what it accomplishes and how it reveals the writer's characteristic mode of thinking in some way.

   Then find a "go-to" sentence of your own in something that you've written. What does this structure reveal to you about how you think? Tip: You can also use The Method to locate "go-to" sentences. Look for repeated conjunctions or subordinators, such as "x; however, y" or "although x, nevertheless, y," or "not only x, but also y."

4. **Discuss the Style of Sentences You Like**. This exercise is a companion to Try This 18.2; it aims to give you more practice at seeing the shapes of sentences. Listed below are five sentences our students like; use these or find your own candidates. As in the Try This, do the following operations:

- identify which of the four types it is
- underline the subject and verb of the main clause(s)
- double-underline the subordinate clauses
- circle the coordinating conjunctions and subordinating conjunctions

In addition, bring to bear the other lenses you've acquired in the latter parts of the chapter. What do you notice about the verbs? The order of clauses? Where do you detect elements of the periodic and cumulative, the antithetical or chiasmic? Write a paragraph or two about the style of each sentence.

   a. "Where is the powerful being who will crush all these reptiles who corrupt everything they touch, and whose venomous bites stir up our citizens, transforming their political assemblies into gladiatorial arenas where each passion, each interest, finds apologists and an army?" (Chaumet, attorney of the Parisian Commune, Sept 5, 1793)

   b. From newspaper baron Lord Northcliffe: "News is what somebody somewhere is trying to suppress. The rest is advertising." (Ben McGrath, "Roid Warriors." *The New Yorker*, 9 March 2009)

   c. "On the all-important question of power—the efficacy of power, the morality of power, the desirability of power—American and European perspectives are diverging." (Kagan, Robert. "Why the United States and Europe See the World Differently." *Policy Review* 113. (2002))

   d. "Republican jibes that the budget was 'socialist' should be treated with the respect they deserve, which is to say none: after a major rise in outlays this year, due to the stimulus package, federal spending as a share of the gross domestic product is projected to fall back to twenty-two percent by 2013, which represents a rise of just one percent over last year's figure." (John Cassidy, "Harder Times." *The New Yorker*, 16 March 2009.)

   e. "Most men gamble with her, and gain all, and lose all, as her wheel rolls." (Ralph Waldo Emerson. "Self Reliance." *The Essential Writings of Ralph Waldo Emerson*. Ed. Brooks Atkinson. New York: Modern Library, 2000).

5. **Analyze the Gettysburg Address**. For many people, Lincoln's Gettysburg Address is one of the best examples of the careful matching of style to situation. Delivered after a long talk by a previous speaker at the dedication of a Civil War battlefield on a rainy day, the speech composed by Abraham Lincoln (some say on the back of an envelope) is a masterpiece of style. Analyze its

sentence structure, such as its use of parallelism, antithesis, and other kinds of repetition. Which features of Lincoln's style seem most important in creating the overall effect of the piece? Or do this with any popular journalist whom you read regularly and who you think has an especially effective style. Or look for another inspirational speech and see if such occasional writing has anything in common. (You can download and print the Gettysburg Address from many sites on the web.)

6. **Do a Full-fledged Stylistic Revision of a Paper**. The best choice might well be an essay you already have revised, resubmitted, and had returned, because in that case, you will be less likely to get distracted by conceptual revision and so can concentrate on stylistic issues. As you revise, try to accomplish each of the following:

   a. Sharpen the diction.

   b. Blend concrete and abstract diction.

   c. Experiment with the order of and relation among subordinate and coordinate clauses.

   d. Choose more knowingly between active and passive voice.

   e. Cut the fat, especially by eliminating unnecessary "to be" constructions.

   f. Vary sentence length and shape.

   g. Use parallelism.

   h. Experiment with periodic and cumulative sentences.

   i. Fine-tune the tone.

Chapter 19

Revising for Correctness: Grammar and Punctuation

THIS CHAPTER ADDRESSES THE ISSUE of grammatical correctness and offers ways of recognizing and fixing (or avoiding) the most important errors. Unlike editing for style, which involves you in making choices between more and less effective ways of phrasing, editing for correctness locates you in the domain of right or wrong. As you will see, there are usually a number of ways to correct an error, so you are still concerned with making choices, but leaving the error uncorrected is not a viable option.

There is more to thinking about grammar than the quest for error-free writing, as Chapter 18 on sentence style demonstrates, with its emphasis on how to analyze writers' syntactical choices and how to think about the relationship between a writer's style and his or her characteristic ways of thinking. Studying the grammar rules in this chapter will enable you to find your way around in a sentence more easily, and thus, to build better sentences.

The first part of this chapter makes the case for learning to recognize a pattern of error in your drafts and learning to prioritize the most serious problems, creating a *hierarchy of error,* rather than treating (and worrying about) all errors equally and all at the same time. Achieving grammatical correctness is a matter of both knowledge—how to recognize and avoid errors—and timing: when to narrow your focus to proofreading.

NINE BASIC WRITING ERRORS

- Sentence fragments
- Comma splices and fused (run-on) sentences
- Errors in subject–verb agreement
- Shifts in sentence structure (faulty predication)
- Errors in pronoun reference
- Misplaced modifiers and dangling participles
- Errors in using possessive apostrophes
- Comma errors
- Spelling/diction errors that interfere with meaning

For each of these, the chapter offers a definition with examples and then talks you through how to fix it—with a little "test yourself" section at the end.

At the end of the chapter, a brief Glossary of Grammatical Terms defines and illustrates many of the key terms used earlier in the chapter and throughout the book. Following this chapter, you will find an appendix that provides solutions to the various "Test Yourself" examples that point up the chapter's lessons.

A great many readers regard technical errors as an inattention to detail that also signals sloppiness at more important levels of thinking. If you produce writing that contains such errors, you risk not only distracting readers from your message but also undermining your authority to deliver the message in the first place.

THE CONCEPT OF BASIC WRITING ERRORS (BWEs)

You get a paper back, and it's a sea of red ink. But if you look more closely, you'll often find that you haven't made a million mistakes—you've made only a few, but over and over in various forms. This phenomenon is what the rhetorician Mina Shaughnessy in a book called *Errors & Expectations* addressed in creating the category of "basic writing errors," or BWEs. Shaughnessy argues that, in order to improve your writing for style and correctness, you need to do two things:

- Look for a *pattern of error,* which will require you to understand your own logic in the mistakes you typically make.
- Recognize that not all errors are created equal, which means that you need to *address errors in some order of importance*—beginning with those most likely to interfere with your readers' understanding.

This chapter's BWE guide, Nine Basic Writing Errors and How to Fix Them, reflects Shaughnessy's view. It does not cover *all* of the rules of grammar, punctuation, diction, and usage, such as where to place the comma or period when you close a quotation or whether or not to write out numerals. Instead, it emphasizes the errors that are potentially the most damaging to the clarity of your writing and to your credibility with readers. We have arranged the error types in a hierarchy, moving in descending order of severity (from most to least problematic).

As in our discussion of style in Chapter 18, the key premises of this chapter are that a sentence is made up of moveable parts and that sentences disclose the relationships among those parts. Keep these premises in mind, and you will see what the errors have in common.

WHY GRAMMAR ERRORS MAKE SOME PEOPLE SO ANGRY

Grammar is a volatile subject. Grammatical errors evoke not just disapproval but anger in some people. Why? Well, clearly correct grammar matters. Readers should not have to struggle to figure out where your sentences begin and end or what goes with what. But the fact that correctness matters—that correctness is necessary to being taken seriously as a writer—does not account for the sheer venom that goes into spotting other people's grammatical errors. *(See Chapter 1, the Short Take entitled A Quick Word on Style Guides.)*

Language use is social and conventional. Conforming to the rules is, in a sense, a sign that you agree to be governed by the same conventions that others conform to. Perhaps this is why the intentional sentence fragment has the impact that it does. Really. The gesture makes the writer's style seem daring. It says, "You and I both recognize that I control the standard conventions with sufficient assurance to break them on purpose, not by accident."

USAGE: HOW LANGUAGE CUSTOMS CHANGE

Errors of grammar are relatively stable and locked down. "The eggs was tasty" is wrong; so is "Obama are President" and "Obama is Presidents." But usage, a kind of troublesome and embarrassing cousin to grammar, is a more vexed subject. According to the *Oxford English Dictionary*, usage has to do with "established or customary use or employment of language, words, expressions, etc." Established by whom? Customary within which what group? Usage, in short, tends to be less clear cut than grammar.

That is why some dictionaries offer brief paragraphs of discussion from a "usage panel"—a group of experts who weigh in on what is proper and improper in language use. Most of the usage guides you will find at the back of grammar handbooks offer a range of examples of usage. At one end of the range, there are examples in which one form is clearly preferred and another disapproved.

Usage: Some Examples of Right & Wrong versus Etiquette

Here is a set of examples, organized on a sliding scale, from clearly distinguished right and wrong to less defensible distinctions.

- **fewer vs. less**: Countable things are fewer: fewer pencils; amounts that can't be counted are less: less support. This is a helpful distinction, one the language needs.

- **good vs. well**: *Good* is an adjective, a part of speech that modifies (describes) nouns and other adjectives. *It was a good movie. Well* is an adverb, a part of speech that modifies a verb or another adverb. *She does not feel well. Good* modifies *movie*; *well* modifies *feel.* This is another helpful distinction; therefore, most people consider this word choice a matter of right and wrong.

- **can vs. may**: *Can* refers to what one is able to do; *may* refers to what one is permitted to do. *He can spit across the classroom, but according to the teacher, he may not.* Again, this distinction conveys a meaningful difference, although in actual practice, the word *may* is starting to lose its clout—it sounds fussy to many contemporary ears.

- **between vs. among**: *Between* refers to two items, *among* to more than two. *The difference between sushi and sashimi is more easily understood than the differences among sushi, sashimi and maki.* In this case, we can clearly see that if you used *between* in both cases, a reader would still be able to make sense of the sentence, but the use of *among* is helpful—it lets us know that more than two items are coming. Still, as you can see, this example of usage is less significant, more a matter of good manners, than *can* vs. *may*. Nonetheless, it is arguably a useful distinction.

- **different from vs. different than**: Some say a writer should not use *different than*, because *than* is comparative, but different already signifies that a comparison is coming, so you should always says *different from*. Let's use this example—and there are others like it—as an emblem of a preference for which there is not really much of a reason.

- **ending a sentence with a preposition**: the prescription that one should not end a sentence with a preposition, or if you will, that a preposition is a part of speech you should not end a sentence with, is a case of rather arbitrary usage. In this same category goes the split infinitive—the practice of locating a word inside a *to* + verb construction, such as *to boldly go where no one has gone before*. In a formal setting—an application to law school, say—you would want to be careful to avoid these usages, even though they are not actually wrong.

Why then do some guardians of the language insist that we not end sentences with prepositions? Is it snobbery? Etiquette? First of all, let's admit that etiquette serves a definite purpose, as anyone who has gone out to dinner and had the misfortune to sit next to a food fight will attest. To be understanding, let's assume that the person who enforces usage distinctions as hard-and-fast rules, even when they are not, is a person who wishes to maintain standards in the face of change. And that too is a position one may (and can!) respect.

But the fact is that the language is always changing, not just with the addition of new words to the standard dictionaries, but also with the circumstances of usage— "the established or customary use or employment of language, words, expressions, etc." Ultimately, a panel of experts cannot control usage, and that is a healthy thing, allowing a language to evolve over time.

When Usage Begins to Change Grammar

Which brings us back to the issue of grammatical correctness, a subject that impelled this digression into usage in the first place (yes, we know it's a fragment). Usage, and more particularly changes in usage, bear on grammar because grammar, although relatively fixed, does not stand still, and the doorway through which grammar changes is the same one through which usage walks.

Here are three common examples of how changing usage appears to be inspiring a change in the grammatical conventions of right and wrong. These changes have not yet occurred, but arguably, they are in the process of occurring.

- **possessive apostrophes:** an increasing number of writers simply leave these out. If one writes, *The cars fender was dented* (not car's) or *Andy Pettittes slider is the best in the American League* (not Pettitte's), virtually every reader will understand the meaning, though not as quickly as the apostrophe would allow.

- *I* **vs.** *me***,** especially in prepositional phrases: This one has to do with what grammarians call the case of pronouns. We use one form of a pronoun when it is in the subject and another when it is the object of a verb or a preposition. For example,

- *My mother and I argue about grammar*—not *My mother and me.* We would not say "*Me argues about grammar.*" *I* is in the subjective case; *me* is in the objective case.
- *According to my mother and me, grammar matters a lot*—not *According to my mother and I.* We would not say *According to I.* "According to" is a preposition, so you have to use the objective case, as the pronoun in question is the object of the preposition.

But increasingly, we hear native speakers saying things such as *Joe and me are going to get a beer* or *For Jill and I, voting is an undeniable civic duty, virtually an ethical imperative.* In the first example, a speaker might say *Joe and me* because it sounds "natural," that is, unpretentious, as unpretentious as having a beer. In the second example, a speaker might say *For Jill and I* because (and we're not sure why this is!), the use of "and I" sometimes sounds classier, more high style, and in a sentence where lofty concepts such as civic duty and ethical imperatives occur, you might wish to sound classy. But "I" in "For Jill and I" must be changed to "me," the objective case, because it is the object of the preposition "For."

- **who versus whom:** This is another version of the pronoun problem. *Who* is subjective case; *whom* is objective case. For example: *I want to know who ate the last slice of pie I left in the refrigerator.* Compare that with *Ask not for whom the bell tolls*—where *whom* is the object of the preposition *for.* Yet increasingly, speakers seem to fear working out the grammar necessary to figure out if the who/whom in question is a subject or an object, so they tend either to eliminate *whom* altogether and just use *who* for every case, or they assume that *whom* is classier, as they do "and I," and they end up misusing *whom.* Here are examples:
  - *Who is Derek Jeter going to sign with, now that he has become a free agent?* This sentence is grammatically incorrect: we need a *Whom* to be the object of the preposition *with—With whom will Jeter sign?*
  - *I read a book by the cognitive therapist whom is most famous for formulating rational emotive therapy.* The loftiness of the topic misleads the writer into using the supposedly classier *whom* even though grammar tells us the pronoun *who* is in the subjective case.

Usage as Cultural Marker

You can think of usage in terms of markers—indicators of something. So, for example:

- usage as marker for informal, conversational versus formal style:
  And then she goes, "that's the silliest thing I've ever heard" versus *And then she says,* . . . And some people disallow contractions as too informal.
- usage as marker for social class:
  Where is he at? versus *Where is he?*
  I ain't going versus *I am not going.*
- usage as gender marker:
  Poetess versus *poet, actress* versus *actor, waitress* versus *waiter* or *wait-person*

Most people have not heard the word *poetess*—how long before the same will be said of actress? (The –*ess* suffix indicating female is now considered sexist by many people because it relegates women to a separate category.)

Try This 19.1: Discover the Rationale for Usage Choices

Research the following pairs of terms. Locate the usage "rules" that govern them, and if you can, uncover the rationale that informs these rules.

Try and / try to

Shall / will

Disinterested / uninterested

Raise / rise

WHAT PUNCTUATION MARKS SAY: A QUICK-HIT GUIDE

These little signs really aren't that hard to use correctly, folks. A few of them will be treated in more specific contexts in the upcoming discussion of BWEs, but here are the basic rules of punctuation for the five basic signs.

The **period** [.] marks the end of a sentence. Make sure what precedes it is an independent clause, that is, a subject plus verb that can stand alone.

The period says to a reader, "This is the end of this particular statement. I'm a mark of closure."

Example: Lennon rules.

The **comma** [,] separates the main (independent) clause from dependent elements that modify the main clause. It also separates two main clauses joined by a conjunction—known as a compound sentence. Information that is not central to the main clause is set off in a comma sandwich. The comma does *not* signify a pause.

The comma says to the reader, "Here is where the main clause begins (or ends)," or "Here is a break in the main clause." In the case of compound sentences (containing two or more independent clauses), the comma says, "Here is where one main clause ends, and after the conjunction that follows me, another main clause begins."

Examples: Lennon rules, and McCartney is cute.

Lennon rules, although McCartney is arguably more tuneful.

The **semicolon** [;] separates two independent clauses not joined by a conjunction. Secondarily, the semicolon can separate two independent clauses joined by a conjunction if either of the clauses already contains commas. In either case, the semicolon both shows a close relationship between the two independent clauses that it connects and distinguishes where one ends and the other begins. It is also the easiest way to fix comma splices (see BWE 2 later in this chapter).

The semicolon says to the reader, "What precedes and what follows me are conceptually close but grammatically independent and thus equal statements."

Example: Lennon's lyrics show deep sympathy for the legions of "Nowhere Men" who inhabit the "Strawberry Fields" of their imaginations; McCartney's lyrics, on the other hand, are more upbeat, forever bidding "Good Day, Sunshine" to the world at large and "Michelle" in particular.

The **colon** [:] marks the end of a setup for something coming next. It provides a frame, pointing beyond itself, like a spotlight. The colon is quite dramatic, and unlike the semicolon, it links what precedes and follows it formally and tightly rather than loosely and associatively. It usually operates with dramatic force. It can frame a list to follow, separate cause and effect, or divide a brief claim from a more expanded version of the claim. The language on at least one side of the colon must be an independent clause, though both sides can be.

The colon says to the reader, "Concentrate on what follows me for a more detailed explanation of what preceded me" or "What follows me is logically bound with what preceded me."

Examples: *Rubber Soul* marked a change in The Beatles' song-writing: the sentimentality of earlier efforts gave way to a new complexity, both in the range of their subjects and the sophistication of their poetic devices.

Nowhere is this change more evident than in a sequence of songs near the album's end: "I'm Looking Through You," "In My Life," "Wait," and "If I Needed Someone."

The **dash** [—] provides an informal alternative to the colon for adding information to a sentence. Its effect is sudden, of the moment—what springs up impulsively to disrupt and extend in some new way the ongoing train of thought. A **pair of dashes** provides an invaluable resource to writers for inserting information within a sentence. In this usage, the rule is that the sentence must read coherently if the inserted information is left out. (To type a dash, type two hyphens with no space between, before, or after. This distinguishes the dash from a hyphen [-], which is the mark used for connecting two words into one.)

The dash says to the reader, "This too!" or, in the case of a pair of them, "Remember the thought in the beginning of this sentence because we're jumping to something else before we come back to finish that thought."

Examples: For all their loveliness, the songs on *Rubber Soul* are not without menace—"I'd rather see you dead little girl than to see you with another man."

In addition to the usual lead, rhythm, and bass guitar ensemble, *Rubber Soul* introduced new instruments—notably, the harpsichord interlude in "In My Life," the sitar spiraling through "Norwegian Wood"—that had not previously been heard in rock 'n' roll.

NINE BASIC WRITING ERRORS AND HOW TO FIX THEM

If you're unsure about some of the terms you encounter in the discussions of BWEs, see the Glossary of Grammatical Terms at the end of this chapter. You'll also find brief Test Yourself questions interspersed throughout this section. Do them: it's easy to conclude that you understand a problem when you are shown the correction, but understanding is not the same thing as actively practicing. There's an appendix to this chapter that—as mentioned earlier—contains answers to these sections, along with explanations.

Some Advice on Proofreading

- Have a separate proofreading phase at the end of your composing process in which you attend only to grammar and punctuation.
- Look at each sentence as a discrete unit. If you have trouble doing this—if you get caught up in the flow of your thinking—try proofreading the paper backward. Start with the last sentence, then the next-to-last, and move all the way from back to front.
- Circle each punctuation mark, and ask yourself why it is there. In this way, you will be more likely to find commas where there should be periods.
- Read your paper out loud with a pencil in hand. Writers are much more likely to notice errors when they hear them. (Many of the BWEs typically make sentences difficult to follow and difficult to read out loud.)

BWE 1: SENTENCE FRAGMENTS

The most basic of writing errors, a *sentence fragment,* is a group of words punctuated like a complete sentence but lacking the necessary structure: it is only part of a sentence. Typically, a sentence fragment occurs when the group of words in question (1) lacks a subject, (2) lacks a predicate, or (3) is a subordinate (or dependent) clause.

To fix a sentence fragment, either turn it into an independent clause by providing whatever is missing—a subject or a predicate—or attach it to an independent clause on which it can depend.

Noun Clause (No Predicate) as a Fragment

A world where imagination takes over and sorrow is left behind.

This fragment is not a sentence but rather a noun clause—a sentence subject with no predicate. The fragment lacks a verb that would assert something about the subject. (The verbs *takes over* and *is left* are in a dependent clause created by the subordinating conjunction *where*.)

Corrections

A world *arose* where imagination takes over and sorrow is left behind. *[new verb matched to "a world"]*

She entered a world where imagination takes over and sorrow is left behind. *[new subject and verb added]*

The first correction adds a new verb ("arose"). The second introduces a new subject and verb, converting the fragment into the direct object of "she entered."

Verbal as a Fragment

Falling into debt for the fourth consecutive year.

"Falling" in the preceding fragment is not a verb. Depending on the correction, "falling" is either a verbal or part of a verb phrase.

Corrections

The company was falling into debt for the fourth consecutive year. *[subject and helping verb added]*

Falling into debt for the fourth consecutive year *led the company to consider relocating. [new predicate added]*

Falling into debt for the fourth consecutive year, *the company considered relocating. [new subject and verb added]*

In the first correction, the addition of a subject and the helping verb "was" converts the fragment into a sentence. The second correction turns the fragment into a gerund phrase functioning as the subject of a new sentence. The third correction converts the fragment into a participial phrase attached to a new independent clause. (See the section entitled Glossary of Grammatical Terms and look under "verbal" for definitions of "gerund" and "participle.")

Subordinate Clause as a Fragment

I had an appointment for 11:00 and was still waiting at 11:30. Although I did get to see the dean before lunch.

"Although" is a subordinating conjunction that calls for some kind of completion. Like "if," "when," "because," "whereas," and other subordinating conjunctions (see the Glossary of Grammatical Terms), "although" *always* makes the clause that it introduces dependent.

Corrections

I had an appointment for 11:00 and was still waiting at *11:30, although* I did get to see the dean before lunch. *[fragment attached to preceding sentence]*

As the correction demonstrates, the remedy lies in attaching the fragment to an independent clause on which it can depend (or, alternatively, making the fragment into a sentence by dropping the conjunction).

Sometimes writers use sentence fragments deliberately, usually for rhythm and emphasis or to create a conversational tone. In less formal contexts, they are generally permissible, but you run the risk that the fragment will not be perceived as intentional. In formal writing assignments, it is safer to avoid intentional fragments.

■ Test yourself 19.1: Fragments

There are fragments in each of the following three examples, probably the result of their proximity to legitimate sentences. What's the problem in each case, and how would you fix it?

1. Like many other anthropologists, Margaret Mead studied non-Western cultures in such works as *Coming of Age in Samoa*. And influenced theories of childhood development in America.

2. The catastrophe resulted from an engineering flaw. Because the bridge lacked sufficient support.

3. In the 1840s the potato famine decimated Ireland. It being a country with poor soil and antiquated methods of agriculture.

Using Dashes and Colons to Correct Fragments

Beyond what the punctuation guide has offered, the particular virtues of the dash and colon as ways to correct sentence fragments deserve brief mention. One way to correct a fragment is to replace the period with a dash: "The campaign required commitment. Not just money." becomes "The campaign required commitment—not just money." The dash offers you one way of attaching a phrase or dependent clause to a sentence without having to construct another independent clause. In short, it's succinct. (Compare the correction that uses the dash with another possible correction: "The campaign required commitment. It also required money.") Moreover, with the air of sudden interruption that the dash conveys, it can capture the informality and immediacy that the intentional fragment offers a writer.

You should be wary of overusing the dash as the slightly more presentable cousin of the intentional fragment. The energy it carries can clash with the decorum of formal writing contexts; for some readers, its staccato effect quickly becomes too much of a good thing.

One alternative to this usage of the dash is the colon. It can substitute because it also can be followed by a phrase, a list, or a clause. It must be preceded by an independent clause. And like the dash, it carries dramatic force because it abruptly halts the flow of the sentence.

The colon, however, does not convey informality. In place of a slapdash effect, it trains a light on what is to follow it. Hence, as in this sentence you are reading, it is especially appropriate for setting up certain kinds of information: explanations, lists, or results. In the case of results, the cause or action precedes the colon; the effect or reaction follows it.

BWE 2: COMMA SPLICES AND FUSED (OR RUN-ON) SENTENCES

A comma splice consists of two independent clauses connected ("spliced") with a comma; a fused (or run-on) sentence combines two such clauses with no conjunction or punctuation. The solutions for both comma splices and fused sentences are the same.

1. Place a conjunction (such as "and" or "because") between the clauses.
2. Place a semicolon between the clauses.
3. Make the clauses into separate sentences.

All of these solutions solve the same logical problem: they clarify the boundaries of the independent clauses for your readers.

Comma Splice

He disliked discipline, he avoided anything demanding.

Correction

Because he disliked discipline, he avoided anything demanding. *[subordinating conjunction added]*

Comma Splice

Today most TV programs are violent, almost every program is about cops and detectives.

Correction

Today most TV programs are violent; almost every program is about cops and detectives. *[semicolon replaces comma]*

Because the two independent clauses in the first example contain ideas that are closely connected logically, the most effective of the three comma-splice solutions is to add a subordinating conjunction ("because") to the first of the two clauses, making it depend on the second. For the same reason—close conceptual connection—the best solution for the next comma splice is to substitute a semicolon for the comma. The semicolon signals that the two independent clauses are closely linked in meaning. In general, you can use a semicolon where you could also use a period.

Cures for the Perpetual Comma Splicer

The comma splice is remarkably common, even among fairly sophisticated writers. It indicates two things: (1) the writer is not distinguishing between independent and dependent clauses and (2) he or she is operating on the so-called "pause theory" of punctuation. All of the clauses in our two examples are independent. As written, each of these should be punctuated not with a comma but rather with a period or a semicolon. Instead, the perpetual comma splicer, as usual, acts on the "pause theory": because the ideas in the independent clauses are closely connected, the writer hesitates to separate them with a period. And so the writer inserts what he or she takes to be a shorter pause—the comma.

But a comma is not a "breath" mark; it provides readers with specific grammatical information, in each of these cases mistakenly suggesting there is only one independent clause separated by the comma from modifying information. In the corrections, by contrast, the semicolon sends the appropriate signal to the reader: the message that it is joining two associated but independent statements. Adding a coordinating conjunction such as "and" would also be grammatically correct, though possibly awkward. *(See the discussion of independent clauses and comma rules at the opening of Chapter 18.)*

Fused Sentence

The Indo-European language family includes many groups most languages in Europe belong to it.

Correction

The Indo-European language family includes many groups. Most languages in Europe belong to it. *[period inserted after first independent clause]*

You could also fix this fused sentence with a comma plus the coordinating conjunction "and." Alternatively, you might condense the whole into a single independent clause.

Most languages in Europe belong to the Indo-European language family.

Comma Splices with Conjunctive Adverbs

Quantitative methods of data collection show broad trends, however, they ignore specific cases.

Sociobiology poses a threat to traditional ethics, for example, it asserts that human behavior is genetically motivated by the "selfish gene" to perpetuate itself.

Corrections

Quantitative methods of data collection show broad trends; however, they ignore specific cases. *[semicolon replaces comma before "however"]*

Sociobiology poses a threat to traditional ethics; for example, it asserts that human behavior is genetically motivated by the "selfish gene" to perpetuate itself. *[semicolon replaces comma before "for example"]*

Both of these examples contain one of the most common forms of comma splices. Both of them are compound sentences, that is, they contain two independent clauses. *(See the section entitled The Compound Sentence in Chapter 18.)* Normally, connecting the clauses with a comma and a conjunction would be correct; for example, "Most hawks hunt alone, but osprey hunt in pairs." In the preceding two comma splices, however, the independent clauses are joined by transitional expressions known as conjunctive adverbs. *(See the Glossary of Grammatical Terms.)* When a conjunctive adverb is used to link two independent clauses, it *always* requires a semicolon. By contrast, when a coordinating conjunction links the two clauses of a compound sentence, it is *always* preceded by a comma.

In most cases, depending on the sense of the sentence, the semicolon precedes the conjunctive adverb and clarifies the division between the two clauses. There are exceptions to this general rule, though, as in the following sentence:

> The lazy boy did finally read a *book, however;* it was the least he could do.

Here, "however" is a part of the first independent clause and qualifies its claim. The sentence thus suggests the boy was not totally lazy because he did get around to reading a book. Note how the meaning changes when "however" becomes the introductory word for the second independent clause.

> The lazy boy did finally read a *book; however,* it was the least he could do.

Here, the restricting force of "however" suggests that reading the book was not much of an accomplishment.

■ Test yourself 19.2: Comma Splices

What makes each of the following sentences a comma splice? Determine the best way to fix each one and why, and then make the correction.

1. "Virtual reality" is a new buzzword, so is "hyperspace."
2. Many popular cures for cancer have been discredited, nevertheless, many people continue to buy them.
3. Elvis Presley's home, Graceland, attracts many musicians as a kind of shrine, even Paul Simon has been there.
4. She didn't play well with others, she sat on the bench and watched.

BWE 3: ERRORS IN SUBJECT–VERB AGREEMENT

The subject and the verb must agree in number, a singular subject taking a singular verb and a plural subject taking a plural verb. Errors in subject–verb agreement usually occur when a writer misidentifies the subject or verb of a clause.

Agreement Problem: plural subject, singular verb

Various kinds of vandalism has been rapidly increasing.

Correction

Various kinds of vandalism *have* been rapidly increasing. *[verb made plural to match "kinds"]*

When you isolate the grammatical subject ("kinds") and the verb ("has") of the original sentence, you can tell that they do not agree. Although "vandalism" might seem to be the subject because it is closest to the verb, it is actually the object of the preposition "of." The majority of agreement problems arise from mistaking the object of a preposition for the actual subject of a sentence. If you habitually make this mistake, you can begin to remedy it by familiarizing yourself with the most common prepositions. (*See the Glossary of Grammatical Terms, which contains a list of these.*)

Agreement Problem: singular subject, plural verb

Another aspect of territoriality that differentiates humans from animals are their possession of ideas and objects.

Correction

Another aspect of territoriality that differentiates humans from animals *is* their possession of ideas and objects. *[verb made singular to match subject "aspect"]*

The subject of the sentence is "aspect." The two plural nouns ("humans" and "animals") probably encourage the mistake of using a plural verb ("are"), but "humans" is part of the "that" clause modifying "aspect," and "animals" is the object of the preposition "from."

Agreement Problem: "each" must take singular verb

The Republican and the Democrat both believe in doing what's best for America, but each believe that the other doesn't understand what's best.

Correction

The Republican and the Democrat both believe in doing what's best for America, but each *believes* that the other doesn't understand what's best. *[verb made singular to agree with subject "each"]*

The word "each" is *always* singular, so the verb ("believes") must be singular as well. The presence of a plural subject and verb in the sentence's first independent clause ("the Republican and the Democrat both believe") has probably encouraged the error.

■ Test yourself 19.3: Subject-Verb Agreement

Diagnose and correct the error in the following example.

> The controversies surrounding the placement of Arthur Ashe's
> statue in Richmond was difficult for the various factions to resolve.

A Note on Dialects and Standard Written English

Some people have trouble recognizing and fixing certain errors because they are not errors in their discourse communities. Different cultures inside the larger culture of English-language speakers use different syntactical forms. This fact has given rise to the phrase "Standard Written English," which names one particular version of English as the norm. People whose language practices constitute a dialect, for example, are told they have to acquire the other dialect—Standard Written English.

The concept of Standard Written English has been controversial. Critics argue that the concept enforces the language practices of privileged groups and discriminates against the practices of less powerful groups in the culture. The best-known instance of this discrimination appears in the matter of subject-verb agreement among some African-Americans who leave off the verb ending -s in the third person singular present tense.

Standard Written English: He walks to town. (singular)

They walk to town. (plural)

Dialect: He walk to town. (singular)

They walk to town. (plural)

Speakers of the dialect do not differentiate singular from plural verb forms with a terminal "–s" in the present tense (only), as in standard written English.

If you look up the term "Ebonics" you can study the debate about whether or not this particular "error" is descended from syntactical patterns in African languages. Like all ethical debates, this one is not easily resolved. In practical terms, however, you should be aware that these two ways of handling subject–verb agreement are recognized by linguists not in terms of right versus wrong but rather in terms of dialect difference.

A *dialect* is a variety of a language characteristic of a region or culture and is sometimes unintelligible to outsiders. The problem for speakers of a dialect that differs from the norm is that they can't always rely on the ear—on what sounds right—when they are editing according to the rules of standard written English. Such speakers need, in effect, to learn to speak more than one dialect so that they can edit according to the rules of standard written English in situations where this would be expected. This adaptation often requires adding a separate proofreading stage for particular errors, like subject–verb agreement, rather than relying on what sounds right.

BWE 4: SHIFTS IN SENTENCE STRUCTURE (FAULTY PREDICATION)

This error involves an illogical mismatch between subject and predicate. If you continually run afoul of faulty predication, you might use the exercises in a handbook to drill you on isolating the grammatical subjects and verbs of sentences because that is the first move you need to make in fixing the problem.

Faulty Predication

In 1887, the release of more information became available.

Correction

In 1887, more *information* became available *for release.* *[new subject]*

It was the "information," not the "release," that "became available." The correction relocates "information" from its position as object of the preposition "of" to the subject position in the sentence; it also moves "release" into a prepositional phrase.

Faulty Predication

The busing controversy was intended to rectify the inequality of educational opportunities.

Correction

Busing was intended to rectify the inequality of educational opportunities. *[new subject formulated to match verb]*

The *controversy* wasn't intended to rectify, but busing was.

■ **Test yourself 19.4:** Faulty Predication
Identify and correct the faulty predication in this example:

The subject of learning disabilities is difficult to identify accurately.

BWE 5: ERRORS IN PRONOUN REFERENCE

There are at least three forms of this problem. All of them involve a lack of clarity about whom or what a pronoun (a word that substitutes for a noun) refers to. The surest way to avoid difficulties is to make certain the pronoun relates back unambiguously to a specific word, known as the antecedent. In the sentence "Nowadays appliances don't last as long as they once did," the noun "appliances" is the antecedent of the pronoun "they."

Pronoun–Antecedent Agreement A pronoun must agree in number (and gender) with the noun or noun phrase that it refers to.

Pronoun Error: Plural Pronoun With Singular Antecedent It can be dangerous if a child, after watching TV, decides to practice what they saw.

Corrections

It can be dangerous if *children,* after watching TV, *decide* to practice what *they* saw. *[antecedent (and verb) made plural to agree with pronouns]*

It can be dangerous if a child, after watching TV, decides to practice what *he or she* saw. *[singular pronouns substituted to match singular antecedent "child"]*

The error occurs because "child" is singular, but its antecedent pronoun, "they," is plural. The first correction makes both singular; the second makes both plural. You might also observe in the first word of the example—the impersonal "it"—an exception to the rule that pronouns must have antecedents.

■ **Test yourself 19.5:** Pronoun-Antecedent Agreement
What is wrong with the following sentence, and how would you fix it?

> Every dog has its day, but all too often when that day happens, they can be found barking up the wrong tree.

Ambiguous Reference A pronoun should have only one possible antecedent. The possibility of two or more confuses relationships within the sentence.

Pronoun Error: more than one possible referent for "they"

Children like comedians because they have a sense of humor.

Corrections

Because children have a sense of humor, *they* like comedians. *[subordinate "because" clause placed first, and relationship between noun "children" and pronoun "they" tightened]*

Children like comedians because *comedians* have a sense of humor. *[pronoun eliminated and replaced by repetition of noun]*

Does "they" in the original example refer to "children" or "comedians"? The rule in such cases of ambiguity is that the pronoun refers to the nearest possible antecedent, so here "comedians" possess the sense of humor, regardless of what the writer may intend. As the corrections demonstrate, either reordering the sentence or repeating the noun can remove the ambiguity.

■ **Test yourself 19.6:** Ambiguous Reference
As you proofread, it's a good idea to target your pronouns to make sure they cannot conceivably refer to more than one noun. What's wrong with the following sentences?

1. Alexander the Great's father, Philip of Macedon, died when he was twenty-six.
2. The committee could not look into the problem because it was too involved.

Broad Reference

Broad reference occurs when a pronoun refers loosely to a number of ideas expressed in preceding clauses or sentences. It causes confusion because the reader cannot be sure which of the ideas the pronoun refers to.

Pronoun Error: use of "this" makes referent unclear

As a number of scholars have noted, Sigmund Freud and Karl Marx offered competing but also at times complementary critiques of the dehumanizing tendencies of Western capitalist society. We see this in Christopher Lasch's analysis of conspicuous consumption in *The Culture of Narcissism.*

Correction

As a number of scholars have noted, Sigmund Freud and Karl Marx offered competing but also at times complementary critiques of the dehumanizing tendencies of Western capitalist society. We see *this complementary view* in Christopher Lasch's analysis of conspicuous consumption in *The Culture of Narcissism. [broad "this" clarified by addition of noun phrase]*

The word "this" in the second sentence of the uncorrected example could refer to the fact that "a number of scholars have noted" the relationship between Freud and Marx, to the competition between Freud's and Marx's critiques of capitalism, or to the complementary nature of the two men's critiques.

Beware "this" as a pronoun: it's the most common source of broad reference. The remedy is generally to avoid using the word as a pronoun. Instead, convert "this" into an adjective, and let it modify some noun that more clearly specifies the referent: "this complementary view," as in the correction or, alternatively, "this competition" or "this scholarly perspective."

■ **Test yourself 19.7:** Broad Reference
Locate the errors in the following examples, and provide a remedy for each.

1. Regardless of whether the film is foreign or domestic, they can be found in your neighborhood video store.

2. Many experts now claim that dogs and other higher mammals dream; for those who don't own such pets, this is often difficult to believe.

A Note on Sexism and Pronoun Usage

Errors in pronoun reference sometimes occur because of a writer's praiseworthy desire to avoid sexism. In most circles, the following correction of the preceding example would be considered sexist.

It can be dangerous if a child, after watching TV, decides to practice what *he* saw.

Though the writer of such a sentence may intend "he" to function as a gender-neutral impersonal pronoun, it in fact excludes girls on the basis of gender. Implicitly, it also conveys sexual stereotypes (for example, that only boys are violent, or perhaps stupid, enough to confuse TV with reality).

The easiest way to avoid the problem of sexism in pronoun usage usually lies in putting things into the plural form because plural pronouns ("we," "you," "they") have no gender. (See the use of "children" in the first correction of the pronoun–antecedent agreement example.) Alternatively, you can use the phrase "he or she." Many readers, however, find this phrase and its variant, "s/he," to be awkward constructions. Another remedy lies in rewriting the sentence to avoid pronouns altogether, as in the following revision.

It can be dangerous if a child, after watching TV, decides to practice *some violent activity portrayed on the screen.*

BWE 6: MISPLACED MODIFIERS AND DANGLING PARTICIPLES

Modifiers are words or groups of words used to qualify, limit, intensify, or explain some other element in a sentence. A misplaced modifier is a word or phrase that appears to modify the wrong word or words.

Misplaced Modifier: modifier appears to modify wrong word

At the age of three he caught a fish with a broken arm.

Correction

At the age of three *the boy with a broken arm* caught a fish. *[noun replaces pronoun; prepositional phrase revised and relocated]*

The original sentence mistakenly implies that the fish had a broken arm. Modification errors often occur in sentences with one or more prepositional phrases, as in this case.

Misplaced Modifier: modifier appears to modify wrong word

According to legend, General George Washington crossed the Delaware and celebrated Christmas in a small boat.

Correction

According to legend, General George Washington crossed the Delaware *in a small boat* and *then* celebrated Christmas *on shore.* *[prepositional phrase relocated; modifiers added to second verb]*

As a general rule, you can avoid misplacing a modifier by keeping it as close as possible to what it modifies. Thus, the second correction removes the implication that Washington celebrated Christmas in a small boat. When you cannot relocate the modifier, separate it from the rest of the sentence with a comma to prevent readers from connecting it to the nearest noun.

A dangling participle creates a particular kind of problem in modification: the noun or pronoun that the writer intends the participial phrase to modify is not actually present in the sentence. Thus, we have the name dangling participle: the participle has been left dangling because the word or phrase it is meant to modify is not there.

Dangling Participle: subject that participle modifies does not appear in the sentence

After debating the issue of tax credits for the elderly, the bill passed in a close vote.

Correction

After debating the issue of tax credits for the elderly, *the Senate passed the* bill in a close vote. *[appropriate noun added for participle to modify]*

The bill did not debate the issue, as the original example implies. As the correction demonstrates, fixing a dangling participle involves tightening the link between the activity implied by the participle ("debating") and the entity performing that activity ("the Senate").

■ Test yourself 19.8: Modification Errors

Find the modification errors in the following examples and correct them.

1. After eating their sandwiches, the steamboat left the dock.
2. The social workers saw an elderly woman on a bus with a cane standing up.
3. Crossing the street, a car hit the pedestrian.

BWE 7: ERRORS IN USING POSSESSIVE APOSTROPHES

Adding *'s* to most singular nouns will make them show possession, for example, the plant*'s* roots, the accountant*'s* ledger. You can add the apostrophe alone, without the "s," for example, to make plural nouns that already end with "s" show possession: the flowers*'* fragrances or the ships*'* berths (although you may also add an additional "s").

Apostrophe Error

The loyal opposition scorned the committees decisions.

Corrections

The loyal opposition scorned the *committee's* decisions.
The loyal opposition scorned the *committees'* decisions. *[possessive apostrophe added]*

The first correction assumes there was one committee; the second assumes there were two or more.

Apostrophe Error

The advisory board swiftly transacted it's business.

Correction

The advisory board swiftly transacted *its* business. *[apostrophe dropped]*

Unlike possessive nouns, possessive pronouns ("my," "your," "yours," "her," "hers," "his," "its," "our," "ours," "their," "theirs") *never* take an apostrophe.

▪ **Test yourself 19.9:** Possessive Apostrophes
Find and correct any errors in the following sentence.
The womens movement has been misunderstood by many of its detractors.

BWE 8: COMMA ERRORS

As with other rules of punctuation and grammar, the many that pertain to comma usage share an underlying aim: to clarify the relationships among the parts of a sentence. Commas separate the parts of a sentence grammatically. One of their primary uses, then, is to help your readers distinguish the main clause from dependent elements such as subordinate clauses and long prepositional phrases. They do not signify a pause, as was discussed in BWE 2.

Comma Error: comma missing after introductory phrase

After eating the couple went home.

Correction

After *eating,* the couple went home. *[comma added before independent clause]*

The comma after "eating" is needed to keep the main clause "visible" or separate; it marks the point at which the prepositional phrase ends and the independent clause begins. Without this separation, readers would be invited to contemplate cannibalism as they move across the sentence.

Comma Error: comma missing after introductory phrase

In the absence of rhetoric study teachers and students lack a vocabulary for talking about their prose.

Correction

In the absence of rhetoric *study,* teachers and students lack a vocabulary for talking about their prose. *[comma added to separate prepositional phrase from main clause]*

Without the comma, readers would have to read the sentence twice to find out where the prepositional phrase ends—with "study"—to figure out where the main clause begins.

Comma Error: two commas needed around parenthetical element

Dog owners, despite their many objections will have to obey the new law.

Correction

Dog owners, despite their many *objections,* will have to obey the new law. *[single comma converted to a pair of commas]*

A comma is needed after "objections" to isolate the phrase in the middle of the sentence ("despite their many objections") from the main clause. The phrase needs to be set off with commas because it contains additional information not essential to the meaning of what it modifies. (Dog owners must obey the law whether they object or not.) Phrases and clauses that function in this way are called *nonrestrictive.*

A Note on Restrictive versus Nonrestrictive Elements

The test of nonrestrictive phrases and clauses is to see if they can be omitted without substantially changing the message that a sentence conveys ("Dog owners will have to obey the new law," for example). Nonrestrictive elements always take two commas— a comma "sandwich"—to set them off. Using only one comma illogically separates the sentence's subject ("dog owners") from its predicate ("will have to obey"). This problem is easier to see in a shorter sentence. You wouldn't, for example, write "I, fell down." As a rule, commas virtually never separate the subject from the verb of a sentence. (Here's an exception: "Ms. Smith, a high fashion model, watches her diet scrupulously.")

Comma Error: two commas needed around parenthetical element

Most people regardless of age like to spend money.

Correction

Most *people,* regardless of *age,* like to spend money. *[comma sandwich added]*

Here, commas enclose the nonrestrictive elements; you could omit this information without significantly affecting the sense. Such is not the case in the following two examples.

Comma Error: restrictive elements should not be enclosed within commas

People, who live in glass houses, should not throw stones.

Correction

People *who live in glass houses* should not throw stones. *[commas omitted]*

Comma Error: no comma setting off restrictive clause
Please return the library book, that I left on the table.

Correction

Please return the library *book that* I left on the table. *[comma omitted]*

It is incorrect to place commas around "who live in glass houses" or a comma before "that I left on the table." Each of these is a *restrictive clause,* that is, it contains information that is an essential part of what it modifies. In the first sentence, for example, if "who live in glass houses" is left out, the fundamental meaning of the sentence is lost: "People should not throw stones." The word "who" is defined by restricting it to "people" in the category of glass-house dwellers. Similarly, in the second example the "that" clause contributes an essential meaning to "book"; the sentence is referring to not just any book but to a particular one, the one "on the table."

So, remember the general rule: if the information in a phrase or clause can be omitted—if it is nonessential and therefore nonrestrictive—it needs to be separated by commas from the rest of the sentence. Moreover, note that nonrestrictive clauses are generally introduced by the word "which," so a "which" clause interpolated into a sentence takes a comma sandwich. ("The dinner, which I bought for $20, made me sick.") By contrast, a restrictive clause is introduced by the word "that" and takes no commas.

■ **Test yourself 19.10:** Comma Errors
Consider the following examples as a pair. Punctuate them as necessary, and then briefly articulate how the meanings of the two sentences differ.

1. The book which I had read a few years ago contained a lot of outdated data.
2. The book that I had read a few years ago contained a lot of outdated data.

BWE 9: SPELLING/DICTION ERRORS THAT INTERFERE WITH MEANING

Misspellings are always a problem in a final draft, insofar as they undermine your authority by inviting readers to perceive you as careless (at best). If you make a habit of using the spellchecker of a word processor, you will take care of most misspellings; however, the problems a spellchecker won't catch are the ones that can often hurt you most. These are actually diction errors—incorrect word choices in which you have confused one word with another that it closely resembles. In such cases, you have spelled the word correctly, but it's the wrong word. Because it means something other than what you've intended, you end up misleading your readers. *(See "Right" and "Wrong" Words: Shades of Meaning in Chapter 17.)*

The best way to avoid this problem is to memorize the differences between pairs of words commonly confused with each other but that have distinct meanings. The following examples illustrate a few of the most common and serious of these errors. Most handbooks contain a glossary of usage that *cites* more of these *sites* of confusion.

Spelling/Diction Error: "It's" versus "Its"

Although you can't tell a book by its' cover, its fairly easy to get the general idea from the introduction.

Correction

Although you can't tell a book by *its* cover, *it's* fairly easy to get the general idea from the introduction. *[apostrophe dropped from possessive and added to contraction]*

"It's" is a contraction for "it is." "Its" is a possessive pronoun meaning "belonging to it." If you confuse the two, *it's* likely that your sentence will mislead *its* readers.

Spelling/Diction Error: "Their" versus "There" versus "They're"

Their are ways of learning about the cuisine of northern India besides going their to watch the master chefs and learn there secrets—assuming their willing to share them.

Correction

There are ways of learning about the cuisine of northern India besides going *there* to watch the master chefs and learn *their* secrets—assuming *they're* willing to share them. *[expletive "there," adverb "there," possessive pronoun "their," and contraction "they're" inserted appropriately]*

"There" as an adverb normally refers to a place; "there" can also be used as an expletive to introduce a clause, as in the first usage of the correction. *(See Beginning With "It Is" or "There Is": Advantages and Disadvantages in Chapter 18.)* "Their" is a possessive pronoun meaning "belonging to them." "They're" is a contraction for "they are."

Spelling/Diction Error: "Then" versus "Than"

If a person would rather break a law then obey it, than he or she must be willing to face the consequences.

Correction

If a person would rather break a law *than* obey it, *then* he or she must be willing to face the consequences. *[comparative "than" distinguished from temporal "then"]*

"Than" is a conjunction used with a comparison, for example, "rather X than Y." "Then" is an adverb used to indicate what comes next in relation to time, for example, "first X, then Y."

Spelling/Diction Error: "Effect" versus "Affect"

It is simply the case that BWEs adversely effect the way that readers judge what a writer has to say. It follows that writers who include lots of BWEs in their prose may not have calculated the disastrous affects of these mistakes.

Correction

It is simply the case that BWEs adversely *affect* the way that readers judge what a writer has to say. It follows that writers who include lots of BWEs in their prose may not have calculated the disastrous *effects* of these mistakes. *[verb "affect" and noun "effects" inserted appropriately]*

In their most common usages, "affect" is a verb meaning "to influence," and "effect" is a noun meaning "the result of an action or cause." The confusion of "affect" and "effect" is enlarged by the fact that both of these words have secondary meanings: the verb "to effect" means "to cause or bring about"; the noun "affect" is used in psychology to mean "emotion or feeling." Thus, if you confuse these two words, you will inadvertently make a meaning radically different from the one you intend.

■ **Test yourself 19.11:** Spelling/Diction Errors
Make corrections as necessary in the following paragraph.

> Its not sufficiently acknowledged that the behavior of public officials is not just an ethical issue but one that effects the sale of newspapers and commercial bytes in television news. When public officials don't do what their supposed to do, than their sure to face the affects of public opinion—if they get caught—because there are dollars to be made. Its that simple: money more then morality is calling the tune in the way that the press treats it's superstars.

GLOSSARY OF GRAMMATICAL TERMS

adjective An adjective is a part of speech that usually modifies a noun or pronoun—for example, *blue, boring, boisterous.*

adverb An adverb is a part of speech that modifies an adjective, adverb, or verb—for example, *heavily, habitually, very.* The adverbial form generally differs from the adjectival form via the addition of the ending "–ly"; for example, *happy* is an adjective, and *happily* is an adverb.

clause (independent and dependent) A clause is any group of words that contains both a **subject** and a **predicate**. An **independent clause** (also known as a **main clause**) can stand alone as a sentence. For example,

> The most famous revolutionaries of this century have all, in one way or another, offered a vision of a classless society.

The subject of this independent clause is "revolutionaries," the verb is "have offered," and the direct object is "vision." By contrast, a **dependent** (or **subordinate**) **clause** is any group of words containing a subject and verb that cannot stand alone as a separate sentence because it depends on an independent clause to complete its meaning. The following sentence adds two dependent clauses to our previous example:

> The most famous revolutionaries of this century have all, in one way or another, offered a vision of a classless society, *although* most historians would agree *that* this ideal has never been achieved.

The origin of the word "depend" is "to hang": a dependent clause literally hangs on the independent clause. In the preceding example, neither "although most historians would agree" nor "that this ideal has never been achieved" can stand independently. The "that" clause relies on the "although" clause, which in turn relies on the main clause. "That" and "although" function as **subordinating conjunctions**; by eliminating them, we could rewrite the sentence to contain three independent clauses:

> The most famous revolutionaries of this century have all, in one way or another, offered a vision of a classless society. Most historians would agree on one judgment about this vision: it has never been achieved.

comma splice   A comma splice consists of two independent clauses incorrectly connected (spliced) with a comma. See BWE 2.

conjunction (coordinating and subordinating)   A conjunction is a part of speech that connects words, phrases, or clauses, for example, *and*, *but*, *although*. The conjunction in some way defines that connection: for example, *and* links; *but* separates. All conjunctions define connections in one of two basic ways. Coordinating conjunctions connect words or groups of words that have equal grammatical importance. The coordinating conjunctions are *and*, *but*, *or*, *nor*, *for*, *so*, and *yet*. Subordinating conjunctions introduce a dependent clause and connect it to a main clause. Here is a partial list of the most common subordinating conjunctions: *after*, *although*, *as*, *as if*, *as long as*, *because*, *before*, *if*, *rather than*, *since*, *than*, *that*, *though*, *unless*, *until*, *when*, *where*, *whether*, and *while*.

conjunctive adverb   A conjunctive adverb is a word that links two independent clauses (as a conjunction) but that also modifies the clause it introduces (as an adverb). Some of the most common conjunctive adverbs are *consequently*, *furthermore*, *however*, *moreover*, *nevertheless*, *similarly*, *therefore*, and *thus*. Phrases can also serve this function, such as *for example* and *on the other hand*. When conjunctive adverbs are used to link two independent clauses, they always require a semicolon:

> Many pharmaceutical chains now offer their own generic versions of common drugs; however, many consumers continue to spend more for name brands that contain the same active ingredients as the generics.

When conjunctive adverbs occur within an independent clause, however, they are enclosed in a pair of commas, as is the case with the use of *however* earlier in this sentence.

coordination Coordination refers to grammatically equal words, phrases, or clauses. Coordinate constructions are used to give elements in a sentence equal weight or importance. In the sentence "The tall, thin lawyer badgered the witness, but the judge interceded," the clauses "The tall, thin lawyer badgered the witness" and "but the judge interceded" are coordinate clauses; "tall" and "thin" are coordinate adjectives.

dependent clause (see clause)

direct object The direct object is a noun or pronoun that receives the action carried by the verb and performed by the subject. In the sentence, "Certain mushrooms can kill you," "you" is the direct object.

gerund (see verbals)

fused (or run-on) sentence A fused sentence incorrectly combines two independent clauses with no conjunction or punctuation. See BWE 2.

independent clause (see clause)

infinitive (see verbals)

main clause (see clause)

noun A noun is a part of speech that names a person (*woman*), place (*town*), thing (*book*), idea (*justice*), quality (*irony*), or action (*betrayal*).

object of the preposition (see preposition)

participle and participial phrase (see verbals)

phrase A phrase is a group of words occurring in a meaningful sequence that lacks either a subject or a predicate. This absence distinguishes it from a clause, which contains both a subject and a predicate. Phrases function in sentences as adjectives, adverbs, nouns, or verbs. They are customarily classified according to the part of speech of their keyword: "over the mountain" is a **prepositional phrase**; "running for office" is a **participial phrase**; "had been disciplined" is a **verb phrase**; "desktop graphics" is a **noun phrase**; and so forth.

predicate The predicate contains the verb of a sentence or clause, making some kind of statement about the subject. The predicate of the preceding sentence is "contains the verb, making some kind of statement about the subject." The simple predicate—the verb to which the other words in the sentence are attached—is "contains."

preposition, prepositional phrase A preposition is a part of speech that links a noun or pronoun to some other word in the sentence. Prepositions usually express a relationship of time (*after*) or space (*above*) or direction (*toward*). The noun to which the preposition is attached is known as the object of the preposition. A preposition, its object, and any modifiers comprise a prepositional phrase. "*With love from me to you*" strings together three prepositional phrases. Here is a partial list of the most common prepositions: *about, above, across, after, among, at, before, behind, between, by, during, for, from, in, into, like, of, on, out, over, since, through, to, toward, under, until, up, upon, with, within*, and *without*.

pronoun A pronoun is a part of speech that substitutes for a noun, such as *I, you, he, she, it, we*, and *they*.

run-on (or fused) sentence   A run-on sentence incorrectly combines two independent clauses with no conjunction or punctuation. See BWE 2.

sentence   A sentence is a unit of expression that can stand independently. It contains two parts, a **subject** and a **predicate**. The shortest sentence in the Bible, for example, is "Jesus wept." "Jesus" is the subject; "wept" is the predicate.

sentence fragment   A sentence fragment is a group of words incorrectly punctuated like a complete sentence but lacking the necessary structure; it is only a part of a sentence. "Walking down the road" and "the origin of the problem" are both fragments because neither contains a **predicate**. See BWE 1.

subject   The subject, in most cases a noun or pronoun, names the doer of the action in a sentence or identifies what the predicate is about. The subject of the previous sentence, for example, is "the subject, in most cases a noun or pronoun." The simple subject of that sentence—the noun to which the other words in the sentence are attached—is "subject."

subordination, subordinating conjunctions   "Subordination" refers to the placement of certain grammatical units, particularly phrases and clauses, at a lower, less important structural level than other elements. As with coordination, the grammatical ranking carries conceptual significance as well: whatever is grammatically subordinated appears less important than the information carried in the main clause. In the following example, Microsoft is subordinated both grammatically and conceptually to Apple:

> Although Microsoft continues to upgrade the operating system and special features on its computers, the more stylish and virus-free Apple MacIntosh computers continue to outclass them.

Here, "although" is a **subordinating conjunction** that introduces a subordinate clause, also known as a **dependent clause**.

verb   A verb is a part of speech that describes an action (*goes*), states how something was affected by an action (*became angered*), or expresses a state of being (*is*).

verbals (participles, gerunds, and infinitives)   Verbals are words derived from verbs. They are verb forms that look like verbs but, as determined by the structure of the sentence they appear in, they function as nouns, adjectives, or adverbs. There are three forms of verbals.

An **infinitive**—composed of the root form of a verb plus *to* (*to be*, *to vote*)—becomes a verbal when it is used as a noun ("*To eat* is essential"), an adjective ("These are the books *to read*"), or an adverb ("He was too sick *to walk*").

Similarly, a **participle**—usually composed of the root form of a verb plus "–ing" (present participle) or "–ed" (past participle)—becomes a verbal when used as an adjective. It can occur as a single word, modifying a noun, as in *faltering negotiations* or *finished business*. But it also can occur in a participial phrase, consisting of the participle, its object, and any modifiers. Here are two examples:

> *Having been tried and convicted,* the criminal was sentenced to life imprisonment.

> *Following the path of most resistance,* the masochist took deep pleasure in his frustration.

"Having been tried and convicted" is a participial phrase that modifies "criminal"; "Following the path of most resistance" is a participial phrase that modifies "masochist." In each case, the participial phrase functions as an adjective.

The third form of verbal, the **gerund**, resembles the participle. Like the participle, it is formed by adding "–ing" to the root form of the verb, but unlike the participle, it is used as a noun. In the sentence "Swimming is extraordinarily aerobic," the gerund "swimming" functions as the subject. Again like participles, gerunds can occur in phrases. The gerund phrases are italicized in the following example: "*Watching a film adaptation* takes less effort than *reading the book* from which it was made."

When using a verbal, remember that although it resembles a verb, it cannot function alone as the verb in a sentence: "Being a military genius" is a fragment, not a sentence.

Assignments for Working With Basic Writing Errors

1. **Chart the BWEs.** Write an example for each of the BWEs, along with a corrected version.

2. **Compose a Grammar and Style Quiz.** Write a paragraph that contains all of the basic writing errors. Not every sentence should contain an error, and you may contain multiple examples of the errors, but make sure you include all nine. Then, append an answer key in which you identify the errors and provide corrections.

3. **Research Online Resources.** Go online to different universities and colleges in search of their writing centers, and then look for the ways these websites handle the problem of grammatical correctness. See as an example OWL at Purdue University. Write a brief summary of what you find there.

4. **Circle Every Punctuation Mark.** Take a short piece of writing, your own or someone else's, published or unpublished. Circle every punctuation mark and explain why it is there. This is a useful exercise to do in pairs or in small groups. As a follow-up exercise, you might underline every independent clause and double-underline every dependent clause, circling the subordinating conjunctions.

CHAPTER 19 APPENDIX

Basic Writing Errors (BWEs) Test Yourself Section Answer Key (With Discussion)

Test Yourself 19.1: Fragments (Page 426)

1. Original example:
Like many other anthropologists, Margaret Mead studied non-Western cultures in such works as *Coming of Age in Samoa.* And influenced theories of childhood development in America.

   Problem: The second sentence is actually a fragment, a predicate in need of a subject.

   Possible correction:
Like many other anthropologists, Margaret Mead studied non-Westerncultures (in such works as *Coming of Age in Samoa*) in ways that influenced theories of childhood development in America.

   Comment: There are many ways to fix this example, but its original form leaves ambiguous whether the fragment refers only to *Mead,* or to *many other anthropologists* as well. The correction offered includes the other anthropologists in the referent and diminishes the emphasis on Mead's book by placing it within parentheses. Although the correction uses a subordinating *that* to incorporate the fragment into the first sentence, it keeps this information in an emphatic position at the end of the sentence.

2. Original example:
The catastrophe resulted from an engineering flaw. Because the bridge lacked sufficient support.

   Problem: The second sentence is actually a dependent clause; *because* always subordinates.

   Possible correction:
The catastrophe resulted from an engineering flaw: the bridge lacked sufficient support.

   Comment: Because the colon has causal force, this is an ideal spot to use one, identifying the "flaw."

3. Original example:
In the 1840s the potato famine decimated Ireland. It being a country with poor soil and antiquated methods of agriculture.

   Problem: The second sentence is actually a fragment, a subject plus a long participial phrase.

   Possible correction:
In the 1840s the potato famine decimated Ireland, a country with poor and antiquated methods of agriculture.

Comment: The cause of this kind of fragment is usually that the writer mistakenly believes that *being* is a verb rather than a participle that introduces a long phrase (modifying "Ireland" in this case). It would also be correct simply to change the period to a comma in the original sentence.

Test Yourself 19.2: Comma Splices (Page 429)

1. Original example: "Virtual reality" is a new buzzword, so is "hyperspace."

   Problem: This is a comma splice—both clauses are independent, yet they are joined with a comma.

   Possible correction: "Virtual reality" is a new buzzword; so is "hyperspace."

   Comment: Because the clauses are linked by association—both naming buzzwords—a semicolon would show that association. A writer could also condense the clauses into a simple sentence with a compound subject, for example, "Both 'virtual reality' and 'hyperspace' are new buzzwords."

2. Original example: Many popular cures for cancer have been discredited, nevertheless, many people continue to buy them.

   Problem: A comma splice results from the incorrectly punctuated conjunctive adverb *nevertheless*.

   Possible correction: Many popular cures for cancer have been discredited; nevertheless, many people continue to buy them.

   Comment: Without the semicolon to separate the independent clauses, the conjunctive adverb could conceivably modify either the preceding or the following clause. This problem is usually worse with *however*.

3. Original example: Elvis Presley's home, Graceland, attracts many musicians as a kind of shrine, even Paul Simon has been there.

   Problem: This is a comma splice—the two independent clauses are linked by a comma without a conjunction. The problem is exacerbated by the number of commas in the sentence; the reader cannot easily tell which one is used to separate the clauses.

   Possible correction: Elvis Presley's home, Graceland, attracts many musicians as a kind of shrine—even Paul Simon has been there.

   Comment: Although one could justly use a semicolon here, the dash conveys the impromptu effect of an afterthought.

4. Original   She didn't play well with others, she sat on the bench and watched.
    example:

Problem: Because the second clause develops the first one, a writer might think that it is dependent on the first; conceptually, yes, but grammatically, no.

Possible   She didn't play well with others; she sat on the bench and watched.
correction:

Comment: If the writer wanted to link the two clauses more tightly, a colon would be appropriate instead of the semicolon.

Test Yourself 19.3: Subject–Verb Agreement (Page 430)

Original   The controversies surrounding the placement of Arthur Ashe's
example: statue in Richmond was difficult for the various factions to resolve.

Problem: The grammatical subject of the main clause (controversies) is plural; the verb (was) is singular.

Possible   The controversies surrounding the placement of Arthur Ashe's
corrections: statue in Richmond were difficult for the various factions to
               resolve (or, The controversy . . . was).

Comment: An error of this kind is encouraged by two factors: the distance of the verb from the subject and the presence of intervening prepositional phrases that use singular objects, either of which a writer might mistake for the grammatical subject of the main clause.

Test Yourself 19.4: Faulty Predication (Page 432)

Original   The subject of learning disabilities is difficult to identify accurately.
example:

Problem: The predicate matches the object of the preposition (learning disabilities) rather than the subject of the main clause (subject).

Possible   Learning disabilities are difficult to identify accurately.
corrections:

Comment: Omitting the abstract opening (The subject of) enables the predicate (are) to fit the new grammatical subject (disabilities).

Test Yourself 19.5: Pronoun–Antecedent Agreement (Page 433)

Original   Every dog has its day, but all too often when that day happens,
example: they can be found barking up the wrong tree.

Problem: The plural pronoun *they* that is the grammatical subject of the second clause does not have a plural antecedent in the sentence.

Possible correction: Every dog has its day, but all too often when that day happens, the dog can be found barking up the wrong tree.

Comment: If a writer vigilantly checks all pronouns, he or she will identify the intended antecedent of the pronoun *they* to be the singular *dog*, and revise accordingly. The sentence would still be incorrect if the pronoun *it* were used instead of the repeated *dog* because *it* could refer to the nearest preceding noun, *day*.

Test Yourself 19.6: Ambiguous Reference (Page 433)

1. Original example: Alexander the Great's father, Philip of Macedon, died when he was twenty-six.

Problem: A reader can't be sure whether *he* refers to Alexander or to Philip.

Possible correction: Alexander the Great's father, Philip of Macedon, died at the age of twenty-six.

Comment: The correction rewords to remove the ambiguous pronoun. This solution is less awkward than repeating *Philip* in place of *he*, though that would also be correct.

2. Original example: The committee could not look into the problem because it was too involved.

Problem: A reader can't be sure whether *it* refers to *the committee* or to *the problem*.

Possible correction: The committee was too involved with other matters to look into the problem.

Comment: As with the previous example, rewording to eliminate the ambiguous pronoun is usually the best solution.

Test Yourself 19.7: Broad Reference (Page 434)

1. Original example: Regardless of whether the film is foreign or domestic, they can be found in your neighborhood video store.

Problem: The plural pronoun *they* does not have a plural antecedent in the sentence.

Possible correction: Regardless of whether the film is foreign or domestic, it can be found in your neighborhood video store.

Comment: Although the sentence offers two options for films, the word *film* is singular and so, as antecedent, requires a singular pronoun (it). It is probably worth noting here that *it* would still be correct even if the original sentence began, "Regardless of whether the film is a foreign film or a domestic film." The rule for compound subjects that use an either/or construction is as follows: the number (singular or plural) of the noun or pronoun that follows *or* determines the number of the verb. Compare the following two examples: "Either several of his aides *or* the *candidate is* going to speak" and "Either the candidate *or* several of his *aides are* going to speak."

2. Original example: Many experts now claim that dogs and other higher mammals dream; for those who don't own such pets, this is often difficult to believe.

Problem: The referent of the pronoun *this* is unclear. Precisely what is difficult to believe—that mammals dream or that experts would make such a claim?

Possible correction: Many experts now claim that dogs and other higher mammals dream; for those who don't own such pets, this claim is often difficult to believe.

Comment: Often the best way to fix a problem with broad reference produced by use of *this* as a pronoun is to attach *this* to the noun to which it refers, as in "this book. As a rule, when you find an isolated *this* in your draft, ask and answer the question "This what?"

Test Yourself 19.8: Modification Errors (Page 436)

1. Original example: After eating their sandwiches, the steamboat left the dock.

Problem: This is a dangling participle—the grammar of the sentence conveys that the steamboat ate their sandwiches.

corrections: After the girls ate their sandwiches, the steamboat left the dock. Or, After eating their sandwiches, the girls boarded the steamboat, and it left the dock.

Comment: The two corrections model the two ways of remedying most dangling participles. Both provide an antecedent (the girls) for the pronoun *their*. The first correction eliminates the participial phrase and substitutes a subordinate clause. The second correction adds to the existing main clause (steamboat left) another one (girls boarded) for the participial phrase to modify appropriately.

2. Original example: The social workers saw an elderly woman on a bus with a cane standing up.

Problem: Misplaced modifiers create the problems in this sentence, which implies that the bus possessed a cane that was standing up. The problem exemplified here is produced by the series of prepositional phrases—"*on* a bus *with* a cane"—followed by the participial phrase *standing up,* which is used as an adjective and intended to modify *woman.*

Possible correction: The social workers saw an elderly woman on a bus. She was standing up with the help of a cane.

Comment: Writers often try to cram too much into sentences, piling on the prepositions. The best remedy is sometimes to break up the sentence, a move that usually involves eliminating prepositions, which possess a sludgy kind of movement, and adding verbs, which possess more distinct movement.

3. Original   Crossing the street, a car hit the pedestrian.
    example:

Problem: The dangling participle (Crossing the street) does not have a word to modify in the sentence. The sentence conveys that the car crossed the street.

Possible   Crossing the street, the pedestrian was hit by a car. Or: As the
corrections: pedestrian crossed the street, a car hit him.

Comment: The first solution brings the participial phrase closest to the noun it modifies (pedestrian). The second converts the participial into the verb (crossed) of a dependent *as* clause and moves *pedestrian* into the clause as the subject for that verb. As in the *steamboat* example, one correction provides an appropriate noun for the participial phrase to modify, and the other eliminates the participle.

Test Yourself 19.9: Possessive Apostrophes (Page 437)

Original   The womens movement has been misunderstood by many of its
example: detractors.

Problem: The possessive apostrophe for *womens* is missing. The trickiness here in inserting the apostrophe is that this word is already plural.

Possible   The women's movement has been misunderstood by many of its
correction: detractors.

Comment: Because the word is already plural, it takes a simple "–'s" to indicate a movement belonging to women—not "–s'" (womens').

Test Yourself 19.10: Comma Errors (Page 439)

Original   The book which I had read a few years ago contained a lot of
paired   outdated data.
examples: The book that I had read a few years ago contained a lot of out-
             dated data.

Problem: In the first example, the modifying clause "which I had read a few years ago" is nonrestrictive: it could be omitted without changing the essential meaning of the sentence. Therefore, it needs to be enclosed in commas—as the *which* signals.

Possible correction:	The book, which I had read a few years ago, contained a lot of outdated data.

Comment: The second example in the pair is correct as it stands. The restrictive clause, "that I had read a few years ago," does not take commas around it because the information it gives readers is an essential part of the meaning of *book*. That is, it refers to not just any book read a few years ago, as in the first example in the pair, but rather specifies the one containing outdated data. "The book that I had read a few years ago" thus functions as what is known as a *noun phrase*.

Test Yourself 19.11: Spelling/Diction Errors (Page 441)

Original example:	Its not sufficiently acknowledged that the behavior of public officials is not just an ethical issue but one that effects the sale of newspapers and commercial bytes in television news. When public officials don't do what their supposed to do, than their sure to face the affects of public opinion—if they get caught—because there are dollars to be made. Its that simple: money more then morality is calling the tune in the way that the press treats it's superstars.

Problems: The paragraph confuses the paired terms discussed under BWE 9. It mistakes

its for *it's* before *not sufficiently.*

effects for *affects* before *the sale.*

their for *they're* before *supposed.*

than for *then* before *their sure.*

they're for *their* before *sure.*

affects for *effects* before *of public opinion.*

its for *it's* before *that simple.*

then for *than* before *morality.*

it's for *its* before *superstars.*

Possible correction:	It's not sufficiently acknowledged that the behavior of public officials is not just an ethical issue but one that affects the sale of newspapers and commercial bytes in television news. When public officials don't do what they're supposed to do, then they're sure to face the effects of public opinion—if they get caught—because there are dollars to be made. It's that simple: money more than morality is calling the tune in the way that the press treats its superstars.

Comment: If you confuse similar words, the only solution is to memorize the differences and consciously check your drafts for any problems until habit takes hold.

Part 2

THE READINGS

Chapter 20

Manners, Communication, and Technology

One of our preliminary titles for this chapter was "How We Live Now." All of the readings in this chapter focus on the relationships between the public and the private, with particular focus on how those relationships are affected by the technologies of the information age—technologies that have brought us closer together in some ways, and further estranged us from each other in other ways.

The writers in this chapter come from disparate backgrounds, but they share a conviction that manners are anything but trivial—not simply a sign of your upbringing, the product of a parent's scolding about which fork to use or how to answer the phone. Rather, manners have to do with the fundamental ways that people in the public sphere interact with one another; they have to do with the boundaries of civility. And so to understand manners is to understand how we live as social beings.

ABOUT THE READINGS IN THIS UNIT

The readings in this unit explore the links among manners, communication, and technology. Christine Rosen starts things off with a historical piece (and position paper) on the cultural impact of the cell phone: "They encourage talk, not conversation." This focus leads her to voice the need for us to reclaim what she calls "social space." Paul Goldberger adopts a complementary view in his short piece on the tendency of cell phones to transport us "out of real space into a virtual realm."

Next, Jeffrey Rosen broadens the focus to consider how individuals today "brand" themselves as part of what he calls "America's culture of self-revelation." The proliferation of weblogs, for example, he interprets as a sign of how the Internet complicates "our ability to negotiate the boundary between public and private." Geoffrey Nunberg does a variation on this theme in his short radio piece on the style of weblogs and the audiences they target and exclude.

The chapter then turns toward the personal essay in the novelist Jonathan Franzen's witty discussion of the mismatch between the outcry against the loss of privacy and the fact that we are "drowning" in it. He demonstrates how the concern with our private lives and those of public figures threatens to overwhelm the public sphere.

At the end of the chapter, we encounter Sam Anderson's rambunctious discussion of multitasking, ADHD, lifehacking, and the perpetual battle between focusing and pursuing the pleasures of (mostly electronic) distraction.

Christine Rosen

Our Cell Phones, Our Selves

A historian by training, Rosen is a senior editor of *The New Atlantis: A Journal of Technology and Society* where this piece first appeared in 2004. Rosen here offers a brief history of the cell phone and begins to chart the implications of its conquest of contemporary culture.

"Hell is other people," Sartre observed, but you need not be a misanthrope or a diminutive French existentialist to have experienced similar feelings during the course of a day. No matter where you live or what you do, in all likelihood you will eventually find yourself participating in that most familiar and exasperating of modern rituals: unwillingly listening to someone else's cell phone conversation. Like the switchboard operators of times past, we are now all privy to calls being put through, to the details of loved ones contacted, appointments made, arguments aired, and gossip exchanged.

Today, more people have cell phones than fixed telephone lines, both in the United States and internationally. There are more than one billion cell phone users worldwide, and as one wireless industry analyst recently told *Slate,* "some time between 2010 and 2020, everyone who wants and can afford a cell phone will have one." Americans spend, on average, about seven hours a month talking on their cell phones. Wireless phones have become such an important part of our everyday lives that in July, the country's major wireless industry organization featured the following "quick poll" on its website: "If you were stranded on a desert island and could have one thing with you, what would it be?" The choices: "Matches/Lighter," "Food/Water," "Another Person," "Wireless Phone." The World Health Organization has even launched an "International EMF Project" to study the possible health effects of the electromagnetic fields created by wireless technologies.

But if this ubiquitous technology is now a normal part of life, our adjustment to it has not been without consequences. Especially in the United States, where cell phone use still remains low compared to other countries, we are rapidly approaching a tipping point with this technology. How has it changed our behavior, and how might it continue to do so? What new rules ought we to impose on its use? Most importantly, how has the wireless telephone encouraged us to connect individually but disconnect socially, ceding, in the process, much that was civil and civilized about the use of public space?

Untethered

Connection has long served as a potent sign of power. In the era before cell phones, popular culture served up presidents, tin-pot dictators, and crime bosses who were never far from a prominently placed row of phones, demonstrating their importance at the hub of a vast nexus. Similarly, superheroes always owned special communications devices: Batman had the Batphone, Dick Tracy his wrist-phone, Maxwell Smart his shoe spy phone. (In the Flash comics of the 1940s, the hero simply outraces

Christine Rosen, "Our Cell Phones, Our Selves", The New Atlantis: A Journal of Technology and Society. Copyright © 2001. Reprinted by permission.

phone calls as they are made, avoiding altogether the need for special communication devices.) To be able to talk to anyone, at any time, without the mediator of the human messenger and without the messenger's attendant delays, is a thoroughly modern triumph of human engineering.

5   In 1983, Motorola introduced DynaTAC, now considered the first truly mobile telephone, and by the end of that year, the first commercial cellular phone systems were being used in Chicago and in the Baltimore/Washington, D.C. area. Nokia launched its own mobile phone, the cumbersome Cityman, in 1987. Americans were introduced to the glamour of mobile telephone communication that same year in a scene from the movie *Wall Street.* In it, the ruthless Gordon Gekko (played by Michael Douglas) self-importantly conducts his business on the beach using a large portable phone. These first-generation cell phones were hardly elegant—many people called them "luggables" rather than "portables," and as one reporter noted in *The Guardian,* "mobiles of that era are often compared to bricks, but this is unfair. Bricks are quite attractive and relatively light." But they made up in symbolic importance what they lacked in style; only the most powerful and wealthiest people owned them. Indeed, in the 1980s, the only other people besides the elite and medical professionals who had mobile technologies at all (such as pagers) were presumed to be using them for nefarious reasons. Who else but a roving drug dealer or prostitute would need to be accessible at all times?

This changed in the 1990s, when cell phones became cheaper, smaller, and more readily available. The technology spread rapidly, as did the various names given to it: in Japan it is *keitai,* in China it's *sho ji,* Germans call their cell phones *handy,* in France it is *le portable* or *le G,* and in Arabic, *el mobile, telephone makhmul,* or *telephone gowal.* In countries where cell phone use is still limited to the elite—such as Bulgaria, where only 2.5 percent of the population can afford a cell phone—its power as a symbol of wealth and prestige remains high. But in the rest of the world, it has become a technology for the masses. There were approximately 340,000 wireless subscribers in the United States in 1985, according to the Cellular Telecommunications and Internet Associate (CTIA); by 1995, that number had increased to more than 33 million, and by 2003, more than 158 million people in the country had gone wireless.

Why do people use cell phones? The most frequently cited reason is convenience, which can cover a rather wide range of behaviors. Writing in the *Wall Street Journal* this spring, an executive for a wireless company noted that "in Slovakia, people are using mobile phones to remotely switch on the heat before they return home," and in Norway, "1.5 million people can confirm their tax returns" using cell phone short text messaging services. Paramedics use camera phones to send ahead to hospitals pictures of the incoming injuries; "in Britain, it is now commonplace for wireless technology to allow companies to remotely access meters or gather diagnostic information." Construction workers on-site can use cell phones to send pictures to contractors off-site. Combined with the individual use of cell phones—to make appointments, locate a friend, check voicemail messages, or simply to check in at work—cell phones offer people a heretofore unknown level of convenience.

More than ninety percent of cell phone users also report that owning a cell phone makes them feel safer. The CTIA noted that in 2001, nearly 156,000 wireless emergency service calls were made every day—about 108 calls per minute. Technological Good Samaritans place calls to emergency personnel when they see traffic accidents or crimes-in-progress; individuals use their cell phones to call for assistance when a car breaks down or plans go awry. The safety rationale carries a particular poignancy after the terrorist attacks of September 11, 2001. On that day, many men and women used cell phones to speak their final words to family and loved ones. Passengers on hijacked airplanes called wives and husbands; rescue workers on the ground phoned in to report their whereabouts. As land lines in New York and Washington, D.C., became clogged, many of us made or received frantic phone calls on cell phones—to reassure others that we were safe or to make sure that our friends and family were accounted for. Many people who had never considered owning a cell phone bought one after September 11th. If the cultural image we had of the earliest cell phones was of a technology glamorously deployed by the elite, then the image of cell phones today has to include people using them for this final act of communication, as well as terrorists who used cell phones as detonators in the bombing of trains in Madrid.

Of course, the perceived need for a technological safety device can encourage distinctly irrational behavior and create new anxieties. Recently, when a professor at Rutgers University asked his students to experiment with turning off their cell phones for 48 hours, one young woman told *University Wire,* "I felt like I was going to get raped if I didn't have my cell phone in my hand. I carry it in case I need to call someone for help." Popular culture endorses this image of cell-phone-as-life-line. The trailer for a new suspense movie, *Cellular,* is currently making the rounds in theaters nationwide. In it, an attractive young man is shown doing what young men apparently do with their camera-enabled cell phones: taking pictures of women in bikinis and e-mailing the images to himself. When he receives a random but desperate phone call from a woman who claims to be the victim of a kidnapping, he finds himself drawn into a race to find and save her, all the while trying to maintain that tenuous cell phone connection. It is indicative of our near-fetishistic attachment to our cell phones that we can relate (and treat as a serious moment of suspense) a scene in the movie where the protagonist, desperately trying to locate a cell phone charger before his battery runs out, holds the patrons of an electronics store at gunpoint until the battery is rejuvenated. After scenes of high-speed car chases and large explosions, the trailer closes with a disembodied voice asking the hero, "How did you get involved?" His response? "I just answered my phone."

Many parents have responded to this perceived need for personal security by 10 purchasing cell phones for their children, but this, too, has had some unintended consequences. One sociologist has noted that parents who do this are implicitly commenting on their own sense of security or insecurity in society. "Claiming to care about their children's safety," Chantal de Gournay writes, "parents develop a 'paranoiac' vision of the community, reflecting a lack of trust in social institutions and in any environment other than the family." As a result, they choose surveillance technologies, such as cell phones, to monitor their children, rather than teaching them (and trusting them) to behave appropriately. James E. Katz, a communications professor at Rutgers who has written extensively about wireless communication, argues that parents who give children cell phones are actually weakening the traditional bonds of authority; "parents think they can reach kids any time they want, and thus are more indulgent of their children's wanderings," Katz notes. Not surprisingly, "my cell phone battery died" has become a popular excuse among teenagers for failure to check in with their parents. And I suspect nearly everyone, at some point, has suffered hours of panic when a loved one who was supposed to be "reachable" failed to answer the cell phone.

Although cell phones are a technology with broad appeal, we do not all use our cell phones in the same way. In June 2004, Cingular announced that "for the fourth year in a row, men prove to be the more talkative sex in the wireless world," talking 16 percent more on their phones than women. Women, however, are more likely to use a cell phone "to talk to friends and family" while men use theirs for business—including, evidently, the business of mating. Researchers found that "men are using their mobile phones as peacocks use their immobilizing feathers and male bullfrogs use their immoderate croaks: To advertise to females their worth, status, and desirability," reported the *New York Times*. The researchers also discovered that many of the men they observed in pubs and nightclubs carried fake cell phones, likely one of the reasons they titled their paper "Mobile Phones as Lekking Devices Among Human Males," a lek being a "communal mating area where males gather to engage in flamboyant courtship displays." Or, as another observer of cell phone behavior succinctly put it: "the mobile is widely used for psychosexual purposes of performance and display."

The increasingly sophisticated accessories available on cell phones encourage such displays. One new phone hitting the market boasts video capture and playback, a 1.2 megapixel camera, a 256 color screen, speakerphone, removable memory, mp3 player, Internet access, and a global positioning system. The *Wall Street Journal* recently reported on cell phones that will feature radios, calculators, alarm clocks, flashlights, and mirrored compacts. Phones are "becoming your Swiss army knife," one product developer enthused. Hyperactive peacocking will also be abetted by the new walkie-talkie function available on many phones, which draws further attention to the user by broadcasting to anyone within hearing distance the conversation of the person on the other end of the phone.

With all these accoutrements, it is not surprising that one contributor to a discussion list about wireless technology recently compared cell phones and BlackBerrys to "electronic pets." Speaking to a group of business people, he reported, "you constantly see people taking their little pets out and stroking the scroll wheel, coddling them, basically "petting' them." When confined to a basement conference room, he found that participants "were compelled to "walk' their electronic pets on breaks" to check their messages. In parts of Asia, young women carry their phones in decorated pouches, worn like necklaces, or in pants with specially designed pockets that keep the phone within easy reach. We have become thigmophilic with our technology—touch-loving—a trait we share with rats, as it happens. We are constantly taking them out, fiddling with them, putting them away, taking them out again, reprogramming their directories, text messaging. And cell phone makers are always searching for new ways to exploit our attachments. Nokia offers "expression" phones that allow customization of faceplates and ring tones. Many companies, such as Modtones, sell song samples for cell phone ringers. In Asia, where cell phone use among the young is especially high, companies offer popular anime and manga cartoons as downloadable "wallpaper" for cell phones.

Cell phone technology is also creating new forms of social and political networking. "Moblogging," or mobile web logging, allows cell phone users to publish and update content to the World Wide Web. An increasing number of companies are offering cell phones with WiFi capability, and as Sadie Plant noted recently in a report she prepared for Motorola, "On the Mobile," "today, the smallest Motorola phone has as much computing power in it as the largest, most expensive computer did less than a generation ago." In his *Forbes* "Wireless Outlook" newsletter, Andrew Seybold predicted, "in twenty-five years there aren't going to be any wired phones left and I think it might happen even much sooner than that—ten to fifteen years." As well, "the phone will be tied much more closely to the person. Since the phone is the person, the person will be the number." It isn't surprising that one of Seybold's favorite movies is the James Coburn paranoid comedy, *The Presidents' Analyst* (1967), whose premise "centered on attempts by the phone company to capture the president's psychoanalyst in order to further a plot to have phone devices implanted in people's brains at birth." Ma Bell meets *The Manchurian Candidate.*

Dodgeball.com, a new social-networking service, applies the principles of web- 15
sites such as Friendster to cell phones. "Tell us where you are and we'll tell you who and what is around you," Dodgeball promises. "We'll ping your friends with your whereabouts, let you know when friends-of-friends are within ten blocks, allow you to broadcast content to anyone within ten blocks of you or blast messages to your groups of friends." The service is now available in fifteen cities in the U.S., enabling a form of friendly pseudo-stalking. "I was at Welcome to the Johnson's and a girl came up behind me and gave a tap on the shoulder," one recent testimonial noted. " 'Are you this guy?' she inquired while holding up her cell phone to show my Dodgeball photo. I was indeed."

Political organizers have also found cell phone technology to be a valuable tool. Throughout 2000 in the Philippines, the country's many cell phone users were text-messaging derogatory slogans and commentary about then-President Joseph Estrada. With pressure on the Estrada administration mounting, activists organized large demonstrations against the president by activating cell phone "trees" to summon protesters to particular locations and to outmaneuver riot police. Estrada was forced from office in January 2001. Anti-globalization protesters in Seattle and elsewhere (using only non-corporate cell phones, surely) have employed the technology to stage and control movements during demonstrations.

Communication Delinquents

The ease of mobile communication does not guarantee positive results for all those who use it, of course, and the list of unintended negative consequences from cell phone use continues to grow. The BBC world service reported in 2001, "senior Islamic figures in Singapore have ruled that Muslim men cannot divorce their wives by sending text messages over their mobile phones." (Muslims can divorce their wives by saying the word "talaq," which means "I divorce you," three times).

Concerns about the dangers of cell phone use while driving have dominated public discussion of cell phone risks. A 2001 study by the National Highway Traffic Safety Administration estimated that "54 percent of drivers 'usually' have some type of wireless phone in their vehicle with them" and that this translates into approximately 600,000 drivers "actively using cell phones at any one time" on the road. Women and drivers in the suburbs were found to talk and drive more often, and "the highest national use rates were observed for drivers of vans and sport utility vehicles." New York, New Jersey, and Washington, D.C. all require drivers to use hands-free technology (headsets or speakerphones) when talking on the cell.

Cell phones can also play host to viruses, real and virtual. A 2003 study presented at the American Society for Microbiology's conference on infectious disease found that twelve percent of the cell phones used by medical personnel in an Israeli hospital were contaminated with bacteria. (Another recent cell phone-related health research result, purporting a link between cell phone use and decreased sperm counts, has been deemed inconclusive.) The first computer virus specifically targeting cell phones was found in late June. As *The Guardian* reported recently, anti-virus manufacturers believe that "the mobile phone now mirrors how the Net has developed over the past two or three years—blighted with viruses as people got faster connections and downloaded more information."

20   With technology comes addiction, and applicable neologisms have entered the lexicon—such as "crackberry," which describes the dependence exhibited by some BlackBerry wireless users. In a 2001 article in *New York* magazine about feuding couples, one dueling duo, Dave and Brooke, traded barbs about her wireless addictions. "I use it when I'm walking down the street," Brooke said proudly. "She was checking her voice mail in the middle of a Seder!" was Dave's exasperated response. "Under the table!" Brooke clarified. A recent survey conducted by the Hospital of Seoul National University found that "3 out of 10 Korean high school students who carry mobile phones are reported to be addicted" to them. Many reported feeling anxious without their phones and many displayed symptoms of repetitive stress injury from obsessive text messaging.

The cell phone has also proven effective as a facilitator and alibi for adulterous behavior. "I heard someone (honest) talking about their 'shag phone' the other day," a visitor to a wireless technology blog recently noted. "He was a married man having an affair with a lady who was also married. It seems that one of the first heady rituals of the affair was to purchase a 'his and her' pair of pre-pay shag phones." A recent story in the *New York Times* documented the use of cell phone "alibi and excuse clubs" that function as an ethically challenged form of networking—Dodgeball for the delinquent. "Cell phone-based alibi clubs, which have sprung up in the United States, Europe, and Asia, allow people to send out mass text messages to thousands of potential collaborators asking for help. When a willing helper responds, the sender and the helper devise a lie, and the helper then calls the victim with the excuse," the report noted. One woman who started her own alibi club, which has helped spouses cheat on each other and workers mislead their bosses, "said she was not terribly concerned about lying," although she did concede: "You wouldn't really want your friends to know you're sparing people's feelings with these white lies." Websites such as Kargo offer features like "Soundster," which allows users to "insert sounds into your call and control your environment." Car horns, sirens, the coughs and sniffles of the sick room—all can be simulated in order to fool the listener on the other end of the call. Technology, it seems, is allowing people to make instrumental use of anonymous strangers while maintaining the appearance of trustworthiness within their own social group.

Technology has also led to further incursions on personal privacy. Several websites now offer "candid pornography," peeping-Tom pictures taken in locker rooms, bathrooms, and dressing rooms by unscrupulous owners of cell phone cameras. Camera phones pose a potentially daunting challenge to privacy and security; unlike old-fashioned cameras, which could be confiscated and the film destroyed, digital cameras, including those on cell phones, allow users to send images instantaneously to any e-mail address. The images can be stored indefinitely, and the evidence that a picture was ever taken can be destroyed.

Will You Please Be Quiet, Please?

Certain public interactions carry with them certain unspoken rules of behavior. When approaching a grocery store checkout line, you queue behind the last person in line and wait your turn. On the subway, you make way for passengers entering and exiting the cars. Riding on the train, you expect the interruptions of the ticket taker and the periodic crackling blare of station announcements. What you never used to expect, but must now endure, is the auditory abrasion of a stranger arguing about how much he does, indeed, owe to his landlord. I've heard business deals, lovers' quarrels, and the most unsavory gossip. I've listened to strangers discuss in excruciating detail their own and others' embarrassing medical conditions; I've heard the details of recent real estate purchases, job triumphs, and awful dates. (The only thing I haven't heard is phone sex, but perhaps it is only a matter of time.) We are no longer *overhearing*, which implies accidentally stumbling upon a situation where two people are talking in presumed privacy. Now we are all simply *hearing*. The result is a world where social space is overtaken by anonymous, unavoidable background noise—a quotidian narration that even in its more interesting moments rarely rises above the tone of a penny dreadful. It seems almost cruel, in this context, that Motorola's trademarked slogan for its wireless products is "Intelligence Everywhere."

Why do these cell phone conversations bother us more than listening to two strangers chatter in person about their evening plans or listening to a parent scold a recalcitrant child? Those conversations are quantitatively greater, since we hear both sides of the discussion—so why are they nevertheless experienced as qualitatively different? Perhaps it is because cell phone users harbor illusions about being alone or assume a degree of privacy that the circumstances don't actually allow. Because cell phone talkers are not interacting with the world around them, they come to believe that the world around them isn't really there and surely shouldn't intrude. And when the cell phone user commandeers the space by talking, he or she sends a very clear message to others that they are powerless to insist on their own use of the space. It is a passive-aggressive but extremely effective tactic.

25   Such encounters can sometimes escalate into rude intransigence or even violence. In the past few years alone, men and women have been stabbed, escorted off of airplanes by federal marshals, pepper-sprayed in movie theaters, ejected from concert halls, and deliberately rammed with cars as a result of their bad behavior on their cell phones. The *Zagat* restaurant guide reports that cell phone rudeness is now the number one complaint of diners, and *USA Today* notes that "fifty-nine percent of people would rather visit the dentist than sit next to someone using a cell phone."

The etiquette challenges posed by cell phones are universal, although different countries have responded in slightly different ways. Writing about the impact of cell phone technology in *The Guardian* in 2002, James Meek noted, with moderate horror, that cell phones now encourage British people to do what "British people aren't supposed to do: invite strangers, spontaneously, into our personal worlds. We let everyone know what our accent is, what we do for a living, what kind of stuff we do in our non-working hours." In France, cell phone companies were pressured by the public to censor the last four digits of phone numbers appearing on monthly statements, because so many French men and women were using them to confirm that their significant other was having an affair.

In Israel, where the average person is on a cell phone four times as much as the average American, and where cell phone technology boasts an impressive 76 percent penetration rate (the United States isn't projected to reach that level until 2009), the incursion of cell phones into daily life is even more dramatic. As sociologists Amit Schejter and Akiba Cohen found, there were no less than ten cell phone interruptions during a recent staging of *One Flew Over the Cuckoos' Nest* at Israel's National Theater, and "there has even been an anecdote reported of an undertaker's phone ringing inside a grave as the deceased was being put to rest." The authors explain this state of affairs with reference to the Israeli personality, which they judge to be more enthusiastic about technology and more forceful in exerting itself in public; the subtitle of their article is "chutzpah and chatter in the Holy Land."

In the U.S., mild regional differences in the use of cell phones are evident. Reporting on a survey by Cingular wireless, CNN noted that cell phone users in the South "are more likely to silence their phones in church," while Westerners "are most likely to turn a phone off in libraries, theaters, restaurants, and schools." But nationwide, cell phones still frequently interrupt movie screenings, theater performances, and concerts. Audience members are not the sole offenders, either. My sister, a professional musician, told me that during one performance, in the midst of a slow and quiet passage of Verdi's *Requiem,* the cell phone of one of the string players in the orchestra began ringing, much to the horror of his fellow musicians.

We cannot simply banish to Tartarus—the section of Hades reserved for punishment of the worst offenders—all those who violate the rules of social space. And the noise pollution generated by rude cell phone users is hardly the worst violation of social order; it is not the same as defacing a statue, for example. Other countries offer some reason for optimism: In societies that maintain more formality, such as Japan, loud public conversation is considered rude, and Japanese people will often cover their mouths and hide their phones from view when speaking into them.

Not surprisingly, Americans have turned to that most hallowed but least effective 30
solution to social problems: public education. Cingular Wireless, for example, has launched a public awareness campaign whose slogan is "Be Sensible." The program includes an advertisement shown in movie theaters about "Inconsiderate Cell Phone Guy," a parody of bad behavior that shows a man talking loudly into his cell phone at inappropriate times: during a date, in a movie, at a wedding, in the middle of a group therapy session. It is a miniature manners nickelodeon for the wireless age. July is now officially National Cell Phone Courtesy Month, and etiquette experts such as Jacqueline Whitmore of the Protocol School of Palm Beach advise companies such as Sprint about how to encourage better behavior in their subscribers. Whitmore is relentlessly positive: "Wireless technology is booming so quickly and wireless phones have become so popular, the rules on wireless etiquette are still evolving," she notes on her website. She cites hopeful statistics culled from public opinion surveys that say "98 percent of Americans say they move away from others when talking on a wireless phone in public" and "the vast majority (86 percent) say they 'never' or 'rarely' speak on wireless phones while conducting an entire public transaction with someone else such as a sales clerk or bank teller." If you are wondering where these examples of wireless rectitude reside, you might find them in the land of wishful thinking. There appears to be a rather large disconnect between people's actual behavior and their reports of their behavior.

Whitmore is correct to suggest that we are in the midst of a period of adjustment. We still have the memory of the old social rules, which remind us to be courteous towards others, especially in confined environments such as trains and elevators. But it is becoming increasingly clear that cell phone technology itself has disrupted our ability to insist on the enforcement of social rules. Etiquette experts urge us to adjust—be polite, don't return boorish behavior with boorish behavior, set a standard of probity in your own use of cell phones. But in doing so these experts tacitly concede that every conversation is important, and that we need only learn how and when to have them. This elides an older rule: when a conversation takes place in public, its merit must be judged in part by the standards of the other participants in the social situation. By relying solely on self-discipline and public education (or that ubiquitous modern state of "awareness"), the etiquette experts have given us a doomed manual. Human nature being what it is, individuals will spend more time rationalizing their own need to make cell phone calls than thinking about how that need might affect others. Worse, the etiquette experts offer diversions rather than standards, encouraging alternatives to calling that nevertheless still succeed in removing people from the social space. "Use text messaging," is number 7 on Whitmore's Ten Tips for the Cell Phone Savvy.

These attempts at etiquette training also evade another reality: the decline of accepted standards for social behavior. In each of us lurks the possibility of a Jekyll-and-Hyde-like transformation, its trigger the imposition of some arbitrary rule. The problem is that, in the twenty-first century, with the breakdown of hierarchies and manners, all social rules are arbitrary. "I don't think we have to worry about people being rude intentionally," Whitmore told *Wireless Week*. "Most of us simply haven't come to grips with the new responsibilities wireless technologies demand." But this seems foolishly optimistic. A psychologist quoted in a story by UPI recently noted the "baffling sense of entitlement" demonstrated by citizens in the wireless world. "They don't get sheepish when shushed," he marveled. "You're the rude one." And *contra* Ms. Whitmore, there is intention at work in this behavior, even if it is not intentional rudeness. It is the intentional removal of oneself from the social situation in public space. This removal, as sociologists have long shown, is something more serious than a mere manners lapse. It amounts to a radical disengagement from the public sphere.

Spectator Sport

We know that the reasons people give for owning cell phones are largely practical—convenience and safety. But the reason we answer them whenever they ring is a question better left to sociology and psychology. In works such as *Behavior in Public Spaces, Relations in Public,* and *Interaction Ritual,* the great sociologist Erving Goffman mapped the myriad possibilities of human interaction in social space, and his observations take on a new relevance in our cell phone world. Crucial to Goffman's analysis was the notion that in social situations where strangers must interact, "the individual is obliged to "come into play' upon entering the situation and to stay "in play' while in the situation." Failure to demonstrate this presence sends a clear message to others of one's hostility or disrespect for the social gathering. It effectively turns them into "non-persons." Like the piqued lover who rebuffs her partner's attempt to caress her, the person who removes himself from the social situation is sending a clear message to those around him: I don't need you.

Although Goffman wrote in the era before cell phones, he might have judged their use as a "subordinate activity," a way to pass the time such as reading or doodling that could and should be set aside when the dominant activity resumes. Within social space, we are allowed to perform a range of these secondary activities, but they must not impose upon the social group as a whole or require so much attention that they remove us from the social situation altogether. The opposite appears to be true today. The group is expected never to impinge upon—indeed, it is expected to tacitly endorse by enduring—the individual's right to withdraw from social space by whatever means he or she chooses: cell phones, BlackBerrys, iPods, DVDs screened on laptop computers. These devices are all used as a means to refuse to be "in" the social space; they are technological cold shoulders that are worse than older forms of subordinate activity in that they impose visually and auditorily on others. Cell phones are not the only culprits here. A member of my family, traveling recently on the Amtrak train from New York, was shocked to realize that the man sitting in front of her was watching a pornographic movie on his laptop computer—a movie whose raunchy scenes were reflected in the train window and thus clearly visible to her. We have allowed what should be subordinate activities in social space to become dominant.

35   One of the groups Goffman studied keenly were mental patients, many of them residents at St. Elizabeth's Hospital in Washington, D.C., and his comparisons often

draw on the remarkable disconnect between the behavior of people in normal society and those who had been institutionalized for mental illness. It is striking in revisiting Goffman's work how often people who use cell phones seem to be acting more like the people in the asylum than the ones in respectable society. Goffman describes "occult involvements," for example, as any activity that undermines others' ability to feel engaged in social space. "When an individual is perceived in an occult involvement, observers may not only sense that they are not able to claim him at the moment," Goffman notes, "but also feel that the offender's complete activity up till then has been falsely taken as a sign of participation with them, that all along he has been alienated from their world." Who hasn't observed someone sitting quietly, apparently observing the rules of social space, only to launch into loud conversation as soon as the cell phone rings? This is the pretense of social participation Goffman observed in patients at St. Elizabeth's.

Goffman called those who declined to respond to social overtures as being "out of contact," and said "this state is often felt to be full evidence that he is very sick indeed, that he is, in fact, cut off from all contact with the world around him." To be accessible meant to be available in the particular social setting and to act appropriately. Today, of course, being accessible means answering your cell phone, which brings you in contact with your caller, but "out of contact" in the physical social situation, be it a crosstown bus, a train, an airplane, or simply walking down the street.

In terms of the rules of social space, cell phone use is a form of communications panhandling—forcing our conversations on others without first gaining their tacit approval. "The force that keeps people in their communication place in our middle-class society," Goffman observed, "seems to be the fear of being thought forward and pushy, or odd, the fear of forcing a relationship where none is desired." But middle class society itself has decided to upend such conventions in the service of greater accessibility and convenience. This is a dramatic shift that took place in a very short span of time, and it is worth at least considering the long-term implications of this subversion of norms. The behavioral rules Goffman so effectively mapped exist to protect everyone, even if we don't, individually, always need them. They are the social equivalent of fire extinguishers placed throughout public buildings. You hope not to have to use them too often, but they can ensure that a mere spark does not become an embarrassing conflagration. In a world that eschews such norms, we find ourselves plagued by the behavior that Goffman used to witness only among the denizens of the asylum: disembodied talk that renders all of us unwilling listeners.

We also use our cell phones to exert our status in social space, like the remnants of the entourage or train, which "led a worthy to demonstrate his status by the cluster of dependent supporters that accompanied him through a town or a house of parliament." Modern celebrities still have such escorts (a new cable television series, *Entourage,* tracks a fictional celebrity posse). But cell phones give all of us the unusual ability to simulate an entourage. My mother-in-law recently found herself sharing an elevator (in the apartment building she's lived in for forty years) with a man who was speaking very loudly into his cell phone. When she asked him to keep his voice down, he became enraged and began yelling at her; he was, he said, in the midst of an "important" conversation with his secretary. He acted, in other words, as if she'd trounced on the hem of his royal train. She might have had a secretary too, of course—for all he knew she might have a fleet of assistants at her disposal—but because she wasn't communicating with someone *at that moment* and he, thanks to his cell phone, was, her status in the social space was, in effect, demoted.

The language of wireless technology itself suggests its selfishness as a medium. One of the latest advances is the "Personal Area Network," a Bluetooth technology used in Palm Pilots and other personal digital assistants. The network is individualized, closed to unwelcome intruders, and totally dependent on the choices of the user. We now have our own technological assistants and networks, quite an impressive kingdom for ordinary mortals. In this kingdom, our cell phones reassure us by providing constant contact, and we become much like a child with a security blanket or Dumbo with his feather. Like a security blanket, which is also visible to observers, cell phones provide the ""publicization' of emotional fulfillment," as French sociologist Chantal de Gournay has argued. "At work, in town, while traveling—every call on the mobile phone secretly expresses a message to the public: "Look how much I'm in demand, how full my life is."" Unlike those transitional objects of childhood, however, few of us are eager to shed our cell phones.

Absent Without Leave

40   Our daily interactions with cell phone users often prompt heated exchanges and promises of furious retribution. When *New York Times* columnist Joe Sharkey asked readers to send in their cell phone horror stories, he was deluged with responses: "There is not enough time in the day to relay the daily torment I must endure from these cell-yellers," one woman said. "There's always some self-important jerk who must holler his business all the way into Manhattan," another commuter wearily noted. Rarely does one find a positive story about cell phone users who behaved politely, observing the common social space.

Then again, we all apparently have a cell phone *alter idem,* a second self that we endlessly excuse for making just such annoying cell phone calls. As a society, we are endlessly forgiving of our own personal "emergencies" that require cell phone conversation and easily apoplectic about having to listen to others'. At my local grocery store around 6:30 in the evening, it is not an uncommon sight to see a man in business attire, wandering the frozen food aisle, phone in hand, shouting, "Bird's Eye or Jolly Green Giant? What? Yes, I got the coffee filters already!" How rude, you think, until you remember that you left your own grocery list on the kitchen counter; in a split second you are fishing for your phone so that you can call home and get its particulars. This is the quintessential actor-observer paradox: as actors, we are always politely exercising our right to be connected, but as observers we are perpetually victimized by the boorish bad manners of other cell phone users.

A new generation of sociologists has begun to apply Goffman's insights to our use of cell phones in public. Kenneth J. Gergen, for example, has argued that one reason cell phones allow a peculiar form of diversion in public spaces is that they encourage "absent presence," a state where "one is physically present but is absorbed by a technologically mediated world of elsewhere." You can witness examples of absent presence everywhere: people in line at the bank or a retail store, phones to ear and deep into their own conversations—so unavailable they do not offer the most basic pleasantries to the salesperson or cashier. At my local playground, women deep in cell phone conversations are scattered on benches or distractedly pushing a child on a swing—physically present, to be sure, but "away" in their conversations, not fully engaged with those around them.

The first time you saw a person walking down the street having a conversation using a hands-free cell phone device you intuitively grasped this state. Wildly gesticulating, laughing, mumbling—to the person on the other end of the telephone, their street-walking conversation partner is engaged in normal conversation. To the outside observer, however, he looks like a deranged or slightly addled escapee from a psychiatric ward. Engaged with the ether, hooked up to an earpiece and dangling microphone, his animated voice and gestures are an anomaly in the social space. They violate our everyday sense of normal behavior.

The difficulty of harmonizing real and virtual presence isn't new. As Mark Caldwell noted in *A Short History of Rudeness* about the first telephones, "many early phone stories involved a bumpkin who nods silently in reply to a caller's increasingly agitated, 'Are you there?' " Even young children know Goffman's rules. When a parent is in front of a child but on the telephone (physically present but mentally "away"), a child will frequently protest—grabbing for the phone or vocalizing loudly to retrieve the parent's attention. They are expressing a need for recognition that, in a less direct and individualized way, we all require from strangers in public space. But the challenge is greater given the sheer number of wireless users, a reality that is prompting a new form of social criticism. As a "commentary on the potential of the mobile phone for disrupting and disturbing social interactions," the Interaction Design Institute Ivrea recently sponsored a project called "Mass Distraction." The project featured jackets and cell phones that only allowed participants to talk on their phones if the large hood of the jacket was closed completely over their head or if they continued to insert coins into the pocket of the jacket like an old fashioned pay phone. "In order to remain connected," the project notes, "the mobile phone user multitasks between the two communication channels. Whether disguised or not, this practice degrades the quality of the interaction with the people in his immediate presence."

Cocooned within our "Personal Area Networks" and wirelessly transported to   45 other spaces, we are becoming increasingly immune to the boundaries and realities of physical space. As one reporter for the *Los Angeles Times* said, in exasperation, "Go ahead, floss in the elevator. You're busy; you can't be expected to wait until you can find a bathroom. ... [T]he world out there? It's just a backdrop, as movable and transient as a fake skyline on a studio lot." No one is an outsider with a cell phone—that is why foreign cab drivers in places like New York and Washington are openly willing to ignore laws against driving-and-talking. Beyond the psychic benefits cell phone calls provide (cab driving is a lonely occupation), their use signals the cab driver's membership in a community apart from the ever-changing society that frequents his taxi. Our cell phones become our talismans against being perceived as (or feeling ourselves to be) outsiders.

Talk and Conversation

Recently, on a trip to China, I found myself standing on the Great Wall. One of the members of our small group had hiked ahead, and since the rest of us had decided it was time to get back down the mountain, we realized we would need to find him. Despite being in a remote location at high altitude, and having completely lost sight of him in the hazy late morning air, this proved to be the easiest of logistical tasks. One man pulled out his cell phone, called his wife back in the United States, and had her send an e-mail to the man who had walked ahead. Knowing that our lost companion religiously checked his BlackBerry wireless, we reasoned that he would surely notice an incoming message. Soon enough he reappeared, our wireless plea for his return having successfully traveled from China to Washington and back again to the Wall in mere minutes.

At the time, we were all caught up in the James Bond-like excitement of our mission. Would the cell phone work? (It did.) Would the wife's e-mail get through to our companion's BlackBerry? (No problem.) Only later, as we drove back to Beijing, did I experience a pang of doubt about our small communications triumph. There, at one of the Great Wonders of the World, a centuries-old example of human triumph over nature, we didn't hesitate to do something as mundane as make a cell phone call. It is surely true that wireless communication is its own wondrous triumph over nature. But cell phone conversation somehow inspires less awe than standing atop the Great Wall, perhaps because atop the Great Wall we are still rooted in the natural world that we have conquered. Or perhaps it is simply because cell phones have become everyday wonders—as unremarkable to us as the Great Wall is to those who see it everyday.

Christian Licoppe and Jean-Philippe Heurtin have argued that cell phone use must be understood in a broader context; they note that the central feature of the modern experience is the "deinstitutionalization of personal bonds." Deinstitutionalization spawns anxiety, and as a result we find ourselves working harder to build trust relationships. Cell phone calls "create a web of short, content-poor interactions through which bonds can be built and strengthened in an ongoing process."

But as trust is being built and bolstered moment by moment between individuals, public trust among strangers in social settings is eroding. We are strengthening and increasing our interactions with the people we already know at the expense of those who we do not. The result, according to Kenneth Gergen, is "the erosion of face-to-face community, a coherent and centered sense of self, moral bearings, depth of relationship, and the uprooting of meaning from material context: such are the dangers of absent presence."

50   No term captures this paradoxical state more ably than the word "roam," which appears on your phone when you leave an area bristling with wireless towers and go into the wilds of the less well connected. The word appears when your cell phone is looking for a way to connect you, but the real definition of roam is "to go from place

to place without purpose or direction," which has more suggestive implications. It suggests that we have allowed our phones to become the link to our purpose and the symbol of our status—without its signal we lack direction. Roaming was a word whose previous use was largely confined to describing the activities of herds of cattle. In her report on the use of mobile phones throughout the world, Sadie Plant noted, "according to the *Oxford English Dictionary,* one of the earliest uses of the word 'mobile' was in association with the Latin phrase *mobile vulgus,* the excitable crowd," whence comes our word "mob."

Convenience and safety—the two reasons people give for why they have (or "need") cell phones—are legitimate reasons for using wireless technology; but they are not neutral. Convenience is the major justification for fast food, but its overzealous consumption has something to do with our national obesity "epidemic." Safety spawned a bewildering range of anti-bacterial products and the overzealous prescription of antibiotics—which in turn led to disease-resistant bacteria.

One possible solution would be to treat cell phone use the way we now treat tobacco use. Public spaces in America were once littered with spittoons and the residue of the chewing tobacco that filled them, despite the disgust the practice fostered. Social norms eventually rendered public spitting déclassé. Similarly, it was not so long ago that cigarette smoking was something people did everywhere—in movie theaters, restaurants, trains, and airplanes. Non-smokers often had a hard time finding refuge from the clouds of nicotine. Today, we ban smoking in all but designated areas. Currently, cell phone users enjoy the same privileges smokers once enjoyed, but there is no reason we cannot reverse the trend. Yale University bans cell phones in some of its libraries, and Amtrak's introduction of "quiet cars" on some of its routes has been eagerly embraced by commuters. Perhaps one day we will exchange quiet cars for wireless cars, and the majority of public space will revert to the quietly disconnected. In doing so, we might partially reclaim something higher even than healthy lungs: civility.

This reclaiming of social space could have considerable consequences. As sociologist de Gournay has noted, "the telephone is a device ill suited to listening...it is more appropriate for exchanging information." Considering Americans' obsession with information—we are, after all, the "information society"—it is useful to draw the distinction. Just as there is a distinction between information and knowledge, there is a vast difference between conversation and talk.

Conversation (as opposed to "talk") is to genuine sociability what courtship (as opposed to "hooking up") is to romance. And the technologies that mediate these distinctions are important: the cell phone exchange of information is a distant relative of formal conversation, just as the Internet chat room is a far less compelling place to become intimate with another person than a formal date. In both cases, however, we have convinced ourselves as a culture that these alternatives are just as good as the formalities—that they are, in fact, improvements upon them.

"A conversation has a life of its own and makes demands on its own behalf," Goffman   55 wrote. "It is a little social system with its own boundary-making tendencies; it is a little patch of commitment and loyalty with its own heroes and its own villains." According to census data, the percentage of Americans who live alone is the highest it has ever been in our country's history, making a return to genuine sociability and conversation more important than ever. Cell phones provide us with a new, but not necessarily superior means of communicating with each other. They encourage talk, not conversation. They link us to those we know, but remove us from the strangers who surround us in public space. Our constant accessibility and frequent exchange of information is undeniably useful. But it would be a terrible irony if "being connected" required or encouraged a disconnection from community life—an erosion of the spontaneous encounters and everyday decencies that make society both civilized and tolerable.

Things to Do with the Reading

1. Talk and conversation offer an organizing contrast (binary) in Rosen's essay. Track the strands attached to each of these key terms and write a paragraph or two about how they suggest what is at stake in this piece. What other binaries figure prominently?

2. What is this piece assuming about the function of manners in a culture? In other words, reason back to premises in regard to Rosen's point of view. Rosen refers, for example, to something she calls "social space." What are some of Rosen's stated—and unstated—assumptions about this space? (See Chapter 4 on uncovering assumptions.)

3. Rosen's essay is a piece of research writing that makes use of a number of other writers and theorists, most notably the sociologist Erving Goffman. What use does Rosen make of this research?

4. **Application:** Near the end of the section "Will You Please Be Quiet, Please?", in the paragraph beginning "Not surprisingly," Rosen cites an etiquette expert, Jacqueline Whitmore, who observes, "Wireless technology is booming so quickly and wireless phones are becoming so popular, the rules on wireless etiquette are still evolving." This idea is worth investigating. Spend a few days observing cell phone behavior; take careful notes. Your goal is to look for trends in cell phone etiquette. What is that etiquette? Where and how do you see it evolving? Write up your results.

   You might extend this project by exploring further the disagreement between Rosen and Whitmore on what Rosen calls "wireless rectitude." Rosen claims at the end of the paragraph that there is a mismatch between people's reports of their behavior and their actual behavior. Develop a few questions about cell phone use and ask them of your friends or peers. Compare the results with your actual observations.

Paul Goldberger

Disconnected Urbanism

Paul Goldberger is the Architecture Critic for *The New Yorker*. Formerly Dean of the Parsons school of design, Goldberger currently holds the Joseph Urban Chair in Design and Architecture at The New School in New York City. He began his career at *The New York Times*, where in 1984 his architecture criticism was awarded a Pulitzer Prize. His most recent book is entitled *Why Architecture Matters* (2009). In this short piece, taken from Metropolismag. com (November 2003), Goldberger considers the impact of the cell phone on our sense of place.

There is a connection between the idea of place and the reality of cellular telephones. It is   1
not encouraging. Places are unique—or at least we like to believe they are—and we strive to experience them as a kind of engagement with particulars. Cell phones are precisely the opposite. When a piece of geography is doing what it is supposed to do, it encourages you to feel a connection to it that, as in marriage, forsakes all others. When you are in Paris you expect to wallow in its Parisness, to feel that everyone walking up the Boulevard Montparnasse is as totally and completely there as the lampposts, the kiosks, the façade of the Brasserie Lipp—and that they could be no place else. So we want it to be in every city, in every kind of place. When you are in a forest, you want to experience its woodsiness; when you are on the beach, you want to feel connected to sand and surf.

This is getting harder to do, not because these special places don't exist or because urban places have come to look increasingly alike. They have, but this is not another rant about the monoculture and sameness of cities and the suburban landscape. Even when you are in a place that retains its intensity, its specialness, and its ability to confer a defining context on your life, it doesn't have the all-consuming effect these places used to. You no longer feel that being in one place cuts you off from other places. Technology has been doing this for a long time, of course—remember when people communicated with Europe by letter and it took a couple of weeks to get a reply? Now we're upset if we have to send a fax because it takes so much longer than e-mail.

But the cell phone has changed our sense of place more than faxes and computers and e-mail because of its ability to intrude into every moment in every possible place. When you walk along the street and talk on a cell phone, you are not on the street sharing the communal experience of urban life. You are in some other place—someplace at the other end of your phone conversation. You are there, but you are not there. It reminds me of the title of Lillian Ross's memoir of her life with William Shawn, *Here But Not Here*. Now that is increasingly true of almost every person on almost every street in almost every city. You are either on the phone or carrying one, and the moment it rings you will be transported out of real space into a virtual realm.

This matters because the street is the ultimate public space and walking along it is the defining urban experience. It is all of us—different people who lead different lives—coming together in the urban mixing chamber. But what if half of them are

Disconnected Urbanism, Paul Goldberger. Reprinted with permission of the author.

elsewhere, there in body but not in any other way? You are not on Madison Avenue if you are holding a little object to your ear that pulls you toward a person in Omaha.

5   The great offense of the cell phone in public is not the intrusion of its ring, although that can be infuriating when it interrupts a tranquil moment. It is the fact that even when the phone does not ring at all, and is being used quietly and discreetly, it renders a public place less public. It turns the boulevardier into a sequestered individual, the flaneur into a figure of privacy. And suddenly the meaning of the street as a public place has been hugely diminished.

I don't know which is worse—the loss of the sense that walking along a great urban street is a glorious shared experience or the blurring of distinctions between different kinds of places. But these cultural losses are related, and the cell phone has played a major role in both. The other day I returned a phone call from a friend who lives in Hartford. He had left a voice-mail message saying he was visiting his son in New Orleans, and when I called him back on his cell phone—area code 860, Hartford—he picked up the call in Tallahassee. Once the area code actually meant something in terms of geography: it outlined a clearly defined piece of the earth; it became a form of identity. Your telephone number was a badge of place. Now the area code is really not much more than three digits; and if it has any connection to a place, it's just the telephone's home base. An area code today is more like a car's license plate. The downward spiral that began with the end of the old telephone exchanges that truly did connect to a place—RHinelander 4 and BUtterfield 8 for the Upper East Side, or CHelsea 3 downtown, or UNiversity 4 in Morningside Heights—surely culminates in the placeless area codes such as 917 and 347 that could be anywhere in New York—or anywhere at all.

It's increasingly common for cell-phone conversations to begin with the question, "Where are you?" and for the answer to be anything from "out by the pool" to "Madagascar." I don't miss the age when phone charges were based on distance, but that did have the beneficial effect of reinforcing a sense that places were distinguishable from one another. Now calling across the street and calling from New York to California or even Europe are precisely the same thing. They cost the same because to the phone they are the same. Every place is exactly the same as every other place. They are all just nodes on a network—and so, increasingly, are we.

Things to Do with the Reading

1. In "Our Cell Phone, Our Selves," Christina Rosen writes of the use of cell phones in public, "It is the intentional removal of oneself from the social situation in public. This removal, as sociologists have long shown, is something more serious than a mere manners lapse. It amounts to a radical disengagement from the public sphere." Locate any statement in Goldberger's essay that connects in some interesting way with Rosen's remark. Then do a focused freewriting (see Chapter 4) on the two together, getting them to interact.

2. How is Goldberger using the term "public space"? The idea of a public sphere and of public space is one that connects not only the readings in this chapter but those in several other chapters as well. You might compare Goldberger's sense of the term with the way public space is valued in the essays by Adam Gopnik, Jane Jacobs, or Mike Davis in Chapter 21.

Jeffrey Rosen
The Naked Crowd

"Why is it that American anxiety about identity has led us to value exposure over privacy? Why, in short, are we so eager to become members of
the Naked Crowd, in which we have the illusion of belonging only when
we are exposed?" This essay by a professor of law at George Washington
University and legal affairs editor of the *New Republic* is excerpted from his
book, *The Naked Crowd: Reclaiming Security and Freedom in an Anxious
Age* (2004).

1   After 9/11, the most celebrated ritual of mourning was the *New York Times*'s Portraits
of Grief. For months after the attack, the *New York Times* published more than 1,800
sketches of those who died in the collapse of the World Trade Centre. Not designed
as obituaries in the traditional sense—at 200 words, there was no space for a full
accounting of the lives that had been cut short—the Portraits were offered up as "brief,
informal, and impressionistic, often centred on a single story or idiosyncratic detail",
intended not "to recount a person's résumé, but rather to give a snapshot of each victim's personality, of a life lived."

The Portraits were intended to be democratic—showing the personal lives of janitors as well as chief executives. Above all, they attempted to recognise the victims as
distinctive individuals, each distinguished from the crowd. "One felt, looking at those
pages every day, that real lives were jumping out at you," said Paul Auster, the novelist,
when interviewed by the *New York Times* about the profiles. "We weren't mourning
an anonymous mass of people, we were mourning thousands of individuals. And the
more we knew about them, the more we could wrestle with our own grief."[1]

Although public criticism of the Portraits of Grief was hard to detect during the
months of their publication, a few dissident voices emerged after the series came to
an end. More than 80 percent of the victims' families agreed to talk to the *New York
Times,* but a handful of them later complained that the Portraits had failed to capture
the people they had known. In an eloquent essay in the *American Scholar,* the literary critic Thomas Mallon echoed this criticism, arguing that in the process of trying
to individualise their subjects, the Portraits of Grief had managed to homogenise
them instead. "To read the Portraits one would believe that work counted for next to
nothing, that every hard charging bond trader and daredevil fireman preferred—and
managed—to spend more time with his family than at the office," Mallon wrote.

American obituaries, to a certain extent, tend to obey the convention of speaking well of the dead (British obituaries are far nastier), but the Portraits of Grief were
not successful on their own terms: instead of recognising the public achievements of
lives that had reached some kind of fulfilment, the Portraits instead trivialised their
subjects by emphasising one or two private hobbies or quirks. As a result, any genuine achievements or complexity of personality were airbrushed away in the narrative
effort to reduce each person to a single, memorable, and democratically accessible
detail. "If Mayor Rudolph Giuliani had perished in the attacks, as he nearly did,"

The Naked Crowd, Jeffrey Rosen. © Jeffrey Rosen. This essay, which appeared in Spiked.com, is an excerpt
from the Naked Crowd: Reclaiming Security and Freedom in an Anxious Age, (Random House, 2004), and
is reprinted by permission.

Mallon concluded, "he would be remembered in the Portraits as a rabid Yankee fan who sometimes liked to put on lipstick."[2]

The homogenising effects of the Portraits of Grief were inherent in the project itself. The *New York Times* instructed its reporters to convey a sense of the victims as distinct individuals by extracting from conversations with their families a single representative detail about their lives that would give readers the illusion of having known them. In each case, complexity and accuracy had to be sacrificed to the narrative imperative of finding a memorable quirk of personality with which the audience could quickly identify.

But the Portraits of Grief were not designed to do justice to the victims in all of their complexity. They were designed as a form of therapy for the families of the victims and as a source of emotional connection for the readers of the *New York Times*. They aspired to give all Americans the illusion of identifying with the victims, and therefore allowing them to feel that they themselves had somehow been touched by the horrific event. What was flattened out in this juggernaut of democratic connection was the individuality of the victims themselves.

This flattening resulted from a broader demand: the crowd's insistence on emotionally memorable images at the expense of genuine human individuality. The crowd, which thinks in terms of images rather than arguments, demands a sense of emotional connection with everyone who catches its fleeting attention. This means that everyone who is subject to the scrutiny of the crowd—from celebrities to political candidates to the families of terrorists' victims—will feel pressure to parcel out bits of personal information in order to allow unseen strangers to experience a sense of vicarious identification.

But revealing one or two personal details to strangers is inevitably a trivialising experience that leads us to be judged out of context. It's impossible to know someone on the basis of snippets of information; genuine knowledge is something that can only be achieved slowly, over time, behind a shield of privacy, with the handful of people to whom we've chosen to reveal ourselves whole.

The sociologist Thomas Mathiesen has contrasted Michel Foucault's Panopticon—a surveillance house in which the few watched the many—with what he called the "Synopticon" created by modern television, in which the many watch the few. But in the age of the internet, we are experiencing something that might be called the "Omnipticon" in which the many are watching the many, even though no one knows precisely who is watching or being watched at any given time. The homogenisation wrought by the Portraits of Grief is a symptom of the identity crisis that Americans are experiencing as they attempt to negotiate the challenges of the Omnipticon—a world in which more and more citizens are subject to the scrutiny of strangers. The challenges of interacting with strangers have increased the pressures on Americans to trade privacy for an illusory sense of security and connection, turning many of us into virtual portraits of grief.

Exposing Ourselves

The British sociologist Anthony Giddens has described the ways that citizens in a risk society can no longer rely on tradition or fixed hierarchies to establish their identity or to give them reliable guidance about whom to trust in a society of strangers.

Confused and anxious about status in a world where status is constantly shifting, we feel increasing pressure to expose details of our personal lives to strangers in order to win their trust, and we demand that they expose themselves in order to win our trust in return. "Trust—in a person or in a system, such as a banking system—can be a means of coping with risk, while acceptance of risk can be a means of generating trust", Giddens writes.[3]

In the past, intimate relationships of trust—such as marriage, friendship, and business associations—were based on rigidly controlled status hierarchies, which brought with them codes of expected behaviours: you could behave one way with your wife and another with your servant and another with your boss, because you had no doubt where you stood in relationship to each of them, and where they stood in relation to you. Today, by contrast, intimacy and trust are increasingly obtained not by shared experiences or fixed social status but by self-revelation: people try to prove their trustworthiness by revealing details of their personal lives to prove that they have nothing to hide before a crowd whose gaze is turned increasingly on all the individuals that compose it.

A world where individuals have to prove their trustworthiness and value every day before the crowd, choosing among an infinite range of lifestyles, behaviours, clothes, and values, is inevitably a world that creates great anxiety about identity. Rather than conforming to preexisting social roles, individuals are expected to find their true selves and constantly to market themselves to a sceptical world. In the 1950s, Eric Fromm wrote about the "marketing orientation" of the American self, in which "man experiences himself as a thing to be employed successfully on the market. ... His sense of value depends on his success: on whether he can sell himself favourably. ... If the individual fails in a profitable investment of himself, he feels that he is a failure; if he succeeds, *he* is a success."[4] Fromm worried that the marketed personality, whose precarious sense of self-worth was entirely dependent on the fickle judgements of the market, would be wracked by alienation and anxiety.

The internet has vastly increased the opportunities for individuals to subject themselves to the demands of the personality market, resulting in ever increasing confusion and anxiety about how much of ourselves to reveal to strangers. The logic of Fromm's marketed self as being extended into a virtual world where the easiest way to attract the attention and winning the trust of strangers is to establish an emotional connection with them by projecting a consistent, memorable, and trustworthy image. In an ideal relationship of trust, self-revelation should be reciprocal. In the age of the internet, however, we are increasingly forced to interact with strangers whom we will never meet face-to-face. As a result, individuals find themselves in more and more situations where they feel pressure to reveal details of their personal lives without being able to gauge the audience's reaction. But the quest for attention from and emotional connection with strangers is fraught with peril.[5]

In 2000, for example, Laurence Tribe, the constitutional scholar from Harvard Law School, posted a personal statement on his family's website. "I'm Larry", Tribe wrote. "I love brilliant magenta sunsets, unagi, Martin Amis" *Time's Arrow*, the fish tank at MGH, T.S. Eliot's "Love Song of J Alfred Prufrock", eating, my stairmaster, looking at the ocean, dreaming about impossible things, *New Yorker* cartoons, the twist in a short story, *The Hotel New Hampshire,* good (and even not-so-good) movies, rereading *The Great Gatsby* and *Ethan Frome,* and Monet and Vermeer.' Several websites devoted to media gossip posted links mocking Tribe's statement for displaying the overly intimate tones of a personal ad. Embarrassed by the public reaction, Tribe tried to remove the statement, but one of the media gossip sites resurrected it from the archives of Google, the popular internet search engine. Tribe was then ridiculed more for his attempt to cover his tracks than for his initial act of self-exposure.

"The website itself was a thing our son helped Carolyn and me put together one   15 Christmas", Tribe emailed me later, reflecting on his experience. "I was having fun letting my hair down, as it were, in just chatting about myself as unselfconsciously as I could, not giving much of a thought to who might read it but probably assuming, naively it now seems, that it wouldn't really be of interest to anybody. When I learned that people were finding it a source of public amusement, I do admit to being nonplussed and unsure of what to do." Tribe's understandable error shows how hard it is to strike a decent balance between personal disclosure and the projection of a consistent image, especially on the internet.

Many citizens, of course, don't care if they embarrass themselves before strangers on the internet, as the proliferation of personal websites shows. It is now commonplace on a website to reveal hobbies, favourite foods and music, and pictures of children, in an effort to create an illusion of intimacy. Even the most intimate moments of life, such as a wedding, are now being posted on the web for public consumption. The private moments offered up for public consumption tend to be generic tropes of informality which, like the Portraits of Grief, have a homogenising effect. Instead of the beginning of a romantic partnership, one often has the impression of watching a particularly excruciating episode of *The Dating Game.* And then there are the reality TV shows, which represent the most absurd examples of the application of the values of the public opinion society to the most intimate activities of life.

One way of understanding privacy is not whether we choose to expose personal information in public—we all do at different times and places—but the ease with which we can return to being private. The internet, however, is complicating our ability to negotiate the boundary between public and private, making it hard to recover a private self that has been voluntarily exposed. Consider the proliferation of weblogs—personal internet journals that often combine political musings with intimate disclosures about daily life. There are more than half a million, according to a recent estimate.[6] Some are devoted exclusively to public affairs, while others are nothing more than published diaries. A website called Diarist.net collects more than 5,000 journals from self-styled "online exhibitionists."[7] Often, these diaries are virtually unreadable examples of self display, dreary accounts of daily navel gazing whose primary function seems to be therapeutic. But they reflect a common but treacherous error: that thoughts appropriate to reveal to friends and intimates are also appropriate to reveal to the world.

In a pluralistic society, people are and should be free to have different instincts about the proper balance between reticence and self-revelation. If exercises in personal exhibitionism give pleasure to the exhibitionists and an illusory sense of emotional connection for the virtual audience, there's no harm done except to the dignity of the individuals concerned, and that's nobody's business but their own. But the growing pressure to expose ourselves in front of strangers has obvious and important consequences for a democracy's ability to strike a reasonable balance between liberty and security. The ease with which we reveal ourselves suggests that in the face of widespread anxiety about identity, people are more concerned with the feeling of connection than with the personal and social costs of exposure. Why is it that American anxiety about identity has led us to value exposure over privacy? Why, in short, are we so eager to become members of the Naked Crowd, in which we have the illusion of belonging only when we are exposed?

From Sincerity to Authenticity

Anxiety about how much of ourselves to reveal to strangers has always been a defining trait of the American character. But the form of the anxiety changed over the course of the nineteenth and twentieth centuries, reflecting changes in society and technology. In the late nineteenth century, conceptions of personal truthfulness changed in a way that the critic Lionel Trilling has described as a change from sincerity to authenticity.[8]

20   By sincerity, Trilling meant the expectation that individuals should avoid duplicity in their dealings with each other: there should be an honest correlation between what is exposed in public and what is felt in private; but not everything that is felt has to be exposed. By authenticity, Trilling meant the expectation that instead of being honest with each other, individuals should be honest with themselves, and should have no compunction about directly exposing strangers to their most intimate emotions. Sincerity requires that whatever is exposed must be true; authenticity requires that everything must be exposed as long as it is deeply felt.

In an age of sincerity, the fine clothes and family crest of an aristocrat were the markers of the self; in an age of authenticity, as the sociologist Peter Berger has noted, "the escutcheons hide the true self. It is precisely the naked man, and even more specifically the naked man expressing his sexuality, who represents himself more truthfully."[9] The motto for the age of sincerity came from the Delphic Oracle: Know Thyself. The motto for the age of authenticity comes from the therapist: Be Thyself.

As self-disclosure became the yardstick of trustworthiness, individuals began to relate to strangers in psychological terms. Politicians, like actors on the stage, came to be judged as trustworthy only if they could convincingly dramatise their own emotions and motivations. "The content of political belief recedes as in public, people become more interested in the content of the politician's life," Richard Sennett writes. "The modern charismatic leader destroys any distance between his own sentiments and impulses and those of his audience, and so, focusing his followers on his motivations, deflects them from measuring him in terms of his acts."[10] The earnest nod, the brow furrowed by concern, and the well-timed tear are now more important for politicians than traditional skills of oratory.

In *The Image*, Daniel Boorstin explored the way the growth of movies, radio, print, and television had transformed the nature of political authority, which came to be exercised not by distant and remote heroes but instead by celebrities, whom Boorstin defined as "a person who is known for his well-knownness." "Neither good nor bad,' a celebrity is "morally neutral," "the human pseudo-event," who has been "fabricated on purpose to satisfy our exaggerated expectations of human greatness."[11] While the heroes of old exercised authority by being remote and mysterious, modern celebrities exercise authority by being familiar and intelligible, creating the impression—but not the reality—of emotional accessibility. Heroes were distinguished by their achievement, celebrities by their images or trademarks or "name brands."

In an age when images were becoming more important than reality, Boorstin lamented the fact that politicians were trying to hold the attention of the crowd by recasting themselves in the mould of celebrities, projecting an image of emotional authenticity through selective self-disclosure. He feared that as synthesised images took the place of complicated human reality, the result would be a proliferation of conformity: politicians would have to alter their personalities to fit with the images that the crowd expected them to present; and the believability of the image would become more important than the underlying human truth.

Boorstin wrote before the development of the internet. But as life increasingly 25 takes place in cyberspace, private citizens are now facing some of the same social pressures and technological opportunities as politicians to expose and market themselves to strangers, with similarly homogenising results. As the internet has increased the circumstances in which ordinary citizens are forced to present a coherent image to strangers, the methodology of public relations is increasingly being applied to the presentation of the self. Ordinary citizens are now being forced to market themselves like pseudo-events, using techniques that used to be reserved for politicians, corporations, and celebrities. In an eerie fulfilment of Boorstin's fears, business gurus today are urging individuals to project a consistent image to the crowd by creating a personal brand.

Personal Branding

The idea of selling people as products began to appear in magazines like *Ad Age* as early as the 1970s; but the idea of personal branding didn't proliferate until the 1990s, when a series of business books emerged with names like *Brand You, The Personal Branding Phenomenon,* and *Be Your Own Brand: A Breakthrough Formula for Standing Out from the Crowd.* To invent a successful brand you have to establish trust with strangers, argues the personal branding guru, Tom Peters. A brand is a "trust mark" that "reaches out with a powerful connecting experience." To connect with colleagues and customers, you have to decide the one thing you want them to know about you and create an "emotional context" by telling stories about yourself. Peters's nostrums are an example of the banalisation of Gustave Le Bon; and *Be Your Own Brand* is in the same vein. It defines a personal brand as "a perception or emotion, maintained by somebody other than you, that describes the total experience of having a relationship with you."

Like the brand of a corporation or product, personal brands are defined by whether people trust, like, remember, and value you: "your brand, just like the brand of a product, exists on the basis of a set of perceptions and emotions stored in someone else's head." To create a strong personal brand that makes and maintains an emotional connection with strangers, individuals are advised to be "distinctive, relevant, and consistent."

To achieve the goals of distinctiveness, relevance, and consistency, branded individuals are urged to simplify the complex characteristics that make up a genuine individual. Following the model of the Portraits of Grief, personal branders urge their clients to write down a list of the adjectives that best describe their personal style and values, and to incorporate three of them in a "personal brand promise" that can easily be remembered. For example, a surgeon who says he is "humble, collaborative, and friendly" promises "the discipline to achieve world-class results"; a writer who claims to be "enthusiastic, energetic, and professional" promises "enthusiasm that will make your day." These brand attributes are so abstract and banal that they are impossible to remember, which is why the entire enterprise seems dubious, even on its own terms; but they neatly achieve the goal of turning individuals into stereotypes, for the purpose of making them intelligible to strangers with short attention spans.

In *The Lonely Crowd*, his classic study of the American self in the 1950s, the sociologist David Riesman distinguished between the inner-directed individual, who derives his identity from an internal moral gyroscope, and the outer-directed individual, who derives his identity from the expectations of the crowd. By measuring individuals in terms of their success on the personality market, the personal branding strategy seems at first to be an apotheosis of outer-directedness. But the personal branding books deny this, emphasising that successfully branded individuals must first look inward, to discover their authentic selves, and then turn outward, attempting to market that self to the world.

30   "Trust is built faster and maintained longer when people believe you are being real, not putting on a false front to cover up what's really going on inside of you," the branding manual counsels. "When it comes to relationships, authenticity is what others say they want most from us. We make the most lasting and vivid impressions when people witness us being true to our beliefs, staying in alignment with who and what we really are."[12] The self constructed by the personal branders, then, is an anxious hybrid of Riesman's two types: a form of marketed authenticity in which the self is turned inside out, and then sold to the world.

Although the phenomenon of personal brand management is in its infancy, it represents the logical application of marketing technologies to the most intimate aspects of the self. But its hazards are already becoming evident; and they have to do with the substitution of image-making for genuine individuality. As early as 1997, the *New York Times* reported that an unhappy bachelor had convened a focus group of the single women who had rejected him. As he watched from behind a one-way mirror, they evaluated his dating performance, and offered advice for improvement. Meeting in the studios of a market research company called Focus Suites, where consumers usually gather to criticise soap or cereal, the women urged him to bolster his confidence and change his wardrobe. "I think it's really alarming that we let a market economy dictate our human relationships," the head of the company told the *New York Times*. "I think it's much more healthy for the human model to dictate to the business world than for the business model to inform human life."[13]

Allowing public opinion to expand into the recesses of the soul, the entrepreneurs of the self insist that personal branding is a spiritual as well as an economic imperative. Nick Shore, the head of a New York advertising agency called the Way Group, is writing a book called _Who Are You: The Search for Your Authentic Self in Business._ Over the phone, Shore told me that his personal "brand DNA" was "a punk rocker in a pinstripe suit—that's how I understand myself." But when I met him at his stylish loft office in the Chelsea Market, he turned out to be a young British man in khakis and a sweater. "The classical distinctions between personal life, professional life, what I do in my family, how I set up my business, how I plan my career" are breaking down, Shore said. "It's this whole postmodern idea of the script to life just basically being thrown away and no one quite knows exactly what they're supposed to do in any given situation. ... If I can't find true worth by looking to the corporation that I work for or by looking to the government or the queen, then ultimately you end up with yourself, you have to find your own truth."

In the 1950s, the organisation man was told to find what the marketplace wants and supply it. But in a talent economy, Shore says, "it's the other way around: find out what you are then go look for the space in the market place that needs that." Successful brands must be authentic because "the marketplace smells a rat," and consumers, in deciding whom to trust, are suspicious of any gaps between the image of the person or product being marked and the underlying reality. "In the old days somebody would look at a business card and say, "oh, this guy's a vice president; I'll put him on a hierarchy." Now they look at your haircut and your shirt and a box of other stuff, and they say, "this is the box this guy fits in." And if what he's doing is not real, if he's only trying to protect an image, they notice."

This leads to the phenomenon of marketed authenticity. "Because consumers are sensitive to inauthenticity, you have to look inside out, not outside in: you have to start from the core and then move outward," Shore said. Only those whose public and private reality are aligned can sustain the attention of the marketplace. Far from trying to capture the authentic self in all of its complexities, however, branding is a technology for the simplification of identity, a response to the short attention spans of the audience. "In marketing terms, it's always been about, strip away, strip away," Shore emphasised. "People are troubled about thinking about more than one thing at once. If you're trying to project something and you try to be penetrative into people's consciousness you have to be absolutely simple and to the point about it all—otherwise people can't hold it." In trying to excavate a person's "brand DNA," Shore says that he is suspicious of long lists of abstract characteristics. "It's too complicated, it's too generic. If I said, you are an "Individualistic Maverick," that can describe all people. But if I tell you that someone's a "Modern-Day Robin Hood," that's pointed. You'll remember "Modern-Day Robin Hood" for 10 years." (A few hours later, when I tried to repeat this slogan to my wife, I had already managed to forget it.)

Although presented in the therapeutic language of self-actualisation, personal 35 branding is ultimately a technology for the rigid control of personal identity. Personal branding claims to help individuals be distinctive, so that they can differentiate themselves from the crowd and become more successful competitors in the marketplace of the self. But in the process of seeking distinctiveness, personal branding is ultimately a recipe for a smothering conformity. Branding confuses distinctiveness and individuality.

Products can be differentiated from each other, with the techniques of advertising and public relations. But the application of branding technologies to the self is based on a category error: individuals can't distinguish themselves from the crowd by measuring their value to the crowd. All of the private attributes of human individuality change shape when they are turned outward and presented to the public: Eros becomes sex; sin becomes crime; guilt becomes shame.

When everything is exposed to the crowd, as John Stuart Mill recognised, individuality is impossible. "As the various social eminences which enabled persons entrenched on them to disregard the opinion of the multitude, gradually become levelled; as the very idea of resisting the will of the public, when it is positively known that they have a will disappears more and more from the minds of practical politicians; there ceases to be any social support for nonconformity," Mill lamented. "It is individuality we war against," he concluded, because of the "ascendancy of public opinion in the State."[14]

We can now appreciate with special force the distinction between the individuality praised by Mill and the individualism lamented by Alexis de Tocqueville, which he defined as the tendency of citizens in a democracy to isolate themselves from each other and to focus obsessively on their own self-interest. Even more than the Victorian era, ours is an age of individualism rather than individuality. The growth of media technologies such as the internet and television have increased the overwhelming authority of public opinion, as citizens in the Omnipticon find more and more aspects of their personal and public lives observed and evaluated by strangers. These technologies tend to encourage citizens to be self-absorbed, as terrifying images from across the country or across the globe give them an exaggerated sense of personal vulnerability.

At the same time, by decreasing the distance between central authorities and individual citizens, these technologies lead people to expect personal protection from national leaders, rather than taking responsibility for their own freedom and security at a local level. The related feelings of personal anxiety and personal helplessness feed on themselves, and the technology now exists to bring about the conformity that Mill most feared.

The Comfort of Strangers?

40   The personal branding movement is based on the same fantasy that underlay the Portraits of Grief, which is the fantasy that people can achieve emotional intimacy with strangers. But there is no such thing as public intimacy. Intimacy can be achieved only with those who know us; and strangers cannot know us; they can only have information about us or impressions of us. To offer up personal information that has been taken out of context, in an effort to create the illusion of emotional connection with strangers, requires us to homogenise and standardise the very qualities that made the information personal in the first place. The family members of the 9/11 victims who offered up details of their mourning to the *New York Times* are not so different from the family members of the victim of a car crash who, moments after the accident, weep on cue for the local news. What is most alarming about these scenes is not the tears but the fact that, even at moments of tragedy, we instinctively look at the camera and talk into the microphone.

The personal branding phenomenon is a crude attempt to provide regulated forms of self-exposure, to maintain some kind of boundary between public and private in a world where self-revelation has become a social imperative. And of course most citizens will never resort to expert assistance in their efforts to present a coherent face to the world. But living in the Omnipticon, where we are increasingly unsure about who is observing us, individuals will have to worry more about acting consistently in public and private, in precisely the way the branding advisors prescribe.

In the 1980s, before the proliferation of the web, the sociologist Joshua Meyrowitz discussed the way the electronic media were changing what he called the "situational geography" of social life.[15] As television made us one large audience to performances that occurred in other places, the old walls that separated backstage areas, where people could let down their hair and rehearse for public performances, from the front-stage areas, where the formal performances occurred, began to collapse. Television made viewers aware of the discrepancy between front- and backstage behaviour (such as the woman who plays hard to get, or the fearful man who acts confident in a reality TV dating show), and it became increasingly hard for people to project different images in public and in private without appearing artificial or inauthentic.

Now that the internet is allowing strangers to observe us even as we observe them, ordinary citizens have to worry more about being caught off guard, like actors with their wigs off. As a form of self-defence, all citizens face the same pressures that confused Laurence Tribe: we will increasingly adopt what Meyrowitz called "middle region" behaviour in public: a blend of the formal frontstage and informal backstage, with a bias toward self-conscious informality. As private concerns like sexual behaviour and depression, anxieties and doubts become harder to conceal, they have to be integrated into the public performance. The result can create an illusion of familiarity—the crazy heavy metal rock star Ozzy Osborne looked cuddlier (though still scatological) as MTV cameras recorded every moment of his domestic life for a reality TV show. But the cuddly domesticated Osborne was far less eccentric, and far less distinctive, than his onstage persona had led audiences to expect.

Like Boorstin, Meyrowitz worried that conformity and homogeneity would result as the electronic media expanded the middle region at the expense of front- and backstage behaviour. In addition to blurring the boundaries between political leaders and followers, Meyrowitz predicted that the electronic technologies of exposure would blur the boundaries between the behaviour of men and women, as well as children and adults. All of these groups speak and act differently when they are segregated from each other; and once the boundaries that separate the groups began to collapse, each of these groups would begin to act more like the others. Now the democratising technology of the internet is fulfilling Meyrowitz's fears: as more personal information about ourselves is available on the web, private figures are feeling the same pressure that public figures have long experienced to expose details of their personal lives as a form of self-defence; and men, women, and children are blurring into a indistinguishable cacophony of intimate exposure.

To the degree that self-revelation to strangers is a bid for relief from anxiety about 45 identity, however, it may not succeed. Social psychologists who have studied the therapeutic effects of emotional disclosure have discovered a consistent pattern: people who receive positive social support for their emotional disclosures tend to feel better as a result, while those who receive negative responses—from indifference to hostility—feel worse.

For example, a nationwide study of psychological responses to 9/11 found that those who sought social support and vented their anxieties without receiving positive reinforcement were more likely to feel greater distress during the six months after the attack than those who engaged in more social coping activities such as giving blood or attending memorial services.[16] This is consistent with studies of Vietnam veterans and survivors of the California firestorms, who actually felt worse after sharing their feelings with strangers who made clear they didn't want to listen. ("Thank you for not sharing your earthquake story," read an especially wounding T-shirt.) Those who shared their pain with unreceptive audiences felt worse than those who didn't talk at all, although not as good as those who shared their pain with a receptive audience.

Studies of the benefits of writing as well as talking about emotional experiences confirm the same insight: emotional disclosure can have therapeutic effects when it helps people to become less isolated and more integrated with social networks, but it can have negative effects when it leads people to vent their feelings in a void, without the support of a receptive audience.[17] This suggests that therapeutic venting on the internet to a faceless audience in an unreciprocated bid for attention and emotional support is unlikely to help, and may well make things worse.

In *The Book of Laughter and Forgetting,* Milan Kundera examines the phenomenon of graphomania—the pathological desire to express yourself in writing before a public of unknown readers. "General isolation breeds graphomania, and generalised graphomania in turn intensifies and worsens isolation," Kundera writes. "Everyone [is] surrounded by his own words as by a wall of mirrors, which allows no voice to filter through from outside." Kundera contrasts the reticence of his heroine, who is mortified by the idea that anyone except for her beloved might read her love letters, with the graphomania of a writer like Johann Wolfgang von Goethe, who is convinced that his worth as a human being will be called into question if a single human being fails to read his words. The difference between the lover and Goethe, he says, "is the difference between a human being and a writer."

In an indifferent and socially atomised universe, "everyone is pained by the thought of disappearing, unheard and unseen" as a result, everyone is tempted to become a writer, turning himself "into a universe of words." But "when everyone wakes up as a writer," Kundera warns, "the age of universal deafness and incomprehension will have arrived."[18] Now, we are living in an age of graphomania; we are experiencing the constant din of intimate typing—in email, in chatrooms, on the web and in the workplace. The clacking noise we hear in the air is the noise of endless personal disclosure. But as Kundera recognised, instead of forging emotional connections with strangers, personal exposure in a vacuum may increase social isolation, rather than alleviate it.

50   Many factors put tremendous pressure on individuals in the Naked Crowd, to expose personal details of their lives and strip themselves bare. The crowd demands exposure out of a combination of voyeurism, desire for emotional connection, fear of strangers, democratic suspicion of reticence as sign of elitism, demand for markers of trustworthiness, and an unwillingness to conceive of public events or to relate to public figures except in personal terms. From the perspective of the individual who is pursuing the attention of the crowd, there is, as Charles Derber has suggested, the hope of gaining a mass audience by self-exposure; the demands of a therapeutic culture, which rewards people who talk about intimate problems in public by casting

them as victims and survivors; the narcissism that leads people obsessively to call attention to their own fears and insecurities about their identity, in a world where identity is always up for grabs; and the expansion of democratic technologies, which create so many new opportunities for individuals to expose themselves before the crowd.[19] Above all, there is the desire to establish oneself as trustworthy in a risk society by proving—through exposure—that we have nothing to hide.

All this suggests little cause for optimism that, in the face of future terrorist threats, the crowd will strike the balance between personal security and personal exposure in a reasonable way. Individuals, as we've seen, don't care much about privacy in the aggregate at all: faced with a choice between privacy and exposure, many people would rather be exposed than be private, because the crowd demands no less. Concerned mainly about controlling the conditions of their own exposure, many people are only too happy to reveal themselves promiscuously if they have the illusion of control.

Anxious exhibitionists, trained from the cradle to believe that there is no more valuable currency than personal exposure, are not likely to object when their neighbors demand that they strip themselves bare. But just as public intimacy is a kind of delusion, so is the hope of distinguishing ourselves from the crowd by catering to the crowd's insatiable demands for exposure. It is impossible to achieve genuine distinction without a certain heedlessness of public opinion. We can turn ourselves into Portraits of Grief only at the cost of looking more like each other. As both spectators and actors in the Naked Crowd, we are too willing to surrender privacy for an illusory sense of emotional connection and security. Perhaps we will realise what a poor bargain we have struck only after it is too late.

Notes

[1] "Closing a Scrapbook Full of Life and Sorrow," Janny Scott, *New York Times*, 31 December 2001

[2] "The Mourning Paper," Thomas Mallon, *The American Scholar*, Spring 2002, p 6–7

[3] *Conversations with Anthony Giddens: Making Sense of Modernity*, Anthony Giddens and Christopher Pierson, Stanford University Press, 1998, p 101

[4] *The Sane Society*, Erich Fromm, Reinhart, 1955, p141–42

[5] *The Pursuit of Attention: Power and Ego in Everyday Life*, Charles Derber, Oxford University Press, 2000, p 81

[6] See "Online Diary: Blog Nation," *New York Times*, 22 August 2002

[7] See the Diarist.net website

[8] *Sincerity and Authenticity*, Lionel Trilling, Harvard University Press, 1972

[9] *The Homeless Mind: Modernisation and Consciousness*, Peter L Berger, Brigitte Berger and Hansfried Kellner, Random House, 1973, p 90

[10] *The Fall of Public Man*, Richard Sennett, WW Norton & Co, 1974, p 196, 265

[11] *The Image: A Guide to Pseudo-Events in America*, Daniel J. Boorstin, Atheneum, 1977, p 57–58

[12] *Be Your Own Brand: A Breakthrough Formula for Standing Out from the Crowd*, David McNally and Karl D Speak, Berrett-Koehler, 2002, p 4, 7, 11, 13, 47

[13] "Hold Me! Squeeze Me! Buy a Six-Pack!," Alex Kuczynski, *New York Times*, 16 November 1997

[14] *On Liberty*, in *On Liberty and Other Essays*, John Stuart Mill, Oxford University Press, 1998, p 82, 79

[15] *No Sense of Place: The Impact of Electronic Media on Social Behaviour*, Joshua Meyrowitz, Oxford University Press, 1985, p 6

[16] "Nationwide Longitudinal Study of Psychological Responses to September 11," Roxane Cohen Silver, E Alison Holman, Daniel N McIntosh, Michael Poulin, and Virginia Gil-Rivas, 288 *Journal of the American Medical Association* 1235, p 1241–1242, 2002

[17] "Patterns of Natural Language Use: Disclosure, Personality, and Social Integration," JW Pennebaker and A Graybeal, 10 *Current Directions In Psychological Science* 92, 2001

[18] *The Book of Laughter and Forgetting*, Milan Kundera, Perennial Classics, 1999, p 127–28, 146, 147

[19] *The Pursuit of Attention: Power and Ego in Everyday Life*, Charles Derber, Oxford University Press, 2000, p xv–xviii

Things to Do with the Reading

1. Binaries are usually a sign of what is at stake in a piece of writing. They are also the place where key terms and often subtle distinctions among them tend to congregate. Consider the distinction that Rosen makes between "the individuality praised by Mill and the individualism lamented by Alexis de Tocqueville." Define the difference, and then track the ways that the concept of individuality is used in the piece. What other key terms get aligned with it? And what are the various terms that are opposed to it? Make two lists.

2. Make a list of other significant binaries in the piece and write about the one that you think is most interesting or revealing. You might consider, for example, sincerity versus authenticity or "heroes of old" versus modern celebrities.

3. It is often productive to think about a piece of writing in terms of its hopes and its fears. In this piece, the fears are fairly clear. For example, the essay ends with a warning. Why does Rosen think that we have struck "a poor bargain" in exchanging "privacy" for "an illusory sense of emotional connection"? To answer this question is to get at what this piece is worried about. Less immediately accessible are its hopes. What are its hopes? Is there a better bargain Rosen would have us strike?

4. Consider *to what extent* Jeffrey Rosen and Christina Rosen might agree on the place of private experience in public life. Imagine the conversation they might have on locating the line between public and private. What would be the primary thing they'd agree on? If it's fair to say that Jeffrey Rosen is concerned with the loss of what he calls "genuine individuality," what is Christina Rosen's primary concern?

5. **Application—Using the Reading as a Lens:** Look at either the self-representation of a current politician (national or local) or a modern hero. In light of Rosen's claims (taken from Boorstin in paragraph 23), what do you notice?

Geoffrey Nunberg

Blogging in the Global Lunchroom

Geoffrey Nunberg is the emeritus chair of the usage panel of the *American Heritage Dictionary*. He is also a professor of linguistics and author of a number of books and articles on the nature of contemporary language practices, as well as a contributor to the National Public Radio show "Fresh Air," where this piece originally appeared in 2004. Nunberg is interested in the stylistic differences between journalistic writing as it appears in newspapers and magazines and the internet world of commentary known as the blogosphere.

Over the last couple of months, I've been posting on a group blog called languagelog.org, 1
which was launched by a couple of linguists as a place where we could vent our comments on the passing linguistic scene.

Still, I don't quite have the hang of the form. The style that sounds perfectly normal in a public radio feature or an op-ed piece comes off as distant and pontifical when I use it in a blog entry. Reading over my own postings, I recall what Queen Victoria once said about Gladstone: "He speaks to me as if I were a public meeting."

I'm not the only one with this problem. A lot of newspapers have been encouraging or even requiring their writers to start blogs. But with some notable exceptions, most journalists have the same problems that I do. They do all the things you should do in a newspaper feature. They fashion engaging leads, they develop their arguments methodically, they give context and background, and tack helpful ID's onto the names they introduce—"New York Senator Charles E. Schumer (D)."

That makes for solid journalism, but it's not really blogging. Granted, that word can cover a lot of territory. A recent Pew Foundation study found that around three million Americans have tried their hands at blogging, and sometimes there seem to be almost that many variants of the form. Blogs can be news summaries, opinion columns, or collections of press releases, like the official blogs of the presidential candidates. But the vast majority are journals posted by college students, office workers, or stay-at-home moms, whose average readership is smaller than a family Christmas letter. (The blog hosting site livejournal.com reports that two-thirds of bloggers are women—I'm not sure what to make of that proportion.)

But when people puzzle over the significance of blogs nowadays, they usually 5
have in mind a small number of A-List sites that traffic in commentary about politics, culture, or technology—blogs like Altercation, Instapundit, Matthew Yglesias, Talking Points, or Doc Searls. It's true that bloggers like these have occasionally come up with news scoops, but in the end they're less about breaking stories than bending them. And their language is a kind of anti-journalese. It's informal, impertinent, and digressive, casting links in all directions. In fact one archetypal blog entry consists entirely of a cryptic comment that's linked to another blog or a news item—"Oh, please," or "He's married to her?"

Blogging in the Global Lunchroom, Geoffrey Nunberg, Center for the Study of Language and Information. Reprinted with permission of the author.

That interconnectedness is what leads enthusiasts to talk about the blogosphere, as if this were all a single vast conversation—at some point in these discussions, somebody's likely to trot out the phrase "collective mind." But if there's a new public sphere assembling itself out there, you couldn't tell from the way bloggers address their readers—not as anonymous citizens, the way print columnists do, but as co-conspirators who are in on the joke.

Taken as a whole, in fact, the blogging world sounds a lot less like a public meeting than the lunchtime chatter in a high-school cafeteria, complete with snarky comments about the kids at the tables across the room. (Bloggers didn't invent the word snarky, but they've had a lot to do with turning it into the metrosexual equivalent of bitchy. On the Web, blogs account for more than three times as large a share of the total occurrences of snarky as of the occurrences of irony.)[1]

Some people say this all started with Mickey Kaus's column in *Slate,* though Kaus himself cites the old *San Francisco Chronicle* columns of Herb Caen. And Camille Paglia not surprisingly claims that her column in *Salon.com* was the first true blog, and adds that the genre has been going downhill ever since.

But blogs were around on the web well before Kaus or Paglia first logged in.[2] And if you're of a mind to, you can trace their print antecedents a lot further back than Caen or Hunter S. Thompson. That informal style recalls the colloquial voice that Addison and Steele devised when they invented the periodical essay in the early 18th century, even if few blogs come close to that in artfulness. Then too, those essays were written in the guise of fictive personae like Isaac Bickerstaff and Sir Roger de Coverly, who could be the predecessors of pseudonymous bloggers like Wonkette, Atrios, or Skippy the Bush Kangaroo, not to mention the mysterious conservative blogger who goes by the name of Edward Boyd.[3]

10   For that matter, my languagelog co-contributor Mark Liberman recalls that Plato always had Socrates open his philosophical disquisitions with a little diary entry, the way bloggers like to do: "I went down yesterday to see the festival at the Peiraeus with Glaucon, the son of Ariston, and I ran into my old buddy Cephalus and we got to talking about old age..."

Of course whenever a successful new genre emerges, it seems to have been implicit in everything that preceded it. But in the end, this is a mug's game, like asking whether the first SUV was a minivan, a station wagon, or an off-road vehicle.

The fact is that this is a genuinely new language of public discourse—and a paradoxical one. On the one hand, blogs are clearly a more democratic form of expression than anything the world of print has produced. But in some ways they're also more exclusionary, and not just because they only reach about a tenth of the people who use the web.[4] The high, formal style of the newspaper op-ed page may be nobody's native language, but at least it's a neutral voice that doesn't privilege the speech of any particular group or class. Whereas blogspeak is basically an adaptation of the table talk of the urban middle class—it isn't a language that everybody in the cafeteria is equally adept at speaking. Not that there's anything wrong with chewing over the events of the day with the other folks at the lunch table, but you hope that everybody in the room is at least reading the same newspapers at breakfast.[5]

Notes

[1] This is a rough estimate, arrived at by taking the proportion of total Google hits for a word that occurs in a document that also contains the word blog:

snarky: 87,700
snarky + blog: 32,600 (37%)
irony: 1,600,000
irony + blog: 168,000 (10.5%)

Of course, the fact that the word blog appears in a page doesn't necessarily mean that it is a blog, but it turns out that more than 90 percent of the pages containing the word are blog pages, and in any case, the effect would be the same for both terms. And while some part of this variation no doubt reflects the status of snarky as a colloquial word that is less likely to show up in serious literary discussions and the like, the effect is nowhere near so marked when we look at the word bitchy:

bitchy: 250,000
bitchy + blog: 43,700 (17.5%)

That is, the specialization to blogs is more than twice as high for snarky as for bitchy, even though both are colloquial items.

[2] Many have given credit for inventing the genre to Dave Winer, whose Scripting News was one of the earliest weblogs, though Winer himself says that the first weblog was Tim Berners-Lee's page at CERN. But you could argue that blog has moved out from under the derivational shadow of its etymon—the word isn't just a truncation of weblog anymore. In which case, the identity of the first "real blog" is anybody's guess—and it almost certainly will be.

[3] James Wolcott makes a similar comparison in the current *Vanity Fair*, and goes so far as to suggest that "If Addison and Steele, the editors of *The Spectator* and *The Tatler*, were alive and holding court at Starbucks, they'd be WiFi-ing into a joint blog." That's cute, but I think it gets Addison and Steele wrong—the studied effusions of Isaac Bickertaff and Sir Roger de Coverly may have sounded like blogs, but they were fashioned with an eye toward a more enduring literary fame. Which is not to say that blogs couldn't become the basis for a genuine literary form. As I noted in a "Fresh Air" piece a few years ago that dealt more with blogs as personal journals:

> There's something very familiar about that accretion of diurnal detail. It's what the novel was trying to achieve when eighteenth-century writers cobbled it together out of subliterary genres like personal letters, journals, and newspapers, with the idea of reproducing the inner and outer experience that makes up daily life. You wonder whether anything as interesting could grow up in the intimate anonymity of cyberspace. (See "I Have Seen the Future, and It Blogs," in Going Nucular, *PublicAffairs*, May, 2004.)

So it's not surprising that a number of fictional blogs ("flogs"? "blictions"?) have begun to emerge, adapting the tradition of the fictional diary that runs from *Robinson Crusoe* to *Bridget Jones' Diary*. As to whether that will ultimately amount to "anything as interesting" as the novel, the jury is likely to be out for a while.

[4] The Pew study found that 11 percent of Internet users have read the blogs or diaries of other Internet users.

[5] For a diverting picture of the blogosphere-as-lunchroom, see Whitney Pastorek's recent piece in the *Village Voice*, "Blogging Off."

Things to Do with the Reading

1. Given that this is a short radio piece, Nunberg doesn't have the time to develop the implications of his observations at much length. So, this piece would be useful for practicing skills described in Chapter 13, especially ways to use a source as a point of departure.

   First, determine what Nunberg's primary claims are in this piece. Locate sentences that you think best capture his main ideas about blogs. (One of these has to do with his analogy between blogs and high school lunchrooms, about which he says, "blogspeak is basically an adaptation of the table talk of the urban middle class: it isn't a language that everybody in the cafeteria is equally adept at speaking.")

   Then go after assumptions and implications. What are some of the implications of the thinking that Nunberg lays out in his final paragraph? And what assumption underlies his final sentence?

2. Put Nunberg's piece into conversation with one or more of the other essays in this unit using the strategy called "similarity within difference" (Chapter 4). Goldberger's piece "Disconnected Urbanism" might be a good choice, and like Nunberg's essay, it's short. First, develop the difference. Then, look past the difference to locate a point of contact, or similarity. Or, if you think the similarity between the two is more obvious than the difference, start with the similarity and then look past the similarity to what you take to be a significant difference.

3. **Application:** Clearly, this piece could launch a more extended project in which you follow-up some of Nunberg's leads and look for trends in blogspeak. With the definition of style from Chapter 18 in mind, you might explore to what extent there is a discernible blog style. You might check out the range of blogs listed on aldaily.com, or alternatively, those listed on Nunberg's own website, http://www-csli.stanford.edu/~nunberg/.

Jonathan Franzen

Imperial Bedroom

Jonathan Franzen is the author of four novels, including the recent *Freedom* (2010), as well as *The Corrections*, which won the National Book Award in 2001. In this essay, taken from his collection *How to Be Alone* (2002), Franzen meditates on the invasion of public space by the private and mourns the eroding of the distinction between the two. He is a gifted stylist and an agile thinker, full of surprising reversals. For example: "The real reason that Americans are apathetic about privacy is so big as to be almost invisible: we're flat-out *drowning* in privacy. What's threatened isn't the private sphere. It's the public sphere."

Privacy, privacy, the new American obsession: espoused as the most fundamental of   1 rights, marketed as the most desirable of commodities, and pronounced dead twice a week.

Even before Linda Tripp pressed the "Record" button on her answering machine, commentators were warning us that "privacy is under siege," that "privacy is in a dreadful state," that "privacy as we now know it may not exist in the year 2000." They say that both Big Brother and his little brother, John Q. Public, are shadowing me through networks of computers. They tell me that security cameras no bigger than spiders are watching from every shaded corner, that dour feminists are monitoring bedroom behavior and water-cooler conversations, that genetic sleuths can decoct my entire being from a droplet of saliva, that voyeurs can retrofit ordinary camcorders with a filter that lets them *see through people's clothing*. Then comes the flood of dirty suds from the Office of the Independent Counsel, oozing forth through official and commercial channels to saturate the national consciousness. The Monica Lewinsky scandal marks, in the words of the philosopher Thomas Nagel, "the culmination of a disastrous erosion" of privacy; it represents, in the words of the author Wendy Kaminer, "the utter disregard for privacy and individual autonomy that exists in totalitarian regimes." In the person of Kenneth Starr, the "public sphere" has finally overwhelmed—shredded, gored, trampled, invaded, run roughshod over—"the private."

The panic about privacy has all the finger-pointing and paranoia of a good old American scare, but it's missing one vital ingredient: a genuinely alarmed public. Americans care about privacy mainly in the abstract. Sometimes a well-informed community unites to defend itself, as when Net users bombarded the White House with e-mails against the "clipper chip," and sometimes an especially outrageous piece of news provokes a national outcry, as when the Lotus Development Corporation tried to market a CD-ROM containing financial profiles of nearly half the people in the country. By and large, though, even in the face of wholesale infringements like the war on drugs, Americans remain curiously passive. I'm no exception. I read the editorials and try to get excited, but I can't. More often than not, I find myself feeling the opposite of what the privacy mavens want me to. It's happened twice in the last month alone.

On the Saturday morning when the *Times* came carrying the complete text of the Starr report, what I felt as I sat alone in my apartment and tried to eat my breakfast

"Imperial Bedroom" from HOW TO BE ALONE by Jonathan Franzen. Copyright © 2003 by Jonathan Franzen. Reprinted by permission of Farrar, Straus and Giroux, LLC.

was that my own privacy—not Clinton's, not Lewinsky's—was being violated. I love the distant pageant of public life. I love both the pageantry and the distance. Now a President was facing impeachment, and as a good citizen I had a duty to stay informed about the evidence, but the evidence here consisted of two people's groping, sucking, and mutual self-deception. What I felt, when this evidence landed beside my toast and coffee, wasn't a pretend revulsion to camouflage a secret interest in the dirt; I wasn't offended by the sex qua sex; I wasn't worrying about a potential future erosion of my own rights; I didn't feel the President's pain in the empathic way he'd once claimed to feel mine; I wasn't repelled by the revelation that public officials do bad things; and, although I'm a registered Democrat, my disgust was of a different order from my partisan disgust at the news that the Giants have blown a fourth-quarter lead. What I felt I felt personally. I was being intruded on.

5   A couple of days later, I got a call from one of my credit-card providers, asking me to confirm two recent charges at a gas station and one at a hardware store. Queries like this are common nowadays, but this one was my first, and for a moment I felt eerily exposed. At the same time, I was perversely flattered that someone, somewhere, had taken an interest in me and had bothered to phone. Not that the young male operator seemed to care about me personally. He sounded like he was reading his lines from a laminated booklet. The strain of working hard at a job he almost certainly didn't enjoy seemed to thicken his tongue. He tried to rush his words out, to speed through them as if in embarrassment or vexation at how nearly worthless they were, but they kept bunching up in his teeth, and he had to stop and extract them with his lips, one by one. It was the computer, he said, the computer that routinely, ah, scans the, you know, the pattern of charges ... and was there something else he could help me with tonight? I decided that if this young person wanted to scroll through my charges and ponder the significance of my two fill-ups and my gallon of latex paint, I was fine with it.

So here's the problem. On the Saturday morning the Starr Report came out, my privacy was, in the classic liberal view, absolute. I was alone in my home and unobserved, unbothered by neighbors, unmentioned in the news, and perfectly free, if I chose, to ignore the report and do the pleasantly *al dente* Saturday crossword; yet the report's mere existence so offended my sense of privacy that I could hardly bring myself to touch the thing. Two days later, I was disturbed in my home by a ringing phone, asked to cough up my mother's maiden name, and made aware that the digitized minutiae of my daily life were being scrutinized by strangers; and within five minutes I'd put the entire episode out of my mind. I felt encroached on when I was ostensibly safe, and I felt safe when I was ostensibly encroached on. And I didn't know why.

THE RIGHT to privacy—defined by Louis Brandeis and Samuel Warren, in 1890, as "the right to be let alone"—seems at first glance to be an elemental principle in American life. It's the rallying cry of activists fighting for reproductive rights, against stalkers, for the right to die, against a national health-care database, for stronger data-encryption standards, against paparazzi, for the sanctity of employee e-mail, and against employee drug testing. On closer examination, though, privacy proves to be the Cheshire cat of values: not much substance, but a very winning smile.

Legally, the concept is a mess. Privacy violation is the emotional core of many crimes, from stalking and rape to Peeping Tommery and trespass, but no criminal statute forbids it in the abstract. Civil law varies from state to state but generally follows a forty-year-old analysis by the legal scholar Dean William Prosser, who dissected the invasion of privacy into four torts: *intrusion* on my solitude, the publishing of *private facts* about me which are not of legitimate public concern, publicity that puts my character in a *false light,* and *appropriation* of my name or likeness without my consent. This is a crumbly set of torts. Intrusion looks a lot like criminal trespass, false light like defamation, and appropriation like theft; and the harm that remains when these extraneous offenses are subtracted is so admirably captured by the phrase "infliction of emotional distress" as to render the tort of privacy invasion all but superfluous. What really undergirds privacy is the classical liberal conception of personal autonomy or liberty. In the last few decades, many judges and scholars have chosen to speak of a "zone of privacy," rather than a "sphere of liberty," but this is a shift in emphasis, not in substance: not the making of a new doctrine but the repackaging and remarketing of an old one.

Whatever you're trying to sell, whether it's luxury real estate or Esperanto lessons, it helps to have the smiling word "private" on your side. Last winter, as the owner of a Bank One Platinum Visa Card, I was offered enrollment in a program called PrivacyGuard®, which, according to the literature promoting it, *"puts you in the know* about the very personal records available to your employer, insurers, credit card companies, and government agencies." The first three months of PrivacyGuard® were free, so I signed up. What came in the mail then was paperwork: envelopes and request forms for a Credit Record Search and other searches, also a disappointingly undeluxe logbook in which to jot down the search results. I realized immediately that I didn't care enough about, say, my driving records to wait a month to get them; it was only when I called PrivacyGuard® to cancel my membership, and was all but begged not to, that I realized that the whole point of this "service" was to harness my time and energy to the task of reducing Bank One Visa's fraud losses.

Even issues that legitimately touch on privacy are rarely concerned with the actual   10 emotional harm of unwanted exposure or intrusion. A proposed national Genetic Privacy Act, for example, is premised on the idea that my DNA reveals more about my identity and future health than other medical data do. In fact, DNA is as yet no more intimately revealing than a heart murmur, a family history of diabetes, or an inordinate fondness for Buffalo chicken wings. As with any medical records, the potential for abuse of genetic information by employers and insurers is chilling, but this is only tangentially a privacy issue; the primary harm consists of things like job discrimination and higher insurance premiums.

In a similar way, the problem of online security is mainly about nuts and bolts. What American activists call "electronic privacy" their European counterparts call "data protection." Our term is exciting; theirs is accurate. If someone is out to steal your Amex number and expiration date, or if an evil ex-boyfriend is looking for your new address, you need the kind of hard-core secrecy that encryption seeks to guarantee. If you're talking to a friend on the phone, however, you need only a *feeling* of privacy.

The social drama of data protection goes something like this: a hacker or an insurance company or a telemarketer gains access to a sensitive database, public-interest watchdogs bark loudly, and new firewalls go up. Just as most people are moderately afraid of germs but leave virology to the Centers for Disease Control, most Americans take a reasonable interest in privacy issues but leave the serious custodial work to experts. Our problem now is that the custodians have started speaking a language of panic and treating privacy not as one of many competing values but as the one value that trumps all others.

The novelist Richard Powers recently declared in a *Times* op-ed piece that privacy is a "vanishing illusion" and that the struggle over the encryption of digital communications is therefore as "great with consequence" as the Cold War. Powers defines "the private" as "that part of life that goes unregistered," and he sees in the digital footprints we leave whenever we charge things the approach of "that moment when each person's every living day will become a Bloomsday, recorded in complete detail and reproducible with a few deft keystrokes." It is scary, of course, to think that the mystery of our identities might be reducible to finite data sequences. That Powers can seriously compare credit-card fraud and intercepted cell-phone calls to thermonuclear incineration, however, speaks mainly to the infectiousness of privacy panic. Where, after all, is it "registered" what Powers or anybody else is thinking, seeing, saying, wishing, planning, dreaming, and feeling ashamed of? A digital *Ulysses* consisting of nothing but a list of its hero's purchases and other recordable transactions might run, at most, to four pages: was there really nothing more to Bloom's day?

When Americans do genuinely sacrifice privacy, moreover, they do so for tangible gains in health or safety or efficiency. Most legalized infringements—HIV notification, airport X-rays, Megan's Law, Breathalyzer roadblocks, the drug-testing of student athletes, laws protecting fetuses, laws protecting the vegetative, remote monitoring of automobile emissions, county-jail strip searches, even Ken Starr's exposure of presidential corruption—are essentially public health measures. I resent the security cameras in Washington Square, but I appreciate the ones on a subway platform. The risk that someone is abusing my E-ZPass toll records seems to me comfortably low in comparison with my gain in convenience. Ditto the risk that some gossip rag will make me a victim of the First Amendment; with two hundred and seventy million people in the country, any individual's chances of being nationally exposed are next to nil.

15   The legal scholar Lawrence Lessig has characterized Americans as "bovine" for making calculations like this and for thereby acquiescing in what he calls the "Sovietization" of personal life. The curious thing about privacy, though, is that simply by expecting it we can usually achieve it. One of my neighbors in the apartment building across the street spends a lot of time at her mirror examining her pores, and I can see her doing it, just as she can undoubtedly see me sometimes. But our respective privacies remain intact as long as neither of us *feels* seen. When I send a postcard through the U.S. mail, I'm aware in the abstract that mail handlers may be reading it, may be reading it aloud, may even be laughing at it, but I'm safe from all harm unless, by sheer bad luck, the one handler in the country whom I actually know sees the postcard and slaps his forehead and says, "Oh, jeez, I know this guy."

OUR PRIVACY panic isn't merely exaggerated. It's founded on a fallacy. Ellen Alderman and Caroline Kennedy, in *The Right to Privacy,* sum up the conventional wisdom of privacy advocates like this: "There is less privacy than there used to be."

The claim has been made or implied so often, in so many books and editorials and talk-show dens, that Americans, no matter how passive they are in their behavior, now dutifully tell pollsters that they're very much worried about privacy. From almost any historical perspective, however, the claim seems bizarre.

In 1890, an American typically lived in a small town under conditions of near-panoptical surveillance. Not only did his every purchase "register," but it registered in the eyes and the memory of shopkeepers who knew him, his parents, his wife, and his children. He couldn't so much as walk to the post office without having his movements tracked and analyzed by neighbors. Probably he grew up sleeping in the same bed with his siblings and possibly with his parents, too. Unless he was well off, his transportation—a train, a horse, his own two feet—either was communal or exposed him to the public eye.

In the suburbs and exurbs where the typical American lives today, tiny nuclear families inhabit enormous houses, in which each person has his or her own bedroom and, sometimes, bathroom. Compared even with suburbs in the sixties and seventies, when I was growing up, the contemporary condominium development or gated community offers a striking degree of anonymity. It's no longer the rule that you know your neighbors. Communities increasingly tend to be virtual, the participants either faceless or firmly in control of the face they present. Transportation is largely private: the latest SUVs are the size of living rooms and come with onboard telephones, CD players, and TV screens; behind the tinted windows of one of these high-riding I-see-you-but-you-can't-see-me mobile PrivacyGuard® units, a person can be wearing pajamas or a licorice bikini, for all anybody knows or cares. Maybe the government intrudes on the family a little more than it did a hundred years ago (social workers look in on the old and the poor, health officials require inoculations, the police inquire about spousal battery), but these intrusions don't begin to make up for the small-town snooping they've replaced.

The "right to be left alone"? Far from disappearing, it's exploding. It's the *essence* of modern American architecture, landscape, transportation, communication, and mainstream political philosophy. The real reason that Americans are apathetic about privacy is so big as to be almost invisible: we're flat-out *drowning* in privacy.

What's threatened, then, isn't the private sphere. It's the public sphere. Much has been made of the discouraging effect that the Starr investigation may have on future aspirants to public office (only zealots and zeros need apply), but that's just half of it. The public world of Washington, because it's public, belongs to everyone. We're all invited to participate with our votes, our patriotism, our campaigning, and our opinions. The collective weight of a population makes possible our faith in the public world as something larger and more enduring and more dignified than any messy individual can be in private. But, just as one sniper in a church tower can keep the streets of an entire town empty, one real gross-out scandal can undermine that faith.

If privacy depends upon an expectation of invisibility, the expectation of *visibility* is what defines a public space. My "sense of privacy" functions to keep the public out of the private *and* to keep the private out of the public. A kind of mental Border collie yelps in distress when I feel that the line between the two has been breached. This is why the violation of a public space is so similar, as an experience, to the violation of privacy. I walk past a man taking a leak on a sidewalk in broad daylight (delivery-truck drivers can be especially self-righteous in their "Ya gotta go, ya gotta go" philosophy of bladder management), and although the man with the yawning fly is ostensibly the one whose privacy is compromised by the leak, I'm the one who feels the impingement. Flashers and sexual harassers and fellators on the pier and self-explainers on the crosstown bus all similarly assault our sense of the "public" by exposing themselves.

Since really serious exposure in public today is assumed to be synonymous with being seen on television, it would seem to follow that televised space is the premier public space. Many things that people say to me on television, however, would never be tolerated in a genuine public space—in a jury box, for example, or even on a city sidewalk. TV is an enormous, ramified extension of the billion living rooms and bedrooms in which it's consumed. You rarely hear a person on the subway talking loudly about, say, incontinence, but on television it's been happening for years. TV is devoid of shame, and without shame there can be no distinction between public and private. Last winter, an anchorwoman looked me in the eye and, in the tone of a close female relative, referred to a litter of babies in Iowa as "America's seven little darlin's." It was strange enough, twenty-five years ago, to get Dan Rather's reports on Watergate between spots for Geritol and Bayer aspirin, as if Nixon's impending resignation were somehow located in my medicine chest. Now, shelved between ads for Promise margarine and Celebrity Cruises, the news itself is a soiled cocktail dress—TV the bedroom floor and nothing but.

Reticence, meanwhile, has become an obsolete virtue. People now readily name their diseases, rents, antidepressants. Sexual histories get spilled on first dates, Birkenstocks and cutoffs infiltrate the office on casual Fridays, telecommuting puts the boardroom in the bedroom, "softer" modern office design puts the bedroom in the boardroom, sales-people unilaterally address customers by their first name, waiters won't bring me food until I've established a personal relationship with them, voice-mail machinery stresses the "I" in "*I'm* sorry, but *I* don't understand what you dialed," and cyberenthusiasts, in a particularly grotesque misnomer, designate as "public forums" pieces of etched silicon with which a forum's unshaved "participant" may communicate while sitting crosslegged in tangled sheets. The networked world as a threat to privacy? It's the ugly spectacle of a privacy triumphant.

A genuine public space is a place where every citizen is welcome to be present and where the purely private is excluded or restricted. One reason that attendance at art museums has soared in recent years is that museums still feel public in this way. After those tangled sheets, how delicious the enforced decorum and the hush, the absence of in-your-face consumerism. How sweet the promenading, the seeing and being seen. Everybody needs a promenade sometimes—a place to go when you want to announce to the world (not the little world of friends and family but the big world, the real world) that you have a new suit, or that you're in love, or that you suddenly realize you stand a full inch taller when you don't hunch your shoulders.

25   Unfortunately, the fully public place is a nearly extinct category. We still have courtrooms and the jury pool, commuter trains and bus stations, here and there a small-town Main Street that really is a main street rather than a strip mall, certain coffee bars, and certain city sidewalks. Otherwise, for American adults, the only halfway

public space is the world of work. Here, especially in the upper echelons of business, codes of dress and behavior are routinely enforced, personal disclosures are penalized, and formality is still the rule. But these rituals extend only to the employees of the firm, and even they, when they become old, disabled, obsolete, or outsourceable, are liable to be expelled and thereby relegated to the tangled sheets.

The last big, steep-walled bastion of public life in America is Washington, D.C. Hence the particular violation I felt when the Starr Report crashed in. Hence the feeling of being intruded on. It was privacy invasion, all right: private life brutally invading the most public of public spaces. I don't want to see sex on the news from Washington. There's sex everywhere else I look—on sitcoms, on the Web, on dust jackets, in car ads, on the billboards at Times Square. Can't there be one thing in the national landscape that isn't about the bedroom? We all know there's sex in the cloakrooms of power, sex behind the pomp and circumstance, sex beneath the robes of justice; but can't we act like grownups and pretend otherwise? Pretend not that "no one is looking" but that *everyone* is looking?

For two decades now, business leaders and politicians across much of the political spectrum, both Gingrich Republicans and Clinton Democrats, have extolled the virtues of privatizing public institutions. But what better word can there be for Lewinskygate and the ensuing irruption of disclosures (the infidelities of Helen Chenoweth, of Dan Burton, of Henry Hyde) than "privatization"? Anyone who wondered what a privatized presidency might look like may now, courtesy of Mr. Starr, behold one.

IN DENIS JOHNSON'S SHORT STORY "Beverly Home," the young narrator spends his days working at a nursing home for the hopelessly disabled, where there is a particularly unfortunate patient whom no one visits:

> A perpetual spasm forced him to perch sideways on his wheelchair and peer down along his nose at his knotted fingers. This condition had descended on him suddenly. He got no visitors. His wife was divorcing him. He was only thirty-three, I believe he said, but it was hard to guess what he told about himself because he really couldn't talk anymore, beyond clamping his lips repeatedly around his protruding tongue while groaning.
>
> No more pretending for him! He was completely and openly a mess. Meanwhile the rest of us go on trying to fool each other.

In a coast-to-coast, shag-carpeted imperial bedroom, we could all just be messes and save ourselves the trouble of pretending. But who wants to live in a pajama-party world? Privacy loses its value unless there's something it can be defined against. "Meanwhile the rest of us go on trying to fool each other"—and a good thing, too. The need to put on a public face is as basic as the need for the privacy in which to take it off. We need both a home that's not like a public space and a public space that's not like home.

Walking up Third Avenue on a Saturday night, I feel bereft. All around me, attrac- 30 tive young people are hunched over their StarTacs and Nokias with preoccupied expressions, as if probing a sore tooth, or adjusting a hearing aid, or squeezing a pulled muscle; personal technology has begun to look like a personal handicap. All I really want from a sidewalk is that people see me and let themselves be seen, but even this modest ideal is thwarted by cell-phone users and their unwelcome privacy. They say things like "Should we have couscous with that?" and "I'm on my way to Blockbuster." They aren't breaking any law by broadcasting these breakfast-nook conversations. There's no PublicityGuard that I can buy, no expensive preserve of public life to which I can flee. Seclusion, whether in a suite at the Plaza or in a cabin in the Catskills, is comparatively effortless to achieve. Privacy is protected as both commodity and right; public forums are protected as neither. Like old-growth forests, they're few and irreplaceable and should be held in trust by everyone. The work of maintaining them gets only harder as the private sector grows ever more demanding, distracting, and disheartening. Who has the time and energy to stand up for the public sphere? What rhetoric can possibly compete with the American love of "privacy"?

When I return to my apartment after dark, I don't immediately turn my lights on. Over the years, it's become a reflexive precaution on my part not to risk spooking exposed neighbors by flooding my living room with light, although the only activity I ever seem to catch them at is watching TV.

My skin-conscious neighbor is home with her husband tonight, and they seem to be dressing for a party. The woman, a vertical strip of whom is visible between the Levelors and the window frame, is wearing a bathrobe and a barrette and sitting in front of a mirror. The man, slick-haired, wearing suit pants and a white T-shirt, stands by the sofa in the other room and watches television in a posture that I recognize as uncommitted. Finally the woman disappears into the bedroom. The man puts on a white shirt and a necktie and perches sidesaddle on the arm of the sofa, still watching television, more involved with it now. The woman returns wearing a strapless yellow dress and looking like a whole different species of being. Happy the transformation! Happy the distance between private and public! I see a rapid back-and-forth involving jewelry, jackets, and a clutch purse, and then the couple, dressed to the nines, ventures out into the world.

[1998]

Things to Do with the Reading

1. Much of the effect of Franzen's piece has to do with its style, and one element of the style is the repetition of certain metaphors. These metaphors are themselves complex nodes of meaning—usually an image that has been introduced and laden with feeling and point of view. In music and in some literary study as well, the use of a repeated image that accumulates meaning as it recurs is known as a *leitmotif*. There are numerous examples of this technique in the essay, but two prominent ones are "tangled sheets" and the "skin-conscious neighbor." Take notes on where and how any of these repeated terms are used in the essay.

2. The sinuous turns of thought in Franzen's essay—which is clearly inductive and does not start with a thesis—make it a rich candidate for analyzing how the thesis evolves in a piece of writing. Familiarize yourself with the discussion of the evolving thesis in Chapter 11 and then do Try This 11.3, Tracking a Thesis, with Franzen's essay. List all of the different versions of his primary claims to arrive at a chart of how the thinking in the piece moves.

3. A primary point made in *Writing Analytically* about conclusions is to culminate, not simply summarize (see Chapter 16). Study the way that Franzen culminates his essay. What do you notice about his final paragraph? How does it proceed? What key terms from the essay does it include? How does it provide judgment, culmination, and send-off?

4. Think about the connection between Franzen's favored sentence shapes and his way of thinking. (See Chapter 2 on "Go To" sentences.) A striking and thus emphatic "go to" sentence shape of Franzen's is called chiasmus, which is described under parallelism in Chapter 18. Here are some examples of chiasmus from his essay:

> "I felt encroached on when I was ostensibly safe, and I felt safe when I was ostensibly encroached on."

> "My "sense of privacy' functions to keep the public out of the private and to keep the private out of the public."

> "Telecommunicating puts the boardroom in the bedroom, "softer' modern office design puts the bedroom in the boardroom (....)"

And here is a variant, not quite chiasmus:

> "If privacy depends upon an expectation of invisibility, the expectation of visibility is what defines a public space."

Ponder the relationship between this chiasmic sentence shape and the way that Franzen's thinking proceeds in general in the essay. What do you notice about the structure of thinking in Franzen's essay that might prompt him to shape his sentences in this way?

5. Style creates what rhetoricians call *persona*—a version of the writer that he or she creates for the purpose at hand. Describe Franzen's persona in this piece, the sort of person he comes off as being on the page and the kind of relationship he seeks to establish with the reader. Determine what features of Franzen's style (word choice, tone, sentence shape) are most significant in creating this persona. Once you have gotten to this point, ask yourself, Why this persona for this piece?

6. **Links:** In their essays, Christina Rosen and Paul Goldberger mourn the loss of public space, as does Franzen. How does Franzen's thinking about public vs. private compare with the viewpoints of the other two writers in this regard? Find sentences about public space from each of the three essays and put these into conversation with each other. What similarities and differences do you find?

Here, for example, is a relevant passage from Rosen: "As trust is being built and bolstered moment by moment between individuals, public trust among strangers in social settings is eroding. We are strengthening and increasing our interactions with the people we already know at the expense of those who we do not."

7. **Application:** Use the essay as a lens to locate interesting instances of what Franzen calls "the panic about privacy." Alternatively, locate examples from your experience of public spaces as Franzen defines the term. Or apply the following remark as a lens to any show on the airwaves: "TV is devoid of shame, and without shame there can be no distinction between public and private."

Sam Anderson

In Defense of Distraction

Sam Anderson is the book reviewer for *New York* magazine. He also occasionally writes longer pieces, such as "In Defense of Distraction," which started out as a book review but then grew into the cover story of the May 2009 issue. Although he writes primarily about books, he has become increasingly interested in broader cultural criticism, for example, the way our reading habits as a culture have continued to change with technology.

I. The Poverty of Attention

I'm going to pause here, right at the beginning of my riveting article about attention, and ask you to please get all of your precious 21st-century distractions out of your system now. Check the score of the Mets game; text your sister that pun you just thought of about her roommate's new pet lizard ("iguana hold yr hand LOL get it like Beatles"); refresh your work e-mail, your home e-mail, your school e-mail; upload pictures of yourself reading this paragraph to your "me reading magazine articles" Flickr photostream; and alert the fellow citizens of whatever Twittertopia you happen to frequent that you will be suspending your digital presence for the next twenty minutes or so (I know that seems drastic: Tell them you're having an appendectomy or something and are about to lose consciousness). Good. Now: Count your breaths. Close your eyes. Do whatever it takes to get all of your neurons lined up in one direction. Above all, resist the urge to fixate on the picture, right over there, of that weird scrambled guy typing. Do not speculate on his ethnicity (German-Venezuelan?) or his backstory (Witness Protection Program?) or the size of his monitor. Go ahead and cover him with your hand if you need to. There. Doesn't that feel better? Now it's just you and me, tucked like fourteenth-century Zen masters into this sweet little nook of pure mental focus. (Seriously, stop looking at him. I'm over here.)

Over the last several years, the problem of attention has migrated right into the center of our cultural attention. We hunt it in neurology labs, lament its decline on op-ed pages, fetishize it in grassroots quality-of-life movements, diagnose its absence in more and more of our children every year, cultivate it in yoga class twice a week, harness it as the engine of self-help empires, and pump it up to superhuman levels with drugs originally intended to treat Alzheimer's and narcolepsy. Everyone still pays some form of attention all the time, of course—it's basically impossible for humans not to—but the currency in which we pay it, and the goods we get in exchange, have changed dramatically.

Back in 1971, when the web was still twenty years off and the smallest computers were the size of delivery vans, before the founders of Google had even managed to get themselves born, the polymath economist Herbert A. Simon wrote maybe

Sam Anderson/New York Magazine. Reprinted by permission.

the most concise possible description of our modern struggle: "What information consumes is rather obvious: It consumes the attention of its recipients. Hence a wealth of information creates a poverty of attention, and a need to allocate that attention efficiently among the overabundance of information sources that might consume it." As beneficiaries of the greatest information boom in the history of the world, we are suffering, by Simon's logic, a correspondingly serious poverty of attention.

If the pundits clogging my RSS reader can be trusted (the ones I check up on occasionally when I don't have any new e-mail), our attention crisis is already chewing its hyperactive way through the very foundations of Western civilization. Google is making us stupid, multitasking is draining our souls, and the "dumbest generation" is leading us into a "dark age" of bookless "power browsing." Adopting the Internet as the hub of our work, play, and commerce has been the intellectual equivalent of adopting corn syrup as the center of our national diet, and we've all become mentally obese. Formerly well-rounded adults are forced to MacGyver worldviews out of telegraphic blog posts, bits of YouTube videos, and the first nine words of *Times* editorials. Schoolkids spread their attention across 30 different programs at once and interact with each other mainly as sweatless avatars. (One recent study found that American teenagers spend an average of 6.5 hours a day focused on the electronic world, which strikes me as a little low; in South Korea, the most wired nation on earth, young adults have actually died from exhaustion after multiday online-gaming marathons.) We are, in short, terminally distracted. And *distracted,* the alarmists will remind you, was once a synonym for *insane.* (Shakespeare: "poverty hath distracted her.")

This doomsaying strikes me as silly for two reasons. First, conservative social critics have been blowing the apocalyptic bugle at every large-scale tech-driven social change since Socrates' famous complaint about the memory-destroying properties of that newfangled technology called "writing." (A complaint we remember, not incidentally, because it was written down.) And, more practically, the virtual horse has already left the digital barn. It's too late to just retreat to a quieter time. Our jobs depend on connectivity. Our pleasure-cycles—no trivial matter—are increasingly tied to it. Information rains down faster and thicker every day, and there are plenty of non-moronic reasons for it to do so. The question, now, is how successfully we can adapt.

Although attention is often described as an organ system, it's not the sort of thing you can pull out and study like a spleen. It's a complex process that shows up all over the brain, mingling inextricably with other quasi-mystical processes like emotion, memory, identity, will, motivation, and mood. Psychologists have always had to track attention secondhand. Before the sixties, they measured it through easy-to-monitor senses like vision and hearing (if you listen to one voice in your right ear and another in your left, how much information can you absorb from either side?), then eventually graduated to PET scans and EEGs and electrodes and monkey brains. Only in the last ten years—thanks to neuroscientists and their functional MRIs—have we been able to watch the attending human brain in action, with its coordinated storms of neural firing, rapid blood surges, and oxygen flows. This has yielded all kinds of fascinating insights—for instance, that when forced to multitask, the overloaded brain shifts its processing from the hippocampus (responsible for memory) to the striatum (responsible for rote tasks), making it hard to learn a task or even recall what you've been doing once you're done.

When I reach David Meyer, one of the world's reigning experts on multitasking, he is feeling alert against all reasonable odds. He has just returned from India, where he was discussing the nature of attention at a conference with the Dalai Lama (Meyer gave a keynote speech arguing that Buddhist monks multitask during meditation), and his trip home was hellish: a canceled flight, an overnight taxi on roads so rough it took thirteen hours to go 200 miles. This is his first full day back in his office at the University of Michigan, where he directs the Brain, Cognition, and Action Laboratory—a basement space in which finger-tapping, card-memorizing, tone-identifying subjects help Meyer pinpoint exactly how much information the human brain can handle at once. He's been up since 3 a.m. and has by now goosed his attention several times with liquid stimulants: a couple of cups of coffee, some tea. "It does wonders," he says.

My interaction with Meyer takes place entirely via the technology of distraction. We scheduled and rescheduled our appointment, several times, by e-mail. His voice is now projecting, tinnily, out of my cell phone's speaker and into the microphone of my digital recorder, from which I will download it, as soon as we're done, onto my laptop, which I currently have open on my desk in front of me, with several windows spread across the screen, each bearing nested tabs, on one of which I've been reading, before Meyer even had a chance to tell me about it, a blog all about his conference with the Dalai Lama, complete with RSS feed and audio commentary and embedded YouTube videos and pictures of His Holiness. As Meyer and I talk, the universe tests us with a small battery of distractions. A maximum-volume fleet of emergency vehicles passes just outside my window; my phone chirps to tell us that my mother is calling on the other line, then beeps again to let us know she's left a message. There is, occasionally, a slight delay in the connection. Meyer ignores it all, speaking deliberately and at length, managing to coordinate tricky subject-verb agreements over the course of multi-clause sentences. I begin, a little sheepishly, with a question that strikes me as sensationalistic, nonscientific, and probably unanswerable by someone who's been professionally trained in the discipline of cautious objectivity: Are we living through a crisis of attention?

Before I even have a chance to apologize, Meyer responds with the air of an Old Testament prophet. "Yes," he says. "And I think it's going to get a lot worse than people expect." He sees our distraction as a full-blown epidemic—a cognitive plague that has the potential to wipe out an entire generation of focused and productive thought. He compares it, in fact, to smoking. "People aren't aware what's happening to their mental processes," he says, "in the same way that people years ago couldn't look into their lungs and see the residual deposits."

I ask him if, as the world's foremost expert on multitasking and distraction, he has found his own life negatively affected by the new world order of multitasking and distraction.

"Yep," he says immediately, then adds, with admirable (although slightly hurtful) bluntness: "I get calls all the time from people like you. Because of the way the Internet works, once you become visible, you're approached from left and right by people wanting to have interactions in ways that are extremely time-consuming. I could spend my whole day, my whole night, just answering e-mails. I just can't deal with it all. None of this happened even ten years ago. It was a lot calmer. There was a lot of opportunity for getting steady work done."

Over the last twenty years, Meyer and a host of other researchers have proved again and again that multitasking, at least as our culture has come to know and love and institutionalize it, is a myth. When you think you're doing two things at once, you're almost always just switching rapidly between them, leaking a little mental efficiency with every switch. Meyer says that this is because, to put it simply, the brain processes different kinds of information on a variety of separate "channels"—a language channel, a visual channel, an auditory channel, and so on—each of which can process only one stream of information at a time. If you overburden a channel, the brain becomes inefficient and mistake-prone. The classic example is driving while talking on a cell phone, two tasks that conflict across a range of obvious channels: Steering and dialing are both manual tasks, looking out the windshield and reading a phone screen are both visual, etc. Even talking on a hands-free phone can be dangerous, Meyer says. If the person on the other end of the phone is describing a visual scene—say, the layout of a room full of furniture—that conversation can actually occupy your visual channel enough to impair your ability to see what's around you on the road.

The only time multitasking does work efficiently, Meyer says, is when multiple simple tasks operate on entirely separate channels—for example, folding laundry (a visual-manual task) while listening to a stock report (a verbal task). But real-world scenarios that fit those specifications are very rare.

This is troubling news, obviously, for a culture of BlackBerrys and news crawls and Firefox tabs—tools that, critics argue, force us all into a kind of elective ADHD. The tech theorist Linda Stone famously coined the phrase "continuous partial attention" to describe our newly frazzled state of mind. American office workers don't stick with any single task for more than a few minutes at a time; if left uninterrupted, they will most likely interrupt themselves. Since every interruption costs around 25 minutes of productivity, we spend nearly a third of our day recovering from them. We keep an average of eight windows open on our computer screens at one time and skip between them every twenty seconds. When we read online, we hardly even read at all—our eyes run down the page in an *F* pattern, scanning for keywords. When you add up all the leaks from these constant little switches, soon you're hemorrhaging a dangerous amount of mental power. People who frequently check their e-mail have tested as less intelligent than people who are actually high on marijuana. Meyer guesses that the damage will take decades to understand, let alone fix. If Einstein were alive today, he says, he'd probably be forced to multitask so relentlessly in the Swiss patent office that he'd never get a chance to work out the theory of relativity.

II. The War on the Poverty of Attention

For Winifred Gallagher, the author of *Rapt*, a new book about the power of attention, it all comes down to the problem of jackhammers. A few minutes before I called, she tells me, a construction crew started jackhammering outside her apartment window. The noise immediately captured what's called her bottom-up attention—the broad involuntary awareness that roams the world constantly looking for danger and rewards: shiny objects, sudden movements, pungent smells. Instead of letting this distract her, however, she made a conscious choice to go into the next room and summon her top-down attention—the narrow, voluntary focus that allows us to isolate and enhance some little slice of the world while ruthlessly suppressing everything else.

This attentional self-control, which psychologists call executive function, is at the very center of our struggle with attention. It's what allows us to invest our focus wisely or poorly. Some of us, of course, have an easier time with it than others.

Gallagher admits that she's been blessed with a naturally strong executive function. "It sounds funny," she tells me, "but I've always thought of paying attention as a kind of sexy, visceral activity. Even as a kid, I enjoyed focusing. I could feel it in almost a mentally muscular way. I took a lot of pleasure in concentrating on things. I'm the sort of irritating person who can sit down to work at nine o'clock and look up at two o'clock and say, "Oh, I thought it was around 10:30.'"

Gallagher became obsessed with the problem of attention five years ago, when she was diagnosed with advanced and aggressive breast cancer. She was devastated, naturally, but then realized, on her way out of the hospital, that even the cancer could be seen largely as a problem of focus—a terrifying, deadly, internal jackhammer. It made her realize, she says, that attention was "not just a latent ability, it was something you could marshal and use as a tool." By the time she reached her subway station, Gallagher had come up with a strategy: She would make all the big pressing cancer-related decisions as quickly as possible, then, in order to maximize whatever time she had left, consciously shift her attention to more positive, productive things.

One of the projects Gallagher worked on during her recovery (she is now cancer free) was *Rapt*, which is both a survey of recent attention research and a testimonial to the power of top-down focus. The ability to positively wield your attention comes off, in the book, as something of a panacea; Gallagher describes it as "the sine qua non of the quality of life and the key to improving virtually every aspect of your experience." It is, in other words, the Holy Grail of self-help: the key to relationships and parenting and mood disorders and weight problems. (You can apparently lose seven pounds in a year through the sheer force of paying attention to your food.)

"You can't be happy all the time," Gallagher tells me, "but you can pretty much focus all the time. That's about as good as it gets."

The most promising solution to our attention problem, in Gallagher's mind, is also the most ancient: meditation. Neuroscientists have become obsessed, in recent years, with Buddhists, whose attentional discipline can apparently confer all kinds of benefits, even on non-Buddhists. (Some psychologists predict that, in the same way we go out for a jog now, in the future we'll all do daily 20- to 30-minute "secular attentional workouts.") Meditation can make your attention less "sticky," able to notice images flashing by in such quick succession that regular brains would miss them. It has also been shown to elevate your mood, which can then recursively stoke your attention: Research shows that positive emotions cause your visual field to expand. The brains of Buddhist monks asked to meditate on "unconditional loving-kindness and compassion" show instant and remarkable changes: Their left prefrontal cortices (responsible for positive emotions) go into overdrive, they produce gamma waves 30 times more powerful than novice meditators, and their wave activity is coordinated in a way often seen in patients under anesthesia.

Gallagher stresses that because attention is a limited resource—one psychologist has calculated that we can attend to only 110 bits of information per second, or 173 billion bits in an average lifetime—our moment-by-moment choice of attentional targets determines, in a very real sense, the shape of our lives. *Rapt*'s epigraph comes from the psychologist and philosopher William James: "My experience is what I agree to attend to." For Gallagher, everything comes down to that one big choice: investing your attention wisely or not. The jackhammers are everywhere—iPhones, e-mail, cancer—and Western culture's attentional crisis is mainly a widespread failure to ignore them.

"Once you understand how attention works and how you can make the most productive use of it," she says, "if you continue to just jump in the air every time your phone rings or pounce on those buttons every time you get an instant message, that's not the machine's fault. That's your fault."

Making the responsible attention choice, however, is not always easy. Here is a partial list, because a complete one would fill the entire magazine, of the things I've been distracted by in the course of writing this article: my texting wife, a very loud seagull, my mother calling from Mexico to leave voice mails in terrible Spanish, a man shouting "Your weed-whacker fell off! Your weed-whacker fell off!" at a truck full of lawn equipment, my *Lost*-watching wife, another man singing some kind of Spanish ballad on the sidewalk under my window, streaming video of the NBA playoffs, dissertation-length blog breakdowns of the NBA playoffs, my toenail spontaneously detaching, my ice-cream-eating wife, the subtly shifting landscapes of my three different e-mail in-boxes, my Facebooking wife, infinite YouTube videos (a puffin attacking someone wearing a rubber boot, Paul McCartney talking about the death of John Lennon, a chimpanzee playing Pac-Man), and even more infinite, if that is possible, Wikipedia entries: puffins, *MacGyver,* Taylorism, the phrase "bleeding edge," the Boston Molasses Disaster. (If I were going to excuse you from reading this article for any single distraction, which I am not, it would be to read about the Boston Molasses Disaster.)

When the jackhammers fire up outside my window, in other words, I rarely ignore them—I throw the window open, watch for a while, bring the crew sandwiches on their lunch break, talk with them about the ins and outs of jackhammering, and then spend an hour or two trying to break up a little of the sidewalk myself. Some of my distractions were unavoidable. Some were necessary work-related evils that got out of hand. Others were pretty clearly inexcusable. (I consider it a victory for the integrity of pre-Web human consciousness that I was able to successfully resist clicking on the first "related video" after the chimp, the evocatively titled "Guy shits himself in a judo exhibition.") In today's attentional landscape, it's hard to draw neat borders.

I'm not ready to blame my restless attention entirely on a faulty willpower. Some of it is pure impersonal behaviorism. The Internet is basically a Skinner box engineered to tap right into our deepest mechanisms of addiction. As B. F. Skinner's army of lever-pressing rats and pigeons taught us, the most irresistible reward schedule is not, counterintuitively, the one in which we're rewarded constantly but something called "variable ratio schedule," in which the rewards arrive at random. And that randomness is practically the Internet's defining feature: It dispenses its never-ending little shots of positivity—a life-changing e-mail here, a funny YouTube video there—in gloriously unpredictable cycles. It seems unrealistic to expect people to spend all day clicking reward bars—searching the Web, scanning the relevant blogs, checking e-mail to see if a co-worker has updated a project—and then just leave those distractions behind, as soon as they're not strictly required, to engage in "healthy" things like books and ab crunches and undistracted deep conversations with neighbors. It would be like requiring employees to take a few hits of opium throughout the day, then being surprised when it becomes a problem. Last year, an editorial in the *American Journal of Psychiatry* raised the prospect of adding "Internet addiction" to the *DSM*, which would make it a disorder to be taken as seriously as schizophrenia.

A quintessentially Western solution to the attention problem—one that neatly circumvents the issue of willpower—is to simply dope our brains into focus. We've done so, over the centuries, with substances ranging from tea to tobacco to NoDoz to Benzedrine, and these days the tradition seems to be approaching some kind of zenith with the rise of neuroenhancers: drugs designed to treat ADHD (Ritalin, Adderall), Alzheimer's (Aricept), and narcolepsy (Provigil) that can produce, in healthy people, superhuman states of attention. A grad-school friend tells me that Adderall allowed him to squeeze his mind "like a muscle." Joshua Foer, writing in Slate after a weeklong experiment with Adderall, said the drug made him feel like he'd "been bitten by a radioactive spider"—he beat his unbeatable brother at Ping-Pong, solved anagrams, devoured dense books. "The part of my brain that makes me curious about whether I have new e-mails in my in-box apparently shut down," he wrote.

Although neuroenhancers are currently illegal to use without a prescription, they're popular among college students (on some campuses, up to 25 percent of students admitted to taking them) and—if endless anecdotes can be believed—among a wide spectrum of other professional focusers: journalists on deadlines, doctors performing high-stakes surgeries, competitors in poker tournaments, researchers suffering through the grind of grant-writing. There has been controversy in the chess world recently about drug testing at tournaments.

In December, a group of scientists published a paper in *Nature* that argued for the legalization and mainstream acceptance of neuroenhancers, suggesting that the drugs are really no different from more traditional "cognitive enhancers" such as laptops, exercise, nutrition, private tutoring, reading, and sleep. It's not quite that simple, of course. Adderall users frequently complain that the drug stifles their creativity—that it's best for doing ultrarational, structured tasks. (As Foer put it, "I had a nagging suspicion that I was thinking with blinders on.") One risk the scientists do acknowledge is the fascinating, horrifying prospect of "raising cognitive abilities beyond their species-typical upper bound." Ultimately, one might argue, neuroenhancers spring from the same source as the problem they're designed to correct: our lust for achievement in defiance of natural constraints. It's easy to imagine an endless attentional arms race in which new technologies colonize ever-bigger zones of our attention, new drugs expand the limits of that attention, and so on.

One of the most exciting—and confounding—solutions to the problem of attention lies right at the intersection of our willpower and our willpower-sapping technologies: the grassroots Internet movement known as "lifehacking." It began in 2003 when the British tech writer Danny O'Brien, frustrated by his own lack of focus, polled 70 of his most productive friends to see how they managed to get so much done; he found that they'd invented all kinds of clever little tricks—some high-tech, some very low-tech—to help shepherd their attention from moment to moment: ingenious script codes for to-do lists, software hacks for managing e-mail, rituals to avoid sinister time-wasting traps such as "yak shaving," the tendency to lose yourself in endless trivial tasks tangentially related to the one you really need to do. (O'Brien wrote a program that prompts him every ten minutes, when he's online, to ask if he's procrastinating.) Since then, lifehacking has snowballed into a massive self-help program, written and revised constantly by the online global hive mind, that seeks to help you allocate your attention efficiently. Tips range from time-management habits (the 90-second shower) to note-taking techniques (mind mapping) to software shortcuts (how to turn your Gmail into a to-do list) to delightfully retro tech solutions (turning an index card into a portable dry-erase board by covering it with packing tape).

When I call Merlin Mann, one of lifehacking's early adopters and breakout stars, he is running late, rushing back to his office, and yet he seems somehow to have attention to spare. He is by far the fastest-talking human I've ever interviewed, and it crosses my mind that this too might be a question of productivity—that maybe he's adopted a time-saving verbal lifehack from auctioneers. He talks in the snappy aphorisms of a professional speaker ("Priorities are like arms: If you have more than two of them, they're probably make-believe") and is always breaking ideas down into their atomic parts and reassessing the way they fit together: "What does it come down to?" "Here's the thing." "So why am I telling you this, and what does it have to do with lifehacks?"

Mann says he got into lifehacking at a moment of crisis, when he was "feeling really overwhelmed by the number of inputs in my life and managing it very badly." He founded one of the original lifehacking websites, 43folders.com (the name is a reference to David Allen's Getting Things Done, the legendarily complex productivity program in which Allen describes, among other things, how to build a kind of "three-dimensional calendar" out of 43 folders) and went on to invent such illustrious hacks as "in-box zero" (an e-mail-management technique) and the "hipster PDA" (a stack of three-by-five cards filled with jotted phone numbers and to-do lists, clipped together and tucked into your back pocket). Mann now makes a living speaking to companies as a kind of productivity guru. He Twitters, podcasts, and runs more than half a dozen websites.

Despite his robust Web presence, Mann is skeptical about technology's impact on our lives. "Is it clear to you that the last fifteen years represent an enormous improvement in how everything operates?" he asks. "Picasso was somehow able to finish the *Desmoiselles of Avignon* even though he didn't have an application that let him tag his to-dos. If John Lennon had a BlackBerry, do you think he would have done everything he did with the Beatles in less than ten years?"

One of the weaknesses of lifehacking as a weapon in the war against distraction, Mann admits, is that it tends to become extremely distracting. You can spend solid days reading reviews of filing techniques and organizational software. "On the web, there's a certain kind of encouragement to never ask yourself how much information you really need," he says. "But when I get to the point where I'm seeking advice twelve hours a day on how to take a nap, or what kind of notebook to buy, I'm so far off the idea of lifehacks that it's indistinguishable from where we started. There are a lot of people out there that find this a very sticky idea, and there's very little advice right now to tell them that the only thing to do is action, and everything else is horseshit. My wife reminds me sometimes: "You have all the information you need to do *something* right now.""

For Mann, many of our attention problems are symptoms of larger existential issues: motivation, happiness, neurochemistry. "I'm not a physician or a psychiatrist, but I'll tell you, I think a lot of it is some form of untreated ADHD or depression," he says. "Your mind is not getting the dopamine or the hugs that it needs to keep you focused on what you're doing. And any time your work gets a little bit too hard or a little bit too boring, you allow it to catch on to something that's more interesting to you." (Mann himself started getting treated for ADD a year ago; he says it's helped his focus quite a lot.)

Mann's advice can shade, occasionally, into Buddhist territory. "There's no shell script, there's no fancy pen, there's no notebook or nap or Firefox extension or hack that's gonna help you figure out why the fuck you're here," he tells me. "That's on you. This makes me sound like one of those people who swindled the Beatles, but if you are having attention problems, the best way to deal with it is by admitting it and then saying, "From now on, I'm gonna be in the moment and more cognizant." I said not long ago, I think on Twitter—God, I quote myself a lot, what an asshole—that really all self-help is Buddhism with a service mark.

"Where you allow your attention to go ultimately says more about you as a human being than anything that you put in your mission statement," he continues. "It's an indisputable receipt for your existence. And if you allow that to be squandered by other people who are as bored as you are, it's gonna say a lot about who you are as a person."

III. Embracing the Poverty of Attention

Sometimes I wonder if the time I'm wasting is actually being wasted. Isn't blowing a couple of hours on the Internet, in the end, just another way of following your attention? My life would be immeasurably poorer if I hadn't stumbled a few weeks ago across the Boston Molasses Disaster. (Okay, seriously, forget it: I hereby release you to go look up the Boston Molasses Disaster. A giant wave of molasses destroyed an entire Boston neighborhood 90 years ago, swallowing horses and throwing an elevated train off its track. It took months to scrub all the molasses out of the cobble-stones! The harbor was brown until summer! The world is a stranger place than we will ever know.)

The prophets of total attentional meltdown sometimes invoke, as an example of the great culture we're going to lose as we succumb to e-thinking, the canonical

French juggernaut Marcel Proust. And indeed, at seven volumes, several thousand pages, and 1.5 million words, *À la Recherche du Temps Perdu* is in many ways the anti-Twitter. (It would take, by the way, exactly 68,636 tweets to reproduce.) It's important to remember, however, that the most famous moment in all of Proust, the moment that launches the entire monumental project, is a moment of pure distraction: when the narrator, Marcel, eats a spoonful of tea-soaked madeleine and finds himself instantly transported back to the world of his childhood. Proust makes it clear that conscious focus could never have yielded such profound magic: Marcel has to abandon the constraints of what he calls "voluntary memory"—the kind of narrow, purpose-driven attention that Adderall, say, might have allowed him to harness—in order to get to the deeper truths available only by distraction. That famous cookie is a kind of hyperlink: a little blip that launches an associative cascade of a million other subjects. This sort of free-associative wandering is essential to the creative process; one moment of judicious unmindfulness can inspire thousands of hours of mindfulness.

My favorite focusing exercise comes from William James: Draw a dot on a piece of paper, then pay attention to it for as long as you can. (Sitting in my office one afternoon, with my monkey mind swinging busily across the lush rain forest of online distractions, I tried this with the closest dot in the vicinity: the bright-red mouse-nipple at the center of my laptop's keyboard. I managed to stare at it for 30 minutes, with mixed results.) James argued that the human mind can't actually focus on the dot, or any unchanging object, for more than a few seconds at a time: It's too hungry for variety, surprise, the adventure of the unknown. It has to refresh its attention by continually finding new aspects of the dot to focus on: subtleties of its shape, its relationship to the edges of the paper, metaphorical associations (a fly, an eye, a hole). The exercise becomes a question less of pure unwavering focus than of your ability to organize distractions around a central point. The dot, in other words, becomes only the hub of your total dot-related distraction.

This is what the web-threatened punditry often fails to recognize: Focus is a paradox—it has distraction built into it. The two are symbiotic; they're the systole and diastole of consciousness. Attention comes from the Latin "to stretch out" or "reach toward," distraction from "to pull apart." We need both. In their extreme forms, focus and attention may even circle back around and bleed into one other. Meyer says there's a subset of Buddhists who believe that the most advanced monks become essentially "world-class multitaskers"—that all those years of meditation might actually speed up their mental processes enough to handle the kind of information overload the rest of us find crippling.

The truly wise mind will harness, rather than abandon, the power of distraction. Unwavering focus—the inability to be distracted—can actually be just as problematic as ADHD. Trouble with "attentional shift" is a feature common to a handful of mental illnesses, including schizophrenia and OCD. It's been hypothesized that ADHD might even be an advantage in certain change-rich environments. Researchers have discovered, for instance, that a brain receptor associated with ADHD is unusually common among certain nomads in Kenya, and that members who have the receptor are the best nourished in the group. It's possible that we're all evolving toward a new techno-cognitive nomadism, a rapidly shifting environment in which restlessness will be an advantage again. The deep focusers might even be hampered by having too much attention: Attention Surfeit Hypoactivity Disorder.

I keep returning to the parable of Einstein and Lennon—the great historical geniuses hypothetically ruined by modern distraction. What made both men's achievements so groundbreaking, though, was that they did something modern technology is getting increasingly better at allowing us to do: They very powerfully linked and synthesized things that had previously been unlinked—Newtonian gravity and particle physics, rock and blues and folk and doo-wop and bubblegum pop and psychedelia. If Einstein and Lennon were growing up today, their natural genius might be so pumped up on the possibilities of the new technology they'd be doing even more dazzling things. Surely Lennon would find a way to manipulate his BlackBerry to his own ends, just like he did with all the new technology of the sixties—he'd harvest spam and text messages and Web snippets and build them into a new kind of absurd poetry. The Beatles would make the best viral videos of all time, simultaneously addictive and artful, disposable and forever. All of those canonical songs, let's remember, were created entirely within a newfangled mass genre that was widely considered to be an assault on civilization and the sanctity of deep human thought. Standards change. They change because of great creations in formerly suspect media.

Which brings me, finally, to the next generation of attenders, the so-called "net-gen" or "digital natives," kids who've grown up with the Internet and other time-slicing technologies. There's been lots of hand-wringing about all the skills they might lack, mainly the ability to concentrate on a complex task from beginning to end, but surely they can already do things their elders can't—like conduct 34 conversations simultaneously across six different media, or pay attention to switching between attentional targets in a way that's been considered impossible. More than any other organ, the brain is designed to change based on experience, a feature called neuroplasticity. London taxi drivers, for instance, have enlarged hippocampi (the brain region for memory and spatial processing)—a neural reward for paying attention to the tangle of the city's streets. As we become more skilled at the 21st-century task Meyer calls "flitting," the wiring of the brain will inevitably change to deal more efficiently with more information. The neuroscientist Gary Small speculates that the human brain might be changing faster today than it has since the prehistoric discovery of tools. Research suggests we're already picking up new skills: better peripheral vision, the ability to sift information rapidly. We recently elected the first-ever BlackBerry president, able to flit between sixteen national crises while focusing at a world-class level. Kids growing up now might have an associative genius we don't—a sense of the way ten projects all dovetail into something totally new. They might be able to engage in seeming contradictions: mindful web-surfing, mindful Twittering. Maybe, in flights of irresponsible responsibility, they'll even manage to attain the paradoxical, Zenlike state of focused distraction.

Things to Do with the Reading

1. What rhetorical choices has Anderson made in his essay? How does the ethos (the kind of persona he creates to tell his readers about the subject) of the piece reveal Anderson's attitude toward both his subject and his audience(s)? Anchor your answer to a few sentences in the essay that you think typify these rhetorical choices. Anderson is known, by the way, for his "imitative reviews," which copy the style of their subjects.

2. Insofar as the essay has a single governing claim—a thesis—what is it? What are the primary claims of Anderson's essay (list these or mark them in the margins)? By what logic does one claim evolve into the next? How, for example, does the piece function as a "defense" of distraction suggested by its title?

3. The Boston Molasses Disaster is mentioned several times in the essay. How does Anderson put it to use rhetorically? What, that is, are the various functions this example serves in helping Anderson achieve his ends?

4. Links: "In Defense of Distraction" is one of a number of recent pieces worrying aloud about the effects of an increasingly electronic environment, especially given our increasing awareness of neuroplasticity—of the effects such technology might have on the way our brains function. Use Anderson's essay as a lens for reconsidering the discussions of technology in the other readings in this chapter. Alternatively, look for points of contact with an essay by Nicholas Carr in *The Atlantic* (2008), "Is Google Making Us Stupid?: What the Internet Is Doing to Our Brains" [http://www.theatlantic.com/magazine/archive/2008/07/is-google-making-us-stupid/6868/], which grew into his book *The Shallows* (2010).

FOR FURTHER RESEARCH: MANNERS, COMMUNICATION, AND TECHNOLOGY

By Kelly Cannon, Reference Librarian

The readings and activities below invite you to further explore the theme of Manners, Communication, and Technology. WARNING: Some essays are polemical; they are intended to promote insight and discussion (or a starting point for your next paper). To access the online readings, visit the *Writing Analytically with Readings* website at www.cengagebrain.com.

Open access

Blumberg, Andrew J. and Peter Eckersley. "On Locational Privacy, and How to Avoid Losing it Forever." *Electronic Frontier Foundation.***" August 2009. 14 Jan. 2011. http://www.eff.org/wp/locational-privacy**
Now Big Brother really is watching you. Your comings and goings are being monitored whether you know it or not.

> Explore: What is EFF? Do you generally agree with the foundation's stance on civil liberties and technology? What makes them trustworthy or not?

Cowen, Tyler. "Three Tweets for the Web." *Wilson Quarterly* **(2009): 54–58. 19 January 2011. http://www.wilsonquarterly.com/article.cfm?aid=1481.**
Multitasking engendered by the internet is not distraction at all, but rather a series of "long strands of continued involvement," the result of voluntary choices a person has made, creating a highly "personalized mix of stimuli."

> Explore: Cowen offers direct counterpoint to other articles referenced in this section of the reader. Note the rhetorical moves Cowen makes, such as comparing Internet multitasking to an intimate marriage. Would you consider this to be "evidence"? Are you persuaded? How so?

***Emily Post Institute Etipedia.* Emily Post Institute, 2011. 11 January 2011. http://www.emilypost.com/etipedia**
Your online etiquette encyclopedia.

> Explore: Navigate the section titled "Communication and Technology." Or search the site for the keyword: "cell phones." How does your online behavior rate with Ms. Post?

Gitlin, Todd. "Uses of Half True Alarms." *New Republic.* **7 June 2010. 11 January 2011. http://www.tnr.com/print/book/review/the-uses-half-true-alarms**
Gitlin gives mixed reviews to the endless technological interruptions typifying the Google era.

> Explore: Consider your own experience. Do you have difficulty paying attention in a long face-to-face discussion? Can you turn off your cell phone easily or set it aside when needed? Viewed another way, do you find you can attend to many conversations at once, all adequately?

Hampton, Keith N., et al. "Social Isolation and New Technology." *Pew Internet and American Life Project.* **Pew Research Center, November 2009. 14 January 2011. http://www.pewinternet.org/~/media//Files/Reports/2009/PIP_Tech_and_Social_Isolation.pdf**

This respected think-tank on the Internet use found that "when we examine people's full personal network— their strong ties and weak ties—Internet use in general and use of social networking services such as Facebook in particular, are associated with having a more diverse social network....This flies against the notion that technology pulls people away from social engagement."

> Explore: Compare the findings of this report with the conclusions drawn by Christine Rosen and Paul Goldberger in their essays, printed above, and another Christine Rosen essay referenced below on virtual friendship. What do you find most convincing about the Hampton report? What is not as strong, or missing as evidence altogether? Do you agree generally with the findings? What from your own experience supports or differs from the findings?

Madden, Mary, et al. "Digital Footprints: Online Identity Management and Search in the Age of Transparency." *Pew Internet and American Life Project.* **Pew Research Center, 16 December 2007. 14 January 2011. http://www.pewinternet.org/~/media//Files/Reports/2007/PIP_Digital_Footprints.pdf.pdf**
The more we contribute information voluntarily to the public or semi-public corners of the Web, the more we are not only findable, but also knowable.

> Explore: Perform a Google Search on your name, adding details like city or high school to distinguish you from others with the same name. What digital footprints have you left for others to find?

Rosen, Christine. "Virtual Friendship and the New Narcissism." *The New Atlantis: A Journal of Technology and Society* **(Summer 2007). 19 January 2011. http://www.thenewatlantis.com/publications/virtual-friendship-and-the-new-narcissism**
Rosen argues that virtual connections may not be all they are cracked up to be; something gets lost in the translation from face-to-face to remote.

> Explore: Compare this Rosen essay with the essays printed above by Christine Rosen and by Paul Goldberger. What stylistic features do the two Christine Rosen essays share? What kind of evidence and rhetoric does Rosen bring to bear in this essay on narcissism and technology? Are you convinced? What does your own experience tell you?

Shea, Virginia. *Netiquette.* **Albion, 2004. 11 January 2011. http://www.albion.com/netiquette/book/index.html**
An online classic, this textbook for proper online behavior espouses 10 core rules.

> Explore: Compare with Emily Post's *Etipedia*, mentioned above. What does Shea place first as the cardinal of her 10 rules? Why?

Proprietary

(Ask your librarian about print or online access to the following resources.)
Hosking, Simon G., Kristie L. Young, and Michael A. Regan. "The Effects of Text Messaging on Young Drivers." *Human Factors: The Journal of the Human Factors and Ergonomics Society* **51.4 (2009): 582 –592.**

This research article confirms earlier studies about the effects of text messaging on driving abilities, and advances some new findings.

> Explore: Sam Anderson references scientific research articles much like this one—though not this one precisely—throughout his essay printed above. What advantages does an article like Anderson's have in persuading a lay audience of claims concerning multitasking over this article? What audience is the Hosking article written for? How do these two types of articles—primary research and popular—work symbiotically to reach and convince a broad audience—even if in the end they reach different conclusions?

Humphreys, Lee. "Social Topography in a Wireless Era: the Negotiation of Public and Private Space." *Journal of Technical Writing and Communication* **35.4 (2005): 367–84.**
In this study, the author explores how callers and bystanders negotiate privacy.

> Explore: This study typifies "empirical research." What is empirical about it? In what section can the results of the research be found? What other elements make this article typical of research performed in the social sciences?

Pauwels, Luc. "A Private Visual Practice Going Public? Social Functions and Sociological Research Opportunities of Web-Based Family Photography." *Visual Studies* **23.1 (2008): 34–49.**
The sharing of family photos on the Internet showcases the blending of public and private spheres engendered by Web 2.0 technology.

> Explore: Look closely at the family websites depicted in this article. Are there hints that these were meant for a wider audience than just family members? What would be the motive of placing these sometimes awkward pictures on the web for all to see? What does this say about the nature of privacy today? To what extent do the conclusions of Pauwel's research corroborate Jeffery Rosen's essay above on "America's culture of self-revelation"?

Chapter 21

Places and Spaces: Cities and Suburbs

The readings in this section call to mind a provocative definition of nostalgia offered by a character in Don Delillo's 1985 novel *White Noise*: "Nostalgia," says the Visiting Lecturer in Communications Murray Jay Suskind, "is a product of dissatisfaction and rage; a settling of grievances between the present and the past" (258). All of the essays in this unit cast a skeptical eye on the future of urban and suburban life in America, and, explicitly or implicitly, they look back with a certain degree of nostalgia to a lost past when life appeared more genuinely democratic—and livable.

The writers all converse in one way or another with what is known as the New Urbanism, a movement seeking to rethink the ways our cities have declined and our suburbs have expanded in the past half-century. There are potent comparisons with the preceding chapter. The interest in public versus private life treated in Manners, Communication, and Technology returns here in the concern with impersonal living spaces—barren suburbs fueled by the car culture and fortressed cities fraught with risk.

ABOUT THE READINGS IN THIS UNIT

"The United States is the wealthiest nation in the history of the world," begins the first essay in this unit, by James Howard Kunstler, "yet its inhabitants are strikingly unhappy." Kunstler's is an ethical call to attention, a plea for us to become citizens rather than simply consumers, by rebuilding the material culture that surrounds us in the public realm, starting at the level of the neighborhood. Jack Gambino's discussion of the landscapes of two contemporary photographers provides graphic illustration of Kunstler's vision. Although the two photographers' work differs widely in focus and tone, it shares a fascination with "creative destruction" that Gambino sees as distinctively modern, and it functions, in both cases, as a kind of visual cultural memory against a past too easily forgotten.

Next, Adam Gopnik offers a wry history of the redevelopment of Times Square in New York City, providing a lens for viewing redevelopment anywhere.

Gopnik's piece provides insight into the actual jostlings for power that accompany redevelopment, in this case, wherein "a question of virtue had to be disguised as a necessity of commerce." We move next from New York City to the Long Island suburbs, a chapter from Rosalyn Baxandall and Elizabeth Ewen's history of how the suburbs happened. Focusing on Robert Moses, their work casts a revealing eye on the vexed politics of urban planning and the way it reinscribes longstanding class privileges as the nation moves from the city to the suburbs.

The chapter concludes with two classic essays on civic space that might be fruitfully compared. A selection from Jane Jacobs' pioneering study of city life analyzes safe versus unsafe neighborhoods. One conclusion she draws about her late 1950s' New York City neighborhood is that "thinning out a city does not insure safety from crime and fear of crime." This line rings ominously against Mike Davis's chilling account of the spatial imperatives militating against the urban poor and the homeless in 1990s' Los Angeles.

James Howard Kunstler

The Public Realm and the Common Good

The author and journalist James Howard Kunstler is an eloquent advocate of what is known as the "New Urbanism"—an urban design movement that arose in the late 1980s. The New Urbanism supports walkable neighborhoods, mixed use and mixed income housing, and a restored sense of community feeling, and it vigorously opposes urban sprawl. The following piece is excerpted from his book *Home from Nowhere: Remaking Our Everyday World for the Twenty-first Century* (1996). In it, Kunstler argues that the development of American towns and cities since World War II has been marked by an absence of respect for what he terms the "public realm," defined as "the physical manifestation of the common good."

The United States is the wealthiest nation in the history of the world, yet its inhabit- 1 ants are strikingly unhappy. Unhappiness is manifest at every level of the national scene. From big city to the remotest rural trailer court, our civic life is tattered and frayed. Unspeakable crimes occur in the most ordinary places. Government can't fulfill its most basic role in guaranteeing the public safety. Our schools, in many cases, barely function. The consensus of what constitutes decent behavior fractured with the social revolutions of the 1960s and has not been restored. Anything goes.

Community, as it once existed in the form of places worth caring about, supported by local economies, has been extirpated by an insidious corporate colonialism that doesn't care about the places from which it extracts its profits or the people subject to its operations.

The Public Realm and the Common Good

American cities are dismal. The majority of American small towns have become dismal. Of course, those two types of places represent America as it developed before World War Two, and their current state must be understood as one of abandonment and dereliction. The newer suburban subdivisions are dismal, too, in their own unique way, as are the commercial highway strips, the malls, the office parks, and the rest of the autocentric equipment of the human habitat. Their architectural shortcomings aside, these places are dismal because the public realm that binds them together is degraded, incoherent, ugly and meaningless. In case the term *public realm* seems vague or mystifying, I shall attempt to define it with some precision.

The public realm is the connective tissue of our everyday world. It is made of those pieces of terrain left between the private holdings. It exists in the form of streets, highways, town squares, parks, and even parking lots. It includes rural or wilderness landscape: stretches of the seacoast, national forests, most lakes and rivers, and even the sky (though "air rights" are sometimes bought and sold in the cities). The public realm exists mainly outdoors because most buildings belong to private individuals or corporations. Exceptions to this are public institutions such as libraries, museums, and

Reprinted with the permission of Simon & Schuster Adult Publishing Group, from HOME FROM NOWHERE: Remaking Our Everyday World for the Twenty-First Century by James Howard Kunstler. Copyright © James Howard Kunstler. All rights reserved.

town halls, which are closed some hours of the day, and airports and train stations, which may be open around the clock. Some places, while technically private, function as quasi-public realm—for instance, college campuses, ballparks, restaurants, theaters, nightclubs, and, yes, shopping malls, at least the corridors between the private shops. Their owners retain the right to regulate behavior within, particularly the terms of access, and so the distinction must be made that they are only nominally public. The true public realm then, for the sake of this argument, is that portion of our everyday world which belongs to everybody and to which everybody ought to have access most of the time. The public realm is therefore a set of real places possessing physical form.

5   The public realm in America became so atrocious in the postwar decades that the Disney Corporation was able to create an artificial substitute for it and successfully sell it as a commodity. That's what Disney World is really about. In France, where the public realm possesses a pretty high standard of design quality and is carefully maintained as well, there is much less need for artificial substitutes, so few people feel compelled to go to EuroDisney (it lost over $1 billion in its first two years of operation). The design quality of everything at EuroDisney is about five notches *beneath* that of the most mediocre French street corner. The quality of the park benches and street lamps in EuroDisney is recognizably inferior to the quality of the park benches and street lamps in ordinary French towns. Even the flower beds lack finesse. They look like berms designed for corporate parking lots. There are more interesting things to eat along nine linear yards of the Rue Buci on the Left Bank than in all the magic kingdoms of EuroDisney.

The design quality of Disney World in Orlando, on the other hand, is about 1.5 notches better than the average American suburban shopping mall or housing subdivision—so Americans love it. Forget about how cheap-looking the benches and lampposts might be —we don't even have sidewalks in most of suburbia (and besides, nobody walks there anyway)—so *any* benches and lampposts seem swell. Americans love Disney World, above all, because it is uncontaminated by cars, except for a few antique vehicles kept around as stage props. By and large, they do not know that this is the reason they love Disney World. Americans are amazingly unconscious of how destructive the automobile has been to their everyday world.

Main Street USA is America's obsolete model for development—we stopped assembling towns this way after 1945. The pattern of Main Street is pretty simple: mixed use, mixed income, apartments and offices over the stores, moderate density, scaled to pedestrians, vehicles permitted but not allowed to dominate, buildings detailed with care, all built to last (though we still trashed it). Altogether it was a pretty good development pattern. It produced places that people loved deeply. That is the reason Main Street persists in our cultural memory. Many people still alive remember the years before World War Two and what it felt like to live in integral towns modeled on this pattern. Physical remnants of the pattern still stand in parts of the country for people to see, though the majority of Americans have moved into the new model habitat called suburban sprawl.

For all its apparent success, Suburban Sprawl sorely lacks many things that make life worth living, particularly civic amenities, which Main Street offered in spades. Deep down, many Americans are dissatisfied with suburbia—though they have trouble understanding what's missing—which explains their nostalgia for the earlier model. Their dissatisfaction is literally a *dis-ease*. They feel vaguely and generally un-well where they are. Nostalgia in its original sense means homesickness. Americans essay to cure their homesickness with costly visits to Disney World. The crude, ineffective palliatives they get there in the form of brass bands and choo-choo train rides leave them more homesick and more baffled as to the nature of their disease than when they arrived—like selling chocolate bars to someone suffering from scurvy—and pathetically, of course, they must return afterward to the very places that induce the disease of homesickness.

Historically Americans have a low regard for the public realm, and this is very unfortunate because the public realm is the physical manifestation of the common good. When you degrade the public realm, as we have, you degrade the common good.

Civic life is what goes on in the public realm. Civic life refers to our relations with   10 our fellow human beings—in short, our roles as citizens. Sometime in the past forty years we ceased to speak of ourselves as citizens and labeled ourselves consumers. That's what we are today in the language of the evening news—*consumers*—in the language of the Sunday panel discussion shows—*consumers*—in the blizzard of statistics that blows out of the U.S. Department of Commerce every month. Consumers, unlike citizens, have no responsibilities, obligations, or duties to anything larger than their own needs and desires, certainly not to anything like the common good. How can this be construed as anything other than an infantile state of existence? In degrading the language of our public discussion this way—labeling ourselves consumers—have we not degraded our sense of who we are? And is it any wonder that we cannot solve any of our social problems, which are problems of the public realm and the common good?

Charm, Sanity, and Grace

During America's financially richest period, we put up almost nothing but the cheapest possible buildings, particularly civic buildings. Look at any richly embellished 1904 firehouse or post office and look at its dreary concrete box counterpart today. Compare the home of a small-town bank president dating from the 1890s, with its masonry walls and complex roof articulation, to the flimsy house of a 1990s business leader, made of two-by-fours, sheetrock, and fake fanlight windows. When we were a far less wealthy nation, we built things with the expectation that they would endure. To throw away money (painfully expended) on something guaranteed to fall apart in thirty years would have seemed immoral, if not insane, in our great-grandfathers' day.

The buildings they constructed paid homage to history in their design—including elegant solutions to age-old problems posed by the cycles of light and weather—and they paid respect to the future through the expectation that they would endure through the lifetimes of the people who built them. They therefore evinced a sense of chronological connectivity—one of the fundamental patterns of the universe—an understanding that time is a defining dimension of existence, particularly the existence of living things, such as human beings, who miraculously pass into life and then tragically pass out of it, perhaps forever—we do not know—our self-awareness of this fate making it tragic.

Chronological connectivity lends meaning and dignity to our little lives. It charges the present with a more vividly conscious validation of our own aliveness. It puts us in touch with the ages and the eternities, suggesting that we are part of a larger and more significant organism. It even suggests that the larger organism we are part of *cares* about us, and that, in turn, we should respect ourselves, our fellow creatures, and all those who will follow us in time, as those preceding us respected us who followed them. In short, chronological connectivity puts us in touch with the holy. It is at once humbling and exhilarating. I say this as someone who has never followed any formal religious practice. Connection with the past and the future is a pathway that literally charms us in the direction of sanity and grace.

The antithesis to this can be seen in the way we have built since 1945. We reject the past and the future, and it shows in our graceless constructions. Our houses, commercial, and civic buildings are constructed with the fully conscious certainty that they will disintegrate in a few decades. There is even a name for this condition: the *design life.* Strip malls and elementary schools have short design lives. They are not expected to endure through the span of a human life. In fact, they fall apart in under fifty years. Since there is not expectation that these things will last, nor that they will speak to any era but their own, we seem to believe that there is no point in putting any money or effort into their embellishment—except for the sort of cartoon decoration that serves to advertise whatever product is sold on the premises. Nor do we care about age-old solutions to the problems of weather and light, because we have technical artifacts to mitigate these problems, namely electricity and central heating. In especially bad buildings, like the average WalMart, there may be no windows. Yet this process of disconnection from the past and future, and from the organic patterns of weather and light, all done for the sake of expedience, ends up diminishing us spiritually, impoverishing us socially, and degrading the aggregate set of cultural patterns that we call civilization. We register these discontinuities as *ugliness,* or the absence of beauty.

15   Our streets used to be charming and beautiful. The public realm of the street was understood to function as an outdoor room. Like any room, it required walls to define the essential *void* of the room itself. Where I live, Saratoga Springs, New York, there once existed a magnificent building called the Grand Union Hotel. It was enormous—the largest hotel in the world in the late nineteenth century—occupying a six-acre site in the heart of town. The hotel consisted of a set of rather narrow buildings which lined the outside of an unusually large superblock. Inside the block was a semipublic parklike courtyard. Any reasonably attired person could walk in off the street, pass through the hotel lobby, and enjoy the interior park. The sides of the hotel that faced the street incorporated a gigantic veranda twenty feet deep, with a roof three stories high supported by columns. This facade functioned as a marvelous street-wall. Its size—a central cupola reached seven stories—was appropriate to the scale of the town's main street, called Broadway. The facade, or street-wall, was active and permeable. The veranda that lined it was filled with people sitting perhaps eight feet above the sidewalk grade, talking to each other while they watched the pageant life of the street. These veranda sitters were protected from the weather by the roof, and protected from the sun by elm trees along the sidewalk. The orderly rows of elm trees performed an additional architectural function. Their trunks were straight and round, like columns,

reiterating and reinforcing the pattern of the hotel facade, while the crowns formed a vaulted canopy over the sidewalk, pleasantly filtering the sunlight for pedestrians as well as the hotel patrons. Notice that the integral soundness of all these patterns worked to enhance the lives of everybody in town, a common laborer on his way home as well as a railroad millionaire rocking on the hotel veranda. In doing so, they supported civic life as a general proposition. They nourished our civilization.

While nothing lasts forever, it was tragic that this magnificent building was destroyed less than a hundred years after it was built. In 1953 America stood at the brink of the greatest building spree in history, and the very qualities that made the Grand Union Hotel so wonderful were antithetical to all the new stuff that America was about to build. The town demolished it with a kind of mad glee. What replaced the hotel was a strip mall anchored by, of all things, a *Grand Union* supermarket. This Grand Union shopping plaza was prototypical of its time. Tens of thousands of strip malls like it have been built all over America since then. It is in absolutely all its details a perfect piece of junk. It is the anti-place.

What had been the heart and soul of the town was now converted into a kind of mini-Outer Mongolia. The strip mall buildings were set back from Broadway one hundred and fifty feet, the setback now comprising a parking lot. The street and the buildings commenced a non-relationship. Since the new buildings were one story high, their scale bore no relation to the scale of the town's most important street. They failed to create a street-wall. The perception of the street functioning as an outdoor room was lost. The space between the buildings and the street now had one function: automobile storage. The street, and consequently, the public realm in general, was degraded by the design of the new strip mall. As the street's importance as a public space declined, people ceased to care what happened in it. If it became jammed with cars, so much the better, because individual cars were understood not merely as "personal transportation" but as *personal home delivery vehicles,* enabling people to physically haul home enormous volumes of merchandise very efficiently, at no cost to the merchandizer—a great boon for business. That is why the citizens of Saratoga in 1953 were willing to sacrifice the town's most magnificent building. It was okay to simply throw away the past. The owners of the supermarket chain that anchored the strip mall didn't live in town. They didn't care what effect their style of doing business would have on the town. They certainly didn't care about the town's past, and their interest in the town's future was limited only to technicalities of selling dog food and soap flakes.

What has happened to the interrelation of healthy, living patterns of human ecology in the town where I live has happened all over the country. Almost everywhere, the larger patterns are in such a sorry state that the details seem almost irrelevant. When my town invested tens of thousands of dollars in Victorian-style street lamps in an effort to create instant charm, the gesture seemed pathetic, because there was no awareness of the larger design failures. It is hard to overstate how ridiculous these lampposts look in the context of our desolate streets and the cheap, inappropriate new buildings amid their parking lots in what remains of our downtown. The lamppost scheme was like putting Band-Aids on someone who had tripped and fallen on his chainsaw.

Burn Your Zoning Laws

It is literally against the law almost everywhere in the United States to build the kind of places that Americans themselves consider authentic and traditional. It's against the law to build places that human beings can feel good in, or afford to live in. It's against the law to build places that are worth caring about.

20   Is Main Street your idea of a nice business district? Sorry, your zoning laws won't let you build it, or even extend it where it already exists. Is Elm Street your idea of a nice place to live—you know, the houses with the front porches on a tree-lined street? Sorry, that's against the law, too. All you can build where I live, in upstate New York, is another version of Los Angeles. The zoning laws say so.

This is not a gag. Our zoning laws comprise the basic manual of instruction for how we create the stuff of our communities. Most of these laws have only been in place since World War Two. For the previous 300-odd years of American history we didn't have zoning laws. We had a popular *consensus* about the right way to assemble a town, or a city. Our best Main Streets and Elm Streets were not created by municipal ordinances, but by cultural agreement. Everybody agreed that buildings on Main Street ought to be more than one story tall, that corner groceries were good to have in residential neighborhoods, that streets ought to intersect with other streets to facilitate movements, that sidewalks were necessary, and that orderly rows of trees planted along them made the sidewalks much more pleasant, that rooftops should be pitched to shed rain and snow, that doors should be conspicuous so you could easily find the entrance to a building, that windows should be vertical to dignify a house. Everybody agreed that communities needed different kinds of housing to meet the needs of different families and individuals, and the market was allowed to supply it. Our great-grandfathers didn't have to argue endlessly over these matters of civic design. Nor did they have to reinvent civic design every fifty years because everybody forgot what they agreed about.

Zoning began as a political response to the obnoxious effect of industry on human settlements. Originally, its intent was to keep factories away from houses, to create separate zones for industry to carry on its noisy and dirty activities. Over the twentieth century, the imposition of motor vehicles brought the obnoxious noise and danger of industry to virtually every doorstep, and so zoning became preoccupied with problems posed by the movement and storage of cars. The problem became so pervasive that zoning completely replaced civic art as the ordering principle of human settlement, especially in the years since 1945.

The place that results from zoning is suburban sprawl. It must be understood as the product of a particular set of institutions. Its chief characteristics are the strict separation of human activities (or *uses*), mandatory driving to get from one use to the other, and huge supplies of free parking. After all, it's called *zoning* because the basic idea is that every activity demands a separate zone of its own. You can't allow people to live around shopping. That would be harmful and indecent. Better not even allow them within walking distance of it. They'll need their cars to haul all that stuff home, anyway—in case you haven't noticed, most supermarkets don't deliver these days. While you're at it, let's separate the homes, too, by income gradients. Don't let the $75,000-a-year families live near the $200,000-a-year families—they'll bring down your *property values*—and, for Godsake, don't let some $25,000-a-year recent college graduate live near any of them, or a $19,000-a-year widowed grandmother on Social Security. There goes the neighborhood! Now, put all the workplaces in a separate office "park" or industrial "park," and make sure nobody can walk to them either. As for nice public squares, parks, and the like—forget it, we can't afford them because we spent all our public funds paving the four-lane highways and collector roads and the parking lots, and laying sewer and water lines out to the housing subdivisions, and hiring traffic cops to regulate the movement of people in their cars going back and forth to these segregated areas.

It soon becomes obvious that the model of the human habitat dictated by zoning is a formless, soulless, centerless, demoralizing mess. It bankrupts families and townships. It causes mental illness. It disables whole classes of decent, normal citizens. It ruins the air we breathe. It corrupts and deadens our spirits.

In the absence of a new widespread consensus about how to build a better every- 25 day environment, we'll have to replace the old set of rules with an explicit new set of rules. Or, to put it a slightly different way, replace zoning laws with principles of civic art.

A Short Course in the General Principles of Civic Art

The pattern under discussion here has been called variously *neo-traditional planning, traditional neighborhood development* (or the *TND*), *low-density urbanism, Transit-Oriented Development* (or the *TOD*), *the New Urbanism,* or just plain *civic art.* Its principles produce a setting that resembles the American town prior to World War Two.[1]

The Neighborhood

The basic unit of planning is the neighborhood. A neighborhood standing alone can be a village or a town. A cluster of neighborhoods becomes a bigger town. Clusters of a great many neighborhoods become a city. The population of a neighborhood can vary, depending on local conditions.

The neighborhood is limited in physical size, with a well-defined edge and a focused center. Human scale is the standard for proportion in buildings and their accessories. Automobiles and other wheeled vehicles are permitted, but do not take precedence over human needs, including aesthetic needs. The neighborhood contains a public transit stop.

The size of a neighborhood is defined as a five-minute walking distance (or a quarter-mile) from the edge to the center, thus a ten-minute walk edge to edge, or one-half a square mile. Chores that may require many separate, tedious car trips in sprawl can be accomplished in a single outing on foot (shop owners may offer home delivery of bulky merchandise). Walking allows a person to visit many different types of shops—thereby promoting small-scale, locally owned businesses, which, in turn, promote manifold civic benefits from the support of local institutions to the physical caretaking of the street. Walking down the street permits casual socializing. Pedestrians make streets safer by their mere presence in numbers. Finally, walking down the street is spiritually elevating. When neighborhoods are used by pedestrians,

a much finer detailing inevitably occurs. Building facades become more richly orna-
mented and interesting. Little gardens and windowboxes appear. Shop windows create
a continuity of public spectacle, as do outdoor cafes, both for walkers and the sitters.
There is much to engage the eye and heart. In such a setting, we feel more completely
human. This is not trivial.

30   The boundaries between neighborhoods are formed by corridors, which both
connect and define them. Corridors can incorporate natural features like streams or
canyons. They can take the form of parks, natural preserves, travel corridors, railroad
lines, or some integral combination of all these things. In towns and cities, a neighborhood or parts of neighborhoods can comprise a district. Districts are composed of
streets or ensembles of streets where special activities get preferential treatment. The
French Quarter of New Orleans is an example of a district. It is a whole neighborhood
dedicated to entertainment in which housing, shops, and offices are also integral. A
corridor can also be a district—for instance, a major shopping avenue between adjoining neighborhoods.

        The neighborhood is emphatically mixed-use and provides housing for people
with different incomes. Commerce is integrated with residential, business, and even
industrial use, though not necessarily on the same street in a given neighborhood.
Apartments are permitted over stores. There is a mixture of housing types.

The Street

The street is understood to be the preeminent form of public space and buildings
that define it are expected to honor and embellish it. In the absence of a consensus
about the appropriate decoration of buildings, an architectural code may be devised to
establish some fundamental unities of massing, fenestration, materials, and roof pitch,
within which many variations may function harmoniously. Buildings also define parks
and squares, which are distributed throughout the neighborhood and appropriately
designated for recreation, repose, periodic commercial uses (e.g., farmers' markets),
or special events such as political meetings, concerts, theatricals, exhibitions, and fairs.

        The street pattern is conceived as a network in order to create the greatest number
of alternative routes from one part of the neighborhood to another. This has the beneficial effect of relieving vehicular congestion. This network can be a grid. Networks
based on a grid must be modified by parks, squares, diagonals, T-intersections, round-
abouts, and other devices that relieve the grid's tendency to monotonous regularity.
The streets exist in a hierarchy from broad boulevards to narrow lanes and alleys.
In a town or city, limited access highways may exist only in a corridor, preferably in
the form of parkways. Cul-de-sacs (dead ends) are strongly discouraged except under
extraordinary circumstances—e.g., where rugged topography requires them. In the
New Urbanism, the meaning of the street as the essential fabric of public life is restored.

        Under the regime of Zoning, all streets were made as wide as possible because the
specialist in charge—the zoning engineer—was concerned solely with the movement
of cars and trucks. In the process, much of the traditional decor that made streets
pleasant for people was gotten rid of. For instance, street trees were eliminated. It is
hard to overstate how much orderly rows of mature trees can improve even the most

dismal street by softening its hard edges and sun-blasted bleakness. Under zoning, street trees were deemed a hazard to motorists and chopped down in many American towns after World War Two.

The practice of maximizing car movement, at the expense of all other concerns, 35 was applied with particular zeal to housing subdivisions. Suburban streets were given the speed characteristics of country highways, though children played in them. Suburbs notoriously lack parks. The spacious private lots were supposed to make up for the lack of parks, but children have an uncanny tendency to play in the street anyway—bicycles don't work too well on the lawn. In the suburbs, where street trees were expressly forbidden, we see those asinine exercises in romantic landscaping that attempt to recapitulate the North Woods in clumps of ornamental juniper. Sidewalks, in a setting so inimical to walking, were deemed a waste of money.

Parallel parking is emphatically permitted along the curbs of all streets, except under the most extraordinary conditions. Parallel parking is desirable for two reasons: (1) Parked cars create a physical barrier, and a psychological buffer, that protects pedestrians on the sidewalk from moving vehicles; and (2) a rich supply of parallel parking can eliminate the need for parking lots, which are extremely destructive of civic fabric. Anyone who thinks that parallel parking "ruins" a residential street should take a look at some of the most desirable real estate in America (as reflected by house prices): Georgetown, Beacon Hill, Nob Hill, Alexandria, Charleston, Savannah, Annapolis, Princeton, Greenwich Village, Marblehead, et cetera. All permit parallel parking.

Civic buildings (town halls, churches, schools, libraries, museums) are placed on preferential building sites such as the frontage of squares, neighborhood centers, and where street vistas terminate, in order to serve as landmarks and to reinforce their symbolic importance.

Can America Become Civilized?

I don't know if we will be able to reinstate a social contract that recognizes both rights and responsibilities in a civic context. It will certainly not be possible unless we restore that context, and I mean in bricks and mortar. There is a vital relationship between the character of our surroundings and the common good. Rights and responsibilities need a civic setting in which to dwell. Such a setting is identical with the physical setting of our lives, an actual place that must be worth caring about.

It is easy to be discouraged. The general political attitude among the suburban well-off is that they have been willing to try almost any expensive social experiment *except* returning to live in towns and cities. In the face of this shunning, the will to behave constructively has been rather conspicuously absent among the urban poor themselves. But the poor nevertheless have responsibilities and obligations too, beginning with civil behavior and extending to useful work. One of the unfortunate side effects of the psychology of entitlement is the notion both among the poor and government officials that jobs must be *given* to idle people, and that they must be *good* jobs—which I take to mean something like professional careers. Nothing could be further from the way the world really operates.

40   It may strike some readers as an unbelievable effrontery to state that the poor
ought to work in menial jobs. I am not arguing that they ought to live in violence and
squalor—just the opposite. Before World War Two this was a nation full of menial
employments, and many people so employed lived more decently than today's poor
do, particularly in the cities where, for all the cities' historic shortcomings, the poor
at least had easy access to a great deal of cultural and civic equipment. Poor people
may have lived in cramped tenements in 1911, but they had access to well-maintained
parks, low-cost public transit, safe streets, free public schools, excellent public libraries, museums, baths, and infirmaries. Most important, this civic equipment was shared
by everybody. People of all stations in life went to parks, museums, and libraries. The
poor *saw* the middle class and the wealthy every day in the public realm of the streets.
They observed their behavior, and were constrained in their own behavior by seeing
them. The poor saw where the rich lived. A boy from Hell's Kitchen could walk ten
minutes across town and stand within a few yards of William H. Vanderbilt's front
door on Fifty-ninth Street and Fifth Avenue with no fear of being hassled by private
security guards. In short, the poor lived in a civic context that included the entire
range of social classes, so that many of the problems of the poor in the cities were also
the problems of the middle class and the rich.
          Today the poor in most American cities live only in the context of the poor. The
only place they see the other America is on television, and then through a wildly distorting lens that stimulates the most narcissistic, nihilistic consumer fantasies. Since
the poor, by definition, can't participate fully in consumer culture, the predictable
result is rage at what appears to be a cruel tease, and this rage is commonly expressed
in crime. What may be equally damaging is that the poor see very little in the way of
ordinary polite conduct, very little civil behavior. They do not see people routinely
going about honorable occupations. What they do see all around is mayhem, squalor,
and disorder, and almost no evidence that it is possible to live a happy life without
being a sports hero, a gangster, or a television star.
          The problems of the cities are not going to be relieved unless the middle class and
the wealthy return to live there. For the moment these classes are off in suburbia. All
the evidence demonstrates that suburbia is becoming unaffordable and unsustainable.
The economy makes them nervous. Companies are shedding employees. They feel
anxious, trapped. For the first time in American history, there is nowhere else left to
go, no place to escape to. What will they do?
          I'm afraid they may misunderstand the crisis of the suburbs, particularly as it man-
ifests itself in the personal catastrophes of lost jobs, declining incomes, falling property
values, family breakups, and misbehavior. Poor people are not the only Americans
afflicted by the psychology of entitlement. Middle-class suburbanites really believe
that they are owed a package of goodies called *the American Dream,* and when they
are suddenly deprived of it, they may get very angry and vote for political maniacs.
          The Republicans are now in charge of things at many levels of government, and
though they have been shouting the loudest about the crisis of "family values," they are
also the chief boosters of suburbia, which is to say, a profoundly uncivil living arrangement. Their chosen way of life is therefore at odds with their most cherished wishes
for a civil society, and so it is unlikely that they are going to be able to solve any of the
social problems they deplore—even the problems of their own children's behavior.

Suburban Moms and Dads wonder why their fifteen-year-old children seem so 45 alienated. These kids are physically disconnected from the civic life of their towns. They have no access to the civic equipment. They have to be chauffeured absolutely everywhere, to football practice, to piano lessons, to their friends' houses, to the library, and, of course, to the mall. All they live for is the day that they can obtain a driver's license and use their environment. Except then, of course, another slight problem arises: they need several thousand dollars to buy a used car and pay for insurance, which is usually exorbitant for teens, often more than the price of their cars. Is it really any wonder that these kids view their situation as some kind of swindle?

Americans are convinced that suburbia is great for kids. The truth is, kids older than seven need more from their environment than a safe place to ride their bikes. They need at least the same things adults need. Dignified places to hang out. Shops. Eating establishments. Libraries, museums, and theaters. They need a public realm worthy of respect. All of which they need access to on their own, without our assistance—which only keeps them in an infantile state of dependency. In suburbia, as things presently stand, children have access only to television. That's their public realm. It's really a wonder that more American children are not completely psychotic.

In order to make American towns and cities habitable again, we will have to take the greater portion of public money now spent on subsidizing car use and redirect it into replacing the civic equipment of the cities that was allowed to be trashed over the past several decades. The cost of doing these things is, fortunately, apt to be less than the cost of continuing to subsidize the suburban automobile infrastructure. For instance, a single new freeway exchange can cost $600,000,000, which is the same cost as building and equipping an entire twenty-mile-long electric trolley line.[2]

Making our cities habitable again will take a rededication to forms of buildings that were largely abandoned in America after World War Two. It will call for devices of civic art that *never* really caught on here, but have always existed in older parts of the world—for instance, waterfronts that are integral with the rest of the city. The human scale will have to prevail over the needs of motor vehicles. There will have to be ample provision for green space of different kinds—neighborhood squares, wildlife corridors, parks—because people truly crave regular contact with nature, especially pockets of repose and tranquillity, and having many well cared-for parcels of it distributed equitably around town improves civic life tremendously.

The transformation I propose will not be possible unless Americans recognize the benefits of a well-designed public realm, and the civic life that comes with it, over the uncivil, politically toxic, socially impoverished, hyper-privatized realm of suburbia, however magnificent the kitchens and bathrooms may be there. I don't believe that we can be an advanced society without cities. Tragically, American cities have become unworthy of the American republic. Our task is to make them worthy, to reconstruct them in a physical form that is worth caring about, and to reinhabit them.

The common good demands a public realm in which to dwell. It can't sustain 50 itself merely in our hearts or memories. This is, finally, the sentimental fallacy of the suburban patriot: that hanging a cast-iron eagle over your garage door proves you care about your country.

Notes

[1] The principles outlined here are derived from a consensus among members of the Congress for the New Urbanism. Other lists of principles exist and have been articulated in various formats by Elizabeth Plater-Zyberk and Andres Duany, Peter Calthorpe, Daniel Solomon, Peter Katz, and Anthony Nelesson. A complementary list, called the Ahwahnee Principles, was drawn up in a 1991 conference at the Ahwahnee Lodge in Yosemite Park. Among the participants were Duany and Plater-Zyberk, Katz, Stefanos Polyzoides, and Elizabeth Moule, architects and planners, and Michael Corbett, a former mayor of Davis, California. The book *Town Planning in Practice*, by Raymond Unwin (1863–1940) republished in 1994 by the Princeton Architectural Press, is also a classic source.

[2] Author's interview with Milwaukee Mayor John O. Norquist, June 1995.

Things to Do with the Reading

1. Apply the Method (aka Looking for Patterns of Repetition and Contrast—see Chapter 2) to Kunstler's piece. Make a list in the margins of the key terms repeated, the strands in which they participate, and the binary oppositions into which they are aligned. Then choose what you consider to be the two most important repetitions, the two most interesting strands, and the two most significant binaries. Finally, choose any ONE of these and write for a paragraph or two about what it means and why it matters to Kunstler's vision.

2. In Chapter 5, we offer as a frame for reading critically the notion of understanding a piece of writing in terms of "the pitch, the complaint, and the moment." Locate Kunstler's piece in this context. (See Try This 5.2.)

3. Kunstler argues that "in the past forty years we ceased to speak of ourselves as citizens and labeled ourselves consumers" (paragraph 10). He then builds an argument on the different implications of these two key terms, *citizen* and *consumer*. What are these implications?

   Note: the words *citizen*, *civic* (as in civic center), and *civilized* play a key role in Kunstler's piece. Look up the etymology (word history) of these terms: how might they enrich your understanding of his point of view?

4. **Application:** Kunstler asserts that "the basic unit of planning is the neighborhood" (paragraph 27). Apply his perceptions to your neighborhood, or one close to you. How is it constructed? How does it locate parking? Public transportation? How does it set up housing—and in what relation to income levels? Where if at all does it attend to what Kunstler terms "human needs" and "aesthetic needs"? What ultimately does Kunstler's lens allow you to discover about your neighborhood?

Jack Gambino

Demolition Zones: Contemporary Photography by Edward Burtynsky and Camilo Jose Vergara

A political scientist looks at two contemporary photographers' representations of urban and industrial landscapes as sites of "creative destruction," commenting, "It is this sense of displacement—of human beings alienated from the environments they have created—that provides the common theme that haunts these two very different photographers."

If you look closely at Camilo Jose Vergara's "Fern Street, Camden" (1988), you'll notice   1
a sign on the side of a dilapidated building:

> *"Danger: Men Working*
> *W. Hargrove Demolition"*

Perhaps that warning captures the ominous atmosphere evoked in the human and natural landscapes of two very different kinds of photographers, Camilo Jose Vergara and Edward Burtynsky. "Danger: Men Working." Watch out—human beings are at work! But the work they present is not so much a building-up as it is a tearing-down—the work of demolition. Of course, demolition is often necessary in order to construct anew: old buildings are leveled for new projects, whether they are the highways and high rises that dominate the contemporary American city or the massive dams now transforming portions of the Chinese countryside. To destroy in order to create: that is a modern formula. Modernity is, after all, a process of "creative destruction," a term used variously to describe the dynamics of modern art, capitalism, and technological innovation. The photographs in this exhibit, however, force us to pay attention to the destructiveness, both deliberate and unintentional, at the very heart of modern creation. What both Burtynsky and Vergara do in their respective ways is to point to the warning signs already posted on the modern landscape. They compel us to wonder whether the process of creative-destruction may not have spun recklessly out of control, producing places that are not just unsustainable in the future, but uninhabitable in the present. Indeed, a common element connecting their photographic visions is the near absence of people in the landscape. While we see the evidence of the transforming power of human production on the physical and social environment, neither Vergara's urban ruins nor Burtynsky's industrial sites actually show us "men working." Isolated figures peer suspiciously out back doors or pick through the rubble, but they appear out-of-place. It is this sense of displacement—of human beings alienated from the environments they themselves have created—that provides the common theme that haunts the work of these two very different photographers.

The dominant theme in Burtynsky's work, as he puts it, is "nature transformed through industry." His photos are large industrial landscapes—quarries, oil refineries, mines, dams—mostly dedicated to the extraction and production of energy resources. Burtynsky's landscapes vividly portray what landscape historian J.B. Jackson called the "engineered landscape"—a landscape developed for "the production, conservation,

Demolition Zones, Jack Gambino. Reprinted with permission of the author.

and use of energy." The Three Gorges Dam is, of course, one of the latest and largest of the modern engineer's remaking of the social and physical environment. Highways are another, more familiar example, with their horizontal forms and parallel lines, similar to the shiny, sleek pipeline cutting its way through the forest in Burtynsky ("Oil Fields #22. Cold Lake, Alberta, Canada, 2001"). [See Figure 21.1.] What better image of the triumph of precision, linearity, efficiency, and clarity? Even the forest appears as a controlled environment, an ecological monoculture made available for easy exploitation. "To the engineer (and the engineer-minded society)," Jackson wrote, "a landscape is beautiful when the energy-flow system is functioning with unimpeded efficiency." A well-engineered highway or pipeline aims for this kind of efficiency. So will Three Gorges Dam, which, when completed, is expected to generate 8.4 billion kilowatts-per-hour of unimpeded energy for China's exploding industrial cities (one ninth of its electricity needs, according to some estimates). This massive attempt at state enforced modernization will not only meet practical energy needs; it will fulfill China's socialist destiny, as proclaimed by former President Jiang Zemin in a 1997 celebration of the Three Gorges Dam. Yet that destiny—"the great feat of conquering, developing and exploiting nature," to quote President Zemin—is hardly an exclusively socialist dream: it's what modernization is all about in capitalist societies as well.

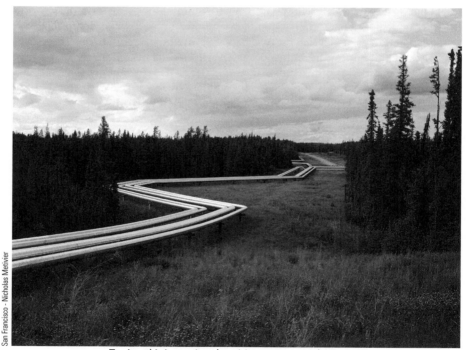

San Francisco - Nicholas Metivier

To view this image in color, visit www.cengagebrain.com

FIGURE 21.1
"Oil Fields #22. Cold Lake, Alberta, Canada, 2001" by Edward Burtynsky

The fact that the process of energy extraction and transfer, once initiated, could be maintained with little direct human presence suggests all the more that the engineer's quest for efficiency culminates in a kind of robotic automatism portrayed in "Oil Fields #13. Taft, California, USA, 2002." [See Figure 21.2.] Earth-moving machines, cranes, and oil derricks largely occupy the industrial landscape Burtynsky portrays. But the engineer's ingenious instruments are not his real subject, as much as their unintentional and unexpected effects. Burtynsky is attracted to the awesome (awful) beauty of the industrial landscapes (something, one suspects, that the engineers may not have noticed), most notably in the chiseled shapes of the quarries of Utah and Vermont.[1] Yet whether they produce the effect of gigantic, abstract sculptures, as in the Vermont quarry, or the semblance of a classical amphitheatre, as in the Utah copper mine, Burtynsky's photos remind us that the beauty of these landscapes cannot be separated from the industrial power that *forcefully cuts* them from the earth. Like all sculptures, they are creative works of violence—a form hammered and chiseled out of rock ("Rock of Ages," 1991). Here Burtynsky suggests a fascination with something deeper than the engineer's desire for efficiency—a fascination with the violence at the

San Francisco - Nicholas Metivier

To view this image in color, visit www.cengagebrain.com

FIGURE 21.2
"Oil Fields #13. Taft, California, USA, 2002" by Edward Burtynsky

heart of the modern creative process. For the remnants of the violence are evident in the denuded forests, the pulverized concrete, the piles of rubble, the incisions in the earth, the jagged debris of partially demolished buildings. The sites of production are necessarily demolition zones.

To many modern architects, urban planners, and engineers, demolition is merely the prelude to a new construction, which, once completed, will cover over (and make us forget) both the physical scars to the land and the emotional scars of displaced people who found themselves in the way. We may join with the modern builders in justifying the violence of means—the sculptor's hammer and chisel—by applauding the greater goods these violent means serve. Sometimes the beauty of the end result does in fact conceal the violent incisions: we may still enjoy Paris' famed boulevard even after acknowledging that its designer, Baron Haussmann, under Louis Napoleon's authoritarian rule, had to *cut* through medieval streets of old Paris, uprooting tens of thousands of urban poor in the mid 19th century. Yet too often modern planners and engineers would justify the creative destruction of habitat as necessary for doubtful utopias: think of Le Corbusier who would have demolished those same 19th-century boulevards to create "a blank piece of paper" for an even more modern city of highways and skyscrapers! Stalin—whose displacement of Russian peasants through forced collectivization reached a level of unprecedented and perhaps unsurpassed brutality—bluntly insisted that "you can't make an omelet without breaking eggs." This was a maxim that Robert Moses, the master planner who ruthlessly leveled New York City neighborhoods to make way for expressways, loved to quote, adding his own: "When you operate in an overbuilt metropolis, you have to hack your way with a meat axe." Here the butcher's axe replaces the sculpture's chisel, but the point is the same—big modern projects require the demolition of existing structures and the displacement of people. The Three Gorges Dam also is a monument to modern ambition—a work in progress, which when completed, will literally *cut* the flow of the Yangtze River, causing it to form a 400 mile long reservoir that will eventually hide, it is hoped, the physical and human scars caused by the demolition of 11 cities and displacement of 1.2 million people.

5   Perhaps Burtynsky's monumental prints remind us that the scars created by such modernization projects cannot be made-over by the engineers' sense of beauty in efficiency. He insists on keeping those scars exposed, even finding a seductive beauty in the jagged edges of demolished buildings and the raw incisions into the surface of the earth.[2] It seems to me, however, that it is a beauty we can only contemplate at a distance, by subtracting ourselves from the scene. We can be struck by the eerie surrealism of "Uranium Tailings" (2002), but we can't imagine human beings walking about in such a landscape. At the same time, he tells us that these inhuman places are part of the industrial infrastructure of a world dependent on energy extraction and consumption. We are made accomplices to those industrial processes and its byproducts: mountains of used tires, rusted hulks of ships, piles of rubble, demolished buildings. His landscapes are thus, as he understands them, a "metaphor for the dilemma of our modern existence: they search for a dialogue between attraction and repulsion, seduction and fear. We are drawn by desire—a chance at good living, yet we are consciously or unconsciously aware that the world is suffering for our success."[3]

His images—especially the series on the Three Gorges Dam—not only bid us to gaze at the human and ecological costs of modernity's creative destructive process, but also warn us that these sites of demolition are never very far from our own safe places. [See Figure 21.3.]

If Burtynsky provokes questions about the seductive beauty of "nature transformed through industry," Camilo Vergara insists that we directly confront urban landscapes transformed by deindustrialization. Vergara's series on the hard luck city of Camden—which is part of a larger project documenting the "process of decline" of the American industrial city—invites us to move closer to inspect the details of places that few of us would call beautiful and most of us would like to avoid. Although we don't see them, the men working in Camden nowadays are doing the work of demolition. This is a bleak, harsh view with little to offer of the awesome industrial monuments found in Burtynsky's work. It is the view most suburbanites (now the majority of Americans) only catch glimpse of as they speed by on the highways and bridges to and from Philadelphia. Yet by placing us "among dereliction and destruction," Vergara calls on us to search for signs of resurgent life—what he calls "the energies of the outmoded."

San Francisco - Nicholas Metivier

To view this image in color, visit www.cengagebrain.com

FIGURE 21.3

"Wan Zhou #4, Three Gorges Dam Project, Yangtze River, 2002" by Edward Burtynsky

The Camden he documents is a site marked by a series of displacements. Once upon a time, the city was home to Walt Whitman and, later, Campbell Soups, and it could boast (despite W.C. Fields' joke that Camden is "the pimple on Philadelphia's ass") that it was "the biggest little city in the nation" making "everything from fountain pens to battleships." With over 105,000 people in the 1920s, it was home to thirteen downtown theatres, an opera company, a major shipbuilding port, an airport with flights to Europe, and a railroad terminus. The factories along the waterfront provided employment to large numbers of European immigrants and African-Americans. On Independence Day, 1926, when President Coolidge participated in the dedication ceremony for the Ben Franklin Bridge (called the Delaware River Bridge back then), the city notables could look forward to what they foresaw as an era of urban growth, with the new bridge making possible the city's "venture in progress."[4]

By now the story of urban decline of old industrial powerhouses like Camden, St. Louis, Detroit, and my hometown, Newark, is a familiar one. Factories moved to more spacious accommodations in the suburbs.[5] The Federal Housing Administration, which underwrote mortgages for families seeking to relocate in the suburbs, virtually wrote off loans to urban dwellers by "redlining" whole neighborhoods as too risky. Moreover, its misguided urban renewal projects during the 1950s and 1960s condemned and demolished entire neighborhoods, displacing thousands of urban families (one out of every 15 families in Camden). Low-income, high-rise apartments were built (the "projects" as they were called), which separated the poor both from the middle class and from places of employment. Many poor but settled neighborhoods were demolished only to be paved into parking lots. Along with the loss of jobs and the increasingly dilapidated housing, the exodus of the white middle class, the deterioration of the downtown commercial district, and mounting racial tensions and riots appeared to doom Camden by the early 1970s.

The irony is that the very structure that would lead to Camden's "venture in progress"—the Ben Franklin Bridge—helped facilitate its undoing. The construction of the bridge itself required the displacement of an entire neighborhood in the city. On and off ramps not only required the bulldozing of established neighborhoods in order to widen access roads, the roads themselves acted as a barrier effectively cutting the city into segments. Like Three Gorges Dam, the bridge was supposed to serve a larger public need by re-engineering the landscape for efficiency and ease of mobility. Such large-scale projects, which embodied the muscular industrial modernity of urban planners and engineers like Moses and Le Corbusier, actually replaced one icon of modernity, the bourgeois city, with another, the automobile. In the new city cars would displace pedestrians, and highways displace the street (Le Corbusier famously declared the "death of the street") as primary urban space. More than anything else, the car and highway transformed the American landscape. As urban problems became more intractable, more Americans fled to the suburbs fulfilling an early prophesy of no less a modernist than Henry Ford: "The ultimate solution [to urban problems everywhere] will be the abandonment of the city, its abandonment as a blunder."[6]

10   The process of urban decay was well underway when Vergara began his documentary project in the 1970s. What his time-series photos help us to see is the "process of decline" unfolding over many years, even decades.[7] The Fern Street series, for

instance, shows the decay and eventual demolition of most of the houses on an urban residential street and their replacement by rubble strewn empty lots. [See Figure 21.4.] Abandoned buildings and vacant lots have become dead spaces, gaps in the urban fabric and depositories for all kinds of junk. It used to be that the city street was the scene of diversity and vitality—think of Jacob Riis' famous shot of Mulberry St. Bend in NY—life may have been tough, but it was teeming with energy. In a more optimistic vein, Jane Jacobs pointed out that the vitality of great American cities was always on the sidewalks where "a constant succession of eyes" of those passing by made the street both vitally interesting and safe.[8] In contrast, Vergara shows us urban scenes largely devoid of people; the isolated figures which emerge here and there only reinforce the sense of loneliness and exhaustion. In contrast, automobiles are present in virtually all of the photos, occupying not only the street, but empty lots and sidewalks as well. Vergara is haunted by the disappearance of a once vibrant "street life," so much so that he can't resist poking about the physical and psychic rubble for ghosts.

Anyone who has visited cities like Camden sees this strange process of the city "emptying out," becoming less densely populated (my hometown went from around 420,000 when I was born, to about 250,000). Abandoned buildings decay, are demolished, and eventually paved into parking lots to accommodate suburban commuters. Many downtowns are nothing more than anonymous office buildings, surrounded by parking lots and a ring of run down houses. The parking lots erase the history of the place; the junk is gone, the buildings cleared, but so are the memories of the people who once lived there. But these empty spaces are for Vergara's lens not Le Corbusier's blank piece of paper; they are haunted places filled with fragmentary evidence of a former human presence. The exteriors of such places—which Vergara usually photographs directly from the street—go mostly unnoticed, both by those who live among them (notice the pedestrian in front of the dilapidated public library) and the suburban commuters. With his camera, he becomes the eyes on the empty streets that most of us overlook. More poignant are the images in which Vergara enters the interiors of dangerous buildings, an intruder who insists on exposing what is hidden inside those demolition zones, as in his eerie portrait of the Camden Public Library. [See Figure 21.5.]

Such photographic intrusion into unoccupied spaces (both physical and mental)—while often appearing merely as objective documentation—is in fact driven by his own sense of the "terrible loss" of urban decline, as he puts it.[9] His abandoned spaces are not only physical "gaps" in the urban fabric (representing the physical displacement of individuals and families), but interruptions in our collective memory and history. This points to an important feature of Vergara's work, and that which makes it more than a sociological record of the process of urban decline: he wants to meditate on the violent contradictions in modernity itself. Vergara, who grew up in a poor agricultural town in Chile and dreamed of a modern life of "Flash Gordon," came to America to study electrical engineering at Notre Dame: "I wanted to believe that science and technology would keep me from being poor."[10] What he discovered in America was not just the landscape of technical innovation and creativity but the contradictory underworld of decay and exhaustion. Modernity is not just about transforming nature and building an industrial civilization; it's about the violence that leaves the human habitat in fragments and a state of disrepair: "I became so attached to derelict buildings that

To view these four images in color, visit www.cengagebrain.com

FIGURE 21.4
Collage of four color photographs, "Fern Street"—photographed by Camilo Jose Vergara "clockwise from top left," in 1979, 1988, 1997, 2004

FIGURE 21.4
Continued

To view this image in color, visit www.cengagebrain.com

FIGURE 21.5
"Camden Library" by Camilo Jose Vergara

sadness came not from seeing them overgrown and deteriorating—this often rendered them more picturesque—but from the violent destruction, which often left a big gap in the urban fabric."[11]

Like Burtynsky, Vergara is intent on showing us demolition sites that contradict the more sanguine representations of the modern landscape. Both remind us that continuous innovation ("development," "modernization") of industrial civilization comes at a price: continuous demolition and displacement. But whereas Burtynsky bids us to keep a distant gaze on the monuments of creative-destruction in order to coolly resist the seduction of industrial power, Vergara wants us to join him as intruders into abandoned libraries and boarded-up houses, not just to expose the violent destruction in our midst, but, more importantly, to fill in the "gaps" in our collective memory. By photographing urban "ruins," Vergara hopes to search out and preserve traces of the "soul" "among the dereliction and destruction." What kind of soul might we find? Certainly not the "soul" in the machines that earlier modernists like Le Corbusier and Henry Ford celebrated. The automobile, of course, dominates the urban landscape, along with utility poles, garbage pails, barred windows and doors. But in Vergara's photos the presence of automobiles (often they, too, are left abandoned among the weeds) reminds us that the assumptions of the modern American dream—mobility based on cheap energy, prosperity defined as unlimited consumption, technology as the ever-expanding control over nature—have exacted a terrible price on the landscape.

But even among the ruins there remain signs of hope and redemption, evidenced by the many churches and religious symbols that fill Vergara's photos. Pentecostal churches have re-occupied numerous structures originally built for other purposes. (In my old Newark neighborhood, Hispanic Pentecostal churches have occupied what were once a delicatessen, a candy store, a firehouse, and a former go-go bar.) But unlike the stone-built churches—built to symbolize stability and permanence, not just of the church itself, but of the whole neighborhood in which it was located—these makeshift churches, whatever personal sense of salvation they provide their members, seem to be as temporary as the buildings surrounding them. They offer an enclave of survival in the urban landscape, but they are inward looking, often windowless structures seeking to defend themselves against the hostile world outside, just like the barred-pink fortress-house Vergara shows us on Fern Street.

Other signs of transcendence are scattered throughout Vergara's urbanscapes—"Jesus" graffitied on a boarded-up house; a billboard advertising "detoxification" treatments ("Procedure Confidential"); a middle school sign proclaiming that "Everybody is Somebody and We Are Rising" (with several of its letters having already dropped to the ground). Christians might read spiritual significance in the mundane storefront sign of the "Penn Fish Co.," the fish as symbol of Christ, the fisher of men. Yet, I don't see Vergara searching for a form of religious redemption in the urban wilderness he documents. His photographs fill in the "gaps" of historical memory by memorializing the fragmentary remains of a past. Abandoned buildings and empty lots become haunted ruins. "Penn Fish Co." thus evokes an era when the urban street formed the backdrop of a contemporary life—a scene of diversity, vitality, and permanence. Vergara knows he's playing with nostalgia in his photos: "I imagine Gary and Detroit as the noisy, dramatic cities they once were and I see myself photographing the ghosts left behind."[12] Like Burtynsky's, there is nothing in Vergara's vision to suggest what we might do to control the creative-destructive processes of modernity; rather, his stark images call upon us to stop, look around us and think what we are doing. In a world that is obsessed with erasing the past, he would have us regain a sense of history by reflecting on the remnants of what we have lost.

Notes

[1] The unintended sculptured forms appear in other of Burtynsky's work, for example, in the series on ship breakers in Bangladesh.

[2] While demolition is shown to be the underside of energy production in his Three Gorges Dam series, Burtynsky also points to another paradigmatic site of industrial modernization: the landfill. Mountains of used tires transform the landscape by "building it up," whereas energy extraction appears as a digging out (mines, quarries). The depletion of resources (abandoned mines) is thus coupled with the accumulation of waste. In his novel, *Underworld,* Don DeLillo also proposed the landfill—where the "waste stream ended"—as a paradigmatic site of industrial America.

[3] "Artist Statement." (http://www.edwardburtynsky.com/)

[4] Quotations from David L. Kirp, John P. Dwyer, Larry A. Rosenthal, *Our Town: Race, Housing, and the Soul of Suburbia,* (New Brunswick, NJ: Rutgers University Press, 1997), pp. 15, 20.

[5] While manufacturing boomed in the outlying suburbs of Camden County during 1950–1970, the city of Camden lost half of its manufacturing jobs. Ibid.

[6] Ibid, 23.

[7] Vergara, *American Ruins* (New York: The Monacelli Press, 1999), p. 12.

[8] Jane Jacobs, *The Death and Life of Great American Cities.*

[9] American Ruins, 23.

[10] American Ruins, 22.

[11] American Ruins, 23.

[12] Op. cit. 24.

Things to Do with the Reading

1. Locate a point of contact between Kunstler's essay and Gambino's—find a significant passage from each. Decide what Kunstler might say about one or more of the images that Gambino discusses and that are included with his essay. Consider, for example, Gambino's treatment of the Ben Franklin Bridge. See "Put Your Sources into Conversation with Another" in Chapter 13.

2. Gambino notes how often human figures are conspicuously absent in Burtynsky's and Vergara's photographs. But there are in fact some people in Burtynsky's "Three Gorges" and in Vergara's "Fern Street." Write about the role that human figures play in terms of how each photograph communicates—perhaps in relation to the absence of human figures in other of their photographs.

3. In much analytical writing the writer does not simply set out to prove a thesis but instead formulates a thesis in order to create a workable space in which a range of related claims might be made about the subject. Gambino's essay is a good place to observe this aspect of essay construction/organization—the evolving thesis in action.

   First, find a sentence that serves as a thesis—the claim that causes the piece to cohere, to possess a sense of direction. (Note: you will find more than one version of this primary claim in an essay.) Then locate interesting claims in the piece that the thesis seems to allow Gambino the space to produce. You'll notice these are connected to the thesis but not necessarily just another version of the same thing. Write down three or four of these, noting where you find them.

4. Look at how Gambino uses the formula that *Writing Analytically* calls "Seems to Be About X" (see Chapter 4) in paragraph 3. Here he says that the engineers' "ingenious instruments are not [Burtynsky's] real subject." As the paragraph progresses, Gambino complicates the essay's thinking, noting "Burtynsky's photos remind us that the beauty of these landscapes cannot be separated from the industrial power that *forcefully cuts* them from the earth." This is a symptom of the essay's fondness for paradox, also evident in the title

of the photo, "Rock of Ages" (an old religious hymn about how some things can be relied on to last forever), and elsewhere in the piece. What do you make of these paradoxes? How do they function to organize the piece? What are the terms of the ambivalence that Gambino is investigating in this essay, and what point of view is he ultimately inviting us to take towards it?

5. **Application:** Imagine that Vergara and Burtynsky planned to spend a week taking photographs in the area around which you live. Where would each of them go to shoot, and why? Be as specific as you can. (Maybe you could take some photographs in one or more of these places yourself.)

Note: You may wish to look ahead to the discussion of contemporary photography in the interview of Joseph Elliott, which opens Chapter 22, "Seeing." It will give you a crash course in thinking about photographs, and in it Elliott discusses Vergara and Burtynsky overtly.

Adam Gopnik

Times Regained: How the Old Times Square Was Made New

Nominally a book review about two recent histories of the revitalization of Times Square in New York City, this essay also offers a resonant analysis of the patterns and politics of urban redevelopment. Adam Gopnik is an essayist, cultural commentator, and an award-winning journalist for The New Yorker.

1   This year marks the hundredth anniversary of the decision to take an hourglass-shaped traffic funnel between Forty-second Street and Forty-seventh Street on Broadway, which had been called Longacre Square, and rename it after the New York *Times,* which had just built its office there. This was less an honor than a consolation prize. The other, then bigger and brighter newspaper, the New York *Herald,* had claimed the other, then brighter and better square, eight blocks south, which still bears its ghostly name. Nine years later, in 1913, the *Times* scurried off to a prim side street and a Gothic Revival bishop's palace, where it has been lifting its skirts and shyly peeking around the corner at its old home ever since.

    No other part of New York has had such a melodramatic, mood-ring sensitivity to the changes in the city's history, with an image for every decade. There was the turn-of-the-century Times Square, with its roof gardens and showgirls; the raffish twenties Times Square of Ziegfeld and Youmans tunes; the thirties Times Square of "42nd Street," all chorus lines and moxie; the forties, V-J "On the Town" Times Square, full of sailors kissing girls; the wizened black-and-white fifties Times Square of "Sweet Smell of Success," steaming hot dogs, and grungy beats; and then the sixties and the seventies Times Square of "Midnight Cowboy" and "Taxi Driver," where everything fell apart and Hell wafted up through the manhole covers. No other place in town has been quite so high and quite so low. Within a single half decade, it had Harpo Marx in the Marx Brothers' valedictory movie, "Love Happy," leaping ecstatically from sign to sign and riding away on the flying Mobilgas Pegasus, and, down below, the unforgettable image of James Dean, hunched in his black overcoat, bearing the weight of a generation on his shoulders.

    Now, of course, we have the new Times Square, as fresh as a neon daisy, with a giant Gap and a Niketown and an Applebee's and an ESPN Zone and television announcers visible through tinted windows, all family retailing and national brands. In some ways, the Square has never looked better, with the diagonal sloping lines of the Reuters Building, the curving Deco zipper, even the giant mock dinosaur in the Toys R Us. There are, of course, people who miss the old Times Square, its picturesque squalor and violence and misery and exploitation. Those who pointed at the old Times Square as an instance of everything that capitalism can do wrong now point to the new Times Square as an instance of everything that capitalism can do worse. Where once Times Square was hot, it is now cold, where once varied, now uniform, where once alive, now dead. Which just proves, as with the old maxim about belief,

Times Regained: First published in The New Yorker, March 2004. Copyright © 2004 by Adam Gopnik, by permission of the author.

that people who refuse to be sentimental about the normal things don't end up being sentimental about nothing; they end up being sentimental about anything, shedding tears about muggings and the shards of crack vials glittering like diamonds in the gutter.

And yet, whatever has been gained, something really is missing in the new Times Square. The forces that created it, and the mixed emotions that most of us have in its presence, are the subject of James Traub's *The Devil's Playground* (Random House; $25.95), which is both an engaged civics lesson and a work of social history. The book begins with an ironic moment—Traub takes his eleven-year-old son to the new Forty-second Street to see the old "42nd Street"—and then spirals back into history, moving decade by decade over the past century.

Traub, a writer for the *Times,* hates city myth but loves city history: on every page 5 you learn something about how the city really happened, and how it really happens now. He is particularly good at wrestling complicated history into a few tight pages. He gives the best account we have of the original sin of New York: the birth, in 1811, of the iron street grid almost before there were any streets. The decision to lay a crisscross of numbers over the city without any breaks for public squares, plazas, or parks—a deliberately brutal nod to the governing principle of commerce—is why we still, sadly, call any awkward and accidental space created by the diagonal of Broadway intersecting an avenue a "square."

Traub also has a gift for filtering social history through a previously invisible individual agent. As always, the vast forces of mass culture turn out to be the idiosyncratic choices of a few key, mostly hidden players. The character of the signs in Times Square, for instance, was mostly the invention of O. J. Gude, the Sign King of Times Square. Gude, a true aesthete with a significant art collection, was the first to sense that the peculiar shape of Times Square—a triangle with sign-friendly "flats" at the base and the apex—made it the perfect place for big electric national-brand signs, or "spectaculars," as they were called, even before the First World War. In 1917, when Gude put up a two-hundred-foot-long spectacular, on the west side of Broadway between Forty-third and Forty-fourth, featuring twelve gleaming "spearmen" who went through spasmodic calisthenics, it was as big an event in American pop culture, in its way, as the opening of "The Jazz Singer," ten years later. Gude also had the bright idea of joining the Municipal Art Society, the leading opponent of big signs, and later helped shape the zoning ordinances that essentially eliminated big electric signs anywhere in midtown *except* in Times Square.

Times Square is famous for what used to be called its "denizens"—Damon Runyon, George S. Kaufman, Clifford Odets, A. J. Liebling—and Traub writes brief lives of a lot of them. But the history of the place isn't really a history of its illuminati; it's a history of its illuminations. Though social forces and neon signs flow out of individuals, they don't flow back into individuals so transparently. George S. Kaufman, to take one instance, was exclusively a creature of the theatre; if, like the galleries in SoHo in the nineteen-nineties, the Broadway theatre had in the thirties picked up and moved to Chelsea, Kaufman would have followed it blindly and would never have been seen on Forty-second Street again. Even Runyon has about as much to do with the history of Times Square as P. G. Wodehouse does with the history of Mayfair: his subject is language, not place, and in all of Runyon's stories it would be hard to find a single set-piece description of Times Square, a single bulb on a single sign. Individual artists help make cities, but cities don't make their artists in quite so neatly reciprocal a way. Dr. Johnson's "London" is a poem; "The London of Dr. Johnson" is a tour-bus ride.

Traub gives no false gloss to the decay of Times Square; it was really bad. The neighborhood declined to a point where, by the mid-seventies, the Times Square precincts placed first and second in New York in total felonies. (Harlem had a third as many.) These were crimes of violence, too: a rape or an armed robbery or a murder took place nearly every day and every night. Stevie Wonder's great 1973 song "Living for the City" has a spoken-word interlude in which the poor black kid from the South arrives on West Forty-second Street and in about five minutes is lured into the drug business. This was a song, but it was not a lie.

Traub's account of the area's transformation is lit from behind by another, still longer and larger one—Lynne B. Sagalyn's masterly *Times Square Roulette: Remaking the City Icon*, just issued in paperback (M.I.T.; $29.95). Sagalyn teaches real estate at the University of Pennsylvania, and her book, the fruit of more than a decade of scholarly labor, is as mind-bendingly detailed an account of the relations of property and culture as one can find outside Galsworthy or Trollope.

10   It's full of eye-opening material, if one can keep one's eyes open long enough to find it. Sagalyn's book is written, perhaps of necessity, in a prose so dense with city acronyms and cross-referential footnotes that it can defeat even the most earnest attention. Nonetheless, its material is the material of the city's existence. Reading it is like reading an advanced-biology textbook and then discovering that its sole subject is your own body.

Traub and Sagalyn agree in dispelling a myth and moving toward a history, and the myth irritates them both—Traub's usual tone of intelligent skepticism sometimes boils over here into exasperation. The myth they want to dispel is that the cleanup of Times Square in the nineties was an expression of Mayor Giuliani's campaign against crime and vice, and of his companion tendency to accept a sterilized environment if they could be removed, and that his key corporate partner in this was the mighty Disney, which led the remaking of West Forty-second Street as a theme park instead of an authentic urban street. As Traub and Sagalyn show, this is nearly the reverse of the truth. It was Mayor Koch who shaped the new Times Square, if anyone did, while the important private profit-makers and players were almost all purely local: the Old Oligarchs, the handful of rich, and mostly Jewish, real-estate families—the Rudins, Dursts, Roses, Resnicks, Fishers, Speyers, and Tishmans, as Sagalyn crisply enumerates them. Mayor Giuliani, basically, was there to cut the ribbon, and Disney to briefly lend its name.

The story follows, on a larger scale than usual, the familiar form of New York development, whose stages are as predictable as those of a professional wrestling match: first, the Sacrificial Plan; next, the Semi-Ridiculous Rhetorical Statement; then the Staged Intervention of the Professionals; and, at last, the Sorry Thing Itself. The Sacrificial Plan is the architectural plan or model put forward upon the announcement of the project, usually featuring some staggeringly obvious and controversial device—a jagged roof or a startling pediment—which even the architect knows will never be built, and whose purpose is not to attract investors so much as to get people used to the general idea that something is going to be built there. (Sometimes the Sacrificial Plan is known by all to be sacrificial, and sometimes, as in "The Lottery," known to everyone but the sacrifice.) The Semi-Ridiculous Rhetorical Statement usually accompanies, though it can precede, the Sacrificial Plan, and is intended to show that the plan is not as brutal and cynical as it looks but has been designed in accordance with the architectural mode of the moment. ("The three brass lambs that stand on the spires of Sheep's Meadow Tower reflect the historical context of the site …" was the way it was done a decade ago; now it's more likely to be "In its hybrid façade, half mirror, half wool, Sheep's Meadow Tower captures the contradictions and deconstructs the flow of …") The Staged Intervention marks the moment when common sense and common purpose, in the form of the Old Oligarchs and their architects—who were going to be in charge in the first place—return to rescue the project from itself. The Sorry Thing itself you've seen. (At Ground Zero, Daniel Libeskind supplied the sacrificial plan, and now he is pursuing all of the semi-ridiculous rhetoric, in the forlorn hope that, when the professionals stage their intervention, he will be the professional called on.)

The only difference in the Times Square project was that, because of its size, it all happened twice. (Actually, there were two dimensions to the remaking of Times Square—the West Forty-second Street projects, and the reclaiming of the Square itself—but each depended on the other, and, though administratively distinct, they were practically joined.) The first Sacrificial Plan appeared in the late seventies, and was called "the City at Forty-second Street." Presented by the developer Fred Papert, with the support of the Ford Foundation and with proposed backing from Paul Reichmann, of Olympia & York, it envisioned a climate-controlled indoor-mall Forty-second Street, with a five-hundred-thousand-square-foot "educational, entertainment, and exhibit center," and a 2.1-million-square-foot merchandise mart for the garment trade, all strung together with aerial walkways and, lovely period touch, equipped with a monorail. Mayor Koch wasn't happy about the plan; "We've got to make sure that they have seltzer"—that it's echt New York—"instead of orange juice," he said. But mostly he worried because someone else would be squeezing the oranges.

Still, the plan did what such plans are meant to do: establish the principle, civic-minded rather than commercial, that something had to be done here, and the larger principle that whatever was done should be on a large scale—the old, outdoor theatre-and-arcade Forty-second Street could be turned into "a consumer-oriented exposition center with people moving across 42nd Street by means of pedestrian bridges," as one early draft of the rhetoric put it. As the initiative passed from the developers to the Koch administration, a further principle was established. The transformation could be made only by large-scale condemnation of what was already there, and the city and state together proposed a new way to link up private and public: the developers would get the right to build on condition that they paid directly for public improvements. The price of your tower on top was a cleaner subway station below.

Still more significant, and what should have been seen as a portent in the first 15 Sacrificial Plan, was the felt need to pull away from the street completely. This was not simply snobbery but self-preservation; Forty-second Street wasn't dying but raving.

The porno shops on West Forty-second Street weren't there because the middle class had fled. They were there because the middle class was there. The people who bought from the porn industry were the office workers who walked by the stores on the way to and from work, and the tourists who wanted to take back a little something not for the kids. The XXX video rooms and bookstores and grind-house theatres were going concerns, paying an average of thirty-two thousand dollars a year in rent; peep shows could gross five million a year. Though the retailers were obviously entangled with the Mafia, the buildings were owned by respectable real-estate families—for the most part, the same families who had owned the theatres since the thirties, the Brandts and the Shuberts. Times Square was Brechtville: a perfect demonstration of the principle that the market, left to itself, will produce an economy of crime as happily as an economy of virtue.

This—the crucial underlying reality in the Forty-second Street redevelopment—meant that the city, if it was to get the legal right to claim and condemn property in order to pass it over, had to be pointing toward some enormous, unquestioned commercial goal, larger or at least more concrete than the real goal, which was essentially ethical and "cultural." For once, the usual New York formula had to be turned right around: a question of virtue had to be disguised as a necessity of commerce. On Forty-second Street, a group of perfectly successful private businessmen in the movie-theatre business were being pushed aside in favor of a set of private businessmen in the tall-building business, and the legal argument for favoring the businessmen in the tall-building business was that they had promised that if you let them build a really tall building they would fix up the subway station.

This produced the Second Sacrificial Plan, of 1983: Philip Johnson and John Burgee's immense four towers straddling either side of Times Square on Forty-second, each with a slightly different pedimented top. The Semi-Ridiculous Rhetorical Statement invoked for this plan was that the pedimented tops "contextualized" the big buildings because they recalled the roofline of the old Astor Hotel, a victim of development twenty years before. They were by far the biggest and bulkiest buildings that had ever been proposed for midtown; Sagalyn gasps at the sheer zoning outrage of it. They had to be that big to establish their right to be at all. The Brandt family, which owned many of the theatres, sued and lost. "The Durst family interests put their name on five lawsuits," Sagalyn reports, "but the rumors of their financial backing of many more are legion." (The Dursts owned various individual lots along the street, which they intended to put together for their own giant building.) After ten years, they lost, too. Forty-seven suits were launched, and the plan withstood them all. The Johnson models, fortresses designed to withstand a siege of litigation, had triumphed. But nobody really wanted to build the buildings.

In the interim between the First Sacrificial Plan and the Second, however, something had changed in the ideology of architecture. A new orthodoxy had come into power, with an unapologetic emphasis on formal "delirium" and the chaotic surface of the city. In Rem Koolhaas's epoch-marking manifesto "Delirious New York" (1978), the buzz, confusion, danger, and weirdness of New York were no longer things to worry about. In fact, they were pretty much all we had to boast of. To an increasing bias in favor of small-scale streetscapes and "organic" growth was added a neon zip of pop glamour. The new ideology was Jane Jacobs dressed in latex and leather.

By what turned out to be a happy accident, this previously academic, pop-perverse set of ideas had influenced minds at the Municipal Art Society—the very group that had fought against the idea of signs and signage in Times Square at the turn of the century. In 1985, after the appearance of the Johnson plan, the Municipal Art Society, under the impeccable direction of the white-shoed Hugh Hardy, took on as its cause the preservation of the "bowl of light" in Times Square and "the glitz of its commercial billboards and electronic signs." After being digested in various acronymic gullets, this campaign produced not only new zoning text (sections ZR81-832 and ZR81-85, as Sagalyn duly notes) but, as an enforcement mechanism, an entirely new unit of measurement: the LUTS, or "Light Unit Times Square." (Each sign had to produce a minimum LUTS reading; the lighting designer Paul Marantz gave it its name.)

And so the Municipal Art Society became the major apostle of a continuing cha-   20
otic commercial environment in Times Square, while the big developers had to make the old Beaux-Arts case for classical order, lucidity, and space—for "trees and clean streets … museums and sidewalk cafés," in the plaintive words of the developer David Solomon. Eventually, in the early-nineties decline, Prudential, which had been holding on to the development on West Forty-second Street, was forced to sell its rights at a discount—to the Durst family, which had been leading the litigation against the plan all along but which, as everyone could have predicted, was there at the finale to develop and build, including 4 Times Square, the big building in which these words are being written.

None of this, however, could have created the new Times Square had it not been for other, unforeseeable changes. The first, and most important, was the still poorly explained decline in violent crime. (Traub tours the Eighth Avenue end of Forty-second with one of the district's privately financed security officers, who points out that there is still plenty of prostitution and drug-trafficking but very few muggings or assaults; even chain-snatching and petty theft are now rare.) This decline allowed for the emergence of the real hyperdrive of the new Square, the arrival of what every parent knows is the engine of American commerce: branded, television-based merchandise directed at "families" (that is, directed at getting children to torture their parents until they buy it). The critical demographic fact, as a few have pointed out, is the late onset of childbearing, delayed here until the habit of New York is set and the disposable income to spend on children is larger. When Damon Runyon was writing, the presence of Little Miss Marker in the Square was the material for a story. Now Little Miss Marker runs the place.

Of all the ironies of the Times Square redevelopment, the biggest is this: that the political right is, on the whole, happy with what has happened, and points to Times Square as an instance of how private enterprise can cure things that social engineering had previously destroyed, while the left points to Times Square as an instance of how market forces sterilize and drive out social forces of community and authenticity. But surely the ghosts of the old progressives in Union Square should be proudest of what has happened. It was, after all, the free market that produced the old Times Square: the porno stores were there because they made money, as part of a thriving market system. Times Square, and Forty-second Street, was saved by government decisions, made largely on civic grounds. Nothing would have caused more merriment on the conservative talk shows than the LUTS regulations—imagine some bureaucrat telling you how bright your sign should be—but it is those lights which light the desks of the guys at the offices of Clear Channel on Forty-second Street, and bring the crowds that make them safe. Civic-mindedness, once again, saved capitalism from itself.

And yet you don't have to have nostalgia for squalor and cruelty to feel that some vital chunk of New York experience has been replaced by something different, and less. Traub ends with the deconstructionist Mark Taylor, who trots out various depressions about the Society of Spectacle to explain the transformation, all of which are marvellously unilluminating. Times Square may be spectacular—that is what its sign-makers have called their own signs for a century—but in the theoretical sense it's not a spectacle at all. It's not filled by media images that supplant the experience of real things. It's a tangible, physical, fully realized public square in which real people stare at things made by other people. The absence of spectacle, in that sense—the escape from the domination of isolated television viewing—is what still draws people on New Year's Eve, in the face of their own government's attempts to scare them away. (Dick Clark, of course, is a simulacrum, but he was born that way.)

Traub toys with the idea that the real problem lies in the replacement of an authentic "popular" culture, of arcades and Runyonesque song-pluggers, with a "mass" culture, of national brands and eager shoppers. But it's hard to see any principled way in which the twenty-foot-tall animatronic dinosaur at the new Toys R Us howls at the orders of mass culture, while O. J. Gude's dancing spearmen were purely Pop. The distinction between popular culture and mass culture is to our time what the distinction between true folk art and false folk art was to the age of Ruskin and Morris; we want passionately to define the difference because we know in our hearts that it doesn't exist. Even fairy tales turn out to be half manufactured by a commercial enterprise, half risen from the folkish ground. The idea that there is a good folkish culture that comes up from the streets and revivifies the arts and a bad mass culture imposed from above is an illusion, and anyone who has studied any piece of the history knows it.

25   All the same, there is something spooky about the contemporary Times Square. It wanders through you; you don't wander through it. One of the things that make for vitality in any city, and above all in New York, is the trinity of big buildings, bright lights, and weird stores. The big buildings and bright lights are there in the new Times Square, but the weird stores are not. By weird stores one means not simply small stores, mom-and-pop operations, but stores in which a peculiar and even obsessive entrepreneur caters to a peculiar and even an obsessive taste. (Art galleries and modestly ambitious restaurants are weird stores by definition. It's why they still feel very New York.) If the big buildings and the bright signs reflect the city's vitality and density, weird stores refract it; they imply that the city is so varied that someone can make a mundane living from one tiny obsessive thing. Poolrooms and boxing clubs were visible instances of weird stores in the old Times Square; another, slightly less visible, was the thriving world of the independent film business, negative cutters, and camera-rental firms.

There is hardly a single weird store left on Broadway from Forty-second Street to Forty-sixth Street—hardly a single place in which a peculiar passion seems to have committed itself to a peculiar product. You have now, one more irony, to bend east, toward respectable Fifth Avenue, toward the diamond merchants and the Brazilian restaurants and the kosher cafeterias that still fill the side streets, to re-create something that feels a little like the old Times Square. (Wonderful Forty-fifth Street! With the Judaica candlesticks and the Japanese-film rental and the two-story shops selling cheap clothes and stereos, lit up bright.) Social historians like to talk about the Tragedy of the Commons, meaning the way that everybody loses when everybody overgrazes the village green, though it is in no individual's interest to stop. In New York, we suffer from a Tragedy of the Uncommons: weird things make the city worth living in, but though each individual wants them, no one individual wants to pay to keep them going. Times Square, as so often in the past, is responding, in typically heightened form, to the general state of the city: the loss of retail variety troubles us everywhere, as a new trinity of monotony—Starbucks, Duane Reade, and the Washington Mutual Bank—appears to dominate every block. We just feel it more on Broadway.

Do we overdraw Times Square history, make it more epic than it ought to be? Piccadilly and Soho, in London, and Place de Clichy, in Paris, are similar places, have known similar kinds of decline and similar kinds of pickup—but without gathering quite the same emotion. We make Times Square do more work than it ought to. Other great cities have public spaces and pleasure spaces, clearly marked, and with less confusion between them. When Diana died, it was Kensington Palace, not Piccadilly, that got the flowers, and in Paris it is the Champs-Élysées, not Place de Clichy, that gets the military parade on the fourteenth of July. Which returns us, with a certain sense of awe, to the spell still cast by the original sin of the 1811 grid plan. We make our accidental pleasure plazas do the work of the public squares we don't have. This is asking a lot of a sign, or even a bunch of bright ones lighting up the night.

Things to Do with the Reading

1. This essay offers a number of models for how to analyze that are worthy of imitating. One is its use of the "Appears to Be About X, but Is Really About Y" gambit (see Chapter 4) to distinguish the "myths" about rebuilding from the "history." Make note of all of the too-easy answers—the misconceptions—that Gopnik points out.

2. Link: The reversals in this essay (mentioned above) also call to mind the fondness for paradox we pointed to in Gambino's piece. How does Gambino's treatment of such complicated notions as "creative destruction" resemble and differ from Gopnik's treatment of the tangled history of Times Square's redevelopment? You might note, by the way, (and analyze) Gopnik's own fondness for verbal paradox, as in his discussion of the responses of the political left and right (see paragraph 22). A sentence in Gopnik that invites linkage to Gambino's perspective is "the transformation [of Times Square] could be made only by large-scale condemnation of what was already there" (paragraph 14).

3. **Link:** In his essay, "The Public Realm and the Common Good," Kunstler has much to say about "civic" matters and about the commercial pressures that have shaped Americans' use of space. Use Kunstler as a lens for looking at Gopnick's essay. What, for example, might Kunstler say about the various plans for Times Square? Also consider how Gopnick's perspective might alter (complicate, qualify) Kunstler's. Useful sentences in Gopnick for this purpose are: "civic-mindedness, once again, saved capitalism from itself" and "Times Square, and Forty-second Street, were saved by government decisions, made largely on civic grounds" (paragraph 22).

4. This essay is full of proper names. See, for example, paragraph 7: Damon Runyan (whose name coined the adjective "Runyonesque," which appears throughout the piece), P.G. Wodehouse, Sr., [Samuel] Johnson, among others. Make a list of names mentioned in Gopnick's piece and then Google them. How are these "allusions" functioning in this essay—what do they provide? Why does Gopnik do this? And what does this way of proceeding suggest about his assumptions about his audience—readers of *The New Yorker*? (See the discussion of ethos in the short take on rhetoric in Chapter 1.)

5. **Application:** Don't let the witty way that Gopnik names the stages of redevelopment lead you to dismiss them as merely comic. The "familiar form" that he educes in four parts—the Sacrificial Plan, the Semi-Ridiculous Rhetorical Statement, the Staged Intervention of the Professionals, and the Sorry Thing Itself—offers a potent lens for examining redevelopment elsewhere. An obvious case in point is New Orleans. How might we apply the four steps to the rebuilding efforts going on there? Do some research in the popular press (and/or Google) on the way that this (or any) major project of urban rebuilding is being talked about and planned. Identify one or more Sacrificial Plans, Semi-Ridiculous Rhetorical Statements, and so forth. Then use your answers to fuel a few pages (or more) of analysis.

   You could also use Gopnick as a lens for examining something more local. Gopnick, like Kunstler, addresses the issue of zoning. Locate a zoning issue where you live and analyze it from Gopnick's and/or Kunstler's point of view.

Rosalyn Baxandall and Elizabeth Ewen

Suburban Birth Pangs

This piece, taken from the authors' book entitled *Picture Windows: How the Suburbs Happened*, documents the rise of Long Island as an example of suburban expansion.

The discussion focuses on the role that urban planner Robert Moses played in the conversion of Long Island from an unregulated and sparsely populated enclave for the rich to a diverse network of communities. The story of the development of Long Island reveals how deeply embedded our national assumptions are about social class, race, and land ownership.

When New York City folk decided to take advantage of their new free weekends by packing a picnic, hopping into a car, and heading to the country for sunshine and space, Long Island seemed a logical destination. Around the turn of the century New York City had built many bridges linking the city to the island by automobile; Long Island therefore was accessible as well as close.[1] Although the landed gentry did everything in their power to keep city people out of their private playgrounds, urban interlopers in their new, affordable Model Ts began to acquire a taste for space, sun, and sea—and some even dared to dream of owning a home on Long Island.

In 1925, for instance, Brooklyn-bred Seth and Peggy Mills inherited a dry goods store, bought a Model T, and began taking day trips to Long Island. As Peggy put it, "In those days it took a long time; the roads were so bad, the car often broke down. But still it was worth it. The sight of those rolling hills, something you'd only see in the pictures, I'll never forget it. Coming from Brooklyn, the countryside seemed endless and you could finally be alone. Even on weekends when we couldn't make the trip, we'd sit around and dream of what it would be like to live there."[2]

Clearly these dreams could not be realized on the elite North Shore, which estate owners considered their personal domain. They went to great lengths to keep it so, building huge walls around their estates and posting armed guards at the borders to prevent errant day trippers from meandering onto the grounds.

Wealthy Long Islanders also made sure the North Shore was difficult to circumnavigate. At their behest, officials in Nassau County allowed all public roads to fall into disrepair. Moreover, private estate roads were built like mazes—winding and deliberately confusing. Most of the North and South Shore beaches were marked CLOSED with large private property signs, and were guarded as well. The only beaches open to the public were rocky, unappealing, and pitifully narrow, and city residents had to pay exorbitant rates to the local towns to use them.

Opulent estate owners also make sure that the journey itself to Long Island was arduous. Northern Boulevard, a main access road through Queens to the North Shore, was the widest highway, 160 feet of macadam (a pavement of small layers of stone, bound with tar). At the city line, it shrank to 18 feet of deteriorating pavement, eventually becoming dirt and dust. Cars had to go single file and watch for gaping holes

From *Picture Windows* by Elizabeth Ewen, © 2000 Perseus Books Group.

and unpaved stretches. Desperate families often tried to picnic at the side of the road, but the ever vigilant guards made their stops brief. The average Sunday journey of thirty-two miles in 1923, from the Queensborough Bridge to Huntington, took four hours. As Robert Caro noted, "when the families of New York City reached Long Island, they found the milk and honey sour indeed."[3]

The robber barons also insured that railroad travel to Long Island was difficult. A wealthy group lead by Charles Pratt, a partner of John D. Rockefeller, bought enough stock in the Long Island Railroad to control the North Shore lines.[4] Following the dictum of a Long Island Railroad vice-president that "population follows transportation," Pratt made sure that the North Shore branches were never electrified, because it would make for faster, more comfortable, and cheaper travel.[5]

As more city residents bought Model Ts, an increasing number of people became frustrated by the inaccessibility of Long Island's vast stretches of pristine beach lands. Mounting pressure for access to Long Island's sun and sand and the relentless intransigence of the rich combined to create an impasse.

The influential urban planner Robert Moses was one of the few men with enough power, guts, know-how, and vision to confront the estate owners and insist that they open up Long Island. Moses had worked in progressive reform organizations such as the Good Government Commission, and had the ear and respect of powerful politicians such as Al Smith, then governor of New York State. In his capacity first as the president of the Long Island Park Commission (1924–1936) and later as park commissioner for the metropolitan area and surroundings (1936–1964), Moses wielded the political power to float special bond issues to finance and appropriate land for highways, water crossings, beaches, and parks.[6] He believed that the public had as much right to recreation and leisure activity as the wealthy.

In 1922, Moses rented a summer bungalow in Babylon with his wife and small children and fell in love "with the town, with the bay, with the whole South Shore."[7] As he commuted on the Long Island Railroad and looked out the window, he saw "thick leafy bands of wood and through the trees the blue waters of ponds and streams." Moses began to explore, looking up the property rights in local libraries and trekking by foot through vast forests and streams. His "eyes" burned with ideas, and he soon discovered that the South Shore contained 3,500 acres of empty, unused land close to the city line not owned by the robber barons or local Long Island governments. It was owned by the government of New York City, which meant that "land could be opened to the cities' people merely by turning a key." Moreover, beyond lay another vast reserve of unused land, reachable only by boat: Jones Beach and Fire Island. Jones Beach seemed remote, but Moses realized that it was a mere twenty-five miles from Times Square.[8]

Moses proposed building two connecting highways to link the city to the beach, and making the beach a public park. The idea was revolutionary. Up to that point, most country parks originally conceived as habitats to be hiked and canoed through and kept in their natural wild state—they could not be reached by automobile and so remained unused. Yet Moses' proposal to make Jones Beach into a park transformed and domesticated the concept of the pristine nature preserve. His plan incorporated baseball diamonds, tennis courts, golf courses, and swimming pools—not exclusively for the rich but for less affluent city people.

Even though Moses wanted to see Long Island more accessible, his desire for democratization was limited. Like most mainstream progressives of the time, Moses made a distinction between the public and the common people. As Frances Perkins, later the secretary of labor under Franklin D. Roosevelt and a longtime associate of Moses, observed:

> He'd denounce the common people terribly. To him they were lousy, dirty people, throwing bottles all over Jones Beach.... He loves the public, but not as people. The public is just the public. It's a great amorphous mass to him; it needs to be bathed, it needs to be aired, it needs recreation, but not for personal reasons—just to make it a better public.[9]

As parks commissioner, Moses had the clout to put his convictions into practice. Although he opened the beach to automobile traffic, making sure there was sufficient parking for huge numbers of cars, he vetoed any plans for making the parks accessible by rapid public transit; Moses wouldn't even extend a Long Island Railroad line to Jones Beach. He made park access to those without cars even more difficult by building bridges across the new parkways so low that chartered buses had to take slow, indirect local roads. Later on, during the Depression Moses charges 50 cents for entry to Jones Beach, in violation of the American tradition of free public parks.

Moses considered African Americans inherently "dirty" and took specific measures to deny them access to the parks. Permits required for buses to enter public parks often were denied to black groups, especially permits for Jones Beach. Most chartered trips were shunted to parks many miles away from the entrance to Jones Beach, and even in those parks buses carrying black passengers were directed to the furthest reaches of the parking areas. Blacks were discouraged by park officials from using the best "white" beaches; and the handful of black lifeguards were stationed at the most distant and least developed beaches. Moses believed that African Americans did not like cold water and had the temperature at the Jones Beach swimming pool deliberately kept ice cold in an effort to keep blacks out.[10]

Despite his undemocratic definition of the people, these actions taken by Moses were still far too democratic for the Long Island elite. While wealthy Long Islanders did not contest the construction of the Southern State Parkway, which provided access to Jones Beach but did not trespass on their vast holdings, the construction of the Northern State Parkway was another story. When the plans of the Long Island State Park Commission called for a parkway to be built in the northern part of Nassau and Suffolk counties—cutting east through their estates—the ruling class issues a clarion call to halt the highways' invasion of their territory.

Declaring that the parkway would allow the Gold Coast to be "overrun with rabble from the city,"[11] estate owners used their powerful connections in Long Island and Albany to pass legislation abolishing the Long Island State Park Commission and its authority to allocate money for construction. Moses, however, had the ear of the Governor, Al Smith, who considered himself one of the rabble and their chief defender. The war was on. The state legislature favored Long Island's elite and passed bill after bill, only to be thwarted by the governor's veto.

After many years of skirmishes, a compromise was struck. The Northern State Parkway was built in spite of the estate owners' opposition, but the highway was routed far from the estates of the most powerful group of landowners. This compromise was costly for both drivers, who now had to go miles out of their way, and taxpayers, who had to finance a land purchase for the 2.3 miles of additional road. This might seem minute, but it illustrates the power of the estate owners: Drivers now had to go 839.5 miles out of their way each year.

The North Shore elite may have won the battle to preserve their dominion, but they lost the war. After the completion of the highways and beaches, an infrastructure that supported the development of housing, industry, leisure, and recreation on the South Shore sprang up seemingly overnight. In 1920 there were no highways on Long Island; but 12 years later there was a modern interconnected parkway system linking the various Long Island communities and allowing easy access to New York City. When Moses became president of Long Island State Park Commission, there was only one underutilized state park. In 1928, only four years later, there were fourteen state parks totaling 9,700 acres—parks that were automobile-accessible and outfitted with modern recreational facilities.[12]

Many people who flocked to Long Island for recreation and a temporary respite from city life decided to settle permanently, especially on the flatter, less well-landscaped South Shore, which was not dominated by powerful elites. At the turn of the century the South Shore of Long Island—which eventually would house the quintessential suburb of Levittown—was still predominantly rural, inhabited by fishermen, farmers, artisans, and tradespeople. Freeport, the second-largest village in Nassau County, was a major South Shore fishing port; oystering, clamming, and whaling were the predominant industries. In 1892, Freeport became an incorporated village, which attested to its economic importance.

By the early 1920s, Freeport has emerged as an open, public resort and summer haven. Located near Astoria, Queens, then the moviemaking capital of the East Coast, Freeport became a vacation center for the aristocracy of the burgeoning entertainment industry. Freeport developed its own entertainment too with summer theaters and a giant amusement park that opened in 1923 on the waterfront. Playland had numerous rides, vaudeville shows, dance halls, and a saltwater swimming pool.[13] Mimicking the industrial elite, the entertainers built large and luxurious mansions and hotels, albeit on a smaller scale. This in turn attracted actors, movie stars, comedians, singers, and stagehands.

By the mid-1920s, Freeport's original working population of artisans and farmers swelled to include European immigrants and a small colony of African Americans who migrated from South Carolina and Georgia to work as domestic servants for rich entertainers and a newly arrived middle class. Recruited or brought to Long Island by relatives or agencies, they settled in small, segregated enclaves, many near the railroad tracks and some in Bennington Park in the center of Freeport. These South Shore communities originally were built through family, church, and kinship ties.

Local resident Louise Simpson, who worked on voter registration forms that included information on where people were born, observed this distinct pattern:

> I realized that they were all from the same area in South Carolina, a lot form Charleston.... Freeport was a hub, it had good transportation for people migrating to do domestic work. For domestics, it was okay, you had one day off and every other Sunday. Freeport got to be a meeting place for people who did domestic work and they were able to find work in the large homes; there were rooming houses, so when they quit a job they could find a room. This is how friendships developed, if you're from my hometown, I'm going to seek you out. You felt comfortable, you knew each other. If you didn't go that route of family and friends, there was this particular family who was sort of like a personnel person for employment. She would go to where she came from in Carolina and bring people up, or tell them to get in touch and their transportation would be paid. Freeport blossomed like that.[14]

Harve Sinklar-Herring, who came from South Carolina, ran such an employment agency. Her first contact with Freeport was in 1927, when she came up with her cousin to work as a domestic servant for the summer. She also found work as a chauffeur and a caterer. Using these skills, she opened a domestic service agency, first in her home and then in a large house that encompassed an office, a dormitory, and a staff of twenty. She recruited and trained women from South Carolina in domestic work. She claims to have had "the only agency like this. I advertised in local papers. I charged employers who hired the women. I charged the domestics room and board while I trained them."[15]

Like other railroad depot towns of the South Shore, Freeport had significant real estate activity. Large tracts of land were bought by speculators, builders, and developers. Freeport participated in a nationwide suburban housing boom. Indeed, Nassau County, including Freeport, was the fastest growing county in the United States in the 1920s.[16] Planned communities and large subdivisions promoted by developers like the Freeport Land Company were aimed at upper-middle-class families, some of whom had vacationed in and around Freeport and were drawn to town life within easy access of the city.

Seth and Peggy Mills could not find a house on the North Shore, so they bought a lot and built a tudor house in Freeport. "We couldn't move to the North Shore, our original dream, but we did find a house within reach of the city with beautiful beaches, quiet streets and flowers and trees," said Peggy. "We felt like we were living rich in miniature."[17] The Mills were part of a trend of new upper-middle-class suburban home owners.

Between 1922 and 1929, six million new homes went up across the nation—twice as many as in any previous seven-year period. Well over half were single-family homes. Rising wages and falling housing prices propelled the construction industry. The suburbs grew twice as rapidly as the center cities in the 1920s; nearly one out of six Americans lived in the suburbs by 1930.[18] The increased availability of mortgages made it easier to borrow money. This growth, however, benefited only the upper and upper middle class. Three quarters of the new housing continued to be marketed to the top third of the household income spectrum, and there was no production at all for the bottom third, categorized as living below "any decent standard."[19] The 1920 census indicated that 46 percent of all American families were home owners, although in metropolitan areas—where the poor lived—fewer families owned homes. New York City had the lowest rate of home ownership with only 12 percent. Residential patterns remained segregated along economic and racial lines.

This segregation reflected deep prejudices that were manifested in Freeport. Freeport's expansion was welcomed by many of its summer visitors and new residents, but many older local Anglo-Saxon residents felt threatened by the flamboyant entertainers and the new immigrants who had come to settle there. The Ku Klux Klan flourished in the 1920s, reflecting and inflaming local fears of immigrants, Catholics, Jews, African Americans, and ethnic entertainers. During the early 1920s, one out of every eight white residents in Nassau and Suffolk counties was a member of the Klan. On July 4, 1924, 30,000 spectators looked on as 2,000 robed Klansmen marched with their floats down Main Street. In Freeport, the Klan's membership included several local ministers, the chief of police, county workers, and a wide array of other townspeople—a list that would have made a civic club or organization proud; but the Klan was no Kiwanis club. It held cross burnings at Christmastime, Lincoln's birthday, and the Fourth of July. It actively tried to keep black people confined to Bennington Park and out of Roosevelt, a neighboring white community.[20]

In her 1993 book *Having Our Say*, Elizabeth (Bessie) Delany provides a rare first-hand account of a confrontation between the Ku Klux Klan and African Americans on Long Island. In the 1920s the Delany sisters had moved to New York City in search of further education and greater opportunities. Bessie was solidly middle class and one of the few female black dentists in Harlem. One Sunday she and her boyfriend were returning from the beach, heading back toward Sag Harbor, a predominantly black seaside resort town:

> We came around the corner of this two-lane road, and there are about twenty men dressed in white robes, hoods and all, stopping cars and searching. You could see that they were making colored people get out of their cars! Well, my eyes popped out of my head, I said, "Aren't you going to stop?" But my friend never answered me. He stepped on the gas and drove around them, up an embankment and everything, and next thing I knew we had just zoomed around them. . . . I believe we simply outran them. Here, all those long years in the South they

[our parents] had managed to keep us Delany children out of the hands of the KKK and they'd almost got their hands on me—on Long Island.[21]

Racism did not only manifest itself through the organizational activities of the Klan. It was deeply inscribed into all the codes that governed who could live where. During the 1920s, restrictive covenants prevented the sale of property to Mexicans, Asians, blacks, and Jews. Although the U.S. Supreme Court struck down municipal and residential segregation laws in 1917, real estate boards and property owner associations concocted contractual "gentlemen's" agreements to prevent class, religious, and racial integration. Economic restrictions such as house prices, codes that prevented the construction of two family houses and apartments, loan and mortgage policies, and minimum lot sizes all kept the suburbs closed to anyone who wasn't white, Protestant, wealthy, or upper middle class.[22] Zoning regulations also determined whether towns would be industrial and working class or residential and suburban.

Even the select segment of the population *not* excluded from the new suburbs by restrictive covenants or zoning encountered problems. The housing industry at the time was small, makeshift, local, and unregulated. At best it was a patchwork that included genuine growth in real estate sales and housing subdivisions, as well as unscrupulous promoters and developers creating speculative profit-making schemes. By the mid-1920s, large auctions of land tracts were opening, promoted for investment speculation. Developers used newly conceived advertising techniques to sell both property and whole communities not yet built.

Lavish brochures and advertising folders, for example, claimed the Biltmore Shores in Massapequa had "paved streets, fine homes, a vast park, modern shops, churches, schools, golf, tennis, yachting and riding clubs, and a splendid fire department and complete administrative system."[23] This was all fiction. When people bought land sight unseen from speculators, they risked getting burned. One group of investors from Dayton, Ohio, tried to sell their Long Island property only to learn it was nothing but worthless land. The unscrupulous activities of the "land sharks" caused one reader of the *New York Times* to write to the editor, "My advice is to leave all Long Island property alone."[24]

According to *Architectural Forum*, much of this fly-by-night development was shoddy. Suburban home construction in Long Island was considered the worst in the nation. Bradley Randall, chief underwriter for New York, did a study of Long Island building and found that "examples of faulty construction most prevalent were two plaster coats instead of three, no fire stopping, insufficient thickness of foundation walls, poor quality timber and flooring ... no collar beams between rafters and other minor sins of commission and omission."[25] One writer in *Architectural Forum* observed that "no phrase more aptly conveys the thought of miserable home development practice than the brand, 'cheap Long Island.'"[26]

Although there was a housing boom in the 1920s—albeit mainly shoddy and speculative—by 1925 it had peaked, followed by a rapid downturn in construction. By 1929, residential housing had dropped 46 percent to 509,000 units. In dollars this meant a decline from $4.5 billion in 1925 to $2.45 billion in 1929.[27] The breakdown of the housing market was the bellwether of the Great Depression.

Suburban housing had accelerated in the early 1920s, but its financing had become precarious. Single-family dwellings typically were purchased through an unsound web of first, second, and even third mortgages generally of short terms and without any built-in orderly system for repayment.[28] As the depression deepened and people lost their jobs, they were sitting ducks for defaults and foreclosures.

With the onset of the Great Depression, credit was frozen and no capital was available for speculation in housing. Upscale 1920s housing based on speculation by unscrupulous promoters failed. The widespread failure of real estate and bond scandals resulted in the loss of new high-priced city apartments and suburban developments. By 1932 the housing decline reached epic proportions. As one scholar noted, "In 1930 total housing production receded to a point 60 percent below the 1922–28 average; by 1931 the rate had descended 69 percent below that average. ... In 1932 foreclosures reached the disastrous level of 250,000 homes."[29]

Unlike European countries, the United Stated had never developed strategies to deal with the issue of housing on a national level. It had no federal housing programs or policies, no public housing for low-income and working-class families, and no financial guarantees to aid the middle class in case of bank credit or mortgage failures. The federal government's lack of federal housing policies reflected the American belief in individualism, private enterprise, and individual home ownership, an ideology eloquently expressed by President Herbert Hoover, who claimed with confidence, "The sentiment for home ownership is so embedded in the American heart that millions of people who dwell in tenements, apartments, and rental rows of solid brick have the aspirations for wider opportunity in ownership of their own home."[30] The sentiment might have been there, but sentiment alone could not build houses—especially when the fledging housing industry had already collapsed.

Notes

[1] Robert A. Caro, *The Power Broker: Robert Moses and the Rise and Foll of New York* (New York: Vintage, 1975), 144–47. Westchester barred its parks to anyone not a resident of the county, and New Jersey was accessible only by privately operated ferries that took a long time. Long Island was accessible by the Brooklyn Bridge (1883), the Williamsburg Bridge (1903), the Queensborough Bridge (1909), and the Manhattan Bridge (1909).

[2] Peggy and Seth Mills, interview by authors, March 1993.

[3] Caro, *Power Broker*, 153.

[4] Ibid, 151.

[5] Dennis P. Sorbin, *The Dynamics of Community Control*, Empire State Historical Publication Series 59 (Port Washington: Ira Friedman Inc., 1968), 113.

[6] On Long Island Moses built the Van Wyck, Long Island, Willowbrook, Northern State, and Seaford-Oyster Bay Expressways, the Wantaugh, Bethpage, Grand Central, Southern State, Meadowbrook, and Cross Island Parkways, and the Cross Bay, Queensborough,

Bronx Whitestone, and Triborough Bridges, and the Robert Moses Causeway, as well as twenty-one parks. See http://www.boone.calstatela.edu/g476winter98KirbyMoses.html.

[7] Caro, *Power Broker*, 157.

[8] Ibid., 157–59.

[9] Ibid., 318.

[10] Ibid., 318–19.

[11] Bernie Bookbinder, *Long Island People and Places Past and Present* (New York: Newsday Books/Harry Abrams, 1983), 202.

[12] Caro, *Power Broker*, 238.

[13] Bookbinder, *Long Island People*, 139.

[14] Louise Simpson, interview by authors, April 1991.

[15] Harve Sinklar-Herring, interview by authors, September 1991.

[16] Jon C. Teaford, *Post-Suburbia, Government and Politics in the Edge Cities* (Baltimore, MD: Johns Hopkins University Press, 1997), 33.

[17] Peggy Mills, interview by authors, March 1993.

[18] Kenneth Jackson, *Crabgrass Frontier: The Suburbanisation of the United States* (New York: Oxford University Press, 1985), 174–75; *Who Built America: From the Gilded Age to the Present*, vol. 11. American Social History Project, ed. (New York: Pantheon Books, 1992), 274–75.

[19] Nathaniel Schneider Keith, *Politics and the Housing Crisis Since 1930* (New York: Universe Books, 1973), 17; Gwendolyn Wright, *Building the Dream: A Social History of Housing in America* (Boston: MIT Press, 1983), 195.

[20] *New York Times*, 19 January 1923, 13 February 1923, 19 March 1923, 29 August 1923, 16 August 1924, 15 December 1924, 11 August 1992, *Newsday*, 7 November 1982. See Jane Gombieski, "Klokards, Kleagles, Kludds, and Kluxers: The Ku Klux Klan in Suffolk County, 1915–1928." *Long Island Historical Journal* 6 (Fall 1993): 41–62, for an informative analysis of the growth of the KKK and its activities on Long Island.

[21] Sarah Delany and Elizabeth Delany, *Having Our Say: The Delany Sisters' First Hundred Years* (New York: Kodansha International, 1993), 139.

[22] Wright, *Building the Dream*, 212.

[23] Edward Smits, *Nassau Suburbia USA* (Garden City, NY: Doubleday, 1974; rev. ed., 1990), 184.

[24] Marilyn E. Weingold, *American Mediterranean: An Environmental, Economic, and Social History of the Long Island Sound* (Port Washington, NY: Kennikat Press, 1974), 91.

[25] *Architectural Forum*, "Sub Divisions and the FHA," May 1935, 487.

[26] Ibid., "Nassau Shores," 465.

[27] Keith, *Politics and the Housing Crisis*, 17.

[28] Ibid., 18.

[29] Ibid., 19.

[30] Richard O. Davies, *Housing Reform During the Truman Administration* (Columbia: University of Missouri Press, 1966), 11.

Things to Do with the Reading

1. Look over the essay, focusing on how the authors use numbers and dates. What is the relation between these kinds of facts and the various firsthand accounts the authors include from ordinary people and from famous ones? Examine how the essay uses different kinds of evidence. (See Kinds of Evidence: What Counts? In Chapter 8.) To what ends does it marshal evidence—to support and advance what claims? How does the piece ultimately wish us to regard the rise of Long Island and more generally, the rise of the suburbs? To what extent can you determine its point of view?

2. **Link**: Among the most notorious remarks about Robert Moses is Francis Perkins' comment that "He'd denounce the common people terribly. To him they were lousy, dirty people, throwing bottles all over Jones Beach. ... He loves the public, but not as people." How does Moses' notion of the public compare with other writers' notions included in this book? How does it compare with the point of view toward the public in Kunstler's essay at the beginning of this chapter, or of Gopnik's? How does the way Jonathan Franzen thinks about the public and the private compare with the way Baxandall and Ewen conceive of them? Locate specific sentences from both "Suburban Birth Pangs" and the essay of your choice and use them to anchor your comparison.

3. **Application**: The essay concludes by distinguishing the United States from Europe, in that it "never developed strategies to deal with the issue of housing on a national level," and the authors assert that "the federal government's lack of housing policies reflected the American belief in individualism, private enterprise, and individual home ownership." They follow this assertion with a quotation from President Hoover identifying home ownership with the American dream.

   How might we use these concluding remarks as a lens for interpreting the state of the housing market in America today? Look up recent commentaries on housing. Check the records on the numbers of foreclosures. How has the credit crisis affected those trying to refinance? How are the banks, who lost millions on poor-risk mortgages, playing a role, making it difficult for some categories of people to get mortgages?

Jane Jacobs

The Uses of Sidewalks: Safety

This piece is excerpted from Jacobs' *The Death and Life of Great American Cities* (1961), a work commonly ranked among the most influential American books on urban planning. In a style of simple eloquence, Jacobs argues against the prevailing approach toward urban renewal in the 1950s, offering a point of view that remains pertinent today: "that the sight of people attracts still other people, is something that city planners and city architectural designers seem to find incomprehensible. They operate on the premise that city people seek the sight of emptiness, obvious order and quiet. Nothing could be less true."

Streets in cities serve many purposes besides carrying vehicles, and city sidewalks—   1
the pedestrian parts of the streets—serve many purposes besides carrying pedestrians. These uses are bound up with circulation but are not identical with it and in their own right they are at least as basic as circulation to the proper workings of cities.

A city sidewalk by itself is nothing. It is an abstraction. It means something only in conjunction with the buildings and other uses that border it, or border other sidewalks very near it. The same might be said of streets, in the sense that they serve other purposes besides carrying wheeled traffic in their middles. Streets and their sidewalks, the main public places of a city, are its most vital organs. Think of a city and what comes to mind? Its streets. If a city's streets look interesting, the city looks interesting; if they look dull, the city looks dull.

More than that, and here we get down to the first problem, if a city's streets are safe from barbarism and fear, the city is thereby tolerably safe from barbarism and fear. When people say that a city, or a part of it, is dangerous or is a jungle what they mean primarily is that they do not feel safe on the sidewalks.

But sidewalks and those who use them are not passive beneficiaries of safety or helpless victims of danger. Sidewalks, their bordering uses, and their users, are active participants in the drama of civilization versus barbarism in cities. To keep the city safe is a fundamental task of a city's streets and its sidewalks.

This task is totally unlike any service that sidewalks and streets in little towns or   5
true suburbs are called upon to do. Great cities are not like towns, only larger. They are not like suburbs, only denser. They differ from towns and suburbs in basic ways, and one of these is that cities are, by definition, full of strangers. To any one person, strangers are far more common in big cities than acquaintances. More common not just in places of public assembly, but more common at a man's own doorstep. Even residents who live near each other are strangers, and must be, because of the sheer number of people in small geographical compass.

The bedrock attribute of a successful city district is that a person must feel personally safe and secure on the street among all these strangers. He must not feel automatically menaced by them. A city district that fails in this respect also does badly in other ways and lays up for itself, and for its city at large, mountain on mountain of trouble.

From THE DEATH AND LIFE OF GREAT AMERICAN CITIES by Jane Jacobs, copyright © 1961, 1989 by Jane Jacobs. Used by permission of Random House, Inc.

Today barbarism has taken over many city streets, or people fear it has, which comes to much the same thing in the end. "I live in a lovely, quiet residential area," says a friend of mine who is hunting another place to live. "The only disturbing sound at night is the occasional scream of someone being mugged." It does not take many incidents of violence on a city street, or in a city district, to make people fear the streets. And as they fear them, they use them less, which makes the streets still more unsafe.

To be sure, there are people with hobgoblins in their heads, and such people will never feel safe no matter what the objective circumstances are. But this is a different matter from the fear that besets normally prudent, tolerant and cheerful people who show nothing more than common sense in refusing to venture after dark—or in a few places, by day—into streets where they may well be assaulted, unseen or unrescued until too late.

The barbarism and the real, not imagined, insecurity that gives rise to such fears cannot be tagged a problem of the slums. The problem is most serious, in fact, in genteel-looking "quiet residential areas" like that my friend was leaving.

10   It cannot be tagged as a problem of older parts of cities. The problem reaches its most baffling dimensions in some examples of rebuilt parts of cities, including supposedly the best examples of rebuilding, such as middle-income projects. The police precinct captain of a nationally admired project of this kind (admired by planners and lenders) has recently admonished residents not only about hanging around outdoors after dark but has urged them never to answer their doors without knowing the caller. Life here has much in common with life for the three little pigs or the seven little kids of the nursery thrillers. The problem of sidewalk and doorstep insecurity is as serious in cities which have made conscientious efforts at rebuilding as it is in those cities that have lagged. Nor is it illuminating to tag minority groups, or the poor, or the outcast with responsibility for city danger. There are immense variations in the degree of civilization and safety found among such groups and among the city areas where they live. Some of the safest sidewalks in New York City, for example, at any time of day or night, are those along which poor people or minority groups live. And some of the most dangerous are in streets occupied by the same kinds of people. All this can also be said of other cities.

Deep and complicated social ills must lie behind delinquency and crime, in suburbs and towns as well as in great cities. This book will not go into speculation on the deeper reasons. It is sufficient, at this point, to say that if we are to maintain a city society that can diagnose and keep abreast of deeper social problems, the starting point must be, in any case, to strengthen whatever workable forces for maintaining safety and civilization do exist—in the cities we do have. To build city districts that are custom made for easy crime is idiotic. Yet that is what we do.

The first thing to understand is that the public peace—the sidewalk and street peace—of cities is not kept primarily by the police, necessary as police are. It is kept primarily by an intricate, almost unconscious, network of voluntary controls and standards among the people themselves, and enforced by the people themselves. In some city areas—older public housing projects and streets with very high population turnover are often conspicuous examples—the keeping of public sidewalk law and order is left almost entirely to the police and special guards. Such places are jungles.

No amount of police can enforce civilization where the normal, casual enforcement of it has broken down.

The second thing to understand is that the problem of insecurity cannot be solved by spreading people out more thinly, trading the characteristics of cities for the characteristics of suburbs. If this could solve danger on the city streets, then Los Angeles should be a safe city because superficially Los Angeles is almost all suburban. It has virtually no districts compact enough to qualify as dense city areas. Yet Los Angeles cannot, any more than any other great city, evade the truth that, being a city, it *is* composed of strangers not all of whom are nice. Los Angeles' crime figures are flabbergasting. Among the seventeen standard metropolitan areas with populations over a million, Los Angeles stands so pre-eminent in crime that it is in a category by itself. And this is markedly true of crimes associated with personal attack, the crimes that make people fear the streets.

Los Angeles, for example, has a forcible rape rate (1958 figures) of 31.9 per 100,000 population, more than twice as high as either of the next two cities, which happen to be St. Louis and Philadelphia; three times as high as the rate of 10.1 for Chicago, and more than four times as high as the rate of 7.4 for New York.

In aggravated assault, Los Angeles has a rate of 185, compared with 149.5 for 15 Baltimore and 139.2 for St. Louis (the two next highest), and with 90.9 for New York and 79 for Chicago.

The overall Los Angeles rate for major crimes is 2,507.6 per 100,000 people, far ahead of St. Louis and Houston, which come next with 1,634.5 and 1,541.1, and of New York and Chicago, which have rates of 1,145.3 and 943.5.

The reasons for Los Angeles' high crime rates are undoubtedly complex, and at least in part obscure. But of this we can be sure: thinning out a city does not insure safety from crime and fear of crime. This is one of the conclusions that can be drawn within individual cities too, where pseudosuburbs or superannuated suburbs are ideally suited to rape, muggings, beatings, hold-ups and the like.

Here we come up against an all-important question about any city street: How much easy opportunity does it offer to crime? It may be that there is some absolute amount of crime in a given city, which will find an outlet somehow (I do not believe this). Whether this is so or not, different kinds of city streets garner radically different shares of barbarism and fear of barbarism.

Some city streets afford no opportunity to street barbarism. The streets of the North End of Boston are outstanding examples. They are probably as safe as any place on earth in this respect. Although most of the North End's residents are Italian or of Italian descent, the district's streets are also heavily and constantly used by people of every race and background. Some of the strangers from outside work in or close to the district; some come to shop and stroll; many, including members of minority groups who have inherited dangerous districts previously abandoned by others, make a point of cashing their paychecks in North End stores and immediately making their big weekly purchases in streets where they know they will not be parted from their money between the getting and the spending.

Frank Havey, director of the North End Union, the local settlement house, says, "I 20 have been here in the North End twenty-eight years, and in all that time I have never heard of a single case of rape, mugging, molestation of a child or other street crime of that sort in the district. And if there had been any, I would have heard of it even if it did not reach the papers." Half a dozen times or so in the past three decades, says Havey, would-be molesters have made an attempt at luring a child or, late at night, attacking a woman. In every such case the try was thwarted by passers-by, by kibitzers from windows, or shopkeepers.

Meantime, in the Elm Hill Avenue section of Roxbury, a part of inner Boston that is suburban in superficial character, street assaults and the ever present possibility of more street assaults with no kibitzers to protect the victims, induce prudent people to stay off the sidewalks at night. Not surprisingly, for this and other reasons that are related (dispiritedness and dullness), most of Roxbury has run down. It has become a place to leave.

I do not wish to single out Roxbury or its once fine Elm Hill Avenue section especially as a vulnerable area; its disabilities, and especially its Great Blight of Dullness, are all too common in other cities too. But differences like these in public safety within the same city are worth noting. The Elm Hill Avenue section's basic troubles are not owing to a criminal or a discriminated against or a poverty-stricken population. Its troubles stem from the fact that it is physically quite unable to function safely and with related vitality as a city district.

Even within supposedly similar parts of supposedly similar places, drastic differences in public safety exist. An incident at Washington Houses, a public housing project in New York, illustrates this point. A tenants' group at this project, struggling to establish itself, held some outdoor ceremonies in mid-December 1958, and put up three Christmas trees. The chief tree, so cumbersome it was a problem to transport, erect, and trim, went into the project's inner "street," a landscaped central mall and promenade. The other two trees, each less than six feet tall and easy to carry, went on two small fringe plots at the outer corners of the project where it abuts a busy avenue and lively cross streets of the old city. The first night, the large tree and all its trimmings were stolen. The two smaller trees remained intact, lights, ornaments and all, until they were taken down at New Year's. "The place where the tree was stolen, which is *theoretically* the most safe and sheltered place in the project, is the same place that is unsafe for people too, especially children," says a social worker who had been helping the tenants' group. "People are no safer in that mall than the Christmas tree. On the other hand, the place where the other trees were safe, where the project is just one corner out of four, happens to be safe for people."

This is something everyone already knows: A well-used city street is apt to be a safe street. A deserted city street is apt to be unsafe. But how does this work, really? And what makes a city street well used or shunned? Why is the sidewalk mall in Washington Houses, which is supposed to be an attraction, shunned? Why are the sidewalks of the old city just to its west not shunned? What about streets that are busy part of the time and then empty abruptly?

25   A city street equipped to handle strangers, and to make a safety asset, in itself, out of the presence of strangers, as the streets of successful city neighborhoods always do, must have three main qualities:

First, there must be a clear demarcation between what is public space and what is private space. Public and private spaces cannot ooze into each other as they do typically in suburban settings or in projects.

Second, there must be eyes upon the street, eyes belonging to those we might call the natural proprietors of the street. The buildings on a street equipped to handle strangers and to insure the safety of both residents and strangers, must be oriented to the street. They cannot turn their backs or blank sides on it and leave it blind.

And third, the sidewalk must have users on it fairly continuously, both to add to the number of effective eyes on the street and to induce the people in buildings along the street to watch the sidewalks in sufficient numbers. Nobody enjoys sitting on a stoop or looking out a window at an empty street. Almost nobody does such a thing. Large numbers of people entertain themselves, off and on, by watching street activity.

In settlements that are smaller and simpler than big cities, controls on acceptable public behavior, if not on crime, seem to operate with greater or lesser success through a web of reputation, gossip, approval, disapproval and sanctions, all of which are powerful if people know each other and word travels. But a city's streets, which must control not only the behavior of the people of the city but also of visitors from suburbs and towns who want to have a big time away from the gossip and sanctions at home, have to operate by more direct, straightforward methods. It is a wonder cities have solved such an inherently difficult problem at all. And yet in many streets they do it magnificently.

It is futile to try to evade the issue of unsafe city streets by attempting to make   30
some other features of a locality, say interior courtyards, or sheltered play spaces, safe instead. By definition again, the streets of a city must do most of the job of handling strangers for this is where strangers come and go. The streets must not only defend the city against predatory strangers, they must protect the many, many peaceable and well-meaning strangers who use them, insuring their safety too as they pass through. Moreover, no normal person can spend his life in some artificial haven, and this includes children. Everyone must use the streets.

On the surface, we seem to have here some simple aims: To try to secure streets where the public space is unequivocally public, physically unmixed with private or with nothing-at-all space, so that the area needing surveillance has clear and practicable limits; and to see that these public street spaces have eyes on them as continuously as possible.

But it is not so simple to achieve these objects, especially the latter. You can't make people use streets they have no reason to use. You can't make people watch streets they do not want to watch. Safety on the streets by surveillance and mutual policing of one another sounds grim, but in real life it is not grim. The safety of the street works best, most casually, and with least frequent taint of hostility or suspicion precisely where people are using and most enjoying the city streets voluntarily and are least conscious, normally, that they are policing.

The basic requisite for such surveillance is a substantial quantity of stores and other public places sprinkled along the sidewalks of a district; enterprises and public places that are used by evening and night must be among them especially. Stores, bars and restaurants, as the chief examples, work in several different and complex ways to abet sidewalk safety.

First, they give people—both residents and strangers—concrete reasons for using the sidewalks on which these enterprises face.

Second, they draw people along the sidewalks past places which have no attrac-   35
tions to public use in themselves but which become traveled and peopled as routes to

somewhere else; this influence does not carry very far geographically, so enterprises must be frequent in a city district if they are to populate with walkers those other stretches of street that lack public places along the sidewalk. Moreover, there should be many different kinds of enterprises, to give people reasons for crisscrossing paths.

Third, storekeepers and other small businessmen are typically strong proponents of peace and order themselves; they hate broken windows and holdups; they hate having customers made nervous about safety. They are great street watchers and sidewalk guardians if present in sufficient numbers.

Fourth, the activity generated by people on errands, or people aiming for food or drink, is itself an attraction to still other people.

This last point, that the sight of people attracts still other people, is something that city planners and city architectural designers seem to find incomprehensible. They operate on the premise that city people seek the sight of emptiness, obvious order and quiet. Nothing could be less true. People's love of watching activity and other people is constantly evident in cities everywhere. This trait reaches an almost ludicrous extreme on upper Broadway in New York, where the street is divided by a narrow central mall, right in the middle of traffic. At the cross-street intersections of this long north-south mall, benches have been placed behind big concrete buffers and on any day when the weather is even barely tolerable these benches are filled with people at block after block after block, watching the pedestrians who cross the mall in front of them, watching the traffic, watching the people on the busy sidewalks, watching each other. Eventually Broadway reaches Columbia University and Barnard College, one to the right, the other to the left. Here all is obvious order and quiet. No more stores, no more activity generated by the stores, almost no more pedestrians crossing—and no more watchers. The benches are there but they go empty in even the finest weather. I have tried them and can see why. No place could be more boring. Even the students of these institutions shun the solitude. They are doing their outdoor loitering, outdoor homework and general street watching on the steps overlooking the busiest campus crossing.

It is just so on city streets elsewhere. A lively street always has both its users and pure watchers. Last year I was on such a street in the Lower East Side of Manhattan, waiting for a bus. I had not been there longer than a minute, barely long enough to begin taking in the street's activity of errand goers, children playing, and loiterers on the stoops, when my attention was attracted by a woman who opened a window on the third floor of a tenement across the street and vigorously yoo-hooed at me. When I caught on that she wanted my attention and responded, she shouted down, "The bus doesn't run here on Saturdays!" Then by a combination of shouts and pantomime she directed me around the corner. This woman was one of thousands upon thousands of people in New York who casually take care of the streets. They notice strangers. They observe everything going on. If they need to take action, whether to direct a stranger waiting in the wrong place or to call the police, they do so. Action usually requires, to be sure, a certain self-assurance about the actor's proprietorship of the street and the support he will get if necessary, matters which will be gone into later in this book. But even more fundamental than the action and necessary to the action, is the watching itself.

Not everyone in cities helps to take care of the streets, and many a city resident or city worker is unaware of why his neighborhood is safe. The other day an incident occurred on the street where I live, and it interested me because of this point. 40

My block of the street, I must explain, is a small one, but it contains a remarkable range of buildings, varying from several vintages of tenements to three- and four-story houses that have been converted into low-rent flats with stores on the ground floor, or returned to single-family use like ours. Across the street there used to be mostly four-story brick tenements with stores below. But twelve years ago several buildings, from the corner to the middle of the block, were converted into one building with elevator apartments of small size and high rents.

The incident that attracted my attention was a suppressed struggle going on between a man and a little girl of eight or nine years old. The man seemed to be trying to get the girl to go with him. By turns he was directing a cajoling attention to her, and then assuming an air of nonchalance. The girl was making herself rigid, as children do when they resist, against the wall of one of the tenements across the street.

As I watched from our second-floor window, making up my mind how to intervene if it seemed advisable, I saw it was not going to be necessary. From the butcher shop beneath the tenement had emerged the woman who, with her husband, runs the shop; she was standing within earshot of the man, her arms folded and a look of determination on her face. Joe Cornacchia, who with his sons-in-law keeps the delicatessen, emerged about the same moment and stood solidly to the other side. Several heads poked out of the tenement windows above, one was withdrawn quickly and its owner reappeared a moment later in the doorway behind the man. Two men from the bar next to the butcher shop came to the doorway and waited. On my side of the street, I saw that the locksmith, the fruit man and the laundry proprietor had all come out of their shops and that the scene was also being surveyed from a number of windows besides ours. That man did not know it, but he was surrounded. Nobody was going to allow a little girl to be dragged off, even if nobody knew who she was.

I am sorry—sorry purely for dramatic purposes—to have to report that the little girl turned out to be the man's daughter.

Throughout the duration of the little drama, perhaps five minutes in all, no eyes appeared in the windows of the high-rent, small-apartment building. It was the only building of which this was true. When we first moved to our block, I used to anticipate happily that perhaps soon all the buildings would be rehabilitated like that one. I know better now, and can only anticipate with gloom and foreboding the recent news that exactly this transformation is scheduled for the rest of the block frontage adjoining the high-rent building. The high-rent tenants, most of whom are so transient we cannot even keep track of their faces,[1] have not the remotest idea of who takes care of their street, or how. A city neighborhood can absorb and protect a substantial number of these birds of passage, as our neighborhood does. But if and when the neighborhood finally *becomes* them, they will gradually find the streets less secure, they will be vaguely mystified about it, and if things get bad enough they will drift away to another neighborhood which is mysteriously safer. 45

In some rich city neighborhoods, where there is little do-it-yourself surveillance, such as residential Park Avenue or upper Fifth Avenue in New York, street watchers are hired. The monotonous sidewalks of residential Park Avenue, for example, are surprisingly little used; their putative users are populating, instead, the interesting store-, bar- and restaurant-filled sidewalks of Lexington Avenue and Madison Avenue to east and west, and the cross streets leading to these. A network of doormen and superintendents, of delivery boys and nursemaids, a form of hired neighborhood, keeps residential Park Avenue supplied with eyes. At night, with the security of the doormen as a bulwark, dog walkers safely venture forth and supplement the doormen. But this street is so blank of built-in eyes, so devoid of concrete reasons for using or watching it instead of turning the first corner off of it, that if its rents were to slip below the point where they could support a plentiful hired neighborhood of doormen and elevator men, it would undoubtedly become a woefully dangerous street.

Once a street is well equipped to handle strangers, once it has both a good, effective demarcation between private and public spaces and has a basic supply of activity and eyes, the more strangers the merrier.

Strangers become an enormous asset on the street on which I live, and the spurs off it, particularly at night when safety assets are most needed. We are fortunate enough, on the street, to be gifted not only with a locally supported bar and another around the corner, but also with a famous bar that draws continuous troops of strangers from adjoining neighborhoods and even from out of town. It is famous because the poet Dylan Thomas used to go there, and mentioned it in his writing. This bar, indeed, works two distinct shifts. In the morning and early afternoon it is a social gathering place for the old community of Irish longshoremen and other craftsmen in the area, as it always was. But beginning in midafternoon it takes on a different life, more like a college bull session with beer, combined with a literary cocktail party, and this continues until the early hours of the morning. On a cold winter's night, as you pass the White Horse, and the doors open, a solid wave of conversation and animation surges out and hits you; very warming. The comings and goings from this bar do much to keep our street reasonably populated until three in the morning, and it is a street always safe to come home to. The only instance I know of a beating in our street occurred in the dead hours between the closing of the bar and dawn. The beating was halted by one of our neighbors who saw it from his window and, unconsciously certain that even at night he was part of a web of strong street law and order, intervened.

A friend of mine lives on a street uptown where a church youth and community center, with many night dances and other activities, performs the same service for his street that the White Horse bar does for ours. Orthodox planning is much imbued with puritanical and Utopian conceptions of how people should spend their free time, and in planning, these moralisms on people's private lives are deeply confused with concepts about the workings of cities. In maintaining city street civilization, the White Horse bar and the church-sponsored youth center, different as they undoubtedly are, perform much the same public street civilizing service. There is not only room in cities for such differences and many more in taste, purpose and interest of occupation; cities also have a need for people with all these differences in taste and proclivity. The preferences of Utopians, and of other compulsive managers of other people's leisure, for one kind of legal enterprise over others is worse than irrelevant for cities. It is harmful. The greater and more plentiful the range of all legitimate interests (in the strictly legal sense) that city streets and their enterprises can satisfy, the better for the streets and for the safety and civilization of the city.

Bars, and indeed all commerce, have a bad name in many city districts precisely 50 because they do draw strangers, and the strangers do not work out as an asset at all.

This sad circumstance is especially true in the dispirited gray belts of great cities and in once fashionable or at least once solid inner residential areas gone into decline. Because these neighborhoods are so dangerous, and the streets typically so dark, it is commonly believed that their trouble may be insufficient street lighting. Good lighting is important, but darkness alone does not account for the gray areas' deep, functional sickness, the Great Blight of Dullness.

Under the seeming disorder of the old city, wherever the old city is working successfully, is a marvelous order for maintaining the safety of the streets and the freedom of the city. It is a complex order. Its essence is intricacy of sidewalk use, bringing with it a constant succession of eyes. This order is all composed of movement and change, and although it is life, not art, we may fancifully call it the art form of the city and liken it to the dance—not to a simple-minded precision dance with everyone kicking up at the same time, twirling in unison and bowing off en masse, but to an intricate ballet in which the individual dancers and ensembles all have distinctive parts which miraculously reinforce each other and compose an orderly whole. The ballet of the good city sidewalk never repeats itself from place to place, and in any one place is always replete with new improvisations.

The stretch of Hudson Street where I live is each day the scene of an intricate sidewalk ballet. I make my own first entrance into it a little after eight when I put out the garbage can, surely a prosaic occupation, but I enjoy my part, my little clang, as the droves of junior high school students walk by the center of the stage dropping candy wrappers. (How do they eat so much candy so early in the morning?)

While I sweep up the wrappers I watch the other rituals of morning: Mr.Halpert unlocking the laundry's handcart from its mooring to a cellar door, Joe Cornacchia's son-in-law stacking out the empty crates from the delicatessen, the barber bringing out his sidewalk folding chair, Mr. Goldstein arranging the coils of wire which proclaim the hardware store is open, the wife of the tenement's superintendent depositing her chunky three-year-old with a toy mandolin on the stoop, the vantage point from which he is learning the English his mother cannot speak. Now the primary children, heading for St. Luke's, dribble through to the south; the children for St. Veronica's cross, heading to the west, and the children for P.S. 41, heading toward the east. Two new entrances are being made from the wings: well-dressed and even elegant women and men with briefcases emerge from doorways and side streets. Most of these are heading for the taxis are part of a wider morning ritual: having dropped passengers from midtown in the downtown financial district, they are now bringing downtowners up to midtown. Simultaneously, numbers of women in housedresses have emerged and as they crisscross with one another they pause for quick conversations that sound with either laughter or joint indignation, never, it seems, anything between. It is time for me to hurry to work too, and I exchange my ritual farewell with Mr. Lofaro, the short, thick-bodied, white-aproned fruit man who stands outside his doorway a little up the street, his arms folded, his feet planted, looking solid as earth itself. We nod; we each glance quickly up and down the street, then look back to each other and smile. We have done this many a morning for more than ten years, and we both know what it means: All is well.

55   The heart-of-the-day ballet I seldom see, because part of the nature of it is that working people who live there, like me, are mostly gone, filling the roles of strangers on other sidewalks. But from days off, I know enough of it to know that it becomes more and more intricate. Longshoremen who are not working that day gather at the White Horse or the Ideal or the International for beer and conversation. The executives and business lunchers from the industries just to the west throng the Dorgene restaurant and the Lion's Head coffee house; meat-market workers and communications scientists fill the bakery lunchroom. Character dancers come on, a strange old man with strings of old shoes over his shoulders, motor-scooter riders with big beards and girl friends who bounce on the back of the scooters and wear their hair long in front of their faces as well as behind, drunks who follow the advice of the Hat Council and are always turned out in hats, but not hats the Council would approve. Mr. Lacey, the locksmith, shuts up his shop for a while and goes to exchange the time of day with Mr. Slube at the cigar store. Mr. Koochagian, the tailor, waters the luxuriant jungle of plants in his window, gives them a critical look from the outside, accepts a compliment on them from two passers-by, fingers the leaves on the plane tree in front of our house with a thoughtful gardener's appraisal, and crosses the street for a bite at the Ideal where he can keep an eye on customers and wigwag across the message that he is coming. The baby carriages come out, and clusters of everyone from toddlers with dolls to teenagers with homework gather at the stoops.

When I get home after work, the ballet is reaching its crescendo. This is the time of roller skates and stilts and tricycles, and games in the lee of the stoop with bottle-tops and plastic cowboys; this is the time of bundles and packages, zigzagging from the drug store to the fruit stand and back over to the butcher's; this is the time when teenagers, all dressed up, are pausing to ask if their slips show or their collars look right; this is the time when beautiful girls get out of MGs; this is the time when the fire engines go through; this is the time when anybody you know around Hudson Street will go by.

As darkness thickens and Mr. Halpert moors the laundry cart to the cellar door again, the ballet goes on under lights, eddying back and forth but intensifying at the bright spotlight pools of Joe's sidewalk pizza dispensary, the bars, the delicatessen, the restaurant and the drug store. The night workers stop now at the delicatessen, to pick up salami and a container of milk. Things have settled down for the evening but the street and its ballet have not come to a stop.

I know the deep night ballet and its seasons best from waking long after midnight to tend a baby and, sitting in the dark, seeing the shadows and hearing the sounds of the sidewalk. Mostly it is a sound like infinitely pattering snatches of party conversation and, about three in the morning, singing, very good singing. Sometimes there is sharpness and anger or sad, sad weeping, or a flurry of search for a string of beads broken. One night a young man came roaring along, bellowing terrible language at two girls whom he had apparently picked up and who were disappointing him.

Doors opened, a wary semicircle formed around him, not too close, until the police came. Out came the heads, too, along Hudson Street, offering opinion, "Drunk ... Crazy ... A wild kid from the suburbs."[2]

Deep in the night, I am almost unaware how many people are on the street unless something calls them together, like the bagpipe. Who the piper was and why he favored our street I have no idea. The bagpipe just skirled out in the February night, and as if it were a signal the random, dwindled movements of the sidewalk took on direction. Swiftly, quietly, almost magically a little crowd was there, a crowd that evolved into a circle with a Highland fling inside it. The crowd could be seen on the shadowy sidewalk, the dancers could be seen, but the bagpiper himself was almost invisible because his bravura was all in his music. He was a very little man in a plain brown overcoat. When he finished and vanished, the dancers and watchers applauded, and applause came from the galleries too, half a dozen of the hundred windows on Hudson Street. Then the windows closed, and the little crowd dissolved into the random movements of the night street.

The strangers on Hudson Street, the allies whose eyes help us natives keep the 60 peace of the street, are so many that they always seem to be different people from one day to the next. That does not matter. Whether they are so many always-different people as they seem to be, I do not know. Likely they are. When Jimmy Rogan fell through a plate-glass window (he was separating some scuffling friends) and almost lost his arm, a stranger in an old T shirt emerged from the Ideal bar, swiftly applied an expert tourniquet and, according to the hospital's emergency staff, saved Jimmy's life. Nobody remembered seeing the man before and no one has seen him since. The hospital was called in this way: a woman sitting on the steps next to the accident ran over to the bus stop, wordlessly snatched the dime from the hand of a stranger who was waiting with his fifteen-cent fare ready, and raced into the Ideal's phone booth. The stranger raced after her to offer the nickel too. Nobody remembered seeing him before, and no one has seen him since. When you see the same stranger three or four times on Hudson Street, you begin to nod. This is almost getting to be an acquaintance, a public acquaintance, of course.

I have made the daily ballet of Hudson Street sound more frenetic than it is, because writing it telescopes it. In real life, it is not that way. In real life, to be sure, something is always going on, the ballet is never at a halt, but the general effect is peaceful and the general tenor even leisurely. People who know well such animated city streets will know how it is. I am afraid people who do not will always have it a little wrong in their heads—like the old prints of rhinoceroses made from travelers' descriptions of rhinoceroses.

On Hudson Street, the same as in the North End of Boston or in any other animated neighborhoods of great cities, we are not innately more competent at keeping the sidewalks safe than are the people who try to live off the hostile truce of Turf in a blind-eyed city. We are the lucky possessors of a city order that makes it relatively simple to keep the peace because there are plenty of eyes on the street. But there is nothing simple about that order itself, or the bewildering number of components that go into it. Most of those components are specialized in one way or another. They unite in their joint effect upon the sidewalk, which is not specialized in the least. That is its strength.

Notes

[1] Some, according to the storekeepers, live on beans and bread and spend their sojourn looking for a place to live where all their money will not go for rent.

[2] He turned out to be a wild kid from the suburbs. Sometimes, on Hudson Street, we are tempted to believe the suburbs must be a difficult place to bring up children.

Things to Do with the Reading

1. Summarize Jacobs' argument, using the technique that *Writing Analytically* calls ranking (see Notice and Focus in Chapter 2). Do this by locating all of the characteristics that Jacobs says a neighborhood has to have to remain safe. Concentrate on the one or two characteristics that Jacobs would say are most important.

2. Write a summary in which you focus on the mistakes that Jacobs says housing authorities and city planners make. Also focus on what Jacobs claims are mistaken assumptions about the causes of unsafe neighborhoods. How, for example, does she dispute the charge that the presence of poor people and minorities make neighborhoods unsafe?

3. Look at Kunstler's attack on the kind of segregation that zoning causes, and locate the common ground between Kunstler and Jacobs in this regard. It is interesting that Jacobs makes little mention of the impact of cars, except perhaps in her discussion of what she calls "pseudo-suburbs." Theoretically, both Kunstler and Jacobs would welcome the arrival of a restaurant in a residential area. How does the car culture complicate both writers' advocacy of mixed use (commercial and residential) areas?

4. Now that you have read this essay, go back to the reference to Jane Jacobs in Gopnik's essay and explain it. Speaking of a change in architectural orthodoxy in New York, Gopnik writes, "The new ideology was Jane Jacobs dressed in latex and leather" (paragraph 18).

5. **Application:** Use Jacobs' essay as a lens for observing and analyzing a neighborhood that you know. You might, for example, station yourself some place in this neighborhood as Jacobs did, on the benches, on the median strip, on upper Broadway, or in front of the White Horse in the Village. What do you notice about the way people behave in this area? Gopnik notes that there is always a close relationship between property and culture. Consider how the neighborhood's architecture and the uses its building serve influence the absence or presence of what Jacobs calls "eyes on the street." You might also consider to what extent there is a "clear demarcation between what is public space and what is private space" (paragraph 26).

Mike Davis

Fortress Los Angeles

This piece is a *polemic* (from the Greek work for warlike) by Mike Davis: a former butcher, a longtime political activist, a professor, and the winner of a lucrative MacArthur Foundation grant—the so-called "genius" award given to the nation's most gifted creative minds. In the following excerpt from his most famous book, an urban study of contemporary Los Angeles entitled *City of Quartz* (1992), Davis examines how cultural attitudes and social class provide the actual material shape of urban design.

In Los Angeles—once a paradise of free beaches, luxurious parks, and "cruising   1 strips"—genuinely democratic space is virtually extinct. The pleasure domes of the elite Westside rely upon the social imprisonment of a third-world service proletariat in increasingly repressive ghettos and barrios. In a city of several million aspiring immigrants (where Spanish-surname children are now almost two-thirds of the school-age population), public amenities are shrinking radically, libraries and playgrounds are closing, parks are falling derelict, and streets are growing ever more desolate and dangerous.

Here, as in other American cities, municipal policy has taken its lead from the security offensive and the middle-class demand for increased spatial and social insulation. Taxes previously targeted for traditional public spaces and recreational facilities have been redirected to support corporate redevelopment projects. A pliant city government—in the case of Los Angeles, one ironically professing to represent a liberal biracial coalition—has collaborated in privatizing public space and subsidizing new exclusive enclaves (benignly called "urban villages"). The celebratory language used to describe contemporary Los Angeles—"urban renaissance," "city of the future," and so on—is only a triumphal gloss laid over the brutalization of its inner-city neighborhoods and the stark divisions of class and race represented in its built environment. Urban form obediently follows repressive function. Los Angeles, as always in the vanguard, offers an especially disturbing guide to the emerging liaisons between urban architecture and the police state.

Forbidden City

Los Angeles's first spatial militarist was the legendary General Harrison Gray Otis, proprietor of the *Times* and implacable foe of organized labor. In the 1890s, after locking out his union printers and announcing a crusade for "industrial freedom," Otis retreated into a new *Times* building designed as a fortress with grim turrets and battlements crowned by a bellicose bronze eagle. To emphasize his truculence, he later had a small, functional cannon installed on the hood of his Packard touring car. Not surprisingly, this display of aggression produced a response in kind. On October 1, 1910, the heavily fortified *Times* headquarters—the command-post of the open shop on the West Coast—was destroyed in a catastrophic explosion, blamed on union saboteurs.

From City of Quartz, Verso Books, 1990. Reprinted by permission.

Eighty years later, the martial spirit of General Otis pervades the design of Los Angeles's new Downtown, whose skyscrapers march from Bunker Hill down the Figueroa corridor. Two billion dollars of public tax subsidies have enticed big banks and corporate headquarters back to a central city they almost abandoned in the 1960s. Into a waiting grid, cleared of tenement housing by the city's powerful and largely unaccountable redevelopment agency, local developers and offshore investors (increasingly Japanese) have planted a series of block-square complexes: Crocker Center, the Bonaventure Hotel and Shopping Mall, the World Trade Center, California Plaza, Arco Center, and so on. With an increasingly dense and self-contained circulation system linking these superblocks, the new financial district is best conceived as a single, self-referential hyperstructure, a Miesian skyscape of fantastic proportions.

5   Like similar megalomaniacal complexes tethered to fragmented and desolate downtowns—such as the Renaissance Center in Detroit and the Peachtree and Omni centers in Atlanta—Bunker Hill and the Figueroa corridor have provoked a storm of objections to their abuse of scale and composition, their denigration of street life, and their confiscation of the vital energy of the center, now sequestered within their subterranean concourses or privatized plazas. Sam Hall Kaplan, the former design critic of the *Times,* has vociferously denounced the antistreet bias of redevelopment; in his view, the superimposition of "hermetically sealed fortresses" and random "pieces of suburbia" onto Downtown has "killed the street" and "dammed the rivers of life."[1]

Yet Kaplan's vigorous defense of pedestrian democracy remains grounded in liberal complaints about "bland design" and "elitist planning practices." Like most architectural critics, he rails against the oversights of urban design without conceding a dimension of foresight, and even of deliberate repressive intent. For when Downtown's new "Gold Coast" is seen in relation to other social landscapes in the central city, the "fortress effect" emerges, not as an inadvertent failure of design, but as an explicit—and, in its own terms, successful—socio-spatial strategy.

The goals of this strategy may be summarized as a double repression: to obliterate all connection with Downtown's past and to prevent any dynamic association with the non-Anglo urbanism of its future. Los Angeles is unusual among major urban centers in having preserved, however negligently, most of its Beaux Arts commercial core. Yet the city chose to transplant—at immense public cost—the entire corporate and financial district from around Broadway and Spring Street to Bunker Hill, a half-dozen blocks further west.

Photographs of the old Downtown in its 1940s prime show crowds of Anglo, black, and Mexican shoppers of all ages and classes. The contemporary Downtown "renaissance" renders such heterogeneity virtually impossible. It is intended not just to "kill the street" as Kaplan feared, but to "kill the crowd," to eliminate that democratic mixture that Olmsted believed was America's antidote to European class polarization. The new Downtown is designed to ensure a seamless continuum of middle-class work, consumption, and recreation, insulated from the city's "unsavory" streets. Ramparts and battlements, reflective glass and elevated pedways, are tropes in an architectural language warning off the underclass Other. Although architectural critics are usually blind to this militarized syntax, urban pariah groups—whether young black men, poor Latino immigrants, or elderly homeless white females—read the signs immediately.

Finding the Analytical Lens

This strategic armoring of the city against the poor is especially obvious at street level. In his famous study of the "social life of small urban spaces," William Whyte points out that the quality of any urban environment can be measured, first of all, by whether there are convenient, comfortable places for pedestrians to sit. This maxim has been warmly taken to heart by designers of the high corporate precincts of Bunker Hill and its adjacent "urban villages." As part of the city's policy of subsidizing the white-collar residential colonization of Downtown, tens of millions of dollars of tax revenue have been invested in the creation of attractive, "soft" environments in favored areas. Planners envision a succession of opulent piazzas, fountains, public art, exotic shrubbery, and comfortable street furniture along a ten-block pedestrian corridor from Bunker Hill to South Park. Brochures sell Downtown's "livability" with idyllic representations of office workers and affluent tourists sipping cappuccino and listening to free jazz concerts in the terraced gardens of California Plaza and Grand Hope Park.

In stark contrast, a few blocks away, the city is engaged in a relentless struggle   10 to make the streets as unlivable as possible for the homeless and the poor. The persistence of thousands of street people on the fringes of Bunker Hill and the Civic Center tarnishes the image of designer living Downtown and betrays the laboriously constructed illusion of an urban "renaissance." City Hall has retaliated with its own version of low-intensity warfare.

Although city leaders periodically propose schemes for removing indigents *en masse*—deporting them to a poor farm on the edge of the desert, confining them in camps in the mountains, or interning them on derelict ferries in the harbor—such "final solutions" have been blocked by council members' fears of the displacement of the homeless into their districts. Instead the city, self-consciously adopting the idiom of cold war, has promoted the "containment" (the official term) of the homeless in Skid Row, along Fifth Street, systematically transforming the neighborhood into an outdoor poorhouse. But this containment strategy breeds its own vicious cycle of contradiction. By condensing the mass of the desperate and helpless together in such a small space, and denying adequate housing, official policy has transformed Skid Row into probably the most dangerous ten square blocks in the world. Every night on Skid Row is Friday the 13th, and, unsurprisingly, many of the homeless seek to escape the area during the night at all costs, searching safer niches in other parts of Downtown. The city in turn tightens the noose with increased police harassment and ingenious design deterrents.

One of the simplest but most mean-spirited of these deterrents is the Rapid Transit District's new barrel-shaped bus bench, which offers a minimal surface for uncomfortable sitting while making sleeping impossible. Such "bumproof" benches are being widely introduced on the periphery of Skid Row. Another invention is the aggressive deployment of outdoor sprinklers. Several years ago the city opened a Skid Row Park; to ensure that the park could not be used for overnight camping, overhead sprinklers were programmed to drench unsuspecting sleepers at random times during the night. The system was immediately copied by local merchants to drive the homeless away from (public) storefront sidewalks. Meanwhile Downtown restaurants and markets have built baroque enclosures to protect their refuse from the homeless.

Although no one in Los Angeles has yet proposed adding cyanide to the garbage, as was suggested in Phoenix a few years back, one popular seafood restaurant has spent $12,000 to build the ultimate bag-lady-proof trash cage: three-quarter-inch steel rod with alloy locks and vicious out-turned spikes to safeguard moldering fishheads and stale french fries.

Public toilets, however, have become the real frontline of the city's war on the homeless. Los Angeles, as a matter of deliberate policy, has fewer public lavatories than any other major North American city. On the advice of the Los Angeles police, who now sit on the "design board" of at least one major Downtown project, the redevelopment agency bulldozed the few remaining public toilets on Skid Row. Agency planners then considered whether to include a "free-standing public toilet" in their design for the upscale South Park residential development; agency chairman Jim Wood later admitted that the decision not to build the toilet was a "policy decision and not a design decision." The agency preferred the alternative of "quasi-public restrooms"—toilets in restaurants, art galleries, and office buildings—which can be made available selectively to tourists and white-collar workers while being denied to vagrants and other unsuitables. The same logic has inspired the city's transportation planners to exclude toilets from their designs for Los Angeles's new subway system.[2]

Bereft of toilets, the Downtown badlands east of Hill Street also lack outside water sources for drinking or washing. A common and troubling sight these days is the homeless men—many of them young refugees from El Salvador—washing, swimming, even drinking from the sewer effluent that flows down the concrete channel of the Los Angeles River on the eastern edge of Downtown. The city's public health department has made no effort to post warning signs in Spanish or to mobilize alternative clean-water sources.

15   In those areas where Downtown professionals must cross paths with the homeless or the working poor—such as the zone of gentrification along Broadway just south of the Civic Center—extraordinary precautions have been taken to ensure the physical separation of the different classes. The redevelopment agency, for example, again brought in the police to help design "twenty-four-hour, state-of-the-art security" for the two new parking structures that serve the *Los Angeles Times* headquarters and the Ronald Reagan State Office Building. In contrast to the mean streets outside, both parking structures incorporate beautifully landscaped microparks, and one even boasts a food court, picnic area, and historical exhibit. Both structures are intended to function as "confidence-building" circulation systems that allow white-collar workers to walk from car to office, or from car to boutique, with minimum exposure to the public street. The Broadway-Spring Center, in particular, which links the two local hubs of gentrification (the Reagan Building and the proposed Grand Central Square) has been warmly praised by architectural critics for adding greenery and art to parking. It also adds a considerable dose of menace—armed guards, locked gates, and ubiquitous security cameras—to scare away the homeless and the poor.

The cold war on the streets of Downtown is ever escalating. The police, lobbied by Downtown merchants and developers, have broken up every attempt by the homeless and their allies to create safe havens or self-governed encampments. "Justiceville,"

founded by homeless activist Ted Hayes, was roughly dispersed; when its inhabitants attempted to find refuge at Venice Beach, they were arrested at the behest of the
local council member (a renowned environmentalist) and sent back to Skid Row. The
city's own brief experiment with legalized camping—a grudging response to a series
of deaths from exposure during the cold winter of 1987—was abruptly terminated
after only four months to make way for the construction of a transit maintenance
yard. Current policy seems to involve perverse play upon the famous irony about the
equal rights of the rich and poor to sleep in the rough. As the former head of the city
planning commission explained, in the City of the Angels it is not against the law to
sleep on the street per se—"only to erect any sort of protective shelter."[3] To enforce
this proscription against "cardboard condos," the police periodically sweep the Nickel,
tearing down shelters, confiscating possessions, and arresting resisters. Such cynical
repression has turned the majority of the homeless into urban bedouins. They are
visible all over Downtown, pushing their few pathetic possessions in stolen shopping
carts, always fugitive, always in motion, pressed between the official policy of containment and the inhumanity of Downtown streets.

Sequestering the Poor

An insidious spatial logic also regulates the lives of Los Angeles's working poor. Just
across the moat of the Harbor Freeway, west of Bunker Hill, lies the MacArthur Park
district—once upon a time the city's wealthiest neighborhood. Although frequently
characterized as a no-man's-land awaiting resurrection by developers, the district
is, in fact, home to the largest Central American community in the United States.
In the congested streets bordering the park, a hundred thousand Salvadorans and
Guatemalans, including a large community of Mayan-speakers, crowd into tenements
and boarding houses barely adequate for a fourth as many people. Every morning at
6 A.M. this Latino Bantustan dispatches armies of sewing *operadoras,* dishwashers, and
janitors to turn the wheels of the Downtown economy. But because MacArthur Park
is midway between Downtown and the famous Miracle Mile, it too will soon fall to
redevelopment's bulldozers.

Hungry to exploit the lower land prices in the district, a powerful coterie of
developers, represented by a famous ex-councilman and the former president of the
planning commission, has won official approval for their vision of "Central City West":
literally, a second Downtown comprising 25 million square feet of new office and retail
space. Although local politicians have insisted upon a significant quota of low-income
replacement housing, such a palliative will hardly compensate for the large-scale
population displacement sure to follow the construction of the new skyscrapers and
yuppified "urban villages." In the meantime, Korean capital, seeking *lebensraum* for
Los Angeles's burgeoning Koreatown, is also pushing into the MacArthur Park area,
uprooting tenements to construct heavily fortified condominiums and office complexes. Other Asian and European speculators are counting on the new Metrorail
station, across from the park, to become a magnet for new investment in the district.

The recent intrusion of so many powerful interests into the area has put increasing
pressure upon the police to "take back the streets" from what is usually represented

as an occupying army of drug-dealers, illegal immigrants, and homicidal homeboys. Thus in the summer of 1990 the LAPD announced a massive operation to "retake crime-plagued MacArthur Park" and surrounding neighborhoods "street by street, alley by alley." While the area is undoubtedly a major drug market, principally for drive-in Anglo commuters, the police have focused not only on addict-dealers and gang members, but also on the industrious sidewalk vendors who have made the circumference of the park an exuberant swap meet. Thus Mayan women selling such local staples as tropical fruit, baby clothes, and roach spray have been rounded up in the same sweeps as alleged "narcoterrorists."[4] (Similar dragnets in other Southern California communities have focused on Latino day-laborers congregated at street-corner "slave markets.")

20   By criminalizing every attempt by the poor—whether the Skid Row homeless or MacArthur Park venders—to use public space for survival purposes, law-enforcement agencies have abolished the last informal safety-net separating misery from catastrophe. (Few third-world cities are so pitiless.) At the same time, the police, encouraged by local businessmen and property owners, are taking the first, tentative steps toward criminalizing entire inner-city communities. The "war" on drugs and gangs again has been the pretext for the LAPD's novel, and disturbing, experiments with community blockades. A large section of the Pico-Union neighborhood, just south of MacArthur Park, has been quarantined since the summer of 1989; "Narcotics Enforcement Area" barriers restrict entry to residents "on legitimate business only." Inspired by the positive response of older residents and local politicians, the police have subsequently franchised "Operation Cul-de-Sac" to other low-income Latino and black neighborhoods.

Thus in November 1989 (as the Berlin Wall was being demolished), the Devonshire Division of the LAPD closed off a "drug-ridden" twelve-block section of the northern San Fernando Valley. To control circulation within this largely Latino neighborhood, the police convinced apartment owners to finance the construction of a permanent guard station. Twenty miles to the south, a square mile of the mixed black and Latino Central-Avalon community has also been converted into Narcotic Enforcement turf with concrete roadblocks. Given the popularity of these quarantines—save amongst the ghetto youth against whom they are directed—it is possible that a majority of the inner city may eventually be partitioned into police-regulated "no-go" areas.

The official rhetoric of the contemporary war against the urban underclasses resounds with comparisons to the War in Vietnam a generation ago. The LAPD's community blockades evoke the infamous policy of quarantining suspect populations in "strategic hamlets." But an even more ominous emulation is the reconstruction of Los Angeles's public housing projects as "defensible spaces." Deep in the Mekong Delta of the Watts-Willowbrook ghetto, for example, the Imperial Courts Housing Project has been fortified with chain-link fencing, restricted entry signs, obligatory identity passes—and a substation of the LAPD. Visitors are stopped and frisked, the police routinely order residents back into their apartments at night, and domestic life is subjected to constant police scrutiny. For public-housing tenants and inhabitants of narcotic-enforcement zones, the loss of freedom is the price of "security."

Notes

[1] *Los Angeles Times*, Nov. 4, 1978.

[2] Tom Chorneau, "Quandary Over a Park Restroom," *Downtown News*, Aug. 25, 1986.

[3] See "Cold Snap's Toll at 5 as Its Iciest Night Arrives," *Los Angeles Times*, Dec. 29, 1988.

[4] *Los Angeles Times*, June 17, 1990.

Things to Do with the Reading

1. Apply the Method and Paraphrase × 3 to the reading (see Chapter 2). What significant words repeat? What strands do you find? What is opposed to what? And so what? How would you paraphrase the first sentence of paragraph 6?

2. Uncover assumptions in the piece; that is, reason back to its premises, the unstated givens upon which Davis' argument rests (see Chapter 4). First, list a few of the unstated assumptions. What, for example, are some of his unstated assumptions about the homeless and the poor in cities? Try reasoning back to premises with the first two sentences of the piece: if Davis believes this, what must he also already believe?

3. **Link:** Bring Davis and Jacobs together by locating difference within similarity (see Chapter 4). Find the most significant point of contact between Davis' and Jacobs' ways of thinking about public spaces in cities. Given that similarity, what is the most revealing difference between the two arguments? Which of Davis' key words does Jacobs' piece usefully illuminate? Consider, for example, the way that the two writers use the word "street."

4. **Application:** Describe Davis' analytical method. List the key words that reveal his way of seeing a city. Then experiment with using his method as a lens for looking at a part of your campus or town. Is there, for example, a place where town or campus authorities have arranged things physically so as to encourage or discourage certain kinds of use and/or certain kinds of people? Note: you don't have to focus on homelessness or poverty. Make your priority thinking about public spaces and how they are managed.

FOR FURTHER RESEARCH: PLACES AND SPACES: CITIES AND SUBURBS

By Kelly Cannon, Reference Librarian

The readings and activities below invite you to further explore the theme of Places and Spaces: Cities and Suburbs. WARNING: Some essays are polemical; they are intended to promote insight and discussion (or a starting point for your next paper). To access the online readings, visit the *Writing Analytically with Readings* website at www.cengagebrain.com.

Open access

"Charter of the New Urbanism." *New Urbanism.* **NewUrbanism.org, 2011. 9 January 2011. http://www.newurbanism.org/newurbanism/principles.html**
Lists the basic tenets of New Urbanism, as viewed by New Urbanism.org, a major not-for-profit concerned with remedies to urban blight and sprawl.

> Explore: How does the website move beyond providing information to promoting action? See, for example, the "Principles" sub-section: "Obstacles to Overcome." Compare the values espoused by New Urbanism with those represented in the claims of Gambino and Kunstler in the essays printed above.

Hetzler, Olivia, et al. "Gentrification, Displacement, and the New Urbanism." *Sociation Today* **4.2 (2006). 11 January 2011. http://www.ncsociology.org/sociationtoday/v42/gent.htm**
This article, published in a peer-reviewed journal, contends that New Urbanism is seriously flawed.

> Explore: What about the presentation of this article strikes you as academic (scholarly) as opposed to popular? What is the argument presented here? What types of evidence are used to support that argument? Are you persuaded? Why or why not? How do the conclusions of this essay compare with those drawn by Mike Davis in his essay above on Los Angeles?

Lubell, Sam. "Welcome to Smallville." *New York Times Magazine* **(2010): 38. 11 January 2011. http://www.nytimes.com/2010/10/03/t-magazine/03remix-lubell-t.html**
Lately the American dream has been looking smaller—much smaller. The fabled McMansion is becoming a thing of the past.

> Explore: If large size is no longer a virtue in homes, what is? Does this shift away from the McMansion in any way resonate with James Howard Kunstler's plea above to begin to alter our material culture at the neighborhood level?

McMahon, Edward T. "The Place Making Dividend." *Planning Commissioners Journal* **(Fall 2010). 9 January 2011. http://pcj.typepad.com/planning_commissioners_jo/ 2010/11/527b.html**
Technology giant Apple had to rethink its architectural design before the Georgetown area of Washington, DC, would let it build a store there.

> Explore: This article quotes novelist Wallace Stegner as saying "If you don't know where you are, you don't know who you are." What about your own community or neighboring communities instills a unique sense of identity in the people who live there through its

architecture and use of space? How do the values of this correspond with or differ from the values espoused by Adam Gopnik in his essay above on redevelopment in New York City?

Neighborhood Scout. **2011. 9 January 2011. http://www.neighborhoodscout.com/**
Developed by Location Inc., a Massachusetts-based company, this website helps people who wish to relocate find the neighborhood that's right for them.

> Explore: Can you find your neighborhood? Do you agree with the assessment of your neighborhood? What qualities does this website think are important to someone who is relocating? Do you agree?

Taylor, Jerry, and Peter Van Doren. "Sprawl for Me, But Not for Thee." *Cato Institute.* **1 January 2000. 9 January 2011. http://www.cato.org/pub_display.php?pub_id=4720**
Contends that urban sprawl is loathed by the very people who cause it.

> Explore: In further examination of the website, how does this one article on sprawl reflect Cato Institute's larger views on the public sphere?

Proprietary

(Ask your librarian about print or online access to the following resources.)
Birch, Dr. Eugenie L, and Susan Wachter. *The Shape of the New American City.* **Sage Publications, Inc, 2009.**
Leading scholars conclude that America will see a resurgence of growth in urban areas and a slow-down of sprawl.

> Explore: What chief factor, based on the several studies contained in this book, is luring people back to cities from the suburbs? Do you see this happening in the cities near you? To what extent does this realignment of values provide hope for the visions of Kunstler and Gambino above?

Cuff, Dana. "The Figure of the Neighbor: Los Angeles Past and Future." *American Quarterly* **56.3 (2004): 559–582.**
Los Angeles is the perfect site for the study of people as neighbors, since its modern residential environment is peppered with housing experiments, each one unique. The continuous population booms, the absence of a historic building fabric (as compared to Boston's Back Bay, for example), and the uniquely strong home-building industry, set L.A. up as a neighborhood laboratory. This article examines four neighborhoods across the city that offer physical evidence of the space between house and city, and the zone between domestic privacy and the public realm.

> Explore: Of the four neighborhoods studied in this article, which ones function most effectively for their residents and why? Are Dana Cuff and Mike Davis in his essay printed above on L.A. writing about the same city? How so?

Ruff, Joshua. "For Sale: The American Dream." *American History* **42.5 (2007): 42–49.**
This article from a history magazine with broad readership takes the reader back in time to post-war suburbia of the 1940s and 1950s. The American dream was not without its thorns.

> Explore: What were the people of Levittown searching for? To what extent does this version of the American dream hold true for you and your peers? How does this essay confirm or contradict the notes of nostalgia in the essays by Gambino and Kunstler above?

Chapter 22

Race, Ethnicity, and the Melting Pot

At the heart of this chapter is the contested concept of the "melting pot"—a phrase that belongs inside quotations as a mark of its uncertain status. To what extent does it actually exist, some merging of diverse peoples into an undifferentiated national whole? To what extent is it a utopian dream? More troublingly, might it be a sham that serves entrenched interests and oppresses others—those to be "melted"?

It is probably accurate to say that matters of race and ethnicity in U.S. history have been powder kegs. They have often found homes in the vitriol of diatribes and jeremiads rather than in more dispassionate and subtle reflection. The writers assembled here offer a kind of tonic response to the usual clamoring. They comprise a community of voices who occupy very different positions but all, in one way or another, see the questions raised by the prospect of assimilation as anything but easy and clear.

ABOUT THE READINGS IN THIS CHAPTER:

Over half of the selections in the unit are first-person narratives: stories by people who chronicle their own divided allegiance to the expectations of their more local ethnic neighborhood on the one hand, and to the lures of a denatured—but really "whiter"?—American dream of assimilation on the other. These narratives are framed by a range of essays that treat matters of race and assimilation from a broader social scientific perspective.

The chapter opens with three of these framing lenses. First, comes a trenchant analysis by Benjamin DeMott of interracial buddy films. DeMott indicts the attempts of modern America to forget about white guilt and thus also to deny the need for affirmative action. Next, Peter Salins offers a brief history of the "melting pot," seen in the context of the tension between assimilation and multiculturalism. Then Peggy McIntosh considers the long-term historical effects of institutionalized racial oppression as she catalogues the nearly invisible privileges that accrue to white folks on the basis of race.

These three rather theoretical pieces contextualize the five first-person memoirs that follow—analyses that spring from personal experience but do not remain there. Richard Rodriguez invites us to imagine a nation transformed by the marriage of Latin culture with the Protestant individualism that has been our country's past. Amy Tan offers a complementary view of the merging of cultures as it emerges in her mother's polyglot speech. Then Henry Louis Gates, Jr. recalls his childhood experience with African American hairstyles: a platform for thinking about identity and difference.

Next, there are two narratives about neighborhoods. Ishmael Reed focuses on the implications of moving into the kind of African American neighborhood in Oakland, California, that his parents had "spent about a third of their lives trying to escape." By contrast, in Marianna Torgovnick's homecoming to her Italian American neighborhood in Brooklyn, the comforts of the neighborhood and the past are undercut by the claustrophobia and potential for violence in the present.

What might the first three writers think of the five memoirists, and vice versa? That analytical project is built into the chapter.

The chapter ends with two pieces, one theoretical and one narrative, that seek to test the limits of the category. Peter Jonas reviews a new study by Harvard political scientist Robert Putnam that complicates the orthodoxy that our differences make us stronger. Finally, Robert McLiam Wilson, the only writer speaking of ethnicity outside the United States (he's Irish), brings matters to a close by challenging many of the assumptions the other writers share. To what extent, he wonders, are national and even some racial identities inevitably fabrications?

Benjamin DeMott

Put on a Happy Face: Masking the Differences between Blacks and Whites

Focusing on the "romance" of black-white friendship represented in popular American films, this piece argues, with angry irony, that "the cleansing social force" of friendship has been embraced by mainstream white culture as an easy out from the responsibility for historically produced and institutionalized racism. "People forget the theoretically unforgettable—the caste history of American blacks, the connection between no schools for longer than a century and bad school performance now," declares Benjamin DeMott, and this essay, which first appeared in *Harper's Magazine* in 1995, seeks to make us remember.

At the movies these days, questions about racial injustice have been amicably resolved. 1 Watch *Pulp Fiction* or *Congo* or *A Little Princess* or any other recent film in which both blacks and whites are primary characters and you can, if you want, forget about race. Whites and blacks greet one another on the screen with loving candor, revealing their common humanity. In *Pulp Fiction*, an armed black mobster (played by Samuel L. Jackson) looks deep into the eyes of an armed white thief in the middle of a holdup (played by Tim Roth) and shares his version of God's word in Ezekiel, whereupon the two men lay aside their weapons, both more or less redeemed. The moment inverts an earlier scene in which a white boxer (played by Bruce Willis) risks his life to save another black mobster (played by Ving Rhames), who is being sexually tortured as a prelude to his execution.

Pulp Fiction (gross through July [1995]: $107 million) is one of a series of films suggesting that the beast of American racism is tamed and harmless. Close to the start of *Die Hard with a Vengeance* (gross through July [1995]: $95 million), the camera finds a white man wearing sandwich boards on the corner of Amsterdam Avenue and 138th Street in Harlem. The boards carry a horrific legend: I HATE NIGGERS. A group of young blacks approach the man with murderous intent, bearing guns and knives. They are figures straight out of a national nightmare—ugly, enraged, terrifying. No problem. A black man, again played by Jackson, appears and rescues the white man, played by Willis. The black man and white man come to know each other well. In time the white man declares flatly to the black, "I need you more than you need me." A moment later he charges the black with being a racist—with not liking whites as much as the white man likes blacks—and the two talk frankly about their racial prejudices. Near the end of the film, the men have grown so close that each volunteers to die for the other.

Pulp Fiction and *Die Hard with a Vengeance* follow the pattern of *Lethal Weapon 1, 2*, and *3*, the Danny Glover/Mel Gibson buddy vehicles that collectively grossed $357 million, and *White Men Can't Jump*, which, in the year of the L.A. riots, grossed $76 million. In *White Men Can't Jump*, a white dropout, played by Woody Harrelson, ekes

Copyright © by Harper's Magazine. All rights reserved. Reproduced from the September issue by special permission.

out a living on black-dominated basketball courts in Los Angeles. He's arrogant and aggressive but never in danger because he has a black protector and friend, played by Wesley Snipes. At the movie's end, the white, flying above the hoop like a stereotypical black player, scores the winning basket in a two-on-two pickup game on an alley-oop pass from his black chum, whereupon the two men fall into each other's arms in joy. Later, the black friend agrees to find work for the white at the store he manages.

WHITE (helpless): I gotta get a job. Can you get me a job?

BLACK (affectionately teasing): Got any references?

WHITE (shy grin): You.

Such dialogue is the stuff of romance. What's dreamed of and gained is a place where whites are unafraid of blacks, where blacks ask for and need nothing from whites, and where the sameness of the races creates a common fund of sweet content.[1] The details of the dream matter less than the force that makes it come true for both races, eliminating the constraints of objective reality and redistributing resources, status, and capabilities. That cleansing social force supersedes political and economic fact or policy; that force, improbably enough, is friendship.

5   Watching the beaming white men who know how to jump, we do well to remind ourselves of what the camera shot leaves out. Black infants die in America at twice the rate of white infants. (Despite the increased numbers of middle-class blacks, the rates are diverging, with black rates actually rising.) One out of every two black children lives below the poverty line (as compared with one out of seven white children). Nearly four times as many black families exist below the poverty line as white families. More than 50 percent of African American families have incomes below $25,000. Among black youths under age twenty, death by murder occurs nearly ten times as often as among whites. Over 60 percent of births to black mothers occur out of wedlock, more than four times the rate for white mothers. The net worth of the typical white household is ten times that of the typical black household. In many states, five to ten times as many blacks as whites age eighteen to thirty are in prison.

The good news at the movies obscures the bad news in the streets and confirms the Supreme Court's recent decisions on busing, affirmative action, and redistricting. Like the plot of *White Men Can't Jump*, the Court postulates the existence of a society no longer troubled by racism. Because black-white friendship is now understood to be the rule, there is no need for integrated schools or a congressional Black Caucus or affirmative action. The Congress and state governors can guiltlessly cut welfare, food assistance, fuel assistance, Head Start, housing money, fellowship money, vaccine money. Justice Anthony Kennedy can declare, speaking for the Supreme Court majority last June, that creating a world of genuine equality and sameness requires only that "our political system and our society cleanse themselves ... of discrimination."

The deep logic runs as follows: *Yesterday white people didn't like black people, and accordingly suffered guilt, knowing that the dislike was racist and knowing also that as moral persons they would have to atone for the guilt. They would have to ante up for welfare and Head Start and halfway houses and free vaccine and midnight basketball and summer jobs for schoolkids and graduate fellowships for promising scholars and craft-union apprenticeships and so on, endlessly. A considerable and wasteful expense.*

But at length came the realization that by ending dislike or hatred it would be possible to end guilt, which in turn would mean an end to redress: no more wasteful ransom money. There would be but one requirement: the regular production and continuous showing forth of evidence indisputably proving that hatred has totally vanished from the land.

I cannot tell the reader how much I would like to believe in this sunshine world. After the theater lights brighten and I've found coins for a black beggar on the way to my car and am driving home through downtown Springfield, Massachusetts, the world invented by *Die Hard with a Vengeance* and America's highest court gives way only slowly to the familiar urban vision in my windshield—homeless blacks on trash-strewn streets, black prostitutes staked out on a corner, and signs of a not very furtive drug trade. I know perfectly well that most African Americans don't commit crimes or live in alleys. I also know that for somebody like myself, downtown Springfield in the late evening is not a good place to be.

The movies reflect the larger dynamic of wish and dream. Day after day the nation's corporate ministries of culture churn out images of racial harmony. Millions awaken each morning to the friendly sight of Katie Couric nudging a perky elbow into good buddy Bryant Gumbel's side. My mailbox and millions of demographically simi-lar others are choked with flyers from companies (Wal-Mart, Victoria's Secret) bent on publicizing both their wares and their social bona fides by displaying black and white models at cordial ease with one another. A torrent of goodwill messages about race arrives daily—revelations of corporate largesse, commercials, news features, TV spe-cials, all proclaiming that whites like me feel strongly positive impulses of friendship for blacks and that those same admirable impulses are effectively eradicating racial differences, rendering blacks and whites the same. BellSouth TV commercials present children singing "I am the keeper of the world"—first a white child, then a black child, then a white child, then a black child. Because Dow Chemical likes black America, it recruits young black college grads for its research division and dramatizes, in TV commercials, their tearful-joyful partings from home. ("Son, show 'em what you got," says a black lad's father.) American Express shows an elegant black couple and an elegant white couple sitting together in a theater, happy in one another's company. (The couples share the box with an oversized Gold Card.) During the evening news I watch a black mom offer Robitussin to a miserably coughing white mom. Here's *People* magazine promoting itself under a photo of John Lee Hooker, the black bluesman. "We're these kinds of people, too," *People* claims in the caption. In [a recent] produc-tion of *Hamlet* on Broadway, Horatio [was] played by a black actor. On *The 700 Club*, Pat Robertson joshes Ben Kinchlow, his black sidekick, about Ben's far-out ties.

What counts here is not the saccharine clumsiness of the interchanges but the bulk   10 of them—the ceaseless, self-validating gestures of friendship, the humming, buzz-ing background theme: *All decent Americans extend the hand of friendship to African Americans; nothing but nothing is more auspicious for the African American future than this extended hand.* Faith in the miracle cure of racism by change-of-heart turns out to be so familiar as to have become unnoticeable. And yes, the faith has its benign aspect. Even as they nudge me and others toward belief in magic (instant pals and no-money-down equality), the images and messages of devoted relationships between blacks and whites do exert a humanizing influence.

Nonetheless, through these same images and messages the comfortable majority tells itself a fatuous untruth. Promoting the fantasy of painless answers, inspiring groundless self-approval among whites, joining the Supreme Court in treating "cleansing" as *inevitable*, the new orthodoxy of friendship incites culture-wide evasion, justifies one political step backward after another, and greases the skids along which, tomorrow, welfare block grants will slide into state highway-resurfacing budgets. Whites are part of the solution, says this orthodoxy, if we break out of the prison of our skin color, say hello, as equals, one-on-one, to a black stranger, and make a black friend. We're part of the problem if we have an aversion to black people or are frightened of them, or if we feel that the more distance we put between them and us the better, or if we're in the habit of asserting our superiority rather than acknowledging our common humanity. Thus we shift the problem away from politics—from black experience and the history of slavery—and perceive it as a matter of the suspicion and fear found within the white heart; solving the problem asks no more of us than that we work on ourselves, scrubbing off the dirt of ill will.

The approach miniaturizes, personalizes, and moralizes; it removes the large and complex dilemmas of race from the public sphere. It tempts audiences to see history as irrelevant and to regard feelings as decisive—to believe that the fate of black Americans is shaped mainly by events occurring in the hearts and minds of the privileged. And let's be frank: the orthodoxy of friendship feels *nice*. It practically *consecrates* self-flattery. The "good" Bill Clinton who attends black churches and talks with likable ease to fellow worshipers was campaigning when Los Angeles rioted in '92. "White Americans," he said, "are gripped by the isolation of their own experience. Too many still simply have no friends of other races and do not know any differently." Few black youths of working age in South-Central L.A. had been near enough to the idea of a job even to think of looking for work before the Rodney King verdict, but the problem, according to Clinton, was that whites need black friends.

Most of the country's leading voices of journalistic conscience (editorial writers, television anchorpersons, syndicated columnists) roundly endorse the doctrine of black-white friendship as a means of redressing the inequalities between the races. Roger Rosenblatt, editor of the *Columbia Journalism Review* and an especially deft supplier of warm and fuzzy sentiment, published an essay in *Family Circle* arguing that white friendship and sympathy for blacks simultaneously make power differentials vanish and create interracial identity between us, one by one. The author finds his *exemplum* in an episode revealing the personal sensitivity, to injured blacks, of one of his children.

"When our oldest child, Carl, was in high school," he writes, "he and two black friends were standing on a street corner in New York City one spring evening, trying to hail a taxi. The three boys were dressed decently and were doing nothing wild or threatening. Still, no taxi would pick them up. If a driver spotted Carl first, he might slow down, but he would take off again when he saw the others. Carl's two companions were familiar with this sort of abuse. Carl, who had never observed it firsthand before, burned with anger and embarrassment that he was the color of a world that would so mistreat his friends."

15   Rosenblatt notes that when his son "was applying to colleges, he wrote his essay on that taxi incident with his two black friends. ... He was able to articulate what he

could not say at the time—how ashamed and impotent he felt. He also wrote of the power of their friendship, which has lasted to this day and has carried all three young men into the country that belongs to them. To all of us."

In this homily white sympathy begets interracial sameness in several ways. The three classmates are said to react identically to the cabdrivers' snub; i.e., they feel humiliated. "[Carl] could not find the words to express his humiliation and his friends *would* not express theirs."

The anger that inspires the younger Rosenblatt's college-admission essay on racism is seen as identical with black anger. Friendship brings the classmates together as joint, equal owners of the land of their birth ("the country that belongs to [all of] them"). And Rosenblatt supplies a still larger vision of essential black-white sameness near the end of his essay: "Our proper hearts tell the truth," he declares, "which is that we are all in the same boat, rich and poor, black and white. We are helpless, wicked, heroic, terrified, and we need one another. We need to give rides to one another."

Thus do acts of private piety substitute for public policy while the possibility of urgent political action disappears into a sentimental haze. "If we're looking for a formula to ease the tensions between the races," Rosenblatt observes, then we should "attack the disintegration of the black community" and "the desperation of the poor." Without overtly mocking civil rights activists who look toward the political arena "to erase the tensions," Rosenblatt alludes to them in a throwaway manner, implying that properly adjusted whites look elsewhere, that there was a time for politicking for "equal rights" but we've passed through it. Now is a time in which we should listen to our hearts at moments of epiphany and allow sympathy to work its wizardry, cleansing and floating us, blacks and whites "all in the same boat," on a mystical undercurrent of the New Age.

Blacks themselves aren't necessarily proof against this theme, as witness a recent essay by James Alan McPherson in the Harvard journal *Reconstruction*. McPherson, who received the 1977 Pulitzer Prize for fiction for his collection of stories *Elbow Room*, says that "the only possible steps, the safest steps ... small ones" in the movement "toward a universal culture" will be those built not on "ideologies and formulas and programs" but on experiences of personal connectedness.

"Just this past spring," he writes, "when I was leaving a restaurant after taking a [white] former student to dinner, a black [woman on the sidewalk] said to my friend, in a rasping voice, 'Hello, girlfriend. Have you got anything to spare?'" The person speaking was a female crack addict with a child who was also addicted. "But," writes McPherson, when the addict made her pitch to his dinner companion, "I saw in my friend's face an understanding and sympathy and a shining which transcended race and class. Her face reflected one human soul's connection with another. The magnetic field between the two women was charged with spiritual energy."

The writer points the path to progress through interpersonal gestures by people who "insist on remaining human, and having human responses. ... Perhaps the best that can be done, now, is the offering of understanding and support to the few out of many who are capable of such gestures, rather than devising another plan to engineer the many into one."

The elevated vocabulary ("soul," "spiritual") beatifies the impulse to turn away from the real-life agenda of actions capable of reducing racial injustice. Wherever that impulse dominates, the rhetoric of racial sameness thrives, diminishing historical catastrophes affecting millions over centuries and inflating the significance of tremors of tenderness briefly troubling the heart or conscience of a single individual—the boy waiting for a cab, the woman leaving the restaurant. People forget the theoretically unforgettable— the caste history of American blacks, the connection between no schools for longer than a century and bad school performance now, between hateful social attitudes and zero employment opportunities, between minority anguish and majority fear.

How could this way of seeing have become conventional so swiftly? How did the dogmas of instant equality insinuate themselves so effortlessly into courts and mass audiences alike? How can a white man like myself, who taught Southern blacks in the 1960s, find himself seduced—as I have been more than once—by the orthodoxy of friendship? In the civil rights era, the experience for many millions of Americans was one of discovery. A hitherto unimagined continent of human reality and history came into view, inducing genuine concern and at least a temporary setting aside of self-importance. I remember with utter clarity what I felt at Mary Holmes College in West Point, Mississippi, when a black student of mine was killed by tailgating rednecks; my fellow tutors and I were overwhelmed with how shamefully wrong a wrong could be. For a time, we were released from the prisons of moral weakness and ambiguity. In the year or two that followed—the mid-sixties—the notion that some humans are more human than others, whites more human than blacks, appeared to have been overturned. The next step seemed obvious: society would have to admit that when one race deprives another of its humanity for centuries, those who have done the depriving are obligated to do what they can to restore the humanity of the deprived. The obligation clearly entailed the mounting of comprehensive *long-term* programs of developmental assistance—not guilt-money handouts—for nearly the entire black population. The path forward was unavoidable.

It was avoided. Shortly after the award of civil rights and the institution, in 1966, of limited preferential treatment to remedy employment and educational discrimination against African Americans, a measure of economic progress for blacks did appear in census reports. Not much, but enough to stimulate glowing tales of universal black advance and to launch the good-news barrage that continues to this day (headline in the *New York Times*, June 18, 1995: "Moving On Up: The Greening of America's Black Middle Class").

25   After Ronald Reagan was elected to his first term, the new dogma of black-white sameness found ideological support in the form of criticism of so-called coddling. Liberal activists of both races were berated by critics of both races for fostering an allegedly enfeebling psychology of dependency that discouraged African Americans from committing themselves to individual self-development. In 1988, the charge was passionately voiced in an essay in these pages, "I'm Black, You're White, Who's Innocent?" by Shelby Steele, who attributed the difference between black rates of advance and those of other minority groups to white folks' pampering. Most blacks, Steele claimed, could make it on their own—as voluntary immigrants have done— were they not held back by devitalizing programs that presented them, to themselves and others, as somehow dissimilar to and weaker than other Americans. This argument was all-in-the-same-boatism in a different key; the claim remained that progress

depends upon recognition of black-white sameness. Let us see through superficial differences to the underlying, equally distributed gift for success. Let us teach ourselves—in the words of the Garth Brooks tune—to ignore "the color of skin" and "look for ... the beauty within."

Still further support for the policy once known as "do-nothingism" came from points-of-light barkers, who held that a little something might perhaps be done *if* accompanied by enough publicity. Nearly every broadcaster and publisher in America moves a bale of reportage on pro bono efforts by white Americans to speed the advance of black Americans. Example: McDonald's and the National Basketball Association distribute balloons when they announce they are addressing the dropout problem with an annual "Stay in School" scheme that gives schoolkids who don't miss a January school day a ticket to an all-star exhibition. The publicity strengthens the idea that these initiatives will nullify the social context—the city I see through my windshield. Reports of white philanthropy suggest that the troubles of this block and the next should be understood as phenomena in transition. The condition of American blacks need not be read as the fixed, unchanging consequence of generations of bottom-caste existence. Edging discreetly past a beggar posted near the entrance to Zabar's or H&H Bagels, or, while walking the dog, stepping politely around black men asleep on the sidewalk, we need not see ourselves and our fellows as uncaring accomplices in the acts of social injustice.

Yet more powerful has been the ceaseless assault, over the past generation, on our knowledge of the historical situation of black Americans. On the face of things it seems improbable that the cumulative weight of documented historical injury to African Americans could ever be lightly assessed. Gifted black writers continue to show, in scene after scene—in their studies of middle-class blacks interacting with whites—how historical realities shape the lives of their black characters. In *Killer of Sheep*, the brilliant black filmmaker Charles Burnett dramatizes the daily encounters that suck poor blacks into will-lessness and contempt for white fairy tales of interracial harmony; he quickens his historical themes with images of faceless black meat processors gutting undifferentiated, unchoosing animal life. Here, say these images, as though talking back to Clarence Thomas, here is a basic level of black life unchanged over generations. Where there's work, it's miserably paid and ugly. Space allotments at home and at work cramp body and mind. Positive expectation withers in infancy. People fall into the habit of jeering at aspiration as though at the bidding of physical law. Obstacles at every hand prevent people from loving and being loved in decent ways, prevent children from believing their parents, prevent parents from believing they themselves know anything worth knowing. The only true self, now as in the long past, is the one mocked by one's own race. "Shit on you, nigger," says a voice in *Killer of Sheep.* "Nothing you say matters a good goddamn."

For whites, these words produce guilt, and for blacks, I can only assume, pain and despair. The audience for tragedy remains small, while at the multiplex the popular enthusiasm for historical romance remains constant and vast. During the last two decades, the entertainment industry has conducted a siege on the pertinent past, systematically excising knowledge of the consequences of the historical exploitation of African Americans. Factitious renderings of the American past blur the outlines of black-white conflict, redefine the ground of black grievances for the purpose of diminishing the grievances, restage black life in accordance with the illusory conventions of American success mythology, and present the operative influences on race history as the same as those implied to be pivotal in *White Men Can't Jump* or a BellSouth advertisement.

Although there was scant popular awareness of it at the time (1977), the television miniseries *Roots* introduced the figure of the Unscathed Slave. To an enthralled audience of more than 80 million the series intimated that the damage resulting from generations of birth-ascribed, semi-animal status was largely temporary, that slavery was a product of motiveless malignity on the social margins rather than of respectable rationality, and that the ultimate significance of the institution lay in the demonstration, by freed slaves, that no force on earth can best the energies of American Individualism. ("Much like the Waltons confronting the depression," writes historian Eric Foner, a widely respected authority on American slavery, "the family in 'Roots' neither seeks nor requires outside help; individual or family effort is always sufficient.") Ken Burns's much applauded PBS documentary *The Civil War* (1990) went even further than *Roots* in downscaling black injury; the series treated slavery, birth-ascribed inferiority, and the centuries-old denial of dignity as matters of slight consequence. (By "implicitly denying the brutal reality of slavery," writes historian Jeanie Attie, Burns's programs crossed "a dangerous moral threshold." To a group of historians who asked him why slavery had been so slighted, Burns said that any discussion of slavery "would have been lengthy and boring.")

30   Mass media treatments of the civil rights protest years carried forward the process, contributing to the "positive" erasure of difference. Big-budget films like *Mississippi Burning*, together with an array of TV biographical specials on Dr. Martin Luther King and others, presented the long-running struggle between disenfranchised blacks and the majority white culture as a heartwarming episode of interracial unity; the speed and caringness of white response to the oppression of blacks demonstrated that broadscale race conflict or race difference was inconceivable.

A consciousness that ingests either a part or the whole of this revisionism loses touch with the two fundamental truths of race in America; namely, that because of what happened in the past, blacks and whites cannot yet be the same; and that because what happened in the past was no mere matter of ill will or insult but the outcome of an established caste structure that has only very recently begun to be dismantled, it is not reparable by one-on-one goodwill. The word "slavery" comes to induce stock responses with no vital sense of a grinding devastation of mind visited upon generation after generation. Hoodwinked by the orthodoxy of friendship, the nation either ignores the past, summons for it a detached, correct "compassion," or gazes at it as though it were a set of aesthetic conventions, like twisted trees and fragmented rocks in nineteenth-century picturesque painting—lifeless phenomena without bearing on the present. The chance of striking through the mask of corporate-underwritten, feel-good, ahistorical racism grows daily more remote. The trade-off—whites promise friendship, blacks accept the status quo—begins to seem like a good deal.

Cosseted by Hollywood's magic lantern and soothed by press releases from Washington and the American Enterprise Institute, we should never forget what we see and hear for ourselves. Broken out by race, the results of every social tabulation from unemployment to life expectancy add up to a chronicle of atrocity. The history of black America fully explains—to anyone who approaches it honestly—how the disaster happened and why neither guilt money nor lectures on personal responsibility can, in and of themselves, repair the damage. The vision of friendship and sympathy placing blacks and whites "all in the same boat," rendering them equally able to do each other favors, "to give rides to one another," is a smiling but monstrous lie.

Notes

[1] I could go on with examples of movies that deliver the good news of friendship: *Regarding Henry, Driving Miss Daisy, Forrest Gump, The Shawshank Redemption, Philadelphia, The Last Boy Scout, 48 Hours I–II, Rising Sun, Iron Eagle I–II, Rudy, Sister Act, Hearts of Dixie, Betrayed, The Power of One, White Nights, Clara's Heart, Doc Hollywood, Cool Runnings, Places in the Heart, Trading Places, Fried Green Tomatoes, Q & A, Platoon, A Mother's Courage: The Mary Thomas Story, The Unforgiven, The Air Up There, The Pelican Brief, Losing Isaiah, Smoke, Searching for Bobby Fischer, An Officer and a Gentleman, Speed,* etc.

Things to Do with the Reading

1. How does this essay use references to time? Look for mention of dates, of terms such as "history" and "long-term" and "centuries-old," as well as various aspects of the present, the contemporary scene. Write a short essay in which you analyze DeMott's argument about historical consciousness in America.

2. What is DeMott's answer to the idea that blacks in America don't need government aid because they should be able to harness "the energies of American individualism" to improve their condition? Write a short essay in answer to this question.

   The following questions may help you to focus. So what that DeMott holds both blacks and whites responsible for projecting these "'positive' erasures of difference" (paragraph 30)? Consider, for example, the message that DeMott says the African American-made miniseries *Roots* sent about the situation of blacks in America and what they should rely on as their best hope for the future.

3. **Link:** Write a short essay in which you use DeMott as a lens for analyzing the representation of black-white relationships and black-black relationships in Ishmael Reed's essay "My Neighborhood," which appears later in this chapter What are the chances DeMott would find Reed unduly "rosy" about black-black relationships?

4. **Links Across Units:** Notice how James Peck (in Chapter 23) defines melodrama against tragedy in his analysis, "September 11—A National Tragedy." In what ways do Peck's anxieties about representations of 9/11 occupy the same ground (sharing assumptions) with DeMott? Find sentences in each essay to

put into conversation with each other. Write a short essay in which you consider the extent to which DeMott's term *romance* means the same thing as Peck does by *melodrama*.

Alternatively, study Kera Bolonik's analysis of *Will & Grace* in her review entitled "Oy Gay!" in Chapter 24. Write an essay in which you ponder the extent to which the deception Bolonik sees in the television show resembles the one DeMott observes in his list of films.

5. **Application:** DeMott cites at least two dozen films that he says present "the long-running struggle between disenfranchised blacks and the majority white culture as a heartwarming episode of interracial unity" (see the footnote after paragraph 6). Using the black-white buddy film *White Men Can't Jump* as a primary example of what he calls the "good will messages about race," DeMott argues that the effect of this cultural trend is to create the illusion that blacks and whites are "all in the same boat," so that all that is needed to solve centuries of disaster for blacks is displays of warmhearted sympathy.

DeMott's essay was published in 1995. Your task is to write an essay in which you update it in one of the following ways:

- Consider the extent to which the trend he describes in movies and other media is still alive and well today. Locate one or more current films or other media that seem to you to send the message of black-white friendship as an indication of sameness and as evidence that one-on-one compassion can solve the problems of race in America.

- Locate one or more films or other media that seem to be representative of a different trend in the way that black-white relationships are being represented now. Determine what you think this new trend offers as a message about the state of black-white relations in America, the situation of blacks in America, and what does or does not need to be done about it.

- Use DeMott's analysis as a model for looking at representational trends depicting marginalized groups besides blacks in contemporary films or other media. Does the trend that you locate seem to fall into DeMott's category of "deceptive romances"? Or, does the trend represent the group in a way that DeMott might be more optimistic about? In either case, what does this representation "say" about the situation of this group in America?

Peter Salins

Assimilation, American Style

This essay offers a brief history of that influential American myth, "the melting pot." It locates the melting pot in relation to such key terms in thinking about race as "assimilation" and "multiculturalism." The piece was written in 1997 by the urban planning scholar Peter Salins, a professor of political science at SUNY at Stony Brook and a former Provost and Vice Chancellor for Academic Affairs of the State University of New York system. Salins is also a senior fellow of the Manhattan Institute's Center for State and Local Leadership. Along with his many academic books and articles, he has also published a number of articles in the popular press on the housing crisis in urban areas.

> California Chinese, Boston Irish, Wisconsin Germans, yes, and Alabama Negroes, have more in common than they have apart. ... It is a fact that Americans from all sections and of all racial extractions are more alike than the Welsh are like the English, the Lancashireman like the Cockney, or for that matter the Lowland Scot like the Highlander.
>
> —John Steinbeck, 1962

Most Americans, both those who favor and those who oppose assimilation, believe 1 that for immigrants to assimilate, they must abandon their original cultural attributes and conform entirely to the behaviors and customs of the majority of the native-born population. In the terminology of the armed forces, this represents a model of "up or out": Either immigrants bring themselves "up" to native cultural standards or they are doomed to live "out" of the charmed circle of the national culture.

The notion is not entirely far-fetched because this is exactly what assimilation demands in other societies. North African immigrants to France are, for example, expected to assimilate by abandoning their native folkways with alacrity. Official French policy has been zealous in making North African and other Muslim women give up wearing their *chador*[1] and, in the schools, instilling a disdain for North African and Muslim culture in their children. To varying degrees, most European countries that have had to absorb large numbers of immigrants since World War II interpret assimilation this way—an interpretation that has promoted national and ethnic disunity.

In America, however, assimilation has not meant repudiating immigrant culture. Assimilation, American style has always been much more flexible and accommodating and, consequently, much more effective in achieving its purpose—to allow the United States to preserve its "national unity in the face of the influx of hordes of persons of scores of different nationalities," in the words of the sociologist Henry Fairchild.

A popular way of getting hold of the assimilation idea has been to use a metaphor, and by far the most popular metaphor has been that of the "melting pot," a

Assimilation, American Style, Peter Salins. REASON MAGAZINE. Reprinted with permission of The Burr Media Group.

term introduced in Israel Zangwill's 1908 play of that name: "There she lies, the great Melting-Pot—Listen! Can't you hear the roaring and the bubbling? ... Ah, what a stirring and a seething! Celt and Latin, Slav and Teuton, Greek and Syrian, black and yellow ... Jew and Gentile. ... East and West, and North and South, the palm and the pine, the pole and the equator, the crescent and the cross—how the great Alchemist melts and fuses them with his purifying flame! Here shall they all unite to build the Republic of Man and the Kingdom of God."

5   For all its somewhat ahistorical idealism, the melting-pot metaphor still represents the standard around which fervent proponents of assimilation have rallied over the years. According to the melting-pot metaphor, assimilation involved the fine-grained intermingling of diverse ethnicities and cultures into a single national "alloy." If taken literally, this metaphor implied two things. The point most commonly taken is that the new human products of the melting pot would, of necessity, be culturally indistinguishable. Presumably every piece of metal taken from a melting pot should have the same chemical composition. Less frequently understood is the metaphor's implication that natives and their indigenous cultural characteristics would also be irreversibly changed—blended beyond recognition—because they constituted the base material of the melting pot.

These two corollaries of the melting-pot metaphor have long invited criticism by those who thought they were inconsistent with the ethnic realities of American society. Critics of the metaphor have spanned the ideological spectrum and mounted several different lines of attack on it. Empiricists submitted evidence that the melting pot wasn't working as predicted and concluded, as did Nathan Glazer and Daniel Patrick Moynihan in *Beyond the Melting Pot* (1963), "The point about the melting pot—is that it did not happen." Other critics rejected the second corollary of the metaphor—that natives were changed by it, too—and saw no reason that native Americans should give up any part of their cultural attributes to "melt" into the alloy. If true assimilation were to occur, the criticism went, immigrants would have to abandon all their cultural baggage and conform to American ways. It is the immigrant, said Fairchild, representing the views of many Americans, "who must undergo the entire transformation; the true member of the American nationality is not called upon to change in the least."

A third strain of criticism was first voiced by sociologist Horace Kallen in the early part of this century. Among the most prolific American scholars of ethnicity, Kallen argued that it was not only unrealistic but cruel and harmful to force new immigrants to shed their familiar, lifelong cultural attributes as the price of admission to American society. In place of the melting pot, he called for "cultural pluralism." In Kallen's words, national policy should "seek to provide conditions under which each [group] might attain the cultural perfection that is proper to its kind."

Kallen introduced the concept in 1916, only eight years after publication of Zangwill's *The Melting Pot*, determined to challenge that work's premises. Cultural pluralism rejects melting-pot assimilationism not on empirical grounds but on ideological ones. Kallen and his followers believed that immigrants to the United States should not "melt" into a common national ethnic alloy but, rather, should steadfastly hang on to their cultural ethnicity and band together for social and political purposes even after generations of residence in the United States. As such, cultural pluralism is not an alternative theory of assimilation; it is a theory opposed to assimilation.

Cultural pluralism is, in fact, the philosophical antecedent of modern multiculturalism—what I call "ethnic federalism": official recognition of distinct, essentially fixed ethnic groups and the doling out of resources based on membership in an ethnic group. Ethnic federalism explicitly rejects the notion of a transcendent American identity, the old idea that out of ethnic diversity there would emerge a single, culturally unified people. Instead, the United States is to be viewed as a vast ethnic federation—Canada's Anglo-French arrangement, raised to the nth power. Viewing ethnic Americans as members of a federation rather than a union, ethnic federalism, a.k.a. multiculturalism, asserts that ethnic Americans have the right to proportional representation in matters of power and privilege, the right to demand that their "native" culture and putative ethnic ancestors be accorded recognition and respect, and the right to function in their "native" language (even if it is not the language of their birth or they never learned to speak it), not just at home but in the public realm.

Ethnic federalism is at all times an ideology of ethnic grievance and inevitably   10
leads to and justifies ethnic conflict. All the nations that have ever embraced it, from Yugoslavia to Lebanon, from Belgium to Canada, have had to live with perpetual ethnic discord.

Kallen's views, however, stop significantly short of contemporary multiculturalism in their demands on the larger "native" American society. For Kallen, cultural pluralism was a defensive strategy for "unassimilable" immigrant ethnic groups that required no accommodation by the larger society. Contemporary multiculturalists, on the other hand, by making cultural pluralism the basis of ethnic federalism, demand certain ethnic rights and concessions. By emphasizing the failure of assimilation, multiculturalists hope to provide intellectual and political support for their policies.

The multiculturalists' rejection of the melting-pot idea is seen in the metaphors they propose in its place. Civil rights activist Jesse Jackson suggested that Americans are members of a "rainbow coalition." Former New York Mayor David Dinkins saw his constituents constituting a "gorgeous mosaic." Former Congresswoman Shirley Chisholm characterized America's ethnic groups as being like ingredients in a "salad bowl." Barbara Jordan, recent chairperson of the U.S. Commission on Immigration Reform, said: "We are more than a melting-pot; we are a kaleidoscope."

These counter-metaphors all share a common premise: that ethnic groups in the United States may live side by side harmoniously, but on two conditions that overturn both assumptions of the melting-pot metaphor. First, immigrants (and black Americans) should never have to (or maybe should not even want to) give up any of their original cultural attributes. And second, there never can or will be a single unified national identity that all Americans can relate to. These two principles are the foundations of cultural pluralism, the antithesis of assimilationism.

While all these metaphors—including the melting pot—are colorful ways of representing assimilation, they don't go far in giving one an accurate understanding of what assimilation is really about. For example, across the ideological spectrum, they all invoke some external, impersonal assimilating agent. Who, exactly, is the "great alchemist" of the melting pot? What force tosses the salad or pieces together the mosaic? By picturing assimilation as an impersonal, automatic process and thus placing it beyond analysis, the metaphors fail to illuminate its most important secrets. Assimilation, if it is to succeed, must be a voluntary process, by both the assimilating immigrants and the assimilated-to natives. Assimilation is a human accommodation, not a mechanical production.

15   The metaphors also mislead as to the purposes of assimilation. The melting pot is supposed to turn out an undifferentiated alloy—a uniform, ethnically neutral, American protoperson. Critics have long pointed out that this idea is far-fetched. But is it even desirable? And if it is desirable, does it really foster a shared national identity? The greatest failing of the melting-pot metaphor is that it overreaches. It exaggerates the degree to which immigrants' ethnicity is likely to be extinguished by exposure to American society and it exaggerates the need to extinguish ethnicity. By being too compelling, too idealistic, the melting-pot idea has inadvertently helped to discredit the very assimilation paradigm it was meant to celebrate.

On the other hand, behind their unexceptionable blandness, the antithetical cultural pluralist metaphors are profoundly insidious. By suggesting that the product of assimilation is mere ethnic coexistence without integration, they undermine the objectives of assimilation, even if they appear more realistic. Is assimilation only about diverse ethnic groups sharing the same national space? That much can be said for any multiethnic society. If the ethnic greens of the salad or the fragments of the mosaic do not interact and identify with each other, no meaningful assimilation is taking place.

Perhaps a new assimilation metaphor should be introduced—one that depends not on a mechanical process like the melting pot but on human dynamics. Assimilation might be viewed as more akin to religious conversion than anything else. In the terms of this metaphor, the immigrant is the convert, American society is the religious order being joined, and assimilation is the process by which the conversion takes place. Just as there are many motives for people to immigrate, so are there many motives for them to change their religion: spiritual, practical (marrying a person of another faith), and materialistic (joining some churches can lead to jobs or subsidized housing). But whatever the motivation, conversion usually involves the consistent application of certain principles. Conversion is a mutual decision requiring affirmation by both the convert and the religious order he or she wishes to join. Converts are expected in most (but not all) cases to renounce their old religions. But converts do not have to change their behavior in any respects other than those that relate to the new religion. They are expected only to believe in its theological principles, observe its rituals and holidays, and live by its moral precepts. Beyond that, they can be rich or poor, practice any trade, pursue any avocational interests, and have any racial or other personal attributes. Once they undergo conversion, they are eagerly welcomed into the fellowship of believers. They have become part of "us" rather than "them." This is undoubtedly what writer G. K. Chesterton had in mind when he said: "America is a nation with the soul of a church."

Notes

[1] *Chadors* are the long black veils worn by Muslim women.

Things to Do with the Reading

1. Salins's essay is good at making the implicit explicit and at uncovering assumptions (reasoning back to premises—see Chapter 4). He is especially interested in the implications of the metaphors that have been used to talk about cultural identity and assimilation in America: melting pot, rainbow coalition, etc. Using Salins's method as a model, write an essay in which you draw out the implications of Jesse Jackson's metaphor—the rainbow coalition. (See Chapter 9 on figurative logic.)

   Here are some supporting questions. How is the rainbow metaphor like and unlike the melting pot metaphor? Next, draw out the implications of Salins's proposed religious conversion metaphor as defined in the last paragraph of the essay. How is this metaphor like and unlike the rainbow and the melting pot?

2. A metaphor is a comparison, a way of thinking by analogy (see Chapter 9 on metaphor). In order to be persuasive and fair, the two things being compared need to have enough in common to justify the comparison. What is compared to what in Salins's conversion metaphor? Write a short essay on what this analogy suggests about Salins's way of thinking about being (and becoming) American?

3. Though Salins's piece is a historical analysis, it also is a problem/solution piece with a point of view. This point of view emerges gradually, but becomes evident when you notice that the critique offered of each idea on assimilation, starting with the melting pot, is essentially the same critique. Write a few paragraphs in which you compare paragraphs 6 and 11, locating and exploring the significance of the common element.

4. Write a rhetorical analysis of the Salins essay (for discussion of rhetorical analyses, see especially Chapters 1 and 3). Locate word choice that seems to you to reveal something about Salins's target audience and the kind of relationship he wishes to establish with these readers. What, for example, does the phrase "native folkways" (in the essay's second paragraph) reveal in this regard?

5. **Links Across Units:** First visit the website for the Manhattan Institute for Policy Research, of which Salins is a fellow. Then write an essay in which you apply the lexicon contained in Chris Borick's "On Political Labels" (in Chapter 23) to the key words in the website's articulation of its mission.

   Here are some ways to prompt your analysis. Where does the website fit in terms of the political categories discussed in Borick's essay? Find language in Borick's essay that would make Salins' point of view identifiable among the categories discussed in "On Political Labels."

6. **Application:** The issues and questions raised in Salins's essay are far from dead. On the basis of the historical definitions Salins provides, spend some time (perhaps a week) observing and making note of the language used in the

media (newspapers, websites, television) for talking about issues of assimilation and cultural identity. What metaphors do you find and what do these reveal about contemporary thinking on this issue? Write a short essay in which you present your results.

Peggy McIntosh

White Privilege and Male Privilege: [...Unpacking the Invisible Knapsack]

In this classic analysis, Peggy McIntosh takes a look at her own "overprivilege" by virtue of her skin color and asks the question, what do I take for granted as a white person in ways that I am blind to? To answer, she inventories herself, arriving at a list of "unacknowledged privileges" that express "unconscious oppressiveness" as she imagines it can be perceived by persons of color. For many years the associate director of the Wellesley College Center for Research on Women, McIntosh now co-directs the National S.E.E.D (Seeking Educational Equity and Diversity) Project on Inclusive Curriculum.

Through work to bring materials and perspectives from Women's Studies into the   1
rest of the curriculum, I have often noticed men's unwillingness to grant that they are overprivileged in the curriculum, even though they may grant that women are disadvantaged. Denials that amount to taboos surround the subject of advantages that men gain from women's disadvantages. These denials protect male privilege from being fully recognized, acknowledged, lessened, or ended.

Thinking through unacknowledged male privilege as a phenomenon with a life of its own, I realized that since hierarchies in our society are interlocking, there was most likely a phenomenon of white privilege that was similarly denied and protected, but alive and real in its effects. As a white person, I realized I had been taught about racism as something that puts others at a disadvantage, but had been taught not to see one of its corollary aspects, white privilege, which puts me at an advantage.

I think whites are carefully taught not to recognize white privilege, as males are taught not to recognize male privilege. So I have begun in an untutored way to ask what it is like to have white privilege. This paper is a partial record of my personal observations and not a scholarly analysis. It is based on my daily experiences within my particular circumstances.

I have come to see white privilege as an invisible package of unearned assets that I can count on cashing in each day, but about which I was "meant" to remain oblivious. White privilege is like an invisible weightless knapsack of special provisions, assurances, tools, maps, guides, codebooks, passports, visas, clothes, compass, emergency gear, and blank checks.

Since I have had trouble facing white privilege, and describing its results in my life,   5
I saw parallels here with men's reluctance to acknowledge male privilege. Only rarely will a man go beyond acknowledging that women are disadvantaged to acknowledging that men have unearned advantage, or that unearned privilege has not been good for men's development as human beings, or for society's development, or that privilege systems might ever be challenged and *changed*.

White Privilege and Male Privilege: A Personal Account of Coming to See Correspondences Through Work in Women's Studies (1988) Working Paper 189, Wellesley Centers for Women, Wellesley, MA. This work may not be reproduced without permission of the author, Peggy McIntosh, mmcintosh@wellesley.edu: 781-283-2520.

I will review here several types or layers of denial that I see at work protecting, and preventing awareness about, entrenched male privilege. Then I will draw parallels, from my own experience, with the denials that veil the facts of white privilege. Finally, I will list forty-six ordinary and daily ways in which I experience having white privilege, by contrast with my African American colleagues in the same building. This list is not intended to be generalizable. Others can make their own lists from within their own life circumstances.

Writing this paper has been difficult, despite warm receptions for the talks on which it is based.[1] For describing white privilege makes one newly accountable. As we in Women's Studies work reveal male privilege and ask men to give up some of their power, so one who writes about having white privilege must ask, "Having described it, what will I do to lessen or end it?"

The denial of men's overprivileged state takes many forms in discussions of curriculum change work. Some claim that men must be central in the curriculum because they have done most of what is important or distinctive in life or in civilization. Some recognize sexism in the curriculum but deny that it makes male students seem unduly important in life. Others agree that certain *individual* thinkers are male oriented but deny that there is any *systemic* tendency in disciplinary frameworks or epistemology to overempower men as a group. Those men who do grant that male privilege takes institutionalized and embedded forms are still likely to deny that male hegemony has opened doors for them personally. Virtually all men deny that male overreward alone can explain men's centrality in all the inner sanctums of our most powerful institutions. Moreover, those few who will acknowledge that male privilege systems have overempowered them usually end up doubting that we could dismantle these privilege systems. They may say they will work to improve women's status, in the society or in the university, but they can't or won't support the idea of lessening men's. In curricular terms, this is the point at which they say that they regret they cannot use any of the interesting new scholarship on women because the syllabus is full. When the talk turns to giving men less cultural room, even the most thoughtful and fair-minded of the men I know will tend to reflect, or fall back on, conservative assumptions about the inevitability of present gender relations and distributions of power, calling on precedent or sociobiology and psychobiology to demonstrate that male domination is natural and follows inevitably from evolutionary pressures. Others resort to arguments from "experience" or religion or social responsibility or wishing and dreaming.

After I realized, through faculty development work in Women's Studies, the extent to which men work from a base of unacknowledged privilege, I understood that much of their oppressiveness was unconscious. Then I remembered the frequent charges from women of color that white women whom they encounter are oppressive. I began to understand why we are justly seen as oppressive, even when we don't see ourselves that way. At the very least, obliviousness of one's privileged state can make a person or group irritating to be with. I began to count the ways in which I enjoy unearned skin privilege and have been conditioned into oblivion about its existence, unable to see that it put me "ahead" in any way, or put my people ahead, overrewarding us and yet also paradoxically damaging us, or that it could or should be changed.

My schooling gave me no training in seeing myself as an oppressor, as an unfairly 10
advantaged person, or as a participant in a damaged culture. I was taught to see myself
as an individual whose moral state depended on her individual moral will. At school,
we are not taught about slavery in any depth; we are not taught to see slaveholders as
damaged people. Slaves were seen as the only group at risk of being dehumanized. My
schooling followed the pattern which Elizabeth Minnich has pointed out: whites are
taught to think of their lives as morally neutral, normative, and average, and also ideal,
so that when we work to benefit others, this is seen as work that will allow "them" to
be more like "us." I think many of us know how obnoxious this attitude can be in men.

After frustration with men who would not recognize male privilege, I decided
to try to work on myself at least by identifying some of the daily effects of white
privilege in my life. It is crude work, at this stage, but I will give here a list of special
circumstances and conditions I experience that I did not earn but that I have been
made to feel are mine by birth, by citizenship, and by virtue of being a conscientious
law-abiding "normal" person of goodwill. I have chosen those conditions that I think
in my case *attach somewhat more to skin-color privilege* than to class, religion, ethnic
status, or geographical location, though these other privileging factors are intricately
intertwined. As far as I can see, my Afro-American co-workers, friends, and acquaintances with whom I come into daily or frequent contact in this particular time, place,
and line of work cannot count on most of these conditions.

1. I can, if I wish, arrange to be in the company of people of my race most of the
   time.

2. I can avoid spending time with people whom I was trained to mistrust and who
   have learned to mistrust my kind or me.

3. If I should need to move, I can be pretty sure of renting or purchasing housing
   in an area which I can afford and in which I would want to live.

4. I can be reasonably sure that my neighbors in such a location will be neutral or
   pleasant to me.

5. I can go shopping alone most of the time, fairly well assured that I will not be
   followed or harassed by store detectives.

6. I can turn on the television or open to the front page of the paper and see people
   of my race widely and positively represented.

7. When I am told about our national heritage or about "civilization," I am shown
   that people of my color made it what it is.

8. I can be sure that my children will be given curricular materials that testify to the
   existence of their race.

9. If I want to, I can be pretty sure of finding a publisher for this piece on white
   privilege.

10. I can be fairly sure of having my voice heard in a group in which I am the only
    member of my race.

11. I can be casual about whether or not to listen to another woman's voice in a group
    in which she is the only member of her race.

12. I can go into a book shop and count on finding the writing of my race represented, into a supermarket and find the staple foods that fit with my cultural traditions, into a hairdresser's shop and find someone who can deal with my hair.

13. Whether I use checks, credit cards, or cash, I can count on my skin color not to work against the appearance that I am financially reliable.

14. I could arrange to protect our young children most of the time from people who might not like them.

15. I did not have to educate our children to be aware of systemic racism for their own daily physical protection.

16. I can be pretty sure that my children's teachers and employers will tolerate them if they fit school and workplace norms; my chief worries about them do not concern others' attitudes toward their race.

17. I can talk with my mouth full and not have people put this down to my color.

18. I can swear, or dress in secondhand clothes, or not answer letters, without having people attribute these choices to the bad morals, the poverty, or the illiteracy of my race.

19. I can speak in public to a powerful male group without putting my race on trial.

20. I can do well in a challenging situation without being called a credit to my race.

21. I am never asked to speak for all the people of my racial group.

22. I can remain oblivious to the language and customs of persons of color who constitute the world's majority without feeling in my culture any penalty for such oblivion.

23. I can criticize our government and talk about how much I fear its policies and behavior without being seen as a cultural outsider.

24. I can be reasonably sure that if I ask to talk to "the person in charge," I will be facing a person of my race.

25. If a traffic cop pulls me over or if the IRS audits my tax return, I can be sure I haven't been singled out because of my race.

26. I can easily buy posters, postcards, picture books, greeting cards, dolls, toys, and children's magazines featuring people of my race.

27. I can go home from most meetings of organizations I belong to feeling somewhat tied in, rather than isolated, out of place, outnumbered, unheard, held at a distance, or feared.

28. I can be pretty sure that an argument with a colleague of another race is more likely to jeopardize her chances for advancement than to jeopardize mine.

29. I can be fairly sure that if I argue for the promotion of a person of another race, or a program centering on race, this is not likely to cost me heavily within my present setting, even if my colleagues disagree with me.

30. If I declare there is a racial issue at hand, or there isn't a racial issue at hand, my race will lend me more credibility for either position than a person of color will have.

31. I can choose to ignore developments in minority writing and minority activist programs, or disparage them, or learn from them, but in any case, I can find ways to be more or less protected from negative consequences of any of these choices.

32. My culture gives me little fear about ignoring the perspectives and powers of people of other races.

33. I am not made acutely aware that my shape, bearing, or body odor will be taken as a reflection on my race.

34. I can worry about racism without being seen as self-interested or self-seeking.

35. I can take a job with an affirmative action employer without having my co-workers on the job suspect that I got it because of my race.

36. If my day, week, or year is going badly, I need not ask of each negative episode or situation whether it has racial overtones.

37. I can be pretty sure of finding people who would be willing to talk with me and advise me about my next steps, professionally.

38. I can think over many options, social, political, imaginative, or professional, without asking whether a person of my race would be accepted or allowed to do what I want to do.

39. I can be late to a meeting without having the lateness reflect on my race.

40. I can choose public accommodation without fearing that people of my race cannot get in or will be mistreated in the places I have chosen.

41. I can be sure that if I need legal or medical help, my race will not work against me.

42. I can arrange my activities so that I will never have to experience feelings of rejection owing to my race.

43. If I have low credibility as a leader, I can be sure that my race is not the problem.

44. I can easily find academic courses and institutions that give attention only to people of my race.

45. I can expect figurative language and imagery in all of the arts to testify to experiences of my race.

46. I can choose blemish cover or bandages in "flesh" color and have them more or less match my skin.

I repeatedly forgot each of the realizations on this list until I wrote it down. For me, white privilege has turned out to be an elusive and fugitive subject. The pressure to avoid it is great, for in facing it I must give up the myth of meritocracy. If these things are true, this is not such a free country; one's life is not what one makes it; many doors open for certain people through no virtues of their own. These perceptions mean also that my moral condition is not what I had been led to believe. The appearance of being a good citizen rather than a troublemaker comes in large part from having all sorts of doors open automatically because of my color.

A further paralysis of nerve comes from literary silence protecting privilege. My clearest memories of finding such analysis are in Lillian Smith's unparalleled *Killers of the Dream* and Margaret Andersen's review of Karen and Mamie Field's *Lemon Swamp*. Smith, for example, wrote about walking toward black children on the street and knowing they would step into the gutter; Andersen contrasted the pleasure that she, as a white child, took on summer driving trips to the south with Karen Fields' memories of driving in a closed car stocked with all necessities lest, in stopping, her black family should suffer "insult, or worse." Adrienne Rich also recognizes and writes about daily experiences of privilege, but in my observation, white women's writing in this area is far more often on systemic racism than on our daily lives as light-skinned women.[2]

In unpacking this invisible knapsack of white privilege, I have listed conditions of daily experience that I once took for granted, as neutral, normal, and universally available to everybody, just as I once thought of a male-focused curriculum as the neutral or accurate account that can speak for all. Nor did I think of any of these perquisites as bad for the holder. I now think that we need a more finely differentiated taxonomy of privilege, for some of these varieties are only what one would want for everyone in a just society, and others give license to be ignorant, oblivious, arrogant, and destructive. Before proposing some more finely tuned categorization, I will make some observations about the general effects of these conditions on my life and expectations.

15   In this potpourri of examples, some privileges make me feel at home in the world. Others allow me to escape penalties or dangers that others suffer. Through some, I escape fear, anxiety, insult, injury, or a sense of not being welcome, not being real. Some keep me from having to hide, to be in disguise, to feel sick or crazy, to negotiate each transaction from the position of being an outsider or, within my group, a person who is suspected of having too close links with a dominant culture. Most keep me from having to be angry.

I see a pattern running through the matrix of white privilege, a pattern of assumptions that were passed on to me as a white person. There was one main piece of cultural turf; it was my own turf, and I was among those who could control the turf. I could measure up to the cultural standards and take advantage of the many options I saw around me to make what the culture would call a success of my life. *My skin color was an asset for any move I was educated to want to make.* I could think of myself as "belonging" in major ways and of making social systems work for me. I could freely disparage, fear, neglect, or be oblivious to anything outside of the dominant cultural forms. Being of the main culture, I could also criticize it fairly freely. My life was reflected back to me frequently enough so that I felt, with regard to my race, if not to my sex, like one of the real people.

Whether through the curriculum or in the newspaper, the television, the economic system, or the general look of people in the streets, I received daily signals and indications that my people counted and that others *either didn't exist or must be trying, not very successfully, to be like people of my race.* I was given cultural permission not to hear voices of people of other races or a tepid cultural tolerance for hearing or acting on such voices. I was also raised not to suffer seriously from anything that darker-skinned people might say about my group, "protected," though perhaps I should more accurately say *prohibited*, through the habits of my economic class and social group, from living in racially mixed groups or being reflective about interactions between people or differing races.

In proportion as my racial group was being made confident, comfortable, and oblivious, other groups were likely being made unconfident, uncomfortable, and alienated. Whiteness protected me from many kinds of hostility, distress, and violence, which I was being subtly trained to visit in turn upon people of color.

For this reason, the word "privilege" now seems to me misleading. Its connotations are too positive to fit the conditions and behaviors which "privilege systems" produce. We usually think of privilege as being a favored state, whether earned, or conferred by birth or luck. School graduates are reminded they are privileged and urged to use their (enviable) assets well. The word "privilege" carries the connotation of being something everyone must want. Yet some of the conditions I have described here work to systematically overempower certain groups. Such privilege simply *confers dominance*, gives permission to control, because of one's race or sex. The kind of privilege that gives license to some people to be, at best, thoughtless and, at worst, murderous should not continue to be referred to as a desirable attribute. Such "privilege" may be widely desired without being in any way beneficial to the whole society.

Moreover, though "privilege" may confer power, it does not confer moral strength.   20 Those who do not depend on conferred dominance have traits and qualities that may never develop in those who do. Just as Women's Studies courses indicate that women survive their political circumstances to lead lives that hold the human race together, so "underprivileged" people of color who are the world's majority have survived their oppression and lived survivors' lives from which the white global minority can and must learn. In some groups, those dominated have actually become strong through *not* having all of these unearned advantages, and this gives them a great deal to teach the others. Members of so-called privileged groups can seem foolish, ridiculous, infantile, or dangerous by contrast.

I want, then, to distinguish between earned strength and unearned power conferred systemically. Power from unearned privilege can look like strength when it is, in fact, permission to escape or to dominate. But not all of the privileges on my list are inevitably damaging. Some, like the expectation that neighbors will be decent to you, or that your race will not count against you in court, should be the norm in a just society and should be considered as the entitlement of everyone. Others, like the privilege not to listen to less powerful people, distort the humanity of the holders as well as the ignored groups. Still others, like finding one's staple foods everywhere, may be a function of being a member of a numerical majority in the population. Others have to do with not having to labor under pervasive negative stereotyping and mythology.

We might at least start by distinguishing between positive advantages that we can work to spread, to the point where they are not advantages at all but simply part of the normal civic and social fabric, and negative types of advantage that unless rejected will always reinforce our present hierarchies. For example, the positive "privilege" of belonging, the feeling that one belongs within the human circle, as Native Americans say, fosters development and should not be seen as privilege for a few. It is, let us say, an entitlement that none of us should have to earn; ideally it is an *unearned entitlement*. At present, since only a few have it, it is an *unearned advantage* for them. The negative "privilege" that gave me cultural permission not to take darker-skinned Others seriously can be seen as arbitrarily conferred dominance and should not be desirable for anyone. This paper results from a process of coming to see that some of the power that I originally saw as attendant on being a human being in the United States consisted in *unearned advantage* and *conferred dominance*, as well as other kinds of special circumstance not universally taken for granted.

In writing this paper I have also realized that white identity and status (as well as class identity and status) give me considerable power to choose whether to broach this subject and its trouble. I can pretty well decide whether to disappear and avoid and not listen and escape the dislike I may engender in other people through this essay, or interrupt, answer, interpret, preach, correct, criticize, and control to some extent what goes on in reaction to it. Being white, I am given considerable power to escape many kinds of danger or penalty as well as to choose which risks I want to take.

There is an analogy here, once again with Women's Studies. Our male colleagues do not have a great deal to lose in supporting Women's Studies, but they do not have a great deal to lose if they oppose it either. They simply have the power to decide whether to commit themselves to more equitable distributions of power. They will probably feel few penalties whatever choice they make; they do not seem, in any obvious short-term sense, the ones at risk, though they are, we are all at risk because of the behaviors that have been rewarded in them.

25   Through Women's Studies work I have met very few men who are truly distressed about systemic, unearned male advantage and conferred dominance. And so one question for me and others like me is whether we will be like them, or whether we will get truly distressed, even outraged, about unearned race advantage and conferred dominance and if so, what we will do to lessen them. In any case, we need to do more work in identifying how they actually affect our daily lives. We need more down-to-earth writing by people about these taboo subjects. We need more understanding of the ways in which white "privilege" damages white people, for these are not the same ways in which it damages the victimized. Skewed white psyches are an inseparable part of the picture, though I do not want to confuse the kinds of damage done to the holders of special assets and to those who suffer the deficits. Many, perhaps most, of our white students in the United States think that racism doesn't affect them because they are not people of color; they do not see "whiteness" as a racial identity. Many men likewise think that Women's Studies does not bear on their own existences because they are not female; they do not see themselves as having gendered identities. Insisting on the universal "effects" of "privilege" systems, then, becomes one of our chief tasks, and being more explicit about the *particular* effects in particular contexts is another. Men need to join us in this work.

In addition, since race and sex are not the only advantaging systems at work, we need to similarly examine the daily experience of having age advantage, or ethnic advantage, or physical ability, or advantage related to nationality, religion, or sexual orientation. Professor Marnie Evans suggested to me that in many ways the list I made also applies directly to heterosexual privilege. This is a still more taboo subject than race privilege: the daily ways in which heterosexual privilege makes some persons comfortable or powerful, providing supports, assets, approvals, and rewards to those who live or expect to live in heterosexual pairs. Unpacking that content is still more difficult, owing to the deeper imbeddedness of heterosexual advantage and dominance and stricter taboos surrounding these.

But to start such an analysis I would put this observation from my own experience: The fact that I live under the same roof with a man triggers all kinds of societal assumptions about my worth, politics, life, and value and triggers a host of unearned advantages and powers. After recasting many elements from the original list I would add further observations like these:

1. My children do not have to answer questions about why I live with my partner (my husband).

2. I have no difficulty finding neighborhoods where people approve of our household.

3. Our children are given texts and classes that implicitly support our kind of family unit and do not turn them against my choice of domestic partnership.

4. I can travel alone or with my husband without expecting embarrassment or hostility in those who deal with us.

5. Most people I meet will see my marital arrangements as an asset to my life or as a favorable comment on my likability, my competence, or my mental health.

6. I can talk about the social events of a weekend without fearing most listeners' reactions.

7. I will feel welcomed and "normal" in the usual walks of public life, institutional and social.

8. In many contexts, I am seen as "all right" in daily work on women because I do not live chiefly with women.

Difficulties and dangers surrounding the tasks of finding parallels are many. Since racism, sexism, and heterosexism are not the same, the advantages associated with them should not be seen as the same. In addition, it is hard to isolate aspects of unearned advantage that derive chiefly from social class, economic class, race, religion, region, sex, or ethnic identity. The oppressions are both distinct and interlocking, as the Combahee River Collective statement of 1977 continues to remind us eloquently.[3]

One factor seems clear about all of the interlocking oppressions. They take both active forms that we can see and embedded forms that members of the dominant group are taught not to see. In my class and place, I did not see myself as racist because I was taught to recognize racism only in individual acts of meanness by members of my group, never in invisible systems conferring racial dominance on my group from birth. Likewise, we are taught to think that sexism or heterosexism is carried on only through intentional, individual acts of discrimination, meanness, or cruelty, rather than in invisible systems conferring unsought dominance on certain groups. Disapproving of the systems won't be enough to change them. I was taught to think that racism could end if white individuals changed their attitudes; many men think sexism can be ended by individual changes in daily behavior toward women. But a man's sex provides advantage for him whether or not he approves of the way in which dominance has been conferred on his group. A "white" skin in the United States opens many doors for whites whether or not we approve of the way dominance has been conferred on us. Individual acts can palliate, but cannot end, these problems. To redesign social systems, we need first to acknowledge their colossal unseen dimensions. The silences and denials surrounding privilege are the key political tool here. They keep the thinking about equality or equity incomplete, protecting unearned advantage and conferred dominance by making these taboo subjects. Most talk by whites about equal opportunity seems to me now to be about equal opportunity to try to get into a position of dominance while denying that *systems* of dominance exist.

30   Obliviousness about white advantage, like obliviousness about male advantage, is kept strongly inculturated in the United States so as to maintain the myth of meritocracy, the myth that democratic choice is equally available to all. Keeping most people unaware that freedom of confident action is there for just a small number of people props up those in power and serves to keep power in the hands of the same groups that have most of it already. Though systemic change takes many decades, there are pressing questions for me and I imagine for some others like me if we raise our daily consciousness on the perquisites of being light-skinned. What will we do with such knowledge? As we know from watching men, it is an open question whether we will choose to use unearned advantage to weaken invisible privilege systems and whether we will use any of our arbitrarily awarded power to try to reconstruct power-systems on a broader base.

Notes

[1] This paper was presented at the Virginia Women's Studies Association conference in Richmond in April 1986, and the American Educational Research Association conference in Boston in October 1986, and discussed with two groups of participants in the Dodge seminars for Secondary School Teachers in New York and Boston in the spring of 1987.

[2] Andersen, Margaret, "Race and the Social Science Curriculum: A Teaching and Learning Discussion." *Radical Teacher*, November, 1984, pp. 17–20. Smith, Lillian, *Killers of the Dream*, New York: W. W. Norton, 1949.

[3] "A Black Feminist Statement," The Combahee River Collective, pp. 13–22 in G. Hull, P. Scott, B. Smith, Eds., *All the Women Are White, All the Blacks Are Men, But Some of Us Are Brave: Black Women's Studies*, Old Westbury, NY: The Feminist Press, 1982.

Things to Do with the Reading

1. McIntosh organizes her essay around a single simile (comparison): "White privilege is like an invisible weightless knapsack of special provisions, assurances, tools, maps, guides, codebooks, passports, visas, clothes, compass, emergency gear, and blank checks." Find and discuss single sentences and short passages in the essay that explain some of the word choice in this simile—"invisible," for example, and "weightless." Also paraphrase both the sentence above and the ones you find. Then write a short interpretive essay

on the items in the backpack as listed in the sentence quoted above and other similar ones. To what does the figurative language in these sentences correspond?

2. McIntosh presents this essay (originally given as a paper at a women's studies conference) as a personal reflection: "This paper is a partial record of my personal observations and not a scholarly analysis. It is based on my daily experiences within my particular circumstances." Even though the piece is written in the first person and includes the author's personal experience, it also employs language characteristics of academic discourse in the social sciences. The more specialized, more academic language allows McIntosh to give her argument greater specificity.

   Do Paraphrase × 3 (see Chapter 2) with the following sentences from the essay and then write a short essay in which you explain what these add to the essay's way of defining white privilege.

   • "Others agree that certain individual thinkers are male oriented but deny that there is any systemic tendency in disciplinary frameworks or epistemology to overempower men as a group" (paragraph 8).

   • "The negative 'privilege' that gave me cultural permission not to take darker-skinned Others seriously can be seen as arbitrarily conferred dominance and should not be desirable for anyone" (paragraph 22).

3. Write a short essay in which you explore McIntosh's analogy between male privilege and white privilege. What features of her experience—as a white woman—does McIntosh posit as analogous to those of white males?

4. **Link:** Write an essay in which you use the following two sentences, one from McIntosh's essay and one from DeMott's, to put these two writers' thinking into conversation. Which key words in each quote are the best indications of common ground between McIntosh and DeMott? (See Chapter 13 on putting sources into conversation with each other.)

   • McIntosh: "Obliviousness about white advantage, like obliviousness about male advantage, is kept strongly inculturated in the United States so as to maintain the myth of meritocracy, the myth that democratic choice is equally available to all" (paragraph 30).

   • DeMott: "Factitious renderings of the American past blur the outlines of black-white conflict, redefine the ground of black grievances for the purpose of diminishing those grievances, [and] restage black life in accordance with the illusory conventions of American success mythology" (paragraph 28).

6. **Application:** Before she offers her list of privileges, McIntosh offers a somewhat disingenuous disclaimer—"This list is not intended to be generalizable"—and then proceeds to invite her readers to undergo the same self-scrutiny she has undertaken: "Others can make their own lists from within their own life circumstances."

This challenge brings to mind two obvious applications: to expand McIntosh's list and/or to corroborate it (that is, find confirming evidence) with your own experience.

Give yourself at least a week. Carry around a special notebook for the purpose. Keep the idea of unacknowledged privilege alive in the back of your mind, as you visit sites where people congregate—a square, a shopping district, a lunchroom—with the conscious project of conducting observation.

At the end of the week, write up your results. Start with a list, but then take the most vivid instances and expand them into brief narratives.

Richard Rodriguez
The Fear of Losing a Culture

Richard Rodriguez provides a distinctively Latin American spin on the concept of the melting pot. He argues that Latin America was "formed by a rape that became a marriage" and goes on to tell his North American audience, "Expect marriage." A teacher, journalist (formerly on PBS), and award-winning essayist, Rodriguez is the child of Mexican American immigrants. He earned degrees at Stanford and Columbia and also did graduate work at UC-Berkeley, before deciding to become a freelance essayist. In addition to his famous 1982 memoir, *Hunger of Memory*, from which this piece is taken, Rodriguez has written three other books, including *Brown*, with a new one on the desert religions forthcoming.

What is culture?   1

The immigrant shrugs. Latin American immigrants come to the United States with only the things they need in mind—not abstractions like culture. Money. They need dollars. They need food. Maybe they need to get out of the way of bullets.

Most of us who concern ourselves with Hispanic-American culture, as painters, musicians, writers—or as sons and daughters—are the children of immigrants. We have grown up on this side of the border, in the land of Elvis Presley and Thomas Edison; our lives are prescribed by the mall, by the DMV and the Chinese restaurant. Our imaginations yet vascillate between an Edenic Latin America (the blue door)—which nevertheless betrayed our parents—and the repellent plate glass of a real American city—which has been good to us.

Hispanic-American culture is where the past meets the future. Hispanic-American culture is not a Hispanic milestone only, not simply a celebration at the crossroads. America transforms into pleasure what America cannot avoid. Is it any coincidence that at a time when Americans are troubled by the encroachment of the Mexican desert, Americans discover a chic in cactus, in the decorator colors of the Southwest? In sand?

Hispanic-American culture of the sort that is now showing (the teen movie, the   5
rock songs) may exist in an hourglass; may in fact be irrelevant to the epic. The U.S. Border Patrol works through the night to arrest the flow of illegal immigrants over the border, even as Americans wait in line to get into "La Bamba." Even as Americans vote to declare, once and for all, that English shall be the official language of the United States, Madonna starts recording in Spanish.

But then so is Bill Cosby's show irrelevant to the 10 o'clock news, where families huddle together in fear on porches, pointing at the body of the slain boy bagged in tarpaulin. Which is not to say that Bill Cosby or Michael Jackson are irrelevant to the future or without neo-Platonic influence. Like players within the play, they prefigure, they resolve. They make black and white audiences aware of a bond that may not yet exist.

TIME Magazine, July 11, 1988. Reprinted by permission.

Before a national TV audience, Rita Moreno tells Geraldo Rivera that her dream as an actress is to play a character rather like herself: "I speak English perfectly well ... I'm not dying from poverty ... I want to play *that* kind of Hispanic woman, which is to say, an American citizen." This is an actress talking, these are show-biz pieties. But Moreno expresses as well the general Hispanic-American predicament. Hispanics want to belong to America without betraying the past.

Hispanics fear losing ground in any negotiation with the American city. We come from an expansive, an intimate culture that has been judged second-rate by the United States of America. For reasons of pride, therefore, as much as of affection, we are reluctant to give up our past. Hispanics often express a fear of "losing" culture. Our fame in the United States has been our resistance to assimilation.

The symbol of Hispanic culture has been the tongue of flame—Spanish. But the remarkable legacy Hispanics carry from Latin America is not language—an inflatable skin—but breath itself, capacity of soul, an inclination to live. The genius of Latin America is the habit of synthesis.

10   We assimilate. Just over the border there is the example of Mexico, the country from which the majority of U.S. Hispanics come. Mexico is *mestizo*—Indian and Spanish. Within a single family, Mexicans are light-skinned and dark. It is impossible for the Mexican to say, in the scheme of things, where the Indian begins and the Spaniard surrenders.

In culture as in blood, Latin America was formed by a rape that became a marriage. Due to the absorbing generosity of the Indian, European culture took on new soil. What Latin America knows is that people create one another as they marry. In the music of Latin America you will hear the litany of bloodlines—the African drum, the German accordion, the cry from the minaret.

The United States stands as the opposing New World experiment. In North America the Indian and the European stood apace. Whereas Latin America was formed by a medieval Catholic dream of one world—of meltdown conversion—the United States was built up from Protestant individualism. The American melting pot washes away only embarrassment; it is the necessary initiation into public life. The American faith is that our national strength derives from separateness, from "diversity." The glamour of the United States is a carnival promise: You can lose weight, get rich as Rockefeller, tough up your roots, get a divorce.

Immigrants still come for the promise. But the United States wavers in its faith. As long as there was space enough, sky enough, as long as economic success validated individualism, loneliness was not too high a price to pay. (The cabin on the prairie or the Sony Walkman.)

As we near the end of the American century, two alternative cultures beckon the American imagination—both highly communal cultures—the Asian and the Latin American. The United States is a literal culture. Americans devour what we might otherwise fear to become. Sushi will make us corporate warriors. Combination Plate #3, smothered in *mestizo* gravy, will burn a hole in our hearts.

15   Latin America offers passion. Latin America has a life—I mean *life*—big clouds, unambiguous themes, death, birth, faith, that the United States, for all its quality of life, seems without now. Latin America offers communal riches: an undistressed

leisure, a kitchen table, even a full sorrow. Such is the solitude of America, such is the urgency of American need, Americans reach right past a fledgling, homegrown Hispanic-American culture for the real thing—the darker bottle of Mexican beer; the denser novel of a Latin American master.

For a long time, Hispanics in the United States withheld from the United States our Latin American gift. We denied the value of assimilation. But as our presence is judged less foreign in America, we will produce a more generous art, less timid, less parochial. Carlos Santana, Luis Valdez, Linda Ronstadt—Hispanic Americans do not have a "pure" Latin American art to offer. Expect bastard themes, expect ironies, comic conclusions. For we live on this side of the border, where Kraft manufactures bricks of "Mexican style" Velveeta, and where Jack in the Box serves "Fajita Pita."

The flame-red Chevy floats a song down the Pan American Highway: From a rolled-down window, the grizzled voice of Willie Nelson rises in disembodied harmony with the voice of Julio Iglesias. Gabby Hayes and Cisco are thus resolved.

Expect marriage. We will change America even as we will be changed. We will disappear with you into a new miscegenation.

Along the border, real conflicts remain. But the ancient tear separating Europe from itself—the Catholic Mediterranean from the Protestant north—may yet heal itself in the New World. For generations, Latin America has been the place—the bed—of a confluence of so many races and cultures that Protestant North America shuddered to imagine it.

Imagine it.   20

Things to Do with the Reading

1. Rodriguez has an interesting fix on the way that Americans react to other cultures. He says that "America transforms into pleasure what America cannot avoid" (paragraph 4) and that "Americans devour what we might otherwise fear to become" (paragraph 14). Try paraphrasing these remarks in their given context, as a way of uncovering their implications. Be alert to figurative language—why, for example, "devour"? Write a short essay on the rhetoric the essay employs to talk about (crossing) cultural boundaries. You might find it useful to focus on the use of figurative language in particular (see Chapter 9).

2. **Link:** In an interview conducted 15 years after the publication of *Hunger of Memory*, Rodriguez said, "I am no more in favor of assimilation than I am in favor of the Pacific Ocean. Assimilation is not something to oppose or favor—it just happens." Write an essay in which you explore how Rodriguez's point of view conflicts with the view of assimilation offered by Peter Salins in "Assimilation, American Style." How might we account for the difference in the two writers' perspectives? What are the assumptions that underlie each of their essays? (For uncovering assumptions, see Chapter 4.)

3. Take the passage at the end of paragraph 16, which reads, "Expect bastard themes, expect ironies, comic conclusions. For we live on this side of the border where Kraft manufactures bricks of 'Mexican style' Velveeta, and where Jack in the Box serves 'Fajita Pita.'" How does the essay condition us to respond to this passage? In what verbal strands (see the Method, Chapter 2) does this language participate? This passage occurs shortly before the conclusion. Write a short essay on the way Rodriguez chooses to bring his ruminations to a close in the final five paragraphs.

Amy Tan

Mother Tongue

In this provocative essay about her mother's "broken" English, the novelist Amy Tan distinguishes at least four different "Englishes" that she learned to speak as a Chinese American daughter called upon to succeed in U.S. schools, to communicate with her mother, and to become a writer. Along the way she provides glimpses into the quandaries that face children for whom standard English is not the language spoken at home: we see how the particular language she learns there does not equip her to navigate standardized tests in which, for example, she must discern whether "a sunset precedes nightfall" is analogous to "a chill precedes a fever."

I am not a scholar of English or literature. I cannot give you much more than personal opinions on the English language and its variations in this country or others.

I am a writer. And by that definition, I am someone who has always loved language. I am fascinated by language in daily life. I spend a great deal of my time thinking about the power of language—the way it can evoke an emotion, a visual image, a complex idea, or a simple truth. Language is the tool of my trade. And I use them all— all the Englishes I grew up with.

Recently, I was made keenly aware of the different Englishes I do use. I was giving a talk to a large group of people, the same talk I had already given to half a dozen other groups. The nature of the talk was about my writing, my life, and my book, *The Joy Luck Club.* The talk was going along well enough, until I remembered one major difference that made the whole talk sound wrong. My mother was in the room. And it was perhaps the first time she had heard me give a lengthy speech, using the kind of English I have never used with her. I was saying things like, "The intersection of memory upon imagination" and "There is an aspect of my fiction that relates to thus-and-thus"—a speech filled with carefully wrought grammatical phrases, burdened, it suddenly seemed to me, with nominalized forms, past perfect tenses, conditional phrases, all the forms of standard English that I had learned in school and through books, the forms of English I did not use at home with my mother.

Just last week, I was walking down the street with my mother, and I again found myself conscious of the English I was using, the English I do use with her. We were talking about the price of new and used furniture and I heard myself saying this: "Not waste money that way." My husband was with us as well, and he didn't notice any switch in my English. And then I realized why. It's because over the twenty years we've been together I've often used that same kind of English with him, and sometimes he even uses it with me. It has become our language of intimacy, a different sort of English that relates to family talk, the language I grew up with.

So you'll have some idea of what this family talk I heard sounds like, I'll quote what my mother said during a recent conversation, which I videotaped and then transcribed. During this conversation, my mother was talking about a political gangster in

"Mother Tongue" by Amy Tan, The Threepenny Review, 1990. Used by permission of Sandra Dijkstra Literary Agency.

Shanghai who had the same last name as her family's, Du, and how the gangster in his early years wanted to be adopted by her family, which was rich by comparison. Later, the gangster became more powerful, far richer than my mother's family, and one day showed up at my mother's wedding to pay his respects. Here's what she said in part: "Du Yusong having business like fruit stand. Like off the street kind. He is Du like Du Zong—but not Tsung-ming Island people. The local people call putong, the river east side, he belong to that side local people. That man want to ask Du Zong father take him in like become own family. Du Zong father wasn't look down on him, but didn't take seriously, until that man big like become a mafia. Now important person, very hard to inviting him. Chinese way, came only to show respect, don't stay for dinner. Respect for making big celebration, he shows up. Mean gives lots of respect. Chinese custom. Chinese social life that way. If too important won't have to stay too long. He come to my wedding. I didn't see, I heard it. I gone to boy's side, they have YMCA dinner. Chinese age I was nineteen."

You should know that my mother's expressive command of English belies how much she actually understands. She reads the *Forbes* report, listens to *Wall Street Week*, converses daily with her stockbroker, reads all of Shirley MacLaine's books with ease—all kinds of things I can't begin to understand. Yet some of my friends tell me they understand 50 percent of what my mother says. Some say they understand 80 to 90 percent. Some say they understand none of it, as if she were speaking pure Chinese. But to me, my mother's English is perfectly clear, perfectly natural. It's my mother tongue. Her language, as I hear it, is vivid, direct, full of observation and imagery. That was the language that helped shape the way I saw things, expressed things, made sense of the world.

Lately, I've been giving more thought to the kind of English my mother speaks. Like others, I have described it to people as "'broken" or "fractured" English. But I wince when I say that. It has always bothered me that I can think of no way to describe it other than "broken," as if it were damaged and needed to be fixed, as if it lacked a certain wholeness and soundness. I've heard other terms used, "limited English," for example. But they seem just as bad, as if everything is limited, including people's perceptions of the limited English speaker.

I know this for a fact, because when I was growing up, my mother's "limited" English limited *my* perception of her. I was ashamed of her English. I believed that her English reflected the quality of what she had to say. That is, because she expressed them imperfectly her thoughts were imperfect. And I had plenty of empirical evidence to support me: the fact that people in department stores, at banks, and at restaurants did not take her seriously, did not give her good service, pretended not to understand her, or even acted as if they did not hear her.

My mother has long realized the limitations of her English as well. When I was fifteen, she used to have me call people on the phone to pretend I was she. In this guise, I was forced to ask for information or even to complain and yell at people who had been rude to her. One time it was a call to her stockbroker in New York. She had cashed out her small portfolio and it just so happened we were going to go to New York the next week, our very first trip outside California. I had to get on the phone and say in an adolescent voice that was not very convincing, "This is Mrs. Tan." And my mother was standing in the back whispering loudly, "Why he don't send me check, already two weeks late. So mad he lie to me, losing me money. And then I said in perfect English, "Yes, I'm getting rather concerned. You had agreed to send the check two weeks ago, but it hasn't arrived."

Then she began to talk more loudly. "What he want, I come to New York tell him front of his boss, you cheating me?" And I was trying to calm her down, make her be quiet, while telling the stockbroker, "I can't tolerate any more excuses. If I don't receive the check immediately, I am going to have to speak to your manager when I'm in New York next week." And sure enough, the following week there we were in front of this astonished stockbroker, and I was sitting there red-faced and quiet, and my mother, the real Mrs. Tan, was shouting at his boss in her impeccable broken English.

We used a similar routine just five days ago, for a situation that was far less humorous. My mother had gone to the hospital for an appointment, to find out about a benign brain tumor a CAT scan had revealed a month ago. She said she had spoken very good English, her best English, no mistakes. Still, she said, the hospital did not apologize when they said they had lost the CAT scan and she had come for nothing. She said they did not seem to have any sympathy when she told them she was anxious to know the exact diagnosis, since her husband and son had both died of brain tumors. She said they would not give her any more information until the next time and she would have to make another appointment for that. So she said she would not leave until the doctor called her daughter. She wouldn't budge. And when the doctor finally called her daughter, me, who spoke in perfect English—lo and behold—we had assurances the CAT scan would be found, promises that a conference call on Monday would be held, and apologies for any suffering my mother had gone through for a most regrettable mistake.

I think my mother's English almost had an effect on limiting my possibilities in life as well. Sociologists and linguists probably will tell you that a person's developing language skills are more influenced by peers. But I do think that the language spoken in the family, especially in immigrant families which are more insular, plays a large role in shaping the language of the child. And I believe that it affected my results on achievement tests, I.Q. tests, and the SAT. While my English skills were never judged as poor, compared to math, English could not be considered my strong suit. In grade school I did moderately well, getting perhaps B's, sometimes B-pluses, in English and scoring perhaps in the sixtieth or seventieth percentile on achievement tests. But those scores were not good enough to override the opinion that my true abilities lay in math and science, because in those areas I achieved A's and scored in the ninetieth percentile or higher.

This was understandable. Math is precise; there is only one correct answer. Whereas, for me at least, the answers on English tests were always a judgment call, a matter of opinion and personal experience. Those tests were constructed around items like fill-in-the-blank sentence completion, such as, "Even thought Tom was _____, Mary thought he was _____." And the correct answer always seemed to be the most bland combinations of thoughts, for example, "Even though Tom was shy, Mary thought he was charming" with the grammatical structure "even though" limiting the correct answer to some sort of semantic opposites, so you wouldn't get answers like, "Even though Tom was foolish, Mary thought he was ridiculous." Well, according to my mother, there were very few limitations as to what Tom could have been and what Mary might have thought of him. So I never did well on tests like that.

The same was true with word analogies, pairs of words in which you were supposed to find some sort of logical, semantic relationship—for example, "*Sunset* is to *nightfall* as _____ is to _____. " And here you would be presented with a list of four possible pairs, one of which showed the same kind of relationship: red is to stoplight, bus is to arrival, chills is to fever, yawn is to boring. Well, I could never think that way. I knew what the tests were asking, but I could not block out of my mind the images already created by the first pair, "sunset is to nightfall"—and I would see a burst of colors against a darkening sky, the moon rising, the lowering of a curtain of stars. And all the other pairs of words—red, bus, stoplight, boring—just threw up a mass of confusing images, making it impossible for me to sort out something as logical as saying: "A sunset precedes nightfall" is the same as "a chill precedes a fever." The only way I would have gotten that answer right would have been to imagine an associative situation, for example, my being disobedient and staying out past sunset, catching a chill at night, which turns into feverish pneumonia as punishment, which indeed did happen to me.

I have been thinking about all this lately, about my mother's English, about achievement tests. Because lately I've been asked, as a writer, why there are not more Asian-Americans represented in American literature. Why are there few Asian-Americans enrolled in creative writing programs? Why do so many Chinese students go into engineering? Well, these are broad sociological questions I can't begin to answer.

But I have noticed in surveys—in fact, just last week—that Asian students, as a whole, always do significantly better on math achievement tests than in English. And this makes me think that there are other Asian-American students whose English spoken in the home might also be described as "broken" or "limited." And perhaps they also have teachers who are steering them away from writing and into math and science, which is what happened to me.

Fortunately, I happen to be rebellious in nature and enjoy the challenge of disproving assumptions made about me. I became an English major my first year in college, after being enrolled as pre-med. I started writing nonfiction as a freelancer the week after I was told by my former boss that writing was my worst skill and I should hone my talents toward account management.

But it wasn't until 1985 that I finally began to write fiction. And at first I wrote using what I thought to be wittily crafted sentences, sentences that would finally prove I had mastery over the English language. Here's an example from the first draft of a story that later made its way into *The Joy Luck Club*, but without this line: "That was my mental quandary in its nascent state." A terrible line, which I can barely pronounce.

Fortunately, for reasons I won't get into today, I later decided I should envision a reader for the stories I would write. And the reader I decided upon was my mother, because these were stories about mothers. So with this reader in mind—and in fact she did read my early drafts—I began to write stories using all the Englishes I grew up with: the English I spoke to my mother, which for lack of a better term might be described as "simple"; the English she used with me, which for lack of a better term might be described as "broken"; my translation of her Chinese, which could certainly be described as "watered down"; and what I imagined to be her translation of her Chinese if she could speak in perfect English, her internal language, and for that I sought to preserve the essence, but neither an English nor a Chinese structure. I wanted to capture what language ability tests can never reveal: her intent, her passion, her imagery, the rhythms of her speech and the nature of her thoughts. Apart from what any critic had to say about my writing, I knew I had succeeded where it counted when my mother finished reading my book and gave me her verdict: "So easy to read."

Things to Do with the Reading

1. **Link:** Imagine that Peggy McIntosh, the author of "White Privilege and Male Privilege," read this essay. Write an essay in which you first identify and discuss passages from both essays that illustrate some common ground. Then determine the biggest difference between these two women writers' points of view, and ask so what (see Chapter 2 on the So what? question.) Then answer it. You might use the heuristic in Chapter 4 that we call Looking for Difference within Similarity.

2. One organizing binary in the essay is between standard English and Tan's mother's English. (See The Method in Chapter 2 and Reformulating Binaries in Chapter 4.) What claims does Tan make for the advantages of her mother's English? Why does she speak it with her non-Chinese husband? Use these questions to develop an essay on the extent to which Tan implicitly critiques standard English, even as she uses it. What is it that Tan seems to believe standard English cannot so easily say?

3. **Link:** Write an essay in which you compare and contrast Tan's complex point of view on assimilation with that of Richard Rodriguez in "The Fear of Losing a Culture." You might begin by finding a passage in Rodriguez that you think Tan might like, and then finding a passage in Tan that you think both links with and differentiates from Rodriguez's point of view. To what extent do both writers complicate the melting pot model of assimilation? If you wish, consider the role that style plays in establishing each author's point of view.

Henry Louis Gates, Jr.

In the Kitchen

In this carefully crafted and subtly inflected memoir, Henry Louis Gates, Jr. uses his own memories of African American hairstyling figuratively—as a way of thinking about more than just hair. Neither an apology nor a diatribe, the piece offers a complex and affectionate parable of assimilation. Henry Louis "Skip" Gates, Jr. is the W.E.B. Du Bois Professor of Humanities at Harvard and director of the W.E.B. Du Bois Institute for Afro-American Research. In 1997, Gates was voted one of *Time Magazine*'s "25 Most Influential Americans." Like a number of other authors included in this book, he too was a winner of a MacArthur "genius" Fellowship.

1   We always had a gas stove in the kitchen, in our house in Piedmont, West Virginia, where I grew up. Never electric, though using electric became fashionable in Piedmont in the sixties, like using Crest toothpaste rather than Colgate, or watching Huntley and Brinkley rather than Walter Cronkite. But not us: gas, Colgate, and good ole Walter Cronkite, come what may. We used gas partly out of loyalty to Big Mom, Mama's Mama, because she was mostly blind and still loved to cook, and could feel her way more easily with gas than with electric. But the most important thing about our gas-equipped kitchen was that Mama used to do hair there. The "hot comb" was a fine-toothed iron instrument with a long wooden handle and a pair of iron curlers that opened and closed like scissors. Mama would put it in the gas fire until it glowed. You could smell those prongs heating up.

I liked that smell. Not the smell so much, I guess, as what the smell meant for the shape of my day. There was an intimate warmth in the women's tones as they talked with my Mama, doing their hair. I knew what the women had been through to get their hair ready to be "done," because I would watch Mama do it to herself. How that kink could be transformed through grease and fire into that magnificent head of wavy hair was a miracle to me, and still is.

Mama would wash her hair over the sink, a towel wrapped around her shoulders, wearing just her slip and her white bra. (We had no shower—just a galvanized tub that we stored in the kitchen—until we moved down Rat Tail Road into Doc Wolverton's house, in 1954.) After she dried it, she would grease her scalp thoroughly with blue Bergamot hair grease, which came in a short, fat jar with a picture of a beautiful colored lady on it. It's important to grease your scalp real good, my Mama would explain, to keep from burning yourself. Of course, her hair would return to its natural kink almost as soon as the hot water and shampoo hit it. To me, it was another miracle how hair so "straight" would so quickly become kinky again the second it even approached some water.

My Mama had only a few "clients" whose heads she "did"—did, I think, because she enjoyed it, rather than for the few pennies it brought in. They would sit on one of

"In the Kitchen" from COLORED PEOPLE: A MEMOIR by Henry Louis Gates, Jr., copyright © 1994 by Henry Louis Gates, Jr. Used by permission of Alfred A. Knopf, a division of Random House, Inc.

our red plastic kitchen chairs, the kind with the shiny metal legs, and brace themselves for the process. Mama would stroke that red-hot iron—which by this time had been in the gas fire for half an hour or more—slowly but firmly through their hair, from scalp to strand's end. It made a scorching, crinkly sound, the hot iron did, as it burned its way through kink, leaving in its wake straight strands of hair, standing long and tall but drooping over at the ends, their shape like the top of a heavy willow tree. Slowly, steadily, Mama's hands would transform a round mound of Odetta kink into a darkened swamp of everglades. The Bergamot made the hair shiny; the heat of the hot iron gave it a brownish-red cast. Once all the hair was as straight as God allows kink to get, Mama would take the well-heated curling iron and twirl the straightened strands into more or less loosely wrapped curls. She claimed that she owed her skill as a hairdresser to the strength in her wrists, and as she worked her little finger would poke out, the way it did when she sipped tea. Mama was a southpaw, and wrote upside down and backward to produce the cleanest, roundest letters you've ever seen.

The "kitchen" she would all but remove from sight with a handheld pair of shears,   5 bought just for this purpose. Now, the kitchen was the room in which we were sitting—the room where Mama did hair and washed clothes, and where we all took a bath in that galvanized tub. But the word has another meaning, and the kitchen that I'm speaking of is the very kinky bit of hair at the back of your head, where your neck meets your shirt collar. If there was ever a part of our African past that resisted assimilation, it was the kitchen. No matter how hot the iron, no matter how powerful the chemical, no matter how stringent the mashed-potatoes-and-lye formula of a man's "process," neither God nor woman nor Sammy Davis, Jr., could straighten the kitchen. The kitchen was permanent, irredeemable; irresistible kink. Unassimilably African. No matter what you did, no matter how hard you tried, you couldn't de-kink a person's kitchen. So you trimmed it off as best you could.

When hair had begun to "turn," as they'd say—to return to its natural kinky glory—it was the kitchen that turned first (the kitchen around the back, and nappy edges at the temples). When the kitchen started creeping up the back of the neck, it was time to get your hair done again.

Sometimes, after dark, a man would come to have his hair done. It was Mr. Charlie Carroll. He was very light-complected and had a ruddy nose—it made me think of Edmund Gwenn, who played Kris Kringle in "Miracle on 34th Street." At first, Mama did him after my brother, Rocky, and I had gone to sleep. It was only later that we found out that he had come to our house so Mama could iron his hair—not with a hot comb or a curling iron but with our very own Proctor-Silex steam iron. For some reason I never understood, Mr. Charlie would conceal his Frederick Douglass-like mane under a big white Stetson hat. I never saw him take it off except when he came to our house, at night, to have his hair pressed. (Later, Daddy would tell us about Mr. Charlie's most prized piece of knowledge, something that the man would only confide after his hair had been pressed, as a token of intimacy. "Not many people know this," he'd say, in a tone of circumspection, "but George Washington was Abraham Lincoln's daddy." Nodding solemnly, he'd add the clincher: "A white man told me." Though he was in dead earnest, this became a humorous refrain around our house—"a white man told me"—which we used to punctuate especially preposterous assertions.)

My mother examined my daughters' kitchens whenever we went home to visit, in the early eighties. It became a game between us. I had told her not to do it, because I didn't like the politics it suggested—the notion of "good" and "bad" hair. "Good" hair was "straight," "bad" hair kinky. Even in the late sixties, at the height of Black Power, almost nobody could bring themselves to say "bad" for good and "good" for bad. People still said that hair like white people's hair was "good," even if they encapsulated it in a disclaimer, like "what we used to call 'good.'"

Maggie would be seated in her high chair, throwing food this way and that, and Mama would be cooing about how cute it all was, how I used to do just like Maggie was doing, and wondering whether her flinging her food with her left hand meant that she was going to be left-handed like Mama. When my daughter was just about covered with Chef Boyardee Spaghetti-O's, Mama would seize the opportunity: wiping her clean, she would tilt Maggie's head to one side and reach down the back of her neck. Sometimes Mama would even rub a curl between her fingers, just to make sure that her bifocals had not deceived her. Then she'd sigh with satisfaction and relief: No kink … yet. Mama! I'd shout, pretending to be angry. Every once in a while, if no one was looking, I'd peek, too.

10   I say "yet" because most black babies are born with soft, silken hair. But after a few months it begins to turn, as inevitably as do the seasons or the leaves on a tree. People once thought baby oil would stop it. They were wrong.

Everybody I knew as a child wanted to have good hair. You could be as ugly as homemade sin dipped in misery and still be thought attractive if you had good hair. "Jesus moss," the girls at Camp Lee, Virginia, had called Daddy's naturally "good" hair during the war. I know that he played that thick head of hair for all it was worth, too.

My own hair was "not a bad grade," as barbers would tell me when they cut it for the first time. It was like a doctor reporting the results of the first full physical he has given you. Like "You're in good shape" or "Blood pressure's kind of high—better cut down on salt."

I spent most of my childhood and adolescence messing with my hair. I definitely wanted straight hair. Like Pop's. When I was about three, I tried to stick a wad of Bazooka bubble gum to that straight hair of his. I suppose what fixed that memory for me is the spanking I got for doing so: he turned me upside down, holding me by my feet, the better to paddle my behind. Little *nigger*, he had shouted, walloping away. I started to laugh about it two days later, when my behind stopped hurting.

When black people say "straight," of course, they don't usually mean literally straight—they're not describing hair like, say, Peggy Lipton's (she was the white girl on "The Mod Squad"), or like Mary's of Peter, Paul & Mary fame; black people call that "stringy" hair. No, "straight" just means not kinky, no matter what contours the curl may take. I would have done *anything* to have straight hair—and I used to try everything, short of getting a process.

15   Of the wide variety of techniques and methods I came to master in the challenging prestidigitation of the follicle, almost all had two things in common: a heavy grease and the application of pressure. It's not an accident that some of the biggest black-owned companies in the fifties and sixties made hair products. And I tried them all,

in search of that certain silken touch, the one that would leave neither the hand nor the pillow sullied by grease.

I always wondered what Frederick Douglass put on *his* hair, or what Phillis Wheatley put on hers. Or why Wheatley has that rag on her head in the little engraving in the frontispiece of her book. One thing is for sure: you can bet that when Phillis Wheatley went to England and saw the Countess of Huntingdon she did not stop by the Queen's coiffeur on her way there. So many black people still get their hair straightened that it's a wonder we don't have a national holiday for Madame C. J. Walker, the woman who invented the process of straightening kinky hair. Call it Jheri-Kurled or call it "relaxed," it's still fried hair.

I used all the greases, from sea-blue Bergamot and creamy vanilla Duke (in its clear jar with the orange-white-and-green label) to the godfather of grease, the formidable Murray's. Now, Murray's was some *serious* grease. Whereas Bergamot was like oily jello, and Duke was viscous and sickly sweet, Murray's was light brown and *hard*. Hard as lard and twice as greasy, Daddy used to say. Murray's came in an orange can with a press-on top. It was so hard that some people would put a match to the can, just to soften the stuff and make it more manageable. Then, in the late sixties, when Afros came into style, I used Afro Sheen. From Murray's to Duke to Afro Sheen: that was my progression in black consciousness.

We used to put hot towels or wash-rags over our Murray-coated heads, in order to melt the wax into the scalp and the follicles. Unfortunately, the wax also had the habit of running down your neck, ears, and forehead. Not to mention your pillowcase. Another problem was that if you put two palmfuls of Murray's on your head your hair turned white. (Duke did the same thing.) The challenge was to get rid of that white color. Because if you got rid of the white stuff you had a magnificent head of wavy hair. That was the beauty of it: Murray's was so hard that it froze your hair into the wavy style you brushed it into. It looked really good if you wore a part. A lot of guys had parts *cut* into their hair by a barber, either with the clippers or with a straightedged razor. Especially if you had kinky hair—then you'd generally wear a short razorcut, or what we called a Quo Vadis.

We tried to be as innovative as possible. Everyone knew about using a stocking cap, because your father or your uncle wore one whenever something really big was about to happen, whether sacred or secular: a funeral or a dance, a wedding or a trip in which you confronted official white people. Any time you were trying to look really sharp, you wore a stocking cap in preparation. And if the event was really a big one, you made a new cap. You asked your mother for a pair of her hose, and cut it with scissors about six inches or so from the open end—the end with the elastic that goes up to the top of the thigh. Then you knotted the cut end, and it became a beehive-shaped hat, with an elastic band that you pulled down low on your forehead and down around your neck in the back. To work well, the cap had to fit tightly and snugly, like a press. And it had to fit that tightly because it *was* a press: it pressed your hair with the force of the hose's elastic. If you greased your hair down real good, and left the stocking cap on long enough, voila: you got a head of pressed-against-the-scalp waves. (You also got a ring around your forehead when you woke up, but it went away.) And then you could enjoy your concrete do. Swore we were bad, too, with all that grease and those flat heads. My brother and I would brush it out a bit in the mornings, so that it looked—well, "natural." Grown men still wear stocking caps—especially older men, who generally keep their stocking caps in their top drawers, along with their cufflinks and their see-through silk socks, their "Maverick" ties, their silk handkerchiefs, and whatever else they prize the most.

20   A Murrayed-down stocking cap was the respectable version of the process, which, by contrast, was most definitely not a cool thing to have unless you were an entertainer by trade. Zeke and Keith and Poochie and a few other stars of the high-school basketball team all used to get a process once or twice a year. It was expensive, and you had to go somewhere like Pittsburgh or D.C. or Union-town—somewhere where there were enough colored people to support a trade. The guys would disappear, then reappear a day or two later, strutting like peacocks, their hair burned slightly red from the lye base. They'd also wear "rags"—cloths or handkerchiefs—around their heads when they slept or played basketball. Do-rags, they were called. But the result was straight hair, with just a hint of wave. No curl. Do-it-yourselfers took their chances at home with a concoction of mashed potatoes and lye.

The most famous process of all, however, outside of the process Malcolm X describes in his "Autobiography," and maybe the process of Sammy Davis, Jr., was Nat King Cole's process. Nat King Cole had patent-leather hair. That man's got the finest process money can buy, or so Daddy said the night we saw Cole's TV show on NBC. It was November 5, 1956. I remember the date because everyone came to our house to watch it and to celebrate one of Daddy's buddies' birthdays. Yeah, Uncle Joe chimed in, they can do shit to his hair that the average Negro can't even *think* about—secret shit.

Nat King Cole was *clean*. I've had an ongoing argument with a Nigerian friend about Nat King Cole for twenty years now. Not about whether he could sing—any fool knows that he could—but about whether or not he was a handkerchief head for wearing that patent-leather process.

Sammy Davis, Jr.'s process was the one I detested. It didn't look good on him. Worse still, he liked to have a fried strand dangling down the middle of his forehead, so he could shake it out from the crown when he sang. But Nat King Cole's hair was a thing unto itself, a beautifully sculpted work of art that he and he alone had the right to wear. The only difference between a process and a stocking cap, really, was taste; but Nat King Cole, unlike, say, Michael Jackson, looked *good* in his. His head looked like Valentino's head in the twenties, and some say it was Valentino the process was imitating. But Nat King Cole wore a process because it suited his face, his demeanor, his name, his style. He was as clean as he wanted to be.

I had forgotten all about that patent-leather look until one day in 1971, when I was sitting in an Arab restaurant on the island of Zanzibar surrounded by men in fezzes and white caftans, trying to learn how to eat curried goat and rice with the fingers of my right hand and feeling two million miles from home. All of a sudden, an old transistor radio sitting on top of a china cupboard stopped blaring out its Swahili music and started playing "Fly Me to the Moon," by Nat King Cole. The restaurant's din was not affected at all, but in my mind's eye I saw it: the King's magnificent sleek black tiara. I managed, barely, to blink back the tears.

Things to Do with the Reading

1. Write a short essay in which you identify the attitude in this piece towards the way that the America in which the author grew up dealt with the "problem" of kinky hair. What sentences in the piece seem most revealing of the point of view that Gates wishes us to take? How in particular does the piece make use of the various meanings of the word "kitchen"?

2. **Link:** The subject of assimilation is a primary thread of this chapter. Write an essay in which you determine how this piece compares with Salins' and Rodriguez's outlooks on assimilation? Consider especially the impact of the essay's final paragraph in this regard.

Ishmael Reed

My Neighborhood

In this piece, Ishmael Reed takes the reader on a meditative tour through the various neighborhoods in which he has dwelled as an adult, using these places as sites for thinking about race and matters of assimilation. Reed has been nominated for the Pulitzer Prize and twice shortlisted for the National Book Award. He has published novels, essays, poems, and stories. The musician Max Roach has called him the Charlie Parker of American fiction, and in the biographical sketch of him in the *Dictionary of Literary Biography*, Henry Louis Gates, Jr. (author of the previous selection) argued that he has "no true predecessor or counterpart" in American letters.

1   My stepfather is an evolutionist. He worked for many years at the Chevrolet division of General Motors in Buffalo, a working-class auto and steel town in upstate New York, and was able to rise from relative poverty to the middle class. He believes that each succeeding generation of Afro-Americans will have it better than its predecessor. In 1979 I moved into the kind of neighborhood that he and my mother spent about a third of their lives trying to escape. According to the evolutionist integrationist ethic, this was surely a step backward, since "success" was seen as being able to live in a neighborhood in which you were the only black and joined your neighbors in trying to keep out "them."

My neighborhood, bordered by Genoa, Market Street, and 48th and 55th streets in North Oakland, is what the media refer to as a "predominantly black neighborhood." It's the kind of neighborhood I grew up in before leaving for New York City in 1962. My last New York residence was an apartment in a brownstone, next door to the building in which poet W. H. Auden lived. There were trees in the backyard, and I thought it was a swell neighborhood until I read in Robert Craft's biography of [the composer] Stravinsky that "when Stravinsky sent his chauffeur to pick up his friend Auden, the chauffeur would ask, 'Are you sure Mr. Auden lives in this neighborhood?' " By 1968 my wife and I were able to live six months of the year in New York and the other six in California. This came to an end when one of the people I sublet the apartment to abandoned it. He had fled to England to pursue a romance. He didn't pay the rent, and so we were evicted long distance.

My first residence in California was an apartment on Santa Ynez Street, near Echo Park Lake in Los Angeles, where I lived for about six months in 1967. I was working on my second novel, and Carla Blank, my wife, a dancer, was teaching physical education at one of Eddie Rickenbacker's camps, located on an old movie set in the San Bernardino Mountains. Carla's employers were always offering me a cabin where they promised I could write without interruption. I never took them up on the offer, but for years I've wondered about what kind of reception I would have received had they discovered that I am black.

Excerpted from the book, *Writin' is Fightin'* by Ishmael Reed. Copyright © 2004 by Houghton Mifflin Company. Permission granted by Lowenstein Associates, Inc.

During my breaks from writing I would walk through the shopping areas near Santa Ynez, strolling by vending machines holding newspapers whose headlines screamed about riots in Detroit. On some weekends we'd visit novelist Robert Gover (*The One Hundred Dollar Misunderstanding*) and his friends in Malibu. I remember one of Gover's friends, a scriptwriter for the *Donna Reed Show*, looking me in the eye and telling me that if he were black he'd be "on a Detroit rooftop, sniping at cops," as he reclined, glass of scotch in hand, in a comfortable chair whose position gave him a good view of the rolling Pacific.

My Santa Ynez neighbors were whites from Alabama and Mississippi, and we got 5 along fine. Most of them were elderly, left behind by white flight to the suburbs, and on weekends the street would be lined with cars belonging to relatives who were visiting. While living here I observed a uniquely Californian phenomenon. Retired men would leave their houses in the morning, enter their cars, and remain there for a good part of the day, snoozing, reading newspapers, or listening to the radio.

I didn't experience a single racial incident during my stay in this Los Angeles neighborhood of ex-southerners. Once, however, I had a strange encounter with the police. I was walking through a black working-class neighborhood on my way to the downtown Los Angeles library. Some cops drove up and rushed me. A crowd gathered. The cops snatched my briefcase and removed its contents: books and notebooks having to do with my research of voodoo. The crowd laughed when the cops said they thought I was carrying a purse.

In 1968 my wife and I moved to Berkeley, where we lived in one Bauhaus box after another until about 1971, when I received a three-book contract from Doubleday. Then we moved into the Berkeley Hills, where we lived in the downstairs apartment of a very grand-looking house on Bret Harte Way. There was a Zen garden with streams, waterfalls, and bridges outside, along with many varieties of flowers and plants. I didn't drive, and Carla was away at Mills College each day, earning a master's degree in dance. I stayed holed up in that apartment for two years, during which time I completed my third novel, *Mumbo Jumbo*.

During this period I became exposed to some of the racism I hadn't detected on Santa Ynez or in the Berkeley flats. As a black male working at home, I was regarded with suspicion. Neighbors would come over and warn me about a heroin salesman they said was burglarizing the neighborhood, all the while looking over my shoulder in an attempt to pry into what I was up to. Once, while I was eating breakfast, a policeman entered through the garden door, gun drawn. "What on earth is the problem, officer?" I asked. He said they got word that a homicide had been committed in my apartment, which I recognized as an old police tactic used to gain entry into somebody's house. Walking through the Berkeley Hills on Sundays, I was greeted by unfriendly stares and growling, snarling dogs. I remember one pest who always poked her head out of her window whenever I'd walk down Bret Harte Way. She was always hassling me about parking my car in front of her house. She resembled Miss Piggy. I came to think of this section of Berkeley as "Whitetown."

Around 1974 the landlord raised the rent on the house in the hills, and we found ourselves again in the Berkeley flats. We spent a couple of peaceful years on Edith Street, and then moved to Jayne Street, where we encountered another next-door family of nosy, middle-class progressives. I understand that much time at North Berkeley white neighborhood association meetings is taken up with discussion of and fascination with blacks who move through the neighborhoods, with special concern given those who tarry, or who wear dreadlocks. Since before the Civil War, vagrancy laws have been used as political weapons against blacks. Appropriately, there has been talk of making Havana—where I understand a woman can get turned in by her neighbors for having too many boyfriends over—Berkeley's sister city.

10   In 1976 our landlady announced that she was going to reoccupy the Jayne Street house. I facetiously told a friend that I wanted to move to the most right-wing neighborhood he could think of. He mentioned El Cerrito. There, he said, your next-door neighbor might even be a cop. We moved to El Cerrito. Instead of the patronizing nosiness blacks complain about in Berkeley, I found the opposite on Terrace Drive in El Cerrito. The people were cold, impersonal, remote. But the neighborhood was quiet, serene even—the view was Olympian, and our rented house was secluded by eucalyptus trees. The annoyances were minor. Occasionally a car would careen down Terrace Drive full of white teenagers, and one or two would shout, "Hey, nigger!" Sometimes as I walked down The Arlington toward Kensington Market, the curious would stare at me from their cars, and women I encountered would give me nervous, frightened looks. Once, as I was walking to the market to buy magazines, a white child was sitting directly in my path. We were the only two people on the street. Two or three cars actually stopped, and their drivers observed the scene through their rearview mirrors until they were assured I wasn't going to abduct the child.

At night the Kensington Market area was lit with a yellow light, especially eerie during a fog. I always thought that this section of Kensington would be a swell place to make a horror movie—the residents would make great extras—but whatever discomfort I felt about traveling through this area at 2 A.M. was mixed with the relief that I had just navigated safely through Albany, where the police seemed always to be lurking in the shadows, prepared to ensnare blacks, hippies, and others they didn't deem suitable for such a neighborhood.

In 1979 our landlord, a decent enough fellow in comparison to some of the others we had had (who made you understand why the communists shoot the landlords first when they take over a country), announced he was going to sell the house on Terrace Drive. This was the third rented house to be sold out from under us. The asking price was way beyond our means, and so we started to search for another home, only to find that the ones within our price range were located in North Oakland, in a "predominantly black neighborhood." We finally found a huge Queen Anne Victorian, which seemed to be about a month away from the wrecker's ball if the termites and the precarious foundation didn't do it in first, but I decided that I had to have it. The oldest house on the block, it was built in 1906, the year the big earthquake hit Northern California, but left Oakland unscathed because, according to Bret Harte, "there are some things even the earth can't swallow." If I was apprehensive about moving into this neighborhood—on television all black neighborhoods resemble the commotion of the station house on *Hill Street Blues*—I was later to learn that our neighbors were just as apprehensive about us. Were we hippies? Did I have a job? Were we going to pay as much attention to maintaining our property as they did to theirs? Neglected, the dilapidated monstrosity I'd got myself into would blight the entire block.

While I was going to college I worked as an orderly in a psychiatric hospital, and I remember a case in which a man was signed into the institution, after complaints from his neighbors that he mowed the lawn at four in the morning. My neighbors aren't that finicky, but they keep very busy pruning, gardening, and mowing their laws. Novelist Toni Cade Bambara wrote of the spirit women in Atlanta who plant by moonlight and use conjure to reap gorgeous vegetables and flowers. A woman on this block grows roses the size of cantaloupes.

On New Year's Eve, famed landscape architect John Roberts accompanied me on my nightly walk, which takes me from 53rd Street to Aileen, Shattuck, and back to 53rd Street. He was able to identify plants and trees that had been imported from Asia, the Middle East, and Australia. On Aileen Street he discovered a banana tree! And Arthur Monroe, a painter and art historian, traces the "Tabby" garden design—in which seashells and plates are mixed with lime, sand, and water to form decorative borders, found in this Oakland neighborhood, and others—to the influence of Islamic slaves brought to the Gulf Coast.

I won over my neighbors, I think, after I triumphed over a dozen generations of   15
pigeons that had been roosting in the crevices of this house for many years. It was a long and angry war, and my five year old constantly complained to her mother about Daddy's bad words about the birds. I used everything I could get my hands on, including chicken wire and mothballs, and I would have tried the clay owls if the only manufacturer hadn't gone out of business. I also learned never to underestimate the intelligence of pigeons; just when you think you've got them whipped, you'll notice that they've regrouped on some strategic rooftop to prepare for another invasion. When the house was free of pigeons and their droppings, which had spread to the adjoining properties, the lady next door said, "Thank you."

Every New Year's Day since then our neighbors have invited us to join them and their fellow Louisianans for the traditional Afro-American good luck meal called Hoppin' John. This year the menu included black-eyed peas, ham, corn bread, potato salad, chitterlings, greens, fried chicken, yams, head cheese, macaroni, rolls, sweet potato pie, and fruitcake. I got up that morning weighing 214 pounds and came home from the party weighing 220.

We've lived on 53rd Street for three years now. Carla's dance and theater school, which she operates with her partner, Jody Roberts—Roberts and Blank Dance/Drama—is already five years old. I am working on my seventh novel and a television production of my play *Mother Hubbard*. The house has yet to be restored to its 1906 glory, but we're working on it.

I've grown accustomed to the common sights here—teenagers moving through the neighborhood carrying radios blasting music by Grandmaster Flash and Prince, men hovering over cars with tools and rags in hand, decked-out female church delegations visiting the sick. Unemployment up, one sees more men drinking from sacks as they walk through Market Street or gather in Helen McGregor Plaza, on Shattuck and 52nd Street, near a bench where mothers sit with their children, waiting for buses. It may be because the bus stop is across the street from

Children's Hospital (exhibiting a brand-new antihuman, postmodern wing), but there seem to be a lot of sick black children these days. The criminal courts and emergency rooms of Oakland hospitals, both medical and psychiatric, are also filled with blacks.

White men go from door to door trying to unload spoiled meat. Incredibly sleazy white contractors and hustlers try to entangle people into shady deals that sometimes lead to the loss of a home. Everybody knows of someone, usually a widow, who has been gypped into paying thousands of dollars more than the standard cost for, say, adding a room to a house. It sure ain't El Cerrito. In El Cerrito the representatives from the utilities were very courteous. If they realize they're speaking to someone in a black neighborhood, however, they become curt and sarcastic. I was trying to arrange for the gas company to come out to fix a stove when the woman from Pacific Gas and Electric gave me some snide lip. I told her, "Lady, if you think what you're going through is an inconvenience, you can imagine my inconvenience paying the bills every month." Even she had to laugh.

20   The clerks in the stores are also curt, regarding blacks the way the media regard them, as criminal suspects. Over in El Cerrito the cops were professional, respectful—in Oakland they swagger about like candidates for a rodeo. In El Cerrito and the Berkeley Hills you could take your time paying some bills, but in this black neighborhood if you miss paying a bill by one day, "reminders" printed in glaring and violent typefaces are sent to you, or you're threatened with discontinuance of this or that service. Los Angeles police victim Eulia Love, who was shot in the aftermath of an argument over an overdue gas bill, would still be alive if she had lived in El Cerrito or the Berkeley Hills.

I went to a bank a few weeks ago that advertised easy loans on television, only to be told that I would have to wait six months after opening an account to be eligible for a loan. I went home and called the same bank, this time putting on my Clark Kent voice, and was informed that I could come in and get the loan the same day. Other credit unions and banks, too, have different lending practices for black and white neighborhoods, but when I try to tell white intellectuals that blacks are prevented from developing industries because the banks find it easier to lend money to communist countries than to American citizens, they call me paranoid. Sometimes when I know I am going to be inconvenienced by merchants or creditors because of my 53rd Street address, I give the address of my Berkeley studio instead. Others are not so fortunate.

Despite the inconveniences and antagonism from the outside world one has to endure for having a 53rd Street address, life in this neighborhood is more pleasant than grim. Casually dressed, well-groomed elderly men gather at the intersections to look after the small children as they walk to and from school, or just to keep an eye on the neighborhood. My next-door neighbor keeps me in stitches with his informed commentary on any number of political comedies emanating from Washington and Sacramento. Once we were discussing pesticides, and the man who was repairing his porch told us that he had a great garden and didn't have to pay all that much attention to it. As for pesticides, he said, the bugs have to eat, too.

There are people on this block who still know the subsistence skills many Americans have forgotten. They can hunt and fish (and if you don't fish, there is a man who covers the neighborhood selling fresh fish and yelling, "Fishman," recalling a period of ancient American commerce when you didn't have to pay the middleman). They are also loyal Americans—they vote, they pay taxes—but you don't find the extreme patriots here that you find in white neighborhoods. Although Christmas, Thanksgiving, New Year's, and Easter are celebrated with all get-out, I've never seen a flag flying on Memorial Day, or on any holiday that calls for the showing of the flag. Blacks express their loyalty in concrete ways. For example, you rarely see a foreign car in this neighborhood. And this 53rd Street neighborhood, as well as black neighborhoods like it from coast to coast, will supply the male children who will bear the brunt of future jungle wars, just as they did in Vietnam.

We do our shopping on a strip called Temescal, which stretches from 46th to 51st streets. Temescal, according to Oakland librarian William Sturm, is an Aztec word for "hothouse," or "bathhouse." The word was borrowed from the Mexicans by the Spanish to describe similar hothouses, early saunas, built by the California Indians in what is now North Oakland. Some say the hothouses were used to sweat out demons; others claim the Indians used them for medicinal purposes. Most agree that after a period of time in the steam, the Indians would rush en masse into the streams that flowed through the area. One still runs underneath my backyard—I have to mow the grass there almost every other day.

Within these five blocks are the famous Italian restaurant Bertola's, "Since 1932";   25 Siam restaurant; La Belle Creole, a French-Caribbean restaurant; Asmara, an Ethiopian restaurant; and Ben's Hof Brau, where white and black senior citizens, dressed in the elegance of a former time, congregate to talk or to have an inexpensive though quality breakfast provided by Ben's hardworking and courteous staff.

The Hof Brau shares its space with Vern's market, where you can shop to the music of DeBarge. To the front of Vern's is the Temescal Delicatessen, where a young Korean man makes the best po' boy sandwiches north of Louisiana, and near the side entrance is Ed Fraga's Automotive. The owner is always advising his customers to avoid stress, and he says goodbye with a "God bless you." The rest of the strip is taken up by the Temescal Pharmacy, which has a resident health advisor and a small library of health literature; the Aikido Institute; an African bookstore; and the internationally known Genova deli, to which people from the surrounding cities travel to shop. The strip also includes the Clausen House thrift shop, which sells used clothes and furniture. Here you can buy novels by J.D. Salinger and John O'Hara for ten cents each.

Space that was recently occupied by the Buon Gusto Bakery is now for rent. Before the bakery left, an Italian lady who worked there introduced me to a crunchy, cookie-like treat called "bones," which she said went well with Italian wine. The Buon Gusto had been a landmark since the 1940s, when, according to a guest at the New Year's Day Hoppin' John supper, North Oakland was populated by Italians and Portuguese. In those days a five-room house could be rented for $45 a month, she said.

The neighborhood is still in transition. The East Bay Negro Historical Society, which was located around the corner on Grove Street, included in its collection letters written by nineteenth-century macho man Jack London to his black nurse. They were signed, "Your little white pickaninny." It's been replaced by the New Israelite Delight restaurant, part of the Israelite Church, which also operates a day care center. The restaurant offers homemade Louisiana gumbo and a breakfast that includes grits.

Unlike the other California neighborhoods I've lived in, I know most of the people on this block by name. They are friendly and cooperative, always offering to watch your house while you're away. The day after one of the few whites who lives on the block—a brilliant muckraking journalist and former student of mine—was robbed, neighbors gathered in front of his house to offer assistance.

30   In El Cerrito my neighbor was indeed a cop. He used pomade on his curly hair, sported a mustache, and there was a grayish tint in his brown eyes. He was a handsome man, with a smile like a movie star's. His was the only house on the block I entered during my three-year stay in that neighborhood, and that was one afternoon when we shared some brandy. I wanted to get to know him better. I didn't know he was dead until I saw people in black gathered on his doorstep.

I can't imagine that happening on 53rd Street. In a time when dour thinkers view alienation and insensitivity toward the plight of others as characteristics of the modern condition, I think I'm lucky to live in a neighborhood where people look out for one another.

A human neighborhood.

Things to Do with the Reading

1. Reed has made a career out of being provocative and hard to peg, and so the issue of tone in his essay is crucial. [For further discussion of tone—the implicit point of view (POV) in a piece towards its subject, see Chapter 17]. This is clearly an essay interested in race and matters of assimilation, but what is its point of view on these matters? Compose a short essay on the function of tone in this essay. Make a list of indirect references and apparent throw-away lines about race in the piece. Then make inferences about these lines—"close read" them—to bring out Reed's POV toward race and assimilation. (See Chapter 5 on close reading.)

2. Track and analyze the ways that the police function as a strand (see Chapter 2 on The Method) in the essay. See especially paragraphs 6, 8, and 20, as well as the essay's last four paragraphs. Write up your results in a short essay.

3. Irony is a complex verbal gesture that generally acknowledges the relative validity of both sides of an issue, as well as the limitations of both positions. The famous critic William Empson once described it with a phrase from *Romeo and Juliet*, "a plague on both your houses." Ishmael Reed is fond of irony, and it provides an interesting way into his essay. Write an essay on how the concept of evolution functions ironically (and unironically) in the piece. How does the fact that Reed is African American and is writing about race and racism add to this irony? See especially the essay's first paragraph, paragraphs 12–15, and paragraph 23.

4. **Link:** Consider paragraphs 25–28 wherein Reed catalogues the names and ethnic origins of shops—mostly shops selling food in his neighborhood. Use Rodriguez's essay as a lens for thinking about Reed's essay, starting with this point of contact between the two essays: food. Write an essay on how Reed's thinking about assimilation fits and does not fit with Rodriguez's. Would Salins see Reed as an "ethnic federalist"?

Note: See the link and application on writing about neighborhoods following the end of the next selection, and also see the question about Reed and Jonas at the end of the next to last selection in this chapter.

Marianna Torgovnick

On Being White, Female, and Born in Bensonhurst

A visit to her old neighborhood in Brooklyn shortly after a racially motivated killing provides the occasion for Marianna Torgovnick to re-evaluate her conflicted attitudes toward her own past. Wandering the neighborhood, she reflects on the legacy of ethnic and gender prejudice in her own family, on the desire it bore in her not only to escape her upbringing but to obscure it, and ultimately, on the cost of doing so. Torgovnick is a professor of English at Duke University with a special interest in cultural studies. A version of this essay appeared in her 1994 book, *Crossing Ocean Parkway: Readings by an Italian American Daughter*, which won the American Book Award.

1   The mafia protects the neighborhood, our fathers say, with that peculiar satisfied pride with which law-abiding Italian Americans refer to the Mafia: the Mafia protects the neighborhood from "the colored." In the fifties and sixties, I heard that information repeated, in whispers, in neighborhood parks and in the yard at school in Bensonhurst. The same information probably passes today in the parks (the word now "blacks," not "coloreds") but perhaps no longer in the schoolyards. From buses each morning, from neighborhoods outside Bensonhurst, spill children of all colors and backgrounds—American black, West Indian black, Hispanic, and Asian. But the blacks are the only ones especially marked for notice. Bensonhurst is no longer entirely protected from "the coloreds." But in a deeper sense, at least for Italian Americans, Bensonhurst never changes.

Italian-American life continues pretty much as I remember it. Families with young children live side by side with older couples whose children are long gone to the suburbs. Many of those families live "down the block" from the last generation or, sometimes still, live together with parents or grandparents. When a young family leaves, as sometimes happens, for Long Island or New Jersey or (very common now) for Staten Island, another arrives, without any special effort being required, from Italy or a poorer neighborhood in New York. They fill the neat but anonymous houses that make up the mostly tree-lined streets: two-, three-, or four-family houses for the most part (this is a working, lower to middle-middle class area, and people need rents to pay mortgages), with a few single family or small apartment houses tossed in at random. Tomato plants, fig trees, and plaster madonnas often decorate small but well-tended yards which face out onto the street; the grassy front lawn, like the grassy back yard, is relatively uncommon.

Crisscrossing the neighborhood and making out ethnic zones—Italian, Irish, and Jewish, for the most part, though there are some Asian Americans and some people (usually Protestants) called simply Americans—are the great shopping streets: Eighty-sixth Street, Kings Highway, Bay Parkway, Eighteenth Avenue, each with its own distinctive character. On Eighty-sixth Street, crowds bustle along sidewalks lined with ample, packed fruit stands. Women wheeling shopping carts or baby strollers

Reprinted with permission. "On Being White, Female, and Born in Bensonhurst," from *Crossing Ocean Parkway*, by Marianna De Marco Torgovnick. The University of Chicago Press.

check the fruit carefully, piece by piece, and often bargain with the dealer, cajoling for a better price or letting him know that the vegetables, this time, aren't up to snuff. A few blocks down, the fruit stands are gone and the streets are lined with clothing and record shops, mobbed by teenagers. Occasionally, the el rumbles overhead, a few stops out of Coney Island on its way to the city, a trip of around one hour.

On summer nights, neighbors congregate on stoops which during the day serve as play yards for children. Air conditioning exists everywhere in Bensonhurst, but people still sit outside in the summer—to supervise children, to gossip, to stare at strangers. "*Buona sera*," I say, or "*Buona notte*," as I am ritually presented to Sal and Lily and Louie, the neighbors sitting on the stoop. "*Grazie*," I say when they praise my children or my appearance. It's the only time I use Italian, which I learned at high school, although my parents (both second-generation Italian Americans, my father Sicilian, my mother Calabrian) speak it at home to each other but never to me or my brother. My accent is the Tuscan accent taught at school, not the southern Italian accents of my parents and the neighbors.

It's important to greet and please the neighbors, any break in this decorum would   5 seriously offend and aggrieve my parents. For the neighbors are the stern arbiters of conduct in Bensonhurst. Does Mary keep a clean house? Did Gina wear black long enough after her mother's death? Was the food good at Tony's wedding? The neighbors know and pass judgment. Any news of family scandal (my brother's divorce, for example) provokes from my mother the agonized words: "But what will I *tell* people?" I sometimes collaborate in devising a plausible script.

A large sign on the church I attended as a child sums up for me the ethos of Bensonhurst. The sign urges contributions to the church building fund with the message, in huge letters: "Each year St. Simon and Jude saves this neighborhood one million dollars in taxes." Passing the church on the way from largely Jewish and middle-class Sheepshead Bay (where my in-laws live) to Bensonhurst, year after year, my husband and I look for the sign and laugh at the crass level of its pitch, its utter lack of attention to things spiritual. But we also understand exactly the values it represents.

In the summer of 1989, my parents were visiting me at my house in Durham, North Carolina, from the apartment in Bensonhurst where they have lived since 1942: three small rooms, rent-controlled, floor clean enough to eat off, every corner and crevice known and organized. My parents' longevity in a single apartment is unusual even for Bensonhurst, but not that unusual; many people live for decades in the same place or move within a ten-block radius. When I lived in this apartment, there were four rooms; one has since been ceded to a demanding landlord, one of the various landlords who have haunted my parents' life and must always be appeased lest the ultimate threat— removal from the rent-controlled apartment—be brought into play. That summer, during their visit, on August 23 (my younger daughter's birthday) a shocking, disturbing, news report issued from the neighborhood: it had become another Howard Beach.

Three black men, walking casually through the streets at night, were attacked by a group of whites. One was shot dead, mistaken, as it turned out, for another black youth who was dating a white, although part-Hispanic, girl in the neighborhood. It all made sense: the crudely protective men, expecting to see a black arriving at the girl's house and overreacting; the rebellious girl dating the outsider boy; the black dead as a sacrifice to the feelings of the neighborhood.

I might have felt outrage, I might have felt guilt or shame, I might have despised the people among whom I grew up. In a way I felt all four emotions when I heard the news. I expect that there were many people in Bensonhurst who felt the same rush of emotions. But mostly I felt that, given the set-up, this was the only way things could have happened. I detested the racial killing, but I also understood it. Those streets, which should be public property available to all, belong to the neighborhood. All the people sitting on the stoops on August 23 knew that as well as they knew their own names. The black men walking through probably knew it too—though their casual walk sought to deny the fact that, for the neighbors, even the simple act of blacks walking through the neighborhood would be seen as invasion.

10   Italian Americans in Bensonhurst are notable for their cohesiveness and provinciality; the slightest pressure turns those qualities into prejudice and racism. Their cohesiveness is based on the stable economic and ethical level that links generation to generation, keeping Italian Americans in Bensonhurst and the Italian-American community alive as the Jewish-American community of my youth is no longer alive. (Its young people routinely moved to the suburbs or beyond and were never replaced, so that Jews in Bensonhurst today are almost all very old people.) Their provinciality results from the Italian Americans' devotion to jealous distinctions and discriminations. Jews are suspect, but (the old Italian women admit) "they make good husbands." The Irish are okay, fellow Catholics, but not really "like us"; they make bad husbands because they drink and gamble. Even Italians come in varieties, by region (Sicilian, Calabrian, Neapolitan, very rarely any region further north) and by history in this country (the newly arrived and ridiculed "gaffoon" versus the second or third generation).

Bensonhurst is a neighborhood dedicated to believing that its values are the only values; it tends toward certain forms of inertia. When my parents visit me in Durham, they routinely take chairs from the kitchen and sit out on the lawn in front of the house, not on the chairs on the back deck; then they complain that the streets are too quiet. When they walk around my neighborhood (these De Marcos who have friends named Travaglianti and Occhipinti), they look at the mailboxes and report that my neighbors have strange names. Prices at my local supermarket are compared, in unbelievable detail, with prices on Eighty-sixth Street. Any rearrangement of my kitchen since their last visit is registered and criticized. Difference is not only unwelcome, it is unacceptable. One of the most characteristic things my mother ever said was in response to my plans for renovating my house in Durham. When she heard my plans, she looked around, crossed her arms, and said, "If it was me, I wouldn't change nothing." My father once asked me to level with him about a Jewish boyfriend who lived in a different part of the neighborhood, reacting to his Jewishness, but even more to the fact that he often wore Bermuda shorts: "Tell me something, Marianna. Is he a Communist?" Such are the standards of normality and political thinking in Bensonhurst.

I often think that one important difference between Italian Americans in New York neighborhoods like Bensonhurst and Italian Americans elsewhere is that the others moved on—to upstate New York, to Pennsylvania, to the Midwest. Though they frequently settled in communities of fellow Italians, they did move on. Bensonhurst

Italian Americans seem to have felt that one large move, over the ocean, was enough. Future moves could be only local: from the Lower East Side, for example, to Brooklyn, or from one part of Brooklyn to another. Bensonhurst was for many of these people the summa of expectations. If their America were to be drawn as a *New Yorker* cover, Manhattan itself would be tiny in proportion to Bensonhurst and to its satellites, Staten Island, New Jersey, and Long Island.

"Oh, no," my father says when he hears the news about the shooting. Though he still refers to blacks as "coloreds," he's not really a racist and is upset that this innocent youth was shot in his neighborhood. He has no trouble acknowledging the wrongness of the death. But then, like all the news accounts, he turns to the fact, repeated over and over, that the blacks had been on their way to look at a used car when they encountered the hostile mob of whites. The explanation is right before him but, "Yeah," he says, still shaking his head, "yeah, but what were they *doing* there? They didn't belong."

Over the next few days, the television news is even more disturbing. Rows of screaming Italians lining the streets, most of them looking like my relatives. I focus especially on one woman who resembles almost completely my mother: stocky but not fat, mid-seventies but well preserved, full face showing only minimal wrinkles, ample steel-gray hair neatly if rigidly coiffed in a modified beehive hairdo left over from the sixties. She shakes her fist at the camera, protesting the arrest of the Italian-American youths in the neighborhood and the incursion of more blacks into the neighborhood, protesting the shooting. I look a little nervously at my mother (the parent I resemble), but she has not even noticed the woman and stares impassively at the television.

What has Bensonhurst to do with what I teach today and write? Why did I need   15
to write about this killing in Bensonhurst, but not in the manner of a news account or a statistical sociological analysis? Within days of hearing the news, I began to plan this essay, to tell the world what I knew, even though I was aware that I could publish the piece only someplace my parents or their neighbors would never see or hear about it. I sometimes think that I looked around from my baby carriage and decided that someday, the sooner the better, I would get out of Bensonhurst. Now, much to my surprise, Bensonhurst—the antipode of the intellectual life I sought, the least interesting of places—had become a respectable intellectual topic. People would be willing to hear about Bensonhurst—and all by the dubious virtue of a racial killing in the streets.

The story as I would have to tell it would be to some extent a class narrative: about the difference between working class and upper middle class, dependence and a profession, Bensonhurst and a posh suburb. But I need to make it clear that I do not imagine myself as writing from a position of enormous self-satisfaction, or even enormous distance. You can take the girl out of Bensonhurst (that much is clear), but you may not be able to take Bensonhurst out of the girl. And upward mobility is not the essence of the story, though it is an important marker and symbol.

In Durham today, I live in a twelve-room house surrounded by an acre of trees. When I sit on my back deck on summer evenings, no houses are visible through the trees. I have a guaranteed income, teaching English at an excellent university, removed by my years of education from the fundamental economic and social conditions of Bensonhurst. The one time my mother ever expressed pleasure at my work was when I got tenure, what my father still calls, with no irony intended, "ten years." "What does that mean?" my mother asked when she heard the news. Then she reached back into her experience as a garment worker, subject to periodic layoffs. "Does it mean they can't fire you just for nothing and can't lay you off?" When I said that was exactly what it means, she said, "Very good. Congratulations. That's *wonderful.*" I was free from the *padrones*, from the network of petty anxieties that had formed, in large part, her very existence. Of course, I wasn't really free of petty anxieties: would my salary increase keep pace with my colleagues', how would my office compare, would this essay be accepted for publication, am I happy? The line between these worries and my mother's is the line between the working class and the upper middle class.

But getting out of Bensonhurst never meant to me a big house, or nice clothes, or a large income. And it never meant feeling good about looking down on what I left behind or hiding my background. Getting out of Bensonhurst meant freedom—to experiment, to grow, to change. It also meant knowledge in some grand, abstract way. All the material possessions I have acquired, I acquired simply along the way—and for the first twelve years after I left Bensonhurst, I chose to acquire almost nothing at all. Now, as I write about the neighborhood, I recognize that although I've come far in physical and material distance, the emotional distance is harder to gauge. Bensonhurst has everything to do with who I am and even with what I write. Occasionally I get reminded of my roots, of their simultaneously choking and nutritive power.

Scene one: It's after a lecture at Duke, given by a visiting professor from Princeton. The lecture was long and a little dull and—bad luck—I had agreed to be one of the people having dinner with the lecturer afterward. We settle into our table at the restaurant: this man, me, the head of the comparative literature program (also a professor of German), and a couple I like who teach French, the husband at my university, the wife at one nearby. The conversation is sluggish, as it often is when a stranger, like the visiting professor, has to be assimilated into a group, so I ask the visitor from Princeton a question to personalize things a bit. "How did you get interested in what you do? What made you become a professor of German?" The man gets going and begins talking about how it was really unlikely that he, a nice Jewish boy from Bensonhurst, would have chosen, in the mid-fifties, to study German. Unlikely indeed.

20   I remember seeing *Judgment at Nuremberg* in a local movie theater and having a woman in the row in back of me get hysterical when some clips of a concentration camp were shown. "My God," she screamed in a European accent, "look at what they did. Murderers, MURDERERS!"—and she had to be supported out by her family. I couldn't see, in the dark, whether her arm bore the neatly tattooed numbers that the arms of some of my classmates' parents did—and that always affected me with a thrill of horror. Ten years older than me, this man had lived more directly through those feelings, lived with and *among* those feelings. The first chance he got, he raced to study in Germany. I myself have twice chosen not to visit Germany, but I understand his impulse to identify with the Other as a way of getting out of the neighborhood.

At the dinner, the memory about the movie pops into my mind but I pick up instead on the Bensonhurst—I'm also from there, but Italian American. Like a flash, he asks something I haven't been asked in years: Where did I go to high school and (a more common question) what was my maiden name? I went to Lafayette High School, I say, and my name was De Marco. Everything changes: his facial expression, his posture, his accent, his voice. "Soo, Dee Maw-ko," he says, "dun anything wrong at school today—got enny pink slips? Wanna meet me later at the park on maybe bye the Baye?" When I laugh, recognizing the stereotype that Italians get pink slips for misconduct at school and the notorious chemistry between Italian women and Jewish men, he says, back in his Princetonian voice: "My God, for a minute I felt like I was turning into a werewolf."

It's odd that although I can remember almost nothing else about this man—his face, his body type, even his name—I remember this lapse into his "real self" with enormous vividness. I am especially struck by how easily he was able to slip into the old, generic Brooklyn accent. I myself have no memory of ever speaking in that accent, though I also have no memory of trying not to speak it, except for teaching myself, carefully, to say "oil" rather than "earl."

But the surprises aren't over. The female French professor, whom I have known for at least five years, reveals for the first time that she is also from the neighborhood, though she lived across the other side of Kings Highway, went to a different, more elite high school, and was Irish American. Three of six professors, sitting at an eclectic vegetarian restaurant in Durham, all from Bensonhurst—a neighborhood where (I swear) you couldn't get the *New York Times* at any of the local stores.

Scene two: I still live in Bensonhurst. I'm waiting for my parents to return from a conference at my school, where they've been summoned to discuss my transition from elementary to junior high school. I am already a full year younger than any of my classmates, having skipped a grade, a not uncommon occurrence for "gifted" youngsters. Now the school is worried about putting me in an accelerated track through junior high, since that would make me two years younger. A compromise was reached: I would be put in a special program for gifted children, but one that took three, not two, years. It sounds okay.

Three years later, another wait. My parents have gone to school this time to make 25 another decision. Lafayette High School has three tracks: academic, for potentially college-bound kids; secretarial, mostly for Italian-American girls or girls with low aptitude-test scores (the high school is de facto segregated, so none of the tracks is as yet racially coded, though they are coded by ethnic group and gender); and vocational, mostly for boys with the same attributes, ethnic or intellectual. Although my scores are superb, the guidance counselor has recommended the secretarial track; when I protested, the conference with my parents was arranged. My mother's preference is clear: the secretarial track—college is for boys; I will need to make a "good living" until I marry and have children. My father also prefers the secretarial track, but he wavers, half proud of my aberrantly high scores, half worried. I press the attack, saying that if I were Jewish I would have been placed, without question, in the academic track. I tell him I have sneaked a peek at my files and know that my IQ is at genius level. I am allowed to insist on the change into the academic track.

What I did, and I was ashamed of it even then, was to play upon my father's competitive feelings with Jews: his daughter could and should be as good as theirs. In the bank where he was a messenger, and at the insurance company where he worked in the mailroom, my father worked with Jews, who were almost always his immediate supervisors. Several times, my father was offered the supervisory job but turned it down after long conversations with my mother about the dangers of making a change, the difficulty of giving orders to friends. After her work in a local garment shop, after cooking dinner and washing the floor each night, my mother often did piecework making bows; sometimes I would help her for fun, but it *wasn't* fun, and I was free to stop while she continued for long, tedious hours to increase the family income. Once a week, her part-time boss, Dave, would come by to pick up the boxes of bows. Short, round, with his shirttails sloppily tucked into his pants and a cigar almost always dangling from his lips, Dave was a stereotyped Jew but also, my parents always said, a nice guy, a decent man.

Years after, similar choices come up, and I show the same assertiveness I showed with my father, the same ability to deal for survival, but tinged with Bensonhurst caution. Where will I go to college? Not to Brooklyn College, the flagship of the city system—I know that, but don't press the invitations I have received to apply to prestigious schools outside of New York. The choice comes down to two: Barnard, which gives me a full scholarship, minus five hundred dollars a year that all scholarship students are expected to contribute from summer earnings, or New York University, which offers me one thousand dollars above tuition as a bribe. I waver. My parents stand firm: they are already losing money by letting me go to college; I owe it to the family to contribute the extra thousand dollars plus my summer earnings. Besides, my mother adds, harping on a favorite theme, there are no boys at Barnard; at NYU I'm more likely to meet someone to marry. I go to NYU and do marry in my senior year, but he is someone I didn't meet at college. I was secretly relieved, I now think (though at the time I thought I was just placating my parents' conventionality), to be out of the marriage sweepstakes.

The first boy who ever asked me for a date was Robert Lubitz, in eighth grade: tall and skinny to my average height and teenage chubbiness. I turned him down, thinking we would make a ridiculous couple. Day after day, I cast my eyes at stylish Juliano, the class cutup; day after day, I captivated Robert Lubitz. Occasionally, one of my brother's Italian-American friends would ask me out, and I would go, often to ROTC dances. My specialty was making political remarks so shocking that the guys rarely asked me again. After a while I recognized destiny: the Jewish man was a passport out of Bensonhurst. I of course did marry a Jewish man, who gave me my freedom and, very important, helped remove me from the expectations of Bensonhurst. Though raised in a largely Jewish section of Brooklyn, he had gone to college in Ohio and knew how important it was, as he put it, "to get past the Brooklyn Bridge." We met on neutral ground, in Central Park, at a performance of Shakespeare. The Jewish-Italian marriage is a common enough catastrophe in Bensonhurst for my parents to have accepted, even welcomed, mine—though my parents continued to treat my husband like an outsider for the first twenty years ("Now Marianna. Here's what's going on with you brother. But don't tell-a you husband").

Along the way I make other choices, more fully marked by Bensonhurst cautiousness. I am attracted to journalism or the arts as careers, but the prospects for income seem iffy. I choose instead to imagine myself as a teacher. Only the availability of NDEA fellowships when I graduate, with their generous terms, propels me from high school teaching (a thought I never much relished) to college teaching (which seems like a brave new world). Within the college teaching profession, I choose offbeat specializations: the novel, interdisciplinary approaches (not something clear and clubby like Milton or the eighteenth century). Eventually I write the book I like best about primitive others as they figure within Western obsessions: my identification with "the Other," my sense of being "Other," surfaces at last. I avoid all mentoring structures for a long time but accept aid when it comes to me on the basis of what I perceive to be merit. I'm still, deep down, Italian-American Bensonhurst, though by this time I'm a lot of other things as well.

Scene three: In the summer of 1988, a little more than a year before the shoot- 30 ing in Bensonhurst, my father woke up trembling and in what appeared to be a fit. Hospitalization revealed that he had a pocket of blood on his brain, a frequent consequence of falls for older people. About a year earlier, I had stayed home, using my children as an excuse, when my aunt, my father's much loved sister, died, missing her funeral; only now does my mother tell me how much my father resented my taking his suggestion that I stay home. Now, confronted with what is described as brain surgery but turns out to be less dramatic than it sounds, I fly home immediately.

My brother drives three hours back and forth from New Jersey every day to chauffeur me and my mother to the hospital: he is being a fine Italian-American son. For the first time in years, we have long conversations alone. He is two years older than I am, a chemical engineer who has also left the neighborhood but has remained closer to its values, with a suburban, Republican inflection. He talks a lot about New York, saying that (except for neighborhoods like Bensonhurst) it's a "third-world city now." It's the summer of the Tawana Brawley incident, when Brawley accused white men of abducting her and smearing racial slurs on her body with her own excrement. My brother is filled with dislike for Al Sharpton and Brawley's other vocal supporters in the black community—not because they're black, he says, but because they're troublemakers, stirring things up. The city is drenched in racial hatred that makes itself felt in the halls of the hospital: Italians and Jews in the beds and as doctors; blacks as nurses and orderlies.

This is the first time since I left New York in 1975 that I have visited Brooklyn without once getting into Manhattan. It's the first time I have spent several days alone with my mother, living in her apartment in Bensonhurst. My every move is scrutinized and commented on. I feel like I am going to go crazy.

Finally, it's clear that my father is going to be fine, and I can go home. She insists on accompanying me to the travel agent to get my ticket for home, even though I really want to be alone. The agency (a mafia front?) has no one who knows how to ticket me for the exotic destination of North Carolina and no computer for doing so. The one person who can perform this feat by hand is out. I have to kill time for an hour and suggest to my mother that she go home, to be there for my brother when he arrives from Jersey. We stop in a Pork Store, where I buy a stash of cheeses, sausages, and other delicacies unavailable in Durham. My mother walks home with the shopping bags, and I'm on my own.

More than anything I want a kind of *sorbetto* or ice I remember from my childhood, a *cremolata*, almond-vanilla-flavored with large chunks of nuts. I pop into the local bakery (at the unlikely hour of 11 A.M.) and ask for a *cremolata*, usually eaten after dinner. The woman—a younger version of my mother—refuses: they haven't made a fresh ice yet, and what's left from the day before is too icy, no good. I explain that I'm about to get on a plane for North Carolina and want that ice, good or not. But she has her standards and holds her ground, even though North Carolina has about the same status in her mind as Timbuktoo and she knows I will be banished, perhaps forever, from the land of *cremolata*.

35   Then, while I'm taking a walk, enjoying my solitude, I have another idea. On the block behind my parents' house, there's a club for men, for men from a particular town or region in Italy: six or seven tables, some on the sidewalk beneath a garish red, green, and white sign; no women allowed or welcome unless they're with men, and no women at all during the day when the real business of the club—a game of cards for old men— is in progress. Still, I know that inside the club would be coffee and a *cremolata* ice. I'm thirty-eight, well-dressed, very respectable looking; I know what I want. I also know I'm not supposed to enter that club. I enter anyway, asking the teenage boy behind the counter firmly, in my most professional tones, for a *cremolata* ice. Dazzled, he complies immediately. The old men at the card table have been staring at this scene, unable to place me exactly, though my facial type is familiar. Finally, a few old men's hisses pierce the air. "*Strega*," I hear as I leave, "*mala strega*"—"witch," or "brazen whore." I have been in Bensonhurst less than a week, but I have managed to reproduce, on my final day there for this visit, the conditions of my youth. Knowing the rules, I have broken them. I shake hands with my discreetly rebellious past, still an outsider walking through the neighborhood, marked and insulted—though unlikely to be shot.

Things to Do with the Reading

1. It's a paradox of effective reading that sometimes you can see more out of the corner of your eye than by staring straight ahead. That is, looking at issues aslant, from one side, rather than directly, can be especially revealing. Write an essay on the functions that Torgovnick's brother, husband, high school boy friends, and the female French professor who has been her friend for five years serve in her larger discussion of ethnicity and the melting pot.

2. A key word in this essay is the often-capitalized "Other." It is used in reference to the visiting lecturer at the end of paragraph 20, for example: "I myself have twice chosen not to visit Germany, but I understand his impulse to identify with the Other as a way of getting out of the neighborhood." Find other references in the essay to the Other, or situations of Otherness, and write an essay on how this concept operates in Torgovnick's struggle to understand Assimilation American Style.

3. Torgovnick explicitly names social class as a barrier between, for example, herself and her parents. In paragraph 16, Torgovnick asserts, "The story as I would have to tell it would be *to some extent* a class narrative" (our italics). To what extent? As you write in response to this question, take care to look for ways that her thinking about class—and about her parents—changes as the essay progresses.

4. **Link:** Write an essay on how Torgovnick's Bensonhurst compares and contrasts with Reed's El Cerrito. What features of El Cerrito might Reed point to as preventing it from having the kind of provinciality that Torgovnick shows us leads to racism and violence in Bensonhurst? To what extent do Reed

and Torgovnick find similar things to celebrate in their largely unassimilated neighborhoods?

5. **Link:** Write an essay analyzing the brief scene in which Torgovnick is treated as an outsider by a group of Italian American men. In this case, they have verbally insulted her primarily for her gender. Where else does gender discrimination appear in the essay? How does it compare as a lens—seeing as a woman—with the lens of race adopted by Reed and Gates in their essays? What are the biggest similarities? And given those similarities, what's the biggest difference? (See Chapter 4 on difference within similarity.)

6. **Link Across Units:** Torgovnick's essay begins with the issue of neighborhood safety as seen by her Italian American parents and neighbors, wherein safety and racism are directly connected. Write an essay in which you put Torgovnick's piece into conversation with Jacobs' essay, "Uses of Sidewalks: Safety" in Chapter 21. What might Jacobs find to praise about Bensonhurst, and why? What's different about the neighborhoods that Jacobs describes that apparently make them safer for strangers and outsiders? How is Bensonhurst different from the neighborhood around the White Horse Tavern that Jacobs describes, and so what?

7. **Application:** Equipped with a notebook or laptop, spend an afternoon wandering around your old neighborhood. Make a point of stopping every half hour or so to free-write on the question, "How has my neighborhood shaped me?" Obviously, the readings in this chapter should have enriched the implications of that question for you, to include such matters as

   • the marks of social class

   • the elements in yourself you have wished to conceal or make over

   • your tastes to this day, but also your "local" prejudices

   • your own ambivalence to your past, that strange mix of reverence and dread that neighborhoods specialize in inspiring

Make at least three entries of 20 minutes or more. (If you are currently living away from your neighborhood, you can write from memory.) Then return to these—type them if you have handwritten them—and revise and expand them. If you carried this project through to some sort of completion, one or more of them might open out into your own personal essay about the complex hold that a neighborhood can claim on who and what we become. See Chapter 1 on freewriting.

Michael Jonas

The Downside of Diversity

With this analysis of a recent controversial survey by Harvard political scientist Robert Putnam, the chapter opens back out to a wider theoretical frame, providing a new context for reconsidering the series of first-person memoirs by Rodriguez, Tan, Gates, Reed, and Torgovnick. It is the first of two concluding readings to this chapter, both aimed at challenging conventional assumptions about the melting pot. The article, which first appeared in the *Boston Globe*, discusses Putnam's findings—suggesting racial and ethnic diversity diminishes rather than increases civic strength. The article also surveys the responses Putnam's findings evoked from both the right and the left, as well as the rhetorical challenges Putnam faced in finding a way to contextualize results that challenged his own vision of the melting pot. The author of the piece, Michael Jonas, is executive editor of *CommonWealth*, a journal published by MassINC, an independent think tank using non-partisan research, civic journalism, and public forums to stimulate debate and shape public policy.

A Harvard political scientist finds that diversity hurts civic life. What happens when a liberal scholar unearths an inconvenient truth?

It has become increasingly popular to speak of racial and ethnic diversity as a civic strength. From multicultural festivals to pronouncements from political leaders, the message is the same: our differences make us stronger.

But a massive new study, based on detailed interviews of nearly 30,000 people across America, has concluded just the opposite. Harvard political scientist Robert Putnam—famous for *Bowling Alone*, his 2000 book on declining civic engagement—has found that the greater the diversity in a community, the fewer people vote and the less they volunteer, the less they give to charity and work on community projects. In the most diverse communities, neighbors trust one another about half as much as they do in the most homogenous settings. The study, the largest ever on civic engagement in America, found that virtually all measures of civic health are lower in more diverse settings.

"The extent of the effect is shocking," says Scott Page, a University of Michigan political scientist.

The study comes at a time when the future of the American melting pot is the focus of intense political debate, from immigration to race-based admissions to schools, and it poses challenges to advocates on all sides of the issues. The study is already being cited by some conservatives as proof of the harm large-scale immigration causes to the nation's social fabric. But with demographic trends already pushing the nation inexorably toward greater diversity, the real question may yet lie ahead: how to handle the unsettling social changes that Putnam's research predicts.

From The New York Times, August 5 © 2007 The New York Times. All rights reserved. Used by permission and protected by the Copyright Laws of the United States. The printing, copying, redistribution, or retransmission of this Content without express written permission is prohibited.

"We can't ignore the findings," says Ali Noorani, executive director of the Massachusetts Immigrant and Refugee Advocacy Coalition. "The big question we have to ask ourselves is, what do we do about it; what are the next steps?"

The study is part of a fascinating new portrait of diversity emerging from recent scholarship. Diversity, it shows, makes us uncomfortable—but discomfort, it turns out, isn't always a bad thing. Unease with differences helps explain why teams of engineers from different cultures may be ideally suited to solve a vexing problem. Culture clashes can produce a dynamic give-and-take, generating a solution that may have eluded a group of people with more similar backgrounds and approaches. At the same time, though, Putnam's work adds to a growing body of research indicating that more diverse populations seem to extend themselves less on behalf of collective needs and goals.

His findings on the downsides of diversity have also posed a challenge for Putnam, a liberal academic whose own values put him squarely in the pro-diversity camp. Suddenly finding himself the bearer of bad news, Putnam has struggled with how to present his work. He gathered the initial raw data in 2000 and issued a press release the following year outlining the results. He then spent several years testing other possible explanations.

When he finally published a detailed scholarly analysis in June in the journal *Scandinavian Political Studies*, he faced criticism for straying from data into advocacy. His paper argues strongly that the negative effects of diversity can be remedied, and says history suggests that ethnic diversity may eventually fade as a sharp line of social demarcation.

"Having aligned himself with the central planners intent on sustaining such social engineering, Putnam concludes the facts with a stern pep talk," wrote conservative commentator Ilana Mercer, in a recent *Orange County Register* op-ed titled "Greater diversity equals more misery."

Putnam has long staked out ground as both a researcher and a civic player, someone willing to describe social problems and then have a hand in addressing them. He says social science should be "simultaneously rigorous and relevant," meeting high research standards while also "speaking to concerns of our fellow citizens." But on a topic as charged as ethnicity and race, Putnam worries that many people hear only what they want to.

"It would be unfortunate if a politically correct progressivism were to deny the reality of the challenge to social solidarity posed by diversity," he writes in the new report. "It would be equally unfortunate if a historical and ethnocentric conservatism were to deny that addressing that challenge is both feasible and desirable."

Putnam is the nation's premier guru of civic engagement. After studying civic life in Italy in the 1970s and 1980s, Putnam turned his attention to the United States, publishing an influential journal article on civic engagement in 1995 that he expanded five years later into the best-selling *Bowling Alone*. The book sounded a national wake-up call on what Putnam called a sharp drop in civic connections among Americans. It won him audiences with presidents Bill Clinton and George W. Bush, and made him one of the country's best known social scientists.

Putnam claims the United States has experienced a pronounced decline in "social capital," a term he helped popularize. Social capital refers to the social networks—whether friendships or religious congregations or neighborhood associations—that he says are key indicators of civic well-being. When social capital is high, says Putnam, communities are better places to live. Neighborhoods are safer; people are healthier; and more citizens vote.

The results of his new study come from a survey Putnam directed among residents in 41 U.S. communities, including Boston. Residents were sorted into the four principal categories used by the U.S. Census: black, white, Hispanic, and Asian. They were asked how much they trusted their neighbors and those of each racial category, and questioned about a long list of civic attitudes and practices, including their views on local government, their involvement in community projects, and their friendships. What emerged in more diverse communities was a bleak picture of civic desolation, affecting everything from political engagement to the state of social ties.

Putnam knew he had provocative findings on his hands. He worried about coming under some of the same liberal attacks that greeted Daniel Patrick Moynihan's landmark 1965 report on the social costs associated with the breakdown of the black family. There is always the risk of being pilloried as the bearer of "an inconvenient truth," says Putnam.

After releasing the initial results in 2001, Putnam says he spent time "kicking the tires really hard" to be sure the study had it right. Putnam realized, for instance, that more diverse communities tended to be larger, have greater income ranges, higher crime rates, and more mobility among their residents—all factors that could depress social capital independent of any impact ethnic diversity might have.

"People would say, 'I bet you forgot about X,'" Putnam says of the string of suggestions from colleagues. "There were 20 or 30 X's."

But even after statistically taking them all into account, the connection remained strong: Higher diversity meant lower social capital. In his findings, Putnam writes that those in more diverse communities tend to "distrust their neighbors, regardless of the color of their skin, to withdraw even from close friends, to expect the worst from their community and its leaders, to volunteer less, give less to charity and work on community projects less often, to register to vote less, to agitate for social reform more but have less faith that they can actually make a difference, and to huddle unhappily in front of the television."

"People living in ethnically diverse settings appear to 'hunker down'—that is, to pull in like a turtle," Putnam writes.

In documenting that hunkering down, Putnam challenged the two dominant schools of thought on ethnic and racial diversity, the "contact" theory and the "conflict" theory. Under the contact theory, more time spent with those of other backgrounds leads to greater understanding and harmony between groups. Under the conflict theory, that proximity produces tension and discord.

Putnam's findings reject both theories. In more diverse communities, he says, there were neither great bonds formed across group lines nor heightened ethnic tensions, but a general civic malaise. And in perhaps the most surprising result of all, levels of trust were not only lower between groups in more diverse settings, but even among members of the same group.

"Diversity, at least in the short run," he writes, "seems to bring out the turtle in all of us."

The overall findings may be jarring during a time when it's become commonplace to sing the praises of diverse communities, but researchers in the field say they shouldn't be.

"It's an important addition to a growing body of evidence on the challenges created by diversity," says Harvard economist Edward Glaeser.

In a recent study, Glaeser and colleague Alberto Alesina demonstrated that roughly half the difference in social welfare spending between the United States and Europe—Europe spends far more—can be attributed to the greater ethnic diversity of the U.S. population. Glaeser says lower national social welfare spending in the United States is a "macro" version of the decreased civic engagement Putnam found in more diverse communities within the country.

Economists Matthew Kahn of UCLA and Dora Costa of MIT reviewed 15 recent studies in a 2003 paper, all of which linked diversity with lower levels of social capital. Greater ethnic diversity was linked, for example, to lower school funding, census response rates, and trust in others. Kahn and Costa's own research documented higher desertion rates in the Civil War among Union Army soldiers serving in companies whose soldiers varied more by age, occupation, and birthplace.

Birds of different feathers may sometimes flock together, but they are also less likely to look out for one another. "Everyone is a little self-conscious that this is not politically correct stuff," says Kahn.

So how to explain New York, London, Rio de Janiero, Los Angeles—the great melting-pot cities that drive the world's creative and financial economies?

The image of civic lassitude dragging down more diverse communities is at odds with the vigor often associated with urban centers, where ethnic diversity is greatest. It turns out there is a flip side to the discomfort diversity can cause. If ethnic diversity, at least in the short run, is a liability for social connectedness, a parallel line of emerging research suggests it can be a big asset when it comes to driving productivity and innovation. In high-skill workplace settings, says Scott Page, the University of Michigan political scientist, the different ways of thinking among people from different cultures can be a boon.

"Because they see the world and think about the world differently than you, that's challenging," says Page, author of *The Difference: How the Power of Diversity Creates Better Groups, Firms, Schools, and Societies*. "But by hanging out with people different than you, you're likely to get more insights. Diverse teams tend to be more productive."

In other words, those in more diverse communities may do more bowling alone, but the creative tensions unleashed by those differences in the workplace may vault those same places to the cutting edge of the economy and of creative culture.

Page calls it the "diversity paradox." He thinks the contrasting positive and negative effects of diversity can coexist in communities, but "there's got to be a limit." If civic engagement falls off too far, he says, it's easy to imagine the positive effects of diversity beginning to wane as well. "That's what's unsettling about his findings," Page says of Putnam's new work.

Meanwhile, by drawing a portrait of civic engagement in which more homogeneous communities seem much healthier, some of Putnam's worst fears about how his results could be used have been realized. A stream of conservative commentary has begun—from places like the Manhattan Institute and "The American Conservative"—highlighting the harm the study suggests will come from large-scale immigration. But Putnam says he's also received hundreds of complimentary emails laced with bigoted language. "It certainly is not pleasant when David Duke's website hails me as the guy who found out racism is good," he says.

In the final quarter of his paper, Putnam puts the diversity challenge in a broader context by describing how social identity can change over time. Experience shows that social divisions can eventually give way to "more encompassing identities" that create a "new, more capacious sense of 'we,'" he writes.

Growing up in the 1950s in a small Midwestern town, Putnam knew the religion of virtually every member of his high school graduating class because, he says, such information was crucial to the question of "who was a possible mate or date." The importance of marrying within one's faith, he says, has largely faded since then, at least among many mainline Protestants, Catholics, and Jews.

While acknowledging that racial and ethnic divisions may prove more stubborn, Putnam argues that such examples bode well for the long-term prospects for social capital in a multiethnic America.

In his paper, Putnam cites the work done by Page and others, and uses it to help frame his conclusion that increasing diversity in America is not only inevitable, but ultimately valuable and enriching. As for smoothing over the divisions that hinder civic engagement, Putnam argues that Americans can help that process along through targeted efforts. He suggests expanding support for English-language instruction and investing in community centers and other places that allow for "meaningful interaction across ethnic lines."

Some critics have found his prescriptions underwhelming. And in offering ideas for mitigating his findings, Putnam has drawn scorn for stepping out of the role of dispassionate researcher. "You're just supposed to tell your peers what you found," says John Leo, senior fellow at the Manhattan Institute, a conservative think tank. "I don't expect academics to fret about these matters."

But fretting about the state of American civic health is exactly what Putnam has spent more than a decade doing. While continuing to research questions involving social capital, he has directed the Saguaro Seminar, a project he started at Harvard's Kennedy School of Government that promotes efforts throughout the country to increase civic connections in communities.

"Social scientists are both scientists and citizens," says Alan Wolfe, director of the Boisi Center for Religion and American Public Life at Boston College, who sees nothing wrong in Putnam's efforts to affect some of the phenomena he studies.

Wolfe says what is unusual is that Putnam has published findings as a social scientist that are not the ones he would have wished for as a civic leader. There are plenty of social scientists, says Wolfe, who never produced research results at odds with their own worldview.

"The problem too often," says Wolfe, "is people are never uncomfortable about their findings."

Things to Do with the Reading

1. There are at least two primary foci to this piece: Putnam's findings and his subsequent struggles with how to present these findings. What, according to Jonas, are the issues at stake in the second focus—the question of presentation? Find the various places where Jonas treats this question, both from Putnam's point of view and that of his detractors. What are the larger issues here—issues involving the ethics of presentation, the partisan nature of all research projects, and the like? Once you have drafted some answers to these questions, write an essay on how, finally, Jonas invites us to regard Putnam and his work.

2. **Link:** Imagine that Ishmael Reed had read "The Downside of Diversity" and sent Putnam "My Neighborhood," and then they arranged to meet. Write an essay in which you discuss what each would find most interesting in the other's work. The following questions might help to guide you.

   How does Reed reflect on what Putnam terms "social capital"? Find sentences in Reed that shed light on how he might respond to Putnam's challenges to the "contact" theory and the "conflict" theory of ethnic and racial diversity. Ultimately, what common ground do the two figures share, and where to they appear to diverge most significantly? (See Chapter 13 on conversing with sources.)

3. **Link:** Imagine that Peter Salins read the article by Michael Jonas, and the two met for conversation. Both writers are affiliated with think tanks—Jonas with MassINC and Salins with the Manhattan Institute (whom Jonas references near the end of his piece). Write an essay in which you imagine what Salins and Jonas might have to say to each other. Locate sentences from both pieces that might justify your answer.

4. **Application:** According to Jonas, "Putnam claims the US has experienced a pronounced decline in 'social capital,'" defined as "social networks—whether friendships or religious congregations or neighborhood associations—that are key indicators of civic well-being." Write an essay in which you assess the status of the social capital of some social network on your campus or in your neighborhood. How would you begin to make a case for the civic health of some particular aspect of your local community? Your report will of necessity be largely anecdotal, comprised largely of what you can observe.

Robert McLiam Wilson

Sticks and Stones: The Irish Identity

In this salty, iconoclastic piece, the Northern Irish novelist Robert McLiam Wilson offers a broadly subversive response to many of the assumptions about both national identity and racial identity shared by the other contributors to this chapter. "Our racial authenticity," Wilson says of the Irish, "is an extremely negotiable commodity"—a flabby myth, prone to marketing and mistruth.

1   I am five foot eleven. I weigh around 170 pounds. I have brown hair, green eyes, and no real distinguishing marks. I'm heterosexual, atheist, liberal, and white. I don't shave as often as I should and I have pale, Irish skin. I smoke and I always wear a suit. I drive a small black car and I don't drink much alcohol. I prefer cats to dogs.

I don't know what that makes me, but I suspect that it makes me what I am.

When I was seventeen, I decided that I wanted to be Jewish. Like most Roman Catholics, I had only the vaguest notion of what this might entail. I stopped being good at sports and frequented the only kosher butcher in the city. (How he blushed for me, the poor man). I could never understand why no one took me seriously. I could never understand why I should not simply decide such questions for myself. Why was I such a goy? Who had decided that this should be so?

Like that of most citizens of Belfast, my identity is the subject of some local dispute. Some say I'm British, some say I'm Irish, some even say that there's no way I'm five foot eleven and that I'm five ten at best. In many ways I'm not permitted to contribute to this debate. If the controversy is ever satisfactorily concluded, I will be whatever the majority of people tell me I am.

5   As a quotidian absolute, nationality is almost meaningless. For an Italian living in Italy, Italianness is patently not much of a distinction. What really gives nationality its chiaroscuro, its flavor, is a little dash of hatred and fear. Nobody really knows or cares what they are until they meet what they don't want to be. Then it's time for the flags and guns to come out.

So when the airport cops ask me what I am, how do I explain that I live in the northeastern segment of an island sliced like a cheap pizza and with as many titles as a bar full of yuppie cocktails—Ireland, Northern Ireland, Britain, Eire, Ulster, etc. How do I explain how little that would tell them?

I suppose I could tell them that I live in a place where people have killed and died in an interminable fight over the names they should call themselves and each other. (In Belfast, sticks and stones may break your bones but names will blow you to pieces on a regular basis.) I could tell them about the self-defeating eugenic templates of racial purity by which no human being still living on the island can be properly deemed Irish. That the English and the Scottish have been here a long time and that we're all smudged by now—café au lait, mulattoes, half-breeds, spicks, wops, and dagos. I could tell them that I don't really understand the question.

Sticks and Stones: The Irish Identity by Robert McLiam Wilson. Reprinted with permission of Antony Harwood, Ltd., Agent for Robert McLiam Wilson.

Irishness is unique amongst the self-conscious nationalisms. A self-conscious Frenchman bores everyone. A self-conscious American is a nightmare. And a self-conscious Englishman makes you want to lie down in a darkened room. But a self-conscious Irishman is a friend to the world and the world listens attentively. The reviews are always good. There's a global appetite for Irishness that is almost without parallel.

Nationalistic self-obsession is corrupt, corrosive, and bogus enough without this extra angle. When well-received, this fake concoction of myth and bullshit is reflected in the mirror of imprecise good will and sentimental foolishness. This in itself produces further distortions which are then seamlessly incorporated into the "genuine" article. Over the years I've watched the fundamental concepts of what it is to be Irish being altered by common-currency American errors. Here in the "old country," when we hear that New Yorkers are marching in green-kilted bagpipe bands (an entirely Scottish phenomenon) on St. Patrick's Day, we immediately look around for somewhere to buy green kilts and bagpipes. Our racial authenticity is an extremely negotiable commodity.

Yet I've always believed that such Americans have it just about right. Their ideas   10
of Irishness are as fake as a hooker's tit, but then so are ours.

To understand all things Irish, you must understand something fundamental. Everyone knows that Ireland is the land of myth. And myth is a beautiful and resonant word. It sounds so profound, so spiritual. There is something visceral in it. Our mythmaking is vital to the self-imposed standardized norms of nationality that are current here at home. Catholics are Irish, so Irish, and Protestants are British, poor things. The common assumption that the Irish language, Irish music, and Irish history are pure Catholic monoliths, and the oft-suppressed expression of the indigenous culture, ignores the truth that the Irish linguistic, musical, and cultural revivals were the product of nineteenth-century Protestant historicism. Everything we say is myth. The lies are old and dusty. The waters are muddy and the truth long gone.

Even our understanding of our own history—you know the kind of thing, perfidious Albion, eight hundred years of oppression, etc.—teems with bullshit. King William of Orange waged war in seventeenth-century Ireland and is still a Catholic-baiting Protestant icon who causes trouble here. No one remembers that he was blessed by the Pope. Wolfe Tone is a much-loved historical rebel leader who sailed with a French army to liberate Catholic Ireland. No one mentions that he was defeated by a Catholic militia. The President of Ireland called on a German minister to express his official condolences after Hitler's suicide at the end of World War II. Nobody wrote any songs about that.

In some ways, the Irish tendency for romancing can be seen as harmless, almost charming. It is, after all, what produces our leprechauns, our fairy rings, all our beguiling fakery. But it also produces people who will murder for lies they only half-believe and certainly never understand—for the Irish have always armed their ideas. We don't have any white lies here anymore. We only have the deadly barbaric type.

Given the wildest differences in latitude and climate, it is remarkable how countries can remind you of one another. In cold March Manhattan, the air is as thick, dark, and injurious as any Berlin winter. In Paris, the rain falls and stains the pale stone with the same dispiriting grace you find in Cambridge on most days of the year. London can look and feel like everywhere.

15   If true of the places, how much truer of the people. *Quod erat demonstrandum* and then some.

We are a pretty poor species. Even the most gifted of us, the wisest and most studious of us, are weak-minded. We toss aside our Pushkin and read Judith Krantz. We watch goofy TV shows and asinine movies. We can't help liking big noises, colored lights, and pictures of naked people.

Our beliefs are often fantastic alloys of fear, self-interest, prejudice, and ignorance. As Tolstoy gloriously demonstrates, our finest moments of heroism, selflessness, and grandeur are usually founded on the meanest egotisms and vanities. Our notion of the sublime is laughable. In acts of worship, many of us pay homage to some form of invisible man who mimics us in the pettiest detail. Apart from our uncharacteristic capacity for love (a mistake, a design flaw), we're a shambles.

It is the things we say that most prove what monkeys we still are. We are driven to generalize, to sweep on through, to prognosticate, to diagnose. Typically male, we say, typically female. That's the problem with rich people, we opine. The poor were ever so. Gentlemen prefer blondes. Fuck right off, I can't help thinking.

Our most outrageous banalities are reserved for questions of race and nationality. This is how the French behave, we say. How do we know? Have we met them all? Have we asked any of them? Millions of people are summoned and dismissed in a few moments of robust fatuousness.

20   I'm five foot eleven. I weigh around 170 pounds. I have brown hair, green eyes, and so on. Irish or British is very far down on my list—somewhere below my favorite color. Nonetheless, I must concede that nationality is tenacious. People have real stamina when it comes to this business. I must further concede that Irishness is a great arena for disquisitions on national identity. Because the Irish conflict is internecine (it has nothing to do with the English anymore), definitions of Irishness have particular charm. Nationalities primarily define themselves by what they're not. The Swiss are not German, the Scottish are not English, and the Canadians are definitely not American. But the Irish make internal distinctions as well. Some of the Irish aren't properly Irish. Some of the Irish aren't even vaguely Irish. In pursuit of the mantle of absolute Irishness, brother kills brother and sisters look on and applaud.

A few years ago I had an apartment on a leafy South Belfast street called Adelaide Park. A police station was being rebuilt across the street from my building (the original had been flattened by a bomb a few years before). It was a controversial building site, naturally. Apart from their well-known attacks on the policemen, soldiers, prison officers, and almost everyone else, the IRA liked to target construction workers who helped build police stations. Thus, the site was guarded round the clock by the police. For nearly six months there were always a couple of cops standing in my driveway, all peaked caps, submachine guns, and high anxiety. This was okay in the spring. It was fine in the summer, and manageable in the fall. But as winter set in, the position of these guys became more and more unpleasant. It was windy and cold, and it rained for months. As night fell, I would look out my apartment window and watch the damp rozzers. It was obviously not a good gig.

For weeks I debated whether or not I should take them cups of coffee. It was more complicated than it might sound. Policemen and soldiers here are very unlikely to accept such things from the public now. Twenty-five years of ground glass, rat poison, and Drano in friendly cups of tea discouraged them from accepting such largesse. Not long before, a woman had handed some soldiers a bomb in a biscuit tin in a charming incident near Derry. Additionally, of course, there might have been swathes of people willing to do me grief for being nice to the police.

Policemen are usually Protestant and I myself am customarily Catholic. They couldn't have known that I was a Catholic, but they would have been suspicious. (In this country, the big haters can't really tell each other apart. How we envy those who hate black or white people—that obvious difference, that demonstrable objection.)

It was a small thing, a minor transaction, an unimportant detail. The weeks passed, the wind blew, and the rain rained. I didn't hand out any coffee.

—*July 1997*

Things to Do with the Reading

1. Wilson's essay is the kind of writing that sometimes gets called a *tour de force* (a feat of strength, power or skill, according to the *OED*). In writing of this sort, authors often deliberately overstate their points, using exaggeration and an aggressively assertive tone to jolt people into seeing absurdity in what they might otherwise wish to guard as cherished positions. There is strategy in this. If the writer tries to take a mile, we might be cajoled by his sheer audacity into giving him an inch, which is perhaps all that he really wanted in the first place.

   Write an essay in which you determine what you think Wilson actually hoped to accomplish, given that his piece is unlikely to cause the Irish (or any other group) to completely give up on "Irishness." Start with paragraphs 16 and 17 and analyze the rhetoric of Wilson's piece. What do these two paragraphs reveal about Wilson's aims and his means of achieving those aims through style? (For more on rhetoric, see especially Chapters 1 and 3.)

2. **Link:** Wilson's essay challenges and interestingly undercuts many of the assumptions about cultural identity that inform previous essays in this chapter. For reasons particular to his own circumstances as a citizen of Belfast (Northern Ireland), Wilson is extremely dubious about the concept of national identity. "Nationalistic self-obsession," he writes, "is corrupt, corrosive, and bogus.... When well-received, this fake concoction of myth and bullshit is reflected in the mirror of imprecise good will and sentimental foolishness. This in itself produces further distortions which are then seamlessly incorporated into the 'genuine' article" (paragraph 9). A repeated word in the essay is "bullshit," part of a strand including "fake," "fake concoction," "myth," "beguiling fakery," "bogus," and "lies." The word "genuine" is placed emphatically in quotes.

Write an essay in which you reflect backward from Wilson's piece to one or more other pieces in this chapter that you think it illuminates. What might Wilson say, for example, about Salins's position on the importance of people choosing to "convert" to being American? Alternatively, how might he respond to Jesse Jackson's rainbow metaphor or to what Salins has to say about ethnic federalism or to Torgovnick's mixed emotions about the cohesiveness and tenacity of Italian American neighborhoods?

3. **Link:** Because of the long-standing civil war in Northern Ireland between Catholics and Protestants—between proponents of a United Ireland and those supporting Northern Ireland remaining under English rule—Wilson worries about the potential of nationalism and cultural identities to fuel violence. "In pursuit of the mantle of absolute Irishness," he writes, "brother kills brother and sisters look on and applaud." In the second to last paragraph of his essay, however, he writes, "In this country, the big haters can't really tell each other apart. How we envy those who hate black or white people—that obvious difference, that demonstrable objection."

    What are we to do about racial identities—whether the product of mythologizing and stereotyping or not—where physical difference and long histories of struggle and oppression come more starkly into play? To what extent can these be willed out of existence? Write a paper in which you bring Wilson, Reed, and Rodriguez into conversation on the issue of cultural and racial difference. To what extent would Rodriguez agree with Wilson on the phoniness and foolishness and even the potential danger of so valuing distinct national identities? What sort of conversation do you imagine Reed would have with Wilson on the same issue?

4. **Application:** It is interesting to consider which of our personal tendencies and traits each of us would choose to include if asked to identify ourselves to others. This is especially interesting to think about in America, which contains so many different racial, national, and ethnic groups, and so many different religions, customs, and regions. Write your own version of Wilson's opening paragraph as a means of generating some thinking about the markers of particular identities in America. The second sentence of Wilson's essay is, "I don't know what that makes me, but I suspect that it makes me what I am." After you have written your paragraph of identifying traits, write a second paragraph in which you try to explain how the information you chose to include in your first paragraph makes you what you are.

FOR FURTHER RESEARCH: RACE, ETHNICITY, AND THE MELTING POT

By Kelly Cannon, Reference Librarian

The readings and activities below invite you to further explore the theme of Race, Ethnicity, and the Melting Pot. WARNING: Some essays are polemical; they are intended to promote insight and discussion (or a starting point for your next paper). To access the online readings, visit the *Writing Analytically with Readings* website at www.cengagebrain.com.

Open Access

"Almost All Millennials Accept Interracial Dating and Marriage." *Pew Research Center.* **1 February 2010. 11 January 2011. http://pewresearch.org/pubs/1480/millennials-accept-interracial-dating-marriage-friends-different-race-generations**
Perhaps the litmus test of the melting-pot theory, interracial dating and marriage find much greater acceptance among millennials than among preceding generations, in a study conducted by the Pew Research Center.

> Explore: Do the results of this survey ring true to you? Find out more about the Pew Research Center. What is it? What is its agenda? Does this agenda support or detract from the validity of the findings? What would Peter Salins think about interracial dating, à la his article extant above?

"Between Two Worlds: How Young Latinos Come of Age." *Pew Hispanic Center.* **Pew Research Center, 11 December 2009. 12 January 2011. http://pewhispanic.org/reports/report.php?ReportID=117**
A long report, summarized at this website, looks closely at how young Latinos navigate two worlds, American and Latin American.

> Explore: Does the behavior of Latin American youth in the majority assert or contradict the melting-pot theory? How so? Why did the Pew Research Center launch the Pew Hispanic Center? Do you think the center is well-positioned to fulfill its mission? Why?

Minority Links. **United States Census Bureau, 7 June 2010. 31 July 2010. http://www.census.gov/newsroom/minority_links/minority_links.html**
Current in-depth statistical reports from the Census Bureau on Asian and Pacific Islander, Black, Foreign-Born, and Hispanic populations in the United States

> Explore: Compare one variable such as "families and living arrangements" across the various ethnic groups. What differences and similarities do you notice?

Le, C. N. "Assimilation and Ethnic Identity." *Asian-Nation: The Landscape of Asian America.* **2010. 12 January 2011. http://www.asian-nation.org/assimilation.shtml**
Looks succinctly yet eloquently at assimilation and the melting pot through the lens of Asian America.

> Explore: How important is it that an essay on this topic be written by someone from the subject community, in this case Asian American? To what extent do the struggles of representation to the larger culture surface? How do such struggles compare with those outlined in the McLiam Wilson essay above?

Noah, Timothy. "Why American Muslims don't join al-Qaida." *Slate Magazine* (27 February 2009). 19 January 2011. http://www.slate.com/id/2211996
Noah conjectures that assimilation à la the melting pot may be what sets American Muslims apart from Muslims in other parts of the world.

> Explore: The author of this conjectural piece refers to a study conducted by the Pew Foundation. Link to this study. Scan the sections of this study and ask yourself, to what extent does it appear to confirm Noah's hypothesis about American Muslims and the melting pot? To what extent does this article confirm Peter Salins' claims about the melting pot vs. multiculturalism in his essay printed above?

Piper, Greg. "Laughter Is the Best Melanin." *Cultural Imperialist.* 2010. 11 January 2011. http://www.culturalimperialist.com/2010/09/race-bottom-nix-mixed-ethnicities
This essay good naturedly takes issue with anyone who would argue that the dilution of racial distinctiveness is a good thing. Piper's view finds its counterpoint in the companion piece "Genetic Carpool" by Jeremiah Lewis.

> Explore: Scroll to the bottom of the page and click on "About Cultural Imperialist." What rhetorical space has this website carved out for itself? To what extent has it been successful in its enterprise, as illustrated by the two opposing articles named above? Compare these arguments with those espoused in the Peter Salins piece.

Thompson, Ginger. "Where Education and Assimilation Collide." *The New York Times.* 15 March 2009. 11 January 2011. http://www.nytimes.com/2009/03/15/us/15immig.html
On the surface, Cecil D. Hylton High School, just outside of D.C., exemplifies assimilation. And yet those who speak English and those who are learning English as a second language exist in two separate worlds, all under the same roof.

> Explore: Click on the interactive map adjacent to the article. What do you think contributes to the high number of ESL students in the following counties? Fairfax County, VA? Chatham County, NC? Todd County, SD? Where does your home county fall in this respect?

Proprietary

(Ask your librarian about print or online access to the following resources.)
Firmat, Gustavo Perez. "On Bilingualism and Its Discontents." *Daedalus* 134.3 (Summer 2005): 89–92.
A Spanish professor whose native language is Spanish but who teaches in the United States reveals some discontent over his bilingual existence.

> Explore: What is at the heart of Firmat's discontent? If you speak a second language, how does this affect your "language loyalty"? Does some of Firmat's discontent correspond with that felt by McLiam Wilson regarding Irish Americanness? What do both essays say about mixed identities?

Haiming Liu, and Lianlian Lin. "Food, Culinary Identity, and Transnational Culture: Chinese Restaurant Business in Southern California." *Journal of Asian American Studies* 12.2 (2009): 135–162.
Food serves as the litmus test here of assimilation, with a paradoxical outcome.

Explore: How does food both permit and restrict assimilation? In your own experience, how does the food you prepare and eat reinforce your sense of who you are?

Utkin, Anatolii. "The Future of the West." *Russian Social Science Review* 45.4 (July/August 2004): 4–27.
A thought-provoking peer-reviewed article forecasting the apocalyptic effect that changing demographics will have on world powers. Europe is losing population rapidly. In the United States, non-European minorities will soon be the majority.

Explore: What does Utkin think of the melting-pot idea? How important is immigrant assimilation in determining the future? Do you agree with the author's prediction, or does it seem extreme? How so? To what extent does Utkin's essay compare with Peter Salins'?

Wilkes, Rima, and John Iceland. "Hypersegregation in the Twenty-First Century." *Demography* 41.1 (2004): 23–36.
A population study that indicates startling differences in segregation geographically and between different minority groups.

Explore: Reflect on how your own community is or is not racially segregated. Does it reflect the trends in this article?

Chapter 23

The Language of Politics and the Politics of Language

This is a chapter about a particular kind of rhetoric—political rhetoric. Its aim is to equip you to analyze political language, attuning you to the characteristic vocabularies of different political orientations, and sensitizing you to the politics of spin. The writers sampled here share the assumption that we inhabit a world of competing voices telling us what to believe and whom to support. And they share the conviction that political language is always partisan: It's never just the facts, though that is the position it most often claims to be presenting.

And so as citizens of a democratic society, we are faced with the challenge of figuring out what others who have political designs upon us "really" believe, or at least, what they are "really" saying. This challenge has been rendered more difficult by the rise in the last few decades of increasingly subtle methods of crafting and wording political positions, methods that build upon what political rhetoricians glean from focus groups and public opinion polls. In this context, the selections in this unit offer a primer in decoding the language of politics that surrounds us.

ABOUT THE READINGS IN THIS CHAPTER

The opening selection, Christopher Borick's "On Political Labels," offers the primary lens through which to read subsequent pieces in this unit, and for that matter, to interpret examples of political speeches wherever you find them. Borick provides a brief history of key terms such as liberal, conservative, and libertarian; charts the ways they overlap; and then offers readers a simple test to measure the gap between the labels they embrace and their actual beliefs. At the end of the essay, Borick includes a "vocabulary of contemporary ideological positions" that can be used to smoke out the political leanings of articles and speeches one is likely to encounter in the popular press. Following this piece are five editorials that readers can use to test out the tools that Borick has provided. What are the key words and phrases in each piece, we ask, that enable you to identify each piece as primarily liberal or conservative?

Next comes a classic essay, George Orwell's "Politics and the English Language." His analysis of the strategies by which political language tends to "defend the indefensible" concludes with a list of prescriptions for writing politically responsible prose. This discussion serves as a frame for the next four pieces, all of which examine the contemporary politics of spin.

First comes an extensive interview with the conservative pollster and image-consultant Frank Luntz conducted on PBS's *Frontline* series about the shaping of public opinion in U.S. politics today. Says Luntz, "We as Americans and as humans have very selective hearing and very selective memory. We only hear what we want to hear and disregard the rest." Such comments invite us to contemplate how Borick and Orwell might interpret Luntz's views on the language of politics.

Next, Matt Bai in "The Framing Wars" focuses on political consultant (and linguist) George Lakoff, the Democratic counterpart to the Republican Luntz. The two figures, Luntz and Lakoff, offer intriguing opportunities for comparison and contrast. Following these two portraits are two brief newspaper accounts of attempts by the Obama administration to seize the linguistic initiative through renaming and redefining political code words—attempts to control the discussion by enforcing the terms by which it will be carried out. The first article, "Buzzwords: Rephrasing Obama's Lexicon," looks at the language of his energy policy; the second, "Obama Subtly Adopts the Language of Business," analyzes the way he, and previous presidents, have talked about "competition" and international business.

The chapter ends, as is customary in these final chapters, by providing a piece with a different slant, designed to get readers to test the limits of the lenses they have been offered. James Peck's "September 11—a National Tragedy?" suggests that while most politicians and members of the press labeled the terrorist attacks as a tragedy, they actually treated the event as a melodrama. He concludes by inviting us to interpret the event as tragedy, but to take that label seriously. Drawing on the history of theater and dramatic theory, Peck argues that tragedy is not only about loss but also about painful self-assessments.

Note: The readings in this chapter will be enriched by the context that Chapter 9, "Analyzing Arguments" provides—especially the section on logical fallacies. In particular, look for examples of ad hominem, bandwagon, equivocation, false analogy, poisoning the well, red herring, slippery slope, straw man, and weasel words. All of these are particularly relevant in analyzing political language.

Christopher Borick

On Political Labels

Written specifically for this book, "On Political Labels" is a primer for decoding the spin now employed by both political parties. The author, Christopher P. Borick, is a professor of political science and the director of an institute of public opinion, that has conducted over 100 large-scale surveys during the past decade, appearing in the *Wall St Journal, Los Angeles Times, London Guardian,* and *Washington Post*. He has also provided analysis for the BBC, National Public Radio's *Morning Edition,* and *CBS* News and NBC *Nightly News*. This piece offers a history of the key terms "liberal" and "conservative." Borick charts the ways that each of these terms is connected to a set of assumptions about what government should be and do. Ultimately, this essay provides a lens for analyzing the rest of the readings in this unit.

Note: Respond to the questionnaires in Boxes 23.1 and 23.2 of this essay as you are reading it for the first time. Do so before you get to the interpretation and the statistics that Borick subsequently provides about them.

In the world of politics labels are a currency. Labels allow politicians to set the public's 1
image of themselves and their opponents and help advance and destroy plans and policies. Even though history shows us that labels are as much a part of politics as waving flags or kissing babies, the meaning of labels remains quite elusive. What does it really mean to call oneself a libertarian, a compassionate conservative, a progressive? Is there actually such a thing as a "Massachusetts Liberal" or "Blue Dog Democrat"? While there are no easy answers to those questions, the legendary Humpty Dumpty of Alice in Wonderland fame offers some insight on the matter. When Humpty tells Alice that there is "glory for you" on your birthday, Alice replies, "I don't know what you mean by glory." Humpty answers, "of course you don't until I tell you … when I use a word it means what I choose it to mean—neither more or less!" This wisdom, while emanating from a fictional egg-shaped character, is used regularly by today's real world political consultants. Wordsmiths such as the Republican political consultant Frank Luntz have crafted careers out of making words mean just what they want them to. Luntz advises his politician clients to change the name of the "estate tax" to the "death tax" and to switch the word "privatize" to "personalize" in an attempt to sway public perceptions. There is evidence that Luntz and others have been successful in making the public believe that words mean what they want them to, and that this success is changing the way politics is done in the United States. But just what changes are taking place and what can you do as a citizen to better understand the use of labels in our political discourse?

To answer this question, it is essential to realize that political labels are often more about emotion than reason. Politicians have long made the assumption that the public lacks the interest and attention to critically analyze government affairs. Constitutional architect James Madison went to great measures to try to limit public control over

On Political Labels, Christopher Borick. Reprinted with permission of the author.

government because he viewed the public as prone to emotional reactions that lacked insight into the complexities of governance. Fearful that public opinion could be shaped through the linguistic trickery of a demagogue, Madison tried to insulate government from direct public pressure through institutions such as the Electoral College and Supreme Court. In the end, Madison simply was not confident enough that the general public had the tools necessary to critically engage the debates pertinent to governing.

In contrast, Madison's counterpart Thomas Jefferson did not share his skepticism about the public's ability to analyze political matters. Instead, Jefferson believed citizens could be educated in a manner that could enhance their ability to make political judgments. In essence, he thought regular citizens, given proper training, could get beyond the emotional trickery of political language and discern broader meaning. While strong arguments can be made for both the Madisonian and Jeffersonian positions, I believe that Jefferson's approach to this matter must be the framework for how we are to think about political labels today. Simply accepting that the public will act on emotion rather than reason, and therefore the government should be insulated from public pressures, is not a very attractive proposition. This approach undermines the central role of the citizen in a democratic system of government, and in some ways creates a self-fulfilling prophecy where citizens have limited need to think analytically about politics. Such an approach to democratic discourse also plays into the hands of political consultants and strategists who want the public to act on emotion rather than reason because emotion is often easier to manipulate.

Thus, I suggest that we take some time to think about political labels in a manner that allows for critical reflection—especially given the threat posed by today's spin doctors. Since in all likelihood you will encounter thousands of political labels over the course of your lifetime as a citizen, it is important to develop a lens that will allow for a productive analysis of a label's use and effects. It is not my purpose to contend that labels have no place in politics or political discourse. Quite the contrary, labels help us organize our thoughts and provide meaningful reference points from which citizens can engage in thoughtful political discussions. But while labels are completely necessary for productive discourse, they can also be used to confuse and control the voting public. Therefore, in the remainder of this article I offer a number of suggestions for you (in your capacity as one of Jefferson's informed citizens) to consider when you are confronted with a label. In particular much of my attention will be directed to the most commonly used political labels in the United States: liberal and conservative. While my suggestions are by no means inclusive, the following list offers some perspective on how you might think about political labels.

1. Think About the Historical Background of the Label

5   One of the first things you should think about when you see or hear a political label is where it came from. Common political labels such as "liberal" or "conservative" have long histories that shed light on their contemporary use. It's important to recognize that a label's meaning differs from place to place and over time. A conservative in Texas may believe much differently from a conservative in New York, just as an American conservative varies in view points from a conservative in Norway. Similarly,

someone calling herself a conservative in 2005 would significantly differ from someone calling himself a conservative in 1905 or even 1975. You may wonder, with such variation over time and place, how can we attach meaning to key political terms at all? While not always easy to see, at least part of the answer can be discovered through an examination of the history of the terms.

Let's look at liberalism for a start. The term liberal can be traced at least back to 17th-century England, where it evolved from debates dealing with the voting franchise among English citizens. Proponents of including greater numbers of Englishmen in elections came to be known as liberals, thanks in part to the writings of John Locke, whose ideas about the social contract helped to build the philosophical underpinnings of this political ideology. Over time liberalism has maintained its focus on public control over government actions, but there have been splits that have led to its current manifestation. In the 18th and 19th centuries, liberalism began to stress the importance of individual freedom and broader rights of the citizenry in terms of limits on government. In essence, this type of liberalism focused on "negative rights" or the restrictions on what government could do to its citizens. The First Amendment of the Constitution includes numerous examples of negative rights. The granting of the right to freedom of speech or the press is achieved through the prohibition of government from creating laws that abridge such freedoms. Thus negating an action of government creates rights for the people.

In the 20th century, however, liberalism became synonymous with the view that government had to be much more active in helping citizens get to the point where they would be able to truly live a free life. In this expanding view of liberalism, government intervention in society is necessary to create a more level playing field on which individuals can then use their freedom to achieve desired goals. Such beliefs have been at the roots of government expansion into social welfare policies such as public housing, food stamps and affirmative action, and have formed the core of government agendas such as Franklin Roosevelt's New Deal and Lyndon Johnson's Great Society.

It is also this focus on active government that has helped transform the term liberal into a derogatory term in contemporary political dialogue. For example, let's look at the title of the recent best selling book *Treason: Liberal Treachery from the Cold War to the War on Terrorism*. As can be seen, author Ann Coulter equates a liberal philosophy with treason against the nation itself. She finds liberalism's focus on protecting individual rights to be detrimental to the security of the United States and a threat to the very survival of the republic. Thus Coulter attaches a scarlet "L" to anyone and anything that places high value on civil rights or civil liberties if those rights and liberties can be seen as undermining national security.

While Coulter uses the term liberal to slam those who believe government is a positive force in society, conservative author Sean Hannity tries to disentangle contemporary liberalism from its historical focus on individual liberty. In his book, *Let Freedom Ring: Winning the War of Liberty Over Liberalism,* Hannity contends that it's conservatism that is really interested in liberty, while it's liberalism that creates an environment where government activity limits individual freedom and autonomy. He sees the regulations and programs that are designed to create level playing fields for citizens as counterproductive to democracy and the vitality of the country. Hannity is reflecting the beliefs of modern conservative thinkers such as Russel Kirk who equate government efforts to achieve equality with severely limiting individualism. Kirk famously stated, "men are created different; and a government which ignores this law becomes an unjust government, for it sacrifices nobility to mediocrity; it pulls down the aspiring natures to gratify the inferior natures." In other words, for conservatives, government is not a force for improving the human condition; rather it's an anchor on the driving force of individual motivation.

10   While someone identifying herself or himself as a liberal may take great exception to the arguments and reasoning of writers like Coulter and Hannity, the core belief that government can be a force for positive social change is a fundamental element of modern liberalism. Liberalism's interest in the equality of citizens may indeed come at the expense of individual liberties. For example, in trying to create a fair playing field for candidates in elections, contemporary liberalism embraces strong government regulations on campaign contributions and spending. The "liberal" defense of such restrictions rests in the notion that the compelling public interest in having elections that are not controlled by those with the greatest financial resources trumps any individual's claim to spend as one chooses. So aspects of freedom are sometimes reduced in the name of equality—in this case, the freedom to spend as much as one wants on a political campaign. Similarly, liberals tend to believe that government should limit the freedom of businesses when such freedom comes into conflict with the public good—such as the right to clean air and clean water.

Unlike liberalism's evolution to the point where authors like Hannity and Coulter use it as a negative label, the history of the term conservative is one of increasing political value. Like liberalism, conservatism has a long history that can be traced back to the 18th century. The Anglo-Irish philosopher Edmund Burke is generally credited with developing the core ideas associated with conservative thought. In particular, Burke espoused a philosophy that rested on individual control of property and small and limited government. These tenets of conservatism are in large part the cornerstone of contemporary conservatism in the United States. In essence, government is often more of the problem than the answer. Here is an example of these beliefs coming out in a famous quote by Ronald Reagan during his presidency. Reagan claimed that most terrifying words in the English language are: "I'm from the government and I'm here to help." The clear animosity to government intervention in Reagan's words symbolizes the core conservative belief that the best government is the smallest government. As we shall see, this conviction is not always upheld, as in the case of defense spending for national security.

While conservatism has consistently focused on the role of limited government and private property rights, self-identified American conservatives are increasingly interested in using government to limit individual behaviors that are considered counter to the traditional values of the nation. In particular, behaviors such as homosexuality and choosing abortion are seen as direct threats to the order of society and thus require government intervention in the lives of individuals. This tendency to embrace government intervention as a means of protecting values has become an accepted principle for many in the United States, but also a persistent point of tension among individuals identifying themselves as conservative. In particular, many contemporary conservatives who have found a home in the Republican Party are uneasy with the inconsistency of endorsing government intervention in some aspects of an individual's life such as reproductive rights, while excoriating government intervention in other areas such as property rights. For some, these inconsistencies in contemporary American conservatism are too great to accept; thus, many individuals identify themselves more as libertarian rather than conservative.

A libertarian generally agrees with the conservative focus on limited government, but can't accept exceptions where government limits freedoms to preserve traditional values. A libertarian stresses the minimal role of government, with functions such as public safety and defense the only necessary roles of government. A quote from the 2004 United States Libertarian Party platform nicely summarizes this philosophy:

> We, the members of the libertarian party challenge the cult of the omnipresent state and defend the rights of the individual. We hold that all individuals have the right to exercise sole dominion over their own lives, and have the right to live in whatever manner they choose, so long as they do not forcibly interfere with the equal right of others to live in whatever manner they choose.

Thus, a libertarian would likely agree with a contemporary conservative on issues like low taxes and fewer government programs, but disagree with policies that might limit individual freedom such as restrictions on marijuana use and abortion. Similarly, libertarians and liberals share a belief in free expression even in controversial areas such as flag burning, yet libertarians would split with their liberal counterparts on topics such as government restrictions on the ownership and use of firearms. In Figure 23.1 below you can see that while the ideologies of liberalism, conservatism, and libertarianism may have distinctive qualities, they also can have areas of commonality.

The shared positions of various ideological positions are often obscured by their   15
differences. Therefore, it is essential to dig deeper beneath broad ideological labels to discern important nuances of thought.

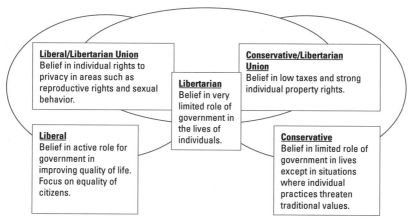

FIGURE 23.1

2. Labels Can Exaggerate Difference

While labels can be used to demonstrate real differences among individuals and political parties, they may mask similarities that cut across ideologies in the United States. It is important to note that American liberals and conservatives have more in common than one might anticipate. For foreign observers of politics in the United States there is often a belief that there is very little difference between Democrats and Republicans and liberals and conservatives. Let's look in particular at the role of government in the area of the economy and taxes. Among conservatives and liberals in the United States there is general agreement that government control of the economy should be limited. While there may be some argument about how government should regulate businesses, there is almost no discussion about government ownership or control of companies. Conversely, in Sweden the government owns 25% of businesses in the country.

Similarly, while it may appear that liberals and conservatives in the United States vehemently disagree on the issue of taxation, the scope of the debate is fairly limited. The highly debated 2003 tax cuts in the United States lowered tax rates in the top bracket from 39.6% to 35%. Compare these tax rates to those in Sweden where the top rate is 47% or France where the richest are taxed at 49% of their income.

Thus while the American liberal and conservative may have real differences, the divide may be exaggerated when labels are being applied in the heat of political debate. It serves the interest of politicians to distinguish differences between themselves and their opponents for voters. It would be a bad political strategy to campaign on the platform that "my opponent and I are in agreement on most issues." Nevertheless, the reality of American politics is that the differences between liberalism and conservatism may not be as great as we are led to believe.

3. The Source of the Label Matters

When a label is applied to something or someone, it's rarely a spontaneous off the cuff remark. In a world where political campaigns are priced in the billions and government budgets are measured in trillions, politics is a high stakes endeavor. Not surprisingly, then, each word used is measured very carefully in an attempt to elicit desired responses from the public. Take for example the term "Massachusetts Liberal" that was used against presidential candidate John Kerry in the 2004 campaign for the White House. During the presidential race the Bush campaign regularly added a Massachusetts qualifier to the time honored liberal label. A good example of the use of this label is a quote by Bush campaign manager Ken Mellman, who, in regard to John Kerry's nomination, stated, "America doesn't need a Massachusetts liberal today." Why would Mellman feel the need to use Massachusetts in this context? The answer is found in the desired effect that he seeks to elicit from voters.

20   Massachusetts is home to a number of prominent politicians such as Senator Ted Kennedy and Representative Barney Frank who have been outspoken proponents of policies that are considered both liberal and contentious. Among these polices are equal rights for homosexuals and preferential treatment for minority individuals in the areas

of education and employment. Furthermore, in a well publicized 2003 decision the Massachusetts Supreme Court ruled to allow gay and lesbian couples to legally marry. With a history of controversial officials and legal precedents, the term *Massachusetts* carried with it a degree of political baggage. By applying the term to John Kerry, Mellman and the rest of the Bush campaign were hoping to attach the polarizing aspects of Massachusetts politics to their Democratic opponent, even if Kerry himself did not support the positions that were synonymous with his home state. Given the number of times that this label was used, we can be confident that at least the Bush campaign thought the label was scoring political points for the conservatives.

Sometimes a politician gives himself or herself a label as part of a broader goal of shaping public perceptions. Such was the case with George W. Bush's self-identification as a "compassionate conservative." While long referring to himself as a conservative, Bush began adding the term compassionate as he began to pursue the White House in the late 1990s. What was the reason for including this new term with the time honored conservative moniker? It seems to me that Bush is using compassionate as a qualifier for conservative. The term conservative, while generally regarded more positively than liberal, has been associated with a cold-heartedness in the past. Conservatives in their zest to keep government out of the public's business were accused of neglecting the needs of the poor and minorities, and being out of touch with the struggles facing the common person. Thus, in packaging himself as a viable presidential candidate, Bush and his handlers sought to qualify conservative with a term that displayed caring and understanding for all Americans.

But what are we to do with labels that are applied by politicians themselves? Just as you probably would question the validity of someone at your college who gave himself his own nickname, you should always question the names that politicians give themselves. When a guy calls himself "Romeo" or "Stud," you would probably think twice before accepting the accuracy of the tag. So, shouldn't you think twice when you come across the "compassionate conservatives" and "new Democrats" of the world?

4. Does the Label Hold Up to Facts?

Another thing to think about regarding labels is their ability to measure reality. Earlier I discussed some of the general tenets of conservatives and liberals in the United States. For example, liberals are generally considered to favor government activity to level the playing field in society. Therefore such policies as affirmative action and a high minimum wage are often thought of as core liberal beliefs. If one's overall ideological stance guides his or her positions on particular issues, we might reasonably expect an individual who self-identifies as a "liberal" to support government policies that are consistent with an active government approach. These expectations can actually be tested fairly easily by looking at public opinion data from surveys of the American public. By asking individuals to state their opinion on key issues that are indicative of broader political philosophies such as liberalism and conservatism, it's possible to measure how consistent their beliefs may be. For example, let's look at the relationship between what label you use to identify your political beliefs and your views on a number of specific political issues. Start by answering the question in Box 23.1.

BOX 23.1 Which of the following best describes your overall political beliefs?

Very Liberal
Somewhat Liberal
Moderate
Somewhat Conservative
Very Conservative

Next, take the survey in Box 23.2 regarding key issues in contemporary American politics. Mark the box that best describes your position on each of the statements that is given.

BOX 23.2 Survey of Political Attitudes

Statement	Agree	Disagree
The practice of abortion should be made illegal.	☐	☐
Prayer should be allowed in public schools.	☐	☐
Burning the American flag should be made illegal.	☐	☐
There should be a national law prohibiting marriage between members of the same sex.	☐	☐
Citizens should be allowed to own assault weapons.	☐	☐
The 10 Commandments should be allowed to be displayed in government buildings.	☐	☐
Affirmative Action policies should be abolished in the United States.	☐	☐
The minimum wage should not be increased.	☐	☐

25   Now, add up the total number of times that you agreed with the statements given. Each check mark in the "agree" column signifies that you support a position that is generally perceived as conservative in the United States. Thus, if you

identified yourself as very conservative and agreed with 8 out of 8 statements presented, your policy positions appear consistent with your self-identified political ideology. However, if you call yourself very conservative and only agree with a few of the statements presented, there appears to be a disconnect between your perception of your ideological standing and the issue positions that define one as conservative. Similarly, if you agreed with most of the statements presented, and call yourself a liberal, then the label might be misplaced.

While the previous exercise may have demonstrated an inconsistency between the label you used to describe yourself and your beliefs on specific issues, many surveys have found that the American public as a whole demonstrates similar inconsistencies. For example, each year I survey hundreds of students at Muhlenberg College to see if the labels they use to describe themselves are consistent with their positions on particular issues. What I have regularly found is that while our self-identified ideological labels may paint a generally accurate picture of our political views, these labels mask key inconsistencies that are common among individuals. In Box 23.3 the responses of self-identified conservative students to the policy questions are presented.

As can be seen in Box 23.3, there is by no means consensus among self-identified conservatives regarding the array of issues that were presented to them. While all of the positions presented in the table are considered conservative viewpoints, many of those students who view themselves as conservative disagree with the conservative stances. For example, the issue of same sex marriage in the United States has been seen as divisive between liberals and conservatives, with conservative Americans supporting bans on marriages between individuals of the same sex. In our surveys we find that while about 2 out of 3 conservatives support a ban on same sex marriage, 1 out of 3 oppose such action. Similarly, while allowing prayer in public schools is seen as a conservative position, about 4 in 10 self-identified conservatives in our surveys oppose such policies.

Clearly, the conservative and liberal labels that are so commonly used in the United States often mask important details about the individuals that the labels are applied to. Public opinion researchers have recognized the inconsistencies that are associated with broad labels, and have thus tried to come up with labels that capture patterns. Labels such as "Reagan Democrat," "Christian Conservative," "Limousine Liberal," and "Country Club Republican," are used to describe individuals who share some of the characteristics of the core label (e.g., conservative, liberal) but differ on other key factors. For example, the term "Country Club Republican" is commonly used to describe individuals who vote Republican because of the party's pro-business and anti-tax positions, yet oppose the party's increasing emphasis on socially conservative issues such as banning abortion or restricting same-sex marriage. In contrast, the label "Christian Conservative" is used to describe individuals whose major goal is for government to intervene in social matters to preserve traditional values (e.g., marriage between a man and a woman). While both "Country Club Republicans" and "Christian Conservatives" would likely identify themselves as conservative when asked in a survey question such as the example from Box 23.1, they by no means share identical ideological perspectives.

BOX 23.3 Policy Positions of Self-Identified Conservative Students

Statement	Agree	Disagree
The practice of abortion should be made illegal.	43%	57%
Prayer should be allowed in public schools.	63%	37%
Burning the American flag should be made illegal.	77%	23%
There should be a national law prohibiting marriage between members of the same sex.	62%	38%
Citizens should be allowed to own assault weapons.	23%	77%
The 10 Commandments should be allowed to be displayed in government buildings.	60%	40%
Affirmative Action policies should be abolished in the United States.	79%	21%
The minimum wage should not be increased.	24%	76%

Survey results drawn from surveys of Muhlenberg College students conducted between 2002 and 2005. Survey conducted by the Muhlenberg College Institute of Public Opinion. The respondents were drawn randomly from the student body and completed the survey via telephone. Sample sizes ranged from 350 to 400 respondents.

5. An Alternative Vocabulary of Ideology

Finally, while labels such as liberal and conservative can be used by political figures to elicit desired reactions from the public, there are other terms to look for when reading literature related to political affairs. There are times when a commentator, speechwriter, or politician does not want to use labels such as liberal or conservative for fear of losing credibility with the general public. Thus, it becomes useful to adopt a language that captures ideological leanings without sounding partisan. For example, if the term *liberal* has indeed taken on a negative connotation for many Americans, it becomes necessary for advocates of liberal policies to adopt other terms in an attempt to persuade the public. Similarly, while politicians don't run from the term *conservative* like they run from the liberal moniker, there are times when it's better to avoid explicit use of any politically charged label.

30   Without using terms that are considered too partisan or controversial, how can individuals still make arguments that rest on strong ideological beliefs? The answer lies in an alternate vocabulary that helps to transmit ideological beliefs without the

partisan baggage. This vocabulary includes terms that capture elements of partisanship without sounding overly divisive, and are thus attractive forms of language for those engaging in political persuasion.

Political language guru Frank Luntz, whom you will read about later in this unit of the book, has regularly advised his Republican clients to avoid words that may sound overtly partisan, and instead embrace language that resonates as more neutral. By no means are Luntz and other political linguists advocating that political figures should abandon partisan positions, but simply that they embrace language that most effectively shapes public perceptions in a way that helps them advance their agenda in a more effective way.

Not only is the choice of words important in shaping public opinion, but also the number of times the words are used. You may have heard the expression, "if you say something enough times, people will start to believe it." For political consultants this adage is a guiding principle that permeates their communication strategies. Repetition of key words is seen as essential to conveying a message that people will remember. This repetition is commonly referred to as staying "on message." Political party leaders regularly encourage their members to uniformly employ language that is considered effective in shaping public perceptions. One of the most prominent examples of staying on message is the use of the term "war on terror." When President Bush was making his case for going to war in Iraq, he framed the military campaign as part of a broader war on terror. While Saddam Hussein and the Iraqi regime had clearly committed atrocities during its tenure, there was no compelling evidence that Iraq had any substantial role in the attacks of 9/11. Nevertheless, in almost every speech where he discussed the invasion of Iraq, the president included the military endeavor as part of the war on terror, often mentioning 9/11 and Saddam Hussein in the same sentence. While never going so far as pinning the attacks directly on the Iraqi dictator, the linguistic connection of the terrorist threat with Iraq helped reinforce the impression that the two were linked. It appears from looking at public opinion polls conducted as the invasion began in 2003 that the White House's framing strategy had paid dividends, with almost half of the American population indicating a belief that Hussein was "personally involved" in the attacks of September 11, 2001. Once again, if you say something enough times, people will believe it.

As with the selection of "war on terror," many other words are regularly employed to achieve partisan ends through less overtly partisan language. Box 23.4 includes a selection of terms that are commonly used by individuals to make ideological arguments. These terms are directly related to the underlying roots of liberalism and conservatism, but may be perceived as more politically neutral. For example, the word *ownership* has become popular in many speeches and articles from self-described conservatives, often in the form of a call to create an "ownership society." The principle of ownership usually resonates among Americans who have come to strive for the day when they can buy that first new car or house. The idea of owning a piece of property can hardly be viewed as a highly ideological or partisan notion when an overwhelming majority of Americans make such action a life goal. The safety of the word helps explain why it has been regularly employed in debates on one of the most controversial topics of the day—Social Security reform. When President Bush advocates allowing Americans to invest part of their Social Security savings in

BOX 23.4 Vocabulary of Contemporary Ideological Positions

Conservative	Liberal
Individualism	Community
Ownership	Equality
Traditional	Progressive
Free Market	Social Justice
Property Rights	Human Rights

individual retirement accounts, he claims his plan is part of the broader "ownership society" that benefits all Americans. The safety and acceptance of the ownership concept helps him to sell an idea that regularly draws high levels of concern and suspicion from a public that has become very attached to Social Security as a key source of retirement income.

Conclusion

As I noted earlier in this article, labels permeate the political discourse in the United States. It has not been my intent to have you believe that labels are necessarily a negative part of politics, but to empower you to better control the effects of labels on your own thoughts about politics and government. I have tried to provide you with a list of things to consider when you are confronted with a political label that can be applied when you are listening to a speech, watching the news or reading an editorial in a newspaper. It is through the process of evaluating political language that you can limit the control that politicians and consultants believe they have over the political discourse in the nation. When Frank Luntz says that most of politics is about emotion he assumes a public that does not reflect upon political language, but instead one that simply responds to feelings. While I don't disagree with his appraisal, I take great offense at the arrogance that it demonstrates. Luntz is practically flaunting the fact that he can consistently trick the public into reacting in ways that he desires by simply changing language to induce emotional rather than reasoned reactions.

35   Luntz assumes a laziness in the electorate that is indeed all too present. However, the control that he wields is very tenuous. By simply looking more closely at political labels, you and your counterparts can diminish the control that Luntz and other language gurus claim over the public. Remember the fate of another character who claimed that he could make words mean just what he wanted to. The arrogant Humpty Dumpty met his end during a fateful fall, with all the king's horses and all the king's men unable to put him together again. A more careful and thoughtful consideration of political language may crack the control that today's masters of the word believe they have.

Things to Do with the Reading

1. Using Borick's discussion of the questionnaires in paragraphs 26–29 as a model, write a short essay in which you interpret the results of your own answers to the questionnaires in Boxes 23.1 and 23.2. Where (if at all) does your self-identification (on the continuum from "Very Liberal" to "Very Conservative" in Box 23.1) diverge from your stance on political attitudes, as ascertained by Box 23.2? How (if at all) do you account for these divergences? How do you "fit" relative to the statistical profile offered in Box 23.3?

2. One source of possible confusion for most people about the terms "liberal," "conservative," and "libertarian" is that each political orientation seems to cherish individual rights, but each defines these rights differently and has different ideas about how these can best be guaranteed. Write a short essay in which you summarize how each group, according to Borick, thinks about the concept of individual rights. Explain as well how they differ from one another. (See Chapter 7 on Summary and on Comparing and Contrasting.)

3. "On Political Labels" seeks to sensitize you to the keywords used by different political orientations (conservative, libertarian, and liberal) by seeing them in historical context. Consider the following list of terms. What would a conservative think of each term? What would a liberal think? What would a libertarian think? Why?

   Level playing field

   National security

   Negative rights

   Property rights

   Write up the results of your thinking in a short essay.

4. Look at the quote from the 2004 United States Libertarian Party platform in paragraph 13 of the essay. Write a short essay in which you ponder how this philosophy might play out (in both theory and practice) if one property owner chooses to erect a fast food restaurant on his or her land next to the property of another individual who wants to preserve quiet, clean air, and privacy.

5. **Link Across Chapters:** Once you have become comfortable with the essay's terminology, use "On Political Labels" as a tool for indexing the political orientation of any other chapter in this book. Compose an essay in which you arrange the writers that you have read in that chapter from most conservative to most liberal, briefly citing the telltale sentences and word choice that allow you to make this kind of discrimination. The chapter on race might be a good place to start. (Consider Salins versus Rodriguez.) The public versus private language in the chapters on Manners and on Places and Spaces could also yield interesting political analysis.

6. **Application:** Use Borick's essay as a lens for analyzing news articles and editorials on matters such as social security, the war in Afghanistan, tax cuts, and healthcare reform. See especially Box 23.4 on the Vocabulary of Contemporary Ideological Positions. *Resist the urge to take a position on any of these issues.* Instead, locate the key terms in your article or editorial that reveal political orientation and explain what they reveal. Once you have "decoded" your chosen piece, write an essay in which you explain what makes it essentially liberal or conservative or libertarian (or some combination of these) in its orientation.

FIVE EDITORIALS

Robert J. Fisher, "In Election, U.S. Should Not Return to 'Rugged Individualism'"

James J. Kirkpatrick, "Justices Amended Constitution on Their Own…"

Richard A. Epstein, "… By Letting Redevelopers Take Little Guy's Property"

John F. Grim, "More than Abortion Is at Stake in Supreme Court Picks"

Paul Krugman, "Losing Our Country"

> What follows are five newspaper editorials to which you can apply Borick's essay on political labels. In effect, you will be trying to decode their politics by using his lexicon.
> The first editorial locates competing attitudes to the American ideal of rugged individualism as a way of understanding contemporary political arguments. The next three editorials concern Supreme Court decisions and the makeup of the Court. The final editorial is a *New York Times* opinion piece on the status of the middle class in early twenty first-century America.

Note: The editorials refer to two eras in twentieth-century America—the New Deal, which was President Franklin Roosevelt's response to the Depression of the 1930s, and the Robber Baron era—a reference to the pre-taxation open market years early in the twentieth century when there were few limits on the methods industrial entrepreneurs could use to amass wealth.

Robert J. Fisher

In Election, U.S. Should Not Return to "Rugged Individualism"

In 1890, the Census Bureau declared that any region in the United States could no 1 longer be classified as a frontier—a region where population density was less than one person per square mile. In 1893, noted historian Frederick Jackson Turner theorized that the passing of the frontier was a defining turning point in American history.

The Turner thesis stated, "Individualism struck its frontier when the pioneer struck his." In other words, economic individualism could only exist with an unlimited supply of free land and natural resources. Turner theorized Americans would have to begin to seek collective and cooperative solutions to economic challenges.

In the 25 years after 1893, the United States experienced two significant periods of economic reform. In a rare nonpartisan effort, three Republican and two Democratic administrations gradually established regulatory controls over railroads, pipelines, communications, environmentally sensitive areas, banking, and the food and drug industries. Establishment of the Federal Trade Commission gave the government controls over business practices in general and institutionalized the nascent antitrust movement.

Robert J. Fisher, "In Election, US Should Not Return to 'Rugged Individualism'," The Morning Call, Oct. 14, 2010. Used by permission.

5   The adoption of the 16th Amendment deliberately legalized the concept of "ability to pay" with respect to taxation. In essence, the government recognized the validity of the Turner thesis by establishing a neo-socialistic economic system for the United States.

Americans have never been comfortable with the decline of individualism. Romanticism of frontier life, today referred to as the "cowboy mentality," has remained an increasingly elusive ideal in American culture while socialism is regarded as a negative and otherworldly concept.

In the 1920s, three Republican presidents, Harding, Coolidge and Hoover, governed under a masculine mantra of "rugged individualism," which included tax cuts, deregulation and isolationist tariff policies.

After the stock market crash of 1929, President Hoover reduced government spending, rejected welfare relief and balanced the budget. The results were catastrophic as unemployment reached 25 percent and homelessness and malnutrition became commonplace. Historians have estimated that as many as 1 million Americans may have died as a result of the Great Depression.

In the 1932 election, Franklin D. Roosevelt ousted Hoover and established the New Deal, which cemented the neo-socialistic economy in place.

Unions were legalized in a deliberate attempt to redistribute income. Banking and stock market regulations were strengthened. The New Deal created Social Security and unemployment insurance and mandated wage and hours standards. Massive deficit spending and a system of "war socialism" during World War II finally ended the Depression and eroded any lingering support for "rugged individualism."

10   In the post-war era, the U.S. economy experienced generally mild recessions alternating with impressive prosperity, particularly in the 1950s and 1990s. The neo-socialistic system matured with the enactment of Medicare/Medicaid, the Environmental Protection Agency, Occupational Safety and Health Administration, the War on Poverty and, most recently, health insurance reform.

Periodically, however, conservative extremists attempted to resurrect "rugged individualism" and castigate neo-socialism as unworkable and even unpatriotic. They seek a return to laissez-faire capitalism whose limitations and failures inspired neo-socialism in the first place.

In the 1980s, "Reaganomics" included a massive tax cut, mainly for upper-income Americans, and deregulation of banking and Wall Street.

This country now has a declining middle class and the largest wage gap in the developed world. The poverty level has risen from 10 percent to 14 percent; more than 45 million Americans lack basic health insurance. Finally, in 2008, the second most serious recession/depression in American history resulted in the current economic crisis.

In 2008, voters enthusiastically elected Barack Obama, an obviously progressive president, presumably to undo damages caused, in part, by the latest flirtation with the ongoing fantasy of "rugged individualism."

15   Now, only two years later, conservative Republicans, pressured by the tea party fringe element, are attempting to convince voters that 125 years of neo-socialism can be reversed.

What exactly is there in the economic record of the last 30 years that suggests this would be desirable or even feasible? One can only imagine what life would be like in the current recession without Social Security, Medicare, unemployment compensation and stimulus spending. America cannot afford another 30 years of naive, wishful thinking about frontier individualism.

The only real choice is to accept the inevitability of the existing economic system and to work constructively to solve problems and make needed improvements.

James J. Kirkpatrick
Justices Amended Constitution on Their Own …

The Supreme Court ended its current term on Monday with more of a whimper than   1
a bang. In the Ten Commandments cases, the justices further muddied the muddy waters of the First Amendment. In a Colorado case, they found no way to compensate a victim of grossly incompetent cops. They refused even to hear the appeal of two reporters who face prison for doing their job. Then they doffed their robes and departed for the summer.

One is reminded of Oliver Cromwell's farewell to the Rump Parliament of 1653: "You have sat too long for any good you have done. Let us have done with you! In the name of God, go!"

The most regrettable decision of a regrettable term came a week ago, in the eminent domain case of *Kelo v. City of New London*. Speaking through Justice John Paul Stevens, the court applied the law according to Humpty Dumpty. To that eminent jurist, words meant only what he chose them to mean, and neither more nor less. Until last week, the words "public use" meant "public use." Now they mean "public purpose or private benefit."

To be sure, this was not the first time the court has effectively amended the Constitution by judicial interpretation. The subtle process dates from the days of John Marshall. Only a few weeks ago the court rewrote the 21st Amendment in order to nullify the liquor laws of Michigan and New York. Last week's plastic surgery on the Fifth was surgery at a more critical level.

Every sixth-grader can identify a public "use." The indispensable power of eminent   5
domain permits governments to build roads, establish parks, erect public buildings and establish public schools. These are *public uses*.

Nothing of the sort was at the heart of last week's decision. The city now may proceed to seize the unoffending home of Susette Kelo, smash it to bits, haul away the debris, and sell the vacant land to the highest bidder. A few doors away, the redevelopers will evict Wilhelmina Dery from the home she has occupied for more than 80 years.

Will the owners receive "just compensation"? Of course, but for Kelo and other owners, the modifying "just" mocks the noun. Their property will not be put to a "public use." It will pass unjustly to private developers. If all goes well, the developers can go to their banks with a bundle. Ms. Kelo and her neighbors can go to—they can go to some other neighborhood, somewhere else.

"Justices amended Constitution on their own…," James J. Kilpatrick, The Morning Call, July 6, 2005. Used by permission.

In his majority opinion for the court, Justice John Paul Stevens smiled upon the city's rose-petaled justification. The city has been slowly losing jobs and population. What to do? Get rid of the owners! Then land could be cleared for the Pfizer corporation to build a $300 million research facility. The city fathers licked their chops. Their eyes rolled around like Mr. Toad's when he saw the motorcar. They saw classy restaurants, retail stores, a marina! There would be 80 new residences, none of which Susette Kelo could afford. What a deal!

To Stevens and his four colleagues, the "narrow view" that "use" means "use" is a view that has steadily eroded over time. A literal interpretation has proved to be "impractical" and "difficult to administer." Mrs. Kelo's eviction must be viewed "in light of the entire plan." This plan "unquestionably serves a public purpose, and the takings satisfy the public use requirement of the Fifth Amendment."

10   Justice Sandra Day O'Connor filed a powerful dissent: "Today the court abandons a long-held, basic limitation on government power. Under the banner of economic development, all private property is now vulnerable to being taken and transferred to another private owner, so long as it might be upgraded—i.e., given to an owner who will use it in a way that the legislature deems more beneficial to the public."

She asked rhetorically: "Are economic development takings constitutional?" She answered without equivocation: "I would hold that they are not."

In a separate dissenting opinion, Justice Clarence Thomas agreed with O'Connor: "If 'economic development' takings are for a 'public use,' any taking is, and the court has erased the Public Use Clause from our Constitution. ... Once one permits takings for public *purposes* in addition to public *uses,* no coherent principle limits what could constitute a valid public use ... "

So ends the court's term. It should have ended when it began nine months ago.

Richard A. Epstein

... By Letting Redevelopers Take Little Guy's Property

1   The dreadful decision of the U.S. Supreme Court in *Kelo v. City of New London* recently held that New London, Conn., could take the homes of ordinary citizens in the name of urban planning. It didn't seem to matter to the five-member majority that the city's porous redevelopment plan did not evince any intelligible purpose, let alone the public use that the Constitution requires.

The good news in the aftermath of *Kelo* is that it has forced people, especially on the political left, to rethink their views on the place of private property. Ever since the decisive and wrongheaded New Deal decisions in the mid-1930s, the Supreme Court has by and large held that the constitutional protections of private property should be read weakly so as to allow governments to act in ways that advance some notion of the common or public good. The underlying liberal vision was that private property was the instrument of individuals of privilege and power, which had to be cut down to size by an alert legislature that had the interests of the little man at heart. The liberal justices on the Supreme Court have accordingly done everything to give their blessing to local land use condemnation and regulation.

"... by letting redevelopers take little guy's property," Richard A. Epstein, The Morning Call, July 6, 2005. Reprinted with permission of the author.

Kelo shows the utter fatuity in that position. There is of course every reason to believe that people with great wealth will use their power and influence to turn legislative decisions in their direction. But it hardly follows that private property is the villain of the piece. In many cases, the system of strong property rights works to protect people of limited wealth from the machinations of others. This defensive use of private property was evident to such philosophers as John Locke and such economists as Adam Smith. It impressed itself on this nation's Founders, who understood the risk that political factions put to the stability of our social order.

Here is one telltale sign of the massive amounts of political favoritism in *Kelo*. One common argument in favor of a broad use of the eminent domain power is that it is necessary to allow developers to assemble large parcels of land for major developments. But in *Kelo* the New London planners were quite happy to slate private homes for destruction while allowing the Italian Dramatic Club (a watering hole for local politicians) to remain untouched, even though it abutted one of the private homes that was taken.

Last year, the Michigan Supreme Court held that its state constitution blocked 5 the use of the eminent domain power for so-called economic development. Other states are now falling into line. With a little bit of hard work, the instinctive revulsion toward the *Kelo* decision could lead to a groundswell of public action. But whatever the future brings, remember that the four dissenters—Rehnquist, O'Connor, Scalia and Thomas—all so-called conservatives, were the defenders of the Constitution and the little man.

John F. Grim

More than Abortion Is at Stake in Supreme Court Picks

Far-right Republicans were incensed that 14 U.S. senators brokered a deal to avoid 1 the "nuclear option" to bar a filibuster on judicial nominations, news reports said. And a Republican activist wrote an op-ed column on June 18 that said 14 "centrist" senators may hold the key to confirming Supreme Court nominees who would overturn *Roe v. Wade.*

Again, the foes of a woman's right to choose show tunnel vision, because a court with just one or two more members who share the aggressive and ideologically extreme philosophy of Justices Antonin Scalia and Clarence Thomas could overturn not only *Roe v. Wade* but also more than 100 high court precedents protecting civil rights, privacy and reproductive choice, the environment, worker rights, consumer rights, religious liberty and much more.

"Courting Disaster 2005," a report by the liberal People for the American Way Foundation, documents how President Bush has picked lawyers and judges who favor a pre-New Deal approach to the Constitution: An era when property rights and states rights were given greater weight than protecting individual rights, and when the courts forbade Congress to address urgent issues of poverty and health care.

Examining the concurring and sometimes angry dissenting opinions of Scalia and Thomas, the report (www.pfaw.org) lists decisions that could be overturned by

"More Than Abortion Is at Stake in Supreme Court Picks," John F. Grim, The Morning Call, July 27, 2005. Reprinted with permission of the author.

more justices with the same philosophy. Some of those cases, their dates and what a reversal would do are:

5   *Ferguson v. Charleston* (2001): Hospitals would be allowed to test pregnant women without their knowledge and consent for drug use and give results to police.

Hill v. Colorado (2000): States would be forbidden to pass laws to protect people approaching health care facilities from harassment.

City of Indianapolis v. Edmond (2000): Police would be free to set up roadblocks and randomly stop motorists to look for drugs.

Lawrence v. Texas (2003): Criminal prosecution of private sexual conduct by consenting adults would be allowed.

Grutter v. Bollinger (2003): Affirmative action in higher education would be forbidden.

10   *Jackson v. Birmingham Bd. of Educ.* (2005): Retaliation against those who complain about illegal sex discrimination in education under federal law would be allowed.

Johnson v. Transportation Agency (1987): Affirmative action for women under Title VII of the 1964 Civil Rights Act would be eliminated.

J.E.B. v. Alabama (1994): Sex discrimination in jury selection would be allowed.

Olmstead v. L.C. (1999): Improper and unnecessary institutionalization of disabled persons would no longer violate the Americans With Disabilities Act.

Hibbs v. Winn (2004): Federal courts would be forbidden to decide challenges to discriminatory and unconstitutional state tax laws.

15   *Zadvydas v. Davis* (2001): The government would be allowed to keep an immigrant who is under a final order of removal in jail indefinitely, even though no other country will accept that person.

Rasul v. Bush (2004): It would be impossible to challenge the indefinite imprisonment of foreign nationals on U.S. territory in Guantanamo, even if they contend they have been tortured or are not combatants.

Chavez v. Martinez (2003) and *Hope v. Pelzer* (2002): The ability to sue law enforcement officials for violating constitutional rights would be severely limited.

Lee v. Weisman (1992) and *Santa Fe Independent School Dist. v. Doe* (2000): True government neutrality toward religion would be eliminated, and government-sponsored prayer at graduation and at other public school events would be allowed.

Kiryas Joel Village School District v. Grumet (1994): School district lines could be drawn to permit one religious sect to predominate.

20   *Rutan v. Republican Party of Illinois* (1990): Government employees could be fired for belonging to the wrong political party.

Alaska Department of Conservation v. EPA (2004): EPA would be stripped of the authority to prevent damaging air pollution by industries when state agencies improperly fail to do so.

Americans deserve high court justices who are fair to all sides, who guard against abuses of power by the executive and legislative branches, and who protect our rights and liberties. Returning the nation to the early 20th century and the days of the robber barons is an exorbitant price to pay to satisfy people who were characterized by U.S. Rep. Barney Frank on the House floor as believing life begins at conception and ends at birth.

Paul Krugman
Losing Our Country

Baby boomers like me grew up in a relatively equal society. In the 1960s America was   1
a place in which very few people were extremely wealthy, many blue-collar workers
earned wages that placed them comfortably in the middle class, and working families
could expect steadily rising living standards and a reasonable degree of economic
security.

But as *The Times*'s series on class in America reminds us, that was another country. The middle-class society I grew up in no longer exists.

Working families have seen little if any progress over the past 30 years. Adjusted
for inflation, the income of the median family doubled between 1947 and 1973. But it
rose only 22 percent from 1973 to 2003, and much of that gain was the result of wives'
entering the paid labor force or working longer hours, not rising wages.

Meanwhile, economic security is a thing of the past: year-to-year fluctuations in
the incomes of working families are far larger than they were a generation ago. All it
takes is a bit of bad luck in employment or health to plunge a family that seems solidly
middle-class into poverty.

But the wealthy have done very well indeed. Since 1973 the average income of the top   5
1 percent of Americans has doubled, and the income of the top 0.1 percent has tripled.

Why is this happening? I'll have more to say on that another day, but for now let
me just point out that middle-class America didn't emerge by accident. It was created
by what has been called the Great Compression of incomes that took place during
World War II, and sustained for a generation by social norms that favored equality,
strong labor unions and progressive taxation. Since the 1970s, all of those sustaining
forces have lost their power.

Since 1980 in particular, U.S. government policies have consistently favored the
wealthy at the expense of working families—and under the current administration,
that favoritism has become extreme and relentless. From tax cuts that favor the rich to
bankruptcy "reform" that punishes the unlucky, almost every domestic policy seems
intended to accelerate our march back to the robber baron era.

It's not a pretty picture—which is why right-wing partisans try so hard to discredit
anyone who tries to explain to the public what's going on.

These partisans rely in part on obfuscation: shaping, slicing and selectively presenting data in an attempt to mislead. For example, it's a plain fact that the Bush tax
cuts heavily favor the rich, especially those who derive most of their income from
inherited wealth. Yet this year's *Economic Report of the President*, in a bravura demonstration of how to lie with statistics, claimed that the cuts "increased the overall
progressivity of the federal tax system."

The partisans also rely in part on scare tactics, insisting that any attempt to limit   10
inequality would undermine economic incentives and reduce all of us to shared misery. That claim ignores the fact of U.S. economic success after World War II. It also
ignores the lesson we should have learned from recent corporate scandals: Sometimes

From The New York Times, June 10 © 2005 The New York Times. All rights reserved. Used by permission
and protected by the Copyright Laws of the United States. The printing, copying, redistribution, or
retransmission of this Content without express written permission is prohibited.

the prospect of great wealth for those who succeed provides an incentive not for high performance, but for fraud.

Above all, the partisans engage in name-calling. To suggest that sustaining programs like Social Security, which protects working Americans from economic risk, should have priority over tax cuts for the rich is to practice "class warfare." To show concern over the growing inequality is to engage in the "politics of envy."

But the real reasons to worry about the explosion of inequality since the 1970s have nothing to do with envy. The fact is that working families aren't sharing in the economy's growth, and face growing economic insecurity. And there's good reason to believe that a society in which most people can reasonably be considered middle class is a better society—and more likely to be a functioning democracy—than one in which there are great extremes of wealth and poverty.

Reversing the rise in inequality and economic insecurity won't be easy: The middle-class society we have lost emerged only after the country was shaken by depression and war. But we can make a start by calling attention to the politicians who systematically make things worse in catering to their contributors. Never mind that straw man, the politics of envy. Let's try to do something about the politics of greed.

Things to Do with the Reading

1. **Link:** Write a paragraph on each editorial in which you use Borick's "On Political Labels" as a lens to identify the language—the key words and phrases—that most clearly enables readers to identify the given editorial as primarily liberal or conservative or libertarian. You may wish to review the discussion of uncovering assumptions in Chapter 4 to help you unearth the various premises that underlie each editorial.

2. Write a brief essay in which you explain how Fisher uses the word "neosocialist" in "In Election, U.S. Should Not Return to 'Rugged Individualism.'" This is an interesting word choice, because *socialist* has been used recently by politicians and the press in an almost entirely negative light. What positive spin does Fisher wish to put on the term, based on what historical precedents and rationale?

3. Throughout Fisher's editorial and in the title, the phrase "rugged individualism" is placed inside quotation marks. Why? What spin does the editorial take on the rights of individuals? Write a short essay in which you analyze how Fisher uses the word, in comparison with how Kilpatrick spins individualism in "Justices Amended Constitution on Their Own ..." Be sure to discuss what individual right the Kilpatrick editorial is defending, and on what grounds.

4. Use the reading strategy in Chapter 5 called finding "the pitch, the complaint, and the moment" to write an analysis of what Epstein is trying to accomplish in "... By Letting Redevelopers Take Little Guy's Property." Against which positions (the complaint) is he arguing? One of these is fairly explicit, but

another is handled more subtly. What potential attack on conservatives is the writer somewhat worried about, and how does he defend against it?

5. In "More than Abortion Is at Stake in Supreme Court Picks" John F. Grim reveals himself from the beginning as an opponent of what he calls "far-right Republicans." He then offers a list of relatively recent high court decisions that he claims could be reversed by a more decidedly Republican (conservative) Supreme Court. The reader is left to decide why a Republican court would make the decisions the writer says it would make. Do so in a short essay. Choose the three cases that you find most interesting, and using Borick's article as a lens, articulate for each legal decision the political philosophy that might cause conservative Supreme Court judges to rule in the way the writer fears. See uncovering assumptions in Chapter 4.

6. Paul Krugman's "Losing Our Country" is filled not only with the key words of the liberal political orientation but with some dire predictions about the direction in which the country is heading. Write a short essay in which you analyze the attacks the writer makes on the policies of the Bush administration and its Republican predecessors. How do these attacks reveal both the writer's liberal orientation and the conservative orientation of the Bush administration?

7. Krugman's editorial anticipates an issue that will occupy many of the subsequent readings in this chapter: the politics of spin, which Krugman attacks as "name-calling." He cites two phrases: "class warfare" and "the politics of envy." Write a brief essay in which you explore why he finds these labels not only objectionable but essentially inaccurate.

George Orwell

Politics and the English Language

The British writer George Orwell has left so emphatic a mark on modern thinking about politics and language that the adjective "Orwellian" has arisen to characterize forms of political oppression, especially those involving the manipulation of language. The dystopian vision of the future in his novel *1984* is probably the source of the adjective that bears his name, but in the influential essay "Politics and The English Language" (1946) Orwell first gives voice to the ominous tendency of modern public prose to obscure its aims.

1   Most people who bother with the matter at all would admit that the English language is in a bad way, but it is generally assumed that we cannot by conscious action do anything about it. Our civilization is decadent and our language—so the argument runs—must inevitably share in the general collapse. It follows that any struggle against the abuse of language is a sentimental archaism, like preferring candles to electric light or hansom cabs to aeroplanes. Underneath this lies the half-conscious belief that language is a natural growth and not an instrument which we shape for our own purposes.

   Now, it is clear that the decline of a language must ultimately have political and economic causes: It is not due simply to the bad influence of this or that individual writer. But an effect can become a cause, reinforcing the original cause and producing the same effect in an intensified form, and so on indefinitely. A man may take to drink because he feels himself to be a failure, and then fail all the more completely because he drinks. It is rather the same thing that is happening to the English language. It becomes ugly and inaccurate because our thoughts are foolish, but the slovenliness of our language makes it easier for us to have foolish thoughts. The point is that the process is reversible. Modern English, especially written English, is full of bad habits which spread by imitation and which can be avoided if one is willing to take the necessary trouble. If one gets rid of these habits one can think more clearly, and to think clearly is a necessary first step towards political regeneration: so that the fight against bad English is not frivolous and is not the exclusive concern of professional writers. I will come back to this presently, and I hope that by that time the meaning of what I have said here will have become clearer. Meanwhile, here are five specimens of the English language as it is now habitually written.

   These five passages have not been picked out because they are especially bad—I could have quoted far worse if I had chosen—but because they illustrate various of the mental vices from which we now suffer. They are a little below the average, but are fairly representative samples. I number them so that I can refer back to them when necessary:

> "(1) I am not, indeed, sure whether it is not true to say that the Milton who once seemed not unlike a seventeenth-century Shelley had not become, out of an experience ever more bitter in each year, more alien [*sic*] to the founder of that Jesuit sect which nothing could induce him to tolerate."
>
> Professor Harold Laski (Essay in *Freedom of Expression*)

"Politics and the English Language" by George Orwell. First published in Horizon, April 1946.

"(2) Above all, we cannot play ducks and drakes with a native battery of idioms which prescribes such egregious collocations of vocables as the Basic *put up with* for *tolerate* or *put at a loss* for *bewilder*."

Professor Lancelot Hogben (*Interglossa*)

"(3) On the one side we have the free personality: by definition it is not neurotic, for it has neither conflict nor dream. Its desires, such as they are, are transparent, for they are just what institutional approval keeps in the forefront of consciousness; another institutional pattern would alter their number and intensity; there is little in them that is natural, irreducible, or culturally dangerous. But *on the other* side, the social bond itself is nothing but the mutual reflection of these self-secure integrities. Recall the definition of love. Is not this the very picture of a small academic? Where is there a place in this hall of mirrors for either personality or fraternity?"

Essay on psychology in *Politics* (New York)

"(4) All the 'best people' from the gentlemen's clubs, and all the frantic fascist captains, united in common hatred of Socialism and bestial horror of the rising tide of the mass revolutionary movement, have turned to acts of provocation, to foul incendiarism, to medieval legends of poisoned wells, to legalize their own destruction of proletarian organizations, and rouse the agitated petty-bourgeoisie to chauvinistic fervour on behalf of the fight against the revolutionary way out of the crisis."

Communist pamphlet

"(5) If a new spirit *is* to be infused into this old country, there is one thorny and contentious reform which must be tackled, and that is the humanization and galvanization of the B.B.C. Timidity here will bespeak cancer and atrophy of the soul. The heart of Britain may be sound and of strong beat, for instance, but the British lion's roar at present is like that of Bottom in Shakespeare's *Midsummer Night's Dream*—as gentle as any sucking dove. A virile new Britain cannot continue indefinitely to be traduced in the eyes or rather ears, of the world by the effete languors of Langham Place, brazenly masquerading as 'standard English.' When the Voice of Britain is heard at nine o'clock, better far and infinitely less ludicrous to hear aitches honestly dropped than the present priggish, inflated, inhibited, school-ma'amish arch braying of blameless bashful mewing maidens!"

Letter in *Tribune*

Each of these passages has faults of its own, but, quite apart from avoidable ugliness, two qualities are common to all of them. The first is staleness of imagery: the other is lack of precision. The writer either has a meaning and cannot express it, or he inadvertently says something else, or he is almost indifferent as to whether his words mean anything or not. This mixture of vagueness and sheer incompetence is the most marked characteristic of modern English prose, and especially of any kind of political writing. As soon as certain topics are raised, the concrete melts into the abstract and no one seems able to think of turns of speech that are not hackneyed: prose consists less and less of *words* chosen for the sake of their meaning, and more and more of *phrases* tacked together like the sections of a prefabricated hen-house. I list below, with notes and examples, various of the tricks by means of which the work of prose-construction is habitually dodged:

Dying Metaphors

5   A newly invented metaphor assists thought by evoking a visual image, while on the other hand a metaphor which is technically "dead" (e.g., *iron resolution*) has in effect reverted to being an ordinary word and can generally be used without loss of vividness. But in between these two classes there is a huge dump of worn-out metaphors which have lost all evocative power and are merely used because they save people the trouble of inventing phrases for themselves. Examples are: *Ring the changes on, take up the cudgels for, toe the line, ride roughshod over, stand shoulder to shoulder with, play into the hands of, no axe to grind, grist to the mill, fishing in troubled waters, on the order of the day, Achilles' heel, swan song, hotbed.* Many of these are used without knowledge of their meaning (what is a "rift," for instance?), and incompatible metaphors are frequently mixed, a sure sign that the writer is not interested in what he is saying. Some metaphors now current have been twisted out of their original meaning without those who use them even being aware of the fact. For example, *toe the line* is sometimes written *tow the line*. Another example is *the hammer and the anvil,* now always used with the implication that the anvil gets the worst of it. In real life it is always the anvil that breaks the hammer, never the other way about: a writer who stopped to think what he was saying would be aware of this, and would avoid perverting the original phrase.

Operators or Verbal False Limbs

These save the trouble of picking out appropriate verbs and nouns, and at the same time pad each sentence with extra syllables which give it an appearance of symmetry. Characteristic phrases are: *render inoperative, militate against, make contact with, be subjected to, give rise to, give grounds for, have the effect of, play a leading part (role) in, make itself felt, take effect, exhibit a tendency to, serve the purpose of, etc., etc.* The keynote is the elimination of simple verbs. Instead of being a single word, such as *break, stop, spoil, mend, kill,* a verb becomes a *phrase,* made up of a noun or adjective tacked on to some general-purposes verb such as *prove, serve, form, play, render.* In addition, the passive voice is wherever possible used in preference to the active, and noun constructions are used instead of gerunds (*by examination of* instead of *by examining*). The range of verbs is further cut down by means of the *-ize* and *de-* formation, and the banal statements are given an appearance of profundity by means of the *not un-* formation. Simple conjunctions and prepositions are replaced by such phrases as *with respect to, having regard to, the fact that, by dint of, in view of, in the interests of, on the hypothesis that;* and the ends of sentences are saved from anticlimax by such resounding commonplaces as *greatly to be desired, cannot be left out of account, a development to be expected in the near future, deserving of serious consideration, brought to a satisfactory conclusion,* and so on and so forth.

Pretentious Diction

Words like *phenomenon, element, individual* (as noun), *objective, categorical, effective, virtual, basic, primary, promote, constitute, exhibit, exploit, utilize, eliminate, liquidate,* are used to dress up simple statements and give an air of scientific impartiality to biased judgments. Adjectives like *epoch-making, epic, historic, unforgettable, triumphant, age-old, inevitable, inexorable, veritable,* are used to dignify the sordid processes of international politics, while writing that aims at glorifying war usually takes on an archaic color, its characteristic words being: *realm, throne, chariot, mailed fist, trident, sword, shield, buckler, banner, jackboot, clarion.* Foreign words and expressions such as *cul de sac, ancien régime, deus ex machina, mutatis mutandis, status quo, gleichschaltung, weltanschauung,* are used to give an air of culture and elegance. Except for the useful abbreviations *i.e., e.g.,* and *etc.,* there is no real need for any of the hundreds of foreign phrases now current in English. Bad writers, and especially scientific, political and sociological writers, are nearly always haunted by the notion that Latin or Greek words are grander than Saxon ones, and unnecessary words like *expedite, ameliorate, predict, extraneous, deracinated, clandestine, subaqueous* and hundreds of others constantly gain ground from their Anglo-Saxon opposite numbers.[1] The jargon peculiar to Marxist writing (*hyena, hangman, cannibal, petty bourgeois, these gentry, lackey, flunky, mad dog, White Guard,* etc.) consists largely of words and phrases translated from Russian, German or French; but the normal way of coining a new word is to use a Latin or Greek root with the appropriate affix and, where necessary, the *-ize* formation. It is often easier to make up words of this kind (*deregionalize, impermissible, extra-marital, nonfragmentatory* and so forth) than to think up the English words that will cover one's meaning. The result, in general, is an increase in slovenliness and vagueness.

Meaningless Words

In certain kinds of writing, particularly in art criticism and literary criticism, it is normal to come across long passages which are almost completely lacking in meaning.[2] Words like *romantic, plastic, values, human, dead, sentimental, natural, vitality,* as used in art criticism, are strictly meaningless in the sense that they not only do not point to any discoverable object, but are hardly ever expected to do so by the reader. When one critic writes, "The outstanding feature of Mr. X's work is its living quality," while another writes, "The immediately striking thing about Mr. X's work is its peculiar deadness," the reader accepts this as a simple difference of opinion. If words like *black* and *white* were involved, instead of the jargon words *dead* and *living,* he would see at once that language was being used in an improper way. Many political words are similarly abused. The word *Fascism* has now no meaning except in so far as it signifies "something not desirable." The words *democracy, socialism, freedom, patriotic, realistic, justice,* have each of them several different meanings which cannot be reconciled with one another. In the case of a word like *democracy,* not only is there no agreed definition, but the attempt to make one is resisted from all sides. It is almost universally felt that when we call a country democratic we are praising it: consequently the defenders of every kind of régime claim that it is a democracy, and fear that they might have to stop using the word if it were tied down to any one meaning. Words of this kind are often used in a consciously dishonest way. That is, the person who uses them has his own private definition, but allows his hearer to think he means something quite different. Statements like *Marshal Pétain was a true patriot, The Soviet Press is the freest in the world, The Catholic Church is opposed to persecution,* are almost always made with intent to deceive. Other words used in variable meanings, in most cases more or less dishonestly, are: *class, totalitarian, science, progressive, reactionary, bourgeois, equality.*

Now that I have made this catalog of swindles and perversions, let me give another example of the kind of writing that they lead to. This time it must of its nature be an imaginary one. I am going to translate a passage of good English into modern English of the worst sort. Here is a well-known verse from *Ecclesiastes:*

> "I returned and saw under the sun, that the race is not to the swift, nor the battle to the strong, neither yet bread to the wise, nor yet riches to men of understanding, nor yet favor to men of skill; but time and chance happeneth to them all."

10   Here it is in modern English:

> "Objective consideration of contemporary phenomena compels the conclusion that success or failure in competitive activities exhibits no tendency to be commensurate with innate capacity, but that a considerable element of the unpredictable must invariably be taken into account."

This is a parody, but not a very gross one. Exhibit (3), above, for instance, contains several patches of the same kind of English. It will be seen that I have not made a full translation. The beginning and ending of the sentence follow the original meaning fairly closely, but in the middle the concrete illustrations—race, battle, bread—dissolve into the vague phrase "success or failure in competitive activities." This had to be so, because no modern writer of the kind I am discussing—no one capable of using phrases like "objective consideration of contemporary phenomena"—would ever tabulate his thoughts in that precise and detailed way. The whole tendency of modern prose is away from concreteness. Now analyse these two sentences a little more closely. The first contains forty-nine words but only sixty syllables, and all its words are those of everyday life. The second contains thirty-eight words of ninety syllables: eighteen of its words are from Latin roots, and one from Greek. The first sentence contains six vivid images, and only one phrase ("time and chance") that could be called vague. The second contains not a single fresh, arresting phrase, and in spite of its ninety syllables it gives only a shortened version of the meaning contained in the first. Yet without a doubt it is the second kind of sentence that is gaining ground in modern English. I do not want to exaggerate. This kind of writing is not yet universal, and outcrops of simplicity will occur here and there in the worst-written page. Still, if you or I were told to write a few lines on the uncertainty of human fortunes, we should probably come much nearer to my imaginary sentence than to the one from *Ecclesiastes*.

As I have tried to show, modern writing at its worst does not consist in picking out words for the sake of their meaning and inventing images in order to make the meaning clearer. It consists in gumming together long strips of words which have already been set in order by someone else, and making the results presentable by sheer humbug. The attraction of this way of writing is that it is easy. It is easier—even quicker, once you have the habit—to say *In my opinion it is a not unjustifiable assumption that* than to say *I think*. If you use ready made phrases, you not only don't have to hunt about for words; you also don't have to bother with the rhythms of your sentences, since these phrases are generally so arranged as to be more or less euphonious. When you are composing in a hurry—when you are dictating to a stenographer, for instance, or making a public speech—it is natural to fall into a pretentious, Latinized style. Tags like *a consideration which we should do well to bear in mind* or *a conclusion to which all of us would readily assent* will save many a sentence from coming down with a bump. By using stale metaphors, similes and idioms, you save much mental effort, at the cost of leaving your meaning vague, not only for your reader but for yourself. This is the significance of mixed metaphors. The sole aim of a metaphor is to call up a visual image. When these images clash—as in *The Fascist octopus has sung its swan song, the jackboot is thrown into the melting pot*—it can be taken as certain that the writer is not seeing a mental image of the objects he is naming; in other words he is not really thinking. Look again at the examples I gave at the beginning of this essay. Professor Laski (1) uses five negatives in fifty-three words. One of these is superfluous, making nonsense of the whole passage, and in addition there is the slip *alien* for akin, making further nonsense, and several avoidable pieces of clumsiness which increase the general vagueness. Professor Hogben (2) plays ducks and drakes with a battery which is able to write prescriptions, and, while disapproving of the everyday phrase *put up with*, is unwilling to look *egregious* up in the dictionary and see what it means. (3), if one takes an uncharitable attitude towards it, is simply meaningless: probably one could work out its intended meaning by reading the whole of the article in which it occurs. In (4), the writer knows more or less what he wants to say, but an accumulation of stale phrases chokes him like tea leaves blocking a sink. In (5), words and meaning have almost parted company. People who write in this manner usually have a general emotional meaning—they dislike one thing and want to express solidarity with another—but they are not interested in the detail of what they are saying. A scrupulous writer, in every sentence that he writes, will ask himself at least four questions, thus: What am I trying to say? What words will express it? What image or idiom will make it clearer? Is this image fresh enough to have an effect? And he will probably ask himself two more: Could I put it more shortly? Have I said anything that is avoidably ugly? But you are not obliged to go to all this trouble. You can shirk it by simply throwing your mind open and letting the ready-made phrases come crowding in. They will construct your sentences for you—even think your thoughts for you, to a certain extent—and at need they will perform the important service of partially concealing your meaning even from yourself. It is at this point that the special connection between politics and the debasement of language becomes clear.

In our time it is broadly true that political writing is bad writing. Where it is not true, it will generally be found that the writer is some kind of rebel, expressing his private opinions and not a "party line." Orthodoxy, of whatever color, seems to demand a lifeless, imitative style. The political dialects to be found in pamphlets, leading articles, manifestos, White Papers and the speeches of under-secretaries do, of course, vary from party to party, but they are all alike in that one almost never finds in them a fresh, vivid, home-made turn of speech. When one watches some tired hack on the platform mechanically repeating the familiar phrases—*bestial atrocities, iron heel, bloodstained tyranny, free peoples of the world, stand shoulder to shoulder*—one often has a curious feeling that one is not watching a live human being but some kind of dummy: a feeling which suddenly becomes stronger at moments when the light catches the speaker's spectacles and turns them into blank discs which seem to have no eyes behind them. And this is not altogether fanciful. A speaker who uses that kind of phraseology has gone some distance towards turning himself into a machine. The appropriate noises are coming out of his larynx, but his brain is not involved as it would be if he were choosing his words for himself. If the speech he is making is one that he is accustomed to make over and over again, he may be almost unconscious of what he is saying, as one is when one utters the responses in church. And this reduced state of consciousness, if not indispensable, is at any rate favorable to political conformity.

In our time, political speech and writing are largely the defense of the indefensible. Things like the continuance of British rule in India, the Russian purges and deportations, the dropping of the atom bombs on Japan, can indeed be defended, but only by arguments which are too brutal for most people to face, and which do not square with the professed aims of political parties. Thus political language has to consist largely of euphemism, question-begging and sheer cloudy vagueness. Defenseless villages are bombarded from the air, the inhabitants driven out into the countryside, the cattle machine-gunned, the huts set on fire with incendiary bullets: this is called *pacification*. Millions of peasants are robbed of their farms and sent trudging along the roads with no more than they can carry: this is called *transfer of population* or *rectification of frontiers*. People are imprisoned for years without trial, or shot in the back of the neck or sent to die of scurvy in Arctic lumber camps: this is called *elimination of unreliable elements*. Such phraseology is needed if one wants to name things without calling up mental pictures of them. Consider for instance some comfortable English professor defending Russian totalitarianism. He cannot say outright, "I believe in killing off your opponents when you can get good results by doing so." Probably, therefore, he will say something like this:

15   "While freely conceding that the Soviet régime exhibits certain features which the humanitarian may be inclined to deplore, we must, I think, agree that a certain curtailment of the right to political opposition is an unavoidable concomitant of

transitional periods, and that the rigors which the Russian people have been called upon to undergo have been amply justified in the sphere of concrete achievement."

The inflated style is itself a kind of euphemism. A mass of Latin words falls upon the facts like soft snow, blurring the outlines and covering up all the details. The great enemy of clear language is insincerity. When there is a gap between one's real and one's declared aims, one turns as it were instinctively to long words and exhausted idioms, like a cuttlefish squirting out ink. In our age there is no such thing as "keeping out of politics." All issues are political issues, and politics itself is a mass of lies, evasions, folly, hatred and schizophrenia. When the general atmosphere is bad, language must suffer. I should expect to find—this is a guess which I have not sufficient knowledge to verify—that the German, Russian and Italian languages have all deteriorated in the last ten or fifteen years, as a result of dictatorship.

But if thought corrupts language, language can also corrupt thought. A bad usage can spread by tradition and imitation, even among people who should and do know better. The debased language that I have been discussing is in some ways very convenient. Phrases like *a not unjustifiable assumption, leaves much to be desired, would serve no good purpose, a consideration which we should do well to bear in mind,* are a continuous temptation, a packet of aspirins always at one's elbow. Look back through this essay, and for certain you will find that I have again and again committed the very faults I am protesting against. By this morning's post I have received a pamphlet dealing with conditions in Germany. The author tells me that he "felt impelled" to write it. I open it at random, and here is almost the first sentence that I see: "(The Allies) have an opportunity not only of achieving a radical transformation of Germany's social and political structure in such a way as to avoid a nationalistic reaction in Germany itself, but at the same time of laying the foundations of a cooperative and unified Europe." You see, he "feels impelled" to write—feels, presumably, that he has something new to say—and yet his words, like cavalry horses answering the bugle, group themselves automatically into the familiar dreary pattern. This invasion of one's mind by ready-made phrases (*lay the foundations, achieve a radical transformation*) can only be prevented if one is constantly on guard against them, and every such phrase anaesthetizes a portion of one's brain.

I said earlier that the decadence of our language is probably curable. Those who deny this would argue, if they produced an argument at all, that language merely reflects existing social conditions, and that we cannot influence its development by any direct tinkering with words and constructions. So far as the general tone or spirit of a language goes, this may be true, but it is not true in detail. Silly words and expressions have often disappeared, not through any evolutionary process but owing to the conscious action of a minority. Two recent examples were *explore every avenue* and *leave no stone unturned,* which were killed by the jeers of a few journalists. There is a long list of flyblown metaphors which could similarly be got rid of if enough people would interest themselves in the job; and it should also be possible to laugh the *not un*-formation out of existence,[3] to reduce the amount of Latin and Greek in the average sentence, to drive out foreign phrases and strayed scientific words, and, in general, to make pretentiousness unfashionable. But all these are minor points. The defense of the English language implies more than this, and perhaps it is best to start by saying what it does *not* imply.

To begin with, it has nothing to do with archaism, with the salvaging of obsolete words and turns of speech, or with the setting up of a "standard English" which must never be departed from. On the contrary, it is especially concerned with the scrapping of every word or idiom which has outworn its usefulness. It has nothing to do with correct grammar and syntax, which are of no importance so long as one makes one's meaning clear, or with the avoidance of Americanisms, or with having what is called a "good prose style." On the other hand it is not concerned with fake simplicity and the attempt to make written English colloquial. Nor does it even imply in every case preferring the Saxon word to the Latin one, though it does imply using the fewest and shortest words that will cover one's meaning. What is above all needed is to let the meaning choose the word, and not the other way about. In prose, the worst thing one can do with words is to surrender to them. When you think of a concrete object, you think wordlessly, and then, if you want to describe the thing you have been visualizing you probably hunt about till you find the exact words that seem to fit. When you think of something abstract, you are more inclined to use words from the start, and unless you make a conscious effort to prevent it, the existing dialect will come rushing in and do the job for you, at the expense of blurring or even changing your meaning. Probably it is better to put off using words as long as possible and get one's meaning as clear as one can through pictures or sensations. Afterwards one can choose—not simply *accept*—the phrases that will best cover the meaning, and then switch round and decide what impression one's words are likely to make on another person. This last effort of the mind cuts out all stale or mixed images, all prefabricated phrases, needless repetitions, and humbug and vagueness generally. But one can often be in doubt about the effect of a word or a phrase, and one needs rules that one can rely on when instinct fails. I think the following rules will cover most cases:

(i) Never use a metaphor, simile or other figure of speech which you are used to seeing in print.

(ii) Never use a long word where a short one will do.

(iii) If it is possible to cut a word out, always cut it out.

(iv) Never use the passive where you can use the active.

(v) Never use a foreign phrase, a scientific word or a jargon word if you can think of an everyday English equivalent.

(vi) Break any of these rules sooner than say anything outright barbarous.

These rules sound elementary, and so they are, but they demand a deep change of attitude in anyone who has grown used to writing in the style now fashionable. One could keep all of them and still write bad English, but one could not write the kind of stuff that I quoted in those five specimens at the beginning of this article.

I have not here been considering the literary use of language, but merely language as an instrument for expressing and not for concealing or preventing thought. Stuart Chase and others have come near to claiming that all abstract words are meaningless, and have used this as a pretext for advocating a kind of political quietism. Since you don't know what Fascism is, how can you struggle against Fascism? One need not swallow such absurdities as this, but one ought to recognize that the present political chaos is connected

with the decay of language, and that one can probably bring about some improvement by   20
starting at the verbal end. If you simplify your English, you are freed from the worst follies
of orthodoxy. You cannot speak any of the necessary dialects, and when you make a stupid
remark its stupidity will be obvious, even to yourself. Political language—and with variations this is true of all political parties, from Conservatives to Anarchists—is designed to
make lies sound truthful and murder respectable, and to give an appearance of solidity
to pure wind. One cannot change this all in a moment, but one can at least change one's
own habits, and from time to time one can even, if one jeers loudly enough, send some
wornout and useless phrase—some *jackboot, Achilles' heel, hotbed, melting pot, acid test,
veritable inferno* or other lump of verbal refuse—into the dustbin where it belongs.

Notes

[1] An interesting illustration of this is the way in which the English flower names which
were in use till very recently are being ousted by Greek ones, *snapdragon* becoming *antir-
rhinum, forget-me-not* becoming *myosotis*, etc. It is hard to see any practical reason for
this change of fashion: it is probably due to an instinctive turning-away from the more
homely word and a vague feeling that the Greek word is scientific.

[2] Example: "Comfort's catholicity of perception and image, strangely Whitmanesque in
range, almost the exact opposite in aesthetic compulsion, continues to evoke that trembling atmospheric accumulative hinting at a cruel, an inexorably serene timelessness ...
Wrey Gardiner scores by aiming at simple bull's-eyes with precision. Only they are not
so simple, and through this contented sadness runs more than the surface bittersweet of
resignation" (*Poetry Quarterly*).

[3] One can cure oneself of the *not un-* formation by memorizing this sentence: A *not unblack
dog was chasing a not unsmall rabbit across a not ungreen field.*

Things to Do with the Reading

1. In the section "Operators or Verbal False Limbs" (paragraph 6) and again in
   the "rules" offered at the end of the essay (paragraph 19), Orwell articulates
   (and justifies) his preference for cutting unnecessary words and avoiding the
   passive voice. With these notions in mind, apply the last section of Chapter
   18, "Cut Extra Words to Achieve Greater Directness," to produce a revision
   of anything you have written. To prepare you, first experiment with Try This
   exercises 18.8, and 18.9 to sharpen your ability to distinguish active voice
   from passive voice and to refine your understanding of what each of these
   options offers a writer.

2. **Application:** Near the end of his essay, Orwell delivers its most famous
   sentence, "In our time political speech and writing are largely the defense
   of the indefensible" (paragraph 14). He illustrates this declaration with a
   series of examples of "euphemism, question-begging, and sheer cloudy
   vagueness," such as use of the term "pacification" to describe "defenseless

villages bombarded from the air, inhabitants driven out into the countryside, the cattle machine-gunned, the huts set on fire with incendiary bullets"
(paragraph 14).

That was a half-century ago. How about now? Visit a wonderful website
for its collection of speeches, American Rhetoric, at http://www.american-
rhetoric.com/. Find a speech that you think Orwell would condemn for
defending the indefensible. Then write an essay in which you produce an
Orwellian analysis of its methods of doing so.

3. **Application:** Orwell's essay also conveys, both explicitly and by implication,
a set of traits that characterize politically responsible language. Review the
essay to extract a list of those traits Orwell approves of in political speech.
Then go to the American Rhetoric website (cited in the previous question)
and locate an example of a speech he would like. Write an essay in which you
point out specific features Orwell would like about it, explaining the reasoning behind your judgment. You might want to start by looking at speeches
by Barbara Jordan, the first African American woman to be elected to the
House of Representatives in Texas. She went on to a high-profile career in
Congress where she came to be recognized as one of America's great ora-
tors. Try to find the speech she gave in Congress on the occasion of the
House Judiciary Committee, of which she was a member, being asked to
speak about their deliberations on the question of impeaching a president
(Richard Nixon). This speech made Jordan a nationally known and admired
speaker. Why?

Interview with Frank Luntz

This interview with the controversial pollster Frank Luntz first appeared on PBS's *Frontline* on December 15, 2003, as part of a series of interviews entitled *The Persuaders*. The series explored the broader influence that the cultures of marketing and advertising have had on American life. In the interview, Luntz discusses his central role in crafting the Contract with America that the Republican Party presented to voters in 1994, as well as his theories about the construction and presentation of messages in political language. A graduate of the University of Pennsylvania with a PhD from Oxford, Luntz is currently the CEO of The Word Doctors, a firm specializing in "message creation and image management." He is also a frequent commentator and political analyst for the Fox News Channel. Most recently, he has instructed Senate Republicans in talking about healthcare, and a leaked 17-page memo he wrote in January 2011 advises the Republican Party about the words to use in the financial regulation debate.

What are you measuring with the dial technology? [A mechanism Luntz uses 1 whereby people in a focus group register their moment by moment responses to a speech or presentation.]

It's like an X-ray that gets inside your head, and it picks out every single word, every single phrase [that you hear], and you know what works and what doesn't. And you do it without the bias of a focus group. People are quiet as they're listening, and they're reacting anonymously. The key to dial technology is that it's immediate, it's specific, and it's anonymous.

It's so immediate, it feels instantaneous.

But it is, because politics is instantaneous. Politics is gut; commercials are gut. You're watching a great show on TV, you now come to that middle break, you decide in a matter of three seconds whether or not you're going to a) flip the channel; b) get up; or c) keep watching. It's not intellectual; it is gut.

Is it the same for political decisions about power companies and politicians, though? 5

We decide based on how people look; we decide based on how people sound; we decide based on how people are dressed. We decide based on their passion. If I respond to you quietly, the viewer at home is going to have a different reaction than if I respond to you with emotion and with passion and I wave my arms around. Somebody like this is an intellectual; somebody like this is a freak. But that's how we make up our minds. Look, this is about the real-life decisions of real-life Americans, who to vote for, what to buy, what to agree with, what to think, how to act. This is the way it is.

You think emotions are more revelatory than the intellect for predicting these decisions?

80 percent of our life is emotion, and only 20 percent is intellect. I am much more interested in how you feel than how you think. I can change how you think, but how

From FRONTLINE/WGBH Boston. Copyright © 1995 - 2011 WGBH Educational Foundation.

you feel is something deeper and stronger, and it's something that's inside you. How you think is on the outside, how you feel is on the inside, so that's what I need to understand.

And this technology can get at that?

10   The great thing about dial technology is you can get a small response on the dial, or you can get a huge jump. You watch with your own eyes: At some points, the lines are way up at the top of the screen or even out beyond. People were practically breaking their dials in agreement at certain points, and at other points, they were flat. It measures intensity. And if you want to understand public opinion, if you want to understand public behavior, if you want to understand the way we operate as Americans and as humans, you've got to understand that one word: intensity.

It can be anything, then, that you're selling.

I'm not going to let you twist the words, because if I say to you that you can sell a politician the way you sell soap—and it may even look that way from the outside—that says to Americans that they shouldn't respect politicians or soap. It really isn't that way. The way you communicate an idea is different than the way you communicate a product. However, the way you measure [the response of the public in both instances] is quite similar. And the principles behind explaining and educating the product or the elected official is similar, even though the actual execution of it is very, very different.

Are there different techniques you use when working with politics versus corporations?

The technique is a little bit different because politics and corporations are a little bit different. But in the end you're still using the same focus groups; you're still using the same dial technology; you're still using the same quantitative data; you're still doing split samples where you ask half a sample one way and the other half a different way. You're still asking and re-asking the questions. You're still showing them visuals to see what they like the best, and you're still showing them or having them listen to audio track to see how they respond. So the actual techniques are the same, but how they are applied is different. And that really is the separation; that's the differentiation between politics and the corporate world.

15   **Was there a eureka moment, watching the responses of these people to the power company's ideas, where you figured out what really worked?**

The eureka moment is two reasons why the output-based standard should be adopted: common sense and accountability. Input-based standards don't encourage energy diversity; they don't create any incentives; they don't produce solar, hydro, nuclear. As a result, companies are actually penalized if they use the cleanest fuels, and it doesn't make sense. It's not substance; it's language. And when they heard the language that they wanted to hear and they were able to apply it to an idea that at least they were open to, you watched a marriage of good communication and good policy. That was the eureka moment: I watched people nod their heads; I watched them look to each other, and they were willing at this point to fight for this position. Now I'll be able to walk to this electricity company on Monday and be able to say to them, "Your policy makes sense, and here's the language to explain it."

And the amazing thing was, it explained a very complicated policy. That's the job of language; that's the job of English. This is not about politics; this is not about selling soap. This is taking very traditional, simple, clear-cut words of the English language and figuring out which words, which phrases to apply at which opportunities, which times.

So what will you say at that Monday meeting?

On Monday I will sit down with a Washington representative of Florida Power & Light and I will tell him that what he wants to do, his goal for his company, is the goal of America; that if he uses this language to explain his principles and his policies, not only will the company benefit, but the public will be appreciative of what they're trying to do. This is a good company, this is a clean company, but it's got all the baggage of every other electric company, of every other power company. We as Americans assume that big companies are bad, and big power companies are even worse. This language, what we saw tonight, is a demonstration that a single company can differentiate itself, can improve its public image.

You believe language can change a paradigm.   20

I don't believe it—I know it. I've seen it with my own eyes. I have seen how effective language attached to policies that are mainstream and delivered by people who are passionate and effective can change the course of history. I watched in 1994 when the group of Republicans got together and said: "We're going to do this completely differently than it's ever been done before. We are going to prove to the American people that we are different." And so instead of a platform, instead of a policy, instead of a mass of different issues and policies, they came up with a "contract," because a contract is different. A contract says that it is a legal document. It says that you put your name on it, and it says that there is enforcement if you don't do it. The word "contract" means something different than "platform." Every politician and every political party issues a platform, but only these people signed a contract.

Was that your idea?

The concept of it was hatched in Salisbury, MD, at a Republican retreat. I was fortunate enough to have been invited to do a presentation about how the American people didn't trust politicians in general and, quite frankly, didn't trust Republicans in particular. And Newt Gingrich was there, and he listened to the presentation, and he said: "We have to do it differently in this election. We have to find a way to communicate that takes all of these policies that we believe in, that the Democrats don't, and articulates that difference. How can we do it?" I presented at that presentation a proclamation. I got the idea from a Massachusetts campaign I was involved with. Gingrich saw that, and he came up with the phrase "contract."

I didn't create the "Contract with America;" I was the pollster for it. I said, "If you're going to do a contract, you've got to make it a contract." For example, "Keep this page to hold us accountable"—that did not exist in the original document. I insisted that that be added, because they wanted to know that you could actually hold these guys accountable. One of the things that you have trouble with politicians, particularly in Washington, is when you get mad at them and you can't touch them; you can't punch them; you can't yell at them. This accountability says, "I can really demand that they do what they promise."

25   This sentence was the one that I had the most trouble keeping in this final document: "If we break this contract, throw us out. We mean it." When has a politician ever said, "If I don't come through with what I promise, boot me"? I said: "You need that sentence in there, and you need it at the very bottom of the document. People will read the top, and they read the bottom, and only if they believe in the top and the bottom will they actually read the text, will they read the substance." This is the enforcement clause, and this is what told people that this was for real.

It's not the "Republican Contract with America," because in 1994, as it is today, Americans don't want partisanship. So you will notice that there are mentions of the word "Republican," but I did not want it in red; I did not want it as the lead line that people would see because it was too overtly partisan. Part of my job is to teach subtlety. I may not be a subtle person—I'm pretty loud and outspoken—but so often subtlety, the quiet voice, actually communicates.

"We listen to your concerns, and we hear you loud and clear." [The contract] is responsive. That's what the public was looking for back in 1994: a politician who was responsive and responding to them. And all of this language was all tested to make sure it would be effective. The whole document is filled with listening, with responsiveness, with accountability.

Who hired you?

The Republican National Committee hired me, and they hired me because they wanted someone who could look members straight in the eye and tell them the truth. There's a problem with political polling in that you have so much pressure to do what your client wants you to do and say what your client wants you to say. I've never felt that pressure. I am independent of the political parties. I came up outside that structure so that I could tell these members: "This document is going to work. People are going to believe you." And they would believe me because they knew that I was not making money from it.

30   **You must admit that language can cloud as well as clarify.**

If it doesn't describe what it's selling, then it is a very poor descriptor. If you've got a bad product, you shouldn't be selling it. And people like me have to have the discipline only to work for clients, corporations, political people, products, services, networks that we believe in and we want to see succeed. I don't believe that good language can obscure a bad product.

What about replacing "global warming" with "climate change"?

What is the difference? It is climate change. Some people call it global warming; some people call it climate change. What is the difference?

Look, for years, political people and lawyers—who, by the way, are the worst communicators—used the phrase "estate tax." And for years they couldn't eliminate it.

The public wouldn't support it because the word "estate" sounds wealthy. Someone like me comes around and realizes that it's not an estate tax, it's a death tax, because you're taxed at death. And suddenly something that isn't viable achieves the support of 75 percent of the American people. It's the same tax, but nobody really knows what an estate is. But they certainly know what it means to be taxed when you die. I argue that is a clarification; that's not an obfuscation.

The language of America changed with the election of Bill Clinton, because with all due respect to my friends on the Republican side, Bill Clinton is the best communicator of the last 50 years. He felt your pain. Now, I'd argue that he caused your pain, but at least he felt it while he was causing it. When Bill Clinton spoke, his words were so good, and they were spoken with such passion. And that biting of the lower lip and the squinching of the eyes—you just couldn't turn away. Bill Clinton made Frank Luntz because Bill Clinton discovered the power and the influence of words. Now, I'd like to think that I apply them to clients, to philosophies, to products and services and corporations that I believe in, that are good. I don't argue with you that words can sometimes be used to confuse, but it's up to the practitioners of the study of language to apply them for good and not for evil. It is just like fire; fire can heat your house or burn it down.

There are words that work, that are meant to explain and educate on policies that work, on products that work, on services that work. I'm not going to ever try to sell a lemon. I don't do that. I work for pharmaceutical companies because my dad was kept alive for a long time on medications thanks to companies like Pfizer. I work for a company like Federal Express because it allows me to get my packages there the next morning. It's a wonderful, innovative corporation. I work for a company like Merrill Lynch because I believe in the financial services and the quality of the product.

I believe in the people who work at the corporations that I work for, and the political people. The best example is Rudy Giuliani. What have I done that's wrong if I provide someone like a Rudy Giuliani or a corporation like a Pfizer language that helps them explain or educate? I've simplified the process for them which allows them to explain. What did they say in there [in the focus group]? They kept coming back to it again and again: What they want from their elected officials, from the CEOs, from the elite of America is clarity. They said it again and again: "Be clear with us. Be straight with us. Common sense; clarity; down the road, look us straight in the eye." That's exactly what I do. I help them do that.

Talk to me about the Healthy Forests Initiative of President Bush. Isn't calling it "Healthy Forests" obfuscating the fact that it entails keeping the forests healthy with widespread logging?

Yes, the Bush administration benefited from the phrase "healthy forest." But what do we know as a fact? If you allow this underbrush to subsume the forest, to get so thick that you can't walk through it, you can't get through it, if you don't touch a twig or a tree and you say, "Oh, let Mother Nature deal with it," then you get these catastrophic forest fires that we saw in Arizona, Colorado and in California. The Native Americans, they know how to thin a forest, and yes, they do take trees out, and what happens? A fire burns, and it stops right where that thinning process took place. But thanks to environmentalists who are extreme and radical in their approach, who say that we must not touch anything at any time in any way, we lose thousands, thousands, hundreds of thousands of acres of forests and all the wildlife that was inside it. And they don't come back again. It takes generations for it to regenerate. So don't tell me about language, because "healthy forests" actually is what it means. And you have to understand the policy, and you've got to understand the product if you want to be able to communicate it. You can't just approach it naively.

40 **Is there a line you won't cross in the creative use of language?**

You cannot lie ever, because a lie destroys the credibility of the product, and credibility is more important than anything. Credibility's even more important than clarity. They have to believe you before they will listen to you. So you can't lie. This is an interesting line, because in my own life, in some of the things I've worked for, I get angry. I am a proponent of the pharmaceutical industry. I believe in these heart medications and these anti-cancer drugs. I'm a supporter of a very famous medication right now, OxyContin, because I think that this is a miracle drug which allows people to get through the day. And this is a medication that some people want to see taken off the market. There are all sorts of lawsuits. I believe that there are things worth fighting for. I believe that there are things worth explaining and educating, even if it takes months or years. The only thing I don't believe in is lying. Beyond that, you can use almost anything. You can use emotion. It is acceptable to bring someone to tears if it explains to them in an emotional way why a product, a service, or a candidate is the right person, is the right thing to do.

Do facts matter?

Of course facts matter. And what we do—and you watched it here—is to give them accurate facts and see which facts matter. My point is that when you're talking issues like the environment, a straight recitation of facts is going to fall on deaf ears, and that industry has been very ineffective. Even by using that word "industry," people think of smokestacks. So often corporate America, business America, are the worst communicators because all they understand are facts, and they cannot tell a story. They know how to explain their quarterly results, but they don't know how to explain what they mean.

I don't understand why people whose entire lives or their corporate success depends on communication, and yet they are led on occasion by CEOs who cannot talk their way out of a paper bag and don't care to. I know some CEOs who are outstanding communicators, and those individuals have a much better time with shareholders, have a much better time with the media, and, most importantly, with their consumers and the general public, because they know how to explain the benefits; they know how to put things in context. But there are so many CEOs that only know how to talk about numbers. Numbers don't mean anything. You talk about billions and tax procedures and all sorts of acronyms, and the only people who understand that are government bureaucrats and accountants. Americans don't want to hear the language of accountants; they want to hear the language of teachers and social workers.

Do you think Republicans do this better than Democrats?

That is brand new. When I started in this business, everybody said the Democrats were the better communicators because they sounded like social workers, and Republicans were awful because they sounded like morticians. In some cases. they actually dressed like morticians. That has changed over the last 10 years. Bill Clinton brought the change in the Democratic Party, and George W. Bush brought a significant change in the Republican Party: that it was not enough to have a superior policy, or it was not enough to have all the facts at your fingertips; it became essential that you be able to communicate that on a one-to-one basis, as individuals on a personal level rather than a philosophical or ideological level.

There are people still in the Republican Party that I believe practice the communication of anger, of disappointment, of regret, of pain, of sorrow, of suffering. That's not what the American people want to hear. For 20 years, the Democrats were effective at the communication of hope and things that are positive. I asked Republicans at one point to do this little test, to turn down the television set in a debate between Republicans and Democrats, just look at the two individuals—which one would you want to hang out with? Which one would you want to have a beer with? Which one would you want as your uncle, or who would you want to hang out with at Thanksgiving? For years the Democratic candidate was the one that smiled; the Republican candidate was the one that was angry. Now, there are always exceptions to this, and I'm sure you can come up with 10 of them. But basically, Republicans practiced the politics of anger, and Democrats practiced the politics of hope. And all that began to change in 1994, and it finally came to fruition in 2000. And now it's the Democrats who are angry and the Republicans who are hopeful.

Who else were the visionaries?

The change in Republican language began with Newt Gingrich in 1994, and while much of his communication still came across as angry and partisan, when Newt was speaking about policy and not talking about those who opposed him, there was none better, and there has been none better. Newt Gingrich had the ability to explain a very complicated process in very clear-cut, common-sense ways, unlike anyone I've ever seen. He explained the difference between taxing and spending. He explained the difference between investment and savings. He explained the difference between a weak foreign policy and a strong one. This is a guy who knew how to articulate a philosophical point of view in a way that just made sense. And if it wasn't coming from Newt Gingrich, you believed it; you absolutely supported it. The problem with Gingrich was he was too angry in some of his communication.

So what we needed was someone with that level of explanatory ability with a gentle heart and a gentle soul, and that's where George W. Bush came in. The Bush that we know now is not the Bush that ran for election in 2000. The one who ran in 2000 talked about education; talked about Social Security; talked about a kinder, gentler conservatism; talked about an inclusive conservatism. And it's exactly what the public wanted.

And you compare that with Al Gore. The Democrats became the party of the cold and the aloof. And in 2004, you look at Howard Dean and John Kerry and to a lesser extent Dick Gephardt; the Democratic Party is now the party of anger. I know that this is what happens when you're an opposition party, but that's not what Republicans did in 1994 or 2000. In '94 they offered a "contract." They offered something positive, and people voted for it. And in 2000 they offered a change, an alternative to Bill Clinton; people voted for it. George Bush attacked Al Gore a lot less than Gore attacked Bush. And now in 2004 the Democrats are making the same mistakes. We don't want our messages screamed at us. We don't want to be yelled at.

How important is keeping the consistency of the message in political language?

The advantage of working for a corporation is that it has only one message, because a product or a service doesn't speak; it's just there, and you can advertise it. The challenge in working in politics, particularly if you're working for a political party, is that everyone's a messenger. I think the best example of this, frankly, is Israel, where you can have 20 members of the Cabinet, and they've got 68 messages between them, because among the 20, all of them think that they're prime minister or will be prime minister or should be prime minister or hate the person who is prime minister. And when you have all these people saying things in a different way, nobody hears anything.

I've got a certain rule that I always teach my staff: It's not what you say; it's what people hear that matters. I may respond to you effectively, but if you edit it in such a way that they only hear the negativity of what I do, then that's all they're going to know. And so they're going to conclude that my profession isn't an honorable profession. And that's why how I say it has as much of an impact on what people think of me as what I say.

55   [Regarding consistency,] there's a simple rule: You say it again, and you say it again, and you say it again, and you say it again, and you say it again, and then again and again and again and again, and about the time that you're absolutely sick of saying it is about the time that your target audience has heard it for the first time. And it is so hard, but you've just got to keep repeating, because we hear so many different things—the noises from outside, the sounds, all the things that are coming into our head, the 200 cable channels and the satellite versus cable, and what we hear from our friends. We as Americans and as humans have very selective hearing and very selective memory. We only hear what we want to hear and disregard the rest.

Republicans use think tanks to come up with a lot of their messages.

The think tanks are the single worst, most undisciplined example of communication I've ever seen. Cato [Institute] still calls it the "privatization of Social Security." Heritage [Foundation] did so until a couple of years ago. Every time you use the words "privatization" and "Social Security" in the same sentence, you frighten seniors, and more of them turn against you. This is a specific and perfect example of the intellectual goo-goo heads who are more interested in policy than they were in success. Changing the word from "privatize" to "personalize," which is the work that we had done, they wouldn't accept it, because to them it was selling an idea short.

They would rather communicate their way and lose the issue than communicate in a sensible way and win. The fact is, ideology and communication more often than not run into each other rather than complement each other. Principle and communication work together. Ideology and communication often work apart.

Tell me about your work for Rudy Giuliani.

Rudy Giuliani hired me because I was recommended by his political consultant and   60
because I love baseball. I hate to admit this, but I brought my baseball card collection
to show him, because I'd heard he was a fanatic Yankee fan, and I figured this would
be a way that we could bond. We ended up talking for 22 minutes. My whole interview
with Rudy Giuliani in 1993 lasted for 22 minutes, and at least 19 of the 22 minutes was
focused on baseball. So I don't know if he got it right or wrong; all I know is that this
was a guy who understood the value of words and understood the value of language,
but even more than that, it's the power of personality. You know, you have asked me
what matters in research and how do you apply different components. What matters
most in politics is personality. It's not issues; it's not image. It's who you are and what
you represent. And this guy, from the very beginning of his administration, even if
people disagreed with what he was doing, they trusted him to do it, and even if they
didn't like him, they respected him.

My job as a pollster is to understand what really matters. Those levers of importance—sometimes they're called levers; sometimes they're called triggers. What causes
people to buy a product? What causes someone to pull a lever and get them to vote? I
need to know the specifics of that. And in politics, more often than not, it's about the
personality and the character of the individual rather than where they stand, and that's
exactly the opposite of what your viewers will think.

Did you help him?

Part of the task is using language and using speeches and using photo ops and using
the power of campaign to convey a specific message. And my job in '93 and '97
was to explain to the campaign what the public wanted and to help explain to the
public that that's exactly what he was offering. A pollster, a marketer, someone who
is the explainer of public opinion, has the ability to inform somebody like Rudy
Giuliani [of] what really matters to the public, and so that makes Rudy Giuliani an
even better candidate.

**Can you talk about how you've applied your approach to the use of language to
corporate America?**

I've done reasonably well over the last 10 years because I took the strategy of lan-   65
guage and politics and applied it to the corporate world, which has never been done
before. Up to this point, the only people who ever communicated were those little
30-second characters, the little Alka-Seltzer guy or the StaPuf, whatever his name is.

And were your ideas well received in corporate America?

Oh, you have no idea. I am amazed at how eager the CEOs of the biggest companies are today to communicate as effectively as possible, to employ the skills and
the language of what you saw right here earlier. They want to know that they can
talk to a shareholder one-on-one, not just through their head but also through

their heart. They want to know that they can reach their consumer not just on an intellectual basis, but on an emotional basis. In fact, I'd argue that CEOs, with all the corporate scandals that have taken place, are more interested in effective communication than even political people, because corporate people are interested in the bottom line, and so for them good words, good phrases, good presentation matter more than anything.

If we're getting information from 200 cable channels, if we're talking to 200 people a day, there are so many different messages that are cluttering our heads. It's the same way in corporate America. If a CEO speaks and no one hears it, it doesn't matter. And so they're looking for people like me to help them cut through the clutter, to help them explain and educate why their product or their service or their company is better. And the challenge for CEOs is that they generally came up through the ranks by being good numbers people. And I have seen 99 out of 100 cases, if you're a good numbers person, you're a bad language person.

What kind of reception do you get from their marketing departments?

70   There are two people that tend to beat up on me. One are the ideologues, particularly in the far left or the far right, who don't want to communicate to everybody; they don't want to be loved; they don't even want to be respected. They want to say it their own way, and they don't like people like me who challenge the way they communicate their policies, their platforms or their principles. The other people who beat me up are the market research people in some of these big companies, because they don't understand language.

The problem with the job and the service that I provide is that I have to be involved in it. I can't write a memo from somebody else's focus group. I can't do this from traditional polling of 1,000 people on the telephone. I have to be able to hear it. Traditional market researchers are cold and calculating and scientific. In this business of language, you have to have a heart, and you have to have emotion, and you have to be willing to become what you are studying, no matter what it puts you through.

So the main point is emotion.

It's all emotion. But there's nothing wrong with emotion. When we are in love, we are not rational; we are emotional. When we are on vacation, we are not rational; we are emotional. When we are happy, we are not [rational]. In fact, in more cases than not, when we are rational, we're actually unhappy. Emotion is good; passion is good. Being into what we're into, provided that it's a healthy pursuit, it's a good thing.

But if emotion is the main point, why go for the words?

75   Because the words provide the emotions.

Words are keys to the emotions?

Yeah. You call it keys, but my job is to look for the words that trigger the emotion. Words alone can be found in a dictionary or a telephone book, but words with emotion can change destiny, can change life as we know it. We know it has changed history; we know it has changed behavior; we know that it can start a war or stop it. We know that words and emotion together are the most powerful force known to mankind.

What new directions do you see for market research like yours?

Part of what market research and the understanding of language that has not been exploited sufficiently is actually in the courtroom. There are jury consultants and there are message consultants for trials, but not to the degree that it's been applied to politics and the corporate world. This is where people are going next, and frankly, this is where I'm going next. There's a lot of money with a lot of big law firms that have a tremendous amount at stake by getting the right language to convince the right jury that my client is either innocent or that the opposition is guilty.

Things to Do with the Reading

1. Another of "the persuaders" interviewed in the PBS series from which this interview was taken commented that the influx of marketing and advertising into politics has created an environment in which "the principal of democracy yields to the practice of demography." How would you paraphrase that remark? (See Paraphrase × 3 in Chapter 2.) And how would Luntz respond to that charge? Write an essay in answer to these two questions. As you do so, review Borick's discussion at the beginning of "On Political Labels" on Madisonian versus Jeffersonian views on democracy. Whose point of view is Luntz closer to and so what?

2. If you were to do The Method on Luntz's interview (see Chapter 2), you would undoubtedly discover repetitions of such terms as the heart, emotion and passion, which comprise a strand we might label "Emotion" (including as well enthusiasm, empathy, feeling, etc.) and which constitute half of an organizing contrast opposed to what Luntz names "Intellect" (See paragraph 8: "80 percent of our life is emotion, and only 20 percent is intellect.")

   Write an essay in which you account for the emphasis Luntz places on emotion. How does the language of emotion figure in the way that Luntz thinks about politics, and more, about winning in the political arena? What, in short, is the logic of his argument about emotion?

3. Toward the end of the interview, in response to a question about working for Rudy Giuliani, Luntz says, "What matters most in politics is personality. It's not the issues; it's not image. It's who you are and what you represent" (paragraph 60). Rhetoricians study the role that a speaker's character plays in his or her ability to persuade others under the category "ethos," a word that comes from the Greek for "character, a person's nature or disposition" (*OED*). (See the section of Chapter 3 entitled "Ethos and Analysis" for a discussion of ethos.)

Write an essay on what we might call the "ethos strand" in the Luntz interview. Note places where Luntz seems to be supplying language or information (especially biographical information) designed to win readers and listeners through winning their support for his character and personality. Consider, for example, what Luntz says in response to the question "Who hired you?" See also the personal information he offers when explaining why he works for pharmaceutical companies. What kind of ethos is Luntz trying to establish? What possible criticisms of Luntz might this ethos help him to deflect? Given that Luntz has a PhD in political science from Oxford, why do you think he refers to intellectuals as "goo-goo heads" in his response to a question about Republican think tanks?

4. **Link:** Write an essay in which you put Orwell's arguments in "Politics and the English Language" into conversation with Luntz's arguments. Consider, for example, what Orwell might say to Luntz on Luntz's assertion, "I don't believe that good language can obscure a bad product."

Luntz does not here define what he means by "good language," but elsewhere in the piece he talks about using "traditional, simple, clear-cut words of the English language." He says that what Americans want is clarity: "Be clear with us. Be straight with us." He also says that his job is "to look for the words that trigger emotion." Presumably, Orwell would agree with these criteria for good language, since he is opposed to language that hides its real intent and that seeks to soften people's response to what is being talked about—the brutality of war, for example. But Orwell also speaks of language "as an instrument for expressing and not for concealing or preventing thought." Luntz says that changing the phrase "estate tax" to "death tax" is a clarification and does not obscure. Would Orwell agree with Luntz that this change is a clarification and that it does not, in Orwell's terms, conceal and prevent thought? Why or why not?

Matt Bai

The Framing Wars

This article, originally a cover story of the *New York Times* Magazine, focuses on the Democrats' answer to the Republicans' Frank Luntz, the linguist George Lakoff, a professor at the University of California, Berkeley, who specializes in metaphor. Political reporter Matt Bai offers an analysis of how the Democrats have attempted to construct a more coherent party narrative and stick to it with reinforced party discipline.

After last November's defeat, Democrats were like aviation investigators sifting   1
through twisted metal in a cornfield, struggling to posit theories about the disaster all around them. Some put the onus on John Kerry, saying he had never found an easily discernable message. Others, including Kerry himself, wrote off the defeat to the unshakable realities of wartime, when voters were supposedly less inclined to jettison a sitting president. Liberal activists blamed mushy centrists. Mushy centrists blamed Michael Moore. As the weeks passed, however, at Washington dinner parties and in public post-mortems, one explanation took hold not just among Washington insiders but among far-flung contributors, activists and bloggers too: the problem wasn't the substance of the party's agenda or its messenger as much as it was the Democrats' inability to communicate coherently. They had allowed Republicans to control the language of the debate, and that had been their undoing.

Even in their weakened state, Democrats resolved not to let it happen again. And improbably, given their post-election gloom, they managed twice in the months that followed to make good on that pledge. The first instance was the skirmish over the plan that the president called Social Security reform and that everybody else, by spring, was calling a legislative disaster. The second test for Democrats was their defense of the filibuster (the time-honored stalling tactic that prevents the majority in the Senate from ending debate), which seemed at the start a hopeless cause but ended in an unlikely stalemate. These victories weren't easy to account for, coming as they did at a time when Republicans seem to own just about everything in Washington but the first-place Nationals. (And they're working on that.) During the first four years of the Bush administration, after all, Democrats had railed just as loudly against giveaways to the wealthy and energy lobbyists, and all they had gotten for their trouble were more tax cuts and more drilling. Something had changed in Washington—but what?

Democrats thought they knew the answer. Even before the election, a new political word had begun to take hold of the party, beginning on the West Coast and spreading like a virus all the way to the inner offices of the Capitol. That word was "framing." Exactly what it means to "frame" issues seems to depend on which Democrat you are talking to, but everyone agrees that it has to do with choosing the language to define a debate and, more important, with fitting individual issues into the contexts of broader story lines. In the months after the election, Democratic consultants and elected officials came to sound like creative-writing teachers, holding forth on the importance of metaphor and narrative.

From The New York Times, © 2005 The New York Times. All rights reserved. Used by permission and protected by the Copyright Laws of the United States. The printing, copying, redistribution, or retransmission of the material without express written permission is prohibited.

Republicans, of course, were the ones who had always excelled at framing controversial issues, having invented and popularized loaded phrases like "tax relief" and "partial-birth abortion" and having achieved a kind of Pravda-esque discipline for disseminating them. But now Democrats said that they had learned to fight back. "The Democrats have finally reached a level of outrage with what Republicans were doing to them with language," Geoff Garin, a leading Democratic pollster, told me in May.

5   In January, Geoff Garin conducted a confidential poll on judicial nominations, paid for by a coalition of liberal advocacy groups. He was looking for a story—a frame—for the filibuster that would persuade voters that it should be preserved, and he tested four possible narratives. Democratic politicians assumed that voters saw the filibuster fight primarily as a campaign to stop radically conservative judges, as they themselves did. But to their surprise, Garin found that making the case on ideological grounds—that is, that the filibuster prevented the appointment of judges who would roll back civil rights—was the least effective approach. When, however, you told voters that the filibuster had been around for over 200 years, that Republicans were "changing rules in the middle of the game" and dismantling the "checks and balances" that protected us against one-party rule, almost half the voters strongly agreed, and 7 out of 10 were basically persuaded. It became, for them, an issue of fairness.

Garin then convened focus groups and listened for clues about how to make this case. He heard voters call the majority party "arrogant." They said they feared "abuse of power." This phrase struck Garin. He realized many people had already developed deep suspicions about Republicans in Washington. Garin shared his polling with a group of Democratic senators that included Harry Reid, the minority leader. Reid, in turn, assigned Stephanie Cutter, who was Kerry's spokeswoman last year, to put together a campaign-style "war room" on the filibuster. Cutter set up a strategy group, which included senior Senate aides, Garin, the pollster Mark Mellman and Jim Margolis, one of the party's top ad makers. She used Garin's research to create a series of talking points intended to cast the filibuster as an American birthright every bit as central to the Republic as Fourth of July fireworks. The talking points began like this: "Republicans are waging an unprecedented power grab. They are changing the rules in the middle of the game and attacking our historic system of checks and balances." They concluded, "Democrats are committed to fighting this abuse of power."

Cutter's war room began churning out mountains of news releases hammering daily at the G.O.P.'s "abuse of power." In an unusual show of discipline, Democrats in the Senate and House carried laminated, pocket-size message cards—"DEMOCRATS FIGHTING FOR DEMOCRACY, AGAINST ABUSE OF POWER," blared the headline at the top—with the talking points on one side and some helpful factoids about Bush's nominees on the other. During an appearance on "This Week with George Stephanopoulos" in April, Senator Charles Schumer of New York needed all of 30 seconds to invoke the "abuse of power" theme—twice.

By the time Reid took to the airwaves in late May, on the eve of what looked to be a final showdown on the filibuster ("This abuse of power is not what our founders intended," he told the camera solemnly), the issue seemed pretty well defined in the public mind. In a typical poll conducted by *Time* magazine, 59 percent of voters said they thought the G.O.P. should be stopped from eliminating the filibuster.

Perhaps feeling the pressure, a group of seven Republicans joined with seven Democrats in a last-minute compromise. Bill Frist, the Senate majority leader, and his team, smarting from crucial defections, had no choice but to back down from a vote. The truce meant that several of Bush's judges would be confirmed quickly, but it marked a rare retreat for Republicans and infuriated conservative activists, who knew that a Supreme Court battle would now be messier than they had hoped.

For their part, Democrats were euphoric at having played the G.O.P. to a draw. 10 The facts of the filibuster fight hadn't necessarily favored them; in reality, the constitutional principle of "checks and balances" on which the Democrats' case was based refers to the three branches of government, not to some parliamentary procedure, and it was actually the Democrats who had broken with Senate tradition by using the filibuster to block an entire slate of judges. ("An irrelevancy beyond the pay grade of the American voter," Garin retorted when I pointed this out.) And yet it was their theory of the case, and not the Republicans', that had won the argument. As Garin explained it, Republicans had become ensnared in a faulty frame of their own making. The phrase "nuclear option"—a term Frist and his colleagues had tried gamely, but unsuccessfully, to lose—had made Dr. Frist sound more like Dr. Strangelove. "It's a very evocative phrase," Garin said. "It's blowing up the Senate. It's having your finger on the button."

Garin was gloating, but it was hard to blame him. On the eve of what promises to be a historic debate over the direction of the nation's highest court, Democrats on Capitol Hill seemed to have starkly reversed the dynamic of last fall's election. Then, they had watched helplessly as George W. Bush and his strategists methodically twisted John Kerry into a hopeless tangle of contradictions and equivocations, using words and imagery to bend him into a shape that hardly resembled the war hero he had been. Now, Democrats believed, they had deciphered the hieroglyphics of modern political debate that had so eluded them in the campaign, and in doing so they had exacted some small measure of revenge. As one of the party's senior Senate aides told me a few days after the filibuster compromise was reached, "We framed them the way they framed Kerry."

The father of framing is a man named George Lakoff, and his spectacular ascent over the last eight months in many ways tells the story of where Democrats have been since the election. A year ago, Lakoff was an obscure linguistics professor at Berkeley, renowned as one of the great, if controversial, minds in cognitive science but largely unknown outside of it. When he, like many liberals, became exasperated over the drift of the Kerry campaign last summer—"I went to bed angry every night," he told me—Lakoff decided to bang out a short book about politics and language, based on theories he had already published with academic presses, that could serve as a kind of handbook for Democratic activists. His agent couldn't find a publishing house that wanted it. Lakoff ended up more or less giving it away to Chelsea Green, a tiny liberal publisher in Vermont.

That book, "Don't Think of an Elephant!" is now in its eighth printing, having sold nearly 200,000 copies, first through liberal word of mouth and the blogosphere and then through reviews and the lecture circuit. (On the eve of last fall's election, I came across a Democratic volunteer in Ohio who was handing out a boxful of copies to her friends.) Lakoff has emerged as one of the country's most coveted speakers among liberal groups, up there with Howard Dean, who, as it happens, wrote the foreword to "Don't Think of an Elephant!" Lakoff has a DVD titled "How Democrats and Progressives Can Win: Solutions from George Lakoff," and he recently set up his own consulting company.

In the 1970s, Lakoff, verging into philosophy, became obsessed with metaphors. As he explained it to me one day over lunch at a Berkeley cafe, students of the mind, going back to Aristotle, had always viewed metaphor simply as a device of language, a facile way of making a point. Lakoff argued instead that metaphors were actually embedded in the recesses of the mind, giving the brain a way to process abstract ideas. In other words, a bad relationship reminds you on an unconscious level of a cul-de-sac, because both are leading nowhere. This results from what might be called a "love as journey" frame in the neural pathways of your brain—that is, you are more likely to relate to the story of, say, a breakup if it is described to you with the imagery of a journey. This might seem intuitive, but in 1980, when Lakoff wrote "Metaphors We Live By," it was considered fairly radical.

15   Through his work on metaphors, Lakoff found an avenue into political discourse. In a seminal 1996 book, *Moral Politics*, he asserted that people relate to political ideologies, on an unconscious level, through the metaphorical frame of a family. Conservative politicians, Lakoff suggests, operate under the frame of a strict father, who lays down inflexible rules and imbues his family with a strong moral order. Liberals, on the other hand, are best understood through a frame of the nurturant parent, who teaches his child to pursue personal happiness and care for those around him. (The two models, Lakoff has said, are personified by Arnold Schwarzenegger on one side and Oprah Winfrey on the other.) Most voters, Lakoff suggests, carry some part of both parental frames in the synapses of their brains; which model is "activated"—that is, which they can better relate to—depends on the language that politicians use and the story that they tell.

The most compelling part of Lakoff's hypothesis is the notion that in order to reach voters, all the individual issues of a political debate must be tied together by some larger frame that feels familiar to us. Lakoff suggests that voters respond to grand metaphors—whether it is the metaphor of a strict father or something else entirely—as opposed to specific arguments, and that specific arguments only resonate if they reinforce some grander metaphor. The best evidence to support this idea can be found in the history of the 2004 presidential campaign. From Day 1, Republicans tagged Kerry with a larger metaphor: he was a flip-flopper, a Ted Kennedy-style liberal who tried to seem centrist, forever bouncing erratically from one position to the other. They made sure that virtually every comment they uttered about Kerry during the campaign reminded voters, subtly or not, of this one central theme. (The smartest ad of the campaign may have been the one that showed Kerry windsurfing, expertly gliding back and forth, back and forth.) Democrats, on the other hand, presented a litany of different complaints about Bush, depending on the day and the backdrop; he was a liar, a corporate stooge, a spoiled rich kid, a reckless warmonger. But they never managed to tie them all into a single, unifying image that voters could associate with the president. As a result, none of them stuck. Bush was attacked. Kerry was framed.

According to Lakoff, Republicans are skilled at using loaded language, along with constant repetition, to play into the frames in our unconscious minds. Take one of his favorite examples, the phrase "tax relief." It presumes, Lakoff points out, that we are being oppressed by taxes and that we need to be liberated from them. It fits into a familiar frame of persecution, and when such a phrase, repeated over time, enters the everyday lexicon, it biases the debate in favor of conservatives. If Democrats start to talk about their own "tax relief" plan, Lakoff says, they have conceded the point that taxes are somehow an unfair burden rather than making the case that they are an investment in the common good. The argument is lost before it begins.

Lakoff informed his political theories by studying the work of Frank Luntz, the Republican pollster who helped Newt Gingrich formulate the Contract with America in 1994. To Lakoff and his followers, Luntz is the very embodiment of Republican deception. His private memos, many of which fell into the hands of Democrats, explain why. In one recent memo, titled "The 14 Words Never to Use," Luntz urged conservatives to restrict themselves to phrases from what he calls, grandly, the "New American Lexicon." Thus, a smart Republican, in Luntz's view, never advocates "drilling for oil"; he prefers "exploring for energy." He should never criticize the "government," which cleans our streets and pays our firemen; he should attack "Washington," with its ceaseless thirst for taxes and regulations. "We should never use the word outsourcing," Luntz wrote, "because we will then be asked to defend or end the practice of allowing companies to ship American jobs overseas."

In Lakoff's view, not only does Luntz's language twist the facts of his agenda but it also renders facts meaningless by actually reprogramming, through long-term repetition, the neural networks inside our brains. And this is where Lakoff's vision gets a little disturbing. According to Lakoff, Democrats have been wrong to assume that people are rational actors who make their decisions based on facts; in reality, he says, cognitive science has proved that all of us are programmed to respond to the frames that have been embedded deep in our unconscious minds, and if the facts don't fit the frame, our brains simply reject them. Lakoff explained to me that the frames in our brains can be "activated" by the right combination of words and imagery, and only then, once the brain has been unlocked, can we process the facts being thrown at us.

This notion of "activating" unconscious thought sounded like something out of 20 *The Manchurian Candidate* ("Raymond, why don't you pass the time by playing a little solitaire?"), and I asked Lakoff if he was suggesting that Americans voted for conservatives because they had been brainwashed.

"Absolutely not," he answered, shaking his head.

But hadn't he just said that Republicans had somehow managed to rewire people's brains?

"That's true, but that's different from brainwashing, and it's a very important thing," he said. "Brainwashing has to do with physical control, capturing people and giving them messages over and over under conditions of physical deprivation or torture. What conservatives have done is not brainwashing in this way. They've done something that's perfectly legal. What they've done is find ways to set their frames into words over many years and have them repeated over and over again and have everybody say it the same way and get their journalists to repeat them, until they became part of normal English."

I asked Lakoff how he himself had avoided being reprogrammed by these stealth Republican words. "Because I'm a linguist, I recognize them," he said. Even to him, this sounded a little too neat, and a moment later he admitted that he, too, had fallen prey to conservative frames now and then. "Occasionally," he said with a shrug, "I've caught myself."

25   In May 2003, Senator Byron Dorgan, the North Dakota Democrat, read *Moral Politics* and took Lakoff to a Democratic Senate retreat in Cambridge, Md. Lakoff had never met a senator before. "I knew what they were up against, even if they didn't know what they were up against," Lakoff says. "They were just besieged. My heart went out to them."

Lakoff gave a presentation, and in the parlance of comedians, he killed. Hillary Clinton invited him to dinner. Tom Daschle, then the minority leader, asked Lakoff if he would rejoin the senators a few days later, during their next caucus meeting at the Capitol, so that he could offer advice about the tax plan they were working on. Lakoff readily agreed, even though he had come East without so much as a jacket or tie. "I went in there, and it was just this beautiful thing," he told me, recalling the caucus meeting. "All these people I'd just met applauded. They gave me hugs. It was the most amazing thing."

Of course, the idea that language and narrative matter in politics shouldn't really have come as a revelation to Washington Democrats. Bill Clinton had been an intuitive master of framing. As far back as 1992, Clinton's image of Americans who "worked hard and played by the rules," for instance, had perfectly evoked the metaphor of society as a contest that relied on fairness. And yet despite this, Democrats in Congress were remarkably slow to grasp this dimension of political combat. Having ruled Capitol Hill pretty comfortably for most of the past 60 years, Democrats had never had much reason to think about calibrating their language in order to sell their ideas.

"I can describe, and I've always been able to describe, what Republicans stand for in eight words, and the eight words are lower taxes, less government, strong defense and family values," Dorgan, who runs the Democratic Policy Committee in the Senate, told me recently. "We Democrats, if you ask us about one piece of that, we can meander for 5 or 10 minutes in order to describe who we are and what we stand for. And frankly, it just doesn't compete very well. I'm not talking about the policies. I'm talking about the language."

Dorgan has become the caucus's chief proponent of framing theory. "I think getting some help from some people who really understand how to frame some of these issues is long overdue," he says, which is why he invited Lakoff back to talk to his colleagues after the 2004 election. Meanwhile, over on the House side, George Miller, a Democrat from the San Francisco area, met Lakoff through a contributor and offered to distribute copies of *Don't Think of an Elephant!* to every member of the caucus. The thin paperback became as ubiquitous among Democrats in the Capitol as Mao's Little Red Book once was in the Forbidden City. "The framing was perfect for us, because we were just arriving in an unscientific way at what Lakoff was arriving at in a scientific way," says Representative Nancy Pelosi, the minority leader in the House.

In fact, though Lakoff started the framing discussion, he was by no means the only   30
outside expert whom Democrats were consulting about language. To the contrary, a
small industry had blossomed. Even before the 2004 election, Pelosi had enlisted John
Cullinane, a software entrepreneur in Boston, to help the caucus develop the wording for a vision statement. Cullinane spent an hour and a half with members of the
caucus one afternoon, while his aide scrawled suggestions on a white board. Among
his recommendations was that they come up with a list that had six parts—either six
principles or six values or six ideas. When we spoke, I asked Cullinane why it had to
be six. "Seven's too many," he replied. "Five's too few."

Then there was Richard Yanowitch, a Silicon Valley executive and party donor,
who worked with Senate Democrats, providing what he calls "private-sector type
marketing." Last December, at Dorgan's request, Reid put Yanowitch in charge of a
"messaging project" to help devise new language for the party. Another adviser who
became a frequent guest on the Hill after the election was Jim Wallis, a left-leaning
evangelical minister who wrote *God's Politics: Why the Right Gets It Wrong and the
Left Doesn't Get it*. In January, after addressing a Senate caucus retreat at the Kennedy
Center, Wallis wrote a memo to the Democratic Policy Committee titled "Budgets
Are Moral Documents," in which he laid out his argument that Democrats needed to
"reframe" the budget in spiritual terms.

What all of these new advisers meant by "framing," exactly, and whether their concepts bore much resemblance to Lakoff's complex cognitive theories wasn't really clear.
The word had quickly become something of a catchall, a handy term to describe anything having to do with changing the party's image through some new combination of
language. So admired were these outside experts that they could hardly be counted as
outsiders anymore. In May, for instance, Roger Altman, Clinton's former deputy trea-
sury secretary, held a dinner for the former president to discuss the party's message
with about 15 of its most elite and influential thinkers, including James Carville, Paul
Begala, the pollster Mark J. Penn and John Podesta, president of the Center for American
Progress, the liberal think tank. Lakoff sat at Clinton's table; Wallis, at the next one over.

Bush's plan to reform Social Security provided, last winter, the first test of the
Democrats' new focus on language and narrative. In retrospect, it shows both the limits of framing and, perhaps, the real reason that Democrats have managed to stymie
critical pieces of the Bush agenda.

Almost as soon as Bush signaled his intention to overhaul the existing program,
Democrats in Congress, enamored of Lakoff's theories, embarked on a search for a
compelling story line. Yanowitch's highly secretive messaging group met for months
on the topic and came up with two "sample narratives" that Democrats might use.
The first, titled "Privatization: A Gamble You Can't Afford to Take," stressed the
insecurity of middle-class families and compared Bush's plan to a roll of the dice.
The second, "The Magical World of Privatization," spun out a metaphor that centered on Bush as "an old-fashioned traveling salesman, with a cart full of magic
elixirs and cure-all tonics." Some of this imagery found its way into the dialogue,
for better or worse; Pelosi and other House members, never too proud to put their
dignity above the greater good, held an outdoor news conference standing next to
a stack of giant dice.

35   As they would later with the filibuster fight and with the Supreme Court, Senate Democrats, under Reid's direction, set up a war room and a strategy group, this one run by Jim Messina, chief of staff for Senator Max Baucus of Montana. Eschewing all the lofty metaphors, the war room stuck to two simple ideas: Bush's plan relied on privatizing the most popular government benefit in America, and it amounted to benefit cuts coupled with long-term borrowing. In addition to keeping members focused on their talking points, Messina's team and its allies—led by two liberal interest groups, MoveOn.org and Campaign for America's Future, with help from the all-powerful AARP—also had to stop senators and congressmen from offering compromise plans that might drive a wedge into the caucus. In this way, Democrats had decided to follow the example of Bill Kristol, the Republican strategist who had urged his party (shrewdly, as it turned out) to refrain from proposing any alternatives to Clinton's doomed health-care plan in 1993. "The minute we introduce a plan, we have to solve the problem" is how one senior Democratic aide explained it to me. "We are the minority party. It's not our job to fix things."

As it happened, this was where Lakoff himself proved most helpful. In a meeting with House Democrats, some of whom were considering their own versions of private accounts, he urged them to hold firm against Bush's plan. "I pointed out that as soon as you allow them to get a privatization frame in people's minds about retirement and Social Security, it becomes an unintelligible difference," he recalled. "People will not be able to tell the difference between your plan and the other guy's." Referring to Pelosi, he added, "Nancy was saying the same thing, and so they stopped." As Democrats stood firm, Bush's idea for private accounts, which was never all that popular with voters to begin with, seemed to slowly lose altitude. A Gallup tracking poll conducted for CNN and *USA Today* showed the president's plan losing support, from 40 percent of voters in January to 33 percent in April.

Bush had tried to recast his proposed "private accounts" as "personal accounts" after it became clear to both sides that privatization, as a concept, frightened voters. But as they did on the filibuster, Democrats had managed to trap the president in his own linguistic box. "We branded them with privatization, and they can't sell that brand anywhere," Pelosi bragged when I spoke with her in May. "It's down to, like, 29 percent or something. At the beginning of this debate, voters were saying that the president was a *president* who had new ideas. Now he's a *guy* who wants to cut my benefits." At this, Pelosi laughed loudly.

What had Democrats learned about framing? In the end, the success of the Social Security effort—and, for that matter, the filibuster campaign—may have had something to do with language or metaphor, but it probably had more to do with the elusive virtue of party discipline. Pelosi explained it to me this way: for years, the party's leaders had tried to get restless Democrats to stay "on message," to stop freelancing their own rogue proposals and to continue reading from the designated talking points even after it got excruciatingly boring to do so. Consultants like Garin and Margolis had been saying the same thing, but Democratic congressmen, skeptical of the in-crowd of D.C. strategists, had begun to tune them out. "Listening to people inside Washington did not produce any victories," Pelosi said.

But now there were people from outside Washington—experts from the worlds of academia and Silicon Valley—who were making the same case. What the framing experts had been telling Democrats on the Hill, aside from all this arcane stuff about narratives and neural science, was that they needed to stay unified and repeat the same few words and phrases over and over again. And these "outsiders" had what Reid and Pelosi and their legion of highly paid consultants did not: the patina of scientific credibility. Culturally, this made perfect sense. If you wanted Republican lawmakers to buy into a program, you brought in a guy like Frank Luntz, an unapologetically partisan pollster who dressed like the head of the College Republicans. If you wanted Democrats to pay attention, who better to do the job than an egghead from Berkeley with an armful of impenetrable journal studies on the workings of the brain?

You might say that Lakoff and the others managed to give the old concept of message discipline a new, more persuasive frame—and that frame was called "framing." "The framing validates what we're trying to say to them," Pelosi said. "You have a Berkeley professor saying, 'This is how the mind works; this is how people perceive language; this is how you have to be organized in your presentation.' It gives me much more leverage with my members." 40

On a recent morning in his Virginia office, seated next to one of those one-way glass walls that you find only in the offices of cops and pollsters, Frank Luntz explained why George Lakoff and his framing theory were leading the Democratic Party astray. In recent years, Luntz's penchant for publicity—he is a frequent commentator on cable television—has earned him no small amount of scorn and ridicule from fellow Republicans; that Lakoff's little book had suddenly elevated Luntz to a kind of mythic villain seemed to amuse him. "In some ways, the Democrats appreciate me more than the Republicans do," Luntz, 43, told me with a trace of self-pity.

The problem with Lakoff, Luntz said, is that the professor's ideology seemed to be driving his science. Luntz, after all, has never made for a terribly convincing conservative ideologue. (During our conversation, he volunteered that the man he admired most was the actor Peter Sellers, for his ability to disappear into whatever role he was given.) Luntz sees Lakoff, by contrast, as a doctrinaire liberal who believes viscerally that if Democrats are losing, it has to be because of the words they use rather than the substance of the argument they make. What Lakoff didn't realize, Luntz said, was that poll-tested phrases like "tax relief" were successful only because they reflected the values of voters to begin with; no one could sell ideas like higher taxes and more government to the American voter, no matter how they were framed. To prove it, Luntz, as part of his recent polling for the U.S. Chamber of Commerce, specifically tested some of Lakoff's proposed language on taxation. He said he found that even when voters were reminded of the government's need to invest in education, health care, national security and retirement security, 66 percent of them said the United States overtaxed its citizenry and only 14 percent said we were undertaxed. Luntz presented this data to chamber officials on a slide with the headline "George Lakoff Is Wrong!!"

"He deserves a lot of credit," Luntz said of Lakoff. "He's one of the very few guys who understands the limits of liberal language. What he doesn't understand is that there are also limits on liberal philosophy. They think that if they change all the words, it'll make a difference. Won't happen."

Luntz's dismissiveness is what you might expect to hear about Lakoff from a Republican, of course. But the same complaint has surfaced with growing ferocity among skeptical Democrats and in magazines like *The Atlantic Monthly* and *The New Republic*. An antiframing backlash has emerged, and while it is, on the surface, an argument about Lakoff and his theories, it is clearly also a debate about whether the party lacks only for language or whether it needs a fresher agenda. Lakoff's detractors say that it is he who resembles the traveling elixir salesman, peddling comforting answers at a time when desperate Democrats should be admitting some hard truths about their failure to generate new ideas. "Every election defeat has a charlatan, some guy who shows up and says, 'Hey, I marketed the lava lamp, and I can market Democratic politics,' " says Kenneth Baer, a former White House speechwriter who wrote an early article attacking Lakoff's ideas in *The Washington Monthly*. "At its most basic, it represents the Democratic desire to find a messiah."

45   In a devastating critique in *The Atlantic's* April issue, Marc Cooper, a contributing editor at *The Nation*, skillfully ridiculed Lakoff as the new progressive icon. "Much more than an offering of serious political strategy, *Don't Think of an Elephant!* is a feel-good, self-help book for a stratum of despairing liberals who just can't believe how their common-sense message has been misunderstood by eternally deceived masses," Cooper wrote. In Lakoff's view, he continued, American voters are "redneck, chain-smoking, baby-slapping Christers desperately in need of some gender-free nurturing and political counseling by organic-gardening enthusiasts from Berkeley."

Lakoff doesn't have much patience for criticism (he's a tenured professor, after all), and he keeps at his disposal a seemingly bottomless arsenal of linguistic and philosophical theories with which to refute such attacks. In response to Cooper's article and another in *The Atlantic*, by Joshua Green, Lakoff fired off a nine-page draft response to a long e-mail list of friends and journalists in which he accused Cooper and Green of living in the "rationalist-materialist paradigm" (that's RAM for short), an outdated belief system that mistakenly assumes the rationality of other human beings. He also pointed out that they had cleverly, but unsuccessfully, tried to trap him in the "guru frame," a story line about one individual who passes himself off as having all the answers to other people's problems.

Lakoff has some valid points. In his writing, at least, he explains framing in a way that is more intellectually complex than his critics have admitted. His essential insight into politics—that voters make their decisions based on larger frames rather than on the sum of a candidate's positions—is hard to refute. And Lakoff does say in *Don't Think of an Elephant!* albeit very briefly, that Democrats need not just new language but also new thought; he told me the party suffers from "hypocognition," or a lack of ideas. What's more, when it comes to the language itself, Lakoff has repeatedly written that the process of reframing American political thought will take years, if not decades, to achieve. He does not suggest in his writing that a few catchy slogans can turn the political order on its head by the next election.

The message Lakoff's adherents seem to take away from their personal meetings with him, however, is decidedly more simplistic. When I asked Senator Richard Durbin of Illinois, the minority whip and one of Lakoff's strongest supporters, whether Lakoff had talked to the caucus about this void of new ideas in the party, Durbin didn't hesitate. "He doesn't ask us to change our views or change our philosophy," Durbin said. "He tells us that we have to recommunicate." In fact, Durbin said he now understood, as a result of Lakoff's work, that the Republicans have triumphed "by repackaging old ideas in all new wrapping," the implication being that this was not a war of ideas at all, but a contest of language.

The question here is whether Lakoff purposely twists his own academic theories to better suit his partisan audience or whether his followers are simply hearing what they want to hear and ignoring the rest. When I first met Lakoff in Los Angeles, he made it clear, without any prompting from me, that he was exasperated by the dumbing down of his intricate ideas. He had just been the main attraction at a dinner with Hollywood liberals, and he despaired that all they had wanted from him were quick fixes to long-term problems. "They all just want to know the magic words," he told me. "I say: 'You don't understand, there aren't any magic words. It's about ideas.' But all everyone wants to know is: 'What three words can we use? How do we win the next election?' They don't get it."

Peter Teague, who oversees environmental programs at the liberal Nathan Cummings Foundation, was Lakoff's most important patron in the days after he wrote "*Moral Politics*." When I spoke with Teague about Lakoff a few months ago, he sounded a little depressed. "There's a cartoon version of Lakoff out there, and everyone's responding to the cartoon," Teague said. "It's not particularly useful. As much as we talk about having a real dialogue and a deeper discussion, we really end up having a very superficial conversation.

"I keep saying to George, 'You're reinforcing the very things you're fighting against.' "

I asked Lakoff, during an afternoon walk across the Berkeley campus, if he felt at all complicit in the superficiality that Teague was describing. "I do," he said thoughtfully. "It's a complicated problem. Of course it bothers me. But this is just Stage I, and there are stages of misunderstanding. People have to travel a path of understanding."

His celebrity may yet prove to be his undoing. When I visited him in Berkeley in April, Lakoff, who until then had done all his work with Washington Democrats on a volunteer basis, had submitted a proposal to leaders in the House for a consulting contract. Although the details were closely guarded, it had something to do with a project to use focus groups to study narrative. In May, House Democrats decided not to finalize the deal after some members and senior aides wondered out loud if Lakoff mania had gotten out of hand. Lakoff, it seemed, was experiencing a common Washington phenomenon to which Frank Luntz could easily relate: the more famous an adviser gets, the more politicians begin to suspect him of trying to further himself at their expense. A friend of Lakoff's suggested to me that we were witnessing the beginning of an all-too-familiar frame: the meteoric rise and dizzying fall of a political sensation.

If that were true, it seemed, then the whole notion of framing might just be a passing craze, like some post-election macarena. It certainly sounded like that might be the case when I visited Harry Reid just before Memorial Day. Reid waved away the suggestion that language had much to do with the party's recent successes. "If you want my honest opinion, and I know you do, I think people make too much out of that," he said. "I'm not a person who dwells on all these people getting together and spending hours and days coming up with the right words. I know that my staff thinks, 'Oh, why don't you tell him about all this great work we've done on framing?' But honestly, that's not it."

55   Reid credited the "team effort" and message discipline of the caucus for its victory on the filibuster issue. At one point, when I asked Reid, a former boxer, about Lakoff's theories, he seemed to equate them with psychotherapy. "I'm not going to waste a lot of time sitting in a room talking about how my parents weren't good to me or something like that," Reid said firmly. "I'm not involved in any of that gimmickry."

After leaving Reid, I walked across the Capitol to see Nancy Pelosi, who told a different story. She assured me that Lakoff's ideas had "forever changed" the way Democratic House members thought about politics. "He has taken people here to a place, whether you agree or disagree with his particular frame, where they know there has to be a frame," she told me. "They all agree without any question that you don't speak on Republican terms. You don't think of an elephant."

I suggested that maybe she and Reid had different views on the value of framing as a strategy. "Oh, no," she said emphatically, drawing out the last word. "He's been a leader on it! The two of us know better than anyone what's at stake here. In fact, he sort of initiated our abuse-of-power frame."

It was hard to know what to make of these conflicting conversations. Perhaps Reid feared that if he admitted to caring about framing, he would be framed as one of those clueless Democrats seeking easy answers. Perhaps Pelosi was covering for him by suggesting they were unified when in fact they weren't. But it seemed more likely that the disconnect between the party's two elected leaders reflected a broader confusion among Democrats about what they actually mean by framing. There is no doubt that having a central theme and repeating it like robots has made Democrats a respectable opposition force in Congress. To Pelosi and a lot of other Democrats, that is the miracle of this thing called framing. To Reid, it is just an intuitive part of politics, and he doesn't need some professor to give it a name or tell him that Democrats haven't been very good at it.

Whatever you call it, this kind of message discipline will be a crucial piece of what will most likely become, in the weeks ahead, a Democratic push to block Bush's designs on the Supreme Court. In order to stop a nominee, Democrats will have to frame the filibuster battle in the public arena all over again, and this time, they will have to convince voters that it is Bush's specific choice for the nation's highest court—and not simply a slate of faceless judges—who represents the reckless arrogance of Republican rule. Even in the hours after O'Connor made her announcement, you could see in Democratic responses the first stirrings of this new campaign. "If the president abuses his power and nominates someone who threatens to roll back the rights and freedoms of the American people," said Ted Kennedy, lifting lines directly from Garin's latest polling memo, "then the American people will insist that we oppose that nominee, and we intend to do so." Meanwhile, Susan McCue, Reid's powerful chief of staff, offered me a preview of the theory to come: "It goes beyond 'abuse of power.' It's about arrogance, irresponsibility, being out of touch and catering to a narrow, narrow slice of their ideological constituency at the expense of the vast majority of Americans."

It is not inconceivable that such an argument could sway public opinion; 60 Americans are congenitally disposed to distrust whichever party holds power. The larger question—too large, perhaps, for most Democrats to want to consider at the moment—is whether they can do more with language and narrative than simply snipe at Bush's latest initiative or sink his nominees. Here, the Republican example may be instructive. In 1994, Republican lawmakers, having heeded Bill Kristol's advice and refused to engage in the health-care debate, found themselves in a position similar to where Democrats are now; they had weakened the president and spiked his trademark proposal, and they knew from Luntz's polling that the public harbored serious reservations about the Democratic majority in Congress. What they did next changed the course of American politics. Rather than continue merely to deflect Clinton's agenda, Republicans came up with their own, the Contract with America, which promised 10 major legislative acts that were, at the time, quite provocative. They included reforming welfare, slashing budget deficits, imposing harsher criminal penalties and cutting taxes on small businesses. Those 10 items, taken as a whole, encapsulated a rigid conservative philosophy that had been taking shape for 30 years—and that would define politics at the end of the 20th century.

By contrast, consider the declaration that House Democrats produced after their session with John Cullinane, the branding expert, last fall. The pamphlet is titled "The House Democrats' New Partnership for America's Future: Six Core Values for a Strong and Secure Middle Class." Under each of the six values—"prosperity, national security, fairness, opportunity, community and accountability"—is a wish list of vague notions and familiar policy ideas. ("Make health care affordable for every American," "Invest in a fully funded education system that gives every child the skills to succeed" and so on.) Pelosi is proud of the document, which—to be fair—she notes is just a first step toward repackaging the party's agenda. But if you had to pick an unconscious metaphor to attach to it, it would probably be a cotton ball.

Consider, too, George Lakoff's own answer to the Republican mantra. He sums up the Republican message as "strong defense, free markets, lower taxes, smaller government and family values," and in *Don't Think of an Elephant!* he proposes some Democratic alternatives: "Stronger America, broad prosperity, better future, effective government and mutual responsibility." Look at the differences between the two. The Republican version is an argument, a series of philosophical assertions that require voters to make concrete choices about the direction of the country. Should we spend more or less on the military? Should government regulate industry or leave it unfettered? Lakoff's formulation, on the other hand, amounts to a vague collection of the least objectionable ideas in American life. Who out there wants to make the case against prosperity and a better future? Who doesn't want an effective government?

What all these middling generalities suggest, perhaps, is that Democrats are still unwilling to put their more concrete convictions about the country into words, either because they don't know what those convictions are or because they lack confidence in the notion that voters can be persuaded to embrace them. Either way, this is where the power of language meets its outer limit. The right words can frame an argument, but they will never stand in its place.

Things to Do with the Reading

1. Write an essay in which you apply the heuristic "Looking for Difference within Similarity" (Chapter 4) to a comparison of George Lakoff and Frank Luntz. Aside from being resident language gurus for their respective parties, what do the two have in common? What assumptions about political language do they share? Then, crucially, what are the most significant differences between them, and so what?

2. In the questions following the Luntz interview, we noted the strand of "emotion" words in Luntz's language, suggesting that this orientation was a revealing (and complicating) aspect of his approach. Write an essay on the status of emotion (and similar words) in Lakoff's program. Luntz opposes the emotional to the intellectual: what is Lakoff's position on this binary? And how does he value each side of it?

3. **Link:** Lakoff argues that people tend to think about political ideologies in terms of what he calls "the metaphorical frame of a family." "Conservative politicians, Lakoff suggests, operate under the frame of a strict father, who lays down inflexible rules and imbues his family with a strong moral order. Liberals, on the other hand, are best understood through a frame of the nurturant parent, who teaches his child to pursue personal happiness and care for those around him" (paragraph 15). What links do you see between these two parental metaphors (and the terms associated with each of them) and the way that Christopher Borick characterizes conservatism and liberalism in "On Political Labels"? How, for example, might the histories of the two parties, as traced by Borick, have inclined them toward these roles?

   Note: Language in the Application that follows provides further key terms for considering these parental metaphorical frames in light of liberal and conservative values as defined by Borick.

4. **Application:** Use the language of "The Framing Wars" to interpret any political conflict or campaign in your immediate environment. Bai defines framing as having "to do with choosing the language to define a debate and, more important, with fitting individual issues into the contexts of broader story lines" (paragraph 3). Locate some "individual issue" in your town or on your campus within the story lines implicit in Lakoff's parenting metaphors. (The front page of college newspapers customarily teams with such issues.) In what ways does one side of the issue or campaign resemble the strict father who, in the words

of columnist Michael Erard, "protects moral dependents, punishes moral inferiors, and aims to raise independent children to fend for themselves in a dangerous world"? Where do you see the other side resembling "the nurturing parent who encourages children's inherent goodness so that they will treat others with fairness and equality."? (Michael Erard, "Frame Wars," *The Texas Observer*, 11/5/2004.) Write an essay, in short, in which you discern how each side is framing the issue.

OBAMA AND THE LANGUAGE OF POLITICS: TWO SHORT ARTICLES

Peter Nicholas and Jim Tankersley, "Buzzwords: Rephrasing Obama's Lexicon"
Michael D. Shear, "Obama Subtly Adopts the Language of Business"

The following brief articles offer a glimpse of the way the Obama administration is engaged in changing labels and words to elicit a more positive response from the electorate. In "Buzzwords: Rephrasing Obama's Lexicon," which appeared in the *Los Angeles Times*, Peter Nicholas and Jim Tankersley discuss the president's substitution of alternative phrases for "cap and trade" and "global warming," two previous code phrases in Democratic energy policy. Then in "Obama Subtly Adopts the Language of Business," a piece written for "The Caucus: The Politics and Government Blog" of the *New York Times*, Michael D. Shear provides a brief history of the phrase "American competitiveness," with special attention to Democratic attempts to appropriate this traditionally Republican term.

Peter Nicholas and Jim Tankersley

Buzzwords: Rephrasing Obama's Lexicon

1   *Scratch "cap and trade" and "global warming," Democratic pollsters tell Obama. They're ineffective. Republicans are also rethinking how to use words to their advantage.*

WASHINGTON—In the debate over his top environmental goals, President Obama is backing away from "cap and trade."

Not the policy. It's the phrase itself, deemed confusing by Democratic pollsters, that has all but disappeared from the president's vocabulary of late.

Now when Obama talks about forcing companies to bid at auction for the right to emit greenhouse gases, he is more apt to mention "market-based" proposals and "clean energy jobs," hinting at a rich new employment source.

5   Control the language, politicians know, and you stand a better chance of controlling the debate. So the Obama administration, in its push to enact sweeping energy and healthcare policies, has begun refining the phrases it uses in an effort to shape public opinion.

Words that have been vetted in focus groups and polls are seeping into the White House lexicon, while others considered too scary or confounding are falling away.

Today, aides in Obama's Council on Environmental Quality will meet with a research and marketing group that is promoting an alternative to the phrase "global warming," which some pollsters say fails to capture the idea of greenhouse gases threatening the environment.

"There is value in trying to get the messaging right," said a senior White House environmental aide, who was not authorized to speak on the record. "Because at the end of the day this is tricky policy.... We want to make sure we're talking in a way that people understand."

Peter Nicholas and Jim Tankersley, "Buzzwords: Rephrasing Obama's Lexicon" http://articles.latimes.com /print/2009/may/11/nation/na-obama-language11 Los Angeles Times May 11, 2009. Used by permission.

Republicans too are rethinking the words they use. The GOP's response to   10
Obama's energy effort is "light-switch tax." Their message is that if Obama gets his
way, Americans will be taxed every time they turn on a light.

As for Obama's healthcare overhaul, consultant Frank Luntz led a briefing for
Republican aides on Capitol Hill last week to suggest phrases that might prove effective against it.

Luntz especially liked the term "rationing," with its connotation of long waits for
medical tests and denial of care.

"The word 'rationing' does induce the negative response you want," Luntz's memo
to GOP congressional staff said.

"As you can see," the memo continued, "'rationing' tests very well against the
other healthcare buzzwords that frighten Americans," such as "socialized medicine"
and "Hillary-care"—a reference to Hillary Rodham Clinton's failed effort to revamp
healthcare when she was first lady in the 1990s.

The San Francisco firm David Binder Research has conducted focus groups for
the Democratic National Committee, which has shared the findings with White
House officials such as senior advisor David Axelrod and Dan Pfeiffer, a deputy communications director. The Democratic committee's expense records show it has paid
the firm $87,500 so far this year.

"The problem in the past for Democrats has been once they get elected they revel   15
in talking to each other in policy-ese," said Geoff Garin, a Democratic strategist. "But
in doing so, they talk in a language that is incomprehensible to people who live and
work outside the bubble."

Results of a recent poll by the Mellman Group were also shared with the White
House. The Washington consulting firm undertook a survey for environmentalists
that polled 800 likely voters in late March. Its 45-page report recommended playing
up the idea that curbing global warming would create jobs.

The survey tested 19 phrases and found "clean energy jobs" had the widest appeal,
with 42% of the respondents "very enthusiastic" about it.

"Cap and trade," by contrast, ranked next to last, with only 7% registering enthusiasm.   20

Few people know that the "cap" in the proposed cap-and-trade system refers to
the limit that the government would impose on industrial emissions of heat-trapping
gases. In order to exceed the caps, polluters would have to buy emission permits from
the government and from other companies—thus, the "trade."

"Cap-and-trade is a term used by policymakers and insiders, and it's not understood by average Americans," one Democratic strategist said.

Another strategist said the term "trade" reminded people of the volatile stock
market, which made them uneasy about the underlying policy.

It seems clear that the White House is absorbing some of these messages. During
Obama's 2008 presidential campaign, his website included a section devoted to energy
and environmental protection. The phrase "cap-and-trade" popped up at several points.

In contrast, Obama's White House website carries an energy section that makes
no mention of "cap-and-trade."

A list of energy policy talking points compiled by Obama's Council on
Environmental Quality is filled with poll-tested messages, such as variations on the
phrase "clean energy jobs."

25   Republicans' use of the "light-switch tax" is meant to make a simple point: Obama's energy plan costs money. Senate Minority Leader Mitch McConnell (R-Ky.) used the term on a television talk show in March. Rep. Michele Bachmann (R-Minn.) and Sen. Judd Gregg (R-N.H.) have invoked it too.

"Republicans want to ensure that the American people see the Democrats' energy cap policy for what it really is—a back-breaking tax on every American in this country who 'dares' use electricity," Brad Dayspring, a spokesman for House Republican Whip Eric Cantor of Virginia, said in an interview Sunday.

Obama privately is advising Democratic members of Congress to pay special attention to the words they use too. Hosting the House Energy and Commerce Committee, the president counseled members to say that the energy and cap-and-trade legislation moving through Congress would create "clean jobs."

"Global warming" is a phrase that also may be in jeopardy. Some Democratic pollsters dislike it; others think that jettisoning a term that has been the subject of a vigorous branding campaign would be risky.

One critic of the phrase is Robert Perkowitz, who is meeting with Obama's Council on Environmental Quality today.

30   Perkowitz said that "90% of people, when they hear about global warming, the first person that comes to mind is Al Gore. And if you like Al Gore, you're excited. But if you don't, then that turns you off to global warming."

Michael D. Shear

Obama Subtly Adopts the Language of Business

1   By focusing his State of the Union address on competitiveness abroad and the investment needed at home to secure it, President Obama is using storied Washington code words that have long histories and double meanings, and are—he hopes—less fraught with political baggage than the alternatives.

Aides say the broad theme of Mr. Obama's speech will be a clarion call for a new focus on America's ability to compete around the world. By using the language of corporate America, the president hopes to reassure those who doubt he is business friendly, but to do so without alienating his core supporters.

The phrase "American competitiveness" is hardly new, and it is definitely not an invention of Mr. Obama's Democratic Party.

In fact, for decades the phrase was the intellectual property of Republican administrations, which used it as a way of signaling their desire to reduce regulatory burdens on business and pave the way to higher profits for corporations struggling to compete with companies in other countries.

5   In 1981, Vice President George Bush called for "strong necessary steps to restore our competitiveness with other nations," as he proposed to do away with environmental and highway safety regulations that he said hampered the American auto industry.

From The New York Times, January 25 © 2011 The New York Times. All rights reserved. Used by permission and protected by the Copyright Laws of the United States. The printing, copying, redistribution, or retransmission of this Content without express written permission is prohibited.

When Mr. Bush became president, his vice president, Dan Quayle, headed a council on competitiveness inside the White House until it was attacked by Democrats as a cover for antiregulatory efforts, defunded in Congress and finally eliminated altogether by President Bill Clinton early in his first term.

In a statement by Vice President Al Gore, the Clinton administration said at the time that they were "sending a clear message to the special interests who used the Council on Competitiveness as a back door to avoid the law. That back door is closed." Mr. Gore said the "Council on Competitiveness was founded on a false choice, that the interests of workers, consumers and the environment conflict with the goal of economic growth."

But Mr. Clinton's White House did not discard the phrase. Rather, the president appropriated it as a new, global justification for the kind of policies he wanted to push through the Congress. In a 1993 speech urging passage of his healthcare plan, Mr. Clinton argued that revamping the healthcare system was necessary because of the impact it would have on the nation's ability to compete around the world.

"Our competitiveness, our whole economy, the integrity of the way the government works and, ultimately, our living standards depend upon our ability to achieve savings without harming the quality of health care," Mr. Clinton said. Competitiveness under Mr. Clinton harked back to the Sputnik era, when the space race spurred federal spending, fueled by a nationalistic, us-versus-them fervor.

Mr. Clinton also harnessed the power of competition to argue for his trade policies.   10 On the day he signed the North American Free Trade Act into law, Mr. Clinton said: "We cannot stop global change. We cannot repeal the international economic competition that is everywhere. We can only harness the energy to our benefit."

The question now is what Mr. Obama intends when he uses that phrase.

Labor unions worry that the president is trying to signal a rapprochement with business—a fear that grew when Mr. Obama last week announced a government-wide review of unneeded regulations. In an article in the *Wall Street Journal*, Mr. Obama wrote that such a review was needed "to remove outdated regulations that stifle job creation and make our economy less competitive."

When Mr. Obama talks about competitiveness, it resonates with business groups that had become suspicious of the president's commitment to private industry after his efforts to reform Wall Street. It is part of a realignment of Mr. Obama's White House that has included the hiring of William M. Daley as chief of staff. And it is a shield against critics who accuse Mr. Obama of having an antibusiness policy agenda.

But Mr. Obama's White House also appears to be leaning toward Mr. Clinton's use of the phrase—a justification for the president's approach to education and infrastructure spending that he says is necessary to compete with China and other rapidly growing economies.

And Mr. Obama is not likely to use the phrase "government spending" to describe   15 what he wants. Instead, he is likely to focus on what he calls "investments" in America's future.

Like competitiveness, that phrase has a long history in presidential communication. Often, it has become a favorite euphemism for Democratic politicians seeking to increase federal spending without raising the specter of negative implications for the nation's long-term debt.

Mr. Clinton used the phrase repeatedly, starting in his inaugural address, when he called for the country to "invest more in our own people, in their jobs, and in their future, and at the same time cut our massive debt."

And Mr. Obama has used it repeatedly during his presidency, often as a way of promising federal spending on his priorities. In a June speech last year at Carnegie Mellon University, Mr. Obama described his broad economic policy.

"It's a foundation based on investments in our people and their future; investments in the skills and education we need to compete," he said. "Investments in a 21st century infrastructure for America, from high-speed railroads to high-speed Internet; investments in research and technology, like clean energy, that can lead to new jobs and new exports and new industries."

20   That message is exactly what worries conservatives, who say Mr. Obama could just as easily substitute "spending" for "investment" in that paragraph.

"With all due respect to our Democratic friends, any time they want to spend, they call it investment, so I think you will hear the president talk about investing a lot Tuesday night," Senator Mitch McConnell of Kentucky, the Republican leader, said on *Fox News Sunday*.

An aide to Mr. McConnell summed up his boss's feelings in a Twitter message later, quoting the senator as saying, "Investment is a Latin term for more Washington spending."

Until Mr. Obama speaks on Tuesday night, people like Mr. McConnell will be left to wonder how the president intends to use phrases like "competitiveness" and "investment." And then everyone can start trying to interpret what he meant.

Things to Do with the Reading

1. **Link:** Compare the two articles in the context of Borick's "On Political Labels" or alternatively, the Luntz interview and the Bai essay on Lakoff. Write a short essay in which you analyze what the various renamings in the two articles have in common. Paraphrase the new terms in order to tease out their implications. And how do the new phrasings fit with the lexicon Borick offers (in Figure 23.1 and elsewhere) for aligning the particular issue named with the traditional beliefs of the party?

2. **Application:** Use the articles by Nicholas and Tankersley and by Shear as models to decode any recent political speeches or other public responses to current events. Use The Method on the speech (see Chapter 2) to identify key repetitions and strands and then write a brief essay in which you "decode" what the key terms appear to mean. Make sure to explore the buried rationale for such political naming. Note how Shear does this in his piece, interpreting evidence to formulate what competitiveness meant for the Republicans as opposed to what the Democrats wish it to mean. Do the same with key terms in the speech or article you choose.

3. Application: Track the response of both parties to any current political event—something dramatic enough to attract commentary from a range of spokespersons with a variety of political orientations. Assemble these responses and then write an essay in which you focus on the nature of the political rhetoric that has been used to discuss the same event. Translate it, as Shear has done, for example, in suggesting that "American competitiveness" is "a way of signaling [Republican] desire to reduce regulatory burdens on business" (paragraph 4). Suggest connotations, as Nicholas and Tankersley have done for Luntz's backing for the term "rationing."

James Peck

September 11th—a National Tragedy?

A director and professor of theater, James Peck feels troubled by the label so casually attached by the press, the politicians, and the rest of us to the September 11th attacks: "a national tragedy." In applying tragic theory to American response to the attack, Peck calls us to distinguish tragic events from just bad stuff happening and reminds us that "we have our own hubris to face." Beyond that, this piece helps us to see how much the label can matter when we talk about what things mean.

It is not the grave we mourn, but the dead.
Clytemnestra, in Euripides' *Iphigenia at Aulis*

1   Since the events of September 11th, I've been pursued by thoughts and images of tragedy. Frequently, I hear the terrorist attacks called "tragic" or "a national tragedy." The lead article in the *New York Times Magazine* the following Sunday, for example, was a collection of short pieces by prominent writers called "Elements of Tragedy." The title alludes to a key passage of Aristotle's *Poetics,* the canonical treatment of Greek tragedy and the most influential book of dramatic theory in the Western world. Subsequently, I've heard the tragic evoked by Sunday morning pundits, politicians of the left, right, and center, rock stars, talk-show hosts, the mayor of New York, professional athletes, my friends and colleagues, preachers, and members of my family. Probably others, too. As a lifelong theater person, this use of the language always triggers specific associations in me. Tragedy, of course is a theatrical genre dating in its origins from the fifth-century B.C. in Athens. The idea of the tragic recalls a long, vexed history in my art form. For many centuries, tragedy was the gold standard of drama, and debates about the definition and meaning of tragedy constitute some of the most vital episodes in the history of the theater. People in my field still make their reputations arguing the grounds or even the possibility of tragedy. Given my intellectual context, I confess to a certain proprietary interest in the way the concept of tragedy is deployed. Usually when I hear current events called tragic, I privately roll my eyes and lament the abuse of a term that is, if not exacting, at least rich, complicated, and possessed of a distinctive critical lineage. A voluminous literature theorizes the limits of tragic form, and I admit it rankles me to hear the word "tragic" used as a generic modifier for anything really bad that happens.

With the events of September 11th, however, I have found myself using the language of tragedy pretty indiscriminately. My immediate reaction to the attacks was precise and striking. Right after learning that the Twin Towers had collapsed, I wanted to read Euripides. I had an urge to go get *Iphigenia at Aulis* from the library and read it. Like scripture—for metaphors, sustenance, moral compass. I had not read this play in several years and still don't know it especially well, but it seemed at the time like my best hope for some kind of framework to apprehend what I was experiencing. I shuffled numbly around my office for a while feeling like this was kind of a silly notion till something else took over and I went about trying to make it through the day. But

September 11th: A National Tragedy? James Peck, from Aftermath: Thinking After September 11th: Occasional Papers of the Center for Ethics and Leadership. Reprinted with permission of the author.

the impulse persisted, and eventually I found my way to the bottom floor of Trexler to browse the Greeks. I can't say and won't boast that reading a few tragedies has clarified much about the socio-political, ethical, and spiritual crisis in which we find ourselves. But I am coming to the conviction that tragedy offers a demanding, stark paradigm that at least accounts for some of the emotional force of these events and may even suggest some generative ways to think about them. Beyond simply capturing a bit of the devastation wrought by the attacks, can the form of tragedy help us narrate, image, or otherwise represent these horrors?

I acknowledge that it may seem frivolous, even blasphemous, to discuss these overwhelming and all too real events in a matrix borrowed from the relatively rarified topic of dramatic form. I do know that life is life and theater is theater. And though I have faith that theater is enormously important, I recognize that it is not quite life. The suffering of the thousands of people who died, lost their loved ones, or lost their livelihoods is quite real. Retaliatory air strikes and civilian casualties in Afghanistan are quite real. It's essential to mark the distance between aesthetic forms and world events. At the same time, it is also the case that we have no choice but to narrate September 11th. In fact, the story is being told all the time—on news reports, in snappily edited video clips, in press conferences, in office conversations while the xeroxing goes on. A truism of contemporary narrative theory states that humans order their world by telling stories about it. We innately turn people into characters and assemble incidents into narratives. We are hardwired to do this. But an array of incidents can be strung together in an endless variety of ways. Who's in our cast of characters? What's the plot? Whose point of view predominates? The choices we make matter because they articulate our perspective on how the world works. They matter, too, because narratives often function as guides for action. Stories are, among many other things, templates of behavior. They propose options and suggest outcomes; they mediate relations between people. What kind of a person can I be? Given the sort of person I am, how might I act? With what likely consequences? What should I expeot from people seemingly unlike myself? In the end, the stories we experience collapse back onto the material world because they shape our deeds. If we are to assimilate the events of September 11th into a meaningful context (or allow them to alter our sense of what a meaningful context might be), we have no choice but to hear them as stories.

I'm suggesting that the form of tragedy might accommodate some of the affective power of September 11th, and even point towards some of its moral claims. It seems fitting to me that the rhetoric of the tragic is so frequently invoked of late. Tragedy is above all a genre of suffering and witness. A form of lamentation, it facilitates mourning and generates memory. In its classical form, tragedy oscillates between a protagonist caught in an unlivable situation and a chorus who collectively responds to his or her anguish. While it does not celebrate or fetishize pain, it places hope in the belief that pain can catalyze insight. Above all, tragedy investigates contradiction. Tragedy stages moments when the systems people live by fall apart and fail them. It examines the inadequacy of familiar categories to provide meaningful accounts of catastrophic experiences. It resists easy resolution, preferring a difficult, even agonizing process of self-recognition to the reassuring comforts of self-deception.

It is both analytic and empathetic. It defers closure in quest of revelation. Tragedy recognizes tensions between individual ambitions and group solidarity, and it often turns its self-scrutinizing impulse to the struggles of civic life. In fact, tragedy has flourished in epochs (Classical Athens, Renaissance England, Absolutist France, Romantic Germany) endeavoring to remake the social order or authorize a social order recently remade. It speaks to adversities faced on the cusp of history; considered historically, it often gives testament to the death of one era as another labors to be born. Tragedy admits the seemingly arbitrary nature of so much human suffering, even as it finds the will to go on living through communal rites that grieve the persistence of this condition.

5   I think this ought to be the tenor of our discourse in the wake of September 11th. As a nation, I believe we would benefit from seeking out the tragic potential in the destruction of the Twin Towers, the attack on the Pentagon, and the crash of a plane in southwestern Pennsylvania destined for an undetermined Washington landmark. A tragic response to September 11th, a tragic witnessing of it, would try to hold at least three contradictory impulses together. First, we need to mourn, and stories of loss seem fundamental. Many people died and many more have seen their lives irrevocably altered. The ripples are endless, from the unremitting absence of dead friends and family members to the slow burn of a faltering economy to the muscle tension that arises at the sight of camouflaged military personnel patrolling the airport with M-16s, to the permanent gap in the Manhattan skyline. I suspect most Americans feel a level of anxiety for their personal safety that they did not experience prior to September 11th. I admit that I do. Degrees of loss differ widely and are by no means commensurate. But loss is widespread and deserves to be marked.

A tragic witnessing of September 11th must also preserve outrage at these callous acts. "Terror is theater," said the leader of the terrorists who kidnapped and murdered Israeli athletes at the Munich Olympics. Human carnage for the sake of good video is indisputably evil. It may turn out to be the greatest, most characteristically postmodern of evils. The attackers need to be (as they have been) resoundingly and unequivocally condemned. A tragic perspective particularly rejects the murder of innocents in the service of signification. Deeply invested in a politics of empathy, tragedy asserts that insight into the order of things arises only through compassion. It demands the imaginative leap of trying to see the world from someone else's position in it, and insists that we act based on these imaginative identifications. Tragedy deals harshly with those who inflict suffering, in order to hold to or advance an idea. It names this unfeeling form of arrogance *hubris,* and punishes it.

Finally, a tragic witnessing of these events should squarely face some awful truths, dwell in the full weight of those truths, and try to see ourselves anew as a result of doing so. The terrorists staged September 11th for maximum semiotic impact. Their message was clear. In their rhetoric, the World Trade Center figures America's global economic power and a certain modernist insouciance; the Pentagon figures America's military power. The attacks construct America as the wealthy superpower it is, and dramatize its destruction. Clearly, these attacks were a despicable criminal act. The perpetrators must be brought to justice through appropriate processes of national and international law. However, they do articulate some partial truths about the United States. We are the principal agents and beneficiaries of globalization. We have the most powerful military in the world and often deploy it in bellicose ways. I think we need to hear that much of the world perceives us in this manner and accept that this perception, while not the whole story, has its basis in US actions. Since becoming the world's lone superpower in 1989, we have moved toward a dangerous and arrogant isolationism in foreign affairs. We have tended toward self-congratulatory smugness, representing ourselves as the victors of history, the champions of an economic system that will inevitably bring peace and prosperity to the entire planet. We have not adequately appreciated other peoples' fears for their material and cultural autonomy, nor have we done enough to temper the material and cultural inequities that have thus far accompanied globalization. We have our own hubris to face.

The cornerstone of Aristotle's theory of tragedy is the dual principle of *peripety* and *recognition*. A peripety is a reversal, a moment when the plot shifts powerfully for better or worse. In tragedies, peripeties are catastrophic, often unbearable. But terrible events do not alone make for tragedy. For Aristotle, the defining feature of tragedy is that peripety leads to recognition. As a result of their bad fortune, tragic characters see themselves in a new light. They recognize some unfortunate, painful, even devastating truth about themselves. From suffering comes insight. Nationally, we have endured peripety but are refusing recognition. We ought to take seriously the view of the United States that generated these evil acts. How did it arise? How is it justified? What can we do to change it? I do not stand with those who believe that if we change, "the terrorists will have won." We have already changed, and inevitably so given the magnitude of events and the levels of loss endured. But how will we change? Will we take up the moral rigor of tragedy and examine ourselves anew? Will we question and alter those policies and practices that inhibit reciprocity in our material and cultural relations with other nations? It is a sad truth that the rest of the world knows much more of us than we know of it. Let us consider the discomfiting possibility that it may also know something of us that we do not yet know of ourselves.

I worry that my discussion may seem tasteless, or worse, coy. Who cares whether we witness September 11th in the spirit of tragedy? I actually think the stakes of the genre are concrete, the consequences of it utterly material. In point of fact, since September 11th, our national policy has been determined by a narrative borrowed from a dramatic form. That form is melodrama. Melodrama is a genre of moral absolutes. It traffics in heroes and villains, white hats and black hats. It dates from the early nineteenth-century and dominated American theater into the early twentieth-century. It remains powerfully with us in film, television, and to some lesser degree theater. Luke Skywalker and Darth Vader are its progeny, as are Buffy and Angel, Rambo, professional wrestling, and soap opera. To its credit, melodrama cares about questions of morality and takes seriously the evil that men do. But it also divides the world into stark, simplistic categories. It thrives on a politics of us and them. Since September 11th, I believe we've been living out a national melodrama. The defining moment of this melodrama came when President Bush cast Osama bin Laden as the villain in a movie Western: "Wanted: Dead or Alive," he announced. I've since seen bin Laden's visage in a mock Old West poster many times in many places. I am not so much concerned with the representation of bin Laden here as I am with the implicit representation of the United States. In this scenario, the US is a hero without blemish crusading for a rugged, frontier justice. I share the President's view that the people involved in planning these attacks should be pursued, captured, and prosecuted. All signs point to al Qaeda. However, our intervention into Afghanistan has come perilously close to state-sponsored vigilantism. We have not acted within the most relevant and authoritative legal framework, seeking an international tribunal under the authority of the United Nations to apprehend these criminals and to prosecute their crimes. We have opted instead to proclaim the post-September 11th world a new place, the rule of law obsolete, and invent new rules of engagement to fight "a new kind of war." To me, this seems more like the plot of a John Ford film than a considered, far-seeing approach to international leadership.

    I don't want to live in a melodrama. Melodrama is pleasing like a Twinkie is pleasing, but like a Twinkie it's a lie. Melodrama makes for dissatisfying theater. More gravely, it makes for disastrous foreign policy. I do not believe that in the long term the "war on terrorism" as we are currently waging it will make us safer. If anything, it will harden the resolve of people sufficiently desperate to kill themselves and murder massive numbers of innocent civilians to voice their opinions. Even more pragmatically, most of the foreign policy analysis I've read since September 11th suggests that a bombing campaign is a grossly ineffective way to combat terrorism. Human intelligence (spying), combined with cross-national cooperation between domestic law enforcement agencies (states the consensus), is far more effective. To defeat terrorism, we need to cultivate friends, not make more enemies. We need to place ourselves within the norms and constraints of international law to demonstrate our genuine desire to be a leader within the community of nations rather than the boss country that unilaterally determines its agenda. Nor do I believe that the war on terrorism as 10 we are currently waging it will lead to a lasting peace. Everything I've ever read on the subject of terrorism suggests that terrorist violence correlates most consistently and most strongly with poverty. The experience of abjection powerfully nurtures feelings of resentment that easily grow into hatred. People turn to terrorism when they believe they have no other means of influencing public affairs. Ultimately, the solution is economic. The best assurance that the US will not again be the object of a comparably horrific terrorist attack is an equitable distribution of global capital that moves wealth more evenly throughout the world and generates genuinely reciprocal forms of cultural encounter. In the wake of September 11th, we should be as powerfully concerned to work toward this goal as we are urgently resolved to bring to justice the perpetrators of these terrible crimes.

    It deeply worries me that the dominant national discourse in the aftermath of September 11th is melodramatic. As I write this, it looks like the Northern Alliance, aided by the US bombing campaign, will win the war in Afghanistan and preside over a broad-based coalition government. I hope this brings some stability to the people of Afghanistan and relieves the poverty and repression that, by all reports, they have endured under the Taliban. When this happens, the melodramatic narrative put in motion by the Bush administration will reach at least a temporary denouement. However, I fear that by donning the white hat we are refusing to hear some necessary lessons of September 11th. I fear we are failing to recognize our role in creating the circumstances that led to such intense hatred of the United States. I fear that by acting above the community of nations we are confirming our enemies' worst view of us. I fear that in turning tragedy into melodrama, we are inviting more terror onto our shores.

I'd like to close by evoking the function of tragedy in Athenian democracy. Throughout the fifth-century B.C. tragedies were performed every spring at the City Dionysia, an annual theater festival sponsored by the state. The City Dionysia was a competition—five comic writers competed for one prize, three tragedians for the other. The tragic writers each staged a tragic cycle comprised of three tragedies and a satyr play. The festival lasted several days (between five and eight, depending upon how you read the evidence), with prizes awarded at the end. Most recent work on Greek theater emphasizes the civic character of theater-going in classical Athens. Theater-going was a privilege of citizenship and the theater a significant institution of political life. Approximately half the voting population of Athens attended the City Dionysia each year. Audience members sat with their tribes, a distribution of spectators that echoed the city's political structure. The judges were similarly appointed, one from each tribe. Wealthy citizens could pay their taxes by sponsoring a production. The performers were not professionals, but were themselves citizens. Rituals performed on the first day framed the festival within Athenian civic discourse. These rituals particularly emphasized Athens' military prowess: generals from each tribe poured libations; the children of those who had died in war were brought on stage; tribute from subject nations was paraded in the arena; names of men who had greatly benefited the city were read aloud.

Given this avowedly patriotic context, the most remarkable thing about the City Dionysia was its frank criticism of Athenian public life. The City Dionysia consistently and ferociously scrutinized the *polis*. Comedy specialized in scurrilous mockery of leading public figures. Tragedy placed local questions into contexts of ultimate concern. Tragedies especially investigated the fissures of civic ideology—the relationships, impulses, and desires that the dominant discourse could not accommodate. I don't want to totally romanticize Athenians; they were, in many ways, a belligerent, exclusionary society. However, I do find it inspiring that they gathered on a yearly basis to collectively consider the contradictions, failures, and inadequacies of their political system. Doing so was in fact an expression of their loyalty to and love of their homeland. It quite literally constituted them as democratic subjects. In this moment of national crisis, I think we would benefit from bringing the same questioning, restless, self-critical spirit to our own national conversation.

I hope we take seriously our casual language, and witness September 11th as a tragedy. Remember the dead. Pursue their killers. Interrogate ourselves.

Things to Do with the Reading

1. Chapter 6 discusses at some length the idea of interpretive context. Peck's essay is a good example of arguing carefully for the appropriateness and usefulness of an interpretive context. Peck invites us to view the events of September 11th in two contexts: tragedy and melodrama. Locate the places in the essay where Peck defends his choice of these interpretive contexts. Then write a brief essay in which you discuss the grounds on which he defends his choice of tragedy as a productive lens.

2. The essay reveals its anxiety about seeming to trivialize a very real event by locating it in the context of dramatic and narrative theory. Look at the shape of Peck's argument to see where it locates its concessions and what these are. Also determine where and how it introduces its more challenging points. How, for example, would the essay differ if Peck rearranged the order of the "three contradictory impulses" announced in paragraph 5? Then write up the results of this analysis in a brief essay. (See Chapter 15 on Concessions and Refutations.)

3. **Link:** Find the keywords in Peck's piece that locate him politically, as defined by Borick. Write a short essay on how the thinking and value system in his piece fit in the categories that Borick lays out.

4. **Application:** Where do you see evidence of melodrama in the national or international news? And what would a rescripting of melodrama into tragedy for this particular event entail? For example, what would the melodramatic and then the tragic readings of Hurricane Katrina be? Write an essay in which you interpret a current event, offering both melodramatic and tragic versions.

FOR FURTHER RESEARCH: THE LANGUAGE OF POLITICS AND THE POLITICS OF LANGUAGE

By Kelly Cannon, Reference Librarian

The readings and activities below invite you to further explore the theme of The Language of Politics and the Politics of Language. WARNING: Some essays are polemical; they are intended to promote insight and discussion (or a starting point for your next paper). To access the online readings, visit the *Writing Analytically with Readings* website at www.cengagebrain.com.

Open Access

American Rhetoric Online Speech Bank. Ed. Michael E. Eidenmuller. 2010. 31 July 2010. http://www.americanrhetoric.com
A searchable collection of thousands of public speeches, with a preponderance of political voices. Speech categories include "Rhetoric of 9/11," "Christian Rhetoric," and "Iraq War Speeches."

> Explore: Can you find a speech with a tendency to "defend the indefensible," as aptly described by George Orwell? (Don't forget to try out the "Cool Exercises" to test your rhetorical savvy.)

FactCheck.org. Annenberg Public Policy Center, University of Pennsylvania, 2010. 11 January 2011. http://factcheck.org
"A nonpartisan, nonprofit, 'consumer advocate' for voters that aims to reduce the level of deception and confusion in U.S. politics."

> Explore: Examine the "About Us" portion of the website. Then look at a number of entries. Does this website live up to its claim of nonpartisanship? How so? Would this site make George Orwell proud? How so?

Martin, Jonathan, et al. "Violence and Politics Merge." *Politico.com*. 9 January 2011. 18 January 2011. http://www.politico.com/news/stories/0111/47294.html
Asks to what extent political rhetoric is to blame for the shooting of Congresswoman Gifford and others in Tucson, Arizona, in January of 2011.

> Explore: The Tucson shootings brought rhetoric into the foreground. President Barack Obama responded with a certain type of rhetoric, Sarah Palin with another. And then there was the shooter himself. What rhetoric, as reported in any news stories you can find, did the shooter employ in his online and handwritten notes? Can rhetoric really lead people to violence? Consider this "tragedy" in light of the tragedy analyzed rhetorically in James Peck's essay above. Are their similarities in the way the media and politicians chose to describe each of these events?

Hardisty, Jean, and Deepak Bhargava. "Wrong About the Right." *Political Research Associates*. 2005. 11 January 2011. http://www.publiceye.org/hardisty/wrong_about_right.html
Originally published in *Nation* magazine, this article contends that the conservative rise to power is not just about rhetoric and framing, but about such things as ideas and organization.

Explore: Is the political orientation of these authors evident? What are the clues? How well do the labels used here correspond with political labels as defined by Christopher Borick above?

Kolbert, Elizabeth. "Firebrand: Phyllis Schlafly and the Conservative Revolution." *New Yorker* **(7 November 2005): 134–38. 11 January 2011. http://www.newyorker.com/ archive/2005/11/07/051107crbo_books**
"Schlafly's denunciatory tone, more than any of her actual campaigns, probably represents her most lasting contribution to American life. While Ann Coulter and Laura Ingraham were still playing tea party, she recognized that deliberation was no match for diatribe, and logic no equal to contempt. She was, in this way, a woman ahead of her time."

Explore: What is the tone of this essay (its attitude toward Schlafly)? Condemnatory? Admiring? What does the rhetoric of this essay reveal about its author, in light of Christopher Borick's definitions?

"Rhetoric of 9-11." *American Rhetoric.* **2011. 18 January 2011. http://www.americanrhetoric. com/rhetoricofterrorism.htm**
Access to over 150 files of key speeches and rhetorical artifacts relating to the September 11th, 2001 terrorist attacks against the Pentagon and World Trade Center. They include speeches and addresses to the nation by American President George W. Bush, British Prime Minister Tony Blair, and other key politicians. Also accessible is a tape of Osama Bin Laden.

Explore: Examine the list of "most access 9/11 rhetoric." What tops the list? Why? How do the "sides" begin to take shape in these most accessed speeches? What would you identify as the most powerful rhetorical moves on either side, those that would most affect the intended audience? Listen to some of the speeches archived by figures renowned as conservative or liberal? What rhetorical aspects do they share with the editorials by Kilpatrick and others printed above that would make them stand out as politically right or left?

Rubin, Lillian B. "Why Don't They Listen to Us?" *Dissent* **52.1 (Winter 2005): 86–91. 17 January 2011. http://www.dissentmagazine.org/article/?article=278**
This article from the liberal press explains why liberals have lost out to conservatives. Conclusion: It's all about rhetoric.

Explore: What aspect of liberal rhetoric does Rubin find most counterproductive? How does this essay stand up to Christopher Borick's definitions of political labels?

Sanders, Skeeter. "Remarks on Arizona Shootings Confirm Palin Is a Demagogue Unfit for the Presidency." '*Skeeter Bites Report.* **18 January 2011. http://www.skeeterbitesreport. com/2011/01/remarks-on-arizona-shootings-confirm.html**
This editorial claims rhetoric will be Palin's undoing.

Explore: How does the rhetoric of this editorial confirm the politics of its author? Do you agree that rhetoric will undo Sarah Palin? Can political success really rise or fall on one's use of the language?

"Top 10 Examples of Liberal Hate." *Human Events Online.* **11 January 2011. 18 January 2011. http://www.humanevents.com/article.php?id=41108**
A leading conservative news source responds to liberals' allegations of hate-filled rhetoric coming from the right.

Explore: Do you agree with Human Events' list? Have you heard such rhetoric? Why have these allegations received so little press? How well do the labels employed here correspond to the definitions provided by Christopher Borick?

Zukin, Cliff. "Sources of Variation in Published Election Polling: A Primer." *American Association for Public Opinion Research.* **October 2004. 17 January 2011. http://aapor.org/ uploads/zukin_election_primer.pdf**
Zukin, a Rutgers University professor of public policy, outlines the major liabilities in polling.

Explore: According to Zukin, how much does the wording of questions in polls play a role in poll results? What factor overall in Zukin's mind most heavily affects the outcome of a poll? Interestingly, Zukin only deals with one type of election polling. What type does Zukin expressly exclude from his article? What strikes you as important about naming this distinction up front? Can polling questions themselves be "liberal" or "conservative"?

Chapter 24

Seeing

An article entitled "The Image Culture" by Christine Rosen (whose essay on cell phones is the first of the readings in this book) begins by reflecting on the deluge of apocalyptic images that washed over us on the television and Internet in the wake of Hurricane Katrina. Rosen goes on to consider the footage of the 9/11 attacks, citing our "saturation" by images. She quotes novelist Don DeLillo: "In our world we sleep and eat the image and pray to it and wear it too" (*The New Atlantis: A Journal of Technology and Society,* Fall 2005).

It has become a virtual cliché that in America the image has come to displace the word, and accordingly, in the schools and in the media, verbal literacy has lost ground to visual literacy. The aim of this chapter is not, however, to defend one side against the other. Rather, our overarching goal is to provide you with a vocabulary for seeing more acutely. This is a cultural as well as a perceptual matter. Inevitably, it involves attention to both the producing and the consuming ends of the so-called Image Culture: how images are created and for what ends, and how we have been conditioned to value and resist them.

We have made "Seeing" the final chapter by design, for it raises topics relating back to the previous four chapters of readings. The readings in these earlier chapters are united by their concern with matters of rhetoric and representation: how issues get phrased and framed and to whom and for what purposes. In this final chapter, the readings focus most insistently on the visual element of this rhetorical framing. The writers encourage us to ponder not only how we see, but how the surrounding culture and the images it offers us affect how we see. You can expect to revisit the issues that drive the earlier chapters—issues of technology, place, race, and power—but this time, with special attention to their life in the Image Culture.

ABOUT THE READINGS IN THIS CHAPTER

The interview that we conducted with photographer Joseph Elliott offers the primary lens for the selections in "Seeing." Elliott distinguishes two primary ways of producing images—staging them and recording them. Attached to each of these approaches are assumptions that Elliott uncovers about how images communicate. Eventually, he elaborates a series of qualified positions within the recorder/stager binary to arrive at a system for classifying a wide range of photographic approaches. Additionally, he offers specific technical advice for apprehending the formal elements of an image—what he refers to as "seeing the hand" of the photographer.

Next comes a classic piece entitled "In Plato's Cave" by the philosopher and cultural critic Susan Sontag. Whereas Elliott values the photographer's role as a recorder of events, Sontag is concerned that the desire to record will supplant the desire to experience and become involved. She worries that photography tends to appropriate (that is, "leach out") real life in a predatory fashion. And because photos tend to look recorded even though they all are staged, she argues, those in power exploit this fact to deceive us. Seeing, after all, tends to be believing.

Barry Lopez's "Learning to See" relocates the ethical discussion to the terrain of nature photography. He also returns the focus to some of the concerns with form discussed by Elliott. Lopez concentrates on the elusive photographic pursuit of light and spatial volume—of "the deep pattern of turbulence" and "indigenous time." The backbone of his essay is a narrative of how he came to give up his career as a photojournalist to concentrate on words rather than images. In the process of telling this story, he offers a striking comparison of the mindsets that go into capturing an event in words versus in pictures—and what each medium inevitably leaves out or keeps us from seeing.

Next, the chapter moves to John Berger's famous analysis of nudes in classical art, taken from his book *Ways of Seeing*. Like the other writers, he is interested in issues of spectatorship and power. His focus rests on the representation of the female form, and in particular, on how the nude functions as a category within which "women have been seen and judged as sights" and so, as Berger comments, "They do to themselves what men do to them. They survey, like men, their own femininity" (paragraph 63).

Susan Bordo's "Beauty (Re)discovers the Male Body" offers a rich comparison with Berger's essay, as it focuses on images of men rather than women. The essay also marks a shift in the chapter's orientation, toward popular culture, as Bordo focuses not on high art but on images from advertising. Her goal, shared with the other writers in this chapter, is to invite us to question our assumptions about the way we see and about how our seeing is shaped by the culture. She takes issue with the conventional idea of the sex object, for example, arguing that "the most compelling images are suffused with "subjectivity'—they speak to us, they seduce us. Unlike other kinds of "objects' (chairs and tables, for example) they don't let us use them in any way we like."

Next, Malcolm Gladwell's "Listening to Khakis" extends Berger's and Bordo's focus on gender through his journalistic study of ad campaigns aimed at men, especially the highly successful Dockers campaign, with its key phrase, "Nice pants." Gladwell's interviewing style gives voice to a range of resonant cultural commentators about how we live now. Some of these voices address how men as opposed to women see—an issue that takes us back to Berger and Bordo. What Gladwell discovers about how those who make ads theorize gender and perception provides rich matter for both analysis and application.

"Seeing" concludes, as most of the book's reading chapters have, with something a little different—in this case, two short pieces that test the flexibility of the chapter's analytical project. In "Oy Gay!" Kera Bolonik provides a revelatory way of thinking about the television sitcom *Will & Grace*, less as a show about gays (as it is usually seen) than about Jews and Gentiles.

The chapter's final essay, X.J. Kennedy's "Who Killed King Kong?" is a mid-twentieth-century review, which, like other readings in the chapter, takes a cultural studies approach to how we see. Written in the era of the Civil Rights movement, Kennedy's review of the original 1933 film *King Kong* invites us to see the volatile issues of race, class, and gender that burble just below the surface of the film. Ultimately, we can use Kennedy not only to contemplate how our own moment has re-envisioned *King Kong* (in Peter Jackson's 2005 remake), but how revisiting any image of the past may open up the way we see now.

Finally, mention should be made of an essay included elsewhere in this anthology that easily could be incorporated here: Jack Gambino's "Demolition Zones: Contemporary Photography by Edward Burtynsky and Camilo Jose Vergara" (Chapter 21). Vergara is frequently mentioned in Elliott's interview as a representative recorder.

Joseph Elliott, David Rosenwasser, and Jill Stephen

Looking at Photographs: Stagers and Recorders—an Interview with Joseph Elliott

Composed specifically for this book, this interview features Joseph Elliott, a noted photographer and a professor of art, on the subject of how photographers see. Elliott offers here a kind of short course on visual literacy from a photographer's point of view as he offers a guided tour through the two primary traditions of thinking about images: as recorded and as staged. In addition, he offers ways of analyzing the work of reigning art photographers in both traditions and suggests how we can expand our powers of observing the world that surrounds us. Since graduating with an M.F.A. from Pratt Institute, Elliott has had his photographs featured in 10 solo exhibits, 12 group exhibits, and many publications. He has also received 15 commissions from the Historic American Buildings Survey as well as numerous grants.

Note: The interviews that follow were conducted over a period of several months and are divided into seven meetings, each with its own title.

The First Meeting: 8/29/05 "The Two Camps"

1   **David:** Our book uses the metaphor of the lens to think about analyzing. Are there primary lenses that you use when you think about photographers?

Joe: I see two camps: staging versus recording. Edward S. Curtis, the photographer of the American West, is a stager. He's not observing but staging. He's a romantic who fabricates a vision of the West. An interesting photographer to compare him to is Timothy H. O'Sullivan. If you Google-image O'Sullivan, you'll see that he's a more dispassionate, severe recorder of the West.

David: So these approaches—staging and recording—are still present today?

Joe: Yes. Gregory Crewdson is a stager you might look at. His work has a cinematic feel. His point of view goes against the purist-observers, the ones who want to approach matters solely in the context of "Let's see what seeing is …"

5   Another stager you might check out is Cindy Sherman, who has photographed herself for years in all manner of costumes and disguises (such as 1970s period dress). You might compare her with Diane Arbus, but with this difference: Arbus *found* the grotesque, but Sherman seems to say, "Let's just invent it." Sherman doesn't derive from Arbus; she draws on 1950s–60s popular culture, advertising images, movies and movie stills. In the current scene it seems as if films are getting more and more "still," and still photographers are getting more and more staged.

Jill: And contemporary recorders?

Looking at Photographs: Stagers and Recorders, Joseph Elliott. Interviewed by David Rosenwasser and Jill Stephen. Reprinted with permission.

Joe: Andreas Gursky is an interesting recorder. His work seems to say, "Let's look at something clearly and make a giant print of it." Although he's a recorder most of the time, sometimes he digitally alters his images in subtle ways, perhaps in search of a more perfect banality. (For other straightforward types like Gursky, see Eggleston, Struth, Shore, and Sternfeld, who are replaying O'Sullivan. You could also think about my work and Vergara's.)

Jill: So you see yourself as a recorder, then?

Joe: I'm interested in a quality of seeing, with the aim to see things well and make a strong image. Then it is a matter of how to construct a frame and where to position the vantage point. I like to control frame and vantage point, as do all straight photographers, but not the object, so I'm not a fabricator. But like the fabricators, any photographer is clearly implicated by the process of taking photos. You are making an object, a photograph; you're creating, not just recording.

The Second Meeting: 10/21/05 "Burning Down the House"

The session begins with brief discussion of Alice in Wonderland *and the notion that that text is not simply words but a hybrid work of words and pictures—in which the pictures are integral—with a long history of illustration, starting with Lewis Carroll's own sketches (circa 1860) and famously followed by John Tenniel, whose illustrations are featured in the first edition.*

Joe: Carroll was also a well-known photographer of young girls in the early days of   10
photography as an art. Have you ever heard of Jock Sturges? Google-image him. He's a kind of modern-day Carroll who photographs children and adolescents, and who has been hounded by the authorities as morally suspicious.

Henry Peach Robinson and Oscar Rejlander were Carroll contemporaries, who we might term "Victorian fabricators."

Most photographers at this time were referred to as camera operators—recorders of images, trying to capture the real in some unmediated, unadulterated way, insofar as that is ever possible for a person with a camera. A photographer is inevitably selecting what to shoot and thus what not to shoot, and he or she is always framing the shot in various ways.

The Victorian fabricators saw themselves as artists. They embraced a belief in photography as an art form. The thought was, if you were going to produce a work of art, you had to make it entirely. You had to be seen as not just taking a picture of something out there and using factory-made materials to make the print. The audience had to be sure that the artist made the whole thing. From the 1870s–1890s the artist-photographer was a pictorialist—a person who had applied the emulsion and had made each photograph as its own object. The finished photos were often fabricated from many separate images, or were impressionistic, soft focused, subtly toned, resembling paintings and drawings.

Queen Victoria purchased a huge photo of the Last Supper done by Rejlander. A third key member of early Victorian photographic circles was Julia Margaret Cameron, who was well known in artistic and literary circles and was a friend of Tennyson.

Digital Image © The Museum of Modern Art/Licensed by SCALA/Art Resource, NY

FIGURE 24.1
"Poling the Marsh Hay, England," 1886 by Peter Henry Emerson and Thomas Frederick Goodall

The discussion moves to contemporary stagers and recorders in the world of art photography.

15   **David:** I saw in an interview with Gregory Crewdson, the stager you told me to Google, that he had traveled to various rust belt cities in the Northeast, and that Pittsfield, Massachusetts, was eager to woo him, once he selected it as a possible site for his next project, Beneath the Roses. In a meeting with town officials, including the mayor and fire chief, he mentioned that he would like to burn down a house for one of his photographs, and "a few hours later they showed us up to 40 possible houses we were welcome to burn down. They were all owned by the city, on schedule for demolition" (See the link to "Desperate House Lives," available on the website for this book).

What's the difference between the photo that resulted and one of a house burning down here in Allentown? If he waited awhile listening to a police channel, he could have found many burning rust belt houses to photograph without employing 7 best boys and a huge production crew.

Joe: First of all, look at the context. Crewdson is a sophisticated Yale professor, top end. He sells in the most fashionable galleries in Chelsea. These factors in combination affect what he decides to shoot and how he decides to shoot it, the kind of art he decides to make. The image is designed in advance of the actual shooting, as it would be in filmmaking or advertising. Control is more complete that way. Racing to a real fire leaves too much to chance. Too much room for error. With such a huge production crew, Crewdson cannot afford to waste time. Crewdson isn't interested in making art using the real; his art isn't about the real.

David: Why burn a house down to make a picture?

Joe: It involves decadence, a level of decadence, the end of some period of American art. Decadence implies something that is over-ripe. It implies money, an affluence that is without striving. You see it in how carefully the water is spread on the ground to simulate recent rain in the photograph of the burning house, and in how big the image is, how lush the image is.

You can understand this better by comparing Crewdson to somebody like Vergara.   20
Vergara offers a counterpoint to this more fashionable art world. He actually photographs burnt out houses in Camden, New Jersey. [*See the Vergara photos in Jack Gambino's essay, "Demolition Zones: Contemporary Photography by Edward Burtynsky and Camilo Jose Vergara" in Chapter 21.*]

Crewdson is also attracted to burnt out rust belt cities, with a decayed past. But we need to focus on what he's looking at, and what world will receive his art.

To view this image in color, visit www.cengagebrain.com

FIGURE 24.2
Untitled (house fire) 1999 by Gregory Crewdson

© Gregory Crewdson. Courtesy Gagosian Gallery

To view this image in color, visit www.cengagebrain.com

FIGURE 24.3
Untitled (pregnant woman) 2001 by Gregory Crewdson

© Gregory Crewdson. Courtesy Gagosian Gallery

To view this image in color, visit www.cengagebrain.com

FIGURE 24.4
Untitled (ray of light) 2001 by Gregory Crewdson

© Gregory Crewdson. Courtesy Gagosian Gallery

The post-modern art world would say that Vergara, the more honest observer, doesn't get it. There is no irony in his work. He thinks real information matters. A gallery owner once told me, "You can't show documentary photographs (like Vergara's). It's not cool."

David: What is the "it" that Vergara doesn't get?

Joe: The idea that it's hopelessly romantic to think you can capture an image in real life, and bring it to people. But there's a step missing here. In the past there was a belief that you could shoot a picture of Omaha Beach as Robert Capa did, and the image would become vitally important to almost everyone. Spielberg's *Saving Private Ryan* fashions a long sequence of the D-Day invasion of Omaha beach based on this single Capa image.

Along these lines, Steichen's 1950s MOMA (Museum of Modern Art) exhibit, *The Family of Man,* tried to show the universal commonalities of all world cultures in an effort to bring people together and promote world peace. Also see Lewis Hine, and the effect of his photos to motivate Congress to pass child labor protection laws.   25

Now that position gets discounted. It's seen as pretentious and as denying that the photographer is part of a world that oppresses anyway. So the thought is, if you cannot deny your complicity, maybe you just have to accept the construct, and make the biggest staged image you can and sell it to the wealthiest buyer you can find.

Lewis W. Hine/George Eastman House/Getty Images

FIGURE 24.5
Portrait of a girl in mill (child labor) by Lewis Hine

Vergara, to return to our previous contrast, occupies a middle ground. His work won't tug at your heartstrings or show you the distended belly of a starving African child, but he'll show you picture after picture of Camden, and want you to *see* the setting as it is.

Another kind of straight photographer, less the anthropologist than Vergara, and more of what we might call a sensationalist, is the legendary Weegee, the 1940s photo journalist who listened to his police scanner in New York City and raced to position himself next to the guy who had jumped out of the window and splattered on the street. You might check out his famous book called *The Naked City*. Weegee anticipates Diane Arbus in some sense, and in another, Crewdson, who *aestheticizes* the crime scene. Arbus makes an art form out of the blunt, unflinching encounter. After we've seen Crewdson, Weegee's photos also seem staged.

David: You were speaking a few moments ago about the ethical position of the photographer, how he or she can get seen as contributing to some kind of oppression. Could you say more about that?

30 **Joe:** I have a friend, Bill Burke, who does what he calls "Docu-art": it looks like documentary investigation but is really an investigation of his own life choices and the resulting situations he finds himself in. In this case, Bill went to Vietnam and Cambodia to take photographs (he had skipped the actual war with a college deferment), and when he returned, he was attacked for "imaging the Other" (people of cultures and ethnicities unlike his own), using the "Other" as fodder for his work; he was accused of parasitism.

Burke's work fits the category of personal documentation, occupying a middle ground between the stagers and the recorders. His images are not staged, but are more consciously self-involved than the documentarians we have been discussing. Other members of this school are Larry Clark, *Tulsa* (teenage heroin addicts, his high school classmates), Sally Mann (her children), and Nan Goldin (street life in New York City in the 80s).

David: How do you categorize your own recent work in Costa Rica on the legacy of gold mining? Do your photos differ from the kind of documentary work that you've been talking about as more consciously self-involved?

Joe: The documentary, in the simplified sense of the word, means making the photographs that will become part of the history of a people or culture; you're trying to have as little influence as possible on the photographed subject. Of course, you do make decisions about what to shoot. You want it to last. You are "recording the site," which goes along with other methods of surveying, mapping, oral history, research, etc.—and otherwise, without the documenting, it could be lost. So you want to preserve it simply and cleanly, to be of use for the future. And the document itself also becomes part of the history.

We could apply this to Vergara's work. He'll have the map of Camden and drive up and down every street in his area of concentration to get total coverage. And he is not after some representative or iconic or symbolic images, but rather a density of images, a collecting.

35 **Jill:** Why does he record that space?

Weegee (Arthur Fellig)/International Center of Photography/Getty Images

FIGURE 24.6
Brooklyn School Children See Gambler Murdered in Street, 1941 aka "Their First Murder" by Arthur Fellig (Weegee)

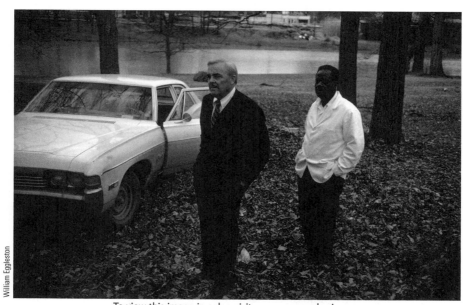

William Eggleston

To view this image in color, visit www.cengagebrain.com

FIGURE 24.7
Untitled (Two men standing by car, Sumner, MS, ca. 1970) by William Eggleston

Joe: Vergara wants to record change over time. He is interested in what happens to a place, the effects of politics, weather, crime, economic decline, etc. Only now, parts of Camden have become gentrified. What happens to the people? He doesn't follow them. (See the four Fern Street photos in Gambino's essay.)

Along these lines, you might look up Milton Rogovin, who returned to the same neighborhood in Buffalo over 20–30 years at regular intervals. He would find the same people and re-photograph them. Also you could look up Mark Klett's re-photographic surveys. He goes to sites that Timothy O'Sullivan, a documenter of the American West, had photographed and sets up his camera to see the site again but also to reveal how O'Sullivan had shaped the shot.

The Third Meeting: 10/28/05 "The Photographer's Hand"

David: At your direction, we've been spending a lot of time looking at books by John Szarkowski, the longtime director of photography at MOMA. How would you categorize him according to your Recorder/Stager categories?

Joe: Szarkowski was an advocate of the straight approach for many years. He seemed to ignore the fabricators. And so he essentially bypassed in his curatorship of MOMA's photographic collection the rise of the post-moderns (like Sherman and Wegman) who say all photographic representations are constructions, are contextualizations, are whatever the photographer makes of it, so let's make up the whole thing!

40   Szarkowski thus missed the boat when it came to including the fabricators in the MOMA collection. And of course, this tradition had been producing work all along—e.g., Ray Metzger, Ralph Eugene Meatyard. In the 1970s Cindy Sherman would have given photos to MOMA for the asking. By the time MOMA came on board, five years ago, they paid a million dollars to catch up.

David: Szarkowski isn't still at MOMA, is he?

Joe: He has retired. Peter Galassi is now curator at MOMA. There is no one curator as influential as Szarkowski had been. But there are now many galleries in Chelsea that show photographers, whereas there were really only two in the mid 1970s, Witkin and Light galleries.

Szarkowski's choices are back in vogue, extolling the straightforward value of the big camera, showing meticulous details, as evident in certain photographers of the 1970s who are again becoming prominent. These include Stephen Shore, Joe Sternfeld, and William Eggleston, all color photographers.

Another change in the photography curatorial scene is that it has become more academy-oriented. Szarkowski was himself a photographer, as Stieglitz and Steichen before him had been. They were not trained in art programs or art history. Now the curators all have that training.

45   **David:** I've been meaning to ask you, how do the recorders view the stagers? And how do the stagers, or, as you sometimes call them, the fabricators tend to view themselves?

Joe: The photo-art world is so diverse that there is a "live and let live" mentality now. The fabricators see themselves as being in some sense more honest, for admitting that they're making it up. This is the implicit argument in Crewdson's work. In his photo of the house on fire, the people on the train track on the other side of the frame are a competing focal point by design. Nothing is an accident in the photo. He wants it to be carefully observed, to invite a close reading. We may think of a photograph having an initial impact, but there's also something else going on, a counterpoint, a set of messages. A lot of this kind of work resembles film-making; the photograph is only a piece of it. The photograph is like a performance piece recorded by a camera that is being used in a straightforward way. Is it a photograph or an installation (or performance piece?) recorded in a photograph?

On the other hand, some of the recorders probably resent the success of the fashionable stagers for being driven by trend rather than the search for truth.

Jill: This reminds me of a remark that Szarkowski makes in *The Photographer's Eye*—that we tend to have faith in what we see in a photograph as real, but in fact the photographer is always "hiding his hand."

Joe: The question to ask beginning students is not, How does the photographer hide his hand? but Where is the photographer's hand? They assume there is no hand! In that famous Alfred Stieglitz photograph "Georgia Engelhard"–it's on the cover of Szarkowski's *Looking at Photographs*—we need to ask why Stieglitz included the edge, with the part of an urn and a rubber tree. *Where is the hand? is the question they need to lead with.* In Crewdson, by contrast, the hand is much easier to see. In the straight-shooters it is less obvious.

The tradition of fabricators is full of other rich examples where we can eas- 50 ily see the hand. Check out the work of Les Krims. His work was part of a 1970s phase in which photographers made little books. One is called "Making Chicken Soup," and features his mother doing exactly that in the kitchen—only she's naked. Another is called "The Incredible Stack'O'Wheat Murders" and features shots of murder scenes, but in each one there is a stack of pancakes. These are precedents for Crewdson.

O. Winston Link's photos of 1950s' steam trains lit by hundreds of flash bulbs are another great precedent for Crewdson. Link in turn reminds us of the train motif in the surreal paintings of De Chirico and Magritte. In their paintings, though, the train, along with clocks, represents Modernism's rebellion against notions of Progress and clock time. But in Link's case the train represents the nostalgic past. The symbol has taken on a different meaning.

David: So in the kinds of photographs you've been talking about, the photographer tries to show his hand ... ?

Joe: At the root of so much of the history of photography as a tradition is the question of where the art lies. Is the art in the making, the fabricating of the image? Is the art in the recording as cleanly and accurately as possible? Is the art an intellectual activity such as Duchamp's urinal, where naming it as art, framing it as art, makes it art? Szarkowski is most faithful to the second item in this list: if you take the machine and use it precisely and consciously, it will produce art. So, for example, he includes anonymous aerial shots taken from bombers in World War II in his book *Looking at Photographs*.

Photography became widely marketable in galleries when the whole process became detached from the hand of the photographer. Some prefer to be called "an artist who works with a camera" rather than "photographer." Photographers who make their own prints in the darkroom are now seen as hopelessly craftsy.

55 **Jill:** This whole discussion is making me think about the effects of digital technology. How does the rise of the computerized image affect the way you think about "the hand"?

Digital Image © The Museum of Modern Art/Licensed by SCALA / Art Resource, NY

To view this image in color, visit www.cengagebrain.com

FIGURE 24.8
"Georgia Engelhard," 1921 by Alfred Stieglitz

Joe: Students who take beginning photography with me love to work in the dark room; it's all about the difference from producing digital images. Traditional photography is simpler, more tangible, more hands-on.

I also teach a course in digital photography. I can teach it coming out of the way I teach black and white—that there are certain roadblocks and limitations. But people don't normally think of it that way. The lens, the ability to capture light, too much or too little, these things are usually taken care of in automatic mode, but the digital camera can be taken back to a manual mode.

Manipulation of the image using Photoshop is not without precedent. Collage and montage, which the Modernists were famous for, anticipate the way a computer cuts and pastes. It's just easier now to amend the image, and it can be done so mindlessly.

Jill: So at least to some people, digitalization has to do with interfering somehow with the original recorded image?

Joe: For Vergara the photograph is evidence, with minimal "interference." It's straight   60
photography. This raises the question, how is evidence affected by "the hand" of the photographer? Photographs are of course all evidence, but evidence of what? And they are all inevitably constructs.

Vergara is coming from the surveyors, the Western survey photographers, a tradition of imperialist mapping. He is standing that tradition on its head by mapping the results of cultural and economic imperialism within American cities.

David: Can you tell us more about the tradition of survey photography? What made it imperialist?

Joe: The photographers—people like Carleton Watkins, O'Sullivan, and A.J. Russell—were hired by the U.S. Geological Survey and by the railroads in order to photograph all of the resources along new routes. Photographers were mapping the stuff that was ready to be taken by new investors. This was part of the exercise of Manifest Destiny in the opening of the West to commerce. So people argued that these new surveys of the West were needed to map our country, but one motivation was to discover the country's resources and know where they were. It's imperialist because you push the Native Americans out of the way.

Vergara comes at the other end of this tradition. His photographs say, well, this is what happened as a result of political and economic decisions that have shaped land use, property values, and people's lives.

Other documentarians were more sensationalist. In the tradition of newspaper   65
photography, for example, the photographs of Weegee convey the circumstances in which they were taken. This is unlike Vergara, whose work is much more distanced. Weegee is more of a raw sensationalist, an inverted Crewdson, almost a sentimentalist. When I look at Weegee's images, it's as if he's saying, "If you can't smell your subject, you're not close enough." They're taken with a big flash to produce that gritty light. There's a coarse tonal range, it's stark: the technology of the newspaper. The gritty light seems to fall off around the edges.

The Fourth Meeting: 11/10/05 Photographs and Paintings

Jill: Last time you were talking about the photographer's hand and the charge from some quarters that darkroom work has become quaint and nostalgic. Could you say more about that?

Joe: Fabricators tend to view the need for the dark room and the artist's hand as quaint—as too "craftsy," too absorbed in the making of "the thing itself." If you are Cindy Sherman and don't make it yourself, your art has moved to the realm of idea. For the postmodern photographer, the dark room is a waste of time. In this context, we might consider Crewdson as an impresario and director, who looks through the lens to make sure the shot is framed the right way but doesn't click the shutter. What the darkroom ace knows is just not that important. Crewdson hires darkroom aces (technicians) to work for him.

Jill: You've been telling us that there are different kinds of recorders and different schools of thought on fabrication. What at base *is* fabrication?

Joe: It is anything beyond point-and-shoot, whether the artist is building an elaborate set, like Crewdson, or cutting up and reassembling collages, like Metzger. You might also check out the work of Ralph Meatyard (an optometrist in Louisville). This collage process is also absorbed into painting, as in the "stuttering" Cubistic painting of *Nude Descending a Staircase* by Marcel Duchamp. Some people think that photography imitated Modernist painting, but the fact is that Modernist painters were influenced by photography. Cubism sees things from a lot of different angles at virtually the same time.

70 **Jill:** So the Cubists were influenced by photography?

Joe: At least by their knowledge of what the camera could do—how it sees.

Jill: Szarkowski points out that Edgar Degas, the French impressionist painter, was also an amateur photographer whose paintings were influenced by the structure of photographs.

Joe: Fabricators come from more than one tradition. One of these is the tradition of late 19th-century photographers like Henry Peach Robinson and Oscar Rejlander and Lewis Carroll, who dressed young girls in costumes. The other tradition comes out of European Modernism, and includes Bauhaus figures such as Moholy-Nagy, Hannah Hoch, and John Heartfield. This latter tradition features a combination of photography and print and drawing, in some cases reframing images from the popular press, as in Dada. You might want to check out Hans Belmer, who did grotesque, reconstructed dolls. His work is interesting in the context of the contemporary photographer Loretta Lux, a subtle fabricator who makes doll-like images of children. At the (Chicago) Institute of Design, Moholy-Nagy reinvents Bauhaus aesthetic, where Metzger is his student.

In the 1930s Bauhaus, there was the conviction that the machine should be used to make art—that intelligent art for the masses could be the product of the machine. But it is not art if no hand is involved (versus Szarkowski's assumption that you can make art without pretense, as in the aerial photographs). Multiple exposures like Metzger's make the constructedness of the image overt; they render the photographic process more self-conscious. If you have a machine and use it thoughtfully, it makes art.

Philadelphia Museum of Art/Fine Art/Corbis

To view this image in color, visit www.cengagebrain.com

FIGURE 24.9
Nude Descending a Staircase #2 by Marcel Duchamp

The Fifth Meeting: 11/18/05 On Portraiture

75   **David:** I spent some time Googling the photographers you mentioned last week. In particular I was intrigued by Loretta Lux [*takes out copies—starting with a portrait of a girl in pigtails*]. What's the difference between this photograph and a snapshot? What do you notice about it?

Joe: First of all, the color. It's so flat; we could call it desaturated. Look at the tonal difference between the complexion of the face and the sky behind her. The difference is very slight. So the effect is to flatten the space. And the sky is straight out of Photoshop. This photograph is constructed in a computer. [*Note: Please see copies of these photos online to apprehend the color.*]

It's interesting to compare Lux's work with Crewdson's. Hers is not like Crewdson's work, which operates in real space. He's limited to what the camera can record. But her work, with that spatial flattening, is comparatively unreal. Crewdson thinks of his art more as a film-maker would. You build a set; you control the lighting. If you went there and looked into the lens, it would look the way the photograph does.

But Lux, if you look at the heads in those portraits of the young boy set against the clouds, they're ever so slightly stretched ... it creates a kind of surrealist effect. The viewer says, "Oh, okay, wait a minute. The space is a little weird in this photograph, isn't it? Why are the colors this way? Why are the heads this way? Am I awake? Or am I dreaming?"

David: So what is Lux getting at?

80   **Joe:** Well, maybe it's something like this: we all like to have our kids have their portraits taken at a studio. She's playing with and calling attention to our sense of what a portrait is. It's fabricated. And it's cheesey. "Why do we go to Wal-Mart and get these portraits made?," her work might be asking.

Her work is getting us to see that the typical child's portrait is staged. It's projecting an idealized image, a serene and perfect vision, not the messy room and screaming kid. The portrait represents what we think things should be like, not what they're really like.

And she's interested in this—our interest in portraits. Portraits and snapshots make up the vast majority of all photos made. People want to look at other people. In Lux, the children are idealized in a surreal way. The image is perfect in its own self-containment, but disorienting, off in ways that are hard to put your finger on.

David: Okay, so you're saying that these photos are satiric; they're sending up the conventions of portraiture. If you look at satire in literary terms, however, it's not only directed at certain targets; it's also coming from some relatively stable point of view. Where is Lux standing for her critique?

Joe: I think that the visual artist does not usually want to go that far. She's satisfied to point it out. What else is it? What is the surrealists' goal? Must it be an avant garde position, something never seen before? Or can her artist's role be that of a barometer, reflecting back to the culture what we are?

85   This can lead us to wonder, are artists really at the forefront of the culture, as a lot of people like to think, or are they rather a barometer bringing out for the rest of us

what is already happening, but which we may not be seeing? Maybe they're barometers rather than initiators.

I took a field trip with the senior art majors last Monday to the studio of a working sculptor. He made a powerful impression on them. The guy was a kind of living caricature of the self-involved, arrogant artist. He claimed that to make an impact you needed to create stuff that had never been seen before, and if he decided any of his own work was derivative, he'd throw it out. He was saying that the artist's role is to be the inventor of culture, not just a cultural analyst using the culture as material to work over.

This reminds me of another book by Szarkowski called *Mirrors and Windows*. The mirrors part suggests that photographs cause the viewer to see himself or herself. The windows help us to see what's out there more carefully, by framing it. In this context, Lux's portraits bounce us back to the conventions normally used to set up a portrait. But her work is twisting this and making us self-conscious of the conventions. But it's subtle, and things we think are natural—children's portraits—are really not natural; they're fabricated.

David: Could you say more about the frame?

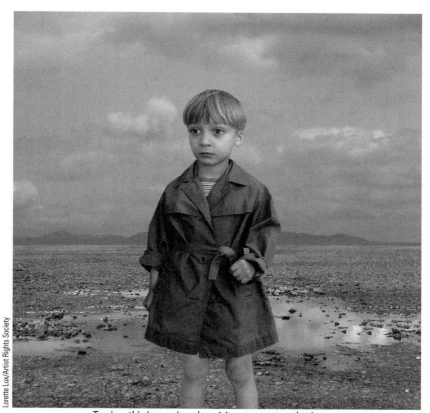

Lorette Lux/Artist Rights Society

To view this image in color, visit www.cengagebrain.com

FIGURE 24.10
Boy in a Blue Raincoat #2 by Loretta Lux

Joe: A frame requires a different kind of seeing, entirely different from the way we normally see. It makes us see and construct in a formal sense that has its own reasons for being; it's about conveying space, about balance, about traditional beauty in the relationship among the parts. Another way to look at it is that it forces us to examine

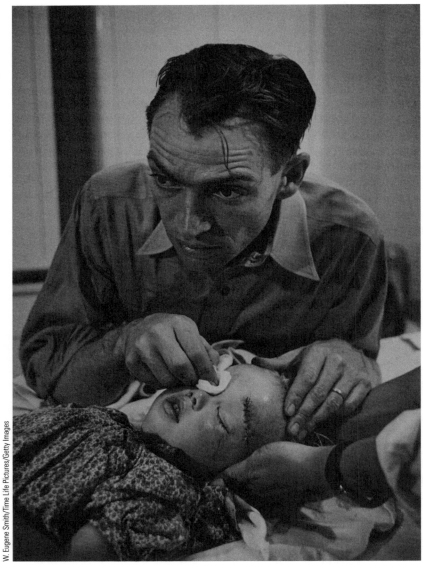

FIGURE 24.11
Untitled (Dr. Ceriani with Injured Child, 1948)—black and white photo by W. Eugene Smith

everything inside the frame. Burtynski and the straightforward photographers induce us to look at what's inside the frame in some dispassionate way—all is equal inside the frame; things included are carefully chosen.

An illuminating comparison in this context might be between Lux and the work   90
of Eugene Smith. [*Joe turns to the portrait of the country doctor, which first appeared in the 1950s in* Life Magazine, *on page 150 of Szarkowski's* Looking at Photographs.] Smith's work has classical form—note how the figure of the doctor is centered, and thrust forward into the frame. He wants us to see a more heroic figure than the rest of us are. But framing gets us to examine carefully what's inside.

Jill: This reminds me of what the contemporary American poet Robert Pinsky has said about artistic truth: that it is not insistent but poised. Poise is a key word for him.

Joe: I would connect the word poise with the work of Walker Evans, Helen Levitt, and Roy deCarava as well as with Eugene Smith. Smith's work is so sculpturesque. It's like Michelangelo. He's a good example of romantic intensification. He's got a journalistic code to obey. But there is fabrication of a sort. "This is why people want to become doctors," his photograph is saying. Smith is interesting to contemplate, because he's so different from Crewdson or Lux.

Jill: Some fabricators overdo romantic intensification on purpose, don't they?

Joe: Yes, like Lux, though I'm not sure that romantic is the correct word for Lux. Lux calls attention to this. Try to compare Lux to another photographer named Reineke Dijkstra, who compares with Gursky and Burtynsky—she's very straight.

[*Joe looks at the famous Andreas Gursky photograph of the candy and other food*   95
items, "99 Cent" (1999).] This photograph is huge—10' × 8'—and you can read the label on every Snickers bar, and all the things inside the frame are equal. He's showing us how we're surrounded with unending crappy stuff. The photograph is making a huge critique in a dispassionate way.

David: Well, who is doing romantic portraiture?

Joe: We have the clearly fabricated portraiture of Edward Curtis; he puts Native Americans up against a sylvan background in all their tribal gear and feathers. And while W. Eugene Smith has been out of fashion for all his romanticizing, at least he is doing it in a real context.

In thinking about portraits, it is interesting to think about the relationship between photographers and their subjects. In the famous Walker Evans' portraits of sharecroppers, the figure of the woman is tight-lipped. She does not want to be photographed, but she is allowing it. The husband is more accommodating, but he is still resisting. But Smith's figures do not resist the camera. They go along with it. They are part of the project.

The Sixth Meeting: 12/2/05 Varieties of Documentarians (Recorders)

Note: The photographers discussed in this interview later appear in a list of categories that Elliott has composed, which is included at the end of these interviews. The boldfaced labels in this interview are taken from that list.

Joe: In contemporary photography we want to be aware of the distance, that a photo is not just a piece of life; it's detached. One of the earlier assumptions was that a little camera could take you *into* life (for example: Brassai, Capa, Weegee).

100   From 1925 until recently, there was the assumption that the small, portable, fast camera could bring us a slice of life, the essence of an event, a decisive moment. That slice of life, Salgado, Cartier-Bresson tradition has come to an end in art photography. And that may be because, why try to catch life in still form? Because it's superseded by video, by the videographers. But when things are moving, you can't meditate on them. We need the camera to stop time.

Jill: So is the small camera/slice of life approach always in the service of what you call recording?

Joe: In the documentary tradition, such as the photographs of W. Eugene Smith, *you are there.* As a photographer you bring the world to people with all the sweat attached. But Smith has also fabricated; he has framed the shot, controlling where we look, and so forth. And he has taken a lot of pictures of this guy. All in all, he has intensified the tools for making us see.

If you wanted to look at other comparable heroic photographs of this sort by Smith, check out the Albert Schweitzer picture, the white doctor in the jungle, bringing hope to these unfortunate lepers. Or there's a similar one of a Pittsburgh steel worker.

Or if you wanted to move to more contemporary documentarians, try Sebastiao Salgado's *Workers* or Eugene Richards, who is grittier. These people are documentarians, but I call them **idea-driven documentarians** because they have a position that shapes the way they execute their photographs.

105   There is another interesting photographer in this category, Lauren Greenfield, who is making a big splash. She focuses on girl culture. She's looking at suburban culture, not at Africa like Salgado or the ghetto, like Richards, who looks at crack addicts in Philly (and gets flak for exploiting their dire situation for his own benefit). She critiques young women's obsession with beauty in the culture. Is she saying this consumption is a bad thing? I don't know. See her image of teenagers in a convertible in California on the way to the beach, in swimsuits.

Jill: You also have a category that you call personal documentarians. How do they differ from the ones you call idea-driven?

Joe: Let's consider Nan Goldin. Her work is a cross between self-portraiture and the totally fabricated world of Cindy Sherman. But Goldin is a participant observer, as in anthropology. Whereas Eugene Smith is supposed to be a fly on the wall, Goldin turns the camera on herself as much as she does on the subcultures she documents. That's why I would call her a **personal documentarian**. The same goes for Sally Mann, who documents her own family. Her kids become actors in their own documentation, so she produces a documentary with the explicit cooperation of the subject.

Or consider Larry Sultan. He is a photographer of identity issues. He does "Pictures from Home," a series of his parents. He is a documentarian *and* a stager, doing photo essays about life in California. His colors and style anticipate Crewdson.

Jill: There are, then, documentarians who cross the line between the two camps, stagers and recorders?

Joe: Yes. And there are fabricators whose work comes out of the documentary tradi- 110
tion of recorders, but in a clearly staged way. Consider Lorna Simpson, an African American who photographs staged re-enactments of black women dressed in colonial costumes as slaves in the house. She is examining identity though these re-enactments—her work offers *pictures of representations: it's a framing of the representation.*

   There is another interesting photographer in this context, An-My Le. She teaches at Bard, went to Yale. She photographs re-enactments of battles in Vietnam; this is a search for identity (she is Vietnamese). She does not use her own family history but someone else's fabrication of that history.

David: This leads to a problem common in post-modernism. Once you get rid of authenticity as a viable concept (since everything is a representation or role), it is extremely difficult to distinguish between kinds or degrees of fabrication in photographs, between Smith and Crewdson.

Joe: Do people no longer care where truth is located?

Jill: Your post-modernist would say it's all images on TV.

Joe: These images really are beautiful, technologically speaking—spectacular, if you 115
choose to look at them.

Jill: How do we deal with those who are captivated by the televised image?

Joe: I pretend the TV world is not out there. The students have the camera, and within that context they'll explore and appreciate the world of black and white, learning to distinguish a good image from a bad one. It's simpler, quieter, bucolic, and they can claim ownership.

Jill: One of my students who is also taking your photography course mentioned that he was told to go shoot, and he started with guys in the middle of the frame and nothing else going on. But soon he learned how much more there was to think about in taking a good photograph.

Joe: Yeah, for example, I do not allow beginning students to crop their images. The frame of the image must be thought through by the artist. It would violate the art to crop; a photograph, they learn, is meticulously put together.

   One of my models here is Eugene Smith, who was an anomaly in the world 120
of *Life Magazine* photographers. In the old days, the magazine would develop and select images from among all those submitted on film by its photographers. But Smith refused. He wanted to select and print the image himself. So he quit *Life*. He wanted the control to exhibit the maximum romantic values, as in the "Country Doctor" series.

David: On that note, what about photographers who are primarily interested in the medium itself?

Sebastiao Salgado/Contact Press Images

FIGURE 24.12

A community above Chimborazo, Ecuador, 1982 by Sebastiao Salgado

To view this image in color, visit www.cengagebrain.com

FIGURE 24.13
Lauren Greenfield, "Ashleigh, 13, with her friends and parents, Santa Monica"

Lauren Greenfield/INSTITUTE

Joe: I know this is a category we haven't discussed—the **Formalists**. It exists between the documentarians and the post-modern stagers. Formalists are mostly interested in how the image is framed and how photographic controls are used to form the image— its design. This category includes small camera explorers like André Kertész and Lee Friedlander, but also artists who work on a more monumental scale, like Edward Weston, Aaron Siskind, and Hiroshi Sugimoto.

David: I've been looking at the photos in the *Blind Spot* magazines you gave me, especially from John Divola's "As Far As I Can Get" series. How would you locate his work?

Joe: His work is a form of fabrication. He is doing a kind of conceptual art move. You set up a lot of parameters with instructions in order to accomplish your art, and then you apply them. Sol Lewitt is an example. Divola does this. So does Ed Ruscha in his "26 Gasoline Stations" series. There is also his small fires series—it includes pictures of the flame on a glass ring, a cigarette, some pieces of paper burning. Another conceptual person is William Wegman, who established a basic collaboration with his dog, and he was determined to operate within that framework. My category for these artists is **Prescribed Process** (more commonly called Conceptual Art).

125 **Jill:** Oh, so the artist makes some rules to follow, and then the photographing becomes a kind of controlled experiment?

Joe: Yes, it's not like Ruscha picked only certain gas stations to photograph because they were beautiful, or whatever, he had decided to photograph them all within a certain space—that was his rule.

The Seventh Meeting: 12/13/05 Writing about Photographs

David: One photographer you've said very little about is … you. We're sitting in this room across from one of the photographs that is part of your Bethlehem Steel series.

Joe: I began making photos at Bethlehem Steel in 1989 and continued until the plant closed in 1999. The motive was fascination with this gargantuan relic of the Machine Age. If I had to categorize the work, I would have to call myself a structural documentarian.

Jill: It's an interesting photograph. There's the protective clothing hanging on the wall. Is that a hat? Did you light the picture?

130 **Joe:** No, the light came in from the window. I got that picture in less than minute. The subject did not know he was being photographed. I just looked over and saw it, and I set up really quickly and took the shot. The foot of another man sneaks into the frame on the lower left. I only noticed this when I printed the photograph. The foot reminds us that there is a world going on outside the frame.

Jill: When I teach poetry-writing, we spend time thinking about how the details in most descriptive writing are implicitly metaphorical—that is, they are both literal and figurative.

David: What do you see as metaphorical in Joe's photograph?

Jill: Well, the man is slightly out of focus, as if in motion; the image reminds us of the passage of time. He is in a box surrounded by his protective clothing, the hat, the gas

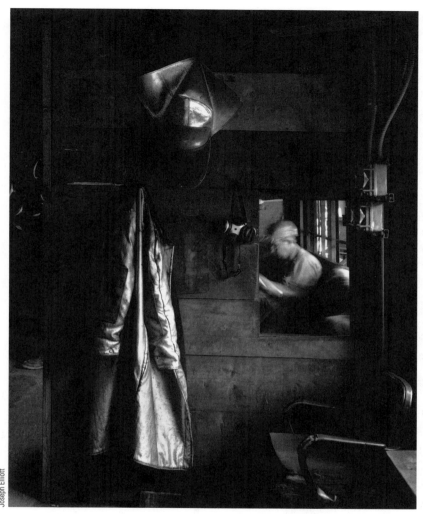

Joseph Elliott

FIGURE 24.14
Blast furnace rest area, Bethlehem, PA, 1992. 20" × 24" gelatin silver print
by Joseph Elliott

mask. So the picture is all about containment and safety, but we also know it's a picture about something—the soon to be closed Bethlehem Steel—about to pass into oblivion.

Joe: Yes, I can see the containment, but if you look at it another way, it is hard to tell where the man is in relation to the space. We could be seeing a mirror reflection of him, or he could be inside the box.

Jill: As we talk I am thinking about how some people are inclined to look for 135 "messages" in photographs, which isn't exactly right. Others decide that they can make of the photograph whatever they wish, which isn't right either.

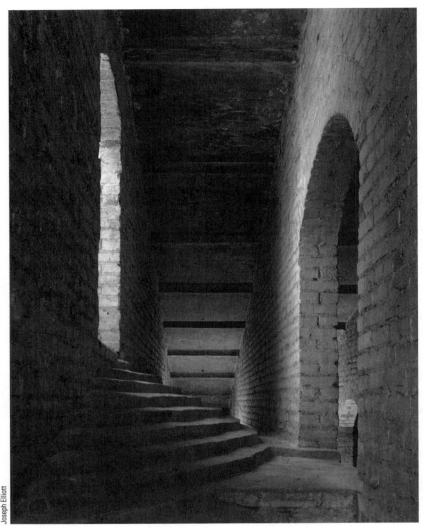

Joseph Elliott

FIGURE 24.15
Attic, Founders Hall, Girard College, Philadelphia, PA, 2000. 20" × 24" gelatin
silver print by Joseph Elliott

Joe: I have been reading a small book called *A Primer for Visual Literacy* by Donis A. Dondis. She says there are three levels on which we can look at a visual image: the representational, the formal, and the symbolic. People often want to jump to the symbolic. But we also need to deal with the other two levels whenever we discuss an image. The levels are not always equally important. As a practitioner I usually stay in the realms of the first two. When I teach beginning students we spend most of our time talking about the second.

Jill: In closing, could you talk to us a little bit about how you look at photographs, and how you teach your students to look at them?

David: How do you begin?

Joe: Well, first, I try to see everything that is in the frame. Too often we engage in unconscious cropping—we look at a piece of the photo instead of taking it all in. In a good photograph, you can't take a piece of it for the whole. It's all important.

One way to get inexperienced viewers to see more is to take a piece of paper and 140 slide it around, cutting off one side or another. Then you re-describe the work: what do you see now that you didn't see before? What does it feel like?

As for other moves, I sometimes give students a cardboard frame, and have them use it to frame the world—to think of the world in terms of framing shots.

Or a viewer can sometimes see more freshly by squinting at the image or turning it upside down. That has the effect of denaturalizing it, so you can see it freshly. Too often inexperienced viewers *get so stuck on the information that they can't see how it is put together.*

The more you look, the finer the distinctions you can learn to see.

Second, there is a kind of memory bank of images that I have access to in my brain when I look at photographs. This comes from a knowledge of the history of photography. I see photographs in the context of other photographs that I have seen.

Third, I try to fit the image roughly into one or more of the categories we have 145 been discussing. What is the cultural, conceptual, political basis for the image? What mode did the photographer choose to express the work?

Jill: Any favorite questions?

Joe: One question I really encourage asking is "Why is this art?" Note that the question is *not* "Is this art?" The implication is that these images are all art. We are looking for what makes them art. It is not our job to judge.

Try asking this question with Ed Ruscha's work, who in "26 Gasoline Stations" does 1950s Americana in canvases 7' × 30' long, featuring smoking rabbits, dogs' heads, phone poles, and other iconic images.

David: Thanks so much for talking to us, Joe.

Jill: Yes, and we'll be sure to call you before we burn down any houses.

Joseph Elliott's Photo-Categories

Note: Some artists fall into more than one category.

Stagers (Fabricators)
  Prescribed Process
    Edward Muybridge
    Sol LeWitt
    Bernd and Hilla Becher
    Ed Ruscha
    John Divola
    William Wegman

Tableaux, Constructed in front of the camera or in the computer
- Julia Cameron
- Peter Henry Emerson
- Edward Curtis
- Gregory Crewdson
- Cindy Sherman
- Loretta Lux
- Philip Lorca di Corcia
- Jeff Wall
- Almost all advertising images (GAP and Apple have used existing images of famous personalities, re-contextualizing them)
- John Heartfield
- An-My Le
- Lorna Simpson (records other people's tableaux)
- Larry Fink
- David LaChapelle

Recorders (Observers)
  Detached Documentarians
- Timothy O'Sullivan
- Eugene Atget
- August Sander
- Walker Evans
- Alfred Stieglitz
- Joel Sternfeld
- Edward Burtynsky
- Camilo Jose Vergara
- William Eggleston
- Joseph Elliott
- An-My Le

  Idea-driven Documentarians, lead with ideological frame
- Eugene Smith
- Dorothea Lange
- Weegee
- Larry Fink
- Sebastio Salgado
- Diane Arbus
- Lauren Greenfield (Girl Culture)
- Arlene Gottfred
- Eugene Richards

Personal Documentarians
    Nan Goldin
    Larry Sultan
    Robin Schwartz
    Bill Burke
    Sally Mann

Formalists
    Walker Evans
    Edward Weston
    Ray Metzger
    Hiroshi Sugimoto
    Lee Friedlander

Works Cited or Recommended

Robert Adams, *On Beauty in Photography*
Roland Barthes, *Camera Lucida: Reflections on Photography*
Vicki Goldberg, *Photographers on Photography*
Lincoln Kirsten, *American Photographs: The 1939 Walker Evans MOMA Exhibition Catalogue*
Janet Malcolm, *Diana & Nikon: Essays on the Aesthetic of Photography*
October Magazine, "The Judgment Seat of Photography" (on Szarkowski's influence)
Aaron Scharf, *Art and Photography*
John Szarkowski, *American Landscapes: Photographs from the Collection of the Museum of Modern Art*
John Szarkowski, *Looking at Photographs*
John Szarkowski, *Mirrors and Windows*
John Szarkowski *The Photographer's Eye*
Alan Trachtenberg, *Reading American Photographs: Images as History: Mathew Brady to Walker Evans*

Things to Do with the Reading

1. Experiment with applying Elliott's primary categories—stagers versus recorders—by writing a short analysis of the photograph by Eggleston. Which features of this photograph might cause you to see it as staged, and why? Which features might cause you to see it as essentially documentary (recorded), and why? You might also try this experiment with Lauren Greenfield's photograph, "Ashleigh, 13, with her friend and parents, Santa Monica." (See the next question for another writing project using the Eggleston photograph.)

2. In the Seventh Meeting Elliott refers to a book entitled *A Primer for Visual Literacy*, by Donis A. Dondis in which the author claims that there are three levels on which we can look at a visual image: the representational, the formal, and the symbolic. Elliott asserts that people too often leap to the symbolic before considering the other two levels. In other words, they leap to some larger (symbolic) meaning that they ascribe to the photo before they have dwelled with the representational details (what it is a picture of) or the formal way that shapes and perspectives are arranged inside the frame.

Use description as an analytical tool for thinking about and writing a short essay on the William Eggleston photograph of two men by a car. First describe the photograph as a representation. What is it a picture of? You might wish to use the method of sliding a piece of paper around the photograph to make sure you don't leave important details out of your description.

Next, write a second description in which you attend to the formal level—the arrangement of elements in the frame, including various kinds of shapes and patterns of light and dark (this will require you to "see past the content").

Finally, use these descriptions to prompt some interpretive leaps about the way the photograph operates symbolically. Which details of the photograph seem to invite a symbolic reading? Why? What unstated claims or positions might this photograph be giving voice?

3. Write an essay comparing Gregory Crewdson and Loretta Lux. Like all good thinkers and writers, Elliott not only creates categories but qualifies them and doesn't allow the categorizing process to cause him to gloss over photographers who don't neatly fit. So, for example, in one of his two primary categories, fabricators (aka stagers), he notes that the works of Gregory Crewdson and Loretta Lux are staged but with interesting differences. Locate this section of the interview (in the Fifth Meeting), choose relevant quotations, and paraphrase them in order to articulate and develop this difference. You should also, of course, study examples of the photographs themselves, or others by Crewdson and Lux.

4. In the third meeting, "The Photographer's Hand," Elliott comments,

> In [Crewdson's] photo of the house on fire, the people on the train track on the other side of the frame are a competing focal point by design. Nothing is an accident in the photo. He wants it to be carefully observed, to invite a close reading. We may think of a photograph having an initial impact, but there's also something else going on, a counterpoint, a set of messages (paragraph 46).

Use these observations as a lens for writing an analysis of the photograph. Here are some questions you might consider. If the photo has competing focal points by design, what is achieved in this way? If the photo has an initial impact but also a counterpoint—more than one, potentially opposed "messages"—what would you say these are? Make sure to share your reasoning about the evidence: why you think particular details mean what you claim they mean. (See Chapter 8, the section called "Giving Evidence a Point: Making Details Speak.") You might also try this with another Crewdson photograph—either another one in this book or one that you locate online.

5. Write a short essay based on Elliott observations in the Third Meeting, "The Photographer's Hand," about looking for the photographer's hand in the Alfred Stieglitz photograph of "Georgia Engelhard." He asks, for example, why Stieglitz included the edge with the part of an urn and a rubber tree. Where is there evidence of the presence of the photographer's shaping influence—his "hand"—in the photograph?

   At the end of the seventh meeting, Elliott describes an exercise in which he has viewers take a piece of paper and slide it around on a photograph, blocking one side or another. He then asks them to re-describe the work each time: "What do you see now that you didn't see before?" Apply this procedure to the Stieglitz photo, and be sure not only to answer Elliott's question but also to ask and answer "So what?" about the difference (see Chapter 2, "Asking "So what?""; also see the next writing project for an extension of this one.)

6. In his famous book *Camera Lucida: Reflections on Photography,* Roland Barthes speaks of the Punctum, which he defines as the single detail in a photograph that "arouses greatest sympathy" and is primarily responsible for the impact of the image on a viewer. In the previous exercise, you were asked to notice as much as you could about the details Stieglitz chooses to frame in his photograph. Barthes' approach is like the technique we call ranking, choosing and arguing for the importance of a single element as a means of prompting an interpretive leap about the whole photograph (see Chapter 2, "Notice and Focus (Ranking)"). Select a Punctum for Stieglitz's "Georgia Englehard" and use it to anchor a short interpretive essay.

7. **Application:** Write a paper about some trend you notice in advertising photography. Here are some questions to help. To what extent do you find evidence of documentary style photography in the world of print advertising? How is it being used, and for what purposes? You might also look for at least one clearly staged advertising photo that you think is representative of staging among advertising photos. And can you find an example of a hybrid, an image that seems to combine staging and recording in the services of advertising some product?

8. **Application:** Elliott discusses the work of Loretta Lux as a commentary on the conventions of portraiture, inviting us to think about what portraits are and why all of us (not just professional photographers) take portraits of people. Elliott refers to these conventions as "idealizing." Apply Elliott's discussion to other portraits—of your own (or family photographs), or of other photographers mentioned in the interview. As you study the portraits you've assembled, try to make a list of what you think the conventions of portraiture actually *are.* Then work out their implications, the meanings attached

to them. Your goal will be to write an essay in which you make some claims about what the photographer of your choice seems to be saying about portraiture. Keep in mind that in Elliott's terms, portraits can be to varying degrees both recorded and staged.

9. **Application:** Near the end of the Sixth Meeting, Elliott discusses those photographers he labels Prescribed Processors—that is, those who "set up a lot of parameters, with instructions to accomplish [their] art" (paragraph 124). John Divola (not included here) photographs a lone runner against a variety of settings in his "As Far as I Can Get" series; Ed Ruscha trains his camera on "26 Gasoline Stations." Try the following experiment with prescribed processing as the basis for a paper: get a camera and then select an object (or subject) and shoot the first 26 that you see. Use the photographs as a subject for analysis. What did you learn about your subject by repeatedly photographing it? How do you see this subject differently now? What did you learn about seeing—and about taking pictures—by doing this project?

10. **Link Across Chapters:** In Chapter 21, James Howard Kunstler writes (in "The Public Realm and the Common Good") that public space has been seriously eroded by contemporary zoning and construction practices. Be a documentarian and try to record in both writing and images what you take to be evidence for the degeneration of what he terms the "public realm," defined as "the physical manifestation of the common good."

Go to places on your campus or in a neighborhood nearby and record (in writing and in photographs) examples of what you take to be good and less good examples of the preservation of public spaces. Use both images and verbal depictions to compose a photo-essay in which you capture what you think to be the essence of one or more of these places.

Susan Sontag

In Plato's Cave

This essay from the influential cultural critic Susan Sontag first appeared as a chapter in her 1977 essay collection *On Photography*, which won the National Book Critics' Circle Award for Criticism in 1977. The art establishment regarded the book with horror, though over time many have come around to acknowledge its stimulating and disturbing discussion of the role of photography in contemporary culture. In an article commemorating the twentieth anniversary of its publication, Michael Starenko claimed that "Perhaps no photography book [. . .] has been analyzed and discussed with more intensity, from so many different and competing perspectives. [. . .] Sontag's claims about photography as well as her mode of argument have become part of the rhetorical "tool kit' that photography theorists and critics carry around in their heads ("Sontag's On Photography at 20," *Afterimage*, March–April 1998)."

Humankind lingers unregenerately in Plato's cave, still revelling, its age-old habit, in mere images of the truth. But being educated by photographs is not like being educated by older, more artisanal images. For one thing, there are a great many more images around, claiming our attention. The inventory started in 1839 and since then just about everything has been photographed, or so it seems. This very insatiability of the photographing eye changes the terms of confinement in the cave, our world. In teaching us a new visual code, photographs alter and enlarge our notions of what is worth looking at and what we have a right to observe. They are a grammar and, even more importantly, an ethics of seeing. Finally, the most grandiose result of the photographic enterprise is to give us the sense that we can hold the whole world in our heads—as an anthology of images.   1

To collect photographs is to collect the world. Movies and television programmes light up walls, flicker, and go out; but with still photographs the image is also an object, lightweight, cheap to produce, easy to carry about, accumulate, store. In Godard's *Les Carabiniers* (1963), two sluggish lumpen-peasants are lured into joining the King's Army by the promise that they will be able to loot, rape, kill, or do whatever else they please to the enemy, and get rich. But the suitcase of booty that Michel-Ange and Ulysse triumphantly bring home, years later, to their wives turns out to contain only picture postcards, hundreds of them, of Monuments, Department Stores, Mammals, Wonders of Nature, Methods of Transport, Works of Art, and other classified treasures from around the globe. Godard's gag vividly parodies the equivocal magic of the photographic image. Photographs are perhaps the most mysterious of all the objects that make up, and thicken, the environment we recognise as modern. Photographs really are experience captured, and the camera is the ideal arm of consciousness in its acquisitive mood.

To photograph is to appropriate the thing photographed. It means putting oneself into a certain relation to the world that feels like knowledge—and, therefore, like power. A now notorious first fall into alienation, habituating people to abstract the

"In Plato's Cave" from *On Photography* by Susan Sontag. Copyright © 1977 by Susan Sontag. Reprinted by permission of Farrar, Straus and Giroux, LLC.

world into printed words, is supposed to have engendered that surplus of Faustian energy and psychic damage needed to build modern, inorganic societies. But print seems a less treacherous form of leaching out the world, of turning it into a mental object, than photographic images, which now provide most of the knowledge people have about the look of the past and the reach of the present. What is written about a person or an event is frankly an interpretation, as are handmade visual statements, like paintings and drawings. Photographed images do not seem to be statements about the world so much as pieces of it, miniatures of reality that anyone can make or acquire.

Photographs, which fiddle with the scale of the world, themselves get reduced, blown up, cropped, retouched, doctored, tricked out. They age, plagued by the usual ills of paper objects; they disappear; they become valuable, and get bought and sold; they are reproduced. Photographs, which package the world, seem to invite packaging. They are stuck in albums, framed and set on tables, tacked on walls, projected as slides. Newspapers and magazines feature them; cops alphabetise them; museums exhibit them; publishers compile them.

5   For many decades the book has been the most influential way of arranging (and usually miniaturising) photographs, thereby guaranteeing them longevity, if not immortality—photographs are fragile objects, easily torn or mislaid—and a wider public. The photograph in a book is, obviously, the image of an image. But since it is, to begin with, a printed, smooth object, a photograph loses much less of its essential quality when reproduced in a book than a painting does. Still, the book is not a wholly satisfactory scheme for putting groups of photographs into general circulation. The sequence in which the photographs are to be looked at is proposed by the order of pages, but nothing holds readers to the recommended order or indicates the amount of time to be spent on each photograph. Chris Marker's film, *Si j'avais quatre dromadaires* (1966), a brilliantly orchestrated meditation on photographs of all sorts and themes, suggests a subtler and more rigorous way of packaging (and enlarging) still photographs. Both the order and the exact time for looking at each photograph are imposed; and there is a gain in visual legibility and emotional impact. But photographs transcribed in a film cease to be collectable objects, as they still are when served up in books.

Photographs furnish evidence. Something we hear about, but doubt, seems proven when we're shown a photograph of it. In one version of its utility, the camera record incriminates. Starting with their use by the Paris police in the murderous roundup of Communards in June 1871, photographs became a useful tool of modern states in the surveillance and control of their increasingly mobile populations. In another version of its utility, the camera record justifies. A photograph passes for incontrovertible proof that a given thing happened. The picture may distort; but there is always a presumption that something exists, or did exist, which is like what's in the picture. Whatever the limitations (through amateurism) or pretensions (through artistry) of the individual photographer, a photograph—any photograph—seems to have a more innocent, and therefore more accurate, relation to visible reality than do other mimetic objects. Virtuosi of the noble image like Alfred Stieglitz and Paul Strand, composing mighty, unforgettable photographs decade after decade, still want, first of all, to show something "out there," just like the Polaroid owner for whom photographs are a handy, fast form of note-taking, or the shutterbug with a Brownie who takes snapshots as souvenirs of daily life.

While a painting or a prose description can never be other than a narrowly selective interpretation, a photograph can be treated as a narrowly selective transparency. But despite the presumption of veracity that gives all photographs authority, interest, seductiveness, the work that photographers do is no generic exception to the usually shady commerce between art and truth. Even when photographers are most concerned with mirroring reality, they are still haunted by tacit imperatives of taste and conscience. The immensely gifted members of the Farm Security Administration photographic project of the late 1930s (among them Walker Evans, Dorothea Lange, Ben Shahn, Russell Lee) would take dozens of frontal pictures of one of their sharecropper subjects until satisfied that they had gotten just the right look on film—the precise expression on the subject's face that supported their own notions about poverty, light, dignity, texture, exploitation, and geometry. In deciding how a picture should look, in preferring one exposure to another, photographers are always imposing standards on their subjects. Although there is a sense in which the camera does indeed capture reality, not just interpret it, photographs are as much an interpretation of the world as paintings and drawings are. Those occasions when the taking of photographs is relatively undiscriminating, promiscuous, or self-effacing do not lessen the didacticism of the whole enterprise. This very passivity—and ubiquity—of the photographic record is photography's "message," its aggression.

Images which idealise (like most fashion and animal photography) are no less aggressive than work which makes a virtue of plainness (like class pictures, still lifes of the bleaker sort, and mug shots). There is an aggression implicit in every use of the camera. This is as evident in the 1840s and 1850s, photography's glorious first two decades, as in all the succeeding decades, during which technology made possible an ever increasing spread of that mentality which looks at the world as a set of potential photographs. Even for such early masters as David Octavius Hill and Julia Margaret Cameron who used the camera as a means of getting painterly images, the point of taking photographs was a vast departure from the aims of painters. From its start, photography implied the capture of the largest possible number of subjects. Painting never had so imperial a scope. The subsequent industrialisation of camera technology only carried out a promise inherent in photography from its very beginning: to democratise all experiences by translating them into images.

That age when taking photographs required a cumbersome and expensive contraption—the toy of the clever, the wealthy, and the obsessed—seems remote indeed from the era of sleek pocket cameras that invite anyone to take pictures. The first cameras, made in France and England in the early 1840s, had only inventors and buffs to operate them. Since there were then no professional photographers, there could not be amateurs either, and taking photographs had no clear social use; it was a gratuitous, that is, an artistic activity, though with few pretensions to being an art. It was only with its industrialisation that photography came into its own as art. As industrialisation provided social uses for the operations of the photographer, so the reaction against these uses reinforced the self-consciousness of photography-as-art.

10   Recently, photography has become almost as widely practised an amusement as sex and dancing—which means that, like every mass art form, photography is not practised by most people as an art. It is mainly a social rite, a defence against anxiety, and a tool of power.

Memorialising the achievements of individuals considered as members of families (as well as of other groups) is the earliest popular use of photography. For at least a century, the wedding photograph has been as much a part of the ceremony as the prescribed verbal formulae. Cameras go with family life. According to a sociological study done in France, most households have a camera, but a household with children is twice as likely to have at least one camera as a household in which there are no children. Not to take pictures of one's children, particularly when they are small, is a sign of parental indifference, just as not turning up for one's graduation picture is a gesture of adolescent rebellion.

Through photographs, each family constructs a portrait-chronicle of itself— a portable kit of images that bears witness to its connectedness. It hardly matters what activities are photographed so long as photographs get taken and are cherished. Photography becomes a rite of family life just when, in the industrialising countries of Europe and America, the very institution of the family starts undergoing radical surgery. As that claustrophobic unit, the nuclear family, was being carved out of a much larger family aggregate, photography came along to memorialise, to restate symbolically, the imperilled continuity and vanishing extendedness of family life. Those ghostly traces, photographs, supply the token presence of the dispersed relatives. A family's photograph album is generally about the extended family—and, often, is all that remains of it.

As photographs give people an imaginary possession of a past that is unreal, they also help people to take possession of space in which they are insecure. Thus, photography develops in tandem with one of the most characteristic of modern activities: tourism. For the first time in history, large numbers of people regularly travel out of their habitual environments for short periods of time. It seems positively unnatural to travel for pleasure without taking a camera along. Photographs will offer indisputable evidence that the trip was made, that the programme was carried out, that fun was had. Photographs document sequences of consumption carried on outside the view of family, friends, neighbours. But dependence on the camera, as the device that makes real what one is experiencing, doesn't fade when people travel more. Taking photographs fills the same need for the cosmopolitans accumulating photograph-trophies of their boat trip up the Albert Nile or their fourteen days in China as it does for lower-middle-class vacationers taking snapshots of the Eiffel Tower or Niagara Falls.

A way of certifying experience, taking photographs is also a way of refusing it —by limiting experience to a search for the photogenic, by converting experience into an image, a souvenir. Travel becomes a strategy for accumulating photographs. The very activity of taking pictures is soothing, and assuages general feelings of disorientation that are likely to be exacerbated by travel. Most tourists feel compelled to put the camera between themselves and whatever is remarkable that they encounter. Unsure of other responses, they take a picture. This gives shape to experience: stop, take a photograph, and move on. The method especially appeals to people handicapped by a ruthless work ethic—Germans, Japanese, and Americans. Using a camera appeases the anxiety which the work-driven feel about not working when they are on vacation and supposed to be having fun. They have something to do that is like a friendly imitation of work: they can take pictures.

People robbed of their past seem to make the most fervent picture takers, at home   15 and abroad. Everyone who lives in an industrialised society is obliged gradually to give up the past, but in certain countries, such as the United States and Japan, the break with the past has been particularly traumatic. In the early 1970s, the fable of the brash American tourist of the 1950s and 1960s, rich with dollars and Babbittry, was replaced by the mystery of the group-minded Japanese tourist, newly released from his island prison by the miracle of overvalued yen, who is generally armed with two cameras, one on each hip.

Photography has become one of the principal devices for experiencing something, for giving an appearance of participation. One full-page ad shows a small group of people standing pressed together, peering out of the photograph, all but one looking stunned, excited, upset. The one who wears a different expression holds a camera to his eye; he seems self-possessed, is almost smiling. While the others are passive, clearly alarmed spectators, having a camera has transformed one person into something active, a voyeur: only he has mastered the situation. What do these people see? We don't know. And it doesn't matter. It is an Event: something worth seeing—and therefore worth photographing. The adcopy, white letters across the dark lower third of the photograph like news coming over a teletype machine, consists of just six words: "... Prague ... Woodstock ... Vietnam ... Sapporo ... Londonderry ... LEICA." Crushed hopes, youth antics, colonial wars, and winter sports are alike—are equalised by the camera. Taking photographs has set up a chronic voyeuristic relation to the world which levels the meaning of all events.

A photograph is not just the result of an encounter between an event and a photographer; picture-taking is an event in itself, and one with ever more peremptory rights—to interfere with, to invade, or to ignore whatever is going on. Our very sense of situation is now articulated by the camera's interventions. The omnipresence of cameras persuasively suggests that time consists of interesting events, events worth photographing. This, in turn, makes it easy to feel that any event, once underway, and whatever its moral character, should be allowed to complete itself—so that something else can be brought into the world, the photograph. After the event has ended, the picture will still exist, conferring on the event a kind of immortality (and importance) it would never otherwise have enjoyed. While real people are out there killing themselves or other real people, the photographer stays behind his or her camera, creating a tiny element of another world: the imagine-world that bids to outlast us all.

Photographing is essentially an act of non-intervention. Part of the horror of such memorable coups of contemporary photojournalism as the pictures of a Vietnamese bonze reaching for the gasoline can, of a Bengali guerrilla in the act of bayoneting a trussed-up collaborator, comes from the awareness of how plausible it has become, in situations where the photographer has the choice between a photograph and a life, to choose the photograph. The person who intervenes cannot record; the person who is recording cannot intervene. Dziga Vertov's great film, *Man with a Movie Camera* (1929), gives the ideal image of the photographer as someone in perpetual movement, someone moving through a panorama of disparate events with such agility and speed that any intervention is out of the question. Hitchcock's *Rear Window* (1954) gives the complementary image: The photographer played by James Stewart has an intensified relation to one event, through his camera, precisely because he has a broken leg and is confined to a wheelchair; being temporarily immobilised prevents him from acting on what he sees, and makes it even more important to take pictures. Even if incompatible with intervention in a physical sense, using a camera is still a form of participation. Although the camera is an observation station, the act of photographing is more than passive observing. Like sexual voyeurism, it is a way of at least tacitly, often explicitly, encouraging whatever is going on to keep on happening. To take a picture is to have an interest in things as they are, in the status quo remaining unchanged (at least for as long as it takes to get a "good" picture), to be in complicity with whatever makes a subject interesting, worth photographing—including, when that is the interest, another person's pain or misfortune.

"I always thought of photography as a naughty thing to do—that was one of my favourite things about it," Diane Arbus wrote, "and when I first did it I felt very perverse." Being a professional photographer can be thought of as naughty, to use Arbus's pop word, if the photographer seeks out subjects considered to be disreputable, taboo, marginal. But naughty subjects are harder to find these days. And what exactly is the perverse aspect of picture-taking? If professional photographers often have sexual fantasies when they are behind the camera, perhaps the perversion lies in the fact that these fantasies are both plausible and so inappropriate. In *Blowup* (1966), Antonioni has the fashion photographer hovering convulsively over Verushka's body with his camera clicking. Naughtiness, indeed! In fact, using a camera is not a very good way of getting at someone sexually. Between photographer and subject, there has to be distance. The camera doesn't rape, or even possess, though it may presume, intrude, trespass, distort, exploit, and, at the farthest reach of metaphor, assassinate—all activities that, unlike the sexual push and shove, can be conducted from a distance, and with some detachment.

20   There is a much stronger sexual fantasy in Michael Powell's extraordinary movie *Peeping Tom* (1960), which is not about a Peeping Tom but about a psychopath who kills women with a weapon concealed in his camera, while photographing them. Not once does he touch his subjects. He doesn't desire their bodies; he wants their presence in the form of filmed images—those showing them experiencing their own death—which he screens at home for his solitary pleasure. The movie assumes connections between impotence and aggression, professionalised looking and cruelty, which point to the central fantasy connected with the camera. The camera as phallus is, at most, a flimsy variant of the inescapable metaphor that everyone unselfconsciously employs. However hazy our awareness of this fantasy, it is named without subtlety whenever we talk about "loading" and "aiming" a camera, about "shooting" a film.

The old-fashioned camera was clumsier and harder to reload than a brown Bess musket. The modern camera is trying to be a ray gun. One ad reads:

> The Yashica Electro-35 GT is the spaceage camera your family will love. Take beautiful pictures day or night. Automatically. Without any nonsense. Just aim, focus and shoot. The GT's computer brain and electronic shutter will do the rest.

Like a car, a camera is sold as a predatory weapon—one that's as automated as possible, ready to spring. Popular taste expects an easy, an invisible technology. Manufacturers reassure their customers that taking pictures demands no skill or expert knowledge, that the machine is all-knowing, and responds to the slightest pressure of the will. It's as simple as turning the ignition key or pulling the trigger.

Like guns and cars, cameras are fantasy-machines whose use is addictive. However, despite the extravagances of ordinary language and advertising, they are not lethal. In the hyperbole that markets cars like guns, there is at least this much truth: except in wartime, cars kill more people than guns do. The camera/gun does not kill, so the ominous metaphor seems to be all bluff—like a man's fantasy of having a gun, knife, or tool between his legs. Still, there is something predatory in the act of taking a picture. To photograph people is to violate them, by seeing them as they never see themselves, by having knowledge of them they can never have; it turns people into objects that can be symbolically possessed. Just as the camera is a sublimation of the gun, to photograph someone is a sublimated murder—a soft murder, appropriate to a sad, frightened time.

Eventually, people might learn to act out more of their aggressions with cameras and fewer with guns, with the price being an even more image-choked world. One situation where people are switching from bullets to film is the photographic safari that is replacing the gun safari in East Africa. The hunters have Hasselblads instead of Winchesters; instead of looking through a telescopic sight to aim a rifle, they look through a viewfinder to frame a picture. In end-of-the-century London, Samuel Butler complained that "there is a photographer in every bush, going about like a roaring lion seeking whom he may devour." The photographer is now charging real beasts, beleaguered and too rare to kill. Guns have metamorphosed into cameras in this earnest comedy, the ecology safari, because nature has ceased to be what it always had been—what people needed protection from. Now nature—tamed, endangered, mortal—needs to be protected from people. When we are afraid, we shoot. But when we are nostalgic, we take pictures.

It is a nostalgic time right now, and photographs actively promote nostalgia. Photography is an elegiac art, a twilight art. Most subjects photographed are, just by virtue of being photographed, touched with pathos. An ugly or grotesque subject may be moving because it has been dignified by the attention of the photographer. A beautiful subject can be the object of rueful feelings, because it has aged or decayed or no longer exists. All photographs are *memento mori*. To take a photograph is to participate in another person's (or thing's) mortality, vulnerability, mutability. Precisely by slicing out this moment and freezing it, all photographs testify to time's relentless melt.

Cameras began duplicating the world at that moment when the human landscape 25 started to undergo a vertiginous rate of change: while an untold number of forms of biological and social life are being destroyed in a brief span of time, a device is available to record what is disappearing. The moody, intricately textured Paris of Atget and Brassaï is mostly gone. Like the dead relatives and friends preserved in the family album, whose presence in photographs exorcises some of the anxiety and remorse prompted by their disappearance, so the photographs of neighbourhoods now torn down, rural places disfigured and made barren, supply our pocket relation to the past.

A photograph is both a pseudo-presence and a token of absence. Like a wood fire in a room, photographs—especially those of people, of distant landscapes and faraway cities, of the vanished past—are incitements to reverie. The sense of the unattainable that can be evoked by photographs feeds directly into the erotic feelings of those for whom desirability is enhanced by distance. The lover's photograph hidden in a married woman's wallet, the poster photograph of a rock star tacked up over an adolescent's bed, the campaign-button image of a politician's face pinned on a voter's coat, the snapshots of a cabdriver's children clipped to the visor—all such talismanic uses of photographs express a feeling both sentimental and implicitly magical: they are attempts to contact or lay claim to another reality.

Photographs can abet desire in the most direct, utilitarian way—as when someone collects photographs of anonymous examples of the desirable as an aid to masturbation. The matter is more complex when photographs are used to stimulate the moral impulse. Desire has no history—at least, it is experienced in each instance as all foreground, immediacy. It is aroused by archetypes and is, in that sense, abstract. But moral feelings are embedded in history, whose personae are concrete, whose situations are always specific. Thus, almost opposite rules hold true for the use of the photograph to awaken desire and to awaken conscience. The images that mobilise conscience are always linked to a given historical situation. The more general they are, the less likely they are to be effective.

A photograph that brings news of some unsuspected zone of misery cannot make a dent in public opinion unless there is an appropriate context of feeling and attitude. The photographs Mathew Brady and his colleagues took of the horrors of the battlefields did not make people any less keen to go on with the Civil War. The photographs of ill-clad, skeletal prisoners held at Andersonville inflamed Northern public opinion—against the South. (The effect of the Andersonville photographs must have been partly due to the very novelty, at that time, of seeing photographs.) The political understanding that many Americans came to in the 1960s would allow them, looking at the photographs Dorothea Lange took of Nisei on the West Coast being transported to internment camps in 1942, to recognise their subject for what it was—a crime committed by the government against a large group of American citizens. Few people who saw those photographs in the 1940s could have had so unequivocal a reaction; the grounds for such a judgment were covered over by the pro-war consensus. Photographs cannot create a moral position, but they can reinforce one—and can help build a nascent one.

Photographs may be more memorable than moving images, because they are a neat slice of time, not a flow. Television is a stream of underselected images, each of which cancels its predecessor. Each still photograph is a privileged moment, turned into a slim object that one can keep and look at again. Photographs like the one that made the front page of most newspapers in the world in 1972—a naked South Vietnamese child just sprayed by American napalm, running down a highway toward the camera, her arms open, screaming with pain—probably did more to increase the public revulsion against the war than a hundred hours of televised barbarities.

30   One would like to imagine that the American public would not have been so unanimous in its acquiescence to the Korean War if it had been confronted with photographic evidence of the devastation of Korea, an ecocide and genocide in some

respects even more thorough than those inflicted on Vietnam a decade later. But the supposition is trivial. The public did not see such photographs because there was, ideologically, no space for them. No one brought back photographs of daily life in Pyongyang, to show that the enemy had a human face, as Felix Greene and Marc Riboud brought back photographs of Hanoi. Americans did have access to photographs of the suffering of the Vietnamese (many of which came from military sources and were taken with quite a different use in mind) because journalists felt backed in their efforts to obtain those photographs, the event having been defined by a significant number of people as a savage colonialist war. The Korean War was understood differently—as part of the just struggle of the Free World against the Soviet Union and China—and, given that characterisation, photographs of the cruelty of unlimited American firepower would have been irrelevant.

Though an event has come to mean, precisely, something worth photographing, it is still ideology (in the broadest sense) that determines what constitutes an event. There can be no evidence, photographic or otherwise, of an event until the event itself has been named and characterised. And it is never photographic evidence which can construct—more properly, identify—events; the contribution of photography always follows the naming of the event. What determines the possibility of being affected morally by photographs is the existence of a relevant political consciousness. Without a politics, photographs of the slaughter-bench of history will most likely be experienced as, simply, unreal or as a demoralising emotional blow.

The quality of feeling, including moral outrage, that people can muster in response to photographs of the oppressed, the exploited, the starving, and the massacred also depends on the degree of their familiarity with these images. Don McCullin's photographs of emaciated Biafrans in the early 1970s had less impact for some people than Werner Bischof's photographs of Indian famine victims in the early 1950s because those images had become banal, and the photographs of Tuareg families dying of starvation in the sub-Sahara that appeared in magazines everywhere in 1973 must have seemed to many like an unbearable replay of a now familiar atrocity exhibition.

Photographs shock insofar as they show something novel. Unfortunately, the ante keeps getting raised—partly through the very proliferation of such images of horror. One's first encounter with the photographic inventory of ultimate horror is a kind of revelation, the prototypically modern revelation, a negative epiphany. For me, it was photographs of Bergen-Belsen and Dachau which I came across by chance in a bookstore in Santa Monica in July 1945. Nothing I have seen—in photographs or in real life—ever cut me as sharply, deeply, instantaneously. Indeed, it seems plausible to me to divide my life into two parts, before I saw those photographs (I was twelve) and after, though it was several years before I understood fully what they were about. What good was served by seeing them? They were only photographs—of an event I had scarcely heard of and could do nothing to affect, of suffering I could hardly imagine and could do nothing to relieve. When I looked at those photographs, something broke. Some limit had been reached, and not only that of horror; I felt irrevocably grieved, wounded, but a part of my feelings started to tighten; something went dead; something is still crying.

To suffer is one thing; another thing is living with the photographed images of suffering, which does not necessarily strengthen conscience and the ability to be compassionate. It can also corrupt them. Once one has seen such images, one has started down the road of seeing more—and more. Images transfix. Images anaesthetise. An event known through photographs certainly becomes more real than it would have been if one had never seen the photographs—think of the Vietnam War. (For a counter-example, think of the Gulag Archipelago, of which we have no photographs.) But after repeated exposure to images it also becomes less real.

35   The same law holds for evil as for pornography. The shock of photographed atrocities wears off with repeated viewings, just as the surprise and bemusement felt the first time one sees a pornographic movie wear off after one sees a few more. The sense of taboo which makes us indignant and sorrowful is not much sturdier than the sense of taboo that regulates the definition of what is obscene. And both have been sorely tried in recent years. The vast photographic catalogue of misery and injustice throughout the world has given everyone a certain familiarity with atrocity, making the horrible seem more ordinary—making it appear familiar, remote ("it's only a photograph"), inevitable. At the time of the first photographs of the Nazi camps, there was nothing banal about these images. After thirty years, a saturation point may have been reached. In these last decades, "concerned" photography has done at least as much to deaden conscience as to arouse it.

The ethical content of photographs is fragile. With the possible exception of photographs of those horrors, like the Nazi camps, that have gained the status of ethical reference points, most photographs do not keep their emotional charge. A photograph of 1900 that was affecting then because of its subject would, today, be more likely to move us because it is a photograph taken in 1900. The particular qualities and intentions of photographs tend to be swallowed up in the generalised pathos of time past. Aesthetic distance seems built into the very experience of looking at photographs, if not right away, then certainly with the passage of time. Time eventually positions most photographs, even the most amateurish, at the level of art.

The industrialisation of photography permitted its rapid absorption into rational— that is, bureaucratic—ways of running society. No longer toy images, photographs became part of the general furniture of the environment—touchstones and confirmations of that reductive approach to reality which is considered realistic. Photographs were enrolled in the service of important institutions of control, notably the family and the police, as symbolic objects and as pieces of information. Thus, in the bureaucratic cataloguing of the world, many important documents are not valid unless they have, affixed to them, a photograph-token of the citizen's face.

The "realistic" view of the world compatible with bureaucracy redefines knowledge—as techniques and information. Photographs are valued because they give information. They tell one what there is; they make an inventory. To spies, meteorologists, coroners, archaeologists, and other information professionals, their value is inestimable. But in the situations in which most people use photographs, their value as information is of the same order as fiction. The information that photographs can give starts to seem very important at that moment in cultural history when everyone is thought to have a right to something called news. Photographs were seen as a way of giving information to people who do not take easily to reading. The *Daily News* still calls itself "New York's Picture Newspaper," its bid for populist identity. At the opposite end of the scale, *Le Monde,* a newspaper designed for skilled, well-informed readers, runs no photographs at all. The presumption is that, for such readers, a photograph could only illustrate the analysis contained in an article.

A new sense of the notion of information has been constructed around the photographic image. The photograph is a thin slice of space as well as time. In a world ruled by photographic images, all borders ("framing") seem arbitrary. Anything can be separated, can be made discontinuous, from anything else. All that is necessary is to frame the subject differently. (Conversely, anything can be made adjacent to anything else.) Photography reinforces a nominalist view of social reality as consisting of small units of an apparently infinite number— as the number of photographs that could be taken of anything is unlimited. Through photographs, the world becomes a series of unrelated, freestanding particles; and history, past and present, a set of anecdotes and *faits divers.* The camera makes reality atomic, manageable, and opaque. It is a view of the world which denies interconnectedness, continuity, but which confers on each moment the character of a mystery. Any photograph has multiple meanings; indeed, to see something in the form of a photograph is to encounter a potential object of fascination. The ultimate wisdom of the photographic image is to say: "There is the surface. Now think—or rather feel, intuit—what is beyond it, what the reality must be like if it looks this way." Photographs, which cannot themselves explain anything, are inexhaustible invitations to deduction, speculation, and fantasy.

Photography implies that we know about the world if we accept it as the camera   40 records it. But this is the opposite of understanding, which starts from *not* accepting the world as it looks. All possibility of understanding is rooted in the ability to say no. Strictly speaking, one never understands anything from a photograph. Of course, photographs fill in blanks in our mental pictures of the present and the past: for example, Jacob Riis's images of New York squalor in the 1880s are sharply instructive to those unaware that urban poverty in late-nineteenth-century America was really that Dickensian. Nevertheless, the camera's rendering of reality must always hide more than it discloses. As Brecht points out, a photograph of the Krupp works reveals virtually nothing about that organisation. In contrast to the amorous relation, which is based on how something looks, understanding is based on how it functions. And functioning takes place in time, and must be explained in time. Only that which narrates can make us understand.

The limit of photographic knowledge of the world is that, while it can goad conscience, it can, finally, never be ethical or political knowledge. The knowledge gained through still photographs will always be some kind of sentimentalism, whether cynical or humanist. It will be a knowledge at bargain prices—a semblance of knowledge, a semblance of wisdom; as the act of taking pictures is a semblance of appropriation, a semblance of rape. The very muteness of what is, hypothetically, comprehensible in photographs is what constitutes their attraction and provocativeness. The omnipresence of photographs has an incalculable effect on our ethical sensibility. By furnishing this already crowded world with a duplicate one of images, photography makes us feel that the world is more available than it really is.

Needing to have reality confirmed and experience enhanced by photographs is an aesthetic consumerism to which everyone is now addicted. Industrial societies turn their citizens into image-junkies; it is the most irresistible form of mental pollution. Poignant longings for beauty, for an end to probing below the surface, for a redemption and celebration of the body of the world—all these elements of erotic feeling are affirmed in the pleasure we take in photographs. But other, less liberating feelings are expressed as well. It would not be wrong to speak of people having a *compulsion* to photograph: to turn experience itself into a way of seeing. Ultimately, having an experience becomes identical with taking a photograph of it, and participating in a public event comes more and more to be equivalent to looking at it in photographed form. That most logical of nineteenth-century aesthetes, Mallarmé, said that everything in the world exists in order to end in a book. Today everything exists to end in a photograph.

Things to Do with the Reading

1. The word "power" repeats frequently in Sontag's essay. Write a three- to four-page paper in which you quote, paraphrase, and more fully explain the relationship between photography and power that Sontag is concerned about.

2. The novelist and critic William Gass wrote of *On Photography* that

   > No simple summary of the views contained in Susan Sontag's brief but brilliant work on photography is possible, first because there are too many, and second because the book is a thoughtful meditation, not a treatise, and its ideas are grouped more nearly like a gang of keys upon a ring than a run of onions on a string.

   The same might be said of just the essay "In Plato's Cave"—that it is too conceptually rich and meditative to allow simple summary. And yet, we can probably improve our ability to understand this densely idea-laden essay if we make a list of the most important statements or claims that Sontag makes. Copy out the five sentences you find most arresting in the piece, each from a different paragraph. Then use these to generate a focused freewrite—an opportunity for your own meditation.

   Here are three possible ways of proceeding. (1) You might write about the single sentence you find most compelling, beginning by paraphrasing it. (2) You might look for some repeated element or contrast that figure in several of your sentences. (3) You might pair any of the sentences with one of the images included in the book, in the essays by Elliott, Berger, or Gambino. (See Chapter 4 on Passage-Based Focused Freewriting.)

3. Write an essay in which you reflect on Sontag's claims about the moral, ethical, and psychological effects of photography. In these contexts Sontag talks both about photography as an activity and photographs as objects that have

some supposed impact on the world. Study paragraphs 29–36 of Sontag's essay, which deal with the impact and ethics of photographs that record atrocities—"the vast catalogue of misery and injustice throughout the world."

In what terms does Sontag reject the often-made defense of photographs of atrocities and exploitation—that they call people's attention to problems and thus inspire people to address them? You might wish to include in your thinking the brief autobiographical account that Sontag provides in paragraph 33 of her first experience at age 12 with photographs of the Holocaust. (It is worth noting in this context that Sontag was a noted human rights activist for more than two decades, serving for several years as president of the American Center of PEN, the international writers' organization dedicated to freedom of expression and the advancement of literature.)

4. Application: Sontag in her role of provocateur loves to make bold claims—for example, that people take photos to opt out of life and to construct a family album of the ever-vanishing extended family. Use your own experience to engage these volatile notions.

Locate either some family photographs or photographs that you have taken as a tourist, select five or six, and then write a short essay on what you think the photographer (possibly you) was trying to accomplish in taking them. Be sure to include your reasoning. Next, consider a few single sentences you've selected from Sontag's commentary on family photographs and vacation photographs (see paragraphs 10–18) and use these as a springboard for some sustained reflection on photography as an activity.

Alternatively, write an essay in which you reflect on and analyze the role of photographs and photo-taking in your life. Notice photos that are prominent in your environment—in your room, in your wallet, on your computer, on your Facebook page. What do you notice about these pictures and your use and placement of them? Be sure to use Sontag's essay as a lens to prompt your own thinking.

Warning: Don't turn this into an agree–disagree exercise. Use Sontag's thinking as starting points for your thinking about the topic, not *primarily* as the impetus to support or refute her position.

5. Application: On the matter of the ethics of photography and its potential to effect social change, do some research on the life and work of one of the photographers that Joseph Elliot describes at the end of the interview as an Opinionated Documentarian or a Personal Documentarian. Try Nan Goldin, Lauren Greenfield, Sally Mann, or Sebastiao Salgado. Find claims in the Sontag essay that you think are interesting and illuminating in the context of your chosen photographer. Try to find not only a range of images by the photographer of your choice but perhaps artistic statements by him or her, as well as short biographies. Write up your results in an essay. Here are some questions to help: What might Sontag praise about this photographer's work? What might make her anxious about it? How might the photographer respond?

Barry Lopez

Learning to See

Barry Lopez is an award-winning writer of both nonfiction and fiction. In this essay he gives an account of his decision to stop pursuing his "other" career, as a landscape photographer. In the process of telling this story, Lopez focuses astutely on an area of photography that neither Joseph Elliott nor Susan Sontag directly addresses: nature photography. His photographic career (which he decided to end in 1981) focused on subjects that included only the land—no people and, for the most part, no animals. But as you will see, the land for Lopez is no inert entity, but the home of small miracles of physics.

1   In June 1989, I received a puzzling letter from the Amon Carter Museum in Fort Worth, Texas, an invitation to speak at the opening of a retrospective of the work of Robert Adams. The show, "To Make It Home: Photographs of the American West, 1965–1985," had been organized by the Philadelphia Museum of Art and would travel to the Los Angeles County Museum and the Corcoran Gallery of Art in Washington, D.C., before being installed at the Amon Carter, an institution renowned for its photographic collections, in the spring of 1990.

Robert Adams, an un-self-promoting man who has published no commercially prominent book of photographs, is routinely referred to as one of the most important landscape photographers in America, by both art critics and his colleagues. His black-and-white images are intelligently composed and morally engaged. They're also hopeful, despite their sometimes depressing subject matter—brutalized landscapes and the venality of the American Dream as revealed in suburban life. Adams doesn't hold himself apart from what he indicts. He photographs with compassion and he doesn't scold. His pictures are also accessible, to such a degree that many of them seem casual. In 1981 he published *Beauty in Photography: Essays in Defense of Traditional Values,* one of the clearest statements of artistic responsibility ever written by a photographer.

If there is such a thing as an ideal of stance, technique, vision, and social contribution toward which young photographers might aspire, it's embodied in this man.

I suspected the Amon Carter had inadvertently invited the wrong person to speak. I'd no knowledge of the history of American photography sufficient to situate Robert Adams in it. I couldn't speak to the technical perfection of his prints. I'd no credentials as an art critic. As an admirer of the work, of course, I'd have something to say, but it could only be that, the words of an amateur who admired Adams's accomplishment.

5   I wondered for days what prompted the invitation. For about fifteen years, before putting my cameras down on September 13, 1981, never to pick them up again, I'd worked as a landscape photographer, but it was unlikely anyone at the Amon Carter knew this. I'd visited the museum in the fall of 1986 to see some of their luminist paintings and had met several of the curators, but our conversations could not have left anyone with the impression that I had the background to speak about Adams's work.

"Learning to See," from ABOUT THIS LIFE by Barry Lopez, copyright © 1998 by Barry Holstun Lopez. Used by permission of Alfred A. Knopf, a division of Random House, Inc.

I finally decided to say yes. I wrote and told the person coordinating the program, Mary Lampe, that though I didn't feel qualified to speak I admired Mr. Adams's work, and further, I presumed an affinity with his pursuits and ideals as set forth in *Beauty in Photography*. And I told her I intended to go back and study the work of Paul Strand, Wynn Bullock, Minor White, Harry Callahan, and others who'd been an influence on my own work and thought, in order to prepare my lecture.

Months later, when I arrived at the museum, I asked Ms. Lampe how they had come to invite me and not someone more qualified. She said Mr. Adams had asked them to do so. I sensed she believed Robert Adams and I were good friends and I had to tell her I didn't know him at all. We'd never met, never corresponded, had not spoken on the phone. I was unaware, even, that it was "Bob" Adams, as Ms. Lampe called him.

"But why did you agree to come?" she asked.

"Out of respect for the work," I said. "Out of enthusiasm for the work." I also explained that I was intimidated by the prospect, and that sometimes I felt it was good to act on things like that.

Ms. Lampe subsequently sent Robert Adams a tape of my talk. He and I later met   10 and we now correspond and speak on the phone regularly. He set the course of our friendship in the first sentence of a letter he wrote me after hearing my presentation. "Your willingness to speak in my behalf," he wrote, "confirms my belief in the community of artists."

He believed from work of mine that he'd read that we shared a sensibility, that we asked similar questions about the relationship between culture and landscape, and that our ethical leanings and our sense of an artist's social responsibility were similar. He later told me that for these reasons he'd given my name, hopefully but somewhat facetiously, to Ms. Lampe, not knowing the curators and I were acquainted and that they would write me.

I've long been attracted to the way visual artists like Robert Adams imagine the world. The emotional impact of their composition of space and light is as clarifying for me as immersion in a beautifully made story. As with the work of a small group of poets I read regularly—Robert Hass, Pattiann Rogers, Garrett Hongo—I find healing in their expressions. I find reasons not to give up.

Though I no longer photograph, I have maintained since 1981 a connection with photographers and I keep up a sort of running conversation with several of them. We talk about the fate of photography in the United States, where of course art is increasingly more commodified and where, with the advent of computer manipulation, photography is the art most likely to mislead. Its history as a purveyor of objective reality, the idea that "the camera never lies," is specious, certainly; but with some artistic endeavors, say those of Cartier-Bresson, Aaron Siskind, or W. Eugene Smith, and in the fields of documentary photography, which would include some news photography, and nature photography, one can assert that the authority of the image lies with the subject. With the modern emphasis on the genius of the individual artist, however, and with the arrival of computer imaging, authority in these areas now more often lies with the photographer. This has become true to such an extent that the reversal that's occurred—the photographer, not the subject, is in charge—has caused the rules of evidence to be changed in courts of law; and it has foisted upon an unwitting public a steady stream, for example, of fabricated images of wildlife.

As a beginning photographer I was most attracted to color and form, to the emotional consequence of line. It is no wonder, looking back now, that I pored over the images of someone like Edward Weston, or that I felt isolated in some of my pursuits because at the time few serious photographers outside Ernst Haas and Eliot Porter worked as I did in color. I wanted to photograph the streaming of light. For a long while it made no difference whether that light was falling down the stone walls of a building in New York or lambent on the corrugations of a wheat field. Ansel Adams was suggested to me early on as a model, but he seemed to my eye inclined to overstate. I wanted the sort of subtlety I would later come to admire in Bob Adams's work and in the aerial photographs of Emmet Gowin.

15   The more I gravitated as a writer toward landscape as a context in which to work out what I was thinking as a young man about issues like justice, tolerance, ambiguity, and compassion, the more I came to concentrate on landforms as a photographer. I valued in particular the work of one or two wildlife photographers shooting *in situ,* in the bush. (I remember enthusiastically contacting friends about John Dominis's groundbreaking portfolio of African cat photographs, which appeared in three successive issues of *Life* in January 1967.) But I was not inclined toward mastering the kind of technical skill it took to make such photographs. More fundamentally, I had misgivings about what I regarded as invasions of the privacy of wild animals. The latter notion I thought so personal an idea I kept it mostly to myself; today, of course, it's a central concern of wildlife photographers, especially for a contingent that includes Frans Lanting, the late Michio Hoshino, Gary Braasch, Tui De Roy, and the team of Susan Middleton and David Liittschwager.

I began photographing in a conscientious way in the summer of 1965. I was soon concentrating on landscapes, and in the mid-1970s, with a small list of publication credits behind me, I made an appointment to see Joe Scherschel, an assistant director of the photographic staff at *National Geographic.* He told me frankly that though my landscape portfolio was up to the standards of the magazine, the paucity of wildlife images and human subjects made it unlikely that he could offer me any assignments. In response I remember thinking this was unlikely to change, for either of us. Discouraged, I started to scale back the effort to market my photographs and to make part of my living that way. I continued to make pictures, and I was glad that much of this work was still effectively represented by a stock agency in New York; but by 1978 I knew photography for me was becoming more a conscious exercise in awareness, a technique for paying attention. It would finally turn into a sequestered exploration of light and spatial volume.

Three events in the late 1970s changed the way I understood myself as a photographer. One summer afternoon I left the house for an appointment with an art director in a nearby city. Strapped to the seat of my motorcycle was a box of photographs, perhaps three hundred images representative of the best work I had done. The two-lane road I traveled winds gently through steep mountainous country. When I got to town, the photographs were gone. I never found a trace of them, though I searched every foot of the road for two days. The loss dismantled my enthusiasm for photography so thoroughly that I took it for a message to do something else.

In the summer of 1976 my mother was dying of cancer. To ease her burden, and to brighten the sterile room in Lenox Hill Hospital in New York where she lay dying, I made a set of large Cibachrome prints from some of my 35-mm Kodachrome images—a white horse standing in a field of tall wild grasses bounded by a white post-and-plank fence; a faded pink boat trailer from the 1940s, abandoned in the woods; a small copse of quaking aspen, their leaves turning bright yellow on the far side of a remote mountain swamp. It was the only set of prints I would ever make. As good as they were, the change in color balance and the loss of transparency and contrast when compared with the originals, the reduction in sharpness, created a deep doubt about ever wanting to do such a thing again. I hung the images in a few shows, then put them away. I knew if I didn't start developing and printing my own images, I wouldn't be entering any more shows.

I winced whenever I saw my photographs reproduced in magazines and books, but I made my peace with that. Time-Life Books was publishing a series then called *American Wilderness,* each volume of which was devoted to a different landscape—the Maine woods, the Cascade Mountains, the Grand Canyon. I was pleased to see my work included in these volumes, but I realized that just as the distance between what I saw and what I was able to record was huge, so was that between what I recorded and what people saw. Seeing the printed images on the page was like finding one's haiku published as nineteen-syllable poems.

The third event occurred around the first serious choice I made as a photogra-   20
pher to concentrate on a limited subject. The subject was always light, but I wanted to explore a single form, which turned out to be the flow of water in creeks and rivers near my home. I photographed in every season, when the water was high in February and March, when it was low in August, when it was transparent in July, when it was an opaque jade in December. In 1980 I began to photograph moving water in moonlight, exposures of twenty-five or thirty minutes. These images suffered from reciprocity failure—the color balance in them collapsed—but they also recorded something extraordinary, a pattern of flow we cannot actually see. They revealed the organizing principle logicians would one day call a strange attractor.

The streaming of water around a rock is one of the most complex motions of which human beings are aware. The change from a laminar, more or less uniform flow to turbulent flow around a single rock is so abstruse a transition mathematically that even the most sophisticated Cray computer cannot make it through to a satisfactory description.

Aesthetically, of course, no such difficulty exists. The eye dotes on the shift, delights in the scintillating sheeting, the roll-off of light around a rock, like hair responding to the stroke of a brush. Sometimes I photographed the flow of water in sunshine at 1/2000 of a second and then later I'd photograph the same rock in moonlight. Putting the photos side by side, I could see something hidden beneath the dazzle of the high-speed image that compared with our renderings of the Milky Way from space: the random pin-dot infernos of our own and every other sun form a spiraling, geometrical shape motionless to our eyes. In the moonlit photographs, the stray streaks from errant water splashes were eliminated (in light that weak, they occur too quickly to be recorded); what was etched on the film instead were orderly, fundamental lines of flow, created by particle after illuminated particle of gleaming water, as if each were a tracer bullet. (Years later, reading *Chaos,* James Gleick's lucid report on chaos theory, I would sit bolt upright in my chair. What I'd photographed was the deep pattern in turbulence, the clothing, as it were, of the strange attractor.)

In the months I worked at making these photographs, I came to realize I actually had two subjects as a photographer. First, these still images of a moving thing, a living thing—as close as I would probably ever come to fully photographing an animal. Second, natural light falling on orchards, images of a subject routinely understood as a still life. The orchards near me were mostly filbert orchards. In their change of color and form through the seasons, in the rain and snow that fell through them, in crows that sat on their winter branches, in leaves accumulated under them on bare dark ground, in the wind that coursed them, in the labyrinths of their limbs, ramulose within the imposed order of the orchard plot, I saw the same profundity of life I found in literature.

This was all work I was eager to do, but I would never get to it.

25   In September 1981 I was working in the Beaufort Sea off the north coast of Alaska with several marine biologists. We were conducting a food-chain survey intended to provide baseline data to guide offshore oil drilling, an impulsive and politically motivated development program funded by the Bureau of Land Management and pushed hard at the time by the Reagan government. On September 12, three of us rendez-voused at Point Barrow with a National Oceanic and Atmospheric Administration research vessel, the *Oceanographer.* They hoisted us, our gear, and our twenty-foot Boston Whaler aboard and we sailed west into pack ice in the northern Chukchi Sea.

Scientific field research is sometimes a literally bloody business. In our study we were trying to determine the flow of energy through various "levels" (artificially determined) of the marine food web. To gather data we retrieved plankton and caught fish with different sorts of traps and trawls, and we examined the contents of bearded seal, ringed seal, and spotted seal stomachs. To accomplish the latter, we shot and killed the animals. Shooting seals located us squarely in the moral dilemma of our work, and it occasioned talk aboard the *Oceanographer* about the barbarousness of science. The irony here was that without these data creatures like the ringed seal could not be afforded legal protection against oil development. The killings were a manifestation of the perversions in our age, our Kafkaesque predicaments.

I was disturbed by the fatal aspects of our work, as were my companions, but I willingly participated. I would later write an essay about the killing, but something else happened during that trip, less dramatic and more profound in its consequences for me.

Late one afternoon, working our way back to the *Oceanographer* through a snow squall, the three of us came upon a polar bear. We decided to follow him for a few minutes and I got out my cameras. The bear, swimming through loose pack ice, was clearly annoyed by our presence, though in our view we were maintaining a reasonable distance. He very soon climbed out on an ice floe, crossed it, and dropped into open water on the far side. We had to go the long way around in the workboat, but we caught up. He hissed at us and otherwise conveyed his irritation, but we continued idling along beside him.

Eventually we backed off. The bear disappeared in gauze curtains of blowing snow. We returned to the *Oceanographer,* to a warm meal and dry clothes.

Once the boat was secure and our scientific samples squared away in the lab, I 30 went to my cabin. I dropped my pack on the floor, stripped off my heavy clothes, showered, and lay down in my bunk. I tried to recall every detail of the encounter with the bear. What had he been doing when we first saw him? Did he change direction then? How had he proceeded? Exactly how did he climb out of the water onto the ice floe? What were the mechanics of it? When he shook off seawater, how was it different from a dog shucking water? When he hissed, what color was the inside of his mouth?

I don't know how long I lay there, a half hour perhaps, but when I was through, when I'd answered these questions and was satisfied that I'd recalled the sequence of events precisely and in sufficient detail, I got up, dressed, and went to dinner. Remembering what happened in an encounter was crucial to my work as a writer, and attending to my cameras during our time with the bear had altered and shrunk my memory of it. While the polar bear was doing something, I was checking f-stops and attempting to frame and focus from a moving boat.

I regarded the meeting as a warning to me as a writer. Having successfully recovered details from each minute, I believed, of that encounter, having disciplined myself to do that, I sensed I wouldn't pick up a camera ever again.

It was not solely contact with this lone bear a hundred miles off the northwest coast of Alaska, of course, that ended my active involvement with photography. The change had been coming for a while. The power of the polar bear's presence, his emergence from the snow squall and his subsequent disappearance, had created an atmosphere in which I could grasp more easily a complex misgiving that had been building in me. I view any encounter with a wild animal in its own territory as a gift, an opportunity to sense the real animal, not the zoo creature, the TV creature, the advertising creature. But this gift had been more overwhelming. In some way the bear had grabbed me by the shirtfront and said, Think about this. Think about what these cameras in your hands are doing.

Years later, I'm still thinking about it. Some of what culminated for me that day is easy to understand. As a writer, I had begun to feel I was missing critical details in situations such as this one because I was distracted. I was also starting to feel uncomfortable about the way photographs tend to collapse events into a single moment, about how much they leave out. (Archeologists face a similar problem when they save only what they recognize from a dig. Years afterward, the context long having been destroyed, the archeologist might wonder what was present that he or she didn't recognize at the time. So begins a reevaluation of the meaning of the entire site.)

I was also disturbed about how nature and landscape photographs, my own and 35 others', were coming to be used, not in advertising where you took your chances (some photographers at that time began labeling their images explicitly: NO TOBACCO, NO ALCOHOL), but in the editorial pages of national magazines. It is a polite fiction of our era that the average person, including the average art director, is more informed about natural history than an educated person was in Columbus's age. Because this is not true, the majority of nature photographers who work out in the field have felt a peculiar burden to record accurately the great range of habitat and animal behavior they see, including nature's "dark" side. (Photographers accepted the fact back then that magazines in the United States, generally speaking, were not interested in photographs of mating animals—unless they were chaste or cute—or in predatory encounters if they were bloody or harrowing, as many were.)

What happened as a result of this convention was that people looking at magazines in the 1970s increasingly came to think of wild animals as vivacious and decorative in the natural world. Promoted as elegant, brave, graceful, sinister, wise, etc., according to their species, animals were deprived of personality and the capacity to be innovative. Every wildlife photographer I know can recount a story of confrontation with an art director in which he or she argued unsuccessfully for an image that told a fuller or a truer story about a particular species of animal in a layout. It was the noble lion, the thieving hyena, and the mischievous monkey, however, who routinely triumphed. A female wolf killing one of her pups, or a male bonobo approaching a female with a prominent erection, was not anything magazine editors were comfortable with.

In the late seventies, I asked around among several publishers to see whether they might have any interest in a series of disturbing photographs made in a zoo by a woman named Ilya. She'd taken them on assignment for *Life*, but very few of them were ever published because she'd concentrated on depicting animals apparently driven insane by their incarceration. I remember as particularly unsettling the look of psychosis in the face of a male lion, its mane twisted into knots. I could develop no interest in publishing her work. An eccentric view, people felt. Too distressing.

So, along with a growing political awareness of endangered landscapes and their indigenous animals in the 1970s came, ironically, a more and more dazzling presentation of those creatures in incomplete and prejudicial ways. Photo editors made them look not like what they were but the way editors wanted them to appear—well-groomed, appropriate to stereotype, and living safely apart from the machinations of human enterprise. To my mind there was little difference then between a *Playboy* calendar and a wildlife calendar. Both celebrated the conventionally gorgeous, the overly endowed, the seductive. I and many other photographers at the time were apprehensive about the implications of this trend.

Another concern I had that September afternoon, a more complicated one, was what was happening to memory in my generation. The advertising injunction to preserve family memories by taking photographs had become so shrill a demand, and the practice had become so compulsive, that recording the event was more important for some than participating in it. The inculcated rationale which grew up around this practice was that to take and preserve family photos was to act in a socially responsible way. The assumption seemed specious to me. My generation was the first to have ready access to inexpensive tape recorders and cameras. Far from recording memories of these talks and events, what we seemed to be doing was storing memories that would never be retrieved, that would never form a coherent narrative. In the same way that our desk drawers and cabinet shelves slowly filled with these "personal" sounds and images, we were beginning, it seemed to me, to live our lives in dissociated bits and places. The narrative spine of an individual life was disappearing. The order of events was becoming increasingly meaningless.

40   This worry, together with the increasingly commercial use to which the work of photographers like myself was being put and the preference for an entertaining but not necessarily coherent landscape of wild animals (images that essentially lied

to children), made me more and more reluctant to stay involved. Some of the contemporary photographers I most respect—Lanting, Hoshino, Braasch, De Roy, Jim Brandenburg, Flip Nicklin, Sam Abell, Nick Nichols, Galen Rowell—have managed through the strength of their work and their personal integrity to overcome some of these problems, which are part and parcel of working in a world dominated more and more by commercial interests pursuing business strategies. But I knew I had no gift here to persevere. That realization, and my reluctance to photograph animals in the first place, may have precipitated my decision that day in the Chukchi.

As a writer, I had yet other concerns, peculiar to that discipline. I had begun to wonder whether my searching for the telling photographic image in a situation was beginning to interfere with my writing about what happened. I was someone who took a long time to let a story settle. I'd began to suspect that the photographs made while I was in a note-taking stage were starting to lock my words into a pattern, and that the pattern was being determined too early. Photographs, in some way, were introducing preconceptions into a process I wanted to keep fluid. I often have no clear idea of what I'm doing. I just act. I pitch in, I try to stay alert to everything around me. I don't want to stop and focus on a finished image, which I'm inclined to do as a photographer. I want, instead, to see a sentence fragment scrawled in my notebook, smeared by rain. I don't want the clean, fixed image right away.

An attentive mind, I'm sure, can see the flaws in my reasoning. Some photographers are doing no more than taking notes when they click the shutter. It's only after a shoot that they discover what the story is. But by trying to both photograph and write, I'd begun to feel I was attempting to create two parallel but independent stories. The effort had become confusing and draining. I let go of photography partly because its defining process, to my mind, was less congruent with the way I wanted to work.

On June 16, 1979, forty-one sperm whales beached themselves at the mouth of the Siuslaw River on the Oregon coast, about one hundred miles from my home. I wrote a long essay about the stranding but didn't start work on it until after I'd spent two days photographing the eclipse of these beasts' lives and the aftermath of their deaths. That was the last time I attempted to do both things.

Perhaps the most rarefied of my concerns about photography that day in the Chukchi was one that lay for me at the heart of photography: recording a fleeting pattern of light in a defined volume of space. Light always attracted me. Indeed, twenty-five years after the fact, I can still vividly recall the light falling at dusk on a windbreak of trees in Mitchell, Oregon. It rendered me speechless when I saw it, and by some magic I managed to get it down on film. The problem of rendering volume in photography, however, was one I never solved beyond employing the conventional solutions of perspective and depth of field. I could recognize spatial volume successfully addressed in the work of other photographers—in Adams's work, for example, partly because so many of his photographs do not have an object as a subject. Finding some way myself to render volume successfully in a photograph would mean, I believed, walking too far away from my work as a writer. And, ultimately, it was as a writer that I felt more comfortable.

I miss making photographs. A short while ago I received a call from a curator at 45 the Whitney Museum in New York named May Castleberry. She had just mounted a show called "Perpetual Mirage: Photographic Narratives of the Desert West" and I had been able to provide some minor assistance with it. She was calling now to pursue a conversation we'd begun at the time about Rockwell Kent, an illustrator, painter, and socialist widely known in the thirties, forties, and fifties. She wanted to hang a selection of his "nocturnes," prints and drawings Kent had made of people under starlit night skies. She was calling to see what I could suggest about his motivation.

Given Kent's leanings toward Nordic myth and legend and his espousal of Teddy Roosevelt's "strenuous life," it seemed obvious to me that he would want to portray his heroic (mostly male) figures against the vault of the heavens. But there were at least two other things at work here, I believed. First, Kent was strongly drawn to high latitudes, like Greenland, where in winter one can view the deep night sky for weeks on end. It was not really the "night" sky, however, he was drawing; it was the sunless sky of a winter day. Quotidian life assumes mythic proportions here not because it's heroic, but because it's carried out beneath the stars.

Secondly, I conjectured, because Kent was an artist working on flat surfaces, he sought, like every such artist, ways to suggest volume, to make the third dimension apparent. Beyond what clouds provide, the daytime sky has no depth; it's the night sky that gives an artist volume. While it takes an extraordinary person—the light and space artist James Turrell, say—to make the celestial vault visible in sunshine, many artists have successfully conveyed a sense of the sky's volume by painting it at night.

The conceit can easily grow up in a photographer that he or she has pretty much seen all the large things—the range of possible emotion to be evoked with light, the contrasts to be made by arranging objects in different scales, problems in the third and fourth dimension. But every serious photographer, I believe, has encountered at some point ideas unanticipated and dumbfounding. The shock causes you to reexamine all you've assumed about your own work and the work of others, especially the work of people you've never particularly understood. This happened most recently for me in seeing the photography of Linda Connor. While working on a story about international air freight, I became so disoriented, flying every day from one spot on the globe to another thousands of miles away, I did not know what time I was living in. Whatever time it was, it was out of phase with the sun, a time not to be dialed up on a watch, mine or anyone else's.

At a pause in this international hurtling, during a six-hour layover in Cape Town, I went for a ride with an acquaintance. He drove us out to Clifton Bay on the west side of Table Mountain. I was so dazed by my abuse of time that I was open to thoughts I might otherwise never have had. One of those thoughts was that I could recognize the physicality of time. We can discern the physical nature of space in a picture, grasp the way, for example, Robert Adams is able to photograph the air itself, making it visible like a plein air painter. In Cape Town that day I saw what I came to call indigenous time. It clung to the flanks of Table Mountain. It resisted being absorbed into my helter-skelter time. It seemed not yet to have been subjugated by Dutch and British colonial expansion, as the physical landscape so clearly had been. It was time apparent to the senses, palpable. What made me believe I was correct in this perception was that, only a month before, I'd examined a collection of Linda Connor's work, a book called *Luminance.* I realized there at Table Mountain that she'd photographed what I was looking at. She'd photographed indigenous time.

I'd grasped Ms. Connor's photographs in some fashion after an initial pass, but 50 I hadn't sensed their depth, their power, what Gerard Manley Hopkins called "the achieve of the thing." With this new insight I wrote her an excited note, an attempt to thank her for work that opened the door to a room I'd never explored.

One of the great blessings of our modern age, a kind of redemption for its cruelties and unmitigated greed, is that one can walk down to a corner book-store and find a copy of Ms. Connor's book. Or of Robert Adams's *What We Brought: The New World,* or Frans Lanting's *Bonobo: The Forgotten Ape,* or, say, Mary Peck's *Chaco Canyon: A Center and Its World,* and then be knocked across the room by a truth one had not, until that moment, clearly discerned.

It is more than illumination, though, more than a confirmation of one's intuition, aesthetics, or beliefs that comes out of the perusal of such a photographer's images. It's regaining the feeling that one is not cut off from the wellsprings of intelligence and goodwill, of sympathy for human plight.

I do not know, of course, why the photographers I admire, even the ones I know, photograph, but I am acutely aware that without the infusion of their images hope would wither in me. I feel an allegiance to their work more as a writer than as someone who once tried to see in this way, perhaps because I presume we share certain principles related to the effort to imagine or explain.

It is correct, I think, as Robert Adams wrote me that day, to believe in a community of artists stimulated by and respectful of one another's work. But it's also true that without an audience (of which we're all a part) the work remains unfinished, unfulfilled. A photographer seeks intimacy with the world and then endeavors to share it. Inherent in that desire to share is a love of humanity. In different media, and from time to time, we have succeeded, I believe, in helping one another understand what is going on. We have come to see that, in some way, this is our purpose with each other.

Things to Do with the Reading

1. **Link:** So what that Lopez repeatedly uses the phrase "making photographs" rather than "taking photographs," which is the more common phrase and the one upon which Sontag offers a powerful critique? Write an essay in which you locate Lopez's word choice in terms of Sontag's observations about cameras as guns and Eliott's commentary on fabrication versus recording.

2. Like Sontag, Lopez has his anxieties about the artistic, psychological, and ethical impact of photography—both as product and as activity. But he also testifies to the importance of photography in his life in strong terms: "I do not know, of course, why the photographers I admire, even the ones I know, photograph, but I am acutely aware that without the infusion of their images

hope would wither in me" (paragraph 53). Write and reflect on Lopez's anxieties about photography, especially in relation to his work as a writer. Then try to negotiate the gap between this anxiety and Lopez's powerful praise for photography as a source of hope.

You might want to Google images from the photographers Lopez feels most strongly about, Linda Connors and Robert Adams, and make your analysis of these part of your essay. On the relationship between photography and writing, see paragraphs 31–34, Lopez's account of the aftermath of his encounter with the polar bear; also see the thinking in paragraph 34 about the way that "photographs tend to collapse events into a single moment."

3. **Link:** It is interesting to consider what Lopez thinks a photograph—at least his idea of photographs—is. Summarize and reflect on Lopez's various accounts of what he was trying to photograph, and then write a short essay in which you locate him in the context of the Elliott interview. What, for example, does Lopez mean when he says "The subject was always light" (paragraph 20)?

4. **Link:** The moral and psychological dimension that was central in the Sontag essay is central in Lopez's essay as well. Although Lopez finds things to worry about in landscape and nature photography, he also offers powerful praise of its recuperative and moral value, as is evident in the following statement: "The more I gravitated as a writer toward landscape as a context in which to work out what I was thinking as a young man about issues like justice, tolerance, ambiguity, and compassion, the more I came to concentrate on landforms as a photographer" (see paragraph 15).

Find points of contact among Sontag, Elliott, and Lopez, and synthesize these into a short paper on photography—what it is, what it can and cannot do, and what it perhaps should and should not do.

5. **Application:** In his essay Lopez relives his arrival at an awareness of tension, in fact, competition, between his two art forms—writing and taking photographs. The result of this awareness is that he stops taking photographs. Why? The essay keeps returning the day in Chukchi when Lopez saw the polar bear. Using Lopez's essay as a model, write a reflective essay on a moment when you came to recognize some kind of incompatibility between two ways you approach the world—two things you like to do, wherein one was starting to interfere with the other. Choose something fairly serious, but not necessarily life-shaking.

6. **Application:** There is an interesting moment in paragraph 23 in which Lopez offers the verbal equivalent of something that he repeatedly tried to photograph (the natural light falling on orchards). This is a form of writing called *ekphrasis*. An ekphrastic piece of writing tries to be the verbal equivalent of a photograph. It strives to create the same mental images and the same emotional/psychological effect as a photograph or painting of the same thing might produce. Much ekphrastic writing takes the form of verbal

re-enactments of paintings or photographs. Ekphrasis offers an illuminating exercise for thinking about visual images. Experiment with ekphrasis in one or both of the following ways:

—Go somewhere that you might feel inspired to take a picture. Write a verbal equivalent of the picture that you would like to take. Take a photograph of the same subject. Write a short essay on what you learned by comparing and contrasting the two. Note: Avoid talking about which was better; concentrate instead on describing and reflecting on the differences.

—Start with a photograph, preferably one of the type that you think Lopez would want to take. This can be a photograph of your own or one that you find by Googling some of the photographers that Lopez cites in his essay. Write a verbal equivalent of the photograph and then reflect (in writing) on what you learned in the process.

John Berger

Images of Women in European Art

Originally produced for television in England, John Berger's book *Ways of Seeing* (1972), from which this essay is taken, focuses on the relationship between the implied spectator or viewer and a work of art. Interested especially in the history of the nude in European painting, Berger demonstrates the ways that these paintings were designed to flatter and enhance the power of male viewers, while inducing the women to see themselves as males would see them. Berger's discussion of nudes is part of a larger cultural and aesthetic discourse on what is called "the gaze." This concept originates with French theorists Jean-Paul Sartre, Simone de Beauvoir, Jacques Lacan, and Michel Foucault and has been extended and applied by other writers, such as the film theorist Teresa de Lauretis. Besides being an art critic, Berger is also an essayist, painter, and novelist.

1   According to usage and conventions which are at last being questioned but have by no means been overcome, the social presence of a woman is different in kind from that of a man. A man's presence is dependent upon the promise of power which he embodies. If the promise is large and credible, his presence is striking. If it is small or incredible, he is found to have little presence. The promised power may be moral, physical, temperamental, economic, social, sexual—but its object is always exterior to the man. A man's presence suggests what he is capable of doing to you or for you. His presence may be fabricated, in the sense that he pretends to be capable of what he is not. But the pretense is always toward a power which he exercises on others.

By contrast, a woman's presence expresses her own attitude to herself, and defines what can and cannot be done to her. Her presence is manifest in her gestures, voice, opinions, expressions, clothes, chosen surroundings, taste—indeed there is nothing she can do which does not contribute to her presence. Presence, for a woman, is so intrinsic to her person that men tend to think of it as an almost physical emanation, a kind of heat or smell or aura.

To be born a woman has been to be born, within an allotted and confined space, into the keeping of men. The social presence of women has developed as a result of their ingenuity in living under such tutelage within such a limited space. But this has been at the cost of a woman's self being split into two. A woman must continually watch herself. She is almost continually accompanied by her own image of herself. Whilst she is walking across a room or whilst she is weeping at the death of her father, she can scarcely avoid envisaging herself walking or weeping. From earliest childhood she has been taught and persuaded to survey herself continually.

"Chapter 3", from WAYS OF SEEING by John Berger, copyright © 1972 by John Berger. Used by permission of Viking Penguin, a division of Penguin Group (USA) Inc.

And so she comes to consider the *surveyor* and the *surveyed* within her as the two constituent yet always distinct elements of her identity as a woman.

She has to survey everything she is and everything she does because how she 5 appears to others, and ultimately how she appears to men, is of crucial importance for what is normally thought of as the success of her life. Her own sense of being in herself is supplanted by a sense of being appreciated as herself by another.

Men survey women before treating them. Consequently, how a woman appears to a man can determine how she will be treated. To acquire some control over this process, women must contain it and interiorize it. That part of a woman's self which is the surveyor treats the part which is the surveyed so as to demonstrate to others how her whole self would like to be treated. And this exemplary treatment of herself by herself constitutes her presence. Every woman's presence regulates what is and is not "permissible" within her presence. Every one of her actions—whatever its direct purpose or motivation—is also read as an indication of how she would like to be treated. If a woman throws a glass on the floor, this is an example of how she treats her own emotion of anger and so of how she would wish it to be treated by others. If a man does the same, his action is only read as an expression of his anger. If a woman makes a good joke, this is an example of how she treats the joker in herself and accordingly of how she as a joker-woman would like to be treated by others. Only a man can make a good joke for its own sake.

One might simplify this by saying: *Men act* and *women appear.* Men look at women. Women watch themselves being looked at. This determines not only most relations between men and women but also the relation of women to themselves. The surveyor of woman in herself is male: the surveyed female. Thus, she turns herself into an object—and most particularly an object of vision: a sight.

In one category of European oil painting women were the principal, ever-recurring subject. That category is the nude. In the nudes of European painting we can discover some of the criteria and conventions by which women have been seen and judged as sights.

The first nudes in the tradition depicted Adam and Eve. It is worth referring to the story as told in Genesis:

> And when the woman saw that the tree was good for food, and that it was a delight to the eyes, and that the tree was to be desired to make one wise, she took of the fruit thereof and did eat; and she gave also unto her husband with her, and he did eat.
>
> And the eyes of them both were opened, and they knew that they were naked; and they sewed fig-leaves together and made themselves aprons. And the Lord God called unto the man and said unto him, "Where are thou?" And he said, "I heard thy voice in the garden, and I was afraid, because I was naked; and I hid myself. "
>
> Unto the woman God said, "I will greatly multiply thy sorrow and thy conception; in sorrow thou shalt bring forth children; and thy desire shall be to thy husband and he shall rule over thee."

What is striking about this story? They became aware of being naked because, as a result of eating the apple, each saw the other differently. Nakedness was created in the mind of the beholder.

The second striking fact is that the woman is blamed and is punished by being made subservient to the man. In relation to the woman, the man becomes the agent of God.

In the medieval tradition the story was often illustrated, scene following scene, as in a strip cartoon. [See Figure 24.16.]

During the Renaissance the narrative sequence disappeared, and the single moment depicted became the moment of shame. The couple wear fig leaves or make a modest gesture with their hands. But now their shame is not so much in relation to one another as to the spectator. [See Figure 24.17.]

Later the shame becomes a kind of display.

15   When the tradition of painting became more secular, other themes also offered the opportunity of painting nudes. But in them all there remains the implication that the subject (a woman) is aware of being seen by a spectator.

She is not naked as she is.

She is naked as the spectator sees her.

Often—as with the favourite subject of Susannah and the Elders—this is the actual theme of the picture. We join the Elders to spy on Susannah taking her bath. She looks back at us looking at her. [See Figure 24.18.]

In another version of the subject by Tintoretto, Susannah is looking at herself in a mirror. Thus, she joins the spectators of herself. [See Figure 24.19.]

20   The mirror was often used as a symbol of the vanity of woman. The moralizing, however, was mostly hypocritical.

You painted a naked woman because you enjoyed looking at her, you put a mirror in her hand and you called the painting *Vanity,* thus morally condemning the woman whose nakedness you had depicted for your own pleasure. [See Figure 24.20.]

The real function of the mirror was otherwise. It was to make the woman connive in treating herself as, first and foremost, a sight.

The judgment of Paris was another theme with the same inwritten idea of a man or men looking at naked women.

But a further element is now added. The element of judgment. Paris awards the apple to the woman he finds most beautiful. Thus Beauty becomes competitive. (Today The Judgment of Paris has become the Beauty Contest.) Those who are not judged beautiful are *not beautiful.* Those who are, are given the prize. [See Figure 24.21.]

25   The prize is to be owned by a judge—that is to say to be available for him. Charles the Second commissioned a secret painting from Lely. It is a highly typical image of the tradition. Nominally it might be a *Venus and Cupid.* In fact it is a portrait of one of the King's mistresses, Nell Gwynne. It shows her passively looking at the spectator staring at her naked. [See Figure 24.22.]

This nakedness is not, however, an expression of her own feelings; it is a sign of her submission to the owner's feelings or demands. (The owner of both woman

Ms 65/1284 f.25v Adam and Eve in the Garden of Eden, from the 'Tres Riches Heures du Duc de Berry' (vellum), Limbourg, Pol de (d.c.1416)/Musee Conde, Chantilly, France/Giraudon/The Bridgeman Art Library International

To view this image in color, visit www.cengagebrain.com

FIGURE 24.16

Adam and Eve in the Garden of Eden; Fall and Expulsion miniature from Les Tres Riches Heures du Duc de Berry by Pol de Limbourg

Bildarchiv Preussischer Kulturbesitz/Art Resource, NY

To view this image in color, visit www.cengagebrain.com

FIGURE 24.17
Fall of Man, ca. 1525 by Jan Gossaert called Mabuse. Oil on oak, 170 × 114 cm

To view this image in color, visit www.cengagebrain.com

FIGURE 24.18

Susannah in Her Bath. Canvas, 167 × 238 cm by Jacopo Robusti Tintoretto

and painting.) The painting, when the King showed it to others, demonstrated this submission and his guests envied him.

It is worth noticing that in other non-European traditions—in Indian art, Persian art, African art, Pre-Columbian art—nakedness is never supine in this way. And if, in these traditions, the theme of a work is sexual attraction, it is likely to show active sexual love as between two people, the woman as active as the man, the actions of each absorbing the other. [See Figure 24.23.]

We can now begin to see the difference between nakedness and nudity in the European tradition. In his book *The Nude,* Kenneth Clark maintains that to be naked is simply to be without clothes, whereas the nude is a form of art. According to him, a nude is not the starting point of a painting but a way of seeing which the painting achieves. To some degree, this is true—although the way of seeing "a nude" is not necessarily confined to art. There are also nude photographs, nude poses, nude gestures. What is true is that the nude is always conventionalized—and the authority for its conventions derives from a certain tradition of art.

What do these conventions mean? What does a nude signify? It is not sufficient to answer these questions merely in terms of the art form, for it is quite clear that the nude also relates to lived sexuality.

To be naked is to be oneself.

30

To view this image in color, visit www.cengagebrain.com

FIGURE 24.19
Susannah Bathing. Oil on canvas (after 1560) by Jacopo Robusti Tintoretto

To be nude is to be seen naked by others and yet not recognized for oneself. A naked body has to be seen as an object in order to become a nude. (The sight of it as an object stimulates the use of it as an object.) Nakedness reveals itself. Nudity is placed on display.

To be naked is to be without disguise.

To be on display is to have the surface of one's own skin, the hairs of one's own body, turned into a disguise which, in that situation, can never be discarded. The nude is condemned to never being naked. Nudity is a form of dress.

In the average European oil painting of the nude, the principal protagonist is never painted. He is the spectator in front of the picture, and he is presumed to be a man. Everything is addressed to him. Everything must appear to be the result of his being there. It is for him that the figures have assumed their nudity. But he, by definition, is a stranger—with his clothes still on.

Consider the *Allegory of Time and Love* by Bronzino. The complicated symbolism which lies behind this painting need not concern us now, because it does not affect its sexual appeal—at the first degree. Before it is anything else, this is a painting of sexual provocation. [See Figure 24.24.]

The painting was sent as a present from the Grand Duke of Florence to the King of France. The boy kneeling on the cushion and kissing the woman is Cupid. She is

To view this image in color, visit www.cengagebrain.com

FIGURE 24.20

Vanity, central panel from the Triptych of Earthly Vanity and Divine Salvation, c. 1485 by Hans Memling

Vanity, central panel from the Triptych of Earthly Vanity and Divine Salvation, c.1485 (oil on panel), Memling, Hans (c.1433–94)/Musee des Beaux-Arts, Strasbourg, France/The Bridgeman Art Library

To view this image in color, visit www.cengagebrain.com

FIGURE 24.21
The Judgement of Paris, 1639 (oil on canvas) by Peter Paul Rubens

To view this image in color, visit www.cengagebrain.com

FIGURE 24.22
Portrait of Nell Gwynne as Venus with her son as Cupid by Sir Peter Lely

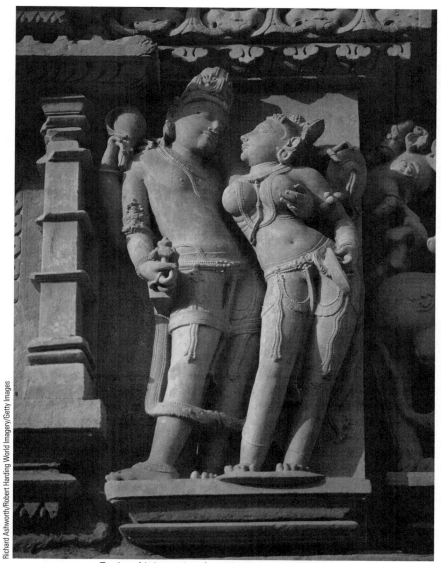

Richard Ashworth/Robert Harding World Imagery/Getty Images

To view this image in color, visit www.cengagebrain.com

FIGURE 24.23
**Detail of 11th century sculpture of Vishnu and Lakeshmi, Parsavantha Temple,
Khajuraho**

To view this image in color, visit www.cengagebrain.com

National Gallery, London/Art Resource, NY

FIGURE 24.24
Venus, Cupid, Time and Love by Bronzino

Venus. But the way her body is arranged has nothing to do with their kissing. Her body is arranged in the way it is, to display it to the man looking at the picture. This picture is made to appeal to *his* sexuality. It has nothing to do with her sexuality. (Here and in the European tradition generally, the convention of not painting the hair on a woman's body helps towards the same end. Hair is associated with sexual power, with passion. The woman's sexual passion needs to be minimized so that the spectator may feel that he has the monopoly of such passion.) Women are there to feed an appetite, not to have any of their own. […]

It is true that sometimes a painting includes a male lover.

But the woman's attention is very rarely directed towards him. Often she looks away from him, or she looks out of the picture toward the one who considers himself her true lover—the spectator-owner.

There was a special category of private pornographic paintings (especially in the eighteenth century) in which couples making love make an appearance. But even in front of these it is clear that the spectator-owner will in fantasy oust the other man, or else identify with him. By contrast the image of the couple in non-European traditions provokes the notion of many couples making love. "We all have a thousand hands, a thousand feet and will never go alone."

Almost all post-Renaissance European sexual imagery is frontal—either literally or metaphorically—because the sexual protagonist is the spectator-owner looking at it.

The absurdity of this male flattery reached its peak in the public academic art of the nineteenth century.

Men of state, of business, discussed under paintings like this. When one of them felt he had been outwitted, he looked up for consolation. What he saw reminded him that he was a man. [See Figures 24.25 and 24.26.]

There are a few exceptional nudes in the European tradition of oil painting to which very little of what has been said above applies. Indeed, they are no longer nudes—they break the norms of the art form; they are paintings of loved women, more or less naked. Among the hundreds of thousands of nudes which make up the tradition, there are perhaps a hundred of these exceptions. In each case, the painter's personal vision of the particular woman he is painting is so strong that it makes no allowance for the spectator. The painter's vision binds the woman to him so that they become as inseparable as couples in stone. The spectator can witness their relationship—but he can do no more: He is forced to recognize himself as the outsider he is. He cannot deceive himself into believing that she is naked for him. He cannot turn her into a nude. The way the painter has painted her includes her will and her intentions in the very structure of the image, in the very expression of her body and her face.

The typical and the exceptional in the tradition can be defined by the simple naked/nude antinomy, but the problem of painting nakedness is not as simple as it might at first appear.

What is the sexual function of nakedness in reality? Clothes encumber contact and 45 movement. But it would seem that nakedness has a positive visual value in its own right: we want to *see* the other naked: The other delivers to us the sight of themselves, and we seize upon it—sometimes quite regardless of whether it is for the first time or the hundredth. What does this sight of the other mean to us, how does it, at that instant of total disclosure, affect our desire?

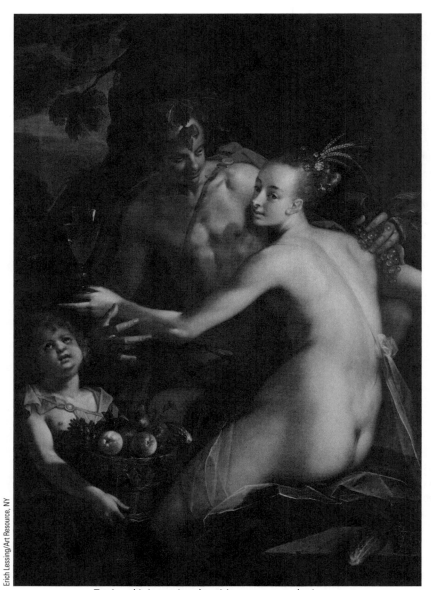

To view this image in color, visit www.cengagebrain.com

Erich Lessing/Art Resource, NY

FIGURE 24.25
Bacchus, Ceres and Amor. Canvas by Hans von Aachen

The Oreads, 1902 (oil on canvas), Bouguereau, William-Adolphe (1825–1905)/Private Collection/Giraudon/The Bridgeman Art Library

To view this image in color, visit www.cengagebrain.com

FIGURE 24.26
The Oreads, 1902 by William-Adolphe Bourguereau

Their nakedness acts as a confirmation and provokes a very strong sense of relief. She is a woman like any other: or he is a man like any other: we are overwhelmed by the marvelous simplicity of the familiar sexual mechanism.

We did not, of course, consciously expect this to be otherwise: Unconscious homosexual desires (or unconscious heterosexual desires if the couple concerned are homosexual) may have led each to half expect something different. But the "relief" can be explained without recourse to the unconscious.

We did not expect them to be otherwise, but the urgency and complexity of our feelings bred a sense of uniqueness which the sight of the other, as she is or as he is, now dispels. They are more like the rest of their sex than they are different. In this revelation lies the warm and friendly—as opposed to cold and impersonal—anonymity of nakedness.

One could express this differently: At the moment of nakedness first perceived, an element of banality enters: an element that exists only because we need it.

50   Up to that instant the other was more or less mysterious. Etiquettes of modesty are not merely puritan or sentimental: It is reasonable to recognize a loss of mystery. And the explanation of this loss of mystery may be largely visual. The focus of perception shifts from eyes, mouth, shoulders, hands—all of which are capable of such subtleties of expression that the personality expressed by them is manifold—it shifts from these to the sexual parts, whose formation suggests an utterly compelling but single process. The other is reduced or elevated—whichever you prefer—to their primary sexual category: male or female. Our relief is the relief of finding an unquestionable reality to whose direct demands our earlier, highly complex awareness must now yield.

We need the banality which we find in the first instant of disclosure because it grounds us in reality. But it does more than that. This reality, by promising the familiar, proverbial mechanism of sex, offers, at the same time, the possibility of the shared subjectivity of sex.

The loss of mystery occurs simultaneously with the offering of the means for creating a shared mystery. The sequence is: subjective—objective—subjective to the power of two.

We can now understand the difficulty of creating a static image of sexual nakedness. In lived sexual experience nakedness is a process rather than a state. If one moment of that process is isolated, its image will seem banal, and its banality, instead of serving as a bridge between two intense imaginative states, will be chilling. This is one reason why expressive photographs of the naked are even rarer than paintings. The easy solution for the photographer is to turn the figure into a nude, which, by generalizing both sight and viewer and making sexuality unspecific, turns desire into fantasy. [See Figure 24.27]

Let us examine an exceptional painted image of nakedness. It is a painting by Rubens of his young second wife, whom he married when he himself was relatively old. [See Figure 24.28.]

We see her in the act of turning, her fur about to slip off her shoulders. Clearly she will not remain as she is for more than a second. In a superficial sense her image is as instantaneous as a photograph's. But, in a more profound sense, the painting "contains" time and its experience. It is easy to imagine that a moment ago, before she pulled the fur round her shoulders, she was entirely naked. The consecutive stages up to and away from the moment of total disclosure have been transcended. She can belong to any or all of them simultaneously.

Her body confronts us, not as an immediate sight but as experience—the painter's experience. Why? There are superficial anecdotal reasons: her dishevelled hair, the expression of her eyes directed toward him, the tenderness with which the exaggerated

To view this image in color, visit www.cengagebrain.com

Danae, 1643 (oil on canvas), Rembrandt Harmensz. van Rijn (1606–69)/Hermitage, St. Petersburg, Russia/The Bridgeman Art Library

FIGURE 24.27
Danae, 1643 by Rembrandt van Rijn

susceptibility of her skin has been painted. But the profound reason is a formal one. Her appearance has been literally recast by the painter's subjectivity. Beneath the fur that she holds across herself, the upper part of her body and her legs can never meet. There is a displacement sideways of about nine inches: her thighs, in order to join onto her hips, are at least nine inches too far to the left.

Rubens probably did not plan this: The spectator may not consciously notice it. In itself it is unimportant. What matters is what it permits. It permits the body to become impossibly dynamic. Its coherence is no longer within itself but within the experience of the painter. More precisely, it permits the upper and lower halves of the body to rotate separately, and in opposite directions, round the sexual center which is hidden: the torso turning to the right, the legs to the left. At the same time this hidden sexual center is connected by means of the dark fur coat to all the surrounding darkness in the picture, so that she is turning both around and within the dark, which has been made a metaphor for her sex.

Helena Fourment in a Fur Wrap, 1636–38, Rubens, Peter Paul (1577–1640)/Kunsthistorisches Museum, Vienna, Austria/The Bridgeman Art Library

To view this image in color, visit www.cengagebrain.com

FIGURE 24.28
Peter Paul Rubens, Helene Fourment in a Fur Coat

Apart from the necessity of transcending the single instant and of admitting subjectivity, there is, as we have seen, one further element which is essential for any great sexual image of the naked. This is the element of banality which must be undisguised but not chilling. It is this which distinguishes between voyeur and lover. Here such banality is to be found in Rubens's compulsive painting of the fat softness of Hélène Fourment's flesh, which continually breaks every ideal convention of form and (to him) continually offers the promise of her extraordinary particularity.

The nude in European oil painting is usually presented as an admirable expression of the European humanist spirit. This spirit was inseparable from individualism. And without the development of a highly conscious individualism, the exceptions to the tradition (extremely personal images of the naked), would never have been painted. Yet the tradition contained a contradiction which it could not itself resolve. A few individual artists intuitively recognized this and resolved the contradiction in their own terms, but their solutions could never enter the tradition's *cultural* terms.

The contradiction can be stated simply. On the one hand the individualism of the 60 artist, the thinker, the patron, the owner: on the other hand, the person who is the object of their activities—the woman—treated as a thing or an abstraction.

Dürer believed that the ideal nude ought to be constructed by taking the face of one body, the breasts of another, the legs of a third, the shoulders of a fourth, the hands of a fifth—and so on. [See Figure 24.29.]

The result would glorify Man. But the exercise presumed a remarkable indifference to who any one person really was.

In the art form of the European nude, the painters and spectator-owners were usually men and the persons treated as objects, usually women. This unequal relationship is so deeply embedded in our culture that it still structures the consciousness of many women. They do to themselves what men do to them. They survey, like men, their own femininity.

Foto Marburg/Art Resource, NY

FIGURE 24.29
Artist drawing a model in foreshortening through a frame using a grid system. Woodcut from Unterweysung der Messung Nuremberg, 1527 by Albrecht Dürer

In modern art the category of the nude has become less important. Artists themselves began to question it. In this, as in many other respects, Manet represented a turning point. If one compares his *Olympia* with Titian's original, one sees a woman, cast in the traditional role, beginning to question that role, somewhat defiantly. [See Figures 24.30 and 24.31.]

65   The ideal was broken. But there was little to replace it except the "realism" of the prostitute—who became the quintessential woman of early avant-garde twentieth-century painting (Toulouse-Lautrec, Picasso, Rouault, German Expressionism, etc.). In academic painting the tradition continued.

Today the attitudes and values which informed that tradition are expressed through other, more widely diffused media—advertising, journalism, television.

But the essential way of seeing women, the essential use to which their images are put, has not changed. Women are depicted in a quite different way from men—not because the feminine is different from the masculine—but because the "ideal" spectator is always assumed to be male, and the image of the woman is designed to flatter him. If you have any doubt that this is so, make the following experiment. Choose an image of a traditional nude. Transform the woman into a man, either in your mind's eye or by drawing on the reproduction. Then notice the violence which that transformation does—not to the image, but to the assumptions of a likely viewer.

Alinari Archives/Fratelli Alinari/Corbis

To view this image in color, visit www.cengagebrain.com

FIGURE 24.30
The Venus of Urbino by Titian

To view this image in color, visit www.cengagebrain.com

FIGURE 24.31
Olympia by Edouard Manet

Things to Do with the Reading

1. Write a paper in which you use Berger's essay as a lens for thinking about representations of women in, for example, fashion photography or on magazine covers aimed at either male or female audiences. Select particular sentences from Berger's essay as starting points. Consider, for example, the sentence, "And so she comes to consider the surveyor and the surveyed within her as the two constituent yet always distinct elements of her identity as a woman." Whatever sentence you choose as your starting point, do *not* write about whether you agree or disagree with Berger. Write so as to deepen your understanding of Berger's ideas and to make them your own.

2. **Link:** Several of the photographers discussed in the interview with Joseph Elliott have made a project of photographing women—Lauren Greenfield's "Girl Culture," for example. What might Berger notice about the Greenfield photograph we have included in this book, the one of the girl on the scale? How might we see the gender of the photographer (female) having a shaping effect in this photograph? Write an essay in which you explore this question as well as analyze the photograph in light of insights you have gained from the Berger essay. There is a mirror in the Greenfield photograph, for

example. So what? For that matter, how do the female figures captured by Greenfield and/or Sally Mann compare with the photograph of the young woman on the porch by Alfred Stieglitz?

3. **Application:** Berger's essay offers not just an interpretation of selected paintings but a rhetorical analysis of a set of conventions in European art. As in all rhetorical analyses, Berger focuses on how the paintings are designed to appeal to an assumed audience, in this case, an audience of male viewers. This kind of rhetorical analysis has come to be housed under the concept of the "gaze"—a word taken from French (Lacanian) psychology and developed by cultural analysts such as Teresa de Lauretis, who writes about women in film. In this mode of analysis attention is focused on the ways in which assumptions about the values and interests of particular viewers have shaped the painting or photograph or advertisement or building (etc.) under consideration. One of the reasons writing teachers so often ask students to write about the visual images in advertising is that the makers of such images can be assumed to be more conscious about their selection of a particular target audience and about the desire to win over that audience.

   Write a paper in which you experiment with this analytical approach by studying something for what it seems to assume about its audience. You might study commercials for products typically aimed at men—beer, for example. It would be interesting to see what is different if you could find a beer commercial (or commercial for some other product typically associated with men) that seems aimed at women.

4. **Application:** Using the Berger essay as a lens, write an essay about one or both of the paintings by Alice Neel—the self-portrait and the painting of her son, Hartley. How might we interpret Neel's self-portrait in the context of the conventions governing the representation of women as nudes in European art? How does the painting speak to some of the conventions noted by Berger in his essay? What features of Neel's painting of her son Hartley read interestingly in the context of portraits of female nudes in European art? Hartley is neither naked nor nude, and yet he is clearly being put on display. What does the painting arguably reveal about Neel's assumptions about her audience? Which features of the painting might be designed to negotiate the possible anxiety among male viewers being invited to gaze at another male? Which features of the painting might reveal that it is the product of the gaze of a female viewer (the painter herself)?

National Portrait Gallery, Smithsonian Institution/Art Resource, NY

To view this image in color, visit www.cengagebrain.com

FIGURE 24.32
Self-Portrait, 1980 by Alice Neel. Oil on canvas, 54" × 40"

National Gallery of Art, Washington, DC

To view this image in color, visit www.cengagebrain.com

FIGURE 24.33
Alice Neel, Hartley, 1965, oil on canvas, 50" × 36"

Susan Bordo

Beauty (Re)discovers the Male Body

With this essay, the chapter makes a turn from high art in the direction of popular culture. In this excerpt from her book *The Male Body* (1999), Susan Bordo offers a compelling history of how advertising has rediscovered the male body. She examines how the pressures of commercial culture have expanded the range of acceptable images of masculinity, at once shaping and satisfying an expanding audience of women and men, straight and gay. Bordo's interpretations take us beyond cultural stereotypes, deftly challenging common cultural assumptions about masculinity, femininity, sexuality, and beauty itself. Susan Bordo is a professor of English and Women's Studies at the University of Kentucky.

Men on Display

Putting classical art to the side for the moment, the naked and near-naked female body became an object of mainstream consumption first in *Playboy* and its imitators, then in movies, and only then in fashion photographs. With the male body, the trajectory has been different. Fashion has taken the lead, the movies have followed. Hollywood may have been a chest-fest in the fifties, but it was male clothing designers who went south and violated the really powerful taboos—not just against the explicit depiction of penises and male bottoms but against the admission of all sorts of forbidden "feminine" qualities into mainstream conceptions of manliness.

It was the spring of 1995, and I was sipping my first cup of morning coffee, not yet fully awake, flipping through *The New York Times Magazine*, when I had my first real taste of what it's like to inhabit this visual culture as a man. It was both thrilling and disconcerting. It was the first time in my experience that I had encountered a commercial representation of a male body that seemed to deliberately invite me to linger over it. Let me make that stronger—that seemed to reach out to me, interrupting my mundane but peaceful Sunday morning, and provoke me into erotic consciousness, whether or not I wanted it. Women—both straight and gay—have always gazed covertly, of course, squeezing our illicit little titillations out of representations designed for—or pretending to—other purposes than to turn us on. *This* ad made no such pretense. It caused me to knock over my coffee cup, ruining the more cerebral pleasures of the *Book Review*. Later, when I had regained my equilibrium, I made a screen-saver out of him, so I could gaze at my leisure.

I'm sure that many gay men were as taken as I was, and perhaps some gay women too. The erotic charge of various sexual styles is not neatly mapped onto sexual orientation (let alone biological sex). Brad Pitt's baby-butch looks are a turn-on to many lesbians, while I—regarded by most of my gay friends as a pretty hard-core heterosexual—have always found Anne Heche irresistible (even before Ellen did). A lesbian friend of mine, reading a draft of my section on biblical S&M, said the same movies influenced her later attraction to butch *women*. Despite such complications,

"Beauty (Re)discovers the Male Body," from THE MALE BODY by Susan Bordo. Copyright (c) 1999 by Susan Bordo. Reprinted by permission of Farrar, Straus and Giroux, LLC.

until recently only heterosexual men have continually been inundated by popular cultural images *designed* with their sexual responses (or, at least, what those sexual responses are imagined to be) in mind. It's not entirely a gift. On the minus side is having one's composure continually challenged by what Timothy Beneke has aptly described as a culture of "intrusive images," eliciting fantasies, emotions, and erections at times and in places where they might not be appropriate. On the plus side is the cultural permission to be a voyeur.

Some psychologists say that the circuit from eyes to brain to genitals is a quicker trip for men than for women. "There's some strong evidence," popular science writer Deborah Blum reports, citing studies of men's responses to pictures of naked women, "that testosterone is wired for visual response." Maybe. But who is the electrician here? God? Mother Nature? Or Hugh Hefner? Practice makes perfect. And women have had little practice. The Calvin Klein ad made me feel like an adolescent again, brought me back to that day when I saw Barry Resnick on the basketball court of Weequahic High and realized that men's legs could make me weak in the knees. Men's legs? I knew that *women's* legs were supposed to be sexy. I had learned that from all those hose-straightening scenes in the movies. But men's legs? Who had ever seen a woman gaga over some guy's legs in the movies? Or even read about it in a book? Yet the muscular grace of Barry's legs took my breath away. Maybe something was wrong with me. Maybe my sex drive was too strong, too much like a man's. By the time I came across that Calvin Klein ad, several decades of feminism and life experience had left me a little less worried about my sex drive. Still, the sight of that model's body made me feel that my sexual education was still far from complete.

I brought the ad to classes and lectures, asking women what they thought of him. Most began to sweat the moment I unfolded the picture, then got their bearings and tried to explore the bewitching stew of sexual elements the picture has to offer. The model—a young Jackson Browne look-alike—stands there in his form-fitting and rip-speckled Calvin Klein briefs, head lowered, dark hair loosely falling over his eyes. His body projects strength, solidity; he's no male waif. But his finely muscled chest is not so overdeveloped as to suggest a sexuality immobilized by the thick matter of the body. Gay theorist Ron Long, describing contemporary gay sexual aesthetics—lean, taut, sinuous muscles rather than Schwarzenegger bulk—points to a "dynamic tension" that the incredible hulks lack. Stiff, engorged Schwarzenegger bodies, he says, seem to *be* surrogate penises—with nowhere to go and nothing to do but stand there looking massive—whereas muscles like this young man's seem designed for movement, for sex. His body isn't a stand-in phallus; rather, he *has* a penis—the real thing, not a symbol, and a fairly breathtaking one, clearly outlined through the soft jersey fabric of the briefs. It seems slightly erect, or perhaps that's his non-erect size; either way, there's a substantial presence there that's palpable (it looks so touchable, you want to cup your hand over it) and very, very male.

At the same time, however, my gaze is invited by something "feminine" about the young man. His underwear may be ripped, but ever so slightly, subtly; unlike the original ripped-underwear poster boy Kowalski, he's hardly a thug. He doesn't stare at the viewer challengingly, belligerently, as do so many models in other ads for male underwear, facing off like a street tough passing a member of the rival gang on the street. ("Yeah, this is an underwear ad and I'm half naked. But I'm still the one in charge here. Who's gonna look away first?") No, this model's languid body posture, his averted look are classic signals, both in the "natural" and the "cultural" world, of willing subordination. He offers himself nonaggressively to the gaze of another. Hip cocked in the snaky S-curve usually reserved for depictions of women's bodies, eyes downcast but not closed, he gives off a sultry, moody, subtle but undeniably seductive consciousness of his erotic allure. Feast on me, I'm here to be looked at, my body is for your eyes. Oh my.

Such an attitude of male sexual supplication, although it has (as we'll see) classical antecedents, is very new to contemporary mainstream representations. Homophobia is at work in this taboo, but so are attitudes about gender that cut across sexual orientation. For many men, both gay and straight, to be so passively dependent on the gaze of another person for one's sense of self-worth is incompatible with being a real man. As we'll see, such notions about manliness are embedded in Greek culture, in contemporary visual representation, and even (in disguised form) in existentialist philosophy. "For the woman," as philosopher Simone de Beauvoir writes, "... the absence of her lover is always torture; he is an eye, a judge ... away from him, she is dispossessed, at once of herself and of the world." For Beauvoir's sometime lover and lifelong soul mate Jean-Paul Sartre, on the other hand, the gaze (or the Look, as he called it) of another person—including the gaze of one's lover—is the "hell" that other people represent. If we were alone in the world, he argues, we would be utterly free—within physical constraints—to be whomever we wanted to be, to be the creatures of our own self-fantasies, to define our behavior however we like. Other people intrude on this solipsism, and have the audacity to see us from their own perspective rather than ours. The result is what Sartre calls primordial Shame under the eyes of the Other, and a fierce desire to reassert one's freedom. The other person has stolen "the secret" of who I am. I must fight back, resist their attempts to define me.

I understand, of course, what Sartre is talking about here. We've all, male and female alike, felt the shame that another pair of eyes can bring. Sartre's own classic example is of being caught peeking through a keyhole by another person. It isn't until those other eyes are upon you that you truly feel not just the "wrongness" of what you are doing, but—Sartre would argue—the very fact that you are doing it. Until the eyes of another are upon us, "catching us" in the act, we can deceive ourselves, pretend. Getting caught in moments of fantasy or vanity may be especially shameful. When I was an adolescent, I loved to pretend I was a radio personality, and talking into an empty coffee can created just the right sound. One day, my mother caught me speaking in the smooth and slightly sultry tones that radio personalities had even in those days. The way I felt is what Sartre means when he describes the Look of another person as the fulcrum of shame-making. My face got hot, and suddenly I saw how ridiculous I must have seemed, my head in the Chock Full O' Nuts, my narcissistic fantasies on full display. I was caught, I wanted to run.

The disjunction between self-conception and external judgment can be especially harsh when the external definitions carry racial and gender stereotypes with them. Sartre doesn't present such examples—he's interested in capturing the contours of an existential situation shared by all rather than in analyzing the cultural differences that affect that situation—but they are surely relevant to understanding the meaning of the Look of the Other. A black man jogs down the street in sweat clothes, thinking of the class he is going to teach later that day; a white woman passes him, clutches her handbag more tightly, quickens her step; in her eyes, the teacher is a potentially dangerous animal. A Latin American student arrives early the first day of college; an administrator, seeing him in the still-deserted hall, asks him if he is the new janitor. The aspiring student has had his emerging identity erased, a stereotype put in its place by another pair of eyes. When women are transformed from professionals to "pussies" by the comments of men on the street, it's humiliating, not so much because we're puritans as because we sense the hostility in the hoots, the desire to bring an uppity woman down to size by reminding her that she's just "the sex" (as Beauvoir put it).

We may all have felt shame, but—as the different attitudes of Beauvoir and Sartre suggest—men and women are socially sanctioned to deal with the gaze of the Other in different ways. Women learn to anticipate, even play to the sexualizing gaze, trying to become what will please, captivate, turn shame into pride. (In the process, we also learn how sexy being gazed at can feel—perhaps precisely because it walks the fine edge of shame.) Many of us, truth be told, get somewhat addicted to the experience. I'm renting a video, feeling a bit low, a bit tired. The young man at the counter, unsolicited, tells me I'm "looking good." It alters everything, I feel fine, alive; it seems to go right down to my cells. I leave the store feeling younger, stronger, more awake. When women sense that they are not being assessed sexually—for example, as we age, or if we are disabled—it may feel like we no longer exist.

Women may dread being surveyed harshly—being seen as too old, too fat, too flat-chested—but men are not supposed to enjoy being surveyed *period*. It's feminine to be on display. Men are thus taught—as my uncle Leon used to say—to be a moving target. Get out of range of those eyes, don't let them catch you—even as the object of their fantasies (or, as Sartre would put it, don't let them "possess," "steal" your freedom). This phobia has even distorted scientific research, as mentioned earlier. Evolutionary theorists have long acknowledged display as an important feature of courting behavior among primates—except when it comes to *our* closest ancestors. With descriptions of hominid behavior, male display behavior "suddenly drops out of the primate evolutionary picture" (Sheets-Johnstone) and is replaced by the concept of year-round female sexual receptivity. It seems that it has been intolerable, unthinkable for male evolutionary theorists to imagine the bodies of their male ancestors being on display, sized up, dependent on selection (or rejection) by female hominids.

Scientists and "ordinary guys" are totally in synch here, as is humorously illustrated in Peter Cattaneo's popular 1997 British film *The Full Monty*. In the film, a group of unemployed metalworkers in Sheffield, England, watch a Chippendale's show and hatch the money-making scheme of presenting their own male strip show in which they will go right down to the "full Monty." At the start of the film, the heroes are hardly pillars of successful manliness (Gaz, their leader, refers to them as "scrap"). Yet even they have been sheltered by their guy-hood, as they learn while putting the show together. One gets a penis pump. Another borrows his wife's face cream. They run, they wrap their bellies in plastic, they do jumping jacks, they get artificial tans.

The most overweight one among them (temporarily) pulls out of the show. Before, these guys hadn't lived their lives under physical scrutiny, but in male action mode, in which men are judged by their accomplishments. Now, anticipating being on display to a roomful of spectators, they suddenly realize how it feels to be judged as women routinely are, sized up by another pair of eyes. "I pray that they'll be a bit more understanding about us" than they've been with women, David (the fat one) murmurs.

They get past their discomfort, in the end, and their show is greeted with wild enthusiasm by the audience. The movie leaves us with this feel-good ending, not raising the question obvious to every woman watching the film: would a troupe of out-of-shape women be received as warmly, as affectionately? The climactic moment when the men throw off their little pouches is demurely shot from the rear, moreover, so we—the audience—don't get "the full Monty." Nonetheless, the film gently and humorously makes an important point: for a heterosexual man to offer himself up to a sexually evaluating gaze is for him to make a large, scary leap—and not just because of the anxieties about size discussed earlier in this book (the guy who drops out of the show, remember, is embarrassed by his fat, not his penis). The "full Monty"—the naked penis—is not merely a body part in the movie (hence it doesn't really matter that the film doesn't show it). It's a symbol for male exposure, vulnerability to an evaluation and judgment that women—clothed or naked—experience all the time.

I had to laugh out loud at a 1997 *New York Times Magazine* "Style" column, entitled "Overexposure," which complained of the "contagion" of nudity spreading through celebrity culture. "Stars no longer have private parts," the author observed, and fretted that civilians would soon also be measured by the beauty of their buns. I share this author's concern about our body-obsessed culture. But, pardon me, he's just noticing this now??? Actresses have been baring their breasts, their butts, even their bushes, for some time, and ordinary women have been tromping off to the gym in pursuit of comparably perfect bodies. What's got the author suddenly crying "overkill," it turns out, is Sly Stallone's "surreally fat-free" appearance on the cover of *Vanity Fair*, and Rupert Everett's "dimpled behind" in a Karl Lagerfeld fashion spread. Now that *men* are taking off their clothes, the culture is suddenly going too far. Could it be that the author doesn't even "read" all those naked female bodies as "overexposed"? Does he protest a bit too much when he declares in the first sentence of the piece that he found it "a yawn" when Dirk Diggler unsheathed his "prosthetic shillelagh" ("penis" is still a word to be avoided whenever possible) at the end of *Boogie Nights*? A yawn? My friend's palms were sweating profusely, and I was not about to drop off to sleep either.

As for dimpled behinds, my second choice for male pinup of the decade is the Gucci series of two ads in which a beautiful young man, shot from the rear, puts on a pair of briefs. In the first ad, he's holding them in his hands, contemplating them. Is he checking out the correct washing-machine temp? It's odd, surely, to stand there looking at your underwear, but never mind. The point is: his underwear is in his hands, not on his butt. *It*—his bottom, that is—is gorgeously, completely naked—a motif so new to mainstream advertising (but since then catching on rapidly) that several of my friends, knowing I was writing about the male body, E-mailed me immediately when they saw the ad. In the second ad, he's put the underwear on, and is adjusting it to fit. Luckily for us, he hasn't succeeded yet, so his buns are peeking out the bottom of the underwear, looking biteable. For the *Times* writer, those buns may be an indecent exposure of parts that should be kept private (or they're a boring yawn, I'm afraid he can't have it both ways), but for me—and for thousands of gay men across the country—this was a moment of political magnitude, and a delicious one. The body parts that *we* love to squeeze (those plastic breasts, they're the real yawn for me) had come out of the closet and into mainstream culture, where *we* can enjoy them without a trip to a specialty store.

But all this is very new. Women aren't used to seeing naked men frankly portrayed as "objects" of a sexual gaze (and neither are heterosexual men, as that *Times* writer makes clear). So pardon me if I'm skeptical when I read arguments about men's greater "biological" responsiveness to visual stimuli. These "findings," besides being ethnocentric (no one thinks to poll Trobriand Islanders), display little awareness of the impact of changes in cultural representations on our capacities for sexual response. Popular science writer Deborah Blum, for example, cites a study from the Kinsey Institute which showed a group of men and women a series of photos and drawings of nudes, both male and female:

> Fifty-four percent of the men were erotically aroused versus 12 percent of the women—in other words, more than four times as many men. The same gap exists, on a much larger scale, in the business of pornography, a $500-million-plus industry in the U.S. which caters almost exclusively to men. In the first flush of 1970s feminism, two magazines—*Playgirl and Viva*—began publishing male centerfolds. Viva dropped the nude photos after surveys showed their readers didn't care for them; the editor herself admitted to finding them slightly disgusting.

Blum presents these findings as suggestive of a hard-wired difference between men and women. I'd be cautious about accepting that conclusion. First of all, there's the question of which physiological responses count as "erotic arousal" and whether they couldn't be evidence of other states. Clearly, too, we can *learn* to have certain physiological responses—and to suppress them—so nothing biologically definitive is proved by the presence or absence of physical arousal.

Studies that rely on viewers' *own* reports need to be carefully interpreted too. I know, from talking to women students, that they sometimes aren't all that clear about *what* they feel in the presence of erotic stimuli, and even when they are, they may not be all that comfortable admitting what they feel. Hell, not just my students! Once, a lover asked me, as we were about to part for the evening, if there was anything that we hadn't done that I'd really like to do. I knew immediately what that was: I wanted him to undress, very slowly, while I sat on the floor and just watched. But I couldn't tell him. I was too embarrassed. Later, alone in my compartment on the train, I sorely regretted my cowardice. The fact is that I love to watch a man getting undressed, and I especially like it if he is conscious of being looked at. But there is a long legacy of shame to be overcome here, for both sexes, and the cultural models are only now just emerging which might help us move beyond it.

Perhaps, then, we should wait a bit longer, do a few more studies, before we come to any biological conclusions about women's failure to get aroused by naked pictures. A newer (1994) University of Chicago study found that 30 percent of women ages eighteen to forty-four and 19 percent of women ages forty-five to fifty-nine said they found "watching a partner undress" to be "very appealing." ("Not a bad percentage," Nancy Friday comments, "given that Nice Girls didn't look.") There's still a gender gap—the respective figures for men of the same age groups were 50 percent and 40 percent. We're just learning, after all, to be voyeuses. Perhaps, too, heterosexual men could learn to be less uncomfortable offering themselves as "sexual objects" if they realized the pleasure women get from it. Getting what you have been most deprived of is the best gift, the most healing gift, the most potentially transforming gift—because it has the capacity to make one more whole. Women have been deprived not so much of the *sight* of beautiful male bodies as the experience of having the male body *offered* to us, handed to us on a silver platter, the way female bodies—in the ads, in the movies—are handed to men. Getting this from her partner is the erotic equivalent of a woman's coming home from work to find a meal prepared and ready for her. Delicious—even if it's just franks and beans.

Thanks, Calvin!

Despite their bisexual appeal, the cultural genealogy of the ads I've been discussing and others like them is to be traced largely through gay male aesthetics, rather than a sudden blossoming of appreciation for the fact that women might enjoy looking at sexy, well-hung young men who don't appear to be about to rape them. Feminists might like to imagine that Madison Avenue heard our pleas for sexual equality and finally gave us "men as sex objects." But what's really happened is that women have been the beneficiaries of what might be described as a triumph of pure consumerism—and with it, a burgeoning male fitness and beauty culture—over homophobia and the taboos against male vanity, male "femininity," and erotic display of the male body that have gone along with it.

Throughout this century, gay photographers have created a rich, sensuous, and dramatic tradition which is unabashed in eroticizing the male body, male sensuousness, and male potency, including penises. But until recently, such representations have been kept largely in the closet. Mainstream responses to several important exhibits which opened in the seventies—featuring the groundbreaking early work of Wilhelm von Gloeden, George Dureau, and George Platt Lynes as well as then-contemporary artists such as Robert Mapplethorpe, Peter Hujar, and Arthur Tress—would today probably embarrass the critics who wrote about them when they opened. John Ashbery, in *New York* magazine, dismissed the entire genre of male nude photography with the same sexist tautology that covertly underlies that *Times* piece on cultural "overexposure": "Nude women seem to be in their natural state; men, for some reason, merely look undressed ... When is a nude not a nude? When it is male." (Substitute "blacks" and "whites" for "women" and "men" and you'll see how offensive the statement is.)

For other reviewers, the naked male, far from seeming "merely undressed," was unnervingly sexual. *New York Times* critic Gene Thompson wrote that "there is something disconcerting about the sight of a man's naked body being presented as a sexual object"; he went on to describe the world of homoerotic photography as one "closed to most of us, fortunately." Vicki Goldberg, writing for the *Saturday Review*, was more appreciative of the "beauty and dignity" of the nude male body, but concluded that so long as its depiction was erotic in emphasis, it will "remain half-private, slightly awkward, an art form cast from its traditions and in search of some niche to call its home."

Goldberg needed a course in art history. It's true that in classical art, the naked human body was often presented as a messenger of spiritual themes, and received as such. But the male bodies sculpted by the Greeks and Michelangelo were not exactly nonerotic. It might be more accurate to say that in modernity, with the spiritual interpretation of the nude body no longer a convention, the contemporary homophobic psyche is not screened from the sexual charge of the nude male body. Goldberg was dead wrong about something else too. Whatever its historical lineage, the frankly sexual representation of the male body was to find, in the next twenty years, a far from private "niche to call its home": consumer culture discovered its commercial potency.

Calvin Klein had his epiphany, according to one biography, one night in 1974 in New York's gay Flamingo bar:

> As Calvin wandered through the crowd at the Flamingo, the body heat rushed through him like a revelation; this was the cutting edge.... [The] men! The men at the Flamingo had less to do about sex for him than the notion of portraying men as gods. He realized that what he was watching was the freedom of a new generation, unashamed, in-the-flesh embodiments of Calvin's ideals: straight-looking, masculine men, with chiseled bodies, young Greek gods come to life. The vision of shirtless young men with hardened torsos, all in blue jeans, top button opened, a whisper of hair from the belly button disappearing into the denim pants, would inspire and inform the next ten years of Calvin Klein's print and television advertisements.

Klein's genius was that of a cultural Geiger counter; his own bisexuality enabled him to see that the phallic body, as much as any female figure, is an enduring sex object within Western culture. In America in 1974, however, that ideal was still largely closeted. Only gay culture unashamedly sexualized the lean, fit body that virtually everyone, gay and straight, now aspires to. Sex, as Calvin Klein knew, sells. He also knew that gay sex wouldn't sell to straight men. But the rock-hard, athletic gay male bodies that Klein admired at the Flamingo did not advertise their sexual preference through the feminine codes—limp wrists, raised pinkie finger, swishy walk—which the straight world then identified with homosexuality. Rather, they embodied a highly masculine aesthetic that—although definitely exciting for gay men—would scream "heterosexual" to (clueless) straights. Klein knew just the kind of clothing to show that body off in too. As Steven Gaines and Sharon Churcher tell it:

> He had watched enough attractive young people with good bodies in tight jeans dancing at the Flamingo and Studio 54 to know that the "basket" and the behind was what gave jeans sex appeal. Calvin sent

his assistants out for several pairs of jeans, including the classic five-button Levi's, and cut them apart to see how they were made. Then he cut the "rise," or area from the waistband to under the groin, much shorter to accentuate the crotch and pull the seam up between the buttocks, giving the behind more shape and prominence. The result was instant sex appeal—and a look that somehow Calvin just knew was going to sell.

So we come to the mainstream commercialization of the aesthetic legacy of Stanley Kowalski and those inspired innovations of Brando's costumer in *A Streetcar Named Desire.* When I was growing up, jeans were "dungarees"—suitable for little kids, hayseeds, and juvenile delinquents, but not for anyone to wear on a date. Klein transformed jeans from utilitarian garments to erotic second skins. Next, Klein went for underwear. He wasn't the first, but he was the most daring. In 1981, Jockey International had broken ground by photographing Baltimore Oriole pitcher Jim Palmer in a pair of briefs (airbrushed) in one of its ads—selling $100 million worth of underwear by year's end. Inspired by Jockey's success, in 1983 Calvin Klein put a forty-by-fifty-foot Bruce Weber photograph of Olympic pole vaulter Tom Hintinauss in Times Square, Hintinauss's large penis clearly discernible through his briefs. The Hintinauss ad, unlike the Palmer ad, did not employ any of the usual fictional rationales for a man's being in his underwear—for example, the pretense that the man is in the process of getting dressed—but blatantly put Hintinauss's body on display, sunbathing on a rooftop, his skin glistening. The line of shorts "flew off the shelves" at Bloomingdale's and when Klein papered bus shelters in Manhattan with poster versions of the ad, they were all stolen overnight.

Images of masculinity that will do double (or triple or quadruple) duty with a variety of consumers, straight and gay, male and female, are not difficult to create in a culture like ours, in which the muscular male body has a long and glorious aesthetic history. That's precisely what Calvin Klein was the first to recognize and exploit—the possibility and profitability of what is known in the trade as a "dual marketing" approach. Since then, many advertisers have taken advantage of Klein's insight. A recent Abercrombie & Fitch ad, for example, depicts a locker room full of young, half-clothed football players getting a postmortem from their coach after a game. Beautiful, undressed male bodies doing what real men are "supposed to do." Dirty uniforms and smudged faces, wounded players, helmets. What could be more straight? But as iconography depicting a culture of exclusively male bodies, young, gorgeous, and well-hung, what could be more "gay"?

It required a Calvin Klein to give the new vision cultural form. But the fact is that if we've entered a brave, new world of male bodies it is largely because of a more "material" kind of epiphany—a dawning recognition among advertisers of the buying power of gay men. For a long time prejudice had triumphed over the profit motive, blinding marketers to just how sizable—and well-heeled—a consumer group gay men represent. (This has been the case with other "minorities" too. Hollywood producers, never bothering to do any demographics on middle-class and professional African-American women—or the issues that they share with women of other races and classes in this culture—were shocked at the tremendous box office success of *Waiting to Exhale.* They won't make that particular mistake again.) It took a survey

Image Courtesy of The Advertising Archives

FIGURE 24.34
Bronzed and beautiful Tom Hintinauss: a breakthrough ad for Calvin Klein—and the beginning of a new era for the unabashed erotic display of the male body

conducted by *The Advocate* to jolt corporate America awake about gay consumers. The survey, done between 1977 and 1980, showed that 70 percent of its readers aged twenty to forty earned incomes well above the national median. Soon, articles were appearing on the business pages of newspapers, like one in 1982 in *The New York Times Magazine,* which described advertisers as newly interested in "wooing ... the white, single, well-educated, well-paid man who happens to be homosexual."

"Happens to be homosexual": the phrasing—suggesting that sexual identity is peripheral, even accidental—is telling. Because of homophobia, dual marketing used to require a delicate balancing act, as advertisers tried to speak to gays "in a way that the straight consumer will not notice." Often, that's been accomplished through the use of play and parody, as in Versace's droll portraits of men being groomed and tended by male servants, and Diesel's overtly narcissistic gay posers. "Thanks, Diesel, for making us so very beautiful," they gush. Or take the ad [. . .] with its gorgeous, mechanically inept model admitting that he's "known more for my superb bone construction and soft, supple hair than my keen intellect." The playful tone reassures heterosexual consumers that the vanity (and mechanical incompetence) of the man selling the product is "just a joke." For gay consumers, on the other hand, this reassurance is *itself* the "joke"; they read the humor in the ad as an insider wink, which says, "This is for *you,* guys." The joke is further layered by the fact that they know the model in the ad is very likely to be gay.

Contrast this ad to the ostentatious heterosexual protest of a Perry Ellis ad which appeared in the early 1990s (and no, it's not a parody):

I hate this job. I'm not just an empty suit who stands in front of a camera, collects the money and flies off to St. Maarten for the weekend.

I may model for a living, but I hate being treated like a piece of meat. I once had a loud-mouthed art director say "Stand there and pretend you're a human." I wanted to punch him, but I needed the job.

What am I all about? Well, I know I'm very good-looking, and there are days when that is enough. Some nights, when I'm alone, it's not.

I like women—all kinds.

I like music—all kinds.

I like myself so I don't do drugs.

Oh yeah, about this fragrance. It's good. Very good.

When I posed for this picture, the art director insisted that I wear it while the pictures were being taken. I thought it was silly, but I said "What the hell? It's their money."

After a while, I realized I like this fragrance a lot. When the photo shoot was over, I walked right over, picked up the bottle, put it in my pocket and said "If you don't mind, I'd like to take this as a souvenir." Then I smiled my best f— you smile and walked out.

Next time, I'll pay for it.

It's that good.

Today, good-looking straight guys are flocking to the modeling agencies, much less concerned about any homosexual taint that will cleave to them. It's no longer necessary for an ad to plant its tongue firmly in cheek when lavishing erotic attention on the male body—or to pepper the ad with proofs of heterosexuality. It used to be, if an advertisement aimed at straight men dared to show a man fussing over his looks with seemingly romantic plans in mind, there had better be a woman in the picture, making it clear just *whom* the boy was getting pretty for. To sell a muscle-building product to heterosexuals, of course, you had to link it to virility and the ability to attract women on the beach. Today, muscles are openly sold for their looks; Chroma Lean nutritional supplement unabashedly compares the well-sculpted male body to a work of art (and a gay male icon, to boot)—Michelangelo's "David." Many ads display the naked male body without shame or plot excuse, and often exploit rather than resolve the sexual ambiguity that is generated.

Today, too, the athletic, muscular male body that Calvin plastered all over buildings, magazines, and subway stops has become an aesthetic norm, for straights as well as gays. "No pecs, no sex," is how the trendy David Barton gym sells itself: "My motto is not "Be healthy'; it's "Look better naked,'" Barton says. The notion has even made its way into that most determinedly heterosexual of contexts, a Rob Reiner film. In *Sleepless in Seattle*, Tom Hanks's character, who hasn't been on a date in fifteen years, asks his friend (played by Rob) what women are looking for nowadays. "Pecs and a cute butt," his friend replied without hesitation. "You can't even turn on the news nowadays without hearing about how some babe thought some guy's butt was cute. Who the first woman to say this was I don't know, but somehow it caught on." Should we tell Rob that it wasn't a woman who started the craze for men's butts?

ROCKS AND LEANERS

We "nouvelles voyeuses" thus owe a big measure of thanks to gay male designers and consumers, and to the aesthetic and erotic overlap—not uniform or total, but significant—in what makes our hearts go thump. But although I've been using the term for convenience, I don't think it's correct to say that these ads depict men as "sex objects." Actually, I find that whole notion misleading, whether applied to men or women, because it seems to suggest that what these representations offer is a body that is inert, depersonalized, flat, a mere thing. In fact, advertisers put a huge amount of time, money, and creativity into figuring out how to create images of beautiful bodies that are heavy on attitude, style, associations with pleasure, success, happiness. The most compelling images are suffused with "subjectivity"—they *speak* to us, they seduce us. Unlike other kinds of "objects" (chairs and tables, for example), they don't let us use them in any way we like. In fact, they exert considerable power over us—over our psyches, our desires, our self-image.

How do male bodies in the ads speak to us nowadays? In a variety of ways. Sometimes the message is challenging, aggressive. Many models stare coldly at the viewer, defying the observer to view them in any way other than how they have chosen to present themselves: as powerful, armored, emotionally impenetrable. "I am a rock," their bodies (and sometimes their genitals) seem to proclaim. Often, as in the Jackson Browne look-alike ad, the penis is prominent, but *unlike* the penis in that ad, its presence is martial rather than sensual. Overall, these ads depict what I would describe as "face-off masculinity,"

Image Courtesy of The Advertising Archives

FIGURE 24.35
Face-off masculinity

in which victory goes to the dominant contestant in a game of will against will. Who can stare the other man down? Who will avert his eyes first? Whose gaze will be triumphant? Such moments—"facing up," "facing off," "staring down"—as anthropologist David Gilmore has documented, are a test of macho in many cultures, including our own.

"Don't eyeball me!" barks the sergeant to his cadets in training in *An Officer and a Gentleman*; the authority of the stare is a prize to be won only with full manhood. Before then, it is a mark of insolence—or stupidity, failure to understand the codes of masculine rank. In *Get Shorty*, an unsuspecting film director challenges a mob boss to look him in the eye; in return, he is hurled across the room and has his fingers broken.

"Face-off" ads, except for their innovations in the amount of skin exposed, are pretty traditional—one might even say primal—in their conception of masculinity. Many other species use staring to establish dominance, and not only our close primate relatives. It's how my Jack Russell terrier intimidates my male collie, who weighs over four times as much as the little guy but cowers under the authority of the terrier's macho stare. In the doggie world, size doesn't matter; it's the power of the gaze—which indicates the power to stand one's ground—that counts. My little terrier's dominance, in other words, is based on a convincing acting job—and it's one that is very similar, according to William Pollack, to the kind of performance that young boys in our culture must learn to master. Pollack's studies of boys suggest that a set of rules—which he calls "The Boy Code"—govern their behavior with each other. The first imperative of the code—"Be a sturdy oak"—represents the emotional equivalent of "face-off masculinity": Never reveal weakness. Pretend to be confident even though you may be scared. Act like a rock even when you feel shaky. Dare others to challenge your position.

The face-off is not the only available posture for male bodies in ads today. Another possibility is what I call "the lean"—because these bodies are almost always reclining, leaning against, or propped up against something in the fashion typical of women's bodies. James Dean was probably our first pop-culture "leaner"; he made it stylish for teenagers to slouch. Dean, however, never posed as languidly or was as openly seductive as some of the high-fashion leaners are today. A recent Calvin Klein "Escape" ad depicts a young, sensuous-looking man leaning against a wall, arm raised, dark underarm hair exposed. His eyes seek out the imagined viewer, soberly but flirtatiously. "*Take Me*," the copy reads.

Languid leaners have actually been around for a long time. Statues of sleeping fauns, their bodies draped languorously, exist in classical art alongside more heroic models of male beauty. I find it interesting, though, that Klein has chosen Mr. Take Me to advertise a perfume called "Escape." Klein's "Eternity" ads usually depict happy, heterosexual couples, often with a child. "Obsession" has always been cutting-edge, sexually ambiguous erotica. This ad, featuring a man offering himself up seductively, invitingly to the observer, promises "escape." From what? *To* what? Men have complained, justly, about the burden of always having to be the sexual initiator, the pursuer, the one of whom sexual "performance" is expected. Perhaps the escape is from these burdens, and toward the freedom to indulge in some of the more receptive pleasures traditionally reserved for women. The pleasures, not of staring someone down but of feeling one's body caressed by another's eyes, of being the one who receives the awaited call rather than the one who must build up the nerve to make the call, the one who

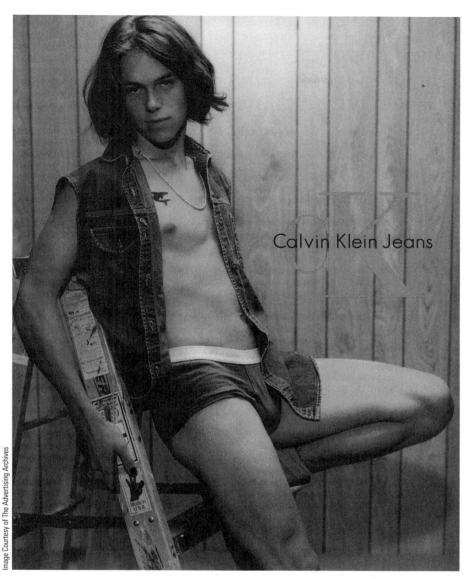

Calvin Klein Jeans

Image Courtesy of The Advertising Archives

FIGURE 24.36
A languid leaner

doesn't have to hump and pump, but is permitted to lie quietly, engrossed in reverie and sensation.

Some people describe these receptive pleasures as "passive"—which gives them a bad press with men, and is just plain inaccurate too. "Passive" hardly describes what's going on when one person offers himself or herself to another. Inviting, receiving, responding—these are active behaviors too, and rather thrilling ones. It's a macho bias to view the only *real* activity as that which takes, invades, aggresses. It's a bias, however, that's been with us for a long time, in both straight and gay cultures. In many Latin cultures, it's not a disgrace to sleep with other men, so long as one is *activo* (or *machista*)—the penetrator rather than the penetratee. To be a *pasivo*, on the other hand, is to be socially stigmatized. It's that way in prison cultures too—a good indication of the power hierarchies involved. These hierarchies date back to the ancient Greeks, who believed that passivity, receptivity, penetrability were marks of inferior feminine being. The qualities were inherent in women; it was our nature to be passively controlled by our sexual needs. (Unlike us, the Greeks viewed women—not men—as the animalistic ones.) Real Men, who unlike women had the necessary rationality and will, were expected to be judicious in the exercise of their desires. But being judicious and being "active"—deciding when to pursue, whom to pursue, making advances, pleading one's case—went hand in hand.

Allowing oneself to be pursued, flirting, accepting the advances of another, offering one's body—these behaviors were permitted also (but only on a temporary basis) to still-developing, younger men. These young men—not little boys, as is sometimes incorrectly believed—were the true "sex objects" of elite Greek culture. Full-fledged male citizens, on the other hand, were expected to be "active," initiators, the penetrators not the penetratees, masters of their own desires rather than the objects of another's. Plato's *Symposium* is full of speeches on the different sexual behaviors appropriate to adult men with full beards and established professions and glamorous young men still revered more for their beauty than their minds. But even youth could not make it okay for a man to behave *too much* like a woman. The admirable youth was the one who—unlike a woman—was able to remain sexually "cool" and remote, to keep his wits about him. "Letting go" was not seemly.

Where does our culture stand today with respect to these ideas about men's sexuality? Well, to begin with, consider how rarely male actors are shown—on their faces, in their utterances, and not merely in the movements of their bodies—having orgasms. In sex scenes, the moanings and writhings of the female partner have become the conventional cinematic code for heterosexual ecstasy and climax. The male's participation is largely represented by caressing hands, humping buttocks, and—on rare occasions—a facial expression of intense concentration. She's transported to another world; he's the pilot of the ship that takes her there. When men are shown being transported themselves, it's usually been played for comedy (as in Al Pacino's shrieks in *Frankie and Johnny*, Eddie Murphy's moanings in *Boomerang*, Kevin Kline's contortions in *A Fish Called Wanda*), or it's coded to suggest that something is not quite normal about the man—he's sexually enslaved, for example (as with Jeremy Irons in *Damage*). Mostly, men's bodies are presented like action-hero toys—wind them up and watch them perform.

Hollywood—still an overwhelmingly straight-male-dominated industry—is clearly not yet ready to show us a man "passively" giving himself over to another, at least not when the actors in question are our cultural icons. Too feminine. Too suggestive, metaphorically speaking, of penetration by another. But perhaps fashion ads are less uptight? I decided to perform an experiment. I grouped ads that I had collected over recent years into a pile of "rocks" and a pile of "leaners" and found, not surprisingly, that both race and age played a role. African-American models, whether in *Esquire* or *Vibe,* are almost always posed facing-off. And leaners tend to be younger than rocks. Both in gay publications and straight ones, the more languid, come-hither poses in advertisements are of boys and very young men. Once a certain maturity line is crossed, the challenging stares, the "face-off" postures are the norm. What does one learn from these ads? Well, I wouldn't want to claim too much. It used to be that one could tell a lot about gender and race from looking at ads. Racial stereotypes were transparent, the established formulas for representing men and women were pretty clear (sociologist Erving Goffman even called ads "gender advertisements"), and when the conventions were defied it was usually because advertisers sensed (or discovered in their polls) that social shifts had made consumers ready to receive new images. In this "post-modern" age, it's more of a free-for-all, and images are often more reactive to each other than to social change. It's the viewers' jaded eye, not their social prejudices, that is the prime consideration of every ad campaign, and advertisers are quick to tap into taboos, to defy expectations, simply in order to produce new and arresting images. So it wouldn't surprise me if we soon find languid black men and hairy-chested leaners in the pages of *Gentlemen's Quarterly.*

But I haven't seen any yet. At the very least, the current scene suggests that even in this era of postmodern pastiche racial clichés and gender taboos persist; among them, we don't want grown men to appear too much the "passive" objects of another's sexual gaze, another's desires. We appear, still, to have somewhat different rules for boys and men. As in ancient Greece, boys are permitted to be seductive, playful, to flirt with being "taken." *Men* must still be in command. Leonardo DiCaprio, watch out. Your days may be numbered.

Things to Do with the Reading

1. This essay exemplifies what Chapter 11 calls "the evolving thesis"—in which a broad opening claim leads the writer to engage evidence that continually reshapes that claim, often in surprising ways. Track the evolving thesis in "Beauty (Re)discovers the Male Body" to help you control the overarching argument, but also to grasp a model of how an evolving thesis can enable a writer to develop her ideas across a range of associations. See if you can make a list of perhaps five sentences that offer the essay's essential claims. Then connect these into a summary of the essay's argument. This exercise could be very helpful as a prelude to more analytical uses of the essay, because writing the summary of claims will enable you to understand and respect the complexity of its argument. Also see Chapter 7 on summary.

2. Link: Write an essay in which you apply Berger's categories *naked* and *nude* to the photos of men in Bordo's article and then consider how and to what extent Bordo is interested in the same binary. Pick any two images in Bordo's article and explain what Berger might see in these images. The treatment of the naked-nude binary is arguably an essential element of similarity and difference between the two writers. See Chapter 2 on Difference within Similarity.

3. **Application:** Look for some kind of depiction of men that is apparently aimed at female viewers, such as pictures of men in women's fashion magazines or in magazines aimed at (mostly female) teenagers. Write an essay in which you examine the assumptions about this female audience suggested by the visual language of your chosen images. How, conceivably, have these assumptions shaped the image?

4. **Link & Application:** John Berger's "Images of Women in European Art" concludes in the final paragraph that

> Women are depicted in a quite different way from men—not because the feminine is different from the masculine—but because the "ideal" spectator is always assumed to be male, and the image of the woman is designed to flatter him.

Berger then invites readers to conduct an "experiment"—to transform the image of traditional female nude into a man and take note of the violence this "transformation does—not to the image, but to the assumptions of a likely viewer." Obviously, Bordo's essay revels in examining just such assumptions. As she notes, "men and women are socially sanctioned to deal with the gaze of the Other in different ways."

Write an essay in which you apply Berger's experiment *in reverse* to Bordo's essay. What is revealed when you take an example of any of the images of men that Bordo examines (or image types, such as the Leaner or the Rock), and you replace it with an image of a woman?

5. **Application:** To what extent does Bordo argue that gender taboos about men appearing as "passive objects of another's sexual gaze" have really changed. Locate images of men (not nudes) in print materials that are local—at your own campus or workplace, for example, or on billboards near where you live. Use these as the basis for a short analytical essay on changing attitudes towards representations of men and masculinity.

Alternatively, do some primary research to see if images of men, clothed or not, in advertising for other kinds of products such as Wall Street, banking, alcohol, cars, etc., display some of the same characteristics that Bordo notices. Your aim here is write a paper in which you try to extend or refine Bordo's analysis, not simply reject it.

6. **Application:** The essay concludes by returning to a subject raised at the beginning: taboos. In the final paragraph Bordo suggests that "advertisers are quick to tap into taboos," and she predicts that ads representing the male body are likely to move increasingly in this direction. Test that prediction by locating a recent ad that taps into a taboo. Write a paper in which you carefully describe and analyze it, keeping its evident audience in mind.

Malcolm Gladwell

Listening to Khakis: What America's Most Popular Pants Tell Us About the Way Guys Think

Named one of the "100 most influential people" by *Time* magazine in 2005, Malcolm Gladwell is the author of many best-selling books on trends, including *The Tipping Point: How Little Things Can Make a Big Difference* (2000), *Blink: The Power of Thinking Without Thinking* (2006), and *Outliers: The Story of Success* (2008). Originally trained as a historian, Gladwell entered journalism as a science writer (for the *Washington Post*) but has become, to use one of the terms that *The Tipping Point* made famous, "a connector" — one who bridges different fields of knowledge. In "Listening to Khakis," which was first published in 1997 in *The New Yorker*, Gladwell explores the success of the ad campaign for Dockers pants, talking with ad designers and social psychologists on the challenges of producing successful fashion advertising for men.

In the fall of 1987, Levi Strauss & Co. began running a series of national television   1
commercials to promote Dockers, its new brand of men's khakis. All the spots—and there were twenty-eight—had the same basic structure. A handheld camera would follow a group of men as they sat around a living room or office or bar. The men were in their late thirties, but it was hard to tell, because the camera caught faces only fleetingly. It was trained instead on the men from the waist down—on the seats of their pants, on the pleats of their khakis, on their hands going in and out of their pockets. As the camera jumped in quick cuts from Docker to Docker, the men chatted in loose, overlapping non sequiturs—guy-talk fragments that, when they are rendered on the page, achieve a certain Dadaist poetry. Here is the entire transcript of "Poolman," one of the first—and, perhaps, best—ads in the series:

"She was a redhead about five foot six inches tall."

"And all of a sudden this thing starts spinning, and it's going round and round."

"Is that Nelson?"

"And that makes me safe, because with my wife, I'll never be that way."

"It's like your career, and you're frustrated. I mean that—that's—what you want."

"Of course, that's just my opinion."

"So money's no object."

"Yeah, money's no object."

"What are we going to do with our lives, now?"

"Well ..."

"Best of all ..."

Malcolm Gladwell, "Listening to Khakis: What America's Most Popular Pants Tell Us About the Way Guys Think," The New Yorker. Reprinted with permission of the author.

[Voice-over] "*Levi's one-hundred-percent-cotton Dockers. If you're not wearing Dockers, you're just wearing pants.*"

"And I'm still paying the loans off."

"You've got all the money in the world."

"I'd like to at least be your poolman."

By the time the campaign was over, at the beginning of the nineties, Dockers had grown into a six-hundred-million-dollar business—a brand that if it had spun off from Levi's would have been (and would still be) the fourth-largest clothing brand in the world. Today, seventy percent of American men between the ages of twenty-five and forty-five own a pair of Dockers, and khakis are expected to be as popular as bluejeans by the beginning of the next century. It is no exaggeration to call the original Dockers ads one of the most successful fashion-advertising campaigns in history.

This is a remarkable fact for a number of reasons, not the least of which is that the Dockers campaign was aimed at men, and no one had ever thought you could hit a home run like that by trying to sell fashion to the American male. Not long ago, two psychologists at York University, in Toronto—Irwin Silverman and Marion Eals—conducted an experiment in which they had men and women sit in an office for two minutes, without any reading material or distraction, while they ostensibly waited to take part in some kind of academic study. Then they were taken from the office and given the real reason for the experiment: to find out how many of the objects in the office they could remember. This was not a test of memory so much as it was a test of awareness—of the kind and quality of unconscious attention that people pay to the particulars of their environment. If you think about it, it was really a test of fashion sense, because, at its root, this is what fashion sense really is—the ability to register and appreciate and *remember* the details of the way those around you look and dress, and then reinterpret those details and memories yourself.

When the results of the experiment were tabulated, it was found that the women were able to recall the name and the placement of seventy percent more objects than the men, which makes perfect sense. Women's fashion, after all, consists of an endless number of subtle combinations and variations—of skirt, dress, pants, blouse, T-shirt, hose, pumps, flats, heels, necklace, bracelet, cleavage, collar, curl, and on and on—all driven by the fact that when a woman walks down the street she knows that other women, consciously or otherwise, will notice the name and the placement of what she is wearing. Fashion works for women because women can appreciate its complexity. But when it comes to men what's the point? How on earth do you sell fashion to someone who has no appreciation for detail whatsoever?

5   The Dockers campaign, however, proved that you could sell fashion to men. But that was only the first of its remarkable implications. The second—which remains as weird and mysterious and relevant to the fashion business today as it was ten years ago—was that you could do this by training a camera on a man's butt and having him talk in yuppie gibberish.

* * *

I watched "Poolman" with three members of the new team handling the Dockers account at Foote, Cone & Belding (F.C.B.), Levi's ad agency. We were in a conference room at Levi's Plaza, in downtown San Francisco, a redbrick building decorated (appropriately enough) in khakilike earth tones, with the team members—Chris Shipman, Iwan Thomis, and Tanyia Kandohla—forming an impromptu critical panel. Shipman, who had thick black glasses and spoke in an almost inaudible laid-back drawl, put a videocassette of the first campaign into a VCR—stopping, starting, and rewinding—as the group analyzed what made the spots so special.

"Remember, this is from 1987," he said, pointing to the screen, as the camera began its jerky dance. "Although this style of filmmaking looks everyday now, that kind of handheld stuff was very fresh when these were made."

"They taped real conversations," Kandohla chimed in. "Then the footage was cut together afterward. They were thrown areas to talk about. It was very natural, not at all scripted. People were encouraged to go off on tangents."

After "Poolman," we watched several of the other spots in the original group—"Scorekeeper" and "Dad's Chair," "Flag Football," and "The Meaning of Life"—and I asked about the headlessness of the commercials, because if you watch too many in a row all those anonymous body parts begin to get annoying. But Thomis maintained that the headlessness was crucial, because it was the absence of faces that gave the dialogue its freedom. "They didn't show anyone's head because if they did the message would have too much weight," he said. "It would be too pretentious. You know, people talking about their hopes and dreams. It seems more genuine, as opposed to something stylized."

The most striking aspect of the spots is how different they are from typical fashion 10 advertising. If you look at men's fashion magazines, for example, at the advertisements for the suits of Ralph Lauren or Valentino or Hugo Boss, they almost always consist of a beautiful man, with something interesting done to his hair, wearing a gorgeous outfit. At the most, the man may be gesturing discreetly, or smiling in the demure way that a man like that might smile after, say, telling the supermodel at the next table no thanks he has to catch an early-morning flight to Milan. But that's all. The beautiful face and the clothes tell the whole story. The Dockers ads, though, are almost exactly the opposite. There's no face. The camera is jumping around so much that it's tough to concentrate on the clothes. And instead of stark simplicity, the fashion image is overlaid with a constant, confusing patter. It's almost as if the Dockers ads weren't primarily concerned with clothes at all—and in fact that's exactly what Levi's intended. What the company had discovered, in its research, was that baby-boomer men felt that the chief thing missing from their lives was male friendship. Caught between the demands of the families that many of them had started in the eighties and career considerations that had grown more onerous, they felt they had lost touch with other men. The purpose of the ads—the chatter, the lounging around, the quick cuts—was simply to conjure up a place where men could put on one-hundred-percent-cotton khakis and reconnect with one another. In the original advertising brief, that imaginary place was dubbed Dockers World.

This may seem like an awfully roundabout way to sell a man a pair of pants. But that was the genius of the campaign. One of the truisms of advertising is that it's always easier to sell at the extremes than in the middle, which is why the advertisements for Valentino and Hugo Boss are so simple. The man in the market for a thousand-dollar suit doesn't need to be convinced of the value of nice clothes. The man in the middle, though—the man in the market for a forty-dollar pair of khakis—does. In fact, he probably isn't comfortable buying clothes at all. To sell him a pair of pants you have to take him somewhere he *is* comfortable, and that was the point of Dockers World. Even the apparent gibberish of lines like "She was a redhead about five foot six inches tall." / "And all of a sudden this thing starts spinning, and it's going round and round."/"Is that Nelson?" have, if you listen closely enough, a certain quintessentially guy-friendly feel. It's the narrative equivalent of the sports-highlight reel—the sequence of five-second film clips of the best plays from the day's basketball or football or baseball games, which millions of American men watch every night on television. This nifty couplet from "Score-keeper," for instance—""Who remembers their actual first girlfriend?'/'I would have done better, but I was bald then, too'"—is not nonsense but a twenty-minute conversation edited down to two lines. A man schooled in the highlight reel no more needs the other nineteen minutes and fifty-eight seconds of that exchange than he needs to see the intervening catch and throw to make sense of a sinking liner to left and a close play at the plate.

"Men connected to the underpinnings of what was being said," Robert Hanson, the vice-president of marketing for Dockers, told me. "These guys were really being honest and genuine and real with each other, and talking about their lives. It may not have been the truth, but it was the fantasy of what a lot of customers wanted, which was not just to be work-focussed but to have the opportunity to express how you feel about your family and friends and lives. The content was very important. The thing that built this brand was that we absolutely nailed the emotional underpinnings of what motivates baby boomers."

Hanson is a tall, striking man in his early thirties. He's what Jeff Bridges would look like if he had gone to finishing school. Hanson said that when he goes out on research trips to the focus groups that Dockers holds around the country he often deliberately stays in the background, because if the men in the group see him "they won't necessarily respond as positively or as openly." When he said this, he was wearing a pair of stone-white Dockers, a deep-blue shirt, a navy blazer, and a brilliant-orange patterned tie, and these worked so well together that it was obvious what he meant. When someone like Hanson dresses up that fabulously in Dockers, he makes it clear just how many variations and combinations are possible with a pair of khakis—but that, of course, defeats the purpose of the carefully crafted Dockers World message, which is to appeal to the man who wants nothing to do with fashion's variations and combinations. It's no coincidence that every man in every one of the group settings profiled in each commercial is wearing—albeit in different shades—*exactly the same kind of pants*. Most fashion advertising sells distinctiveness. (Can you imagine, say, an Ann Taylor commercial where a bunch of thirtyish girlfriends are lounging around chatting, all decked out in matching sweater sets?) Dockers was selling conformity.

"We would never do anything with our pants that would frighten anyone away," Gareth Morris, a senior designer for the brand, told me. "We'd never do too many belt loops, or an unusual base cloth. Our customers like one-hundred-percent-cotton fabrics. We would never do a synthetic. That's definitely in the market, but it's not where we need to be. Styling-wise, we would never do a wide, wide leg. We would never do a peg-legged style. Our customers seem to have a definite idea of what they want. They don't like tricky openings or zips or a lot of pocket flaps and details on the back. We've done button-through flaps, to push it a little bit. But we usually do a welt pocket—that's a pocket with a button-through. It's funny. We have focus groups in New York, Chicago, and San Francisco, and whenever we show them a pocket with a flap—it's a simple thing—they hate it. They won't buy the pants. They complain, "How do I get my wallet?' So we compromise and do a welt. That's as far as they'll go. And there's another thing. They go, "My butt's big enough. I don't want flaps hanging off of it, too.' They like inseam pockets. They like to know where they put their hands." He gestured to the pair of experimental prototype Dockers he was wearing, which had pockets that ran almost parallel to the waistband of the pants. "This is a stretch for us," he said. "If you start putting more stuff on than we have on our product, you're asking for trouble."

The apotheosis of the notion of khakis as nonfashion-guy fashion came several   15 years after the original Dockers campaign, when Haggar Clothing Co. hired the Goodby, Silverstein & Partners ad agency, in San Francisco, to challenge Dockers' khaki dominance. In retrospect, it was an inspired choice since Goodby, Silverstein is Guy Central. It does Porsche ("Kills Bugs Fast") and Isuzu and the recent "Got Milk?" campaign and a big chunk of the Nike business, and it operates out of a gutted turn-of-the-century building downtown, refurbished in what is best described as neo-Erector set. The campaign that it came up with featured voice-overs by Roseanne's television husband, John Goodman. In the best of the ads, entitled "I Am," a thirtyish man wakes up, his hair all mussed, pulls on a pair of white khakis, and half sleepwalks outside to get the paper. "*I am not what I wear. I'm not a pair of pants, or a shirt.*" Goodman intones. The man walks by his wife, handing her the front sections of the paper. "*I'm not in touch with my inner child. I don't read poetry, and I'm not politically correct.*" He heads away from the kitchen, down a hallway, and his kid grabs the comics from him. "*I'm just a guy, and I don't have time to think about what I wear, because I've got a lot of important guy things to do.*" All he has left now is the sports section and, gripping it purposefully, he heads for the bathroom. "*One-hundred-percent-cotton wrinkle-free khaki pants that don't require a lot of thought. Haggar. Stuff you can wear.*"

"We softened it," Richard Silverstein told me as we chatted in his office, perched on chairs in the midst of—among other things—a lacrosse stick, a bike stand, a gym bag full of yesterday's clothing, three toy Porsches, and a giant model of a Second World War Spitfire hanging from the ceiling. "We didn't say "Haggar Apparel' or "Haggar Clothing.' We said, "Hey, listen, guys, don't worry. It's just *stuff*. Don't worry about it.' The concept was "Make it approachable.' " The difference between this and the Dockers ad is humor. F.C.B. assiduously documented men's inner lives. Goodby, Silverstein made fun of them. But it's essentially the same message. It's instructive, in this light, to think about the Casual Friday phenomenon of the past decade, the loosening of corporate dress codes that was spawned by the rise of khakis. Casual Fridays are commonly thought to be about men rejecting the uniform of the suit. But surely that's backward. Men started wearing khakis to work because Dockers and Haggar made it sound as if khakis were going to be even easier than a suit. The khaki-makers realized that men didn't want to get rid of uniforms; they just wanted a better uniform.

The irony, of course, is that this idea of nonfashion—of khakis as the choice that diminishes, rather than enhances, the demands of fashion—turned out to be a white lie. Once you buy even the plainest pair of khakis, you invariably also buy a sports jacket and a belt and a whole series of shirts to go with it—maybe a polo knit for the weekends, something in plaid for casual, and a button-down for a dressier look—and before long your closet is thick with just the kinds of details and options that you thought you were avoiding. You may not add these details as brilliantly or as consciously as say, Hanson does, but you end up doing it nonetheless. In the past seven years, sales of men's clothing in the United States have risen an astonishing twenty-one percent, in large part because of this very fact—that khakis, even as they have simplified the bottom half of the male wardrobe, have forced a steady revision of the top. At the same time, even khakis themselves—within the narrow constraints of khakidom—have quietly expanded their range. When Dockers were launched, in the fall of 1986, there were just three basic styles: the double-pleated Docker in khaki, olive, navy, and black; the Steamer, in cotton canvas; and the more casual flat-fronted Docker. Now there are twenty-four Dockers and Haggar and everyone else has been playing a game of bait and switch: lure men in with the promise of a uniform and then slip them, bit by bit, fashion. Put them in an empty room and then, ever so slowly, so as not to scare them, fill the room with objects.

* * *

There is a puzzle in psychology known as the canned-laughter problem, which has a deeper and more complex set of implications about men and women and fashion and why the dockers ads were so successful. Over the years, several studies have been devoted to this problem, but perhaps the most instructive was done by two psychologists at the University of Wisconsin, Gerald Cupchik and Howard Leventhal. Cupchik and Leventhal took a stack of cartoons (including many from *The New Yorker*), half of which an independent panel had rated as very funny and half of which it had rated as mediocre. They put the cartoons on slides, had a voice-over read the captions, and presented the slide show to groups of men and women. As you might expect, both sexes reacted pretty much the same way. Then Cupchik and Leventhal added a laugh track to the voice-over—the subjects were told that it was actual laughter from people who were in the room during the taping—and repeated the experiment. This time, however, things got strange. The canned laughter made the women laugh a little harder and rate the cartoons as a little funnier than they had before. But not the men. They laughed a bit more at the good cartoons but much more at the bad cartoons. The canned laughter also made them rate the bad cartoons as much funnier than they had rated them before, but it had little or no effect on their ratings of the good cartoons. In fact, the men found a bad cartoon with a laugh track to be almost as funny as a good cartoon without one. What was going on?

The guru of male-female differences in the ad world is Joan Meyers-Levy, a professor at the University of Chicago business school. In a groundbreaking series of articles written over the past decade, Meyers-Levy has explained the canned-laughter problem and other gender anomalies by arguing that men and women use fundamentally different methods of processing information. Given two pieces of evidence about how funny something is—their own opinion and the opinion of others (the laugh track)—the women came up with a higher score than before because they added the two clues together: they integrated the information before them. The men, on the other hand, picked one piece of evidence and ignored the other. For the bad cartoons, they got carried away by the laugh track and gave out hugely generous scores for funniness. For the good cartoons, however, they were so wedded to their own opinion that suddenly the laugh track didn't matter at all.

This idea—that men eliminate and women integrate—is called by Meyers-Levy 20 the "selectivity hypothesis." Men are looking for a way to simplify the route to a conclusion, so they seize on the most obvious evidence and ignore the rest, while women, by contrast, try to process information comprehensively. So-called band-width research, for example, has consistently shown that if you ask a group of people to sort a series of objects or ideas into categories, the men will create fewer and larger categories than the women will. They use bigger mental bandwidths. Why? Because the bigger the bandwidth the less time and attention you have to pay to each indi-vidual object. Or consider what is called the invisibility question. If a woman is being asked a series of personal questions by another woman, she'll say more if she's facing the woman she's talking to than she will if her listener is invisible. With men, it's the opposite. When they can't see the person who's asking them questions, they suddenly and substantially open up. This, of course, is a condition of male communication which has been remarked on by women for millennia. But the selectivity hypothesis suggests that the cause of it has been misdiagnosed. It's not that men necessarily have trouble expressing their feelings; it's that in a face-to-face conversation they experi-ence emotional overload. A man can't process nonverbal information (the expression and body language of the person asking him questions) and verbal information (the personal question being asked) at the same time any better than he can process other people's laughter and his own laughter at the same time. He has to select, and it is Meyers-Levy's contention that this pattern of behavior suggests significant differences in the way men and women respond to advertising.

Joan Meyers-Levy is a petite woman in her late thirties, with a dark pageboy haircut and a soft voice. She met me in the downtown office of the University of Chicago with three large folders full of magazine advertisements under one arm, and after chatting about the origins and the implications of her research she handed me an ad from sev-eral years ago for Evian bottled water. It has a beautiful picture of the French Alps and, below that, in large type, "Our factory." The text ran for several paragraphs, beginning:

> You're not just looking at the French Alps. You're looking at one of the most pristine places on earth. And the origin of Evian Natural Spring Water.
>
> Here, it takes no less than 15 years for nature to purify every drop of Evian as it flows through mineral-rich glacial formations deep within the mountains. And it is here that Evian acquires its unique balance of minerals.

"Now, is that a male or a female ad?" she asked. I looked at it again. The picture baffled me. But the word "factory" seemed masculine, so I guessed male.

She shook her head. "It's female. Look at the picture. It's just the Alps, and then they label it "Our factory." They're using a metaphor. To understand this, you're going to have to engage in a fair amount of processing. And look at all the imagery they're encouraging you to build up. You're not just looking at the French Alps. It's "one of the most pristine places on earth' and it will take nature "no less than fifteen years' to purify." Her point was that this is an ad that works only if the viewer appreciates all its elements—if the viewer integrates, not selects. A man, for example, glancing at the ad for a fraction of a second, might focus only on the words "Our factory" and screen out the picture of the Alps entirely, the same way he might have screened out the canned laughter. Then he wouldn't get the visual metaphor. In fact, he might end up equating Evian with a factory, and that would be a disaster. Anyway, why bother going into such detail about the glaciers if it's just going to get lost in the big male bandwidth?

Meyers-Levy handed me another Evian advertisement. It showed a man—the Olympic Gold Medal swimmer Matt Biondi—by a pool drinking Evian, with the caption "Revival of the fittest." The women's ad had a hundred and nineteen words of text. This ad had just twenty-nine words: "No other water has the unique, natural balance of minerals that Evian achieves during its 15-year journey deep within the French Alps. To be the best takes time." Needless to say, it came from a men's magazine. "With men, you don't want the fluff," she said. "Women, though, participate a lot more in whatever they are processing. By giving them more cues, you give them something to work with. You don't have to be so literal. With women you can be more allusive, so you can draw them in. They will engage in elaboration, and the more associations they make the easier it is to remember and retrieve later on."

25   Meyers-Levy took a third ad from her pile, this one for the 1997 Mercury Mountaineer four-wheel-drive sport-utility vehicle. It covers two pages, has the heading "Take the Rough with the Smooth," and shows four pictures—one of the vehicle itself, one of a mother and her child, one of a city skyline, and a large one of the interior of the car, over which the ad's text is superimposed. Around the border of the ad are forty-four separate, tiny photographs of roadways and buildings and construction sites and manhole covers. *Female.* Next to it on the table she put another ad—this one a single page, with a picture of the Mountaineer's interior, fifteen lines of text, a picture of the car's exterior, and, at the top, the heading: "When the Going Gets Tough, the Tough Get Comfortable." *Male.* "It's details, details. They're saying lots of different stuff," she said, pointing to the female version. "With men, instead of trying to cover everything in a single execution, you'd probably want to have a whole series of ads, each making a different point."

After a while, the game got very easy—if a bit humiliating. Meyers-Levy said that her observations were not anti-male—that both the male and the female strategies have their strengths and their weaknesses—and, of course, she's right. On the other hand, reading the gender of ads makes it painfully obvious how much the advertising world—consciously or not—talks down to men. Before I met Meyers-Levy, I thought that the genius of the famous first set of Dockers ads was their psychological complexity, their ability to capture the many layers of eighties guyness. But when I thought about them again after meeting Meyers-Levy, I began to think that their real genius lay in their heroic simplicity—in the fact that F.C.B. had the self-discipline to fill the allotted thirty seconds with as *little* as possible. Why no heads? The invisibility rule. Guys would never listen to that Dadaist extemporizing if they had to process nonverbal cues, too. Why were the ads set in people's living rooms *and* at the office? Bandwidth. The message was that khakis were wide-bandwidth pants. And why were all the ads shot in almost exactly the same way, and why did all the dialogue run together in one genial, faux-philosophical stretch of highlight reel? Because of canned laughter. Because if there were more than one message to be extracted men would get confused.

* * *

In the early nineties, Dockers began to falter. In 1992, the company sold sixty-six million pairs of khakis, but in 1993, as competition from Haggar and the Gap and other brands grew fiercer, that number slipped to fifty-nine million six hundred thousand, and by 1994 it had fallen to forty-seven million. In marketing-speak, user reality was encroaching on brand personality; that is, Dockers were being defined by the kind of middle-aged men who wore them, and not by the hipper, younger men in the original advertisements. The brand needed a fresh image, and the result was the "Nice Pants" campaign currently being shown on national television—a campaign widely credited with the resurgence of Dockers' fortunes.

In one of the spots, "Vive la France," a scruffy young man in his early twenties, wearing Dockers, is sitting in a café in Paris. He's obviously a tourist. He glances up and sees a beautiful woman (actually, the supermodel Tatjana Patitz) looking right at him. He's in heaven. She starts walking directly toward him, and as she passes by she says, "*Beau pantalon.*" As he looks frantically through his French phrase book for a translation, the waiter comes by and cuffs him on the head: "Hey, she says, "Nice pants.' " Another spot in the series, "Subway Love," takes place on a subway car in Chicago. He (a nice young man wearing Dockers) spots her (a total babe), and their eyes lock. Romantic music swells. He moves toward her, but somehow, in a sudden burst of pushing and shoving, they get separated. Last shot: she's inside the car, her face pushed up against the glass. He's outside the car, his face pushed up against the glass. As the train slowly pulls away, she mouths two words: "Nice pants."

It may not seem like it, but "Nice Pants" is as radical a campaign as the original Dockers series. If you look back at the way that Sansabelt pants, say, were sold in the sixties, each ad was what advertisers would call a pure "head" message: the pants were comfortable, durable, good value. The genius of the first Dockers campaign was the way it combined head and heart: these were all-purpose, no-nonsense pants that connected to the emotional needs of baby boomers. What happened to Dockers in the nineties, though, was that everyone started to do head and heart for khakis. Haggar pants were wrinkle-free (head) and John Goodman-guy (heart). The Gap, with its brilliant billboard campaign of the early nineties—"James Dean wore khakis," "Frank Lloyd Wright wore khakis"—perfected the heart message by forging an emotional connection between khakis and a particular nostalgic, glamorous all-Americanness. To reassert itself, Dockers needed to go an extra step. Hence "Nice Pants," a campaign that for the first time in Dockers history raises the subject of sex.

"It's always been acceptable for a man to be a success in business," Hanson said, 30 explaining the rationale behind "Nice Pants." "It's always been expected of a man to be a good provider. The new thing that men are dealing with is that it's O.K. for men to have a sense of personal style, and that it's O.K. to be seen as sexy. It's less about the head than about the combination of the head, the heart, and the groin. It's those three things. That's the complete man."

The radical part about this, about adding the groin to the list, is that almost no other subject for men is as perilous as the issue of sexuality and fashion. What "Nice Pants" had to do was talk about sex the same way that "Poolman" talked about fashion, which was to talk about it by not talking about it—or, at least, to talk about it in such a coded, cautious way that no man would ever think Dockers was suggesting that he wear khakis in order to look *pretty*. When I took a videotape of the "Nice Pants" campaign to several of the top agencies in New York and Los Angeles, virtually everyone agreed that the spots were superb, meaning that somehow F.C.B. had managed to pull off this balancing act.

What David Altschiller, at Hill, Holiday/Altschiller, in Manhattan, liked about the spots, for example, was that the hero was naïve: in neither case did he know that he had on nice pants until a gorgeous woman told him so. Naïveté, Altschiller stressed, is critical. Several years ago, he did a spot for Claiborne for Men cologne in which a great-looking guy in a bar, wearing a gorgeous suit, was obsessing neurotically about a beautiful woman at the other end of the room: "*I see this woman. She's perfect. She's looking at me. She's smiling. But wait. Is she smiling at me? Or laughing at me? … Or looking at someone else?*" You'd never do this in an ad for women's cologne. Can you imagine? "I see this guy. He's perfect. Ohmigod. Is he looking at me?" In women's advertising, self-confidence is sexy. But if a man is self-confident—if he knows he is attractive and is beautifully dressed—then he's not a man anymore. He's a fop. He's effeminate. The cologne guy had to be neurotic or the ad wouldn't work. "Men are still abashed about acknowledging that clothing is important," Altschiller said. "Fashion can't be important to me as a man. Even when, in the first commercial, the waiter says "Nice pants," it doesn't compute to the guy wearing the nice pants. He's thinking. What do you mean, "Nice pants'?" Altschiller was looking at a videotape of the Dockers ad as he talked—standing at a forty-five-degree angle to the screen, with one hand on the top of the monitor, one hand on his hip, and a small, bemused smile on his lips. "The world may think they are nice, but so long as he doesn't think so he doesn't have to be self-conscious about it, and the lack of self-consciousness is very important to men. Because "*I don't care.*' Or "Maybe I care, but I can't be *seen* to care.' " For the same reason, Altschiller liked the relative understatement of the phrase "nice pants," as opposed to something like "great pants," since somewhere between "nice" and "great" a guy goes from just happening to look good to the unacceptable position of actually trying to look good. "In focus groups, men said that to be told you had "nice pants' was one of the highest compliments a man could wish for, "Tanyia Kandohla told me later, when I asked about the slogan. "They wouldn't want more attention drawn to them than that."

In many ways, the "Nice Pants" campaign is a direct descendant of the hugely successful campaign that Rubin-Postaer & Associates, in Santa Monica, did for Bugle Boy Jeans in the early nineties. In the most famous of those spots, the camera opens on an attractive but slightly goofy-looking man in a pair of jeans who is hitchhiking by the side of a desert highway. Then a black Ferrari with a fabulous babe at the wheel drives by, stops, and backs up. The babe rolls down the window and says, "Excuse me. Are those Bugle Boy Jeans that you're wearing?" The goofy guy leans over and pokes his head in the window, a surprised half smile on his face: "Why, yes, they *are* Bugle Boy Jeans."

"Thank you," the babe says, and she rolls up the window and drives away.

35   This is really the same ad as "Nice Pants"—the babe, the naïve hero, the punch line. The two ads have something else in common. In the Bugle Boy spot, the hero wasn't some stunning male model. "I think he was actually a boxboy at Vons in Huntington

Beach," Larry Postaer, the creative director of Rubin-Postaer & Associates, told me. "I guess someone"—at Bugle Boy—"liked him." He's O.K.-looking, but not nearly in the same class as the babe in the Ferrari. In "Subway Love," by the same token, the Dockers man is medium-sized, almost small, and gets pushed around by much tougher people in the tussle on the train. He's cute, but he's a little bit of a wimp. Kandohla says that F.C.B. tried very hard to find someone with that look—someone who was, in her words, "aspirational real," not some "buff, muscle-bound jock." In a fashion ad for women, you can use Claudia Schiffer to sell a cheap pair of pants. But not in a fashion ad for men. The guy has to be *believable.* "A woman cannot be too gorgeous," Postaer explained. A man, however, can be too gorgeous, because then he's not a man anymore. It's pretty rudimentary. Yet there are people who don't buy that, and have gorgeous men in their ads. I don't get it. Talk to Barneys about how well that's working. It couldn't stay in business trying to sell that high-end swagger to a mass market. The general public wouldn't accept it. Look at beer commercials. They always have these gorgeous girls—even now, after all the heat—and the guys are always just guys. That's the way it is. We only reflect what's happening out there, we're not creating it. Those guys who run the real high-end fashion ads—they don't understand that. They're trying to remold how people think about gender. I can't explain it, though I have my theories. It's like a Grecian ideal. But you can't be successful at advertising by trying to re-create the human condition. You can't alter men's minds, particularly on subjects like sexuality. It'll never happen."

Postaer is a gruff, rangy guy, with a Midwestern accent and a gravelly voice, who did Budweiser commercials in Chicago before moving West fifteen years ago. When he wasn't making fun of the pretentious style of East Coast fashion advertising, he was making fun of the pretentious questions of East Coast writers. When, for example, I earnestly asked him to explain the logic behind having the goofy guy screw up his face in such a—well, goofy—way when he says, "Why, yes, they *are* Bugle Boy Jeans," Postaer took his tennis shoes off his desk, leaned forward bemusedly in his chair, and looked at me as if my head came to a small point. "Because that's the only way he could say it," he said. "I suppose we might have had him say it a little differently if he could actually *act.*"

Incredibly, Postaer said, the people at Bugle Boy wanted the babe to invite the goofy guy into the car, despite the fact that this would have violated the most important rule that governs this new style of groin messages in men's-fashion advertising, which is that the guy absolutely cannot ever get the girl. It's not just that if he got the girl the joke wouldn't work anymore; it's that if he got the girl it might look as if he had deliberately dressed to get the girl, and although at the back of every man's mind as he's dressing in the morning there is the thought of getting the girl, any open admission that that's what he's actually trying to do would undermine the whole unself-conscious, antifashion statement that men's advertising is about. If Tatjana Patitz were to say *"Beau garçon"* to the guy in "Vive la France," or the babe on the subway were to give the wimp her number, Dockers would suddenly become terrifyingly conspicuous—the long-pants equivalent of wearing a tight little Speedo to the beach. And if the Vons boxboy should actually get a ride from the Ferrari babe, the ad would suddenly become believable only to that thin stratum of manhood which thinks that women in Ferraris find twenty-four-dollar jeans irresistible. "We fought that tooth and nail," Postaer said. "And it more or less cost us the account, even though the ad was wildly successful." He put his tennis shoes back up on the desk. "But that's what makes this business fun—trying to prove to clients how wrong they are."

* * *

The one ad in the "Nice Pants" campaign which isn't like the Bugle Boy spots is called "Motorcycle." In it a nice young man happens upon a gleaming Harley on a dark back street of what looks like downtown Manhattan. He strokes the seat and then, unable to contain himself, climbs aboard the bike and bounces up and down, showing off his Dockers (the "product shot") but accidentally breaking a mirror on the handlebar. He looks up. The Harley's owner—a huge, leather-clad biker—is looking down at him. The biker glowers, looking him up and down, and says, "Nice pants." Last shot: the biker rides away, leaving the guy standing on the sidewalk in just his underwear.

What's surprising about this ad is that, unlike "Vive la France" and "Subway Love," it *does* seem to cross the boundaries of acceptable sex talk. The rules of guy advertising so carefully observed in those spots—the fact that the hero has to be naïve, that he can't be too good-looking, that he can't get the girl, and that he can't be told anything stronger than. "Nice pants"—are all, in some sense, reactions to the male fear of appearing too concerned with fashion, of being too pretty, of not being masculine. But what is "Motorcycle"? It's an ad about a sweet-looking guy down in the Village somewhere who loses his pants to a butch-looking biker in leather. "I got so much feedback at the time of "Well, God, that's kind of *gay,* don't you think?'" Robert Hanson said. "People were saying, "This buff guy comes along and he rides off with the guy's pants. I mean, what the hell were they doing?' It came from so many different people within the industry. It came from some of our most conservative retailers. But do you know what? If you put these three spots up—"Vive La France,' "Subway Love,' and "Motorcycle'—which one do you think men will talk about ad nauseam? "Motorcycle.' It's No. 1. It's because he's really cool. He's in a really cool environment, and it's every guy's fantasy to have a really cool, tricked-out fancy motorcycle."

40   Hanson paused, as if he recognized that what he was saying was quite sensitive. He didn't want to say that men failed to pick up the gay implications of the ad because they're stupid, because they aren't stupid. And he didn't want to sound condescending, because Dockers didn't build a six-hundred-million-dollar business in five years by sounding condescending. All he was trying to do was point out the fundamental exegetical error in calling this a gay ad, because the only way for a Dockers man to be offended by "Motorcycle" would be if he thought about it with a little imagination, if he picked up on some fairly subtle cues, if he integrated an awful lot of detail. In other words, a Dockers man could only be offended if he did precisely what, according to Meyers-Levy, men don't do. It's not a gay ad because it's a guy ad. "The fact is," Hanson said, "that most men's interpretation of that spot is: You know what? Those pants must be really cool, because they prevented him from getting the shit kicked out of him."

Things to Do with the Reading

1. Link: This essay is interesting in the context of Bordo's essay because it analyzes the ways Docker ads seek to negotiate taboos among men about how they are represented. Write an essay in which you first look for common ground between Bordo's essay and Gladwell's. Where, in the analysis of which images, are Bordo's and Gladwell's perspectives on the representation of men most similar? Where do they differ most? How might you account for the differences? (See Chapter 4, "Looking for Difference within Similarity".)

2. What reasons does the essay offer for the differences between men and women in the two experiments it describes—one testing men's and women's ability to remember detail and the other testing the response of men versus women to canned laughter when assessing the humor of cartoons? Write an essay in which you first explain the use Gladwell makes of these experiments in his analysis of men's versus women's response to advertising. Then locate some print ads in magazines, and answer the question that Joan Meyers-Levy repeatedly poses to Gladwell: "Is that a male or a female ad?"

   Gladwell concludes his analysis of male-oriented fashion advertising campaigns not with summary but with a final and culminating example. Inclusion of the word "integrating" makes the link with a binary (selective versus integrating) that advertisers consider when designing ads for either gender. Begin an essay by explaining how Gladwell's final paragraph (about response to the "Motorcycle" commercial) ties together and culminates the essay's main ideas. According to the essay, why was the ad successful with male viewers?

   Then further develop your essay by comparing and contrasting two current commercials of your choice—one that you think operates in the way Gladwell defines, and another like the motorcycle ad that you think crosses the boundaries of "guy-ad" acceptability.

3. Link: Throughout this book we have argued that interpretation always takes place inside particular interpretive contexts and that more than one plausible interpretive context may apply to the same data (see Chapter 6.) Compare the conclusions Gladwell arrives at about headlessness in the early Dockers ad campaign with the conclusions that Berger might arrive at about the same feature. Berger, in his essay on the nude in European art, theorizes that the image of the female nude in European paintings was designed to flatter a presumed male viewer. He argues that as a result of this tradition women come to see themselves in a divided way—as both spectacle and spectator. Use this interpretive context to write an essay in which you offer an alternative explanation of headlessness in the early Docker ads and of the importance of guy fashion being represented as "non-fashion." What might Berger say to the claim from Gladwell's essay that "A woman cannot be too gorgeous. A man, however, can be too gorgeous, because then he's not a man anymore" (paragraph 35)?

4. **Application:** Gladwell's analysis offers interesting ideas about ad design— about how ad makers act on theories about gender and perception ("processing") in order to target male or female audiences. Do your own primary research with advertisements in order to illustrate, test, and possibly extend Gladwell's analysis. Look for ads for the same product or kind of product in magazines (mainstream) aimed primarily at women and in magazines aimed primarily at men. Write an essay in which you locate what seem to you to be significant differences and then determine the extent to which the "selectivity" and "integration" hypotheses presented in Gladwell's essay could account for the differences.

   Alternatively, write an essay in which you test one of the following assertions by surveying current fashion ads aimed at men: (1) "Most fashion advertising sells distinctness. ... Dockers was selling conformity" (paragraph 13). (2) "What 'Nice Pants' had to do was talk about sex the same way that 'Poolman' talked about fashion, which was to talk about it by not talking about it ..." (paragraph 31).

Kera Bolonik

Oy Gay!

In this piece Kera Bolonik, a freelance writer for *New York Magazine*, Salon. com, and many other publications, uses a review of the TV sitcom *Will & Grace* to anchor a cultural analysis of the representation of Jews and gays on television. Along the way she manages to survey the formulaic "neurotic Levites and their sane-to-a-fault bemused Protestant spouses" — a formula she praises *Will & Grace* for challenging.

Without baring flesh, exchanging fluids or even shedding blood, *Will & Grace* has become the craftiest, if not the most radical, show in the history of network television—though not merely for its unabashed depiction of gay existence, or the risqué, multi-entendre-filled dialogue its writers slyly sneak under the censors' radar.   1

Will & Grace is revolutionary for something so utterly conventional it would warm the hearts of *bubbes* and *zeydes* across America's urban landscapes: sliding a portrait of a twenty-first-century Jewish American's life into a sitcom about a gay man and his best gal pal. Who in America would want to watch a show explicitly about a Jewish woman living in New York? Sounds like *Rhoda Redux*. But pair a single woman with a gay man and suddenly, you've got a winning formula.

Actually, it's downright brilliant. There hasn't been a program this overtly Jewish since *The Goldbergs,* a popular show from 1949 to 1955 that depicted the travails of a hard-working Jewish family of Bronx tenement-dwellers. For starters, the show's name is taken from the "I-Thou" treatise by twentieth-century Jewish philosopher Martin Buber, which described the ongoing dialogue between man and God. And *Will & Grace* is the first prime-time sitcom *ever* to feature a wedding between a Jewish woman and a Jewish man. When American viewers watched the nuptials between interior decorator Grace Adler (Debra Messing) and Southern Jewish doctor Marvin "Leo" Markus (Harry Connick Jr.) last year, they were bearing witness to more than just a sweeps ploy. Those "I do's" doubled as "I don'ts" to decades' worth of assimilationist portrayals of Jews. Two simple words in that context spoke volumes: More than upholding an age-old tradition that would make parents *kvell,* they communicated to Middle America that a Jewish main character does not need a gentile foil to validate his or her presence on television.

It could've been so easy for the redheaded Manhattan transplant from Schenectady to live out her boob-tube destiny in sexless wedded bliss with her *goyishe* gay best friend, Will Truman (Eric McCormack). They're symbiotic, they love and respect each other, they share man problems and they even considered having a baby together. But co-creators Max Mutchnick and David Kohan decided to thumb their collective nose at television's love affair with interfaith marriage—which, by the way, is *so* 1990s—and delivered Grace a Hebraic knight on a white horse in Central Park just as she was en route to the obstetrician's office to be inseminated with Will's sperm. A few short months later, there stood bride and groom under a *chuppah* amid a sea of white *kippot* for the entire nation to behold.

Reprinted with permission from the November 17, 2003 issue of The Nation. For subscription information, call 1-800-333-8536. Portions of each week's Nation magazine can be accessed at http://www.thenation.com.

5   Until Leo galloped into Grace's life that fateful afternoon, couch potatoes had been barraged with neurotic Levites and their sane-to-a-fault, bemused Protestant spouses for more than ten years. There was nice Jewish boy Paul Buchman and his wispy WASP wife, Jamie Stemple, on *Mad About You;* nasal nanny Fran Fine, the Barbra Streisand-loving borough girl, and her haughty English boss, Maxwell Sheffield, on *The Nanny;* and hippie-dippy Dharma Finkelstein and her buttoned-up blue-blooded hubby, Greg Montgomery, in *Dharma & Greg.* On *Friends,* Ross and Monica Geller are the children of a couple who married outside the faith, and both brother and sister follow suit (Ross does so again and again.). Jerry never married on *Seinfeld,* but neither did he date Jewish women in a city that boasts a surplus of eligible *madelach.* And to think, back in 1972 Jews and Catholics protested the Meredith Baxter and David Birney comic vehicle *Bridget Loves Bernie* for its depiction of a marriage between an Irish Catholic woman and a Jewish man (it was subsequently canceled). This is what you call progress?

Apparently, it *was* a step up. Before the 1990s, the Jew was relegated to a secondary character, at best—Juan Epstein (*Welcome Back, Kotter*), Natalie Green (*The Facts of Life*), Abner and Gladys Kravitz (*Bewitched*), Alex Rieger (*Taxi*)—if their Jewishness was even explicitly articulated. They were the nosy neighbors, the class clowns, the voice of reason and the best friends, and were frequently asexual or spectacular failures in the love department. Rhoda Morgenstern was a rare case, her popularity as a sidekick allowing her to spin off from *The Mary Tyler Moore Show* in 1974 to have her very own sitcom.

Still, a Jew cast as a sitcom lead was usually stuck playing the quirky partner of a straitlaced gentile, the fact of a character's Judaism almost always serving as shorthand for "neurotic," "funny" or "eccentric." (Perhaps the sole, and remarkable, exception is the case of *Seinfeld,* where the show's namesake was both the Jew and the straight man, while his "non-Jewish" friends were the oddballs.) Yet even as Jews vacated the minor-character role, another group was waiting to be typecast. Gays and lesbians (and the occasional transgendered person) turned up all over the tube: Roseanne's gay boss Leon in *Roseanne;* bed-and-breakfast owners Ron and Erick in *Northern Exposure;* Paul's lesbian sister Debbie in *Mad About You;* Ross's lesbian ex-wife Carol on *Friends,* to name just a few.

Will & Grace is the antidote to this long legacy of marginalizing and stereotyping of Jews and gays. Grace Adler and Will Truman are *both* nutty—the two are as competitive as they are insecure and self-deprecating—and enjoy their vanity as much as they do their geeky qualities (Will has a penchant for puns, Grace loves to sing badly). Yet neither Will nor Grace has anything on secondary characters like Jack McFarland (Sean Hayes), a manic Himbo with huge theatrical aspirations, pop-celebrity obsessions and delusions of grandeur, who recognizes little outside his microcosmic world of bad cabaret and gym bunnies; and Grace's gin-soaked assistant, Karen Walker (Megan Mullally), a rich bitch who knows the boldfaced names in all the New York society pages, but most days can barely remember her own. These two, along with Karen's devoted, acid-tongued maid, Rosario Salazar (Shelley Morrison), set the comedy in motion with their outrageous dysfunctions and interactions as Karen and Jack affectionately grope each other, "charge themselves some happy" at Barney's and Hermes, prank-call Marlo Thomas and torture Karen's fleet of servants.

All four friends, plus the deadpan Rosario, are fluent in queerspeak, trading bawdy quips, wicked in-jokes and pop-cultural references. But only the Upper West Side-dwelling

Will understands Grace's self-referential humor, which is largely shaped by her Jewish experience. She dubs Will "Uncle Hachel" when he's being a jerk, drops casual mentions of her summers at Camp Ramah and has been known to intone a self-pitying prayer "*Borchu et adonai*, I'm gonna die alone." Jack and Karen would seem to have encountered only one Jew in their life—Grace—so they are often puzzled by her comical asides. But Grace does not become the butt of the joke; rather, we laugh at Karen and Jack for their ignorance about things Jewish. These two *über*-gentiles are the eccentrics for a change.

It would be so simple for Mutchnick and Kohan to posit the "straight" pair against 10 the wacky duo. But there is one crucial difference between Will and Grace—one steeped in cultural mores—that threatens to propel one forward in life and leave the other behind. Will cleaves to his WASP reserve out of fear, preferring denial and decorum to confrontation, which can prove paralytic for him. He is out to his parents, for example, but can't bring himself to acknowledge his father's infidelities, even as he meets the mistress. Grace is the product of a theatrical Jewish mother who knows no bounds (or boundaries), and if it isn't confidence that allows it, she at least has the chutzpah to take leaps of faith.

Last year's season finale of *Will & Grace* intimated that the honeymoon between the newlywed Markuses might have been drawing to a close, though the new season shows the couple negotiating their new life together. But the survival of Grace's marriage hardly even matters. The fact that she did it at all demonstrated to her gang that she was ready to reconfigure her friendship with Will so that she could pursue sexual and emotional fulfillment through a marriage built on romance. More so, it conveyed to millions of viewers that, as *Will & Grace* blazes trails by offering fully realized, nonstereotypical gay characters, it is simultaneously an extremely entertaining sitcom about a Jewish gal from Schenectady who is as American as (the Big) Apple Pie.

Things to Do with the Reading

1. Write an essay in which you explain Bolonik's analysis of how the television show *Will & Grace* presses viewers to revise—to re-see—stereotypes about Jews and gays. Because Will and Grace seem often to behave in ways that confirm gay and Jewish stereotypes, what, according to Bolonik, did the show do in order to invite viewers to see these characters differently?

2. **Application:** Bolonik's review makes repeated reference to the language of stereotypes—both "queerspeak" and the occasional Hebrew phrase and summer camp allusion—and locates these astutely in the context of audience reception for a network sitcom. Indeed, references to other sitcoms that situate ethnic and gendered stereotypes are scattered throughout the piece. We get very little, however, about how *Will & Grace* offers *visual representation* of these groups. Write an essay in which you track the imaging of members of both mainstream and outlier groups in any other television sitcom, with the aim of analyzing how the show predisposes us to see. What are the primary elements of its visual vocabulary? So what that it invites us to see as it does?

X.J. Kennedy

Who Killed King Kong?

This essay, originally published in *Dissent* in Spring 1960, offers an analysis of the causes for the continued popularity of the original 1933 film of *King Kong* with various audiences, including African Americans. Other readings in this chapter have focused on ways that cultural forces shape the way we see. In this final reading of the chapter, we end with Kennedy's lively evocation of some of the most famous visual moments in American film history—King Kong tossing subway cars filled with commuters, King Kong carrying a small screaming blonde woman across the tops of buildings, King Kong swatting the small air planes seeking to knock him off his refuge at the top of the Empire State building. In a final twist on this chapter's scrutiny of "Seeing," Kennedy's review invites readers to consider how images connect with and shape the self-image of their viewers. It is provocative to see the context in which the poet and essayist X.J. Kennedy published his views of the reception of *King Kong* in 1960 in a leftist journal. And it is similarly provocative now to compare that reading to the ones that might be produced post 9/11 about a destructive force unleashed in New York City.

1   The ordeal and spectacular death of King Kong, the giant ape, undoubtedly have been witnessed by more Americans than have ever seen a performance of *Hamlet, Iphigenia at Aulis,* or even *Tobacco Road.* Since RKO-Radio Pictures first released *King Kong,* a quarter-century has gone by; yet year after year, from prints that grow more rain-beaten, from sound tracks that grow more tinny ticket-buyers by thousands still pursue Kong's luckless fight against the forces of technology, tabloid journalism, and the DAR. They see him chloroformed to sleep, see him whisked from his jungle isle to New York and placed on show, see him burst his chains to roam the city (lugging a frightened blonde), at last to plunge from the spire of the Empire State Building, machine-gunned by model airplanes.

Though Kong may die, one begins to think his legend unkillable. No clearer proof of his hold upon the popular imagination may be seen than what emerged one catastrophic week in March 1955, when New York WOR-TV programmed *Kong* for seven evenings in a row (a total of sixteen showings). Many a rival network vice-president must have scowled when surveys showed that *Kong*—the 1933 B-picture—had lured away fat segments of the viewing populace from such powerful competitors as Ed Sullivan, Groucho Marx and Bishop Sheen.

But even television has failed to run *King Kong* into oblivion. Coffee-in-the-lobby cinemas still show the old hunk of hokum, with the apology that in its use of composite shots and animated models the film remains technically interesting. And no other monster in movie history has won so devoted a popular audience. None of the plodding mummies, the stultified draculas, the white-coated Lugosis[1] with their shiny pinball-machine laboratories, none of the invisible stranglers, berserk robots, or menaces from Mars has ever enjoyed so many resurrections.

Who Killed King Kong? X.J. Kennedy. Originally published in Dissent Magazine in 1961. Reprinted with permission of the author.

Why does the American public refuse to let King Kong rest in peace? It is true, I'll admit, that *Kong* outdid every monster movie before or since in sheer carnage. Producers Cooper and Schoedsack crammed into it dinosaurs, headhunters, riots, aerial battles, bullets, bombs, bloodletting. Heroine Fay Wray, whose function is mainly to scream, shuts her mouth for hardly one uninterrupted minute from first reel to last. It is also true that *Kong* is larded with good healthy sadism, for those whose joy it is to see the frantic girl dangled from cliffs and harried by pterodactyls. But it seems to me that the abiding appeal of the giant ape rests on other foundations.

Kong has, first of all, the attraction of being manlike. His simian nature gives   5 him one huge advantage over giant ants and walking vegetables in that an audience may conceivably identify with him. Kong's appeal has the quality that established the Tarzan series as American myth—for what man doesn't secretly image himself a huge hairy howler against whom no other monster has a chance? If Tarzan recalls the ape in us, then Kong may well appeal to that great-granddaddy primordial brute from whose tribe we have all deteriorated.

Intentionally or not, the producers of *King Kong* encourage this identification by etching the character of Kong with keen sympathy. For the ape is a figure in a tradition familiar to moviegoers: the tradition of the pitiable monster. We think of Lon Chaney in the role of Quasimodo, of Karloff in the original *Frankenstein*. As we watch the Frankenstein monster's fumbling and disastrous attempts to befriend a flower-picking child, our sympathies are enlisted with the monster in his impenetrable loneliness. And so with Kong. As he roars in his chains, while barkers sell tickets to boobs who gape at him, we perhaps feel something more deep than pathos. We begin to sense something of the problem that engaged Eugene O'Neill in *The Hairy Ape*: the dilemma of a displaced animal spirit forced to live in a jungle built by machines.

King Kong, it is true, had special relevance in 1933. Landscapes of the depression are glimpsed early in the film when an impresario, seeking some desperate pretty girl to play the lead in a jungle movie, visits souplines and a Woman's Home Mission. In Fay Wray—who's been caught snitching an apple from a fruitstand—his search is ended. When he gives her a big feed and a movie contract, the girl is magic-carpeted out of the world of the National Recovery Act. And when, in the film's climax, Kong smashes that very Third Avenue landscape in which Fay had wandered hungry, audiences of 1933 may well have felt a personal satisfaction.

What is curious is that audiences of 1960 remain hooked. For in the heart of urban man, one suspects, lurks the impulse to fling a bomb. Though machines speed him to the scene of his daily grind, though IBM comptometers ("freeing the human mind from drudgery") enable him to drudge more efficiently once he arrives, there comes a moment when he wishes to turn upon his machines and kick hell out of them. He wants to hurl his combination radio-alarmclock out the bedroom window and listen to its smash. What subway commuter wouldn't love—just for once—to see the downtown express smack head-on into the uptown local? Such a wish is gratified in that memorable scene in *Kong* that opens with a wide-angle shot: interior of a railway car on the Third Avenue El. Straphangers are nodding, the literate refold their newspapers. Unknown to them, Kong has torn away a section of trestle toward which the train now speeds. The motorman spies Kong up ahead, jams on the brakes. Passengers hurtle together like so many peas in a pail. In a window of the car appear Kong's bloodshot eyes. Women shriek. Kong picks up the railway car as if it were a rat, flips it to the street and ties knots in it, or something. To any commuter the scene must appear one of the most satisfactory pieces of celluloid ever exposed.

Yet however violent his acts, Kong remains a gentleman. Remarkable is his sense of chivalry. Whenever a fresh boa constrictor threatens Fay, Kong first sees that the lady is safely parked, then manfully thrashes her attacker. (And she, the ingrate, runs away every time his back is turned.) Atop the Empire State Building, ignoring his pursuers, Kong places Fay on a ledge as tenderly as it she were a dozen eggs. He fondles her, then turns to face the Army Air Force. And Kong is perhaps the most disinterested lover since Cyrano: his attentions to the lady are utterly without hope of reward. After all, between a five-foot blonde and a fifty-foot ape, love can hardly be more than an intellectual flirtation. In his simian way King Kong is the hopelessly yearning lover of Petrarchan convention. His forced exit from his jungle, in chains, results directly from his single-minded pursuit of Fay. He smashes a Broadway theater when the notion enters his dull brain that the flashbulbs of photographers somehow endanger the lady. His perilous shinnying up a skyscraper to pluck Fay from her boudoir is an act of the kindliest of hearts. He's impossible to discourage even though the love of his life can't lay eyes on him without shrieking murder.

10   The tragedy of King Kong then, is to be the beast who at the end of the fable fails to turn into the handsome prince. This is the conviction that the scriptwriters would leave with us in the film's closing line. As Kong's corpse lies blocking traffic in the street, the enterpreneur who brought Kong to New York turns to the assembled reporters and proclaims: "That's your story, boys—it was Beauty killed the Beast!" But greater forces than those of the screaming Lady have combined to lay Kong low, if you ask me. Kong lives for a time as one of those persecuted near-animal souls bewildered in the middle of an industrial order, whose simple desires are thwarted at every turn. He climbs the Empire State Building because in all New York it's the closest thing he can find to the clifftop of his jungle isle. He dies, a pitiful dolt, and the army brass and publicity-men cackle over him. His death is the only possible outcome to as neat a tragic dilemma as you can ask for. The machine-guns do him in, while the manicured human hero (a nice clean Dartmouth boy) carries away Kong's sweetheart to the altar, O, the misery of it all. There's far more truth about upper-middle-class American life in *King Kong* than in the last seven dozen novels of John P. Marquand.

A Negro friend from Atlanta tells me that in movie houses in colored neighborhoods throughout the South, *Kong* does a constant business. They show the thing in Atlanta at least every year, presumably to the same audiences. Perhaps this popularity may simply be due to the fact that Kong is one of the most watchable movies ever constructed, but I wonder whether Negro audiences may not find some archetypical appeal in this serio-comic tale of a huge black powerful free spirit whom all the hard-working white policemen are out to kill.

Every day in the week on a screen somewhere in the world, King Kong relives his agony. Again and again he expires on the Empire State Building, as audiences of the devout assist his sacrifice. We watch him die, and by extension kill the ape within our bones, but these little deaths of ours occur in prosaic surroundings. We do not die on a tower, New York before our feet, nor do we give our lives to smash a few flying machines. It is not for us to bring to a momentary standstill the civilization in which we move. King Kong does this for us. And so we kill him again and again, in much-spliced celluloid; while the ape in us expires from day to day, obscure, in desperation.

NOTES

[1] Bela Lugosi, an actor in many horror movies.

Things to Do with the Reading

1. Get a copy of the 1933 version of *King Kong* and watch it. From the perspective of today, which of the claims that Kennedy makes from his own contemporary perspective—one that is now nearly fifty years old—seem least credible, and why? And which arguably are still pertinent interpretations of the original *Kong*? In short, which features of the cultural climate now would require a writer to update and adjust the 1960 lens?

2. The Kennedy essay offers the opportunity to think about how all research needs to be conditioned by a sense of history. In other words, to some extent, "Who Killed King Kong?" is a piece that tells us at least as much about 1960, when it was written, as it does about 1933, when the film was produced. What does the review tell us about 1960—or at least about political attitudes on the left in 1960? (See Chapter 5, the section titled "The Pitch, The Complaint, and The Moment.")

3. **Application:** One interesting analytical project is to study several versions of a film—the original and its remake(s). The fact that the film gets remade speaks to something enduring in its vision of things, something that might be called mythic or transhistorical. But the remake also suggests the desire to update that vision, or at least, it suggests that a new version of the vision might prove newly marketable.

   There are at least three full-fledged versions of *King Kong*: Merian C. Cooper's 1933 original, John Guillerman's 1976 version, and Peter Jackson's 2005 remake. For more data on these see http://www.aboyd.com/kong/index2.html and http://www.kongisking.net/index.shtml.

   Write an essay in which you analyze how the remake reshapes the earlier version. What, at the level of representation, remains essentially the same in the way the remake sees the essential story? What has changed most dramatically, and how do you interpret the way that the film is attempting to induce viewers to see themselves differently? Alternatively, you might treat a film and its sequel.

4. "Monster" movies, for lack of a better term, have been with us for a long time—Dracula, the Mummy, Frankenstein, Godzilla. And new "monsters," along with quasi-monstrous superheroes continue to appear—Buffy the vampire slayer, lots of vampires in all walks of life and death, Spiderman, Batman, and so forth. Images of Godzilla flattening buildings in Japanese cities and Spiderman scaling glass-walled high rises in New York are part of our collective visual imaginations. Pick some fairly current monster or supernatural superhero and write an essay in which you analyze it as a reflection of how we see ourselves or would like to see ourselves or are afraid to see ourselves at this moment in time.

5. **Application:** Select a film that has enjoyed significant popularity, and using Kennedy's essay as a model, write an essay in which you analyze the reasons for the film's popularity with a particular audience. Kennedy is particularly effective at describing key scenes in evocative ways, which bring out the affective power of striking cinematic images. As you analyze your chosen film, target its most powerful images and interpret them in ways that bring out their shaping power.

For further research: Seeing

—By Kelly Cannon, Reference Librarian

The readings and activities below invite you to further explore the theme of "Seeing." WARNING: Some essays are polemical; they are intended to promote insight and discussion (or a starting point for your next paper). To access the online readings, visit the *Writing Analytically with Readings* website at www.cengagebrain.com.

Open Access

"Documenting America: Photographic Series." *American Memory.* **Library of Congress, 1998. 30 December 2011. http://memory.loc.gov/ammem/fsowhome.html**
Includes some of the more renowned photographs and photographers from the Depression-era documentary project associated with the Farm Security Administration.

> Explore: Find out more about the Farm Security Administration. What prompted the taking of these photographs? To what extent do these images appear "staged" or "recorded" according to Joseph Elliott's and Susan Sontag's analyses of photography in the essays printed above?

Johnston, Mike. "Evidence, Not Proof." *The Luminous Landscape.* **7 March 2004. 3 January 2011. http://www.luminous-landscape.com/columns/sm-04-03-07.shtml**
Discusses the practical and much-debated matter of how photographers enlist cooperation from their subjects.

> Explore: Click on the "discussion" link embedded in the essay. What question is at the center of this discussion? Consider this essay in light of Sontag's thought that all photography is to some extent staged.

"Edward S. Curtis's The North American Indian." *American Memory.* **Northwestern University Library and Library of Congress, 2001. 30 December 2011. http://memory.loc.gov/ammem/award98/ienhtml/curthome.html**
A renowned collection of photographs of North American Indians taken in the early 1900s, these striking images have collectively exerted tremendous influence on pop culture's perception of American Indians.

> Explore: To what extent do you think Curtis accomplished his goal to accurately document "the old time Indian, his dress, his ceremonies, his life and manners"? How so? To what extent do these images appear "staged" or "recorded" according to Joseph Elliott's and Susan Sontag's analyses of photography in the essays printed above?

Kipnis, Laura. "The Eloquence of Pornography." *Frontline.* **PBS, 2002. 1 January 2011. http://www.pbs.org/wgbh/pages/frontline/shows/porn/special/eloquence.html**
Eloquent essay proposing that pornography "insists on a sanctioned space for fantasy."

> Explore: According to this essay, what does pornography enable us to see that society would prefer to keep invisible? Compare this essay with the John Berger essay on the female nude.

Rosen, Christine. "The Image Culture." *The New Atlantis: A Journal of Technology and Society* **10 (Fall 2005): 27–46. 19 January 2011. http://www.thenewatlantis.com/publications/the-image-culture**

Historical survey of the technology of the image, beginning with the daguerreotype, and then chronicling the rise of photography and film, up to "the MTV effect" (the discontinuous barrage). Along the way, dispassionate history begins to give way to jeremiad.

> Explore: How does Rosen's point of view resemble but also differ from that of Susan Sontag in the essay included in this chapter?

SandLotScience.com. 2005. 30 December 2011. http://www.sandlotscience.com
Click on any of the links to the "Optical Illusion Tours." Contains over 100 optical illusions.

> Explore: Go to the website's "reading room" to find some of the most recent scientific research on what constitutes an optical illusion.

Proprietary

(Ask your librarian about print or online access to the following resources.)
Barthes, Roland. ["Chapters 25–29."] *Camera Lucida: Reflections on Photography*. New York: Hill and Wang, 1981. 63–72.
In this somewhat difficult piece, the author sorts through old photographs, trying to find one that captures the essence of his memory of his mother.

> Explore: Look through Barthes' entire book *Camera Lucida*. Find the image that most appeals to you. What is it specifically about the image that draws you in, what Barthes calls its punctum?

Colbert, Charles. *Seeing What I Like & Liking What I See*. Pendaya Publications, 1991.
Contains 120 "mind-eye" photographs, mostly landscapes, taken by the author, representing a stunning visual feast.

> Explore: What pattern runs through some or all of the images that makes them visually interesting? How much do these images confirm Barry Lopez's claims regarding the photographer's quest for light and spatial volume in the essay printed above?

Elkins, James. "How to Look at a Postage Stamp." *How to Use Your Eyes*. New York: Routledge, 2000. 2–11.
Looks back to old postage stamps designed by people who "knew that there is no reason to make everything easy to see." These old stamps are "tiny worlds" in themselves.

> Explore: Visit the online stamp collection with the Writing Analytically with Readings website link. Click on each stamp to make it as large as possible. To what extent do these old postage stamps support Elkins' contention that stamps are "tiny worlds"?

Frisby, John P. "Pictures in Our Heads." *Seeing: Illusion, Brain and Mind*. New York: Oxford, 1980. 8–25.
A psychologist scientifically examines what goes on inside our heads when we see.

> Explore: In a single sentence, what would you say is the author's main conclusion? (In other words, what does the author think of the "inner screen" theory?)

Hartnell, Anna. "Katrina Tourism and a Tale of Two Cities: Visualizing Race and Class in New Orleans." *American Quarterly* 61.3 (2009): 723–747. http://0-search.ebscohost.com. library.muhlenberg.edu/login.aspx?direct=true&db=aph&AN=44655157&site=ehost-live&scope=site

Discusses how the site of hurricane Katrina has become a tourist attraction. The difference between the tourist gaze and that of the residents could hardly be more striking, highlighting racial and economic differences.

> **Explore:** Have you been to see a disaster site, or would you go? Why or why not? How do the ethical concerns raised in this essay about seeing resonate with those discussed in the essays above by Sontag and Lopez?